THE MAKING OF THE

OXFORD ENGLISH DICTIONARY

THE MAKING OF THE
Oxford English Dictionary

PETER GILLIVER

OXFORD

UNIVERSITY PRESS

OXFORD

UNIVERSITY PRESS

Great Clarendon Street, Oxford, OX2 6DP,
United Kingdom

Oxford University Press is a department of the University of Oxford.
It furthers the University's objective of excellence in research, scholarship,
and education by publishing worldwide. Oxford is a registered trade mark of
Oxford University Press in the UK and in certain other countries

© Peter Gilliver 2016

The moral rights of the author have been asserted

First Edition published in 2016

Impression: 1

Published in the United States of America by Oxford University Press
198 Madison Avenue, New York, NY 10016, United States of America

British Library Cataloguing in Publication Data
Data available

Library of Congress Control Number: 2015959816

ISBN 978–0–19–928362–0

Printed in Great Britain by
Clays Ltd, St Ives plc

For Robin, *sine quo non*

CONTENTS

PREFACE

The Making of the O.E.D. would be a good subject for a book
in due course—by some retired lexicographer.[1]

There are already numerous histories of the *Oxford English Dictionary*; indeed, such accounts began to be written long before the first edition of the Dictionary was completed in 1928.[2] There is even one history called 'The Making of the *Oxford English Dictionary*'.[3] The Dictionary itself, in both its first and second editions, included an account of its compilation,[4] and much historical material is available on the *OED*'s own website.

It nevertheless seemed to me, sometime in the late 1990s, that there was room for another history. I had already begun to explore some of the Dictionary's archives in relation to my interest in the work done by J. R. R. Tolkien as one of Henry Bradley's assistants just after the First World War;[5] subsequently I also contributed a biographical appendix[6] to a volume of essays on the Dictionary (mainly with reference to the first edition). The absorbing task of researching the latter revealed to me just how much more there was to say about the thousands of individuals whose combined efforts created the *OED* than was available in the existing published histories. The fact that I was one of these individuals, and indeed belonged to a small and fortunate subgroup of them—I have been a member of the Dictionary's staff since 1987—made me realize that I could bring a distinctive perspective to writing about the project. Most people encounter and interact with the *OED* as readers, consulting individual entries or definitions; my main mode of interaction with it over nearly thirty years has been as a lexicographer, constantly engaged in creating and remaking its text. First-hand

---

[1] Comment, apparently by Robert Burchfield, in an unsigned memo to Dan Davin dated 2 July 1975 (OUPA(u)).

[2] The first account which was available as a separate publication was arguably the pamphlet issued by OUP in 1913 entitled 'A Brief Account of the Oxford Dictionary': see p. 334 n. 18. Numerous earlier accounts appeared as magazine articles or sections of longer works, including many published before the Dictionary itself began to be issued.

[3] A short pamphlet by John Cowley with this title, originally issued as an insert in the *Clarendonian* (a magazine for OUP employees, of which he was then editor), was printed by the Press in 1972 for publicity purposes; copies are preserved in OUPA.

[4] The history included with the reissue of the first edition (Craigie 1933a) was reprinted with only minor modifications in the second edition.

[5] In 1992 I gave a conference paper on my findings, subsequently published as Gilliver (1995).

[6] Gilliver (2000).

experience of what the process of compiling or revising *OED* entries of all kinds can involve has, I believe, enabled me to inhabit the minds of those who have done similar work before me in a way that nothing else could have done. Anyone who pores over the slips from which the first edition of the Dictionary and its Supplements were compiled will have a strong sense of looking over the shoulders of those earlier workers; but a practising lexicographer stands a better chance than most of understanding the nature of their work and the issues they faced.

In any case, there was at that time no single full-length book available which told the whole history of the Dictionary. Even *Caught in the Web of Words*, the superb biography of James Murray by his granddaughter Elisabeth[7]—the only book which had been recommended to me by way of preliminary reading when I was appointed to the staff—is only a partial history in many respects: it offers (understandably) only a very brief account of the decades following the death of Murray in 1915, and of course is first and foremost a biography of one man rather than a history of the project.[8] And it was a history of the Dictionary as a project which I particularly wanted to read; and which, I eventually realized, I might be suitably qualified to write. Moreover, in the four decades since the publication of *Caught in the Web of Words* much additional documentation about the *OED* has come to light, both in the remarkable archives of the Dictionary itself and elsewhere. Some of this information has been made use of in a number of more recent books, which have generally focused on a particular aspect of the Dictionary, or a particular period of its history.[9]

It has been, as I have said, my intention to write a project history, tracing the development of the original idea of the *OED* from its earliest roots through the various stages of its realization, down to (more or less) the present day. I have not, for the most part, sought to supplement this with detailed assessment or analysis of the content of the Dictionary; these matters could fill several further volumes in themselves, and I have thought it best not to clutter my historical narrative with such material. There are, however, a couple of exceptions to this.

Firstly, I thought it would be of interest to include an examination of the lexicographical output of the first phase of the Dictionary's history, namely the work of the 'sub-editors' under the editorship of Frederick Furnivall during the 1860s and 1870s; this

---

[7] Elisabeth Murray's book—justly described by Anthony Burgess as 'one of the finest biographies of the twentieth century'—drew extensively on an earlier, unpublished memoir of Murray by her own father, Harold, a copy of which is held in OUPA. Perhaps surprisingly, both *Caught in the Web of Words* and Harold Murray's memoir were both turned down by OUP, the latter on two occasions. A much earlier proposal for a biography of James Murray, made by his former assistant P. J. Philip (see p. 312 n. 120), was also rejected by the Press (OED/B/3/2/7 12 Aug. 1915 Cannan to Oswyn Murray; OD 22 Oct. 1915).

[8] It is a matter of great regret to me that none of the other three Editors of the first edition of the Dictionary have left papers of anything like the richness of those left by James Murray, on which much of the detailed information given in *Caught in the Web of Words* is based (and of which I have likewise made extensive use); the sparseness of material relating to Henry Bradley is particularly unfortunate.

[9] Among the more important recent academic studies are those by Charlotte Brewer, Lynda Mugglestone, and Sarah Ogilvie (see Bibliography). An entertaining general account, dealing mainly with the first edition, is Winchester (2003).

examination—which is more of an analysis of how the Dictionary might have been than of how it actually emerged—appears as one of two 'interludes' placed in between the chapters of the main chronological narrative. A second, non-chronological interlude sets out the various stages of the process of compiling a Dictionary entry.

Secondly, from time to time I have found that a particular word can form the basis of an exploration of a particular topic (such as an aspect of editorial policy) which seems called for at a particular point, or may simply be of interest in itself. This material is presented in the form of 'capsules',[10] interspersed throughout the text but kept separate from the main narrative.

In quoting letters and other documents I have in all cases retained the writer's original spelling and punctuation.

ACKNOWLEDGEMENTS

It would have been impossible for me to write this book without the help of a great many people and organizations, and I wish here to record my gratitude to them all. I owe a particular debt to Martin Maw: not just because, as the archivist of Oxford University Press, he has given me the kind of access to the collections in his care that most researchers could only dream of, but also because of his encouraging me to think, when I spoke to him a decade and a half ago about my feeling that it was time someone wrote a new academic history of the *OED*, that I might be the person to do it. He and all of his colleagues in the OUP archives have been unfailingly helpful to me for over a decade. The *OED*'s own archives form a self-contained and important part of the Press's archives, and I am immensely grateful to Bev McCulloch for constant assistance in all matters relating to the records of the Dictionary and the Press's other lexicographical projects, as well as to her maternity cover, Jennifer Mason; I wish also to thank their colleagues Katharine Davis, Fran Bourke, and (formerly) Tom McCulloch.

First and foremost among the many other archivists and librarians that have aided me in various ways, I must place Colin Harris and the staff of Special Collections in the Bodleian Library, in particular for their help with using the papers of James Murray; I have made valuable discoveries in many of Oxford University's network of libraries, and I am grateful for all the assistance I have received. I have also received invaluable help from many of Oxford's archivists: my particular thanks go to Simon Bailey and Alice Millea of Oxford University Archives, Penelope Baker of Exeter College, Robin Darwall-Smith of University and Magdalen, Emma Goodrum of Worcester, Clare Hopkins of Trinity, Amanda Ingram of Pembroke, Rob Petre of Oriel, Julian Reid of Merton and Corpus Christi, Mike Riordan of Queen's and St John's, Sean Rippington

---

[10] The term, and the concept, is borrowed from Norman Davies's *Europe: A History* (1996).

of St Peter's, and Anna Sander of Balliol; and also to Sally Speirs of St Anne's College library. Outside Oxford, I am happy to record my gratitude to: Mark Stevens of Berkshire Record Office; Sheena Ebsworth, Records Manager, Broadmoor Hospital; the British Library; the staff of Cambridge University Library; Jacqueline Cox of Cambridge University Archives; Hannah Westall of Girton College, Cambridge; Guildhall Library Manuscripts Section; Archives and Special Collections, King's College London; the archives of University College London; Dr Pamela Taylor, archivist of Mill Hill School; the custodians of the John Murray Archive (now held in the National Library of Scotland); Mike Bott, Verity Andrews, and Alex Fisher of Reading University Library; Michelle Gait of the Special Libraries and Archives Department, University of Aberdeen; the National Library of Scotland; Edinburgh University Library; Rachel Hart of the Special Collections Division, University of St Andrews; Robin Adams and Jane Maxwell, of the Manuscripts Department of Trinity College Dublin; Patricia Moloney of the National Folklore Collection at University College Dublin; Steve Mendoza, Library of the University of California at Berkeley; Jessica Westphal of the University of Chicago Library; Julia Gardner, Special Collections Research Center, University of Chicago; Sue Hodson of the Huntington Library, San Marino, California; the Library of the University of Michigan; Carol Leadenham of the Hoover Institution Archives at Stanford University; Sharon Thayer of the Bailey-Howe Library, University of Vermont; Alexander Turnbull Library, National Library of New Zealand. To those institutions in this list who have also granted permission to quote from the materials in their care I am also most grateful.

This book necessarily draws extensively on material in the archives of Oxford University Press; all material from these archives is reproduced by permission of the Secretary to the Delegates of Oxford University Press.[11] Much material is also quoted from the papers of James Murray in the Bodleian, and I am grateful to Oswyn and John Murray for permission to do so. I have also been very fortunate in being given access to some of the personal papers of other lexicographers who feature in this history, and my thanks are likewise due to James Wyllie for the access he has given me to his father's papers, and to Elizabeth Burchfield for giving me such free access to her husband's papers. I am also grateful to the Council of the Philological Society for allowing me to consult and quote from the Society's records.

I owe another debt of gratitude to Elizabeth Burchfield and many others, for so freely giving of their reminiscences, which have enriched my knowledge of the more recent years of the Dictionary's history. In fact living memory extends further back than might be expected, and for answering many questions about his work in the 1950s I am particularly grateful to Alan Horsman. Recollections, and answers to many questions, have been generously provided by many other members of the Dictionary's staff, including many

---

[11] Access to recent unpublished archival material in the OUP archives is generally governed by a 30-year closure rule; I am especially grateful to the Secretary to the Delegates of Oxford University Press for granting me permission to study and cite from those more recent records.

who are still my colleagues: Bob Allen, Liz Ashdowne, Tony Augarde, Andrew Ball, Julian Barnes, Richard Beatty, Tim Benbow, Lesley Brown (formerly Burnett), Andrew Buxton, Margot Charlton, Jill Cotter, Jean Pierre de Rosnay, Graeme Diamond, Philip Durkin, Laura Elliott, Anthony Esposito, Ewen Fletcher, Andreas Gröger, Roland Hall, Philip Hardie, Denny Hilton, Richard Holden, David Howlett, Deborah Honoré, Alan Hughes, Veronica Hurst, Rosamund Ions, Jane Johnson, Elizabeth Knowles, the late Jeanne Lindley, Elizabeth Livingstone, Blaise Machin, Eleanor Maier, Jeremy Marshall, Katherine Connor Martin, Inge Milfull, Rosamund Moon, Bernadette Paton, Judy Pearsall, Kay Pepler, Jennie Price, Michael Proffitt, Nick Rollin, Rosemary Sansome, Sam Schad, Penny Silva, Jon Simon, John Simpson, Katrin Thier, Freda Thornton, Jeffery Triggs, Bill Trumble, Anne Wallace-Hadrill, Yvonne Warburton, Bill Waterfield, Nick Wedd, Edmund Weiner, Sally Wheeler (née Hilton), and Jelly Williams. I have also been fortunate to draw on the memories of others, employed by OUP and elsewhere, who became closely involved with the *OED*, including Richard Charkin, Peter Glare, the late Adam Kilgarriff, Paul Luna, and Eric Stanley.

It should also be mentioned that colleagues engaged in revising the text of the Dictionary have also made numerous valuable observations to me about the nature of that text, and the inferences that can be drawn about the methods adopted by their predecessors. This is only one of the many ways in which my research has benefited from being surrounded by other lexicographers. For this and for other reasons, I would like to thank my employers, Oxford University Press, for making it possible for me to research and write this book while continuing to work on the *OED* as a lexicographer (a job which still, after nearly thirty years, strikes me as the best job I could have anywhere).

Invaluable help of a different kind has also been forthcoming from many *OED* colleagues, namely comments on drafts of various portions—in some cases nearly all—of my text. In this capacity I would like to thank Eleanor Maier, Fiona McPherson, Kate Wild, and especially Jonathan Dent, Denny Hilton, Michael Proffitt, John Simpson, and Edmund Weiner. I would also like to thank the two readers appointed by OUP for their extremely thorough and well-informed criticisms of my text. Responsibility for any remaining errors or shortcomings in the text of course remains mine.

It is a pleasure to record my debt to various fellow scholars. In particular, those who choose to make a serious study of dictionaries and their history form a small band; many are, or have been, practising lexicographers as well. I have been fortunate indeed to get to know so many of them, and to share information, compare notes, consult, and on occasion simply co-enthuse about our favourite subject with Michael Adams, Richard Ashdowne, the late Richard Bailey, Anne Bello, Charlotte Brewer, John Considine, Jonathon Green, Joan Houston Hall, Toni Healey, Alan Kirkness, Elizabeth Knowles, Robert E. (Bob) Lewis, Iseabail Macleod, Manfred Markus, Rod McConchie, Lynda Mugglestone, Sarah Ogilvie, Darrell Raymond, Allen Reddick, Susan Rennie, Ammon Shea, Simon Winchester, Steven Wood, and especially Chris Stray, to whom I owe a particular debt of thanks for reading the entire draft text at a late stage. Among other historians of scholarship and publishing I would like to thank Simon Eliot, Roger Louis, Angus Phillips, Keith Robbins, and Helen Spencer.

For other help and information of various kinds I would like to thank: Mary Alden, Cynthia Barnhart, Roderick Braithwaite, Robert Bruce, Jennie Burgess of the Birchington Heritage Trust, Jeremy Campbell-Grant, Alice Chandler of the Office of the President at the University of Chicago, Tony Comer, Susan Falcone, Eileen Finlayson, Paul Gannon, Tim Gell, Daniel Grimley, Will Hale, Michael and Mary Holder, Amanda Laugesen, Jennie McGregor-Smith, Don Montague, Desmond Morris, Chris Nash, Christine Robinson, Karen Thomson, and Andrew Willett.

At OUP I would like to thank John Davey, my original editor, and also his successor, Julia Steer, together with all those who saw the book through the various stages of production. I am grateful to Deborah Protheroe and Robert Faber for much-needed help and advice with illustrations.

Finally, I owe more than any words—in or out of the *OED*—can say to my partner, Robin Darwall-Smith. His support and encouragement have sustained me in my work since long before the start of this project; in fact I doubt that I would have undertaken it without him. I certainly could not have finished it without him. Along the way he has uncomplainingly, indeed enthusiastically shared in its ups and downs, helping with the research, reading chapter after chapter, offering valuable insights, talking through knotty problems, and in between reminding me how much more there is to life. Neither of us anticipated that it was going to take thirteen years, but throughout that time he has been a constant source of … well, everything really. This book is dedicated to him, with my love.

LIST OF ILLUSTRATIONS

FIGURE ACKNOWLEDGEMENTS

Every effort has been made to trace copyright owners, and apologies are extended to anyone whose rights have inadvertently not been acknowledged. Omissions or inaccuracies of copyright detail will be corrected in subsequent printings where possible.

The photograph of Frederick Furnivall (Figure 1a) was supplied by Charlotte Brewer.

For permission to reproduce the photographs of Henry Hucks Gibbs (Figure 4) and Fitzedward Hall (Figure 9) I am grateful to John Murray.

For permission to reproduce the photograph of Henry Bradley (Figure 13) I am grateful to Jennie McGregor-Smith.

For permission to reproduce the photograph of the Scriptorium (Figure 14) I am grateful to Oswyn Murray.

The image of Philip Lyttelton Gell (Figure 15) was supplied by Anna Sander.

The photograph of the printing plate (Figure 18) was supplied by Sarah Ogilvie.

The image of printing sheets of the Dictionary (Figure 19) is taken from the film *The Oxford University Press and the Making of a Book*, produced by the Federation of British Industries in 1925, and is reproduced with the permission of the Confederation of British Industry.

The photograph of Craigie and Bradley in the Dictionary Room (Figure 23) was supplied by Rachel Hart of the University of St Andrews Library, and appears courtesy of the University of St Andrews Library.

The photograph of James Wyllie (Figure 33) was supplied by Charlotte Brewer, and is reproduced from an original in the possession of Peter Glare with his permission.

The photograph of the *Compact OED* (Figure 35) was supplied by Jean Pierre de Rosnay.

The photograph of *Countdown* (Figure 38) was supplied by Gyles Brandreth, and is reproduced courtesy of Rex Features.

The photograph of the LEXX editing system (Figure 39a) was supplied by Mike Cowlishaw, and appears with his permission.

The photographs of John Simpson and Edmund Weiner with *OED2* (Figure 40), and of the launch of *OED Online* (Figure 41), are reproduced courtesy of PA Images.

The photographs of Michael Proffitt (Figure 44) and the *OED* staff in 2015 (Figure 46) were supplied by Keith Barnes of Photographers Workshop.

Images held in the archives of Oxford University Press (Figures 1b, 2, 3, 5, 6, 7, 8, 10, 16, 17, 20, 22, 24, 25, 26, 27, 28, 29, 30, 31, 34, 36, 37, 39b, and 43) are reproduced by permission of the Secretary to the Delegates of Oxford University Press.

LIST OF CAPSULES

Beginnings: to 1861

UNCERTAINTY surrounds the question of exactly when the *Oxford English Dictionary* can be said to have begun: an uncertainty arising, appropriately enough, from difficulties of definition. The publication of the first instalment of the Dictionary in 1884 is one kind of beginning; another is the appointment of James Murray as Editor in 1879; but there are beginnings of various kinds long before this. If the 'Committee to collect unregistered words in English' which came into being in the summer of 1857, under the auspices of the Philological Society, might be regarded as the Dictionary's first shoots, its roots extend much further back through the early years of the nineteenth century, and beyond.

During the decades around 1800 the study of language in Britain, and especially England, was preoccupied with such philosophical questions as the origin of language and the idea of a universal grammar, and, as Hans Aarsleff has shown,[1] was prevented from fully absorbing the empirical, evidence-based methods of the 'new philology' (as increasingly practised in Continental Europe) by the pervasive influence of the rather different ideas to be found in the two volumes of John Horne Tooke's *The Diversions of Purley* (1786–1805).[2] This strange combination of philology and philosophy put forward the thesis that underlying whole groups of words there were certain fundamental units of meaning, and proceeded to etymologize several thousand words on this basis

---

[1] The following paragraphs owe much to Aarsleff (1967), still unsurpassed as a survey of language study in England during the late eighteenth and early nineteenth centuries. His other more detailed analyses of the early history of the *OED* (Aarsleff 1962; 1990) are also of great value. In regard specifically to the application of historical principles to lexicography, John Considine's recent examination of the origins and development of the historical approach (Considine 2015a) is invaluable; see also the first chapter of Zgusta (2006), which includes perceptive assessments of the most important historical dictionary projects conceived during the nineteenth century. Momma (2012) also gives a good account of the impact of the 'new philology' on the study of English, including a chapter on the Philological Society and several of the key figures in the history of the *OED*. For a useful guide to key events in the history of lexicography in general, with a particular focus on English, see Considine (2015b).

[2] For a more sympathetic assessment of some of Horne Tooke's linguistic ideas, see Bergheaud (1979).

The Making of the *Oxford English Dictionary*. First edition. Peter Gilliver.
© Peter Gilliver 2016. First published 2016 by Oxford University Press.

(*heaven* 'some place, any place *Heav-en* or *Heav-ed*', *bacon* derived from 'to bake', and so forth).[3] On the Continent, by contrast, interest in the relationships between languages—partly stimulated, ironically, by the observations of a British philologist, Sir William Jones, on the relationship of Sanskrit to various European languages—was interacting productively with the burgeoning Romantic enthusiasm for language as the embodiment of national identity, notably in Germany and the Scandinavian countries. By the 1820s something of the new historical approach had begun to percolate across the Channel, often through the personal influence of visiting German scholars, as for example with the visit of the pioneering comparative philologist Franz Bopp to London in 1819–20, and the appointment in 1828 of Friedrich August Rosen, a pupil of Bopp, to the chair of oriental languages at London University. The year 1828 also saw the creation of England's first university professorship in English language and literature, also in London. Something of a watershed was reached in the year 1830, when an English translation of the *Grammar of the Anglo-Saxon Tongue* by the great Danish linguist and literary scholar Rasmus Rask, carried out by his former pupil Benjamin Thorpe, was published, along with N. F. S. Grundtvig's prospectus for a series of editions of Anglo-Saxon texts, *Bibliotheca Anglo-Saxonica*. As Aarsleff has observed, the *Oxford English Dictionary*

is unthinkable without the rapid absorption of Continental scholarship by English philologists and their intensive study after 1830 of early English language and literature; and, equally important, without the complete departure from the powerful Tooke tradition, from philological speculation, from random etymologizing, and from the notion that the chief end of language study is the knowledge of mind.[4]

In view of this late development in England of the particular kind of evidence-based approach to language study with which the *Oxford English Dictionary* is imbued, it is hardly surprising that, taken in order, the significant milestones in English dictionary-making—a process influenced by commercial pressures as well as the desire for scholarly respectability—during the early nineteenth century do not suggest anything like an inevitable progress in the direction of the *OED*.[5] However, the Dictionary was not, by any means, independent of the British lexicographical context from which it emerged; on the contrary, it stands firmly in a succession of (completed and uncompleted) dictionary projects conceived in the early nineteenth century which, notwithstanding their regrettable distance methodologically from contemporary

---

[3] Horne Tooke even began work on a dictionary of his own, and to this end constructed indexes of the words to be found in a number of key texts. Details of the project, which never came to anything, are given in Read (1937: 354–5).

[4] Aarsleff (1967: 165).

[5] Thus Aarsleff, implicitly taking issue with the historical picture presented by James Murray in his 1900 Romanes Lecture (see below, p. 287): 'It has been said that the *OED* is lineally descended from a long succession of English dictionaries, as if by a process of natural evolution, but this is not true' (Aarsleff 1990: 160).

projects in other countries, can be seen as striving towards at least two of the same goals: unprecedented comprehensiveness of coverage, and what may be called a historical outlook. Some other lexicographical projects in other languages which were of considerable significance as methodological forerunners also merit brief consideration.

Formidable though the reputation of Samuel Johnson's *Dictionary of the English Language* continued to be during the decades following publication of the first edition in 1755, it was not without its critics.[6] Even before Johnson's death in 1784, various individuals had proposed to improve on it by compiling either a supplement to it or an entirely new dictionary of their own.[7] A striking early example from outside Britain is the *Neues grammatisch-kritisches Wörterbuch der englischen Sprache* by the prolific German philologist Johann Christoph Adelung, published in two volumes in 1783 and 1796; based on Johnson's fourth edition, this was described on its title page as 'expanded with many words, meanings and examples'.[8] Adelung's great achievement in the lexicography of his own language, his *Grammatisch-kritisches Wörterbuch der hochdeutschen Mundart* (1793–1801), was also an importantly innovative work of historical lexicography, in that his declared principle for the arrangement of the different meanings of each word was that they should be ordered 'in conformity with how they appear to have developed from each other'.[9]

Perhaps the most famous, and certainly one of the most ambitious, of the attempts to improve on Johnson was that by Herbert Croft, who in a series of public announcements during the 1780s and 1790s held out the prospect of a new dictionary which would correct Johnson's errors and include thousands of words which he had overlooked.[10] In a striking prefiguring of subsequent developments, one of his first announcements appeared in 1787 under the heading 'Oxford Dictionary of the English Language'. Croft had strong connections with Oxford: he had studied at University College—the college which became a favourite haunt of Johnson in his later years—and, by another remarkable coincidence, the University granted him space to accommodate his

---

[6] Detailed surveys of the reception of Johnson's dictionary are given in Sledd and Kolb (1955) and Noyes (1955). Particularly interesting among the early critics—who also included Horne Tooke—was Archibald Campbell, who argued that the dictionary fell 'infinitely short' of what ought to have been its aim, namely to include 'a distinct treatise on every word that is, or ever has been in use'—although he conceded that this was, like the philosopher's stone, 'impossible to obtain' (Campbell 1767: xxxiv–xxxv).

[7] A very full account of the numerous ventures launched as responses to Johnson, and of other projected English dictionaries between 1755 and 1828 (the year of publication of Noah Webster's great dictionary), is given in Read (1937).

[8] Original German: 'mit vielen Wörtern, Bedeutungen und Beyspielen vermehrt'. Adelung also published a careful consideration of the 'relative merits and demerits' of Johnson's dictionary (an English translation of which, by A. F. M. Willich, appeared in 1798 as the third of *Three Philological Essays*). His assessments are discussed in Considine (2014c: 41–3); his main criticisms were that Johnson was insufficiently comprehensive, that his etymological knowledge was 'shallow', and that he tended to subdivide meanings too finely.

[9] Translation from Considine (2015a), who observes that 'the diachronic element in his [German] dictionary was stronger than that in any previous general monolingual dictionary had been' (p. 167).

[10] A full account of Croft's project is given in Congleton (1968).

many volumes of working papers, in the building later known as the Old Ashmolean Museum.[11]

Croft's grandiose plans ultimately came to nothing; in 1795 he was even forced to flee the country because of debts. Other would-be successors to Johnson managed to get as far as publishing at least part of their work, including George Mason (*A Supplement to Johnson's English Dictionary*, 1801) and John Pytches (who brought out the first instalment of his *New Dictionary of the English Language* in 1807). A particularly interesting case is that of Jonathan Boucher (1738–1804), an English clergyman who spent considerable periods in America, and who devoted the last fourteen years of his life to the compilation of a Johnson supplement focusing particularly on 'provincialisms' and 'archaisms'; he issued a proposal to print his projected 'Linguæ Anglicanæ Veteris Thesaurus' in 1802, but only the first part (80 pages, covering the letter A) was ever published. Boucher's interest lies in the fact that he was much admired, and his work was drawn upon, by Henry Todd in his compilation of what was to become the 'official' revised version of Johnson, published in eleven parts between 1814 and 1818 and running to five volumes. Todd modestly described his own contribution to the work as 'dust in the balance' compared to Johnson's, and describes Boucher's published specimen as illustrating 'how much remains to be done, in order to have a perfect view of the English Language';[12] but the new edition, which almost immediately became known as 'Todd's Johnson', was quickly recognized as effectively superseding earlier editions.

The use of illustrative quotations was a celebrated feature of Johnson's dictionary, although of course he was not the first lexicographer to include them.[13] An important innovation in the use of quotations was made by the Scottish antiquary John Jamieson in his *Etymological Dictionary of the Scottish Language* (1808); Jamieson's stated aim in this dictionary was to give 'the oldest printed or MS. authorities' for every word and meaning,[14] and on this basis his work has been asserted to be 'the first dictionary on historical principles of any variety of English'.[15] While there is no clear evidence that it exercised a direct influence on the genesis of the *OED*, his pioneering approach to the use of quotations—an approach very close to that adopted in the *OED*—is clear.[16]

---

[11] *Gentleman's Magazine* Aug. 1787, pp. 651–2; *Morning Post* 20 Feb. 1788, p. 1. On Johnson and University College see Darwall-Smith (2008: 287–90). For the significance of the Old Ashmolean see below, p. 291.

[12] Todd (1818: vol. 1, Advertisement, sig. Av).

[13] Read (1986) credits the dictionary of Italian produced by the Accademia della Crusca (first edition 1612) as an influential model for Johnson in its inclusion of quotations with references, while noting examples of quotations in lexicographic works dating as far back as the first century AD. Further on quotations in dictionaries see Considine (2015a).

[14] From Jamieson's Preface to Vol. I, p. v.

[15] Aitken (1992: 902). In fact the method adopted by Jamieson in ordering material within his dictionary entries is only partly historical, in that although he always included the earliest evidence for a word, the sense illustrated by it is not always placed first. Further on Jamieson and his dictionary see Rennie (2012) (particularly, on his approach to historical lexicography, pp. 120–3).

[16] See further Considine (2014b). The *Etymological Dictionary of the Scottish Language* was of course well known to the later compilers of the *OED*; one of the earliest serious dictionary-related projects of one of them, James Murray, was a planned (but never completed) phonetic key to Jamieson's work (*CWW* p. 51).

Only a few years after the publication of Jamieson's dictionary, another notable English dictionary was just beginning to appear. In the spring of 1817 a prospectus was issued for a new and exceptionally compendious encyclopedia, the *Encyclopædia Metropolitana*, which was to include (along with much else) 'a Philosophical and Etymological Lexicon of the English language, or the History of English Words', with the quotations arranged chronologically.[17] This grand project was largely conceived by Samuel Taylor Coleridge, one of the small group of English scholars who at that date knew something of Continental philological thinking (he had studied philology at the University of Göttingen in 1798–9); however, the task of compiling the 'Lexicon' was taken over at an early stage by the schoolmaster and aspiring philologist Charles Richardson.[18] The entries of this 'Lexicon' began to be published in 1818 as a component of the *Encyclopædia*; Richardson then revised this material slightly and republished it in two volumes in 1835–7 as the *New Dictionary of the English Language*. The dictionary suffers from Richardson's Horne Tookean ideas about the history of language (which led him, for example, to present groups of words in aggregated entries according to the primitive 'root' from which they were all considered to derive); it was nevertheless much admired, and its extensive collections of chronologically arranged quotations provided an important pointer to what might be done in this respect.[19]

The dictionary which arguably has the strongest claim to have influenced the *OED* methodologically—which, indeed, was explicitly acknowledged as a direct inspiration at an early stage—is, perhaps unsurprisingly, the work of a German scholar; and it was concerned, not with English or indeed any Germanic language, but with classical Greek. The first volume of Franz Passow's *Handwörterbuch der griechischen Sprache* appeared in 1819, but it was only in the fourth edition (1831) that he was able to bring to something like fruition his original plan, which he had first discussed nearly twenty years earlier. It was, however, in the introduction to the second edition of 1826 that Passow first stated his now famous dictum that a dictionary should represent 'the life history of each individual word',[20] by means of quotations showing when each word and meaning was first used.[21] Passow's approach was carried still further—and brought

<hr />

[17] The original version of the prospectus is reproduced in Snyder (1940).

[18] Coleridge had undertaken to provide the first few pages of the 'Lexicon' by Oct. 1817 (18 June 1817 Coleridge to T. Curtis and R. Fenner; *Collected Letters*, ed. E. L. Griggs, 1959, vol. IV, p. 741); it is not clear whether he had done so before the work was reassigned to Richardson, whose recent *Illustrations of English Philology* (1815) had been highly critical of Johnson's dictionary. For more on Coleridge's contribution to the *Encyclopædia Metropolitana* see Collison (1966). McKusick (1992) provides a more general discussion of Coleridge's influence on the genesis of the *OED*.

[19] For a recent assessment of Richardson's dictionary see Reddick (2009). See also Zgusta (2006: 19–26, 47–51).

[20] Passow (1826: xvi) (original German: 'die Lebensgeschichte jedes einzelnen Wortes'). Passow had already articulated a version of this principle in his 1812 essay *Über Zweck, Anlage und Ergänzung griechischer Wörterbücher* (discussed in Considine 2015a). His words were closely echoed by Wilhelm Grimm (see below) when he proposed that the *Deutsches Wörterbuch* would contain the 'natural history' (*Naturgeschichte*) of the individual words of the language (Grimm 1847: 118).

[21] For an investigation of the independent genesis of both Jamieson's and Passow's version of the 'historical principle' in the application, in a lexicographical context, of contemporary ideas about the

to an English-speaking readership—in Henry Liddell and Robert Scott's great *Greek-English Lexicon*, itself based on Passow's work. In the Preface to the first edition (1843) of their work, Liddell and Scott enthusiastically associated themselves with the 'plan [...] marked out and begun by Passow; viz: *to make each Article a History of the usage of the word referred to*';[22] the method was christened 'the historical principle', and given a further powerful boost, by J. R. Fishlake in his very favourable review of Liddell and Scott's *Lexicon* in the *Quarterly Review*.[23]

By the 1840s, then, the historical approach to lexicography which was to be adopted in the *OED* was beginning to gain acceptance among English linguists. At the same time, on an emotional level, a groundswell of what might be called lexicographic nationalism had been building up for some time. Of course national sentiment had long played a significant part in lexicography, in England as elsewhere: describing Johnson's as a 'national Dictionary' had become commonplace, and those who sought to replace or improve upon his work had often claimed patriotic motives.[24] A fresh call to arms had been issued in 1834 by the orientalist (and lexicographer of Malay) William Marsden, in a pamphlet entitled 'Thoughts on the Composition of a National English Dictionary', in which he proposed that the work he had in mind might best be prepared under the auspices of 'a Society composed of persons distinguished for their learning, judgment, taste, and knowledge of the English language'.[25] Marsden's (admittedly rather prescriptive) proposals were not taken up, but something was evidently in the air, as a similar call was made the following year by Richard Garnett, in

study of development in other fields (including literary and cultural history, geology, palaeontology, and biology), see Considine (2014b); further on the development of the historical approach in English lexicography, see Read (1986). Considine (2015a) also traces occasional prefigurings of these historical principles in the work of earlier French and German lexicographers, which, remarkably, can be found as far back as 1690, when Pierre Bayle, in his preface to Furetière's *Dictionnaire Universel*, envisaged a dictionary whose entries would use quotations to illustrate words, and deal with 'the history of words [...] the period of their reign and of their decadence, with the changes of their meaning' (Considine's translation).

A striking early reference to the same concept in an English context occurs in an essay by Thomas De Quincey published in 1823, in which he mentions the idea that 'one condition of a good dictionary would be to exhibit the *history* of each word; that is, to record the exact succession of its meanings' (De Quincey 1823: 493). Interestingly, De Quincey regards this as something which has 'already [...] been said more than once in print'; he may be thinking of Coleridge, whose thoughts on etymology he goes on to discuss.

[22] Liddell and Scott (1843: xx). On the history of the *Greek–English Lexicon* see Stray (2010), and further Stray et al. (forthcoming).

[23] *Quarterly Review* Mar. 1845, p. 306. Fishlake is identified as the author of the review in the *Gentleman's Magazine* of July 1847, p. 37.

[24] Thus Herbert Croft, in a circular about his proposed dictionary distributed in 1789 (and reproduced in the *Gentleman's Magazine* of November 1790, p. 991), aspires 'to make it such a national dictionary as a great people may expect'; and a later article in the *Monthly Review* of December 1798 lamenting the lack of interest his project has stimulated owns to taking 'a patriotic interest in his enterprise' (p. 498). John Pytches similarly refers to his 'great National Dictionary of the English Language' in an advertisement in the *Morning Chronicle* of 16 Jan. 1817, p. 2.

[25] Marsden (1834: 5); I am grateful to Rod McConchie for this reference. In fact Marsden had in mind (and named in his pamphlet) an existing learned society, the Royal Society of Literature.

a lengthy comparative review of three dictionaries (Todd's Johnson, the first two parts of Richardson's dictionary, and a London reprint of Noah Webster's 1828 *American Dictionary of the English Language*) which also reviewed the state of English lexicography, drawing unfavourable comparisons with the work of Continental scholars. He concluded with a plea that the subject might be 'treated with something of the same rigorous and scientific application of principles and copious induction of particulars, that have been exercised upon some of the sister tongues. Much has been done and is still doing by the Germans and Danes, which ought to excite our emulation, and which we may turn to our own advantage.'[26] A still greater challenge to national pride came in 1838 with the start of work on the first of the great nineteenth-century national historical dictionaries, Jakob and Wilhelm Grimm's monumental *Deutsches Wörterbuch*, which was soon followed by similarly ambitious projects in other languages.[27]

One last strand in this confluence of linguistic aspirations has its roots in the antiquarian enthusiasm for collecting items of regional dialect, an enthusiasm which at least since the early eighteenth century had been finding published expression in dialect glossaries.[28] The feature of this tradition which is of interest in the present context is the way in which, certainly from the early nineteenth century, it embraced the idea of collaboration, and in particular the idea that the lexis of particular regions, as collected and presented by individual scholars, could then be aggregated into some kind of national compilation of 'archaic and provincial words'—a formula, used in the titles of several dialect glossaries,[29] which clearly reflects the widespread view that in regional dialects could be found preserved traces of older components of the language. As early as 1829 one such glossarist, the Yorkshireman Joseph Hunter, commenting on the recent publication of a number of dialect glossaries, looked forward to the time when 'all these fragments shall have been gathered up and prepared for the use of critics on our early writers, and especially of those persons who may hereafter undertake the arduous task of preparing a systematic and historical Dictionary of the English Language'.[30] Belief in the benefits to be derived from the gathering up of what has been

---

[26] Garnett (1835: 330).

[27] The commencement of work on the *Deutsches Wörterbuch* was noticed in the *Foreign Quarterly Review* of Jan. 1839, p. 253, although its first volume did not appear in print for another fourteen years. Émile Littré made the first proposals for what would become his four-volume *Dictionnaire de la langue française* in 1841, although the idea was to lie dormant for several years; the great *Woordenboek der Nederlandsche Taal* (published 1864–1998) grew out of proposals made at a conference in Ghent in 1849. Alan Kirkness has written extensively on the history and methodology of the *Deutsches Wörterbuch*; see in particular Kirkness (1980), on the early period (down to the death of Jakob Grimm in 1863), and (in English, with much interesting detail about the surviving source materials from this period) Kirkness (2015). For an overview of the whole project down to the present see Kirkness (2012).

[28] On this topic see also Gilliver (2011). Penhallurick (2009) usefully surveys the history of dialect dictionaries.

[29] The earliest seems to have been the posthumous edition of Jonathan Boucher's collections; the antiquaries Joseph Hunter and Joseph Stevenson prepared these for publication in 1832–3 under the title 'Boucher's Glossary of Archaic and Provincial Words'.

[30] Hunter (1829: xx).

called 'scattered erudition'[31] can also be seen in the success of the journal *Notes and Queries*, which began to appear in 1849 and quickly became an important forum for the sharing of information among antiquarians and, significantly, students of the history of English.

When the Philological Society was founded in the spring of 1842,[32] it might be supposed from its stated objects—'the investigation of the Structure, the Affinities and the History of Languages; and the Philological Illustration of the Classical Writers of Greece and Rome'—that the study of English dialects, and the compilation of a dictionary of these, would not have been of particular interest to its members. However, although it is true that from the beginning papers on classical and comparative philology were regularly read to the Society, the English language rapidly emerged as a major preoccupation: a development which is hardly surprising given the presence among the Society's original members of so many key figures in the field of English language study. These include the lexicographers Joseph Bosworth and Charles Richardson, the Anglo-Saxonists John Kemble and Benjamin Thorpe, and also the professor of English language and literature at University College London, Robert Latham, who may have chosen the subject of 'the dialects of the Papuan or Negrito race' for the very first paper to be read before the Society, but who would have been better known to his audience as the author of *The English Language* (1841), a voluminous, well-informed, and extremely popular account of its subject.[33] Many other founder members were also alumni of Trinity College, Cambridge, including four—J. C. Hare, Henry Malden, Connop Thirlwall, and William Whewell—who in the early 1830s had formed a short-lived 'Etymological Society' at Cambridge, of particular interest because, as Whewell later recalled, it had conceived 'a grand, but I fear hopeless, scheme of a new Etymological Dictionary of the English language'.[34] Finally there was Richard Garnett, who in 1843 read to the Society what was to be the first of a series of papers on 'the Languages and Dialects of the British Islands'. It is also noteworthy that in 1843 Jakob and Wilhelm Grimm were both made honorary members.[35]

Consequently, when in January 1844 George Cornewall Lewis, another founder member (and the compiler of a well-received glossary of Herefordshire dialect), wrote to the Society's Council drawing their attention to 'a subject of great importance,

---

[31] I owe this apt phrase to John Considine (private communication), who also drew my attention to the flourishing of *Notes & Queries* as another manifestation of enthusiasm for collaborative research in the mid-nineteenth century.

[32] For an account of the early history of the Philological Society—and of an earlier, short-lived society of the same name, formed in 1830 by Friedrich Rosen (see p. 2 above) and two of his colleagues at University College London—see Marshall (2006).

[33] Latham's book was imbued with the 'new philology' of Rask and Grimm, as he readily acknowledged in his Preface, in which he also expressed 'the anxious wish and firm hope, that the very foundation of accurate Etymology, the study of existing processes, should be begun by Englishmen, continued by Englishmen, and exhausted by Englishmen' (Latham 1841: viii). He would soon become equally well known as an ethnologist, with a particular interest in human origins.

[34] 6 Feb. 1852 W. Whewell to Edwin Guest, printed in ProcPS 20 Feb. 1852, pp. 133–42.

[35] ProcPS 24 Mar. 1843, p. 77; 8 Dec. 1843, p. 149.

namely, the compilation of a dictionary devoted to the archaic and provincial terms of the English language', he would have been confident of receiving a sympathetic hearing.[36] Indeed, at the meeting which considered his letter, it was observed that the Society 'possessed within itself facilities for carrying such an object into effect, which were not probably at the command of any single individual', and the Council made it known that they were happy to receive, from all quarters, 'any information which might tend to illustrate the past or present condition of our provincial dialects': in particular, any lists of local dialect words, such as were being collected by many enthusiasts, and which might be made use of in compiling such a dictionary. A few months later—stung into further action, perhaps, by an article in the *Edinburgh Review* which specifically called upon the Society to undertake the compilation of 'an Archaic Dictionary of the English Language'[37]—they took the further step of issuing a circular inviting all and sundry to send in their observations on local dialect, with the intention that these would be incorporated in 'a Dictionary of British Provincialisms, on a more extensive scale than has hitherto been accomplished'.[38] This initiative ultimately came to nothing, although for a few years manuscript dialect glossaries were presented at the Society's meetings;[39] but the idea that the lexicographical efforts of individuals might be seen as contributions to some grand collective project gained some currency. Some were even moved to use newly grandiose language to describe the idea. In 1846 a new work on Cornish dialect was described in the *Gentleman's Magazine* as 'another welcome little contribution towards a "Dictionarium totius Anglicitatis"'; and in 1848 A. B. Evans, the compiler of a glossary of Leicestershire dialect, suggested that such works 'may assist the labours of some great Lexicographer [...] who shall, it is hoped, at no very distant day, compile a work, now greatly to be desired, if not indispensable in a language like the English [...]: I mean a "*Thesaurus, sive Lexicon, totius Anglicitatis*", or, *Complete Glossary of the English language*.'[40]

---

[36] *Ibid.* 26 Jan. 1844, p. 169. Cornewall Lewis had also been a contributor to the *Philological Museum*, a short-lived journal (1831–3) which had also published articles by members of the Cambridge Etymological Society. See Stray (2004), esp. pp. 302–5.

[37] *Edinburgh Review* Apr. 1844, p. 471. The call came in the course of a long article on 'Provincialisms of the European Languages'; the author is identified as C. H. Hartshorne in the *Wellesley Index to Victorian Periodicals*.

[38] The only copy of the circular, dated 20 August 1844, which I have been able to locate is bound into a volume of the Society's *Proceedings* in the possession of the Library of the University of Michigan; I am grateful to the librarians at Michigan for sending me a scanned image of this copy. The circular's contents were reproduced in various contemporary journals (see e.g. *Critic* Aug. 1844, p. 53; *Archaeological Journal* 2 (1845), pp. 88, 116).

[39] Glossaries of Kent and Hampshire dialect were presented at the meeting on 9 May 1845, followed by others in 1845, 1846, 1847, and 1850; thereafter provincialisms were only occasionally mentioned among the 'Philological Scraps' printed in the Society's *Proceedings*. As late as 1855 a work on Norfolk dialect was submitted to the Society 'in consequence of the Circular requesting that Members should collect peculiar words current in their respective districts' (*TPS* for 1855, p. 29).

[40] *Gentleman's Magazine* Aug. 1846, p. 178; Evans (1848: xi–xii). These Latin expressions are an allusion (explicitly in Evans's case) to Jacopo Facciolati and Egidio Forcellini's comprehensive *Totius Latinitatis Lexicon* of 1771.

Enthusiasm for such a national project, and for the idea of collective endeavour, lingered among some members of the Philological Society; and in February 1852 it was given something of a boost by the arrival of a letter from William Whewell describing the earlier activities of the Cambridge Etymological Society, and its ambition to compile 'a new Etymological Dictionary'. The letter provoked 'a long and interesting conversation as to the best mode of promoting the objects of English scholarship'; the Cambridge approach of dividing the lexicon into classes of words which individual members would undertake to investigate—another implementation of the cooperative ideal—was praised as promising 'advantages that could not be expected from the isolated efforts of individuals'.[41]

One Philological Society member who might have been expected to respond enthusiastically to talk of collaborative scholarly endeavour—one, indeed, whose response to almost anything seems to have been characterized by passionate enthusiasm—was the man whose involvement with the *Oxford English Dictionary* during much of the later nineteenth century was arguably to be greater than that of any other individual. Frederick Furnivall, who had joined the Society in 1847, was one of the most extraordinary characters to be found in the world of Victorian men of letters, a world which frequently found him impossible to deal with but which owed a great deal to the energy with which he pursued various projects, notably the founding of numerous literary societies, including the Early English Text Society, for which he edited a prodigious number of Middle English and early modern texts. His boundless but frequently unfocused energy, which landed him in many scrapes during his own lifetime, has led many writers into rather over-coloured descriptions of him; one which captures something of the spirit of the man without tipping over into caricature is that by John Gross, of 'one of the great rock-blasting entrepreneurs of Victorian scholarship, the kind of man who if his energies had taken another turn might have covered a continent with railways'.[42] In 1852 the young Furnivall's energies were still largely taken up with Christian socialism, workers' education, and the cooperative and labour movements (while he was also practising, without much enthusiasm, as a barrister); but he was becoming increasingly interested in literary matters, and was soon to become a prominent member of the Philological Society, becoming its joint secretary in 1853.

Despite the Philological Society's 'long and interesting conversation' of February 1852, there were no specific new proposals to revive the flagging national dictionary project. The lack of a suitable editor may have been a problem, although there were a number of active and successful lexicographers among the Society's members who

---

[41] ProcPS 20 Feb. 1852, p. 142. Interestingly, the *Proceedings* for 1852 make no mention of the publication of the eagerly anticipated (and well-received) first instalment of the *Deutsches Wörterbuch* in the summer of that year.

[42] Gross (1969: 169). Benzie (1983) remains the standard biography of Furnivall, though it was severely criticized by Aarsleff (1985), not least for its uncritical use of earlier accounts given in Munro et al. (1911).

might have undertaken the task. One such was Charles Richardson, who though in his late seventies was still an active scholar; however, the book that he produced in 1854 gives grounds for relief that he did not do so. Entitled *On the Study of Language*, it was an exposition of the principles of Horne Tooke's *Diversions of Purley*—principles of which he proudly professed to have made 'constant, and I trust not unsuccessful' use in the compilation of his own dictionary, which was still being regularly reprinted.[43] He was also at work on a supplement to his dictionary, which appeared in 1856.[44] It may be significant in this context that an interleaved copy of 'Richardson's English Dictionary' (presumably including the new supplement) was presented to the Philological Society in February 1857 by its publishers, Bell and Daldy, 'on the condition that they might be allowed to use any notes made in it'.[45] There is no surviving documentation to indicate whether this was with a view to collecting material for a new edition—to be edited by Richardson or a successor—or whether it was in connection with the Society's own ambitions for a national dictionary. Either way, it is tempting to see a connection between this and the more significant events that took place at meetings of the Society over the next few months; however, as the fate of this interleaved dictionary is unknown, one can only speculate.

Of more definite significance was the admission to the Philological Society at its next two meetings of two new members: another young barrister with linguistic interests, and the recently appointed Dean of Westminster. The first of these was the 26-year-old Herbert Coleridge, the exceptionally brilliant grandson of the poet, who, as James McKusick has observed, 'was deeply instilled with a knowledge of his grandfather's accomplishments and determined to carry on his legacy in the field of historical linguistics';[46] while still a schoolboy at Eton he had already begun to learn various modern languages, including Icelandic.

The second new member of the Society is someone whom it is something of a surprise not to find among its founder members, given his close association with his fellow Trinity College alumni Hare, Kemble, and Thirlwall. It is true that Richard Chenevix Trench was not resident in London until the spring of 1857, having previously held the rectorship of Itchen Stoke in Hampshire; but he had been a regular visitor, not least in his capacity as professor of divinity at King's College London. He had known Furnivall at least since 1853, and possibly long before then through his friendship with F. D. Maurice, whom he had known since his undergraduate days.[47]

---

[43] Richardson (1854: xiii).

[44] Richardson may perhaps have been pushed into producing a supplement by the appearance in 1855 of a supplement to John Ogilvie's very successful two-volume *Imperial Dictionary* (1847–50).

[45] *TPS* for 1857, p. 139. Richardson himself had presented a copy of his dictionary to the Society in 1844 (ProcPS 9 Feb. 1844, p. 181).

[46] *TPS* for 1857, p. 139 (meetings of 19 Feb. and 5 Mar.); McKusick (2009: 584). Coleridge, like Furnivall, specialized in conveyancing, and may have known him professionally.

[47] The standard biography is Bromley (1959). Trench, Kemble, and Maurice were also all members of the secret Cambridge Society known as the Apostles, who were at the time much influenced by Coleridge.

FIGURE 1 The Unregistered Words Committee: (a) Frederick Furnivall, (b) Herbert Coleridge, (c) Richard Chenevix Trench.

As might be expected, Trench had a number of theological works to his name; but he had also written two immensely successful books on language, *On the Study of Words* (1851) and *English Past and Present* (1855), which had played an important role in popularizing language study in Britain,[48] as well as winning him considerable prominence in the field. For Trench philology and theology were intimately bound up with one another: the study of words was for him 'a source of moral and religious instruction and contemplation'.[49] At the time of his joining the Philological Society he had almost completed work on another book, *A Select Glossary of English Words Used Formerly in Senses Different from their Present*, in which he set out to exploit the instructive potential he saw in the study of how words might change in meaning.[50] The semantic changes undergone by each word selected were copiously illustrated with quotations taken from texts he had examined in the course of an extensive programme of reading. In many cases the earlier meanings were ones which he had been unable to find in any dictionary.

It is hardly surprising that such an eminent figure was elected to the Society's Council at its 'Anniversary Meeting' on 21 May.[51] Coleridge was also made a Council

[48] Hans Aarsleff suggests that 'without that popularity it seems unlikely that the *New English Dictionary* would have been able both to get the readers it needed and to arouse the general interest which sustained it' (Aarsleff 1967: 235).

[49] Aarsleff (1990: 154). Trench's approach to the study of language, which can also be found in the writings of Hare and Maurice, and which unsurprisingly owes much to Coleridge's concept of words as 'living growths, offlets, and organs of the human soul', has even been called 'Broad Church philology' (Morris 2004).

[50] Although not published until 1859, Trench's book was, according to his Preface, completed 'in all essential parts' two years earlier.

[51] *TPS* for 1857, pp. 139–40. The 'Anniversary Meetings', which were effectively AGMs, were so called in commemoration of the Society's inaugural meeting on 18 May 1842.

member, having lost no time in making his mark, with two papers to his name, the first ('On the termination -*let* in English') being delivered only a month after joining the Society.

The precise sequence of events which followed is hard to reconstruct, but it seems that at some point in May 1857 a new conception of the Society's long-cherished idea of a national dictionary came into being. This was probably at, or shortly after, the Anniversary Meeting, at which a general discussion took place on the present state of English lexicography, a topic never far from the thoughts of Society members like Furnivall. It would have been natural for Trench to say something in such a discussion about his experiences in collecting evidence of unrecorded meanings for his own *Select Glossary*; and even more natural for Furnivall, with his passionate belief in the value of collective effort, to consider how much more might be done in this regard if a large number of people could be mobilized and organized to do further research of the same kind. He evidently made some kind of specific proposal along these lines to Trench, who wrote to him a few days later:

I [. . .] shall be very glad to share in so good a work. I will between this & that think over the books which seem to me likely to render up the amplest harvest of words, which as yet have been unregistered. I am sure the incomings may be very large, though doubtless they cannot be gathered in without industry & pains.[52]

Trench was unable to attend the Society's next meeting on 4 June, but on 18 June it was announced that the Society's Council had appointed Coleridge, Furnivall, and Trench (see Figure 1) 'as a Committee to collect unregistered words in English', and that the Committee would report to the Society at its next meeting in November.[53] By 'unregistered' was meant that a word (or meaning) was not to be found either in Richardson's newly supplemented dictionary, or in Todd's edition of Johnson. This was explained, along with instructions for how evidence was to be collected—namely by reading and excerpting selected texts—in a circular issued by the new Unregistered Words Committee in July, which was reprinted in various public journals,[54] and whose wording clearly evoked both Furnivall's co-operativist philosophy and the nationalist sentiment of the Society's earlier grand project. Noting how far the dictionaries of Johnson and Richardson fell short of being 'a "*Lexicon totius Anglicitatis*"', it invited volunteers to take part in 'the collection of materials towards the completion of this

---

[52] MP 29 May 1857 Trench to FJF. This seems to corroborate the provisional acknowledgement of Furnivall's role made in the 'Historical Introduction' to the *OED* which was published with the first Supplement in 1933: '[the appointment of the Unregistered Words Committee was] apparently as the result of a suggestion made by F. J. Furnivall to Dean Trench in May' (Craigie 1933a: vii).

[53] *TPS* for 1857, p. 141.

[54] For example in the *Athenaeum* of 25 July and *Notes & Queries* of 1 August. The notice in the *Literary Gazette* of 8 August (p. 759) presented the circular under the heading 'The Proposed New English Dictionary'. A copy of the original July version of the circular itself is preserved in JMA, and a proof and revise of the August version (see below) in OUPA (OED/B/1/1/1).

truly national work', a task whose success would be dependent on it being 'undertaken by several persons, acting in concert on a fixed and uniform system'. A long list of 'Works and Authors [...] suggested for examination' was included (although it was 'not by any means intended to limit the discretion of Collectors in this respect'); remarkably, over 40 individuals—less than a third of whom were members of the Society—were listed as having already volunteered to take up particular texts for reading.[55] Two pages of the circular were given over to 'Rules and Directions for Collectors', evidently with a view to establishing the necessary 'fixed and uniform system'.

Despite the professedly grand scope of this new project, its initial focus, as set out in the circular, was strikingly restricted in comparison with what came later. The search for words was to be '*primarily* directed to the less-read authors of the 16th and 17th centuries [...] The vast number of genuine English words and phrases, scattered over such works as the Translations of Philemon Holland, Henry More's Works, Hacket's Life of Williams, &c., which have not hitherto found their way into our Dictionaries [...] would probably pass the belief of most persons who have never been engaged in the perusal of these old works, or have never tested the incompleteness of our Dictionaries by their aid.' There was also to be a defined canon of literature: in order for an author's works to be taken up, he or she had first to be 'admitted to the rank of a Dictionary authority'. Not that this was to be a 'literary' canon: Hakluyt's Voyages, Pepys's diaries, and a Declaration by Charles I appeared alongside poems, plays, essays, and translations in the list of works already undertaken, and the list of suggested reading included the Paston Letters, State papers, and accounts of Parliamentary debates. Moreover, once an author or work had been admitted, 'all unregistered words, *without exception*, used by that author, or in that work, ought to be registered'—a stipulation with intimidating practical implications.

The initial response of the public was encouraging. By August Herbert Coleridge, who had been appointed the Committee's secretary, could report that almost all the works listed in the circular, and many more, had been undertaken by volunteers, 'and every day brings four or five fresh offers of co-operation.' This was recounted in a letter published in the *Athenaeum* on 8 August, in which Coleridge displays (not for the last time) what appears to be extraordinary optimism regarding the task ahead: the collection of material could be brought to a close after two years, after which 'the difficulty of arranging the crude mass into dictionary order will be comparatively

---

[55] The appeal to individuals had begun as early as 11 July, when Coleridge sent a proof copy of the circular to the pioneering photographer Henry Fox Talbot, inviting him to take up one of the works listed. This was evidently part of a concerted campaign by the Committee, which, as Coleridge explained to Fox Talbot, was 'anxious to shew as large a list of "works undertaken" as possible' (11 July 1857 HC to H. Fox Talbot; 'Correspondence of William Henry Fox Talbot' project (online: foxtalbot.dmu.ac.uk), document 10049). Fox Talbot, a founder member of the Society and indeed a keen amateur etymologist, does not seem to have accepted Coleridge's invitation.

light'.[56] The optimism is, however, less reckless than it seems. In the same letter Coleridge writes approvingly of the Supplement to Richardson's Dictionary: it is 'an excellent model for such a work as that which we proposed, and to the external form of that publication we desire as nearly as possible to assimilate our own.' It is clear that Coleridge, at least, was still envisaging a dictionary of comparatively limited scope. Most of the entries in Richardson's Supplement consist simply of a headword followed by one or more quotations; there are a small number of completely new entries, and some which add additional cognates or a cross-reference, but the great majority of the entries have no etymologies or definition, and as such must have been fairly straightforward to compile. The *Athenaeum* letter also included a list of those works which had already been taken up for reading, and a new list of further suitable works from the early modern period.

Whether or not Coleridge's concept of the work differed from that of Furnivall and Trench, the Committee were already beginning to revise their ideas. Only a few days after Coleridge's letter appeared in the *Athenaeum*, a revised version of the circular was issued, noting that 'owing to the great amount of friendly cooperation which the Committee have received since the first issue of the proposal, the scheme has assumed far larger dimensions than was at first anticipated'; the Committee now aspired to 'a thorough investigation [...] of *all* the early English literature, from Robert of Gloucester down to the end of the 17th century'. Nor was the project to be limited to the medieval and early modern periods:

although [...] the Committee wish principally to direct the attention of Contributors to the Elizabethan and earlier times, they will gladly receive the results of any examination of the chief classics of the present century, such as Wordsworth, Coleridge, Shelley, Byron, Walter Scott, Southey, and the leading writers of the Victorian era (except Sir A. Alison), provided only that such examination be *complete*, so as not to leave the work hereafter to be done over again by any future Lexicographer.[57]

The wording is strongly suggestive of Furnivall: one wonders whether Trench or Coleridge had the same enthusiasm for such an expansion of horizons.

---

[56] *Athenaeum* 8 Aug. 1857, pp. 1007–8. Coleridge was in fact responding to a concern expressed the previous week by the literary scholar J. O. Halliwell-Phillipps (writing as 'A Student'; 1 Aug., pp. 976–7) that 'in attempting too much, a risk of failure may be incurred'. The writer's suggestion that occasional volumes be published, containing 'the best portions of the materials selected as they come to hand' and indexed, was dismissed. Halliwell-Phillipps, who had himself compiled a successful dictionary of 'Archaic and Provincial Words', subsequently loaned several books for the use of the Dictionary (Spevack 2001: 280).

[57] While the exclusion of the prolix historian Sir Archibald Alison might have been made because someone had already offered to read his works, Alison is not mentioned in any of the various lists of texts being read that date from this period. The approximately 270 quotations from his works that eventually appeared in the first edition of the Dictionary appear to have been largely contributed by the Somerset schoolmaster Arthur Henry Coombs, who began reading sometime after 1879.

cradlehood

Some of the quotation slips sent in to the Unregistered Words Committee in 1857 by the first cohort of volunteer readers, and quoted by Herbert Coleridge in his report, are still preserved among the slips that subsequently formed part of the printer's copy for the first edition of the Dictionary as eventually published decades later. For example, when James Murray came to work on words beginning with *cr-* in 1892 he found awaiting him a quotation for the rare word *cradlehood* which had been excerpted from Thomas Nashe's *Lenten Stuffe* thirty-five years earlier by one of the very earliest volunteer readers for the Dictionary (see Figure 2). The Yorkshire clergyman and topographer Jonathan Eastwood had undertaken to read several texts within weeks of the formation of the Committee, and is listed in the July Circular as the reader of tracts by Nashe and others. Although this seems to have been the only quotation available to Murray for the word, he decided that its continuing currency needed to be illustrated by a concocted 'modern' quotation (see p. 144); thus the published entry concludes with '*Mod.* From the stage of cradlehood to extreme old age'. Among other quotations contributed by Eastwood which were mentioned in Coleridge's report, and which went on to appear in Dictionary entries for the words in question, are examples of the rare word *losthope* ('an abandoned person') and of the word *ignorant* used in the obsolete sense 'unknown'. Coleridge's 1857 report also occasionally cited quotations which he had himself collected, such as the quotation for *dromundaries* (referring to a kind of ship more usually called a *dromon* or *dromond*), which Coleridge took from Christopher Watson's 1568 translation of Polybius, and which went on to be included by Murray in his entry for *dromedary* in 1897.

The first of the Philological Society's winter meetings took place on 5 November. However, contrary to what had been advertised, the report of the Unregistered Words Committee was not given at this meeting. Coleridge, as the Committee's secretary, would eventually present this report four weeks later; but on 5 November he made way for the first part of a quite different paper by Trench, entitled 'On some Deficiencies in our English Dictionaries'. The second part followed on 19 November.[58]

What was the reason for this change of plan? Trench was, after all, a member of the Unregistered Words Committee, and at first glance it is hard to see why the Committee should have decided that a paper written by one of their number should displace their no doubt eagerly anticipated report. Trench does seem to have been less involved with the practical work of the Committee—recruiting and corresponding with volunteers, and processing the flood of paper slips on which they sent in their quotations—than Furnivall and Coleridge during the summer and autumn of 1857. This was perhaps to

---

[58] *TPS* for 1857, p. 141. It is possible that Trench was not present to read the first part of his paper himself: Coleridge is named as the reader of the paper at the 5 November meeting in one contemporary account, although this was admittedly in a foreign journal (*Archiv für das Studium der neueren Sprachen und Literaturen* 23 (1858), pp. 208–10) and may have been garbled.

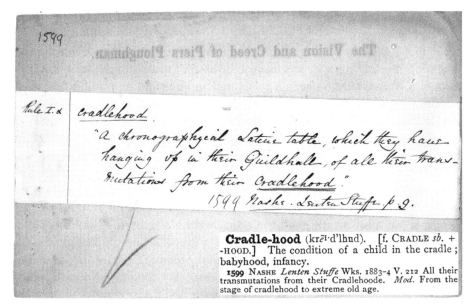

FIGURE 2   One of the first quotation slips, contributed by Jonathan Eastwood in 1857 for the word *cradlehood*, and subsequently used in the Dictionary entry for the word when eventually published (see inset).

be expected: as a newly appointed Dean of Westminster he must have had much else to deal with during this time. A sense of distance, almost of semi-detachment, is even to be found in the opening pages of his paper, in which he does not identify himself as a member of the Committee, describing himself only as '[t]aking a lively interest in this effort', and insisting that his views have been formed without so much as looking at any of the material so far collected.[59]

This is not to say, however, that Trench should be seen as taking up a different position from that of his fellow Committee members. On the contrary, the opening words of the report that was eventually read on 3 December[60] make it clear that the Committee were of one mind: 'We propose [...] to request the Society to consider the statements and views contained in that [i.e. Trench's] paper, although emanating from

[59] Trench (1857: 1–2). Cf. also Walter Skeat's later recollection (in Munro et al. 1911: 174–5): 'the commencement of the work [...] received, at the first, much efficient support from such advisers [*sic*] as Dr. Guest and Archbishop Trench. The two men who made themselves chiefly responsible for the work of collection were Herbert Coleridge and Furnivall.'

[60] The draft text of the report (hereafter UWC Report) is preserved in OUPA at OED/B/1/1/2. This 38-page manuscript, although largely in Coleridge's hand, was evidently circulated to Furnivall for comment, as there are pencilled comments by Furnivall which Coleridge has taken up in some rewritten passages. None of the annotations can confidently be assigned to Trench, so he may not have been involved in this round of rewording. The report was clearly written out after Trench had delivered both parts of his paper.

one of us only, as an expression of the unanimous opinion of the whole Committee.' It may rather have been a case of strategic division of labour: Trench—whose reputation as a published writer on language was such that any pronouncement he chose to make on the subject of lexicography was likely to be listened to attentively—would deliver a theoretical disquisition, backed up by his own findings, and the position he had set out could then be further substantiated by the practical findings of the two younger men. The fact that the task with which the Committee had been entrusted was, as all three of them were aware, likely to be vast made it all the more important that the matter be presented to the Society in the most effective (and least intimidating) way possible.

Trench's paper, then, was unquestionably crucial in preparing the ground for the next stage in the Philological Society's grand project. However, the fact that the text of his paper was subsequently published, whereas the Unregistered Committee's joint report was not, may have concealed from posterity the collective nature of some of the thinking which went into the earliest versions of the future *OED*'s theoretical under-pinning. Trench's role in the history of the Dictionary has certainly on occasion been overstated; accordingly, both 'On some Deficiencies' and the Committee's December report merit careful examination.

Trench lists the 'Deficiencies' he has identified under seven heads, and subjects each to a lengthy exposition, illustrated with copious examples. This detailed discussion is prefaced by a more general statement of what, in Trench's view, should be regarded as 'the true *idea* of a Dictionary', namely that it should be 'an inventory of the language [...] a historical monument, the history of a nation contemplated from one point of view'. This much-quoted passage is at least as important, in terms of its impact, as any of the 'Deficiencies' that follow. This is true even though, as Aarsleff has observed, there was nothing particularly new in it. Enthusiasts for the 'new philology' had been advocating an evidence-based approach to language study to English readers long before Trench's own earlier books had helped to focus popular attention on the history of English in particular; and among those with a classical education Liddell and Scott's Greek dictionary had shown what could be achieved by applying this approach to lexi-cography. Indeed, the wording of the Committee's original circular, and the manner in which they had gone about their work, shows clearly that there was already widespread acceptance of the importance of collecting objective data as a first stage in the compi-lation of the projected '*lexicon totius Anglicitatis*'. In his characterization of the ideal dictionary as 'an inventory of the language', and of the lexicographer as 'an historian of [the language], not a critic', Trench was, in a way, simply restating and rejustifying the terms of the project upon which the Committee had already embarked, in language which vividly brought home both the validity of the approach and its full implications. The latter were further emphasized in the concluding section of the paper, in which, having established the desirability of comprehensiveness as an ideal, he spelt out what this could mean in practice: only by the marshalling of a veritable army of volunteers could the whole historical record of English lexis be adequately trawled—a process which he memorably described as 'this drawing as with a sweep-net over the whole surface of English literature'—thereby bringing together the raw material for 'that complete inventory of our English tongue [...] which we ought not to rest satisfied until we possess.'[61]

Modern readers will have no difficulty with Trench's statement of his overall lexicographical ideal; indeed, so much of the historical lexicography carried out during the century and a half since he wrote his paper has sought to put these descriptive principles into practice that it is hard to imagine them being questioned. The same is true of some, but not all, of the seven categories with which his paper is mainly taken up.[62] These categories are: (i) the patchy and inconsistent way in which obsolete words are registered; (ii) the inclusion of only some of the members of 'families or groups of words'; (iii) the failure to record the earliest known instances of the occurrences of many words, and of the latest known instances of words now obsolete; (iv) the omission of important senses of some words, including in some cases the earliest sense; (v) the lack of attention paid to the distinguishing of synonymous words; (vi) the failure to include 'many passages in our literature [...] which might be usefully adduced in illustration of the first introduction, etymology, and meaning of words'; and (vii) the inclusion in dictionaries of some words 'which have properly no claim to find room in their pages'.

The assertion that a historical dictionary should aim to include words and senses throughout the period covered, and in each case to give the earliest documentation available—which is effectively equivalent to the first, third, and fourth categories combined—would be hard to disagree with.[63] (Of course, the Unregistered Words Committee had already specifically noted the desirability of collecting antedatings, postdatings, and unrecorded senses in their July circular.) That being said, Trench makes an important and distinctly problematic point in his discussion of the first category. Having asserted the importance of adequately registering obsolete words, he then declares that '*provincial* or *local* words stand [...] on quite a different footing': such words, indeed, 'have no right to a place in a Dictionary of the English tongue'

---

[61] Trench (1857: 4, 6, 57) ('drawing with a sweep-net' is Trench's gloss of the Greek word σαγηνεύειν, which he cites in connection with a story in Herodotus' *Histories* of how a group of Persian soldiers scoured an island by traversing it in an unbroken line from coast to coast); Aarsleff (1967: 261). In his 1860 revision of his paper, Trench was still more explicit about the practical implications of comprehensiveness (p. 69): 'If, therefore, we count it worth while to have all words, we can only have them by reading all books; this is the price which we must be content to pay.'

[62] Zgusta (1989: 226) identifies eleven 'requirements' made by Trench (by subdividing some of the main 'Deficiencies'), and claims that five of them are not adhered to in *OED*, although in several cases his interpretation seems questionable, as for example his assertion that *OED* does not include completely obsolete senses of a word.

[63] It is in his discussion of the fourth 'Deficiency' that Trench perhaps comes closest to a statement of Passow's idea of the 'life history' of a word, though significantly it is not to Passow but to an insight of Samuel Coleridge (from his *Aids to Reflection*) that he refers: 'It is one of the primary demands which we make upon a Dictionary, that it should thus present us with the history of words, the significant phases of meaning through which they have travelled. It was a remark of Coleridge, that you might often learn more from the history of a word than from the history of a campaign; and this is true' (Trench 1857: 34).

unless they were once in general use, in which case, having now 'retreated to remoter districts', they merit inclusion 'not [...] in right of what they now are, but of what they once have been'.[64] A dictionary compiled on this basis would surely fall far short of being a '*lexicon totius Anglicitatis*'. Trench's second point, that each documented member of a 'family' of words (meaning the group of words formed on a given head-word by suffixation or compounding) merits separate consideration, seems reasonable enough, and his fifth point, as to the desirability of distinguishing synonyms, would no doubt be widely accepted as a general lexicographical principle; but the sixth and seventh categories are more problematic. Did he really mean, on the one hand, that there are certain quotations which a dictionary simply *must* include, and on the other that there are areas of vocabulary which are beyond any dictionary's remit?

Trench divides the quotations in his sixth category into three types, namely those illustrative of 'the first introduction, etymology, and meaning of words. [...] There are passages for one cause or another so classical, in respect of certain words, that it would be a manifest defect if they were omitted.' (Again, the Unregistered Words Committee had already noted the value of evidence illustrating incompletely naturalized forms.) To a modern historical lexicographer this privileging of particular instances of words seems very odd indeed. Admittedly the earliest known example of a word or sense has a special claim for inclusion; but the value, as historical evidence, of quotations which 'consciously discuss, or unconsciously reveal' etymology, and those which contain 'happy definitions or explanations', is arguably lessened by their self-conscious nature. Such quotations are of course very evident in the pages of Richardson's Dictionary, and perhaps it is too much to expect Trench to break free at one bound from the idea, explicitly espoused by both Richardson and Johnson, that quotations should serve such purposes. But the idea that the generous inclusion of such 'happy' quotations is the mark of a good dictionary is certainly a long way from the neutral recording of a word's history.[65]

It is arguably in Trench's final category that we find the greatest departure from the principles on which the *OED* was eventually based.[66] The remark that 'a Dictionary ought to know its own limits' can of course be understood in a practical sense; indeed James Murray said something similar in his 'General Explanations' nearly thirty years later.[67] But Trench's delimitation of the bounds of his ideal Dictionary was not practical, but ideological. His detailed discussion of this point makes this clear: there were, he observed, words which by their very nature did not qualify for inclusion. He makes the point several times, and with some force: such words are 'foreign and extraneous matter [...] mere intruders and interlopers'; lexicographers should 'throw overboard that which never had any claim to make part of their cargo'. He reserved especial contempt for technical words, the inclusion of which was 'the most mischievous shape

---

[64] *Ibid.* 12.
[65] *Ibid.* 39, 41, 42.
[66] *Ibid.* 44–51.
[67] Murray (1884: vii): 'practical utility has some bounds, and a Dictionary has definite limits.'

which this error [of over-inclusiveness] assumes'; such words were 'not for the most part, except by an abuse of language, words at all, but signs; having been deliberately invented as the nomenclature, and, so to speak, the algebraic notation of some special art or science, and having never passed the threshold of this, nor mingled with the general family of words.' The incorporation of such words could often be attributed to 'barren ostentation'; they were 'disfigurements of the work which they profess to complete. Let such be reserved for a technological lexicon by themselves; such a supplement to the Dictionary of the Academy has lately been published in France; but in a Dictionary of the language they are a mere incumbrance, troubling the idea of the book, occupying precious room to which they have no manner of claim, and which will be abundantly needed for that which has.' He went on to criticize Johnson and Webster in turn for including such words—citing as examples many which could hardly be excluded by any dictionary aspiring to comprehensiveness, including *zeugma*, *steatoma*, *acroteria*, and *zygomatic*. (Richardson is applauded for having 'thrown overboard far the greater part of this rubbish', but even he has succumbed to the supposedly specious claims of words such as *oedematous*.)

The surviving records give no indication of which parts of Trench's paper engendered most discussion, but it certainly met with a warm reception; indeed, the Society immediately prevailed upon him to publish it.[68] An atmosphere of heightened anticipation must surely have surrounded the Unregistered Words Committee's postponed report, which was finally read by Coleridge on 3 December. This meeting, however, was the occasion for another unexpected announcement, namely that 'a larger scheme, for a completely new English Dictionary'—rather than a supplement to existing dictionaries—'might shortly be submitted to the Society'. In consequence of this momentous announcement, the Committee's report, rather than being formally adopted, was 'received and laid on the table'.[69] There is no definite record of who made the announcement, but although it has sometimes been thought to be Trench, the weight of evidence seems to favour giving the credit to Furnivall.[70]

---

[68] *TPS* for 1857, p. 141. Although the earliest printed copies of Trench's paper are dated 1857 on the title page, the wording of its closing pages strongly suggests that it was not issued until January 1858.

[69] *TPS* for 1857, p. 142.

[70] Aarsleff, for example, credits Trench as the source of 'the chief impulse to the making of the new dictionary' (1967: 258), citing a passage from James Murray's 1900 Romanes Lecture, in which, however, Murray notes only that 'from this impulse [i.e. that given by Trench in his paper] arose the movement which, widened and directed by much practical experience, has culminated in the preparation of the Oxford English Dictionary' (Murray 1900: 45–6). Murray's version of events was of course second-hand, as he did not join the Philological Society until 1868. In a longer account (in Munro et al. 1911: 122–6) he was more explicit about his lack of first-hand knowledge, but did set down what he knew about the project's origins. He recorded the connection of Coleridge and Trench with 'the initial impulse in the society's work of collecting materials for a new English dictionary', but notes: 'I have always understood [...] that this extension of the scheme from a mere supplement to a new dictionary was mainly urged and carried by Dr. Furnivall, that it was not favoured by Dr. Trench, and that, at first at least, Mr. Coleridge was not very keen about it. Furnivall had even then done work at Early English (which Trench's studies did not specially include) and he realized more than his colleagues how much that was not supplemental but altogether new, needed to be done.' Further evidence is to be found in a very late alteration to the wording

The Committee's report, then, might be said to have been overtaken by events; but as a complementary document to 'On some Deficiencies', it deserves attention. In its opening pages, in particular, there is much that rounds out our knowledge of the lines along which Trench, Coleridge, and Furnivall had been thinking during this crucial period in the genesis of the Dictionary. As already noted, it begins with a formal association of the whole Committee with the views expressed in Trench's paper; this was made the starting point for the exposition of a 'lexicographical Creed', which sought to clarify and expand upon the key questions of inclusiveness and authority. Trench had been explicit on the first of these: the maker of the Dictionary which he envisaged was bound 'to collect and arrange all the words, whether good or bad, whether they commend themselves to his judgment or otherwise, which, with certain exceptions hereafter to be specified, those writing in the language have employed. [...] The *delectus verborum*, on which so much, on which nearly everything in style depends, is a matter with which *he* has no concern. [...] The lexicographer is making an inventory; that is his business.'[71]

On this subject of inclusiveness Coleridge's text echoes and expands upon Trench's:

we are prepared on the one hand to maintain, that no word for which authority can be cited (we shall define our sense of 'authority' hereafter) should be refused admission into the Dictionary, and on the other, to deny that the functions of the Lexicographer and the critic are in any way compatible with each other [...] the mere merit of a word in an artistic or æsthetic point of view is a consideration, which the Lexicographer cannot for a moment entertain.

Trench's view of a dictionary as 'the history of a nation contemplated from one point of view' is brought in explicitly as making completeness essential:

Every word whatever its pretensions to acceptance may be, illustrates more or less the particular phase through which the language is passing at the time of its production, and these phases of language are almost invariably found to be reflexes of the sequence of events successively taking place in the external world. Thus History and Philology go hand in hand and throw

of the Unregistered Words Committee's report: in a passage (f. 33) where Coleridge had written 'we profess to write, not a Dictionary *de novo*, but a *Supplement* to existing Dictionaries', 'profess' is altered to 'professed', apparently by Furnivall—perhaps suggesting that Coleridge was made aware of the 'larger scheme' only when he was going through Furnivall's last-minute changes to his text. As noted above (p. 17 n. 60), evidence is lacking for any involvement of Trench with the report at this point. Aarsleff (1985) further argues against Furnivall's claims, observing that Trench is given the credit in the 1933 'Historical Introduction' to the *OED* (which however was written long after the event and again without first-hand knowledge), and suggesting that Furnivall's shortcomings as a scholar disqualified him from carrying out such a scheme (which, while this may have been the case, does not make him incapable of conceiving it).

[71]   Trench (1857: 4–5). Trench went on to mention three categories of 'exceptions': provincial language, technical vocabulary, and ephemeral compound epithets of the type 'heaven-saluting'/'flower-enwoven'—although he wisely hedged his bets by conceding that in each category there are some words which do merit inclusion.

mutual light upon each other [...] if once the principle of selection is admitted [...] it is clear, that the outlines of the philological image will be broken into and marred of their distinctness in a thousand points, and that the corroborative evidence of historical event which language often supplies,—evidence of the highest value by reason of its undesignedness,—must be in great danger of being almost wholly annihilated.

In a discarded passage Coleridge waxed eloquent on the failure of previous dictionaries to achieve this ideal:

hitherto the only principle [of inclusion] consistently adopted has been a principle of the purest caprice. For example the three words 'semiustulation,' 'sanguification,' and 'chylification' occur in one page of Burton's Anatomy of Melancholy; Johnson and Richardson agree in admitting the last two [...] while they equally agree in rejecting the first [...]. We think ourselves entitled to ask on behalf of 'semiustulation' and his numerous companions, what natural deformity or inconcinnity they possess, which does not in at least an equal degree affect the claims of Ogdoastic, Immarcescible, Obdormition, enterocele &c &c.[72]

Even in the final text, the Committee refused to accept the proposition that anything more than a single instance should be required for inclusion: an idealistic position which their successors would find impossible to maintain in practice.

The question of authority, however, was one which Trench had not addressed. The Committee's July 1857 circular had proposed requiring each author (and, by implication, each variety of text) to be formally considered before being 'admitted' as a 'Dictionary authority'; by December they had evidently abandoned this position in favour of one which, while much more extreme, had at least the merit of being consistent with the position on inclusiveness. In fact, as the report observed, it was a natural consequence of it:

If all English words for which written authority can be produced are *of right* to be admitted into the Lexicon, it follows that the literary merit or demerit of any particular writer, like the comparative elegance or inelegance of any given word, is a subject upon which the Lexicographer is bound to be almost indifferent: he has to give as nearly as he can the date of the word's entrance into, or perhaps more strictly speaking, of its earliest appearance in the language, and for a chronological purpose of this kind a madrigal or chapbook will serve as well as a Canto of the Fairy Queen, or a play of Shakspere. Logically therefore we cannot refuse to throw the doors of our Lexicographical temple open to the Bavii and Mavii of our Literature, as well as to the Varii and Virgils.[73]

---

[72] UWC Report, ff. 2–4. In due course all seven of the unusual words mentioned by Coleridge were entered in the first edition of the *OED*.

[73] *Ibid*. f. 6. Bavius and Mavius (more usually Maevius) were poets of Augustan Rome whose later reputation depends chiefly on Virgil's reference to the feebleness of their poetry in his third *Eclogue*; 'Varii' is a reference to Lucius Varius Rufus, whose poetry was admired by Virgil and Horace.

The 'almost' in this passage Coleridge proceeded to explain: there were certain books which the lexicographer should be able to reject as ineligible. Coleridge's description of the most significant class of such books is most interesting:

those, which may be termed in a Lexicographical point of view, 'books with a purpose', as dictionaries, and glossaries of all kinds, and works written to illustrate dialectic peculiarities, which in reality are little else than glossaries in disguise; and works on scientific subjects which necessarily require & presuppose an artificial terminology, and assumed a license of adding to their stock of verbal symbols (we cannot call them *words*) quite ad libitum. [...] in a language like our own, [...] we are justified, we think, in refusing a place to words, which the confraternity of writers have ignored, and which can boast no better sanction for the fact of their very questionable existence, than what arises from their being found in such Refuges for the Destitute as the Promptorium Parvulorum and the Dictionary of Bailey.[74]

The Dictionary would have been very different if this insistence on excluding 'artificial' evidence, and especially on the discounting of 'works on scientific subjects', had been adhered to.

Following this disquisition on theoretical matters, the report proceeded to give the promised account of the Committee's practical activities. By 3 December 77 individuals had come forward to offer help in reading texts, and '116 works, or in some cases, parts of works' had been undertaken; 26 readers had actually submitted their work. However, a long list of 'works of primary importance' remained to be taken up, including the Chronicles of Hardyng, Holinshed, and others, and many English translations of the classics (Holland's Livy, Hall's Homer, etc.). The Committee acknowledged that in order to help with the project, in addition to access to the necessary books, helpers would above all need 'the leisure, requisite for work of this kind (though much more may be done in a very limited time than most persons suppose)'.[75] Over half the report is given over to examples of the material which contributors had so far sent in, arranged according to a scheme of categories derived from the seven headings of 'On some Deficiencies'.

The penultimate section of the report is concerned with etymology, a matter which the Committee had—quite deliberately—entirely passed over in their earlier circular. They were well aware of the scarcity of people qualified to contribute anything of value in this area, and had sought to pre-empt 'a flood of etymological trifling, nine-tenths of which would be totally useless'; moreover, since the original intention had been to

---

[74] *Ibid.* f. 7. The *Promptorium Parvulorum* was a fifteenth-century English–Latin glossary, the earliest known. Coleridge's opposition to the inclusion of words attested only in dictionaries can be traced back to a letter to James Halliwell-Phillipps on 5 September 1857, in which he proposes that 'except under very special circumstances no word, which has nothing but Dictionary authority to support it in a *living* language, should be admitted' (Halliwell-Phillipps papers, Edinburgh University Library, 'Letters of Authors' vol. 63, no. 10). For the views of one of Coleridge's successors on words of this type see below, p. 120.

[75] UWC Report, f. 8.

compile a supplement, rather than a complete dictionary *de novo*, a large proportion of suitable etymological material was already to be found in Richardson and Johnson/Todd, and it was supposed that the additional etymological work could be carried out by the Committee, with regular reference to the members of the Society at large in cases of difficulty. This collective approach was considered greatly preferable to 'the mischief arising from the etymological bias of a single mind being allowed to run rampant through the Dictionary'.[76]

The report concludes with two practical recommendations as to the way forward. The first is perhaps surprising: that Todd's edition of Johnson be abandoned as a basis of comparison for the new Dictionary. There were certainly conceptual disadvantages in using two dictionaries for comparison; a Dictionary compiled on this basis 'would not supply accurately the deficiencies of either'. But the rejection of Johnson in favour of Richardson would seem to have been on methodological grounds:

no one who has once distinctly conceived the true idea of a Dictionary can doubt that upon the foundation of Johnson no really valuable superstructure can ever be raised [...] it is upon Richardson that they must build if they wish to erect an edifice instead of augmenting the confusion of a vast and shapeless ruin.

Todd's edition was moreover out of print (a new edition had recently been proposed).[77]

The second recommendation was of much greater consequence, and not only in terms of the scope of the project. The original 1857 circular had proposed that reading be concentrated on texts of the sixteenth and seventeenth centuries, and the examples cited in the report showed that the Committee and its helpers had done so (with a small number of quotations from earlier sources, including *The Owl and the Nightingale* and various works printed by Caxton). Any dictionary entries compiled from this limited evidence, however, would clearly fail in the agreed aim of allowing each word to tell its entire story. Thus it would be necessary to trawl 'the earliest writers' before anything useful could be published. It was important that 'the *absolutely earliest* quotation [be] assigned to every word, not merely the earliest within certain arbitrary limits.' Such an expansion into earlier literature had its practical problems: comparatively few readers were able to cope with the language of these texts, and many of those ready to do so (such as the Committee itself) were still fully occupied with the later period. The report proposed that the Committee be empowered to form subcommittees to consider how best to trawl the literature of each period; the hope was expressed 'that our list of collectors may speedily be so far increased as to leave our hands comparatively free to encounter in propriis personis the greater difficulties of our earlier literature.'[78] The wording here suggests that Coleridge, for one, was keen to start grappling with the earlier texts.

[76] *Ibid.* ff. 33, 34.
[77] *Ibid.* f. 35.
[78] *Ibid.* ff. 36, 37. *in propriis personis*: in our own persons.

The report's final appeal is for more volunteers to join the ranks. In making this request, and acknowledging the contributions of those who have already volunteered, the work of the brothers Grimm is cited as a basis for an interesting comparison: 'while 83 students are sufficient to exhaust, or nearly to exhaust the literature of Germany, it would take twice that number to do proportionate justice to the infinitely more noble literature of England.'[79] Furnivall often included such patriotic appeals in the prospectuses through which he launched his various literary societies; the Committee evidently felt that 'so national a work' (as Coleridge's concluding paragraph calls it) could count on the support of all comers.

And of course the work would have even stronger claims to be 'national' if it were to be directed towards the compilation of an entire dictionary, rather than a mere supplement. The announcement of the 'larger scheme', whatever form it took, must have set the Society buzzing. Whether for this or some other reason, at the next meeting on 17 December—most unusually—no formal paper was given; instead, the distinguished orientalist Theodor Goldstücker 'made some remarks on the Etymological requirements of an English Dictionary'; it seems from an annotation made by Coleridge in the report of the Committee that he may have offered to undertake the etymological component of the new project.[80] No detailed record of Goldstücker's remarks survives, and there is no sign that his offer came to anything; but there must surely have been further discussion of the Society's newly expanded lexicographical ambitions.

The stage was set, then, for the momentous meeting on 7 January 1858, at which six 'resolutions [...] relating to the undertaking of a New English Dictionary', moved by Furnivall, were passed.[81] The resolutions were: that a new and comprehensive dictionary should be prepared, 'instead of the Supplement [...] now in course of preparation'; that two committees should be given charge of the work, a 'Literary and Historical' committee (this being in effect the old Unregistered Words Committee renamed) and an etymological one consisting of Hensleigh Wedgwood and Henry Malden; that existing and new contributors should be invited to assist with the work; that Furnivall and Coleridge should be empowered to negotiate with publishers; that the two Committees should be allocated the subscriptions of 'all Members who have joined or shall join the Society through the Unregistered Words Committee or the New Dictionary Committee', to help defray the costs of the project; and, finally and rousingly, that the Society would 'afford every assistance in its power to enable its Committees to make a Dictionary worthy of the English Language'.

---

[79] *Ibid.* f. 37.

[80] *TPS* for 1857, p. 142; UWC Report, f. 33. A considerably larger role is assigned to Goldstücker in a report on the Dictionary which appeared in the *Jahrbuch für romanische und englische Literatur* in 1861 (vol. III, pp. 241–4; signed 'H.B.'), in which he is described as having made the proposal to compile a comprehensive dictionary rather than a supplement; however, the report contains a number of inaccuracies, and the attribution of the idea to Goldstücker is probably another error.

[81] *Athenaeum* 13 Feb. 1858, p. 212. Two drafts of the resolutions in Furnivall's hand survive in OUPA (OED/B/1/1/2 and OED/B/1/1/5); the earlier of the two is postmarked 6 January, recording when Furnivall sent it to his fellow Honorary Secretary, Thomas Hewitt Key.

The new resolutions had immediate practical implications for those who were already reading for the Dictionary, as they would now have to abandon the use of Richardson and Johnson for purposes of comparison. Coleridge and Furnivall seem to have prepared for this: a letter sent to one reader, the naturalist John Lubbock, on the day after the Resolution was passed is signed by both men but written in another hand (presumably that of a clerk assigned to write multiple copies). The letter asks Lubbock to 'extract for us all words &c. not in the Bible & Shakspere instead of Richardson & Johnson trusting to your memory in case you have not Concordances to hand. We hope to send you full details of the new plan in about a month's time.'[82] In the event these 'full details' would take rather longer to prepare. At the Society's next meeting on 21 January—at which Trench took the chair—the text of a possible circular about the Dictionary was read out by Furnivall (who had almost certainly drafted it) and discussed.[83] But no circular appeared; evidently the Society felt it could not make a full public announcement until various matters had been settled. One such matter may have been the etymological policy for the new Dictionary, a matter on which there were evidently strongly differing opinions among the Society's members. Hensleigh Wedgwood and Henry Malden were natural enough choices for the Etymological Committee—Wedgwood, in particular, could hardly have failed to be selected[84]—but there were also several other members who wished to contribute, two of whom, John Davies and James Kennedy, addressed the Society specifically in 1858 on the subject of the 'etymological deficiencies' of current dictionaries (the titles of their papers evidently chosen to match Trench's).[85]

The fourth of the Society's six resolutions, that concerned with publishing the Dictionary, mentioned the names of David Nutt, a London publisher and bookseller, and A. Asher & Co., a Berlin bookselling firm, as preferred candidates. Negotiations with both firms were already well advanced; indeed, they may even have been persuaded to offer to publish the projected Dictionary even before the 7 January meeting.

[82] BL MS Add. 49638 f. 95 8 Jan. 1858 HC/FJF to John Lubbock.

[83] TPS for 1858, pp. 198–9. The mere fact of the six resolutions having been passed was of course immediately public knowledge, and was widely noticed in the public prints (e.g. Times 19 Jan. 1858, p. 12).

[84] Hensleigh Wedgwood (1803–91), another founder member of the Philological Society, had acquired considerable eminence in the field of English etymology. He regularly read papers to the Society on particular etymologies, and had argued as early as 1844 that the collection of such 'materials for an etymology of the English language' was a task 'peculiarly adapted [...] for the cooperation of the members of the Philological Society' (ProcPS 22 Nov. 1844, p. 2); his own Dictionary of English Etymology began to appear in 1859. However, although many of his etymologies are sound, he was led into numerous blunders by his conviction that the origins of human language lay in interjections, and it has been suggested that it would have been a disaster if he had become the Dictionary's principal etymologist (Liberman 2009: 276). Henry Malden (1800–76), professor of Greek at University College London, and another former member of the Cambridge 'Etymological Society', was also well qualified.

[85] TPS for 1858, pp. 199 (4 Mar.), 201 (20 May). Neither paper was published in the Society's Transactions, although Kennedy's later appeared (under the title 'Hints on the Formation of a New English Dictionary') in a posthumous collection of his essays, in which his main recommendation was that the Society ought to secure the help of 'persons well acquainted with all the languages that can be supposed to have had any connexion with the English', in order that the Dictionary could give an adequate account of the origins of every word (Kennedy 1861: 163).

Two drafts survive[86] of an agreement between Furnivall, Coleridge, and these two firms in which reference is made to their 'offer [...] to publish at their own risk a new English Dictionary' as having been one of the factors which encouraged the Society to pass their six resolutions. Unfortunately David Nutt seems to have developed cold feet, and his name soon dropped out of negotiations; so Furnivall wrote to the publisher John Murray, whom he had met some years earlier, to ask whether he was 'inclined to treat with the Philological Society for the publication—after 6 years or so—of their new & complete English Dictionary'.[87] Murray responded courteously but cautiously, expressing a (prophetic) concern that the scope of the project was 'so gigantic as not only to render its execution most difficult—but to render its success nearly impossible'.[88] His idea of the kind of dictionary that was needed soon turned out to be very different from that envisaged by the Philological Society (or at least by its representatives), with obsolete words rigorously excluded, and a more inclusive approach to scientific vocabulary than Trench would have countenanced;[89] and by May he had realized that the project was simply too much of an unknown quantity. 'To bind myself absolutely,' he admonished Furnivall, 'to publish a work w[hi]ch I have not seen & regarding the contents of w[hi]ch I am to have no control is contrary to any thing of previous occurrence in my literary experience. [...] I can only hope that the Society may find another publisher who does not look at these terms in the serious light that I do.' He duly returned Furnivall's draft contract unsigned.[90]

The search for a publisher may well have been what delayed the issue of a full prospectus for the Society's Dictionary, which did not appear until August 1858. Although no surviving copies of this have been traced, it is possible to deduce from quotations in newspapers and magazines that it made reference to 'arrangements hav[ing] been made for an early publication in parts'. A month later it was reissued, now with the title of 'Proposal for the Publication of a New English Dictionary', and with the publisher named as Asher & Co.[91]

---

[86] In OUPA (OED/B/1/1/2) and MP; neither is dated, but the latter appears to be the earlier version. Other papers relating to negotiations with Nutt and Asher are in MP.

[87] JMA 8 Feb. 1858 FJF to John Murray. The firm of John Murray was best known for travel books, memoirs, and history, but it also published some dictionaries and language textbooks.

[88] JMA 25 Feb. 1858 John Murray to FJF and HC. Murray thought that the Dictionary might extend to four volumes of the same size as Richardson's two (each of which contained a little over 1,200 pages), a guess (as he described it) which soon became established as a convenient rough estimate in Furnivall's subsequent negotiations with Murray and other publishers.

[89] JMA 4 Mar. 1858 John Murray to FJF (noting that 'words of Science, art &c [are] daily coming into increased use, in conversation & in newspapers', and that their omission 'would impair the utility of the Dictionary among general readers').

[90] MP 12, 13 May 1858 John Murray to FJF.

[91] *Critic* 21 Aug. 1858, p. 491; this report was widely reprinted. Cf. Coleridge (1860: 72): 'it was not till August, 1858, that we felt ourselves in a position to announce the plan of a New Dictionary as a certainty [...]. A new and much-enlarged prospectus was shortly afterwards brought out.' The latter seems to have been issued in late September or early October—following Furnivall's return from a holiday in Normandy (Munro et al. 1911: xxxvi)—to judge from the renewed flurry of public notices at this time, including one (*Morning Post* 1 Oct. 1858, p. 2) which mentions the 'Proposal' by name. No copies of this autumn version of the 'Proposal' have been traced, but the version issued in December (see below) again seems to have

The text of the 'Proposal' attests to a great deal of deliberation on the part of the Dictionary's two supervisory Committees; it gives a greatly enhanced level of detail about the nature of the work that was now envisaged. This includes a restatement of several key points of the 'lexicographical creed' (supplemented by a reference to Trench's 'On some Deficiencies'), with a few further clarifications and changes of emphasis. Perhaps the most significant new points were two relating to chronology: firstly, that the scope of the dictionary was to extend back to the middle of the thirteenth century, this being considered to be the time of the 'definite appearance of an English type of language, distinct from the preceding semi-Saxon' (p. 3);[92] and secondly, that for the purpose of collecting quotation evidence, the history of English was to be divided into three periods: (1) from the beginnings to 1526 (the date of the first printed English New Testament), (2) from 1526 to 1674 (the date of the death of Milton), and (3) from 1674 to the present day. This somewhat arbitrary threefold[93] division, which was to structure the work of the Dictionary for much of the next two decades, had been arrived at for practical reasons. Although quotations had continued to flow in from the army of contributors—whose numbers had now swelled to over 100—volunteers were invited to undertake the reading of more texts in all three periods. The aim of the Dictionary would then be, as a minimum, to give at least one instance of each word in whichever of these three periods it was known to occur (although the Proposal gives the compilers licence to include more examples where a word's importance warranted it).

For each of the three periods it was proposed to provide readers with a baseline (or 'basis of comparison'), in the form of a wordlist; the absence of an item of vocabulary from the wordlist could then be the prompt for a reader to supply a quotation for it. For the second period two widely available publications could be used to form an aggregate wordlist, namely Alexander Cruden's concordance to the Authorized Version of the Bible and Mary Cowden Clarke's concordance to Shakespeare; and for the third period, the Literary and Historical Committee announced their intention to issue 'a list of Burke's words'—apparently on the basis of a careful examination of his writings which had been undertaken by a protégé of Furnivall's named William Rossiter—to serve a similar purpose. For the first period it was anticipated that readers would be in particular need of a sound basis of comparison; fortunately Coleridge, who had a particular interest in the period, had been working for some time on something

been largely identical, apart from the name of the publisher. All quotations are taken from the December text unless otherwise stated. A heavily corrected manuscript draft of the 'Proposal', which can be securely dated to before 1 July 1858, is in OUPA at OED/B/1/1/2.

[92] For a discussion of the term 'Semi-Saxon' as used during the nineteenth century, and contemporary ideas about the different phases into which the history of English should be divided, see Matthews (1999: xxvii–xxxii).

[93] A division into five periods was also considered (as can be seen from the manuscript draft of the 'Proposal'), perhaps reflecting a desire to go one better than Charles Richardson, who in his dictionary had set himself the aim of including a quotation for every word (or group of words) from each of four periods (Richardson 1836: 'Preface', 51). Furnivall apparently never had much confidence in such divisions, and 'thought that Coleridge attributed far too much importance to the influence on the language of the Scripture versions' (as stated by James Murray, in Munro et al. 1911: 126).

which would fit the bill admirably, and which was now far advanced, despite bouts of illness (he had been suffering from tuberculosis for some years). The English of the thirteenth century, insofar as it was available to be read, was now considered to have been trawled sufficiently thoroughly by readers that Coleridge could announce in the Proposal his intention to issue 'an alphabetical list of all A.D.1250–1300 words'. (He was well aware that availability of such material was the real problem, and complained that even some of the texts that had been edited for publication had been issued in limited editions by more or less exclusive private clubs, and 'might, for all that the public in general is the better for them, just as well have remained in MS.') It was hoped that, armed with this late thirteenth-century wordlist, those readers who were prepared to tackle Middle English could then concentrate on the remainder of the first period.[94]

The remainder of the 'Proposal' is given over to practical matters: no less than three sets of Rules and Regulations, and periodized lists both of works already read, and of works suggested for further reading.[95] The 'Rules and Directions for Collectors' cover much the same ground, though in much greater detail, as those given in the Unregistered Words Committee's 1857 Proposal; these are now supplemented by rules for 'all persons [...] desirous of contributing to the Etymological portion of the work', and a highly detailed set of 'Mechanical and Practical Regulations'—governing the choice of edition read, standards for transcription and bibliographical citation, and even the size of paper to be used—which were no doubt compiled in response to problems already caused by inconsistency among existing contributors.[96]

No sooner had the 'Proposal' appeared, however, when the Dictionary encountered another hitch: the withdrawal of Asher & Co. from their undertaking to publish it. The details are again unclear, but at the Philological Society's first meeting of the new session, on 4 November, Furnivall announced that the Dictionary was to be published, not by Asher & Co., but by Nicholas Trübner (and in December the 'Proposal' was reissued with Trübner named as publisher). However, at least he could also announce that Coleridge's 'Glossary of Early English' would be 'ready for press by Christmas'; and on 27 January 1859 it was announced that this work, too, would be published by Trübner.[97]

---

[94] 'Proposal', pp. 5–6.

[95] It is notable that, in the lists of works already undertaken, work on the third period seems barely to have started: only five items are listed as having been taken up (one being 'Burke's Works' as undertaken by William Rossiter).

[96] Contributors were now requested to write each quotation on 'a separate half-sheet of note-paper'. The original 1857 'Proposal' had specified 'ordinary small quarto letter paper', but allowed the option of writing two or more quotations on each piece, which might then be cut up into assorted shapes and sizes; in fact any such lack of uniformity in size or shape severely hinders the efficient sorting and filing of paper slips. On later stipulations as to slip size see p. 261 n. 3.

[97] *TPS* for 1858, p. 201; *TPS* for 1859, p. 292. (This new version of the 'Proposal' was advertised as available in December 1858, although the imprint gives the date as 1859.) Nicholas Trübner was in fact a close business associate of David Nutt. His agreement to publish Coleridge's glossary, dated 19 January 1858, is in MP.

Another Trübner advertisement in the *Athenaeum* of 1 January 1859 (p. 26) went so far as to announce that 'the Philological Society's New Dictionary of the English Language' was to be published 'in 4to. Parts, at 5s. each'. One wonders how many readers wrote in to apply for copies.

By this stage Coleridge was indeed putting the finishing touches to his text; on 29 January he wrote to Sir Frederic Madden asking his opinion on the interpretation of certain passages to be cited in the Glossary, and two days later Furnivall reported to Madden that the Glossary was 'at the printers'.[98] In the same letter Furnivall sought Madden's advice about the problem of inaccessible early texts, regarding which he had conceived the beginnings of a solution:

Can you tell me of any early English M.S. (in London), before 1300 if possible, which would take up from 100 to 150 octavo pages, & which we could print as a Supplement to our Philological Society's Transactions. We shall have above 100 pages to spare this year, and I should like to make them available for some Early English matter.

Over the next few months both Committees continued to grapple with the materials being sent in by the ever-swelling army of contributors. In April a collection of queries, regarding the interpretation of certain Middle English passages and the etymology of particular words, was circulated; several Society members and other contributors responded with suggestions, which Coleridge reported on 28 April.[99] These queries gave rise to further papers, including two by Wedgwood and one by Furnivall. From the references given by Furnivall in his paper—a curious piece 'on an unregistered sense of the word *thing* and its base *the*'—it is clear that he had already begun to transcribe some of the early (mainly thirteenth-century) texts recommended to him by Madden, including Robert Mannyng of Brunne's poem *Handlyng Synne*.[100] Meanwhile Coleridge's Glossary, 'the foundation-stone of the Historical and Literary portion of the Philological Society's proposed English Dictionary',[101] finally appeared in June, publication having been delayed by the illness of its compiler, and was discussed at a Philological Society meeting on 23 June.[102]

The new glossary (now entitled 'A Glossarial Index to the Printed English Literature of the Thirteenth Century') was generally well received, although it suffered from comparison with Trench's *Select Glossary*, which appeared at almost exactly the same time and which, as a rather more readable book by an already distinguished author, received considerably more attention. A review in the *Athenaeum* expressed regret that Coleridge's book contained little more than 'a catalogue of words', accompanied by bare references, as opposed to the lengthy quotations given by Trench: a rather unfair criticism given that Coleridge's glossary was really no more than a tool for the

---

[98] BL MS Egerton 2847, ff. 22–3 29 Jan. 1859 HC to Madden; ff. 32–3 31 Jan. 1859 FJF to Madden.

[99] The responses were printed in *TPS* for 1859, pp. 67–74.

[100] *Ibid.* 125–6. Other texts mentioned in Furnivall's paper—the scholarship of which is condemned as 'deeply incompetent' by Aarsleff (1985: 176)—include a poem from MS Egerton 613 and some saints' lives in Harl. MS 2277.

[101] Coleridge (1859: iii) (from Coleridge's 'Preface', dated 13 June 1859).

[102] *TPS* for 1859, p. 294. At the meeting Furnivall also read extracts from *Handlyng Synne*. Although his edition of this important early fourteenth-century text, for the Roxburghe Club—ironically, one of the very printing clubs whose exclusivity had been criticized in the 'Proposal'—did not appear until 1862, much of his work on it was done in 1859.

Dictionary's readers, and was not intended to provide entertainment and edification of the kind that readers might reasonably expect from Trench's very differently conceived work.[103] A more serious shortcoming was the shortness of the list of works quoted: barely thirty texts, even including Furnivall's as yet unpublished transcriptions of thirteenth-century texts. One reviewer regretfully suggested that 'the greater part' of the potentially available literature of the period 'still lies buried in manuscript in our public and private libraries'.[104]

Although the *Glossarial Index* was concerned only with the first of the three periods given in the 'Proposal'—indeed, with the earliest portion of that period—Coleridge had made a real start on the task of processing all of the quotation evidence so far collected. At much the same time as the publication of his glossary, he issued a list of nearly 1000 words beginning with A, noting against each word the 'deficiencies' of the collections to date in respect of the second and third periods, i.e. whether a quotation was still needed for either period, or both.[105] The response was encouraging: by the following May he was able to report that 'barely 300 words [from this list] now remain without quotations from one period or the other'.

Another significant development during the summer of 1859 was the Dictionary's acquisition of a transatlantic dimension. The appearance of the 'Proposal', and even of the original 1858 prospectus, had generated a certain amount of interest in America,[106] and several interested scholars had made offers of help, among whom was George Perkins Marsh, professor of English literature at Columbia College in New York, who agreed to act as the project's American secretary.[107] On 9 August a circular was issued in Marsh's name, inviting American readers to make their contributions through him. The circular announced a new division of labour: it had been agreed that 'the entire body of English literature belonging to the eighteenth century' should be reserved for American readers, on the basis that texts of earlier periods were less accessible in America. The circular included revised versions of the lists of works already taken up, and of those suggested for reading; a 'list of American works to be read and excerpted' would shortly be issued; and work on an index of the works of Burke was still ongoing. Similar lists of texts also appeared in a slightly revised version of the 'Proposal' which appeared soon after the American circular; the work being done by readers, including many new ones, is attested by the considerably expanded section on 'Works of

---

[103] *Athenaeum* 2 July 1859, p. 12. A much briefer but more positive notice in the *Literary Gazette* of 17 September described the *Glossarial Index* as 'a valuable and much wanted work' which had 'already received the approbation of several savants competent to judge' (p. 284).

[104] *Gentleman's Magazine* Sept. 1859, p. 297.

[105] This four-page leaflet, mentioned in Coleridge (1860: 75) as having been 'circulated among members and contributors' during the latter part of 1859, is extremely scarce; I am grateful to the Library of the University of California at Berkeley for providing me with a scan of the only copy known to me.

[106] The *New York Times* of 2 November 1858, for example, reported the appearance of the prospectus in an article headed 'Dictionary Making' (p. 4).

[107] Lowenthal (2000) provides a full account of the life and achievements of Marsh (1801–82), who was later to distinguish himself as a pioneer of environmentalism. In early 1859 he was preparing for publication a series of lectures on the English language which he had just finished giving at Columbia College.

the Second Period [...] already undertaken', although the third period still remained largely untouched (readers may have been discouraged because the promised index to the vocabulary of Burke was still not ready).[108]

When the Philological Society reconvened in November 1859, there was much progress to report. The task of doing so fell once again to Coleridge, who was also increasingly finding himself treated as the Dictionary's *de facto* editor in respect of the numerous questions of policy upon which he was asked to pronounce. He accordingly put it to the Society that it was time to choose an editor *de jure*; it was perhaps no surprise to many that the unanimous choice of the Society's Council was to offer the position to Coleridge himself.[109] He promptly set to work establishing the editorial policy of the Dictionary in considerably more detail. The starting point was a document, drafted by Coleridge and shown to both Furnivall and Trench, before being presented to the Society on 24 November under the title of 'Canones Lexicographici'.[110] A committee was appointed to consider the issues raised, and draw up 'Rules for the guidance of the Editor'.[111] The rules were discussed at length over the course of the next five months, first by the appointed committee, and then at three general meetings of the Society, following the last of which, they were published, both separately and (later) as a supplement to the Society's (delayed) *Transactions* for 1857.[112] The published document by no means represented a consensus among members of the Society: at the very meeting (10 May 1860) at which the text of the 'Canones' was finally settled, a thoroughly dissenting view was set out in a paper by Derwent Coleridge, uncle of the Dictionary's editor, who sought to reassert the 'judicial or regulative authority' of the office of the lexicographer, who should be allowed 'a liberty of selection', advocated the giving of only comparative information in etymologies, and made various other suggestions which were not taken up.[113]

In fact the 'Canones Lexicographici' set out a vision of the Dictionary which had moved on considerably from the visions of Trench's 'On some Deficiencies', of Coleridge's 'Report', or even of the Society's 'Proposal'. The vision, however, was one which would surely have been too grandiosely ambitious ever to be realized; the main interest of the 'Canones' today arguably lies in the divergences between the dictionary which they envisage and the *OED* as it eventually began to emerge over two decades

[108] An incomplete copy of the American circular is preserved at OED/B/1/2/1. Copies were advertised as available from the New York publisher J. S. Redfield as well as from Marsh (*American Publishers' Circular and Literary Gazette* 14 Jan. 1860, p. 14).

[109] Coleridge described his election in two undated letters to Henry Hucks Gibbs (GL MS 11021/19 ff. 359–61, 363–5). See also Coleridge (1860: 76–7) and ProcPS 10 and 24 Nov. 1859, p. 295.

[110] HL 24 Nov. 1859 Trench to FJF.

[111] *TPS* for 1859, pp. 295–6. The committee consisted of Trench, Theodor Goldstücker, Thomas Hewitt Key, Thomas Watts, Hensleigh Wedgwood, Furnivall, Francis Pulszky, and (according to the published 'Canones') Coleridge himself.

[112] At least one interim version of the 'Canones' was printed prior to publication of the final version; there are significant differences between the versions, mainly in regard to matters of etymology. Quotations from the 'Canones' are given from the text as printed in *TPS*.

[113] D. Coleridge (1860: 154, 157).

later. The scope of the 'Main Dictionary', it is true, was largely the same as that described in the earlier documents (although with a significantly more inclusive approach to dialect); but this was now conceived as merely the first component of a three-part work, of which the second was to contain both a 'Vocabulary of Technical and Scientific Terms' and a comprehensive listing of proper names (including Christian names, surnames, and place-names), and the third was to be an 'Etymological Appendix', in which every 'root' and 'primitive base' from which the words of the Main Dictionary had been derived was to be discussed, along with 'prefixes' and 'affixes', these terms being described in terms which show only too clearly how far the Etymological Committee's ideas were from what we would regard as good philology today (in that, for example, the initial *b* of *brow* was to be regarded as 'really' a prefix). Still more ambitiously, the opening paragraph of the 'Canones' declared the aim of the Dictionary to be to record 'every word in the language for which sufficient authority, whether printed or oral, can be adduced'—although the matter of how the 'sufficiency' of oral evidence is to be assessed is passed over in silence. Indeed in general the 'Canones' are concerned rather too much with expansive statements of general policy; it was presumably to be left to Coleridge to find ways of putting the principles into practice.

Before the Editor could begin to tackle such editorial questions, however, there was still a considerable amount to be done by way of collecting evidence. In particular there was the pressing matter of a 'basis of comparison' for the third period, to complement those already available to readers for the first and second periods; Coleridge decided that he could not wait for William Rossiter to produce his promised index to Burke, and instead set about compiling something rather larger himself, following on from the list of words in A which he had issued in the summer. He announced his intention to do so in an open letter to Trench, dated 30 May 1860 and published as an appendix to a new edition of Trench's 'On some Deficiencies' which was published around this time.[114] This letter also gives a usefully detailed report of progress, and as such is an important source of information about the state of the project at this point.

Coleridge was able to report, with some pride, that eighty-nine volunteers were currently at work collecting quotations, in addition to three who had died, forty-three who had completed their assigned texts, and fifteen who had been given up as 'hopeless' on account of their failure to send any material.[115] He was realistic about the variable quality of his readers, of whom fifteen were described as 'of inferior merit' and only thirty as producing work which '[left] nothing to be desired in any respect'; and he lamented that even with conscientious and skilled readers there remained the problem

---

[114] The new edition of Trench's paper contains many small revisions, as well as updates to reflect the changed circumstances (notably the expansion of the Philological Society's plan from a supplementary to a comprehensive dictionary, 'no patch upon old garments, but a new garment throughout'), but his argument remained in all essentials unchanged.

[115] Coleridge sent out a circular in May to all those who had undertaken reading, asking when he could expect to receive their contributions, so that 'the preparation of the Work [i.e. the Dictionary] for the press should be commenced with as little delay as possible' (partial copies preserved at OED/B/4/1/2).

of inaccessibility of many of the most valuable texts. (The response from American readers, under Marsh's secretaryship, was apparently disappointing: by March only 40 texts had been taken up for reading,[116] and no quotations from them had been received.) However, he contrasted the effectiveness of his band of contributors with the rather less happy experiences of the Grimm brothers—who had admitted that only six of the eighty-three individuals reading for their *Deutsches Wörterbuch* could be regarded as satisfactory—and went so far as to assert that the current numbers were 'quite sufficient to do all that yet remains to be done'. Such optimism is remarkable, especially considering that reading in the third period had still hardly started.[117] But his optimism extended beyond the collection of evidence to include his own task of compiling entries, on which he can barely have started. Making the proviso that he has responsibility only for the 'literary and historical portion' of the work, the etymological component being 'left in abeyance'—differences of opinion on etymological matters had evidently still not been resolved—Coleridge ends his letter with an astonishing prediction: 'I confidently expect, unless any unforeseen accident should occur to paralyze our efforts, that in about two years we shall be able to give our first number to the world. Indeed, were it not for the dilatoriness of many contributors [...] I should not hesitate to name an earlier period.'[118] A reported remark regarding the set of pigeonholes which he had had made to house the accumulating quotation evidence reflects a similarly sanguine assessment of the timescale: he is supposed to have said that when these fifty-four pigeonholes—capable of holding perhaps 100,000 quotations—were full, it would be 'time to begin making the dictionary'.[119] This might seem like optimism of the most irresponsible kind; Furnivall, more understandingly, attributed it to 'the hope that sometimes inspires the last stage of consumption'.[120] For Coleridge was now very ill: indeed, he had been advised in late 1859—around the time of his appointment as Editor—that 'recovery was hopeless'.[121] Perhaps he was simply desperate to believe that he would at least see something in print during whatever years of life remained to him.

There is certainly a feverishness about Coleridge's level of activity during 1860. He now turned once again to questions of inclusion; his immersion in the evidence of the third period during the compilation of the 'Basis of Comparison' had led him to patrol, as others after him would do repeatedly, what might be regarded as the outer reaches

---

[116] *New-York Daily Tribune* 10 Mar. 1860, p. 6.

[117] Coleridge gives no figure for works taken up by readers in the third period, stating merely that 'little in a direct way has yet been done'; for the first and second periods he reports 139 and 276 works, respectively, as having been taken up (Coleridge 1860: 74–5).

[118] *Ibid.* 77–8.

[119] James Murray claimed (in Munro et al. 1911: 128) to have heard this reported by Furnivall.

[120] Furnivall (1861), 'Preliminary Notice'.

[121] Tuckwell (1900: 119). According to Tuckwell it was upon receiving this news that Coleridge declared that he 'must begin Sanskrit to-morrow'. These, then, were not his 'last words', as has been reported; in fact he made considerable progress in the study of Sanskrit during the last eighteen months of his life (Considine 2014a: 91).

of 'Anglicity'. He concluded that questions about whether to include some of this marginal vocabulary were best settled by consultation. In November he read a paper to the Philological Society 'On the exclusion of certain words from a dictionary', in which he identified five categories of word whose admissibility he felt to be questionable: (i) nonce-words formed by humorous analogy (which he termed 'vocabular parodies'), such as the mock-titles *devilship* and *knaveship*; (ii) 'quaint' words formed using the prefix *be-*, such as *be-stockinged*, and playful diminutives in *-kin* and the like; (iii) even more exuberant *jeux d'esprit* (or 'literary fungi', as he called them) of a type favoured by some recent writers, such as Southey's *sinequanonniness*, Carlyle's *Correggiosity*, and Thackeray's *snobonomer*; (iv) the less common analogues of familiar words formed by varying the suffix, as *psychologer* for *psychologist* and the like; and (v) imperfectly naturalized foreign expressions like *ne plus ultra* and *smorzando* (even when rendered in Greek, like οἱ πολλοί). Regarding the fourth category Coleridge waxed eloquent (and prescriptive):

> I do strongly protest against the reception of words, which not only are not wanted, but by virtue of their malformation either mean nothing at all, or mean something totally different from that intended by the ingenious author. [...] A great writer may pardonably enough take a license [*sic*] once now and then with his language, but if every one who writes a book is to consider himself at liberty to snip pieces out of words or to add syllables to them according to his or her notions of rhythm, every new publication will soon have to be accompanied with its glossary, just as it is now with its index or table of contents.

Coleridge's exasperation at the hosts of (in his view) unworthy words which he was being obliged to consider even led him to wonder 'whether all three-volume novels, sermons, tracts and newspapers are of right to claim admittance, or can in fact be cited for any useful purpose whatever': a view in striking contrast to his earlier embracing of 'the Bavii and Mavii of our Literature'. But in fact he had an alternative solution to suggest: all the words which fell into his five categories could be listed in a separate sequence, and 'not admitted into the columns of the Main Dictionary *at present*'; they could then be considered for 'promotion' into the main text by the editor of a second edition.[122] He could hardly have known how far into the future he was looking by using these words.

In a note appended to the published version of Coleridge's paper, Furnivall records that the meeting took a very different view. Apart from the third category, where it was agreed that 'word-puns, such as *hepistle, shepistle*' could be excluded, all of the classes identified by Coleridge were deemed suitable for inclusion, not exclusion; indeed, regarding the fourth category, it was agreed that it was important for a dictionary such as the one now contemplated to record both the prevalent and the less common words.[123]

---

[122] Coleridge (1861a: 41–2).

[123] *TPS* for 1860–1, pp. 43–4. With regard to Coleridge's fourth category, an interesting case in point was recalled by T. H. Key in the discussion: 'at the first Meeting of this Society, in 1842, the members were about equally divided on the question, whether *philologer* [...] or *philologist* was the right form.'

At the Society's third meeting of 1861 'the first part, A.–D., of the 3d Period, Basis of Comparison [...] was laid on the Table'.[124] Coleridge must have been fully occupied with its compilation over the preceding months, as it not only contains an indication of very nearly all the quotations sent in for words in A–D by contributors working in the Third Period, but incorporates a considerable amount of further trawling by Coleridge himself. In his Preface he declared that the planned index to Burke had had to be abandoned; instead, he had himself extracted 'a number of words large enough to serve as a foundation, from the writings of Dryden, Wordsworth and Tennyson', and then added to these 'all, or nearly all the contributions for this Period already in the Editor's hands.'[125]

The 'Basis of Comparison' is designed very specifically for use by those reading for the Dictionary, and as such its entries are even simpler than those in the earlier 'Glossarial Index', consisting simply of a headword followed by the briefest of indications of what has already been collected, usually consisting of a single source, occasionally two. The very first entry, for example, reads simply 'Aback, adv. S T C', meaning that an example of the word *aback* has been found in a text by S. T. Coleridge: surely an instance of familial piety on the part of Herbert Coleridge, whose grandfather in fact figures prominently among the sources cited. The most frequently cited author of all is Burke, suggesting that William Rossiter's abandoned project had at least supplied some usable material. But Coleridge was also happy to use evidence from non-literary sources: there are references to recent scientific writing—Darwin and Herbert Spencer are listed as authorities on the very first page—and periodicals such as the *Times*, the *Quarterly Review*, and the *Cornhill Magazine*. He was later asked: 'Why have you quoted a newspaper as the authority for a word when you might have quoted Tennyson?' His response was, 'Because some contributor had sent me a quotation for the word from a newspaper, and nobody had sent me one from Tennyson. If you will send me the Tennyson one, I will use it in the Dictionary.'[126]

Coleridge also gives precise instructions as to how each contributor can use the 'Basis' as a means of 'very considerably diminishing the toilsomeness of the task he has undertaken'. The writing out of quotations in full for every word noted in a given book (unless it was very short) was of course time-consuming; for the time being, Coleridge suggested, contributors need only make a brief note for themselves of items 'likely to be required', each with a page reference. They should then go through their list, and for each word in A–D that was not given in the Basis, copy out a full quotation. Then, 'when the publication of the Dictionary has made progress, another portion of the Basis, of equal magnitude, will be issued'—whereupon readers could go through their old wordlists, this time for the letters E–H; and then again for I–L, and so on. Coleridge was evidently still envisaging publication in the imminent future, and had

---

[124] *TPS* for 1860–1, p. 307 (14 Feb. 1861). This publication was one of the first to be printed by the Victoria Press, set up in early 1860 by Emily Faithfull and run entirely by women.

[125] Coleridge (1861b: 4).

[126] Reported in Furnivall (1861), 'Preliminary Notice'.

even gone so far as to have a specimen page printed, containing entries from *affect* to *affection*.[127]

The tragic next event in the history of the Dictionary is well known. Coleridge's tuberculosis had already placed obstacles in the way of his 'Glossarial Index'; it now deprived the Dictionary itself of its Editor, who died on 23 April 1861, at the age of only 31.[128] An 'unforeseen accident' had occurred; although it would not 'paralyze [the] efforts' of those concerned with driving forward the Dictionary, Coleridge's successors would soon discover just how far the project was from publication.

POSTSCRIPT: COLERIDGE'S *NACHLASS*

In fact Coleridge had gone further than preparing his printed specimen. Among the materials which were to be passed on to James Murray in 1879, as will be described in Chapter 4, were a number of slips in Coleridge's hand, showing that he had begun to compile a full sequence of complete entries in A; the surviving material—which James Murray made direct use of when he came to begin work on the letter A—shows that Coleridge had reached as far as the word *abrupt*: several dozen, probably over a hundred entries which he had worked up into something like a publishable form, including definitions, etymologies, and indications of which quotations were to be given for each word and sense.[129] Coleridge had thus had ample opportunity to encounter, and provisionally settle, many issues of editorial policy. We can see something of his conclusions in the two pages of Coleridge's entries (from *A* to *aback*) which Furnivall printed as an appendix to Part III of the 'Basis of Comparison' in 1862, which together with the fragmentary manuscript material constitute an instructive indication of how the Dictionary might have looked had Coleridge survived.

Arguably the most obvious difference between Coleridge's entries and their counterparts in the Dictionary as eventually published is one of presentation. All the definitions in each entry are placed in a block before the quotations, which are then given in a numbered chronological sequence, with each definition keyed to

---

[127] Craigie (1933a: x). I know of no surviving copy of the specimen.

[128] According to Elisabeth Murray, his final attack was 'brought on by a chill caused by sitting in damp clothes during a Philological Society lecture' (*CWW* p. 136). For a discussion of the various accounts of Coleridge's death and the events leading up to it, see Considine (2014a).

[129] A few of Coleridge's slips were incorporated directly—almost always with substantial alterations— by James Murray into his printer's copy, which is preserved today in the OUP archives as 'NED copy'; a rare case of a Coleridge definition surviving more or less unchanged is that for *abatis*. Many more were discarded but not thrown away altogether, and therefore survive among the separate sequence of slips known as 'NED superfluous'. None of his slips for words in *abs-* survive, although from the large number of quotations beyond this point which are written out in his hand, it would seem that he had done at least some preliminary work on words as far as *afflation*. Some of the completed entries presumably formed the basis of the paper on 'Extracts from the Dictionary-Articles left by the late Herbert Coleridge' which was read to the Philological Society, probably by Furnivall, on 24 April 1862 (*TPS* for 1862–3, p. 329). Furnivall also used the entries as the basis for some specimen entries of his own: see p. 60 below.

cleane drawne out.—(1577)—*Hounshed.   Desc. Britain.*
B. 2, c. 22, p. 213.

ABACK, adv.   [also written ' o bak' *divisim.*
    Etym. A.S. *on-bæc,* Old Norse, *á bak,* or *á baki*].
        a. 1. (denoting motion) Backwards, towards
                that which lies behind (1, 2, 4, 5,
                6, 9, 11, 12).
            2. (denoting rest) On or in that which is
                behind; behind (3, 8, 10).
        Phr. ' Take *aback,*' signifying to surprise by
                something novel and unexpected (11).
            ' Put *aback,*' to rebuke, check suddenly
                (7).
    The leading idea is that of a forward motion in a
given course being suddenly arrested.   The earlier
form of the phrase, that with ' put,' implies something unpleasant in the arrest to the thing or person
arrested; the other denotes simple surprise.

1   He not thurs the i-meinde smak
            Wether he shall avorth the *abak.*
                (c. 1270)—*Owl and Night,* 822, 3.

2.   Twei grete dragones out of *this* stones come,
        That on was red, *the other* wyte, *tho* gonne to fy*g*te faste
        Strong batail, and *the* fuyr out of *the* mou*th* caste,
        So *that the* white was aboue, as *the* folk y-seye,
        And drof *the* rede al *abak* out of *the* put ney.
                (1300) – *Robert of Gloucester, p.* 131.

    3. Jeroboam was dampnid, for he held *the* peple *abak* by
two kalfis, *that thei* worschipid not God in Jerbm̄,—(15th
cent. early)—*Apol. for Lollards, p.* 75.

    4. Of *theis* [disciplis] sum are iuel, and gon *o bak* ; and
Judas was His disciple chosun, and His apostil, and mani
of His disciplis went *a bak.*—*Ibid.* p. 82.

    5. He [Crist] turnid and seid to Peter, Go *o bak* after
Me, Sathanas.—*Ibid.* p. 56.

    6. For lacke of māhod draweth hī ever *abacke.*—(1420)—
Lydgate.   Chron. of Troy, Bk. i. c. 5.

    7. If eny man wolde seie here that in tho daies no lay
persoon ou*g*te geve eny hous or feeld to the clergie . . . . .
certis this seiyng may be at fulle Putt *Abak* and be rebukid.
—(c. 1449)—*Pecocke.   Repressor.* p. 290.   Part iii. ch. 3.

    8.   And when tyme is, to put thyselfe in prease,
            And when tyme is, to holde thyselfe *abacke.*
            For tyme well spent can never have lacke.
                    Skelton.   On Tyme, 22.

    9.   Why dost withdraw thy hand *abacke*
                And hide it in thy lap
            O plucke it out and be not slacke
                To give thy foes a rap.
(c. 1540) *John Hopkins.   Psalm* lxxiv. v. 11, *Metr. Version.*

    10. Keep your self in the love of Christ, and stand far
a-back from the pollutions of the world.—(1637) – *Ruther-
foord's Letters.   Epistle* viii.

    11.   A beauty hovers still, and ne'er takes wing ;
            But with a silent charm compels the stern
            And tort'ring genius of the bitter spring,
            To shrink *aback* and cower upon his urn.
        S. T. Coleridge.   The Two Founts.   Poems, p. 340.

    12. Thus occupied, the observation of Quirk had com-
pletely *taken* Gammon *aback* ; and he lost his presence of
mind.—*S. Warren.   Ten Thousand a-Year.* Vol. i. ch. 4.

FIGURE 3   Coleridge's entry for *aback* as printed by Furnivall in 1862.

the quotations by numerical references: a scheme which had been specified in the 'Canones Lexicographici', and which arguably owes much to the layout of entries in Richardson's dictionary. In addition to such presentational differences, there are also many differences of content. There are many inconsistencies, as for example the fact that some of the smaller printed entries lack anything that could be called an etymology; this may merely be a reflection of the unfinished state of the material. In fact what etymological material does survive is something of an embarrassment in the glimpse it reveals of the etymological approach that was (at least by Coleridge) considered appropriate at this stage. The fullest etymology is that given for the exclamation *ah*, which is traced to 'AK or AH, denoting sorrow or pain, a root which reappears constantly, as Gr[eek] ἄχος, Eng. *ache*, A.S. *ace*, etc. The first usage therefore, and the only one which is etymologically justifiable, of *Ah*, is as an exclamation of pain or grief—mere surprise being indicated by Ha! or the compound Ah ha!'

Surely the most important difference, however, is the paucity of Coleridge's quotation evidence, and the consequent sparseness of the set of meanings which they illustrated. The largest entry to survive in printed form, for the archaic preposition *a*, contained only eighteen quotations, which were taken as representing four meanings; by contrast, James Murray was later able to present the reader with entries for two distinct prepositions, divided into fifteen and three senses respectively, and containing well over a hundred quotations. The situation for *aback* (see Figure 3) is similar, with twelve quotations in Coleridge's entry compared with twenty-nine in Murray's. There was evidently a very long way indeed to go before Passow's principle 'that every word should be made to tell its own story'—to which Coleridge had recommitted himself in his open letter of May 1860[130]—could be realized.

---

[130] Coleridge (1860: 72).

2

Furnivall's Dictionary: 1861–1875

Two days after Coleridge's death, Trench wrote to Furnivall: 'Should not the Philological soon meet, & consider what ought now to be done—I fear the keystone of our arch has been withdrawn & that we remain an arch no longer.'[1] In fact Furnivall announced Coleridge's death at the scheduled meeting of the Society that took place that evening, although the published record of this meeting makes no mention of any discussion about the Dictionary's future.

But the torch had been passed on. Furnivall, visiting Coleridge only just before he died, had promised to carry on his work.[2] On 27 April Trench wrote of 'how rejoiced I am that you are so minded; & that there is to be no interruption of the work'.[3] Quotations of course continued to arrive from the Dictionary's readers, and Furnivall immediately began to take delivery of them himself.[4] It is not clear exactly when he was formally appointed Editor, but by the Society's Anniversary Meeting in May, at which he reported on 'the present condition of the Collections for the Society's Dictionary, and the course he proposed to pursue with regard to the scheme', he was evidently recognized *de facto* as the person in charge of the project.[5]

Furnivall's view of the prospects for early publication of the Dictionary was very different from Coleridge's, and his assessment of the 'condition of the Collections' was

---

[1] HL 25 Apr. 1861 Trench to FJF.

[2] John Duke Coleridge, 'The late Herbert Coleridge', *Macmillan's Magazine* Nov. 1861, pp. 56–60.

[3] HL 27 Apr. 1861 Trench to FJF.

[4] A note by Furnivall dated 2 May 1861 records his having picked up several new collections of quotations 'from H.C.'s house' (OUPA, OED/B/1/2/11).

[5] *TPS* for 1860–1, p. 309. The meetings of the Philological Society seem to have concerned themselves remarkably little with the Dictionary during the rest of 1861: the announcement of Coleridge's death and the report by Furnivall on 23 May are the only mentions of the project in the Notices of the Society's meetings for 1861.

almost certainly a gloomy one. He seems to have taken, as his first task, the preparation of Part II of the Basis of Comparison for the third period, which appeared in
September, covering the letters E to L, and whose Preface contrasts starkly with the
optimism of Coleridge's to Part I. Coleridge had, it is true, acknowledged the incompleteness of the materials collected so far, observing that the wordlist he had been able
to assemble 'presents a somewhat uneven and heterogeneous appearance'—though he
argued that it was better to publish the list as it was than to delay its appearance still
further. Furnivall clearly regarded 'uneven' as a considerable understatement. Indeed,
comparison of any part of Coleridge's list with any of the comprehensive dictionaries
then available shows how patchy the evidence was.[6]

But the incompleteness of the materials for the third period was not the only problem. In preparing his entries for words beginning with A, Coleridge had hoped to be
able to fill up the gaps in these from his own reading, but Furnivall realized that this
was hopelessly optimistic:

I was (and am) convinced that nothing would supply the deficiencies but the work of our
contributors for two years on new and revised Bases of Comparison for the first Two Periods
at least, and the having in hand some material for our Etymological Committee to get into
finished shape. With this conviction I have determined to put aside all idea of printing the First
Part of the Dictionary for four or five years unless some great unexpected help is forthcoming.

Such a drastically revised view of the situation necessitated a new plan of action; and
Furnivall, of course, had ideas on how best to prepare the way for the compilation
of the Dictionary proper. Once he had completed the Basis of Comparison for the
third period, he proposed to compile 'Two Concise Dictionaries of Early and Middle
English, which shall include severally all the materials sent in for the First and Second
Periods, and serve as new Bases of Comparison for those Periods'. This elaborate
scheme for the production of purely preparatory material must have alarmed the
Philological Society, who until recently had been offered the prospect of imminent
publication of the Dictionary itself.

Furnivall's Preface to Part II of the Basis of Comparison is more optimistic on the
subject of the Dictionary's etymological component. Carl Lottner, an etymologist of
some repute, had been commissioned to prepare 'an Etymological Analysis of all the
words in the latest English Dictionary—Worcester's', and had already nearly finished
the letter C.[7] Furnivall then describes his view of the next stage in the compilation
process, which shows just what a lengthy task he saw as lying ahead. The two Concise

---

[6] For example, the *Imperial Dictionary* (1847–50) contained dozens of words which should appear, but
do not, in the first column of the first page of the list, including *aardvark, Aaronic, abacist, abaft, abasement,
abatable, abattoir, abecedarian, abele, aberdevine*, and *aberrancy*.

[7] The American Joseph E. Worcester (1784–1865) compiled several dictionaries, of which the *Dictionary
of the English Language* (1860) was arguably the most important. Carl Lottner's work for Furnivall had
already been brought to the attention of the public in a short article in the *Athenaeum* of 29 June 1861
(p. 865), in which he was said to have 'completed the A's' in Worcester's dictionary.

FIGURE 4   Henry Hucks Gibbs.

Dictionaries, together with Lottner's etymological material, would form the basis for two years' further work by the Dictionary's contributors, after which 'the Editor whoever he may then be, will be in a somewhat fitting position for producing a work worthy of the Society'. In fact Trübner went so far as to announce that both Concise Dictionaries were now 'in the Press', together with Lottner's 'Etymological Analysis' (edited for publication by Furnivall, 'Editor of the Philological Society's Proposed New English Dictionary').[8]

Fragmentary and incomplete the evidence for the third period undoubtedly still was, but in compiling Part II of the Basis of Comparison Furnivall evidently had more material to draw on than Coleridge. 'Mr. Rossiter's Index to Burke's Works' must now at last have been in some consultable form, since it is mentioned in the Preface, as are other 'contributors', including over a dozen whom Furnivall acknowledges by name, among them Henry Hucks Gibbs (Figure 4), a wealthy merchant banker (and director of the Bank of England) who would go on to become one of the Dictionary's greatest supporters.[9] There were also three names marked as 'U.S.'—the first publicly identified

[8] All three publications are mentioned in a 'List of New Publications for 1861' issued by Trübner & Co.
[9] Gibbs had been reading for the Dictionary at least since July 1860, as seen from a letter of that date to James Halliwell-Phillipps (Halliwell-Phillipps papers, Edinburgh University Library, 'Letters of Authors', vol. 79, no. 73).

American contributors to the Dictionary.[10] Nor was it only in the third period that contributors continued to be active: reading in the second period was also still going on, as can be seen from the expanding lists given in the several versions of a printed 'List of Books already read, or now being read, for the Philological Society's New English Dictionary' which Furnivall issued during the summer.[11]

In his Preface to Part II of the Basis of Comparison, published in September 1861, Furnivall promised that Part III would follow 'early' in 1862. In this he was only slightly optimistic: his Preface to Part III is dated 15 March 1862.

In the intervening months, however, ideas about what form the next stage of work on the Dictionary should take had changed considerably, as may be seen from a resolution passed by the Philological Society in February.[12] The resolution makes no mention of separate Concise Dictionaries for the first and second periods; instead, it envisages a single work, to be prepared 'as a preliminary to the Society's proposed new English Dictionary and as a new basis of comparison for all the other Periods'. Another resolution passed on the same occasion marks an important innovation in the way the editorial work was to be carried out: it authorized Furnivall 'to entrust the quotations in his possession, and the sub-editing of any parts of the concise Dictionary to such of the contributors to the Dictionary or other Volunteers as he shall think fit'. In the event, no Concise Dictionary would ever see the light of day, but the idea, and the extension of the principle of cooperation beyond the collection of quotations to the actual compilation of entries, amounted to a complete reconception of the project, with far-reaching consequences.[13]

Furnivall enthusiastically announced the new dispensation in his Part III Preface. He also promised to prepare a specimen of the proposed Concise Dictionary, to be printed for further consideration by the Society, who were evidently still cautious about a venture which—'Concise' or not—was still bound to be lengthy and expensive. Furnivall, however, had no such reservations: while the Society might reasonably wish to see what a book was to be like before putting its name to it, he was confident that the book would appear, with or without the Society's name attached, 'as a working book, an abridged first edition of the new Dictionary originally proposed'. In fact he mentions having already made arrangements with a publisher, although it is not clear who this can have been.

The extent to which the Concise Dictionary was to be 'a working book' is clear from the explicit way in which it would acknowledge the incompleteness of the materials collected so far. The Philological Society's February resolution provided for the

---

[10] The three Americans are 'Mr. Bacon', 'Mr. Johnson', and 'W. Sargeant [*sic*; *recte* Sargent]'. Of these the most prolific by far was Winthrop Sargent of Natchez, Mississippi, whose contributions (from works by Washington Irving) had in fact begun to reach Coleridge before his death.

[11] Copies of three versions, with various dates in June and July 1861, are preserved at OED/B/1/2/2.

[12] ProcPS 27 Feb. 1862, p. 328.

[13] It has become a commonplace to cite the *OED* as an early successful implementation of the kind of mass collaborative compilation now generally known as crowdsourcing. See for example O'sullivan (2009: 47–56).

inclusion of 'words, senses of words, idioms, etc., known to exist, but for which authority has not yet been sent to the Editor [...] marked with a *, or other sign, to denote
the want of an authority'. Furnivall further spelled out what this was to mean in his
Preface: there was a need for a book which would show '[w]hat are our known defects,
what we have not that other Dictionaries and Glossaries have, and which shall afford
our Contributors a less meagre frame to fill up with their newly-found words, idioms,
etc., than the Bases [of Comparison] they are at present working on'.

For the man at the centre of the enterprise, and providing much of the driving force,
Furnivall remains strikingly modest about the editorial role he envisages for himself.
He undertakes to sort the quotation materials into' alphabetical and chronological
order, and to prepare a few sample entries for the guidance of intending sub-editors;
but these entries are to be 'models, or rather suggestions, for Sub-editors to work by'.
Knowing as he did the magnitude of the task that lay ahead, how could he imagine that
a coordinating Editor would have so little to do? He was of course still taking delivery
of quotations from existing readers and sending them new texts.[14] And he had other
literary preoccupations: he was still seeking out unpublished Early English texts and
persuading others to prepare editions of them (while editing some of them himself).[15]

It is true that the Bases of Comparison for the first and third periods had done
no more than list the range of evidence collected for each word; and if the Concise
Dictionary were to be no more than a 'new Basis of Comparison', a 'working book'
of a very preliminary kind, then he could hope to get away with doing comparatively
little editorial work. But it is clear from the February Resolution that the Philological
Society expected considerably more than this: the Concise Dictionary was to be 'as far
as possible, an abstract of what the larger Dictionary should be; and shall contain the
Pronunciation, Critical marks [i.e. labelling], Etymologies, Roots, Prefixes, Suffixes,
Definitions, and Synonyms of the Words registered in it; with short quotations [...]
for all words for which passages have been sent in'. This clearly represented a huge
volume of editorial work. The smallness of the part that Furnivall saw for himself in
this becomes more understandable when we remember the faith that he placed in the
virtues of cooperation: he may have been anticipating that the sub-editors would be
able to write the entries for him, and to do this so well that only light editing would be
needed. Such confidence in the abilities of his (as yet unidentified) sub-editors would

[14] Benzie (1983: 95) quotes correspondence in July and November 1861 with one such contributor,
William Carew Hazlitt.

[15] In December 1861 Furnivall completed the Preface to his edition of *Handlyng Synne*, which was
published by the Roxburghe Club the following year, while in early 1862 his *Early English Poems and Lives
of Saints* appeared as a supplement to the Philological Society's (delayed) *Transactions* for 1858. An edition
by Whitley Stokes of the fifteenth-century *Play of the Sacrament* appeared as an appendix to *TPS* for
1860–1; and in April 1862 the Society's Council decided, apparently at Furnivall's prompting (see BL MS
Egerton 2847 ff. 262, 267–8), to publish Richard Morris's edition of the *Liber Cure Cocorum* on a similar
basis. The Society published two further such editions of early texts in 1863 and 1864. The publication of
this series of early texts by the Society constitutes an immediate precursor to the work of the Early English
Text Society: see p. 48.

be entirely characteristic, but it was also seriously misplaced. The Part III Preface invited all those 'with qualifications for the task' to volunteer for sub-editing; precious few of those who came forward would turn out to be suitably qualified for the work that was needed.

Meanwhile, and notwithstanding the numerous appeals already made elsewhere, Furnivall issued a new appeal for further collection of quotations. For the second period there was urgent work outstanding: most of 'the extracts for Shakespeare's and the Bible words' still needed to be written out. For the third period, Furnivall, fresh from the task of sorting everything that had so far been sent in, was only too aware of what still needed to be read. Readers were exhorted 'to take one book at least by [a long list of poets, novelists, dramatists, historians, and essayists follows; Mill, for some reason, appears in italics], and the host of other writers of whose books none have been yet read'. Furnivall's inclusive view of the Dictionary's remit receives its most eloquent description:

We have set ourselves to form a National Portrait Gallery, not only of the worthies, but of all the members, of the race of English words which is to form the dominant speech of the world. No winged messenger who bears to us the thoughts and aspirations, the weakness and the littleness, of our forefathers; who is to carry ours to our descendants; is to be absent,—

Fling our doors wide! all, all, not one, but all,

must enter: for their service let them be honoured; and though the search for them may sometimes seem wearisome, and the labour of the ingathering more irksome still, yet the work is worthy and the aim unselfish. Let us, then, persevere.[16]

Whatever the response to these appeals, the task of processing the ongoing Dictionary reading was certainly keeping Furnivall busy enough: too busy to make much progress through A as regards the compilation of dictionary entries.[17] As if the work of processing quotations, and pressing on with the editing of Early English texts, were not enough, in May he became the Philological Society's sole Honorary Secretary—Thomas Hewitt Key, who had shared this task with him since 1853, was elected a Vice-President of the Society, and gave up his Secretaryship—which can only have added to his administrative workload.

But interested parties did begin to come forward to offer themselves as sub-editors. By the autumn Furnivall had been able to allocate letters of the alphabet to fourteen volunteers; almost all were people who had already helped the project by extracting

[16] Circular to members of the Philological Society, 9 Nov. 1862, pp. 3–4 (quoted in *CWW* p. 137); the quoted line of poetry is from Tennyson's *The Princess*. Furnivall's anxiety that no opportunity be missed to recruit contributors is seen at the end of the Part III Preface, where what would have been a blank quarter-page is filled with another exhortation to 'Every one into whose hands this [pamphlet] may fall' to send in extracts.

[17] The account of the Dictionary work which Arthur Munby found Furnivall engaged in when he visited him in May 1862 (Hudson 1974: 123–4, quoted in *CWW* p. 138) mentions 'arranging and writing out words', but this may well mean the writing out of quotations rather than the editing of entries.

quotations—including Henry Hucks Gibbs, Charlotte Yonge (a cousin of Gibbs), and W. M. Rossetti—although by no means all were members of the Philological Society. In September Furnivall sent them a substantial circular headed 'The Concise Dictionary. Letter to Sub-Editors', together with a specimen page showing 'the abstract of the full articles proposed for the Concise Dictionary'.[18]

One sub-editor, at least, was quick off the mark. The letter B was allocated to William Gee, a banker living in Boston (Lincolnshire), who soon after taking delivery of the quotations decided—no doubt in consultation with Furnivall—to prepare and publish a complete list of all of the words for which he had evidence, together with an indication of the evidence—not just for a single period, as with the earlier Bases of Comparison, but for all three. This was issued in the summer of 1863 as 'A Vocabulary of Words Beginning with the Letter B': a 96-page pamphlet listing approximately 18,000 items.

Having set his first cohort of sub-editors to work, Furnivall reapplied himself to the question of securing a publisher. In December 1862 he wrote to John Murray with a fresh proposal for publication, 'not for the large Dictionary, but for one of the size of Liddell & Scott, 1600 pages 4to., something like the Specimen which I enclose'.[19] Furnivall enthusiastically talked up the new project, on which 'twenty Subeditors, mostly University men, are now at work'—and, amazingly, forecast that copy would all be ready within three years. At the same time, plans were afoot for a scheme to raise the funds needed to complete 'the large Dictionary'—to be headed, allegedly, by the Prince of Wales and the Duke of Devonshire. Furnivall was evidently determined not to lose sight of the original grand project.

The response from Murray was encouraging. While he had some reservations over matters of presentation, and retained the doubts that he had expressed four years earlier about the inclusion of obsolete words, in general the new proposal struck him as acceptable. Negotiations took place over the next few months; Murray was still referring to a 'draft agreement' at the end of March, but from subsequent correspondence it is clear that a contract—a personal one with Furnivall—must eventually have been signed, with Furnivall committed to deliver copy for the Concise Dictionary on or before 1 January 1866.[20] Although by April 1863 Murray was already sending Furnivall money, the two men continued to disagree over how the scale of the book was to be kept within acceptable limits. Furnivall persisted in his view that obsolete and archaic words should be covered; Murray, who felt that these would 'impede rather than aid' the project, was more concerned that at least a few words of quotation should be included to illustrate each word and sense, while Furnivall felt that bare references, presented

---

[18] The 'Letter to Sub-Editors' is dated 15 September 1862, but copies of the same letter were sent to those sub-editors who volunteered at a later date. Charlotte Yonge seems to have started work in November 1862; Furnivall's letter to her of 11 November 1862, explaining that the materials for N have not been fully alphabetized, survives in MP. He also comments, with typical optimism: 'should you find N not enough for you, I have no doubt that there will be another letter to spare in course of time.'

[19] JMA 19 Dec. 1862 FJF to JM.

[20] HL 31 Mar. 1863 JM to FJF.

in a highly condensed form, would suffice. Furnivall's estimate that the inclusion of quotation text would increase the extent of the text by a third was dismissed by Murray with the comment that 'a volume 1/3^d larger than L[iddell] & S[cott's] Lexicon seems to me quite out of the question—no one w^d accept such a bulk of paper as *a volume*.'[21] The two men evidently saw the Concise Dictionary very differently: Furnivall regarded it as the forerunner of the great national project, with which any publisher ought to be proud to associate himself, while Murray, ever the businessman, insisted that the book had to be made attractive to something more than a tiny number of potential purchasers. The difference is clear from a letter Murray wrote two years later:

[Y]our work to succeed must be a practical Dicty i.e. one of words in use [...] the archaeology of our language must be the matter of a second work. If you satisfy the public with the first, a portion of them will come to you for the second. If you mix the two you will please no party.[22]

The fact that the two men could disagree so profoundly, and at such a late stage, about the nature of the book they were engaged upon hardly boded well for the success of the project.

However, during the first year or two at least of the contract with Murray the project did advance on the twin fronts of sub-editing and the collection of yet more quotations. Furnivall reported progress to Philological Society members in a series of circulars; the first, dated 9 November 1862, listed the names of the first fourteen sub-editors, and noted that 756 works or authors had been read and excerpted, with another 271 in hand. He does not appear to have produced a comparable report in 1863—perhaps because for once even he found himself too busy: this was, after all, the time when, after failing to persuade the Philological Society to continue funding the publication of new editions of Early English texts, he persuaded some other members of the Society to join him in founding another society to carry on this work.[23] The Early English Text Society was founded early in 1864, and must have given Furnivall plenty to do; however, for the circular issued to Philological Society members in October of that year, he did manage to put together a report on the preceding two years' activities, with over 1,100 works now read—quotation slips arrived constantly, averaging 'more than

[21] JMA 7 Apr, 1863 FJF to JM; HL 10 Apr. 1863 JM to FJF.

[22] JMA 4 Aug. 1865 JM to FJF (copy).

[23] For a full account of the founding and early work of the Early English Text Society, see Singleton (2005). As Singleton points out, although it seems certain that the making available of early texts for the use of the Dictionary's contributors was an important objective of the EETS, explicit evidence of this is wanting: James Murray, writing some years later (in Munro et al. 1911: 132), recalled that it had been '[o]ne of the great objects, perhaps originally the greatest, in founding the E. E. T. S., although in the original prospectus it was for good reasons put second to the publication of works of the Arthurian Cycle', but it is not mentioned as an object in any of the EETS's published records before 1900. I have been unable to improve on the indirect evidence found by Singleton, namely the remark by Whitley Stokes in his edition of the *Play of the Sacrament* (see p. 45 n. 15) that he hoped his text 'may prove a useful quarry for the dictionary of the Philological Society'.

a packet a day, excluding Sundays'—and more in hand. The customary appeal for new volunteer readers is made, but the lengths to which Furnivall is now willing to go to make things easier for potential readers suggest an element of desperation. Certainly the quotation evidence was still alarmingly fragmentary—Furnivall complained, for example, that there were still no examples at all of such ordinary words as *imaginable*, *imaginative*, and *immerse*—but the circular invites those disinclined to take the trouble to copy out quotations in full simply to mark up suitable passages in a book or journal, which can then be passed on to be copied out as a purely clerical task. Even the chore of repeatedly writing out the date and title could now be done away with: a letter from Furnivall in the *Athenaeum* of 3 December offers to provide slips pre-printed with this information. More disturbingly, a list is given of books waiting to be 'marked and cut up'.[24] The practice of cutting up the pages of books, which Furnivall countenanced for some years, had the one advantage of eliminating copying errors, but it is distressing to see among the quotation slips collected for the Dictionary a large number of cannibalized pages from some extremely old books, some from as early as the mid-sixteenth century.[25]

The state of play in the autumn of 1864 as regards sub-editing was rather more mixed. Furnivall, seeking as ever to put the best slant on things, reported that almost all of the sub-editors 'are able to promise their work complete before or by the 1st of October next'; but even he had to acknowledge that there were some serious exceptions to this rosy picture. Henry Hucks Gibbs lost his right hand in a shooting accident; he was determined not to let this stand in the way of his work for the Dictionary—his left-handed contributions, sloping as sharply to the left as his earlier writing had to the right, continued for another four decades—but it did curtail his sub-editing of the letter C; some work had been done in L, but it had yet to be abridged for the Concise Dictionary; and the letters M, R, T, and W had been, or were in danger of being, abandoned by their respective sub-editors.

During 1865 some, at least, of the sub-editors made progress. Furnivall himself apparently did resume work on at least one (!) dictionary entry, as in May he read a paper to the Philological Society on 'the derivation of *abash*'.[26] Two of the other sub-editors, Charlotte Yonge and T. H. Sheppard, made more visible progress, in the form of 'Vocabularies' for their own letters, on the model of William Gee's for B. Both lists—Charlotte Yonge's (anonymously published) list for N, and Sheppard's for the letters U and V—were apparently issued in May or June. In each 'Vocabulary' Furnivall

---

[24] All of the books listed, '& 20 others', had been taken within weeks of the circular being issued, according to an annotated copy in JMA.

[25] For example, among the unused quotations for the word *ready* are cuttings from a 1549 volume of translations of Erasmus' paraphrases of the New Testament, and the 1557 edition of the works of Sir Thomas More.

[26] *TPS* for 1865, Notices of Meetings, p. 5. Furnivall gave several other papers in 1864–5, on topics including the language of Laȝamon (4 Nov. 1864), the early use of *who* in the nominative (20 Jan. 1865), and the romance *Sir Generides* (1 Dec. 1865). Thereafter his name does not figure again (except in the lists of Society officers) in the accounts of meetings until 1867.

(as ever) squeezed in a 'Preliminary Notice', announcing the usual list of books 'in hand for cutting up', but also reporting further gaps in the sub-editing team.[27]

By the time of his circular the following October Furnivall was obliged to state in even starker terms the alarming state of the project:

The Concise Dictionary [...] is by no means in the state that could be wished [...] from the reports of the Sub-editors that have just reached me, it is evident that the work cannot be completed for the next year (though several letters are promised before the end of the winter), and Mr. Murray's forbearance must be asked for at least that time.

(The 'forbearance' required of Murray was by this stage considerably more than Furnivall had indicated in December 1864, when he had breezily assured him of his 'good hopes of placing the MS. in [Murray's] hands by the time agreed on, though part of it will want further revision, for which the issue [of the Dictionary] in Parts will give time'.[28]) The ranks of volunteer readers had continued to swell, but as far as sub-editing was concerned things had if anything deteriorated, with several further letters in need of a sub-editor.

Such a chaotic state of affairs, only months before the copy for the whole Dictionary was due to be handed over, must have been a matter of considerable concern to John Murray. Unfortunately, after August 1865, when Murray wrote to ask about the progress of the Concise Dictionary, there is a gap of nearly a year and a half during which no records survive of any communication between the two men. However, it is at least clear that the deadline of 1 January 1866 came and went without the arrival of any Dictionary copy at Murray's offices.

How much did the Philological Society care about Furnivall's management of the task with which it had entrusted him? As far as the membership at large were concerned, the only indication we have is the negative evidence provided by the published notices of the Society's meetings. Remarkably, the Dictionary does not figure explicitly at all in these records between April 1862, when Coleridge's draft entries were discussed, and November 1868 (except for a brief mention at the Anniversary Meeting in May 1868 when Furnivall 'stated generally the condition in which the Society's Dictionary material was'[29]). Several members of the Society's Council during these years were figures who had interested themselves in the Dictionary from its earliest days, including some members of the committee that had been established in 1859 to

---

[27]   No other 'vocabularies' like those compiled by Gee, Sheppard, and Charlotte Yonge were published. The only other such publication to survive is a single sheet listing words in the first part of the letter I, compiled by William Woodham Webb and issued on his behalf by Furnivall sometime during the 1860s. A copy is held in OUPA at OED/B/1/2/1; the inadequacy of Webb's materials may be judged from the fact that he lists a large number of words for which he has no evidence at all apart from other dictionaries, including such relatively common words as *Icelandic*, *icily*, and *idealistic*.

[28]   JMA 20 Dec. 1864 FJF to JM.

[29]   ProcPS 15 May 1868, p. 11.

draw up the 'Canones Lexicographici'. But of the original triumvirate, only Furnivall now remained actively involved. Trench had been nominated to succeed Richard Whately as Archbishop of Dublin in December 1863, which effectively removed him from the picture. He was evidently doubtful about the merits of Furnivall's 'Concise Dictionary', as he had withdrawn his support for it by February 1863.[30] Nor had any of the old 'Canones' committee volunteered their services as sub-editors. Only Hensleigh Wedgwood could be said still to be doing anything of use to the Dictionary, with a steady succession of papers to the Philological Society on etymological topics.[31]

During 1866 there is some evidence that even Furnivall's own efforts may have slackened. Perhaps the lapse of the agreement with John Murray might be expected to be followed by something of a drawing of breath; but other reasons are not hard to find. 1866 was a terrible year for him personally: his baby daughter Ena died, and he suffered heavy financial losses in the collapse of the Overend and Gurney bank, in which he had invested most of his inheritance from his father.[32] The flourishing Early English Text Society took up much of the energy he had to spare, although even here his work was affected: his preface to his edition of *The Book of Quinte Essence*, dated 16 May 1866, pleads as an excuse for its brevity 'the loss of our sweet, bright, only child, and other distress'.

Further evidence of a loss of momentum at this time may be found in the corpus of the *OED*'s newspaper quotations. It is fairly clear that Furnivall's practice of taking quotations from his daily reading of the newspapers was on a scale not matched by that of any of his fellow contributors; of course only a small fraction of the newspaper quotations he contributed were made use of, but from searches of the *OED* database and the paper slips in the archives it is clear that throughout the 1860s (and later) quotations from Furnivall's usual choice of newspapers constitute a high proportion of all periodical quotations available to the later *OED* editors. Working on the reasonable assumption (and one which is borne out by checks of the slips themselves, for the 1860s and 1870s at least) that the yearly count of newspaper quotations *used* in the Dictionary correlates fairly closely with those supplied by Furnivall, it would seem that in 1866 his extraction of newspaper quotations declined by something like 50 per cent compared to the previous year; the figure drops even lower in subsequent years (apart from a possible slight rally in 1869).

Evidence of the progress of the Dictionary during the later 1860s is hard to find, and what little there is—mainly in the form of Furnivall's annual Philological Society

---

[30] On a letter from Furnivall of 14 February (JMA), John Murray subsequently noted: 'Feb 19 Mr. F. called—Dean of West has withdrawn from C Dict.'

[31] Key, now a Vice-President of the Society, was continuing to interest himself in etymological matters, but by this stage his rather exotic views were hardly helping the project (the *ODNB* describes him as having become 'something of an embarrassment' to the Society). Goldstücker was probably busy with his monumental (and hopelessly impractical) revision of Horace Wilson's Sanskrit–English dictionary.

[32] It is suggested in John Munro's memoir of Furnivall (in Munro et al. 1911: xlii) that Henry Hucks Gibbs and the bibliophile Henry Huth gave him financial assistance at this time.

circulars—is generally not encouraging.[33] In October 1867 he claimed that seven editors had finished, or nearly finished, one or more of the letters assigned to them, and that all the other letters were 'in progress, except W, the sub-editor of which [...] died about a year ago'; the reading of books was 'kept up by a faithful few', but he had failed to find a new sub-editor for W, and the letters I, J, P, R, and S were all in need of additional sub-editing help. Before the month was out another sub-editor, Robert Rogers, had given up.[34] The 1868 circular reported only that replies from sub-editors 'shew a favourable state of progress' and that 'of our readers a few faithful ones keep on'. In November he gave a progress report at a Philological Society meeting, 'together with a calculation by the Rev. G. Wheelwright, showing that about one-third of the work had been sub-edited'—a profoundly discouraging admission given that the whole text of the Concise Dictionary was supposed to have been ready for the printers nearly three years earlier.[35] In 1869 he reported 'a steady rate of progress' in sub-editing; in 1870, while sub-editing is still going on, there are now only 'four or five faithful readers'.

Members of the Philological Society could at least count on learning something about the Dictionary's progress, either from Furnivall's circulars or at the Society's anniversary meeting.[36] Outside this circle, news of the project was only erratically reported. For example, the *Athenaeum*, which in 1864 had sympathetically reported on the project's need for more help following Henry Hucks Gibbs's shooting accident, does not seem to have mentioned the Dictionary at all in 1865; and in 1866 the project is only briefly mentioned in the course of a correspondence about the word *bonfire*, initiated by the Dictionary sub-editor Robert Griffith. At about the same time a contributor to *Notes & Queries* wondered 'if the Philological Society's Dictionary is to be an accomplished fact; and if so, *when?*' He does not seem to have received a reply.[37]

On 2 February 1867 the *Athenaeum* carried a report that the number of quotations sent in for the Dictionary now exceeded half a million. The work of the sub-editors was mentioned; it was anticipated that the Philological Society would appoint a committee to revise their work—Furnivall is not mentioned, let alone named as Editor—and that it would be another two or three years before the Concise Dictionary could be published. In August one 'L.L.L.' wrote to *Notes & Queries*: 'Many books have been read [for the Dictionary], and thousands of extracts made for the purpose. I am very anxious to gather some fruit from these labours. Will some one who has authority in this undertaking report progress?' This time the enquiry did evoke a response—

---

[33] Few copies of these circulars survive; the quotations given here from those of 1867–9 are as reproduced in Wheelwright (1875).

[34] KCLFP 30 Oct. 1867 Rogers to FJF.

[35] TPS for 1868–9, Appendix, p. 12.

[36] The Dictionary was occasionally mentioned in the Society's own publications: for example, Henry Wheatley, in his *Dictionary of Reduplicated Words in the English Language* (published in 1866 as a substantial appendix to *TPS* for 1865), acknowledged the assistance of 'Mr. Furnivall and several of the Dictionary readers' in providing him with some of his quotation evidence. Wheatley's *Dictionary* dealt with words such as *fiddle-faddle*, *gew-gaw*, and *hanky-panky*; an appeal to Dictionary readers to send their quotations for such words to Wheatley had been included in T. H. Sheppard's 'Vocabulary' for U and V in 1865.

[37] *Athenaeum* 6 and 13 Oct. 1866, pp. 433, 473; *Notes & Queries* 8 Sept. 1866, p. 199.

although not from Furnivall, but from a recent recruit to the ranks of his sub-editors, Walter Skeat, who was to go on to become one of the greatest English scholars of his generation, and a great friend and supporter of the Dictionary. Skeat assured 'L.L.L.' that 'what was undertaken some years ago is being pushed on *now* as vigorously as ever […]. The thousands, say rather tens of thousands of extracts, are all duly sorted as they come in, and they are coming in still.' This was of course only a report on the collection of data; regarding sub-editing, Skeat struggled to match Furnivall's usual optimism—'parts of most of the letters are nearly ready for press'—but urged those with 'patience, industry, accuracy, and *leisure*' to contact Furnivall if they could offer help. A further letter from Skeat on the subject of collecting quotations, published a month later, notes: 'The thing most needed at this moment is a good collection of *common* words, as used by writers of the *present* century.'[38] The same practical request was made in Furnivall's October circular; and a report on the progress of the Dictionary, apparently based on the circular, appeared in the *Athenaeum* on 9 November.

Only six months later, however, the *Athenaeum* printed a brief and rather puzzling item asking 'What has become of the Philological Society?' After describing the Society's original proposal to compile the Dictionary—the plan for which was wrongly ascribed to Goldstücker—the item continued:

What has become of it? Is it being shaped for publication? If so, when will the first part appear? Such inquiries are pressed on our notice from time to time by gentlemen who were induced by us to enter on the toil of reading books and making extracts. We begin to feel that these complaints are not wholly unreasonable.

Furnivall's lengthy and irritated response was published the following week, pointing out the *Athenaeum*'s own recent coverage of the project; more interestingly, however, he mentions that—besides the fact that the 'two dozen sub-editors' have not yet finished their work—publication will have to wait until 'some more of the many important questions yet remaining unsettled in the domain of English Philology are settled': he instances the ongoing work of Alexander Ellis on early English pronunciation, and that of Richard Morris on case structure, one to be published by the Philological Society, the other by the Early English Text Society. In juxtaposing these different areas of research, Furnivall was evidently seeking—wishfully or otherwise—to suggest that all of them were in some way part of a grand enterprise. A further letter published a week later, this time from the literary scholar C. Mansfield Ingleby, sought to cast further doubt on the Dictionary's prospects, again from what seems a rather ill-informed position: Ingleby claimed that, whereas progress reports had been published annually during Coleridge's editorship,

now for years past not a single report has been issued; and to judge from my own experience, the general belief is, that the project will not be carried out. […] If your inquiry shall awaken

---

[38] *Athenaeum* 2 Feb. 1867, p. 158; *Notes & Queries* 31 Aug. 1867, p. 169, 28 Sept., p. 256, 2 Nov., p. 358.

the Council of the Philological Society from their long trance, you will have conferred an obligation on all persons interested in the success of that magnificent enterprise.[39]

The 'general belief' seemed likely to prove correct: during the next few years the project showed precious few signs of life, and in fact reached its very lowest ebb. In 1869 the *Pall Mall Gazette* commented that 'we fear there is nothing but an account of unfulfilled promise to be recorded [regarding the Dictionary]'; and in 1870 Furnivall, anonymously reviewing Robert Latham's new edition of Johnson in the *Athenaeum*, wrote bitterly of the unwisdom of entrusting the work of compilation to 'volunteers— volunteers who had other work to do, and could only give hours of scanty leisure, burdened with other engagements, to what should be the business of their lives. And so the Philological Society's Dictionary lags, and will lag, until the English people do for it what the German people have done for their dictionary.'[40] On 21 April 1871 the Philological Society's Council did rouse itself from its 'trance' to the extent of appointing 'a Committee [...] to enquire into the state of the Society's Dictionary'[41]— but this seems to have been no more than a response to financial difficulties. The Council meeting at which this committee was instituted had just heard a report from the Treasurer, Danby Fry, on the Society's financial position, which had recently deteriorated because of the cost of producing its publications, some of which had been exceptionally expensive. As a consequence the Society's available funds had dwindled to the point where Fry thought it necessary to point out the significant amounts of money still being expended on account of the Society's intended Dictionary: over £50 in the last four years. 'Perhaps,' Fry suggested, 'it might be advisable to appoint a Committee to inquire and report upon this subject, with a view to the future.'[42] The new committee does not seem to have made any reports, and the Dictionary once again disappears from the records of the Council.

John Murray might be expected—given the substantial sum he had already invested in the project—to be a continuing source of badgering regarding the Dictionary's pro-

---

[39] *Athenaeum* 2 May 1868, p. 629; 9 May, p. 662; 16 May, p. 698. In Furnivall's brief reply to Ingleby's letter, published in the *Athenaeum* of 30 May (p. 764), he observes with understandable waspishness that Ingleby—a one-time reader and supplier of quotations—had been a regular recipient of the circulars reporting on the Dictionary, and that Furnivall had written privately to him only recently.

[40] *Pall Mall Gazette* 25 May 1869, p. 11; *Athenaeum* 26 Feb. 1870, p. 289. Striking negative evidence may be seen in the extensive discussion in the pages of *Notes & Queries* of the idea of collecting materials for a national glossary of dialect—and, indeed, of forming a society to do so—following a proposal (made apparently in ignorance of the Philological Society's abortive scheme of the 1840s) by W. Aldis Wright (12 Mar. 1870, p. 271); at no point in the ensuing correspondence, which continued until 1872, is the Philological Society's Dictionary mentioned, even though the correspondents included several active members of the Society. One of these, Walter Skeat, went on to found the English Dialect Society in 1873.

[41] The minutes of Council meetings, which survive from the start of 1868, make no mention at all of the Dictionary before the appointment of this Committee. No minutes of the Society's 'Ordinary Meetings' survive before 1872.

[42] PSCM: MS note (on a loose page) 21 Apr. 1871 from D. P. Fry, addressed 'To the Council of the Philological Society'. The Council minutes for 21 April record that the Committee was to consist of Goldstücker, Russell Martineau, Joseph Payne, Fry, and Furnivall.

gress; but by this stage he had evidently given up hope of publication. In 1870 he had complained to Furnivall: 'There is no doubt the whole affair of the Concise Dictionary is a mess.' He had so far advanced to Furnivall a total of £600, and he suggested to Furnivall that, in the absence of any real prospect of a finished Dictionary, the raw materials so far collected should be returned to him 'as some slight security for my outlay'. Furnivall, while not agreeing to this, at least remained conscious of his debt to Murray; in 1872 he had offered 'to edit for [Murray] gratis, *next year*, 3 little Early English schoolbooks' as a way of compensating Murray for his outlay.[43]

The new committee may not have taken any conclusive action, but it may have been at its prompting that in October 1871 Furnivall included, in his annual circular, an appeal for 'a fresh editor for the whole work', in addition to the 'fresh sub-editors for A, I, J, N, O, P, W' that were also needed. The young philologist Henry Sweet—at this point studying classics at Oxford—had, it seems, already refused the task; his cousin Henry Nicol was persuaded to take it on, but he was 'a sick man with much work of his own on hand and he did nothing'.[44] In October 1872 Furnivall admitted in his circular to Philological Society members that 'the progress in the Dictionary work has been so slight that no fresh report in detail is needed'.[45] Indeed, the Dictionary is not even mentioned in the lengthy report of recent philological activities undertaken by Society members and others delivered by Alexander Ellis in his Presidential Address on 16 May 1873—even though this report incorporated a long section drafted for Ellis by Furnivall, which included a survey of recent work in 'English Lexicography'.[46]

Ellis did refer to the Dictionary at the Society's Anniversary Meeting the following year; he described it, however, as 'merely one of the things we have tried to do [...] Several things, indeed, make me inclined to think that a Society is less fitted to compile a dictionary than to get the materials collected.' The lack of an individual editor, he argued, was the real problem: the examples of Johnson and Littré showed that 'the personal efforts of the man who wants to do the work and get it done would appear to be necessary for bringing about the result'. Ellis went on to acknowledge that it was no longer reasonable to look to Furnivall, busy as he was with his 'labours [...] to further the study of our older literature', to take on the editorship, and appealed directly to Henry Sweet to do so. It is perhaps unsurprising that the appeal fell on deaf ears: Sweet was at this time busy with his pioneering work in English phonetics (his *History of English Sounds* appeared in 1874).[47]

---

[43] JMA 5 July 1870 JM to FJF (copy); 18 Nov. 1872 FJF to JM. The issue of the money owing to Murray was to drag on for several years, and even came to figure in the later negotiations with Macmillan to publish the Dictionary: see p. 88 n. 28.

[44] MP 21 Jan. 1882 FJF to JAHM; *CWW* pp. 139–40.

[45] Circular 23 Oct. 1872, quoted in Wheelwright (1875: 3).

[46] *TPS* for 1873–4, pp. 201–52; Furnivall's report is included in the section on 'Early English', pp. 235–47.

[47] *TPS* for 1873–4, pp. 354–5. Another gloomy public assessment of the state of the project had appeared in the *New York Times* a few months earlier, in the form of a letter from Fitzedward Hall, who had already supplied thousands of quotations (and who would once again become an invaluable contributor a few

During 1873 and 1874 Furnivall was also finding it difficult to devote much time to the Dictionary. The demands of his other projects were greater than ever: the Chaucer Society, which he had founded in 1868, had a heavy schedule of publications including his own massive 'Six-Text' edition of the Canterbury Tales; in full swing too were the Ballad Society and the New Shakspere Society, founded in 1868 and 1873 respectively; and of course the Early English Text Society was as busy as ever. It was a challenge even to someone of Furnivall's boundless energy; and what with running, or helping to run, all these societies, in addition to editing several texts for publication by them, he evidently found it impossible to do anything significant as regards helping the Dictionary to progress. During these years he does not even seem to have issued his annual circulars; thus not even interested parties, like the remaining sub-editors and readers, received any news of the project.[48] The Philological Society's next President, Richard Morris, once more omitted any reference to the Dictionary in his Presidential Address in May 1875;[49] Ellis's words about the Dictionary being 'merely one of the things we have tried to do' appeared to be coming true; and nobody in the Society seemed to have the inclination, or the energy, to protest. But some months before Morris's address a strong protest was in preparation, from a different and unexpected quarter, and one which was to have far-reaching consequences.

The Rev. George Wheelwright, vicar of the small Surrey parish of Crowhurst, was apparently never a member of the Philological Society. However, he had been working at the Dictionary for some time, having been signed up in 1862 to sub-edit the letter F; by 1871 Furnivall reported this letter as 'done and half revised', making Wheelwright one of the more industrious sub-editors. Having heard no report on the progress of the Dictionary since Furnivall's circular of October 1872, he was becoming increasingly concerned that all his efforts, and those of the other sub-editors, were in danger of going to waste. In late 1874 he assembled a specimen of Dictionary entries, based on his own sub-editing, and made arrangements with the Clarendon Press to have copies of it printed (privately, at his own expense) for distribution. The specimen subsequently acquired a four-page preamble, expressing Wheelwright's frustration at what he saw as the stagnation of the project, and the complete twelve-page pamphlet appeared in the spring of 1875 under the title 'An Appeal to the English-Speaking Public on behalf of A New English Dictionary'.[50] The pamphlet begins by tracing the history of the project,

years later: see below, p. 128), but who now declared that the 'mighty undertaking' was 'now, I fear, at a standstill' (Hall 1874).

[48] Indeed, the only outward sign of life in 1874 which I have found anywhere is in a brief item by Henry Hucks Gibbs in *Notes & Queries* of 21 Feb., pp. 141–2; in the course of a discussion of some unusual words beginning with *col-*, Gibbs quotes from 'the Dictionary slips of the Philological Society, for which I am editing part of "C"'—the present tense indicating that Gibbs, at least, regarded the project as ongoing.

[49] *TPS* for 1875–6, pp. 1–142.

[50] The pamphlet is dated 5 March 1875, but was probably not in circulation much before 29 May, when it was noticed in the *Academy* (p. 554), which also mentioned that the Cambridge classicist and antiquarian J. E. B. Mayor (who had a long-standing interest in the lexicography of Latin) had suggested the formation of 'a separate Dictionary Society' to take up the work. The printing of Wheelwright's specimen was already under consideration in September 1874; Wheelwright even entertained thoughts of asking the Delegates

quoting extensively from Coleridge's 1860 letter to Trench and from Furnivall's series of annual circulars. Wheelwright mentions Furnivall's promise to the dying Coleridge to see the work through to its completion, reproduces Furnivall's accounts of the state of progress of the various letters, and reports that, according to his own rough calculations, 'nearly half (say four-tenths) of the whole work has been completed' by the sub-editors.[51] He concludes with several rather flowery paragraphs of expostulation, asserting (with an optimism worthy of Furnivall) how little remains to be done, and attributing part of the project's present difficulty to the fact that 'so little is known about it in the world at large'—for which reason he has chosen to address his words to 'all who speak our common mother-tongue, for assistance and co-operation in carrying on this good work to its proper end and completion. [...] Many a little makes a mickle. Nothing but the voluntary principle, the sacred fire of co-operation burning in many hearts can bring our stout bark to the haven where we would be.' Wheelwright is careful to distance the Philological Society from his actions in issuing the pamphlet; Furnivall may likewise have known nothing of it, although his name and address are given as the point of contact for those wishing to offer help.

In view of later events it is worth saying a little more about the organization which had printed Wheelwright's pamphlet. The Clarendon Press was the Press of the University of Oxford; it had a long history as a printer of books and other materials for the University, but during the mid-nineteenth century had become increasingly active as a publisher.[52] It was run by a Delegacy of academics appointed within the University. Wheelwright evidently hoped to interest the Press in the Philological Society's Dictionary, and was advised to contact Bartholomew Price, the Secretary to the Delegates (the Press's senior executive officer). This was good advice: Price had been Herbert Coleridge's tutor, and was well aware of his former pupil's involvement with the project. In February 1875 he observed to Wheelwright that '[t]he Work in its totality is a very large undertaking [...] I should be glad if it could be completed.' Price arranged for copies of the 'Appeal' to be sent to the Delegates of the Press, and suggested sending three copies to 'each of the Common or Combination Rooms at Oxford & Cambridge'.[53]

of the Clarendon Press if they would publish the Dictionary, but was advised that there was no point in applying to them until an editor had been found (FL 24 Sept. 1874 H. Frowde to Keningale Cook, 30 Dec. 1874 Frowde to Wheelwright).

[51] The extent to which the project really was grinding to a halt is shown by the fact that as long ago as 1868 Wheelwright had provided Furnivall with the only slightly smaller figure of one-third of the total to report in his circular (see above, p. 52).

[52] The names 'Oxford University Press' and 'Clarendon Press' have been used interchangeably, the latter having come into use after the University moved its printing activities into the Clarendon Building in Broad Street in 1713. In the early twentieth century, when OUP began publishing books through its London office, 'Clarendon Press' began to be used specifically with reference to books from Oxford. After the London office closed in the 1970s OUP continued to use 'Clarendon Press' as an imprint for some Oxford publications considered to be of particular academic importance.

[53] FL 30 Dec. 1874 Frowde to Wheelwright; SL 18 Feb., 24 May 1875 B. Price to Wheelwright. Curiously, when the *Academy* mentioned the 'Appeal' only a few days later (see p. 56 n. 50) it commented that 'the Oxford Press cannot be convinced that the work when finished will sell enough to pay them for the outlay necessary to finish it'.

Had Wheelwright confined himself to issuing an expostulatory pamphlet, it seems likely that, as with Ingleby's letter seven years earlier, the protest would have come to nothing.[54] But he did not let it rest there. On 2 September he sent a copy of the 'Appeal' to Henry Hucks Gibbs with a covering letter according to which he was 'pressing Mr Furnivall hard to make up his mind & do something to put an end to the intolerable suspense under which we now groan'—and had persuaded Furnivall to attach copies of the 'Appeal' to the issue of the Philological Society's Transactions that was due to be sent out in October. He also began to contemplate the possibility of publishing more of his sub-editing—perhaps the whole of the letter F—by subscription. He persuaded Archbiship Trench to give his public support to this scheme, which he hoped might serve as 'a beacon to the future editor of F. whenever the day shall arrive for the publication of the Full Dicty in all its glory'. Incidentally, Wheelwright's private opinion as to the chances of getting this done on a voluntary basis was rather different from that stated in his 'Appeal': 'if anyth[in]g is certain, it is this—that the Voluntary Fire has burned itself out, & if aught is to be done in the future it must be the result of money payment.' The cost of doing things at one's own expense was very much on his mind at this time, as he was still in debt to the Clarendon Press, and had (unsuccessfully) applied to the Delegates for subsidy.[55]

The alarming implications of Wheelwright's plan were obvious to Gibbs, and no doubt to the Philological Society's Council, who discussed the Dictionary on 5 November. A scheme to publish part of the Dictionary independently of the Philological Society, with the public support of Archbishop Trench, was bound to be embarrassing. The Council discussed 'the possibility of raising a fund of from 300 to 500 £ a year to pay an Editor of the Society's Dictionary for 10 years'; but the discussion was inconclusive, and no resolutions were made.[56]

Tragically, George Wheelwright was not to see his plans progress any further; he died suddenly, early in December.[57] But he had once again stirred the Council of the Philological Society from their 'long trance'; and this time the apparently comatose Dictionary would wake up in earnest.

---

[54] Wheelwright had 2,000 copies of the 'Appeal' printed (OED/B/1/2/1 17 May 1875 Wheelwright to Frowde), but it is unclear how widely he was able to circulate it. The absence of any reference to it, or to Dictionary matters, in the minutes of the Philological Society's Council before the summer break suggests that copies had not reached Society members by then.

[55] GL MS 11021/19 ff. 937–4 2 Sept. 1875 Wheelwright to HHG; ff. 949–52 4 Nov. 1875 Wheelwright to HHG; OD 28 May 1875.

[56] PSCM 5 Nov. 1875.

[57] *Pall Mall Gazette* 10 Dec. 1875, p. 8 (reporting his death); MP 10 Jan. 1876 Mary Wheelwright to FJF.

Interlude

The work of Furnivall's sub-editors

NEARLY fifteen years elapsed between the death of Coleridge and the revival of interest in the Dictionary provoked by George Wheelwright's pamphlet.[1] As we have seen, Furnivall did not regard himself as Editor for all of this period; but he was at least the project's presiding genius. Quite apart from the contract which he entered into to edit the Concise Dictionary for John Murray, he did supervise a group of co-workers who between them produced a significant body of lexicographical work: less, perhaps, than Furnivall at times claimed—and, as we shall see, of distressingly varied quality—but substantial enough to warrant proper assessment. Indeed, it is intriguing to wonder what kind of dictionary would have appeared if Furnivall and his sub-editors had succeeded in producing a complete text.

In total, approximately forty people came forward at various times in response to Furnivall's repeated appeals for sub-editors, although some of them may never have actually started work. They varied enormously in their qualifications and abilities. In 1863 Furnivall had sought to reassure John Murray that they were 'mostly University men', and this continued to be the case; but a degree was no guarantee of lexicographical aptitude. Some sub-editors evidently became involved simply through personal acquaintance: Henry Hucks Gibbs, for example, was a cousin of Charlotte Yonge—the only woman among Furnivall's sub-editors—as was John Duke Pode, who briefly undertook the letter W; while John Smallpeice and Joseph Middleton were lecturers at St Bees Theological College, and appear to have been recruited by Edward Hadarezer Knowles, a clergyman with close ties to the college. At least four other sub-editors were Dublin alumni, including two of the earliest, W. F. Grahame and the Shakespeare scholar Edward Dowden (who at the time of his recruitment was still an undergraduate).

The earlier generation of volunteer readers, many of whom now volunteered as sub-editors, had varied considerably in the quality of their work; and Furnivall's circular

---

[1] This is a much expanded version of my earlier paper (Gilliver 2008).

The Making of the *Oxford English Dictionary*. First edition. Peter Gilliver.
© Peter Gilliver 2016. First published 2016 by Oxford University Press.

letter to his sub-editors dated 15 September 1862 explicitly acknowledges that he expected the same to be true of sub-editing:

If you find that tracing the etymologies beyond the first parents of the words requires too much time and research, leave it alone, I can get it done afterwards. The chief things that I want from Sub-editors are, the arrangement and classification of the extracts (including the definitions and tracing of the meanings), and the supplying of deficient words and senses for the Concise Dictionary.

This circular letter is an important document, as it contains the only practical editorial guidance for the sub-editors which ever appeared in print. It was accompanied by a page of specimen entries compiled as a model—covering the words *afatement*, *afayte*, *affect*, and *abide*—and a four-page list of all the quotations so far collected for these words.[2] Furnivall realized that his volunteers would need more guidance than this— the sample entries in particular had been 'drawn up (in some haste) partly on the model of the friend who was taken from us, and of whose work I have left as much as I could'—and he invited comment on any editorial matters not fully dealt with. Some dialogue of this sort did take place, but it is clear from the great variation in approach among sub-editors that Furnivall made no attempt to update them about any new editorial practices which emerged. Walter Skeat voiced his concern about diverging practices among sub-editors in November 1865, in a letter written shortly after he had started work on the letter R.[3] He urged Furnivall to examine samples of each sub-editor's work and provide feedback: 'I am sure every subeditor would be only *too glad* to have his work tested, for his own satisfaction, & mistakes might be thus nipped in the bud. My idea is—you would thus have one or two unpleasant surprises—but better *now* than *hereafter*.'[4] As Elisabeth Murray notes in *Caught in the Web of Words*, her classic biography of her grandfather, it was he who was to have the unpleasant surprises: there is no evidence that Furnivall did any systematic monitoring of the kind suggested. Indeed, apart from answering some initial queries, he seems to have left the sub-editors largely to their own devices.

Some of the sub-editors may not even have written any entries at all, contenting themselves with attempting to fill the gaps in the illustrative material for their assigned letter. William Gee, who was assigned the letter B and who may have been the first sub-editor to make a start, certainly took a rather 'minimal' approach to sub-editing: there is no evidence that he wrote any etymologies, or divided any word into numbered senses, although the large number of quotations in his hand which survive for words

---

[2] Furnivall evidently compiled his 1862 guidelines with a careful eye to the Philological Society's 'Canones Lexicographici', although of course these had been published in 1860, before the idea of the Concise Dictionary, or the use of sub-editors, had been conceived.

[3] Skeat probably became acquainted with Furnivall through the Early English Text Society; he was not one of the Society's founding members, but by January 1865 he was a member of its committee. He did not join the Philological Society until 1 December 1865.

[4] MP 17 Nov. 1865 Skeat to FJF (photocopy).

in B, taken from a wide range of sources, attest to his efforts in this direction. The only signs of his 'lexicographical' efforts are the catchwords on his quotation slips, which are often given a part of speech and sometimes (especially with polysemous words) a brief definition. (He did of course compile and issue the wordlist for the letter B in 1863.)

For those who wished to do more than this, Furnivall supplied a useful additional resource to accompany the collected quotation evidence: a set of pages pulled out of over thirty other dictionaries, including both foreign-language dictionaries, on which to draw when compiling etymologies, and dictionaries of modern English, to help with 'supplying deficient words'—the latter being necessitated by the serious incompleteness of the quotation material. It was clear (as Furnivall had already discussed in his Preface to Part III of the Basis of Comparison for the third period) that the Concise Dictionary's list of headwords would have to include those whose existence was only vouched for by their being recorded in other dictionaries; indeed, Furnivall now warned his sub-editors that 'very many such gaps will be found in our material'—gaps which they should fill as best they could.

But it was with the quotations already available that Furnivall instructed his sub-editors to start their work. The method he sets out does not differ in most of its essentials from the methods of the OED's lexicographers, in James Murray's time or today (the main difference being, as discussed further below, in the ordering of senses within an entry). Each quotation for a word should be read through, in order to establish its part of speech, and the sense in which it was used; to each bundle of quotations for a particular word or sense should then be attached a definition (or similar 'remarks'). The next stage was the organization of senses into 'logical succession', from which a 'full scheme'—intended for the 'full' Dictionary—could be drawn up; some sub-editors did this on separate paper, but most seem simply to have pinned their definitions to the front of the relevant bundle of slips. Finally, an entry for the Concise Dictionary was to be written out, consisting of headword, pronunciation, part of speech, variant forms and inflections, etymology, and then one or more definitions, each accompanied by references to up to three quotations, one for each of the three periods—or by a numbered asterisk (*1, *2, *3) if no quotation evidence for a period was available.

The sub-editors, then, would generate two kinds of documentation: the fully written-out 'Concise' dictionary entries, and the 'full scheme', sometimes in the form of similarly written-out entries, more often as slips attached to the individual bundles of quotations. The quotations themselves, being raw, unprocessed lexicographical data, were of intrinsic value, and were bound to be made use of by the next generation of people to work on the Dictionary—James Murray and his assistants (and the teams headed by Bradley, Craigie, and Onions in due course), and the new team of sub-editors recruited by Murray—but it also made sense for these later workers to re-use, wherever possible, the lexicographical work of Furnivall's sub-editors. This they certainly did, and in a way which renders a full assessment of the earlier phase more or less impossible. In some cases the paper on which definitions, or other notes, had been written was simply turned over and used as scrap paper; at least some of the time, however, a new definition was written on the back of the earlier sub-editor's notes on the same word, suggesting that the later workers did find them of some use. This is even more evident in the rather smaller number of cases where the original definition slip was retained, with modifications of wording and style. Where use has been made of the early material in this way, it is possible to recover fragments of the early sub-editing by careful examination of these later materials, in the same way that surviving fragments of Coleridge's editing have been identified.

There are, however, five sub-editors whose work on Furnivall's Concise Dictionary survives in coherent form. Henry Hucks Gibbs completed a large part of the letter C in the form of bound volumes. Some of these were cannibalized for use by Murray's sub-editors and assistants—sections of particular entries were cut out and adapted for use as 'Dictionary slips'—but five largely complete volumes survive. As a kind of appendix to Gibbs's work, there is a single volume of entries for words beginning with *conc-*, prepared under Gibbs's direction (and in identical format) by George White of Torquay. There are several bundles of slips for words beginning with *bo-*, sub-edited by the Cardiff solicitor Robert Griffith; and some entries for part of the letter R, written out on sheets of foolscap by Walter Skeat.[5] Finally, there is the section of the letter F which George Wheelwright had printed up as part of his 1875 'Appeal'. Bearing in mind how few of Furnivall's original sub-editors were said by Murray to have brought their work to a conclusion,[6] it may be that this represents a high proportion of the 'written-up' entries that were ever compiled; the body of material, supplemented where possible by fragments of the work of other sub-editors, is certainly sufficient to give some indication of the editorial practice—or range of practices—adopted for Furnivall's Dictionary.

PRESENTATION AND SCALE

The first point to make is that there was very little about this Dictionary that was 'Concise': in fact it was arguably only in the decision to include limited numbers of quotations, and to give these in limited form, that it differed from the 'Full' Dictionary

---

[5] Henry Hucks Gibbs is mentioned in Furnivall's earliest list of sub-editors, in his Philological Society circular of November 1862; and he evidently continued with his sub-editing at least until 1869, since his entry for *coacher* 'a coach-horse' is illustrated by a quotation from the *Daily News* of 7 August 1869 (and it is clear from the manuscript that this was not a later addition). George White's sub-editing can be dated to early 1865, from the date of a letter discussing his initial attempts (GL MS 11021/19 ff. 499–502 10 Mar. 1865 White to HHG). Skeat's work can similarly be dated to late 1865; Griffith seems to have started a little later, as much of his sub-editing is written on re-used printed stationery dated 1867. All of this sub-edited material is preserved in OUPA at OED/B/1/3.

[6] Murray claimed that only '[t]hree or four of the more earnest sub-editors' completed their assigned task of preparing entries for the Concise Dictionary (Munro et al. 1911: 131). Compare Furnivall's rather more optimistic claim in his 1871 circular that nine sub-editors had finished or nearly finished.

as originally envisaged. There was certainly no intention that conciseness should mean selectivity about what vocabulary should be included: Furnivall evidently expected that every word or sense for which a quotation was available, or for which an entry was given in one of the dictionaries supplied to the sub-editors, would be covered. Indeed, his circular authorized the inclusion of a word solely on the basis that a sub-editor knew of its existence; this accounts for many of the words listed which are marked '*1 *2 *3' (indicating the lack of contextual quotations from any of the three periods), and for which no dictionary authority is given. The coverage, moreover, was to be uniformly thorough: every entry, even for simple derivatives and compounds, was to contain a pronunciation (or more than one), an account of recorded spelling variants and inflections, and an etymology, followed by definitions for each sense, together with constructional information, phrases and idioms, synonyms, and proverbial uses. Furnivall's directions conclude with a characteristic invitation:

Lastly, having finished the strict business of an Article, I exhort you, for the Full Dictionary, to indulge in a little chat with your Reader, noting for him the chief points of interest in the history you have set before him, moralizing shortly on them if you will, and giving any additional facts to bring out the full meaning and value of your word […] Being good sense and well put, as of course it will be, Editor and Publisher will be only too glad to find room for it.

Furnivall's weakness for 'chats' and 'moralizing' will be familiar to anyone who has read the prefaces to his editions for the Early English Text Society. No evidence survives that any of the sub-editors went so far as to 'chat':[7] there would be more than enough for them to do without that.

One sub-editor, at least, was alarmed by the sheer scale of the text that would result from applying Furnivall's directions comprehensively to the available evidence. Skeat's concerns about this are set out in the letter, already mentioned, in which he urged Furnivall to monitor the sub-editing: 'Some method of *abbreviation* ought to be found, I think, or else it seems hardly fair to expect one to go on doing a work which can hardly be printed, or, if printed, cannot *sell* because of its *cost*.' Skeat's anxiety was based on more than general impressions: the letter goes on to give detailed calculations, based on the extent of corresponding portions of Ogilvie's *Imperial Dictionary* and the new (1864) edition of Webster: 'the net result [of my calculations] is that the C[oncise] D[ictionary] will be *at least* equal to 8 such huge treble-columned volumes as the Impl Dictionary has 2 of—& if you print in double-columned 4to, you can't make less than 10 vols; of which I should have to write *half* a one.'[8]

The treatment of compounds is an obvious area where 'abbreviation' might be appropriate. The first noun for which Henry Hucks Gibbs encountered multiple

---

[7] The occasional brief 'obs[ervation]' is to be found in Skeat's entries, as for example at *Re-baptize*, where he comments '*Obs.* The spelling *rebaptise* [which he has given as a possible variant] is incorrect.'

[8] MP 17 Nov. 1865 Skeat to FJF (photocopy).

compounds was *cabbage*; he realized that not all of these would require a full entry, and elected merely to list them, after a rather expansive preamble:

And, like all other substantives in English, it may be used, in composition, to imply that the substantive with which it is compounded has some relation, in use, size, colour, or otherwise, to a cabbage such as *Cabbage*-daisy, *Cabbage*-bark-tree, *Cabbage*-leaf, *Cabbage*-palm, [...] *Cabbage*-shoestring, *Cabbage*-butterfly (the caterpillar feeding on the cabbage), Cattle-*cabbage*, and the like.

Most of the compounds are undefined, no pronunciation or etymological informa-tion is given, and the only documentation is a single 1833 quotation for *cabbage-net*. Later lists of compounds are similarly brief (and all have much shorter preambles), although there is inconsistency as to definition and documentation. At *cloth*, for example (see Figure 5), a bare list is given, with only a few definitions and no quotations or references; whereas at *cloud* the briefest of references provide some documentation ('*Cloudbank* sb Skeat 1864', '*Cloudberry* sb Coxe 1780'), and a few definitions have been inserted later. This condensed style was presumably arrived at by discussion with Furnivall; and Gibbs also used it to accommodate derivatives, such as *coalery* and *coalless*, which he included (without definition) in a list containing mainly compounds like *coal-axe* and *coal-barge*. Of course, space would only be saved by this method if the entry for the compound in the main alphabetical sequence were limited to a simple cross-reference; in fact Gibbs was inconsistent, and in later volumes there is an increasing tendency to give a fairly full entry (as with all four of the *coal*-words just mentioned, for example). A similar approach—arguably even closer to the condensed style later developed by Murray for both compounds and derivatives—may be seen at the end of the entry for *fable* (noun) in George Wheelwright's printed sample of F, where a section headed 'Compounds' contains brief entries for *fabledom, fable-framing, fable-maker, fable-monger,* and *fable-weaver,* all without pronunciation or etymology (except in the case of *fabledom,* where Wheelwright has included a sprawling, incompletely edited note on the terminal suffix *-dom*). By contrast, both George White (under direction from Gibbs) and Skeat consistently use a full entry style even for such relatively unimportant compounds as *concert-giver* and *rebel-race*; and Griffith, evidently applying Furnivall's guidelines to the letter, supplies even an ephemeral formation such as *boy-bridegroom* with a pronunciation, a note of the genitive and plural forms, and an etymology ('boy sb.; bride sb.; groom sb. q.v.').[9] The same full treatment is accorded to phrases such as *board of guardians* and *board of trade,* although Griffith falls far short of doing this for every word.

---

[9] None of the other sub-editors seem to have been as assiduous as Griffith in giving the genitive form for nouns, although even he is far from consistent. The same is true in regard to Furnivall's stipulations for other parts of speech, which were impractically thorough: for verbs, any irregular tenses and participles were to be given, and for adjectives, the comparatives and superlatives, but also 'the feminines and plurals' (although Furnivall anticipated that these would generally be obsolete).

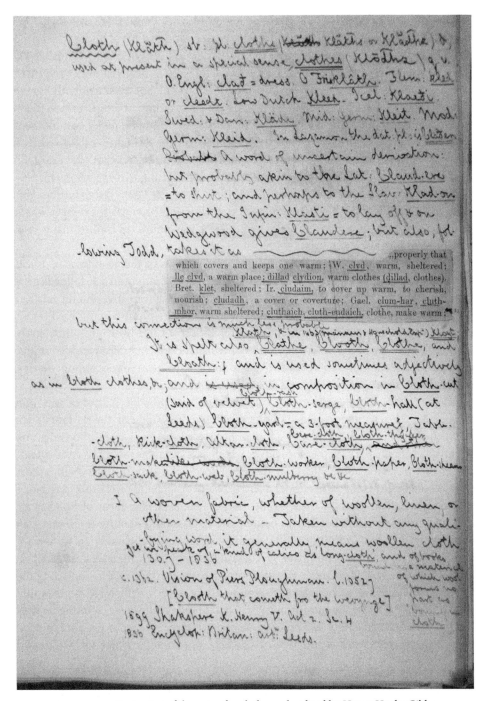

Sub-editors would also often deal with compounds with a prefixed first element. The 'Canones Lexicographici' had anticipated that these would be listed under the second element in the third, separate Part of the Dictionary (the 'Etymological Appendix'), while compounds in Part I (the 'Main Dictionary') were to be given under their first element; Furnivall's circular gave no guidance on this point, but it was evidently agreed that both kinds of compounds might be considered together, to judge from William Gee's 1863 'Vocabulary' for the letter B, which lists (for example) *ballot box* and *deed box* under *box*, as well as *box-barrow*, *box-bed*, etc. The sub-editors followed suit, although they varied in the thoroughness of their treatment; so that (for example) Griffith, working in B, gave his usual full entries not only for *boy-bridegroom* and *boy-harlot*, but also *cabin-boy*, *collier-boy*, *cow-boy*, etc., whereas Gibbs did mention *altar-cloth*, *table-cloth*, and the like in his entry for *cloth*, but only briefly. The extent to which Furnivall left his sub-editors to their own devices was bound to lead to many such variations in practice.

A little condensation of a different kind was possible in the treatment of verbs. Furnivall, working presumably on the basis of Coleridge's drafts (and also following the practice of some contemporary dictionaries), specified that transitive and intransitive uses of verbs should be given as separate headwords; the point is reinforced by his sample entries. The policy results in some repetition (of headword, pronunciation, and sometimes etymology). Griffith follows the instruction, but Gibbs and Skeat give a single headword, followed by transitive and intransitive uses (often, but not always, grouped by transitivity).

Another area where considerable condensation was possible is that of variation in spelling. The 'Canones Lexicographici' of 1860 had allowed for variants such as *ait/ayot/eyot* to be listed under a single headword of the Editor's choosing, and Furnivall's sample entry for the verb *afayte*, which lists variant forms *affayty* and *affaite*, shows that he made some efforts in this direction. Following this lead, sub-editors often conflated different forms under a single headword, giving brief cross-references in the alphabetical place.[10] Thus Griffith writes '*Boucher* obs. form of butcher sb. q.v.', and similarly refers *boulster* to *bolster*; and Gibbs could identify *cauderne* as an obsolete form of *cauldron*, and could even (having charge of the materials for both C and K) list *kadi* as a variant of *cadi* ('a Turkish Judge of a low rank'). Skeat groups a range of diverse spellings under the headword *Rebeck* (see Figure 6)—including the (alphabetically and morphologically) remote *ribibe*, which William Craigie would later regard as distinct enough to merit a separate entry. However, working as they were in isolation, generally having only the materials for one letter (or part of it) at their disposal, there were bound to be cases where, not knowing which form of a word

---

[10] In fact the first mention of a 'cross-reference' style of entry—which Furnivall's circular does not allow for—is in a discussion of just such spelling variants in Skeat's November 1865 letter to Furnivall, where he asks for the liberty to 'reject writing out words again, when they merely are new *spellings*, in which case one might write, e.g. *Rawntree*; see *Rawntry*. &c.'

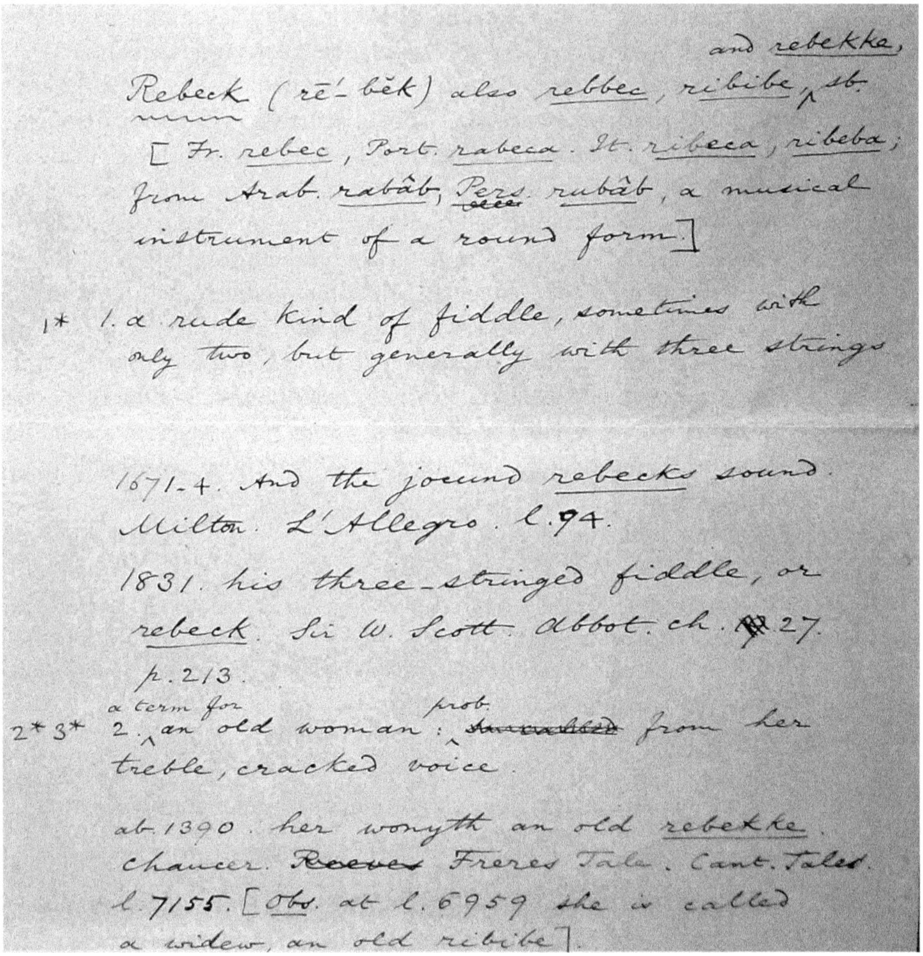
and rebekke,
Rebeck (rē-bĕk) also rebbec, ribibe, sb.
[Fr. rebec, Port. rabeca. It. ribeca, ribeba; from Arab. rabâb, Pers. rubâb, a musical instrument of a round form.]
1* 1. a rude kind of fiddle, sometimes with only two, but generally with three strings
1671-4. And the jocund rebecks sound. Milton. L'Allegro. l. 94.
1831. his three-stringed fiddle, or rebeck. Sir W. Scott. Abbot. ch. 27. p. 213.
2* 3* 2. a term for an old woman: prob. ~~so called~~ from her treble, cracked voice.
ab. 1390. her wonyth an old rebekke. Chaucer. ~~Reeves~~ Freres Tale. Cant. Tales. l. 7155. [Obs. at l. 6959 she is called a widew, an old ribibe].

FIGURE 6 Entry for *rebeck* as sub-edited by Walter Skeat.

was to be taken as the headword, they felt obliged to give the form they were looking at the benefit of the doubt.

It was in the different ways in which quotations should be presented that there was the greatest possibility for variation. Furnivall's original idea had been to give only bibliographical references, and it was only in response to pressure from John Murray that he conceded that a few words of context should be included. His circular to sub-editors urged them to make quotations 'as short as you possibly can', and the last entry on his specimen page, for *abide* used as a transitive verb, includes two quotations in this style: one from the Towneley Mystery Plays ('that shal thou sore abite') and one from Shakespeare's *Julius Caesar* ('if it be found so, some will dear abide it'). When Robert Griffith began sub-editing in B, he gave bare references; but when he passed his first bundle of entries to Furnivall for comment, Furnivall went through the first few slips adding brief contexts. Eight or nine words was the maximum (e.g. 'boaking as if I'd bring my pluck up', for *boak* 'to vomit'), and much of the time the extracts were so short as to be of doubtful value: the entry for *boa-constrictor*, for example, is hardly enhanced by the addition of the extract 'a large boa-constrictor' (from Henry Gouger's *Two Years' Imprisonment in Burmah*). The extent to which Griffith took Furnivall's advice is clear from his subsequent sub-entries, many of which are 'illustrated' by even less informative quotations—the limit being reached in examples such as 'þe bouh' (for *bough* 'arm or large branch of a tree') and 'brace it' (for *brace* 'enclose, fasten up'). Gibbs had a better sense of the utility of quotations, sometimes giving only three words of context but allowing himself ten or twelve when the sense required it (e.g. 'great firme boughs..spreading themselves at the top into very sharp cags', for *cag* 'stump'). Other sub-editors were considerably more liberal. Cornelius Paine, the sub-editor of the first part of R whose work Skeat used as a model (and whose entries survive among the later *OED* slips in reasonable quantity), often gave twenty or thirty words of context; Skeat initially followed this lead, but, realizing the implications in terms of scale, asked Furnivall for guidance, in the 1865 letter already quoted:

Either that the manner in which Mr Paine & myself have been making the abstracts is far *too full and long*, (in which case I had better begin to curtail & abridge my articles *at once* before I go too far:–[)] or else, on the other hand, your dictionary will be far more enormous than one would suppose could possibly *sell*—far too large to be printed at anything but a frightful expenditure of money, far too large to be called, in any sense, a *Concise* Dictionary.

The quotations in Skeat's own surviving sub-editing are of much the same length as Gibbs's.

INCLUSION: THE 'LEXICON TOTIUS ANGLICITATIS'

It was all very well for the 'Canones Lexicographici' to commit the Dictionary to recording 'the existence of every word in the language for which sufficient authority, written or oral, can be adduced'; but when such a broad statement of principle was brought to bear on the actual evidence, decisions had to be taken about what it should mean in practice. As long ago as 1860 (see p. 36), Coleridge had asked for guidance regarding several categories of potentially omittable vocabulary, most of which he was advised to include. In some areas Furnivall and his sub-editors therefore had a lead to follow; in following it they were sometimes more inclusive than James Murray and his colleagues would be. In other areas there was no such guidance.

One area of uncertainty related to what James Murray would later refer to as the limits of 'Anglicity'. Foreign words mentioned by English writers, for example, were often noted by readers, but only sparingly included by Murray; Gibbs regularly included such non-naturalized words as *caçadores* ('a class of Spanish troops') and *calamander* ('a kind of hard wood from Ceylon'), of which only the latter was given by Murray. On occasion Furnivall himself was clearly in doubt. Among Robert Griffith's first bundle of entries is a slip for the word *boab* ('a gate keeper'), illustrated by a quotation from Mary Whately's *Ragged Life in Egypt* (1863), on which Furnivall has written '?English yet'. (The word is still not in the *OED*.) Griffith subsequently annotated many words with a similar query, including *bouillabaisse*, *boulê* (from Greek βουλή), *boustrophedon* ('hardly Engl.'), *boyar* (and *boyard*), *Brahma* (though not *Brahmin* or *Brahmahood*), and *boulevard* (which was marked 'qu. Eng.' but divided into two senses, for the first of which, 'bulwark', he had no English documentation; neither did Murray, who elected simply to mention this as the original meaning of the French word). It is hard to discern any consistency: *bourgeoisie* is queried, but not *bourgeois* (perhaps the latter was viewed differently because of its having two distinct meanings—a social class and the name of a size of type); nor is *bourguinon* (thus spelt; 'one of the kinds of white vine', with a quotation from Markham's *The Countrey Farme*) or *braciato* ('a brewer', illustrated from Stow's *Survey of London*).[11] On the other hand, Gibbs does not seem to have made any such annotations, even against a word so 'obviously foreign' as *caçadores*; and there are no such queries among Skeat's entries, which admittedly lie in an alphabetical range containing few candidates.

There was less argument about the 'Anglicity' of regional vocabulary, of the kind covered in dictionaries such as Halliwell's *Dictionary of Archaic and Provincial Words* (1847; 8th edition, 1874) and Jamieson's *Etymological Dictionary of the Scottish Language* (1808; Supplement, 1825). The Committee who formulated the 'Canones Lexicographici' had chosen to go beyond the Philological Society's 'Proposal' and include 'provincialisms', irrespective of whether they were attested by 'the otherwise indispensable passport of a quotation'; the policy is reflected in the innumerable words listed in the 'Vocabularies' of Gee, Yonge, and Sheppard for which 'H.' or 'J.' is given as the authority. Much of the surviving sub-editing shows a similarly inclusive attitude towards provincialisms, including many entries for words for which no contextual evidence was available. Of course, such evidence can be hard to come by for regional vocabulary, and the later editors of the *OED* were also often obliged to include dialect words for which only glossarial evidence could be cited; but Furnivall's sub-editors were often more liberal in this respect, including many items not given in the *OED*. Thus Griffith includes *brab* 'spike-nail', recorded in Halliwell as Yorkshire dialect; Gibbs lists *cobnobble* 'to beat (Halliwell)'; and Skeat has *rebaghle* 'reproach', taken from Jamieson—none of these were later included in the *OED*.

---

[11] Griffith had the advantage of being able to work from a wordlist which had already received the imprimatur of print, namely Gee's 'Vocabulary'; various small details suggest that many of his headwords were copied onto slips directly from the published list. Of the B words mentioned here, only *boab*, *boulê*, *braciato*, and *Brahmahood* do not appear in Gee's list. A rather slavish copying of Gee would also account for the fact that Griffith's tendency to deal with 'compounds' not beginning with B extended to tackling *vambrace*, and even *embrace*, under *brace*: both of these appear in the 1863 'Vocabulary'.

Another category of words to which Furnivall's sub-editors showed comparative generosity is that of words derived from proper names by suffixation, which in general have a distinctively English form but which constitute such a large group that Murray felt obliged to limit their coverage.[12] *Caditanian* ('of or belonging to Cadiz'), for example, was included by Gibbs but not by Murray;[13] the same is true of *Californian*, which Gibbs accorded two separate entries, one each for the adjective and the noun— although he had no quotations at all for the adjective, and apparently only one (of 1861) for the noun. Similarly, Griffith includes *Bracarense* (from the Portuguese city of Braga), illustrated by a quotation from Donne. There are even some proper names, such as *Calcutta*, *Cathay*, and *Calleis* (an early English spelling of *Calais*)—of which only *Cathay* was later included by Murray.

DOCUMENTATION

Of course, before a sub-editor could begin to deliberate over whether a word was eligible for inclusion, it was necessary that his or her attention be drawn to its existence. Furnivall's directions allow for the inclusion of words purely from personal knowledge ('any non-technical word that you know to exist'), and Gibbs, for one, seems to have taken him at his word; at least, some of the numerous entries in his volumes for which no documentation (either quotations, or mention in another dictionary or glossary) is given are for words with which he sounds to have been familiar, such as *coach-dog* ('A handsome white dog spotted with black, kept chiefly as an attendant on the carriage'). But such apparent instances of personal knowledge are rare; in general the sub-editors took documentation, printed or (occasionally) in manuscript, as their starting point. Of course the resurgence in reading for the Dictionary which took place under James Murray's direction presented the later lexicographers with vastly more evidence to consider. A reasonable question, then, is: how handicapped were Furnivall and his collaborators by the limited extent of their documentation?

As the quotation slips collected during the pre-Murray period were merged with those collected later, and are not easily distinguishable from them, it is not possible to reassemble the exact corpus of evidence available to a sub-editor such as Gibbs. However, an impression of some sort may be gained by comparison of the documentation mentioned in his sub-edited entries with that given in the corresponding entries in *OED*. Gibbs is the only sub-editor whose work survives in sufficient quantity to make this a meaningful exercise; as a sample for this purpose I looked at just under 250 items in the last of his surviving volumes, in the alphabetical range *co* to *coarrange*. (In this context a word counts as an 'item' if it appears with a single meaning; each

---

[12] On Murray's difficulties with this category see p. 122 below.
[13] The word was eventually added to the Dictionary, in the form *Gaditanian*, in 1972.

sense of a polysemous word is counted separately, as are subordinate lemmas such as compounds and phrases.)

The greater richness of the documentation available to James Murray and his colleagues is immediately apparent in the sheer number of items covered: although exact counting is difficult, in the alphabetical range covered by Gibbs's 246 items, the first edition of the *OED* has well over 500. No really substantial words are omitted, but in many cases *OED* gives several senses of a word for which Gibbs was only able to document one (e.g. *coagulum* and *coal-man*, for each of which he records only the first of *OED*'s senses); and there many more words for which he seems to have had no evidence at all—mostly compounds (*coach-building*, *coal-fire*, etc.), but also some less common derivatives (*coachfulness*, *coadjutrixship*, *coalitional*, etc.) and a large number of words formed with *co-* (*co-admiration*, *co-affirmation*, *co-angelical*, etc.).

However, Gibbs also dealt with some fourteen items which were not included by Murray, a perhaps surprising number. In a few cases he had no documentation for a word as such, but (like other lexicographers before and since) regarded its existence as implied by the evidence for a related word; this often happens with adjectives in *-ed*, which Gibbs took as implying the existence of a corresponding verb (*coally*, for example, a verb not recorded in *OED*, though its entry for *coallied* quotes the same 1740 source as does Gibbs). Other entries are for items of regional vocabulary, often citing Halliwell as authority, as in the case of the verb *coaken* 'to strain in vomiting'; the inclusive attitude towards 'provincialisms' of this early phase of the project has already been noted.[14] Occasionally, however, a word is included for which 'ordinary' quotation evidence is given: examples include *coal-shadow* (citing Elizabeth Barrett Browning) and an obscure adjective *coaching* (used by Wycherley in *The Plain-Dealer* (1677): 'pert Coaching Cowards'). The reasons for these terms being omitted during the later phase of the project can only be guessed at.

The incompleteness of Gibbs's documentation is also apparent in the number of cases where his earliest quotation is antedated by that given in the first edition of *OED*. In some respects he did well: there are 107 items for which, even after a great deal of further reading, his first quotation has not been improved upon. But in 88 other cases the later entries do antedate him (115 if we include cases where he gave no documentation at all): usually by 50 years or less, but in over twenty cases by a century or more—the most extreme case being the bird name *coal-mouse*, given by Gibbs with a quotation from a 1657 source, but recorded in *OED* with a first quotation from Ælfric's glossary of approximately 650 years earlier. The inaccessibility of early material was clearly a particular handicap:[15] the sample includes no quotations at all earlier than Chaucer, whereas the *OED* entry for *coal* alone begins seven of its subsenses with a quotation from the thirteenth century or earlier.

---

[14] In fact *coaken* was recently added, as a spelling variant, to the revised *OED* entry for the word *querken*, which has a range of meanings including 'choke' as well as 'retch'.

[15] On this difficulty see above, pp. 30–1.

Thus in omitting entries, in giving a single meaning to words where several could later be discerned, and in failing to date the first appearance of so many words, the work of Furnivall's sub-editors makes clear how incomplete was the evidence that they had to work with. But even if all the evidence collected later had been available to them, there is some doubt as to whether their ideas about meaning and sense development would have enabled them to extract from this evidence the information about the history of words which later historical lexicographers would expect.

NOT VERY HISTORICAL PRINCIPLES

The stipulation, in the Philological Society's 'Proposal' of 1859, that 'the historical principle will be uniformly adopted' might seem to pre-echo the 'historical principles' invoked on the title page of the later Dictionary, but this is deceptive. Of course, the principle (which the 'Proposal' goes on to state) that the Dictionary should 'show [...] the development of the sense or various senses of each word from its etymology and from each other' represents an innovation of great significance; but it is instructive to examine the expansion of this point which appeared in the 'Canones Lexicographici' the following year. The 'Canones' specify that the various meanings of a word are to be 'deduced [i.e. traced] logically from the Etymology, and so arranged as to show the common thread or threads which unite them together'. Furnivall's circular offers a further slight expansion: having grouped the quotations for a word according to its several meanings, the sub-editor 'will then see in what logical succession the different senses proceed from the etymological meaning', and use this logical succession as a basis for writing out the complete entry. And, in a later passage:

[Definitions] should be arranged as they follow in mental succession from the etymological meaning of the Catchword, being separated into divisions (A, B, C, etc.), sections (α, β, γ, etc.), and sub-sections (*a, b, c*, etc.; or *a, z, y*, etc.; *b, z, y*, etc.), as required. The concrete meaning should always precede the abstract, and the name of the bodily action that of the mental one.

The last sentence makes explicit what the earlier references to 'logical' or 'mental' succession only imply: that the order of senses is not to be dictated by the chronological sequence in which they are earliest documented.[16] The Horne Tooke approach to historical lexicography had, it seems, still to be cast off.

---

[16] It is interesting to compare the organizing principle proposed, and initially adopted, by Johnson in his *Plan of an English Dictionary* (1747), which posits a canonical sequence for the various meanings of a single word, beginning with the 'natural and primitive signification'. However, in matching the actual examples of usage collected to this normative system, Johnson encountered such difficulties that he was ultimately forced to admit in the Preface to his *Dictionary* that it was 'not always practicable'. Johnson's working methods are discussed in detail in Reddick (1996: esp. ch. 2).

The idea that a logically coherent account of a word's history should be used as the guiding organizational principle is very much in keeping with similar statements in other dictionaries of the period;[17] it is perhaps the most significant way in which the Dictionary as conceived at this stage by Furnivall differed from what it later became under James Murray and his colleagues. It is clearly true that the sparseness of the quotation evidence available to the early sub-editors was such that it could not be relied on as an indicator of the order in which the senses of a word developed; nor, however, was it safe to suppose that the history of such development would always conform to some universal schema. Furnivall's own entry for the noun *affect* illustrates the hazards of such an approach: the sense 'pretence, hypocrisy', recorded from the fourteenth century, is described explicitly as 'the earliest sense in English'—but appears as the last sense of all in the entry, in division B, following six senses grouped under A 'a making-towards, or tendency-to something' (this definition being clearly motivated directly by the component parts of the Latin word *affectus* from which the word derives).

The attempts of sub-editors to devise 'logical successions' from the 'etymological meanings' of words often led them to structure entries in ways which fail to represent actual historical development. A good example of this is Henry Hucks Gibbs's entry for *cadence*. The word derives ultimately from Latin *cadere* 'to fall'; accordingly, Gibbs begins with 'I. First it signifies Falling; thus 1. literally—as of the Sun setting', this first sense being illustrated by a quotation from *Paradise Lost*. From this Gibbs proceeds, 'logically', to 'II [...] a just and agreeable falling, as 1. the rhythmical close of a sentence [...] 2. Of Music [etc.].' His earliest quotation, from Chaucer's *House of Fame*, appears at the sense numbered II.3 ('Rhythm, simply, or Rhythmical sound, or peculiar national Accent'). In fact, as Murray later noted in the *OED* entry, the English word was first borrowed, not from Latin, but from French and Italian, and in the musical and prosodic senses which had developed in these languages; the use of English *cadence* in a sense which consciously echoed the original physical sense of the Latin etymon was a later, seventeenth-century development, which James Murray would later place in a separate branch. Skeat's organization of the entry for the verb *rebate* is similarly 'unhistorical': he begins with the physical sense 'I. 1. lit[erally] to beat back, to blunt, dull the edge of', illustrated from *Measure for Measure*, goes on with '2. to beat back, beat off by fighting', illustrated from a 1590 source, and only reaches his earliest quotation (from the Coventry Mystery Plays) with '3. to abate, lessen, diminish, heal, put aside'. Again, the source of the borrowing—in this case French *rabattre*—could furnish a number of different meanings, which did not arrive in English in the 'logical' order presented.

---

[17] Webster asserts in his 1828 *Dictionary*, for example, that 'There is a primary sense of every word, from which all the other have proceeded; and whenever this can be discovered, this sense should stand first in order' (Introduction, sig. G2r). Richardson goes further still in the introduction to his *New Dictionary of the English Language*: 'The lexicographer can never assure himself that he has attained the meaning of a word, until he has discovered the thing, the sensible object [...] the sensation caused by that thing or object (for language cannot sever them), of which that word is the name. To this, the term *meaning* should be strictly and exclusively appropriated' ('Preliminary Essay', p. 43).

The fact that these 'logical successions' are at variance with the historical evidence of the quotations does not mean that Furnivall and his sub-editors were unaware of the mismatch between logic and history. Instead, like many of their lexicographical contemporaries, they evidently regarded their task as something other than simply recording the historical sequence—which, as Murray and his successors have found, often requires a more complex explanation. But until the primacy of the historical record became established, in an important sense the Dictionary would remain 'unhistorical'.

It was a different matter when it came to the range of quotation evidence for a given word or sense. Furnivall was explicit about this in his circular: 'The earliest authority for every meaning must be referred to, and the latest authority for every obsolete meaning.' He reiterated the point in his feedback to Griffith on the latter's entry for *boa*: an 1863 quotation illustrating the use of the word to mean an article of dress has been struck through and replaced with another from Dickens's *Sketches by Boz* of 1836, together with the comment 'give first use'. This attitude to quotations seems to have remained consistent, as similar comments can be traced right back to the report of the Unregistered Words Committee in 1857. There is some evidence, however, that other sub-editors did not consistently adhere to this policy. From time to time in Gibbs's volumes, and rather more frequently in George White's continuation of his work, a range of dates is written against a word or sense—sometimes added later, but clearly often written at the same time as the rest of the entry—which must denote the range of quotation evidence available at the time. Usually, but not always, the starting date is the same as the date of the first quotation given in the entry. Thus the first sense in the entry for *cockney*, defined as 'a fondling child tenderly brought up and Cocker'd',[18] is marked with a date range '1531–1693'; but whatever Gibbs's 1531 quotation was— probably the passage from Elyot's *Boke called the Governour* later given in the *OED* entry—he chose not to include it, giving instead a 1592 quotation from Nashe, perhaps because the latter illustrated the sense of the word more clearly. Similarly *cockroach* is dated '1693–1861' but illustrated only by an 1840 quotation from Thomas Hood.

When it came to quotations from the second period, Furnivall's circular was strikingly prescriptive: 'Shakspeare first, and then the Authorised Version of the Bible, being preferred to all other authorities'—provided, presumably, that a quotation from the first period had already been given, making it unnecessary to give the earliest available second-period example. Without knowing exactly which quotations the sub-editors had at their disposal, it is impossible to say how consistently they followed this rule; but, looking through Gibbs's entries (the largest available sample) at the cases where quotations from the first and second periods are given, it is remarkable how seldom the latter is taken from a source other than Shakespeare or the Bible. Precedent, of a kind, for the restriction can be found in earlier comments expressing

---

[18] This definition is quoted directly from the 1706 edition of Edward Phillips's dictionary *A New World of Words*.

a preference for literary quotations (e.g. that by Coleridge on preferring Tennyson to newspapers, p. 37), but Furnivall has gone much further. It may be that he was simply giving preference to sources which the Dictionary's readers were most likely to be able to consult; but the policy is certainly an innovation, and one which was not carried through in the Dictionary's later phases.

PRONUNCIATION

Although the 'Canones Lexicographici' stipulate that pronunciation, including changes in pronunciation, should be recorded, none of Coleridge's surviving entries in A gives any information about pronunciation. Furnivall accordingly came up with his own scheme for the representation of pronunciation, which is set out in some detail in his 1862 circular. It is a straightforward enough system (and one which the sub-editors generally managed to implement): most sounds are represented by the letters of the alphabet, denoting their usual sounds, with a few additional marks, such as a curve over certain digraphs (c͡h, d͡h, n͡g, o͡w, etc.) to indicate that they are to be interpreted in a particular way. Certain sounds may be represented in more than one way: for example, the vowels in *mine* and *aye* are represented, respectively, by the symbol ī and the linked digraph a͡i. The use of *r* after vowels is not explained, as may be seen from Furnivall's representation of the regular pronunciation of *creature* as 'crē'-tūr' (where the symbol ū is said to represent the vowel in *new*); and no symbol is given for the neutral vowel sound now usually represented as ə. However, these shortcomings hardly mark Furnivall's system out as worse than the respelling-based systems used in some contemporary dictionaries. It would be some years before the innovations of Alexander Ellis, Alexander Melville Bell, Henry Sweet, and James Murray himself would pave the way for a more precise method for the representation of pronunciation.

ETYMOLOGY

When Carl Lottner was commissioned by Furnivall to prepare etymological analyses of words for the Dictionary (see above, p. 42), his brief had been to separate each word into 'its several prefixes, suffixes, and root'.[19] Furnivall reiterated this method to his sub-editors in his circular the following year, whose guidelines on etymology are worth quoting at length:

---

[19] Part II of the Basis of Comparison (1861), Preliminary Notice.

First comes the native or foreign word from which the Catchword is immediately derived. If that foreigner-1 should be from a daughter language like French, the word in the parent (say Latin) language, or foreigner-2, from which the first was derived, must be given; and if foreigner-2 should be from a third (say in Greek), then foreigner-3 too must be given; also, each foreigner must be translated [...] Secondly, the ultimate foreigner must be analyzed, and its several components—prefixes, base, and suffixes—separately accounted for. Thirdly, the derivation of the base should be given, if possible, resulting in the Root. (For imsonic (*im-* imitate, *son-* sound) roots we shall be able to account; the rest will remain to us what elements do to the chemist; but I believe that more roots will prove to be *imsons* than is supposed by pooh-poohers of the bow-wow theory [...]). Fourthly, the analogues of the native or foreign parent of the Catchword, in its family—whether Gothic, Classical, or other—should be given in large number in the preparatory papers for the Full Dictionary, and in small number (say three or four), in the Concise one.[20]

This general statement can be supplemented by some of the comments he made on the work of his sub-editors, in particular two remarks on the flyleaf of the first volume of Gibbs's work: firstly, that the '1st parent [is] to be given 1st'—really a reiteration of the policy stated in the circular—and, secondly, that 'all words [are] to have etymologies'. Furnivall illustrates this by etymologizing the rare noun *calculer* as 'calcule + er'; and in his correction of Griffith's etymology for *boa-constrictor* he explains the second element as '*constricto*[r] [from] con = cum, with, *stric* bind, *to* p[ast] part[iciple,] *r* er'. Griffith's confidence seems to have been shaken by Furnivall's comments, as many of his later entries simply leave a gap, evidently in the expectation that Furnivall would 'get it done afterwards' as his circular had suggested—although for compound words formed from English elements he was happy enough to write out an etymology, of the type illustrated by *boy-bridegroom* (see p. 64 above).

  To chop Latin words such as *constrictor* into tiny chunks does suggest a distinctly naïve approach to etymology on Furnivall's part.[21] But the principle that every word should be fully etymologized was arguably ahead of its time. None of the other available dictionaries with a substantial etymological component went this far: it was common to give no etymologies at all for the 'suffixed' members of a group of words, reserving all etymological information for the main (unsuffixed) form. (The extreme position is represented by Richardson, who presented such groups of words as single entries.) Nor were Furnivall's editors very successful at implementing the policy. Gibbs gives 'full' etymologies for some suffixed words (e.g. *caliphship* 'from *Caliph* sb + *-ship*', *callously* 'From *callous* adj + *-ly*'), but his practice is patchy and inconsistent (e.g. the ending of *calibration* is not explained, and *calculable* is given no etymology at all).

---

[20] Furnivall's terms *imson* and *imsonic* do not seem to have been taken up by anyone else.

[21] It may be that Furnivall's method was derived directly from the etymological work done for him by Carl Lottner. A small number of surviving slips, in what I believe to be Lottner's handwriting, carry out very similar 'analysis': for example, a slip for *abducent* lists 'ab- from', 'duc lead, draw', '-ent affix of pres. prtp.', together with the Sanskrit word *duh* 'milk, draw out', a cognate of the Latin root. However, it is equally possible that Lottner was following a procedure set out for him by Furnivall.

As for the anatomization of the more remote roots of a word, Gibbs hardly seems to have grasped the point: *calcine*, for example, is given as deriving from 'Fr. *calciner* from Lat. *calci-* (*calx*) = Lime', with no explanation of the -*in*- component.

Gibbs's etymologies are deficient in other respects. While it is clear from the frequent listing of cognates that he was making some use of other sources[22]—including, presumably, the dictionary extracts supplied by Furnivall—these often appear as simple lists, without any sense of organization to illustrate a sequence of borrowing; sometimes the immediate source of the word (Furnivall's 'foreigner-1') is placed first, but without proper comment, as for example at *cause* (noun), where he has written simply 'Fr. *cause*. Span: Ital: Prov: Port: and Latin *causa*'. The surviving fragments of other sub-editors' etymologies suggest an even lower level of competence. Some, like Griffith, were happy enough to recognize their limits by leaving gaps; others might hazard a partial guess, like Joseph Middleton's 'Quatuor – vir Lat:' (for *quadrivirate*).

From the frustratingly small (and etymologically uninteresting) range of entries worked on by Skeat there is at least some evidence of a more organized and coherent approach: the etymology for the adjective *rebel*, for example (to which he refers the noun), is given as '[Fr. *rebelle*, It. *ribelle*, from Lat. *rebellis*, rebellious; which from *re*, and *bellum*, war.]'—an orderly progression which closely resembles the corresponding etymology in the *OED*. However, he hardly goes further than other sub-editors in implementing Furnivall's direction to etymologize every word in full. He seems to regard some suffixes as more in need of explanation than others: thus *rebelliously* and *rebelliousness* are fully etymologized, while the etymology of *rebellious* is given simply as '[rebellion, sb.]'. Similarly, the etymology for both *re-baptizer* and *re-baptizing* is given simply as '[rebaptize, vb.]', and that for *re-barbarization* as '[re-barbarize, vb.]'.

PREPARATIONS FOR PRINT; INCONSISTENCIES

Furnivall's 1862 circular is clear about the need to prepare copy that could be used directly by the printer: sub-editors should leave 'a good margin' around their 'Concise' entries, so that newly discovered quotations and other relevant material could be incorporated easily. Several annotations by Furnivall on the flyleaf of Gibbs's first volume, concerned as they are with matters of presentation and the ordering of entries ('v[er]b with noun of same meaning', 'sb. [=substantive] to precede verb'), show that he continued to regard the entries as 'print-ready'. Gibbs did likewise: against his entry for *caboc*, for example, which appears out of alphabetical sequence, he has written the

---

[22] Gibbs often explicitly acknowledges his sources: at *catafalque*, for example, he cites 'Diez' (i.e. F. C. Diez's etymological dictionary of the Romance languages) as the source of the proposed derivation from 'O[ld] Span[ish] *catar* = to look at […] and *falco* for *palco* a scaffold or stage'. In his later entries he relies heavily on Wedgwood's etymological dictionary, sometimes even pasting excerpts from Wedgwood's text into his own.

instruction 'Print before Caboceer'. But as the years went by, the sub-editors would often find themselves obliged, not merely to add new material to their text, but to revise what they had written in the light of it, making for an increasingly messy manuscript. Gibbs's work shows this most clearly, with additional quotations (and sometimes whole entries) added in the margins, and senses renumbered in many larger entries.

There were some components of the text which Furnivall's editorial policy made particularly liable to need alteration. Mindful, perhaps, of John Murray's views on obsolete words, he decided that obsolete headwords should appear in small capitals (with bold Clarendon type for current headwords), and instructed his sub-editors to mark up their text with underlining indicating the appropriate typeface. The problem with this was, of course, that if later evidence turned up for a word which had been marked as obsolete, the markup would have to be altered. Similarly, because of the policy of including the earliest quotation for every word and sense, these would constantly have to be crossed out as new antedatings came to light. In some cases sub-editors may simply have failed to keep up with the new material, with the result that their text must gradually have become a less and less accurate reflection of the evidence.

But the fact is that, however thorough the sub-editors were in incorporating newly acquired evidence, the lack of communication between them—or with Furnivall— made for such divergence in editorial practice as to make the resulting text hopelessly inconsistent. Some aspects of this, such as the wide variation in the length of the quotations, have already been mentioned; there were also innumerable small aspects of style. Skeat cited two such inconsistencies in support of his plea to Furnivall for better monitoring:

You say, in your letter to sub-editors, that words should have their senses distinguished by A, B, C, but Mr Paine, not noticing this, has invariably put I, II, III. Again, when I refer to words, I don't know whether to say, 'see *Ray*', or 'see *ray*'; or 'v. *ray*.' so that—as things stand—I have come to the conclusion I had best do no more till work has been inspected, & all existing mistakes of subeditors (of the character, I mean, which *pervade* their *whole* work) have been pointed out.

Other examples are, as Skeat suggests, easy to come by. In etymologies of words formed from several components, for example, where Gibbs uses a plus sign (e.g. 'cave sb. + tiger sb.' for *cave-tiger*), Skeat writes 'and' in full, and Griffith puts just a semicolon; where these components are (or are expected to be) headwords, Griffith and Skeat write 'q.v.' but Gibbs does not; and the underlining used to indicate whether these forms are to appear in roman, italic, or small capitals is not even consistent within the work of a single sub-editor. (Of course, each sub-editor, unable to be sure how a particular word outside his or her allocated range would be treated, would sometimes feel obliged to provide each instance of it with a full gloss—such as '*ness*, noun-ending of abstract quality', written out by Skeat at both *rebelliousness* and *rebelness*— rather than a simple cross-reference.) Gibbs sometimes introduces his etymologies with 'From'; Griffith and Skeat do not—but their etymologies are enclosed in square brackets, whereas Gibbs's are not. Every component of the sub-editors' work is marred by similar variation—not important in terms of the readability of individual entries, but fatally compromising the integrity of the text as a whole. Skeat immediately realized this, and warned Furnivall that the sub-editors were in danger of 'throwing their time away utterly by writing out things in a way which could not be printed from'.

AN INCOMPLETE DICTIONARY

Such questions of presentation are, however, academic. The fact is that only a very small proportion of the alphabet was ever digested and written up by Furnivall's sub-editors to a point at which printing was even a possibility.

Was this an enormous missed opportunity? It is clear that some, at least, of the sub-editors shared Furnivall's enthusiasm for the Dictionary, and were both capable of hard work and willing to expend the enormous quantities of time required. It is also all too obvious that Furnivall simply did not adequately supervise their work. His talent for finding volunteers and persuading them to 'do something for the Dictionary' was invaluable; and some kinds of work—notably the collection of quotations—could be done reasonably satisfactorily with little or no further input, provided the initial instructions were good enough.[23] But the compilation of dictionary entries was surely another matter; and Furnivall's faith in the ability of a disparate group of sub-editors, working from a brief circular (supplemented in some cases by a little initial feedback), to produce work of a publishable and consistent standard without careful monitoring—of the kind that Skeat had urged in his 1865 letter—was clearly misplaced. Some of the sub-editors, indeed, produced work of such questionable value that those using the material in later years might have wished that nothing had been attempted at all. Furnivall's attempts to secure enough sub-editors to cover the whole alphabet are understandable, particularly in view of his contractual obligations to John Murray; but it might have been better to concentrate on training a smaller group of sub-editors, and on redirecting their efforts as best suited their different levels of expertise. A man of Furnivall's temperament was perhaps unlikely to adopt such an approach; but if he had, then the Philological Society's Dictionary—or, at least, a condensed, preliminary version of it—might perhaps have begun to appear in print a decade or more before the publication of James Murray's first fascicle.

There are, however, various reasons to be relieved that this never came to pass. As Skeat had warned, if publication had followed anything like the mode of presentation

---

[23] A similar methodology characterizes the editing of texts by volunteers working for the EETS and other publishing societies with which Furnivall was associated. The consequences of assigning texts to be edited by individuals qualified only by 'enthusiasm for the subject, available time, and a willingness to work' are discussed in Singleton (2005).

seen in the surviving samples, the scale of the project would surely have been so vast as to stand no chance of ever being completed. The documentation available to the sub-editors was hopelessly impoverished by the inaccessibility of texts for the whole of the Old English and Middle English periods. The state of etymological knowledge in England would have rendered this component of the Dictionary of little value, even supposing that competent scholars could have been found to attempt it. Finally, the organization of entries according to a 'logical' or 'mental' succession of senses would have made for something very different from what we understand today by a 'historical dictionary'.

Nevertheless, it must be acknowledged that the best of Furnivall's sub-editors did much work which James Murray and his successors would find useful. Of the definition slips which were eventually sent to press, a small but significant number still bear the sub-editor's original draft, often reworded slightly but sometimes preserved unchanged. And even if the actual content of the sub-editors' draft entries for the Concise Dictionary was used sparingly or not at all, their organization of the quotation evidence into senses and subsenses—identified by brief definitions on slips attached to each bundle—would have been of great value, as anyone who has attempted to sort a large number of examples of a word in this way can appreciate. The accumulation of further quotations over the ensuing decades would of course considerably expand the corpus of evidence; but it is generally far easier to allocate additional quotations into an existing sense scheme (even one which requires modification) than to devise one *de novo*. Ironically, this interfiling of later quotations, and the discarding of most of the sub-editors' brief definition slips, has now rendered this component of their work effectively invisible; but to ignore the value of their work is to misrepresent their contribution. Substantial work, of a useful kind, was done during Furnivall's editorship, even if from several points of view it is as well that more was not completed.

3

Manoeuvres: 1876–1879

As 1876 began, the Dictionary remained prominent in the discussions of the Council of the Philological Society. Early in February they discussed an offer, made by one W. J. Anderson of Markinch in Fife, to take on the Editorship; whether the offer was in response to a personal approach from Gibbs or some other member of the Council, or whether a copy of Wheelwright's 'Appeal' had found its way into Anderson's hands (he was a sub-editor), is unclear. However, when Anderson was asked to prepare some specimen entries, it became apparent that he was not up to the task. Furnivall observed that 'he actually doesn't know the difference between an intrans. & trans. vb.'[1]

The recipient of the postcard in which Furnivall made this damning assessment was James Murray (see Figure 10, p. 143), who at last makes his appearance in the story of the dictionary with which he came to be so closely identified. This remarkable man, despite his lack of a formal university education, had acquired a considerable reputation in the field of English philology in the twelve years since his arrival in London from Scotland, particularly in the area of dialect studies. His monograph *The Dialect of the Southern Counties of Scotland*, published by the Philological Society in 1873, had been very well received, and in 1874 he had been awarded an honorary LL.D. from Edinburgh University in recognition of his contributions to philology: a striking achievement for a man who had left school at 14. His knowledge extended to many languages beyond English: already by 1866, when he made an (unsuccessful) application for a post in the British Museum, he could claim some proficiency in over twenty languages. Furnivall's description of him, in his testimonial supporting the proposal to award him the doctorate at Edinburgh, gives an impressive account of his accomplishments:

I consider him the first living authority on our Northern Dialects [...] He takes also first rank among the phoneticists of the day [...] Whatever paper turns up at our [Philological Society]

---

[1] MP 18 Feb. 1876 FJF to JAHM.

The Making of the *Oxford English Dictionary*. First edition. Peter Gilliver.
© Peter Gilliver 2016. First published 2016 by Oxford University Press.

Meetings, Sanscrit, Persian, Russian, Mr Murray has always knowledge of the subject, & something pertinent to say of it.[2]

He had been introduced to the phonetician Alexander Ellis, and through him to the Philological Society, by Alexander Melville Bell in 1868, and had been a member of the Society's Council since May 1869. Thus by 1876 he would have known of the great Dictionary project and its vicissitudes; indeed, he had been present at the Council meeting in 1871 when it constituted the Committee 'to enquire into the state of the Society's Dictionary'.[3] By this time he was an assistant master at the recently re-established Nonconformist boys' school at Mill Hill, a few miles outside London, a post he had been offered in 1870 by his fellow Society member R. F. Weymouth.[4] He had also edited several texts for the Early English Text Society, and collaborated with Furnivall and others on the preparation of other editions.

Anderson's offer also came to the attention of another distinguished philologist, Walter Skeat, who as we have seen had become involved with the Dictionary as one of Furnivall's sub-editors. By 1876, however, he was heavily involved with the activities of the English Dialect Society (which he had founded in 1873), and with his editing of *Piers Plowman*.[5] He had also published several books with the Clarendon Press, and Bartholomew Price regularly consulted him for advice on philological and lexicographical matters; in fact as long ago as 1871 Price had been so impressed by a glossary which Skeat had provided for an anthology of fifteenth- and sixteenth-century English that he had informally sought to persuade him to undertake the compilation of a large-scale English dictionary, 'based on the soundest philological principles', such as the Delegates of the Press had often been encouraged to publish. Price's proposal envisaged Skeat as 'workman and superintending editor, together with such a staff of collaborateurs as you yourself might select', and assumed that he was in a position to make use of the Philological Society's materials. In 1872 he again urged: 'Can't you undertake the Philological Dictionary?' Skeat was thus well aware that at least one of the key figures at the Clarendon Press was both sympathetic to the Dictionary and realistic about the resources that such a project would require.[6]

---

[2] MP JAHM draft application to British Museum, [20 Nov. 1866], testimonial from FJF, 26 Mar. 1874 (copy by JAHM); both quoted in *CWW* (pp. 70, 118). In addition to his doctorate, Murray also held an external BA degree from London University, study for which he had completed in 1873.

[3] Murray joined the Philological Society in June 1868, by which time he was already acquainted with Furnivall. On his friendship with Ellis, and their collaboration in phonetics and dialect studies, see *CWW* pp. 72–6.

[4] In addition to his headmastership of Mill Hill, Weymouth was also a distinguished philologist and biblical scholar, probably best remembered today for his pioneering *New Testament in Modern Speech* (1902); he had been a reader for the Dictionary since the Coleridge era. Some information about Murray's time at Mill Hill, and his relationship with Weymouth, may be found in Roderick Braithwaite's idiosyncratic '*Strikingly alive…': the history of the Mill Hill School foundation 1807–2007* (Andover: Phillimore, 2006).

[5] For more information on Skeat's life and work, see Brewer (1996), esp. pp. 91–113.

[6] SL 30 Oct., 21 or 22 Dec. 1871, 25 June 1872 B. Price to Skeat. Price mentions in a letter to Max Müller of 3 November 1871 that he has had a response (presumably in the negative) from Skeat, which is not preserved.

At the Council's 18 February meeting (when Anderson's offer was discussed), Furnivall was tasked with contacting Price. In the end, however, it seems to have been decided that the approach should be made by Skeat; his commission was to try to persuade the Press to put up money to provide '£500 a year for at least 10 years' to pay an Editor—a subsidy very much along the lines proposed at the Council's meeting in November.[7]

Before he could approach Price, however, Skeat felt it would be sensible to identify someone prepared to take on the task of editing the Dictionary. Having gathered from Furnivall that Murray would be willing to do so, he wrote to him, setting out his own ideas about what might be feasible: a dictionary without quotations or elaborate etymologies, and indeed with only brief definitions, with the main emphasis on quotations, 'in fact, something like Richardson, multiplied by 6 or 10, & with the quotations in better order. Such a scheme might work: a more ambitious one won't. What do you think of it—& are you willing to try?'[8]

In fact Furnivall had (as ever) rather overstated things. He later recalled that Murray had expressed a 'wish [...] to take up the Dict'—a wish which he delightedly passed on to friends in the Society—but Elisabeth Murray has suggested that this must have been a chance remark, not intended to be taken seriously.[9] Certainly Skeat was soon apologizing to Murray for the misunderstanding. He also approached Nicol again, whom he found '*does* seem disposed to take it up, but looks forward to doing other things first. It is a great pity no one is to be had *at once*!' Notwithstanding his own feeling that 'some one ought to *move* in the matter', however, he decided it would be best to hold off from contacting the Clarendon Press until he next had the opportunity to go to Oxford and speak to Price personally.[10]

The delay was to have profound consequences. In early April, before Skeat had had a chance to visit Oxford, James Murray received a letter from the publisher Alexander Macmillan, who had been given his name by Richard Morris in connection with 'a philological work we want done'. Macmillan is likely to have been well aware at this point of the Philological Society's proposal; he may even have discussed it with Bartholomew Price, with whom he was in regular contact in his capacity as 'publisher to the University' for OUP's 'learned side', a position he had held since 1863.[11] However,

---

[7] PSCM 18 Feb., 3 Mar. 1876.

[8] MP 9 Mar. [1876] Skeat to JAHM. This is one of several letters from Skeat which Elisabeth Murray dates to 1877, but for which internal evidence strongly suggests a year earlier.

[9] MP 21 Jan. 1882 FJF to JAHM; *CWW* p. 140. In his letter Furnivall recollects that he had first asked Henry Sweet to take on the Dictionary, and on his refusal had turned to Nicol, but that during a conversation 'in Regent's Park Rd.' Murray had said that he would prefer to do it, and that Furnivall informed the Council of this, having 'got the others to see, with me, that you were the likelier man'.

[10] MP 23 Mar. [1876] Skeat to JAHM; 21 Jan. 1882 FJF to JAHM; 6 Apr. 1876, Skeat to [JAHM]. During March 1876 Skeat was in regular correspondence with Price in regard to two different publishing projects: an anthology of selections from Chaucer, and a *List of English Words, the etymology of which is illustrated by comparison with Icelandic*, published as a kind of Appendix to Cleasby and Vigfusson's great Icelandic–English dictionary—which had itself been published in 1869–73 by the Clarendon Press, at some expense (see Knowles 2013: 611–13).

[11] On Macmillan's professional connections with OUP see Hammond (2013: 282–95).

the proposed 'philological work' turned out to be something quite different: Harpers, the American publisher, had approached Macmillan with a proposal that they should work together on the publication of a new English dictionary in one large volume. The idea was to produce 'something like Webster, in bulk, and as far superior to him in quality as possible'; Macmillan wondered whether Murray would be prepared to take on the editorship of this project, in collaboration with a distinguished American scholar, probably William Dwight Whitney or Francis Child. Macmillan's nephew Maurice, newly graduated from Cambridge, was to provide editorial assistance.[12]

Murray immediately wrote to Skeat to ask how far he had got with the Clarendon Press; it was clear to both men that, while the Harper–Macmillan proposal fell far short of the Philological Society's aspirations, the opportunity to exploit it for the Society's benefit should not be lost.[13] In his reply Skeat gave an account of his lack of progress with Oxford, explaining however why he felt that for the moment it would be better if he did not become directly involved in negotiations with Macmillan.[14]

The letter also reveals much else about the project and its personalities. In regard to the need for confidentiality, Skeat emphasized that '[i]f it can be managed without Mr. Furnivall till all is fairly in order, it will certainly be best. Without doubt, he will publish all he knows about it at the earliest opportunity. I have told him plainly, often, that this is often annoying: but, though he is at heart one of the best of men, he will not take *that* hint.' Furnivall would of course eventually have to become involved, as the only man through whom the sub-editors could be contacted; Skeat was well aware of the great gaps in their work, but he agreed with Murray that 'the *collection of material is simply invaluable, and must on no account be ignored.* [...] Why, it has taken 10 to 15 years to get the results together: & they only want arranging in some places.' He was excited by the new proposal: 'if you & [Macmillan] can actually *do* something in the matter, it will be a great thing for England.'

Encouraged by Skeat's letter, Murray immediately wrote to Macmillan to outline a scheme whereby he might be able to undertake the proposed dictionary, and a meeting was arranged to talk over details.[15] But there was little chance of keeping the project from Furnivall, who knew Macmillan well, and who now threw himself into negotiations with relish. In early June he met with Macmillan and J. R. Green (a popular historian, and a valued Macmillan author) to discuss the project, and

---

[12]   MP 3 Apr. 1876 Alexander Macmillan to JAHM, 16 May 1876 William Jack (for Macmillan) to JAHM, 6 June 1876 FJF to JAHM; OED/B/3/1/2 11 Nov. 1878 JAHM to Price. Macmillan had written to Morris on 27 March asking to see him in confidence on a very important matter which he thought would interest him (BL MS Add. 55399 p. 149), presumably shortly after receiving the approach from Harpers; he had apparently first approached Henry Sweet, who had however declined (Murray 1943: 75). The requirement for an American editor, who may have been expected to have no more than an honorary role, is likely to have been due to the need to secure American copyright for the work (see further below, p. 100).

[13]   Strangely, in a long autobiographical letter which Murray wrote in 1903 (later published as Murray 1957), he claimed to have known nothing about the Philological Society's project at this time, and that it was Macmillan who mentioned it to him. Murray's presence at earlier Council discussions of the Dictionary shows that this cannot have been the case.

[14]   MP 6 Apr. 1876 Skeat to JAHM.

[15]   MP 13 Apr. 1876 A. Macmillan to JAHM; 18 Apr., 3 May 1876 G. Macmillan to JAHM.

suggested various modifications to bring Macmillan's proposals more into line with the Philological Society's scheme. His report to Murray on the meeting was full of optimism, some of which was to prove sadly misplaced:

McM quite agreed about the historical usage of all words being shown, but said he must have a large admission of technical words [...]. This point I yielded with pleasure, as I always meant to smuggle in as many scientific words as possible [...]. McM. agreed at once to the 4 vols. 4to., & the publication in Parts. I said that I thought the work down to the end of R. might be done in 3 years, & then the publication begin, S–Z being prepared while the prior Parts were appearing.

Regarding remuneration, Furnivall mentioned the plan to approach the Clarendon Press for £500 a year—Macmillan was planning to pay his nephew £200—but advised Murray that he 'mustn't ask too much at starting. There'll be pay hanging to future abridgments & the big book, & a share in the royalty.'[16] The reference to the 'big book' shows that, for Furnivall, any mere four-volume dictionary was still only to be seen as a stepping-stone to the Society's original grand project.

Whether Macmillan had in fact agreed to a dictionary on such a scale is doubtful. There were certainly precedents, notably Émile Littré's recently completed four-volume *Dictionnaire de la langue française*, which Furnivall may well have mentioned; but this would be an enormous expansion of what Harpers had originally proposed, and Macmillan was careful to explain to Harpers that, while Littré had been mentioned as a basis for calculations, nothing definite had been fixed as to size. However, he pointed out that only the prospect of a dictionary compiled on a substantial scale would persuade the Philological Society to agree to allow their materials to be used, even if profits could only be expected to come from abridgements of this.[17]

Discussions continued over the summer, and by early September a partner in Macmillan's firm, George Craik, was able to report from New York that matters had been settled to Harpers' satisfaction.[18] Craik returned with a contract committing the two publishers to a book of 4,000 quarto pages—equivalent to rather less than three volumes of the size of Webster's Dictionary—and Murray was asked to prepare a specimen. To his doubts about being able to do the material justice if restricted to this scale Furnivall breezily responded: 'I shouldn't be afraid about the space, because it's a thing to be enlarged afterwards. Also if McM. sees the thing goes well he'll extend it. [...] 4000 pages 'll let you do a good deal. Afterwards we can turn it into 12000 or 20,000, if the Gods are propitious.' Once again this was almost certainly unrealistic: William Jack, another Macmillan partner who conducted much of the negotiations with Murray, was at pains to emphasize that this page limit was the most that could possi-

[16] MP 6 June 1876 FJF to JAHM.
[17] BL MS Add. 55399 6 June 1876 F. Macmillan to Harpers. Macmillan again mentions Whitney, 'a man who is in sympathy with English scholarship & whose name would carry weight', as a possible American editor.
[18] MP 12 Sept. 1876 A. Macmillan to JAHM.

bly be agreed to, and later asserted that Murray had never mentioned anything larger than three Webster volumes (about 4,400 pages).[19] Nevertheless, Murray set to work on his specimen, selecting a range of words beginning with *car-*, for which he could draw on some of the most finished sub-edited material, namely that done by Henry Hucks Gibbs.

However, none of what had taken place over the summer had yet been formally considered or approved by the Philological Society. Furnivall now called a special meeting of the Society's Council, to be held on 20 October, and at a meeting with Macmillan on the 16th he obtained a formal statement of the terms of the proposed project insofar as they concerned the Society (as distinct from Murray as an individual). These were: that the dictionary for which the Society's materials were to be made available would be of 4,000 pages of the size of Webster; that the dictionary's editor was to be mutually agreed by Macmillan and the Society; that the Society would receive a royalty of 20 per cent of any profits; and that the Society would not use their material to compile any larger dictionary until five years after the completion of the 4,000-page work. There was also a clause authorizing the publication of abridgements.[20] The Council was ready to agree to all of these proposals—with the exception of the moratorium on publishing the full Dictionary. If the editing and publication of Macmillan's book—the 4,000 pages of which were evidently not considered capable of accommodating an adequate representation of the accumulated material—was likely to take ten years, this would place the full Dictionary out of reach for fifteen, a prospect which many were not prepared to accept. Accordingly, it was resolved to return, more or less, to the point where things had stood before the approach from Macmillan: Skeat was to be asked to try to persuade the Clarendon Press to undertake publication of the full Dictionary, or, failing that, a larger abridgement of 6,000 pages. The Macmillans were to be informed of this, and negotiations would only be resumed with them if they consented to an increased number of pages.[21]

For the Macmillans this was disastrous news. They had put a great deal of effort into persuading Harpers to accept the idea of a 4,000-page dictionary—nearly three times what had originally been contemplated—and now it now seemed that for the Philological Society this was not big enough; and, what was worse, that they were proposing to offer their materials to another publisher. Furnivall was clearly regarded as the driving force behind the Council's decision, but he was not the only Council member who considered 4,000 pages inadequate: both Ellis and Nicol made exactly this point in letters to Murray.[22]

Murray, however, was already at work on his specimen, and Macmillan were unwilling to let all their efforts come to nothing without a struggle. Angry as he was at the

---

[19] OED/B/1/1/6 signed contract dated 21 Sept. 1876 between Harper Brothers and Macmillan & Co.; MP 9 Oct. 1876 FJF to JAHM, 10 Oct. 1876 W. Jack to JAHM; BL MS Add. 55400 25 Oct. 1876 Jack to FJF.

[20] BL MS Add. 55400 17 Oct. 1876 W. Jack to FJF, with memorandum of points made at the meeting held on the previous day.

[21] PSCM 20 Oct. 1876.

[22] MP 24 Oct. 1876 AJE to JAHM; 24 Oct. 1876 H. Nicol to JAHM.

sudden demand for an increase in scale—which he was sure would never be agreed to by Harpers—William Jack sought to reassure Furnivall that it had never been their intention to exclude the 'Big Dictionary', and that indeed if the abridged work now under consideration were to be a success then Macmillan would surely be interested in undertaking it, and well placed to do so. In the event it was agreed that Murray should continue work on the specimen, not on the basis of an absolute limit of 4,000 pages, but 'in the most compressed form which [he] could conscientiously recommend'. It was further agreed that an estimate of the full extent of a complete Dictionary on this basis should be made, and that Murray, Furnivall, and other interested parties would then see what could be done to compress it to a scale which the publishers could accept.[23]

By the start of November Murray had prepared a specimen, according to which he thought that a worthwhile dictionary could be accommodated within 4,800 pages. Over the next few weeks Macmillan produced a series of proofs for him—nine in all—presenting the text in an increasingly compressed form, in an attempt to bring the scale down to mutually acceptable levels. Interested parties were sent versions of the proofs and asked for suggestions as to methods of compression. Mainly this was a question of type size and spacing—even the largest type used anywhere in the specimens is smaller than that later used in the *OED*'s definitions, and some of the quotations are almost unreadably small—but the later proofs also experiment with the replacement of recent quotations from newspapers by the brief comment 'Modern' (probably as a result of a suggestion by William Jack).[24] The results of this process, and Murray's further discussions with Macmillan, were most encouraging: at the Council's meeting on 17 November Murray was able to report that Macmillan 'had agreed to give 4,400 pages & possibly more if he required it; they seemed inclined to give way to him on such points as he required.' Furnivall, Sweet, Morris, and Ellis were appointed as a committee to resume negotiations with Macmillan; this time, it was to be hoped, everything would go smoothly.[25]

But smoothness was perhaps not to be expected when Furnivall was involved. At the same time as the new committee was seeking a meeting with Macmillan, he was negotiating elsewhere. Skeat had declared himself unwilling to approach the Clarendon Press about the 'Big Dictionary' (although he was ready to try for a 6,000-page version); Furnivall now approached another publisher, H. S. King. It is not clear what proposals were discussed, but King (who was also a banker) estimated the likely cost as £10,000, an amount which his company was not willing to put up; he suggested that some of the capital could instead be raised by issuing debentures of £50 apiece, if fifty 'gentlemen interested in the English Language' could be found. Furnivall informed the 'Dictionary Committee' of his doings on 22 November. All this was of course taking

[23] MP 10 Oct. 1876 W. Jack to JAHM; BL MS Add. 55400 25 Oct. 1876 Jack to FJF.

[24] Copies of the proofs prepared by Macmillan are preserved in MP, some with annotations by Furnivall and Skeat.

[25] PSCM 17 Nov. 1876.

place without Macmillan's knowledge; Furnivall urged Murray to keep it that way, and explained his plan: 'Even if King declines, I shall make his terms an ultimatum to McM. & demand the throwing-over of Harpers. Or go to [the publishers] Bradbury & Evans.'[26]

The Macmillans continued in ignorance of the Philological Society's discussions for several weeks, and became increasingly anxious that the settlement which they believed to be so near would be delayed until after Christmas. But the letter which they received from Furnivall on 14 December shattered their illusions. In it he laid down, in the name of the Society, a new set of terms and conditions, which differed so substantially from those which had previously been discussed that no agreement was possible. The main change was in the share of the profits allocated to the Society: Furnivall now rejected the previous figure of 20 per cent, which indeed he now claimed had never been formally accepted. This was not at all how Macmillan viewed matters: as William Jack complained to Murray, '[a] more ingenious perversion of the spirit in which we supposed our famous interview to have taken place it is difficult to imagine.' Be that as it may, Furnivall now demanded for the Society a full one-third of the profits.[27]

This time the breach was to be irreparable. Macmillan's reply to Furnivall's letter was formal, and distinctly chilly in tone compared to earlier correspondence, and made it clear that the additional conditions offered 'no prospect of any practicable arrangement'.[28] Furnivall in turn replied that he regarded Macmillan's letter as 'practically closing the negociations', and on 15 December the Council authorized the Dictionary Committee to approach 'one of the Universities' (i.e. Oxford or Cambridge), thus bringing matters back to the point where they had stood ten months earlier.[29]

Given his boundless enthusiasm for the Dictionary, it is ironic that Furnivall must take such a large part of the responsibility for the disastrous end to the negotiations with Macmillan. It is true that the Council (or the Dictionary Committee) were kept informed—for the most part—of his doings and communications on their behalf; but one can judge where Macmillan regarded the blame as lying from the letter to Harpers in which they returned a signed copy of the ill-fated joint agreement between the two publishers, and regretfully anticipated that nothing would now come of it:

[26] PSCM 3 Nov., 1 Dec. 1876; MP 23 Nov. 1876 FJF to JAHM, 26 Nov. 1876 JAHM to AJE, 29 Nov. 1876 JAHM to AJE.

[27] MP 15 Dec. 1876 FJF to Macmillan (copy), 18 Dec. 1876 W. Jack to JAHM. Furnivall's letter naming the new terms is not preserved, but the figure of one-third was recalled in correspondence two years later following a Council meeting at which Murray disclosed that Macmillan had offered him (as editor) a 25% share in the profits; an astonished Furnivall wrote apologetically to Macmillan explaining that had he known this, he would never have argued that the Society should receive a further one-third: 'I am certain that so avaricious & dishonourable a notion could never have enter[e]d the heads of any of us' (BL MS Add. 55255 25 Jan. 1879 FJF to A. Macmillan).

[28] BL MS Add. 55401 14 Dec. 1876 Macmillan & Co. to FJF. The letter also mentions some other conditions stipulated by Furnivall which Macmillan were prepared to accept, including an undertaking to pay him the £610 he still owed John Murray; in fact the Philological Society Council had agreed at their October meeting that Furnivall should have this money reimbursed to him.

[29] MP 15 Dec. 1876 FJF to Macmillan (copy); PSCM 15 Dec. 1876.

when we first came to you with the scheme of publishing the Philological Society Dictionary, it was after a great deal of consultation with leading members of the Council and with the very man who is now we believe the chief cause of trouble, and although we had no agreement with them in writing [...] we felt that we had every right to believe that the Society would readily accede to the proposals we then made verbally, as soon as we were ready to make them in the shape of a formal offer.

As Alexander Macmillan commented wryly to Murray: 'It is a pity that his pretty playful ways should ever be intruded into serious business.' On the other hand, it may ultimately have been for the best. As Elisabeth Murray has observed, Macmillan was too small a business to have been able to finance a project on anything like the scale that the Dictionary eventually attained; and if, on the other hand, the proposal to publish a work in three or four volumes had gone ahead, using the Philological Society's materials, probably nothing larger would ever have come of them.[30]

Murray may himself have been relieved that Macmillan's proposals were after all to come to nothing. The work he had put into preparing the specimen entries had brought home the magnitude of the task, and he seems to have begun to think that he might in the end find it too burdensome. Certainly the breakdown of negotiations allowed him to give serious consideration to a quite different career move: some weeks earlier he had been invited to apply for the Principalship of Huddersfield College. However interested he might have become in lexicographical matters, he was still a schoolmaster, and an enthusiastic and successful one, and a Principalship was an attractive next step, not least financially. Furnivall had suggested that Murray might be able to combine the Huddersfield post with editing the Dictionary, by engaging a '3rd Sub Ed[ito]r' to do the preliminary work and spending two hours a day on 'final revision', while still allowing his name to appear on the title page, 'for fame & ultimate profits' sake'; but Murray would have no truck with such pluralism. On 2 February 1877 the Council heard that 'Dr Murray having declined the offered Headship of Huddersfield College, [Furnivall] had written to the Syndics of the Cambridge University Press asking them to take up the Society's Dictionary.'[31]

In fact Furnivall had not waited for Murray to make up his mind. Having decided that Cambridge, not Oxford, was to be offered the glittering prize of the Dictionary (he was after all a Cambridge man), before Christmas he had already written to two interested parties: first to William Aldis Wright, one of the Syndics of the Cambridge University Press, and then to C. J. Clay, University Printer, urging them to 'take up a big thing that 'll ultimately bring you a lot of profit & do you great credit'. Furnivall's letter to Clay, displaying his usual breathless enthusiasm and cavalier approach to facts, set out an elaborate (and hugely optimistic) vision: the Dictionary could be printed up to

---

[30] BL MS Add. 55401 21 Dec. 1876 Macmillan & Co. to Harper & Brothers; MP 19 Dec. 1876 A. Macmillan to JAHM; *CWW* p. 144.

[31] MP 18 Dec. 1876 W. Jack to JAHM; 23 Nov. 1876 FJF to JAHM; 9 Jan. 1877 Robert Bruce (of Huddersfield College) to JAHM; PSCM 2 Feb. 1877.

the letter I in three years if Cambridge would pay Murray and two sub-editors £600 a year; completion in four quarto volumes would take ten years, with 'Abridgments in 4to., 8vo, square f[ools]cap 8vo for schools'; an 'American house' (presumably Harpers!) would be willing to share the initial outlay, as would Trübner or H. S. King; Macmillan was allegedly still keen to be the publisher, but was trying to 'screw' (i.e. drive a hard bargain with) the Philological Society, hence the approach to Cambridge (with the intention of trying Oxford if they were to turn it down). Using information from the French lexicographer Émile Littré about the sales of his great dictionary and its abridgements, Furnivall predicted worldwide sales of 100,000 for the main Dictionary and 'millions' in its abridged versions.[32] After meeting Furnivall in London, Clay advised him to write more formally to James Cartmell, the chairman of the Syndics, who speedily rejected the idea, perhaps simply because it involved Furnivall. As Skeat later told Murray, 'somehow, he isn't believed in at the universities [...]. It has arisen from his odd prefaces, &c. & modes of expression.'[33]

Cambridge, then, would not publish the Dictionary. Nor would Alexander Macmillan; but he was still very much a supporter of it in principle. Early in March he wrote to Bartholomew Price in Oxford with the news that he had been discussing the whole business of the Dictionary with his partners, and that it seemed possible that they might be able to 'cede the matter' to the Clarendon Press. He had asked Murray to come for a talk, apparently in order to establish 'whether the *impracticable* party [i.e. Furnivall] cannot be got rid of or evaded'. Price responded favourably, and the news regarding Furnivall was apparently also satisfactory. On 24 March Macmillan wrote to Murray: 'I think there is a chance that Oxford might be induced to take up the Dictionary & I have told Prof. Price that we will lend him all the aid we can. Could you or Mr Sweet come & see me about it?'[34] Evidently Sweet did go to see him, for on 20 April 1877 he wrote what was to prove to be a momentous letter to Price, setting out the nature of the Dictionary and some suggestions as to the terms on which the Society and the University Press might aim to reach agreement.[35]

The Dictionary Committee clearly realized the importance of giving the new proposal the best possible chance of success; it was, after all, not at all clear where else they might try if it failed. Accordingly, Sweet's letter, written on behalf of the Committee,

---

[32]   23 Dec. 1876 FJF to C. J. Clay, quoted in McKitterick (2004: 104–6). Originally Furnivall had asked Skeat to approach the Syndics (MP 20 Dec. 1876 FJF to JAHM), but he seems to have demurred. According to McKitterick, Furnivall's subsequent letter to James Cartmell (1 Feb. 1877) set out a significantly different proposal, for a dictionary in three volumes, with an additional assistant and a separately remunerated American editor.

[33]   PSCM 2 Mar. 1877; MP [n.d.; autumn 1877] Skeat to JAHM.

[34]   BL MS Add. 55402 7 Mar. 1877 A. Macmillan to JAHM; 8 Mar. 1877 A. Macmillan to Price, 24 Mar. 1877 A. Macmillan to JAHM.

[35]   OED/B/3/1/1 20 Apr. 1877 H. Sweet to Price (reproduced in *CWW* pp. 342–6). This may have been an exceptionally propitious time for Sweet to approach the Press about the Philological Society's project, as only a few weeks earlier he had helped Price out by advising as to how the revision of Joseph Bosworth's dictionary of Anglo-Saxon—pages of which were already going through the press—might be completed following the death of its editor (SL 12 Dec. 1876, 9 Feb. 1877 Price to Sweet).

was worded with great care to present the Dictionary—or, rather, a 6,400-page 'abridg-ment' of the Dictionary as originally conceived—in the best possible light. As on many previous occasions, the description of the state of the materials was optimistic: half the alphabet was said to have been sub-edited, the slips for the other half all sorted.[36] Much emphasis was placed on the importance of 'fullness of citations', which made a unique virtue of one thing which the Philological Society could unquestionably offer, namely the immense mass of quotations which had been collected over the preceding decades. The 'historical method' was also emphasized: the financial success of Littré's French dictionary, once again mentioned as a reassuring precedent, was attributed to 'its fullness of citations and its historical and scientific character'. The Delegates were, accordingly, being offered 'a share in what promises to be a very safe and remunera-tive [undertaking]'; the money they were being asked to invest was compensated by the value of the Society's materials, and by 'the absence of risk and certainty of large returns in the future'.

The fact that the Committee had elected to propose an abridged version of the Dictionary, along the lines of (although larger than) what had so nearly been agreed with Alexander Macmillan, is of particular interest in view of what later became of the project. It was estimated that something like 18,000 pages would be required 'to utilize [...] fully' the accumulated materials;[37] it was 'only on such as scale as this that a thoroughly full and satisfactory work on the plan contemplated by the Society could be produced'. No doubt at Furnivall's suggestion, the suggested terms included provision for the Society to use the materials for the preparation of 'a dictionary not less than twice the size' in due course if the Delegates declined to undertake it; Sweet specifically distanced himself from this in his covering letter, declaring that he was 'certain that such a work will never be undertaken'.

Notwithstanding Price's previously expressed support for the project, his imme-diate reaction—reasonably enough given the financial implications—seems to have been one of caution, even scepticism. He assured Sweet that the proposals were 'very important' and would be given 'careful and favourable consideration'; but the fact that Murray, the proposed editor of the Dictionary, was already three years behind schedule with a much smaller project for the Press—an anthology of 'Specimens of Lowland Scotch and Northern English', for which copy should have been delivered in 1874— was grounds for doubt about his ability to manage a much larger project.[38]

---

[36] As Lynda Mugglestone has pointed out (2005: 225), these estimates were probably based on those given by George Wheelwright in his 1875 'Appeal'.

[37] This figure is probably predicated on the actual use of *all* the quotations collected up to this point.

[38] SL 23 Apr. 1877 Price to H. Sweet; MP 26 Apr. 1877 FJF to JAHM; CPCO 112 agreement with JAHM to publish 'Specimens of Lowland Scotch & Northern English', dated 30 Jan. 1874. The book was never published (see p. 127), although it was announced in the *Academy* of 24 October 1874 (p. 454) as 'nearly ready for press'. It seems that Murray may have taken the project over from an earlier author, a Mr Burgess, who had contracted to produce a collection of 'Specimens of the Early Scottish Language' in 1867 (OD 23 July 1867).

Unsurprisingly, Price promptly consulted Alexander Macmillan about the new proposal. He sent him Sweet's papers for comment with the most carefully neutral of covering letters: '[I] shall be much obliged for any observations you may make on them. I do not tell you what I think, so that you may be quite free.' Macmillan's assessment was blunt: 'The terms may be such as the delegates in the interests of scientific philology might accept but they certainly are not business terms.' He saw potential difficulties in the division of authority between the Press and the Society, 'a body that must be fluctuating', although he conceded that the Society was making an effort to be fair and reasonable.[39]

Price arranged for the proposals to be considered by the Delegates at their next meeting on 11 May.[40] Meanwhile, Furnivall, determined to secure the strongest support for the project, wrote to Archbishop Trench, extolling Murray's virtues as 'one of the best men in philology among us', and asking him to put in a good word with the Dean of Christ Church—and Delegate of the Press—Henry Liddell (who at this point was also busy revising the *Greek–English Lexicon*). Trench promptly did so, praising Murray's *The Dialect of the Southern Counties of Scotland* both for its philological merits and as 'a piece of excellent English prose'.[41] He also took soundings, as did Sweet, from 'influential friends at Oxford', and Sweet reported to the Society's Council on 4 May that 'he thought the Society's proposals [...] would be favourably considered'.[42]

Liddell was unable to attend the meeting on 11 May, but he wrote to Price, concurring with Trench as to Murray's abilities, and suggesting that he be asked to provide some sample entries, using Littré's dictionary as a model, to illustrate the nature of the work envisaged (and to demonstrate his competence to do it). Following the meeting Price invited Sweet to meet him at the Athenaeum, where he informed him that the Delegates desired to see samples of the material at three different stages: the sorted quotation slips, the draft entries prepared by the sub-editors, and a specimen of finished text prepared by Murray.[43] Furnivall promptly wrote to all the sub-editors he knew of. More than a dozen of them responded, some sending their material direct to Price, others to Furnivall or Sweet (who both passed it on to Price) or to Murray; many of their letters express delight that the project seemed likely to be taken up again. Price was soon obliged to write to both Furnivall and Sweet, pleading that he now had plenty of samples, and that no more need be sent. Macmillan also supplied Murray with copies of the printed specimen pages made up for him in 1876, which he sent

---

[39]   SL 30 Apr. 1877 Price to A. Macmillan; OED/B/3/1/1 1 May 1877 A. Macmillan to Price.

[40]   Not 1 May, as stated in *CWW* (p. 150).

[41]   OED/B/3/1/1 26 Apr. 1877 FJF to Trench, 27 Apr. 1877 Trench to Liddell. Trench's acquaintance with Murray's book was extremely recent: it was only two months earlier that he had written to Macmillan asking to borrow a copy. Macmillan bought a copy, and sent it to Trench on indefinite loan (BL MS Add. 55401 24 Feb. 1877 A. Macmillan to Trench). This could have been coincidence: the two men were regular correspondents at this time. But it is tempting to suppose that Trench's request may have been prompted by an approach from Furnivall.

[42]   PSCM 4 May 1877.

[43]   OED/B/3/1/1 10 May 1877 Liddell to Price; SL 12 May 1877 Price to A. Macmillan; 12 May 1877 Price to H. Sweet; PSCM 18 May 1877.

on to Price together with the handwritten copy from which these had been prepared, which dealt with many words not printed in the specimen and which Murray proudly informed Price contained 'much [...] new not only to Lexicography, but to English Literary History'. This was, of course, no substitute for a fresh specimen, which would take rather longer, especially as Murray's time until the end of July was largely taken up with examinations and other Mill Hill responsibilities.[44]

The Macmillan specimen was circulated to two senior Delegates, Liddell and Mark Pattison (Rector of Lincoln College), in advance of the Delegates' next meeting. The minutes of this meeting record merely that consideration of the Dictionary was 'adjourned for further enquiry'; but Price reported to Macmillan that the Delegates had made 'considerable criticism [of the Dictionary] of a character not altogether favourable'. Following another meeting with Sweet he was a little more positive: 'the prospect is favourable, although there may be great difficulties ahead.'[45] One of Furnivall's Oxford moles, T. H. Sheppard (chaplain of Exeter College, and sub-editor of the letters U and V), was also encouraging, commenting that Price was 'always a strict economist, & nothing will induce him to believe it [the Dictionary] will pay, but I can see that some of the Delegates are for proceeding'.[46]

More Delegates were now asked to comment on the Macmillan specimen, including William Stubbs, Regius Professor of Modern History, and the Savilian Professor of Geometry, H. J. S. Smith. Many of their criticisms, which were communicated to Sweet by Price, had already been anticipated, including the extent to which proper names, transparent formations on suffixes, and items of regional vocabulary were to be included (the treatment of all of these in the specimen was evidently considered over-generous), and the acceptability of newspaper quotations as evidence. Sweet emphasized to Murray the importance of giving the Delegates' suggestions full consideration, but for the pragmatic reason that 'when we have once got over their chief objections they will leave the Editor entirely to himself'; he commented reassuringly that the length of their list of criticisms was really only intended 'to show their sharpness & wideawakeness'. Following another meeting of the Dictionary Committee, Sweet wrote deferentially to Price, accepting almost all of the Delegates' detailed criticisms and pointing out that the Macmillan specimen had been prepared in order to settle questions of printing, rather than as a model in terms of editorial policy.[47]

Given his earlier involvement, Walter Skeat's absence from these discussions is noticeable; but he had not been idle. Based as he was in Cambridge, however, it was more difficult for him to obtain reliable information about the negotiations with

[44] SL 5 June 1877 Price to FJF, Price to H. Sweet; BL MS Add. 55402 18 May 1877 A. Macmillan to JAHM; OED/B/3/1/1 29 May, 24 July 1877 JAHM to Price.
[45] OD 1 June 1877; SL 30 May 1877 Price to M. Pattison, 4, 9 June 1877 Price to A. Macmillan.
[46] MP [June 1877] T. H. Sheppard to [FJF].
[47] OED/B/3/1/1 11 June 1877 H. J. S. Smith to Price; SL 11 June 1877 Price to M. Pattison, 21 June 1877 Price to Liddell; 23 July 1877 Price to JAHM; MP [29 June 1877] Sweet to JAHM; OED/B/3/1/1 14 July 1877 Sweet to Price.

Oxford. Under the mistaken impression that the Clarendon Press had definitely declined to take on the Dictionary, he decided that, as the great project now seemed to be a lost cause, he would see whether the Press could be persuaded to take on a project of his own: a dictionary of English etymologies, on which he appears to have been working for some time. His proposal reached Price in time for it to be considered by the Delegates at their last meeting before the long vacation; their response was very favourable, and Skeat was also asked to prepare a specimen. The distinguished philologist Friedrich Max Müller was among the Delegates present; he had not been present on the previous occasions when the Philological Society's Dictionary had been discussed, but evidently took a particular interest in Skeat's proposal.[48]

Price had asked Murray to send in his new specimen in time for it to be considered when the Delegates reconvened on 19 October. In the event it was not until the beginning of October that the manuscript of the specimen was ready, and the preparation and correction of proofs and revises took another two months.[49] Proofs of the specimen, which consisted of entries for the words *arrow, carouse, castle*, and *persuade*, were sent to various people for comment, including Alexander Ellis, Gibbs, Furnivall, and Max Müller. Murray was particularly anxious to give proper consideration to the comments of Max Müller, as a Delegate whose views were likely to be influential. His advice, however, was contradictory: having recommended that conjectural etymologies should not be given, he then put forward a speculative etymology of *arrow*, which if included alongside the two already given by Murray would make for an excessively long entry. Murray turned for counsel to Ellis, who advised him to follow Max Müller's general advice and omit speculative etymologies: 'I think you'll be driven wild by conj[ectura]l etyms. M.M. can't object to your following his advice & cutting down.'[50]

One clear reason for Max Müller's advocacy of briefer etymologies was the favourable response met by Skeat's proposed etymological dictionary. His specimen had come before the Delegates on 2 November and, as Max Müller informed Murray, had been 'as good as accepted'. Skeat, too, realized that the two projects might complement each other, with his book dealing with the etymology and form of words, leaving full definitions and the development of meaning within English to Murray.[51]

Instead, however, of acting to complement the Dictionary, Skeat's project now threatened to damage its prospects with the Clarendon Press. Murray's specimen was considered by the Delegates at their meeting on 30 November, the same meeting at which they gave formal approval to Skeat's proposal. Although they found the specimen satisfactory in many respects, there were two problem areas: they were doubtful about the merits of giving information on pronunciation—in view of what they considered to be 'the present uncertain state of the science of Phonetics'—and they felt

---

[48] MP [n.d.; probably late 1877] Skeat to JAHM; OD 14 July 1877; SL 17, 27 July 1877 Price to Skeat; MP 6 Nov. 1877 F. Max Müller to JAHM.

[49] OED/B/3/1/1 2 Oct. 1877 JAHM to Price; OD 30 Nov. 1877.

[50] MP 16 Nov. 1877 F. Max Müller to JAHM, 17 Nov. 1877 JAHM to [AJE], 19 Nov. 1877 AJE to JAHM.

[51] MP 6 Nov. 1877 Max Müller to JAHM; [n.d.; probably Nov. 1877] Skeat to [JAHM].

that the decision to publish Skeat's dictionary would render the etymological component largely unnecessary. The latter point greatly alarmed Murray, who had given a
great deal of thought to the matter, and who told Price that the Dictionary 'has always
been intended to give the full *history* of each word both *in* English, & in coming into
English. If the Delegates think of the conventional style "Lat[in] *per* through & *suadeo*
I advise" [as an etymology for *persuade*] which *tells nothing*, and implies what is false,
I for one should not think the work worth doing.' The Delegates also asked for lists of
books which had been read for the Dictionary, and the names of those who had done
the reading.[52]

The question of etymologies sufficiently unsettled Murray that he began once again
to express doubts about the whole idea of undertaking to edit the Dictionary. He
seems to have put the whole project on hold, instead devoting January and February
to work on the article 'English Language' which he had been commissioned to write
for the *Encyclopaedia Britannica*.[53] In early March Furnivall, on a visit to Cambridge,
sought to persuade Skeat to write to Oxford pressing the case for full etymologies.
Skeat agreed that this was important, but held off from writing, fearing that it would
damage his own credit with the Press, and still uncertain about Murray's commitment
to the editorship.[54]

As Elisabeth Murray has noted, in later years Murray rather overstated the extent
and duration of his hesitancy over the editorship.[55] An account he wrote in 1903 suggests that he spent 'the most anxious fortnight [he] ever passed or ever may', and that
prior to this point he had not really considered himself as definitely committed to the
work;[56] but he had of course been assumed—with his knowledge—to be the preferred
candidate for the post since the start of negotiations with the Clarendon Press, and the
period of indecision must surely have been rather less than the twelve days between
Skeat's letter of 6 March (asking him whether he was 'prepared to go on & really to *do*
the Big Dictionary') and Furnivall's postcard of 18 March[57] reporting that he had sent
off the lists of readers and books read (which even Furnivall would hardly have done
if Murray was still hesitating). Nevertheless, it was certainly a momentous decision,

[52] MP 4 Dec. 1877 Price to JAHM; OED/B/3/1/1 5 Dec. 1877 JAHM to Price; SL 17 Dec. 1877 Price to
Sweet.
[53] MP 8 Jan., 14 Mar. 1878 Thomas Baynes to JAHM.
[54] MP 6 Mar. [1878] Skeat to [JAHM].
[55] *CWW* pp. 155, 363. Elisabeth Murray ascribes the dramatization of actual events to her grandfather's
liking for 'a good story', and also cites as an interesting parallel the agony of indecision undergone by Émile
Littré when deciding whether to undertake the comprehensive version of his *Dictionnaire*. Littré was
already sixty-one—twenty years older than Murray was in March 1878—and was given only twenty-four
hours to decide; he could not sleep, and only at daybreak was he finally able to make his decision
(Littré 1880: 394).
[56] Murray (1957: 19).
[57] MP 18 Mar. 1878 FJF to JAHM. This postcard also makes reference to a 'revis'd Specimen', suggesting
some attempt at compromise in respect of the etymological question, although no revised specimen
survives. Furnivall writes of having sent the lists to 'my Delegate'—almost certainly Liddell, whom
Furnivall had visited a few days earlier: he reported on their conversation to the Council of the Philological
Society on 15 March (PSCM).

committing him as it did to years of dedicated work, forsaking any ambitions he might have for better academic or teaching appointments. In the end it may well have been, as he claimed, his wife, Ada, who helped him to come to a decision, saying that he should 'do one big thing instead of a number of small ones'—and that that 'big thing' should be the Dictionary.[58]

By 24 March Murray's indecision seemed to be over. He had written a 'capital diplomatic letter', which he passed to Furnivall for comment before it went on to Oxford; this presumably expressed willingness to compromise on the points required by the Delegates. Furnivall was pragmatic about this (as well as showing a rather thicker skin than Murray's was to prove): 'seeing that Oxford is our only hope, & that a little humouring & teaching them will bring 'em round to let you do just what you like, I am sure that it's best to put up with a little undeserved fault-finding at first.'[59]

Murray was now invited to Oxford to meet the Delegates. Meanwhile the lists of readers and books read were dispatched to Max Müller.[60] Furnivall was informed of all this—probably before Murray—by a Delegate (probably Liddell), who apparently advised him that there was still dissatisfaction regarding the treatment of etymologies. He nevertheless sought to reassure Murray that the meeting was likely to be more of a confidence-building measure than an interrogation: 'Don't feel nettled at it. When once confidence is established the Dicty 'll go on.' However, he did advise Murray to prepare a formal statement of the Dictionary's proposed policy on etymology, pronunciation, and various other editorial matters, for the benefit of Delegates who 'haven't evidently got up the facts, & don't know much of the Histy. of English'.[61]

Whether the Delegates were as ignorant as Furnivall thought is doubtful. Certainly Liddell and Max Müller were the most expert in philological matters (and of course Liddell knew at first hand about the practicalities of compiling a large dictionary), but the others who assembled in a lecture room in Christ Church on 26 April were no novices when it came to overseeing the publication of dictionaries. In the months preceding the meeting with Murray, several other substantial dictionary projects had been considered by the Delegacy, including the revision of Monier Monier-Williams's dictionary of Sanskrit, a proposal from the distinguished Hebrew scholar Adolf Neubauer to compile a Hebrew dictionary, and of course Skeat's etymological dictionary; and there was also the new edition of the late Joseph Bosworth's dictionary of Anglo-Saxon. In fact T. N. Toller, the man eventually selected to complete Bosworth's work, 'attended in conference' at the very same meeting of the Delegates, immediately after Murray. As Price remarked a few weeks later to George Grove of Macmillan, who

---

[58] HJRM p. 95.
[59] MP 24 Mar. 1878 FJF to JAHM.
[60] OD 25 Mar. 1878; MP 26 Mar. 1878 Price to JAHM, 26 Mar. 1878 Price to Max Müller.
[61] MP 26, 28 Mar. 1878 FJF to JAHM.

had written to him with a proposal for a dictionary of the Indian language Manipuri, 'Our Delegates are great Dictionary men.'[62]

The meeting seems to have been a friendly affair. Writing to his wife a few hours later, Murray likened it to the long-anticipated Congress of Berlin, 'with myself as Russia, the Dons as England, Max Müller as Bismarck, and the result—nothing yet'.[63] Some matters which remained to be resolved had been set out by Max Müller in a printed note (marked 'Private.—For the Delegates of the Press only') which was circulated to the Delegates.[64] In this document, having declared himself unworried about the project's commercial aspects, Max Müller expressed doubts about the thoroughness of the reading, and stipulated limits to the extent of the etymologies, in a way which shows his view of the complementary nature of Skeat's dictionary:

[the etymology of a word] should in no case go beyond the immediate feeders of the English language. We want for Saxon words their antecedents in Early English and Anglo-Saxon; for Romance, the antecedents in Norman-French and Latin; everything else belongs to an Etymological, not to an Historical Dictionary of the English Language.

His note was accompanied by a list of recommendations as to additional works to be read.

Max Müller was very enthusiastic about the project in principle; indeed, he regarded the undertaking as something 'in which one might almost say the national honour of England is engaged'. He was anxious to minimize duplication of etymological content between the two dictionaries, but it was accepted that in a dictionary on the scale of that proposed by the Philological Society the etymologies would have to be adequately detailed. After he and Murray had met to discuss the matter, the Philological Society's Council agreed that etymologies along the lines suggested in Max Müller's report would be acceptable, provided that Murray could make a further request for fuller etymologies 'if he found they could be advantageously & safely introduced'. Greatly relieved, Max Müller reported back to Price, who was at last authorized by the Delegates to open negotiations with the Dictionary Committee, and with Murray, as to terms.[65] (Rather curiously, the Delegates' doubts about pronunciation still lingered; but Murray irritably dismissed their view (as conveyed by Price) that phonetics was still in a state of flux, suggesting that 'some of the Delegates must be conjuring up a ghost and then trembling at it'.[66])

---

[62] OD 26 Apr. 1878; SL 13 May 1878 Price to G. Grove. For a general account of the Press's dictionary publishing during the nineteenth century, see Knowles (2013).

[63] 26 Apr. 1878 JAHM to Ada Murray (copy, now lost; quoted in HJRM p. 105; the letter is also quoted in CWW pp. 156–7, where it is misdated 24 Apr.).

[64] A copy of this note is pasted into the Delegates' Order Book; the Delegates had presumably seen it in advance of the meeting on 26 April, although it is only referred to in a minute of 10 May.

[65] PSCM 3 May 1878; OED/B/3/1/2 4 May 1878 Max Müller to Price; OD 10 May 1878.

[66] MP 16 May 1878 JAHM to Price (quoted at length in CWW pp. 157–8).

Two separate (though interdependent) negotiations now began: between the Press and Murray, and between the Press and the Philological Society. The negotiations with Murray advanced quickly: after discussing details by letter, Murray and Price met in London on 19 June, and two days later the Delegates approved the terms of a draft agreement.[67] Murray was extremely accommodating in his terms: he sought only such remuneration 'as would actually leave me not a loser by withdrawing my time from other paid work', and observed that as he already devoted a considerable amount of time to unpaid work 'in the interests of English Literature' (he estimated an hour a day), he would henceforth be willing to spend a comparable amount of time working gratis on the Dictionary instead. On the basis that work on the Dictionary would occupy five hours per day, his estimate of the amount that he would need to compensate him for giving up some of his paid work—while still, he hoped, continuing to teach at Mill Hill—was £400 per annum; and the costs of 'assistance', which he was to pay for himself, he estimated at £300–350 for a 'Subeditor' and two clerks plus expenses. He also proposed that he should be paid at a reduced rate during the three years of preparatory work which he believed would be necessary before copy could begin to be sent to press. Finally, he asked for 'a fair share in the profits' to compensate him for abandoning all prospects of promotion by binding himself to the project for what he believed would be ten years.

We now know, of course, that the anticipated profits from the project never materialized, making the tortuous negotiations over their distribution somewhat academic; but at the time they mattered a great deal. The original proposal submitted to Price in April 1877 had suggested that any profits be equally split between the Delegates and the Philological Society, and that the latter should negotiate with Murray regarding the proportion of their share that should be passed on to him. Murray now proposed that his own percentage should be fixed beforehand; his suggested figure was 25 per cent. Price's proposal as to how the 25 per cent should be found—namely by setting the Society's share of the profits at 15 per cent, the Delegates retaining 60 per cent—did not go down well with Furnivall, who maintained that it would be fairer to allocate Murray and the Society each 20 per cent; it is not clear what was agreed at this stage, but the Society—or Furnivall, at least—seems to have proceeded on the assumption of a 60/20/20 split.[68]

Division of the profits was only one of several points of dispute in the negotiations with the Philological Society, which ultimately dragged on for the better part of a year

---

[67] OED/B/3/1/2 29 May 1878 JAHM to Price, memorandum 19 June 1878 of a meeting between Price and JAHM; MP 15 June 1878 Price to JAHM; OD 21 June 1878.

[68] MP 24 June 1878 Price to JAHM; SL 24 June 1878 Price to FJF. These letters propose a 60/25/15 split, not 60/20/20 as stated in *CWW* p. 364. Furnivall subsequently stated that that the 60/20/20 split had indeed been agreed; he also later claimed that Price had originally not envisaged a share of the profits for Murray at all, but only a straight salary, as was the case with the editors of the Press's Icelandic and Latin dictionaries (Vigfusson and Nettleship). Murray, on the other hand, maintained that Macmillan had offered him a 25% share of the profits, and that he would never have undertaken the editorship of the Dictionary without an assurance of 'a substantial share' of the profits (PSCM 20 Dec. 1878, 24 Jan. 1879).

and became more than a little bad-tempered. This was perhaps only to be expected given some of the personalities involved. Furnivall liked nothing better than an argument, particularly a legal one, and was moreover suspicious of the motives of the Delegates; his suspicions were shared by Henry Sweet, and apparently also by Sweet's father, George, who was a solicitor (and who had drafted the terms proposed to Price in April 1877). Another sticking-point was the matter of how and by whom a replacement Editor might be appointed should it prove necessary; the fact that the Delegates wished the responsibility to rest with them was viewed by Sweet as revealing their main object, namely 'depriving the Socy of all control of the material & the way in which it is worked up'. Claiming to know something of Oxford's 'low state of morality as regards jobbery & interest', he sourly warned Murray that he should 'be prepared for a good deal of vexatious interference & dictation hereafter, liable to be enforced any moment by summary dismissal. You will then see your materials & the assistants trained by you utilized by some Oxford swell, who will draw a good salary for doing nothing.' Despite Liddell's assurance to Furnivall that there was 'no thought of [...] putting an Oxford man in [Murray's] place', the Philological Society's Council ultimately concluded that the matter was of sufficient importance that it should be covered by an arbitration clause.[69] Matters were further complicated—and protracted—by uncertainty as to what procedure should be used to enable the Philological Society to become a body that could enter into a contract with the Delegates; an initial proposal to register the Society under the Friendly Societies Act was eventually abandoned in favour of incorporating it under the Joint Stock Companies Act as a company limited by guarantee.

The extended negotiations were increasingly frustrating for Murray, and also left him in an awkward position as regards his existing employment: since the Delegates were not prepared to sign their contract with Murray as Editor until matters had been resolved with the Philological Society, he could not yet make any firm arrangements to reduce his Mill Hill commitments. Nor could he make any real start on the work, or engage any assistants (although Furnivall had already identified one possible candidate, a protégé of his called Sidney Herrtage).[70] It was not until November that the agreement with the Society was ready to be put to the Delegates; it now fell to Price to settle some outstanding matters with Murray. He wrote asking for a fresh estimate of the time Murray would need before he could begin to supply copy for press, the total time needed to complete the work, and the total amount of remuneration he would require now that it had been decided that he should be entirely responsible for engaging and paying assistants.[71] There were also two interesting additional questions: how did Murray propose to treat 'scientific and provincial terms', and what did he propose

---

[69] MP 7 July 1878 H. Sweet to JAHM, 9 July 1878 FJF to JAHM; PSCM 12 July 1878.

[70] OED/B/3/1/2 28 July 1878 FJF to P. Williams (copy). Herrtage's name had already been mentioned at Murray's 19 June meeting with Price.

[71] MP 9 Nov. 1878 Price to JAHM.

to do regarding the engagement of an American collaborator (with a view to securing American copyright, as with the ill-fated Macmillan project)?[72]

The latter question puzzled Murray, who had rather expected the Press to establish what was needed to secure American copyright. He now explained the arrangement that Macmillan and Harpers had proposed in 1876, whereby an American collaborator would add extra quotations to the text, and perhaps revise the etymologies. (He was less than enthusiastic about the idea of such a collaborator being named on the Dictionary's title page.) His response to Price's other questions offers an interesting glimpse of his views on some key editorial questions at this early stage:

As to the inclusion of provincial terms *as* provincial terms, I say *No*; mainly because we *cannot* give them all or half of them, & therefore it would be foolish to pretend to do so. But I would be as *liberal as possible* in their inclusion, whenever there is any plea for bringing them in, as quasi-literary use, etymological interest, [or] representation of forms once literary. As to scientific terms I say Include all adjectives & verbs, all nouns with *connotation*, all nouns with *denotation* merely that have an English form, and as to those with a Latin or Greek form trust the Editor and those whom he consults [...]: the Editor will include *Geranium*, *Molybdenum*, *Cicada*, he will not (as at present minded) include *Chamaerops*, *Amphisbaena*, or *Palinurus*; but can give no general rule as to where the line can be drawn. But he is perfectly willing to comply with any practical plan of the Delegates on this point—short of one which would exclude *Hippopotamus*, *soda*, *rhombus*, and *stratum*. [...] Another difficult point is Geographical Adjectives as Caspian, Persian, English, Papuan, Parisian, French, Oxonian. I should be glad to have the opinion of the Delegates on these words.

He also confidently declared that his own 'general, and, in some things, minute scientific studies' would enable him to deal adequately with all such vocabulary without the need of paid specialist assistance. As for the questions about time and money, he restated his previous estimate of three years before beginning to send copy to press, and ten years overall; but his figure for his own remuneration had now increased considerably. The reason for this was partly practical: whereas in June he had assumed that he would only need to give up six hours of teaching, he now learned that if Mill Hill were to be able to recruit a part-time replacement, it would have to be for a minimum of ten hours a week (resulting in the loss of an additional £50 of income). He was also, however, motivated by the advice of friends and colleagues that, since he could now only look forward to receiving 20 per cent of the anticipated profits in eventual compensation for his loss of prospects in binding himself to the project, he should ask for a larger salary in the short term. This brought the annual figure for his remuneration to

---

[72] The idea of an American editor had certainly been mentioned early on in negotiations with the Press (e.g. OED/B/3/1/1 14 July 1877 H. Sweet to Price). Price would in any case have been acutely conscious of the importance of controlling access to the American market for such a major dictionary, having only recently reached an agreement with Harpers for the distribution of Liddell and Scott's *Greek–English Lexicon* in the USA and Canada; for details of this, and of similar negotiations in regard to Lewis and Short's *Latin Dictionary*, see Stray (2013: 454–8).

£500 or £600; when the cost of assistants was included, this resulted in a revised figure of £900 per annum, or £9,000 over the anticipated lifetime of the project.[73]

On 29 November the Delegates met to consider Murray's proposals, and Murray attended to provide clarification. Everything was approved; but £9,000 was a considerable increase on the figure of £6,500 mentioned in the original proposal of 20 April. Looking for ways to recoup some of the extra outlay, the Delegates turned to their draft Agreement with the Philological Society, and in particular to the Society's proposed share of the profits. Their conclusion was communicated to Furnivall by Price in a letter which argued, not entirely convincingly, that because the Philological Society's material required 'more work to be done on it before it is ready for the Press than the Delegates had supposed', it was therefore of less value; and that in consequence it was desirable to reduce the Society's share of the profits from 20 to 15 per cent.[74]

Furnivall exploded. The figure of 15 per cent had of course been suggested back in June, but he had not accepted it then, and he saw no reason to do so now. He dashed off a furious note to Price, pointing out that Murray's increased estimates resulted entirely from reassessment of his own position, not of the Society's materials, and predicting that the Council would not consent to 'the further reduction you propose'. Notwithstanding Price's insistence that agreement with the Society was, and had always been made clear as being, conditional on the agreement of terms with Murray, Furnivall regarded Price's reopening of negotiations as very sharp practice: 'Even Macmillan did not seek to beat us down as you are doing, & he's a Scotchman & a tradesman.' (He was even ruder about him to Murray: 'It's that mean old skunk Bat Price, damn him!') Sure enough, the Council, meeting on 6 December, declared that their draft Agreement, specifying a 20 per cent share of profits, should stand; and they appointed Furnivall and Murray as a Committee to meet the Delegates about the matter.[75] Furnivall wrote to Liddell, asking him to exercise his good offices among the Delegates, who he assumed had been railroaded into their decision by Price; Liddell replied that the vote of the Delegates had been unanimous.[76]

Murray was also appalled at the turn of events. The Council's opposition to the proposed reduction in their share of the profits meant that further negotiation would be necessary; and he had already provisionally arranged to reduce his school commitments from Christmas. As changes in arrangements at Mill Hill could only practically be made at the start of a new term, any but the briefest delay would mean that the commencement of work on the Dictionary would have to be postponed until Easter. In any case, the negotiations had now been going on for long enough, and he was anxious to start: he had even begun to think about 'purchasing fitting up & pigeon-holing an Iron-room'. He begged Price to meet with the Society's Council and '*try* to make

---

[73] OED/B/3/1/2 11, 14, 25 Nov. 1878 JAHM to Price; MP 19 Nov. 1878 Price to JAHM.

[74] OD 29 Nov. 1878; SL 2 Dec. 1878 Price to FJF.

[75] OED/B/3/1/2 2 Dec. 1878 FJF to Price; SL 3 Dec. 1878 Price to FJF; MP 3 Dec. 1878 FJF to JAHM; PSCM 6 Dec. 1878.

[76] OED/B/3/1/2 7 Dec. 1878 FJF to Liddell; 9 Dec. 1878 Liddell to FJF (draft).

a settlement'. Max Müller commiserated with him about the delay, but urged that it would be best to accept the new terms and begin work, not least because the prospects of the project making a profit were so far off as to be of little practical concern.[77]

It was on 13 December that nine Delegates met to reconsider the question of profits, and to hear directly from both Furnivall and Murray.[78] Furnivall rehearsed, at length, a number of points made on previous occasions, concluding with an appeal to the Delegates which also echoed the language of his earlier protest to Price:

Why do you deal thus with us? We are (in the main) University men, as you are [hardly a tactful remark in the presence of Murray] [...] Why, because you have the capital, or the command of it, why screw us? I won't insult the understanding of any one among you by supposing that you think the result of the Dictionary will not be a certain success. [...] why offer us a lower rate of profit than even the 3 hard-headed Scotchmen & tradesmen, Macmillan, Craik & Jack, offerd us?

Murray, addressing the Delegates in his turn, confined himself to describing the embarrassing position that their decision had put him in, of being entitled to a greater share of the profits than the Society itself, and urging them to restore the 5 per cent. Furnivall and Murray then withdrew; after three-quarters of an hour's deliberation they were called back to be told that the Delegates had resolved to abide by their decision to reduce the Society's share of profits to 15 per cent.[79] They did, however, agree to two other appeals which Murray now made relating to the immediate expenses that he now realized he would soon be put to: they would make available to him any Clarendon Press books that he might need, and they would arrange to have printed at their expense any blank slips for the use of readers for the Dictionary, and any 'lists of desiderata' (appeals for further evidence for particular words), provided Murray would supply the paper.[80]

The Delegates' confirmation of their decision, after listening at length to requests that they should reconsider, should surely have been enough; but it seems that Furnivall was still prepared to take the matter further. Quite what his proposed next step was

<hr/>

[77] OED/B/3/1/2 4 Dec. 1878 JAHM to Price; MP 5 Dec. 1878 Max Müller to [JAHM].

[78] OD 13 Dec. 1878. The formal minutes of the meeting give only brief details of the discussion; a much fuller (though no doubt highly partial) account was given by Furnivall to the Philological Society's Council a week later (PSCM 20 Dec. 1878).

[79] OED/B/3/1/2 note [13 Dec. 1878] recording the Delegates' vote (presumably the means by which the decision was communicated to Furnivall and Murray). This time the vote was carried by a majority of 6 to 3, not unanimously as on 29 November.

[80] Elisabeth Murray suggests (*CWW* p. 163) that Murray regarded this as 'grudging and unhelpful'. In a letter to Furnivall of 14 December (pasted into PSCM 20 Dec.) Murray does indeed express disappointment that the Delegates, having heard about his likely startup expenses, did not volunteer 'any initial aid', but this cannot refer to his requests for help in kind, as Furnivall's report to the Council suggests that he did get everything he asked for; it is more likely that he had been hoping for an actual cash subvention. As he wrote to Furnivall: 'Probably I shall have to expend £250 at once on starting, which is of course somewhat different from the original idea of being willing to give one's work merely.'

to be is unclear, but it elicited a letter from Murray[81] refusing to be a party to such proceedings—and making a further, self-sacrificial offer: he was prepared to reduce his share of the profits to 17½ per cent and give the extra 2½ per cent to the Society, thus restoring parity between the two parties. He also informed Price of his intention to make this offer. Price, commendably, deplored it: 'the work you are undertaking deserves every farthing of the money you are to receive [...]."Thou shalt not muzzle the ox that treadeth out the corn."' He also had a compromise of his own to suggest: that the Society should accept the reduced percentage, but write formally to the Delegates expressing the 'hope and expectation' that as and when substantial profits materialized, they would see fit to award a greater share to the Society.[82]

All these matters came before the Philological Society's Council on 20 December. After his lengthy account of what had been said to and by the Delegates, Furnivall reported Murray's offer of a reduced percentage; Murray in turn read out Price's suggestion. Henry Sweet, furiously condemning the 'grasping & unconscientious' attitude of the Delegates, proposed a motion effectively refusing to cooperate any further with the Press and, when this found no seconder, sulkily refused to take part in any further votes. Furnivall put forward a resolution to accept Murray's compromise proposal, though with much fulmination in typical Furnivallian style ('vigorously denouncing the conduct of the Delegates', 'bound in honour & good faith to keep their deliberately approv'd Agreement'); the day was eventually carried by the orientalist Edward Brandreth, who 'did not see the good of throwing more hard words at the Delegates. Mr Furnivall had given them a fair dose.' He also made the point that at the previous Council meeting, which had been better attended, it had been 'practically decided' to accept the 5 per cent reduction; accordingly, he moved a simple amendment replacing all of the wording with the bland resolution to 'accept the reduction of 5 p.c. in its share of profits, required by the Delegates'. This was carried 4–2; a disgusted Furnivall suggested that 'as the majority had taken the kicking of the Delegates so quietly, they might like to lick the Delegates' boots' by sending them the letter that Price had suggested. Nobody, it seems, had the stomach for any more discussion, and no such letter was agreed upon: Furnivall sent the briefest of notes to Price informing him of the Council's decision to accept the reduction to 15 per cent of profits, and Price could at last instruct the Press's solicitor to draft the necessary legal papers.[83]

The news that nothing—apparently—now stood in the way of the Dictionary must have been an enormous relief to all parties; perhaps especially to Murray, conscious not only that the start of term at Mill Hill was impending, but also of his obligations as an examiner in English for London University, which meant that for a week in mid-January he would be completely immersed in examination work. Although he could not formally commit himself to work on the Dictionary until he had seen and approved

[81] 14 Dec. 1878 JAHM to FJF (the letter pasted into PSCM 20 Dec.: see preceding note).
[82] MP 19 Dec. 1878 Price to JAHM.
[83] PSCM 20 Dec. 1878; OED/B/3/1/2 20 Dec. 1878 FJF to Price; SL 23 Dec. 1878 Price to P. Williams.

the final version of his contract, some preparatory arrangements could be made. Over the Christmas period he obtained specifications for the 'iron house' which he planned to use as his workroom, bought a large quantity of paper for printing slips, and ordered £10 or £15 worth of reference books; Price also provided him with catalogues of the Clarendon Press's own books to select from.[84] Work went ahead on the preparation of a one-page specimen of the Dictionary, to be appended to the Agreements with Murray and the Philological Society; and on 2 January 1879 another milestone was passed when the Society was incorporated as a limited company.[85] News also began to leak out about the impending settlement: the *Athenaeum* of 28 December had announced that the Clarendon Press had agreed to publish 'the English Etymological Dictionary [*sic*]' under Murray's editorship.[86]

Murray received his first intimation that matters might yet not run entirely smoothly on 17 January, the day of the Philological Society's first meeting of the new year. Immersed as he was in his London examination work, he arrived late for the Council meeting—where it emerged that there was to be a further delay. The Council had been advised by George Sweet that the newly incorporated Society could not simply rubber-stamp the dealings of its unincorporated predecessor with the Clarendon Press: a special General Meeting would have to be called, to allow members to consider the matter properly. What was worse, a summary of the sequence of events to date, to be drawn up by Henry Sweet, was to be printed and distributed to members, to enable them to come to an informed conclusion. Three Council members were all for delaying the General Meeting for as long as possible, but Murray was having none of it: the meeting eventually agreed on the date of 7 February. This was in any event dreadful news for Murray, who would now surely have to delay starting work in earnest until the end of the spring term. Desperate as he was to confer with Price about this turn of events, he was prevented from getting away by his examination work, which could take up sixteen or eighteen hours a day. He decided to leave matters until after the Council meeting scheduled for the following Friday, 24 January: a meeting of unprecedented storminess and bitterness, as recorded by Furnivall in his minutes, and also in two letters to Price which Murray wrote on the evening of the meeting (one of which, marked 'Private', went much further than the other in expressing his hurt and frustration).[87]

The starting-point for the bitter arguments on 24 January—which went on for so long that the Society's ordinary meeting (which normally followed the Council meeting) had to be abandoned—was Henry Sweet's draft account of the negotiations to

---

[84] OED/B/3/1/3 25 Jan. 1879 JAHM to Price; MP 31 Dec. 1878 Price to JAHM.

[85] OED/B/3/1/3 20 Jan. 1879 P. Williams to Price.

[86] *Athenaeum* 28 Dec. 1878, p. 856. A notice correcting the *Athenaeum* announcement appeared in the *Academy* of 4 Jan. 1879 (p. 8), probably at the instigation of Furnivall or Sweet: 'some of the terms proposed have been so strongly protested against by the [Philological] society and so sharply debated that, until the execution of the agreements, any announcement on the matter is premature.'

[87] PSCM 17, 24 Jan. 1879; OED/B/3/1/3 25 Jan. 1879 (two letters) JAHM to Price.

date with the Clarendon Press, proofs of which had gone out to Council members in advance. Sweet had seized on the opportunity presented by his commission from the Council to produce 'a short account of the circumstances that had led to the change in the Society's constitution & its proposed Agreement with the Delegates': his draft statement was (to quote Murray's private letter to Price) 'a document of the most offensive character [...] an elaborate and ex-parte arraignment of the agreement with the Delegates, and an invitation to the Members of the Society to upset everything'. Richard Weymouth, who in addition to being Murray's superior at Mill Hill was also a Council member, was concerned that a copy of the draft statement might have reached Price, and wrote to express his 'utter repudiation' of the document.[88] Sweet himself, however, felt that nothing less full than his draft would allow members to form a fair view of the matter, and argued forcefully to this effect at the meeting. His final paragraph also cited the 'strong difference of opinion' between Council members over whether to accept the 5 per cent reduction in profits as justification for placing the whole unedifying sequence of events before the members of the Society.[89]

There was certainly a difference of opinion within the Council, but it was evidently not an even split. Horrified by the hostile tone of Sweet's draft, and its exhaustive account of the dispute with the Press, Council members turned out in unprecedented numbers—two rising from their sickbeds, and others travelling 200 or 300 miles to attend—to ensure that no final spanner could be thrown in the works by the three individuals who still felt that the precious 5 per cent should not be given up: Sweet, Furnivall, and Henry Nicol. These three all spoke against a proposal by Weymouth to issue a much shorter statement, omitting the entire latter half of Sweet's draft and replacing it with a brief mention of the Delegates' proposal to make the 5 per cent reduction and the Council's decision 'after long discussion' to accept this. They were the only Council members to oppose the proposal, which was carried 11–3.[90] Finally, the exhausted Council members agreed that a motion to approve the contract with the Press, and to set the Society's seal to it, should be put from the chair at the meeting on 7 February. Furnivall, still relishing the cut and thrust of debate even after such a long and ill-tempered meeting, gave notice that he would move an amendment to this motion, restating the view that the Society was 'fairly entitled to the 20 per cent.'—although, significantly, he felt that 'in order not to stay the progress of the Dictionary' the contract should be accepted as it stood. His commitment to the Dictionary itself had finally won out over his (still passionately held) view that the Delegates had behaved dishonourably.

On 31 January the Delegates of the Clarendon Press assembled for their first meeting of the new year. They were informed of the Council's decision (on 20 December); they must also have known of the special General Meeting of the Society scheduled

---

[88] OED/B/3/1/3 25 Jan. 1879 Weymouth to Price (also marked 'Private').

[89] PSCM 24 Jan. 1879. A copy of Sweet's original draft is pasted into the minutes.

[90] In Murray's 'Private' letter to Price he confided that he would have withdrawn from the project if the Council had come to any other decision.

for the following Friday, and Price may also have hinted at the difficulties within the Council. No doubt in the hope of pre-empting Furnivall's threatened amendment, the Delegates passed a resolution very much along the lines envisaged by Price in his suggested compromise (and without any 'boot-licking' letter from the Council): they 'venture[d] to express a confident expectation, that should the profits [from the Dictionary] eventually be larger than they now estimate, their successors will entertain favourably any application made to them by the Society for an increase in its share of the profits'. Price informed both Murray and Furnivall that this had been formally entered in the minutes.[91] On the same day the Council met to finalize details for the special General Meeting: it was agreed that Alexander Ellis, one of the Society's Vice-Presidents, should take the chair, so that Murray (who as President would ordinarily have done so) should be able to speak freely.[92]

Both Murray and Weymouth had assured Price that the outcome of the Special General Meeting was not in doubt, but Murray had warned that 'the obstructives threaten to obstruct to the end'. Sure enough, notwithstanding the Delegates' under-taking about future profits (which was communicated to the meeting), Furnivall pro-posed his amendment, and orated in his usual vein ('the Delegates had not kept good faith with the Society [...] deliberate defiance of their deliberatly approv'd Contract [...] calld on the Meeting to affirm the Society's undoubted right'). Sweet was his usual bilious self, declining to second Furnivall's amendment only because it did not go far enough; he read out the 'wrecking' resolution that had fallen without a seconder on 20 December, but explained contemptuously that 'seeing how many Members had made up their minds to accept the Delegates' terms, he would not trouble the Meeting by proposing any Resolution'.[93]

Indeed, even before Furnivall had spoken, the prevailing feeling of the meeting must have been clear. Ellis, opening the meeting from the chair, had urged that by approving the contract with the Press 'the Society's long-contemplated Dictionary would, tho' only in its Concise Form, *become a fact*'. Murray had then spoken in support of acceptance with a brief narrative of his own, beginning with the approach from Macmillan nearly three years before. His explanation of how he thought the 7,000-page limit now envisaged would 'enable the work to be done well' gives some interesting editorial details: his starting-point was to be 'A.D. 1131, when at least 3 fourths of the Anglo-Saxon vocabulary died out';[94] he intended to give one quotation for 'every century for every meaning of every word in which it existed'; and he hoped

---

[91] OD 31 Jan. 1879; MP 5 Feb. 1879 Price to JAHM; SL 5 Feb. 1879 Price to FJF,.

[92] PSCM 31 Jan. 1879. Murray had been elected President of the Society in May 1878.

[93] PSOM 7 Feb. 1879.

[94] The most likely reason for the choice of 1131 is that it marks the point in the Peterborough Chronicle (a version of the Anglo-Saxon Chronicle and one of the most important sources for the history of the transition between Old and Middle English) at which the work of the first scribe ends, the remainder of the manuscript being in the hand of a scribe writing in a noticeably later form of English. This reflects a significant shift in scholarly ideas about the 'starting point' of English from those of the 1858 'Proposal', which had envisaged a starting point of approximately 1250 (see p. 29).

to persuade the Delegates that 'ultimate Etymologies' could eventually be given in a separate volume. To any members still dissatisfied with the Society's share of the profits, he repeated his offer to give up 2½ per cent of his share, an offer which Henry Hucks Gibbs thereupon insisted should be rejected. Other long-time supporters of the project, including Morris and even the 76-year-old Hensleigh Wedgwood, spoke in support of acceptance. Furnivall's amendment was lost; the Resolution to affix the newly incorporated Society's seal to the contract with the Clarendon Press was carried.

It would take many of the parties involved a long time to recover from the ill-feeling and resentment that had been generated by such protracted and bitter argument. For Furnivall, however, bygones were immediately to be bygones. As he made clear (with typical bluntness) to Murray in a letter written a few days later, he was still convinced of the rightness of his case—commenting as explanation for his actions that 'as you seemed to us rather to act as President of the Delegates than of the Soc^y, we tried to look after the latter'—but now that the Society had voted so heavily in favour of acceptance, he wished to 'get the joint work forward. [...] I count the matter as done with.' Even before the meeting he had been badgering Murray about various things that he thought he should be getting on with: 'When are you going to have the Dict^y slips &c? Isn't your room ready for Herrtage to start work? [...] Every day lost now 'll be felt hereafter.' Murray had in fact begun to make inquiries about the legal aspects of erecting a shed in the garden of his house at Mill Hill.[95] Meanwhile, the final legal arrangements were being made: the Press's solicitors drew up both contracts in their final form, and Furnivall arranged for a 'plain seal' to be cast for the Society.[96] Murray also asked the Delegates to appoint 'a Committee [...] to confer with him from time to time on literary questions'; this they did, appointing Dean Liddell, Mark Pattison, and Max Müller.[97]

And so at last, on 1 March 1879, just over three years after the original proposal to approach the Clarendon Press, two agreements were sent out from Oxford, formally executed by the Vice-Chancellor, to the Philological Society and to Murray (the latter with the first quarterly cheque for £175). Two days later, when the sealed agreement with the Society arrived back in Oxford, Price wrote to the Press's solicitor, Peter Williams: 'We may all congratulate each other on the settlement thus far of our transactions with the Philological Society.' By contrast, his letter to Murray acknowledging

---

[95]   MP 2, 12 Feb. 1879 FJF to JAHM, 11 Feb. 1879 T. Scrutton to JAHM.

[96]   PSOM 21 Feb. 1879. It was originally proposed to date the agreement retrospectively to 2 January 1879, but this was unacceptable to Murray, who commented that '[t]he time is too valuable to have it shortened by an hour, even at being paid for time past. [...] It must bear [the] date when it is signed' (OED/B/3/6/3 fragment of letter 14 Feb. 1879, JAHM to [Price?]). The single specimen dictionary page attached to the contracts—shortened from the earlier *arrow/carousel/castle/persuade* specimen—was also altered at a very late stage, so as to include the older word *castle* as well as *persuade*, apparently at Furnivall's insistence (PSCM 21 Feb. 1879; SL 22 Feb. 1879 Price to JAHM, 25 Feb. 1879 Price to P. Williams). The agreement with the Philological Society is reproduced in *TPS* for 1877–9 (Appendix III), pp. xlix–lix.

[97]   OD 21 Feb. 1879.

receipt of his signed agreement got straight down to business, promising to arrange for some slips to be pre-printed to Murray's specification, and to find out from Charles Mount, a retired clergyman who had offered to do some reading, what he might be able to do. The next stage of work on the Dictionary was already under way, and congratulations would have to wait.[98]

[98] SL 3 Mar. 1879 Price to P. Williams; MP 5 Mar. 1879 Price to JAHM. Murray's signed duplicate copy of the Agreement with the Delegates, dated 1 March 1879, is preserved in MP.

4

The road to *Ant*: 1879–1884

A SIGH of relief from all parties, now that the protracted difficulties of negotiation were behind them and the real work of compiling and publishing the Dictionary could begin, would have been understandable. It would, however, have been premature. Three years of preparatory work were expected to elapse before the first instalment could be brought before the public; these three years were to stretch to five, and during those five years the project would be assailed by an almost continuous stream of unanticipated difficulties, several of which would prove serious enough to threaten its very existence before a single page had been published. Problems began immediately, with the realization of just how much more of the basic preliminary work remained to be done than had been thought; they multiplied when James Murray began his editorial work in earnest, and found himself confronted with the 'triple nightmare' (in Elisabeth Murray's vivid phrase) of time, space, and money. Matters were made worse by the loss of key members of Murray's staff, in one case under potentially scandalous circumstances. The development of the Dictionary's editorial policy brought its Editor into conflict with members of the Philological Society and the academic establishment of Oxford, the latter represented especially by the formidable figure of Benjamin Jowett. There were obstacles too for the Dictionary as a publishing venture, as the Press vainly struggled to share the growing costs with foreign publishers, and threats loomed of some important rival publications. Even the eventual publication of Part I, in a context of growing national awareness of the project, would constitute no guarantee of the Dictionary's future, which in the spring of 1884 remained uncomfortably uncertain.

Before Murray could properly begin the task of editing the Dictionary in earnest, he needed a place to work; or rather, a place where the Dictionary's working materials could be housed. The sheer volume of quotation slips and sub-edited material which already crowded Furnivall's house in Primrose Hill could hardly be accommodated in Sunnyside, the house in Mill Hill where the Murrays now lived, without engulfing his family in paper; and of course more material would be forthcoming from readers and

The Making of the *Oxford English Dictionary*. First edition. Peter Gilliver.
© Peter Gilliver 2016. First published 2016 by Oxford University Press.

FIGURE 7   The Scriptorium at Mill Hill. The two assistants (far left and right) are probably Sidney Herrtage and Fred Ruthven; the boy standing beside James Murray is his son Harold. The original set of pigeonholes commissioned by Herbert Coleridge (see p. 35) stands next to him.

sub-editors. A separate building would be necessary. The idea of renting an adjoining cottage was dismissed on grounds of the risk of fire; Murray's wife suggested that they erect a shed in their front garden. As Sunnyside was rented for Murray by Mill Hill School, permission had to be sought from the owners and the school governors to erect this large corrugated iron construction, measuring thirty by sixteen feet; as Murray later recalled, 'we called it first in sport, and then in earnest, the Scriptorium.' (See Figure 7.) Work began even before the contracts with OUP had been signed, and the new building was lined with deal and fitted out with pigeonholes (1,029 of them) and shelving by Murray's brother-in-law Herbert F. P. ('Fred') Ruthven.[1]

Before the Scriptorium was complete Murray had also engaged his first assistant: a former civil engineer and amateur literary scholar named Sidney Herrtage. He had studied at Trinity College Dublin, and for some years had been one of the small group of individuals who circulated within Furnivall's benevolent orbit: he joined the Philological Society in 1876 and began doing small tasks for Furnivall, such as indexing volumes of the Society's Transactions, and thereafter was entrusted with the editing

---

[1] Powell (1879: 181); MP JAHM, text of a lecture on dictionaries given to the London Institution in 1910, p. 19; JAHM, 1879 Presidential Address to Philological Society (*TPS* for 1877–9), p. 568. Ironically, the Mill Hill Scriptorium was eventually destroyed by fire in 1902; the man with the job of informing Murray, the school treasurer Richard Buckland, quailed at the prospect and wrote to Ada instead, asking her to be the intermediary (MP 5 Dec. 1902 R. W. B. Buckland to Ada Murray).

of various volumes for the Early English Text Society.[2] In March 1879 he worked in the British Museum, reading and excerpting some Middle English texts and early printed books for the Dictionary; and on Lady Day (25 March) he joined Murray in the Scriptorium.[3] As Furnivall pointed out, there was also a need for a 'Secretary-&-Sorter', a role which Fred Ruthven agreed to take on. Furnivall may have had another protégé in mind, for he subsequently accused Murray of engaging Ruthven purely for 'family reasons', and within a few months was urging that he be transferred to the task of reading books in the Museum.[4]

27 March was the day fixed for the delivery of materials from Furnivall's house. From a somewhat panicky letter from Furnivall, written that evening, it seems that no van came to collect the papers; but by the following day the whole miscellaneous assortment of material had been sent off to Mill Hill.[5] In total it amounted to one and three-quarter tons of paper, mainly in the form of quotation slips, but also including the work of a few sub-editors who had returned what they had done to Furnivall when they abandoned their task, together with the bound volumes of dictionary extracts with which they had been supplied. The extent to which Furnivall had failed to keep track of just what the accumulating piles of material contained is evident from the letter he wrote to Murray after it had been dispatched:

You shd have all the A slips pickt out first—they're in packets, except such as are in the 2 or 3 G[eorge] Eliot packets, whose slips want written catchwords. [...] Subeditors' work of D, E, O, Ra & S are in packets (D.), bag (E.), boxes, O (? Hamper), Ra. S. S is probably not sorted, & is a heavy letter. [...] Some of the outer slips have got torn, & 'll need mending. You've probably laid in a supply of gum.[6]

Murray of course knew that the quality of the sub-edited work would be variable, but it was only when he had taken delivery of it that he could really make an assessment; Furnivall's vague comment that 'S is probably not sorted', however, gave him some inkling of how bad things might be. In fact it took over a month to rationalize the materials, and even then some parts of the alphabet were still missing. On 10 May he wrote in some irritation to Furnivall:

---

[2] Herrtage appears as 'B.A.' on the title pages of several of his EETS volumes, and Murray described him as 'M.A. Trin. Coll. Dublin' in his 'Report of Work done and Progress made in connexion with the New English Dictionary to 1st March 1880' (OED/B/3/1/4; hereafter '1880 Report to Delegates'), although in fact he only spent two years in Dublin and did not proceed to a degree (information from Trinity College Dublin).

[3] JAHM, '1880 Report to Delegates'. Herrtage was housed in a nearby cottage which Murray had rented for him (Powell 1879: 182).

[4] MP 19 Aug. 1879, 23 Feb. 1880 FJF to JAHM.

[5] Murray's son Harold recalled the 'mountain of boxes, baskets, portmanteaus, sacks and other receptacles—even a [baby's] bassinet—which grew on the floor of the Scriptorium while Ruthven built the great nests of pigeon-holes round the walls', the family of live mice that was discovered in one sack, and the dead mice found in others (HJRM pp. 115–16).

[6] MP 27, 28 Mar. 1879 FJF to JAHM.

[W]e either *have* or know of the existence of all, except *H, Q, Pa. Q* stated in your report of *1862* to be taken by *Rev. T. Sheppard*, has never been heard of since. *Is it lost?* [...] Why do you tacitly drop it in every report, not even saying 'No Report'. [...] Some of the letters being in utter confusion, and requiring a month or more to sort, we may find sections wanting. There are some cruel jokes in your reports. G 'done', 'nearly done', 'will be done in 1872'—a mass of utter confusion, which will take many weeks to put even in alphabetical order. It was nearly burnt you remember as rubbish by Mrs Wilkes after her husband's death: fortunately she bethought her of informing you first. Would you ask this man Crane & ?Holme if they do not care to go on, to give us B & O back? [...] I am sorely troubled about H, Q & Pa.[7]

In the event 'this man Crane' did not carry on with his sub-editing, but half a dozen others did.[8] The letter Q was soon tracked down, and returned by the man who had volunteered to do it twenty years earlier, but who had hardly touched the materials for many years, believing that the project had been abandoned.[9] H too was located, having been similarly undertaken and then neglected by George Marsh, the American secretary from the Coleridge era, who had in fact been living in Italy since 1861, and who promised to send his consignment (from Florence) to the courageous lexicographer who had now undertaken 'this great emprize'.[10] Other materials Murray had to seek out for himself, journeying to 'distant parsonages and country houses' to retrieve the sub-edited (or untouched) material.[11] The hunt was made considerably more difficult by the fact that a notebook in which Furnivall had kept a list of sub-editors' names and addresses could not be found. Furnivall was convinced he had passed it to Price or Murray in 1877, but it eventually turned up in his own possession in late 1880; in the meantime Murray had been obliged to rely on Furnivall's memory in identifying the sub-editors and retrieving the materials from them (or, in some cases, their surviving relatives).[12]

Some letters had passed through the hands of several volunteers. I and J, for example, were originally undertaken by William Woodham Webb, who presumably abandoned the work when he left England to serve in the Franco-Prussian War.[13] His

---

[7] MP 10 May 1879 JAHM to FJF.

[8] In his 1880 Presidential Address to the Philological Society, Murray mentions six 'old sub-editors' as continuing with the work: C. Y. Potts of Ledbury, Joseph Brown of Kendal (eventually to become the longest-serving sub-editor of all), Crane, W. J. Anderson (see p. 81 above), T. H. Sheppard of Oxford, and J. Smallpeice of St. Bees (*TPS* for 1880–1, p. 130). The Cardiff solicitor Robert Griffith seems also to have carried on with the latter part of B, or at least planned to do so, as he is mentioned in a similar list in 1879 (*TPS* for 1877–9, p. 569). Although William Crane did no further sub-editing, it proved to be extremely difficult to persuade him to part with the materials entrusted to him; after personal visits from Murray and Fred Ruthven, and recourse to the Press's solicitors, the materials were finally 'returned [...] untouched' in November 1881 (OED/B/5/7/1 notebook recording dispatch and receipt of sub-editing; see also *CWW* p. 182).

[9] MP 14 May 1879 J. E. Middleton to JAHM (quoted in *CWW* p. 176).

[10] MP 4 May 1879 G. P. Marsh to FJF. Marsh's materials eventually arrived in August (JAHM, '1880 Report to Delegates').

[11] MP JAHM, London Institution lecture (1910), p. 19.

[12] MP 21, 24 May 1877, 28 Mar., 10 May 1879 FJF to JAHM.

[13] Woodham Webb's later work as a reader for the Dictionary, specializing in medical texts, is examined in McConchie (1997: 189–95).

materials subsequently passed to S. C. Morgan, the vicar of Harrow, who in 1876 had been instructed by Furnivall to send them to Murray (so that they could be assessed in relation to the Macmillan project); Morgan, who was on the point of moving house, packed everything up in a hamper with directions to Mill Hill, but this never arrived, and the hamper, now rather the worse for wear, was still at the vicarage six months later, whence it seems to have been retrieved by Murray or Furnivall. However, at least part of I had been reassigned by Furnivall some years earlier to the botanist G. S. Boulger, who as late as 1881 still had some materials for I, 'untouched for some years'.[14] The materials for *Pa* had suffered a worse fate: the sub-editor who had last undertaken it, an Irish clergyman (who had left his living on the disestablishment of the Church of Ireland), had died in 1869, and the papers had passed to his brother, who then passed them to someone else for safe keeping. They were eventually tracked down to a stable in County Cavan, but had not in fact been kept safely: most of them had been used to light fires or rub down horses, and Murray had to appeal for assistance in re-reading early texts to replace the lost quotations.[15]

But the chief problem with the sub-edited material was not that some of it was missing, but rather that so much of what there was fell so far short of the standard expected. Reporting on progress to the Philological Society in May 1879, Murray did his best to be positive, but he could not conceal the incompleteness of the materials:

With gladness I say that one or two of the letters, and sections of letters, are in excellent order, and really sub-edited, in a true sense of the word. This refers especially to F, K, parts of C and R; in a less degree to A, E, N, parts of O and U; of others of the letters it may be said that the slips have received *some* amount of alphabetic arrangement; of one or two unhappily […] I have to report that they are in primitive chaos, and will take the labour of months to reduce even to alphabetical order.[16]

The fact that the letter A was not satisfactorily done was of course a serious and immediate problem, with obvious implications for how long it would take to get Part I of the Dictionary ready for publication.[17]

In addition, there was still much to be done as regards reading, notwithstanding the efforts of the preceding two decades. Murray would have realized this during his preparation of specimen entries, first for Macmillan and then for OUP; as early as his meeting with the Delegates in December 1878 he had been careful to secure

---

[14]   MP 14 Nov. 1876 S. C. Morgan to FJF, 21 May 1877 FJF to JAHM, 23 May 1877 Morgan to FJF, 26 May 1877 Morgan to JAHM, 2 June 1877 Morgan to [JAHM], 29 Aug. 1881 G. S. Boulger to [JAHM]. Boulger had confined himself to alphabetizing the material.

[15]   JAHM, 1880 Presidential Address (*TPS* for 1880–1), p. 129; PSOM 26 Nov. 1880; *Leisure Hour* (1883); *Literary World* 19 Apr. 1901, p. 365; CWW p. 177.

[16]   JAHM, 1879 Presidential Address (*TPS* for 1877–9), p. 569.

[17]   Among the slips for entries in the letter A in the OUP archives are draft entries of an early date in several different hands (one of which is Herbert Coleridge's), suggesting that a number of people had made some attempt to work on the letter before it reached Murray.

their assistance in the pre-printing of slips for use by readers of particular texts, and from the beginning of March 1879 he was sending Price details of slips to be printed, including some for works by Goldsmith, Dickens, and Carlyle.[18] Herrtage was also reading early texts in the British Museum; Furnivall also sent out 250 circulars (many of which were returned marked 'Gone, and left no address') to former readers asking them to inform Murray which of the works formerly assigned to them they expected to finish reading;[19] but a full assessment of the material forwarded by Furnivall—which included unsorted quotations as well as sub-edited entries—confirmed just how much still needed to be done before the work of reading could be considered anything like complete. Accordingly, Murray prepared an 'Appeal to the English-speaking and English-reading Public to read books and make extracts for the Philological Society's New English Dictionary': a four-page pamphlet, accompanied by 'Directions to Readers', giving exact instructions as to what kinds of words to look for and how to set out quotations, and a list of books for which readers were still wanted. The 'Appeal' was dated 'April, 1879', and approved in proof by the Society's Council on 18 April, but publication had to be delayed until it could be submitted to the Delegates; copies were finally printed at the end of the month.[20] However, the *Athenaeum* of 26 April included an article reproducing most of its key points (perhaps Murray, a regular contributor, had passed a copy of the text to the editor), and within a few days copies of the 'Appeal'—issued in the name of the Philological Society's Dictionary Committee— were being sent out to all corners of the English-speaking and English-reading world, and its contents were widely reproduced in journals on both sides of the Atlantic. Within two months it was necessary to publish a second edition, and a third followed in January 1880.

In addition to its stated purpose, the 'Appeal' also served as a kind of prospectus, setting out in some detail both the project's intentions and the work done to date. Of course the last comparably substantial statement about the Dictionary to have been placed before the public was George Wheelwright's call to arms of four years earlier, and the close similarity in the wording of the title suggests that the 'Appeal' may also have been intended to function as a riposte to this. It summarized the history of the project, suggesting that it had never entirely stagnated ('a faithful few, especially some half-dozen of the Sub-editors, [...] have never ceased reading and working'); it noted the 'vast store' of accumulated material, the new agreement with the Clarendon Press, the appointment of Murray, the ten-year timescale, and the plan to issue a first part in 1882. As to size, the potential of the materials to yield 'a work of twelve quarto volumes of 2000 pages each' is mentioned, but the agreed plan to condense this to something under 7,000 pages ('of the size of M. Littré's French Dictionary') is clearly stated, this

---

[18]　MP 3 Mar. 1879, 7 Mar. 1879 Price to JAHM.

[19]　OED/B/2/1/3 printed circular from FJF to readers, n.d.

[20]　PSCM, 18 Apr. 1879; SL 22 Apr. 1879 Price to JAHM; MP 28 Apr. 1879 Price to JAHM. Two proof versions, stamped 17 and 21 April 1879, are preserved in MP.

being 'sufficient to satisfy all the requirements of present English scholarship, and to place our language lexicographically abreast of any modern tongue'. (Murray's contract stipulated that there should be 'not less than six thousand nor more than seven thousand'; it would soon become apparent to all parties that the full maximum figure would be needed, although a figure of 6,400 pages, which went back to Sweet's original letter to Price in 1877, continued to be mentioned on occasion.)

The precise terms in which Murray appealed for help with the reading indicate a careful assessment of what he had inherited from Furnivall. The literature of the earliest period, up to the invention of printing, was, perhaps optimistically, considered to have been so thoroughly examined (and further reading was already being done) that 'little outside help is needed'. Very few early printed books had been read, however, and help was also needed in reading a few works of the late sixteenth century; the seventeenth century had been rather less well explored; and, although books of recent date, being widely available, had been taken up by many, there was plenty more to do, particularly among books of the last ten years (Murray proudly recorded that his own pupils at Mill Hill had extracted 5,000 quotations from modern works in the last month). The real *terra incognita*, however, was the eighteenth century, assigned to American readers in Coleridge's appeal of twenty years earlier but in the event hardly touched, except for Burke's writings.[21] All were now invited to tackle works from the eighteenth century, and indeed of any period. (Within a few months, however, problems arose because of the time taken for letters to cross the Atlantic, which meant that readers on one continent might have a long wait before they could find out whether a particular work had already been taken up on the other; Murray therefore reverted to the old policy of leaving the eighteenth century to the Americans.[22]) 'American and Colonial readers' were also asked to tackle texts which illustrated their distinctive regional vocabularies. Interestingly, readers were informed that '*Local Dialects*, English or American, will *not* be included [in the Dictionary]', for the reason that the work of the new English Dialect Society was only now revealing how little was known about the subject; it was envisaged that in ten years' time work could commence on 'a Dialect Dictionary uniform with this work, so that the two together may constitute a *corpus totius Anglicitatis*, a full repertory of all English Speech from New Zealand to California.'[23] In all of this Murray offered to make a prospective reader's task easier by supplying

---

[21] Murray may subsequently have regretted the statement that Burke's works need not be read. According to Furnivall (MP 28 Apr. 1879 FJF to JAHM), the indexes to Burke prepared by William Rossiter were sent out to sub-editors for their use, but not all of them were returned.

[22] *Athenaeum* 13 Sept. 1879, pp. 337–8. According to this account a new printed reference list of eighteenth-century texts already read or undertaken had been issued for the use of the Americans.

[23] There does seem to have been considerable interest in the idea of a dictionary of English dialect, no doubt fostered by the success of the English Dialect Society; such interest, in fact, that Skeat felt himself obliged to publish an article in *Notes & Queries* (31 May 1879, pp. 421–2) urging that no such project be launched at present, it being more important that the dictionary now launched under Murray's editorship should be the focus of all available effort.

pre-printed slips. Finally, an appeal was made for additional sub-editors to pre-process the material into a state ready for the Scriptorium.

The 'Directions to Readers', explaining what to look for and how to set out a quotation slip, differed significantly from those previously issued. The instruction in the 1859 'Proposal' to note words *not* appearing in specified lists had led readers to concentrate on unusual words at the expense of the more common ones: for example, as Murray commented, 'of *Abusion*, we found in the slips about 50 instances: of *Abuse* not five.'[24] The unusual words were now still to be picked up on ('*every* word that strikes you as rare, obsolete, old-fashioned, new, peculiar, or used in a peculiar way'), but in addition, readers were asked to take 'as many quotations as convenient' for ordinary words. In a later reprint of the 'Directions' Murray explained the need for the latter kind of evidence:

> If Readers will kindly remember that the Dictionary is to contain *all* English words ordinary and extraordinary, [...] and that it is these quotations that we ask them to supply by their reading, they will at once see why we ask them to give us [...] as many *good, apt, pithy* quotations for ordinary words as their time and patience permit. [...] [Q]uotations for common words in their common sense and construction need only be made when they are *good*, that is when the Reader can say, 'This is a capital quotation for, say, *heaven*, or *half*, or *hug*, or *handful*; it illustrates the meaning or use of the word; it is a suitable instance for the Dictionary.'[25]

The need for clarification had been borne in on him by the queries he had received from some readers, such as whether it was necessary to make a quotation for every instance even of such words as *the*: a reasonable question, given that any instance of any word constituted evidence that might be of use. Murray's response was a pragmatic one: useful as it might be in theory to have access to every word in a text (in the manner we take for granted with electronic texts today), the total concordancing by hand necessary to achieve it would be soul-destroyingly dull for all but the most obsessive reader. In fact he did decide that some effort of this sort would be of use, and set his assistants to making 'complete verbal indexes of a large number of books at convenient intervals', although it is unclear whether these were ever completed.[26]

By 16 May 1500 copies of the 'Appeal' had been distributed, and 165 people had responded with offers of help.[27] Such a response after barely a fortnight was impressive, but it fell far short of what Murray had hoped for. The 'Appeal' had 'confidently asked for'

---

[24] JAHM, 1879 Presidential Address, p. 572.
[25] OED/B/4/1/1 copies of two versions of 'Directions to Readers for the Dictionary'.
[26] JAHM, 1879 Presidential Address, p. 572.
[27] *Ibid.* p. 570. Offers of help had begun to come in even before the appearance of the *Athenaeum* article, thanks to an article about the Dictionary in the *Mill Hill Magazine* of April 1879 which gave details of the proposed appeal, and urged Old Millhillians to emulate Murray's own pupils and undertake some reading (Powell 1879). This they certainly did: there are several letters from Old Boys in MP dating from mid-April (e.g. one of 18 April from J. L. Whyte), and their contributions were warmly acknowledged in a later issue of the *Magazine* (Mar. 1880, p. 178).

a thousand readers, working for three years so as to bring the materials to a sufficient level of completeness; but even a year later the total figure was only 754.[28] Murray told the Society of his disappointment at the poor response of its own members, only seven of whom initially undertook to help. Nevertheless, the first three years of reading would ultimately bring in something like 900,000 quotations: a considerable addition to the two million that he had acquired in March, even if it was still to prove insufficient when it came to compiling entries.[29]

And the compilation of entries began straight away, notwithstanding the deficiencies in the material (and the sadly incomplete nature of the sub-editing of A).[30] On 16 May Murray reported to the Society that he had completed draft entries as far as the end of *ab-*, having been 'trying to bottom *Abyss*' that very afternoon.[31] This is the equivalent of 47 printed pages of what would eventually be published as Part I, although at this stage the entries only existed in the form of bundles of slips: numerous editorial and typographical matters had to be settled before material could be sent for typesetting.

Murray had been provided, at his own request, with a committee of Delegates with whom he might 'confer [...] on literary questions';[32] but from the start he also discussed editorial issues at meetings of the Philological Society, which soon became known as 'Dictionary Evenings'. In May, for example, he addressed the issue of compound words, observing that he had found 'the question of questionable compounds' a difficult one. His proposed approach was to divide compounds into three categories: the most important, which merited treatment as separate headwords, the less important, which could be entered under their first or second element, and 'loose, imperfect or obvious combinations', which need only be 'mentioned (some of them)', with a few sample quotations by way of illustration.[33] Issues such as this were bound to arise as soon as the theoretical principles which the Dictionary was intended to embody were put into practice.

A key issue was of course the ideal of the *lexicon totius Anglicitatis*: the principle that any word for which evidence could be found should be included. As a characterization of the ideal dictionary such a principle was all very well, but two related questions arose as soon as one began the process of transforming the quotation evidence into dictionary entries: did everything which a reader had identified as meriting a quotation actually count as a word, worthy of inclusion? And was the same kind of 'inclusion' appropriate for all words? Others had wrestled with such problems before: Coleridge had raised questions about various marginal categories at the very beginning of his editorship,

---

[28] JAHM, 1880 Presidential Address, p. 121.
[29] The figure of 2 million slips initially is given in Murray's 1880 report to the Delegates; that of 900,000 additional quotations (out of 'about a Million' slips sent out) was given in his report to the Philological Society on 20 January 1882 (ProcPS 20 Jan. 1882, p. 73). The count of readers did in fact reach four figures by 1884.
[30] OED/B/3/1/6 23 Mar. 1883 HHG to Liddell.
[31] JAHM, 1879 Presidential Address, p. 572.
[32] See above, p. 86.
[33] JAHM, 1879 Presidential Address, p. 582.

and similar questions had arisen during Murray's own work on the specimen entries for Macmillan. Both aspects of the question of inclusion would continue to manifest themselves in various forms throughout this initial preparatory period, and beyond.

In the second edition of the 'Appeal' Murray was able to announce that there was now once again support for the project from across the Atlantic: Professor Francis March, of Lafayette College in Pennsylvania, a prominent figure in American philology, had agreed to take on the task of co-ordinating those Americans who had volunteered to read.[34] Under his secretaryship an impressive number of Americans volunteered to read for the Dictionary, including far more academics working in the field than did so in Britain.[35]

The level of American involvement in the project was to become a matter of considerable interest in Oxford. It had of course been an American publisher, Harpers, whose approach to Macmillan in 1876 had set in motion the chain of events which led eventually to the signing of contracts with OUP; and throughout negotiations the desirability of providing Murray with an American collaborator, as being a key element in securing American copyright in the work, had been recognized. In November 1878, having established that Murray was open at least in principle to the idea of collaboration,[36] Price had informed Harpers—with whom he was in regular correspondence regarding many other joint publishing ventures, including Liddell and Scott's *Greek–English Lexicon*—that he wished also to discuss 'the large English Dictionary' with them; and shortly after the signing of the agreements with Murray and the Philological Society he wrote again with full details of the work ('intended to be *the* Dictionary of all English-speaking nations'), and invited proposals as to terms on which a joint venture could proceed.[37]

However, it soon became clear that securing American copyright in the *OED* for Harpers—a precondition for their collaboration[38]—would be difficult, particularly following the notorious 1879 ruling by Judge Arthur Butler which allowed the pirating in America of the *Encyclopaedia Britannica*.[39] Discussions continued for several years: in late 1881, R. R. Bowker, Harpers' London agent, sought legal advice on the possibility of securing American copyright on the basis that Murray would be prepared to delegate a substantial part of the editing to Francis March. It was also noted that an American

---

[34] March had been the first holder of a chair in English language and comparative philology in America, had published books on Anglo-Saxon and English, and was active in the American Philological Association, notably as chairman of a committee on spelling reform. He had long known of the Philological Society's project, and had indeed written about it, offering a few quotations, as early as 1860; and already in 1868 he was advocating the Dictionary as a suitable home for the lexicographical findings of individual scholars (March 1860; 1868: 78).

[35] Murray had in fact targeted such academics very early on: on 9 May 1879 Price wrote to Alexander Macmillan asking on his behalf for a list of 'English Professors or other influential persons in the various Colonial Universities' (SL).

[36] See above, p. 100.

[37] SL 13 Nov. 1878 Price to Harper & Brothers, 7 Apr. 1879 Price to J. W. Harper, Jr.

[38] SL 27 Aug. 1879 Price to Harper.

[39] Kogan (1958: 65).

citizen, Henry Phillips of Philadelphia, had done one small portion of the sub-editing while he was in England. Unfortunately the legal advice received was that a work which was a mixture of the work of Americans and non-Americans could not be fully copyrighted.[40] Even after this, OUP continued to seek to persuade Harpers to enter into some kind of partnership (and thereby share the considerable costs of the project). In this Price had an ally in Bowker, who was convinced that Harpers should not pass up the opportunity for involvement in the Dictionary, and was prepared to work hard for it: he told J. W. Harper that 'if it would do any good [he] would […] even go home and back by balloon, for this is the most important thing of the next quarter-century.'[41] In late 1882 a deal was nearly secured, but it finally came to grief over Harpers' fear of being sued by other American dictionary publishers for infringement of copyright— the 'War of the Dictionaries' was still fresh in memory—as OUP would not guarantee to cover any legal costs that Harpers might incur in such an eventuality.[42]

During the latter part of 1879 Murray was concentrating on preparing as much Dictionary copy as possible. The time and effort taken up by the initial collection of materials, the preparation and issue of the 'Appeal', and the resulting immense quantity of correspondence had left precious little time for actual editing: by mid-September he had only reached *ad-*.[43] But the importance of collecting an adequate body of evidence was borne in on him all too clearly by the process of attempting to compile sound dictionary entries from what he was still describing even three years later as 'a by-no-means-complete chronological series of examples'.[44] Murray was soon appealing, as Furnivall's sub-editors had done before him, for particular help in augmenting his evidence for the words currently in hand. A list of words in A for which further quotations were needed appeared in *Notes & Queries* on 25 October, and in December a similar list of words (from *abacist* to *adjust*) was issued as a separate pamphlet, and sent to every person known to be already reading for the Dictionary.[45] These lists—generally referred to as 'lists of wants' or 'desiderata'—brought in significant contributions of evidence, although they were never as successful as Murray had hoped, as he lamented in 1896: 'If every reader would make it his ambition to supply one desideratum at least, it would be of material service to the work.'[46]

In the first of his lists Murray drew particular attention to those words for which his only evidence so far was a mention in another dictionary. Furnivall's sub-editors

---

[40] OED/B/3/1/5 copy of opinion by F. N. Bangs, dated 9 Jan. 1882.

[41] 23 June 1882 R. R. Bowker to Harper, quoted in Fleming (1952: 143).

[42] SL 30 Jan. 1883 Price to Harper & Brothers. For a brief account of the 'War of the Dictionaries', waged during the middle decades of the nineteenth century over the relative merits of the dictionaries compiled by Noah Webster and Joseph Worcester (and charges of copying between them), see Landau (2009: 195–7).

[43] *Athenaeum* 13 Sept. 1879, p. 338.

[44] MP 17 Nov. 1882 T. Hallam to JAHM (quoting Murray's words).

[45] JAHM, '1880 Report to Delegates'.

[46] Preface to the Dictionary fascicle *Depravative–Distrustful*. Many of the later desiderata lists were compiled by John Dormer, an enthusiastic reader and later also sub-editor for the Dictionary.

had been ready enough to accept such evidence, and draft entries accordingly; but Murray was prepared—notwithstanding the incompleteness of his data—to be at least suspicious if a word's existence was asserted by a dictionary but not attested by a contextual example. He had noticed how, of the many words listed by some earlier lexicographers for which he had no independent evidence, many also appeared to have been included in later dictionaries regardless of their currency; even Johnson would sometimes include a word with only a reference to 'Dict.' as authority. He felt strongly that the new Dictionary should not simply follow suit, but should indicate whether a word had achieved any genuine currency, or was merely 'a Dictionary-maker's "essay"', one of the 'mere "dummies" appropriated by each successive compiler to swell his apparent stock-in-trade'.[47] He experimented with various ways of indicating the status of these words, eventually settling on the label '*rare*$^{-0}$' or '*Obs.*$^{-0}$' (the zero indicating no actual examples of usage), a choice which had the advantage of taking up minimal space. Although entries for such words continued to mention their inclusion in earlier dictionaries, Murray often spared the blushes of his immediate predecessors by merely noting that they were to be found 'in mod. Dicts.'[48]

The case of technical terminology, however, was different. Here Murray was quite ready to accept the authority of a specialist glossary and include a word on that basis alone, even in the absence of any contextual quotations. Thus the architectural term *abaciscus* is given an entry, with two separate senses whose definitions are taken straight from a dictionary by the architect Joseph Gwilt, but with no other supporting documentation; the legal term *abandum* is given similar treatment, with a quoted definition (from Tomlins's *Law Dictionary* of 1809) and no quotation, as is the medical term *abevacuation* (here two definitions are quoted, from Mayne's *Expository Lexicon* (1851) and the great medical dictionary of the New Sydenham Society, much cited in the *OED* as '*Syd. Soc. Lex.*'). Entries of this kind appear to show that the Dictionary materials were sparse indeed when it came to specialist language; but it may be that Murray deliberately omitted any examples. The preamble to the first list of desiderata comments that 'it is not essential so to illustrate the mere nomenclature of the sciences', suggesting that such items constituted a distinct lexical category for which Murray felt that briefer treatment was acceptable.[49] The drawing of such a boundary between classes of words would soon prove, as in so many other cases, to be problematic.

The readers who received the first list of desiderata were also sent a new specimen Dictionary entry, which was printed in December 1879 from the materials for the word *address* (verb and noun).[50] Copies of the specimen (see Figure 8) were also made

---

[47] JAHM, 'The Philological Society's Dictionary. Special quotations wanted. List I. Dec. 1879', preamble. Copies of this and later lists of desiderata are preserved in OUPA.

[48] For a more detailed discussion of early stages in the development of this and other aspects of editorial policy, see Gilliver (2010a).

[49] The wording in the original draft of this list (in MP) is more emphatic: 'the Editor [...] does not bind himself to illustrate purely technical terms.'

[50] MP 6 Nov. 1879 FJF to JAHM; SL 27 Dec. 1879 Price to JAHM; *Mill Hill Magazine* Mar. 1880, p. 178.

ADDRESS (a-dres') *v.* also 4–5 Adress(e) [ad. (14th c.) Fr. *adress-er*, older *adrescer*, *adrecer*, *adrecier* = mettre à droit ; f. *à* to + *dresser*, O. Fr. *drecier* :-late pop. Lat. *drictiare* :- *directiare* ; f. *drictum*, *dirictum* : – *directum*, right, straight, direct ; see DRESS. For change of *a-* to *ad-* in 15th c. Fr. (where it was subseq. abandoned), and in Eng. (where retained), see AD- 2.]

Prim. sig. to straighten : — I. to make anything straight ; then, to put things 'straight' or right ; to put in order ; to order, prepare ; to array, clothe. II. to make straight the *course* of anything, to direct, to dispatch ; to direct a letter, direct one's speech or oneself to, speak to. III. to direct oneself with preparation to a task, to apply oneself.

I. To make (a thing) straight or right. Mostly *Obs.*

1. *trans.* To straighten up, to erect ; to raise, to set up. *refl.* To raise oneself, to stand erect, *lit.* and *fig.* *Obs.*

c. 1375. BARBOUR, *Bruce*, vi. 173, How he sa hardyly Addressyt hym againe thaim all. 1483. CAXTON, *Golden Legende*, fo. lxxxvii. col. 2, The first day that he was wasshen and bayned he addressid hym right up in the bassyn. 1620. SHELTON, *Don Quixote*, III. i. I. 116, He arose, remaining bended in the midst of the way, like unto a Turkish Bow, without being able to address himself.

2. To put (things) "straight," or "to rights," to set in order : to order, arrange, or array (a body of troops, etc.). *Obs.*, but cf. DRESS.

1375. BARBOUR, *Bruce*, xiv. 265, His men adressit he thame agane. 1523. LORD BERNERS, *Froissart*, I. ii. 2, [He] achyued many perilous aventures, and dyuers great batelles addressed. 1601. HOLLAND, *Pliny*, I. 445, Put to their shifts, and forced for to addresse themselues, and range a nauall battell in order.

2a. To right what is wrong ; to redress (wrongs), reform (abuses). *Obs.*

1525. LORD BERNERS, *Froissart*, II. lxxx.

[lxxvi.] 238, I say not this to you, bycause ye sholde address my wrongs . . . by hym ye maye be addressed of all your complayntes.

3. *trans.* To order or arrange for any purpose : to prepare, make ready. *Refl.* To prepare oneself. (Const. *obj.* simply, or with *to, unto, for.*) *Obs.*, but see III. *infra.*

1393. GOWER, *Conf.* v. 5021, This lord of Rome it name [*i.e.* took] And therupon him hath adressed. 1485. CAXTON, *Paris and V.*, 40, Eche departed fro other for tadresse suche thynges as to them shold be necessarye. 1598. CHAPMAN, *Iliad*, v. 730, And Hebe, she proceeds T' address her chariot. 1633. HALL, *Hard Texts*, 315, Those of Media addressed their Target for a present defence. 1684. BUNYAN, *Pilg. Prog.* II. 201, He addressed himself to go over the River.

3a. (*with refl. pron. suppressed*). To prepare. *Obs.*

1513. GN. DOUGLAS, *Æn.* VI. iv. 2, Sibillais commandment Enee addressis performe incontinent. *c.* 1607. SHAKS. *Tr. and Cr.* IV. iv. 148, Let vs address to tend on Hectors heeles.

4. *Esp.* To prepare or make ready with the *proper attire;* to accoutre, array, apparel, or attire, for any special purpose or occasion ; *in later usage, simply* to clothe. (Constr. to address *a person in ;* also of *clothes* addressing *a person.*) *Obs.* but see the contracted form DRESS.

1393. GOWER, *Conf.* i. 1722, As he her couthe best adresse In ragges, as she was to-tore. *c.* 1425. WYNTOUN'S *Cronykyl*, VI. ii. 38, Thaire ryng, thaire sceptyre, and thare crownys ar devotly blest Or thai in-to thaim be addresst. 1513. GN. DOUGLAS, *Æn.* IV. iv. 40. [He] wmquhile thaim gan balmyng and anoint, And into gold addres, at full gude poynt. 1567-9. JEWELL, *Defense of the Apology*, 349, Tecla sometime addressed her selfe in Mans apparell. 1628. HALL, *Cont.* Lib. xxi. 80, That soule which should be addressed, a fit Bride for thine holy and glorious majestie. 1678. Fr. QUARLES, *Arg. and Parth.* 63, A Pilgrims weed her liveless limbs addrest from head to foot.

4a. To put on (a garment), to don. (Also with *on.*) *Obs.* or *Arch.*

1513. GN. DOUGLAS, *Æn.* XI. x. 2, Turnus hym self, als fers as ony gleid, full bissely addressyt on his weid. 1835. BROWNING, *Paracelsus*, iii. 81, I have addressed a frock of heavy mail.

FIGURE 8   Part of the Dictionary specimen prepared in 1879, showing the start of the entry for *address* (verb).

available to members of the Philological Society, and it was discussed at length at the Society's Dictionary Evening on 16 January 1880.[51] The entries as presented in the specimen had now to a large extent reached the form in which they would appear in the first portion of the Dictionary when this came to be printed, although many details, of both content and presentation, would change; the Dictionary Evening afforded a valuable opportunity for Murray to present his editorial approach to the Society's members and receive feedback regarding various points of policy and style.

Particular attention was given to the bounds to be observed in this 'lexicon totius Anglicitatis'. Murray defended the decision not to include words which had already become obsolete by 1100 (although the full history of any word surviving beyond that would be given); he sought, but did not receive, guidance as to how far he should go in including words derived from geographical and personal names, like *English* and *Lutheran*; and 'the limits of inclusion as to slang, obscene, and erotic words' were discussed, although the conclusions are not recorded. In general Murray seems to have found the discussions frustratingly inconclusive. It was arguably a mark of the Society's confidence in him that, as Hensleigh Wedgwood observed, they felt they 'must leave to the Editor an enormous discretionary power, and trust to his doing his best with each point of difficulty as it arose'; but definite guidance would have made his work easier, and he complained to Henry Nicol that the meeting had 'not [been] linguistically profitable'.[52]

African

When it came to devising criteria for deciding whether to include particular categories of word, few categories gave Murray more trouble than that of words derived from geographical and personal names by the addition of a suffix. They were clearly English in form, and many of them were moreover included by other contemporary dictionaries, but they were of course just as unlimited in number as the names themselves (which there was at least precedent for excluding, on the grounds that they were names rather than words). He seems initially to have considered a thoroughly inclusive policy, as is seen from the existence of draft entries for words such as *Aberdonian*, but the implications of such an approach seem to have given him pause. After extensive consultation it was decided that, as it was 'impracticable to include [them] *all*', it would be better to omit them all (as he told an unnamed correspondent some years later: draft letter 24 Dec. 1906, in MP). Consequently *Aberdonian* was dropped, as was *Adriatic*, and also *African*. Murray later came to regret this decision, describing it in the Preface to Vol. I (p. ix) as 'a too rigid application of first principles'. It seems to have been when he encountered the evidence for

Continued ➤

---

[51] ProcPS 16 Jan. 1880, pp. 18–19; *Athenaeum* 17 Jan. 1880, p. 87. A version of the specimen was printed in the Philological Society's *Transactions*, as an appendix to Murray's Presidential Address (*TPS* for 1877–9, pp. 622–4). No copy of the original specimen has been located.

[52] MP 20 Jan. 1880 H. Nicol to [JAHM].

American—and also for *Americanize* and *Americanism*, for which the case for inclusion was too strong to ignore—that he began to question the policy; but by then it was too late to reconsider *African*, as the relevant pages of the Dictionary were already in type. In due course Murray came up with a rationale for selective inclusion: 'a proper noun, or adjective thence formed, is included, not for its own sake and as a proper noun, etc., but because it either has other uses, or has derivatives for the explanation of which it is of importance' (Preface to Vol. I, p. ix). The inconsistency of including *American* (which had to be included in order to explain *Americanize* and *Americanism*) but not *African* was noticed within weeks of publication by Charles Doble, who wondered whether it was 'by accident or design' (SL 29 Mar. 1884 Doble to JAHM); it was of course the former, and nothing could be done about it. The policy of including such words only on the grounds of evidence of extended meaning, or the existence of derivatives, was fairly consistently applied thereafter, although there is some evidence of the development of a more inclusive approach as the years passed, with *Orcadian* being included in 1903 despite there being nothing in the entry (for adjective and noun) beyond its straightforward meaning, and subsequently others, including *Sidonian* (1910), *Venezuelan* (1916), and *Styrian* (1919). An entry for *African* was finally added in the 1933 Supplement, which also found room for *Aberdonian*, and indeed many other words of this type.

For a more detailed discussion of this category see Gilliver (2010a: 222–5).

One of the most important issues to be discussed was that of the arrangement of senses within an entry. The old 'Canones Lexicographici' had stipulated that a word's meanings should be 'deduced logically from the Etymology', and Furnivall had reiterated to his sub-editors that senses should be presented in 'logical succession [...] from the etymological meaning'.[53] Murray found, however, that applying this principle could be problematic, particularly with words borrowed from Latin or French, where the source word might already have developed numerous senses in the parent language, any of which might be borrowed into English in any sequence—leading to a historical ordering which might not be at all 'logical'. Indeed, it was often the case with such loanwords that a figurative or developed sense was the first to be borrowed, this being the one which filled a lexical gap in English, whereas for the 'radical' or original meaning there might be no such gap. This had happened, for example, with *advent*, first borrowed into English around 1100 as a word for the period before Christmas, whereas Murray's earliest evidence for the 'radical' sense of an arrival dated from the eighteenth century. The printed specimen of *address* provided a good illustration of the problem. For the verb Murray had been able to devise a structure that was both 'logical'—in that the first of the three branches was closest in meaning to the Latin word *directiare* from which the English word was thought ultimately to derive—and 'historical' in that the earliest-attested senses were all in branch I, and the ordering of senses within each branch was chronological (to within a few years). For the noun, however, while some

---

[53] See above, p. 72.

'logic' (in terms of one definition following on from another) could be discerned in his proposed sequence of eight senses, this did not match the chronological order of their earliest quotation, according to which sense 6 ('dutiful or courteous approach to any one') would have come first, followed by sense 2, and so on. This disparity may have been partly due to the mixed origins of the noun, which was in some cases a borrowing from a corresponding French noun, in others a nominalization of the English verb.[54]

Murray was vindicated in his questioning of the 'logical' approach a few months later, when a paper to the Philological Society (in which he presented his draft of the entry for *aisle*) elicited a forthright letter from Henry Nicol, in which he insisted that the relevant information as far as a historical dictionary of English was concerned was the sequence of senses of a word as they were believed to have occurred in English: 'the logical arrangement of *advent*, for instance, shows nothing as to English, but gives only its *historical* development in *Latin*, whose proper place is not in an Engl. dicty, but in a Latin one. In fact, *for English*, the "logical" arrangement in such a case is illogical.'[55]

Murray nevertheless maintained the view that logic, of some sort, must dictate the way in which the various senses of a word had developed; the problem lay in the incompleteness of the documentation. This was not merely a consequence of the fact that so much reading was still going on (so that newly acquired quotations were continually necessitating a rethink of the structure of an entry). As he was later to write in the introduction to the dictionary: 'If the historical record were complete [...] the simple exhibition of these [i.e. senses in order of their first use] would display a rational or logical development. The historical record is not complete enough to do this, but it is usually sufficient to enable us to infer the actual order.' This was an important elaboration of the 'historical principle' to which the Dictionary had been committed as long ago as the 1858 'Proposal', and a significant departure from the 'Canones'.[56]

In March Murray submitted his first annual report of progress to the Delegates.[57] The quotation slips for the first half of the alphabet had now been sorted into alphabetical order, the work being mainly carried out by Miss Skipper and Miss Scott, 'two young

---

[54] The ordering of the senses of the noun is one of the significant respects in which the published version of this material differed from the specimen. The senses—which eventually numbered eleven, evidence for three further senses having subsequently come to light—were eventually organized into two branches headed 'Preparation' and 'Direction', although there was still no imposition of a strict chronological sequence, with the first sense of the second branch ('The action of directing or dispatching (to a person or place)') attested only by a quotation of 1882, a more recent date than that of any of the six senses that followed it.

[55] MP 6 June 1880 Nicol to JAHM.

[56] Murray (1884: xi). Notwithstanding Murray's assertion, the idea of a 'logical' ordering of senses continued to be appealing, and throughout the first edition of the Dictionary entries may be found in which the fact that something other than (actual or inferred) chronology has provided the rationale for the arrangement of senses is implicitly acknowledged by a note that a particular sense, not placed first in an entry, is 'the earliest sense in Eng[lish]'. The last such comment appears in the entry for the verb *try*, published in 1915, the year of Murray's death. On the eventual abandonment of inferred chronological order see p. 578 below.

[57] JAHM, '1880 Report to Delegates'. This is unfortunately the only one of Murray's reports to the Delegates to survive.

women of fair education belonging to the village'; the complete alphabetization of the materials inherited from Furnivall would not be completed for another two years.[58] The process of compiling dictionary entries was begun by Herrtage, who worked through the quotations for each word in much the same way as Furnivall's sub-editors: dividing the material provisionally into senses and subsenses, and making bundles for each word or subsense, consisting of a draft definition followed by all the relevant quotations in chronological order. He also carried out research to fill at least some of the remaining gaps in the evidence. At this stage there was no selection of which quotations would be included in the published entry: each bundle contained all the available quotations, and new ones were added in by unpinning the bundle and interfiling them. These 'little *fasciculi*' were then reviewed by Murray, who revised and completed Herrtage's draft text. No mention is made in Murray's report of the use made of the work of the sub-editors, probably because the standard of sub-editing in A was not good enough for it to be made use of directly. (Some new sub-editors had been taken on, but they had been set to work on other letters.)

Murray was also at pains to acknowledge the work of others. He warmly acknowledged the work done by Francis March, secretary of the American readers, who he estimated must have dealt with nearly a thousand items of correspondence, and recommended March as the obvious first choice 'if the question of an American editor's name were to become a practical one'. He also singled out the work of three of the most exceptional suppliers of quotations: two are unnamed, but the 'medical man' who has supplied 8,000 quotations can be identified as T. N. Brushfield, the superintendent of Brookwood Asylum, and the similarly prolific 'literary lady', who supports herself by her pen' as the children's author Jennett Humphreys.[59] The one reader to be named was the obscure but remarkable Thomas Austin. A former Exeter College servant, now looking for work—in October he had written to Price asking to be considered for 'literary work'—he had so far contributed 12,250 quotations. Murray considered the work of this apparently uneducated man to be 'of scholarly excellence', and felt 'almost embarrassed by the greatness of the work which he has done for the Dictionary'.[60]

A rather greater source of embarrassment in Murray's report must surely have been his admission that there were serious problems with the rate at which he was moving through the alphabet. This could be assessed by reference to the corresponding pages in another large dictionary, such as the 1864 edition of Webster's dictionary; according to this yardstick, the point he had reached in the compilation of entries—*agedness*—represented approximately a third of the letter A. Herrtage's preparatory work had

---

[58] On 20 May 1881 Murray reported to the Philological Society that almost all of the 'old slips' were now sorted, leaving only a separate sequence of quotations acquired subsequently to be integrated with the older material (PSOM).

[59] Brushfield and Humphreys are named, along with Austin and a dozen or so of the other most valued readers, in Murray's 1880 Presidential Address (*TPS* for 1880–1, p. 122). Brushfield remained a very prolific contributor: he is credited in *ODNB* with an overall total of over 72,000 quotations.

[60] SL 27 Oct. 1879 Price to Austin. Price does not seem to have taken the hint and offered Austin any work.

reached a little further, nearly to the end of *al*. He reassured the Delegates that he did not expect there to be any difficulty in getting the early sections of the Dictionary ready in time; but he now professed the view that it would simply not be possible 'as a physical feat' to complete it in ten years (although he still thought it could be done in less than fifteen). Surprisingly, the Delegates seem not to have reacted to this warning sign: Price, writing to Murray following the meeting at which his report was read out, informed him simply that they were satisfied with it.[61]

By early 1880, however, another side of the 'triple nightmare' was beginning to be of serious concern to Murray, namely the fact that the project was proving far more expensive than anticipated. He seems to have been extremely reluctant to mention this to the Press, perhaps fearing that the prospect of increased costs at such an early stage might lead it to abandon the project; but he had already begun to express his concerns both to his friends and to the Philological Society. Already in December 1879 he had commented to the Society that the costs of paying assistants, purchasing books, printing, postage, and carriage were such that his own work as Editor 'was gratuitous, & would be so for the first 3 years'.[62] He was soon obliged to make economies, such as discontinuing payment to H. R. Helwich for his reading of early texts.[63] The ever-optimistic Furnivall sought to reassure him, pointing out that the first year was no guide to the likely costs in subsequent years, and suggesting that he could easily make the necessary economies by ceasing to pay his brother-in-law for clerical work and by cutting down on printing and postage;[64] but finances remained difficult.

Worse still, for the first time in his life Murray's health began to suffer. Severe headaches caused him to be absent from school in February; despite the urgings of Weymouth that he should have a few days of '*entire* rest', or even a month if necessary, it was only in April that he was persuaded to take a short holiday in Chepstow with a former pupil.[65] Thereafter he did make some attempt to cut down on other commitments, for example by not preparing the customary full report on the Philological Society's activities during the year when giving his Presidential Address in May.[66] (He was still committed, however, to a number of other books, including a 'Primer of the English Language' for Macmillan, an expansion of his *Encyclopaedia Britannica* article on the

---

[61] MP 30 Mar. 1880 Price to JAHM.

[62] PSOM 5 Dec. 1879. In the matter of books Price did what he could to help: in addition to making the Press's own books freely available, he also made a request (unfortunately unsuccessful) to the Master of the Rolls for a set of the valuable 'Rolls Series' of early historical texts to be donated for the use of the Dictionary, and persuaded the Royal Society to loan a complete run of its *Philosophical Transactions* (OD 13 Dec. 1878; SL 19, 24 May 1879 Price to W. Hardy, 22 Dec. 1880 Price to JAHM).

[63] MP 16 Feb. 1879 H. R. Helwich to JAHM. Helwich seems to have been the only reader working at this time who was paid for his contributions, presumably because of his skill at reading early texts. Payment was in fact later resumed at some point (MP 3 May, 18 Oct. 1882 Helwich to JAHM).

[64] MP 23 Feb. 1880 FJF to JAHM.

[65] MP 23 Feb. 1880 Weymouth to Ada Murray; *CWW* pp. 198–9.

[66] JAHM, 1880 Presidential Address, p. 118.

English language into book form, an edition of the romance *The Taill of Rauf Coilyear* for the Early English Text Society—promised to Furnivall at least since 1878—and of course the anthology of specimens of Lowland Scots that he was supposed to be doing for OUP. In the end, perhaps unsurprisingly, none of these projects materialized: the last heard of the Primer was a plaintive request from Macmillan in January 1881 for a sample of anything he had done; no expansion of his *Britannica* article was ever issued; the editing of *Rauf Coilyear* was eventually completed by Herrtage; and the Lowland Scots volume remained in limbo until Murray's contract with OUP was finally cancelled in 1891. Murray also failed to produce an article on the 'Scottish Language' for the *Encyclopaedia Britannica* which he had promised as a companion piece to the one on the English language.[67])

For the rest of 1880 the compilation of entries continued steadily. In May Murray's editing had reached *al-*; and by the autumn he was corresponding with the botanist James Britten about *amaranthus* and *ambrosia*, and appealing for information about the history of the word *ammunition*.[68] An appeal for additional sub-editors met with some success, with the recruitment of six new volunteers by the end of the year. It was now becoming clear that the rate of production was heavily dependent on the quality of sub-editors: Murray and Herrtage could work much faster—and at no additional cost—if material had been prepared to a consistently high standard before it arrived in the Scriptorium. Among the new recruits was a former Mill Hill teaching colleague of Murray's named Alfred Erlebach; the fact that he was assigned to sub-edit the latter part of A suggests that Murray must have had particular confidence in his abilities. Gustavus Schrumpf, a Wolverhampton schoolmaster, also sub-edited a few entries in A, including the difficult preposition *at*. Some of the new volunteers began by preparing small specimens of work and returning them to Murray for detailed comment.[69] Experience had shown him the importance of close supervision in ensuring consistency of work done by such a disparate group; in fact he continued with the practice of allocating only short alphabetical ranges, and also of providing his sub-editors with feedback. Costly though this was in terms of his own time, he regarded it as justified because by keeping tighter control of their work he could ensure that what reached him in the Scriptorium was of more consistent quality (and could be worked

[67] MP 18, 22 Jan. 1881 A. Macmillan to JAHM, 29 Aug. 1881 Fred Ruthven to JAHM, MP 19 Dec. 1891 H. Boyd to JAHM, 14 Mar. 1878 T. Baynes to JAHM, 30 June 1885 W. R. Smith to [JAHM].

[68] ProcPS 21 May 1880, p. 34; MP 25 Sept., 30 Oct. 1880 J. Britten to JAHM; PSOM 26 Nov. 1880. Details of Murray's early consultation of specialists are unfortunately sparse, because the large volumes into which all of his early correspondence was pasted are now lost: see *CWW* p. 181 and n. 28. Some idea of the scale of what has been lost is given by a notebook preserved in MP containing an index of correspondents, maintained until 1893: the running number assigned to each letter had reached 10,000 by the summer of 1885, and the second sequence which was started at this point was well over 2,000 by 1893. By 1882 there were already some 5,000 letters, held in thirteen volumes (Humphreys 1882: 451); by 1894 there were more than 13,000 in thirty-two volumes (Hjelmqvist 1896: 118).

[69] JAHM, 1880 Presidential Address, pp. 130–1; MP 3 Nov. 1880 W. Gregor to JAHM, 5 Nov. 1880 G. A. Schrumpf to [JAHM].

FIGURE 9   Fitzedward Hall, 1862.

up more quickly); the reassuring sense of progress and contact with the Editor may also have encouraged some sub-editors to carry on with the task.[70]

During the year he also began to communicate with various individuals who would go on to become some of the Dictionary's most valuable helpers, including Fitzedward Hall (see Figure 9), a distinguished American-born oriental scholar and philologist who had settled in England, and the historian Edith Thompson.[71] Also in early 1880 special appeals were made for help with scientific words. The members of several scientific societies were asked to help with the collection of evidence for these, and an appeal for quotations was printed in some specialist journals:

We want to know when and by whom *Armadillo* and *Wombat*, *Teak* and *Tulip*, were first used in English; who invented (introduced, or translated) *acinaciform, achene, marsupial, mesoblast, parthenogenesis, biology*, and all the other words of scientific nomenclature. We are glad of notes as to the origin of such descriptive names as *Arrow-root* and *Adjutant*, or the meaning of such adopted ones as *Gutta Percha*.[72]

Important editorial issues continued to arise and be discussed with Philological Society colleagues during the year (notwithstanding the fact that during much of 1880 the

---

[70] JAHM Dictionary Report, in *TPS* for 1880–1, p. 267. The renewed focus on sub-editing may have been stimulated by the fact that Furnivall had at last discovered his notebook with sub-editors' contact details (MP 3 Nov. 1880 FJF to JAHM).

[71] MP 16 Apr. 1880 Edith Thompson to Macmillan, 5 Oct. 1880 JAHM to [Skeat]. Hall had in fact been an extremely prolific contributor of quotations in the pre-Murray era: he claimed to have contributed approximately 200,000 quotations to the Dictionary between 1860 and 1871 (Hall 1874). (He seems to have become something of a recluse after 1869, a disastrous year for him in which he was first suspended from membership of the Philological Society over accusations of misconduct and then forced to leave his position as librarian of the India Office following allegations that he was a drunkard and a foreign spy (*CWW* p. 305). In fact Murray had collaborated with Hall already in the 1860s on another scholarly project, the editing of the works of Sir David Lyndesay for the EETS; but it was only in October 1880 that contact between the two men was renewed. Edith Thompson was the author of a popular *History of England* (1873) for schools; she and her sister Elizabeth would continue to contribute to the Dictionary until their deaths half a century later, both by supplying quotations and, later, by reading proofs.

[72] ProcPS 16 Jan. 1880, p. 18. The appeal from the Council appeared on the outer wrapper of an issue of the *Journal of the Linnean Society* (Botanical section) dated 30 March 1880, a copy of which is preserved at OED/B/4/2/2.

Society's main concern seems to have been with spelling reform). Murray continued to wrestle with the question of comprehensiveness, in regard not only to compounds but also to loanwords from foreign languages, and technical terms from the vocabulary of particular subjects: in his Presidential Address in May he declared that the 'limiting line of English speech [...] could *not* be found or fixt in a Dictionary'.[73] He would continue to develop and refine his ideas about this 'limiting line' over the next few years; and decisions about whether a particular word lay within or outside this boundary would continue to be problematic.

There were also smaller, but thoroughly practical points of editorial practice, which once settled would have to be observed throughout the Dictionary. The terminology used to describe particular linguistic features and processes had to be chosen carefully. For example, in his 1880 Presidential Address Murray declared a preference for the word *echoism* over *onomatopoeia* (on the basis that the latter had 'neither associative nor etymological application to words imitating sounds'); and in the published text of his address he invited suggestions both for the phenomenon whereby a word lost its initial vowel—for which he suggested the word *aphesis*—and for the kind of word which is invented for use on a particular occasion.[74] To invent new terminology was a bold step, and one that Murray subsequently found himself having to defend to Dean Liddell; but the fact that no existing terms exactly met his requirements does point up the pioneering nature of the work on which he was now engaged.[75] After experimenting for some time with other possibilities, including *casual* and *mot d'occasion*, Murray eventually settled on *nonce-word*—this being itself another coinage.

The question of how to refer to words invented 'for the nonce' might seem an unimportant one, but the category had always been a troublesome one: Coleridge had been unhappy about including the playful formations he referred to as 'vocabular parodies' and 'literary fungi'. In fact Murray included many nonce-words in the early pages of the Dictionary, such as *a-Christism*, *addressy*, and *agathokakological*, but by no means all of those for which he had evidence: for example, although a quotation by Swift illustrating his coinage *academico-philosophical* survives among the unused Dictionary slips, no entry for the word was included. An even nearer miss was *anglimania* (used frivolously in an 1835 issue of *Blackwood's Magazine* to denote a passion for angling), an entry for which was drafted, and even sent to the typesetters, but eventually omitted from the published text.

A rather more ominous development, only referred to indirectly in Murray's 1880 address, was the appearance of the first instalment of a work which was to become a

---

[73] ProcPS 21 May 1880, p. 34. Irregular spellings such as 'fixt' occur frequently in much of the Philological Society's official documentation around this time, reflecting the various spelling reforms approved by the Society.

[74] JAHM, 1880 Presidential Address, pp. 136, 175–6. An entry for *aphesis* duly appeared in Part II of the Dictionary, with a note that the word had been 'Suggested by the Editor in 1880', but without quotations; evidence, including a quotation from Murray's 1880 Address, was only added in 1972 in the relevant volume of the second Supplement. An entry for *echoic*, with a quotation from the same source, was included when the relevant section of the Dictionary appeared in 1891.

[75] MP 3 Dec. 1881 Liddell to JAHM.

threat to the Dictionary project in more ways than one. Robert Hunter's *Encyclopaedic Dictionary*, published by Cassell, was eventually to run to seven octavo volumes; as its title declared, it aimed to be a new type of dictionary, and to 'treat certain subjects with something of the exhaustiveness adopted in an Encyclopædia';[76] but in its scale, if in nothing else, it certainly implied competition with the Philological Society's planned work. Fortunately Murray was able to hold up for ridicule, as an example of how prone dictionaries were to copy ignorantly from each other, an entry in the new volume, which had appeared in October 1879.[77] Having encountered an entry in the fifteenth-century English–Latin glossary *Promptorium Parvulorum* which translated the Middle English *a-ȝen wylle* 'unwillingly' by its Latin equivalent *invite*, Hunter unwisely gave an entry defining *a-yen-wylle* as 'To invite'.[78] Although Hunter is allowed to remain anonymous, as 'a [...] recent Dictionary-maker', his identity is clear from the exact reproduction of the *Encyclopaedic Dictionary* entry in Murray's Address.[79] The exposure of such an egregious error no doubt helped to show that academically the new work was no rival to the Philological Society's Dictionary; but the launching of a publication which many might nevertheless see as comparable to it must have been uncomfortable, both for Murray and for the Press.

During the latter part of 1880 the Dictionary began to acquire a more prominent public profile. There had of course been occasional articles about the Philological Society's project, and mentions in the public prints, throughout its first quarter-century—not to mention the various pamphlets and public statements issued by Coleridge, Furnivall, and the Society—and the resumption of work in earnest had garnered some public attention in 1879;[80] but during 1880 there was a significant increase in coverage. A journal which took particular interest in the project was *Notes & Queries*: it had carried Murray's first list of 'desiderata' in October 1879, and more followed in January and February 1880.[81] In June Skeat contributed an article on the importance of giving precise references (by page or line) to the vaguely referenced quotations given in earlier dictionaries such as Johnson and Richardson; and in October a longer account of the project, with much detail about the progress of the reading and

---

[76] R. Hunter, *Encyclopaedic Dictionary*, vol. I (London: Cassell, Petter, Galpin & Co., [1879]), verso of title page.

[77] Hunter et al. (1997: 30).

[78] This blunder was also pointed out by Herrtage in an article on 'Blunders in our English Dictionaries' in *Notes & Queries* 21 Aug. 1880, p. 142. Hunter himself later claimed that the mistake was due to a copyist's error and not to ignorance on his part (MP 5 Dec. 1888 Hunter to JAHM).

[79] The passage inveighing against copying between dictionaries in general, and Hunter in particular, must have been a late addition to the Address, as it is not present in Murray's manuscript draft (in MP).

[80] Murray himself contributed an important early article in the *Athenaeum* (13 Sept. 1879, pp. 337–8), reprinted copies of which he subsequently requested for promotional use (one is attached to his '1880 Report to Delegates'). The article was anonymous, but Murray's authorship has been traced in Richard Bailey's useful bibliography of *OED*-related articles (Bailey 2000b). Another version of Murray's article appeared in the *Academy* on the same day (pp. 194–5).

[81] *Notes & Queries* 25 Oct. 1879, p. 329; 10 Jan. 1880, p. 33; 28 Feb. 1880, p. 173.

the working methods in the Scriptorium, appeared under the pseudonym 'Curiosus'.[82] Henceforth the magazine's columns were to contain many contributions. The fact that in July Murray had arranged to have the interior of the Scriptorium photographed may be evidence of a deliberate effort to publicize the project; or it may show that public interest was already beginning to generate requests for such images.[83] In any event there was certainly a stream of visitors to the Scriptorium over the summer: mainly German and American scholars, but also W. E. Gladstone, who was a regular visitor to Mill Hill (and who expressed the sorrowful conviction that he would never see the completion of the Dictionary).[84] Among the Americans was the classical scholar Basil L. Gildersleeve, whose account of his visit in the *Nation* was one of several articles in the American press; interest in Germany was fostered by an article in the journal *Anglia* by another friend of the project, the literary scholar Lucy Toulmin Smith.[85]

As 1881 began even the completion of the letter A seemed an uncomfortably remote prospect. Murray, still working on entries in *an-*, did not dare to spend time preparing a full report for the first Philological Society meeting of the year, as he had done the previous January, and instead spoke from brief notes.[86] Tasks other than the actual editing of the Dictionary continued to occupy much of his time: in particular the supervision of the fifteen sub-editors, the preparation of a second 'List of Wants' (for words from *adjunctive* to *allongation*), and correspondence with readers as the start of the third and final year of 'preliminary reading' approached. An impressively industrious group of twenty-five readers—headed by the indefatigable Thomas Austin—had accounted for fully one-third of all new quotations; but it was not these who caused the trouble: 'the most extensive readers required the least attention, and wasted least of the editor's time.' Murray and Herrtage were also still finding the evidence for the more ordinary words to be sparse.[87] This must have been embarrassing for Murray, in view of his comments in his report to the Delegates in March 1880 that ordinary words were now 'well represented' and that the focus should now shift to the reading and excerpting of works that would yield quotations for scientific and technical language.[88] Help with such specialist terms was now forthcoming from the members of various learned societies, but more was needed; and he now also appealed to Philological Society members to look out for 'rare ordinary words', especially derivatives formed on the common suffixes (*-ble*, *-ive*, etc.). But even when Murray was able to get down to

[82] Skeat (1880), 'Curiosus' (1880). The level of knowledge of the project in the latter suggests that 'Curiosus' was probably Herrtage or Fred Ruthven.

[83] MP 10 July 1880 H. T. Trew (photographer) to JAHM.

[84] 'Curiosus' (1880: 263). At this point Gladstone had just begun his second term of office as Prime Minister.

[85] Gildersleeve (1880); Smith (1880).

[86] Preserved in MP.

[87] ProcPS 14 Jan. 1881, p. 45; PSOM 14 Jan. 1881. Austin's tally of quotations now stood at 19,200.

[88] Murray also commented on the completeness of the materials for general vocabulary in his Presidential Address in May (*TPS* for 1880–1, p. 125).

some actual editing, the need to keep within the agreed limit of 7,000 pages forced him to work more slowly than he might otherwise have done: illustrative quotations had to be shortened, and poor examples substituted for good ones which happened also to be long; and the drafting and redrafting of etymologies 'to be brief [...] without being obscure' was very time-consuming.

One of the factors tending to expand the space required was the sheer number of compounds. Notwithstanding his earlier classification of them into three levels of importance, the accumulated evidence for even the least important kind of compound was such that, for many words, 'pages might be filled with combinations possessing no difficulty, nor special historical interest.' Murray now felt that it would be desirable to produce a specimen entry for a word with many compounds, as a basis for discussion as to the best way of presenting them; he suggested as suitable candidates *all* and *alms* (the former being enormously productive of compounds, and therefore a good basis for consultation 'as to where an end is forcibly to be put to them'), but he was doubtful of being able to afford the printing costs.[89] In fact the ongoing negotiations with Harpers were also creating an urgent need for a new specimen. Accurate estimates of production costs were heavily dependent on the Dictionary's typography, many details of which had not been settled; a specimen would be a convenient way to establish these. Price accordingly urged Murray to send in the copy for *all* and *alms*.[90]

In fact the copy for *all* and *alms* had not yet been finalized to the point where it could be sent to Oxford. Murray was still compiling entries without making a final selection of quotations, because of the continuing influx of new and important quotation evidence: it would be wasteful of effort to make a provisional selection, only to receive additional quotations subsequently which demanded inclusion. And now, notwithstanding Price's anxious request, he could not afford to spend time on such selection. A more pressing need was to compile the information required for his annual report to the Delegates. He sent out questionnaires to his sub-editors, asking them (as Furnivall had done before him) to report progress.[91] The news, which he also reported to the Philological Society in his annual Presidential Address in May, was good in parts: sub-editing of A (by Herrtage and Erlebach) was now complete, and B nearly so, which offered prospects of better progress in the Scriptorium. Murray himself had prepared entries as far as the end of *an*. However, the overall picture was much worse: the original estimate that the Dictionary materials were in an advanced enough state of preparation to enable the book to be completed in ten years was, he

---

[89]   JAHM Dictionary Report, in *TPS* for 1880–1, p. 268; MP JAHM, MS notes for PS meeting 14 Jan. 1881.
[90]   MP 22 Jan. 1881 Price to JAHM.
[91]   MP 10 Mar. 1881 W. J. Löwenberg to JAHM, E. C. Hulme to JAHM, 11 Mar. 1881 A. P. Fayers to JAHM, T. Henderson to [JAHM], 14 Mar. 1881 W. Gregor to [JAHM]; MP 29 Mar. 1881 Price to JAHM (acknowledging receipt of Murray's report, which, curiously, was not presented to the Delegates until 20 May). Five completed copies of the 1881 questionnaire to sub-editors survive in OED/B/5/7/2.

told the Society, 'utterly fallacious', as it was now clear that much of the old sub-editing had been done incompletely, badly, or not at all.[92]

At last, in late May, copy for *all* and *alms* began to be sent to the printers. On 15 June Murray visited Oxford to discuss a proof of the entries for *alms* and related words with Liddell, Pattison, Max Müller, and William Stubbs; revises were circulated, and on the 24th the specimen pages were displayed at a meeting of the Philological Society.[93]

There was much to discuss in relation to the new specimen besides typography. In particular there was the great difficulty of keeping the Dictionary to the agreed size. Murray described the situation to Henry Hucks Gibbs, in one of what was to be a long series of letters to him confessing worries about the project.[94] The text of Webster's 1864 dictionary was a useful yardstick: comparison of the amount of space taken up in his own entries with that taken up by the corresponding entries in Webster showed him how much his text had to be compressed in order to stay within the agreed limit of 7,000 pages. Such condensation was not only difficult, but also immensely time-consuming: 'it would be much easier & quicker to make [the Dictionary] a work of 14,000 pp. than of 7,000.' This apparently struck one of the Delegates, Mark Pattison, who wondered about the possibility of extending the size of the Dictionary in order to facilitate the task of editing. When he expressed concern about the financial implications of this, Murray, perhaps rashly, assured him that he would be happy to produce a work of 20,000 pages for the same amount as had been agreed for 7,000; whereupon Pattison said 'we must see about it', and they parted, leaving Murray convinced that when—as he now thought would be inevitable—it became necessary to ask for an extension, Pattison was the man to approach.

Further resolution of the outstanding issues had to wait until after the summer break. It was not until October that things began once again to move, with a visit to Oxford by Henry Hucks Gibbs, whose role as a key player in the fortunes of the Dictionary now emerges. His combination of personal wealth (the Gibbs family was one of the richest in the country), business acumen, and Oxford contacts[95] uniquely qualified him to exert influence where it mattered; he also cared a great deal personally about the Dictionary as a project, and was sympathetic but businesslike in his relationship with Murray. In October, meeting Liddell in Oxford on other business, he tackled him on the subject of enlargement. He found him encouragingly receptive, and apparently in favour of an extension; this may have been a result of lobbying from Pattison, but Liddell had also formed his own view, from examination of the specimens, that more space was needed

---

[92] JAHM Dictionary Report, in *TPS* for 1880–1, p. 266.

[93] MP 26, 28 May, 10 June 1881 Price to JAHM; SL 9 June 1881 Price to Pattison, 24 June 1881 C. E. Doble to JAHM, ProcPS 24 June 1881, p. 65. The *alms* specimen was seen at the meeting on 24 June by Albert S. Cook, a visiting American scholar, who subsequently reproduced part of it (Cook 1881).

[94] GL MS 11021/21 ff. 404–7 5 July 1881 JAHM to HHG.

[95] He was a member of Exeter College, but his family were also closely associated with Keble College, which received substantial benefactions from various family members; Gibbs himself served on the college's Council for over thirty years (Cameron and Archer 2008: 22, 52).

if the quotations were to be long enough to illustrate sense-development adequately. Gibbs concurred with his view that 'quality [of quotations] is more important than number' (and cited the entertainment value of the much longer quotations in Richardson's dictionary as a good model); he also passed on to Murray, with his own endorsement, Liddell's desire that quotations from 'the ephemeral literature of the day' should be kept to a minimum—'as little D[aily] T[elegraph] as possible'. This last was soon to become a thorny point of contention; interestingly, Murray's initial response was to agree, saying that he only admitted newspaper quotations when he could not help it, and that for the single such quotation in the *alms* specimen he now had a 'better' replacement. Gibbs was also encouraged by a meeting with Price, whose positive response boded well for the chances of securing the Delegates' approval, since, as he commented to Murray, 'they as a body do what Mr Price advises' (though he added that Price 'does what the Dean of Christch[urch] advises'). Finally, he could also report that Max Müller, a key Delegate, was philosophical about matters of scale: 'The work would extend itself willy nilly.'[96]

The ground was thus carefully laid for Murray to raise the subject of enlargement. From his discussion of the matter with Gibbs, it seems likely that he decided to ask for an extension to 10,000 pages, equivalent to approximately six times the scale of Webster's 1864 dictionary (rather than 7,000 pages, or four and a half times Webster); the *alms* material was considerably larger than this, representing an expansion on Webster by a factor of 11 (or, '*after all condensation*', 10), but, as he explained to Gibbs, it was 'an important word with much history annexed'. Looking at a larger sample of words, he estimated that a scale of six times Webster represented the absolute minimum within which the aims of the Dictionary could be achieved.

Murray now wrote to Price, alluding (against Gibbs's advice) to the sympathetic remarks made by Pattison four months earlier. Price was by this stage extremely anxious to have all typographical matters settled, so that he could make arrangements for casting the new type that would be needed (including new founts for the pronunciation).[97] It was arguable, however, that the final details of typography depended on the Dictionary's permitted extent; and so on 28 October the request for enlargement came before the Delegates. They agreed to rather less than Murray had hoped: the Dictionary might now occupy six volumes of 1,400 pages. Price's letter informing Murray of the decision presented it as an increase from 6,400 to 8,400, but given the now general expectation of a work of 7,000 pages, it represented rather less than this: only 1,400 pages more, and still only five and a half times Webster. The Delegates' willingness to consider even this extension may have been due to an assurance from

---

[96]   GL MS 11021/21 ff. 421–7 20 Oct. 1881 JAHM to HHG; MP 18 Oct. 1881 (incomplete) HHG to JAHM.

[97]   SL 25 Oct. 1881 Price to JAHM. The cost and labour involved in setting up even the *alms* specimen had been considerable; indeed, Price seems to have given instructions that no work was to be done on the larger *all* specimen until the typography had been settled. In fact it is possible that no *all* specimen was ever prepared, as no proof survives in MP or OUPA, and the copy was subsequently returned to Murray (SL 26 May 1882 Doble to JAHM).

Murray that the project's editorial expenses would not be increased: an assurance he would soon have cause to regret. Price represented the Delegates as taking the view that 'it is not expedient to limit you to such a quantity as would lead to the injury of the Book'; Murray took a different view, commenting to Gibbs that 8,400 pages was '*just* too little'.[98]

Only a few days after hearing of the Delegates' decision, Murray received some unwelcome news from a quite different quarter. The politician and literary scholar John Frederick Stanford had for some years been collecting material for a dictionary of the foreign words and phrases that had been borrowed into English; in 1874 he had even sought, unsuccessfully, to persuade the Philological Society that his material should be absorbed into those for its own Dictionary, or failing that used as the basis for a separate work.[99] At his death in 1880 he left a bequest of £5,000 towards the costs of completing his project, which put rather a different complexion on the matter; the University of Cambridge, to which the bequest was offered in the first instance, appointed a syndicate to consider it. One of the syndicate's members was Skeat, who contacted Price privately, and apparently advised that a recommendation should be made to reject the bequest so that it could then be offered to Oxford. However, when the matter was put to a meeting of the university's Congregation, the syndicate's recommendation was defeated by a huge majority—chiefly as a result of lobbying by, of all people, Furnivall, who travelled to Cambridge to argue for a dictionary along the lines envisaged by Stanford. Skeat now wrote to Murray with news that another serious historical dictionary, of some sort, was now being seriously contemplated by Cambridge. He was hopeful that the new project's terms of reference could be framed so that it would complement, rather than compete with, Oxford's dictionary; but Murray was still put out. 'I cannot see,' he complained to Skeat, 'what use a Dictionary of a section of modern English will be to anybody. [...] It is in no spirit of jealousy, but with a pure desire not to see work done twice over, when once doing it is a task hard enough, that I question the advisableness of your project.' In the end Skeat (who turned down an invitation to edit the new work) managed to devise a scheme which concentrated for the most part on foreign words that had not yet become fully naturalized in English. The words in this sometimes hard-to-define category lay towards the margins of the '*corpus Anglicitatis*' that Murray was aiming to cover; but the prospect of such well-funded competition from Cambridge must have been distinctly uncomfortable.[100]

In January 1882 it was time once again to report on progress to the Philological Society. With the projected three years of preliminary reading nearly at an end, nearly 900,000 quotations had been sent in, bringing the total to about two and a half million. Murray was evidently satisfied with the completeness of the reading

[98] MP 4 Nov. 1881 Price to JAHM; 15 Feb. 1882 JAHM to HHG.
[99] ProcPS 4 Dec. 1874.
[100] *TPS* for 1882–4, pp. 7–9; SL 2 Mar., 1 July 1881 Price to Skeat; MP 16 Nov. 1881 Skeat to [JAHM], JAHM to Skeat, 28 Oct. 1882 Skeat to JAHM. Further on the relationship between the *OED* and the *Stanford Dictionary*, see Gilliver (2010b: 68–71) and Ogilvie (2010).

for the last three centuries, and even made a few comments characterizing them: 'The eihteenth century was one of bondage to Addison, etc.: it coind few new words. The nineteenth century was like the sevnteenth in its adventurousness & licence.'[101] The sixteenth century, however, was still poorly covered, and further reading was needed to establish the earlier histories of many words currently known only from their occurrences in Spenser and Shakespeare. The three most helpful readers were singled out for special thanks; of these the most prolific was still the indefatigable Thomas Austin, but prodigious quantities of quotations had also been supplied by Job Pierson, a Presbyterian minister from Michigan, and a Mr William Douglas of London.

It was also time to report on the editing of the Dictionary itself. Murray had just received a revised version of the *alms* specimen, in which various typographic devices had been used both to compress the text slightly and to improve its readability.[102] He predicted that printing of the first Part would begin in March; but Furnivall's minutes record a much gloomier forecast for the completion of the whole work: 'The Dictionary might be out by 1900 A.D., but probably not much before.'[103]

Murray's frankness to his Philological Society colleagues about the likelihood of a much longer timescale is surprising in view of his anxiety, expressed in letters to Gibbs at this time, that the Delegates should not hear of it. Some of them will surely have read the *Academy*, which reported Murray's doubts about completing the book before the end of the century;[104] but the matter was not discussed in his ongoing correspondence with Price over the new agreements with himself and the Society made necessary by the extension in number of pages. Discussion of contractual matters was perhaps bound to be protracted and difficult when it involved Furnivall, who on being sent a draft of the agreement with the Society promptly made various revisions, including one 'binding the Delegates' to 8,400 pages as a minimum; Murray crossly chided him for 'quarrelling with people who are better as friends than as enemies', and distanced himself from Furnivall's wording, explaining to Price that this was 'simply his cantankerousness, and fondness of quarrelling', although he did mention that he was still hopeful of a further extension to 10,000 pages.[105]

But there was another difficulty. Under the original agreement Murray was to be paid a total of £9,000, of which £2,100 would be paid for the three years of initial preparation—this being paid in quarterly instalments of £175, the last of which had

---

[101] ProcPS 20 Jan. 1882, p. 73 (supplemented from PSOM). On the irregular spellings found in this passage see p. 129 n. 73.

[102] MP 13 Jan. 1882 Price to JAHM, 18 Jan. 1882 AJE to JAHM. Copies of three versions of the *alms* specimen survive in OUPA(u) and MP.

[103] The account of this meeting published later in the Society's *Proceedings* (p. 73) gives slightly different information about timescale: 'at the rate of 36 words a day it [the Dictionary] would take 13½ years, and 36 words a day was far beyond the power of any man, to investigate, explain and write.'

[104] *Academy* 4 Feb. 1882, p. 81 (an anonymous note, in which however Furnivall's hand is surely betrayed by his resort to a rowing metaphor—he was a fanatically keen oarsman—in appealing once again for sub-editors: 'A good pull and a strong pull for a few months now might see all the work sub-edited this year').

[105] MP 25 Jan. 1882 JAHM to FJF, 4 Feb. 1882 JAHM to Price (copies).

been paid in December 1881—and the remaining £6,900 at the rate of £1 for each page passed for press (any remaining balance being paid on completion). Enlargement of the book to 8,400 pages would imply a total payment of £10,500; but Murray had promised that editorial expenses would remain unaltered. How, Price asked, should the system of payment be altered?[106]

It is hard to disagree with his granddaughter's assessment that Murray was 'extraordinarily lacking in hard-headedness'. His first response to Price's query is arguably further evidence of his lack of financial good sense—or, more charitably, of his determination to honour his contractual obligations irrespective of whether he could afford to do so.[107] He proposed that, instead of being paid an amount for each page of the new Dictionary, he should be paid according to his progress through the alphabet, measured by the pages of Webster's dictionary of 1864: if for each of Webster's 1,534 pages he were to receive £4 10s., this would total almost exactly £6,900. This had the (supposed) advantage that it was independent of the actual scale he worked at: if the Delegates were to agree to a size of six times Webster, then he would be paid £4 10s. for six pages of new text, or fifteen shillings per page; if the scale remained at 5½, he would receive the same payment for 5½ pages, or £9 for 11 pages.

Price, however, preferred to express things in terms of the pages of the new Dictionary, and to refer back to the agreed maximum of 8,400 of these pages; and the Delegates duly resolved to ask Murray to accept fifteen shillings per page.[108] From the point of view of the work they were getting out of their Editor, this was of course excellent value for money: for the same outlay that had originally been agreed for the compilation of 7,000 pages, they were now to get 8,400. But this would of course be more than offset by the increased production costs of the larger work.

The unwisdom of Murray's assurance that editorial costs would not increase was now brought into sharp relief. He had of course argued that being allowed to exceed the agreed scale would enable him to work more quickly; but even allowing for this, he knew that the work of completing the Dictionary would take him considerably longer than he had so far admitted to the Delegates. His best estimate was that he could complete no more than 33 words per day, and that he was averaging 81 words for each page of Webster. This implied that the maximum rate of work was the equivalent of 1¼ columns of Webster per day; so that (allowing for Sundays, holidays, and illness) the complete Dictionary would take something like thirteen and a half years—on top of the three years of preliminary work. Even this figure did not allow for the fact that some words took much longer—*approve*, for example, had taken him three-quarters of a day—nor for the time that would be required to read and correct proofs and revises, of which he had as yet no experience.[109] If he really was to receive no more than £6,900

---

[106] MP 3 Feb. 1882 Price to JAHM.

[107] *CWW* p. 209; MP 4 Feb. 1882 JAHM to Price (copy).

[108] SL 8 Feb. 1882 Price to P. Williams; OD 10 Feb. 1882.

[109] Calculations taken from MP 12 Feb. 1882 JAHM to HHG. Cf. also the slightly different calculations given above (p. 136 n. 103).

for all of his remaining work as editor, then his annual income would fall a very long way short of the £900 a year on which he had originally persuaded himself that he could undertake the task. He had been prepared to find himself worse off financially after the initial three years (for which he had agreed to accept £700 a year); but he now faced the prospect of working for another thirteen or more years, on an annual income of £500 or less—out of which he would still have to find £350 for his assistants' salaries and other expenses, leaving a quite inadequate amount for the support of a wife and seven children (with an eighth on the way).

Murray turned, once again, to Gibbs, pouring out his worries—and his calculations—in a long letter, the first of three written in four days.[110] His prime concern, he said, was the fact that he had so far withheld from the Delegates his conclusions about the time that the Dictionary would take, seeing it as advisable to refrain from mentioning such problems 'till we get the work fairly launched'; whereas once one or two Parts had been published, and the value of the work was clearly recognized (and when the Press could no longer so easily go back on its commitment), it might be easier to persuade them to take measures to speed things up—and even to suggest that they find him a post of some sort in Oxford, which he could combine with his Dictionary work.[111] This strategy, however, was now becoming unsustainable. He had already spent far more on the Dictionary than he had intended, partly goaded by Furnivall, with his continual urgings that this or that ought to be done; now, with no more preliminary payments, and no prospect of payment per page for a couple of months, he was having to borrow against the small amount of money he had managed to put away for his children's education. It is clear from his letters to Gibbs that this hopeless financial position worried him at least as much as his scruples about not being honest with the Delegates about the timescale:

when it comes to facing the future upon less than £500 a year, I am filled with perplexity, and at times my heart quite fails me. It has done so a good deal of late; and the state is not favourable to work. [...] [I]t is certain that we have all underestimated the cost to *somebody*, at which the work must be done, and that it is I on whom the consequences fall, & whom they threaten to crush.[112]

Gibbs took rather a different view. He initially even doubted whether Murray should feel obliged to stick to the limits set by the Delegates: 'Do you consider yourself *in*

---

[110] MP 12, 15 Feb. 1882 JAHM to HHG; a third letter of 13 February is mentioned by Gibbs in his reply (17 Feb. 1882, in MP), but does not survive. In the first of these letters Murray states that he has been meaning to approach Gibbs for some time, but 'I have not felt since Christmas that I could spare a moment for anything but work, work, work!'

[111] The idea of a post at Oxford had been mentioned over a year earlier by Furnivall, who sent Murray a cutting from the *Athenaeum* ('Notes from Oxford', 11 Dec. 1880, p. 778) reporting on a proposal to allow colleges to award fellowships to 'persons engaged in some literary and scientific work', and suggesting that he ask Price to secure 'a Fellowship that'll relieve you from the worry & drag of Mill Hill School' (MP 11 Dec. 1880 FJF to JAHM). Cold water was poured on the idea by Max Müller, who advised Furnivall: 'Things move slowly—very slowly—at Oxford' (MP 17 Dec. 1880 Max Müller to FJF).

[112] MP 12 Feb. 1882 JAHM to HHG.

honour bound to confine yourself strictly to the number of pages authorised? It is impossible that you can guarantee the doing so without marring your later work [...] if it is only "penalty" which deters you, I say Esto peccator et pecca fortiter.'[113] But as Murray explained, the fact that a yardstick such as Webster was available meant that he could not be so cavalier:

I consider myself in honour & duty bound to confine the work to whatever limits [the Delegates] prescribe, and by constantly seeing, say every 10 pages, that I am marching at even ratio with Webster to secure that the result is attained. I am not quite marching through an untrodden region—there are abundance of footsteps before me, and it means merely following one of these predecessors & taking 4, 5 or 6 steps for his *one*. [...] It is precisely this fact that the space can be estimated [...] *as it passes through the press*, & that I cannot plead ignorance if I transgress, that makes me anxious to have a limit of 10,000. That I *can* pledge myself not to exceed, & that would give me elbow-room; i.e. I should *not* have to play *Procrustes* with every quotation, from the constant terror of outrunning my space.[114]

Much of Murray's anxiety was due to a feeling that his position, and the future of the project, were still acutely vulnerable. From his dealings with Price, and with Max Müller, the Delegate he knew best, he had gained the impression that the Delegates as a body were dubious about investing so much money in a project over which they had so little control, and whose editor was an unknown quantity to them. Gibbs, who had better knowledge of several of the Delegates (including the influential figure of Liddell), could be more reassuring: he was confident that if the case were put to the Delegates as Murray had put it to him, they would grant more time, a limit of 10,000 pages, and more money. He gently chided Murray for his tentativeness: '[the Delegates] know that one should not muzzle the ox that treadeth out the corn [as Price had remarked three years earlier] both for his own sake and because the corn does not get so well trodden. [...] [Y]ou say it would be unreason to ask them to give more money. But surely it is not so if they get more money's worth!'[115] However, he insisted that he would only act as Murray thought best: he was prepared to speak with or write to Liddell, or Murray himself could approach the Delegates formally, but the choice was to be Murray's.

Murray was still nervous about asking for yet more money, so soon after the Delegates had effectively sanctioned greater expenditure by approving the increase in size: he worried that this would make the Dictionary 'seem like a *fifth* thing that never can be satisfied, a great abyss that will never cry "Enough!" '[116] Eventually he was persuaded to compose a letter to Liddell. Both men agreed, however, that it would be as well not to take the matter any further until a substantial body of material—perhaps

---

[113] MP 11 Feb. 1882 HHG to JAHM (Latin: 'Be a sinner and sin boldly').
[114] MP 15 Feb. 1882 JAHM to HHG.
[115] MP 17 Feb. 1882 HHG to JAHM.
[116] MP 25 Feb. 1882 JAHM to HHG. The reference to 'a *fifth* thing that never can be satisfied' is a Biblical allusion (to the *four* insatiable things mentioned in Proverbs 30: 15–16), and not, as Elisabeth Murray rather curiously misreads it (*CWW* p. 211), an instance of a supposed Scotch dialect word '*fifch*'.

thirty pages—had been set up in type; this would constitute a sounder basis from which to estimate scale, as well as illustrating fully the nature of the text as Murray believed it should be done.[117]

There was thus every reason to finalize the Dictionary's typographical details (as Price had been urging Murray to do for over a year). Murray arranged to visit Oxford to do this, bringing with him the first batch of copy;[118] but at the last minute he encountered a serious hitch. James Lecky, one of his more persistent correspondents on the subject of how pronunciation was to be represented in the Dictionary, wrote to Furnivall protesting in the strongest terms about the notation Murray had devised.[119] Furnivall referred the matter to the Society's Council, commenting breezily to Murray how 'comforting' it was that 'you fonetic folk can't agree';[120] and Murray was asked to present his proposals formally at a meeting of the Society. He could be forgiven for feeling immense frustration at this further postponement of the start of printing; he pointed out that the scheme had been arrived at through 'three years' incessant trial and practical experience', without the help from Society members that he had anticipated.[121] In the end he had decided that no currently available system quite met the Dictionary's requirements, and had therefore devised one of his own. There was much vigorous discussion at the meeting, both on what pronunciation should be given in the Dictionary and on the system used to represent it. It was decided that Murray must be allowed to adopt whichever scheme he thought most practical; but Henry Sweet, who had argued against Murray's approach, was unwilling to let matters rest, and continued the discussion by letter, even suggesting that as it was impossible, in the current state of knowledge, to give all the known pronunciations (both current and historical) of each word, it would be better to give none at all. He boldly advised Murray to

sieze [*sic*] every opportunity of lightening your present work [...] What is wanted now, is the *material*. When you have gone through all that, and got it in print before you, you will be able [...] to look at general questions of etymology, prn[n] &c in quite a different light, and to embody your results in the one-vol abridgment.

The idea appalled Furnivall: 'to turn out *the* Dicty without a detail—the pronunciation— that all other decent Dicts give, wd be a profession of incompetence that would disgrace us all.' In any case Murray's contract committed him to including some pronunciation

[117] MP 27 Feb. 1882 HHG to JAHM.
[118] MP 25 Feb. 1882 JAHM to HHG.
[119] For a full discussion of the development of the phonetic notation used in the Dictionary, see MacMahon (1985).
[120] MP 1 Mar. 1882 FJF to JAHM.
[121] ProcPS 17 Mar. 1882, p. 77. In his 1881 Presidential Address he had specifically appealed for someone who would 'save me the time of thinking this matter out, by giving a broad and practical consideration of the question' (*TPS* for 1880–1, p. 268).

information. When it was put to Sweet that, with his undoubted expertise, he could take on this component of the work himself, he demurred. Murray also pointed out that the incompleteness of current knowledge could not be used to justify omitting pronunciation, any more than any of the other components of the Dictionary:

for etymology, history, sematology, explanation are all *subjective*, some of them *more* subjective even than the pronunciation. [...] All that you urge against phonetic statements, can be urged with far greater force against sematological ones: for there I am absolutely a pioneer; nobody has yet *tried* to trace out historically the sense-development of English words. [...] I shall have to do the best I can at defining probably 80,000 words that I never *knew* or *used* or *saw* before.[122]

In the end Sweet did not press his objections, and Murray went ahead with his own system; but the protracted argument had delayed the start of typesetting by several weeks, with the first six bundles of copy arriving in Oxford on 19 April.[123]

The debate over pronunciation was just one component of a combination of tribulations which now once again threatened to overwhelm Murray. He was still worried about his finances, and seems to have mentioned this to Furnivall, whose reaction was characteristic: still convinced that Fred Ruthven's services could be dispensed with ('if he hadn't been your brother-in-law, he'd have had to go long ago'), he also produced a flurry of suggestions as to where additional money might be found, amongst which was the idea of seeking to raise further funds by an appeal to Society members and the general public, and thereby to 'shame Oxford into further advances'.[124] In fact Gibbs may also have been bringing his own influence to bear on the matter, as on the same day that Murray was addressing the Society on pronunciation, the Delegates voted to increase his rate per page from fifteen to seventeen shillings; it is hard to imagine them doing this other than in response to prompting of some sort.[125] The increase was of course welcome, but it was only the promise of more money, and did not address Murray's immediate and pressing need for funds. In April he arranged a loan of £100 from his friend and former Mill Hill colleague Robert Harley, which brought temporary relief from worries about his financial situation;[126] but he remained thoroughly despondent about the project in general. His friends did their best, in their various ways, to raise his spirits. Miss Jemima Brown, a reader who had just started to

---

[122] MP 22 Mar. 1882 Sweet to JAHM; 30 Mar. 1882 FJF to JAHM; 27 Mar. 1882 Sweet to JAHM; 29 Mar. 1882 JAHM to [Sweet].

[123] MP 19 Apr. 1882 J. Griffiths to JAHM. Dating information for many stages in the printing process, from the dispatch of copy to the printer through to the signing off of clean sheets, was recorded in a large logbook (OED/B/5/7/3); from about the middle of 1883 the bundles of 'copy' slips were also date-stamped by the printers on receipt.

[124] MP 19 Mar. 1882 FJF to JAHM.

[125] OD 17 Mar. 1882; SL 21 Mar. 1882 Price to P. Williams. New agreements were drawn up with Murray and the Philological Society formalizing the new rate of payment, and also the new page limit; the Society's seal was put to the new agreement on 5 May (PSCM).

[126] MP 4 Feb. 1885 JAHM to Price (copy).

incorporate the newly accumulated quotation slips for *Pa* with the fragments retrieved from County Cavan, urged him to take a proper summer holiday, somewhere on the Continent—'where posts are few and *As* cannot pursue you'—and told him that she had long remembered him in her prayers, while Furnivall combined sympathy with heartiness: 'I know your feeling well. "Chuck it all up" has come to me a fair number of times. But I think this depends very much on bodily health. If you could get a good gallop or other refreshing rest or change, the old strong *will* 'ud revive. [...] Cheer up. All 'll go well yet.'[127]

But at last printing could begin in earnest. On 5 May Murray was able to show a proof of part of the Dictionary's first entry to members of the Philological Society.[128] Two weeks later he had even better news to report: now that some forty pages of the Dictionary were in type, the indications were that 8,400 pages would be sufficient after all.[129] At the same meeting Murray was also elected President of the Society, for the second time: a post which he took up with great reluctance, and only because the Council thought it fitting that when Part I of the Dictionary was issued, it should be edited by the Society's President.

The appearance for the first time of a substantial quantity of Dictionary entries was the occasion for far more than an encouraging forecast as to scale. In their compilation Murray had taken a multiplicity of editorial decisions, big and small; the proof stage of the first batch of work was effectively the last time that these decisions could be reconsidered before they became irrevocable, and had to be put into practice consistently across the rest of the text. Murray could therefore expect that many interested parties would have comments to make about the textual form which he had given to their idea of the Dictionary. In fact from the beginning he himself gladly sent proofs to Gibbs for comment; but comments also came in from other quarters, not all of them welcome.

One of the first criticisms of the new entries came from Price. He advised Murray that he should 'entirely leave out or be very sparing with extracts from today's newspapers. Our people think they are hardly quotable for the literary use of a word.'[130] The use of such quotations had of course already been queried by Liddell and Gibbs, but Price's comments stung Murray into a fuller justification of his approach:

I never use newspaper quotations, in preference to those from other sources—or when I have or can get others [...] I shall be glad to have special criticism on instances, rather than general

---

[127] MP 30 Apr. 1882 J. E. A. Brown to JAHM, 30 Apr. 1882 FJF to JAHM.

[128] PSOM 5 May 1882 (referring to 'the first Article (on A)'—whether the initial letter or the indefinite article is not clear).

[129] PSOM 19 May 1882; JAHM Dictionary Report, in *TPS* for 1882–4, p. 6. Murray had not had time to prepare, as he had intended, a full account of the preliminary reading now that three years had elapsed since the issuing of the Appeal, and his 19 May report to the Society is in fact very brief.

[130] SL 8 June 1882 Price to JAHM.

FIGURE 10   James Murray, photographed by Elliot and Fry of London sometime between 1882 and 1885; in his hand is a page of Dictionary galley proof.

expression of prejudice (for it is no more) against such quotations. So long as I do not *found definitions* on uses of words found only in newspapers—or at least do not do so without saying, 'In modern loose use' or something of the sort, I believe that I am doing what every true English scholar will approve. If I cannot illustrate current modern usage in any other way, I *must* use the current writing of the day. The only other thing is for me to concoct quotations myself to illustrate such modern usages. And surely it is better to show that the *Daily News* or *Pall Mall Gazette* uses words in such & such senses, than merely to state on my own authority, that such is the current modern usage. [...]

    To the philologist & historian of language—newspaper quotations are the *most valuable* of current instances—they show how the language grows—they make visible to us the actual steps which for earlier stages we must reconstruct by inference. The staid historian or preacher of a university sermon likes to know that a word or phrase is above all suspicion of *parvenuism* before he admits it to his pages. We cannot then get any help as to the history of language from

him: its history is half done before he uses it. I'll be glad to know *who* really objects to these, &
on what grounds; & to fight him on the general question; & I am bold to say that I shall have all
the English scholarship of the world on my side. [...]

Perhaps Sir Garnet Wolseley—not quite unknown to academic Oxford—might not have
used 'A 1.' in annotating Herodotus, but the Eng. lang. is not dedicated exclusively to annotating
Herodotus or translating Kant.[131]

The opening comment about not using newspaper evidence when something else was
available might seem to place Murray among what might be called the 'canonicalists',
but his own 'democratic' approach is clear enough from what follows, which
goes considerably further than Herbert Coleridge's comments about chapbooks,
madrigals, and 'the Bavii and Mavii of our Literature' in its recognition of the validity
of a quotation as evidence regardless of its source. Not that this eloquent defence was
enough to prevent the issue from continuing to be raised, by the Delegates and others,
for decades to come; but for the moment, at least, Murray does seem to have allowed
himself to use newspaper quotations freely.[132]

Another point of interest is Murray's reference to the possibility of 'concoct[ing]
quotations' where nothing from a canonical source was available. This means of
supplementing the body of collected quotations for a word had been authorized during
the earlier negotiations with the Press;[133] despite his understandable reluctance to make
use of the expedient, he had already been obliged to do so on numerous occasions,
especially in entries for some of the commonest words, for which all the reading had
still failed to supply adequate evidence to illustrate recent use. (In one of the earliest
of these, in the entry for *a* (the indefinite article), Murray allowed himself to add a
personal touch: correcting proofs at his wife's bedside a few days after the birth of their
daughter Elsie on 1 May, and lacking a modern instance of the use of *a* preceded by
an adjective when used with *as*, he added 'As fine a child as you will see', which duly
appeared on page 2 of the published Dictionary.[134]) There are also occasional instances

---

[131] MP 9 June 1882 JAHM to Price (copy). A quotation by the distinguished soldier Garnet Wolseley,
taken from *Reynolds's Newspaper*, appears in the Dictionary entry for *A1* 'prime, first-class' alongside
examples from Dickens and Harriet Beecher Stowe. By an odd coincidence (pointed out to me by Chris
Stray) Wolseley himself became such a byword for reliability that his own name—in the form 'all Sir
Garnet'—became almost a synonym for *A1*. An entry for this expression was added to the Dictionary in
1972.

[132] Part I of the Dictionary contains, as of course do its successors, a great many quotations from
newspapers such as the *Daily News*, the *Daily Telegraph*, and the *Pall Mall Gazette*; for a small but
significant number of words, such as *abdicator*, *abjective*, *able-bodiedness*, and *abolished*, a single
newspaper quotation is the only evidence given.

[133] The option to concoct quotations to illustrate modern usage is mentioned by Furnivall as having
been conceded by the Delegates (PSCM 20 Dec. 1878).

[134] Reported in 'In the Dictionary Margin' (*Times* 25 Oct. 1929, p. 17), a collection of Dictionary facts
and anecdotes taken from the papers of Alfred Erlebach. Murray reported to the Philological Society in
May 1882 that he had been obliged to resort to the 'very unsatisfactory' expedient of adding invented
examples of *about* and *above*, after spending precious hours searching vainly for examples in existing
texts, and urged readers to send in more modern instances of uses and constructions of common words
(*TPS* for 1882–4, pp. 6–7).

of invented quotations for much rarer words. An unusual example is *abdicable*, a word included in a list of addenda to Webster's Dictionary published in 1879; Murray seems to have regarded this as a reliable, evidence-based source, and included the word despite having no quotations of his own, but he decided to flesh out the entry with the invented example 'Such responsibilities are not abdicable at will'. In the case of *alation*, recorded in an entomological sense by Craig's *New Universal Dictionary* of 1847, Murray presumably drew upon his own personal knowledge of botanical terminology to add '*Mod. Bot.* The alation of the stem is more conspicuous in other species of the pea.'—a sense for which he apparently had no other evidence.

Murray was evidently very nettled by Price's criticism about newspaper quotations—which he took to be on behalf of the Delegates—as he wrote about it to Gibbs and, perhaps unwisely, to Furnivall. Gibbs promised to write to Dean Liddell about the matter, although he still held to a more prescriptive view than Murray's, feeling that newspapers contained 'slipshod and hasty writing, sometimes betraying ignorance and almost always haste in the writers', and that quotations from them should only be used when no alternative was available.[135] Furnivall hardly helped matters by writing directly to Price, informing him that the matter was settled 'long ago, during my Editorship' in favour of making full use of such evidence: indeed, he argued, 'how many of [the Delegates] are to say that the authority of Jn. Morley in the *Pall Mall*, Andrew Lang in the *Daily News*, M. Pattison in the *Academy* &c isn't as good as that of an Oxford Lecturer or Don?' Price's surely rather disingenuous response was that it was not the Delegates who had made the criticism (though Murray could be forgiven for taking Price's 'our people' in this sense); he also made Furnivall's letter the pretext for a tart request that communications about the Dictionary should be between himself and Murray, 'without the intervention of a third person'. Murray took the point, regretting Furnivall's 'imprudence and meddlesomeness [...] there are some men to whom it is not safe to tell anything whatever, unless you wish to reap vexation from your confidence'; but he took the opportunity to reiterate his own view:

your letter [...] came to me practically as an injunction not to use some of the straw which I had for my bricks, but to leave off work & go over all the land of Egypt for stubble—which I really had not time to do. I cannot find quotations *when I want them*: I must use those I have. With better straw I could no doubt make better bricks; but my business is to do the best I can with what I have.[136]

Furnivall's aggressive championing of Murray's position on newspaper quotations arose, of course, from his passionate devotion to the project as he envisaged it; and when his vision came into conflict with Murray's, he was just as ready to dispense criticism. At the same time as he was defending Murray to Price, he was also protesting to Murray about

135 MP 14 June 1882 HHG to JAHM.
136 OED/B/3/1/5 12 June 1882 FJF to [Price]; MP 14 June 1882 Price to JAHM; OED/B/3/1/5 15 June 1882 JAHM to Price.

the treatment of derivatives such as *abider*, which he felt should be dealt with in the same detail as the parent word: if *abide* had been shown to have several subsenses, then the Dictionary should also show which of these subsenses were also attested for *abider*. Murray had opted for a more condensed treatment, recording that *abider* occcurs 'in the various senses of the verb';[137] but this was not good enough for Furnivall, who suspected the Delegates of having forced the condensed treatment on Murray in order to save space, and threatened to make a public protest if they did not reconsider. Murray wrote in some irritation to Price ('Mr. F. J. Furnivall [...] has an itching for annoying people [...] there is no saying what he might do in one of his mad fits'), pointing out that in fact he had so little evidence for derivatives of this kind that nothing more than brief treatment was possible. He had little respect for Furnivall's judgement: 'He speaks of himself as a former "Editor"; he never 'edited' one word—only superintended the Reading.' The matter was referred to the Delegates at their next meeting in October, and the page containing the entry for *abider* was held back pending resolution of the dispute.[138]

The injured tone of Murray's letter, and of others written around this time, might be taken as a sign that all was not well in the Scriptorium. In fact matters could hardly be worse: on top of all the criticisms of his editorial approach, Murray now found himself having to deal with a betrayal of trust by the one person he arguably relied upon more than anyone in Dictionary matters: his assistant Sidney Herrtage.

Herrtage's betrayal was of an extremely serious kind: he had begun to work for a rival project. After criticism of the treatment of earlier periods of English in Cassell's *Encyclopaedic Dictionary*, Robert Hunter had approached Herrtage with an offer of work; he had not only accepted, but had begun to make use of the materials in the Scriptorium in his work for Hunter. When this was discovered, Murray had little option but to dismiss him.[139] It also emerged that some expensive books had gone missing from the Scriptorium, and the finger of suspicion pointed at Herrtage, who may even have had some kind of mental breakdown. Furnivall was apologetic but defensive about his protégé, attributing the thefts to 'partial insanity [...] a kind of kleptomania for books'. By the end of July Murray had managed to find a replacement, in the form of his sub-editor and former Mill Hill colleague Alfred Erlebach. Herrtage moved away from Mill Hill, and apparently made some kind of recovery; some of the books were returned (probably by his wife, who may have been unaware of his behaviour).[140] Although Murray had reported the matter to the Philological Society,

---

[137] Quoted in MP 11 June 1882 FJF to JAHM.

[138] OED/B/3/1/5 24 July 1882 FJF to [Price]; MP 19 June 1882 JAHM to Price (copy); SL 9 Aug. 1882 Doble to Price.

[139] JP I. H64 ff. 11–12 (notes by Jowett on a conversation with JAHM 4 Sept. 1884). Herrtage went on to write most of the definitions in the *Encyclopaedic Dictionary*; the earliest public mention of his involvement with the project which I have found is in the *Academy* of 20 May 1882 (p. 357).

[140] OED/B/3/1/5 31 July 1882 JAHM to Price; MP 12 June, 7, 12 Aug. 1882 FJF to JAHM. Furnivall was determined to see the best in Herrtage despite his faults ('he is a man with 2 sides to his character, & to one of these I hope to hold'), though I have found no evidence that he criticized Murray for treating him too

it was apparently hushed up: in August the *Athenaeum* reported that he was still working with Murray, while a brief item in the *Academy* (actually written by Furnivall) described him as fully taken up with work on Hunter's dictionary, a confusion drawn to Murray's attention by Charles Doble, Price's Assistant Secretary (who may also have been in the dark).[141]

The shortage of manpower in the Scriptorium will not have helped Murray with the work of reading and correcting proofs and revises, which was proving to be agonizingly slow. It was often only when an entry had been set up that he could properly assess the arrangement of senses, and identify which quotations could safely be omitted in order to save space. The arrival of new quotations for a word after it had been set up in type often necessitated substantial revision and restructuring of an entry. The effect of this slow progress on Murray's finances was disastrous. His loan from Robert Harley had been secured in the expectation that he would soon be receiving payment from Oxford, but by mid-June not a single sheet had been passed for press.[142] Meanwhile, there was an immediate need for funds to pay his assistants, and the project's other ongoing expenses; and his own personal savings were exhausted.

Henry Hucks Gibbs was now the recipient of another anguished appeal from Sunnyside: this time not from Murray but from his wife, Ada. Alarmed at her husband's despondency, she now took the initiative and wrote to Gibbs about the situation. Meanwhile Murray, unaware of his wife's action, had written to Price to ask for an advance of £50, on the basis that text to the value of rather more than that was now at least in type. His letter arrived in Oxford a day too late, the Delegates having dispersed for the summer vacation, though Price promised to convene a meeting to consider the matter.[143] Gibbs, however, responded immediately, and positively: he would see what he could achieve by talking to Liddell, about either the amount or the timing of payments from the Delegates, and was also ready to lend money to meet immediate need from his own funds, to be repaid when money was forthcoming from Oxford. Murray gratefully accepted both offers. Within a week, Gibbs had arranged for a loan of £100; he also wanted to know the exact details of Murray's situation, as information to present to Liddell as soon as he had returned from holiday in Yorkshire.[144]

Murray's figures prompted puzzlement, and some reproach, from the more businesslike Gibbs. The expected annual expenses of the project had been significantly understated, and the agreement to accept a reduced payment of £700 p.a. for the first

---

harshly as Elisabeth Murray suggests (*CWW* p. 368 n. 6). In fact Murray did not cut himself off entirely from Herrtage: the two men continued to serve together as members of the Early English Text Society's management committee for several years.

[141] *Athenaeum* 12 Aug. 1882, p. 203; *Academy* 12 Aug. 1882, p. 117; MP 15 Aug. 1882 Doble to JAHM, 22 Aug. 1882 FJF to JAHM (admitting authorship of the *Academy* piece, and urging that the full details of the case be kept quiet). Doble had been Assistant Secretary since 1879.

[142] ProcPS 19 Jan. 1883, p. iii; SL 22 June 1882 Doble to JAHM.

[143] MP 26 June 1882 Price to JAHM.

[144] MP 25 June 1882 HHG to Ada Murray; OED/B/3/1/5 27 June 1882 JAHM to HHG; MP 28 June, 1 July 1882 HHG to JAHM.

three years had left Murray in a position of being unable to fund it to the level required, other than by drawing on his own resources. In fact the amount of paid editorial assistance had fallen well short of that which would have enabled him to work most efficiently. Finally, Murray had not fully appreciated the effect of the hiatus between the last preliminary payment and the first payment for copy (a period which had also turned out to be longer than expected). Gibbs was more confident of Price's good business sense, and of his awareness of the unwisdom of false economies.

Before Gibbs could act, however, another of Murray's friends quite independently took a hand. Alexander Ellis had been aware of Murray's financial problems at least since February, and had even considered how supporters of the project might be mobilized to help, but illness had prevented him from doing anything about it. Now, however, a visit to Mill Hill confirmed that the situation had worsened significantly, and he secured Murray's (perhaps reluctant) approval for a radical plan: to launch a public appeal for funds to supplement the income promised to the Editor by the Clarendon Press. He wrote to Price enclosing a draft statement which he proposed to issue, explaining that the fact that more copy was not now coming through was not due to any dilatoriness on Murray's part, but rather to the fact that the amount of time required for preparatory work should have been four, not three years—the latter figure being a reasonable estimate, but one which could not have been regarded as reliable before proper work had been done. 'Should this appeal prove unsuccessful,' he wrote, 'I, for one, should recommend Dr Murray to resign the editorship unless the Delegates thought proper to intervene.' He also cheekily asked whether the Press would be prepared to print the Dictionary specimen which he proposed to attach to the appeal.[145]

This did not go down well with Price. Couched as it was in reasonable terms, Ellis's letter was nevertheless clearly a challenge to the Press, who would be seen as short-changing the project if the appeal should become public. An opportunity to discuss the new proposal would be afforded by the meeting of those Delegates still available which had now been called for 19 July. Meanwhile Ellis had busied himself in finding supporters for the appeal. He reported to Ada Murray that numerous Philological Society friends had responded positively, mostly with undertakings to subscribe money; and he wrote again to Price, informing him of the growing list of subscribers, and offering to meet the Delegates himself. Price dissuaded him, 'knowing', as he commented to Liddell, 'how much the Delegates dislike interviews and how little generally comes from them'. In the event Ellis decided against a trip to Oxford, mainly on the advice of Gibbs, now returned from Yorkshire, who had had a long and satisfactory discussion with Liddell.[146]

---

[145] MP 14 Feb. 1882 AJE to JAHM; GL MS 11021/22 ff. 873–6 4 July 1882 AJE to HHG; OED/B/3/1/5 1, 14 July 1882 AJE to Price.
[146] MP 6 July 1882 AJE to Ada Murray; SL 13 July 1882 Price to Liddell.

Price managed to assemble seven Delegates for the meeting on 19 July. They agreed to advance Murray £100 on account of Part I of the Dictionary, by way of relieving the immediate financial crisis; but the matter evidently required further discussion. Murray was summoned to another meeting 'to confer [...] as to the most economical and expeditious mode of passing the Dictionary through the press, and to consider the position of the Editor, the cost of corrections, and the arrangements for future progress generally'. On 26 July Murray met a still rather small gathering of Delegates, who questioned him as to the project's expenses; they authorized him to draw another £200 'in respect of Part I', but concluded that the whole matter of his remuneration needed serious consideration, at a full meeting of the Delegates early in Michaelmas term. They also refused to be party to any public appeal, and 'strongly object[ed]' to the appeal as drafted.[147] Ellis, satisfied that serious consideration was now to be given to financial matters, called an end to his action, crediting Gibbs with having been mainly responsible, through his interview with Liddell, for bringing about such a positive outcome (though the length and distinction of the list of supporters and subscribers which he had supplied to Price must surely also have played some part).[148]

Amid all this drama editorial work on the Dictionary was pushing on. Progress through the alphabet had to be maintained; compositors had to be supplied with copy; there were proofs and revises to read and correct; but now it was essential to start making up pages, so that they could be 'plated', i.e. electroplates could be made of the complete pages of type, which could then be redistributed for re-use. Even at this late stage, however, new material was still turning up which had to be incorporated. The rare word *aa*, denoting a stream or watercourse, was spotted in July by Charles Doble in a newly published volume on the muniments of Magdalen College; this necessitated the creation of a new entry on page 4 of the Dictionary, running to five lines of text. Fortunately Erlebach was already proving to be an excellent replacement for Herrtage, to the extent that in August he was entrusted with the running of the Scriptorium when Murray and his family took a short holiday in Keswick.[149] Perhaps this was just as well, for it seems that around this time Fred Ruthven gave notice that he also wished to leave. Murray had known for some time that he wished to leave, apparently because of his wife's illness, but the blow when it came was no less keenly felt for being long anticipated. By early October a replacement had been found in the form of an assistant named John Mitchell, the son of an old Hawick acquaintance, who fortunately turned out to be capable of far more than clerical assistance.[150]

---

[147] OD 19, 26 July 1882. Murray was also asked to supply a statement of his expenses over the last three years, and an estimate of what they were likely to be in future (OED/B/3/1/5 31 July 1882 JAHM to Price).

[148] MP 1 Aug. 1882 AJE to JAHM.

[149] SL 14 July 1882 Doble to JAHM; OED/B/3/1/5 31 July 1882 JAHM to Price. Erlebach was a real asset to the project: Harold Murray mentions his 'great natural gifts in sematology', but also 'his capacity for solid work, and above all the sunniness of his disposition' (HJRM p. 160).

[150] *CWW* p. 218; OED/B/3/1/5 8 Nov. 1882 JAHM to Price. Fred Ruthven seems to have left the Scriptorium in November or December; the Ruthvens subsequently emigrated to Australia, where they continued to read for the Dictionary.

Now reassembled for Michaelmas term, the Delegates appointed the promised committee to consider Murray's remuneration. This comprised Liddell, Max Müller, and Mark Pattison—the same triumvirate which had been appointed three and a half years earlier 'to confer [...] on literary questions' (although precious little use had been made of them)—plus the mathematician H. J. S. Smith. Their terms of reference were evidently broader than merely financial, for they immediately found themselves considering, not the question of payment, but the disagreement between Furnivall and Murray regarding the treatment of derivatives. Price, having pointed out to Furnivall that neither the Delegates nor the Philological Society had any authority to interfere with Murray's editorial work in this way, nevertheless consulted one or two Delegates, including Pattison, who seems to have shared Furnivall's view that the treatment of derivatives should not be scamped. It would appear that in the specific case of *abider* Furnivall was able to get his way, as the published entry is divided into three senses, but the general point was evidently not pressed: the entry for the noun *absolver*, for example, has a single definition, followed by a single paragraph of quotations illustrating meanings corresponding to several of the subsenses into which the parent verb has been subdivided. Furnivall, at any rate, was mollified, although it was only four months later that he formally withdrew his protest.[151]

Furnivall soon had something to say on the subject of finances as well. A week after the Delegates had appointed their new committee, Murray briefed the Philological Society's Council on his financial position. This galvanized Furnivall into action. Having failed to persuade Gibbs to tackle his Oxford contacts, he wrote to Price himself, in typically forthright terms:

You may judge of my surprise when Dr Murray told us at the Philolog. Soc. Council on Friday night that the present situation was this: Received from Oxford since last Nov^r [actually December] £200. Spent £500. Borrowd £200. All savings gone. Fresh Assistant obliged to be engaged, to push the work on. More money to be borrowd to pay him. Will not you ask the Delegates for some prompt help for Dr M. He's working till 1 every morning. Won't the Delegates give him £2 a page, & let him draw the money as each 50 pages is returnd for press?

He was also trying to find twenty-five subscribers to put up £10 a year each, to supplement Murray's income; and, more dramatically, he had written to Gladstone, now once again Prime Minister, asking whether Murray could be given a Civil List pension of £250.[152]

Here, once again, was Furnivall's 'well-meaning indiscretion', as Murray described it in a pained letter to Price, explaining that there had been another misunderstanding. It was true that he did not expect the £300 approved by the Delegates would be sufficient for the expenses of completing Part I—he had just drawn a second £100, and would shortly be applying for the remaining £100—and that he was therefore

---

[151] OD 27 Oct. 1882; SL 28 July, 5 Aug. 1882 Price to FJF, 8 Aug. 1882 Price to Doble; OD 16 Feb. 1883.
[152] MP 5 Nov. 1882 HHG to FJF; OED/B/3/1/5 6 Nov. 1882 FJF to Price.

anticipating having to borrow more from Gibbs; but he did not see it as appropriate to approach the Press for further funds until Part I was out. Perhaps this was further evidence of Murray's timidity, or naïvety, in money matters; but he was conscious that in voting him £300 the Delegates had already gone beyond what his contract entitled him to. His creditors were not pressing him for repayment; what mattered now was getting Part I ready, and how he did so was up to him.[153] He asked Price not to trouble the Delegates with Furnivall's letter. In fact Price had already sent Furnivall a chilly response, pointing out that funds authorized by the Delegates were still available on application by Murray, and recommending that he suspend his action. He also sent Murray the final £100, with a note confirming that he now intended to let the financial question rest until Part I was ready for publication.[154]

Something like 170 pages of the Dictionary were now in type. Proofs were being read regularly by Gibbs, who had now been joined in the task by Fitzedward Hall, and also by James Platt, another remarkable amateur linguist, who had recently joined the Philological Society, and who had already impressed Murray with his knowledge of Old English.[155] Proofs were also sent to others as the need arose. In late November, for example, Murray encountered the problem of compounds in its most intractable form yet, with the hundreds of formations beginning with *after-*. Even in their most condensed form—a list of very briefly defined lemmas in a single paragraph of text, followed by an alphabetically arranged block of quotations—the 'special combinations' of *after-* took up nearly two columns; and it was difficult for a reader to find the quotation evidence for a given compound in the long block of small type. He sent the proofs to Alexander Ellis, in the hope that he could find a way of shortening the material; Ellis could offer nothing in this regard, but he did suggest a way of improving readability, namely by placing an asterisk against the lemma in each quotation. This was a small presentational innovation, which of course could not be applied retrospectively—dozens of pages had now been 'plated'—but it was adopted for *after-*; Murray thereafter made use of it increasingly, initially only in the largest blocks of compounds, but eventually as a matter of course in all but the smallest compound blocks. In small ways the form of the Dictionary was continuing to evolve.[156]

1882 came to a close with an unexpected indication of support for the Dictionary, in the form of a letter to Furnivall from Downing Street. His quixotic appeal to Gladstone for a Civil List pension was now receiving careful consideration, and enquiries were being made into Murray's work. Ellis, prompted by a delighted Furnivall, wrote to two influential friends, Trench and Prince Louis-Lucien Bonaparte, to solicit their support,

---

[153] OED/B/3/1/5 8 Nov. 1882 JAHM to Price.

[154] MP 7 Nov. 1882 Price to FJF; 11 Nov. 1882 Price to JAHM.

[155] Platt read two papers on Old English topics at a Society meeting on 2 December 1881, at which Murray was present; the two men entered into correspondence soon afterwards, and after another paper of Platt's the following November Murray acknowledged the help of this 'rizing yung scholar' in respect of the Old English component of the Dictionary (ProcPS 17 Nov. 1882, p. ii).

[156] MP 24, 27 Nov. 1882 AJE to JAHM.

as well as writing to Gladstone himself. The results were encouraging: on 30 December Ellis sent Murray copies of both the Prince's enthusiastic encomium and Gladstone's positive (if non-committal) reply.[157] Trench also wrote in support. Murray, as usual, was extremely anxious to avoid giving the Delegates any cause for offence; so, aware as he was that the question of his remuneration was nominally under consideration in Oxford, he wrote to Gladstone suggesting that it would be as well to postpone further consideration of the matter until the publication of Part I. However, the prospect of state subsidy must surely have been heartening.[158]

At the Philological Society's January Dictionary Evening there was at last real progress to report.[159] The project was of course terribly behind schedule—the first Part of the Dictionary had been advertised for 1882—but at least publication was now within sight: 176 pages, exactly half of the expected size of Part I, were now ready for press. The printers had reached *alert*; the completed text reached as far as *age*, and dealt with 4,100 words, as compared to 2,023 in the same range of Webster. The main words had been subclassified and counted, as being obsolete (about a third of the total), 'aboriginal English' (only 187), formations on foreign roots, fully naturalized loanwords, and 'denizens' (incompletely naturalized foreign words, marked with the 'tramlines' symbol (‖): an infinitely expandable category, of which 153 had been included). The 'able quiet work' of the thirty active sub-editors was acknowledged, and the proofreading of Gibbs, Hall, and Platt; a year after the end of the main reading programme, quotations were still being sent in by about 100 readers, many of whom were mentioned, as well as several scholars whose help in particular fields would be recognized again and again on future occasions: Lucy Toulmin Smith for research into particular words in the British Museum, Paul Meyer and Gaston Paris for help with French etymologies, Skeat of course, James Britten in botany, Henry Watts and Henry Roscoe in chemistry, Frederick Pollock in law, and Russell Martineau for unspecified assistance. Even Murray's wife was credited with the contribution of the earliest known example of *aged* in the sense 'of a specified age', from a transcript of a memorial brass of 1637 in Cornelius Nicholson's *Annals of Kendal* (1861).[160] A new assistant, however, was needed to join the existing editorial team of Erlebach and Mitchell (and the indefatigable Ellen Skipper, still hard at work sorting the incoming slips into order[161]). 'Another Mr. Erlebach', Murray observed, 'would be an enormous help to the Dictionary.'

---

[157] MP 19 Dec. 1882 Horace Seymour (Gladstone's secretary) to FJF; 30 Dec. 1882 AJE to JAHM. Prince Louis-Lucien, nephew of Napoleon, was a distinguished linguist, with a particular interest in Basque; he had known Murray since being introduced to him by Ellis in 1870, and the three men had worked together on the classification of English dialects.

[158] MP 8 Jan. 1883 AJE to JAHM (enclosing a copy of 5 Jan. 1883 Gladstone to Trench), 20 Jan. 1883 Horace Seymour to JAHM.

[159] ProcPS 19 Jan. 1883, pp. iii–vi.

[160] The quotation appears to have been taken from the published transcript, and not, as stated in ProcPS, directly from the brass itself.

[161] The sorting done by Murray's children (on which see p. 262 below) is not mentioned.

Notwithstanding the need for another assistant, at least the text of the Dictionary was beginning to materialize. Less positively, it was around this time that the negotiations with Harpers finally collapsed. Price immediately began negotiations with Macmillan, who were also in a position to sell the Dictionary in America; these were ultimately successful.[162] He was also keen to secure a German agent for the Dictionary, but the terms demanded by T. O. Weigel of Leipzig proved unacceptable.[163]

Even as Murray and his assistants were pressing on towards the end of Part I, he was still preoccupied with the uncertain future. In March, trying to carry on with editorial work in spite of a bout of influenza, he wrote to Furnivall about his worries, which related both to finance (he had just borrowed another £100 from Gibbs, and needed more) and the inadequate rate of progress (a new assistant, James Johnston, had been engaged, but had not yet started work).[164] Furnivall, full of enthusiasm and sympathy as ever, urged Murray to 'get right away for a week's *walk* at Easter on the South Downs or in Derbyshire; & then things 'll look cheerier'; he offered to send on Murray's letter to Gladstone, copying it to Price (Murray seems to have managed to dissuade him from this); and he also wrote to Gibbs about the situation. His ideas for solving the problem were nothing if not radical: he suggested that Gibbs should try to persuade the Clarendon Press to raise the rate of pay to '3 or 4 guineas a page', but also that he should put forward to them the idea that the Dictionary should be 'done in quarters, they [the Delegates] finding Ed[ito]rs, with your advice, for the last 3 quarters—say, Erlebach, Smythe Palmer, Davies, or such of the best subeds. as you name.'[165]

Gibbs decided that it was time to act. He arranged for a third loan of £100 to Murray, and reassured him: 'I mean to see you through Part 1, so you may be easy as to paying your way till you have it out with Oxford.'[166] Then, armed with figures supplied by Murray as to the actual costs of Part I, and his loss of income since taking up the editorship, he approached Liddell, and then Price. There was no mention of the idea

[162] SL 30 Jan. 1883 Price to Harper & Brothers; 31 Jan. 1883 Price to F. Macmillan; 27 Dec. 1883 Price to H. Frowde (in regard to the delivery of 2,000 copies of Part I of the Dictionary with Macmillan's imprint).

[163] SL 7 Aug. 1883–13 Feb. 1884 (*passim*) Price to T. O. Weigel. Nicholas Trübner, the Philological Society's publisher, also applied unsuccessfully to be the Press's Continental agent, apparently citing an old agreement with Furnivall and Herbert Coleridge (SL 16 Jan. 1884 Price to Frowde, 17 Jan. 1884 Price to N. Trübner). A discount arrangement for sales to Germany was subsequently made with Alfred Asher and Company, but this was abandoned after only a few months because of insufficient volume of trade (SL 19 Jan., 13 Feb., 12 June 1884 Price to Asher & Co).

[164] MP 1, 14 Mar. 1883 HHG to JAHM.

[165] MP 9 Mar. 1883 FJF to JAHM. The third and fourth suggested editors had both recently published books which drew attention to their philological endeavours. T. Lewis O. Davies's *Supplementary English Glossary* (1881) was a collection of words and meanings not to be found in four standard dictionaries, very much along the lines of the Philological Society's original 1857 plan; Furnivall had written to Murray about 'that Mr Davies, of Southampton' over five years earlier (MP 24 Oct. 1877 FJF to JAHM), and once Davies became aware of the revival of the Philological Society's project, he readily placed his collected quotations at Murray's disposal. Smythe Palmer was already a well-known writer about language in the popular manner of Trench, whose work he greatly admired (he was later the editor of new editions of several of Trench's works); his latest book was *Folk-Etymology* (1882), a useful collection of 'verbal corruptions'.

[166] MP 13, 14 Mar. 1883 HHG to JAHM.

of dividing the editorship; instead, he seems to have put forward once again the idea of a subscription. Price's response was, as usual, non-committal: the matter would be put to the Delegates, but no new scheme could be implemented until the publication of Part I, which Murray had given him to understand might be ready in October.[167]

However, discussion soon began of another idea (which had of course been mooted long before by Furnivall): that of moving the whole project to Oxford. The benefits of such a move were obvious: progress was bound to improve if Murray was to spend his whole time working at the Dictionary, rather than fitting it in around his school commitments; it would also help enormously if a larger body of good sub-editors could be assembled, and these ought to be findable in Oxford, which had already supplied two of the better ones (C. B. Mount and T. H. Sheppard). The idea of moving the project to a place where a closer watch could be kept on progress must also have appealed to the Press.

Gibbs was soon discussing the idea of a move with Price, apparently initially at a meeting which Price had arranged so that the two men could consider the question of a prospectus for the Dictionary. The issue of money came up, of course; Gibbs wished to ensure that any move to Oxford should be on terms which would see Murray better settled financially, and he pressed Price on the subject of whether there was a suitable post in the University. Price gave him to understand that there were reasonable prospects of a place being found soon; indeed the new Merton Professorship of English Language and Literature, created by statute only the previous year, was mentioned (Price was soon having to dissuade Gibbs from lobbying one of the electors, Edward Bond of the British Museum, until nearer the time of the election).[168]

But at this juncture a new figure begins to intrude. A few months later Murray complained to Ingram Bywater, a classicist and Delegate who had become a regular consultant on questions of Greek etymology, that 'the greatest mischief in the world is wrought by your well-meaning people, who are so conscious of their own rectitude that it is impossible to make them see that they may be all wrong.'[169] The subject of the complaint was not, as might be supposed, Furnivall, but the University's new Vice-Chancellor, Benjamin Jowett (see Figure 11), of whom the *Times* had commented more positively at the time of his appointment: 'Nothing is too great for his energy, nothing is too small for his attention.'[170] As *ex officio* chairman of the Delegates since October he had already heard a great deal about the Dictionary; he had, for example, been in the chair in October when the committee to consider Murray's remuneration was appointed. However, his formidable energies were initially directed elsewhere

---

[167] MP 14, 21 Mar. 1883 HHG to JAHM; SL 21 Mar. 1883 Price to HHG.

[168] SL 21 Mar., 24 Apr. 1883 Price to HHG. In the event the Merton chair was not advertised until 1885, due to the time required for Merton College to secure funding for it; the post went to the philologist A. S. Napier (Martin and Highfield 1997: 299).

[169] Reported in GL MS 11021/21 ff. 513–17 8 Nov. 1883 JAHM to HHG. Bywater had been commenting on particular Greek etymologies at least since 1881 (SL 4 Aug. 1881 Doble to Bywater).

[170] *Times* 10 Oct. 1882, p. 9.

THE ROAD TO *ANT*: 1879–1884   155

rime

Spelling reform had long been a matter of interest to many of those involved in the Dictionary, including many members of the Philological Society, which in 1881 went so far as to issue a pamphlet of 'Partial Corections [*sic*] of English Spelling' which had been 'aproovd of' by the Society (MacMahon 1985: 107). Murray had been much involved in the Society's discussions of the subject, and his own enthusiasm for the cause of reform during the early years of his Editorship of the Dictionary led him to take a markedly prescriptive approach in selecting which spelling of certain words to use. Among the headwords in A for which Murray seems to have opted for the more 'logical' spelling over the more widely used one are *aline* (for *align*) and *ax* (for *axe*). In his Preface to Volume I of the Dictionary several years later he described spellings such as *ax*, *connexion*, and *rime* (p. x) as 'intrinsically the best'. The choice of particular spellings—both in headwords and in other editorial text—effectively committed the Dictionary, at least in theory, to using these spellings throughout the text; and some of Murray's decisions made for difficulties decades later.

His preference for *rime* over *rhyme* was to be particularly problematic. The spelling *rhyme* had long been established as standard—to the extent of being given by dictionaries as the headword form—but at some point during the preparation of Part I of the *OED* Murray decided, no doubt for reasons similar to those which the Philological Society had given for recommending it in 1881, that *rime* should be used. Thus, for example, in the etymology of the entry for the word *amound*, a rare synonym of *amount*, it is suggested that the form of the word may have been chosen 'for rime'. The decision ran counter to his own natural inclination, as *rhyme* was his own usual spelling, and he had to school himself to use *rime* instead: even as late as the entry for the adverb *ay*, the printer's copy for the etymology shows that, in writing the word which was eventually printed as 'rimes', he began to write 'rhymes' but corrected himself in the act of writing. Furthermore, in implementing the change in those entries which had been written prior to the decision, he and his assistants failed to spot every instance. Thus the published entries for *abysm* and *anathem* contain the uncorrected forms 'rhyming' and 'rhymes' respectively; a few instances of the more familiar spelling can even be found in Part II (e.g. in the entries for the verbs *astone* and *astony*). Thereafter, however, *rime* was consistently used in editorial text; and this placed William Craigie in an awkward position when he began to edit the relevant portion of the letter R nearly thirty years later. He came to the quite reasonable conclusion that the form of the word used in the headwords of the relevant entries—and also in the definitions and other editorial text—should be *rhyme* (and *rhymed* and so on), these being the spellings overwhelmingly favoured in contemporary usage; but Murray was insistent that *rime* should be used. After some vigorous argument (discussed in Mugglestone 2005: 171–2) a rather awkward compromise was reached: there were to be two separate sequences of entries, one to deal with the *rhyme*-spellings and the other the *rime*-forms—but, in order to be consistent with the rest of the Dictionary, the definitions and other editorial text used the latter. The text remained in this unsatisfactory state—with

Continued ➤

some headwords given a spelling at variance with their definitions (*rhymeful* 'abounding in rimes', *rhymer* 'one who makes rimes or verses', and the like)—until the entries were revised for the third edition of the Dictionary just over a century later.

It seems that not all spellings were as rigorously policed as that of *rime*. While Murray was consistent in his preference for *ax* over *axe*, his fellow Editors did not always follow suit: thus Bradley and Onions used 'axe' or 'battle-axe' in various definitions (e.g. in their entries for *fleur-de-lis, gisarme, sagaris, stybill,* and *wifle*). The spellings *aline* and *alinement* were soon almost entirely abandoned: Murray himself—after having stated in his entry for '*Aline, align*' that there was 'no good reason for retaining the unetymological *g*' in the word, and similarly declared *alinement* to be preferable to *alignment* in that the latter was 'a bad spelling of the Fr[ench word]'—went on to use (or, perhaps, fail to correct the use of) 'alignment' in two definitions at *dress* (verb) and another at *pivot*, although he did very occasionally retain his 'preferred' spelling (as in the mentions of 'alinement' and 'alining' in the entries for *track* v.[1] and *tram* v.[2] respectively). The other Editors consistently used the spelling *align-*: first Bradley at *line* and *lining*, and later Craigie (rather more emphatically) in both the headword form and the definition of the word *realignment*. Onions, commenting many years later on his having never used *aline* or *alinement*, noted it as 'one of the unfortunate examples of Murray's spelling-reforming craze (which he got out of, and of course should never have indulged in in a historical dictionary [...])' (SOED/1952/24 7 Nov. 1952 CTO to DMD).

within the university, and it was only in April 1883 that he turned his attention to the Dictionary. The October committee had so far put forward no proposals; their deliberations would not have been helped by the death of H. J. S. Smith in February. In April the Delegates appointed a new committee, this time comprising Liddell, Max Müller, Bywater, the lawyer William Markby, and Jowett himself, with the considerably broader remit of 'consider[ing] the execution of the Dictionary and the arrangements with Dr Murray'. Jowett, clearly alarmed at a project whose costs now seemed likely to exceed £20,000, demanded to see the Press's accounts, and 32 pages of Dictionary proofs were sent to members of the new committee (Price also sent copies to Pattison, the one member of the October committee who had been left off the new one).[171]

Whether or not it was Jowett who galvanized the new committee into action, it certainly lost no time. On 4 May Price informed Gibbs that the Delegates had 'come to the conclusion that some new arrangement must be made with Dr Murray', and that they wished Price to consult Gibbs before communicating with Murray.[172] At their meeting the following week Gibbs learned that the idea of moving to Oxford was now to be seriously considered; he worked with Price to produce figures for the likely impact of a move on costs and productivity. Gibbs thought that on the whole a move was likely to improve things—after all, at Mill Hill 'great part of [Murray's] time must

---

[171] OD 20 Apr. 1883; SL 3 May 1883 Price to Pattison, Price to Liddell. The figure of '£20,000 or more' appears in notes made by Jowett shortly after the Delegates' meeting on 20 April (JP I. H57 f. 53v).
[172] SL 4 May 1883 Price to HHG.

FIGURE 11   Benjamin Jowett (engraving, after the 1871 portrait by D. F. Laugée).

be given to Priscian and the ferule'—but he was still doubtful that the improvement would be such as to allow Murray to get through the Delegates' target figure of 700 pages a year, even with the help of another assistant (in addition to James Johnston, who had now joined the team in the Scriptorium). After their meeting Gibbs realized that they had in fact underestimated the editorial costs significantly; but his revised figures did not reach Price in time for the Delegates' meeting on 11 May, at which it was agreed to offer Murray £1 per page returned for press, plus '£300 a year on condition of his residing at Oxford'. Even if Murray achieved the ambitious figure of 700 pages a year, this would still fall well short of the figure of £1,250 which Gibbs had estimated as necessary to pay for assistants' salaries and other expenses (now estimated at £600) and to recompense Murray for the loss of income resulting from his completely giving up his teaching position at Mill Hill.[173]

---

[173] OED/B/3/1/6 10 May 1883 HHG to Price; OD 11 May 1883. Gibbs's letter notes that even payment of 25s. per page would not be enough; 27s. would just do it.

On 30 May Price met Murray in London to discuss what might be achieved by a move to Oxford. Murray was evidently reluctant to give a firm undertaking on the matter without careful thought, as at the Delegates' meeting two days later Price was unable to present any definite proposals (although the Delegates did agree to advance Murray another £100). Murray was at pains to make clear that he personally found the idea attractive; but he was apprehensive that the Delegates might have inflated expectations of the difference such a move would make. Freedom from teaching responsibilities would increase the time he could devote to the work, but not by much: his school work now occupied him for twenty hours a week, whereas his weekly workload for the Dictionary was something like fifty-seven hours. As he explained in a detailed letter to Price: 'I have of late been straining every nerve to get Pt. I ready; whether I could work permanently 13 hours a day, I do not know; it has not injured me in any way yet.' His assistants were also working flat out to transform the work now being sent in by sub-editors into copy, to be completed and finalized by Murray; any additional assistants taken on in Oxford would require a good deal of training before they could be of much service. And then there was the question of money. Quite apart from the cost of renting a house in Oxford (as opposed to his free use of one in Mill Hill), a move to Oxford would mean giving up a salary of £350, income from various other sources (private pupils, lectures, examining), not to mention being able to educate his three sons at Mill Hill for a nominal amount. Accordingly, Murray could not see his way to coming to Oxford for less than £750 a year. On top of this there was the cost of assistants, which in fact was almost certain to rise in any case: Alfred Erlebach, his best assistant, who it seems had taken on Dictionary work while recovering from the illness which had forced him to resign his teaching post, was now fully recovered, and therefore able to consider alternative employment which would pay rather better than the £150 a year which Murray currently paid him. The loss of Erlebach would be for Murray 'a calamity of the first magnitude'; and he was sure that he could only be retained with a salary of £250.[174]

However, having set out the terms on which he might be prepared to come to Oxford, Murray perhaps unwisely observed that his obligations at Mill Hill made it almost impossible for him to do so before the spring of 1884. Accordingly, at their next meeting the Delegates resolved to postpone further consideration of future arrangements until Part I was out.[175] Somewhat taken aback, Gibbs and Murray both wrote again to reiterate Murray's continuing financial difficulty, notwithstanding the

---

[174] MP notes by Ada Murray (apparently for use by JAHM at his meeting on 30 May 1883); 7 June 1883 J. Legge to JAHM; OED/B/3/1/6 9 June JAHM to Price. Murray did in fact increase Erlebach's salary to £250 in the summer of 1883 (MP 17 Jan. 1884 JAHM to Price (copy)).

[175] OD 15 June 1883. Strangely, although Price informed Gibbs of the Delegates' decision straight away—and arranged to meet him in London to discuss it (SL 18 June Price to HHG)—it was another two weeks before he wrote to Murray (MP 29 June 1883 Price to JAHM).

latest £100 advance; but the long vacation had begun, and the few Delegates who assembled on 7 July felt that the matter would have to wait.[176]

The end of lexicographical work on Part I was now tantalizingly close. On 18 May Murray reported to the Philological Society that the text was finalized as far as *alternate*, with proofs reaching into *an-*; he predicted that July would see the completion of Part I (at this stage expected to extend to *ap-*), although the Press seemed likely to wish to postpone publication until October. On 1 June the Delegates gave approval for 5,000 copies to be 'put to press'.[177] But another important task was now engaging Murray's attention: the drafting of a prospectus for the Dictionary. In May Doble supplied

---

alamite

Surely one of the more surprising ways in which the Dictionary's inclusive aspirations are manifested is the fact that it includes entries for some words despite the fact that their meaning is entirely unknown. One of the first such words is *alamite*, for which Murray had only a single fifteenth-century quotation, from the will of the Nottinghamshire worthy Sir Thomas Chaworth. The will refers to cushions made of 'tappisserwerk [i.e. tapestry] with alamitez'. If this last word was to be included in the Dictionary, what could Murray do to find out the meaning? Henry Hucks Gibbs, commenting on a range of proofs including the draft entry for this word, recommended that he should 'abandon to future investigators' all such rare and obscure words, 'which now tire your brain and use up valuable time'—and, he might have added, space (MP 14 Mar. 1883 HHG to JAHM). In the end Murray decided to include an entry for the headword *alamite*, with its solitary quotation—and nothing else: no etymology, and not even the most speculative definition. Other such entries followed, including *aquile*, *battleage*, *capoche*, and many more. (In later entries it became more usual to be explicit, with a note such as 'Of uncertain etymology and meaning'.) Some of these words are well-known cruxes in the interpretation of Shakespeare and other writers; in other cases the original source is little-known. Subsequent research has sometimes cast light on the meaning, and a few of the entries in the revised *OED* now give a (sometimes tentative) definition: for the word *muggle*, for example, attested in early seventeenth-century works by Thomas Middleton and Thomas Young, and included in the first edition of *OED* with the note 'Origin and meaning obscure', the meaning 'young woman' or 'sweetheart' is now offered as most likely, with a possible derivation from Italian *moglie*. (This is not to be confused with the (apparently) etymologically distinct earlier word *muggle* 'a tail', nor with the two other homonyms which now appear alongside these two in *OED3*, one meaning 'marijuana' and the other 'a person who possesses no magical powers', the latter being a celebrated coinage of the author J. K. Rowling.)

---

[176] OD 7 July 1883; SL 16 July 1883 Price to HHG.
[177] ProcPS 18 May 1883, p. xvii; OD 1 June 1883.

Murray with a 'skeleton Prospectus', providing a framework into which he could insert the detailed information which he alone could provide. On 15 June the draft reached Oxford; but Price's wish that the text should be finalized before the Long Vacation proved hopelessly optimistic. In fact with the preparation of the Prospectus a new, and almost disastrous, chapter opened in the saga of Murray's troubled relations with his publishers.[178]

Price was soon soliciting comments on Murray's draft text. He sent a proof to Macmillan, who approved of it, and asked to have 'at least 10,000 copies [...] for distribution in America' when it was ready; he also consulted several Delegates.[179] Long Vacation notwithstanding, the Delegates of the April committee met on 25 July to consider a revised text, and Murray was asked to attend another special meeting six days later. His invitation to Oxford this time came from Jowett himself, together with an offer of dinner and accommodation at Balliol College; Price urged him to accept, commenting that Jowett 'takes a great deal of interest in the Dictionary, has many views about it and would like to become personally acquainted with the Author.'[180]

Some, but far from all, of Jowett's 'many views' no doubt became apparent to Murray during his visit to Oxford. A revised version of the Prospectus was discussed at the meeting on 31 July; the minutes record that Murray 'undertook to consider the Delegates' alterations in the Prospectus, and any suggestions for the editing and preparation for press of the subsequent parts of the Dictionary which they might submit to him.'[181] What they do not mention is that these 'suggestions' had been under consideration by the Delegates for some time, as a result of the April committee's scrutiny of the Dictionary proofs. Within a week of receiving these, the committee compiled a list of trenchant criticisms of the Dictionary, which was presented to the Delegates on 11 May. A revised version, now headed 'Rules to be followed in preparing for the Press the copy of subsequent Parts of the English Dictionary', was considered at the meeting on 25 July; and this was subsequently redrafted as 'Suggestions for guidance in preparing copy for the Press'.[182] It was not until mid-August that the final version of this incendiary document was printed and sent to Murray. In the meantime he was to receive unwelcome reminders of the scrutiny to which his work was being subjected, and the desire of Jowett and his colleagues to intervene in it. Among the very last corrections to the text of Part I—which finally went to press on 10 August—were several arising from comments by 'a Delegate' (actually Liddell) who had been looking through the proofs. Murray's mood will not have been improved by the arrival of a revised draft of the Prospectus, much altered by the various members of the Delegates'

---

[178] MP 28 Apr., 22 May, 7, 15 June 1883 Price to JAHM. Doble's 'skeleton Prospectus' is preserved in MP.

[179] BL Add MS 55416 12 July 1882 F. Macmillan to Price; SL 3 July 1883 Doble to Bywater, 16 July 1883 Price to Max Müller, 16 July 1883 Price to Liddell. Macmillan had ceased to be the Press's London publisher in 1880, but continued to act as its agent in America.

[180] MP 28 July 1883 Price to JAHM.

[181] OD 31 July 1883.

[182] Copies of the committee's report of 10 May and of the draft 'Rules to be followed' are preserved in OUPA (Markby papers, box C/2); several copies of the 'Suggestions' also survive in OUPA.

committee, and by no means to his liking. (He promptly submitted a list of objections to Doble, and persuaded Gibbs to take up some other details with Liddell.)[183]

But his dissatisfaction with the Prospectus was as nothing to his reaction to the 'Suggestions'. On Jowett's instruction, these were formally communicated to him by Price, even though he was now on holiday in Dinan (with Doble deputizing for him, and keeping him informed by daily letters). Jowett also wrote personally to Murray, enclosing some proofs annotated by Liddell together with his own lengthy comments. That Price and his deputy were apprehensive about the likely reaction of their Editor is evident from their correspondence: '[Liddell and Jowett] appear to wish to have [the Suggestions] communicated to Dr. Murray,' wrote Doble to Price on 14 August; 'and I suppose I may do so if the V[ice] C[hancellor] gives me final instruction to that effect. His own remarks are very sweeping.' In fact Jowett was prepared, not merely to advise Murray about his future editing, but even to discard some of the work already done, as not being in accordance with his own conception of the Dictionary: he discussed the idea of printing without page numbers, 'so that there might be no difficulty on the score of pagination if at any time it were thought desirable to cancel portions of Part I'. The idea was abandoned when Doble explained that printing, with page numbers, had already (just) begun.[184]

While Jowett was plainly the driving force behind the issuing of the Suggestions, it should be stressed that they are not simply a distillation of his views. The Vice-Chancellor had worked closely with Dean Liddell, who shared his concern about the scale of the Dictionary, and who assured Gibbs that all the Delegates were of the same view, in a letter in which he made clear his own particular aversion to technical terminology:

in a few columns, I find Abdicative—Abdition—Abequitate—Ablactate—Ablacted—Ablastemic—Ablastous—Abone—Abrodieletical.—words wh[ich] I should hope would never establish themselves. These *merely* technical words, if introduced at all, should be greatly abridged. [...] The chief object of the Dictionary is surely literary; & though it may be thought expedient to comprehend technical words, these ought to be reduced to a minimum of space, I think.[185]

The desire to reduce scale underlay several of the Suggestions, but the methods proposed suggested a mixture of ignorance about the practicalities of editing and

---

[183] SL 9 Aug. 1883 Doble to JAHM, 11 Aug. 1883 Doble to Liddell, Doble to Price, 13 Aug. 1883 Doble to JAHM, 17 Aug. 1883 Doble to JAHM; MP 23 Aug. 1883 Liddell to HHG. Doble explained to Murray that many of the changes had been made in the light of the Delegates' desire 'that the claims of the Dictionary should be under-, rather than over-stated, and that something more than full justice should be done to [Murray's] predecessors'.

[184] SL 18 Aug. 1883 Price to JAHM; 14, 15 Aug. 1883 Doble to Price. Compare also SL 18 Aug. 1883 Price to Doble: 'I have written to Dr Murray directly from this place [i.e. Dinan], and enclosed to him a copy of the suggestions [...]. I shall be surprised if there is not a considerable amount of unfavourable comment and of objection from the Philological Society.' Four pages of the proofs annotated by Liddell (and counter-annotated by Murray) are preserved in MP.

[185] MP 23 Aug. 1883 Liddell to HHG.

misunderstanding of the Dictionary's methodology. The recommendation to use no quotations dating from later than 1875, for example, might seem reasonable, until one realized that such a quotation was often the only available evidence that a word was still in use, so that a special hunt would have to be made for a slightly earlier quotation; while the suggestion that in order to illustrate a common word or sense it would be sufficient to give one or two of the earliest examples and then state that its use 'continues to the present day' constituted a rejection of the entire principle of illustrating, rather than commenting on usage. Some Suggestions, while evidently aimed at 'improving' the Dictionary, could only be complied with by spending even longer over the work; interestingly, this was Murray's main objection to the idea that quotations for 'modern literary words' should be taken from 'great writers' rather than newspapers wherever possible. As he commented to Gibbs, 'much of our time is actually spent in endeavouring to get *famous quotations* instead of those we have. Nearly all the "famous quotations" in the Dicty. have been specially hunted for by me & my assistants.'[186] The recommendation that scientific terminology and slang need only be included if it was known to occur 'in literature' was of course problematic in the absence of a definition of 'literature'. Alexander Ellis, commenting on a copy of the Suggestions sent to him by Murray, declared simply: 'The writers of this did not at all understand the dictionary.'[187]

Murray was similarly forthright, in a commentary on the Suggestions which he sent to Gibbs, apparently with a view to forwarding it to the Delegates. Gibbs, however, alarmed by the document's furious tone ('gratuitous impertinence [...] Absurd [...] suicidal'), offered instead a much more diplomatically worded letter of his own: 'Will the enclosed be of any use to you? It is mainly your "thunder" but it contains my own opinion exactly. [...] You may want to send [your version] in—yet some of the expressions are *too strong*.'[188] Gibbs's letter is a model of tact, acknowledging 'the very laudable and desirable' time- and money-saving aims of the Suggestions, and attributing to the Delegates 'no other wish than to make the work as perfect as possible', while 'deprecat[ing]' some of them for reasons similar to Murray's (but more gently, and with more by way of explanation). Murray had in fact already written to Jowett— in terms notably more deferential and less bad-tempered than his draft commentary— focusing principally on suggestions for cutting material, and acknowledging that he was now finding it necessary to strive for greater conciseness than he had at first in order to 'keep within "5 times Webster" [...] this unfortunately does not lessen the work or shorten the time of preparation.'[189] He apparently wrote Jowett a second letter, responding more fully to the Suggestions, in early September, during a fortnight spent in Somerset with his good friend Fred Elworthy. This was by no means a holiday, as he also sent the final sheet of Part I to press, and drafted the lengthy preliminary matter

---

[186] MP JAHM, notes (n.d. but ante 28 Aug. 1883) on the Suggestions, headed 'Comments'.
[187] MP copy of the Suggestions annotated by AJE.
[188] MP 28 Aug. 1883 HHG to JAHM; JAHM 'Comments' on the Suggestions.
[189] MP 24 Aug. 1883 JAHM to Jowett (copy).

FIGURE 12   Murray's 'circle of the English language', as printed in the 'General Explanations' of 1884.

that was to accompany it: a Preface, and a description of the Dictionary's approach eventually entitled 'General Explanations', with its famous representation of the 'circle of the English Language' (see Figure 12).[190]

Murray visited Oxford on his way back from Somerset, and passed the final pages of Part I for press. He also dropped off the copy for the preliminary matter, together with a corrected proof of the Prospectus, which Price (now back in Oxford) was now desperate to print: the disagreements over its content had led to the abandonment of the original idea of issuing it in advance, but with publication of Part I still scheduled for October, finalization of all these documents was now a matter of urgency.[191] Of course the matter of money was also still unresolved, and Murray found himself obliged to apply for a further £150 to cover the cost of his assistants' salaries. (He was now one assistant down once more: James Johnston—who had unfortunately proved incapable of producing work which could be relied upon without rechecking—had left for Edinburgh, and Murray felt it imprudent to replace him while his finances continued so uncertain. It was around this time that he borrowed a fourth £100 from

---

[190] MP JAHM notes (apparently intended for his own reference when giving an account of events to the Philological Society's Council on 25 October 1883). Among the last-minute changes to the Dictionary text was a correction of an error in the definition of the heraldic term *abased*, noted by Liddell on his proofs (MP 4 Sept. 1883 JAHM to HHG). Murray's initial drafts of the Preface and General Explanations are preserved at OED/B/5/3/1.

[191] SL 11 Aug. 1883 Price to H. Frowde. Copies of Part I were sent to London in early October so that trial could be made of different kinds of binding (FL 11 Oct. 1883 Frowde to Price). Various proofs of the Prospectus survive in MP, including several copies of the version sent to Murray in August, which he had sent to various friends for comment; Gibbs wrote '1 October' in the blank space for publication date on his copy. The imminent appearance of Part I was widely anticipated (e.g. the *Pall Mall Gazette* reported on 5 October (p. 5) that it would be published 'during the present month').

Gibbs.[192]) Jowett arranged for the necessary payment; in fact he had had the foresight to obtain an unsigned cheque for £100 from Price before the latter's departure for France, ready to be paid promptly should Murray find himself in need.[193] This generous concern for the Editor, however, was combined with an apparent readiness to consider all options, even including discharging him.[194]

Whether or not Jowett entertained any serious idea of discharging Murray, he still needed to be convinced that the work of compiling the Dictionary was being done effectively and efficiently. On 17 October, probably at the instigation of Henry Hucks Gibbs, he paid a visit to the Scriptorium. Murray's notes on the occasion suggest that he was not impressed with the Vice-Chancellor: 'showed him everything as well as his patience would allow, not very great—jumping at conclusions'.[195] In fact, as Elisabeth Murray observes, it may have been unwise to interpret the rapid thinking of someone with Jowett's remarkable intellect as impatience; but Gibbs, who accompanied Jowett on his visit, did find him to be rather less well informed about the Dictionary than he ought to have been. Both Jowett and Murray also became 'rather heated', and Gibbs found himself keeping the peace. Difficult as the meeting must have been for all parties—Murray told Gibbs that Jowett's visit had left him 'very depressed'—it did at least bring some matters into sharp focus.[196] Jowett was firmly of the opinion that the Dictionary should be completed in ten years, as stipulated in Murray's contract; he was also determined that the text could and should be 'condensed' by a less inclusive approach to scientific terminology and a more limited treatment of derivatives. These points had of course been made in the 'Suggestions', and Murray pointed out that in his most recent work he had been trying to comply with these, although inevitably at the cost of additional time. He was less willing to implement another 'Suggestion', namely that Greek and Latin etymologies should trace words no further than their immediate etymons; however, he seems to have been unable completely to counter all the criticisms of a consummate (and university-trained) classical scholar such as Jowett, who could point to errors picked up in earlier proofs by Bywater, and who apparently secured Murray's agreement that classical etymologies should henceforth be submitted to Bywater for review.[197]

Jowett, then, was determined to have the Dictionary done his way, which meant the implementation of as many of the 'Suggestions' as possible, and the enforcement of the original timescale: 'the burden of his song to the last,' as Murray lamented to Gibbs, 'was "ten years, and condensation".' He asked Murray to prepare and submit

---

[192] MP 17 Jan. 1884 JAHM to Price (copy), 26 Aug. 1884 JAHM to Jowett (draft).

[193] SL 31 July 1883 Price to Jowett.

[194] SL 28 Sept. 1883 Price to Jowett (confirming payment of the full £150 to Murray): 'I think you are quite right in making the payment to him: Discharge him if you will: but treat him liberally while you have him.' Jowett would have had an opportunity to check the terms on which Murray might be discharged when he examined his Agreement with the Delegates in August (SL 15 Aug. 1883 Doble to Price).

[195] MP JAHM notes for PS Council meeting of 25 Oct. 1883.

[196] CWW, p. 225; GL MS 11021/21 ff. 505a,e 20 Oct. 1883 JAHM to HHG.

[197] JP I. H59 p. 102.

within two days (for the upcoming Delegates' meeting) a scheme for completing the Dictionary in ten, or at a pinch twelve years, complete with cost estimates for the two different scenarios of continuing at Mill Hill and moving to Oxford. But was there any way of achieving the joint goals of 'ten years' and 'condensation'? The only options that Murray and Gibbs could suggest involved a considerable increase in costs. One possibility was to take on additional high-quality assistants, capable of working without supervision and of producing copy which needed a minimum of input from Murray; another, more radical idea was to divide the whole work between two Editors, who could work in parallel on separate parts of the text. Both options, obviously, would be expensive; but Jowett was prepared to countenance this. His notes for the Delegates' meeting set out his view of the future in unambiguous terms: Murray was to come to Oxford, and to finish the Dictionary in ten years; a second Editor was to be appointed—he jotted down the names of John Nichol, professor of English at Glasgow, and the writer and folklorist Andrew Lang (both former pupils of his)—and also perhaps a 'Council of Superintendents' to keep a watching brief. He was also evidently prepared to contemplate another unthinkable, namely the abandonment of the whole project if it could not be done on what he considered an acceptable basis.[198]

Murray can have been in no doubt as to the seriousness of the situation; but he refused to be rushed. He called a special meeting of the Philological Society's Council to discuss the 'Suggestions'—and the more general question of whether ways could be found of shortening the Dictionary which would also make for significant saving of time—and he informed Price that any scheme such as Jowett had requested would take longer than a couple of days to draw up if any estimates contained in it were to be relied on. His letter, while polite, shows signs of considerable irritation:

The time which the Dicty. is taking is a very serious trouble to *me*, as I had looked forward to many years of useful work beyond it, and I have every interest in doing everything possible to shorten the time. Since receiving the 'Suggestions' of the Delegates, I have endeavoured in my more recent work to carry out the purport of them, which I fully accept. Many of them are, in fact, the Rules of Practice by which I and my assistants have acted from the first: if we have failed in their application, it has generally been that in the time at our disposal, it has not been possible to consider every point so fully or so calmly as might be desired; or that necessity shut us up to the course we took. These Suggestions have the double aim of saving time & space, and of improving the Dictionary [...]. I hope it will not be considered presumptuous of me to point out that these two purpose[s] largely cancel each other; the Dictionary can be made better in quality only by *more* care, *more* work, *more* time; it can be accelerated in production by less attention to details, less attempt at symmetry, at ideal perfection. [...] The attempt to carry out some of the 'Suggestions' has indeed been one considerable source of delay.

---

[198] JP I. H59 p. 104. Murray apparently reported to Furnivall that Jowett had spoken to him of 'considering whether it was worth while to carry the Dicty on' (OED/B/3/1/6 23 Oct. 1883 FJF to [Price]).

The decision to consult the Council was not, however, simply a delaying tactic: more seriously, he doubted whether there was any practicable method of meeting Jowett's demands, and if he was going to say so, he was going to need backing. As he confided to Gibbs:

My own opinion, after consulting with my assistants, is that *no amount* of mere omission of *scientific terms*, or *derivatives* will make this possible: the bulk of the time and labour is expended on the actual literary words, the verbs and nouns of many senses, and difficult logical arrangement: the derivatives easily follow when their primitives are once done, & the scientific words take no considerable time, and their omission will effect no considerable saving of time.

No wonder the Vice-Chancellor's visit had left him depressed.[199]

In fact Murray had for several months been presenting entries for some of the less important words formed from scientific prefixes in a new condensed form, in which the lemmas and definitions (and some very brief etymologies) ran on continuously without line breaks, with quotations thereafter, in much the same style as had been adopted for compounds.[200] He now adopted an almost identical style for derivatives, beginning with a group derived from *archbishop* (*archbishopess, archbishophood, archbishopship, archbishopling, archbishoply*), which he was thereby able to squeeze into a mere inch and a half of text, instead of the two inches or more that five separate entries would have required. Gibbs, concurring that this was probably 'as much as can and ought to be done' as regards compression of the text, nevertheless urged Murray to try to come up with an estimate of the space that could be saved by the omission of 'all scientific (medical &c) terms that were not in common literary use. I doubt it would not be very great, & I should like to be able to shew that it would only be some small portion of a volume.' More positively, he had received an invitation from Jowett to come and discuss the Dictionary at length in early November: ' "I am very desirous" he says "that we should proceed with it if possible." '[201]

However, Jowett's next action came closer than anything yet to scuppering the entire project. On the evening after Jowett's visit Murray had sent off to Oxford what he believed to be the final text of his Preface and Introduction to the Dictionary. Six days later, however, an envelope arrived from the Vice-Chancellor containing a fresh set of proofs of the Prospectus, some of the preliminary matter, and even the title page of the Dictionary—all substantially altered. Jowett's covering letter referred to 'alterations which some of the Delegates think must be made'; in fact a new committee of Delegates (Jowett, Liddell, Pattison, and Stubbs) had been appointed to consider

---

[199]   OED/B/3/1/6 18 Oct. 1883 JAHM to Price; GL MS 11021/21 ff. 505a,e 20 Oct. 1883 JAHM to HHG.

[200]   Doble had sent Murray a specimen showing such lemmas 'printed continuously' in July (SL 9 July 1883 Doble to JAHM). The first blocks of such words to be printed were those formed on the scientific prefixes *anis-* and *aniso-*.

[201]   MP 21 Oct. 1883 HHG to JAHM.

what revisions might be needed—and to 'confer with Dr Murray thereon'[202]—but Murray may well have been right in regarding the changes as in large part Jowett's own work. Certainly the manner of their dispatch to Mill Hill—with no explanation about the new committee, and without returning Murray's original draft—suggests that Jowett had taken matters into his own hands.

Murray was once again furious. He wrote a private letter to Price, objecting to most of the changes that had been made, and protesting much more at the manner in which this had been done. The Prospectus, he conceded, might reasonably be altered by others now that it had been agreed that it should be issued without attribution; but

the *Preface* is my own, and while I am [...] very willing to reconsider any statement, expression, or word, to which any of the Delegates object, & to exclude anything which they on reasonable grounds wish excluded, I emphatically object to anybody altering it without consulting me, and to its being sent to me with these alterations in print, as now done. I will write my own Preface, or it shall remain unwritten.[203]

The title had in fact been fixed as early as May 1882, when the first page of the main text of the Dictionary was in proof, as 'A New English Dictionary on a Historical Basis';[204] Jowett now saw fit to alter this to 'A New English Dictionary showing the History of the Language from the Earliest Times', a revision which Murray dismissed as 'both weak and erroneous. We do not, & *cannot*, show in a Dictionary the History of the Language—only that of those *words* which are treated therein. [...] And we do not tell the history of the Vocabulary even, *"from the Earliest Times"*; we exclude nine-tenths of the Earliest English words & deal only with those which survived 1150. The whole clause is absurd in the extreme.' He also took particular exception to a change made in the concluding lines of the Prospectus, where the new Dictionary is set in the context of the great lexicographical achievements of Johnson and others: 'New knowledge accumulates, and new Editors enter on the task of the old, with advantages due, not to themselves, but to time.' Murray was always suspicious that some of his Oxford masters regarded his lack of a university education as making him unsuitable for the work of editing the Dictionary; now, more sensitive than ever, he interpreted the remark as 'an intentional slap to remind me that I am only a poor casual Editor [...] Dr Johnson [...] was a great man of letters and of literary genius; I am only a poor hard-working philologist. But even as a poor bricklayer may build a better wall than a philologist, [...] so a poor philologist, who knows his business, may make a better

---

[202] OD 19 Oct. 1883.

[203] SL 18 Aug. 1883 Price to Doble; MP 23 Oct. 1883 JAHM to Price (draft).

[204] Murray's original handwritten draft of the title page survives in MP, with annotations by Liddell (and can be dated from a reference to it in SL 25 May 1882 Price to JAHM). The wording was needed as a heading for the first page of Dictionary entries, which was indeed printed with the words 'on a historical basis'; this page was left unaltered even when the first edition of the Dictionary was reprinted in 1933. Interestingly, Skeat's etymological dictionary, completed in 1882, was described on its title page as 'arranged on an historical basis'.

Dictionary than the greatest man of letters, who knows philology no more than he knows crystallography or trilinear coordinates.' To Gibbs, whom he consulted about how to respond, he was more blunt: 'I consider [the passage] to be an intended snub, and I shall resign forthwith [...] if it is not at once withdrawn & explained. [...] I mean to put my foot down now.'[205]

Price, however, could prickle too. Accustomed as he was to being the channel for all communication between Murray and the Press, he was clearly unsettled by Jowett's readiness to act unilaterally. He coldly informed Murray that his position as Secretary to the Delegates made it impossible for him to reply fully to letters marked as private, but that in any case 'the Board has no knowledge of any letter written to you by any member of the Committee'. Murray accordingly wrote afresh without the 'Private' marking, restating his grievances at greater length, and reiterating that 'it would, of course, be impossible for me to continue work which seemed to be deliberately depreciated in the Prospectus'.[206] He was no doubt fortified by the three thoroughly supportive resolutions passed unanimously by the Philological Society's Council at their special meeting: no significant abridgements, they declared, could be implemented 'without destroying the essential character of the Dictionary & its original Plan as exprest in the Contract'; no significant reduction in time or labour could be effected even by the minor abridgements (such as those involving derivatives and technical terms) that were possible; in fact, only an increase in the editorial staff would appreciably accelerate the work's completion.[207]

Murray's letter was laid before the Delegates when they met to consider the deadlock on 2 November. They also considered two letters from Furnivall, in which he pointed out that, regardless of what they chose to do regarding the Editor, the Press's separate contract with the Philological Society meant that it was obliged to complete the Dictionary according to the 'original scheme' irrespective of cost—'unless either the Ph. Society releases them from the Contract, or the Delegates go thro' the Bankruptcy Court'—and that in his view the only way to achieve this in ten years was to split it into four.[208] It was clear, however, that the most urgent priority was to reach an

---

[205] GL MS 11021/21 f. 507a [24? Oct. 1883] JAHM to HHG.

[206] MP 24 Oct. 1883 Price to JAHM; [27 Oct. 1883] JAHM to Price (copy).

[207] PSCM 25 Oct. 1883. Notwithstanding the position adopted in the three resolutions, the Council did give serious consideration to how the Dictionary might practicably be abridged; proofs of some entries in *an-* were distributed to Council members, and letters from several of them, with some specific suggestions for condensation, survive in MP (28–30 Oct. 1883). Furnivall also sent copies to Skeat in advance of the Council meeting, but unfortunately gave him the impression that a decision to shorten the text had already been taken; Skeat's no-nonsense comments on how this could be achieved caused Murray considerable offence, and Skeat was obliged to apologise for 'seem[ing] to make silly suggestions [...] Please consider my remarks as unsaid' (MP 27 Oct. 1883 Skeat to [JAHM]). His marked-up proof survives in MP, with such forthright remarks as '*rubbish!* mere tradesman's make-up' (against the word *anerithmoscope*) and 'omit these foolish words' (against *angeled* and *angelence*). Annotations of these early proofs, by Skeat and others, are briefly discussed in Mugglestone (2005: xi–xvii).

[208] OED/B/3/1/6 20, 23 Oct. 1883 FJF to [Price]. In his second letter Furnivall argued that the Press's obligations also meant that the 'Suggestions' could not be seriously considered. He reserved particular scorn for 'that infinitely ridiculous "Suggestion" that the 2 earliest instances of a word—say A[nglo] Saxon,

accommodation with the Editor. Jowett consented to write to Murray, explaining (rather after the event) that the new versions of the Prospectus and preliminary matter had been put into print merely 'for convenience', and that while the committee felt that some alterations were needed they were 'far from insisting on the particular ones we have submitted to you'; he also invited him to come to Oxford on 6 November and talk the matter through.[209]

Gibbs's arrival in Oxford on 3 November, as earlier invited by Jowett, now proved to be extremely timely. Aware, as Elisabeth Murray observes, of 'the danger when two strong-willed men start a tug-of-war'—though in fact Jowett was assisted at his end of the rope by Liddell—he was now uniquely well placed to mediate. Although unable to remain in Oxford long enough to see Murray, he wrote to him about the progress of his discussions with the Vice-Chancellor and Dean. He found them 'sincerely sorry that they did anything to hurt your feelings', and willing to admit that 'it was an indiscretion on their part to rewrite your preface'. He had himself gone through the Prospectus with them, including the supposed 'intentional slap', which turned out to have been an insertion by Liddell: '[t]he Dean said he put in those unlucky words only as a sort of profession of modesty, & the V.C. said it was only what the Dean wd put into his own Dictionary—I said yes, but then the Dean would be speaking of *himself*, but your Prospectus is speaking of some one else!' This left the title page, Preface, and other introductory matter to be settled by Murray; Gibbs, aware of his friend's propensity for stubbornness, advised a policy of 'defending your own words where they need defence, and not sticking too closely to anything that is of no moment one way or other.' Other matters also requiring discussion, notably the question of finance, were left for a later occasion, but Gibbs took the opportunity to promote the idea of expanding Murray's team, 'to double or treble Mr Erlebach', as in his view the only feasible way forward. He was also assured by Liddell that if Murray were to move to Oxford, 'some office in the University' could probably be found for him.[210]

But Gibbs's diplomacy was to no avail. Despite his assurance that the discussion would be 'in the most friendly and the least arrogant spirit', the meeting with Jowett's committee proved to be a grinding battle of wills over the disputed text. Murray gave a vivid description of the encounter (which he had originally hoped would be over in an afternoon) to Gibbs:

We had a sederunt of 4 hours on Tuesday afternoon, another of 4½ hours (9 to 1.30) on Wednesday morning, and still another of more than an hour on Wednesday afternoon, till the

---

which no Delegate (?) & few readers could translate—shd be given & then "this usage continues to the present day" [...] Was *Liddell & Scott* done on this plan? Or any other known Dicty?'

[209] OD 2 Nov. 1883; MP 2 Nov. 1883 Jowett to JAHM. A copy of this letter, in Jowett's hand, is pasted into the Delegates' Order Book, perhaps suggesting that Price had pointed out the difficulties caused by his unilateral action, and was now insisting upon having an exact record of what was communicated to Murray. Even the Vice-Chancellor could be brought to book on occasion.

[210] MP 4 Nov. 1883 HHG to JAHM. Gibbs also mentioned that he was now confident of Gladstone's intention to approve a substantial pension for Murray in due course.

V.C. had to rush off in a cab, and I to run for my train; and we had got only to page x, and the rest is adjourned *sine die*! Indeed there is no particular reason why it should not last till a new V.C. comes in. Prof. Jowett said in his letter that their alterations were mere suggestions [...] but it soon became evident to me that they were suggestions, which he was simply determined that I *should* swallow willing or unwilling. We simply had to fight every word, my *wishes* going for nothing; and only when I could absolutely convince him that my words were better, would he yield anything. I expected that they would at certain parts, at least, have said, 'Dr. Murray, we think we can leave this mere detail to you; we have expressed our wishes or stated our difficulties, and shall be glad if you will do as much as you can to meet them'. But there was not an iota of such a spirit shown; dead through every line we must go, and I must be forced to accept either what he had written, or something else which he proposed instead [...]. They must be his words & not mine. The whole was done in such a whirl that one had hardly time to collect one's thoughts, & I often simply ceased protesting, from sheer vexation & weariness.[211]

Such behaviour on the part of the committee—and Jowett in particular—is hard to explain, particularly as it did not relate to the text of the Dictionary itself. It is not as if the original drafts of the Preface and 'General Explanations', preserved in the Murray Papers, are full of egregious errors or infelicities of style; they had, after all, been read, as Murray had pointed out to Price, by 'four gentlemen intimately acquainted with the history of the scheme', and by 'two literary critics' (one of whom was evidently Fitzedward Hall, surely a byword for grammatical and stylistic propriety).[212] With the fruits of so much of his own and others' labour so nearly ready for publication, and after all the sacrifices (not least financial) which he had made, Murray emerged from the meeting bruised and frustrated. He had in fact been considering resignation for some weeks; he now warned Price and Bywater, who were the last to leave, that he might well do so in a few days. Protests from Bywater, who ran with him to Oxford station, that 'everybody had to stand this sort of thing from Jowett', were unavailing; and further discussion with his wife on his return to Mill Hill finally decided him. 'I cannot do what I have been doing', he told Gibbs, 'without enthusiasm and whole-heartedness: the result of all this despicable squabbling over my English, as if it were a school-boy's essay, has been utterly to chill & freeze me, and make me loathe the whole matter [...] I say: I will do it no more.' Indeed he already knew what he would do instead: he had twice been approached about the possibility of 'an English or Teutonic Professorship in an American College', and he was now minded to let his American friends know that he was available. 'The future of English scholarship lies in the United States, where the language is studied with an enthusiasm unknown here, and which will soon leave us far behind. I think I could help on that future.'

It now fell to Henry Hucks Gibbs to save the Dictionary. Matters could hardly have been more serious: as he warned Furnivall, 'The V.C., a most energetic man in all he undertakes, has, I fear, upset the Coach. Murray wont stand their tutelage & will resign

---

[211] GL MS 11021/21 ff. 513–17 8 Nov. 1883 JAHM to HHG.
[212] MP [27 Oct. 1883] JAHM to Price (copy).

if he hasn't done so.' He wrote to Murray, counselling him to keep the matter private—
'[s]ome of our friends are hot-headed and might unintentionally make mischief'—
and also wrote to Jowett and Liddell, warning them of the danger that Murray might
resign, the disastrous consequences that this would have for the project, and the
importance of allowing Murray sufficient editorial freedom.[213] Jowett still insisted that
the Preface and preliminary matter 'would have done serious injury to a great work
if sent out in their original form', and that he did not see why Murray considered this
a resigning matter; but the response of both men seemed to Gibbs to indicate that an
accommodation might still be reached.[214] Murray, however, was still deeply wounded,
and doubtful in particular as to whether Jowett could be trusted not to interfere any
further. He had even received a personal letter from the Vice-Chancellor, of which he
was equally suspicious:

It is the old story; 'we think a great deal of you; we are anxious to help you all we can; and to
make the Dictionary perfect' which means 'we are *determined* to help you, and *determined* that
you *shall accept* the help, whether you want it or not'. [...] *The way to help me is to let me alone*
and I mean to tell Prof. Jowett so plainly, at whatever cost.[215]

Gibbs wrote afresh to Jowett and Liddell, reiterating that 'suggestions' were all that
was required, and pointing out that 'the Preface and Explanations [...] are of much
less importance than the substance of the Dictionary. I can scarcely believe that you
will sell one single copy more or less because the Preface is well or ill written.' Obvious
though all this may now seem, the entrenched positions of both sides at the time
were such that perhaps only someone with Gibbs's influence could say it. As he later
remarked, 'I didn't hesitate to prescribe, though the dose was bitter.'[216]

The prescription worked. Whether it was Gibbs's letters, or something said privately
at the meeting of the full Board of Delegates on 16 November—the minutes of which
refer only to a decision on the format of Part I[217]—or simply a realization that he had
met his match, the Vice-Chancellor now decided that Murray should be allowed to
have his way. Not that this would be the end of Jowett's troublesome tendency to act
independently: indeed, his chosen method of communicating his change of heart to
Murray was independent with a vengeance. On the morning of 19 November Murray

---

[213] GL MS 11021/21 f. 534c 10 Nov. 1883 HHG to FJF; MP 12 Nov. 1883 HHG to JAHM. In fact Murray
had already told others of his intention to resign. Alexander Ellis wrote: 'It may be—I think it is—the best
thing for your health & well-being to give up [...] the thing, after you have resigned can't be kept out of
the papers' (MP 8 Nov. 1883 AJE to JAHM; quoted at length in *CWW* pp. 226–7). He also received a
warmly supportive letter from Fitzedward Hall, sympathizing with him in 'the vexation which you are
suffering from impertinent officiousness', and assuring him that the Philological Society would stand by
him (MP 10 Nov. 1883 F. Hall to JAHM).
[214] MP 12 Nov. 1883 HHG to JAHM, enclosing letters from Jowett and Liddell (11 and 12 Nov.
respectively; copies in MP, originals in GL MS 11021/21 ff. 521–4).
[215] GL MS 11021/21 ff. 526–8 13 Nov. 1883 JAHM to HHG.
[216] GL MS 11021/21 ff. 529–34 14 Nov. 1883 HHG to Jowett (copy); f. 605 undated note by HHG.
[217] OD 16 Nov. 1883.

received a letter from the Vice-Chancellor, containing the text of a 'Resolution of the Delegates' and informing him that he was free to make whatever corrections he wished. The remarkable thing about the 'Resolution' is that it was never passed by the Delegates. As a shocked Murray later reported to Gibbs, it was 'a bogus resolution (!) simply concocted by V.C. himself to cover his retreat. It never came before any Court, the Delegates know nothing of it, and [Price] had never seen it!'[218]

Jowett's capitulation must have been welcome news to Murray, arriving as it did after he had spent some time wrestling with the supposedly 'final' text of the Prospectus; in fact he was in the process of drafting a letter to Price declaring himself unable to bring it into a state fit for publication.[219] Now, interpreting Jowett's letter as 'a full surrender', he set about revising the disputed text once more, reinstating his own wording where necessary, but diplomatically retaining as much as possible of what the Delegates had suggested. The one outstanding matter was the title of the Dictionary. The old form of the title had read 'A New English Dictionary on a Historical Basis; founded chiefly on materials collected by The Philological Society'; this had been criticized by Jowett and Liddell on the rather obscure grounds that 'it looks awkward to have "on a h. *basis*" and then *founded* on something else'. (Fitzedward Hall also disliked this wording, but for the different reason that the combination of the word *a* with the initial *h* of *historical* 'grates on my ear painfully'.) Murray had already expressed his dissatisfaction with the alternative put forward by Jowett; nor did he approve of Liddell's suggested modification 'A New English Dictionary arranged so as to show the continuous history of the Words'. The objection to the combination of *basis* and *founded* was raised by none of the friends and colleagues he consulted, who when it was pointed out to them thought it 'purely hypercritical'. Fortunately someone suggested that the words 'on historical principles' would eliminate all grounds for objection, while still making explicit reference to the Dictionary's most distinctively novel feature; and so, once the matter had been put once more to the Delegates, 'A New English Dictionary on Historical Principles' was accepted.[220]

The correction of the Prospectus and preliminary matter was a complex and difficult task, and it was not until early December that these were finally ready for press.[221] Jowett's intervention had therefore set the project back by something like six

---

[218] GL MS 11021/21 f. 534e 3 Dec. 1883 JAHM to HHG.

[219] MP 19 Nov. 1883 JAHM to Price (copy). Two drafts of this letter, the second dated 17 November, are also preserved.

[220] MP 4 Nov. 1883 HHG to JAHM; proof of title page and preliminary matter, with annotations by Fitzedward Hall; 19 Nov. 1883 JAHM to Price (copy); OD 30 Nov. 1883. The title page as printed to Jowett's specification in October (and amended by Liddell) is reproduced in Mugglestone (2005: 156).

[221] GL MS 11021/21 f. 534e 3 Dec. 1883 JAHM to HHG. Murray's offer to come to Oxford to approve the final corrections, thereby saving a little time, made for one final bit of comedy: Jowett, on hearing at the Delegates' meeting on 30 November that he was to be in Oxford, was eager to have one last conference with him, but another Delegate adroitly suggested that any Delegates with outstanding points should raise them instead with Doble, who could settle them separately with Murray (which he did: SL 3, 5 Dec. 1883 Doble to JAHM). Evidently the risks of bringing Jowett and Murray together were now recognized.

weeks. For Murray the struggle had been extremely painful; but it brought significant benefits. His friend Fred Elworthy, who by chance visited Jowett the day after his capitulation, observed that '[the Delegates] will think many times before quarrelling with you', and Falconer Madan, sub-librarian at the Bodleian, 'quite chuckled' when Murray told him of his having withstood Jowett over his Preface—Jowett having acquired a reputation as a meddler with the details of the Library's management. Fitzedward Hall, too, congratulated him on his victory: '[The Delegates] have, I hope, found out that it is prudent to let you alone.'[222]

The delay had other consequences. Murray had hoped not to have to raise the subject of money again until Part I was out, but he was now obliged to do so. Part II was now well under way, with copy as far as *apropros* sent to the printers by the end of November, and 16 pages (ending at *anti-Gallic*) passed for press;[223] but pro-rata payment for this at seventeen shillings per page fell far short of Murray's outgoings. The Delegates approved his application for an advance of £150,[224] but this was no more than a stopgap: with publication of Part I imminent, the need to find a long-term solution to the project's finances would soon become impossible to ignore. (Publication of Part I was now slated for sometime in January: the need to ensure simultaneous or near-simultaneous publication on both sides of the Atlantic, in order to safeguard copyright, meant that publication would have to wait until copies could be shipped to America.[225])

For Price, and no doubt for Jowett and the other Delegates, the crucial issue was the rate of production. Murray was now asked to state what was needed, in terms of additional assistance, to guarantee 500, or if possible 600 pages per year: fewer than the 700 which Price had proposed to Gibbs a few months previously, but still a very tall order. It would require him and his assistants to prepare entries for forty-five words every day, with definitions, etymologies, quotations, and the correct historical development of senses and subsenses; to read six columns of first proof every day—which usually entailed rewriting of definitions and reorganization of senses—together with six columns of the first revises, considering the extensive comments made by various readers, and six columns of second revises; and, every four days, to pass eight pages for press. As he remarked to Gibbs: 'this is an appalling amount of work: manifestly beyond the power of any one man to do in a day—and *every* day. And what parts of it can I leave out, & yet be responsible to the public for?' Delegation of any of this work would require assistants with considerable skill and aptitude, who (if they

---

[222] MP 19 Nov. 1883 F. T. Elworthy to JAHM; MP 27 Dec. 1883 Hall to JAHM.

[223] A bound volume of date-stamped page proofs for the start of Part II (up to the end of A) survives in OUPA.

[224] OD 14 Dec. 1883.

[225] SL 10 Dec. 1883 Price to F. Macmillan (anticipating publication 'say six weeks hence'). The situation as regards United States copyright at this time made it necessary, in order to secure copyright in a book, to issue the American edition within ten days of publication in the UK. For further details see Nowell-Smith (1968: 64–84) (I am grateful to Chris Stray for this reference). Specifically on the application of contemporary copyright law to the first edition of the *OED* see also Cooper (2015).

could be found) would probably balk at the pay and conditions on offer at Mill Hill, not to mention the prospect of moving there.[226]

Gibbs—whom Price also consulted—realized that the task of compiling the Dictionary from the materials now collected was just as much of an unknown quantity as had been the initial 'preparatory' period, and that any scheme formulated for doing this should therefore be regarded as experimental, and certainly not used as the basis for rigid contractual terms in regard to timescale or cost. Instead, he advised Murray to start from first principles: to work out what he thought would be needed to achieve 500 pages a year while still maintaining the Dictionary's standards, and then to propose that the Delegates should allow him to 'try it for a year, supplying you with the needful and trusting to you to work with as few [assistants] and at as little cost as may be: subject to revision at the end of the year, when, if you find that contrary to expectation the coach is over-horsed you can diminish your assistance & consequently the cost. Or if the strain should prove too great you can then either reduce the standard of the work [...] or diminish the quantity of work per annum.' He was not keen on the alternative scheme of a 'double or treble staff', which he thought would damage the quality of the work.[227]

Unfortunately Murray simply could not see any way of guaranteeing even 500 pages a year. As he explained to Price, this might conceivably be possible if his whole time were devoted to the Dictionary, and given the availability of enough assistants of the requisite calibre, but he could offer no figures on the likely costs or feasibility of doing this at Mill Hill. The best that he could offer, based on the best that he had been able to achieve with his current team (namely 250–270 pages in a year), was that 'with a *very good* and a *good* assistant, say equal to my present two, it might be possible to increase it by one-half, or, say, to reach 400 pages a year'. Even this would require him to reduce his scrutiny of the printed text, confining himself to looking through the initial proofs and the final page proofs. Although hardly the kind of estimate Price had been hoping for, Murray's letter was read to the Delegates on 25 January, and the matter was once again deferred.[228]

For there were now more positive things to consider. Publication of Part I had been fixed for 29 January,[229] and decisions had to be taken regarding who should receive presentation copies, where to send advance copies for review, and the more general

---

[226] MP 17 Dec. 1883 Price to JAHM; GL MS 11021/21 ff. 536–40 26 Dec. 1883 JAHM to HHG.

[227] SL 8 Jan. 1884 Price to HHG; MP 28 Dec. 1883 HHG to JAHM.

[228] MP 17 Jan. 1884 JAHM to Price (copy); OD 25 Jan. 1884. The absence from these discussions of any explicit mention of a move to Oxford is striking. Elisabeth Murray claims (*CWW* p. 232) that it was Jowett who wanted Murray to move, and that the Delegates insisted that a proposal for accelerating the work should come first. There was, however, a widespread expectation that Murray would come to Oxford, and indeed to be found an academic position: Fred Elworthy, for example, visiting Jowett in November, commented that he 'look[ed] forward to visiting Professor Murray here before long' (MP 19 Nov. 1883 Elworthy to JAHM).

[229] The exact date appears to have been fixed as late as 11 January (SL 17 Jan. 1884 Price to F. Macmillan, formally recording 'our conversation on Friday last'). The date of publication in America was 1 February.

question of advertising the new work. A distinctly unwelcome development was the announcement by Cassell of an issue of their *Encyclopaedic Dictionary* in monthly instalments (with the obvious intention', as Jennett Humphreys observed, that 'the masses will confound the two debuts');[230] but there was still substantial public interest, including a long anticipatory article in the *Times*, which hailed 'a work of the utmost importance to the scientific study of the English language'.[231] Review copies—over seventy in total—were sent to every national newspaper (and a great many local ones) in Britain, to the important weeklies and monthlies, and to newspapers and literary journals across Europe, America, India, and Australia; copies of Part I were also presented to the Royal Library at Windsor, to the Prime Minister, the Poet Laureate, the President of the United States, and various professors, libraries, and learned societies (as well as to various friends and supporters of the Dictionary, including Trench, Gibbs, and Skeat). 50,000 copies of the troublesome Prospectus—and 100,000 of a shorter, one-page version—were requested by Henry Frowde, the manager of the Press's London business, and were soon being distributed to booksellers, librarians, university professors, headmasters, school inspectors, and the memberships of numerous learned societies. Frowde also paid for a version of the smaller prospectus to be printed as an advertisement in about forty newspapers and journals.[232]

Among the first 'ordinary' people to see the new Dictionary were the members of the Philological Society, who at their annual Dictionary Evening on 18 January were able to examine three advance copies of Part I. At last, twenty-six years after the Society had passed its 'resolutions [...] relating to the undertaking of a New English Dictionary', the labours of so many were bearing visible fruit. Murray read extracts from his Introduction, and—looking forward to Part II—discussed numerous entries from the latest proofs. Celebration, rather than foreboding about the project's uncertain future, was in order, and he concealed his worries, referring only to the urgent need for more sub-editors to prepare material in advance of the Scriptorium and thereby accelerate progress. Furnivall, moving a vote of thanks, congratulated the Society, and 'looked back [...] to the little room in Somerset House where the Dictionary Committee was first appointed, and thought of the dead friends who were with him then [...]; Mr. Wedgwood was, he thought, the only survivor besides himself.' Murray, replying, paid particular tribute to the work of Herbert Coleridge, commenting that upon reading his letters he 'had often sighed to think that he and others were not spared to see the fruit of their labours'. However, he went on to suggest that it was as well that the Dictionary had *not* been completed at the time of its first conception: had it been, the progress made in English

---

[230] MP 25 Jan. 1884 J. Humphreys to JAHM. The *Athenaeum* of 12 January 1884, for example, carried a full-page advertisement (p. 72) announcing the availability of the *Encyclopaedic Dictionary* in monthly parts, the first of which would be ready on 25 January.

[231] *Times* 26 Jan. 1884, p. 6. Other newspapers carried articles in advance of the publication of Part I: the *Liverpool Mercury* of 28 January, for example, hailed 'a work as great as Littré's', and rather rashly looked forward to '[w]hen the work is completed—and it is now so far advanced that no accident can interfere with its publication' (p. 5).

[232] FL 28 Dec. 1883, 29 Jan., 7 Feb. 1884 Frowde to Price, 13 Feb. 1884 Frowde to JAHM.

and Old French philology in the last fifteen years was such that members 'would all by this time have been ashamed of it, and agitating to do it over again'. As for the possibility that further progress in the subject would in turn render his own work obsolete, he was much more sanguine:

There was a period in the history of every science during which permanent progress was made, and results acquired never to be surrendered, for they were of the nature of actual discovery of *fact*. This stage English Philology had now passed through, and now for the first time was it possible to bring its results to bear upon English lexicography, in the form presented to the Society this evening.[233]

Even the businesslike Price was willing to offer congratulations. Not that he suspended business, even on the day of publication: a letter informing Murray of the ten complimentary copies of 'the Opus Magnum' that the Delegates had voted to present to him continued with queries about the presentation of copies to sub-editors and other helpers, and about the arrangements to be made to allow Philological Society members to purchase copies at half price. The letter concluded with Price's congratulations 'on the sending out into the world this first portion of the great Work of your life. It will carry your name all over the known World.'[234] The irony of this compliment will not have been lost on Murray, who had come so close to removing his name from the whole enterprise only weeks before publication; and the uncertainty which had dogged the first five years of the Dictionary's relationship with the Clarendon Press was far from over.

---

[233] ProcPS 18 Jan. 1884, pp. v–vi (supplemented from PSOM).
[234] MP 29 Jan. 1884 Price to JAHM.
    There remains some uncertainty as to the exact publication date of Part I. Confirmation that it was indeed published on 29 January would appear to be provided by the notices that appeared in newspapers (e.g. *Times, Morning Post, Standard*) announcing its publication on that day; however, only three months later, in his Presidential Address to the Philological Society in May, Murray himself gave the publication date as 1 February (*TPS* for 1882–4, p. 508). It seems unlikely that he would have got it wrong, but the newspaper evidence, together with the date of Price's congratulatory letter, is compelling.

5

The Dictionary divides:
1884–1887

O N 5 February 1884, a week after the publication of Part I, Ada Murray gave birth to a baby girl. Alfred Erlebach marked the occasion by supplementing the quotations for sense 6 of *arrival* with the invented example 'The new arrival is a little daughter.' Within the Murray household this was no doubt cause for celebration; but the proud father was also much preoccupied with his literary progeny. How would this other 'new arrival' be received? And what were the prospects for its future?

Notices of the Dictionary[1] followed swiftly upon the pre-publication articles and publicity—although it must have been disturbing to find it often competing for coverage with, and in some newspapers entirely displaced by, the latest instalment of the *Encyclopaedic Dictionary*.[2] It must have been a relief to all concerned that, when they did begin to appear, the reviews were so uniformly favourable. Indeed the chorus of acclamation was almost deafening, not just in Britain but around the world. The *Boston Daily Advertiser* acclaimed 'what will surely be the best dictionary of all modern languages', and the *New York Times* 'this greatest of English books'; comparably favourable reports appeared in the Australian, German, and even Italian papers. Murray himself, reviewing the reviewers as part of his Presidential Address to the Philological Society in May, observed with satisfaction that 'the general design and plan of the Dictionary [...] has received general, one may say, virtually unanimous approbation [...] the work is hailed as a genuine contribution to English scholarship.'[3] With the

---

[1] A small selection of the vast quantity of published responses to the fascicles of the first edition is surveyed by Bivens (1981); a longer list appears in Bailey (2000b).

[2] For example, on 30 January 1884 the *Leeds Mercury* noticed the latest half-volume of the *Encyclopaedic* but made no mention of the new Dictionary, which eventually received a brief notice on 4 February. Similarly the *Graphic* and *Jackson's Oxford Journal* of 2 February mentioned the *Encyclopaedic* but not Part I.

[3] Murray's discussion of reviewers' comments is printed, along with the rest of his Presidential Address, in *TPS* for 1882–4, pp. 520–8.

The Making of the *Oxford English Dictionary*. First edition. Peter Gilliver.
© Peter Gilliver 2016. First published 2016 by Oxford University Press.

perspective of history it might seem unsurprising that the Dictionary's historical methods, familiar as they have become through their employment in the compilation of many similar works, should have met with approval; but at the time it was by no means certain, and endorsement of what was, for English lexicography at least, something of a new departure must have been welcome. The Dictionary's comprehensiveness and style were widely praised, as was its typography, a fact which must have been pleasing to Murray, who had taken such trouble to make its pages 'eloquent to the eye', as he put it in his Preface.[4] The fact that for French and German comparable dictionaries already existed was not lost on the reviewers, many of whom compared the new Dictionary favourably with the work of Littré and the brothers Grimm. With or without such comparisons, the appeal to national pride was irresistible to many ('truly a national work', declared the *Spectator*). Others invested it with still wider significance: C. W. Ernst, who was to become an enthusiastic supporter of and contributor to the Dictionary, interpreted it as a sign that '[t]he English-speaking world is now prepared to meet German philology on terms of equality'.[5]

Not that the acclaim was universal. Particular elements of the Dictionary's approach excited criticism, often in opposing directions from different critics, neatly pointing up the impossibility of pleasing everybody. One of the most serious criticisms came from a Cambridge scholar, Charles Fennell, writing anonymously in the *Athenaeum*.[6] Fennell, who had been appointed editor of the *Stanford Dictionary*, chose to remind his readers of Richard Chenevix Trench's deprecation of including too many 'purely technical words', and suggested that Murray had fallen into this error, even to the extent of having included two of the words singled out by Trench as having been unwisely included by Johnson (*aegilops* and *acroteria*). He was not alone in finding the Dictionary too inclusive of such vocabulary; but, as Murray pointed out, 'a very different opinion has been expressed by various men of science, each of whom would like rather more indulgence shown to the vocabulary of his own particular department.' Other critics were concerned with different parts of the boundary of the 'circle of the English language': Franz Stratmann, a distinguished lexicographer of Middle English, suggested that words from early periods which had left no trace in modern English need not be covered,[7] while *John Bull*

---

[4] The innovative features of the *OED*'s typography, and its position in the development of dictionary typography, are discussed in detail—by someone who was much involved with some later phases of its design—in Luna (2000). See also *CWW* pp. 197–8.

[5] *Spectator* 16 Feb. 1884, p. 222; *Unitarian Review* July 1884, p. 25. The Boston-based writer C. W. Ernst (1845–1919) became a regular correspondent of Murray, and is thanked for his contributions in a number of Prefaces to the Dictionary. Information taken from his own annotated copy of the *OED* was drawn upon by William Craigie during the compilation of both the 1933 Supplement and the *Dictionary of American English* (Mathews 1955).

[6] The review of Part I, which was spread over two issues of the *Athenaeum* (9 Feb. 1884, pp. 177–8, and 16 Feb. 1884, pp. 211–12), is identified as by Fennell, as are other reviews in the *Athenaeum* down to 1915, in Bailey (2000b). For a fuller discussion of Fennell's criticisms of Part I see Bailey (2000a: 213). Although considerable animosity between Murray and Fennell was to develop later (see p. 213), at this stage relations between the two lexicographers seem to have been cordial, to judge from the congratulatory tone of a letter sent by Fennell in March (see below, p. 180).

[7] *Anglia* 7(2) (1884), pp. 1–2. Poignantly, Stratmann ended his review by wishing Murray health and strength to complete his work; he himself was dead within a year.

queried whether *acrobatically* should have been included with only a single quotation by Rhoda Broughton: 'It may be matter of question how far the right of coining words claimed Virgilio Varioque can properly be conceded to the female novelist.'[8] The use of contemporary newspaper quotations came in for similar censure: a criticism which Murray singled out in his May address to the Philological Society as 'by far the silliest the Dictionary has elicited', pointing out that nobody seemed to object to quotations from older newspapers.[9]

When it came to such methodological criticisms, Murray was well prepared with justification—having already had to respond to just about every possible criticism from those involved with the project during the five years of editorial work that had preceded publication—and in his May address he dealt confidently with these criticisms, which after all were effectively swamped by the general praise for the Dictionary's approach. Particular errors and omissions were another matter. He sought to dismiss the additional words and senses, and earlier examples of particular words, which reviewers had unearthed as 'surprisingly few', and with some justification; and reviewers often said as much.[10] But he was still acutely sensitive to anything which could be taken as implying that his work was less thorough than it might have been. In this he was taking a very different view of the Dictionary from that of Furnivall, who barely a week after publication sent to the *Academy* a list of the additional material for Part I that he had already accumulated, trusting that they would go to form 'a very valuable Appendix to the Dictionary [...] Such a work can never be entirely complete.'[11] Murray's struggles to make the Dictionary as complete as possible, and his own insecurities, sometimes led him to over-react to such criticisms, as when after a few correspondents had sent items to *Notes & Queries*—once again suggesting that

---

[8] *John Bull* 9 Feb. 1884, pp. 94–5 (*Virgilio Varioque*: Latin for 'for [the poets] Virgil and Varius'; an allusion to Horace's *Ars Poetica*). In contrast, Lucy Toulmin Smith noted in the *Bibliographer* (June 1884, p. 2) that novelists (male and female) could be 'useful for the colloquisms [*sic*] they preserve'. In fact Rhoda Broughton's use of *acrobatically* (in her 1880 novel *Second Thoughts*) was not a coinage: the recently published revised entry for the word includes an example from twenty years earlier.

[9] Murray's extended defence of his use of newspaper quotations, given in his May Address, reveals some continuing ambiguity as to the relative merits of newspapers and more canonical sources. Although he states that the general principle in selecting quotations was 'to take that which was intrinsically the best for its purpose, without any regard to its source or authority', he goes on to say that he had 'allowed the question of authorship to be of weight'—while observing that in many cases the question of choice simply did not arise: faced with a usable newspaper quotation, he and his assistants could not afford to spend time searching to find a substitute from a literary source. The implication is, however, that given the time he might have preferred to make such a search. Interestingly, Murray does not avail himself of the opportunity to cite the distinguished precedent of Jamieson's dictionary, whose extensive use of quotations from Scottish newspapers is discussed in Rennie (2012: 140–1, 176–8).

[10] For example *Notes & Queries* (1 Mar. 1884, p. 179): 'The instances of omission that reward a long and close search are advanced as proofs of the care with which the task has been accomplished, and not with the idea of censure.' An exception was the *Spectator*, where omissions and antedatings found after 'some minutes' search in a few books we chanced to take up' were presented as demonstrating that the Dictionary was 'far from being an "exhaustive work"'.

[11] *Academy* 9 Feb. 1884, pp. 96–7. Furnivall's list, which he had been compiling for 'a few weeks', included 'only five' words not in Part I (*abusant, accoucheurship, amorce, Anglo-Saxonising*, and *amalgamationist*), together with a few antedatings and material for additional senses.

they could go in an Appendix—he testily suggested that it would have been better had the items been sent in to him in time to be made use of. Such blemishes in the Dictionary were, he argued, 'due not to me and to those who *have* worked, but to those who *have not*. Only those who forget that *everybody* was asked to read, and that the "readers" were those who generously and gratuitously complied with the request, will think of charging those who did what they could with the derelictions of those who did nothing.' He once again urged anyone who made such discoveries to send them to the Scriptorium directly: 'we are by no means at the eleventh hour.'[12]

The public reaction, then, to the first fruits of the project's labours, was overwhelmingly positive, and a morale-boosting vindication of the approach of Murray and his co-workers. One particularly pleasing review appeared in the *Academy*, a literary journal, above the name of Henry Bradley (see Figure 13).[13] This former correspondence clerk for a Sheffield cutlery firm had, like Murray, acquired considerable skill in numerous languages by private study. He had been contributing articles and reviews on philological topics to various literary magazines for several years;[14] he had received the invitation to review Part I only a few days after moving to London. His review—written using one of the unopened packing cases in his new London house as a desk[15]—was warmly appreciative, while still making some pertinent criticisms. More importantly, it demonstrated impressive philological knowledge and percipience on the part of the reviewer, to the extent that some immediately began to wonder how Bradley's talents might be made use of in contributing to subsequent Parts of the Dictionary.

So much for the critical success of Part I. Equally important, if not more so, for the future of the project was the question of its commercial success. Here, too, the news was excellent: two days after publication Henry Frowde could report that he had sold 750 copies of Part I, and expected to dispose of the rest of his initial order of 1,500 within a week. Less than a month later he had ordered another 1,500 copies. Macmillan had ordered 2,000 copies for the American market, and these too were soon reported by Charles Fennell to be 'going off "like hot cakes"'.[16]

Large orders for Part I were of course encouraging, but they fell a long way short of the project's costs. The particular component of these costs that now clamoured for attention was Murray's remuneration, the present level of which was evidently unsustainable. The idea of securing a Civil List pension, consideration of which had

---

[12] *Notes & Queries* 19 Apr. 1884, p. 310.

[13] *Academy* 16 Feb. 1884, pp. 105–6, and 1 Mar. 1884, pp. 141–2.

[14] Bridges (1928: 10) lists a review of a book on place names by Isaac Taylor in *Fraser's Magazine* (Feb. 1877, pp. 166–72) as Bradley's first significant scholarly article, although he had written before this in the *Sheffield Independent* on the subject of place names, which remained a particular interest. Canon Taylor became a close friend, and in 1883 provided him with letters of introduction to various University figures when he visited Oxford. In May 1882 he had written an article for the *Academy* pointing out some errors in Littré's dictionary, after which he became a regular reviewer of glossaries for the magazine.

[15] Bridges (1928: 12).

[16] FL 8, 31 Jan., 29 Feb. 1884 Frowde to Price; MP 26 Mar. 1884 C. A. M. Fennell to JAHM.

FIGURE 13   Henry Bradley (undated photograph, probably 1870s or 1880s).

been postponed at Murray's request, could now be revisited. Liddell approached Downing Street, and received an encouraging response;[17] and a few weeks later Murray was informed that he had been awarded a pension of £250 a year. This was excellent news, not merely from a financial point of view but also because, as Furnivall said, the award 'set the national stamp on the work', and arguably strengthened the public expectation that the Press would see the project completed properly.[18]

[17] OED/B/3/1/6 26 Feb. 1884 Liddell to Price (on the back of a letter from Gladstone's secretary Horace Seymour). Liddell also revived the suggestion that an academic post might be found for Murray if he came to Oxford, supplying him with a further £150 or £200 a year in return for 'a *diminished* number of lectures on English Language'.
[18] MP 20 Mar. 1884 Horace Seymour to JAHM; 24 Mar. 1884 FJF to JAHM. A further boost to Murray's morale came in the form of an invitation to Edinburgh for the celebration of the University's tercentenary

Ready money, however, remained a problem. The first instalment of the Civil List pension was, it turned out, not due until 1 July, leaving Murray hardly able to pay his assistants' salaries and other expenses; but the Delegates were not forthcoming with any further advances. Instead, the deferred matter of the Dictionary's 'future management and more speedy publication' was referred to a new committee, and Murray was asked for additional details about how output was to be increased. An interim payment of £200 was eventually forthcoming, but apparently only after representations from Gibbs, who was once again about to play a key role.[19]

On 28 May Murray visited Oxford for a meeting with the Delegates of the new committee: Jowett, Liddell, Bywater, William Markby, and the businesslike bursar of New College, Alfred Robinson. The picture of the project's requirements that now emerged was considerably more costly, but probably more realistic. The public had to be convinced that Parts would appear regularly; to achieve this, a guarantee to publish two Parts a year was needed, and Price was authorized to open negotiations with Murray and the Philological Society about how to achieve this—after an initial consultation with Gibbs. It was arranged that the two men should confer on 16 June, and then meet Murray at the Bank of England (of which Gibbs was a director) the following day.[20]

How was the necessary acceleration to be achieved? There was support among the Delegates for the option of appointing a second, independent Editor, but Murray and Gibbs were doubtful that this could be made to work. At the meeting with Price Murray proposed an alternative, but still radical scheme. He would move to Oxford as soon as possible, giving up his remaining teaching commitments, and receiving in compensation the substantially larger salary of £750 (of which £250 would come from the Civil List pension); and he would enlarge his staff of assistants to eight (three 'first-class', three 'second-class', and two 'third-class' or clerical), with salaries totalling £1,375. Together with various minor expenses this made up an annual cost of £1,750. In return for this considerably increased expenditure, the Press required a guarantee to produce enough copy for two Parts per year. This was certainly ambitious: only a few days earlier Murray had told the Philological Society's Council that he could not see how to produce more than three Parts in two years, 'even with a double staff'.[21] Price secured his agreement that such a rate might be feasible, but as soon as the meeting was over Murray's doubts resurfaced. Even in Oxford, finding assistants who could really do the work would be a terribly unpredictable business: 'you can engage navvies,' he wrote to Gibbs, 'and you can engage assistant schoolmasters, but you can only *try* men in the *hope* that they may turn out Dictionary helpers, and in many cases find them of no use; and what becomes, while you are trying them, of the 8 cols. a day,

---

in April, an enjoyable occasion at which he met old friends and new (the latter including Robert Browning), and was pleasantly surprised to find himself something of a public figure (*CWW* pp. 234–5).

[19] OD 25 Apr. 1884; MP 28 Apr. 1884 FJF to JAHM ('*Damn* those Oxford Delegates! It *is* too bad of 'em to leave you stranded like this'), 3 May 1884 Price to JAHM.

[20] OD 6 June 1884; SL 11 June 1884 Price to HHG; MP 12 June 1884 HHG to JAHM.

[21] PSCM 6 June 1884.

and two parts a year […]?' What was worse, Erlebach, his most valued assistant, was apparently reluctant to move to Oxford, and help with the complete reorganization of work that would be necessary—a reorganization which Murray recognized that he himself might find uncongenial: 'many people can do things very well themselves, and cannot superintend others: perhaps I am one of them.'[22] In his carefully worded statement of the undertaking he was willing to give, he declared that he *expected* to be able to produce 700 pages a year once he had put together his new team, and would 'engage to do so unless prevented by unforeseen difficulties'.[23]

The caveat about 'unforeseen difficulties' would prove to have been wise; but it was not acceptable to the Delegates, who decided that only an absolute guarantee of progress could justify the vastly increased expenditure that was now proposed; Murray was informed that the project's commercial viability depended on 'the regular publication of successive Parts at short intervals of time'.[24] In fact such was the pessimism of some Delegates about the rate achievable even by an enlarged team that, rather than commit the Press indefinitely to the increased expenditure, they recommended including a provision for abandoning the project entirely if the target was not met.[25] There was also the matter of securing the Philological Society's consent to any variations in the agreement with them; Furnivall, as the Society's secretary, was told by Murray to expect something from Price, but no communication was forthcoming. He wrote impatiently to Murray: 'As there were once heavy-arst Xtians, so there are now Delegates of like kind.'[26]

Unfortunately for Murray, the protracted (and still incomplete) negotiations, together with the three months' notice that he was obliged to give at Mill Hill, meant that it was now unlikely that he could move to Oxford before Christmas—and that effectively meant not before Easter, as moving house at Christmas was fraught with difficulties. He also felt unable to give the Delegates the absolute guarantee they were looking for: 'I really cannot do more,' he told Price, 'than say "I'll work my hardest, and try to get assistants who will do the same […]." But I cannot ruin myself absolutely for the Dictionary.' If an absolute promise was required, he would simply have to withdraw from the Editorship.[27]

---

[22] GL MS 11021/23 ff. 935–8 18 June 1884 JAHM to HHG.

[23] A copy of Murray's undertaking, with the figures for expenses quoted above, is pasted into the Delegates' Order Book; it is dated 18 June 1884. The same figures are given in a note apparently written by Price and signed by Murray during the meeting on 17 June, preserved in OUPA (OED/B/3/1/6).

[24] OD 20 June 1884; MP 1 July 1884 Price to JAHM.

[25] An early draft of the resolution passed on 20 June, written partly by Jowett and partly by Markby (OED/B/3/1/6), includes a provision for revising the agreement with the Philological Society 'to allow [the Delegates] to discontinue the work'. Markby wrote to Price in similar vein on 1 July (OED/B/3/1/6), and Alfred Robinson went further in a letter to Markby (OUPA, Markby papers, box C/2: dated 'Tuesday', i.e. probably 8 July 1884), suggesting that the proposed scheme, by guaranteeing the Editor's salary for as long as the book remained unfinished, would mean 'the maximum of expense & the minimum of copy', in that Murray would be encouraged to prolong the work indefinitely.

[26] MP 9 July 1884 FJF to JAHM. The allusion is to William Bunyan's 1768 pamphlet *An Effectual Shove to the Heavy-Arse Christian*.

[27] MP [2 July 1884] JAHM to Price (draft, or perhaps a copy; partly quoted in *CWW* p. 239). In this letter Murray twice makes a telling slip, referring to a requirement for 500 pages a year, rather than 700.

Consultation with the Press's solicitor now suggested that the Delegates might be well advised to be explicit about the experimental nature of Murray's proposed scheme of a single enlarged staff. A resolution was passed whereby the expenditure of £1,750 was to be guaranteed for no more than two years, but Price was instructed to sound Gibbs out about the matter before Murray was informed. Gibbs, now increasingly irritated by the Delegates' shifting position, declared that Murray could not be expected to 'break up his establishment and quit his situation and his livelihood for a two years engagement', and also that he too considered it unreasonable to require an unconditional promise from Murray regarding a task which was so dependent on others. He was confident that the Delegates would be persuaded: as he told his son Vicary, 'Those 'coons [i.e. raccoons] will come down.'[28]

But such confidence was misplaced. Jowett and the other Delegates who were doubtful that the necessary acceleration could be achieved by a single editorial team—and were now apparently under the mistaken impression that Murray was reluctant to leave Mill Hill—finally lost patience, and voted to abandon Murray's scheme, instructing him instead to 'continue work as heretofore', while they made arrangements to engage a second Editor. This unexpected step caused some to wonder whether the Delegates had identified a particular person for this job, but this does not seem to have been the case. Furnivall wrote urging Murray, for his own sake, to accept the idea of a second Editor: 'The Society won't get its Dicty so well done as if you did it all; but it will see the Dicty finisht in 10 or 12 years from now, & you left alive to work on.' He even suggested that Murray could 'touch up' the other Editor's work when he had finished his own.[29]

Bewildered at the Delegates' misunderstanding of his position, and no doubt put out at the idea that he should be left simply to carry on with one half of the Dictionary while others made arrangements for the remainder, Murray wrote explaining that he was quite prepared to come to Oxford in 1885 provided he was enabled to give the requisite three months' notice. In response the Delegates substituted a more provisional arrangement whereby Murray would continue 'until further arrangements are made', with a staff made up to its full complement (including a replacement for Johnston, whose post had been vacant since August 1883); he was also asked to look for a second Editor to work 'either under him or in conjunction with him'.[30]

While all these negotiations were going on, Murray and his staff were of course pressing on with the work of the Dictionary. In addition to preparing copy for the printers—which had reached *atmosphere* by the time Murray left for a holiday in Edinburgh at the start of August—and reading and correcting proofs, there was also the supervision of the preparatory work still being done by the sub-editors, not only in A but throughout the alphabet, with the aim of bringing all the material inherited from

[28] OD 17 July 1884; OED/B/3/1/6 22 July 1884 HHG to Price; GL MS 11021/22 ff. 426–9 24 July 1884 HHG to Vicary Gibbs.
[29] OD 24 July 1884; MP 29 July 1884 Skeat to JAHM, FJF to JAHM.
[30] OD 31 July 1884.

Furnivall up to a workable standard. Moreover, although much of A had been put into provisional shape two or three years earlier by assistants, it now needed to be revised to take account of the additional quotations that had accumulated: a task Murray entrusted to four experienced sub-editors, Charles Mount (the reader recruited by Price in 1879), the schoolmaster William Brackebusch, Edward Gunthorpe of Sheffield, and W. M. Rossetti.[31] Finally, quotations were still being sent in in their thousands by readers old and new,[32] and these too had to be acknowledged, and queries dealt with. A holiday would no doubt have been welcome.

Not that Murray could escape Dictionary business even in Scotland: Jowett, keen to 'take energetic steps' about a second Editor, wrote suggesting a meeting in Mill Hill on his return. When they met on 4 September, Murray had two names to suggest: Henry Bradley, whose review in the *Academy* had so impressed him, and Anthony Mayhew, the chaplain of Wadham College, a contributor of quotations for the Dictionary and an able philologist, whom Murray had been hoping to recruit for some kind of etymological work if he moved to Oxford, although Skeat thought him lacking in stamina. He even wondered whether Skeat himself might be willing to take on the work, but confessed to considering him 'wanting in judgment' and 'easily turned this way & that'. In fact Bradley had already approached Murray in June expressing interest in doing work on the Dictionary, and when the two men had met to discuss the possibility Bradley's philological knowledge and general scholarship had impressed him still further. Murray now began to give thought to how a system of two editorial teams might be made to work; for example, could each Editor take a Part in turn?[33]

But Oxford could not be expected to keep pace with Jowett's enthusiasm. Once again all parties had to wait for the University to reawaken after the long vacation; it was not until October that the names of Mayhew and Bradley could be put to the Delegates. Price, after visiting Mayhew himself, wrote to ask Murray for a formal statement of his opinion of the two men, and a recommendation as to how he might work with them. Murray's reply gave a favourable opinion of the scholarly capabilities of both, although he thought that Erlebach might be 'a better man all round' than either of them; he reserved judgement on their competence to head a 'second company of workers', and suggested that it might be best, initially at least, for all three of them to work together at achieving the required rate of production, dividing into two 'companies' after a year

[31] The work of these 're-sub-editors' (see further below, p. 263) is acknowledged in Murray's 1884 Presidential Address (*TPS* for 1882–4, p. 520).

[32] Many of the continuing readers were mentioned by Murray in his report to the Philological Society in January 1885, including H. R. Helwich of Vienna, still sending in large numbers of quotations from *Cursor Mundi* and other early texts, and Samuel Major, a Bath accountant who until his recent death had regularly sent in 50 slips per day, not to mention Furnivall, 'who goes on constantly' (ProcPS 23 Jan. 1885, p. vii).

[33] MP 24 Aug. 1884 Jowett to JAHM; JP I. H64 f. 11 (notes by Jowett on a conversation with JAHM 4 Sept. 1884); OED/B/3/1/6 27 Oct. 1884 JAHM to Price; MP 11 June 1884 HB to JAHM. In fact Bradley had been recommended to Murray as a possible assistant as early as March 1884, by the Oxford Celtic professor John Rhŷs and others (SL 10 Mar. 1884 Doble to JAHM); Doble, indeed, had first-hand knowledge of him as a writer and reviewer for the *Academy* from his time as editor of that journal in 1878–80.

or so if that then seemed preferable. He was certainly not yet ready to see either of them taking full responsibility (and credit) for a Part; but he was prepared to try the experiment, and was in fact keen to come to Oxford as soon as possible—provided that he could be confident that in giving up his position at Mill Hill he could expect terms at least as advantageous in Oxford. The impression is of someone anxious to indicate his willingness to cooperate, but still unconvinced of the feasibility of having two Editors.[34]

He may have been encouraged to take a positive approach by the fact that, in addition to being willing to fund the Dictionary (and its Editor) adequately henceforth, the Delegates were prepared to do something about the position in which Murray had been left by the overspend of the project's first five years. Already in June Gibbs had remonstrated with Price about the private debts (to himself and Robert Harley) which Murray had incurred, now amounting to £500; Price had floated the idea of a private subscription among Murray's friends, and the Delegates indicated that they would be prepared to contribute to such a fund (although the idea of a public appeal seems to have horrified them). Furnivall was distinctly unimpressed: he foresaw that if the excess costs of Part I were paid for by a circle of friends, the Delegates might assume that they would be willing to subsidize later Parts in the same way, and he advised Murray to insist, on threat of resignation, on a guarantee to meet all his expenses subsequent to Part I. Such financial hard-headedness would have been out of character for Murray; but he did mention his debts, and his strong desire to start paying them off, to Jowett, and at their mid-October meeting the Delegates agreed to pay off the £100 he owed to Harley.[35]

On 31 October the Delegates met again, and this time seem to have accepted Murray's misgivings about an immediate splitting of the editorial staff. Not that the idea was dropped; it was recognized, however, that in any case a potential second Editor would have to spend some time working under Murray's supervision. Accordingly, it was decided simply to go back to the scheme proposed in June, with Murray working in Oxford with a single expanded team of assistants, on the understanding that a second Editor could be appointed later if this should prove necessary.[36]

Frustrating as it may have been to find themselves in the same position after over four months of wrangling, Murray and Gibbs were relieved that the way forward was clear at last. Murray undertook to be in Oxford by Easter 1885 at the latest, and

[34]   OD 17 Oct. 1884; MP 24 Oct. 1884 A. L. Mayhew to JAHM, 25 Oct. 1884 Price to JAHM; OED/B/3/1/6 27 Oct. 1884 JAHM to Price. Mayhew also regarded it as obvious that Murray should be brought to Oxford and endowed with 'a Dictionary Fellowship' at a college.

[35]   OED/B/3/1/6 29 June 1884 HHG to Price; SL 1 July 1884 Price to HHG; OD 31 July 1884; SL 12 Aug. 1884 Price to HHG; MP 14 Aug. 1884 FJF to JAHM; OD 17 Oct. 1884.

[36]   OD 31 Oct. 1884; MP 9 Nov. 1884 Price to JAHM. It was also agreed to make financial provision for Murray in the event of his becoming incapacitated: this weighed heavily with Murray, who was always anxious about financial security for himself and his family.

immediately set about finding both a suitable house in Oxford and suitable additional assistants.[37] He had in fact been trying out a cousin of Gibbs named Remmett as a possible assistant, but he unfortunately failed to live up to expectations; Frederic Bumby, a graduate of Owens College, Manchester, proved more satisfactory. Jowett, anxious to help (and to promote his own protégés), was also soon suggesting possible names. As for the two figures who had already been mentioned in connection with more high-level work, Mayhew turned out to be fully occupied, while Bradley had just agreed to deputize as editor of the *Academy*, and would not now be free to do Dictionary work until the end of March. He was, however, keen to be considered, and suggested that Murray send him some work by way of a trial.[38]

The search for accommodation in Oxford was made more difficult by Murray's straitened finances. Excess expenditure on the Dictionary had cost him several hundred pounds, and even after the Delegates had paid off his debt to Robert Harley, he was still unable to afford anything suitable. He visited Oxford in early December, and identified a possible house in Woodstock Road; the Delegates, who had already voted him £100 towards the cost of moving house, now agreed to loan him £500.[39] Unfortunately, thanks to a delay in closing a deal while he negotiated over another house (which proved to be too small), the Woodstock Road possibility fell through, and on New Year's Eve Murray returned home from another visit to Oxford 'wearied, baffled, and beaten', and very worried that he, his family, and the Dictionary, would be left houseless after Easter. The only possibility he had seen was on the large (and expensive) side, and would not be ready before early May: 'a house now building where the tram-cars stop in the Banbury Road'—very much on the edge of town, in fact: the development of the North Oxford estate belonging to St John's College was not yet complete.[40]

The cost of the new house, which was expected to be £1,850, turned out to be less of a problem than Murray might have feared: several members of the Philological Society's Council had offered to lend him the money he needed. He gratefully accepted a loan of £1,600 from Skeat, and the purchase of 78 Banbury Road was soon settled.[41] However, there were difficulties in relation to the erection of a new Scriptorium. Murray's initial suggestion that it be placed in the front garden was objected to by the Bursar of St John's, and his prospective neighbour, Albert Venn Dicey (the University's professor of English law), protested at an alternative site in the kitchen garden on the grounds

---

[37] MP 20 Nov. 1884 JAHM to Price (copy). On Gibbs's advice, Murray pointed out that if he moved to Oxford and still failed to achieve two Parts a year, the cost of then dividing the project into two would be greater than the £1,750 now agreed (MP 16 Nov. 1884 HHG to JAHM). Initially Murray's decision to leave Mill Hill was kept secret, as Weymouth was worried about the effect this would have on the school's reputation (SL 22 Nov. 1884 Price to HHG), but news inevitably leaked out, and was reported in the *Athenaeum* of 27 December (p. 860).

[38] HJRM p. 154; MP 13 Dec. 1884 Mayhew to JAHM, 24 Nov., 6 Dec. 1884 HB to JAHM.

[39] OD 28 Nov. 1884, 12 Dec. 1884.

[40] OED/B/3/1/7 1 Jan. 1885 JAHM to Price.

[41] MP 19 Jan. 1885, [?Sept. 1885] Skeat to JAHM; OED/B/3/1/7 21 Jan. 1885 JAHM to Price.

FIGURE 14   The Scriptorium in the garden of 78 Banbury Road, Oxford (undated photograph).

that the building would 'injure his outlook'. Eventually Murray had to agree to sink it more than two feet into the ground, so that (as he complained to Price) 'no trace of such a place of real work shall be seen by fastidious and otiose Oxford, "where even men who work, do it in secret, & pretend openly to be merely men of the world". (A genuine quot[atio]n from one of the most widely known men in Oxford.)'[42] As a consequence, the new Scriptorium (see Figure 14), although slightly larger than the one at Mill Hill, was permanently damp, suffered from poor ventilation, and in winter was extremely cold; the effect upon those working in what Furnivall was to refer to as 'that horrid corrugated den' can be imagined.[43]

It was with distinctly mixed feelings that Murray rose to give his report on the year's progress at the Philological Society's first meeting of 1885. It was pleasing that

[42] Hinchcliffe (1992) 180; MP 6 May 1885 JAHM to [Price] (draft); St John's College Archives, minutes of Estates Committee 8 May 1885 (ref. ADM II.A.2 p. 233). Elisabeth Murray tentatively attributes the quotation to Max Müller (*CWW* p. 247).

[43] *Oxford Magazine* 2 Dec. 1885, p. 413 (which gives the dimensions as 30′ × 17′); MP 29 Nov. 1892 FJF to JAHM. For a view of the interior of the new Scriptorium, probably dating from sometime after 1905, see Figure 22, p. 309. Murray presented the original Scriptorium to Mill Hill School for the use of the pupils; it was moved into the school grounds, and used for quiet study until it accidentally burned down in 1902 (see p. 110 n. 1). It was replaced with a more substantial building, still known today as the 'Murray Scriptorium'.

arrangements for the move to Oxford had at last been settled, but the 'distractions and interruptions' of recent months had badly hampered progress. Although material 'in the printers' hands' now reached to *baffle*, only 200 pages of Part II had actually been passed for press; the text as far as *baffle*—another 68 pages—still had to be proofread, and a further 84 pages beyond that (up to *batten*) had still not been completed even as printer's copy. To achieve two 352-page Parts a year he and his assistants would have to work something like three times as fast, whereas the end of A was proving to contain many particularly challenging words, including the difficult prepositions *as* and *at*, which along with *back* were to be the longest entries in Part II. He appealed for more volunteers to swell the ranks of sub-editors and re-sub-editors, as it was now clear that material prepared to a high standard before it reached the Scriptorium could be processed much more quickly.[44]

By this stage Murray should also have been taking steps to expand his own paid staff; but he hesitated, apparently because he still regarded his own finances as too precarious to allow him to take on the extra commitment. A significant factor in this was his outstanding debt of £400; Gibbs, who as creditor was far from pressing Murray for repayment, nevertheless felt that an application might reasonably be made to the Press to free him from this debt, and Murray duly wrote to Price. Unfortunately, at the same time Furnivall took up the cudgels on Murray's behalf, writing a thoroughly intemperate letter to Jowett on the subject, which Gibbs blamed for the Delegates' decision to take no action in the matter, at least until Price had discussed it with Murray.[45] In fact Murray, ever reluctant to impose on the Delegates, suggested that they wait until the Philological Society had considered what they could do. Meanwhile, reassured by Price that funding for assistants would be forthcoming, he began to make enquiries, although actual appointments would have to wait until he was in Oxford. He also began to send some B entries to Bradley, for 're-sub-editing' and etymological work; Bradley proved to be exceptionally good at investigating difficult etymologies, and at drafting etymological copy, which Murray was soon making use of with little alteration.[46]

Following a meeting of the Society's Council on 6 February, the idea of a public appeal for contributions—soon christened the 'Murray Indemnity Fund'—was resurrected. After taking legal advice, Price rejected the assertion—made by both Skeat (now the

---

[44] ProcPS 23 Jan. 1885 (supplemented from PSOM). It was at this meeting that Henry Bradley was proposed for membership of the Philological Society.

[45] MP 20 Dec. 1884 HHG to JAHM; 30 Dec. 1884 Price to JAHM; 6 Jan. 1885 FJF to JAHM; OD 23 Jan. 1885; MP 3 Feb. 1885 HHG to JAHM.

[46] OED/B/3/1/7 4 Feb. 1885 JAHM to Price; MP 26 Mar. 1885 Price to JAHM. A notebook (OED/B/5/7/1) recording material sent to sub-editors notes Bradley's first consignment, 'Bath–Batze to re-sub-edit and write etymologies', as sent on 23 Feb. 1885; in the original copy slips his handwriting can indeed be seen in the etymology and definitions of *bath* and subsequent entries, but later on in B appears largely in the etymologies of difficult words. Murray acknowledged his etymological contributions in the Preface to Part II.

Society's President) and Furnivall—that the Press's contract obliged them to pay all the project's costs, including the debts incurred by Murray; but he indicated to Skeat that the Delegates would not object to a public appeal. A circular was prepared (and its wording toned down at the request of Murray, who was clearly very uncomfortable at the whole idea); and it was arranged that the names of the Delegates would appear on the first public issue, as subscribers in their private capacities, thereby showing their 'personal feeling towards the work and Dr Murray'.[47] They contributed £60 in total, and the requisite £400 was raised almost as soon as the circular was issued; in fact the Fund ultimately raised enough to give Murray an additional £180 as well as paying off his debt to Gibbs. This was surely, as Skeat commented to Price, 'a hearty and well-omened welcome to Oxford'.[48] (Less well-omened was the inflammatory article which appeared in the *Oxford Review*, under the heading 'How *not* to treat a man of letters', while the circular was still in proof, accusing the Delegates of 'taking advantage of legal technicalities to escape moral obligations', of 'miserable parsimony and sharp practice', and of 'cheese-paring', and reminding them that they were 'something more than tradesmen'. Anonymous it may have been, but the hand of Furnivall is surely unmistakable.[49])

The new house in Oxford, which the Murrays also named Sunnyside, was ready for occupation (together with the new Scriptorium) in June; on 5 June the Philological Society wished Murray 'God speed', and on 10 June he travelled to Oxford ('with the furniture, the older children and the pet doves'), while Ada and the assistants remained behind to pack up the contents of the Scriptorium. The rest of the family rejoined him the following day.[50]

The search for assistants now began in earnest. Unfortunately, in this respect the timing of Murray's arrival, at the start of the long vacation, could not have been worse. The first to join the team in the Scriptorium was not an Oxford man: R. H. Lord, the nephew of Murray's old friend Robert Harley, who began work on 1 July. Lord, another alumnus of Owens College, vindicated his uncle's recommendation of him, and proved a reliable assistant; less so were some of the others identifed through the appeal that went out to figures in Oxford. An unnamed Oxford BA recommended by W. W. Jackson, the Rector of Exeter College, proved 'an utter numb-skull […] a most lack-a-daisical, graspless fellow born to stare at existence', who had to be got rid of after only a few days, as did several others.[51] Fortunately he did soon manage to secure the

[47]   MP 8, 12 Feb. 1885 AJE to JAHM, 16 Feb. 1885 FJF to JAHM, 25 Apr. 1885 AJE to HHG; OED/B/3/1/7 11 Feb. 1885 FJF to [Price], 23 Feb. 1885 Skeat to Price; OD 6 Mar. 1885; SL 12 Mar., 9 May 1885 Price to Skeat.

[48]   MP 19 May 1885 AJE to FJF; PSCM 6 Nov. 1885; OUP/PUB/11/4 19 May 1885 Skeat to Price. Various versions of the 'Murray Indemnity Fund' circular are preserved in MP. On Furnivall's advice, Murray used some of the surplus money to buy a pair of tricycles (*CWW* pp. 326–7, with illustration of the 'Humber tandem tricycle').

[49]   *Oxford Review* 6 May 1885, quoted in *CWW* pp. 248–9.

[50]   PSOM 5 June 1885; *CWW* p. 243 (which quotes Ada's touching letter to her husband from the empty house in Mill Hill, where 'the bed was *so* hard & *so* lonely').

[51]   MP 2 June [1885] R. H. Lord to JAHM; OUP/PUB/11/5 13 July 1885 JAHM to Doble. Among those who were asked about possible help for the Dictionary were, in Oxford, Arthur Napier, the newly

services of three other men who proved capable of editorial work: Charles Balk and Walter Worrall, who would both ultimately figure among the Dictionary's longest-serving workers, and the Balliol graduate Charles Crump, who had been invalided back from India after only six months in the Civil Service. A clerical assistant, George Parker, started work on 18 July.[52]

Finally there was G. F. H. Sykes, the principal of Forest House School in Essex. He had also been a master (and pupil) at Mill Hill, although he had left before Murray arrived and was in fact an older man. He evidently came to Murray's notice in connection with an event which he had long dreaded: the decision by Alfred Erlebach, his trusted senior assistant—and by now a close personal friend—that he must honour a long-standing promise to his brother Henry to take over the running of Sykes's school. Murray had hoped to persuade him to continue with the Dictionary for a year after the move to Oxford, but in the end he only agreed to stay for a few months. Already in May Sykes had accepted an offer of work on the Dictionary, but he did not move to Oxford until August—which was to be Erlebach's last month: he left at the start of September.[53] This did not by any means mark the end of his assistance to the Dictionary, as he became one of the small group of individuals who read and commented on all of Murray's proofs, and on occasion even returned to the Scriptorium to deputize for Murray when he went on holiday.[54]

Erlebach's departure would have been a great loss at any time; coming when it did it was a calamity. All of Murray's calculations as to the rate of production achievable in Oxford had been predicated on the assumption that Erlebach would be at his side; now, quite apart from the time wasted trying and rejecting possible assistants, the whole business of reorganizing the project and developing new working methods would have to be done without his most experienced assistant. Not that the Press could be expected to make allowances for his loss: the first salary payment to reach Murray after his arrival in Oxford was accompanied by the observation that the Delegates 'enquire with great anxiety as to the weekly progress of the Dictionary', and 'earnestly hope' that two Parts a year would soon be achievable.[55]

appointed Merton professor of English, John Earle, the professor of Old English, and Charles Plummer of Corpus Christi College (29 May 1885 FJF to Napier, Napier papers, English Faculty Library, Oxford; SL 23 June 1885 P. L. Gell to C. Plummer, 14 July 1885 Gell to Earle), and beyond, Edward Dowden of Dublin (an old friend of the Dictionary from early days) and T. N. Toller of Manchester, then at work on his revision of Bosworth's Anglo-Saxon dictionary (SL 14 July 1885 Gell to Dowden, Gell to Toller).

[52] MP Notebook recording payments to assistants and other expenses (which gives the dates of appointment of many assistants). I have not been able to find any mention of Balk prior to his appointment; however, it may be that he was already known to the Press, or to Murray, as in the 1881 census returns for Oxford he is listed as a 'lexicographer'. He was of German parentage; his father apparently came to Ipswich as an engineer, and took British citizenship. Walter Worrall, the son of the minor Liverpool painter Joseph Edward Worrall, had an Oxford classics degree, and may have been recommended by the classicist Robinson Ellis, who was soon to become Murray's closest friend in Oxford.

[53] MP 27 May 1885 G. F. H. Sykes to [JAHM].

[54] Harold Murray recalled that Erlebach 'year after year [...] took charge of the Scriptorium' when Murray took a summer holiday, apparently down to his death in 1899 (HJRM p. 161).

[55] MP 16 July 1885 Gell to JAHM.

FIGURE 15   Philip Lyttelton Gell, photographed around the time of his appointment as Secretary to the Delegates in 1884.

The writer of these chivvying words was a new figure in the history of the Dictionary, and one whose role has been portrayed in the blackest terms by its previous historians. Philip Lyttelton Gell (see Figure 15), who had been appointed in the summer 1884 to take over from Price as Secretary to the Delegates, and who took up his post a year later,[56] was another Balliol man, and a friend (and later literary executor) of Benjamin Jowett. He was very much an outsider, having never worked for the Press nor been a Delegate, and at the time of his appointment was working for the London commercial publishers Cassell and Galpin (the publishers of Robert Hunter's *Encyclopaedic Dictionary*, as Murray was no doubt displeased to observe); as such he no doubt suited Jowett's purposes as someone who might help him to modernize the Press. He is, however, generally regarded as having been a disastrous Secretary. Peter Sutcliffe, while recording that he was 'remembered as idle, quarrelsome, and incompetent', concedes that his reputation may have suffered in retrospect from his being disliked in some quarters simply because he was 'Jowett's man'.[57] He was certainly prone to making enemies, and to making a poor initial impression: Lucy Toulmin Smith, who was editing a volume of mystery plays for the Press, complained to Murray that he 'show[ed] more zeal on behalf of his employers than on the side of the author'.[58] As far as his relationship with the Dictionary is concerned, it is notable that his first communication with Murray was, or at least purported to be, a representation of the wishes of the Delegates. It is certainly true that during his most difficult years at the Press he found himself having to deal with several exceptionally active Delegates who profoundly disagreed with his modernizing ideas. (They were his ideas as well as Jowett's, and persisted long after Jowett was succeeded as Vice-Chancellor by James Bellamy in the autumn of 1886.) The

---

[56] Gell's appointment was engineered by Jowett during the long vacation of 1884, at a time when he could count on being backed up in his choice of candidate by the few Delegates who were still in Oxford (Sutcliffe 1978: 67–9). Price was evidently persuaded of Gell's merits, as he declared his intention to take him on as Assistant Secretary as soon as possible (SL 27 Aug. 1884 Price to F. Macmillan); he finally stepped down as Secretary in June 1885. For further assessments of Gell and his Secretaryship see Curthoys (2013: 68–9), Eliot (2013b: 109–10), and Whyte (2013: 64–6).

[57] Sutcliffe (1978: 66).

[58] MP 29 July 1885 L. T. Smith to JAHM.

Delegates were, in any case, his masters, and if they had strong views about the course to be taken, there was little enough he could do to change them; and it was perhaps unfair, if understandable, that Murray sometimes blamed the messenger rather than the authors of the message.

The importance of achieving a regular issue of Parts, and thereby sustaining public confidence in the Dictionary, had of course been emphasized by others before Gell. Indeed, in May, just before he took over as Secretary, the Delegates had decided that in advertising Part II of the Dictionary explicit assurance should be given that future Parts would appear at the rate of two per year.[59] By the time Gell took up the Secretaryship over a year had elapsed since the publication of Part I; if such confidence was to be publicly expressed, it was surely reasonable to enquire of Murray whether it was well founded. Murray responded to Gell's letter with an explanation of how the 'toilsome & vexatious business' of finding assistants had held up progress, and an assurance that he was sparing no effort in securing 'the best help which the funds at my disposal will secure. But all this takes much time.'[60]

In fact it was not until the autumn that the text of Part II was complete.[61] Its 352 pages extended into the letter B as far as *batten*; and it was already clear that the second letter of the alphabet would be even more challenging than the first. Murray's estimates of the rate of production had assumed that words of especial difficulty were uniformly distributed across the alphabet, but unfortunately this was not the case: B contained a much higher proportion than A of words with histories extending back to the medieval period, which often took much longer than those which began in the Renaissance or later, because of the particular difficulty of their etymologies or because the history of the different senses was significantly harder to establish. Murray's former assistant J. B. Johnston had joined Gibbs and Fitzedward Hall as a regular reader of the proofs, and (whatever his shortcomings in the Scriptorium had been) soon proved an invaluable finder of additional quotations to complete the illustrative record for more recent vocabulary; but incorporating comments from such sources took time. It was not until November that Part II was finally published.[62] On 10 November the University of Oxford conferred the honorary degree of MA upon Murray; he had been proposed by Jowett, with whom relations had definitely improved. As Master of Balliol, he had welcomed Murray and his wife to one of the college's famous Sunday concerts as soon as they had arrived in Oxford, and the two men, perhaps surprisingly, became close

[59] OD 22 May 1885. Sure enough, a statement that the Delegates 'confidently hope' to issue succeeding Parts 'at intervals of six months only' was included in many of the advertisements for Part II.

[60] OUP/PUB/11/5 17 July 1885 JAHM to Gell.

[61] Copy for what were to be the last entries in Part II was delivered to the printers on 24 July, but of course there then followed two rounds of proof correction; Murray also took a short holiday in August. Discussion of the distinctively Oxford word *battels*, one of the very last in the Part, extended well into September (see various letters in MP).

[62] Advance copies of Part II were sent to Furnivall in time for them to be seen at the Philological Society's meeting on 6 November (PSOM 6 Nov. 1885).

friends, to the extent that when in 1886 Murray's sixth son (and tenth child) was born he was christened Arthur Hugh Jowett.[63]

The reception of Part II was more muted than that for Part I, but was once again overwhelmingly favourable; many reviewers took particular notice of the entries to which Murray had drawn attention in his Preface as being of particular difficulty, interest, or simply length. However, the slowness with which the Dictionary was appearing was widely commented on: fairly typical was the reviewer in *John Bull* who anticipated that it was only 'our "nati natorum et qui nascentur ab illis" who have any chance of seeing it in its completed shape'.[64] The contrast with the *Encyclopaedic Dictionary*, which with the half-volume issued in January 1886 (the ninth) extended into P, must have been uncomfortable.

Surely even more uncomfortable was the news about the Dictionary's finances which Furnivall communicated to the Philological Society's Council in January, just before Murray's annual progress report: the latest accounts from the Press showed a loss of over £7,000 on the book up to 30 June 1885. Admittedly this did not show the benefit of sales from Part II, but these hardly improved the picture: American orders had sunk to 1,000, a decline which Gell attributed entirely to the delay in the appearance of Part II. The reasons that it had taken Murray over a year and a half to complete what he had expected to require a year would have been clear enough to all parties; and certainly it would be hard to deny that such matters as the departure of Erlebach and the problems in finding suitable assistants could not have been anticipated. (In January he took on a new assistant, Arthur Maling, who was ultimately to prove one of the best, but it would be some time before his worth became apparent.) But the fact that Murray and his team had faced unforeseen difficulties would hardly cut ice with the public, who had after all been told to expect Part III early in 1886. And as far as Gell—and, presumably, the Delegates—were concerned, the arrangements needed to ensure the production of two Parts a year were, or should be, now in place.[65]

Alarmed that things were so obviously not going according to plan, the Delegates appointed another committee.[66] One of its members was Bartholomew Price, who although now retired from the Secretaryship had been appointed a perpetual Delegate, and who once again took a leading role. The committee's preferred option was evidently the appointment of a second Editor, to start work independently on Part IV, and their

[63] MP 19 Oct. 1885 Jowett to JAHM; *Times* 11 Nov. 1885, p. 6; *CWW* p. 244. W. W. Merry, the University's Public Orator, in presenting Murray for the degree—a task which he told him had never given him more 'unmixed satisfaction' (MP 12 Nov. 1885 Merry to JAHM)—compared his work to that of the sixteenth-century lexicographer Robert Estienne, and described him as a 'worthy disciple of the prince of lexicographers'.

[64] *John Bull* 12 Dec. 1885, p. 819 (the Latin, a quotation from the *Aeneid*, reads '[our] sons' sons and those born of them'). Perhaps surprisingly, Henry Bradley was once again the reviewer for the *Academy* (28 Nov. 1885, pp. 349–50), despite his close involvement; he was at least careful not to discuss any of his own etymologies in his review, which was once again both thorough and favourable. The task of reviewing the Dictionary for the *Academy* was subsequently taken up by Skeat.

[65] PSCM 22 Jan. 1886; SL 19 Oct. 1885 Gell to JAHM. Several reviews of Part II—no doubt drawing on publicity material—refer specifically to the prospect of publication of the next Part early in 1886.

[66] OD 29 Jan. 1886.

preferred candidate Henry Bradley. Price began to negotiate with Bradley about possible terms—and also with Murray, whose attitude to the idea of a second Editor was still far from enthusiastic: when he learned that Price had been authorized to offer Bradley a salary of £400, he seems to have suggested spending the money on enlarging his own (still under-strength) staff, and then when Price firmly discounted this as an option, argued strongly that the setting up of a second team at this stage would not achieve the desired increase in output, and that it would make more sense initially for Bradley to join the existing team and help to complete Part III. In March Bradley received an offer of work with another publisher, which added a further note of urgency.[67]

At least all parties could agree that Bradley would be an asset to the Dictionary. He had already proved his worth as a researcher and drafter of etymologies; and the Delegates were convinced that engaging him offered the best chance of achieving the goal of two Parts a year. Murray, faced with the continuing slow progress of Part III— only 56 pages had been passed for press by 12 March—could hardly deny that drastic action was needed; he seems to have remained dubious as to the wisdom of assigning Bradley a separate portion of the text, but as the Delegates were evidently set upon this course, he was determined to have his say as to what arrangement would work best. And so on 13 April Bradley travelled to Oxford, to spend two days learning about the working arrangements and discussing possible forms of collaboration. He agreed, or at least was willing to be persuaded, that it would be best for him to start with a section of Part III, rather than striking out independently. At the conclusion of his visit Murray wrote (and Bradley approved) a letter setting out the new dispensation: three of Murray's assistants would transfer to Bradley's staff, preparing material to send to him in London in exactly the same way that it was prepared for Murray (Bradley had made it clear that his wife's health made it imperative that he remain in London, at least for the time being). The remaining two assistants would work on the copy produced by both these teams, rendering it stylistically consistent and generally ready to go to the printers. Bradley's team would start at *bra-*, and aim to complete the letter B. Both men expressed regret that the drive for speed would mean a drop in editorial standards, but Bradley observed pragmatically that 'it may be possible to pay too high a price even for perfection of execution'.[68]

There was one further matter to be settled, namely the amount of time that Bradley was prepared to give to the Dictionary. Although it would of course be desirable for him to give all his time to it, he was involved in a number of other projects. One was a popular history of the Goths, which he had contracted to write for another publisher; another, rather surprisingly, was a Clarendon Press project. In March 1885, following the death of the lexicographer Franz Stratmann, Furnivall had suggested to Price that the Press undertake to publish the new edition of his dictionary of Middle English,

---

[67] OD 12 Mar. 1886; MP 25, 27 Mar. 1886 Price to JAHM; OED/B/3/1/7 24 Mar. 1886 HB to [Price].
[68] MP 7 Apr. 1886 HB to JAHM, 17 Apr. 1886 JAHM to Price (draft); OED/B/3/1/7 17 Apr. 1886 HB to [Price].

which Stratmann had been preparing when he died. The proposal met with a positive response from the Delegates, including the historian and Scandinavian scholar Frederick York Powell, who warmly recommended Bradley as a suitable editor; in September he was invited to undertake the editing of Stratmann's manuscript, and in October he was formally appointed to a task which it was anticipated would take him about a year (an estimate which the Delegates would soon find cause to regret; perhaps they had been too ready to believe Furnivall's description of the manuscript as 'ready for the press').[69]

In view of these other commitments it is hardly surprising that Bradley felt obliged, at least initially, to limit his work with Murray to four days a week; but this proposal, and the general collaborative scheme put forward by Murray and Bradley, was approved by the Delegates, and Bradley was engaged for a year, starting on 1 June at a salary of £400, with the prospect of £500 for full-time work if all proved satisfactory. Only £100 of this was to come out of the funds allocated for assistants, the remainder being new money; the Delegates were evidently prepared to pay for speed.[70] For his part, Bradley was well aware of what he was taking on, but he was optimistic: 'The task before me is certainly an arduous one,' he wrote to Gell, 'but I shall spare no pains in endeavouring to justify the flattering opinion which the Delegates have formed of my competence for the work.' The materials for words beginning with *bra-* were soon being dispatched to London, and by July some of Bradley's copy had begun to reach the printers.[71]

But where was Part III? Notwithstanding the public declarations that Parts would now be appearing every six months, rather more than that time had now elapsed since the publication of Part II, and enquiries about the promised Part were beginning to come in. The Delegates were also becoming alarmed. Already in May, when informing Murray officially of Bradley's appointment, Gell had written of their 'anxiety' that only half of Part III had been passed for press at a time when the whole of it should have been ready; and, rather more disturbingly, suggested that by September (the latest possible date when publication of the Part could be countenanced) it would be clear 'whether a sufficient rate of progress can be guaranteed to warrant the further subsidies of the Delegates'.[72] The fact that five weeks later only a single additional sheet

---

[69] PBED 23428 9 Mar. 1885 FJF to [Gell], [n.d.; late 1885] York Powell to Gell; SL 19 Sept. 1885 Gell to HB; OD 23 Oct. 1885.

[70] Murray was at this point being paid a salary of £500, in addition to his Civil List pension of £250. It may be worth mentioning, for comparison, that the average income of an Oxford college fellow at this time was of the order of £600 p.a. (Feather 2013: 349).

[71] OD 7 May 1886; SL 25 May 1886 Gell to HB; OED/B/3/1/7 26 May 1886 HB to [Gell]; PSCM 4 June 1886.

[72] MP 17 May 1886 Gell to JAHM. At Gell's request, his assistant Charles Doble wrote privately to Murray at the same time, to soften the impact of this rather stern letter, and assure him that he recognized the 'great concessions' had had made to meet the Delegates' wishes. Doble himself hoped that the new arrangement would make it unnecessary for there to be any more of 'these harassing communications from the Delegates' (MP 17 May 1886 Doble to JAHM).

(8 pages) had been passed served to increase their anxiety to near consternation, as Gell informed Murray in another stern letter which noted that the rate of progress 'appears to [the Delegates] to have been scarcely if at all accelerated by the substantial financial resources they have placed at your disposal'.[73] Murray responded with 'pain & vexation', and considerable defensiveness: 'I have done my utmost to ensure the progress of the work; and I do not think that anyone could have done more.' He noted that the lack of completed sheets was not entirely attributable to slowness on his part: proof corrections for a further two sheets had in fact been returned to the printers, and he was not responsible for their delay. There was also the unprecedented difficulty of B to contend with. He invited the Delegates to consider some of the research that had had to be done in order to produce some of the challenging entries so far completed: 'the words *Be, Bear, Beat, Bend, Bid, Bite, Begin*; the prepositions *Before, Behind, Below, Between, Betwixt, Beyond*; the words *Best, Better, Beware, Bias*; the treatment of the vast material under *Be-* pref[ix] & *Bi-* prefix; and the terrible word *Black* & its derivatives'—the last of which had taken his experienced sub-editor Charles Mount three months, and had required another month's work in the Scriptorium. 'It is an embittering consideration for me,' he concluded, 'that while trying to do scholarly work in a way which scholars may be expected to appreciate, circumstances place me commercially in the position of the *bête noire* of the Clarendon Press, who involves them in ruinous expenditure.' Alarmed by Gell's warnings, he in turn warned George Sykes that he anticipated 'serious action on [the Delegates'] part', to the extent that it seemed unlikely that Sykes could expect to be employed on the Dictionary beyond the following Michaelmas. Murray, it turned out, was disappointed in how Sykes had turned out, and now felt that after all he would never be an adequate replacement for Erlebach.[74]

Bête noire Murray may have felt himself to be in some quarters in Oxford, but his contributions to scholarship were certainly being recognized elsewhere. In May he heard of a proposal from the University of Durham to award him an honorary DCL; Jowett urged him to accept, and at the end of June he did so, borrowing a full-dress gown for the occasion from Canon J. T. Fowler, a friend and valued Dictionary contributor.[75]

In late July the Delegates enacted that 5,000 copies of Part III should be 'put to press'.[76] Not, of course, that it was ready; but they were evidently expecting it to be

---

[73] MP 23 June 1886 Gell to JAHM.

[74] MP 24 June 1886 JAHM to Gell (copy); 24 June 1886 JAHM to Sykes (copy).

[75] MP 14 May 1886 Jowett to JAHM, 15 June 1886 W. K. Hilton to JAHM (informing him of the decision to offer him the degree; it was conferred on 29 June), 17 June 1886 J. T. Fowler to JAHM. According to Elisabeth Murray (*CWW* p. 292), the original initiative for the award came from an old friend of Murray's, Canon William Greenwell. Joseph Fowler, whom Greenwell had introduced to Murray, was a voluminous reader for the Dictionary, gave advice on many individual words, and later joined the small group of individuals who systematically read the proofs for all four Editors.

[76] OD 23 July 1886.

complete at some point during the long vacation. In this they were sadly mistaken: by mid-September only 200 pages had been passed for press, and by the time of the first regular meeting of the Michaelmas term five weeks later this had only increased to 224.[77] Worse still, it turned out that, thanks to a miscalculation, the work of Bradley's first two months made no contribution to the completion of Part III. The decision to set him to work on words beginning with *br-* was based on the assumption that these would fall within Part III, which had been expected to extend to the end of B or thereabouts. This was a reasonable assumption: given that Murray's general rule was to limit the scale to six times that of Webster's dictionary, a third 352-page Part might be expected to extend roughly to the point reached on page 176 of Webster, namely *burnisher*. Unfortunately, in late August Gell learned from Murray that, due to a somewhat expanded scale compared to Webster, Part III would end around the end of *bo-*, so that all of Bradley's work to that point would form part of Part IV. Bradley was quickly reassigned to the latter part of *bo-*, but valuable time had been lost; the illness of Sykes, Murray's senior assistant, made for further delay, and Bradley's capacity for work had been badly affected by worry about the precarious health of his wife following the birth of a daughter.[78] Gell, responding to a request from Henry Frowde for prospectuses for Part III, was forced to admit that he could not see how the Part could be ready before the New Year: 'It is a terrible business.'[79] Terrible, and expensive: as Gell pointed out to Murray, the vastly increased expenditure on assistants seemed to have made no difference to the time taken to produce a Part, while the appointment of Bradley had perhaps advanced the appearance of Part III by about a month.[80]

Murray was also finding it a terrible business. The reorganization of the work cannot have been easy, given his own acknowledged reluctance to delegate; but what was more worrying was that he was finding Bradley's work far from satisfactory. Of course, it was only to be expected that at this stage Murray should be scrutinizing Bradley's copy (and providing feedback) before it went on to the printers, and also that he should find it necessary to make further revisions to Bradley's entries; but, as he complained to Gibbs, he regarded the resulting text as hardly fit to appear under his own name, but rather 'what I should describe as "the work of Mr Bradley, with some of its most objectionable features improved by Dr Murray, but not what the latter would himself do"'. This may be as much a reflection of Murray's inability to accept that there was more than one valid way of compiling an entry as of any genuine problem with Bradley's work, but it certainly shows the strength of his feeling about the matter. In any case, it was clear that the Delegates had more or less made up their minds to appoint Bradley; and he was inclined not to oppose the idea, as this would be a way of

---

[77] OD 17 Sept., 22 Oct. 1886.

[78] SL 20 Aug. 1886 Doble to HB, 25, 28 Aug. 1886 Gell to HB; MP 3 Sept. [1886] Sykes to JAHM, 18 Aug. 1886 HB to JAHM (reporting that his wife 'was for a long time after [the birth] hanging between life & death'). Bradley had in fact sent in copy as far as *brasque* (MP 3 Sept. [1886] Gell to JAHM).

[79] FL 26 Oct. 1886 Frowde to Gell; 30 Oct. 1886 Gell to Frowde.

[80] MP 16 Nov. 1886 Gell to JAHM.

making clear to the public that the work done by a man whom he regarded as no better fitted to the role than some of his own assistants was not his responsibility.[81]

By the end of November 1886 the final copy for Part III (which as anticipated ended at *Boz*) had at last gone to the printers. Last-minute printing problems caused a further slight delay, and it eventually appeared in March, by which time a significant portion of Part IV was already compiled in slip form, and even in proof.[82] This work had of course been carried out on the collaborative method; and it turned out that, notwithstanding delicate enquiries from Gell, Bradley was still reluctant to start working independently. The saving of time that would result from Murray ceasing to revise Bradley's work was obvious, but Bradley felt that quality would suffer if he did so.[83] The Delegates had little alternative but to accept that a complete division of the project would have to wait a little longer. It may have been some consolation that the letter C was expected to be less difficult, and that Part IV might consequently be ready only eight months after Part III; six months was of course what they had been hoping for, but Gell encouragingly told Murray that such a comparatively short turnaround 'would go far towards restoring

---

bondmaid

Murray was fiercely proud of the systems he developed for keeping track of the vast quantities of slips that flowed between the Dictionary's various centres of operations, as is seen by his furious over-reaction in 1901 (see p. 293) to a remark by Bradley alluding to the possibility of material going astray. But already by this point he knew of one occasion when the mislaying of slips for a particular word had actually led to its being omitted from the Dictionary. The word was *bondmaid*, which failed to appear in Part III in 1887. Murray's sense of shame at this oversight even fourteen years later is discernible in a draft letter to an unknown correspondent (although he conveniently neglected to mention it when expostulating to Bradley only a few months later): the entry 'was undoubtedly prepared in MS. for the printer, and one can only surmise that the "copy" for it was in some unaccountable way lost either here or at the Press, and that not one of the 30 people (at least) who saw the work at various stages between MS. and electrotyped pages noticed the omission. The phenomenon is absolutely inexplicable, and with our minute organization one would have said absolutely impossible; I hope also absolutely unparalleled' (MP 13 Aug. 1901 JAHM to 'Dear Sir'). The omission—which seems not to have excited any adverse comment by reviewers—was eventually remedied in the 1933 Supplement.

---

[81] GL MS 11021/24 ff. 397–401 6 Nov. 1886 JAHM to HHG. Gibbs later commented that Bradley's work on the Dictionary had 'quite falsified Murray's dreary anticipations', while noting that 'Furnivall & some members of the Philological Socy think him better than Murray. I dont' (MS 11021/24 f. 795).
[82] SL 7 Jan. 1887 Doble to JAHM, 12 Feb. 1887 Gell to Frowde.
[83] SL 12 Jan. 1887 Gell to HB; OED/B/3/1/8 19 Jan. 1887 HB to [Gell]. Furnivall urged an even more radical approach, with each volume of the Dictionary entrusted to a separate Editor; his suggestion was welcomed by the Delegates, but it does not seem to have been put to Murray or Bradley, perhaps unsurprisingly given the latter's hesitancy (OD 3 Dec. 1886; SL 7 Dec. 1886 Doble to FJF).

public confidence in the ultimate appearance of the Dictionary'. He reiterated, however, that 'the work is *wanted* by students *now*', and worried that the pursuit of perfection could still lead to its never being completed; and the Delegates put down a marker that once Part IV was finished, arrangements must then be made for Bradley to tackle some part of the Dictionary independently.[84]

Murray gave his annual report to the Philological Society on 21 January. He of course made no mention of his doubts about Bradley, and indeed gave an optimistic assessment of the state of the project, which with a full complement of assistants should be able to do in eight months what had previously taken twelve. He gave a vivid account of the difficulties involved in establishing the arrangement of senses in a large entry such as *break*, starting with a vast mass of quotations: 'You sort your quotations into bundls on your big table, and think you ar getting the word's pedigree riht, when a new sense, or three or four new senses, start up, which upset all your scheme, and you ar obliged to begin afresh, oftn three or four times.' Work was also slowed by deficiencies in the accumulated database of quotations: Murray observed that '[n]o word that takes up 3 inches of space will have complete quotations at first'. Much research in the Bodleian was needed to fill in some of the gaps, and to verify some of the older quotations in their original editions.[85]

As usual, Murray used his report to acknowledge the contributions of many individuals who had helped in various ways. One figure who appears for the first time among those publicly thanked for supplying quotations should be mentioned, as he must be one of the most famous of all the contributors to the first edition: William Chester Minor.[86] The strange story of this profoundly disturbed American surgeon and Civil War veteran, who after being committed to Broadmoor for the fatal shooting of a man in Lambeth somehow came to hear about the Dictionary, and began to send in quotations and in due course to correspond with Murray, has often been told, and has indeed become a matter of legend; at this point Dr Minor was simply acknowledged as having

---

[84] MP 31 Jan. 1887 Gell to JAHM; OD 4 Mar. 1887.

[85] ProcPS 21 Jan. 1887 (supplemented from PSOM).

[86] The fullest account of Minor's contribution to the Dictionary is given by Winchester (1998); a reconsideration of his case, and of his time at Broadmoor, is given by Stevens (2013), who draws on a fuller range of archival sources. See also Knowles (1990), and Kendall (2011), which discusses his earlier work on the 1864 edition of Webster. Although Winchester estimates the date of Minor's first contact with Murray as 1880 or 1881, it is only from June 1883 that he is listed as a correspondent in the index to Murray's lost correspondence files (see p. 127 n. 68). His first contact with the Dictionary may possibly have been through one of the lists of desiderata which regularly appeared in *Notes & Queries*. Although he had not previously been mentioned by Murray in his addresses to the Philological Society, he had appeared in a list of readers published in 1884 as an appendix to Murray's Presidential Address, where he was credited with having supplied approximately 3,200 quotations, taken from over a dozen mainly sixteenth- and seventeenth-century sources (*TPS* for 1882–4, p. 626). Minor would go on to contribute tens of thousands more quotations; Murray regularly paid tribute to his efforts in his addresses to the Philological Society, notably in 1899, when he made the remarkable claim that '[s]o enormous have been Dr. Minor's contributions [...] that we could easily illustrate the last 4 centuries from his quotations alone' (MP 1899 Address, quoted in Knowles (1990: 33)—although the evidence of the Dictionary 'copy' suggests that he and his colleagues did nothing of the kind in practice.

supplied 1,000 quotations during the past year. Murray's report makes no mention of his curious working methods, which involved the manual compilation of exhaustive word indexes to the books in his collection, enabling him to send in needed quotations for particular words at the point when entries were being edited; this method required considerable (indeed obsessive, in Minor's case) investment of effort, but as a result a much higher proportion of his contributions were used than those of readers who simply supplied quotations which they considered likely to be useful. This puts into context Minor's figure of 1,000, which might seem to be dwarfed by, for example, the figure of 15,000 quotations contributed during the year by Murray's son Harold, or the 28,000 from William Douglas, or the 46,599 (!) slips supplied by H. R. Helwich from a single work, the long (and dialectally important) Middle English poem *Cursor Mundi*. Absent from the lists, but of enormous value as a supplier of additional quotations while he read the Dictionary proofs, was Fitzedward Hall, who was now devoting four hours a day to the task: Murray gratefully recorded in the Preface to Part III that 'there is scarcely a page which he has not thus enriched by his contributions.'[87]

The publicity machine attendant upon the appearance of a Part was now becoming streamlined. The daily papers ceased to be targeted quite so much—indeed, coverage in the dailies was well down on Part II—and the focus turned to the 'literary class', which Doble felt ought to be persuadable that 'it is really useless to give an opinion on any literary or etymological point' without first consulting the Dictionary. Thousands of prospectuses were accordingly distributed to the leading clergy, members of learned societies and county families, MPs, librarians, and so on. Discouragingly, Frowde reported considerable cutbacks in orders from booksellers, once again attributable to the slow progress of the work.[88] For his part, Murray in his new Preface provided a much longer list of words of particular interest, enabling '[b]usy journalists, with no noticeable qualifications for reviewing a dictionary' (as Richard Bailey has put it), to make their notices both entertaining and learned-looking with the minimum of effort.[89]

In his prefatory note to Part III Murray acknowledged the contribution made by Bradley, both in regard to the etymologies throughout and as a collaborator on the section *bore–bounden*. He remained doubtful, however, about the quality of Bradley's editing as he moved into Part IV—which of course began with the *br-* entries on which Bradley had cut his editorial teeth—and duly subjected the copy to painstaking, and time-consuming, scrutiny: in the seven weeks following 1 February 1887 he passed only two sheets (16 pages) for press, while during the same period he seems not to have prepared any copy of his own. This was obviously an unsustainable way to proceed. Gell pointed out to Murray that the Delegates had only authorized the considerable

[87] For more on Fitzedward Hall's work—later described by Murray as 'one of the most splendid instances of disinterested scholarly work ever known' (OED/B/3/9/4 28 July 1897 JAHM to Hall)—see Knowles (2000). Hall's approach had some similarity to Minor's, in that he compiled word indexes on scraps of paper, but of course with a better sense of which words would be worth indexing.

[88] MP 10 Feb. 1887 Doble to JAHM; FL 17 Feb. 1887 Frowde to Gell.

[89] Bailey (2000a: 216).

blue

The earliest quotation included in the first edition of the *OED* for the use of the noun *blue* to denote the honour bestowed on someone who represents the University of Oxford or Cambridge in a sporting contest is one from the *Daily News* of 18 January 1882, in which one 'Ainslie, of Oriel [College]' is described as someone who 'may be successful in winning his blue'. A cutting bearing the quotation was made and sent in by Frederick Furnivall, who regularly read the paper, and the quotation duly appeared in the entry for *blue* when the relevant section of the Dictionary was published in 1887. By this time the man mentioned in the quotation, Ralph St John Ainslie, had left Oxford for a career as a schoolmaster. (By an odd coincidence, during his time as a music master at Sedbergh School Ainslie became a close friend of H. W. Fowler, who would later of course achieve renown as a lexicographer; in fact a caricature of Fowler by Ainslie, who was a talented artist, graces the cover of Jenny McMorris's biography of him.)

However, the prediction made by the *Daily News*—which would surely have sunk into obscurity had it not found its way into the *OED*—never came to pass: although Ainslie had captained his college's boat club, and rowed three times in the Trials for the University Eight, he never did row for Oxford, and therefore never won his blue. The emphasis given to his failure to live up to the promise of that 1882 quotation by its appearance in the *OED* apparently rankled with the disappointed Ainslie, who often recounted the story; it is even mentioned in his obituary, and was described by a contemporary as the 'one fly in his ointment'. There is now a postscript to the sad story (which was unearthed by Jenny McMorris in 1999, and recounted in *OED News*): Ainslie would perhaps have been relieved to know that in the revised version of the *OED* entry for *blue* which was published in 2013, an earlier quotation (from the *Cambridge Review* of 30 March 1881) is given for this particular sense—and that the quotation which caused him such embarrassment, being no longer needed, has been dropped.

increase in expenditure in the expectation of faster progress, and invited him to propose any method that might make for 'a less vexatious discrepancy between expenditure & results'. A letter written to Bradley at the same time is more revealing about Gell's view of things. He advised Bradley to do as little work as possible on 'any article upon which experience tells you Dr Murray is likely to have especial views', as a means of minimizing duplication of effort; he also suggested that he keep a record of the extent to which his entries were altered by Murray. He anticipated that when the Delegates reconvened after Easter they would conclude that 'the present arrangement is *not* a practicable one', and would therefore wish to be able to convince the Philological Society that Bradley should be entrusted with his own section of the Dictionary; the matter would in any case shortly come to a head, as Bradley's initial year was due to come to an end, and it would be as well for him to be able to point to 'a solid mass of work'.[90]

By May very little had changed. Bradley was continuing to send material to Oxford, but Murray was allowing very little of it to pass out of his hands; the rate at which

---

[90]   MP 23 Mar. 1887 Gell to JAHM; SL 25 Mar. 1887 Gell to HB.

pages were passed for press had now fallen to four pages a week ('a snails pace—very unsatisfactory', James Bellamy noted on 13 May, when the Delegates appointed yet another committee). As Gell bitterly observed to Bradley: ' "Cooperation" evidently can do nothing to help Dr Murray.' He arranged to meet Bradley to discuss options, noting that it was now 'more than ever obvious that the time has come when we must make our choice between independent editorship & the indefinite postponement of the work.'[91] The Delegates agreed to extend the temporary arrangement with Bradley until such time as Murray had passed 'a substantial portion' of Bradley's work for press; Gell urged Murray to do exactly this, fearing that otherwise the Delegates might 'take some serious & critical resolution'.[92] During July and August Murray kept the printers supplied with a steady flow of copy—including large quantities of the letter C, where the competent sub-editing done by Gibbs two decades earlier made for good progress—but the subsequent reading and correction of proofs continued to be time-consuming. July proved to be a miserable month: not only was Murray ill at the start of the month, but two of his assistants gave notice. Frederic Bumby left in August to take up a teaching post in Nottingham, and Lord in September, apparently to go into the ministry. By September Murray was desperately in need of a holiday; having had none in 1885 or 1886, he now allowed himself a fortnight, some of which he spent doing examination work in order to make a little much-needed extra money.[93]

Meanwhile Gell, anxious that Bradley should be enabled to show his worth (and doubtful that Murray would pass enough of his material to satisfy the Delegates by the end of the long vacation), had opened another front. He asked Bradley—who had now also engaged the former sub-editor Edward Gunthorpe as an assistant of his own in London—to prepare a specimen of his own work towards the end of the letter B, completely independently of Murray. The copy was to be sent directly to Gell; Murray was not informed of the range of words Bradley had selected (from *butter* to *buttock*) until after it was in proof, and he was instructed not to revise the proofs until Bradley had pronounced himself satisfied with them.[94]

When the Delegates reconvened in October, the case for appointing Bradley as second Editor had begun to look compelling. The rate at which pages of the Dictionary were being finalized had hardly risen above the 'snail's pace' of May: only 4½ pages a week on average since the Delegates' last meeting in July. After examining Bradley's specimen, as evidence of what he could do without Murray's help, the Delegates were convinced, and Gell informed Bradley that it was now proposed—subject to the Philological Society's approval—to appoint him as 'independent Editor of a portion of the Dictionary'. Bradley was now quite ready to take on this role, and did not anticipate any opposition from the Philological Society in the matter. However, he suggested that, notwithstanding the Delegates' evident desire to make him an Editor on equal terms

[91]   ODA, OD 13 May 1887; SL 16 May 1887 Gell to HB.
[92]   OD 27 May 1887; MP 6 June 1887 Gell to JAHM.
[93]   MP 8, 15 July 1887 Gell to JAHM; HJRM p. 168; OED/B/3/1/8 16 Nov. 1887 JAHM to Gell.
[94]   SL 20 June, 8 July, 10, 20 Aug. 1887 Gell to HB.

with Murray, to do so would be quite inappropriate: as he diplomatically explained to Gell, even if he were to end up editing half the Dictionary,

the merits of that half will still be very largely due to Dr Murray, and I think this ought to be explicitly recognised. The way in which I wish the matter to go before the public is that Dr Murray is still chief editor of the dictionary, but that it has been found necessary to *depute* certain portions of the editing to me.

He was also willing to be paid by results (30 shillings per page), instead of a regular salary, on the understanding that with appropriate assistance he could complete one Part per year; such a system had of course been disastrous in Murray's case, but it suited Bradley's circumstances, in that it afforded him flexibility as to how he divided his time between the Dictionary and other work, and left open the question of whether and when he might move to Oxford, regarding which he had various reasons for hesitating (notably his wife's delicate health).[95]

As the business of setting up Bradley with suitable assistance promised to be costly, it must have seemed only reasonable to look for retrenchment elsewhere. The current cost of Murray's team was rather more than he had estimated in 1884 as necessary to achieve an output of one Part a year; and so Gell now informed him that the Delegates wished to reduce expenditure on his team to something like the earlier level. It was perhaps unfortunate that he chose to do this at the same time as notifying Murray of the proposal to appoint Bradley; but both points were evidently at the Delegates' behest.[96]

Given Murray's persistent doubts about Bradley's ability to fulfil the role of Editor, he can hardly have welcomed the suggestion that he should cut back on his own team at the same time as being asked to help work out what kind of assistance Bradley should have. His closest confidants, however, discouraged him from further opposition to the plan. Gibbs shared his concerns about the effect of the split on the 'unity' of the work, but was pragmatic enough to recognize that such unity depended on the by no means certain matter of Murray living to see the project through to completion. For Furnivall, of course, completion of the work in a reasonable time was more important than striving for perfection, and the appointment of a second—and even a third and fourth—Editor was an acceptable response to the problem of slowness of production, which was 'ruining the book financially'. Just how far his view of the project still differed from Murray's can be seen from his instancing of Skeat's etymological dictionary as a model: the edition published in 1882 showed signs of haste, and Skeat was now revising it, but 'the 1st edn has been of great service. No first try can produce a perfect work.' Furnivall was happy to let his son wait for the second edition of the Philological Society's Dictionary, and his grandson for the third.[97]

---

[95] SL 1 Nov. 1887 Gell to HB; OED/B/3/1/8 8 Nov. 1887 HB to Gell. The decision to offer Bradley the Editorship was formally approved by the Delegates at their meeting on 4 November (OD), endorsing the recommendations made at a meeting of the Press's Committee on Publications a week earlier.

[96] MP 3 Nov. 1887 Gell to JAHM.

[97] MP 7, 9 Nov. 1887 FJF to JAHM, 10 Nov. 1887 HHG to JAHM.

While Murray was still considering his response, Gell wrote to Furnivall, enclosing Bradley's specimen, and setting out in detail the Delegates' reasons for now proposing to the Philological Society that he should be appointed as second Editor. He dwelt at length on the costs of the project, which had now risen to appalling levels: editorial expenses had risen from £1 per page to something like £8 per page, and the debt against the book was now in excess of £12,000.[98] With Furnivall he was pushing at an open door: the Honorary Secretary replied that his only regret was that the Delegates was not proposing to appoint '2 more joint Ed[ito]rs, so as to bring out 4 Parts a year'. Furnivall also questioned the extent to which the division of the project would adversely affect the quality of the work. Imperfections in the published Parts had of course been pointed out by reviewers, and Furnivall listed some of those which he had found himself: substantial antedatings of various words, omissions, and 'hundreds of like things'. He admitted that his own former suspicion of the Delegates had been transformed into 'genuine admiration' by their willingness to fund the project so generously; now that they had given the present plan a fair trial and found it unworkable, they were quite justified in seeking an alteration.[99]

But of course the decision was not up to Furnivall, but to the Society's Council. Bradley's specimen was duly circulated, and created a generally favourable impression. Gibbs, who it seems had already been sent a copy by Price, concluded that Bradley 'might pass, & would probably improve'; he also recognized that the Delegates had probably already made up their minds. Murray, still convinced that Bradley would not be up to the job, complained to Gibbs that the specimen was in fact useless as a guide to his competence, as it contained no words of particular difficulty and had in any case been prepared for Bradley by Walter Worrall, now one of the most reliable assistants; a better indication could have been obtained from 'bad work at a difficult word or set of words, by one's worst assistant, who has manifestly broken down at it, and which one has to buckle to and do over again'—this being the kind of work he was constantly having to do. With Bradley, he felt, there was a serious risk that some of his work would prove so poor that he would be unable to continue to be associated with it.[100] The fact that when he finally replied to Gell he made no mention of Bradley, but only of his willingness to co-operate with 'any one whom the Delegates and the Philological Society may find competent to fill the position', suggests that he may still have been hoping that Bradley would be dropped; but at their meeting on 18 November the Council voted to approve Bradley's appointment. 'All life is a compromise,' as Furnivall commented to Murray; but this compromise may have been particularly hard to bear.[101]

There were already other compromises to be made, in regard to the requirement to curtail expenditure on Murray's own staff; and this had now to be considered along with all the other practicalities to be decided. Bradley—who for the time being at least would continue to work in London—would of course need additional assistance; while new assistants might be suitable for some aspects of the work, it would make good

---

[98] SL 12 Nov. 1887 Gell to FJF; PSCM 18 Nov. 1887.
[99] OED/B/3/1/8 14 Nov. 1887 FJF to [Gell].
[100] MP 12 Nov. 1887 HHG to JAHM; GL MS 11021/24 ff. 533–5 14 Nov. 1887 JAHM to HHG.
[101] OED/B/3/1/8 16 Nov. 1887 JAHM to Gell; MP 18 Nov. 1887 FJF to JAHM.

sense for one of Murray's experienced assistants to transfer to Bradley's staff, while continuing to work in the Scriptorium. The assistant whom Murray agreed to release was George Sykes, whom Gell assured Bradley was 'the best man we could offer you—steady & solid'. Sykes was immediately set to work preparing material in the letter E, which had been settled on as the point at which Bradley's Editorship should start. Steps were also taken to find a place for Bradley and his team to work; negotiations with the Trustees of the British Museum eventually resulted in a room being reserved there for his use, but this did not become available until February.[102]

Even more drastic reorganization was in the air. Furnivall's idea of further sub-dividing the Dictionary into individual letters, each edited by a separate editor, had evidently found favour with the Delegates, and in December Gell approached one of Furnivall's suggested names, the philologist Joseph Wright, who had recently returned from studies in Germany and was now working in London. Wright had in fact written the Press earlier in the year to ask about the possibility of working for Murray as an assistant, but nothing had come of it; Gell now wrote to ask whether he would be interested in working with Bradley, commenting that it had now been decided to 'break up the work of the Dictionary' and holding out the possibility that he might be allocated his own volume in due course. Wright turned out to be unavailable, and had in fact already become involved in another lexicographical project, the *English Dialect Dictionary*, of which he would soon become editor.[103]

How much of these negotiations reached Murray's ears is unclear. He was in any case desperately trying to see what could be done with the resources he was to be left with. Gell had quoted to him his own assessment of January 1884 that a staff of two 'first-class' assistants and two others, at a total cost of £650, might be sufficient to produce something like a Part a year; but these calculations had of course assumed the continuing availability of Alfred Erlebach—and indeed the securing of another, equally able assistant—whereas he did not regard any of his current assistants as adequately filling the gap left by Erlebach's departure. In any case, the expenditure to which he was now to limit himself would necessitate considerable retrenchment, including the dismissal of one of his existing assistants, the abandonment of the final round of proof correction, and probably even the giving up of Erlebach's valuable services as a proofreader. Worse still, he would be forced to take much more information second-hand from other dictionaries, without independent investigation; the implications for the standard of the resulting work were such that he could readily anticipate being in due course obliged to dissociate himself from it. Gell's response, reassuring as it may have been in various respects—the willingness of the Delegates to take on all office expenses, to pay the wages of Parker as a general clerical assistant for the project as a whole, and to find additional funds to pay for Erlebach's proofreading—was also

---

[102]   SL 5 or 6 Dec. 1887 Gell to HB; OED/B/3/1/8 25 Feb. 1888 Gell to HB.

[103]   OED/B/3/1/8 15 Nov. 1887 FJF to [Gell] (re 'the German plan'); SL 10 May, 1 Dec. 1887 Gell to J. Wright; OD 20 Jan. 1888; Wright (1932: 352–3).

uncompromising: Murray had often described himself as 'the neck of the bottle', and a reduced staff would still be able to supply him with enough prepared material to keep him fully occupied. Murray was eventually permitted to retain his four remaining editorial assistants (Mitchell, Balk, Worrall, and Maling) at their current salaries for another three months, and in fact they remained thereafter.[104]

And so from the beginning of 1888 the Dictionary acquired a new home, in Bradley's house in Bleisho Road, Lavender Hill. A circular was issued on behalf of the Delegates, announcing the new dispensation, and expressing the hope that volunteers would now extend their assistance to Bradley as well as Murray. At the same time a more systematic procedure for monitoring the progress of the two separate editorial teams was introduced, with printed forms to be completed each month, recording for each Editor the amount of work done at each stage from preparation of copy through to the final passing of pages for press. Gell was evidently determined to keep a close eye on progress from now on.[105] But would the experiment work?

---

[104] MP 3 Nov. 1887 Gell to JAHM; OED/B/3/1/8 16 Nov. 1887 JAHM to Gell; MP 30 Nov. 1887 Gell to JAHM; OD 13 Dec. 1887. The exact amount per year that the Delegates were prepared to allow Murray is unclear: Gell's letter of 3 November suggests that it was £1,125 (including Murray's own salary of £500), while on 30 November he mentions a maximum of '£1,000 a Part' for editorial expenses.

[105] Completed monthly progress report forms, the earliest dated 1 Feb. 1888, are preserved in OUPA (OED/B/5/7/4), as are copies of the circular announcing Bradley's appointment, dated February 1888 (OED/B/2/4/4). Although the number of pages finally passed for press was frequently taken as a 'headline figure', a more representative picture of progress is given by the 'approximate total' given on the forms, this being an aggregate figure for the amount of material that had passed through each of the constituent processes, and consequently tending to average out some short-term imbalances between subtasks, such as concentration on passing of sheets for press at the expense of composition of fresh copy.

6

Storm and stress:
1888–1897

Looking about him on 1 January 1888, his first day as the Dictionary's second Editor, Bradley could have been forgiven for feeling discouraged by just how far the facilities and personnel at his disposal fell short of what Murray could command. His 'staff', such as it was, consisted of one assistant in Oxford (Sykes) and one man helping to check references in London (Gunthorpe); and it remained to be seen how much of the voluntary assistance available to Murray would also be given to him. The search for additional assistants, to work with Sykes in Oxford, met a hitch when it emerged that Sykes was intimidated by the idea of training an assistant himself, and would prefer them to receive at least their initial training from Bradley in London. Sykes came up with the alternative of taking some of his work home and getting his family to assist him, an unconventional expedient to which (in the absence of other assistance) the Delegates assented. Fortunately Erlebach agreed to read Bradley's proofs as well as Murray's, although he stipulated a higher rate of pay for the former as being likely to require more work; Gibbs and Fitzedward Hall also agreed to continue their invaluable work with both sets of proofs.[1] By the end of his first month Bradley had completed copy as far as *ear-mark*—which would eventually become the first eight pages of his first Part—but nothing had got beyond the first stage of proof; more could hardly be expected, given that his team was still incomplete, but considering what was needed to finish a Part in the year—four columns (1⅓ pages) of copy drafted, another four sent to press, four corrected and revised, and four returned in final *every day*—it was not an auspicious start. For Murray on a personal level, the year also started badly—his mother died in Hawick on 7 January—but at least editorially he made good progress, and by the time of the Philological Society's annual Dictionary Evening he was approaching the end of *car-*.[2]

[1] OED/B/3/1/8 10 Jan. 1888 HB to Gell; OD 20 Jan. 1888; SL 28 Jan. 1888 Gell to HB; GL MS 11021/24 ff. 547–9 30 Jan. 1888 HB to HHG; MP 10 Jan. 1888 Hall to [JAHM].
[2] ProcPS 20 Jan. 1888, p. v.

Furnivall, meanwhile, continued to campaign for the engagement of additional Editors. His latest candidate was a Balliol graduate named Peirce de Lacy Johnstone, who had retired from the Indian Civil Service for health reasons and was now living in Oxford, and who had declared himself willing to work unpaid in the Scriptorium for three months (he had a pension) with a view to demonstrating his ability to take on a volume.[3] It was soon agreed that Johnstone should be attached to Bradley's staff; Gell was realistic about the limited amount that he would be able to learn in three months, but encouraged Bradley to try him out, initially with some sub-editing before seeking to gain admission into the Scriptorium for him.[4]

Bradley's need for additional help of some kind was in fact becoming acute. Not only was his staff still under strength numerically, but the one person on whom he depended for prepared material—George Sykes—was proving to be another 'bottleneck'. Already in February Bradley found himself having to explain to the Delegates that Sykes was unable to keep him supplied with material from which to prepare copy. The arrival of Johnstone did not help matters—he frequently sent in apologies for not coming to the Scriptorium, and Bradley feared that he 'does not seem to be greatly in earnest about the work'—and by the middle of April the total output of Bradley's team amounted to 8 pages passed for press, with another 27 pages in proof. This contrasted starkly with the 8 pages a week which, as Gell informed Bradley, Murray was now completing 'with great regularity'. The problem was not merely the quantity of work coming through from the Scriptorium: it now emerged that Murray had always found Sykes's work to need more revision than that of his other assistants. Bradley successfully argued that the conditions under which he had agreed to work, and to be paid by results, had so far not been fulfilled, and that it was therefore unreasonable to pay him on this basis; instead, the Delegates agreed to revert to paying him a regular salary, at least for the time being.[5] Meanwhile, the search for assistants to work with Bradley was stepped up: Gell and Doble began to consult their academic contacts as to suitable young men. ('[W]e cannot have too good a man,' Gell wrote to Samuel Butcher of Edinburgh, 'but we look for the necessary qualities rather than particular attainments.'[6])

---

[3]   OD/B/3/1/8 29 Jan. 1888 FJF to [Gell]; MP 31 Jan. 1888 FJF to JAHM. Another name mentioned by Furnivall at this time as a potential third Editor was that of Percy Andreae, a London literary writer, but although he went to see Gell about the possibility (PSCM 17 Feb. 1888), nothing further came of it.

[4]   SL 9 Feb. 1888 Gell to FJF, Gell to HB.

[5]   OD 17 Feb. 1888; SL 17 Mar. 1888 Gell to HB; OED/B/3/1/8 11 Apr. 1888 HB to Gell; OD 27 Apr. 1888.

[6]   SL 12 Apr. 1888 Doble to W. Minto, 27 Apr. 1888 Gell to S. H. Butcher. Among the various names considered as possible assistants in 1888 was that of Thomas Austin, the prolific supplier of quotations, a frustratingly obscure figure. One of the few substantial pieces of evidence about the sad story of his life is a letter from a rather discomposed Bradley, in which—after acknowledging the enormous value of his quotations, which was such that often more than a quarter of the usable quotations for a word were in his handwriting—he refers obliquely to 'accusations' made by him about Murray as being 'founded on impressions received when (as he has himself told me) he was not sane [...] the tone of Austin's letters to me leaves me in doubt whether he has even yet completely recovered [...] somebody had told me he was considered "rather crazy", but I did not know that this was meant literally' (MP 6 June 1888 HB to JAHM). It is not clear how much longer he continued to supply quotations after 1888; he did, however, continue to do literary work for Furnivall, who over the next five years acknowledges his help in the preparation of various EETS volumes. Sadly, this is the last record we have of him doing scholarly work of any kind; he is recorded in later Oxford censuses as a labourer and, in 1911, as a tripe-dresser's assistant.

May brought better news, in the form of the publication of Part IV, which extended as far as *cass*. It was made available in two sections, the first ending with the end of the letter B, so that Volume I (which it had been agreed should contain A and B) could be neatly completed; the writing of separate prefaces, as well as the Preface for Volume I, occupied Murray rather longer than he would have liked, but at least it could at last be said that the Dictionary's first volume was complete. Another small milestone was passed in June with what appears to be the first official use of the title by which the Dictionary has come to be best known. Although 'New English Dictionary' was to remain the official title throughout the history of the first edition, and continued to be widely used, Clarendon Press advertisements now began to use the name 'Oxford English Dictionary' in advertising matter for the first time.[7] (The Dictionary had also already begun to be referred to informally as 'Murray's', a fact which Murray admitted finding 'extremely annoying', declaring to one correspondent that it was '[o]ne of [his] chief regrets [...] that the names of all workers at the Dictionary cannot figure before the public as much as [his] own'.[8]) The change of title seems to have gone unremarked by contemporary reviewers, who were more interested in the prediction in the Preface to Volume I that, now that Bradley and 'a staff of assistants' were at work on a third volume, production should now proceed at twice the previous speed.

Of course, 'staff' continued to be something of an overstatement. Whatever Sykes's shortcomings as an assistant—and Bradley was at pains to reassure Gell that he had 'done all that any man could do'[9]—there was only one of him. To make matters worse, Murray's able assistant John Mitchell had also given notice, apparently because of problems with his eyesight (though there is some suggestion that his real reasons for leaving may have been financial).[10] Fortunately there were soon some new names to conjure with: Bradley had received an application from Arthur Strong, an orientalist at work in Oxford (helping Monier Monier-Williams with his Sanskrit dictionary), and Murray decided to take on one of Samuel Butcher's recommendations, a minister's son recently graduated from Glasgow named George Morrison.[11] By August the new assistants were both at work; and, having recovered from a severe bout of illness, Johnstone also at last began to work steadily, with Sykes reviewing Strong's and Johnstone's work before sending it on to London.[12]

---

[7] The title appears, for example, in Press notices announcing the publication of Part IV in the *Athenaeum* of 16 June 1888, and the *Times* and *Pall Mall Gazette* of 21 June 1888. It was soon widely adopted; for example, the *Washington Post* of 17 July observed (p. 7) that 'the Oxford English Dictionary is apparently the name by which it is intended to be known to history'. Well before this the fact of Oxford's association with the project had led to it being sometimes referred to as the 'Oxford Dictionary'.

[8] MP 20 Apr. 1886 JAHM to 'Dear Sir' (draft).

[9] OED/B/3/1/8 29 June 1888 HB to Gell.

[10] MP 24 May 1888 Gell to JAHM.

[11] SL 14 July 1888 Gell to JAHM, 20 July 1888 Gell to G. H. Morrison. The second of these letters is of particular interest in giving the hours of work in the Scriptorium (9 till 6 on weekdays, with an hour for lunch, and 9 till 1 on Saturdays).

[12] SL 22 June 1888 Gell to Sykes, Gell to Johnstone.

Despite the increase in manpower, however, Bradley's rate of progress remained painfully slow. By late September barely 70 pages of E had been typeset. The problem lay once again, it appeared, with Sykes, who had now received a large quantity of material from his two trainees, but had passed on hardly any of it to Bradley. Gell was convinced that Johnstone and Strong were abler men than Sykes, and shared their frustration at being effectively forced to work at the pace of the older man; but it may simply have been that their work needed considerable overhauling before it was worth sending on. Bradley was certainly aware of shortcomings in the work of both of the new assistants; but Johnstone, apparently confident of his ability to work independently, was growing impatient, and Gell urged Bradley to consider accepting work directly from him and Strong. Whether he agreed to do so or not, progress began to improve, and by the time the Delegates reconvened three weeks later Bradley had managed to send another 20 pages to the printers. Murray, meanwhile, was impressed by George Morrison, who seemed likely to develop into an acceptable replacement for Mitchell; the departure of his junior assistant, Parker, at the end of July, was a further blow, but he could report to the Delegates that he had reached *cast*.[13]

With the arrival of autumn a new difficulty arose: the conditions in the Scriptorium, and in particular the effect of the heating apparatus on the atmosphere, which Arthur Strong declared 'pestilential almost beyond endurance'. Strong had now begun to produce good work for Bradley, but found the conditions so inimical to his health that he was obliged to take two lengthy periods of time off work, and now asked to be permitted to do at least some of his work at home. Murray himself was also seriously ill during October.[14] There was of course nothing to be done about the root cause of the problem, namely the fact that the Scriptorium was half-buried in the ground; this was not the last of Strong's complaints about the matter, nor would he be the only assistant to protest.

As 1888 drew to a close the Dictionary's prospects were looking as gloomy as ever. More text had certainly been edited during the year—approximately 380 pages in total—but this amounted to considerably less than the two Parts which the public had been led to expect.[15] The reduced total was hardly surprising given that neither Editor had had a full complement of assistants. Bradley, in particular, had been obliged to manage for two-thirds of the year with only one Scriptorium assistant, while at the same time trying to complete his revision of Stratmann: far from ideal circumstances for his first year as an independent Editor.[16] He was also becoming increasingly

---

[13] SL 26, 28 Sept. 1888 Gell to HB, 1 Dec. 1888 Gell to Johnstone; OD 19 Oct. 1888; MP 6 July 1888 Gell to JAHM.

[14] OUP/PUB/11/6 15 Nov. 1888 Strong to [Gell]; MP 24 Oct. 1888 R. Ellis to JAHM.

[15] SL 12 Jan. 1889 Gell to FJF. It is notable that in this letter Gell anticipates that once the two Editors have fully staffed and operational teams the output should rise to 600 pages a year, not 700 as previously projected: perhaps he (and the Delegates) had now accepted that this was all that could realistically be hoped for.

[16] Completion of Stratmann's dictionary was evidently a matter of some urgency for the Delegates, who were even willing to consider allowing Bradley to reduce his work on the *NED* to a minimum if this would allow Stratmann to be cleared out of the way quickly (SL 18 Jan. 1889 Gell to HB).

pessimistic about Johnstone's ability to produce work of the required standard. In fact Johnstone now began to fade from the picture, having never lived up to expectations: in February 1889 he demanded to be allowed to produce a substantial specimen 'without interference', as a demonstration of his competence to be appointed as an independent Editor, but although he was allocated a 16-page section at the start of F, no specimen was ever satisfactorily completed.[17] Murray, for his part, had not even been able to find anyone to replace George Parker as a junior assistant. He had even begun to contemplate the radical step of engaging 'a little feminine assistance' to fill the gap, a suggestion welcomed by Gell, who observed, 'There are many philologists among them [women] nowadays.'[18] It would be some years before this idea became a reality.

Murray and Bradley were both present to report their progress, and to appeal for new assistants, at the Dictionary Evening on 18 January 1889. Their audience was no doubt aware that the final section of Robert Hunter's *Encyclopaedic Dictionary* had appeared only the previous month;[19] as if this was not enough reminder of the competition, Furnivall had brought along some specimen pages of another rival publication which promised to be even more of a threat to the Philological Society's project. Plans for the *Century Dictionary*, an American project based on a substantial revision of the latest edition of the *Imperial Dictionary*, had been announced as long ago as 1883; the editor-in-chief, William Dwight Whitney of Yale, was an honorary member of the Society.[20] Furnivall gleefully pointed out 'some of [the] many faults' of the specimens; but this first sight of such a formidable publication must have been the cause of some disquiet.

One year into the new regime, Murray now at last seemed to be settling into a steady routine. His staff was smaller than it had been in 1887, but with Balk, Worrall, Maling, and the very promising Morrison, he made good progress with Part V, and during the first few months of 1889 he managed a monthly average of roughly 20 pages, even though he was still reading and commenting on all of Bradley's proofs.[21] Better still, Mitchell, whose loss had been so keenly felt, returned to the Scriptorium

---

[17]   SL 1 Dec. 1888 Gell to Johnstone; OED/B/3/1/8 18 Feb. 1889 Johnstone to Gell; OED/B/3/1/8 21 Feb. 1889 HB to Gell; SL 17 June 1889 Gell to Johnstone, 1 July 1889 Gell to JAHM. Johnstone was paid an honorarium of 20 guineas for his work; he was not acknowledged by name in any of Bradley's Prefaces in E or F.

[18]   MP 7 Jan. 1889 Gell to JAHM. The idea of engaging female assistants had been suggested to Murray several years earlier by his friend Edward Arber, on the grounds that they were 'more conscientious [than men], and cheaper' (MP 24 Dec. 1884 Arber to JAHM).

[19]   Hunter et al. (1997: 31). The completed *Encyclopaedic Dictionary* was advertised in the *Times* of 10 December 1888.

[20]   PSOM 18 Jan. 1889. For a full account of the origins of the *Century Dictionary* see Bailey (1996). The project was certainly known to Murray by 1886 (MP 26 June 1886 FJF to JAHM).

[21]   Differences of approach between the two Editors were sometimes referred elsewhere, as in December 1888, when Bradley consulted the Philological Society's Council about whether word pairs such as *empair* and *impair* were best dealt with in a single entry, with a cross-reference from the less common spelling; Murray seems to have felt that they should be treated separately. The Council decided in Bradley's favour (PSCM 7 Dec. 1888, MP 7 Dec. 1888 FJF to JAHM, HB to JAHM).

sometime in 1889; perhaps Murray had managed to increase his salary. By contrast, Bradley's average was rather less than 10 pages per month. He was of course diverting some of his energies into pushing Stratmann's dictionary on towards completion; and he still lacked a full complement of assistants. Unfortunately Arthur Strong, whose work was now beginning to be of real value, continued to suffer from health problems, and in April he resigned, again citing the conditions in the Scriptorium. His successor, a barrister named M. L. Rouse, failed after only five weeks, and was in due course replaced by Frederick Arnold, a schoolmaster (and former acquaintance of Gell at King's College London), who started work in September and who was soon making reasonable progress—though he too would fail, rather more spectacularly, in due course. Steps were also taken to improve the heating and ventilation in the Scriptorium, in the hope that the coming winter would not prove too much for anyone else.[22]

The fact that after one year in his new role Bradley was struggling to meet expectations is perhaps hardly surprising. But 1889 also marked a more ominous anniversary for Murray: it was now ten years since he had signed the original contract with the Delegates, and while all parties had long ago given up hope that the Dictionary would be completed after ten years as originally envisaged, the amount so far published was such a small fraction of the whole—barely two letters of the alphabet published, and two others in preparation but far from finished—that Murray could have been forgiven for despairing of ever finishing the task. The now completed *Encyclopaedic Dictionary* stood as a reproach, and reviewers, even those who readily admitted that it could not compare with the Oxford project for thoroughness, acclaimed it as likely to be the best dictionary available for some time to come.[23]

Nor was the *Encyclopaedic Dictionary* the only publication to cause problems. The *Century Dictionary* was clearly likely to constitute even more serious competition; and reports reached Oxford that another another long-anticipated dictionary, the *Stanford Dictionary of Anglicised Words and Phrases*, was nearing completion. In June some early proofs of the Dictionary were sent from Cambridge, apparently anonymously, to Charles Doble, who noticed some suspicious similarities between entries in them and corresponding entries in the published Dictionary; on seeing the proofs Murray furiously claimed that the editor, Charles Fennell, was 'systematically appropriating' his own work.[24] Further proofs were obtained from Anthony Mayhew, who had Cambridge contacts, and who also identified examples of what he regarded as 'bare-faced plagiarism'. The matter was referred to the Delegates, and a diplomatic but very

---

[22] SL 27 Apr. 1889 Gell to Strong, 13 Sept. 1889 Doble to JAHM; OD 3 May, 18 Oct. 1889.

[23] Thus, for example, the *Birmingham Daily Post* of 20 April 1889, p. 6.

[24] SL 4 June 1889 Doble to JAHM; OUP/PUB/11/29 5 June 1889 JAHM to Doble. Fennell had in fact presented some sample entries from the Stanford dictionary at a Philological Society meeting in April 1886; Murray, who was present and who saw some provisional proofs, complained about Fennell's methods to his Cambridge contacts, after which Fennell took care to ensure that further information about his work did not reach Oxford.

determined letter was sent to C. J. Clay, the University Printer at Cambridge, pointing out the extensive use made by Fennell of OUP's published materials, and delicately suggesting that 'nothing could be further from the intention of the Syndics than to sanction any undue use, or any disparaging treatment, of a work which represents such unsparing labour and such a large financial outlay as the New English Dictionary, much less any distinct infringement of copyright'.[25] Cambridge University Press took the hint, and after spending several months investigating the matter undertook to guard against excessive use of the *OED*.[26]

All this was, however, hardly more than a dry run for what was to happen in regard to the *Century Dictionary*. The first volume of this great dictionary was published in America in May 1889, but British publication was delayed until October, apparently because a dockers' strike in London prevented copies from being unloaded.[27] A dictionary which claimed to be unprecedentedly inclusive—the figure of 200,000 words was widely mentioned—and which, moreover, promised to appear in monthly instalments posed a serious commercial threat to the *OED*, and so there was every incentive for Murray and Bradley to find fault with it. The *Academy*, apparently oblivious to the difficult position it might put him in, invited Bradley (who was still a regular contributor[28]) to review the first volume; Bradley refused, but consulted Murray about the best response to the threat. He had seen an advance copy in the British Museum, and could see just how much appeared to have been simply copied from the published sections of the *OED*; but he doubted the wisdom of seeking an injunction preventing publication, as Murray had apparently suggested. More generally, he realized that it might be difficult to make a charge of plagiarism stick: if the facts in a dictionary entry were true, or the quotations valid, then provided the *Century* compilers claimed (whether truthfully or not) to have reinvestigated and verified them, there was little that could be done. Other friends whom Murray consulted, including the distinguished jurist (and regular consultant on legal vocabulary) Frederick Pollock, were also doubtful about legal action; Furnivall, tactless as ever, commented that Whitney 'had a world-wide reputation before any philologist had heard of' Murray, and could therefore surely be assumed to have worked out for himself some of the lexicographical details which Murray believed had been copied. He sympathized with Murray's indignation, but argued that there was satisfaction to be gained from the way in which the facts that had been so painstakingly established by Murray were being taken up by others.[29] In fact the

[25] SL 10 July 1889 Doble to Price, 9 Aug. 1889 Doble to C. J. Clay.
[26] OD 29 Nov. 1889. Fennell later insisted that he had proved to the Syndics that the charge of plagiarism was false, but that they had given the undertaking in order to prevent a quarrel between the two Presses (24 Mar. 1890 Fennell to W. D. Whitney, quoted in Barnhart 1996: 117–18).
[27] Bailey (1996: 9); *Pall Mall Gazette* 21 Oct. 1889, p. 3.
[28] He continued to write and review regularly for the *Academy* until 1896.
[29] MP 18 Oct. 1889 HB to JAHM, 20 Oct. 1889 F. Pollock to JAHM, 19, 26 Oct.1889 FJF to JAHM. Furnivall also wrote to Gell declaring that the *Century*'s use of *OED* material was fair, and advising against legal proceedings (OUP/PUB/11/8 26 Oct. 1889 FJF to Gell).

new dictionary explicitly acknowledged its debt to its Oxford counterpart, both in its preface and in the printing of the letters 'N.E.D.' after several dozen definitions, and some quotations, to indicate their immediate source.

Murray did succeed in mobilizing opposition of a different sort. He does not appear to have written to the papers himself, as Bradley had suggested, but several friends to whom he had complained took it upon themselves to use what influence they had to ensure that the relevant points would be made in reviews of the *Century*. A sympathetic Henry Daniel of Worcester College (commenting 'What thieves these Americans are') contacted the reviewer for the *Times*; Russell Martineau undertook to write to R. H. Hutton of the *Spectator*; and, more significantly, Gell and Doble agreed that critics should be alerted to how much the *Century* owed to the British project.[30] Some of the ensuing reviews clearly show the effects of the 'steer' thus given: the *Pall Mall Gazette*, for example, commented how the compilers of the new dictionary had '"conveyed" freely' from the *OED*, producing a work which 'is not creditable to Professor Whitney, is not creditable to the Century Company, and is not creditable to American scholarship'.[31]

Notwithstanding this careful media manipulation, the delay in publication of the first instalment of the *Century Dictionary* probably did damage the prospects of Part V of the *OED*, which was finally approved for publication by the Delegates on 1 November ('A dead loss,' James Bellamy noted in the Delegates' agenda book), and which finally appeared in early December, at a time when the rival publication was still fresh in the public's mind.[32] *Cast–Clivy* had proved to contain more intractable material than any of the preceding four Parts, and Murray had been obliged to do without a summer holiday once again; his good rate of progress during the first half of the year had proved impossible to maintain.[33] But as far as the daily press was concerned it received very little notice. Murray's worst fears about the decline of public interest in the project seemed to be coming true.

He was also continuing to find Bradley's work unsatisfactory. He still read all of his proofs, keeping a watchful eye not just on the quality but also on the extent of the text; and in December 1889 he wrote confidentially to Gell to express concern about the excessive scale of Bradley's entries in E. After looking into the matter, Gell warned Bradley that he was indeed running ahead of Murray, and using rather more pages of text per page of Webster than was desirable (the scale achieved by Part II, only slightly more than six times Webster, being 'the Standard to be aimed at'). Henry Hucks Gibbs, who also scrutinized Bradley's proofs, concurred: there was potential for substantial cutting down, both in terms of over-elaborate subdivisions

---

[30] MP 18 Oct. 1889 C. H. Daniel to JAHM, 22 Oct. 1889 R. Martineau to JAHM; SL 28 Oct. 1889 Gell to FJF, 31 Oct. 1889 Doble to JAHM.

[31] *Pall Mall Gazette* 31 Oct. 1889, p. 3.

[32] ODA 1 Nov. 1889.

[33] PSOM 24 Jan. 1890.

of sense and of over-generous use of illustrative quotations.[34] Neither Editor enjoyed having to 'apply the press', as Gibbs called it. It was time-consuming—'It takes a long time to be short', as Bradley himself had put it—and the quotations were the essence of the work: Murray memorably described the task of shortening or eliminating them as 'a sorrowful necessity [...] like shearing Samson's locks'.[35] But he had learnt that the commercial imperatives of the Press required it to be done, and Bradley was going to have to learn as well. After nearly two years as Editor, he was still very much on probation: Gell even sent some of Bradley's entries, in confidence, to Arthur Napier, the Merton professor of English, for review, observing darkly that 'if the quality [of them] is in any way defective, it would be essential to consider our steps.' Fortunately Bradley seems to have made the grade, and no 'steps' were taken.[36]

In January 1890 the epidemic of 'Asiatic flu' that was sweeping Europe reached England, and Oxford did not escape. The Press was badly affected, and the Dictionary was no exception: first various assistants, and then in February Murray himself succumbed.[37] In his case the attack was followed by a severe period of depression, during which he once again began to entertain thoughts of resignation. Financial difficulties continued to worry him, as did the *Century Dictionary*, whose regular instalments continued to attract favourable notices; it seemed all too likely that it would 'seize the market', as one reviewer had predicted.[38] An indication of how needled he felt by the American rival may be seen in a letter published in the *Academy* about the word *cock*, in which he rather mockingly drew attention to a blunder made by the *Century* in its rewording of the *Imperial Dictionary*'s definition of *cock-feather*.[39]

In March matters took a rather bizarre turn for the worse, in the shape of the breakdown of Bradley's assistant Frederick Arnold, who was discovered to be suffering from delusions. He had become convinced that his landlady was trying to poison him, and on 19 March he accused Murray of joining the conspiracy. He was promptly expelled from the Scriptorium, and resigned shortly afterwards. Two of Murray's assistants, Morrison and Mitchell, offered to put in extra hours, but once again Bradley

---

[34] SL 16 Dec. 1889 Gell to JAHM, 31 Dec. 1889 Gell to HB; MP 29 Dec. 1889 HHG to JAHM.

[35] PSOM 18 Jan. 1889, 24 Jan. 1890.

[36] SL 2 Jan. 1890 Gell to A. S. Napier. In fact Bradley explained that his expansiveness in *en-* as compared with Webster was to a large extent due to including material which in Webster was entered under *in-*, and assured Gell that he expected to be able to bring the overall scale down (SL 2 Jan. 1890 Gell to JAHM).

[37] Horace Hart reported on the Press's experience of the outbreak in a letter to the *Times*, published on 5 Feb. 1890 (p. 6). Murray's progress report to the Delegates for February recorded only 8⅔ pages—the first time his figure had fallen below Bradley's.

[38] MP 5 Mar. 1890 E. L. Brandreth to JAHM; *Graphic* 23 Nov. 1889, p. 623.

[39] *Academy* 15 Mar. 1890, p. 189. Murray was no doubt rather more pleased with a review of Part V a week later which began by denouncing 'the copious use—or abuse, as some might be tempted to call it—made of its earlier pages by a recent American Dictionary of greater pretension than merit' (*Times*, 22 Mar. 1890, p. 15). The *Century* was not named, but Henry Daniel's protest about American 'thieves' would appear to have been effective.

was left short-staffed.[40] The episode may have been what finally persuaded Murray to accept that he needed a holiday if he was to avoid a breakdown himself; or it may have been an offer from a friend, the eccentric classicist Robinson Ellis, to pay for a joint trip to the Continent. The two men visited France, Belgium, and Germany, and Murray returned greatly refreshed.[41] For Bradley, by contrast, the late spring brought further misfortune: in May he was called away to Sheffield by the deaths of his brother and sister, and then was himself detained by illness, and although he managed to return to London and do some editorial work in June, he too was obliged to take a holiday abroad to recuperate.[42] The experiment of a second Editor was looking more and more like a failure.

Nor could the first Editor be said to be progressing with leaps and bounds. During the second half of 1890 Murray and his staff do at least seem to have been spared any further untoward incident, and in August he secured the services of a new clerk, Frederick Sweatman, who was to prove immensely reliable;[43] but they now found themselves tackling some extremely challenging vocabulary, including the enormous verb *come*. The monthly figures reported to the Delegates following Murray's holiday showed an improvement on the previous year's, but were still well short of the rate required to achieve one Part a year. By the end of the year only 224 pages of Part VI had been passed for press. However, Bradley was now at last free to concentrate on the *OED*, having finally completed his work on Stratmann's dictionary.[44] His rate of progress improved markedly, and by January 1891 completion of his first fascicle was sufficiently close that the end point could at last be estimated. This was just as well, as customers were once again beginning to be uneasy about the non-appearance of any Part of the Dictionary for over a year.[45]

---

[40] SL 20 Mar. 1890 Gell to JAHM, Gell to J. B. Mayor, 26 Mar. 1890 Gell to JAHM; OUP/PUB/11/10 23 Mar. 1890 F. S. Arnold to Gell. Other letters in OUPA suggest that Arnold may have spent a period in the Warneford Asylum following his outburst. He subsequently returned to teaching, and eventually became a professor at the Royal Oriental Institute in Naples.

[41] *CWW*, p. 267. Murray's prickliness on the subject of the *Century Dictionary* was, however, undiminished: his letter about the origin of the word *cockney*, published in the *Academy* on 10 May (pp. 320–1), ridiculed Whitney's etymology in such derisive terms ('I think I know Somerville Hall girls, perhaps even Extension Students, who would irreverently laugh at it as impossible') that Francis March, Murray's valued American coadjutor, was moved to warn him of the risk of alienating the *OED*'s American supporters (MP 30 May 1890 March to JAHM). For more on the *cockney* letter (which contained several other criticisms of the *Century*) and its aftermath, see Liberman (1996: 41–4).

[42] PSOM 16 May 1890; SL 10 June 1890 Gell to HB, OED/3/5/4 28 June 1890 Doble to HB. Bradley's misfortunes caused him to be absent from the Philological Society's Anniversary Meeting in May, at which he was elected President, just as Murray had been in advance of the publication of his first Part.

[43] Sweatman was a former 'Bodley boy'—a lad of humble background who had been given the chance of improving his education through work in the Bodleian Library.

[44] The dictionary, which soon became known as 'Stratmann–Bradley', was published in December 1890.

[45] FL 16 Jan. 1891 Frowde to Gell.

Congressionalist

Once the copy for a particular alphabetical range of Dictionary entries had gone to the typesetters, it became more difficult to insert additional material than when it still only existed as a sequence of paper slips; but such late insertions remained possible until quite an advanced stage in the production process. When a word which had been omitted was suddenly brought to public attention while proofs were still being corrected, it must have been tempting to see what could be done to insert it, rather than simply file the new evidence to be considered, at some uncertain future date, for inclusion in the projected (but still theoretical) Supplement, while hoping that the omission of a newly topical word would go unnoticed. One early instance of Murray apparently yielding to this temptation is the word *Congressionalist*. Whether there had been any evidence for this word when the relevant bundles of copy were being got ready for the printers in the spring of 1891 is uncertain, but it is clear that at this stage no entry was included. However, during 1891 reports about a civil war in Chile began to appear in the newspapers with increasing frequency. The war had broken out in January when the Chilean navy, supported by members of the Chilean National Congress, had begun to organize armed resistance against the party of President José Manuel Balmaceda; this group consequently became known as the Congressionalist faction, or Congressionalists. Quotations soon began to accumulate in the Dictionary files for the word *Congressionalist*, including one taken from the *Pall Mall Gazette* of 4 March by Furnivall; and Murray decided to insert an entry for the word in proof. His definition—'A supporter of a congress; a member of a congressional party'—made no mention of Chile, but the two quotations included with it (Furnivall's, and another from the *Times* of 26 February, which despite being slightly earlier in date was inadvertently placed second) related to the Chilean Congressionalists. The fascicle containing the entry, *Clo–Consigner*, was published in October, making *Congressionalist* one of a relatively small number of words to have an entry published in the same year as its first quotation.

It was not the first such entry, however: that distinction belongs to the rather less topical *barring engine*. The entry for this word was published in 1885, apparently as the result of a suggestion of the patent officer R. B. Prosser, who presumably noticed the term (denoting a recently invented engine used to start large mill engines) in his professional reading. The *OED* entry for the word included a solitary quotation from the magazine *The Engineer*. Other 'late additions' followed, including *chokage* and *chorism* (both published in 1889), *degeomorphization* (1894), and *diabolist* (1895), each illustrated by a single quotation from the year of publication. One of the last entries of all to be added to the first edition of the Dictionary was the noun *work-out*: the single quotation for this—illustrating its use in a boxing context—that appeared in February 1928 as part of the final fascicle of the Dictionary was taken from the issue of the *Daily Express* published on 27 May 1927, by which time the copy for words beginning with *wor-* had already begun to go to press. The same newspaper article also furnished an example of the corresponding use of the verb *to work out*, which was likewise squeezed in at the last minute. On similar 'last-minute' additions to the 1933 Supplement and Volume I of the revised Supplement see below, pp. 409 (*body-line bowling*) and 491 (*Doppler-shift, float*).

On 3 March 1891 Bradley was awarded an honorary MA by Oxford University.[46] The views of the Clarendon Press on his editorial achievements, however, were rather more mixed than might be supposed from this public honour. Gell, responding to yet another letter from Furnivall urging the appointment of a third Editor, commented that the experiment with Bradley had been 'so disappointing' that the Delegates were unlikely to sanction any further outlay; indeed, he seems to have lost all confidence in Bradley, not as an editor *per se*, but as someone able to obtain, train, and retain suitable assistants. 'The real backbone of Bradley's part', he commented, 'is Dr Murray's old assistant Sykes—without him Bradley would be I fear unable to organize or maintain a staff of any kind. He could be merely "Finisher".'[47]

However, the experiment could hardly be pronounced a failure until its first results had been published; and all attention was now focused on the completion of Bradley's Part (the first of Volume III). After some discussion, a form of title page was arrived at which declared Bradley's status without diminishing Murray's: the Dictionary as a whole was announced as 'edited by' Murray, with Bradley's name appearing underneath as the editor of Volume III Part I. Unfortunately, another problem surfaced in connection with Bradley's Preface which was sufficiently serious to delay publication by some weeks. Amongst those whom Bradley acknowledged by name as having assisted him with particular entries was Charles Fennell, who had supplied him with several early quotations for the word *eureka*. Both Gell and Doble realized that, in view of the protests that had been made over Fennell's use of *OED* material in the *Stanford Dictionary*—and the still real possibility of legal action being taken once the latter was published—it could be extremely awkward if the Delegates were placed under any obligation to him such as that which Bradley's proposed acknowledgement might imply. They therefore instituted a frantic search for other instances of *eureka* which could be substituted in place of at least some of those supplied by Fennell; Doble himself managed to find several, and appeals were made to various scholars, including Henry Liddell.[48] In the end, although replacements were found for some of Fennell's quotations, what remained was such that Bradley felt obliged to acknowledge 'several references for the article *Eureka*' as having come from Fennell; this was evidently a sufficiently minimal acknowledgement to satisfy the Delegates, but publication of Bradley's fascicle—now ending at *every*—was as a result delayed until mid-July, despite having been announced for several weeks earlier.[49]

The standoff between the *OED* and the *Stanford Dictionary* contrasts starkly with Murray's willingness to collaborate with another lexicographer engaged on a quite different project. J. S. Farmer seems to have begun work on his extensive dictionary of English slang in 1888, and was certainly already in correspondence with Murray by then.

---

[46] This was apparently at Doble's suggestion (SL 23 Dec. 1890 Doble to Gell).

[47] SL 21 Feb., 24 Mar. 1891 Gell to FJF. Remarkably, Charles Fennell was among the names put forward by Furnivall as a possible third Editor (OD 6 Mar. 1891).

[48] SL 14 May 1891 Doble to HB, 21 May 1891 Gell to HB, 27 May 1891 Doble to A. H. Bullen, 28 May 1891 Gell to Liddell.

[49] SL 9, 17 June 1891 Doble to HB, 7 July 1891 Doble to Sykes.

The two men were soon discussing particular slang expressions, and for a time Farmer even sent him proofs of his own dictionary entries; in return Farmer was permitted to consult the 'copy' for the *OED*. In 1891 he may also have been allowed to consult the Dictionary's accumulated quotation evidence for obscene and taboo terms that it had not been possible to use; he was certainly later permitted to consult the Dictionary 'copy' for some parts of the alphabet.[50]

---

content

With pronunciation as with other facts about a word, the *OED*'s approach from the beginning was descriptive: to record how a word was pronounced, rather than prescribing how it should be pronounced. However, reliable information about the most common pronunciation (or pronunciations) of a word was often hard to come by. James Murray illustrated this difficulty in his Presidential Address to the Philological Society in 1879 (*TPS* for 1877–9, p. 574) by describing how, when he asked at a recent meeting of the Society's Council about the pronunciation of *caviare*, he was given three different versions by his colleagues, none of which matched his own—which he had learned from dictionaries, and which matched that of Swift, who rhymed the word with *cheer* and even spelled it *caveer*. (The three other pronunciations all gave the third syllable as rhyming with *car*, but with the stress varying between the first and third syllable, and in one case with the final *e* pronounced as a fourth syllable.) All four pronunciations were included, along with several others, in a detailed note in the entry when it was eventually published in 1889. Writing to an unnamed correspondent in 1895 Murray restated his commitment to acknowledging such variation: 'it is a free country, and a man may call a *vase* a *vawse*, a *vahse*, a *vaze*, or a *vase*, as he pleases' (quoted in *CWW*, p. 189).

When dealing with the noun *content* in 1891, Murray was sufficiently exercised by the question of how it was most commonly pronounced that he issued a public request (published in the *Academy* 3 Oct. 1891, p. 287) asking readers to send him postcards reporting how they would pronounce the word in each of four sample sentences (which included the word in both its singular and plural forms). 'The younger generation is said to accent the word differently from the older,' he wrote. 'Is it so?' The response was impressive: a few weeks later he was able to report in a follow-up article (*Academy* 21 Nov. 1891, pp. 456–7) that nearly 400 individuals—described as 'educated men and women of all classes'—had provided replies. In his Dictionary entry for the word there was only room for a brief summary of his findings, which were reported in detail in the article. His hunch that there was an age-related component to the variation had been confirmed by the poll: the original pronunciation with stress on the second syllable was used less by younger people, though it was still widespread (whereas today it has entirely disappeared).

Continued ➤

---

[50] MP 25 May 1891 FJF to JAHM, 3 June 1891, 30 Sept. 1901 Farmer to JAHM. For more about the collaboration between Murray and Farmer see Gilliver (2010b: 79–82). See also p. 297.

Similar polling was sometimes resorted to in relation to other components of Dictionary entries. For example, Henry Bradley's entry for *grey*, published in 1901, reported the results of an extensive survey initiated by Murray about the word's spelling, which showed the picture of how *gray* and *grey* were used to be a complex one, with some respondents using both forms to convey different meanings or in different applications. In 1905 a meeting of the Philological Society were asked to vote on whether Murray should use *pigmy* or *pygmy* as the headword spelling of his entry for the word; a narrow majority favoured *pigmy* (PSOM 1 Dec. 1905), but Murray subsequently went against this, and opted for *pygmy* (though he gave *pigmy* as an alternative headword). It seems to have been a good decision: usage since 1905 has shifted substantially in favour of *pygmy*.

Despite Murray's misgivings, Bradley's first fascicle met with an extremely positive critical reception, typified by Skeat in the *Academy*, who declared that he had 'nothing but hearty praise to bestow upon this instalment of the work', and urged the public to buy copies. The *Times*, too, had 'nothing but praise', although it was less than enthusiastic about the range of words which Bradley had had to deal with: '[w]e have got [...] into a scientific stratum of the language [...] many pages and columns of the present part are largely filled with words of uncouth aspect which none but scientific experts ever require to use.' The review in the *Athenaeum*, while generally favourable, took the opportunity to make some sniping criticisms of Murray; the animus of the anonymous reviewer (Fennell once again) evoked protests, unsurprisingly, from Murray, but also displeased Charles Doble, who proposed that the *Athenaeum* be dropped from the list of regular recipients of review copies.[51]

By July 1891 the text of Murray's latest Part was nearly complete. He was still preoccupied by the threat posed by other dictionaries, and by the need to demonstrate the *OED*'s thorough superiority; and in his Preface he found a pretext for veiled criticism of rival publications, and of the *Century Dictionary* and the *Encyclopaedic Dictionary* in particular, namely the great number of 'bogus words [...] which have been uncritically copied by one compiler after another, until, in recent compilations, their number has become serious'—so serious that it had now been decided that, rather than waste space on recording these errors, Murray and his colleagues would begin compiling a 'List of Spurious Words', to be published after their main text was

---

[51] *Academy* 29 Aug. 1891, pp. 167–8; *Times* 16 July 1891, p. 4; *Athenaeum* 16 Jan. 1892, pp. 78–81; SL 21 Jan. 1892 Doble to JAHM. Fennell's review invited Murray to acknowledge Bradley as 'at least his own equal' as an Editor, and commented on Bradley's repetition of 'those errors in Dr. Murray's system which have increased the unwieldiness of the work without enhancing its value' (these being, apparently, the inclusion of too many marginal items of vocabulary, in the areas of scientific jargon, modern coinages, and Old English words which early fell out of use). By contrast, he described Bradley's etymological work as 'as nearly as possible immaculate'.

complete.[52] Murray's Preface announced this new departure, and discussed one such error in detail—the spurious word 'cherisaunce'—in a way that allowed him to criticize Richardson's *Dictionary* (the first to make the mistake), the *Encyclopaedic*, a dictionary of plant names which had compounded the error, and the *Century*, whose entry for the word managed to combine all the previous errors. Only Richardson was referred to by name, but the identity of the other works was clear enough; and Murray evidently took some satisfaction in exposing the 'errors thus sown broadcast by works laying claim to scholarly editorship'.[53]

Part VI (*Clo–Consigner*) appeared in October 1891. The short gap since the publication of Bradley's *E–Every* may have helped to convey the impression that the *OED* was at last moving up a gear; but compared to the now almost complete *Century Dictionary*, it was still progressing painfully slowly, as some reviewers observed: 'Will any of our grandchildren live to see it reach Z?' A note of fatigue could be detected even in some favourable notices, such as that in the *Glasgow Herald*: 'Praise of the work is, and has long been, superfluous. Complete as it is, there is probably no laudatory epithet in its columns which has not been already bestowed upon it. There is certainly none which it does not deserve.'[54] At least there was welcome news for the Press on the financial front: for the first time the sales of the two Parts issued during the year exceeded the money paid out to the Editors and their staffs.[55] In the autumn Bradley increased his Oxford staff by taking on two junior assistants, Wilfred Lewis and Henry Bayliss, who thankfully proved to be of more enduring service than most of their predecessors, and who in fact went on to become two of the Dictionary's longest-serving workers.[56] At the same time, however, he seems to have lost the services of his London assistant, Edward Gunthorpe, who was obliged to give up his post by persistent problems with his eyesight; Bradley seems to have made arrangements with Sykes to take up some of Gunthorpe's work.[57]

---

[52]   Murray had earlier referred to these 'bogus words' in a brief article in *Notes & Queries* (20 Apr. 1889, p. 305), noting an entry in Jamieson's dictionary which had been based on a misreading (and which he pointed out had been ignorantly copied in the *Encyclopaedic Dictionary*).

[53]   The criticism was not so veiled in earlier drafts of the Preface: direct references to the *Century* were only eliminated after Fitzedward Hall—himself no friend of W. D. Whitney, and thoroughly unimpressed by his 'catch-dollar imposition'—had suggested a wording which allowed him to avoid 'stooping to recognize [its] existence' (MP 27 July 1891 Hall to [JAHM]). Both Murray and Bradley (and their assistants) were of course now making regular use of the *Century*; but if Bradley had found any errors in his competitors' dictionaries, he chose not to mention them in the Preface to *E–Every*.

[54]   *Pall Mall Gazette* 3 Oct. 1891, p. 3; *Glasgow Herald* 15 Oct. 1891, p. 9.

[55]   OED/B/3/1/6 19 Jan. 1892 FJF to [Gell].

[56]   OED/B/3/1/6 18 Nov. 1891 G. F. H. Sykes to [Gell]. Like Sweatman, both Lewis and Bayliss were former 'Bodley boys'. Lewis, the son of an Oxford college servant, had first been put forward by Sykes in 1889, but the salary on offer had been insufficient to tempt him away from his post at the library of the Oxford Union (SL 19 Mar. 1889 Gell to Sykes, OD 17 May 1889). Bayliss was a gardener's son, and has left more evidence of a sense of humour—not something for which lexicography offers much scope—than any other assistant; see for example p. 302 below.

[57]   OUP/PUB/11/29 3 Apr. 1892 JAHM to Gell.

act

It is surely some kind of testimony to the growing authority of a dictionary when it begins to be cited in court. The earliest instance I have been able to find of an *OED* definition being cited in a court case dates from 1891; and the case in question was not in a British court, but in an Australian one. In the case of Ballantyne v. The Mutual Life Insurance Company of New York, which reached the Supreme Court of the province of Victoria in December 1891, the interpretation of the phrase 'die by his own act', as used in an insurance policy taken out by a man who subsequently shot himself while of unsound mind, was the subject of dispute. In giving his opinion, Chief Justice George Higinbotham cited 'Murray's New English Dictionary', which, he claimed, defined the 'primary meaning' of the word *act* as 'a deed, a performance of an intelligent mind' (*Victorian Law Reports* (vol. XVII, 1892), p. 536). The quotation, however, was both inaccurate and incomplete. Sense 1 of *act* had been defined in Part I of the Dictionary as 'A thing done; a deed, a performance (of an intelligent being)'. Moreover, sense 1b of the same entry explicitly allowed for the possibility of acts not directed by the conscious will of a sane person (as in 'the act of a madman'). Thus the whole question of whether an act was necessarily volitional or not—on which Higinbotham's argument depended—could arguably not be settled by reference to a dictionary as inclusive as the *OED*.

It was not until some years after this that the *OED* began to be regularly cited in court. In many cases there was of course a good reason for continuing to prefer other dictionaries, namely the fact that there was as yet no *OED* entry for the words under discussion. The earliest use in a British court may be in 1894, when the *Times* reported (14 Feb., p. 13) that the definition of *bonus* had been quoted in relation to a dispute over 'bonus' shares issued by the Eddystone Marine Insurance Company.

1892 began less promisingly. The winter had brought another influenza outbreak, and in January Murray found himself so behind with work, thanks to illness among his assistants, that he was obliged to postpone his annual report to the Philological Society. He then once again succumbed himself, to a rather worse attack than in 1890; this became a serious bout of pneumonia, which left him with a permanent susceptibility to lung trouble.[58] He was still ill on 4 March, the day fixed for his rescheduled report to the Philological Society, and so Bradley (having read his own annual report at the previous meeting) read it on his behalf—with quite unforeseen and nearly disastrous consequences. Furnivall, taking notes on the report for the minutes, was struck by the fact that six sub-editors were mentioned as having worked on the C material for Murray, by contrast with Bradley's acknowledgement of the solitary figure of P. W. Jacob—who had died in 1889—for the material in E. Furnivall had long been uncomfortable about the imbalance between Murray and Bradley in terms of assistants—which of course went a long way towards explaining the latter's much slower rate of progress—and

[58] HJRM pp. 175–6; SL 29 Jan. 1892 Gell to Bywater ('Dr. Murray has frightened us all'); MP 25 Feb. 1892 W. Gregor to JAHM (commiserating with him for having lost 'five weeks' work').

was further disturbed by this apparent indication that Bradley was also being stinted of sub-editing help. He rather overstated this in the report of the meeting which he sent (as usual) to the *Athenaeum*, listing all Murray's sub-editors while lamenting that Bradley 'had not the help of a single one'.[59] This public implication that Murray was being unfair to his fellow Editor led to an angry exchange of letters between an indignant Murray and an unrepentant Furnivall, who had apparently heard a member of Murray's family boast of his being further advanced with his new Part than Bradley, and who insisted that he was being 'ungenerous, if not unfair'.[60] Murray, standing on his dignity, concluded that he must resign from the Philological Society, and was only persuaded to withdraw his resignation after personal appeals from Bradley and other members of the Society's Council, together with a Council resolution regretting the wording of the *Athenaeum* report.[61] The Council evidently accepted Murray's explanation, namely that the fact that C had been worked on by seven sub-editors did not mean that the labour expended on it was any more than that expended on E by P. W. Jacob; there does, however, appear to be something of an imbalance, in that Jacob completed his work (in fact a revision of his first sub-editing of the letter) in 1885, leaving Bradley or his assistants to deal with several years' worth of incoming material, while the re-sub-editing of portions of C took place much closer to the point of their being edited in the Scriptorium. Furnivall, for his part, was ready to declare a cessation of hostilities, but some of his suspicions about Murray's dealings with Bradley remained.

Bradley's delicate negotiations with Murray took place amid some considerably more protracted negotiations between himself and the Press over his own position. Although it was now over four years since his appointment as the Dictionary's second Editor, his contractual arrangements remained on a strangely provisional footing: the original scheme of payment by results had been suspended, but nothing permanent had been substituted. Bradley had now come to the conclusion that unless he could secure a stable annual salary of £500—which had after all been held out to him as a prospect when he was first engaged as Murray's assistant—he would not be able to afford to continue with the work. In January he had, with characteristic diffidence, asked Gell to raise the matter with the Delegates. Perhaps surprisingly, they almost immediately agreed to increase his salary to £500.[62] It certainly seems to have surprised Gell, who it will be remembered entertained serious doubts about the idea of Bradley as a second Editor; and when on looking into the matter further it became apparent that Bradley could not undertake to produce more than half a Part a year, the Delegates

---

[59] PSOM 4 Mar. 1892; HJRM, p. 176; *Athenaeum* 12 Mar. 1892, p. 348.

[60] MP 7 Mar. 1892 FJF to JAHM, 8 Mar. 1892 JAHM to FJF, 14 Mar. 1892 FJF to JAHM.

[61] MP 14 Mar. 1892 HB to JAHM, B. Dawson to JAHM; PSCM 18 Mar., 1 Apr. 1892. It would of course have been acutely embarrassing for Bradley personally if Murray had chosen to resign from the Society during his own Presidency, and he begged Murray to consider at least delaying his resignation until after the Anniversary Meeting in May, when he would be stepping down as President.

[62] OED/B/3/2/1 22 Jan. 1892 HB to Gell; OD 12 Feb. 1892. The Delegates also agreed to pay him an honorarium of £75 for his work on Stratmann, which had gone on for so much longer than expected (OD 26 Feb., 11 Mar. 1892).

decided that after all it would be preferable to return to the original idea of payment by results. They were not ungenerous in the terms now offered: the rate per page was to be doubled, from 30 shillings to £3, and the allowance of £625 p.a. for payment of Bradley's assistants would continue even though the output from this team was to be half what had previously been anticipated. Gell made clear, however, that the Delegates (and, no doubt, he himself) felt that the money he spent on assistants could be more effectively spent, and observed that Murray's assistants were helping him to achieve much faster progress for more or less the same money.[63] Bradley, for his part, did not see how he could do what was required of him on the terms offered, and negotiations dragged on into May.

Before they could be concluded, something seems to have snapped. Bradley had suffered from indifferent health for some years, no doubt exacerbated by the strain of completing Stratmann.[64] It may have been that the stresses of trying to secure a financially stable future for himself (and for the Dictionary, insofar as it involved him), coming as they did on top of tensions in his relationship with Murray over the *Athenaeum* incident, proved just too much. The fact that he had also been working largely on his own in London since the loss of his assistant Gunthorpe can hardly have helped. Whatever the exact cause, by the time of the Philological Society's Anniversary Meeting in May he was showing signs of nervous exhaustion. Alarmed by his 'sadly low state', Furnivall arranged for him to be examined by two doctors (his nephew, the surgeon Herbert Furnivall Waterhouse, and a nerve specialist), who advised that unless he was given an extended period of complete rest he was likely to 'go out of his mind, sink into melancholia, or get paralysis of the brain'.[65] Bradley was immediately authorized—indeed ordered—to take three months' holiday on full pay, and deliberations over his terms of employment were suspended.[66] Henry Hucks Gibbs and some other members of the Philological Society subscribed to pay for a two-week cruise along the coast of Norway; this was followed by several weeks spent with friends in Yorkshire and Durham. Thanks to the welcome news that a Civil List pension of £150 had been secured for Bradley, he was able to complete his recuperation with a holiday in Switzerland (this time accompanied by his wife, who had herself also been extremely ill).[67] Meanwhile, Murray undertook to see some of Bradley's material through the press; effort was concentrated on clearing off the end of E.[68] By early

[63] OD 11 Mar. 1892; SL 16 Mar., 7 Apr. 1892 Gell to HB.

[64] Furnivall reported that Bradley regularly worked until 3 a.m. while completing Stratmann, often putting in over 60 hours a week (MP 18 Mar. 1892 FJF to JAHM).

[65] MP 16 May 1892 FJF to JAHM; OUP/PUB/11/14 16 May 1892 FJF to Gell. A friend of Bradley's had recently been admitted to Bethlem Royal Hospital (the original 'Bedlam') under similar circumstances, which Furnivall observed had added to his distress.

[66] FC 19 May 1892; SL 21 May 1892 Gell to HB.

[67] July 1892 HB to Vivian Lennard, reprinted in Bridges (1928: 15–16). The Civil List pension seems to have been a suggestion of Furnivall's (SL 18 Jan. 1892 Gell to FJF); it was initially set at £100 p.a., but was increased to £150 following further representations from Gibbs and Furnivall (Bridges 1928: 16).

[68] OUP/PUB/11/14 18 May 1892 FJF to Gell; MP 2 June 1892 Gell to JAHM.

September Bradley was back at work, much improved after his rest, but it was clear that neither he nor Murray would complete a Part before the end of the year.

Soon after Bradley's return, however, another dictionary appeared with which the *OED* might uncomfortably be compared. Charles Fennell's *Stanford Dictionary* was published in September, and was acclaimed in the *Times* as 'worthy, within its range, to take rank with the great Oxford Dictionary'.[69] Murray, still indignant about the (unacknowledged) extent to which the early entries had drawn on his own work, declared himself thoroughly unimpressed by the later parts, describing the scholarship as 'disappointingly poor', and singling out the 'utterly puerile and ignorant treatment' of the word *cholera*. He found, to his satisfaction, that in a sample of entries in his own Part V, the *OED* 'beat' Fennell (in the sense of having found earlier evidence) ten times more often than it was 'beaten'. He identified the real problem as being with the dictionary's concentration on the debatable category of incompletely naturalized words, which he conceded was not Fennell's fault; however, he recognized that the remonstrances of the Delegates did seem to have had some effect on the use made of *OED*, and it was decided to take no further action.[70] One other consequence of the completion of the *Stanford* was that its editor became free to take up other work. Fennell himself, apparently willing to bury his own animosity towards Murray, had written to Gell in May—at exactly the time of Bradley's breakdown—enquiring whether the Press might wish to engage him as a co-editor of the *OED*; Gell delicately informed him that the Delegates 'do not under present circumstances feel able to avail themselves of your services'. Furnivall raised the matter with Gell again in October, urging that Fennell should be taken on as a third Editor, and also that Fennell's able young assistant, Frederick Hutt, would make a useful addition to Bradley's staff.[71]

Taking on a third Editor was the very last thing on Gell's mind; indeed he and the Delegates were beginning to wonder if it was feasible to continue with two, or even one. With Bradley's return to work the review of his position which had begun before his breakdown resumed. Bradley had now come to the conclusion that the arrangement proposed to him in the spring was workable, and confirmed that he was prepared to move to Oxford; but when the matter came before the Delegates in November, the alarming state of the Dictionary's finances persuaded them that a more radical reconsideration of the project was called for. As of mid-June the total costs amounted to nearly £33,000, of which only about £10,000 had been recouped in sales. The last year had been more expensive than ever, with nearly £3,600 expended in return for the printing of roughly 320 pages (only 280 of which had been passed

---

[69] *Times* 16 Sept. 1892, p. 10.

[70] OUP/PUB/11/29 20 Oct. 1892 JAHM to Gell; SL 15 Nov. 1892 Gell to JAHM. The awkwardness of the dictionary's scope was also noted by Mayhew in his generally favourable review for the *Manchester Guardian* (27 Sept. 1892, p. 9).

[71] OD 27 May 1892; SL 8 June 1892 Gell to Fennell; OUP/PUB/11/14 18 Oct. 1892 FJF to Gell. Furnivall also suggested that Sykes's services ought to be dispensed with, remarking that he 'never ought to have been put on poor B[radley]'s shoulders'. In the event Hutt was not taken on.

for press): thus, as Gell complained to Furnivall, progress 'has probably never been so slow in comparison with the expenditure'. (Progress in the ensuing four months had of course been worse still because of Bradley's absence.) It was apparently not the expense as such which most concerned the Delegates, so much as the poor value for money: it made no business sense that 'the more they endow the Dictionary the slower proportionately it goes'. In such circumstances it is perhaps unsurprising that some voices began to urge the discontinuation of the entire project. Whether, as Elisabeth Murray suggests, the principal voice was Gell's is doubtful; but there was evidently enough support for the Dictionary among the Delegates that they decided to hold off from this drastic step pending one last attempt to accelerate progress. A committee, headed once again by Bartholomew Price, was appointed to confer with Murray about possible means of increasing the rate of production, and 'the question of the continuance of the work' would only be considered if the committee concluded that publication could not be accelerated. Further consideration of Bradley's position was also postponed pending the committee's report.[72]

With the Dictionary's very existence now under threat, minds were concentrated wonderfully on the question of acceleration, and suggestions came in from every quarter. Murray consulted Gibbs, Bradley, and Furnivall (and through him the other members of the Philological Society's Council, which considered the matter at a special meeting); Gell also had his own ideas, which were communicated through Furnivall to the Council.[73] Each of these individuals viewed the problem from a different perspective. For Murray the key question was: '*How can the character of the Dictionary be so altered or modified, as to make it possible for its Editors to produce a Part in the year?* What can be sacrificed of its *contents*, and what in the *quality* of the work, to render this result possible?' He saw the matter in terms of a number of editorial compromises, to be made if sanctioned by the Council: should he simply omit words and meanings in certain marginal categories, such as compounds of transparent meaning, straightforward figurative uses of words, or obscure items for which he had only one quotation, or only the authority of a dictionary such as the *Century* or the *Stanford*? Or, in the last case, should he simply include an item, with or without explicitly acknowledging the dictionary in question? Bradley was more analytical: the choice of strategies for acceleration depended on whether it was the assistants who were unable to prepare enough work to keep the Editor fully occupied, or the Editor who was unable to keep pace with his assistants. In the former case, sub-editors might be

[72] OD 18 Nov. 1892; SL 22 Nov. 1892 Gell to FJF; MP 7 Dec. 1892 Gell to FJF; *CWW* p. 268. Further on Dictionary finances during the 1890s see Knowles (2013: 618–21). In fact in 1891 the Press had finally accepted that the Dictionary should be categorized as an 'unremunerative' rather than a 'remunerative' publication, a change which, as Knowles observes, enabled its finances to be viewed in a more understanding light. This was perhaps just as well, as the 1890s were to prove difficult times for the British economy in general, and in such hard times the Press was obliged to take a more rigorous look at finances (Eliot 2013b: 110–11).

[73] OED/B/3/1/6 1 Dec. 1892 JAHM to FJF (copy), 2 Dec. 1892 HHG to JAHM; MP 7 Dec. 1892 Gell to FJF, 12 Dec. 1892 HB to JAHM.

able to help by weeding out marginal material; in the latter, the areas where most time could be saved were etymology (where suitable authorities could be simply quoted, with acknowledgement, rather than conducting original research) and specialist terminology (where time-consuming correspondence with experts could be eliminated if suitable specialists could be found to draft the entries properly in advance). Gibbs was, as ever, businesslike but reassuring: he recognized Murray's horror of anything less than perfection, and the unpalatable prospect of merely copying other authorities, but trusted that the 'prudence & [...] amour propre' of the Delegates would not allow them to countenance shoddy work. He also voiced once again his own strictures against 'long-tailed Greek & Latin compounds' and 'foreign words' generally. Gell was less concerned with questions of editorial policy than with the inefficiency of the current situation; he confided to Furnivall his own conviction that only by transporting the entire enterprise to rooms within the Press itself, with a telephone connection to a separate unit at the Bodleian Library, could the work be conducted effectively.[74] He was also acutely conscious of the constant distractions caused by visitors to the Scriptorium, which had become a 'show place'.[75]

It is hard to reconcile the surviving evidence with Elisabeth Murray's colourful account of this crisis, which temptingly portrays Murray as 'fighting Gell and the Delegates for the survival of the ideal Dictionary', upset by the 'treachery' of the Philological Society (carried along by Furnivall as 'Gell's ally') in agreeing to editorial compromises which he could never contemplate, but then discovering that at the last minute, thanks to the influence of Bartholomew Price, 'the sting had been drawn' from the Delegates' attack.[76] The resolutions passed by the Council at their meeting on 16 December certainly contained recommendations with which Murray disagreed, including Furnivall's favourite idea of appointing a third Editor; nor will he have appreciated Furnivall's insistence that 'the Research view must give way to the Business one'.[77] By the time the Delegates' 'Dictionary Committee' had submitted its report—which was duly communicated to Murray, Bradley, and Furnivall—a new name was under consideration as a third Editor: that of Charles Plummer, the chaplain

---

[74] Gell was an enthusiast for the telephone, and had had one installed in his own office in the early 1890s (Sutcliffe 1978: 76).

[75] The Scriptorium had been something of a tourist attraction since Mill Hill days: in 1883 the professor of English at Harvard, F. J. Child, had advised students visiting England that it was one of the three places to visit, along with Westminster Abbey and the Tower of London (*CWW* p. 186). In 1890 Sykes had even prepared a 'Visitors' Guide to the Scriptorium', and even submitted it (with Murray's approval) to the Delegates for publication; Gell, showing considerable restraint, informed Sykes of the Delegates' disinclination to publish his 'interesting little Guide', suggesting that it might help the progress of the Dictionary if Murray could arrange to limit such visits to outside working hours (OD 21 Feb. 1890; SL 24 Feb. 1890 Gell to Sykes). The handwritten 'Guide' was still to be seen in the Scriptorium in 1894 (Hjelmqvist 1896: 120).

[76] *CWW* pp. 269–71.

[77] PSCM 16 Dec. 1892; OED/B/3/1/6 27 Dec. 1892 FJF to Gell; MP 28 Dec. 1892 FJF to JAHM. Furnivall was at this point still urging Gell to engage Fennell, who, remarkably, had attended the Council meeting.

of Corpus Christi College, and a noted Anglo-Saxon scholar.[78] The report included six recommendations identifying 'matters of secondary or subsidiary importance' on which editorial labour could be minimized. The recommendations will have come as little surprise to Murray or Bradley, focusing as they did on scientific and technical words,[79] non-naturalized loanwords, and the amount of original research to be done in etymologies, together with a new 'marginal' category of words of recent origin (post-1880). The recommendations were couched in the most measured terms, with appeals to the Editors to apply them with great discretion, and Murray and Bradley both indicated their readiness to comply with them; but all parties will have been well aware that action of a more radical kind was needed. The committee's five recommendations for 'expediting the machinery by which the Dictionary is produced' (including the appointment of a third Editor), which had appeared in the original version of the report, were postponed for consideration at the Delegates' next meeting.

Murray had his own ideas as to how to 'expedite the machinery'. He had now managed to build up enough of a buffer of copy ahead of the printers that many more problematic entries could be sorted out before copy was sent in, thereby making for significant time-saving at the proof and revise stages. He now also suggested one further step that he might take to speed up his own work: to cease looking over Bradley's work. He was still finding enough in his copy to comment on, as regards 'divergence of principles or their application': a case in point was *eye*, in the etymology of which Bradley had included a lengthy account of the possible ultimate origins of the word which, in Murray's view, 'transgresse[d] a limit strongly & strenuously laid down by the Delegates, and embodied at their requirement in the *General Principles*, and [...] must never be done again'. Of greater concern, however, was Bradley's tendency to include too many illustrative quotations. Murray acknowledged that he himself still found the task of thinning out quotations a difficult one, and even suggested that it might be helpful if a sheet of his entries was looked at from time to time by a Delegate, who with an independent eye might pick out further opportunities for 'retrenchment'; but Bradley's expansiveness (or 'over-setting', as it came to be known) was, he thought, a much more serious problem, as could be seen by the scale of the letter E, which '*ought* to have been got into one part'. A directive from the Delegates enjoining severe cutting-down of quotations might, he suggested, be in order, especially by way of compensating for his ceasing to look through Bradley's proofs.[80]

[78] OD 10 Feb. 1893; SL 13 Feb. 1893 Gell to FJF, Gell to JAHM, Gell to HB. Plummer's name was apparently not mentioned to Murray, Bradley, or Furnivall at this stage.

[79] The view that scientific and technical words were still receiving too much attention was widely shared: when members of the Philological Society's Council were invited to assess the treatment of words beginning with the three scientific prefixes *chloro-*, *chrono-*, and *chryso-* in Part V, their recommendations as to what could be omitted were enough to bring 9 columns of text down to 1½ (PSCM 13 Jan., 3 Feb. 1893).

[80] OUP/PUB/11/29 8 Nov. 1892 JAHM to Doble; OED/B/3/1/11 23 Feb. 1893 JAHM to Gell. The published entry for *eye* included a severely shortened etymological note.

The Delegates jumped at Murray's suggestion of abandoning his reading of Bradley's proofs (although they elected to leave it to Murray to give a parting piece of advice to his errant fellow Editor about his over-setting). They also approved the Dictionary Committee's suggestions for increasing the efficiency of the Scriptorium machine: establishing regular consultants for advice in particular subject areas, the use of pre-printed query forms, and the provision of a shorthand clerk for Murray's use. But further consideration of the two ideas relating to Bradley's work—bringing him to Oxford, and expanding his staff—was deferred.[81] He seems to have been ill again in February—not as seriously as in 1892, but enough to affect his progress badly—and the Delegates may have decided to wait until matters were on an even keel once again before trying anything new. Even the idea of drawing up a contract to formalize his current arrangements was shelved.[82]

In fact something of a freeze seems to have descended upon the project in the spring of 1893. First Murray and then Bradley made enquiries about the possibility of securing extra money for their staffs, beyond the £625 p.a. which had been approved; in each case the Delegates insisted that no increase could be countenanced except in recognition of an increase in the rate of production. One exception of this kind had already been made in the case of George Sykes, who in 1889 had pressed for an increase in his salary: the Delegates had responded by offering him 'payment by results', in the form of a bonus for each page of Bradley's text that was passed for press.[83] This bonus was paid in addition to Bradley's regular allowance for assistants; and now when Murray applied for an increase for his valued assistant Frederick Sweatman, who it seems was threatening to seek a better-paid job elsewhere, he was told that the Delegates would only countenance a similar scheme, whereby for every page passed for press in excess of a suitable norm (Gell initially suggested 200 pages per year) Murray would receive an additional £2, to be distributed among his assistants as he saw fit.[84] When Bradley made a similar application, on behalf of his assistants Lewis and Bayliss, the Delegates were similarly unforthcoming: they refused to go above his £625 allowance, and do not even appear to have proposed a comparable bonus scheme.[85]

The aim of the bonus scheme was of course to give the assistants an incentive to work more quickly; and some may have regarded it as a fairly generous one, in that considerably more than 200 pages per year had been anticipated from each Editor for

[81] OD 24 Feb. 1893; MP 27 Feb. 1893 Gell to JAHM. The idea of engaging a third Editor was also deferred, the approach to Charles Plummer having evidently come to nothing. The news that Bradley was to remain in London must have come as a particular disappointment to Furnivall, who had successfully persuaded the Philological Society's Council to recommend a move, and had anticipated 'charming little Burne-Jonesy Maggie'—Bradley's daughter—becoming 'one of the belles of Oxford' (OED/B/3/1/6 27 Dec. 1892 FJF to Gell).
[82] FC 2 Mar. 1893; OD 10 Mar. 1893.
[83] OD 8, 29 Nov. 1889. Sykes's bonus, initially 5 shillings per page, was later raised to 7s. 6d. (OD 6 Feb. 1891).
[84] OD 24 Feb., 10 Mar. 1893; MP 6, 11 Mar. 1893 Gell to JAHM.
[85] SL 4 Apr. 1893 Gell to HB; OD 28 Apr. 1893; SL 2 May 1893 Gell to HB.

some time. But of course the number of pages passed for press depended, not on the industry of the assistants, but on the work done by their Editor. Murray, recognizing that this would not give his staff the reliable increase in salary they were looking for, elected to augment their pay himself by the amount of bonus which he anticipated would accrue during the year. This was liable to leave him out of pocket if, as regularly happened, the actual page count fell short of his estimate.[86]

By early April Murray had passed the last pages of Part VII (*Consignificant–Crouching*) for press; and the end of the huge letter C was in sight, with only 4 feet of slips left (out of 160).[87] The passing of yet another milestone seems to have given him little satisfaction: he lamented to Skeat, who had invited him and his wife to Cambridge for a break over Easter, that he felt 'all sort of enthusiasm and "go" crushed out of me'.[88] The Delegates, too, were conscious of the great financial burden that the Press was carrying: Part VII was calculated to have cost over £3,500.[89] The comparative scale of each Editor as compared to Webster had once again come to their attention, ironically as a result of Murray's protests about Bradley's expansiveness: it now emerged that Murray's scale in C was nearly nine times Webster, while Bradley in E had so far averaged 7.4. Both were of course in excess of the agreed scale of six. A resolution that 'the attention of the Editors be called from time to time to any increase beyond the present scale' laid down a clear marker, although the absence of a specific demand that the scale be brought back down to six is notable. Murray was also finding other things to worry about. Convinced that Fennell would write another critical review for the *Athenaeum*, he went so far as to suggest to Gell that the Press threaten to withdraw its advertising from the magazine if their notice of the new Part was unduly critical. Gell saw at once the indefensibility of this approach, and told Murray that the Press 'could not dream of fighting the "*Athenaeum*" with such rude (I might say brutal) bludgeons'; but he did at least write to the magazine's editor with the comment that some of the previous notices showed signs of partiality, and

---

[86] *CWW* p. 272; HJRM pp. 181–2. Initially part of the costs of Sweatman's pay increase were given to Murray by the Philological Society (PSCM 14 Apr. 1893), after Murray had disclosed that he did not have the money. He was in fact still struggling financially, and in the summer even found himself unable to pay his accounts; he predicted gloomily to Furnivall that he would soon become insolvent, 'and then the crash will come'. He was only enabled to take a summer holiday through donations from Gibbs and other friends (MP 5 July 1893 JAHM to FJF, 10 July 1893 B. Dawson to JAHM, 11 July 1893 FJF to JAHM).

[87] PSOM 14 Apr. 1893.

[88] MP 24 Mar. 1893 Skeat to JAHM, 29 Mar. 1893 JAHM to Skeat. Skeat had done his best in his invitation to jolly Murray along, suggesting that he could keep abreast of the *cu*-words he was now working on: 'I could find enough talk to *cumber* you. You could come by a *curvilinear* railway. Bring a *cudgel* to walk with. We will give you *culinary* dishes. Your holidays shall *culminate* in sufficient rest; we can *cultivate* new ideas, & *cull* new flowers of speech. We have *cutlets* in the *cupboard*, & *currants*, & *curry*, & *custards*, & (naturally) *cups*. […] Write & say you'll CUM!' Murray declined Skeat's invitation for the somewhat surprising reason that Ada had declared the Scriptorium in need of a spring-clean, an operation for which she insisted that her presence was required.

[89] OD 12 May 1893. The Delegates even contemplated making a fresh appeal to the government for funding, but the idea was later abandoned (OD 9 June 1893).

expressing the hope that future reviews would be entrusted to critics of unquestioned neutrality.[90] In the event his request was unavailing, as the review of Parts VI and VII which eventually appeared in the *Athenaeum* was once again by Fennell, who took the opportunity to point out a few entries in the *Stanford Dictionary* in which he 'beat' Murray in terms of earliest quotations (while conceding that many of Murray's entries were better). His opening paragraph is a curious combination of praise and dissatisfaction: 'The quality of the work is so excellent and the quantity is so vast that one would gladly have both diminished by seven or eight per cent. in consideration of more rapid progress.'[91]

From time to time Murray's own readiness to take up the cudgels on his own behalf in the public prints led him into rather undignified public spats, in which an element of petulance emerges which can have done him and the Dictionary no favours. One such spat was touched off in the pages of the *Athenaeum* in the summer of 1893. A correspondent, J. P. Owen, had dared to suggest that the treatment of the words *cram* and *cramming* (in their slang senses, relating to intensive coaching or tuition) was misleading in that it overlooked the evidence for a Cambridge origin of the usage. Murray, outraged, wrote that this was 'absolutely the very first time that the epithet "misleading" has been applied to the treatment of any word in the Dictionary', and ridiculed the accusation as 'so delicious that, with Mr. Owen's leave, I will use his words as a quotation for *mislead*, and hand them down in the Dictionary, that posterity may not forget the one discerning man who has detected in our exhibition of the facts a base attempt to mislead the unwary'. He went on to justify the Dictionary's treatment of the words, which he claimed (with some justification) had been selectively quoted. Owen, in turn, wrote with further evidence, and a pained comment that Murray's jibe about his 'delicious' charge 'might be more naturally expected from a young lady when some one has inadvertently stumbled against her daintily shod footlet, than from a mighty scholar, whom undiscriminating admirers have impelled to assume the god and to launch his thunderbolts in order to prove that his extremities are not made of clay'. Quite what the Delegates, and others in Oxford, made of this unseemly squabble can only be imagined.[92]

[90] MP 27 May 1893 Gell to JAHM; SL MP 27 May 1893 Gell to editor of *Athenaeum*. Fennell had of course not been publicly identified as the reviewer, but his identity was widely surmised.

[91] *Athenaeum* 2 Dec. 1893, pp. 765–6. The late appearance of this review, six months after the publication of Part VII, may be accounted for by the withholding of review copies from the *Athenaeum* (see above, p. 221).

[92] *Athenaeum* 15 July 1893, pp. 96–7; 29 July, p. 161. Another unseemly public quarrel, this time involving Henry Sweet, took place in the pages of the *Academy* at the start of the great crisis of 1896 (see below). Sweet's rather implausible claim that Murray owed a recent discovery regarding the obscure verb *deche* entirely to a conversation with him in 1894—which led Sweet to accuse him of 'decking [himself] with borrowed philological plumes'—provoked a lengthy riposte from Murray in which he ridiculed Sweet's argument, and likened him to both Achilles sulking in his tent and a berserk warrior 'belabouring friend and foe, and damaging himself not a little' (*Academy* 22, 29 Feb. 1896, pp. 158, 178). For an account of yet another such quarrel, with the anthropologist E. B. Tylor in 1892 over the word *couvade*, see Bailey (2000a: 220–3).

put-up job

The Liberal statesman (and four times Prime Minister) W. E. Gladstone was an enthusiastic supporter of the *OED*, and an occasional correspondent of James Murray. He may also have been the first person to mention the Dictionary in a British parliamentary debate. During a debate in the House of Commons in 1893, the Chancellor of the Exchequer, George Goschen, referred to a parliamentary manoeuvre by the Solicitor General as 'a put-up job'; Gladstone, in a sarcastic riposte to Goschen's remark, observed: 'There is a most comprehensive dictionary of the English language now being prepared with the greatest care and ability by gentlemen to whom I need not refer, and I wonder whether it will include among the new treasures of the English language a "put-up job."' If, he suggested, the name of the author of the expression were also to be given, 'the value of the phrase will, no doubt, be very much enhanced' (*Hansard* (Commons) 5 Dec. 1893, vol. 19, col. 518). The phrase was hardly new—it had been an underworld slang term for a pre-planned crime for some decades—but it was still unusual (though not unprecedented) in a parliamentary context, and certainly 'unparliamentary' enough for Gladstone to be able to make something of it. The exchange was reported in several newspapers; among them was the *Westminster Gazette*, where a (slightly garbled) version of Goschen's remarks caught the eye of Frederick Furnivall. In fact his cutting eventually formed part of the copy for the entry for *put-up* when this was compiled in 1909, and the quotation appeared in the published version of the entry—complete with Goschen's name—when the fascicle *Prophesy–Pyxis* was published in September of that year. The earliest available example of the expression was, and remains, a quotation from *Oliver Twist*.

Once Part VII was off his hands, Murray did begin to make better progress, and by the time of his tussle with Owen he had made a start on the letter D.[93] But, as he well knew, speed came at a cost, not least in terms of scale; and it was now apparent that the letter C alone was going to be larger than A and B combined. This meant that it would not be practicable to include C and D in Volume II, as originally planned, and Gell now proposed to bring the volume to an end with a shorter fascicle extending only to the end of C (which seemed likely to run to just over 100 pages). This in turn had implications, which may not have been welcome to Murray: if Volume III was to contain D and E, as now seemed sensible, the work of the two Editors would for the first time appear together within a single volume. It was agreed that the title page would have to make the division of responsibility quite clear.[94] Bradley, for his part, may well have been grateful for another likely consequence, namely the need to issue

[93] In August Skeat sent Murray a poem congratulating him on having 'conquered [his] ABC', and expressing mock anxiety that he would now be passing on to '*dabble* and *dawdle* and *doze*' and 'words that begin with a d—!'. The poem appeared in the *Academy* on 19 August 1893 (p. 150), and is reprinted (with slight differences) in *CWW* pp. 273–4. Another, longer poem written at the same time, lamenting the 'dismal, dreary dose' of D words that lay ahead (but hailing the 'dogged determination' that would see the task through), was not published. Both poems eventually appeared in *Notes & Queries* 21 Dec. 1897, p. 482.

[94] MP 22, 27 Sept. 1893 Gell to JAHM; SL 27 Sept. 1893 Gell to HB. The change also necessitated the alteration of those plates of the letter F which had already been cast, so that the pagination for what would now be Volume IV would start at 1 (MP 19 Dec. 1893 H. Hart to JAHM).

another short fascicle extending only to the end of E (and of Volume III): he was still struggling to improve his speed, and it would be some time before enough of his copy would be passed to make up another 352-page Part. The stark contrast between the outputs of the two Editors was becoming a matter of serious concern: in November Bradley received a very stern letter from Gell, reporting that his progress over the five months to the end of September (42 pages composed, as compared with 106 supplied by Murray) was causing the Delegates 'the gravest apprehension as to the future. [...] The literary expense per page incurred in your Part during these five months exceeds anything we have ever reached before, and anything which we could afford, permanently to support.' Bradley promised to strive for more rapid progress, and did manage to come closer to Murray's output during the next three months—probably helped by his taking on another Oxford assistant, Arthur Sewall, in December— but a substantial gap remained.[95] Murray's latest fascicle appeared on 4 December; *Everybody–Ezod* would not appear for another three months. This brought Bradley's total published output, after over six years, to 488 pages. The current arrangements with the Dictionary's second Editor were certainly looking unsustainable.[96]

The publication of Murray's reduced fascicle may have been forced on the Press by the revised division of volumes, but it proved to be so popular that the Delegates began to wonder whether it might in fact be a good idea to continue to publish smaller fascicles. The greater frequency with which these would be ready would keep the Dictionary in the public eye on a more regular basis, and the lower prices might bring it within reach of a larger market. Murray and Bradley seem to have approved of the idea, and it was eventually decided to issue 'sections' of 64 or 72 pages, costing 2s. 6d., commencing in October. It was proposed that sections should be issued on a quarterly basis: a clear recognition that the production of a 352-page Part each year could no longer be looked for.[97]

Whether or not the new bonus scheme had been an incentive, 1893 proved to have been a productive year for Murray and his staff: 216 pages were passed for press, earning them a £32 bonus.[98] Less auspiciously, January 1894 also saw the first instalment of yet another potential rival dictionary. Volume I of Funk and Wagnalls' *Standard Dictionary of the English Language* had been published in America in December 1893, and approving reviews were soon appearing in the British press.[99] While not

[95] SL 7 Nov. 1893 Gell to HB; OD 17 Nov. 1893, 19 Jan. 1894 (reporting 34 pages of Bradley's work composed in the three months to 2 January, as against 43 pages from Murray).

[96] Murray's new fascicle was described as 'Part VIII, Section 1', Henry Frowde having advised that it might be considered misleading to describe as a 'Part' something which was less than half the length of its predecessors (MP 2 Nov. 1893 Doble to JAHM). It was also much cheaper, at 3s. 6d., compared with 12s. 6d. for previous Parts. *Everybody–Ezod* was slightly longer (144 pages), and sold for five shillings.

[97] OD 19 Jan., 8 June 1894. For further information about *OED* Sections and Parts see p. 467.

[98] MP 22 Mar. 1894 Gell to JAHM.

[99] For example *Daily News* 28 Feb. 1894, p. 6. Murray was sent a complimentary copy of Volume I by Isaac Funk, the dictionary's editor-in-chief (MP 22 Jan. 1894 Funk to JAHM). A rather less complimentary notice appeared in the *Times* (20 Jan. 1894, p. 6), ridiculing the definition of *golf*, but also mentioning Murray's own 'rather guarded statement that "the specimen pages of the Standard Dictionary had, on examination, appeared to him to be as well done as was practicable within the necessarily small compass of a single-volume [*sic*] dictionary"'.

pretending to match the *OED* in comprehensiveness, the *Standard* was nevertheless another dictionary comparable in size to the *Century*, and in fact covered an even larger vocabulary. It had also been produced with impressive efficiency: compilation of the first of two volumes had taken only three years, and its companion appeared less than a year later. The Delegates had already recognized its potential as a competitor in 1891, when they refused a request to supply the publishers with advance sheets of the *OED*. They could not, however, compete with the American publishers in terms of expenditure, which was reported to approach $1 million (over £200,000).[100]

In March Bradley's section *Everybody–Ezod* finally appeared, to very little fanfare. The inefficiency of having his staff divided between London and Oxford was continuing to frustrate Gell, who complained to Henry Liddell that the arrangement was 'not I think a practical one'.[101] Murray was also still keeping a suspicious eye on Bradley's work, and in June he complained once again about the increasing scale of F. Doble, deputizing in Gell's absence, remonstrated with Bradley in terms which are of particular interest in the light of later events. The Delegates, he said, 'ha[d] long recognised that the old estimate of N.E.D.:Webster::6:1 is entirely superseded', but they regarded a scale of *eight* times Webster as an operating maximum, which was why he was bringing the current scale of F (currently running at over nine times Webster) to Bradley's attention. Bradley gave a fresh undertaking to compress his text wherever possible—promising in particular to cut down on numbers of quotations and on the coverage of technical vocabulary—but also renewed a plea for additional staff: he still had a smaller team of assistants than Murray, and no doubt reminded Gell of the effort that condensation required.[102]

Before any steps could be taken to add to Bradley's staff, however, Murray was to lose the services of one of his best assistants. In late June Walter Worrall, who seems to have been chronically prone to headaches, suffered a complete breakdown in health, apparently as a direct consequence of conditions in the Scriptorium (Doble reported that he had often said that 'the Scriptorium is killing him'). He left almost immediately to stay with his family in Liverpool, and Gell recommended three months' complete rest; it was decided that, as he would not be able to return to work in Oxford, he should join Bradley in London, working only limited hours on the Dictionary, and taking up other literary work by way of variety.[103] Meanwhile Murray was obliged to get his junior assistant Frederick Sweatman—who had just graduated BA—to take over some of the more difficult preparatory work formerly done by Worrall; this in turn meant that another junior assistant would have to be taken on.[104] Fortunately Murray was

---

[100] OD 24 Apr. 1891. Funk and Wagnalls had secured the services of Francis March, who had organized so much of the *OED*'s American reading, as a consulting editor.

[101] SL 5 Mar. 1894 Gell to Liddell.

[102] SL 19 June 1894 Doble to HB; MP 26 June 1894 Doble to JAHM.

[103] OUP/PUB/11/21 3 July 1894 Doble to Gell; SL 6 July 1894 Gell to JAHM, 9 July 1894 Doble to Gell; MP 4 Aug. 1894 JAHM to Worrall (draft); OD 19 Oct. 1894.

[104] SL 16 July 1894 Doble to Gell. Murray also appealed for help to Anthony Mayhew, who however declared himself committed to other projects for at least six months (MP 6 July 1894 Mayhew to JAHM).

soon given the name of a promising young Yorkshireman, Ernest Speight, by Joseph Wright, and negotiations began to secure his services.[105]

Within days of Worrall's breakdown there was further vexing news. Once again it involved Charles Fennell, who now had another project to unveil to the world: it was announced in the *Athenaeum* that he was to edit a new 'National Dictionary of English Language and Literature', and subscriptions were invited to cover the costs of this grand enterprise. The new dictionary was to be published in three large volumes, as well as in monthly parts; its vocabulary was to be drawn from 'full indexes of several carefully selected authors', and thousands of quotations had already been collected, including 'large numbers [...] dated earlier than the earliest given in any dictionary'. Among those who had already indicated their willingness to subscribe were numerous scholars and Cambridge notables, including Skeat.[106] Such an announcement could hardly have been better calculated to annoy Murray; he was described as 'very angry' by Charles Doble, who was also anxious to prevent the sort of 'pillaging' of the *OED* that had been detected in the early pages of the *Stanford Dictionary*.[107] Fortunately, although Fennell had got as far as producing a prospectus and specimen page, his project failed to attract enough financial support, and apparently fizzled out after only a few months.[108]

By late August Murray must have been thoroughly looking forward to his holiday on the North Wales coast. It was to be cut short, however, by tragedy. Murray had only just arrived in Penmaenmawr when he received a telegram from Oxford informing him that an accident had befallen John Mitchell, his most senior assistant, who was holidaying in Snowdonia. Murray dashed (by train, carriage, and on foot) to where Mitchell had been climbing, but only arrived in time to see his body being brought down: he had fallen, and been killed, in an attempt to negotiate a particularly difficult climb.[109] Mitchell was the last remaining assistant who had worked on the Dictionary since the Mill Hill days, and in addition to being immensely experienced in the project's working methods had become a close friend of Murray, who in a Dictionary Preface written nearly a year later wrote with uncharacteristic frankness of the 'unspeakable grief' felt by all those working in the Scriptorium at the loss.[110]

[105]　SL 24 July 1894 Doble to Gell.
[106]　*Athenaeum* 7 July 1894, p. 34.
[107]　SL 9 July 1894 Doble to Gell.
[108]　The last reference to it which I have been able to trace is a letter by A. L. Mayhew in the *Athenaeum* of 13 April 1895, p. 476. Further on the 'National Dictionary' proposal see Ogilvie (2012: 126–7). A rather more gratifying interaction with a very different 'national dictionary' also took place in the summer of 1894, when the Scriptorium received a visit from the Swedish linguist Theodor Hjelmqvist, on behalf of a projected new historical dictionary of Swedish under the auspices of the Svenska Akademi. Hjelmqvist, who would go on to work on the Swedish dictionary for many years, spent several weeks in Oxford collecting information on the *OED*'s working methods; he went on to visit the offices of the *Deutsches Wörterbuch* in Göttingen and the *Woordenboek der Nederlandsche Taal* in Leiden. He published a detailed account of his findings (Hjelmqvist 1896) which is a valuable source of information about the state of all three projects.
[109]　*Times* 1, 3, 5 Sept. 1894.
[110]　Preface to fascicle *D–Depravation* (dated June 1895).

The death of a key assistant had less impact on the progress of the Dictionary than might have been expected. Bradley, who as luck would have it was currently well supplied with prepared copy, made his own junior Oxford assistants available; Ernest Speight joined Murray's own staff in September; and, more valuably, Alfred Erlebach returned to the Scriptorium for a short period.[111] Publication of the first of the new shorter fascicles, *D–Deceit* and *F–Fang*, which had been scheduled for October, did in fact have to be delayed, but only by a month. Murray was able to follow his section with another, *Deceit–Deject*, before the end of the year, thus cementing in the public's mind the idea that the Dictionary was now at last settled into a regular publication schedule.[112]

Speight was not the only new occupant of the Scriptorium at this time. In August the Delegates had received an application for work on the Dictionary from the English scholar John Lawrence, who evidently came with strong recommendations; he had started trial work by October, with a view to his eventually becoming a third Editor. Unfortunately he soon proved not to be up to the work, and following a damning assessment of his work by Bradley his services were soon dispensed with. Both Editors were now becoming familiar with the failure of even the most highly recommended individuals to live up to expectations; most aspects of work on the Dictionary required aptitude of a very particular kind, which few outsiders could judge.[113]

But help was unquestionably needed. Once Erlebach had returned to his teaching, Murray was once again short of an experienced assistant, and of course the gap left by Worrall's departure was still unfilled. In January 1895 he arranged with Sykes that Arthur Sewall, who after over a year working for Bradley was proving a capable assistant, should begin to prepare copy for him. It might be supposed that Bradley would be annoyed at losing an assistant after all the effort of training him, but in fact he could not afford to keep him: his other junior assistants were demanding a pay increase, and with the absolute limit on expenditure still being enforced by the Delegates he could only afford this by making savings elsewhere.[114]

Bradley's progress through F was still poor, with a quarterly total of only 26 pages composed in January 1895 as against Murray's figure of 60; and he was still tending to over-set. He had been reminded of this by Gell in December, and apparently gave suitable assurances, but by May his scale was giving cause for concern. Murray, consulted as to what could be done, pointed out that the bonus scheme, although

---

[111] MP 9 Sept. 1894 HB to JAHM. Murray's account book (MP) records payment to Erlebach for 'supplying Mr Worralls place during part of Aug[us]t'.

[112] SL 11, 20 Oct. 1894 Gell to HB. The section *Deceit–Deject*, published in December 1894, was the first whose title page bore the now familiar name 'Oxford English Dictionary', although officially it remained the 'New English Dictionary'.

[113] OED/B/3/1/6 24 Aug. 1894 J. Lawrence to Delegates; OD 19 Oct. 1894; SL 31 Jan. 1895 HB to Lawrence, 4 Feb. 1895 Gell to HB. Lawrence subsequently held the chair of English literature at Tokyo Imperial University.

[114] MP 19 Mar. 1895 HB to JAHM. The cost of engaging John Lawrence had been borne separately by the Delegates.

intended to encourage output, actually gave Sykes (Bradley's main preparer of copy) an incentive to be expansive; he suggested that if, instead of being based on pages produced, it was tied to progress made through the alphabet, as measured by equivalent pages of Webster, then Sykes would have an additional reason to be as concise as he could.[115]

As for Bradley's speed, Gell had long been convinced that the problem lay with the division of his staff between Oxford and London, and that he could only really manage his assistants effectively if he moved to Oxford. The possible benefits of such a move had been acknowledged by Bradley—so that Gell was perplexed when in the spring of 1895 he did indeed move house, but only to Wandsworth Common.[116] The Delegates decided that it was time to take another serious look at the idea of a move to Oxford. Fortunately there was now a possible location: a house (known as North House) situated within the Press's main Walton Street premises, which had until recently been occupied by the widow of the former superintendent of the Press, Thomas Combe. The matter was not put to Bradley until September, perhaps because of negotiations with the current tenant; meanwhile Bradley's speed, and his expansiveness, did not improve. Nor was Murray doing particularly well: his quarterly total, as reported to the Delegates in May, was only 43 pages, barely half his figure for the corresponding period of 1894.[117] Illness among his assistants seems to have been the cause, and there was also a new assistant to train. For the first time this was a woman: Mary Dormer Harris, who had studied English at Lady Margaret Hall.[118]

At least the quarterly publication model made it easier to preserve a public appearance of steady progress, whatever the project's internal ups and downs. A new section from Bradley (*Fanged–Fee*) appeared at the end of March; and in April Murray was able to report to the Philological Society that over 200 pages of D and F—more than enough for a section from each Editor—had been printed off beyond what had already been published.[119] June saw the appearance of Murray's next section, *Deject–Depravation*, which it was decided would also mark the end of Part VIII. In the autumn both Editors were able to bring out a section, with Bradley's (*Fee–Field*) marking the completion of his second Part.[120]

---

[115] SL 14, 20 Dec. 1894 Gell to HB; OD 25 Jan. 1895; OUPA Minutes of Committee on Publications 24 May 1895; OD 14 June 1895; SL 21 Mar. 1896 Gell to T. Fowler. The suggestion was taken up; in informing Sykes of the change, Gell mentioned that 'the proportion authorised is 8 pp. of the *N.E.D.* to 1 page of *Webster*' (SL 16 July 1895 Gell to Sykes).

[116] Bridges (1928: 17); SL 11 Apr. 1895 Gell to HB.

[117] OD 3, 17 May, 14 June 1895; SL 20 Sept. 1895 Gell to HB.

[118] Field (2002: 34–6). Murray had in fact offered a position to a young woman named Beatrice Martley a few months earlier, when he was apparently considering taking on two female assistants (because, according to Martley, 'he can hardly engage *one* female assistant without being sure of getting the other— He fears a tête-à-tête in the scriptorium might be rather embarassing [*sic*]'). Martley may even have done a little work in the Scriptorium, but it seems that she was unable to take up the offer (correspondence, Nov.–Dec. 1894, at OED/B/2/4/5).

[119] PSOM 5 Apr. 1895.

[120] Press coverage of each new issue had rather tailed off with the change to quarterly publication of small sections, and even the double issue generated only moderate interest: the notice in the *Times* ran to barely a third of a column, noting that '[t]he general character of the Dictionary is now so well established in the estimation of all competent scholars that it is unnecessary to dwell on it once more at length' (*Times* 4 Oct. 1895, p. 4).

September also marked the arrival of another new assistant in the Scriptorium. In the summer of 1894, while he was visiting Birmingham to preside over the Oxford Local Examinations there, Murray had been introduced by his friend Edward Arber (professor of English at Mason Science College, a predecessor of the University of Birmingham) to a young student then completing his MA, Charles Talbut Onions.[121] The son of a designer and embosser in metal, Onions could hardly claim a glittering academic record—in his first degree, in French, he had only obtained third-class honours—but he must have performed impressively during a visit to Oxford in April, as he was subsequently invited to join Murray's staff. He effectively succeeded Mary Harris, who left after only six months, apparently to work as Joseph Wright's assistant on the *English Dialect Dictionary*.[122]

October brought the Delegates' annual review of the Dictionary's finances. The realization that the 'literary expenditure' of Bradley's output was now running at £11 per page—more than twice as much as Murray's—no doubt increased their determination that some drastic step must be taken. Bradley was at last formally requested to make arrangements to bring his work to Oxford. Negotiations now began as to the terms on which North House might be offered to him; but before anything could be settled, the Dictionary had plunged into yet another crisis, possibly the most severe in its history.[123]

By way of a kind of prelude to the real crisis, the winter of 1895 brought two untoward incidents. The first was the resignation of Ernest Speight. On 22 November the Delegates were informed that Speight 'had left Dr Murray's staff without notice'; and a few days later Gell received his letter of resignation, in which he declared himself 'physically and mentally incapable of continuing to work with Dr Murray, under the existing conditions', and urged that the Scriptorium be inspected 'not only at regular times, but in all its conditions. It must be obvious that all is not right, when so many workers are compelled either to leave the place or to take prolonged intervals of rest.' Evidently there was more to this than the mere coldness and dampness of the Scriptorium in winter; the Delegates evidently thought so, as Murray was asked for an explanation.[124] The request reached Murray when he was still smarting from an entirely different reverse: his application for a fellowship at Exeter College had failed.[125] This was not the

---

[121] For a later photograph of Onions see Figure 25, p. 323. This would seem an appropriate point to mention that, contrary to what has sometimes been alleged, Charles Onions did not pronounce his surname with the stress on the second syllable, as if spelled *O'Nions*, as some of his namesakes have certainly done; at least, numerous individuals who knew him in Oxford over many years have assured me that he pronounced it in the same way as the vegetable (although, as he was no doubt aware, the surname, which is of Celtic origin, and the name of the vegetable are etymologically unrelated).

[122] MP 7 Apr. 1895 R. Ellis to JAHM; HJRM p. 186; Wright (1932: 383). Mary Harris was presumably the assistant whom Onions later recalled as having been 'pumped' by Joseph Wright about the *OED*'s 'technique and general procedure' (OUP/PUB/11/8 21 May 1938 CTO to RWC).

[123] SL 28 Oct. 1895 Gell to HB; OD 8 Nov. 1895, FC 14, 28 Nov. 1895.

[124] OUP/PUB/11/23 25 Nov. 1895 Speight to Gell; OD 6 Dec. 1895; SL 10 Dec. 1895 Doble to JAHM.

[125] MP 24 Dec. 1895 W. Stubbs (as Bishop of Oxford) to JAHM. Murray's draft letter of application for the Exeter fellowship is also preserved in MP. It has been suggested (Ogilvie 2012: 93) that a contributory factor in Murray's being turned down may have been his association with Jowett, still a divisive figure in Oxford.

first time that he had applied for a college fellowship: there had been an unsuccessful attempt to make him a fellow of Merton in 1892.[126] As well as giving him the academic status within Oxford that he had always sought, the Exeter fellowship, with its annual stipend of £200, would also have gone a long way towards solving various difficulties: it would, for example, have enabled him to offer better rates of pay to his staff and thereby improve retention rates. (He described the retention problem to Gibbs as 'chronic and acute [...] I continually lose experienced assistants, who take all their knowledge with them, and have to begin with new men.') He had been able to assemble an impressive array of referees in support of his application, including William Stubbs (now Bishop of Oxford), Robinson Ellis, Ingram Bywater, Henry Hucks Gibbs, and a new friend, Herbert Warren, the President of Magdalen. However, in the event the fellowship was awarded to the historian W. H. Stevenson, ironically a valued contributor to the Dictionary who had been a regular reader of Bradley's proofs for several years. Murray grumbled to Warren: 'Alas! I was born too soon! People will just begin to appreciate the Dictionary, when it is too late for *me*.' And in similar vein he wrote to Gibbs (in a letter congratulating him on the news that he was to be made Lord Aldenham): 'I believe it is vain to hope that any College will help the Dictionary [...] the majority of the Fellows "care for none of these things".' Distinguished though some of his supporters were, there were evidently not enough of them in Oxford.[127]

   He could at least take some pride in the fact that, notwithstanding the setbacks of the early part of the year, he had been able to send 240 pages to the printers during 1895, taking him to the end of *dis*: a target he had set himself at the start of the year. He had only managed this through a 'desperate effort', as he told Gibbs, working 80 to 90 hours a week for the last four months of the year. Completion of the letter D, and with it Volume III, was now in sight; and this in turn brought new difficulties. Which letter should he tackle next? Volume IV was to have included F, G, and H (and indeed had already been announced as such), but such was the scale of Bradley's work on F that it seemed unlikely that it would be possible to include all three letters in a single volume. Murray now once again drew the Delegates' attention to Bradley's tendency to over-set, commenting bluntly that he wished 'to wash [his] hands entirely of vol. IV, and to leave to the Delegates and Mr Bradley to do the best they can with it', as the scale on which it was proceeding was 'entirely opposed to [his] wishes as Editor-in-chief'.

---

[126] MP 14 Feb. 1892 Jowett to Ada Murray, 8, 27 Oct. [1892] J. Burnet to JAHM, 8 Oct., 29 Dec. 1892 A. S. Peake to JAHM. There may also have been an attempt in 1891 by his friend Robinson Ellis, then Vice-President of Trinity College, to get him made an honorary fellow of Trinity (MP 25 May 1891 R. Ellis to JAHM).
   [127] MP JAHM, draft application for fellowship ([July 1895]); 24 Dec. 1895 W. Stubbs to JAHM; 4 Jan. 1896 JAHM to H. Warren (as President of Magdalen); GL MS 11021/27 ff. 370–1 11 Jan. 1896 JAHM to HHG. Exeter College may have been unwilling to award Murray a funded fellowship, but there were certainly enough members of the University willing to grant him recognition in other ways: on 25 February he was awarded the degree of MA by decree of Convocation, probably at the instigation of the President of Corpus Christi College, Thomas Fowler (MP 12, 17 Feb. 1896 T. Fowler to JAHM; *Times* 27 Feb. 1896, p. 10). This differed from his earlier honorary MA in that it conferred the right to vote in Convocation.

Should he, then, go on to the letter I, leaving Bradley to carry on with G and H—a task which, he could not resist pointing out, would take Bradley fifteen and a half years at his present rate—or should H be reallocated to Volume V? The question was more urgent than it might seem, as although it would be some months before Murray and his assistants completed D, the preliminary work by volunteer sub-editors would have to begin soon. Murray asked that a committee of two Delegates be appointed to consider the matter.[128] Over the next few months he would have ample opportunity to savour the irony that it was thus his own complaint, and his own suggested remedy, that precipitated the crisis.

Gell was at this point in the South of France, convalescing after a breakdown in his health. The Delegates were, of course, perfectly capable of acting in the absence of their Secretary, though in retrospect it might have been better if they had waited. Murray may have been pleased to find that Bartholomew Price had now taken charge of much of the Press's business, as he seems to have looked back on Price's Secretaryship as something of a halcyon period;[129] if so, he will have been unprepared for the drastic nature of the Delegates' response to his complaints. On 7 February they appointed a committee as he had requested, consisting of Ingram Bywater and the medievalist Frederick York Powell; but they also decided that Bradley should be informed that 'his connexion with the Dictionary should close' unless the remainder of F was kept 'within due scale'.[130]

The Delegates' response certainly seems to have surprised and even alarmed Charles Doble, who urged Price to hold off from informing Bradley of their 'very strongly-worded resolution'. Bradley was in fact anxiously awaiting a reply from the Press in regard to his proposed move to Oxford. Doble duly wrote to him with the cryptic information that the Delegates were now contemplating 'an exhaustive examination of their whole relations to the Dictionary', in the light of which decisions about such comparatively minor matters as the terms of his accommodation would have to wait. This must have been worse than no reply at all for Bradley, who had evidently been expecting negotiations to proceed quickly and who had already been seriously inconvenienced by the delay.[131]

When Murray came to the Press to discuss the distribution of the remaining letters of the alphabet, Bywater received something of a shock. Despite his long-standing

---

[128] MP 27 Jan. 1896 JAHM to [?] (probably Doble, Gell, or Price) (copy). Murray had another reason for wishing to do the letter H, namely the fact that he had already done considerable preparatory work on various pronouns and related words (*he*, *her*, etc.).

[129] MP 9 Feb. 1895 JAHM to J. Churton Collins (copy). In this letter Murray inveighed against the Delegates in general, who he felt took on membership of the Delegacy without appreciating how much effort was required to do the job properly; he particularly disliked the way in which the dispersal of Delegates over the summer months made for a tendency to deal with matters 'in a hasty or summary manner' when they reconvened in October. He noted that his own relations with them had been 'satisfactory enough' for some years, although he suspected that he and the Dictionary were regarded as something of a 'white elephant, an honour that they would gladly dispense with'.

[130] OD 7 Feb. 1896. At this meeting the Delegates also considered (and apparently found satisfactory) a letter from Murray giving his account of the circumstances of Ernest Speight's departure.

[131] SL 10 Feb. 1896 Doble to Price, 13 Feb. 1896 Doble to HB; OED/B/3/1/10 18 Feb. 1896 HB to Doble.

interest in the project, and his position as a regular consultant for both Editors on particular editorial points, he seems to have remained oblivious to the gradual expansion of the text—as edited by both Murray and Bradley—well beyond its original agreed limits. As far as he was concerned, the target scale was rather less than six times Webster, this being necessary to keep the page limit to the figure of 8,400 that had been agreed in 1881. Of course he knew that Bradley was exceeding this scale—after all, it had been Murray's complaint about this that had brought the meeting about—but he now learned that Murray too, after having managed to keep to six times Webster in the letter A, had expanded well beyond this: 'He has never at any time observed the conditions laid down in his agreement.'[132] He now suggested to the Delegates that the issue of Bradley's scale was secondary to the question whether they were prepared to allow Murray to 'go on with the work to the end on its present scale', in disregard of his contractual obligations.

This sudden and ill-informed attack on the Dictionary's chief Editor might seem out of character for a man who had given him and the project so much support over the years: Bywater it was who in 1883 had sought to soothe Murray's anger at Benjamin Jowett's interfering, as the two men ran together to Oxford station, and he had been named as a referee by Murray only a few weeks earlier. However, it should be remembered that Bywater had a long record of being particularly concerned that the Dictionary should be a *commercial* success: he had kept a close eye on the effective advertising of early Parts,[133] and had been a member of almost all of the subcommittees appointed by the Delegates over the years to consider how best to expedite production. While no doubt willing to accept the project's scholarly credentials, he may have been frustrated that it was proving to be very far from the profitable venture which it had appeared to be when the Press took it on: even two decades later he would complain to Murray that the Delegates had been 'grievously mislead [*sic*] from the very first'.[134] Moreover, his fellow member of the latest subcommittee (and of many of its predecessors), York Powell, seems to have been no friend of Murray, whom he was to dismiss in a letter to Gell a few months later as 'an old fool [. . .] driveling on [. . .] in pure and conceited ignorance'.[135]

The Delegates were evidently in an uncompromising mood. Having already voted to threaten Bradley with the ultimate sanction, they now elected to turn the screw on both Editors to an unprecedented degree. At Bywater's suggestion, they resolved that the 'normal scale' of the Dictionary was henceforth to be six times Webster (with occasional allowance made for a scale of seven if a particular section could be shown to require it), and that both Murray and Bradley should be required to give an

---

[132] OD 21 Feb. 1896, with pasted-in report (written by Bywater) of the subcommittee appointed at the previous meeting.

[133] SL 3 Nov. 1885 Gell to Bywater.

[134] MP 10 May 1914 Bywater to JAHM.

[135] The letter, which relates to the question of providing the Taylorian Institution with free copies of the Dictionary, pulls no punches: 'It isn't the first time [Murray] has written himself down an ass,' York Powell continued, 'nor will it be the last that he will do so' (OUPA(u) 7 Dec. 1896 F. York Powell to Gell).

undertaking to keep rigorously to this limit. If they refused to do so, the Delegates agreed—privately in the first instance, although the fact soon leaked out—that they would now 'proceed to consider the question of suspending the publication of the Dictionary for such time as may be thought advisable'.[136]

Both Murray and Bradley were horrified. Murray declared that a reduction to six times Webster could not be achieved without abandoning just about everything that was of distinctive value in the Dictionary; Bradley, tactfully overlooking the fact that the new demand had been precipitated by Murray's criticism of his own work, agreed. Both men realized that the achievement of a scale of six in A had been due to the peculiar character of that letter, in which modern words derived from Greek and Latin—which could be dealt with much more concisely than those with Germanic or earlier French etymologies—predominated to an unusual extent.[137] A united response was needed: first Bradley and then Murray wrote to the Delegates, each arguing that enforcement of a scale of six times Webster would deprive the Dictionary of almost all its historical character—making it, indeed, hardly more than a glorified *Century Dictionary*. For his part, Murray could report that since his meeting with Bywater he and his assistant Charles Balk (who had become particularly skilled in finding ways to save space) had been trying to achieve the required compression in the latest proofs, but in vain: far from being able to cut 28 lines from every column of text, as would be necessary, they had been unable to cut 28 lines in a whole sheet. Both Murray and Bradley threw out the challenge to the Delegates: could anyone take the proofs and demonstrate how they could be brought down to a scale of six times Webster without compromising the historical principles on which the Dictionary's reputation depended? Murray, after years of agonizing over the subject of scale, was convinced that a scale of eight represented 'the lower limit' of what could be achieved consistently with these principles; and if he was to be required to go beyond this, he would have to 'bow to the inevitable and give up the struggle'.[138] Other forces were also mobilized in support of their position, including the Council of the Philological Society, who informed Gell (now back from sick leave) that they were ready to send a deputation to the government, and to make a public appeal for support, 'rather than have the book spoilt'.[139] Fitzedward Hall also launched into the fray, declaring that unless Murray and Bradley could be allowed to continue 'untrammelled' by the Delegates' new limit,

---

[136] OD 21 Feb. 1896.

[137] MP 26 Feb. 1896 HB to JAHM.

[138] OED/B/2/2/1 printed copies of letters 2 Mar. 1896 HB to [Doble], 5 Mar. 1896 JAHM to Gell. Bradley provided Murray with a copy of his own letter for reference (preserved in MP); the full text of Bradley's letter, taken from the printed version, is reproduced in *Dictionaries* 11 (1989), pp. 221–7.

[139] SL 9 Mar. 1896 Gell to J. R. Magrath (quoting a letter from Furnivall). The scheme for public support had already been gone into in some detail; Edward Arber had envisaged an appeal, launched jointly in the name of the Press and the Society, for 2,000 individuals to pay 5 guineas each for three years in return for a copy of the Dictionary, this being enough to clear the debt of approximately £30,000 which OUP had incurred, but on the understanding that the Press would bear all future expenses in anticipation of profits from cheap editions and abridgements (King's College London, Skeat–Furnivall Library, Dictionaries 2/2/7, 5 Mar. 1896 Arber to FJF; I am grateful to Charlotte Brewer for this reference).

it would be better to cease publication of the Dictionary entirely at the end of the letter F, 'and [let] its completion await happier days'.[140]

The problem for the Delegates, as Gell now found himself having to explain, was that the information which had led them to take up such an extreme position in his absence was at best incomplete, at worst actually wrong.[141] While Bywater may have been technically correct in saying that there was no contractual justification for the expanded scale on which the Editors were working, there was no question that a scale in excess of six times Webster had been unofficially sanctioned for some time. Gell could point to the Delegates' decision in May 1893 not to demand a reduction to anything less than 7.4; the following year Doble had acknowledged to Bradley that the Delegates had 'long recognised' that the old 6:1 ratio had been 'entirely superseded', and that eight was now accepted as the working maximum; and 8:1 had even been fixed as the proportion from which Sykes's revised bonus was to be calculated.[142]

Gell's role in this crisis, then, was not at all as portrayed by Elisabeth Murray, that of a man still smarting from his 'defeat of 1893', and seizing on the chance to 'reopen the whole question of the future of the Dictionary'. Indeed, it could be argued that he was instrumental in saving the project from collapse.[143] He wrote to J. R. Magrath, the Vice-Chancellor, warning him of the Philological Society's readiness to make a public protest, suggesting that the Delegates might wish to reconsider their action 'before this crusade commences'. York Powell seems also now to have realized that 8:1, rather than 6:1, was the only limit to which the Delegates could credibly demand adherence.[144] A meeting of the Committee on Publications on 13 March afforded an opportunity to take informal soundings from key Delegates. Meanwhile any suggestion of disunity had to be concealed from the Editors and from the Philological Society. Gell wrote diplomatically to both Bradley—who was now desperately anxious to know where things stood in regard to his invitation to move to Oxford—and Furnivall that he had been instructed to inform them 'that "the subject is under the consideration of a Committee"'. One suggestion, however, had been taken up immediately: Murray and Bradley were informed that first proofs of the Dictionary were now to be scrutinized

---

[140] OED/B/2/2/1 printed copy of letter 16 Mar. 1896 Hall to [Gell]. Hall had been informed of the Delegates' proposed restrictions by Bradley, who suggested that his comments 'would have considerable weight with the Delegates' (OED/B/3/9/5 13 Mar. 1896 HB to Hall).

[141] Gell later diplomatically suggested that the problem had been that 'it is not possible for the busy men on the B[oard] to have the knowledge of the whole detail which it is my business [to] possess' (SL 30 Apr. 1896 Gell to T. Fowler).

[142] See above, pp. 231, 235, 238 n. 115.

[143] CWW p. 275. It should also be borne in mind that 1896 was an exceptionally demanding year for Gell in other respects, with the opening of the Press's New York branch, the erection of new buildings in Oxford to house its expanding printing business, and the setting-up of a new insurance scheme for Press employees; in addition to his own illness at the start of the year, he also lost the services of Doble as Assistant Secretary for several months (Sutcliffe 1978: 99–100).

[144] SL 9 Mar. 1896 Gell to Magrath.

by another committee (Bywater and York Powell again, plus the classicist and Provost of Oriel College, D. B. Monro), with a view to compression.[145]

The Delegates next met in full session on 20 March. It is not clear that by this stage anyone other than Bywater still believed that a scale of 6:1 was achievable or desirable; even he may have begun to regret the suggestion. But he was still convinced that 'curtailment' of some sort, by both Editors, would be 'distinctly for the good of the Dictionary [...] it will remove superfluous foliage but none of the essential parts of the tree.' He had even drafted a letter, to be sent by the Vice-Chancellor to the Philological Society, setting out this view, and giving a list of ways in which the 'curtailment' should be achieved (much of which repeated the recommendations of the 'Dictionary Committee' of February 1893).[146] However, the wind was rather taken out of his sails by Gell, who read to the assembled Delegates various extracts from their minutes and other documents which showed their implicit acceptance of a scale of 8:1 over the course of several years.[147] The meeting seems to have ended in a kind of stalemate: Bywater's letter was rejected as 'not in all points represent[ing] the unanimous opinion of the Delegates'; it was agreed to send Murray and Bradley some proofs which had been marked up by the new committee, but it proved impossible to agree on the text of the committee's formal report on the matter, and further discussion was held over until after the vacation. In addition, the meeting now gave approval for final arrangements to be made with Bradley in regard to his move to North House. Gell, acutely aware that the future of the project was still very much in the balance, was careful to make the offer of the house (rent-free) conditional upon the Delegates being 'satisfied with the progress made in the N.E.D.'[148]

Another reason for the inconclusiveness of the Delegates' meeting may have been that Gell was waiting to hear from the Philological Society, whose Council held a meeting on the evening of the same day. He had already indicated to Magrath that he was hopeful of engineering a 'united action' of the Delegates and the Society around an agreed scale of 8:1; and so it was to prove. The Council passed several resolutions which, while supportive of the Editors' argument that this was 'the straitest limit within which [the Dictionary's] thoroughness & character can be maintained', recognized the reasonableness of seeking to keep the project within acceptable bounds; they even offered, if the 8:1 limit was agreed, to work with the Delegates to secure more public funding for the 'truly National work'.[149]

---

[145] SL 14 Mar. 1896 Gell to HB, Gell to FJF; MP 7 Mar. 1896 Gell to JAHM, SL 7 Mar. 1896 Gell to HB.

[146] OD 20 Mar. 1896. Bywater's draft letter to the Philological Society is preserved at OED/B/3/1/11.

[147] SL 21 Mar. 1896 Gell to T. Fowler.

[148] SL 23 Mar. 1896 Gell to HB. Gell was evidently embarrassed about the delay in the negotiations over North House, which he informed Bradley were due to 'the emergence of absolutely fundamental questions in connexion with the Dictionary'. In fact the negotiations over exact terms were to drag on for several months; the cost of providing a bathroom, for example, was eventually met by the Delegates, but without hot water (OD 5 June 1896).

[149] PSCM 20 Mar. 1896.

Bywater was not yet ready to climb down, however, or even to let the matter rest until after the vacation. Unusually, another meeting of the Delegates was called for 27 March, only a day before the end of term; this time a version of his report was approved, and sent to both Murray and Bradley in the form of a letter from Gell, together with the proofs as revised by Bywater and his committee. Significantly, the letter made no mention of a specific scale—evidently there was more to be discussed on that score—but it did make a number of detailed recommendations. Americanisms were not to be included unless they had been used by 'authors of note', slang only if it had 'passed into general literary use', and recent coinages were not to be sought (the words *fooldom* and *foolometry*, coined respectively by John Ruskin and the rather less famous Lionel Tollemache, were cited as egregious examples); illustrative quotations were to be limited to one per century except in special cases, and those illustrating 'archaistic revivals' were generally to be omitted (except where the word in question had been 'restored to literary use'); where quotations for technical terms from 'technical treatises' were simply definitions, they could simply stand in place of the Dictionary's own definitions; etymologies were to be kept short by the elimination of remote etymons and parallel forms in other languages; finally there was a severe injunction to all involved to show far greater restraint in the subdivision of meanings, a matter upon which the Delegates apparently felt that 'more time and expense [was being] wasted than in any other direction'. Very little in this list was entirely new; several of the recommendations, indeed, were essentially repetitions of points made in the report of February 1893, which perhaps Bywater felt had not been taken sufficiently to heart. The tone, however, was distinctly peremptory: the Delegates, or at least those who had voted for the report to be sent, felt that 'it ha[d] become necessary to lay down more definitely the principles on which the compilation of the Dictionary ought to proceed, with a view to their being brought to the notice of all who take part in the work'.[150]

Stern injunctions to brevity were unlikely to cut much ice with either Murray or Bradley, who were both as stern with themselves as anyone could be. The real point at issue was *how* brief they must be; and Bradley found to his satisfaction that the excisions made in the proofs which he had been sent provided further evidence that a Webster scale of 6:1 was simply unachievable. By the exhaustive application of their recommended techniques for compression (mainly the elimination of Americanisms and slang, and some abbreviating of quotations and definitions), the Delegates had only been able to reduce the scale of his proofs to a scale of 8.72 times Webster. Bradley wrote to Gell, accepting for the most part the Delegates' recommendations—though he did point out that the Dictionary had already been criticized for its poor coverage of Americanisms, and that its etymologies ought not to be any *less* thorough than those in the *Century Dictionary*—but observing that the marked-up proofs seemed to imply that the 6:1 requirement had been effectively withdrawn, and that on that basis he

---

[150] MP 2 Apr. 1896 Gell to JAHM; SL 2 Apr. 1896 Gell to HB (the two letters are almost identical). A copy was also sent to Furnivall, to be considered by the Philological Society.

would be happy to accept the terms on offer for his move to Oxford.[151] Murray talked it over with Gell in similar terms, though through press of work he had been unable to commit his response to paper (he was struggling with the unprecedented difficulties presented by the verb *do*, and was moreover once again understaffed, with Onions off sick for several weeks). Gell was now privately quite ready to dismiss Bywater's proposal of a 6:1 limit as an 'unconsidered guess'; compression was of course to be striven for, but as he remonstrated to York Powell, 'To hear some people talk, one would imagine it was child's play.'[152]

The prospects for bringing the crisis to an end were now looking more favourable—which was just as well, as rumours about the proposed abandonment or drastic curtailment of the Dictionary were beginning to circulate, and notices to appear in the papers.[153] A formal response from the Philological Society was still needed, but fortunately the Council were due to meet on 17 April. They heard from Bradley about the cutting-down of his proofs, and were happy to echo his inference that the Delegates now recognized a limit of 8:1—to which Murray and Bradley were quite ready to pledge themselves—to be the narrowest that could reasonably be required. A forthright resolution to this effect was passed *nem. con.*; rather remarkably, this was retrospectively toned down by Furnivall in response to a plea from Gell that its original wording might 'stir up strife in certain quarters'.[154] The Society's ordinary members were then treated to the Chief Editor's annual report on the Dictionary, which a harassed Murray had come to London to deliver 'unwillingly & under protest [...] feeling very unwell & unfit', but at least able to report that *do* was now at last in proof. (The 12,000 accumulated quotation slips for the word—the organization of which had obliged him to spill out from the Scriptorium and use his own drawing-room floor—had still proved inadequate, with nearly half of the quotations printed in the entry's 17 columns having to be searched out by his assistants.) He recounted the difficulties caused by the failure or departure of assistants; but regarding the project's more serious troubles he seems to have preserved a careful silence.[155]

To bring those troubles to an end only Murray's written response to the Delegates was now wanting. Unfortunately, when they reconvened for their first meeting of

---

[151] OED/B/3/1/10 11 Apr. 1896 HB to JAHM. Bradley discussed some of the words cut out of his proofs (including *flummadiddle*, *flummox*, *flunk*, and the theatrical sense of *fluff*) at a meeting of the Philological Society's Council, who passed resolutions supportive of the inclusion of such words, as well as Ruskin's *fooldom* (PSCM 17 Apr. 1896); *foolometry*, however, did not garner any support, and was not included. Curiously, Lionel Tollemache, the coiner of *foolometry*, later claimed that the word had indeed been included in the Dictionary (Tollemache 1908: 297).

[152] SL 17 Apr. 1896 Gell to York Powell.

[153] The earliest may be the *Saturday Review* of 18 April 1896 (pp. 393–4), which declared that such a step would be 'nothing less than a national calamity and an indelible disgrace to the University'.

[154] PSCM 17 Apr. 1896; SL 21 Apr. 1896 Gell to FJF. The Council endorsed Furnivall's provisional alteration of the resolution at their next meeting (PSCM 22 May 1896).

[155] HJRM p. 190; PSOM 17 Apr. 1896; MP JAHM notes for 1896 Dictionary Evening. Murray had in fact written to Furnivall asking to be excused from preparing and delivering his report, but due to a misunderstanding the notice that he would be speaking at the meeting was issued regardless, and Murray, anxious not to disappoint, felt obliged to attend.

Trinity Term, there was no sign of a letter. The reason for his silence was simple: Murray had finally buckled under the strain. He had been putting in over eighty hours a week solidly since the autumn; the entry for *do* would have posed a formidable and taxing challenge at any time; and the illness and departure of various assistants had exacerbated the situation. The additional stress of the crisis over the scale of the Dictionary had proved to be the final straw. In the week preceding his trip to London to report to the Philological Society he realized that he was in a highly, even a dangerously nervous state, close to breakdown—'My brain would not work', as he told Gell[156]—and that he absolutely had to get away for a rest. Four days at Malvern, with plenty of vigorous walking in the Malvern Hills with Ada, had the desired effect; even before his return to Oxford, he was returning to the fray with a forthright preliminary riposte to the marked-up proofs he had received, which he testily pointed out were of little use because the Delegates had opted to examine first proofs, rather than revises or finals:'These would be on the scale of eight times Webster, and what I want to know, is *what further can be done*, after I have done with them.' On his return to Oxford he followed this up with a more detailed response, along similar lines to Bradley's: apart from a few particular quibbles, the Delegates' recommendations for compression were 'precisely what [he had] been regularly trying to do; but of course the difficulty lies in the application to individual cases as they arise'. He was ready to do what he could by way of compression, for 'a little longer', and then, 'if it is thought best, give it up'.[157]

In fact it was not going to be necessary to 'give it up'. Gell was now desperate that the Delegates should relinquish the position they had taken by passing their February resolutions, and thereby bring to an end a stand-off which was now all over the public press.[158] The desirability of keeping scale to a minimum was accepted by all parties; Murray and Bradley had undertaken to abide by a limit of eight times Webster; there was general recognition that this was the narrowest possible scale consistent with the Dictionary's historical principles and reputation; so the resolution which called for a limit of six must now be rescinded. On 8 May the Delegates voted to do precisely this, not even substituting a limit of eight: instead, in view of the fact that Murray and Bradley had now undertaken to draw up a scheme mapping out in detail the rest of the alphabet, and the page limits for each volume—something which Bywater and York Powell had been tasked with doing in February—they authorized both Editors to 'proceed on the present lines' until this scheme had been submitted.[159] Greatly relieved, Gell informed both Editors of the news, which he hoped would 'terminate the somewhat protracted crisis'. Bartholomew Price undertook to draft a suitable notice for the newspapers, to put paid to reports of

---

[156] OED/B/2/2/1 printed copy of letter 23 Apr. 1896 JAHM to [Gell].

[157] OED/B/2/2/1 printed copy of letter 30 Apr. 1896 JAHM to Gell.

[158] For example, the *Glasgow Herald* deplored the prospect of the Dictionary being 'nipped in the bud by this chilling breeze of Oxford economy' (28 Apr. 1896, p. 6).

[159] SL 30 Apr. 1896 Gell to H. Gerrans, Gell to T. Fowler; OD 8 May 1896. A recommendation referring explicitly to the limit of eight times Webster had been made by the Committee of Publications, based on wording suggested to Fowler by Gell, but this was rejected by the Delegates in favour of a vaguer resolution to 'reconsider the scale' once the scheme for the remaining volumes had been submitted.

the Dictionary's demise.[160] Yet another committee was appointed (Monro, Bywater, and York Powell again) to 'supervise the New English Dictionary', probably to the irritation of Gell, who grumbled to the Vice-Chancellor that '"Dictionary Committees" have been appointed again and again during the last ten or twelve years,—generally on the spur of the moment,—but they have hitherto invariably died away.'[161] This latest committee seems to have been no different, and indeed has left no trace of its activities other than considering drafts of the page scheme for the Dictionary's remaining volumes—which, significantly, it was now accepted would be ten in number. This scheme continued to be agonized over for the next three months; a version was eventually printed and formally submitted to the Delegates, whereupon the matter was deferred indefinitely: a characteristically inconclusive postscript to the crisis.[162] Meanwhile, the Philological Society offered to appoint a committee to whom particular entries could be referred in cases where cutting down was required (or rather, as Furnivall suggested, to act as a further deterrent to expansion); there is no indication that the offer was taken up.[163] The scale of eight times Webster was now universally accepted as something which the Editors would do their utmost to adhere to.

And so, at last, various bits of interrupted business could be picked up again. (Characteristically, Furnivall immediately returned to the question of a third Editor, his latest candidate being the barrister Walter Cohen, who however withdrew before he could be seriously considered.[164]) In particular, preparations for Bradley's relocation to Oxford resumed; alterations were made to North House, and a room in the Press was fitted out as a place for Bradley to establish his editorial team, and the Bradley family moved in on 29 July.[165] (From this time, for a few years, the Press's premises were therefore home to two separate lexicographical workshops, as Joseph Wright and his assistants had been working here on the *English Dialect Dictionary* since the previous summer. Wright had issued the first section of his dictionary only a few weeks before Bradley arrived in Oxford.[166]) Of course work on the Dictionary itself had continued throughout the crisis, although the output of both Editors had been much reduced; fortunately the buffer of text which had now built up was large enough for sections

---

[160] 9 May 1896 Gell to JAHM; SL 9 May 1896 Gell to HB. Announcements confirming the continuation of the Dictionary along its established lines began to appear in the press in late May.

[161] SL 5 May 1896 Gell to Magrath.

[162] SL 15 June 1896 Gell to Bywater; OD 31 July 1896 (with copy of 'Proposed Scheme' pasted in). Unsurprisingly, the scale of the remaining portion of the Dictionary as proposed in this 'Scheme' proved to be increasingly optimistic. The alphabetical ranges and maximum page extents stipulated for Volumes IV to X were as follows (actual figures as published in parentheses): IV (F–G) 1,000 (1,160); V (H–K) 1,100 (1,274); VI (L–N) 1,232 (1,625); VII (O–Q) 1,300 (1,756); VIII (R–Sn) 1,250 (2,078); IX (So–T) 1,300 (2,234); X (U–Z) 820 (1,664)—with the last volume anticipated as having room in addition for a Supplement of approximately 450 pages.

[163] PSCM 5 June 1896; OED/B/3/1/10 6 June 1896 FJF to Gell ('We thought the *in-terrorem* Committee might perhaps be of use, tho' nothing shd ever be referd to it').

[164] SL 14 May 1896 Gell to FJF; OD 22 May, 17 July 1896.

[165] SL 22 July 1896 Gell to HB, OED/B/3/2/1 24 July 1896 HB to Gell. Harold Murray states that Gell would have liked to move Murray's Scriptorium into the Press at the same time, but that Murray, suspicious that this would 'fetter his independence', declined to move (HJRM p. 196).

[166] *Clarendonian* Summer 1974, pp. 44–5 (on Wright's 'Dialect Room').

to be issued by Bradley and Murray in March and June respectively. In October both Editors issued a section, with Bradley's (*Fish–Flexuose*) being his first with an Oxford dateline, although the copy had gone to press long before he had left London.

Notwithstanding this public impression of continuing steady production, work on the Dictionary was seriously behind for the year: partly because of the distractions of the crisis over scale, but also because of illness among Murray's assistants. On 5 September, when he returned from a much-needed three weeks' holiday in Criccieth,[167] he found himself facing the prospect of needing to do roughly twice as much work in the remaining third of the year as he had done in the first two-thirds if he was to complete the letter D in 1896 as he had hoped to do.[168] It was a matter for some pride that he did in fact manage to get to the end of D less than three months later, simply by working between 80 and 90 hours a week for almost the whole of the next eleven weeks (interrupted only by two days of influenza). On 24 November, at 11 p.m., he wrote on the final slip for *dziggetai* (a mule-like quadruped): 'Here endeth D. Τῷ Θεῷ μόνῳ δόξα [to God alone be the glory].' The last proofs were passed for press a few weeks later. In a report on the marathon year that was read out to the Philological Society's Council in December, he acknowledged the great part played by his assistants in achieving this goal, singling out Charles Balk; however, the bundles of copy for the latter part of D suggest that rather more of the work of drafting the definitions had been done by Arthur Maling and Charles Onions, who were evidently becoming extremely dependable.[169] Murray's daughter Hilda, now studying at Oxford University as a Home Student, also contributed some paid work for the Dictionary for the first time, as did a Kendal friend, R. J. Whitwell; and he also took on a schoolboy, Hereward Price, as a clerical assistant.[170] Bradley had also settled into Oxford well, and was invited to become a member of Exeter College in October (Murray's reaction to his being welcomed into the college where he himself had only recently sought unsuccessfully to gain admittance as a fellow may be imagined).[171] The new Editor and his team began to generate an encouraging quantity of proofs; Bradley was soon also thinking of employing his daughter in his 'Dictionary Room' at the Press. Gell welcomed the suggestion, declaring his own belief that 'the Dictionary will be finished by some of these Ladies who do so well in English Studies at Oxford'.[172] All of

---

[167] The holiday was apparently subsidized by Robinson Ellis, after Murray had mentioned in his April report to the Philological Society that he could not afford a holiday this year after having had one in 1895 (MP 6 Aug. 1896 R. Ellis to JAHM; other information from HJRM p. 194 and *CWW* p. 296).

[168] The post-holiday backlog was a regular occurrence: Murray had lamented to Fitzedward Hall in 1894 that the pile of accumulated proofs, correspondence, and other work that awaited him on his return from a fortnight's break made him 'sit down and weep, and vow that I will never go away again'. On this occasion, as he confided to Hall, there was the additional worry—unfounded, as it turned out—that the Delegates might after all make further impracticable resolutions about the Dictionary when they reconvened after the long vacation (OED/B/3/9/4 29 June 1894, 21 Sept. 1896 JAHM to Hall).

[169] A partial copy of Murray's report to the Council (quoted in *CWW* pp. 296–7, and more fully in HJRM pp. 194–6) is preserved in MP.

[170] Hereward Price's father, Charles Price, had been a pupil at Mill Hill School, and had done a little reading for the Dictionary; he subsequently went as a missionary to Madagascar, where Hereward was born.

[171] Minutes of Exeter College Governing Body meeting of 23 Oct. 1896 (Exeter College archives).

[172] SL 21 Dec. 1896 Gell to HB. Eleanor Bradley started work as her father's assistant early in 1897.

this additional man- and womanpower seems to have been approved without a murmur; it was not as though anyone could possibly have forgotten about the project's mounting losses—which by the end of the year were approaching £40,000—but the Delegates may well have been content for the Dictionary to be allowed to go its own way for a while.[173]

---

disproportionableness

In his introductory note to the Dictionary section *Disobst.–Distrustful*, published at the end of 1896, Murray observed of the 21-letter word *disproportionableness* that it was 'reputed to be the longest word (in number of letters) in the language'. The statement, which was picked up in several reviews of the section, proved to be a rash one. The question of which is the longest word in the English language has long been a matter of popular discussion, and it was quickly pointed out by various correspondents that other, longer words were available. One famous candidate, which had been included by Thomas Blount in his 1656 dictionary *Glossographia*, was *honorificabilitudinity* (22 letters), itself an adaptation of the medieval Latin word *honorificabilitudinitas*, which had already become well known as an exceptionally long word by the time of Dante, and which Shakespeare used in the even longer inflected form *honorificabilitudinitatibus* in *Love's Labour's Lost*. This word duly appeared in the OED section *Hod–Horizontal* in 1899. In fact two even longer words had already been published in the first two Parts of the Dictionary. One of these, *anthropomorphologically*, was pointed out by a correspondent to Murray, who publicized the discovery in *Notes & Queries* (10 April 1897, p. 297). The other, *acetylorthoamidobenzoic*, although entered as a lemma in Part I of the Dictionary, is no more than an example of the kind of very long word that can readily be formed from chemical prefixes and suffixes to denote a particular chemical compound; some even longer chemical names subsequently appeared in the first edition of the Dictionary, the longest being *diethylsulphonemethylethylmethane*, which appeared in the definition of the drug name *Trional*.

Only a few months after *disproportionableness*, Henry Bradley included, without comment, the even longer word *floccinaucinihilipilification* in his section *Flexuosity–Foister*. This is also a deliberately invented word, apparently concocted in the eighteenth century from a list of Latin words sharing certain grammatical features (*floccus, naucum, nihil, pilus*) that appeared in a widely used Latin grammar (the 'Eton Latin Grammar', then already long in use at Eton and incorporating material—including this list—which can be traced back to an early sixteenth-century text, the *Institutio Compendiaria Totius Grammaticae*). The word is first recorded in a letter of 1741 by the writer William Shenstone; it remained the longest word mentioned in the OED—apart from chemical formations like *diethylsulphonemethylethylmethane*—until 1982, when the even longer (and equally factitious) word *pneumonoultramicroscopicsilicovolcanoconiosis* was added in Volume III of the Supplement.

Continued ➤

---

[173] SL 18 Nov. 1896 Gell to W. Markby (reporting expenditure to date of approximately £52,000 as against cumulated sales of £15,000).

In 1900 Murray once again risked a comment about one of the long words included in the latest section of the Dictionary: *incircumscriptibleness*, he pointed out for the benefit of those interested in such things, 'has as many letters as *honorificabilitudinity*'. This led to the appearance of a poem addressed—erroneously—'To the Longest Word' in the *Pall Mall Gazette* of 9 April (p. 2), which apostrophized this 'Septisyllabic, immense, amplitudinous, Largest, leviathan, limitless word' (and which contrived to conclude its last line with the word).

As 1897 began Murray had made a good start on the letter H.[174] (At some point during the crisis it had been agreed that G should be left to Bradley, who had in fact started to prepare copy for G in August.) Although it would be some months before the final section of D was published, thoughts now began to turn to the preparations for publication of Volume III. A Preface for the volume would be required—to be written by Murray but on behalf of both Editors—and it was decided that this time there should be a considerably expanded set of statistics, including a comparative table showing just how far the *OED* surpassed various other dictionaries (Johnson, Cassell's *Encyclopaedic*, the *Century*, and Funk and Wagnalls' *Standard*) in terms of numbers of entries and quotations. This was almost certainly suggested by Robert Leonard, who had just been taken on by Henry Frowde to set the Press's publicity department on a more professional footing, and who visited Murray in January to consider ways of boosting public interest in the Dictionary.[175] A new Press journal, *The Periodical*—essentially a vehicle for promoting the Press's publications—was one of his first ventures; the first issue had appeared in December 1896, and the second contained several items about the Dictionary, including statistical tables for the letters A–E and an advance puff for Bradley's next section, which was duly published at the end of March.

In fact Bradley's output for the first three months of 1897 was, unprecedentedly, greater than Murray's. However, while the move to Oxford had indeed been a great success as far as Bradley's productivity was concerned,[176] his overtaking Murray was principally due to the fact that Murray and his assistants had spent most of January doing preparatory and investigative work on the whole of Volume V (H–K), the sub-edited materials for which now filled over 40 yards of shelving. A key part of the preparatory work was the incorporation in slip form of the relevant material from 43 dictionaries, glossaries, and wordlists, either by copying out or by cutting them

---

[174] The New Year was marked by the arrival of another of Skeat's jolly poems, celebrating Murray's assault on 'the terrible aspirate, The H that appals the Cockney crew, Lancashire, Essex, and Shropshire too. [...] We all rejoice, on this New Year's day, To hear you are fairly upon your way To Honour and Happiness, Hope, and Health—I would you were nearer to Worldly Wealth!' This was published in the *Daily News* on 30 January (p. 5), and as with Skeat's other 'dictionary poems' was widely reprinted; a copy in Skeat's hand, probably the original, survives in MP.

[175] FL 14 Jan. 1897 Frowde to JAHM.

[176] Bradley reported to the Philological Society that the move had enabled him nearly to double his rate of production (PSOM 5 Nov. 1897).

up and pasting them on to slips: experience had shown the value of integrating as much information as possible into a single sequence of slips, and thereby minimizing the number of additional sources that had to be consulted entry by entry as editing progressed.

Murray also took the opportunity presented by the start of a new volume to do some radical thinking. The importance—to all parties—of progressing through the alphabet as quickly as possible was of course something of which he was acutely conscious; but perhaps the approach of his own sixtieth birthday in February was another reminder of time's winged chariot. In any case, he seems to have been dissatisfied with his estimate that, based on recent rates of progress, he and his staff would require five years to complete Volume V; and in May he had a bold proposal to put to Gell. If the Delegates were prepared to let him spend the funds agreed for five years' worth of his assistants' salaries in just four years, then he thought it might be possible to complete the volume in that time; he proposed to spend the extra money on engaging qualified specialists to work in advance on the terminology of particular subjects, and also a suitably qualified scholar (German for preference) to pre-draft the etymologies. Entries for specialist terminology had long proved to be exceptionally time-consuming, and he thought that much time and effort could be saved by calling upon experts in advance, rather than consulting them as particular entries cropped up. By this method, he pointed out, the Press would also save a year of his own salary; finally, he regarded it as highly desirable that Volume V should be finished by the end of 1900: 'Into the next century I cannot presume to look very far, and I prefer at the present moment not to look at all, but to do as much as is possible for me, if I am spared to the end of 1900.'[177]

When Gell came to put Murray's novel proposal to the Delegates, it was unfortunate that it coincided with the resurgence of an old problem.[178] While the progress of both Editors in terms of pages was encouragingly rapid, there was also a report from Charles Doble that they were both exceeding the agreed scale of eight times Webster: Bradley's scale so far in F was nearly 10, and Murray's in H nearly 12. In view of recent history, it might seem extraordinary that the Delegates not only refrained from issuing any warnings to either Murray or Bradley about over-setting, but also authorized both Editors to experiment with obtaining 'special assistance in articles on technical words', as Murray had suggested. They did not, however, respond favourably to Murray's scheme for compressing five years' work into four, having no doubt spotted

---

[177] OED/B/3/1/11 6 May 1897 JAHM to Gell. As early as 1891 Murray had suggested engaging the patent officer R. B. Prosser to work on technical words—possibly gratis, as he had a pension—after Prosser had privately expressed criticisms of some of Bradley's entries in E; the idea was approved by Gell, but failing eyesight may have prevented Prosser from making much of a contribution (MP 8 Aug. 1891 Prosser to JAHM; OUP/PUB/11/29 12 Aug. 1891 JAHM to Doble; MP 18 Aug. 1891 Gell to JAHM, 23 Nov. 1891 Prosser to JAHM).

[178] Also unfortunate was the fact that Murray had aired his ideas about compressing the work at a meeting of the Philological Society, and that the report of the meeting supplied (probably by Furnivall) to the *Athenaeum*, which suggested somewhat airily that it only required the Press to 'afford a couple of extra assistants', came to the Delegates' attention (*Athenaeum* 1 May 1897, p. 580).

the obvious flaw that it would require Murray himself, as the 'neck of the bottle', to work 25 per cent faster—a pretty tall order in view of the ridiculously long hours he had already been working in the latter parts of 1895 and 1896. Gell did have an idea as to how the compressed timescale could be made to work without putting Murray under intolerable additional strain, namely by delegating most of the responsibility for some part of the volume—perhaps the letter I, which Murray expected to be comparatively straightforward—to a suitably competent assistant. He did suggest this to Murray, but perhaps without much confidence; delegating had never been Murray's strong point. But in the course of the discussions the Delegates were reminded of another strategy, which had often been considered: could they not resume the search for a third Editor? Individual Delegates now began once again to make inquiries.[179]

The name of William Alexander Craigie[180] was first mentioned as a possible Editor to Charles Cannan, a recently appointed Delegate. Neither he nor the man who suggested him, the chemist D. H. Nagel, was acquainted with this young Scotsman, the son of a Dundee gardener who had gained degrees from St Andrews and Oxford and shown an exceptional affinity for Scandinavian languages; but Nagel's father, who lived in Dundee, knew of his reputation, and it was soon confirmed by Monro (Craigie had studied at Oriel College) and York Powell. After graduating from Oxford, and spending a year studying Icelandic in Copenhagen, he had returned to St Andrews as an assistant to the professor of Latin, Alexander Roberts. He must have been rather surprised when, in late May, he received a letter from Monro, offering him an immediate trial engagement working on the Dictionary, and holding out the possibility that if all went well he might be appointed a third Editor. Craigie's response was enthusiastically positive; he even undertook to postpone his honeymoon—he was on the point of getting married—in order to come to Oxford as soon as possible.[181]

When this was brought up at the Delegates' meeting on 4 June, Gell was horrified. This was the first that he had heard of Craigie, let alone that he had been invited to join Murray's staff without Murray having been consulted or even informed.[182] The likely reaction of the extremely touchy Chief Editor did not bear thinking of. However, now that Craigie had already received an invitation to Oxford, it would be impossible to back out without causing Monro considerable embarrassment. The decision that the formal offer to Craigie should be of a position as Bradley's rather than Murray's assistant savours distinctly of damage limitation; but the Delegates were evidently determined on their candidate, for the offer—of a position starting in mid-July—was

[179] SL 6 May 1897 Gell to JAHM; OD 7 May 1897; MP 11 May 1897 Gell to JAHM.

[180] For later photographs of Craigie see Figure 23, p. 311, and Figure 24, p. 322.

[181] Wyllie (1961: 275); 31 May 1897 WAC to Jessie Hutchen (Craigie Papers, University of St Andrews, Special Collections Division, ref. ms36847); SL 9 June 1897 Gell to WAC.

[182] The two men had in fact met previously, according to Craigie, who later recalled being taken by Monro to visit Murray in the Scriptorium in 1892 (Craigie 1928: [1]).

to be explicitly 'with a view to [Craigie's] ultimate engagement as a third Editor', on terms comparable to those originally offered to Bradley.[183]

The extremely delicate task of informing Murray of the appointment now fell to Gell, who delayed writing until the arrival of Craigie's letter of acceptance made it unavoidable.[184] Murray's response was, predictably, one of extreme umbrage. He could not decide, he declared, whether the Delegates' failure to consult him was an intentional slight, or a denial of his particular status in relation to the project; either way, it was quite unacceptable. Moreover, it was not at all clear that 'further subdivision' of the work was the best way of expediting its completion; and even if it was, there were men on the existing staff (both his own and Bradley's) whose skills and experience made them likely to be far more effective than any stranger could be for some years. He was also concerned that the recruitment of an outsider at a high salary might so 'disgust' his best assistants that they would leave, with disastrous consequences for the project. But the worst thing about the whole thing was the Delegates' apparent decision that the future of the Dictionary was now to be provided for without consulting him; if this was to be the case, then he 'must at once sever [his] connexion with the Dictionary'.[185]

As his granddaughter observes, Murray 'threatened resignation so often that the Delegates had probably ceased to take the possibility seriously'.[186] On this occasion, however, they must have recognized that their action had placed him in an extremely difficult position, and steps were taken to placate him. A new subcommittee—Price, York Powell, the historian and jurist C. L. Shadwell, and the Vice-Chancellor, John Magrath— was appointed to confer with him; their expression of 'regret' at his being so left out of the loop with regard to Craigie's appointment will have mollified him somewhat, and he reconciled himself to the idea of a three months' trial, on the understanding that he would be fully consulted before any further steps were taken. Further placation came in the form of recognition that there were certain components of the work done by Murray (and his assistants) which pertained to the Dictionary as a whole, including Bradley's portion as well as his own, and which merited an additional payment.[187]

July brought the publication of the section *Doom–Dziggetai*, which at 140 pages was more than twice the size of a regular section: with Murray now well into H, and a large buffer of material ready for publication, it was thought that the Press could afford to complete Volume III with a flourish. Indeed, considerably more than a flourish: it was decided, at Murray's suggestion, that in this Diamond Jubilee year it would be a

---

[183] OD 4 June 1897. The word 'ultimate' was amended by Gell to 'possible' in the minutes.

[184] MP 14 June 1897 Gell to JAHM.

[185] MP 15 June 1897 JAHM to Gell (draft). Harold Murray claims that his father specifically mentioned Onions as one of the names he might have put forward, 'thus foreshadowing his appointment as fourth Editor in 1914' (HJRM p. [201a]).

[186] *CWW* p. 277.

[187] OD 18 June, 9 July 1897. It took the Delegates over six months to reach a decision as to the appropriate remuneration for Murray's 'work performed as General Editor of the Dictionary': an annual payment of £50 was eventually approved in January 1898 (OD 21 Jan. 1898). Also from about this time work done by various of Murray's assistants on Bradley's portion of the Dictionary begins to be accounted for separately.

fitting tribute to ask Queen Victoria to accept the dedication of the Dictionary to her.[188] This move was of more than ceremonial significance: as Peter Sutcliffe has observed, it 'bestowed upon the work an aura of permanence and sanctity, and made its unfolding as inexorable as progress itself'—and its wording publicly committed the university to an indefinite association with the project.[189] Finally, the Vice-Chancellor conceived the idea of a grand dinner at Queen's College to celebrate the completion of Volume III, the guest list for which he invited Murray to compile from among those who had given most help to the Dictionary. This was a shrewd move: Magrath had got the measure of Murray during the 1896 crisis, and in particular he was aware of his strong sense that the importance of the project was not properly appreciated by the university. The dinner, he suggested, should give him 'an indication that more people sympathise with you in your self denying labours than perhaps in moments of depression, disappointment or annoyance you have been fully able to realize'.[190]

Welcome as this gesture was, it was hardly going to solve all the Dictionary's problems overnight. Indeed, the path to 12 October—the day chosen for the dinner— was darkened by various difficulties, some with roots that ran deep. Murray's doubts about the 'Craigie experiment' persisted, and will hardly have been lightened by the fact that Bradley's frantic rush to get another double section ready for publication in advance of the dinner had not left him enough time to make a proper assessment of Craigie's work, or even to help with his training as much as he would have liked.[191] Murray's own constant driving of himself had left him severely run down—so much so that in July, while on a visit to Birmingham, he fainted in the street, cutting his head and ending up in hospital—and although a holiday in Wales restored his health, on his return he was badly behind with his proofs. Moreover, the beginning of H had proved to be (as he wrote to Fitzedward Hall) 'the most difficult and laborious section of the Dictionary, that I have ever had to do', making 1897 'a killing year for me'.[192] And then there was the matter of the title page of Volume III, which afforded Murray an opportunity to insist on his seniority over Bradley in a manner which arguably did him little credit. This was the first volume to contain the work of both Editors, and a form of words had to be found which fairly reflected their relative position and contribution. Bradley had always recognized the pre-eminent position which Murray occupied, but Murray had a long record of touchiness on the subject.[193] Now, even

[188] OD 18 June 1897; MP 21 June 1897 Gell to JAHM. The idea of dedicating the Dictionary to the Queen had first been floated nearly two years earlier (OD 25 Oct. 1895).

[189] Sutcliffe (1978: 93). The dedication read: 'To the Queen's most excellent majesty this Historical Dictionary of the English Language is by her gracious permission dutifully dedicated by the University of Oxford A.D. MDCCCXCVII.'

[190] MP 13 July, 9 Aug. 1897 Magrath to JAHM.

[191] OED/B/3/2/1 7 Oct. 1897 HB to Gell.

[192] OED/B/3/9/4 28 Aug. 1897 JAHM to Hall; *CWW* p. 331.

[193] An early slip, to which Murray seems to have reacted with indignation, is the announcement in the *Academy* of 22 May 1886 (p. 361)—almost certainly supplied by Furnivall—that Bradley was to be 'associated as joint-editor' with Murray. Bradley responded with an exceptionally understanding letter, in which he acknowledged the difficulty of Murray's position and his 'unvarying kindness' under 'peculiarly trying' circumstances (MP 31 May 1886 HB to JAHM).

though the final section of D had been published in July—and Volume III announced for the same month—discussion over the wording of the title page delayed publication of the volume until long after its advertised date, indeed until a few days after the October dinner. The final wording listed Murray first, with the two constituent letters, and the names of their respective Editors, beneath. Furnivall, who must have seen an advance copy, was disgusted by Murray's attitude: he had of course long regarded Bradley as joint Editor, and considered that Murray had long been in the habit of 'running him down at Oxford'. Such was his indignation that he refused an invitation to stay at Murray's house on the night of the dinner—'I don't feel that I can come to your house on the old friendly footing'—and, to rub salt in the wound, informed him that there were those in the university who regarded him as 'no gentleman' because of his treatment of Bradley.[194]

On 12 October, however, the friends of Murray, and of the Dictionary, were out in force. The dinner at Queen's College was a very splendid occasion, widely reported in the newspapers.[195] On the guest list were almost all of the Dictionary's assistants (including Craigie) and many of the most valued readers, sub-editors, and other helpers. (Notably absent, as would have been expected at an occasion of this type at the time, were any women: not even the Editors' wives or daughters were invited, nor the invaluable Misses Brown and Thompson. Another notable absentee was the reclusive Fitzedward Hall, the Vice-Chancellor's mention of whom however called forth 'such a unanimous and hearty outburst of applause as was not evoked by any other name'.[196] Henry Hucks Gibbs was unable to attend, as for rather different reasons was Dr Minor.) After dinner the guests heard from fourteen speakers, including not only the two Editors and other luminaries, but also a few less prominent individuals, such as Murray's senior assistant Charles Balk and the durable sub-editor Edward Brandreth. Furnivall took the opportunity to lambaste Oxford and Cambridge for their recent decisions against admitting women to full university membership; Bradley was generous in his praise of Murray's abilities; Sir William Markby, displaying a convenient forgetfulness of his and other Delegates' former scepticism about the enterprise, asserted that the Press 'ha[d] never hesitated in the performance of [...] a great duty which we owe to the University and the nation' nor 'felt any doubt as to [the Dictionary's] ultimate completion'. Murray himself spoke at length, not only about the history of the OED but also about his lexicographical predecessors: he and his colleagues took strength from their awareness of forming part of 'a continuous chain, which, adorned here & there with illustrious

[194] MP 12 Oct. 1897 FJF to JAHM. He also quoted a denunciation from an unnamed Delegate of Murray's 'insensate jealousy' in regard to Bradley.

[195] E.g. Times 13 Oct. 1897, p. 10, Daily News 14 Oct. 1897, p. 2; The Periodical Dec. 1897, pp. 1–4; other sources cited in CWW p. 374 n. 54. Quotations from speeches are taken from these, and also (in the case of Murray) from his own notes (preserved in MP).

[196] OED/B/3/9/5 13 Oct. 1897 HB to Hall. Hall turned down the invitation, but received a report of the dinner a few days later from Murray, who characteristically bemoaned the loss of the three working days which the dinner and associated arrangements had cost him (OED/B/3/9/4 20 Oct. 1897 JAHM to Hall; CWW p. 305).

names, formed elsewhere of less conspicuous links, loses itself in the far off haze of antiquity'. The completion of the third volume of the Dictionary was also, of course, a suitable occasion to contemplate the task of completing the remaining seven; and here, perhaps moved by the spirit of the occasion to an uncharacteristic burst of optimism, he took issue with the date of 1918 now being mooted as a plausible date by which the Dictionary might be completed. His own calculations, he declared, suggested that completion might reasonably be expected in 1910—and even hoped for, if the Delegates would allow him the 'additional strength' he had asked for, by 1908. There was now at last a machine for producing the Dictionary with the utmost efficiency compatible with its high lexicographical standards, and the Press now appeared more committed than ever to ensuring that it continued to operate. Optimism, however, had often proved to be rash before, and this occasion was no exception.

---

dump

The fact that Murray's 'Appeal' for volunteers to read for the Dictionary had an American secretary, in the person of Francis March, is well known, and of course there had been American contributors long before 1879. It is less well known that an attempt was also made to coordinate the rather smaller group of people who volunteered to read for the Dictionary in Australia. In the autumn of 1889 James Murray approached R. T. Elliott, a classicist who had recently joined the Philological Society, about the possibility of his doing some sub-editing for the Dictionary; he expressed interest (MP 12 Sept. 1889 R. T. Elliott to JAHM), but within weeks had left Britain to take up a position at Trinity College, Melbourne. However, he retained a keen interest in the Dictionary, and shortly after arriving in Melbourne—where he was soon in touch with another enthusiast from England, E. H. Sugden—he published a letter in the Melbourne *Argus* (11 July 1890, p. 7), reporting to Australian readers Murray's concern that 'he had hitherto received very little indeed from Australians, and that, consequently, Australian words and usages must be very scantily represented, unless he receives more help from Australians in the shape of illustrative quotations'. Readers were encouraged to send their contributions to himself or Sugden, to be forwarded to Murray. His letter also gave notice of a public meeting with a view to properly coordinating the work of collection: a suggestion which appears to have come from a third Dictionary supporter, E. E. Morris, who coincidentally was also in Melbourne (*Argus* 27 May 1890, p. 6). A further appeal for Australian assistance, issued by Sugden, appeared in the August 1890 issue of the *Melbourne University Review*. Unfortunately, this initiative did not lead to any coordinated programme of reading of Australian sources, although a few individuals did send quotations and suggestions directly to Oxford. Similar appeals were made by both Morris and Elliott in 1892 at the meeting of the Australian Association for the Advancement of Science in Hobart, but to no avail (Morris (1892: 178–9; *Hobart Mercury* 13 Jan. 1892, p. 4).

Continued ➤

Murray's request for Australian help did bear fruit, however. E. E. Morris had begun to collect quotations himself in response to the appeal from England, and by the time he spoke in Hobart he had decided that his materials might form the basis of a book in their own right. This eventually appeared as *Austral English* (1898), a pioneering dictionary of Australian and New Zealand vocabulary, which Morris acknowledged in his Introduction had been inspired by the *OED*, and whose contents he placed at the disposal of his lexicographical colleagues on the other side of the world by supplying them with duplicates of all of the quotations he had collected; these can still be seen among the copy slips for many entries. He also sent proofs of his work to Murray, whose comments on them are occasionally quoted in Morris's text (e.g. in the entry for *creek*). The proofs also furnished Murray and his colleagues with a valuable pre-publication version of the dictionary, which they lost no time in making use of: the *OED*'s entry for the verb *dump*—published in July 1897—gives a quotation for the sense from one of Morris's own definitions, for which the citation is given as '1896 [*sic*] Morris *Austral English*', and at much the same time Bradley inserted into the proof of his entry for *fossick* (also published in 1897) the first quotation given in *Austral English* for the word, acknowledging '(Morris)' as his source. *Austral English* would go on to be a valuable source of both information and quotations for Australian and New Zealand words throughout the compilation of the first edition.

It should be mentioned, though, that the *OED* was receiving enough evidence for Australianisms to include some entries well before the appearance of Morris's book, and even before the earlier appeals made by Elliott and Sugden (both of whom also made substantial contributions to the corpus of quotations from which *Austral English* was compiled). Among the Australian items in Part II of the Dictionary are uses of *bail* (noun and verb) with reference to a framework used for securing the head of a cow, and *banker* 'a river full to the brim', and terms of Australasian natural history appear even earlier, such as *death adder*, briefly mentioned at *adder* (though subsequently dealt with in more detail at *death*).

Method: from quotation slip to published entry

So far this account of the making of the *OED* has been concerned mainly with the fortunes of the project as a whole, and its external relations with the Clarendon Press, the Philological Society, and other bodies and individuals. But at the heart of this project—first in James Murray's Scriptorium at Mill Hill (and its Oxford successor), then in Henry Bradley's London workshop, then in the room fitted out for him within the buildings of the Clarendon Press, and in the Dictionary's various other homes—was a remarkable machine, which would be described by the University's Chancellor as 'the largest single engine of Research working anywhere at the present time'.[1] For a full appreciation of the output of this machine it is essential to understand its constituent components and processes, which by 1897 had reached a form which remained unchanged in all essentials throughout the period of compilation of the first edition of the *OED*. It is true that the number of drivers of the machine, already two since 1888, had not yet reached its maximum. (It is not giving away much to reveal that Craigie would soon become the third to take the controls; it is giving away a little more to mention that there would eventually be a fourth Editor, in the person of Charles Onions.) The methods employed by each Editor's team, however, were essentially identical, and the system for distributing the work of compilation between separate Editors, working independently, was already established.[2]

---

[1] Curzon (1909: 185). The observation may have originated with Charles Cannan, who made a very similar comment to Murray four years earlier (OED/B/3/2/3 23 Jan. 1905 [Cannan] to JAHM: 'The Dictionary do you not think must now be the largest single engine of research working anywhere in the world?').

[2] Mugglestone (2000) contains much further discussion of methodology; see especially the chapters by Knowles, on readers and sub-editors, and Silva, on definition and entry structure.

QUOTATIONS

The raw material on which the Dictionary was based had of course been accumulating even before the *New English Dictionary* had been conceived. Directions for the writing-out of quotation slips are given on the first circular issued by the Philological Society's Unregistered Words Committee in 1857, and the collection of quotations had begun even before this. The instructions given in the 1857 circular are much the same as those given in Murray's 'Appeal' of twenty-two years later, and indeed the same method is still used today by those who continue to contribute quotations on paper: the text of the quotation itself together with a full bibliographical reference indicating exactly where the quotation was found, written on a slip of paper headed with a 'catchword' indicating the word being illustrated.[3]

The beauty of this system was and remains its flexibility: anyone who came across an instance of a word, in any context, which they considered worthy of the Dictionary's attention could write out a quotation slip and submit it. Slips, furthermore, could be used to record evidence found in less conventional sources, not just printed text or even manuscripts: quotations collected for, and used in, the first edition of the *OED* include ones taken from an eighteenth-century inscription on a house in Hawick ('All was Others. All will be Others'; quoted at *Other*) and the label on a container of sweets ('Lemon pennets', at *Pennet*). For those who undertook to read through an entire text looking for useful quotations, an element of the drudgery could be removed by having slips pre-printed with the bibliographical details of the text in question, leaving only the quotation text itself and its exact location to be written out by the reader: an expedient which Frederick Furnivall resorted to as early as 1864. Murray does not seem to have continued Furnivall's alarming practice of inviting readers to cut up the pages of books into slip-sized pieces—despite the saving of readerly effort and the minimizing of copying errors which this of course represented—although some contributors, notably Furnivall himself, continued to take cuttings from newspapers and other inexpensive texts in this way.

Control of which sources were read, and how, during the project's early years was patchy at best. Murray was critical of the materials which he inherited in 1879 in various respects, commenting to Fitzedward Hall in 1899: 'I often wish I had made a

---

[3] The 1857 instructions do not mention a catchword as such, but the example quotations given in the circular begin with a catchword, and the earliest slips surviving from this period are so marked. The original instructions were also particularly insistent that quotations should be written on one side of a piece of 'ordinary small quarto letter paper'; at the time of the 1879 'Appeal' readers were directed to write on 'a half-sheet of note-paper'; in 1928 the size was given as 'about [*sic*] 6⅝ × 4¼ inches' (Craigie et al. 1928: 15); by 1931 this had been simplified to '6" by 4"—not larger' (OED/B/3/10/3 19 Feb. 1931 J. M. Wyllie to KS), and 6 × 4 inches remained the standard size thereafter until the introduction of A6 as part of the European range of 'A' paper sizes in the 1980s. Just about the only significant difference between the oldest slips and those produced today is that originally the bibliographical reference was placed after rather than before the text of the quotation; the change seems to have been made by Murray, following his experiments with format for the abortive Macmillan project.

bonfire of the old and begun anew.' It was certainly true that, of the quotations actually used in Dictionary entries, only a small proportion (perhaps as low as 10 per cent) were from the materials collected by readers working under Coleridge's or Furnivall's direction—so that the declaration which appeared, at Furnivall's insistence, on the Dictionary's title page that it was 'founded mainly on the materials collected by the Philological Society' arguably overstates the part played by the Society.[4] In some cases the same source came to be read several times by different readers, resulting in the accumulation of multiple copies of the same quotation (although different readers might also light on different words in the same text); other readers elected to look only for words beginning with a particular letter, a 'most pernicious and deceptive practice'[5] which could pass undetected until someone noticed that a book which had allegedly been read thoroughly was no longer showing up in the quotation files. Many readers also proved to be unreliable copiers of quotations, or to have failed to give accurate or complete bibliographical details, or simply to have terrible handwriting. Reverification of quotations thus became an important task: see below.

All of the quotations had then to be sorted, first alphabetically according to their catchwords, then chronologically for each word. Given that the number of readers was already in three figures when Furnivall took over the editorship, it is hardly surprising that he failed to keep on top of this task, so that when the accumulated materials—now amounting to well over a million quotations—passed to Murray in 1879, a great deal of sorting remained to be done. The two women engaged by Murray to complete the sorting of this material eventually did so after more than two years; then there was the matter of incorporating the continuing influx of further quotations, which had never entirely stopped, and which of course increased enormously after the launch of the 1879 'Appeal'. Murray later acknowledged that much of the sorting had been carried out by his own children, all eleven of whom were enlisted to help, mostly as soon as they had learned to read;[6] various other volunteers, including some sub-editors, also undertook the sorting (alphabetical or chronological) of batches of material which were posted to them.[7]

---

[4] OED/B/3/9/4 11 Apr. 1899 JAHM to Hall; *CWW* p. 169. However, as Elizabeth Knowles has rightly observed in her detailed survey of the work of both readers and sub-editors, 'allowance must be made for Murray's tendency to doubt the probity of systems other than his own' (Knowles 2000: 23).

[5] As reported by Murray to the Philological Society in March 1892 (*TPS* for 1891–4, p. 275). Furnivall retorted tartly, and not unreasonably, that 'we of old were not, & you now, w[oul]d not be silly enough to refuse slips for any 1 letter sent from a book. We took em, & said please send the other letters in due course. And if folk didn't do so, we were powerless. [...] Beggars can't be choosers; & no one beggar has a right to blame another for the poor case he is in' (MP 28 Oct. 1892 FJF to JAHM).

[6] Harold Murray recalled: 'The work was purely mechanical, but we liked it because we were paid at a fixed rate per hour, and appreciated the independence which the possession of money of our own earning gave us. [...] The tedium of sorting was often relieved, I fear, by reading the quotations, and we all owed an unusual extent of vocabulary in early years to this somewhat scrappy form of reading' (HJRM pp. 120–1). For recollections of other Murray children see *CWW* pp. 178–80.

[7] In the notebook (OED/B/5/7/1) recording batches of material sent out to and received from sub-editors, several individuals are listed as being sent material for sorting only.

SUB-EDITING AND RE-SUB-EDITING

The idea of saving editorial effort by having the accumulated quotation evidence pre-processed by sub-editors had of course been Furnivall's; it was more important than ever now that the number of quotations ran into millions rather than thousands. Already in 1881 Murray estimated that, if he were to spend only half a minute looking at each quotation slip—and of course many would take longer—he would need something like three years to get through even a third of the accumulated material.[8] Some of Furnivall's sub-editors had agreed to continue their work when the Editorship passed to Murray, but many more were needed. Appeals for fresh sub-editors became a regular part of his reports to the Philological Society, and continued at least until 1899; indeed, sub-editing itself continued for many years, although only a handful of sub-editors worked on beyond 1900.[9] There was also the problem that, if a range of material was sub-edited significantly in advance of the point at which the Editor and his assistants could begin work on it in earnest, further quotations would accumulate, and need to be incorporated with the older material, a process which Murray called 're-sub-editing'. The organization of this work, across the whole alphabet, continued to be overseen by Murray even after the division of the Editorship. Copies survive of Murray's guidelines for both sub-editing and re-sub-editing;[10] from the picture which emerges of the tasks which his volunteers were directed to carry out, it is clear that his idea of what they could be expected to achieve was significantly more limited than Furnivall's had been. The sub-editor, having carried out any outstanding sorting, would be faced with a chronological sequence of quotations for a given word; for anything more complex than a word with a single meaning, he or she was then to identify its individual subsenses, and group the slips for each meaning together, attaching them to a slip bearing his or her draft of the definition. The same applied to phrasal and compound uses as well as to subsenses. The individual senses were then to be arranged in what seemed the best order; the complete material for a word would be preceded by a 'top slip' showing the headword together with its variant spellings. (Deciding which form of the word to give as the headword was by no means always a simple matter; and sub-editors were expected to write cross-reference slips for the variants, placed in the appropriate alphabetical place, so that a reader looking a word up under a variant spelling would be directed to the entry.) Sub-editors were encouraged to do their best to remedy deficiencies among their materials, aiming to provide at least one quotation per century. Re-sub-editors essentially revised the work of the sub-editors, incorporating the new quotations that had accumulated and modifying the definitions

---

[8] JAHM Dictionary Report, in *TPS* for 1880–1, p. 261.
[9] PSOM 13 Jan. 1899; OED/B/5/7/1 sub-editing log. The last sub-editor of all was William Robertson Wilson, whose final batch of sub-edited material in W was returned to Oxford in August 1919; this by no means marked the end of his contribution to the Dictionary (see below, p. 285).
[10] OED/B/5/1/1, 2.

and sense order where necessary; in general they were working relatively close in time to the point when the materials came to be worked on in Oxford. In some parts of the alphabet, however, no re-sub-editing was done, with the result that an Editor and his assistants could find themselves faced with literally decades of new material that had not been incorporated.

Unfortunately, there was no way of knowing in advance whether a volunteer sub-editor would actually be any good at the task. The success rate proved to be rather poor, and incompetently sub-edited material could be more troublesome than material which had not been sub-edited at all. Murray's assessment in 1910 was that '[o]ut of nearly 40 who have tried [sub-editing], it would be difficult to pick out 8 [...] whose help has been appreciably worth the trouble'.[11] This is in line with the recollection of one of Murray's later assistants, G. W. S. Friedrichsen, who commented:

Some of these [sub-editors] were excellent, as Rev. C. B. Mount, and the sisters Toulmin-Smith [*sic*; *recte* Thompson]; many were indifferent. [...] I don't think any of us three [*sc.* himself and two colleagues, Arthur Maling and F. A. Yockney] made much use of the Sub-Editors' work; we usually dissembled [*sic*] all the sections, arranged the slips in chronological order, and started *de novo*, perhaps glancing at the definitions to see whether there were any good ideas.[12]

DRAFTING AND SELECTION BY IN-HOUSE ASSISTANTS AND EDITOR

It was only when the assistants, working alongside Murray (and later the other Editors), began to work on the sub-edited material that entries really began to take shape. On the rare occasions when they found themselves dealing with the work of a really competent sub-editor, there was still much work to be done. Even when the quotations had been sensibly divided into senses and good definitions written, there was still the matter of making a suitable selection of quotations for each word and sense—a task which sub-editors were explicitly instructed not to attempt, and which thus gave the assistants an important role in shaping the text—and of writing the pronunciation (in the system specially devised by Murray), applying 'house style'

---

[11] MP JAHM, Dictionary Report, 6 May 1910, quoted in *CWW* p. 200.

[12] 27 May 1971 Friedrichsen to RWB, quoted in Burchfield (1973b: 2). The inadequacies of the sub-editor James Bartlett were occasionally annotated with tart comments by another assistant, the waggish Henry Bayliss, as for example where Bartlett has written 'I feel quite incompetent to tackle the formidable early forms of the word [shake]' and Bayliss has added 'I move to delete all after "incompetent"'. (Knowles (2000: 25–6) identifies the annotations as being by Henry Bradley, but the presence of Bayliss's initials 'H.J.B.' shows this not to be the case.)

to the list of variant spellings which sub-editors were supposed to provide (and incorporating any additional forms found among the new quotations), and, in almost all cases, drafting the etymology.[13] However, from the bundles of slips which formed the 'copy' for the Dictionary it is clear that the assistants did far more than this.[14] Only a small fraction of the top slips which had been supplied by the sub-editors made it to this stage, and most of the replacement slips were written by the assistants rather than by the Editor in charge of them. In a few instances the text on the fresh slips was simply a rewritten version of the sub-editor's draft, altered only to bring it into line with house style: even the best of the sub-editors do not seem to have mastered the minutiae of the Dictionary's style (and many of them, after all, had sent in their work long before that style had been established). Most of the time, however, as described by Friedrichsen, the assistants would change the wording of definitions—and of course write new ones for items which the sub-editor had not had to consider—and also devise an entirely new sense structure for an entry when the evidence warranted it (as very often it did). Quotations were generally not rewritten, but they still had to be brought into house style: this was a demanding task, requiring thorough knowledge of the Dictionary's system of abbreviated short-titling, and some of the assistants specialized in doing this, such as Frederick Sweatman, who also did a great deal of the important work of reverifying quotations. There was also the matter of filling gaps in the quotation evidence, which remained considerable even in the work of the best sub-editors;[15] Murray described the quotations collected up to this stage as supplying 'only the torso' of an entry, leaving 'the head, hands & feet' still to be added.[16] The assistants did a great deal in this regard, checking the few available concordances of standard authors, the word indexes in editions of early texts such as those published by the Early English Text Society, and generally anywhere else they could think of.[17] For most ordinary words, however, the body of quotation evidence was such as to allow for some element of selection; assistants were expected to make their selection according to various criteria, choosing 'those [quotations] which best illustrate the different heads and intentions of a definition,

[13] A few of the sub-editors would attempt to provide etymologies, but hardly any of them proved to be capable of doing so for more than the simplest formations; in most cases the first draft of an etymology would be written by an assistant, although for the more difficult etymologies it was not unusual for them to leave a blank to be filled in by the Editor.

[14] For a full account of the work of the assistants see Gilliver (2004), from which some of the following detail is drawn. See also Craigie et al. (1928), esp. pp. 10–17.

[15] Murray told the Philological Society in 1884: 'For more than five-sixths of the words we have to search out and find additional quotations [...] for *every* word we have to make a general search to discover whether any earlier or later quotations, or quotations in other senses, exist' (Presidential Address, in *TPS* for 1882–4, pp. 515–16).

[16] PSOM 13 Jan. 1899.

[17] A printed list of 'Resources for the addition of quotations and completion of the sense-history of words', evidently produced in the late 1880s, attests to the frequency with which such research was needed (copies in OUPA at OED/B/5/1/4). Among the concordances available were those to the Bible and the works of Shakespeare, Pope, Shelley, Cowper, and Tennyson (Hjelmqvist 1896: 105).

or the phrases and grammatical constructions noted therein', and aiming to include at least one quotation per century.[18]

The end result of an assistant's work was a completed draft entry, or sequence of entries, in the form of a sequence of slips. (The initial slips of the copy for the entry for *dictionary* are shown in Figure 16.) These slips would then be presented to the Editor, together with any material which the assistant had provisionally rejected. This would consist mainly of additional quotations, but an assistant could also recommend a word for omission, for various reasons: as already noted, from an early stage the *OED* was not exhaustively inclusive, and such marginal items as poorly established foreign borrowings could be marked '?omit' by an assistant, generally if the supporting quotation evidence was also poor. The final decision, as with all other aspects of the Dictionary's text, rested with the Editor, but on many matters it was the assistant who was the first to make a provisional choice, whether it be about the inclusion of a particular quotation, or a particular meaning, or a particular word.

The making of such decisions must inevitably have involved discussion between assistants and their Editors, and among the assistants themselves. While direct evidence of oral discussions does not survive, assistants would often annotate their slips with queries, and comments justifying their decisions, which constitute a kind of written counterpart to this spoken dialogue. Such dialogues could take place between assistants—when, for example, the work of a new assistant was gone over by a more senior one, and passed back with alterations and comments for training purposes—or between assistant and Editor, and in certain circumstances between Editors. The copy produced by Craigie in the first year or so after his appointment as Editor, for example, was gone over and commented on by Murray, mainly in the form of observations written on the back of the slips, as for example on a slip for the prefix *quadri-* where he recommended omitting Craigie's observations about the origin of the corresponding Latin prefix on the grounds that they were 'Latin philology not for us to discuss'.[19]

The range of specialist knowledge required at all stages in the process of compiling a dictionary entry was enormous. Often enough some additional information was needed to complete a definition or an etymology which the combined expertise of

---

[18] Craigie et al. (1928: 15–16). This account of the Dictionary's methods goes on to say that 'it is incumbent upon [the Editor] to scrutinize every quotation whether selected by the assistant or not', but there is clear evidence (discussed in Gilliver 2004) that at least some of the time the Editors trusted their assistants' judgement without actually rechecking every rejected slip. The aim of including one quotation per century can be traced back to 1877, when this was mentioned by Henry Sweet as having been agreed with OUP as a desirable level of illustration (OED/B/3/1/1 14 July 1877 Sweet to B. Price). Craigie was later reported as having aimed to include two quotations per century, although 'this rule [...] was often violated' (Mathews 1974: 220).

[19] No such comments can be seen on the copy for the entries in *su-* which marked Onions's first work as an independent Editor; but by this point he had acquired considerable experience as, effectively, a finalizer of copy (see p. 312).

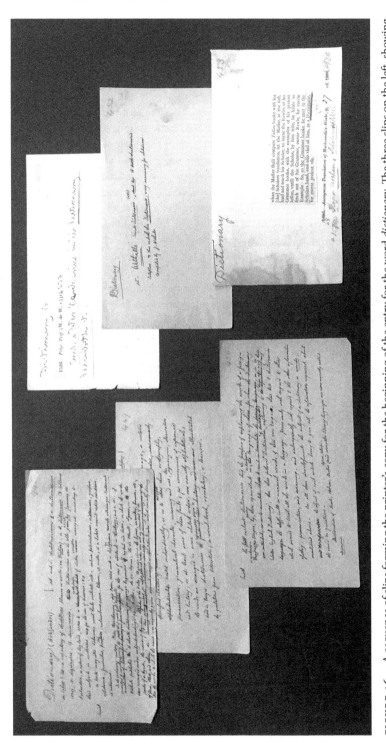

FIGURE 16 A sequence of slips forming the printer's copy for the entry for the word *dictionary*. The three slips on the left, showing the headword, etymology, and the definition of the first sense, are in the hand of James Murray; as is the second of the quotation slips on the right; the quotation of 1526 is in the hand of Henry Hucks Gibbs, and the final quotation, cut out from a reprint of Roger Ascham's *Scholemaster*, appears to have been supplied during the 1860s or early 1870s, in that the bibliographical citation is placed after the quotation text (whereas after Murray became editor in 1879 the order was reversed). The text of the entry and the selection of quotations underwent significant change before publication: material was moved between the etymology and the definition, and several additional sixteenth-century quotations were added.

the Editors and their assistants, and the reference works at their disposal, could not furnish. Consequently the Editors found themselves writing an enormous number of letters to anyone who might be able to help.[20] Murray vividly portrayed the range of his own correspondence in a lecture:

I write to the Director of the Royal Botanic Gardens at Kew about the first record of the name of an exotic plant; to a quay-side merchant at Newcastle about the *keels* on the Tyne; to a Jesuit father on a point of Roman Catholic Divinity; to the Secretary of the Astronomical Society about the primum mobile or the solar constant; to the India Office about a letter of the year 1620 containing the first mention of *Punch*; to a Wesleyan minister about the itineracy; to Lord Tennyson to ask where he got the word *balm-cricket* and what he meant by it; to the *Sporting News* about a term in horse-racing or pugilism or the inventor of the word *hooligan*; [...] to the Deputy Keeper of the Rolls for the exact reading of a historical M.S. which we have reason to suspect has been inaccurately quoted by Mr Froude; to a cotton manufacturer for a definition of Jaconet or a technical term of cotton-printing; to Thomas Hardy to ask what is the meaning of a word *terminatory* in one of his novels; to the Editor of the New York *Nation* for the history of an American political term; to the administrator of the Andaman Islands for the exact reference to an early quotation which he has sent for the word Jute, or the history of *Talapoin*; to the Mayor of Yarmouth about the word *bloater* in the herring fishery; to the chief Rabbi for the latest views upon the Hebrew *Jubilee*; to a celebrated collector of popular songs, for the authorship of 'We dont want to fight, But by Jingo if we do,' which gave his name to the political *Jingo*. In fact a lexicographer if he wants to be accurate, has to be a universal enquirer about everything under the Sun, and over it.[21]

During the early years of Murray's residence in Oxford the volume of his correspondence was such that the Post Office placed a pillar box immediately outside his house for his convenience.[22] Often the first person approached with a query was unable to answer it, and on occasion a dozen or more letters still failed to elicit the relevant information. (Murray recounted one amusing instance of a circular chain of enquiries, initiated by his letter about the origin of the word *aphis* to the Zoological Secretary of the Linnean Society, who wrote to a colleague, who in turn wrote to a third correspondent; at his request a fourth correspondent wrote to Murray himself to ask for the answer to the question, because 'he knows that I know *you* and that *you* know

---

[20] Onions later suggested that the letter-writing approach was favoured particularly by Murray, who 'always preferred to consult the expert instead of going to his works or to the literature of the subject' (OED/B/3/2/17 14 June 1928 CTO to RWC).

[21] MP JAHM, text of 1910 lecture to the London Institution (the source text is in the hand of Murray's wife, Ada, but with various alterations by Murray himself; for a slightly different version of the passage see *CWW* p. 201).

[22] *CWW* p. 213. The pillar box is unusual in that it does not bear the royal cypher; this was apparently due to an oversight by the manufacturers (Handyside of Derby), and is a feature of many pillar boxes dating from the period 1879–87.

everything'.[23]) On the other hand, certain correspondents proved to be so reliable that they became regular consultants; the assistance of hundreds of these individuals is scrupulously acknowledged in the Prefaces to the Dictionary's Parts and Sections. Some of the most durable consultants were those who gave advice on etymologies, including Paul Meyer for Romance languages and Eduard Sievers for Germanic languages, as well as the remarkable James Platt, whose extraordinary facility with many exotic languages was of particular value.[24]

Another important task was the verification of quotations, many of which had been taken from an edition of the work published subsequent to the first (and which could not be assumed to occur in the first edition unless this was checked), and many more of which had been inaccurately copied or cited, or were simply illegible; few indeed were the contributors whose handwritten quotations could be taken completely on trust. Quotations copied from earlier dictionaries such as Johnson and Richardson could also prove suspect.[25] Some of the checking could be carried out by the Dictionary staff, some of whom became particularly expert users of the resources of the Bodleian Library. Many quotations, however, were from rare or unique texts, printed or manuscript, and checking might necessitate a trip to the British Museum, the Public Record Office, or other repositories; here, too, the Editors came to rely on a small number of trusted researchers. Another important task, carried out at a very late stage in the preparation of copy, was the careful reassessment of each slip of copy according to how much printed text it would generate (its 'extent'), with a view to seeing whether, by shortening a quotation by a word or two, or similar expedients, a line could be saved; given the constant drive to keep the scale of the Dictionary within tight limits, it was crucial to make the best possible use of every fraction of an inch of space. The person principally responsible for this was Murray's senior assistant Charles Balk, whose calculations of the exact amount of space taken up by a particular quotation can sometimes be seen on slips in the copy.[26]

---

[23] *CWW* p. 202 (quoting the same 1910 lecture).

[24] On the correspondence of Sievers with the Dictionary's Editors see Durkin (2011); on James Platt see Platt (1910). Judging from the surviving documentation supplied by Sievers and Meyer during the 1880s (OED/B/3/6/1,2), they were consulted by Murray in regard to just about every difficult Germanic or Romance etymology; as late as the 1898 prefatory note to *H–Hod* Murray was thanking them both for their 'constant help' in this regard. Bradley's prefaces also regularly acknowledge the help given by Sievers and Meyer.

[25] Ultimately it proved impossible to verify all quotations taken from Johnson, Richardson, and similar dictionaries; Murray adopted a policy of identifying such 'second-hand' quotations with a label—'(J.)' for Johnson, '(R.)' for Richardson, etc.—showing the source from which they had been taken. For *OED3* it has proved possible to convert many of the outstanding quotations of this type; for an account of the work done on quotations taken from Johnson, see Silva (2005). Work on the remainder is ongoing at the time of writing.

[26] It was later claimed that this practice was discontinued at some point after Craigie was appointed Editor, but Balk was certainly still projecting the extent of copy for Murray as late as 1909 (Wyllie (1961: 279–80); OED/C/2/1/4 3 Aug. 1909 Balk to CTO).

PROOFS AND REVISES

The next stage was the transformation of handwritten copy into printed text. Before being sent to the printers, the slips in each bundle of copy were numbered (generally from 1 to 1,000) so that the sequence could be straightforwardly reconstructed if a bundle was dropped; each bundle was date-stamped on arrival at the Press. The work of typesetting would then be handed out to various compositors (whose names still survive, written on the copy slips).[27] The text was first printed in single columns as galley proofs (see Figure 17), or galleys; these were read and corrected, and new proofs ('revises') printed. A 'second revise' could be (and, during the early years, generally was) produced following another round of reading and correction; a particularly troublesome sequence of entries could occasionally warrant 'third revises'. After this, the corrected columns of type were 'made up' into three-column pages, from which printing plates would be made, thereby freeing up the individual pieces of type to be re-used. Correction 'in plate', although possible to a limited extent, was much more expensive than when the text was still in type, and was therefore kept to a minimum. Eight pages of the dictionary were printed on a single 'sheet', which it was the Editor's responsibility to 'pass for press'. It was of paramount importance to keep the various stages of this whole process running at more or less the same speed: concentrating too much effort on the production of proofs and revises could lead to type being 'locked up', rendering further composition impossible until type was released.

Proofreading the *OED* was very far from being a process of correcting simple typographic errors. Comments from the small inner circle of readers[28] who read the proofs extensively, and replies to particular queries from specialist consultants, could result in drastic, transformative changes to the text.[29] Definitions could go through a succession of rewordings, in the light of clearer or more elegant alternatives put forward by the readers, or they could be discovered to be simply incorrect. The selection of quotations illustrating a particular word or sense could be similarly reconsidered; new quotations were often found at this late stage which demanded to

[27] For most of its first edition the work of typesetting the *OED* was shared out among two or three teams of compositors ('companionships', or ''ships'). For a reminiscence of the work of the 'ships from Dave Faulkner, a printer who joined the Press in 1903, see Belson (2003: 50). Belson's list of those who gave distinguished service to the Press in the late nineteenth and twentieth centuries (pp. 213–78) mentions several of the more durable workers on the *OED*, including William Sheppard, who was one of the four men who began typesetting the Dictionary in 1882, and James Gilbert, who spent 44 of his nearly 48 years of service working on it (on his retirement see p. 385).

[28] Each Editor had his own slightly different inner circle. The key proofreaders from the beginning were Henry Hucks Gibbs and Fitzedward Hall: among those who joined them were several former assistants (Erlebach, Frederic Bumby, J. B. Johnston, G. R. Carline, and G. W. S. Friedrichsen). Other proofreaders who are repeatedly acknowledged in the Prefaces to the Dictionary include A. Caland, J. T. Fowler, H. Chichester Hart, W. W. Jenkinson, Russell Martineau, Skeat, Edith Thompson, W. H. Stevenson, and W. Sykes. The Editors also read each other's proofs: Hjelmqvist (1896: 128) mentions that Murray read Bradley's work in revise, but also that Bradley read Murray's 'finals'.

[29] Many examples of the changes that took place at proof stage are discussed in Mugglestone (2005).

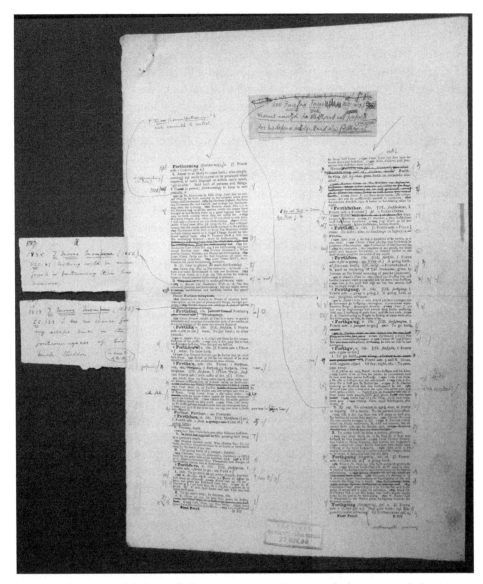

FIGURE 17   Page of first proof, showing entries in the range *forthcoming* to *forthgoing*; two additional quotations supplied by Fitzedward Hall can be seen pasted on to the left.

be incorporated, principally as a result of exhaustive targeted searches by the readers— some of whom (like Fitzedward Hall, Murray's former assistant James Johnston, and later the Shakespeare scholar Henry Chichester Hart) were especially adept at this kind of research—but also simply through the continuing influx of quotations from those individuals who continued to read fresh sources for the Dictionary. Antedatings (quotations which were of earlier date than those previously known) were regarded as having a particularly urgent claim to be included; sometimes this could necessitate a complete rethink of the structure of an entry, as for example when a sense which had previously been thought to be a late development was shown by the arrival of an antedating to be the earliest sense. Nor was it unusual for entire words or senses which had previously been overlooked (or excluded because the evidence appeared marginal) to have their importance belatedly recognized, and thus also to demand inclusion. Of course, the constraints of printing from plates (see Figure 18 for an example) made the inclusion of new material particularly difficult. Occasionally space could be made within an existing column by further application of 'compression' (such as saving a line by shortening a quotation), but generally the only way to include any substantial item at this stage was by excluding something else: sometimes this could mean the loss of a quotation; sometimes, however, the lexicographers were forced to omit an entire entry for a word or sense. An ironic example is the (admittedly rare) word *lexicographing*, included on the first proof with the definition 'The writing of dictionaries' and a single quotation from W. H. Pyne's *Wine and Walnuts* (1823), but subsequently excised (and still not reinstated).

Printing and binding brought other constraints. It was only really practicable to issue sections made up of a whole number of sheets or half-sheets (see Figure 19); it was therefore highly desirable that the text of each section should as nearly as possible run to a multiple of 4 pages. Any overrun would necessitate the printing of another half-sheet, with a consequent significant wastage of paper, while if the text fell short, the unused part of the half-sheet would likewise be wastefully blank. These constraints could lead to some truly Procrustean efforts at compression: in 1915 Murray, observing that a portion of S edited by Craigie ran to an odd number of pages, advised that cutting 10 or 11 lines on each of the previous 32 pages would enable a further page to be saved, thus avoiding the need for a blank page (which, as he declared to Charles Cannan, 'of course cannot be tolerated'). He had done much the same himself many times, and, somewhat chillingly, offered to help out on this occasion: 'If Dr Craigie is not prepared for such a "massacre of the innocents," I should be prepared to do it for him as tenderly as possible.'[30]

Finalizing the text of a Dictionary in one part of the alphabet—and giving it the permanence of print—involved making many decisions about material that would have to appear in later entries: a cross-reference to another entry, for example, would effectively commit the Editors to using that spelling of the word in question as its headword, necessitating a decision—often long in advance of the compilation of the relevant entry—about which spelling to use. Similarly, consistency demanded that a word used in a definition, or indeed an etymology, should be spelled in the same way

---

[30] OED/B/3/2/7 25 Feb. 1915 JAHM to Cannan.

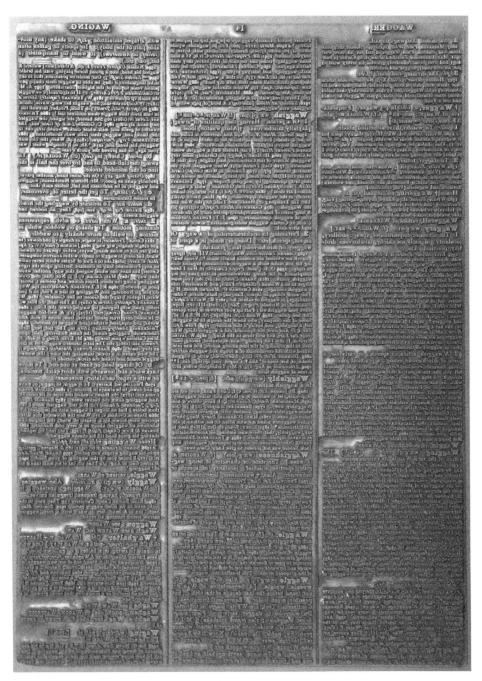

FIGURE 18   Printing plate for the page *Wagger–Waging*.

FIGURE 19   Printing sheets of the Dictionary in 1925.

when it came to be entered in the Dictionary. Careful record had to be kept as to decisions of this kind, perhaps by placing slips in the files for the target words; at least, no evidence survives to suggest that decisions about such matters were recorded in some separate document. Consistency also required that quotations from any given text should be cited, as far as possible, in the same way throughout; here the evidence does survive, in the form of ledgers recording agreed forms of bibliographical citation for thousands of individual texts. Similar files are maintained down to the present day by the *OED*'s bibliographers.

The publication of a section of the Dictionary (see Figure 20) did not, of course, always have to mean that the last word had been said on its contents. Additional information could come to light following publication—indeed often as a direct result of it, in the form of findings noted by reviewers—and, although in most cases these were simply filed for later consideration in a Supplement to the Dictionary (whatever form that might take), a small number of the most significant items were published in the form of addenda and corrigenda appended to the Prefaces of later sections. These emendations were among those taken up into the body of the Dictionary for the corrected Reissue of 1933.

FIGURE 20   Finishing Dictionary fascicles in the bindery at OUP. The fascicle being finished appears to be *Wise–Wyzen*, the last to be issued (in 1928).

DIVERGENCES

Each of the Editors of the first edition of the Dictionary was striving to create a stylistically homogeneous text, implementing a consistent editorial approach, and they succeeded to such a remarkable extent that the fact of there being different Editors for different portions of the text is often overlooked. They were, nevertheless, individuals, each with his own approach, and there are bound to be differences between them. Nor is the fact of such divergence of approach the only cause of variation within the text of the Dictionary. Each individual Editor went through a process of learning his craft, and this learning curve is reflected in differences between the beginning and the end of each Editor's output. There is also the fact that the range and quantity of the evidence available at the start of compilation differed enormously from that available during the later years: so much so that even if Murray and his colleagues had maintained an absolutely unchanging approach in their analysis of this evidence, the resulting Dictionary entries would show variation. Nor should it be forgotten that, while each Editor bore full responsibility for the sections of the Dictionary which appeared under his Editorship, most of the text was drafted by assistants, much of whose work was of necessity left unchanged by their Editor, who after all was severely limited in the amount of time he could devote to revising or recasting material.

Full consideration of the differences between different parts of the text, and the work of different Editors (or even individual members of their staffs), could easily form the subject of a book in itself; it would require careful analysis, not only of the published Dictionary text, but also of the unused material. A few tentative observations, however, can be made, partly on the basis of statements made about the work of individual Editors (mainly by their fellow Editors) during the compilation process, and partly on the basis of the experiences of individuals who have engaged closely with the text— most notably of those lexicographers who have done so during the last two decades in the course of revising it (or, in earlier years, supplementing it).

Murray does seem to have managed, much of the time, to achieve a higher degree of compression in his portions of the text than the other Editors, at least to judge by the scale of his text as compared to Webster's 1864 dictionary.[31] Concision in definition and shortening of quotations could both contribute to compression, but the kind of concision at which Murray seems particularly to have excelled is the distillation of a range of uses of a word into a single, appropriately broad definition, rather than describing the various uses separately. In aiming at this he was acting on advice which he had been given by Henry Liddell, and which he quoted to Craigie in 1902 when giving him feedback on his editing: '*Everybody* can make distinctions: it is the *lexicographer's* business to make broad definitions which embrace them; the synthetic power is far above the analytic.'[32] (Corroboration, of an impressionistic kind, of this aspect of Murray's work was to come decades later, when those working on the revised Supplement to the Dictionary noticed, as they moved from the letter S—which had been edited by Bradley, Craigie, and Onions—into Murray's work in T, that the definitions in the latter tended to have a great deal more packed into them.[33])

The Dictionary's third Editor, William Craigie, can be seen as something of an outlier when his work is viewed from another perspective, namely the structuring of entries. One of the most distinctive features of those parts of the text which were edited by him, as compared to Murray, Bradley, and Onions, is his tendency to use grammatical or syntactic features, particularly transitivity, as a basis for his structuring of large entries. Verb entries in which the transitive senses have been grouped into one branch and the intransitive senses into another separate branch may be encountered anywhere in the text, but they are far more common in the portions edited by Craigie. This preference has become evident during the work of the current revision programme.

---

[31] Figures for the Webster scale achieved by each Editor began to be reported regularly to the Delegates after 1897 (OD *passim*).

[32] OED/B/3/8/5 3 Dec. 1902 JAHM to WAC.

[33] Edmund Weiner, personal information.

One consequence of structuring a large entry in this way is that many pairs of transitive and intransitive senses are separated from each other in a way which obscures their close interrelationship; today's revisers, taking the view that transitivity is not usually a historically meaningful basis for structuring the senses of a verb, are often obliged to recast the structure of such an entry completely, so as to bring the semantically related transitive and intransitive uses together. In 1909 Craigie was criticized by Murray for using just such a structure in his very long entry for the verb *run*; in the event he stuck with a transitivity-based structure, which was only abandoned when the entry was revised in 2010–11.[34] Craigie's editorial practice can also be seen to diverge from that of the other Editors in other minor respects: he is, for example, by far the most prolific user of the label '*rare*-1' to indicate that only a single instance of a word or sense was available, and also by some way the most sparing user of the labels '*nonce-word*' and '*nonce-use*'. Taken together, these perhaps begin to suggest an approach to lexicography that sets him slightly apart from his fellow Editors;[35] but doubtless the individuality of all four of them could be shown to express itself in various ways.

---

[34] Further on the entry for *run*, both as originally edited and as revised, see Gilliver (2013).

[35] It may be relevant here to mention that Craigie was later judged to be 'the weakest of the four editors' by Stefanyja Olszewska, who worked as his assistant on the first Supplement and subsequently became a particularly expert user of the Dictionary, as well as an important contributor to the second Supplement (Brewer 2007: 269 n. 30).

7

And then there were four: 1897–1915

WHILE the road from the grand dinner at Queen's to the completion of the first edition of the Dictionary would prove to be far from smooth, the period following the completion of Volume III is relatively free from that sense of lurching from crisis to crisis which characterized much of the preceding two decades. Old problems and tensions would resurface from time to time, and there was no shortage of new untoward incidents; but the project does at last seem to have developed enough momentum to carry it through these.

The fact that this transition to calmer waters coincided with a change of personnel at the head of the Press suggests that some credit may be due to the man who took over the helm. A few months after the dinner Philip Lyttelton Gell suffered another, even more catastrophic breakdown, and again went to the South of France to convalesce; his duties were carried out, first by another Delegate, the mathematician H. T. Gerrans, then by Gerrans and Charles Cannan together as 'pro-Secretaries', and then, from September 1898, by Cannan alone.[1] Cannan was a remarkable figure, unwilling to suffer fools gladly and with an intimidating capacity to 'blight a man's confidence by silence';[2] but he also had a great talent for diplomacy—as evidenced by the warm relationship he managed to strike up with the perennially tricky Furnivall— and Harold Murray may be right in crediting him with having 'by his urbanity and unfailing good humour introduced a new note into the relations of the Delegates to the Dictionary'.[3] Some credit is also due to the Vice-Chancellor, J. R. Magrath, whose

---

[1] The full story of Gell's departure—regarding which his close friend Alfred Milner commented, 'I don't think there is any fate so enviable as that of being unjustly "sacked" in a civilized country'—is told in Sutcliffe (1978: 97–106), and again (more briefly but with some additional details) in Sutcliffe (2000: 655) and Whyte (2013: 65–6).

[2] Sutcliffe (1978: 107).

[3] HJRM p. 208.

The Making of the *Oxford English Dictionary*. First edition. Peter Gilliver.
© Peter Gilliver 2016. First published 2016 by Oxford University Press.

relations with Murray following the crisis of 1896–7 developed into warm friendship, and whose contribution to smoothing relations with the Press went far beyond being the man behind the celebratory dinner (an occasion marked by Skeat with another of his poems, which ended with 'Three cheers for Queen's and good Magrath!'[4]).

A key factor in the public impression of smooth progress lay in the decision to issue small quarterly sections rather than the larger, and more irregular, Parts. Under this system it was fairly easy for each Editor to build up a buffer of edited material beyond that required for the next section to be published, which could conveniently absorb at least some of the inevitable fluctuations in output. In good times the Press could issue a double section, and on occasion even a triple section; in bad times the expectations of the public could be satisfied with a single section. Skeat, who was as aware as anyone of difficulties and points of friction beneath the surface, commented approvingly on the 'regularity' of the Dictionary, comparing it to 'Sam Weller [in *The Pickwick Papers*] when he got talking of a grievance [...] "like a new barrow with the wheels well greased"'.[5]

But points of friction there certainly were; and Murray found himself rubbing up against two of them within days of the dinner at Queen's. The first of these concerned William Craigie, whose three months' trial ought by now to have ended.[6] Murray had been given to understand that he would be consulted before any further steps were taken; but he now heard from Magrath that the Delegates, having received a hurried (though admittedly favourable) assessment from Bradley, were now minded to extend Craigie's engagement for a further three years, the second of which they wished him to spend working under Murray's direction. Murray himself had still had no opportunity to evaluate Craigie's work, and took exception to being once again left out of the decision-making process. Privately he was in fact still doubtful about the whole principle of the split Editorship, which he regarded the Press as wilfully persisting with in spite of his own protestations that additional money would be better spent securing the best assistants. As he later commented to Gibbs: 'No practical man would for a moment approve of the present method of working, with three separate sets of workers, doing three independent pieces. It was simply childish, after the experiment had failed so greatly, in the case of the second staff, to proceed to constitute a third.'[7] He was also concerned at the effect of Craigie's proposed salary of £300 on his existing assistants, four of whom he declared to be worth far more to the project than Craigie would be for two years at least; he now anticipated that it would be harder than ever to turn down the requests he expected them to make at the year's end for an increase in salary (they were all currently receiving less than half what Craigie was being offered).[8] Magrath reassured him that there was nothing

---

[4] Quoted in HJRM p. 205. Magrath stepped down as Vice-Chancellor in 1898.
[5] MP 30 June 1898 Skeat to JAHM.
[6] Craigie had started work on 12 July (OD 8 Oct. 1897).
[7] GL MS 11021/30 ff. 741–3 15 Apr. 1904 JAHM to HHG.
[8] OD 8 Oct. 1897; OED/B/3/1/11 22 Oct. 1897 JAHM to Gell.

to stop him applying to the Delegates for additional funds to prevent valued assistants from leaving, and that the money available for bonuses was also unaffected by the offer to Craigie;[9] but before Murray's feathers could be smoothed, they were further ruffled by the appearance of an advertisement for the Dictionary in the *Oxford University Gazette* which he regarded as calculated to detract from his unique position. In fact, as Gell wearily pointed out, the wording of the advertisement, which described the Dictionary as 'edited by Dr. James A. H. Murray and Mr. Henry Bradley', was not new; however, previously Bradley's name had appeared beneath Murray's, whereas the new advertisement placed the two Editors' names alongside each other, a change of emphasis which the ever status-conscious Murray pounced on as 'in the opinion of many persons [...] unjust to me'.[10] Magrath was able to mollify Murray on this point too, with the news that the offending format would be discontinued; but Murray was careful to insist on the retention of 'the style hitherto in use' (with his primacy clearly asserted) on the title pages and covers of the Dictionary itself. More importantly, he did indicate his acquiescence in the proposed arrangement with Craigie, at least for the next two and three-quarter years; but his insistence, in the same letter, that all title pages and covers should continue to recognize his position 'as Editor of the whole work' suggests that he may still have been suspicious of the plans which some, at least, of the Delegates might have for 'their' new recruit.[11]

On the subject of assistants' salaries Magrath soon proved to be as good as his word, and in January 1898 the Delegates not only approved increases for Balk, Maling, Onions, Sweatman, and Price, but agreed to reimburse Murray for some additional money which he had felt obliged to pay his assistants for their 'extra exertions' during the previous year. They also finally approved a figure of £50 as the annual payment to Murray for his particular duties as 'General Editor'. As luck would have it, both Editors were in turn able to report that their output had increased markedly: the text composed during January amounted to exactly 50 pages, an almost unprecedented total, coming on top of better-than-average figures for the two preceding months.[12] Of course, there was more than one way of producing large quantities of text, and over the next few months it became clear that neither Murray nor Bradley was

---

[9] MP 2 Nov. 1897 Magrath to JAHM.

[10] OD 29 Oct. 1897; OED/B/3/1/11 29 Oct. 1897 JAHM to Gell. Among others who noticed the change was Anthony Mayhew, who wrote to him 'with heartfelt sympathy' at what he considered a 'cruelly unjust' misleading of the public (MP 1 Nov. 1897 Mayhew to JAHM). The offending advertisement appeared on p. 90 of the *Oxford University Gazette* of 26 October; ironically, it was a full-page advertisement, whereas earlier advertisements (e.g. in the issue of 9 June) had occupied half a page or less.

[11] MP 2 Nov. 1897 (bis) Magrath to JAHM; OED/B/3/1/11 5 Nov. 1897 JAHM to Magrath. Furnivall's report for the *Athenaeum* of the Philological Society's November Dictionary Evening, with its reference to the 'third editor for the "Dictionary" [...] now in training under Mr. Bradley', can hardly have improved Murray's temper (*Athenaeum* 13 Nov. 1897, pp. 677–8). Furnivall continued to refer to Craigie in these terms (e.g. 'will probably become the third editor': *Athenaeum* 21 Jan. 1899, p. 87), only desisting when formally requested to do so by the Delegates (OD 27 Jan. 1899).

[12] OD 21 Jan., 11 Feb. 1898.

managing to stay within the agreed limit of eight times Webster; but no action was taken.[13] The new key players at the Press were evidently happy to let well alone for the time being.

After all, there was now a serious prospect of a third Editor; and Craigie was continuing to make a good impression. In June Bradley submitted a favourable report on his work to the Delegates, and declared that he saw no objection to his being immediately transferred to the Scriptorium for the training under Murray's supervision that he regarded as an essential preliminary to beginning to work independently. Murray concurred, and proposed taking him on in September with a view to setting him loose on a trial portion of J or K in the spring or summer of 1899.[14] Sure enough, it was arranged that, after a holiday visiting Copenhagen, Craigie would begin work in the Scriptorium on 15 September. Murray also took a proper summer holiday in 1898, for the second time touring the Continent with Robinson Ellis.[15] (A reminder of the watchful eye he kept on Bradley's work came on the eve of his departure, when he pointed out that his next double section, if made the usual length of 128 pages, would have to come to an end in the middle of the entry for *get*, 'a calamity so great, that any means of preventing it is preferable'. It was decided to limit the section to 120 pages, ending at *Germanizing*, and to compensate by adding 8 pages to Bradley's next section.[16])

The immediate effect of Craigie's move to the Scriptorium was, of course, a drop in output, as Bradley was deprived of an exceptionally able assistant, while a significant component of Murray's time now had to be spent in training. However, no sooner had the transfer taken place than Cannan began to contemplate a new project. Smoothly though the Dictionary was now running, it was still proving horrendously expensive; and Cannan was doubtless not alone in wondering whether the time had come for seeking to recoup some of the Press's losses by means of some other publication making use of the same material. From the start of the project it had been anticipated that it would be through abridgements and other spin-offs, rather than the big Dictionary itself, that money might be made; and in December he persuaded the Delegates that he should now investigate the question of abridgements seriously. Meanwhile Bradley

[13] In March the Delegates agreed to draw Bradley's attention to complaints about his excessive use of quotations from 'contemporary writers' (OD 11 Mar. 1898), but no mention is made of the fact that his Webster scale was running at nearly 10, nor that Murray's was even higher. One of the complainers may have been Bywater, who in his proposed list of methods of 'curtailment' of two years earlier (see p. 191) had included a suggestion that quotations from 'contemporary journals and society novels' be simply omitted, and the word 'Modern' put in their place.

[14] OD 10 June 1898; OED/B/3/1/11 typed notes of interviews between HB and Gerrans, 14 June 1898, and between JAHM and Gerrans, 15 June 1898.

[15] MP 22 June 1898 Gerrans to JAHM; OUP/PUB/11/26 9 Sept. 1898 WAC to 'Dear Sir'; HJRM p. 207 (recording his father's visits with Ellis to various cities in Belgium, France, Switzerland, Germany, and Holland).

[16] OUP/PUB/11/26 2 Aug. 1898 JAHM to Doble.

managed to engage a replacement for Craigie in the form of a Miss A. M. Turner; and Murray was approaching the end of his long struggle with the intractable letter H.[17]

In January 1899 Bradley suffered another breakdown in health, and was ordered to take a month's leave. This provided an unexpected early opportunity for Craigie to show his mettle. Murray suggested that, in order to maintain the flow of work from Bradley's team to the compositors, Craigie should try his hand at getting some of the prepared material into the form of final copy for the printer, with Murray himself going over the proofs. This of course meant a diversion of effort from his own work, and a consequent drop in the output of the Scriptorium; but at least both teams were able to keep going, and the buffer of text ready for publication meant that both Murray and Bradley were still able to bring out a section at the end of March.[18] A less welcome consequence of the arrangement was that Murray, on looking over the proofs of Bradley's huge entry for the verb *go*—the last of which he had sent to the printers only just before his breakdown—concluded that it was rather more huge than it needed to be: Bradley, it seemed, was still over-setting, at least in Murray's view. Initially two Delegates, Magrath and York Powell, agreed to see what they could do to reduce the entry to a more acceptable length, but they soon recognized the extreme difficulty of the task, and elected to leave it to Murray as being the only person capable of doing it within a reasonable time.[19] Even after the best efforts of both Editors, the published entry for *go* extended to just short of 12 pages, making it over 30 times as long as the corresponding entry in Webster (1864).

Craigie seems to have performed satisfactorily as a deputy for Bradley, who returned to work as planned after a holiday in Devon. However, when he was signed off again only a few weeks later—this time because of gout—Murray declared that Craigie could no longer be spared from the Scriptorium, for the rather peculiar reason that he was now 'bereft of Onions'. Sure enough, Onions seems to have left the Scriptorium, and Oxford, rather suddenly in early April.[20] What could this mean?

In fact no explanation for Onions's sudden departure has come to light. Harold Murray refers to 'a temporary break-down', and suggests that it was partly to do with inadequate heating and ventilation in the Scriptorium;[21] however, it is clear that there was more to the matter. Murray, in a carefully reticent letter to Cannan, observed that it would be difficult for Onions to return to Oxford, because

it is generally known that 'something queer' has happened [...] For myself, I could doubtless take him back, asking no questions, and fully believing that all that is said to

[17] OD 2 Dec. 1898; FC 8 Dec. 1898; PSOM 13 Jan. 1899.

[18] SL(P) 26 Jan. 1899 Cannan to JAHM; OED/B/3/9/4 10 Feb. 1899 JAHM to F. Hall; SL 6 Mar. 1899 Doble to JAHM.

[19] SL 4 Feb. 1899 Cannan to JAHM, copy of letter 11 Feb. 1899 Magrath to JAHM. A few pages of the *go* proofs with Murray's annotations survive in OUPA; the shortenings he indicated mainly involved the elimination of quotations he regarded as unnecessary.

[20] SL 12 Apr. 1899 Cannan to York Powell; OD 21 Apr. 1899. Murray's own notebook recording payments to assistants (in MP) shows that Onions was paid less than two weeks' salary in the second quarter of 1899.

[21] HJRM p. 210. In 1895 the conditions in the Scriptorium had of course seen off Ernest Speight (see above, p. 239), who coincidentally was a close friend of Onions.

have happened has been a grave error of judgement, into which no thought of evil entered; but I have to consider my other collaborators; and Mr Balk hesitates as to how he could be received.[22]

Cannan was similarly delicate in a letter to Henry Frowde, noting that Onions had left the Scriptorium 'owing to "private reasons"'.[23] In the tantalizing absence of further details one can only speculate. One possibility which seems to fit the available evidence is that Onions made some kind of outburst in the Scriptorium. Murray's mention of his assistant Charles Balk suggests that it may have had something to do with him; it should be remembered that anti-German feeling was running high in England at this time,[24] and Balk was of German parentage. On the other hand, Murray may simply be referring to the importance of consulting Balk as his most senior assistant. Another possibility is that someone had made an accusation of some kind of misconduct, which was generally felt to be unfounded but which involved something so scandalous that the accusation alone would be enough to damage his, and the Dictionary's, reputation. Whatever the nature of the misdemeanour, it must surely have constituted a serious blot on what had until then been an excellent record. Even more intriguing, however, is the fact that only five months later Onions was re-engaged—as Bradley's assistant.[25] Bradley was certainly in need of additional skilled help: on top of his own absences earlier in the year, during the summer illness deprived him of his senior assistant Sykes (who was now seventy) for some months, with a disastrous effect on his output.[26]

Alarm of a very different kind blew up in May. The publishers of the *Times*, having already had some success offering their readers a special edition of the *Encyclopaedia Britannica*, now announced that, thanks to an arrangement with the Century Company, readers could purchase the *Century Dictionary* at a bargain price (between £13 and £18, depending on choice of binding), payable by monthly instalments. The advertisements for this scheme dwelt on the vast sums of money that had been expended by the dictionary's original publishers, and pointed out that the *OED*— the only dictionary with which the *Century* might be compared—was still very incomplete; it was also alleged that the Oxford dictionary was 'not intended for the use of the public at large', being (it was implied) full of 'recondite information of use

---

[22] OED/B/3/2/1 31 May 1899 JAHM to Cannan.

[23] 31 May 1899 Cannan to Frowde.

[24] During the late 1890s widespread but sporadic British anti-German sentiment had intensified, especially following the sending of the notorious 'Kruger Telegram' by the German Kaiser in 1896, congratulating the Boers on repelling the Jameson Raid on the Transvaal.

[25] FC 22 Sept. 1899 (recording payment to Onions for '2 w[ee]ks to Sept 30').

[26] SL 6 July 1899 Doble to HB; FC 12 Oct. 1899. During May, June, and July Bradley's output averaged 6 pages per month, barely a quarter of Murray's figure in the same period, which hardly seem to have been affected by Onions's departure. In July Murray engaged the Oxford classics graduate A. H. Mann to replace him, and later in the year his daughter Elsie joined the staff, specializing in verification of quotations in the Bodleian Library; at the same time, however, he also lost the services of her older sister Hilda, who had been assisting with etymological work, but who now took up a lectureship at Royal Holloway College (HJRM pp. 210–11).

only to philologists', and lacking the *Century*'s pictorial illustrations and encyclopedic information.[27]

The *Times* offer threatened to be extremely damaging to sales of the *OED*. Fortunately, word of it reached Cannan in advance, and he was able to persuade the Delegates to respond with uncharacteristic speed. Barely a week after the *Century* offer had first been publicly advertised, the Press announced (in the *Times* and elsewhere) a reissue of the *OED* in monthly instalments, together with an offer (for a limited period) to supply the whole of the Dictionary—which of course was still less than half-finished—for a single down payment of £17.[28] It was also announced that Volumes IV and V would both be completed before the end of 1900, and the remaining five volumes would be completed by 1909. The Press even issued a speculative photograph of the completed Dictionary, with the anticipated 12–13,000 pages evenly distributed across ten uniform volumes.[29] The monthly reissue, priced at 3s. 6d. per instalment, was widely welcomed as bringing the Dictionary within reach of a larger public. Whether or not the new payment options would prove to be commercially sensible for the Press in the long term, the prompt response does seem to have seen off the threat from the *Times*: Cannan was soon able to report to Murray that 'we have succeeded pretty well',[30] and to another correspondent that 'The Times people are described as being "very much worried".'[31]

The recipient of the latter comment was William Little, the former Vice-President of Corpus Christi College (and Cannan's former tutor), whom he had succeeded in interesting in the new moneymaking idea he had brought before the Delegates six months earlier: the compilation of an abridged version of the Dictionary.[32] Little had by this time retired to Cornwall, having been forced to give up a career at the bar when

[27] Quotations are from the large advertisement which appeared in the *Times* on 9 May; a full-page advertisement introducing the offer had appeared the previous day.

[28] SL 1 May 1899 Cannan to York Powell; OD 12 May 1899. An announcement of the new offers appeared in the *Times* on 16 May (p. 9), and was also widely printed elsewhere. The *Times* advertisement gave great prominence to comparative charts showing the *OED*'s superiority to the *Century* in size, and neatly used the *Times* itself to vouch for the quality of the larger work, with eleven separate quotations from its own reviews. A reissue of the Dictionary in smaller sections had in fact been briefly contemplated in 1894, but the idea was abandoned on the advice of Henry Frowde (OD 2 Nov. 1894).

[29] The photograph appeared on the front page of the *Periodical* of September 1899; volumes VI–X are shown as edited jointly by Murray and Bradley (with, of course, no mention of Craigie).

[30] SL 14 June 1899 Cannan to JAHM. The *Times* continued to advertise the *Century Dictionary* offer aggressively for several months, and various special payment schemes continued to appear for some years, even after the publication of the two-volume Supplement to the *Century* in 1909 (which indeed was included in subsequent offers). The Press ended its own offer of the complete *OED* for a single down payment on 31 December 1899.

[31] SL 23 June 1899 Cannan to W. Little. The issue in monthly parts seems to have continued until the end of 1907, by which time it had almost caught up with the standard issue; by 1909 sales were reported to have 'practically ceased' (ML 7 Jan. 1909 HSM to Cannan).

[32] A definitive history of the 'Abridged'—which came to be known as the *Shorter OED*—has yet to be written. The fullest available accounts are to be found in the prefaces to the various editions of the *Shorter* itself, and some additional details in McMorris (2001), although in these sources the project's inception is dated to 1902.

he became completely deaf; it may have been no more than a desire to find rewarding employment for his former tutor that lay behind Cannan's approaching him. Cannan's initial ideas—communicated to Little in 'great secrecy'—were for three different spin-off publications: a basic spelling and pronunciation dictionary ('for the illiterate'), a dictionary for students with some historical content, and possibly 'a dictionary to compete with Webster & the Century; two vols, or one very thick volume—the English Liddell & Scott', containing 'as much of the big book as possible'. Murray was also consulted, and Little was soon preparing specimens, corresponding roughly to the two largest of the three proposals; but it would be some months before they progressed as far as being considered by the Delegates.[33]

Meanwhile, and notwithstanding Bradley's difficulties, sections continued to appear regularly; Murray, indeed, made unprecedented progress during much of 1899, publishing two double sections in consecutive quarters: the end of H at the end of June, and *I–In* three months later. Even more satisfactorily, in the latter section it proved possible to keep the 'Webster scale' down to less than eight. Murray's success can be partly attributed to the fact that much of the material in I was turning out to be relatively straightforward (with notable exceptions, including the formidable word *in*, and the suffix *-ing*, which required three weeks of research). He was also no doubt feeling the benefit of having Craigie on his team, once his period of deputizing for Bradley had come to an end. However, it also seems that Murray was putting himself under greater pressure than ever. He was still desperately keen to reach the end of Volume V by the end of 1900, 'so as to start next century on the mountain top', as he explained to his old friend Edward Arber, '& advance each year down-hill-ward to the end'. As a result, he looked back on 1899 as a year when he had worked 'harder, more desperately, more unremittingly than ever I have done in my life'; and 1900 would have to be the same, if he was to achieve his personal goal.[34]

The final year of the nineteenth century began inauspiciously, with depressing news of the fighting in South Africa (war had been declared against the Boers on 11 October), and another epidemic of influenza; Sykes fell ill, and Miss Turner resigned her post on account of her mother's ill health, leaving Bradley so short-staffed that Craigie was once again released from the Scriptorium to help prepare copy for him.[35] It was now well over a year since Craigie had begun to work for Murray, but the prospect of his promotion to third Editor had apparently receded, with Bradley in need of his services more than ever. Things were not going well for the Dictionary's second Editor on a number of fronts—not the least of which was financial. Since his move to

[33] SL 6, 11, 12, 19 Apr., 15 May 1899 Cannan to W. Little.
[34] MP Photocopy of letter 14 Jan. 1900 JAHM to E. Arber. In fact the work had not been entirely unremitting, in that he had managed to find time for holidays in Bournemouth and North Wales during the year (HJRM p. 210). His continuing work as an examiner for the Oxford Local Examinations also took him to Birmingham for a few days in July.
[35] FC 18 Jan. 1900; MP 18 Feb. 1900 WAC to JAHM. At around the same time Murray secured the services of another junior assistant, a young graduate from St Andrews named E. J. Thomas.

Oxford Bradley had found himself substantially worse off than he had been in London; he now reminded Cannan of the salary of £500 which he had been led to expect on his first appointment—which was £100 more than he was currently receiving—and alluded delicately to having declined various offers from other publishers.[36] Acutely conscious as he was of the disparity between his own rate of progress and Murray's, he nevertheless argued that the fact that he could not match Murray's quite exceptional health and powers of work should not be held against him. The Delegates' first thought was to see whether money could be obtained from elsewhere; and Cannan sought a meeting with Furnivall to discuss the idea of requesting an increase in Bradley's Civil List pension. Perhaps surprisingly, Furnivall was not in favour of the idea: it emerged that he had already approached Arthur Balfour (as First Lord of the Treasury) some time earlier, on his own initiative, and met with 'a very determined refusal'.[37] He also agreed with Cannan that only an increase in Bradley's output could really justify an increase in the salary he received from the Press; and Bradley was duly informed that this was what was required.[38]

At his meeting with Furnivall Cannan learned that the Philological Society was also going through something of a rough patch financially; and Furnivall had a radical proposal of his own for addressing this. A significant component of the Society's expenditure went on the printing of its *Transactions*, and Furnivall was hopeful that the Press could be persuaded to help out in this regard, perhaps by printing some of the *Transactions* itself. In return, he was prepared to suggest that the Society give up its entitlement to a share in the profits from the Dictionary. Furnivall might seem to be one of the least likely people to make such a proposal, given how vigorously he had fought to maximize the Society's share of profits in the negotiations with the Press of twenty years earlier; but his views of the project's financial prospects had changed, as year by year the accounts he presented to the Society showed the Press's ever-increasing expenditure—which in November 1899 had stood at over £60,000[39]—and by now he seems to have concluded that the Society's entitlement was unlikely to be of any value for some time, if ever. He might have hesitated in making his proposal if he had known of the ongoing discussions about the 'Abridged'; or perhaps the Society's needs were too pressing.[40] In any event, formal negotiations were entered into, resulting

---

[36]   OED/B/3/2/2 26 Jan., 21 Feb. 1900 HB to Cannan. Bradley also asked for pay rises for his two assistants Lewis and Bayliss, which were eventually granted a year later.

[37]   OD 23 Feb. 1900; OED/B/3/2/2 MS notes by Cannan on a meeting with FJF on 6 Mar. 1900. Furnivall's approach to Balfour was probably made in late 1897, after he had made another unsuccessful attempt to persuade the Delegates to increase Bradley's salary (OED/B/3/2/1 2 Nov. 1897 FJF to Gell; OD 19 Nov. 1897). The Delegates eventually decided against making their own approach (OD 9 Mar. 1900).

[38]   OED/B/3/2/2 MS memo by Cannan, marked as 'Read to Mr B[radley]' on 17 Mar. 1900.

[39]   PSOM 3 Nov. 1899.

[40]   Furnivall was certainly still enthusiastic about the general idea of 'abridgements' of the Dictionary, and in May had even persuaded Onions, at the time of his mysterious departure from Oxford, to put himself forward as someone who could be employed on one or other such project (OED/B/3/2/1 31 May 1899 Cannan to Frowde); but he does not seem to have known about the work being done by Little.

some months later in a settlement whereby the Society surrendered all rights in the Dictionary in return for an undertaking by the Delegates to contribute £50 a year for ten years towards the publication of the *Transactions*.[41] Cannan was relieved to find that the Society's willingness to give up its rights extended to the annual accounts: he had become increasingly uncomfortable about the publicity given to the growing debit balance by Furnivall's regular reporting of it.[42]

By the summer of 1900 the Dictionary appeared at last to have entered relatively smooth, even pleasant waters. Both Editors were now making good progress; Bradley was approaching the end of G, and was beginning to contemplate Volume VI, beginning with L—and was prepared to undertake to keep the new volume within reasonable bounds (eight and a half times Webster). He was also ready to release Craigie for a proper trial as an independent Editor, with responsibility (subject to final approval of the text by Murray) for entries in the letter K.[43] Murray, meanwhile, was rapidly approaching J. Little's work on the Abridged was continuing—it was decided around this time that he should work at the larger of his two proposed dictionaries—and Cannan was discussing specimens with Bywater and York Powell.[44] Public recognition of the Dictionary, and its chief Editor, also came in several different forms. On 22 June Murray gave the prestigious Romanes Lecture in Oxford's Sheldonian Theatre, on 'The Evolution of English Lexicography';[45] and the Dictionary received international exposure at the Exposition Universelle in Paris, where a ten-volume dummy of the Dictionary (see Figure 21) formed part of the Press's exhibit, as did a display of a whole volume suspended by a single strip of the Press's famous India paper.[46] The summer also saw a visit to the Scriptorium from Mark Twain, who was pleased to be told by Murray that he was the most distinguished literary visitor since Gladstone.[47]

Despite the generally good progress—which continued for the rest of the year, making 1900 the second year in succession in which the Press published over 500 pages of the Dictionary—old problems did resurface from time to time. One such problem was Bradley's persistent tendency to over-set. His 'Webster scale' as he approached the

[41] OD 27 Apr., 4 May, 15 June 1900; SL 12 Sept. 1900 Cannan to FJF.

[42] SL 9 May 1900 Cannan to Freshfields (solicitors). Murray, when consulted about possible consequential revisions to his own agreement with the Press, chose to retain his right to a share of the profits, but Cannan regarded this as 'largely [...] for sentimental reasons' (SL 27 Aug. 1900 Cannan to Freshfields).

[43] MP 23 May 1900; OD 1 June 1900.

[44] OD 11 May 1900; SL 12 May 1900 Cannan to Bywater.

[45] The first Romanes Lecture was given by Gladstone in 1892; among the distinguished figures who followed in subsequent years were T. H. Huxley and Holman Hunt. Thanks to his having matriculated from Balliol College in 1896, Murray was the first resident member of the University to be invited to give the lecture, which was immediately published by the Clarendon Press. A century later, in Michigan in 2001, his successor John Simpson paid tribute to Murray by entitling his own lecture—given on the occasion of the completion of the *Middle English Dictionary*—'The revolution of English lexicography' (published as Simpson 2002).

[46] As shown in a photograph of the exhibit in the *Periodical* of July 1900, p. 3.

[47] MP 23 June 1900 JAHM to Herbert Warren.

FIGURE 21   Dummy copy of the Dictionary in ten volumes, as exhibited at the Exposition Universelle in Paris, 1900 (photograph from the *Periodical* of September 1899).

end of Volume V had remained high—consistently over 10 throughout 1899 and 1900—and in early September, as he was just making a start on what he had promised would be a more compact volume, Cannan arranged for a few of the last proofs of the volume to be scrutinized by D. B. Monro, who found various quotations that he felt could be dispensed with, and made other suggestions for compression. Bradley evidently took the hint, and managed to bring in a Webster scale of precisely 8 for September; but he was unable to sustain this, and by the following month his scale had slipped back up to over 11.[48] Cannan also proposed another limit for the Editors to abide by: that they should not include any quotations later in date than 31 December 1900 (and therefore, of course, not accept any words or meanings whose evidence began after that date). The idea of such a guillotine was not new, of course—the notorious 'Suggestions' of 1883 had included a proposed latest date of 1875—but this time Murray was apparently in favour of the idea.[49] By this stage he must already have been resigned to the fact that the first five volumes of the Dictionary would not be completed by the end of the

[48] SL 11 Sept. 1900 Cannan to HB; OD 28 Sept., 12 Oct. 1900. The letter L eventually ran to 528 pages, making a Webster scale of almost exactly 10.

[49] SL 26 Sept. 1900 Cannan to HB.

year; but a limit such as Cannan was suggesting would at least constitute one way of preventing the task before him from growing ever bigger.

It was not only Murray who was anxious to finish Volume V as quickly as possible. It had, after all, been publicly announced that this would be achieved by the end of 1900, and the embarrassment to the Press would grow in proportion to the time by which this deadline was missed. Craigie had, as agreed, been entrusted with a large share of responsibility for the letter K, but in the increasingly urgent effort to complete the volume he had found himself having to do work which, as he put it to Cannan, 'could more economically have been done by ordinary assistants'.[50] As the year came to a close he was beginning to wonder whether he would ever work as an independent Editor, as had been proposed to him three years previously. Cannan was also keen to settle the matter; but the response he received from Murray was less than positive. He said he was unable to give an immediate answer, as there was the difficult question of how the Scriptorium might be modified to accommodate Craigie together with the additional staff he would require. In fact Murray was preoccupied by another matter: Fitzedward Hall, having taken to his bed in early December with pneumonia, was now seriously ill.[51] Hall's previous bouts of ill health had always alarmed Murray, who knew better than anyone the enormous difference which his contributions made to the Dictionary: during one such illness, in 1893, he had commented to Hall that he 'really dread[ed] to think of the falling-off in our work, which the failure of your help would mean'.[52]

---

appendicitis

In 1903 James Murray declared (*Notes & Queries* 31 Jan., p. 90) that he had received 'more letters about the omission of *appendicitis* [from the *OED*] than about any word in the language'. In accounting for its absence—seeing in the story 'a reminder of the fates of words, and not less of the chances of lexicographers'—he described how, when he was preparing the relevant section of the Dictionary in 1883, there was among the quotations for words beginning with *app-* 'a single reference, from a recent medical source', for the word; he consulted an unnamed 'distinguished medical professor'—later revealed to be Henry Acland, then Regius Professor of Medicine at Oxford—as to the current standing of the term. He reported Acland's assessment that *appendicitis* 'was a name recently given

Continued ➤

---

[50] OED/B/3/2/2 14 Dec. 1900 WAC to [Cannan].

[51] OED/B/3/2/2 27 Dec. 1900 JAHM to Cannan; MP 17 Dec. 1900 Hall to JAHM (also listing various other afflictions, including catarrh, asthma, and a hernia: 'That any poor devil with such a complication of ills should not soon give up the ghost seems incredible').

[52] OED/B/3/9/4 7 Dec. 1893 JAHM to Hall. Elisabeth Murray notes (*CWW* p. 305) that in this letter Murray abandoned the usual formula 'yours truly' for 'yours very affectionately'; he also writes that for many years he has 'looked upon [Hall] as a senior relative of [his] own, and regarded [him] with tender affection and reverence'.

to a very obscure and rare disease' and that it 'was purely technical or professional, and had even less claim to inclusion in an English dictionary than hundreds of other Latin or Latinized Greek terms of which the medical lexicons are full, and which no one thinks of as English'. This chimed with Murray's own view that 'words in *-itis* are not (in origin) English in form, but Græco-Latin, and thus do not come within the scope of an English dictionary, unless, like *bronchitis*, they happen to be in English use', and when Part II of the Dictionary appeared in 1885 it included no entry for *appendicitis*. (Curiously, Parts I and II had both included other words with the same suffix, including *amygdalitis* and *arteritis*, neither of which could be said to be as much 'in English use' as *bronchitis*.) However, during the 1890s appendicitis became an increasingly common diagnosis, first in the United States and then in Britain. A key event in the history of the word—and one which surely accounted for many of the letters which Murray received—took place in the summer of 1902, when the coronation of Edward VII had to be postponed due to the new King having succumbed to this very condition. By the time the coronation took place on 9 August 1902, following an operation by Sir Frederick Treves to drain the inflamed appendix, the word was on everyone's lips; inevitably the absence of *appendicitis* from the famously comprehensive *OED* became a matter of public comment, and the word soon became one of the most well-known omissions from the Dictionary. Although a full entry for the word would not appear until three decades later, in the 1933 Supplement to the Dictionary, Murray did manage to include a mention of it in his entry for the suffix *-itis*, published in 1901.

There is, however, a curious anomaly in Murray's 1903 version of the story. A search in the OUP archives has failed to bring to light any sign of the single instance of *appendicitis* which he claimed to have seen in 1883, nor of his correspondence with Henry Acland. It is of course entirely possible that both the quotation slip and the correspondence have simply gone missing. However, some other rather different correspondence does survive, suggesting that Murray's recollection of the episode may have been at fault. A letter of October 1900 from Hollis French, an engineer based in Boston, Massachusetts, refers to his having been informed by OUP's New York office that 'Dr. Murray would be glad to have information in regard to the earliest uses of the words "appendicitis" and "vermiform appendix"'. French passed on to the Press a letter from the Boston physician Reginald H. Fitz, who is usually credited with coining *appendicitis* in a medical paper of 1886; this paper was duly quoted in the entry for the word in the 1933 Supplement (correspondence preserved at MISC/275/11, 12). It remains possible that an earlier writer had independently coined the word, and that this usage had been brought to Murray's attention: after all, the suffix *-itis* was already in widespread use in medical contexts by 1883. However, even after extensive research no examples of the word earlier than 1886 have yet been found.

In January 1901 Murray did at last give his approval to the appointment of Craigie as the Dictionary's third Editor. He had come to the conclusion, however, that it simply would not be possible to reorganize or enlarge the Scriptorium in such a way as to accommodate a second editorial team. Neither was there sufficient room alongside Bradley, in his room within the Press itself; so new premises would be required.

Cannan approached the Vice-Chancellor, Thomas Fowler, about the possibility of accommodating both Bradley and Craigie in the large room which occupied most of the ground floor of the Old Ashmolean building in Broad Street (now the Museum of the History of Science), and which had until recently been used for University offices. Authorization to use the space was soon secured, and on 25 March, after extensive alterations (including the installation of electric lighting), Bradley and Craigie took up residence in the new 'Dictionary Room'.[53] The new premises had various advantages, notably close proximity to the Bodleian Library, which greatly facilitated the task of reverifying and searching for quotations. Craigie was initially appointed third Editor on a salary of £350, which as he took no time in pointing out was less than he had been given to expect in 1897; he seems to have been mollified by an assurance that the matter would be reviewed soon.[54] He also insisted that he would need a staff of at least four assistants if he was to make decent progress;[55] but initially he had to make do with two. Murray's most recently engaged assistant, E. J. Thomas, was assigned to him straight away, and was joined in the Old Ashmolean by another young Scottish graduate named John Ramsay. It was not until the autumn that he managed to find his third and fourth assistants, Lawrence Powell (another 'Bodley boy', like Bayliss and Lewis) and Ethelwyn Steane, the daughter of a local wine merchant; both proved to be excellent choices.[56]

Murray, meanwhile, was dealing with the consequences of the catastrophe he had feared. Fitzedward Hall died on 1 February, a devoted friend of the Dictionary to the end: the last time he held a pen was to sign a card accompanying a packet of proofs which he had been unable to go through in his accustomed way.[57] Bradley was also well aware of Hall's contribution, and concluded his affectionate obituary for the *Athenaeum* by saying that '[t]he loss of so laborious and so profoundly skilled a helper is a misfortune the magnitude of which it is hardly possible to estimate'.[58] Murray and Bradley were now both deprived of Hall's own critical eye; but a large part of the value of his proofreading lay in the additional quotations he was able to supply from his own enormous collections. It was clear that the considerable effort that would now be required to make use of these collections in their surviving form would be amply justified. Murray appealed for volunteers to write out in full the quotations for which Hall had left only references, a task which he estimated would require rather more than 12,000 person-hours. Approximately 100 individuals came forward, and

---

[53] SL 18 Jan. 1901 Cannan to T. Fowler (as Vice-Chancellor); OD 25 Jan. 1901; SL 14 Feb. 1901 Cannan to Hill Upton & Co.; FC 9 May 1901.

[54] OD 8 Feb. 1901; OED/B/3/2/2 14 Feb. 1901 WAC to Cannan; OD 22 Feb. 1901. Craigie's salary was duly raised to £400 in November (OD 1 Nov. 1901).

[55] OED/B/3/2/2 18 Feb. 1901 WAC to Cannan. For a view of the interior of the Dictionary Room in the Old Ashmolean in 1907, see Figure 23, p. 311.

[56] FC 5 Sept. 1901.

[57] MP 3 Feb. 1901 R. D. Hall to JAHM.

[58] *Athenaeum* 16 Feb. 1901, p. 211.

Murray found himself organizing another reading programme, which took over a year to complete, and which he estimated as having cost him three months of his own time—although this is a task which he could surely have forced himself to delegate.[59]

Murray also continued to keep a close eye on the work of the new third Editor, who set to work on Volume VIII (beginning at Q), as the materials for Volume VII were already earmarked for the Scriptorium. He carefully reviewed Craigie's finalized copy, covering it with comments and suggestions for Craigie's consideration before it went to the compositors. Many of the suggestions, inevitably, were to do with compression: the second Editor had consistently struggled to achieve what was required in this respect, and Murray clearly thought it important for the third Editor to appreciate its importance from the start. 'No one knows so well as I do', he told Craigie, 'how it grieves one to have to do this [i.e. cut out quotations]; but I have had to steel my heart, clench my teeth & do it, for years; & you will also find it, I doubt not, the most painful part of your work.' He pointed out that the Press was now publicly committed to finishing the Dictionary within stated limits—and, indeed, was accepting payment for it on this basis—and he delicately suggested that if Craigie thought that this could not be achieved, he should say so forthwith.[60] Craigie took the hint, and managed to achieve a scale of 6.4 in his first two months—better than either Murray or Bradley;[61] but over-setting was to prove just as much of a challenge for him as for the two senior Editors. Bradley, indeed, was continuing to exceed his agreed limit for Volume VI, to the frustration of Cannan, who commented to Furnivall that 'his quotations amount to "short stories" besides being too numerous'.[62] He remonstrated once again to Bradley himself, but does not seem to have pressed the matter: Bradley was having other difficulties. He had been called away suddenly to Sheffield by the illness of his wife's mother, and he was also worried about the possibility of losing his senior assistant, Walter Worrall, who in November was hurriedly granted an increased salary (of £150 p.a.).[63]

---

[59] For a full account of this enterprise see Knowles (2000), esp. pp. 33–6. Work on Hall's materials continued until the summer of 1902 (OED/B/3/8/5 28 Oct. 1902 JAHM to WAC). Organized reading had of course ceased long before this, although the flow of quotations into the Dictionary offices never entirely dried up: in 1893 50,000 quotations had been sent in, and even as recently as 1897—the last year in which Murray reported on this point to the Philological Society—the annual figure was over 15,000 (PSOM 13 Apr. 1894, 23 Apr. 1897).

[60] OED/B/3/8/5 10 May 1901 JAHM to WAC (incomplete; supplemented by an extended quotation from the letter in HJRM pp. 218–19). Murray also advised Craigie to make his etymologies as concise as possible, and—ironically as one Scotsman to another—to keep his coverage of Scots words to a minimum.

[61] Among the quotations which Craigie had included in his copy was a 1901 quotation for the noun *quack*. Murray must have marked this for excision—perhaps Craigie had been unaware of the embargo on quotations later than 1900—and it was duly omitted from the first proof; but it reappears in the revise, and survived into the published entry. It is possible that Henry Hucks Gibbs, who had supplied the original quotation, noted its omission when reading the proofs, and re-suggested it. Other 1901 quotations soon joined it, and the ban on post-1900 quotations rapidly became a dead letter.

[62] SL 11 Oct. 1901 Cannan to FJF.

[63] SL 10, 14, 24 Oct. 1901 Cannan to HB, OD 1 Nov. 1901.

Bradley's remarkably equable disposition generally enabled him to cope with the most trying circumstances without complaint, but his exceptional worries in the autumn of 1901 may account for the uncharacteristically testy tone of his letters to Murray at this time, in the course of one of the very few recorded direct quarrels between the two men. After querying some of the alterations made to his copy by some of Murray's assistants—who still carried out some bibliographical standardization of the work of all three Editors, as being more experienced in this task than anyone working in the Old Ashmolean—Bradley complained that portions of his copy were 'constantly getting lost at the Scriptorium'. Such a criticism was bound to evoke an indignant response, but Bradley can hardly have been prepared for the reply he received, in which Murray asserted that the organization of materials in the Scriptorium was such that, in the opinion of himself and his assistants, it was 'so inconceivable as to be utterly impossible, that even a single slip could be permanently lost'. The sense of extreme irritation suppressed beneath a determination to be calm and reasonable is palpable in Bradley's reply:

I am much obliged by your letter, and am sorry to have—very unintentionally—added to your worries at this time of pressure. [...] I cannot discuss the question whether it is possible for copy to be lost at the Scriptorium. All I wish to say is that I believe my assistants are honestly convinced that they have known this to happen, and frequently.

He went on to declare that a system 'so perfect in method that accidental disappearance of slips is *impossible*' was simply outside his experience.[64] A less tactful man would probably have simply retorted that the idea was ridiculous.

Such frictions could of course be kept internal; and in fact as far as the public face of the Dictionary was concerned, 1901 proved to be another good year. The number of pages published during the year once again exceeded 500, in spite of various inhibiting factors, including the drain on Murray's time caused by his oversight of Craigie's work, the disruption of the move to the Old Ashmolean, an uncharacteristic bout of ill health for Murray in the spring, and the exceptional difficulty of a few words in the early part of O, including the mind-bending challenges of the preposition *of*. The year saw the completion of both Volumes IV and V at last; and there was also further public recognition for Murray. He was elected a member of Oxford's Board of Studies for the Honours School of English—a position he occupied for the next decade[65]— and in June the University of Glasgow awarded him an honorary LL.D., during their

[64] MP 21 Nov. 1901 HB to JAHM; [n.d., evidently Nov. 1901] JAHM to HB (draft; quoted at length in *CWW* p. 288); 25 Nov. 1901 HB to JAHM. The situation was not improved by Charles Balk, who, apparently stung into making his own defence of the Scriptorium staff, wrote to Bradley himself, in terms which the latter thought he would regret 'when in a calmer mood'.

[65] *CWW* p. 293. In 1909 he unexpectedly failed to be re-elected to the (biennial) position as he had been on previous occasions, but was instead co-opted for two years a month later (MP 8 Feb. 1909 A. S. Napier to JAHM, 13 Mar. 1909 E. S. Craig to JAHM).

450th anniversary celebrations.[66] The title pages of his portions of the Dictionary now displayed an impressive list of degrees. Bradley, by contrast, was still obliged to be content with 'Hon. M.A., Oxon.'; his first honorary degree from another university, a Ph.D. from Heidelberg, was to follow in 1903. He was also President of the Philological Society for the second time, having been re-elected in 1900; and a growing list of other publications was also contributing to his reputation as a philologist.[67] Craigie could hardly be expected to have started to acquire honorary degrees, although it is rather more surprising that he was not yet even a member of the Philological Society; this was rectified in January 1902.[68]

---

of

In his introduction to the section *O–Onomastic*, published in 1902, Murray noted that prepositions were 'among the most difficult words with which the lexicographer has to deal', and—having wrestled with several tough prepositions in this section alone—he singled out *of* as the most difficult of them all. A few years later he recalled it as a 'tremendous pièce de Resistance [...] which nearly killed me', while at the same time placing it among the entries which had given him his greatest satisfaction (MP notes by JAHM for a lecture, undated but probably 1906). And in 1909, writing to Furnivall of his apprehensions about tackling *take*, he declared *of* to have been 'the most difficult word in the Dictionary'. Warming to his theme, he went on: 'The trouble with primary, elemental, verbs & prepositions, is that you cannot explain them in words. Their meaning is known to every one by use; but any attempt to put it into other words is doomed to failure, & really ludicrous. They are the *postulates* of lexicography, and if I had to do a dictionary again, I should give a List of Words first of all, which the Dictionary will not pretend to explain, but assume to be known to everybody. [...] The definitions of these words are merely make-believe—ingenious ways of showing how in a very round about, & to most people unintelligible way, you can *approximate* to the meaning of the words themselves which nobody needs to be told' (21 Sept. 1909 JAHM to FJF (King's College London,

Continued ➤

---

[66] *CWW* p. 292. Elisabeth Murray quotes the story told by one of the other Glasgow honorands, Constance Jones (Mistress of Girton College, Cambridge), of how Murray took care to wear four different hoods at different times during his visit, 'by way of compliment to the University that was giving him another'.

[67] He had assisted Leon Kellner in his revision of Richard Morris's *Historical Outlines of English Accidence* (1895), and in 1900 he completed an edition of Caxton's *Dialogues in French and English* for the Early English Text Society; his book on the history of the Goths also continued to be popular (4th edition 1898). He was also still regularly writing articles and reviews for the literary magazines, and had begun to contribute to the *Dictionary of National Biography*.

[68] PSOM 10 Jan. 1902. Honour of a different kind was bestowed on Furnivall during the year, with the publication by the Clarendon Press of *An English Miscellany*, a Festschrift on the occasion of his seventy-fifth birthday; among the nearly fifty contributions were items by Bradley and Craigie (although, perhaps surprisingly, nothing by Murray), and also Skeat's much reprinted mock-Chaucerian tribute ('A Clerk there was of Cauntebrigge also, That unto rowing haddè longe y-go').

Skeat–Furnivall Library, ref. Dictionaries 2/2/10; I am grateful to Charlotte Brewer for this reference). This is surely more of an expression of frustration at the difficulty of his task than a genuine statement of opinion: the history of such words could hardly be omitted from a dictionary of the comprehensiveness of the *OED*, even if the description of their sense development often had to be couched in terms of metalanguage—describing how the word in question is used—rather than substitutable definitions of the more usual type. The entry for *of* which appeared in 1902 is certainly a fine example of the historical lexicographer's craft, with the main body of the entry—63 main senses, arranged in 17 branches—preceded by more than a column of introductory text, discussing the word's Germanic precursors and the various factors influencing the development in meaning away from an original sense 'away, away from', including the use of the word to render the Latin prepositions *ab*, *de*, and *ex* and (especially) French *de*.

   In constructing the entry for *of* Murray worked closely with his experienced assistant Arthur Maling, who seems to have had a particular facility for difficult function words of this kind. Surviving rough notes on the structure of the entry (in OUPA(u)), amounting to several dozen slips and larger sheets of paper, show how the two men worked together, puzzling out how the hundreds of different uses and constructions could be organized and classified, and commenting on each other's proposed arrangements of the material.

Murray's struggle with prepositions and other difficult words in O continued to hamper his progress in 1902, as did changes in his staff: Mann left in July, and his replacement, William Landells, quickly succumbed to ill health, leaving the following year. Bradley's team also suffered from illness, with Worrall off sick in the summer.[69] It became impossible to avoid a dip in the project's visible progress, and only 400 pages were published in 1902, although these did include Craigie's first published section— the whole of the letter Q—which was generally well received; and at least the Press was able to maintain the regular quarterly issue of sections without a break. The flow of honours for Murray also continued: he was invited to be a founding member of the new British Academy, and in May he received a D.Litt. from the University of Wales.

   The summer of 1902 brought a serious distraction for two of the Editors, and a headache for Cannan, in the form of a threatened lawsuit over one of the Dictionary's definitions. The electrical engineer and inventor Henry Wilde, who had made significant contributions to the development of devices for the generation of electricity, had become preoccupied with the idea that he was being deprived of his rightful place in the history of this technology. He was particularly troubled by what he regarded as an erroneous account of the earliest use of the expression *dynamo-electric machine*, which had appeared in a classic text on the subject by the distinguished physicist Silvanus Thompson. Thompson had been consulted by Murray in 1896 when he was preparing

---

[69] SL 25 July 1902 Cannan to HB. In September Murray's daughter Rosfrith also joined the staff, working on the task of standardizing the bibliographical references to quotations, which for the sake of consistency was done for all three Editors in the Scriptorium (HJRM pp. 221–2).

the *OED* entry for *dynamo-electric machine* (and the now more familiar shortened form *dynamo*); his account of the early use of the expression was quoted in the published entry, and Murray had acknowledged his help with these and related words in his Preface to Volume III. In 1902 Wilde, who had by this time already quarrelled publicly with various bodies over the matter, took the strange step of launching a libel suit against Thompson on the grounds that in his writings he had not adequately acknowledged Wilde's role in the origin of the terms.[70] In June, before this case—which was eventually thrown out—had come to court, Wilde directed his solicitors to write to Murray, threatening legal action over the Dictionary articles for *dynamo* and *dynamo-electric*. Whatever the merits of the case, a reasonably conciliatory response was called for: not only was the Press keen to avoid a lawsuit, with the attendant publicity, but Wilde was also a significant benefactor of the University. Cannan wrote to assure Wilde's solicitors that Murray would 'not neglect any suitable opportunity of correcting any lexicographical inaccuracy in the account of Dynamo and Dynamo-electric', and agreed with Wilde's suggestion that the publication of the related term *magneto-electric* might afford such an opportunity.[71] This brought Bradley into the picture, as the Editor who would in due course be responsible for the letter M, and there was further time-consuming correspondence for both Editors before the matter was finally settled.[72]

The autumn brought further dispiriting news. Dr Minor, the Dictionary's assiduous contributor from inside the walls of Broadmoor, had continued to supply quotations for both Murray and Bradley for many years, but of late his output had diminished considerably, to the extent that in 1901 Murray had considered paying him a visit, to try to 'refresh his interest'.[73] Murray now learned that Minor's health had begun to break down, and that he now recognized that he would not be able to continue to extract quotations from the books in his possession by using the exhaustive word indexes which he had compiled—and which he was now persuaded to part with, together with some of the books, so that some use could be made of them.[74] Minor continued to keep in touch with Murray, and to take some interest in the Dictionary, but with the disappearance of Minor's handwriting from among the new quotations arriving in Oxford an era had definitely come to an end, and another valuable source of material had dried up.

---

[70] A full account of the affair of 'Wilde v. Thompson' is given in Thompson and Thompson (1920); there are also numerous letters relating to the matter in OUPA.

[71] SL 4 July 1902 Cannan to Slatter, Heelis, & Williamson (solicitors).

[72] A brief statement about the early history of the word *dynamo-electric* was included in Bradley's entry for *magneto-electric*, although the relevant section (*M–Mandragon*) was not published until 1904. According to Harold Murray (HJRM p. 222), a corrective note was printed in the relevant instalment of the Dictionary as reissued in monthly sections, which as luck would have it was published in the summer of 1902, but I have been unable to verify this.

[73] OED/B/3/8/5 28 July 1901 JAHM to WAC. Minor was initially reluctant to start collecting evidence for Craigie's benefit, because of the difficulty of reading for three distinct sections of the alphabet at once, but he seems to have been persuaded, as many of his quotations survive among the materials for Q.

[74] OED/B/3/9/6 3 Oct. 1902 JAHM to J. J. Thompson. The exploitation of Minor's materials, which turned out to be a considerably smaller task than had been the case with Fitzedward Hall's quotations, is described in Knowles (2000: 36–7).

quaint

In stating that 'none of the ancient "four-letter" words was included' in the first edition of the *OED* (Burchfield 2004: 937), the editor of the Supplement to the Dictionary made a curious error in describing the work of his predecessors. In fact entries for many of the words usually referred to as 'four-letter words' appeared in the first edition, including *arse*, *cock* (=penis), *fart*, *piss*, *shit*, *turd*, and *twat*, as well as longer words in the same category such as *ballock* (now more usually *bollock*) and the derogatory sense of *bitch*. However unacceptable such words might have become (at least in polite society) by the time the Dictionary came to be compiled, the evidence of their use in earlier periods, often extending over several centuries, was readily available, and they were felt by contemporary scholars to merit treatment in the Dictionary no less than any other word. Their taboo status in polite society was generally indicated by labelling such as 'Not now in decent use' or '*Obs.* in polite use'; in some cases the quotation evidence was also presented in a reduced form, with only the reference given for some quotations (and not the actual quotation text).

There were, however, limits to what the Dictionary's publisher could allow it to print. There was a danger that the respectability of the Press, as an authorized publisher of the Bible, could be called into question by the inclusion of material which was considered to be indecent—however respectably scholarly the context—in one of its other publications. Murray was provided with further illustration of the difficulties facing lexicographers in dealing with such material in 1891, when John Farmer, the compiler of a large dictionary of slang (see p. 219), took his printers to court over their refusal to print the volume C–F—which they had refused to print because of its inclusion of entries for *cock*, *cunt*, and *fuck*—and lost his case. In fact Murray, who supported Farmer's contention that they should be included, was at this point also contemplating the accumulated quotation evidence for the second of these three words (he had already included the first, with quotations for the relevant sense given only as references). His assistant Arthur Maling had written on the top slip for the word 'I suppose this will be omitted'; and indeed Murray decided, after extensive consultation, that it could not be included in the *OED*. Its omission was criticized—though without using the word itself—in at least one review of the section *Crouchmas–Czech* (*National Observer* 30 Dec. 1893, pp. 164–5). The equally taboo word *fuck* was also omitted by Henry Bradley a few years later. The failure of the 1933 Supplement to remedy both omissions was deplored in a review by Alan Ross, who ascribed the exclusion of these and other taboo words to 'the perpetuation of a Victorian prudishness (inacceptable [*sic*] in philology beyond all other subjects)' (Ross 1934: 129); it was not until the first volume of the revised Supplement that full *OED* entries for both words appeared (see p. 479).

But the lexicographers of the first edition had in fact managed, in a way, to include both words—though not in the place where most readers would look for them. The word *quaint* (in various spellings) had been used in Middle and Early Modern English as a punning or euphemistic substitute for *cunt*; and William Craigie, when editing the

Continued ➤

letter Q, included an entry for it, although in place of a definition he simply referred readers to a quotation from Florio's *Worlde of Wordes* (1598), which defines the Italian word *becchina* as 'a womans quaint or priuities'. And in 1926 an entry for the obsolete word *windfucker* appeared in the section *Wilga–Wise*, almost the last to be published, having apparently been added in proof. The word, which has been used both as a name for the kestrel and as a general 'term of opprobrium', was listed without comment, or any explanation of the origin of its second element. In much the same spirit, an entry for the obsolete Scottish word *wanfucked*—glossed as 'Misbegotten'—was drafted a few years earlier by Wilfred Lewis, but this failed to make it into the published text; only Lewis's top slip survives in the superfluous materials. An entry for the word appeared in the *Dictionary of the Older Scottish Tongue* in 2002. (Further on *OED*'s treatment of various types of taboo words, see Mugglestone 2007.)

Bradley, meanwhile, was struggling with his old problem. Although his monthly tally of pages was now generally respectable, and sometimes exceeded Murray's, his scale compared to Webster was often by some way the worst of the three; from time to time Cannan was moved to remonstrate with him about his over-setting.[75] In November, however, the malady appeared to have spread: while Bradley's Webster scale was still over 15, Craigie's had jumped to the alarming figure of 19. Murray was asked to investigate.[76] He still saw himself as having some responsibility for all parts of the Dictionary—regardless of whose name was on the title page of a particular volume—and consequently took the matter extremely seriously. His comments on Bradley's entries for *loosely* and *looseness* and Craigie's for *ramify* were passed on by Cannan, who also took the matter seriously, and promised to 'put such pressure on [Bradley] as may be necessary to convince him, if he slides back'; both Editors were reported to have achieved some compression as a result of Murray's criticisms.[77]

But Murray's criticisms of his fellow Editors did not end there. His attention was now directed—perhaps by Craigie's original sponsor Monro, now taking renewed interest in Dictionary matters as Vice-Chancellor—to the entries for *railroad* and *railway*; and the result was a kind of explosion. Murray had stressed the virtues of brevity to both the other Editors on many occasions, and the excesses (as he saw them) of entries like *railroad* and *railway* now struck him as almost a personal slight: as Elisabeth Murray puts it, he 'waxed almost hysterical at [the other Editors'] "scandalous", "unbearable" and "heart-rending" waste of the space which he felt he had saved only for them to squander'.[78] His choice of remedial action was to write

---

[75] For example, on a range of material in *lo*-: 'there is a deal in it which is surely otiose [...] I must plead with you most earnestly for reduction' (SL 15 July 1902 Cannan to HB).

[76] OD 7, 14 Nov. 1902.

[77] SL 20 Nov. 1902 Cannan to HB, 27 Nov. 1902 Cannan to JAHM.

[78] *CWW* p. 285 (quoting a letter of 29 Nov. 1902 to Cannan, now lost).

a long, distinctly schoolmasterly letter to Craigie—which he showed to Cannan—pointing out sorrowfully that the offending entries were 'not in accordance with the principles and method of the Dictionary', specifically in their excessive treatment of compounds. (Craigie had certainly erred on the expansive side: he had devoted over a column to the compounds of *railway*, which he later managed to reduce by more than a third, although Murray had suggested that a reduction of three-quarters ought to be achievable.) Within the letter's ten (!) pages Murray included much by way of guidance (none of which can have been news to Craigie) as to how text might be compressed: by omitting or shortening quotations, by giving dialect and Scottish vocabulary only the most minimal treatment, and in the larger entries by rewording definitions more inclusively and avoiding excessive subdivision of senses. Nor was he content merely to advise: he had felt it necessary to take the unusual step of advising the Secretary that he could not sanction the printing of the relevant sheet until the necessary compression had been achieved. Remarkably, and notwithstanding the strong language to which he resorted—referring, for example, to the inclusion of the 1894 quotation 'It was a railway porter' as the only evidence for this compound as 'ineptitude [...] which might make the irreverent scoff'—he still assured Craigie that his criticism (and his embargoing of printing) was done 'with the most friendly feeling [...] no part of my work is so onerous and unpleasant to me as that of looking through your copy [...] I should be infinitely glad to have done with it [...] And if you would earnestly set yourself to making my work unnecessary, it might soon be done.'[79]

The principles of compression set out in this letter were also passed on to Bradley, together with some criticisms of some of his own entries made by the Vice-Chancellor, who also worked through some of Craigie's entries with him. Valid though Murray's criticisms may have been—and it is undeniable that the scales to which the three Editors were working were seriously at variance—Bradley and Craigie would have had to be inhuman not to feel some resentment at the implication that their work was not to be trusted. Craigie, indeed, seems to have been stung into pointing out instances of over-setting in Murray's work, and Murray was duly called to account for the scale of a few entries in K and O.[80] Accusations and counter-accusations continued into January; relations between the Editors seem to have reached something of a low point.[81]

Cannan may seem at this point to be acting as a stern taskmaster; but his activities in another area show that his determination to ensure the best possible supporting

[79] OED/B/3/8/5 3 Dec. 1902 JAHM to WAC (quoted at slightly greater length in *CWW* p. 288).

[80] SL 4 Dec. 1902 Cannan to York Powell, 29 Dec. 1902 Cannan to JAHM, Cannan to HB.

[81] The Delegates also continued to keep a watchful eye on scale, and to issue warnings from time to time, but they were rather inconsistent. In March 1903, for example, it was agreed to point out to both Murray and Bradley that they had been over-setting—to the extent, in each case, of a Webster scale of 12 over the previous two months (OD 6 Mar. 1903)—but no other warnings were issued on the numerous other occasions during 1903 when one or other of the Editors exceeded the agreed figure of 8. In fact it was only rarely that all three Editors managed to stay within this limit in the same month.

framework for the project continued undiminished. In November 1902 he had begun to discuss with Henry Boyd, the Principal of Hertford College (and former Vice-Chancellor), the perennial topic of funding the Dictionary; his mind may well have been focused on the subject by the size of the debt against the project, which at the end of March—when publication of the envisaged ten-volume work had just passed the half-way point—stood at just over £59,000.[82] Boyd had also served as Master of the Drapers' Company, one of the old London livery companies, which under his influence had made significant benefactions to both Oxford and Cambridge universities; he had now begun to wonder whether one or other of the London companies, or perhaps some wealthy individual, might be persuaded to make a donation towards the costs of the Dictionary. Cannan responded enthusiastically to the idea, undertaking that in return for a gift of—say—£5,000 towards the cost of a particular volume of the Dictionary, the Delegates would be prepared to 'commemorate the benefaction in all copies of that volume for ever' with an appropriately worded inscription.[83] Boyd began to put out feelers, and in February wrote to Henry Hucks Gibbs, ostensibly for advice about which companies or individuals might be approached, but also in the hope that the wealthy Gibbs might himself consider making a donation. Gibbs, who had of course helped the Dictionary out financially in the past, did not take the bait on this occasion ('though I dressed it as carefully as I could', Boyd lamented to Cannan); but an idea had been planted, and in due course Gibbs consulted his son Alban, a member of the Goldsmiths' Company, about the possibility of approaching them.[84] It would be another two years before this initiative bore fruit.

Cannan was also always keeping an eye out for help of a more practical kind. In September 1902, having turned down a proposal from Furnivall that the Press publish a concordance of the works of Thomas Kyd by another of his protégés, a railway porter named Charles Crawford, Cannan wondered whether he might be of use to the Dictionary, and when Bradley mentioned that it would be helpful to have the letter M re-sub-edited immediately in advance of the work done on it in the Old Ashmolean, he suggested Crawford. Unfortunately Crawford declared the task to be beyond him, and returned to his work on Elizabethan drama.[85] Similarly, when he discovered that Richard Greentree, a brilliant but somewhat unstable Balliol scholar who had been assisting Sidney Lee with the *Dictionary of National Biography*, was short of work, he

[82] SL 24 Nov. 1902 Cannan to Boyd (two letters, one enclosing a full balance sheet for the Dictionary; another copy of this is in OED/B/3/2/2).

[83] OED/B/3/2/2 13 Dec. 1902 Cannan to Boyd.

[84] GL MS 11021/30 ff. 574–5 15 Feb. 1903 Boyd to HHG; OED/B/3/2/2 19 Feb. 1903 HHG to Boyd, 22 Feb. 1903 Boyd to Cannan; MP 14 Apr. 1904 HHG to JAHM. Boyd also approached J. A. Kingdon, a former master of the Grocers' Company, without success (OED/B/3/2/2 3 Mar. 1903 Boyd to Cannan).

[85] SL 8, 29 Sept. 1902 Cannan to FJF, 9 Oct. 1902 Cannan to JAHM, 13 Oct. 1902 Cannan to C. Crawford; OED/B/3/2/2 25 Oct. 1902 C. Crawford to [HB]. Crawford went on to publish several works of literary scholarship, including concordances of both Kyd and Marlowe.

suggested him as an assistant for Craigie. The suggestion was taken up, but Greentree proved unsuitable and left after only a few months.[86] An unsolicited application, from a museum curator (and contributor of quotations to the Dictionary) named James Dallas, proved rather more successful. He was taken on with some relief by Bradley, whose team was showing distinct signs of wear: Sykes retired in 1903, and Worrall continued to be in indifferent health.[87] In the spring of 1903 there were even signs that the ever-resilient Murray (who celebrated his sixty-fifth birthday in February) was beginning to feel his age, when he was 'very poorly' with influenza for a fortnight.[88]

1903 in fact turned out to be what Cannan called a 'second lean year'—although when he mentioned this to Murray as the year drew to its close his tone was mild, and appreciative of 'the difficulties'. His assessment related not to the amount published during the year, which again topped 500 pages, but to the amount of Dictionary text which the Editors had produced: at around 480 pages, this fell somewhat short of the 516 pages which he had hoped for once Craigie was fully up to speed.[89] The 'difficulties' were various. Both Murray and Bradley had had to wrestle with particularly intractable material: for Bradley there was the beginning of M, including the massive verb *make*— the preliminary work for which had been done by Onions, who was proving to have a particular talent for tackling difficult verbs—while Murray began the year struggling with *over* and its compounds and finished it in *Pa*, the one part of the alphabet for which the original materials had been lost. Illness also had its impact on both Murray and Bradley, and on their staffs; and there was considerable disruption associated with changes in the staff. In May Cannan began looking once again for possible assistants, on behalf of both Craigie—who needed a replacement for Greentree—and Murray, whose assistant Arthur Sewall was about to leave after eight years in the Scriptorium, and who was also temporarily without his junior Price, who was about to take his finals.[90] Cannan made enquiries in various quarters, including—apparently for the first time—the University's Appointments Committee, to whom he tellingly observed that with a salary of only £100 the job would probably best suit 'either a young person without prospects, or an older man who is disgusted with some impossible profession'.[91]

[86] SL 3 Dec. 1902 Cannan to E. Caird (as Master of Balliol); FC 22 Jan., 28 May 1903. Greentree had joined the Malayan Civil Service after graduating, but had resigned after his erratic behaviour had begun to give cause for concern (Heussler 1981: 116–17).

[87] OED/B/3/5/4 8 Sept. 1902 J. Dallas to HB; OD 16 Oct. 1903; OED/B/3/2/2 26 Nov. 1903 HB to Cannan.

[88] OED/B/3/2/2 15 Mar. 1903 JAHM to Cannan.

[89] SL 23 Dec. 1903, 4 Jan. 1904 Cannan to JAHM.

[90] Price had been studying as a non-collegiate student since 1899; he took his BA in November 1903.

[91] SL 21 May 1903 Cannan to M. B. Furse. Cannan also wrote to his old friend Charles Lowry (now headmaster of Sedbergh School), to President Warren of Magdalen, and to the professors of Greek at Glasgow and St Andrews, J. S. Phillimore and John Burnet (all in SL); among the names suggested by Lowry was that of H. W. Fowler, who of course began to edit the *Concise Oxford Dictionary* a few years later, as well as working on the Abridged (OED/B/3/2/2 22 May 1903 Lowry to Cannan, quoted in McMorris 2001: 54).

Among the 'young persons' who applied Murray selected Henry Rope, who had graduated from Christ Church with a second in English the previous year, and who in due course proved an able assistant (and one of the most durable contributors to the Dictionary)—but who, in the short term, required training, to the detriment of progress.[92] The same was true of the new assistant who was eventually also found for Craigie, a former headmaster called Frederick Ray, and also of George Carline, the young man who joined Bradley's staff.[93]

---

radium

One of the most famous omissions from the first edition of the *OED*—now perhaps even more well-known than *appendicitis* (see p. 289)—is *radium*. In fact Craigie did prepare an entry for the word in 1902, which had quickly come to prominence despite its very recent coinage (the name had been proposed, in a French context, in 1898); his entry defined it as 'A recently-discovered metal having luminous properties', and included a single quotation from 1900. When Murray noticed the entry as he looked through Craigie's proof sheets, he wrote to his colleague cautioning that the categorical statement that this alleged new substance was a metal 'may turn out to be a regrettable blunder', in that further investigation might show it to be something else entirely. Murray's letter (which was bound into an office copy of the Dictionary, and is still preserved in the *OED* offices) goes on to point out that the name of another supposed new metal, namely *polonium*, is similarly problematic; at the time of this letter Murray was still working on the letter O, but he ends his letter 'I certainly shall omit *Polonium* as at present advised.' Craigie evidently took the hint, and no entry for *radium* was included in the Dictionary when the relevant section (*R–Reactive*) appeared in 1903. By this time, as luck would have it, the properties of radium had been confirmed by later experimenters, and the word had become so well known that when the section was reviewed in the *Athenaeum*, the anonymous reviewer (once again Charles Fennell) could make the barbed mock-apology that the appearance of his review had been delayed by 'the demoralizing perplexity produced by the astounding omission of "radium"' (*Athenaeum* 19 Dec. 1903, p. 821).

The matter of the omission of *radium* seems to have become the subject of discussion among the rest of the Oxford staff, and even of amusement, as is seen from a spoof entry for the word which has survived in the *OED* archives (OED/B/5/5/9). The handwriting is that of Bradley's assistant Henry Bayliss, whose thorough familiarity with the Dictionary

Continued ➤

---

[92] See Gilliver (2004) for a discussion of Rope's training, with some illustrations. Murray also briefly engaged Ritchie Girvan, an English graduate from Glasgow who had recently been studying in Leipzig with Murray's friend Eduard Sievers; he was transferred to Craigie's staff, but after only a few months he left to take up work in the English department at Glasgow, where he subsequently became Professor of English (SL 20 June 1903 Cannan to JAHM).

[93] SL [30 Nov. 1903] Cannan to WAC, FC 3 Dec. 1903.

can be seen from the fine detail of his elaborate and affectionate parody: the etymology traces the word to roots in such languages as 'Preh[istoric]' and 'Antediluv[ian]', and the quotations—from Chaucer's 'Dustman's Tale' and Goldsmith's 'The Inhabited [as opposed to Deserted] Village'—indicate the thoroughness of his knowledge of the most regularly cited sources. The quotation from Pepys's diary should also be mentioned ('And so to bed. Found radium an excellent pick-me-up in the morning'). The first page of Murray's 1902 letter to Craigie, and Bayliss's spoof entry, are reproduced in Gilliver (2004: 59, 61); an immaculately typeset version of the spoof entry also appears in the *Oxford Book of Parodies* (2010).

There is a further irony in the fact that in 1906, when Murray did finally reach *polonium*, the certainty of scientific opinion on the matter left no doubt that he should include it after all. A suitable entry for the word duly appeared in 1907; *radium* had to wait until the 1933 Supplement for inclusion.

It was, however, in 1903 that substantial progress began to be made on another front, with the start of work in earnest on the Abridged. Specimens and sample entries had been in circulation—in confidence—for some time, initially among interested parties within the Press (and the two Editors of the main Dictionary), and in January 1902 the circle was widened to include Skeat, but it was only in April 1903 that the Delegates agreed to open negotiations over terms. Murray's approval of Little's work in March ('I *like* the last Specimen [...] The man who did it has some "gumption"') may well have weighed heavily in the balance. Provisional terms were agreed in May, and Little probably began full-scale editing in late June or early July; by November he had reached *ad*.[94] Cannan, reading through the proofs, noticed the absence of the noun *adenoid*, a word which had entered the language only after the relevant Part of the *OED* had been published: 'As boys constantly have them removed they must be *sbs* [i.e. nouns ('substantives')]; I suppose the name has come in. Will you notice any such omissions[?]'[95] Other conspicuous absences soon joined *adenoid*, and it was soon clear that any dictionary compiled from the *OED* strictly by abridgement would be vulnerable to the charge of failing to include many words which had by now become part of the language. The matter was not, however, a pressing one, as Little was still working in manuscript, to which it would be relatively straightforward to make additions at any time. Moreover, while his progress was respectable—he had completed A by May 1904[96]—he was working on his own, and publication was consequently still a remote prospect.

[94] SL 25 Jan. 1902 Cannan to Skeat, SOED/1902 28 Jan. 1902 Skeat to [Cannan], SL 8 Feb. 1902 Cannan to Little, OED/B/3/2/2 15 Mar. 1903 JAHM to Cannan; OD 24 Apr., 29 May 1903; SL 15 June, 13 July 1903 Cannan to Little.

[95] SL 2 Nov. 1903 Cannan to Little.

[96] OD 6 May 1904.

forgo

Horace Hart was appointed as the manager of OUP's printing business in Oxford in 1883, shortly before the appearance of Part I of the Dictionary. He presided over the transformation of OUP's printing during his three decades as Controller, but he is probably best known today for *Hart's Rules for Compositors and Readers at the University Press, Oxford*, still widely used as a style guide on matters of spelling, hyphenation, punctuation, and the like. The *Rules* were first produced as a broadsheet for internal use at the Press in 1893, and went through many versions before the 'fifteenth edition' was offered for sale to the public in 1904. From the beginning Hart consulted Murray, and later also Bradley, about particular spellings, and many early editions of the *Rules* contain footnotes recording the opinions of one or other Editor regarding a particular word—though sometimes with a counter-comment from Hart himself, as for example with *axe*, where after quoting Murray's observation in the *OED* entry that the spelling *ax* was 'better on every ground', he declared in favour of 'the commoner spelling' on the grounds that 'authors generally still call for [it]'. The recommendation to use *forgo* rather than *forego* was accompanied by an account of an exchange with W. E. Gladstone, who, having called for an instance of the former spelling to be corrected, was sent a copy of Skeat's *Etymological Dictionary of the English Language*, in which the spelling *forego* is condemned as being 'as absurd as it is general', on the grounds that the first element of the word is not *fore-* (as in *foregoing* and *foregone*) but the etymologically distinct prefix *for-* (also found in *forget* and *forsake*). This, however, was not enough for Gladstone: as Hart records, 'it was only after reference to Dr. J. A. H. Murray that Mr. Gladstone wrote to me, "Personally I am inclined to prefer forego, on its merits; but authority must carry the day. *I give in.*"'—testimony to the high regard in which Murray's views on such prescriptive matters were held. It should be pointed out, however, that the *OED* entry for the word—edited by Bradley, although Murray must have had the opportunity to comment on it—makes no such recommendation: the headword is given in two forms, and while the entry is placed alphabetically under *forgo*, there is no prescription as to which form should be preferred. (For more on the history of *Hart's Rules* see Ritter (2004).)

1904 proved to be a year of steadier progress, although not without its struggles: Murray described it as 'inherently the most difficult year's work I have ever had', including as it did the extremely difficult word *pass* ('which came near driving me mad'), and many other words requiring unusually extensive research.[97] He also lost another assistant, Hereward Price, who left in August, and for whom he failed to find a replacement until the winter. He nevertheless managed to exceed 200 pages edited during the year, and published an unprecedented 'triple section' (actually 168 pages),

---

[97] MP 24 Dec. 1904 JAHM to E. Arber. Murray told Arber that he 'could have written two books with less labour' than the entries for the two words *pelican* and *penguin*.

Pargeter–Pennached, in December.[98] Bradley and Craigie could not match this, but both published a double section during the year; Bradley's was slightly short of the regular 128 pages, but these did include *make*—the longest entry in the Dictionary so far—and his achievement is all the more impressive given that his very successful popular book *The Making of English* was published in March.[99] At the same time Onions, drawing on his work on the Dictionary's grammatically complex entries, published a more specialized book, *An Advanced English Syntax*, which was also well received. Craigie began the year with the welcome news that the Delegates had decided to increase his salary to £450, and ended it with recognition from another part of the University, when he was appointed Taylorian lecturer in the Scandinavian languages.[100] He also took on an additional assistant during the year, another non-collegiate student named J. H. Smithwhite.

---

tonk

An illustration of the extent to which James Murray had become a national figure by 1904 is provided by an article which appeared in the humorous magazine *Punch* on 8 June. The article purported to consist of extracts from the catalogue for 'Mr. Punch's Autograph Sale', with excerpts from the letters offered for sale. A letter from Murray to the famous golfer Robert Maxwell was the second item featured (following one from the former Governor of Madras, Grant Duff). The extract from Murray's (fictitious) letter begins, in a tolerable pastiche of his style: 'Being anxious to render my Dictionary complete in the terminology of pastime, I have been recommended to apply to you for enlightenment in reference to certain words with which my unassisted intelligence is unable adequately to cope.' It then proceeds to discuss the possible origin of the word *tonk*, giving as an example a quotation (so far untraced, and probably also fictitious) from a report on a golf match in which another golfer, Edward Blackwell, is said to have 'hit a tremendous tonk on the fifteenth tee'. Other queries about golfing terminology follow, regarding 'the exact meaning of *foozle, fluff,* and *flub*', and the acceptability of '*plusser*, i.e. a *plus* man'. (The catalogue entry ends with a note that the letter was purchased by the famous sportswoman Lottie Dod for thirty shillings.)

Continued ➤

---

[98] He still managed to take his usual summer break, travelling once again to the Continent with Robinson Ellis; on this occasion their route took them to France and Switzerland, including Murray's memorable ascent of the Pic de la Croix de Belledonne in the worst August snowstorm in living memory, from which he emerged with his large beard frozen into 'one huge icicle' (*CWW* pp. 325–6).

[99] The book had been announced as in preparation as early as 1900, as part of J. M. Dent's 'Temple Primers' series; Bradley's preface attributes its late appearance to a combination of illness and the near-impossibility of writing anything while simultaneously editing the Dictionary. He was, however, having some success in doing just this, contributing numerous articles to the 11th edition of the *Encyclopaedia Britannica* (on subjects ranging from Beowulf and Caedmon to riddles and slang), whereas Murray had had to enlist the help of his daughter Hilda in revising his article on the English language, a task which he had in any case come to regret undertaking at all (*CWW* p. 301).

[100] SL 1 Jan. 1904 Cannan to WAC; OD 25 Nov. 1904. The Taylorian lectureship required Craigie to give two lectures a week during term-time; the Delegates granted him permission to accept the post provided he made arrangements to 'prevent any reduction of the time now spent upon the Dictionary'.

In fact no entry for *tonk* was included in the section *Tombal–Trahysh* when this eventually appeared in 1913. It is not known whether Murray knew of the 1904 *Punch* reference, or indeed any evidence for the word. (He and his fellow Editors were certainly not averse to including golfing terminology: entries had already appeared for *foozle* and many other golfing terms.) *Tonk* was included, as both a noun and a verb, in the 1933 Supplement to the Dictionary, but with no quotations earlier than 1910. The noun was for some reason dropped by Robert Burchfield when revising the Supplement, and did not appear in the second edition in 1989; it was reinstated in the second Additions volume in 1993, but still without the 1904 evidence. Burchfield was unable to antedate the 1922 example of the verb given in the 1933 Supplement entry, although his entry (which appears effectively unchanged in *OED Online*) added later quotations, including some for an extended sense 'to beat'.

The most significant event of 1905 as far as the Dictionary was concerned was surely the decision by the Goldsmiths' Company to make a donation of £5,000 towards the costs of the project (which now stood at over £100,000). The good news reached Murray in January, though it was not until May that the Company formally made its offer to the University.[101] Such a handsome gift of course required proper acknowledgement; but the choice of wording for this had some unexpected and rather awkward consequences.[102] The Goldsmiths' gift was offered towards the cost of producing a volume of the Dictionary; the decree thanking them accepted it as a contribution specifically for the sixth volume, and a page recording the gift would be printed for inclusion in the completed volume. When Murray learned of this, he immediately took exception, pointing out that of the three volumes currently under way, the one likely to be completed first was not Bradley's Volume VI but his own Volume VII;[103] unfortunately it proved impossible to change the wording. Of course, the object of the gift was clearly the Dictionary as a whole, and Murray had no reason to feel slighted; but, as luck would have it, the news came at a time of particular frustration at his own lack of funds. He and Ada had long cherished the desire to travel to South Africa in 1905, taking advantage of the British Association's decision to hold a meeting there, especially as this would allow them to visit two of his children who had moved there;[104] but it became clear that the costs of the trip would be beyond his means.

[101] OED/B/3/2/3 23 Jan. 1905 [Cannan] to JAHM (copy); MP 24 Jan. 1905 Alban Gibbs to JAHM.

[102] OD 26 May 1905. The wording of the proposed decree was published in the *Oxford University Gazette* of 30 May (p. 605); the decree was passed *nemine contradicente* in Convocation on 6 June, and announced in the *Gazette* on the same day (p. 632).

[103] OED/B/3/2/2 30 May 1905 C. C. J. Webb to Cannan, 31 May 1905 Cannan to Webb (two letters, in the earlier of which Cannan resignedly refers to having heard that 'Murray was loose' and the need to 'tie him up').

[104] Murray's son Wilfrid had moved to Cape Town in 1897 to join the Colonial Civil Service, and now had a young family, as did his daughter Ethelwyn, who had gone to South Africa in 1900 to marry her fiancé. For information on their families see Ruthven-Murray (1986: 70–4, 83–4).

He was also once again having staff difficulties: he had been obliged to allow Balk, his senior assistant, to reduce his hours by two afternoons a week, and at the same time had taken on two new assistants, which as usual meant spending time on training.[105] Now he unburdened himself to his friend J. R. Magrath, bitterly complaining that he and his staff deserved to be paid at a higher rate than Bradley's and Craigie's teams, given that they consistently produced more Dictionary text than either (indeed, in the first five months of 1905 he had signed off more than the other two Editors combined). He himself had received no salary increase in the twenty years since he had come to Oxford, apart from the £50 agreed in 1898 for his duties as 'General Editor'; the time was long overdue, he felt, for both salaries and bonus arrangements to be reviewed in the light of the difference in productivity. 'Or', he wondered, 'would [the Delegates] prefer me to take my ease, produce no more than others, and let the work hang on for another 20 years, until I having no prospect of seeing the end of it, give it up in disappointment and despair?'[106]

Magrath, who as chairman of the Finance Committee—the subgroup of Delegates which under Cannan's Secretaryship had come to wield much of the real power within the Press—had considerable influence, took Murray's complaints seriously, and secured the Delegates' agreement to an immediate grant of £100 to Murray, to enable him to travel to South Africa, and an undertaking to review financial arrangements later in the year. Murray was pleased to accept the Delegates' gift, but stressed that the review was what really mattered; and he does seem to have been as keen that the other Editors be enabled to match his speed as he was for his own productivity to be properly acknowledged.[107]

Murray and his wife sailed from Southampton on 29 July; the Scriptorium was shut up for a month, and all his assistants were given twice their usual summer break. While in South Africa Murray received an honorary D.Litt. from the University of Cape Town, played a full part in the British Association's busy schedule of activities, and also indulged in some characteristically vigorous sightseeing, climbing Table Mountain, visiting Victoria Falls, bathing in the Zambezi, and exploring the Matobo Hills. He was to remember the visit—which lasted ten weeks in all—as 'the happiest

---

[105] OED/B/3/2/3 MS note dated 1 Mar. 1905; OD 3 Mar. 1905. One of the new assistants, replacing Price, was F. A. Yockney, another former librarian from the Bodleian; the other was Alfred Gough, a graduate of London and Oxford who had lectured at the University of Kiel, and who worked mainly on etymologies. Henry Rope also left Murray's staff during 1905, to take up a post at the University of Breslau, although he subsequently returned to the Dictionary as Craigie's assistant (see p. 312 n. 120).

[106] JAHM to Magrath, undated but evidently June 1905, quoted in HJRM p. 235. Murray seems to have written at least two letters to Magrath in June 1905, but none now survive in MP or OUPA. Elisabeth Murray refers (CWW pp. 272, 286) to one of 14 June 1905 in which Murray complains that the bonus scheme was only a way of saving the Delegates money, and is apparently envious of Bradley's rent-free accommodation and other supposedly generous terms of employment.

[107] OD 16 June 1905; OED/B/3/2/3 MS note by Cannan dated 19 June 1905; HJRM p. 235. Murray also received a postal order towards the cost of his holiday from, of all people, Dr Minor (MP 25 July 1905 Minor to JAHM).

experience of his later life'. Back in Oxford, the promised 'review' got under way in his absence in the form of consultation with Bradley and Craigie as to what sort of bonus scheme might offer the best incentive to productivity among their assistants.[108] It was also decided that Craigie and his staff should break off from work on the letter R and begin instead on the letter N, which which Volume VI was to conclude; after all, the sooner the completed volume could be brought before the public, with its special page acknowledging the Goldsmiths' munificence,[109] the sooner some other body or individual might be persuaded to emulate them. (Murray had approached the millionaire philanthropist Andrew Carnegie just before his departure for the Cape, but without success: Carnegie declared that, while pleased to have Murray's autograph to add to his collection, his sympathies lay more with the *Century Dictionary* as being more committed in its principles to the ideal of spelling reform, of which he was a passionate advocate: 'I consider every letter dropped from a word as a gain.'[110])

On Murray's return from South Africa he of course joined in the discussions over productivity, which soon assumed the proportions of a full-scale review of the project. To add further complexity, both Craigie and Onions had further financial matters to raise. Craigie's proved relatively straightforward: he was having some difficulty in regard to his house on the Iffley Road, and following an enquiry as to whether the Press could help him secure something more permanent, the Delegates agreed to loan him £1,200 (later increased to £1,400) to buy or build a suitable property.[111] Onions was also after security, but of a different kind: he now chose to remind the Press that on his re-engagement by Bradley in 1899 he had been led to expect an increase in his salary, but that he was still being paid the same as when he left Murray's staff. Bradley was seriously concerned: his most able assistant was evidently getting itchy feet, and after the success of his recent book he might well be the recipient of generous offers from elsewhere. On the other hand, an increase in Onions's salary might well go down badly with Lewis and Bayliss, whose admittedly less academic contributions he regarded as irreplaceable, and whose claims for a pay increase he felt were even stronger.[112]

The innovations which eventually emerged from the project review form an impressive group; together they say much for the changed attitude of the Press to the Dictionary, not least in its readiness to agree to increased expenditure if this

---

[108] HJRM p. 238; FC 5 Aug. 1905.

[109] For the Goldsmiths' Company themselves, and a few other privileged persons, this page was printed in gold (*CWW* p. 292).

[110] MP 13 July 1905 A. Carnegie to JAHM. Carnegie was no enemy of the *OED*, however: in 1899 he made his gift of £250 to the Inverness Free Library conditional upon their purchasing a copy of the Dictionary (*Periodical* Dec. 1899, p. 5).

[111] FC 21 Sept., 30 Nov. 1905; OD 8 June 1906. Craigie used the loan to build a house, 'Craigielea', at 15 Charlbury Road.

[112] OED/B/3/2/3 22 Nov. 1905 CTO to Cannan, 29 Nov. HB to Cannan.

FIGURE 22   The Scriptorium at 78 Banbury Road, Oxford. Not all of the assistants seen here can be securely identified; the figure standing on the left appears to be F. A. Yockney (which dates the photograph to 1905 or later), and Frederick Sweatman is sitting next to him. Behind him is Murray's daughter Rosfrith.

was likely to bring completion closer. Onions was to be given a trial as a more or less independent Editor, working at a separate section of the letter M—though with Bradley retaining overall editorial responsibility—on a higher salary; pay increases were approved to keep Lewis and Bayliss happy; one-off additional payments were made to each of the editorial teams 'in respect of the year 1905'; and a completely revamped, two-part bonus scheme was proposed.[113] Previously bonuses had only become due when the yearly page tally exceeded 200 pages, or equivalently 25 pages of Webster; the target was now reduced to 12 pages of Webster, thus ensuring that there would be a significant productivity-related payment. As a further incentive to completion, the immediate bonuses awarded each year would be matched by an undertaking to pay an equal amount when the Dictionary was finished (referred to as a 'deferred contingent bonus'). Murray, while happy enough that more money was being made available for bonus payments, stuck firmly to his view that his own salary should be increased in recognition of 'the much greater work, which the experience

[113] FC 15 Dec. 1905; OD 26 Jan. 1906. Carline and Powell, assistants to Bradley and Craigie respectively, subsequently also received pay increases (FC 25 Jan. 1906).

of many years proves that I have always done'; and eventually the Delegates conceded the point generously, with a £100 increase that brought his salary to the substantial figure of £650.[114]

Finally, another attempt was to be made to address a long-standing desideratum: the idea of finding specialists to work in advance on scientific vocabulary, which all of the Editors found particularly time-consuming. The idea had a long history, going back at least to 1891,[115] and had been mooted regularly since then. For individual words all three Editors had of course long been in the habit of consulting specialists, but systematic preliminary work across whole subject areas was another matter. In fact the geologist and palaeontologist S. S. Buckman had recently begun to do work of this kind for Murray, who thought highly of his work, and recommended that the other Editors make use of him.[116] He was now put forward as someone suitable to do such work on a more regular basis, working in Oxford alongside the editorial staff, but the experiment was unsuccessful—it proved hard to keep him continuously supplied with work, and his definitions, while expert, required to be reworded—and he was not taken on.[117] The search for a suitable expert continued, and promising individuals continued to be put forward, but no long-term solution to the problem was ever found; ultimately the Editors had to rely on their own expertise, and regular consultation with specialists as the need arose.[118]

From the start of 1906, then, the Dictionary might be said to have started firing on four cylinders; there is certainly a sense of increased momentum. Some of this momentum was supplied by Onions, who in January started work—with only clerical assistance, provided by an Oxford grocer's son named J. W. Birt—on the range of words beginning with *mis-*. He seems to have been allowed to send his entries to the printers without intervention by Bradley, although from the proof stage onwards Bradley still retained control; his contribution significantly increased Bradley's tally of pages.[119] All of the sections published in the year were double sections, the last of which (*Mesne–Misbirth*) included some of Onions's first batch of words.

Indeed, for at least a few years the history of the Dictionary can at last be characterized as one of steady progress uninterrupted by major incidents. The occasional

[114] 16 Feb. 1906 JAHM to Cannan (lost; quoted in HJRM p. 238); OD 23 Feb. 1906.
[115] See above, p. 253.
[116] OED/B/3/2/3 MS note by Cannan on an interview with JAHM, [3 or 4 July 1905].
[117] OED/B/3/2/4 24 May 1906 Cannan to JAHM, JAHM to Cannan, 25 May 1906 Cannan to Buckman. Responding to Craigie's complaint that Buckman could not write definitions, Murray commented: 'I begin after much experience, to think that no science man can. The most they can do is to supply us with the *facts*, which [...] we can mould into Dictionary shape.'
[118] One of Murray's most valuable science consultants after the experiment with Buckman was the chemist Henry H. Robinson, a special research assistant at the Imperial Institute, who advised on many chemical and biochemical terms.
[119] OED/B/3/2/3 22 Dec. 1905 CTO to Cannan.

To ᵭʳ W A Craigie.

photo by HBG

JUNE 1907

FIGURE 23   Two Editors conferring: Craigie (left) and Bradley (right) in the Dictionary Room, Old Ashmolean, 1907.

assistant would come and go, but without seriously impeding progress;[120] the illness of an Editor or an assistant might temporarily cause a dip in output,[121] but all three editorial teams seemed to have developed the ability to cope. Certainly the steady flow of quarterly double—and even occasional triple—sections continued without a break. The experiment with Onions had proved such a success that it was repeated, this time with Craigie as the beneficiary, Onions being assigned the words beginning with the prefix *non-*. Thereafter he seems to have become a kind of roving senior assistant for both Bradley and Craigie, taking responsibility—at a further increased salary—for further ranges in M and R.[122] In 1908 his progress was separately reported to the Delegates, making him seemingly a fourth Editor in all but name—Bradley and Craigie certainly fully acknowledged his independent contributions in their Prefaces[123]—and in 1909 he even helped Murray out, bringing his particular abilities to bear on the immense verb *put* during the protracted absence through illness of Murray's assistant Sweatman.[124] However, for the time being the Press held off from formally promoting him.

The final section of Volume VI, *Movement–Myz*, was published in September 1908: ahead of Volume VII, despite Murray's prediction, but of course this had only been achieved by dint of a considerable redistribution of editorial effort (including the assignment of N to Craigie, who had completed the letter in 1907). Now, at last, the page acknowledging the 'munificence' of the Goldsmiths' Company could be published; and it remained unique, as no other institution or individual was persuaded to follow their example. At over 1,600 pages Volume VI was easily the largest to date; its size arguably stood as a reproach to the over-setting of both its contributing Editors. The Webster scale in L, M, and N was consistently in excess of 10, and in the later portions of M Bradley

---

[120] In 1907 Murray took on P. J. Philip, a former medical student from Edinburgh, who however left the following year, going on to become a successful journalist. The etymologist Alfred Gough left in May 1908, and was replaced a few months later by George Friedrichsen, who proved very promising but also left after only two years, although he became a much-valued proofreader, and also sometimes returned to the Scriptorium to help out with etymological work when assistants were on holiday. (On Friedrichsen's later re-engagement with Oxford lexicography see p. 330.) In 1907 Craigie lost two assistants (Ramsay and Smithwhite), but also engaged the man who was to become his most trusted assistant, George Watson of Jedburgh. Henry Rope, Murray's former assistant, who had joined Craigie's staff in 1908, left in 1910; in 1911 Craigie took on E. N. Martin, an Oxford carpenter's son. Bradley's assistant James Dallas left in 1908; the most valuable addition to his staff during this period was a Cambridge graduate named Charlton Walker, who began work in the Old Ashmolean in 1909. A year later he also engaged Percy Dadley, formerly of the Bodleian, who went on to work as Onions's assistant. Various other assistants worked only for a few months, or even weeks.

[121] Murray was laid low in early 1907 by a very serious bout of pneumonia, but without any noticeable impact on his monthly tally as reported to the Delegates; later that year, during his summer holiday in Wales, he was injured in a cycling accident (*Manchester Guardian* 27 Aug. 1907, p. 6), but without any lasting ill effects.

[122] FC 20 Dec. 1906.

[123] After *non-* Onions went on to work on *mult-* and *my-* for Bradley, and *rh-* for Craigie; Bradley's Preface to *S–Sh* refers to 'several extensive portions of the work' as having been 'specially prepared' by Onions.

[124] OED/B/3/8/6 7, 13 May 1909 JAHM to CTO. Sweatman was absent almost continuously for six months in 1909 (MP 2 Mar. 1910 JAHM to Hereward Price (photocopy)).

came close to a scale of 11, notwithstanding regular remonstrations from Cannan. These had reached a peak in early 1908, when, alarmed by news of a scale of nearly 20 for a stretch of words in *mud-*, he instructed the printers to hold off from making Bradley's corrections until he gave the signal, while at the same time going through the entries himself to see how the text might be shortened. He set out many specific suggestions for curtailment in a characteristically amiable letter which can nevertheless have left Bradley in no doubt as to what was expected of him, observing dryly that if *mud hole*—one of several compounds of *mud* for which he advised omission or briefer treatment—was to be defined as 'a salt water lagoon in which whales are captured', then 'a Dictionary might be defined as a "bottomless pit in which thousands of pounds are lost" '.[125]

1908 had of course been the year named by Murray in 1897, in the heady days of the great dinner at Queen's College, as the time by which he believed the Dictionary might be finished. This was not to be; but in some respects it did prove a good year, not the least of which was the conferring of a knighthood upon the Dictionary's chief Editor. On learning that he was to be offered this honour, Murray was initially inclined to refuse, for a peculiar combination of reasons. Partly he felt that knighthoods had become somewhat debased currency in recent years, and that to be made a plain knight 'as if I were a brewer or a local mayor' did not really constitute recognition of his scholarly work as, say, the Order of Merit would have done; partly he feared that it might be more of a burden than a blessing, encouraging tradesmen to put their prices up (and even that it might lead him to shift his own staunchly Liberal political views in the direction of Toryism); but mainly, as Elisabeth Murray astutely observes, because 'to accept [the knighthood] would destroy the image of martyrdom which he had built up for himself and which was in a curious way a help in sustaining him in his task'. Having resigned himself to not—as he thought—being properly appreciated in Oxford, and learned 'not to care a scrap for either blame or praise', he now confessed to his son Harold that he was reluctant to 'come down from this position and accept the honour of this generation; I should prefer that my biographer should have to say "Oxford never made him a Fellow or a D.C.L., and his country never recognized his work, but he worked on all the same, believing in his work and his duty." '[126] Eventually, however, the urgings of various friends, and the realization of the difference that it would make to his wife, persuaded him to accept, and on 21 July he was invested by the King at Buckingham Palace. Another honour came in September when a Litt.D. degree

---

[125] OED/B/3/2/4 18 Feb. 1908 Cannan to H. Hart (as Controller), Cannan to HB. Cannan also drew Bradley's attention to what he regarded as dangerously excessive use of quotations from the *Century Dictionary*. His remonstrations about scale—and the embargo—had some effect: in the published text the Webster scale of the *mud-* words was brought down to approximately 11.

[126] *CWW* pp. 293–4 (quoting various letters from Murray). Interestingly, his son Oswyn, who was by this time a senior official at the Admiralty, thought it not unlikely that, if he refused, he would in due course be offered the Order of Merit (MP 11 June 1908 Oswyn Murray to JAHM).

was conferred upon him at Trinity College Dublin.[127] The Press, and the University, must have enjoyed basking in the reflected glory of such accolades; there was no longer any reason to doubt the esteem in which the Dictionary was held, and even Murray had probably ceased to do so. Further confirmation of the special status of the project came in the pages of a brief history of the University Press by Murray's old friend Falconer Madan, also published in 1908, which acclaimed the Dictionary as 'that crowning work—over-topping perhaps all others, except the Bible', and 'the greatest literary work ever produced at Oxford'.[128]

Whether the Dictionary's Editors or publisher would have concurred with Madan's prediction that the Dictionary would be completed by 1912 is more doubtful. By the end of 1908 Bradley had moved on to the letter S, which proved to be tougher going than even M had been; his progress was further slowed by the departure of his assistant James Dallas for health reasons. The autumn of 1909 brought further disruption, when Bradley and his family moved out of North House to a property in North Oxford.[129] (The fact that at the same time his salary was raised to £500 is evidence of the Press's continuing confidence in his abilities, although Cannan continued to badger him on the subject of scale, notwithstanding Bradley's plea that 'in S. there seems to be a run on the class of words that Webster treats meagrely'.[130]) In 1909 Murray also moved on to a more difficult letter, T, and his progress rate underwent a similar dip.[131] Moreover, he was now over seventy, and despite his continuing prodigious capacity for work, he could have been forgiven for beginning to wonder whether he would 'live to see Zymotic' (the daily good wish of visitors and correspondents alike, as he had once commented to Fitzedward Hall).[132] In his progress reports to the Philological Society—which he had resumed in 1906, after leaving the Society's Dictionary Evenings to Bradley and Craigie for five years—he began to dwell increasingly on the number of key Dictionary figures who had been lost to the project through illness or death; and by 1909 it made a melancholy roster.[133] The most serious among recent losses was Henry Hucks Gibbs, whose multifarious contributions to the Dictionary stretched back over decades, and who had continued his close reading of the proofs of all three Editors until only a few weeks before his death in September 1907. Bradley and

---

[127] *London Gazette* 28 July 1908, p. 5530; *Times* 5 Sept. 1908, p. 3. In 1907 Craigie had also been awarded an LL.D. by St Andrews (*Times* 4 Apr. 1907, p. 3).

[128] Madan (1908: 20, 21).

[129] OD 15 Oct. 1909.

[130] OED/B/3/2/5 18 July 1910 HB to Cannan.

[131] Murray apparently made his first start on T at *Ti*, where it had been decided that Volume X would start, it having long been his ambition to edit the final volume of the Dictionary himself. However, he soon found that he was constantly having to make reference to words in *ta-* and *te-*, to the extent that he was forced to postpone further work on *Ti* and go back to the start of the letter (and thus to Volume IX); accordingly, it was agreed that Volume X would be shared between the Editors, with Bradley and Craigie undertaking V–W (*Athenaeum* 28 May 1910, p. 645).

[132] OED/B/3/9/4 7 Dec. 1893 JAHM to Hall. In fact *zymotic* was not to be the Dictionary's last word: see p. 353.

[133] *Athenaeum* 29 May 1909, p. 651 (reporting Murray's speech to the Society on 7 May).

Craigie also had good reason to mourn the death in 1908 of Henry Chichester Hart, who had added innumerable quotations to their proofs from his close study of sixteenth- and seventeenth-century writers. Other losses amongst the sub-editors were equally serious, including Bartholomew Price's early recruit Charles Mount—described by Murray as his 'greatest helper in Oxford',[134] but now struck down by illness—regular Philological Society Council member Edward Brandreth (who had also been a proofreader, and checked many quotations in the British Museum), the industrious James Bartlett, and Jemima Brown, who had become a close personal friend of Murray, and left him a small legacy which significantly reduced his financial worries.[135] That left only Joseph Brown—the last of Furnivall's sub-editors, now nearly seventy—and William Robertson Wilson, only a couple of years younger, who had been contributing to the Dictionary since 1879.[136] Without fresh sub-editors, the editorial teams in Oxford would soon find themselves having to tackle alphabetical ranges which had not been sub-edited or re-sub-edited for years; this was bound to slow progress, as the task of interfiling and reviewing all of the material which had accumulated since a range was last sub-edited was always time-consuming. Indeed, there is evidence that there had not been enough sub-editors to go round for some time: reference is made both by Bradley in his Preface to the letter L, dated 1903, and by Craigie in the Prefaces to N and Q–R, to the large volume of material that had accumulated after the last period of sub-editing, which in some cases had been over twenty years earlier. This would go some way towards explaining why Bradley and Craigie found it impossible to match Murray's rate of progress. However, although some new volunteer proofreaders came forward to join those who remained, including the essayist Logan Pearsall Smith and Murray's former assistant Frederic Bumby, there was no attempt to recruit new sub-editors. As Murray observed at the Philological Society in May 1910, 'only experienced men are any good at the work at this stage.'[137]

Murray dwelt once again in his 1910 report to the Society on the passing of the Dictionary's helpers; and he had every reason to do so. Not only had the project been deprived of another key proofreader, a Dutchman named Caland who had read all the proofs for over a decade; perhaps more seriously, the Editors had also lost James Platt, who had dealt with so many of their queries regarding loanwords from the more exotic languages of the world, and whose unique linguistic talents were irreplaceable.[138] For Murray himself there was the indisposition of his wife Ada following two (fortunately successful) operations for cataracts in 1909; she had always been an enormous source

---

[134] MP notes by JAHM for a Dictionary Evening on 1 May 1908.

[135] HJRM pp. 241–2.

[136] Robertson Wilson, a Presbyterian minister of Dollar, Clackmannanshire, had been among the first wave of volunteers to respond to Murray's 1879 'Appeal'; he had begun work as a sub-editor by March 1881.

[137] Quoted in *Athenaeum* 28 May 1910, p. 645.

[138] Some help with words from Asian languages was subsequently given by C. O. Sylvester Mawson, who had done similar work for the *Century Dictionary* and for the 1909 revision of Webster, and who coincidentally wrote offering his services only a few weeks before Platt's death (MP 21 Dec. 1909 C. O. S. Mawson to JAHM).

of practical help and moral support, and he now keenly felt the lack of her help. Worst of all, in April came the terrible news that the seemingly indestructible Furnivall—who, now in his eighties, was still a keen rower, and still sent in his daily package of quotations culled from the newspapers—had bowel cancer, and was unlikely to last more than another six months. Matter-of-fact as ever, he sent out many letters and postcards informing friends of his illness, including one to Murray which, remarkably, maintains his usual breezy tone: 'Yes, our Dicty men go gradually, & I am to disappear in 6 months. [...] It's a great disappointment, as I wanted to see the Dicty finished before I die. But it is not to be. However, the completion of the work's certain. So that's all right.'[139] Murray, terribly shocked ('Alas! My friends seem to be dying daily,' he wrote to his daughter Hilda), wrote to Furnivall with admiration for the older man's calmness and fortitude, and—equally characteristically—seeking to boost his morale with an appetizing lexicographical prospect: 'Would it give you any satisfaction to see the gigantic [entry] TAKE in final [proof]? before it is too late?'[140] Furnivall died on 2 July, the last of the men who had been present at the Dictionary's conception over half a century earlier. His contribution to the project, in a multiplicity of ways, was incalculable; it is remarkable that he also found the time and energy to make so many other contributions to the culture of his time. His obituary in the *Times* summed him up well when it observed that he would be 'regretted by hundreds in all ranks of life, from the most eminent of English and foreign men of letters to the waitresses in the teashop in New Oxford-street, whither, after a long day's work in the British Museum, the white-bearded, grey-shirted old scholar went to enjoy a hearty meal'.[141]

The Dictionary, being greater than any one individual, was nevertheless affected by so many losses, though admittedly also by other factors. The progress reported to the Delegates during 1910 amounted to barely 420 pages, nearly 70 pages down on the previous year. Some of this could be attributed to the fact that S and T were both proving exceptionally intractable (Craigie, having at last finished R, had started at *Si* in February); rather more could be attributed to the fact that Craigie had spent three months in Iceland.[142] This was just the latest manifestation of an increasing degree of involvement by the Dictionary's third Editor in the philological study of other Germanic languages, which now extended well beyond the requirements of his

---

[139] MP 15 Apr. 1910 FJF to JAHM.

[140] 17 Apr. 1910 JAHM to Hilda Murray (lost; quoted in *CWW* p. 304); MP 17 Apr. 1910 JAHM to FJF. Onions later recounted the story of the Philological Society meeting at which Furnivall broke the news of his cancer: 'Sir James Murray sitting there with tears streaming down his face, Furnivall himself (it appears) quite cheerful' (KCLFP box 4, 3 Nov. 1948 CTO to Miss White).

[141] *Times* 4 July 1910, p. 12. Furnivall continued to work for the Dictionary right up to the end. A newspaper cutting taken by him from the *Westminster Gazette* of 29 June 1910, to illustrate a new sense of the word *factorial*, formed the basis of an entry in the 1972 *Supplement*. I have not been able to trace the original copy for an instance of the new word *escalator* in the *Daily News* of 2 July 1910, which was added in the 1933 *Supplement*, but as the *Daily News* was a paper from which he took many quotations, it is possible that this was also his contribution.

[142] MP 7 June 1910 WAC to JAHM.

Taylorian lectureship: he had edited a collection of Icelandic ballads, published by the Clarendon Press in 1908, and had made a substantial editorial contribution to a students' dictionary of Icelandic, also published by the Press in 1910.[143] Since 1908 his Dictionary Evenings at the Philological Society had featured, not just a report on the *OED*, but also observations on some of the other dictionaries of Germanic (and later also Celtic) languages then in preparation across northern Europe. He was becoming well known in academic circles in Scandinavia—his trip to Iceland was only the latest of several visits to the region—and in 1909 he also began to give his support to a campaign to secure proper recognition of the Frisian language.[144] It was of course good for the Dictionary to cultivate and maintain contacts with other scholars, but Craigie's activities in this regard must surely have significantly reduced his output as Editor, as well as perhaps giving some reason to doubt his commitment to the project.[145]

It must have been something of a relief for the Press to observe considerable productivity in another of their lexicographical enterprises: not from William Little, working away in Cornwall, whose abridgement of the *OED* was still some way off the point reached by the main Dictionary, but from the brothers Henry and Frank Fowler, who had for some years been working at two still shorter versions of the Dictionary.[146] It was in the autumn of 1906, a few months after the publication of the Fowlers' immensely successful book of observations on English usage, *The King's English*, that Cannan's assistant Humphrey Milford had written to them with the 'quite mad suggestion' that they might like to try their hand at 'cheap dictionaries—to sell at 1/ and 2/ probably', drawing upon the *OED* so far as it was published, and thereafter upon the materials collected for it.[147] The brothers responded with enthusiasm, and more importantly produced some trial material which was pronounced very promising by Henry Bradley, who as the author of *The Making of English* was evidently deemed a better judge than Murray of what kind of book was wanted for this mass market, and whose verdicts on some earlier attempts by other proposed abridgers had been distinctly unfavourable.[148] Work proceeded on both dictionaries until 1908, when it seemed that the Fowlers might be unable to write the kind of elementary school textbook that the smaller dictionary was envisaged as being, and they were persuaded to abandon it; the larger book soon grew (in the way that dictionaries often do) well beyond the point where

---

[143] *Athenaeum* 21 Nov. 1908, p. 652. The *Concise Dictionary of Old Icelandic* was edited by the Icelander Geir T. Zoëga, who however acknowledged in his preface that Craigie had 'revised the whole of the manuscript and proofs'.

[144] Wyllie (1961: 285).

[145] In fact the University was still happy to invite the Dictionary's senior Editor to take on additional commitments. In November 1910 Murray was invited to give a course of lectures on the English language (MP 20 Nov. 1910 W. Raleigh to JAHM). He proceeded to give five lectures the following term. The invitation may have been prompted by the success of a lecture he had given to the London Institution on 31 October, which was widely and favourably reported (e.g. *Times* 3 Nov. 1910, p. 12).

[146] For more information on the Fowlers' various publications for the Press, see McMorris (2001).

[147] ML 13 Oct. 1906 HSM to H. W. Fowler.

[148] McMorris (2001: 75–7).

two shillings could continue to be regarded as a viable price. The fact that the Fowlers lived in Guernsey did not prove as much of an obstacle as might be supposed: they did not in fact utilize the unpublished materials for the entries in S–Z for which there were no *OED* entries to draw on, but instead compiled their own entries on the basis of other small dictionaries sent out to them by the Press, together with what they could get 'from [their] own heads'.[149] The new dictionary was eventually published on 16 June 1911 as *The Concise Oxford Dictionary of Current English*, price three shillings and sixpence, 'adapted', according to the title page, 'from The Oxford Dictionary'; the reviews were almost uniformly excellent, and the *Concise* rapidly became an enormous publishing success, selling nearly 10,000 copies during the first month, and over 40,000 by March 1912. Thus began the powerful symbiotic relationship between the two sides of English lexicography at OUP: the benefit to the Press of investing such vast sums in the *OED* itself was reaped from the smaller dictionaries which explicitly identified themselves as drawing upon the same lexical data as the larger work, at least part of the cost of which the Delegates could at last hope to defray with the revenue from its mass-market companions. (This was perhaps just as well: by 1911 the Press had spent £150,000 on the *OED*, against which could be set a figure of rather less than £60,000 in sales.[150])

And 'companions', plural, was what Cannan and Milford felt it should be. They had never abandoned the idea of the one-shilling dictionary, and even as the Fowlers were being persuaded to abandon it in 1908, other possible editors were being put forward, including Murray's former Scriptorium assistant Ernest Speight, whom Milford— notwithstanding his dismissive description of him as '[a] hack [...] a scholarly kind of person who has failed as a publisher'—believed to have sufficient experience of elementary schools to know what was required. However, the idea was abandoned, apparently because of Murray's anticipated hostility to the appointment—it seems that his relations with Speight were little better than they had been at the time of the latter's sudden departure from the Scriptorium—and the project languished, for want of a writer 'possessing equal qualifications, viz. (1) penury (2) leisure (3) willingness to work (4) fair scholarship (5) experience'.[151] But it never ceased to be discussed; indeed, in January 1911, with the *Concise* nearly ready for publication and looking very promising, Milford even drew up a list of no fewer than six possible condensed versions, ranging from the one-shilling 'Elementary or Small' to the thirty-shilling 'Abridged'.[152] However, although the Fowlers declared themselves ready to start on 'the 1/- dictionary' in June 1911, and Frank Fowler began work on what later became the *Pocket Oxford Dictionary* soon thereafter, it would be some years before another dictionary was forthcoming from Guernsey.[153] Towards the end of 1911 the Press

[149]   *COD*, Preface, p. iv.
[150]   OED/B/3/2/5 22 Aug. 1912 RWC to W. Osler.
[151]   ML 30 Apr., 8 May 1908 HSM to Cannan. Other names mentioned included Walter Skeat's daughter Bertha, and one of Murray's daughters (ML 28 Jan. 1910 HSM to Cannan).
[152]   ML 17 Jan. 1911 HSM to Cannan.
[153]   MEU/1/12 11 June 1911 H. W. Fowler to [RWC].

issued a very different book which was unquestionably the offspring of the *OED*: Onions's *Shakespeare Glossary*, in the compilation of which he had drawn heavily on the Dictionary's published entries and unpublished materials, having been permitted time away from *OED* work in order to do so. A measure of the confidence which the Delegates had in Onions's work even before publication is provided by the fact that they chose to bring out an edition on India paper at the same time. Their confidence was justified: the *Glossary* was extremely well received,[154] and quickly became a standard work of reference for Shakespeare scholars.

Strangely, none of the reviewers of the *Concise Oxford Dictionary* seem to have commented on one feature which seemed to contradict its claim to be 'adapted' from the *OED*: the significant number of items it contained which were not to be found in the larger dictionary. Whatever decision William Little had taken at this point regarding such items, the Fowlers had evidently come to the conclusion that to leave them out of their dictionary would detract from its claim to be an up-to-date dictionary of current English. Accordingly, the *Concise* included entries for many items not in the 'parent' dictionary. In A, in particular, there were many which illustrated only too clearly how much the world had moved on since the Dictionary's first fascicles had appeared: not only *adenoids* and *appendicitis*, but a welter of terms relating to innovations in transport, including *aerodrome*, *automobile*, and *aviator*.

The *OED*'s lexicographers had long maintained a 'Supplement' file, to which observations about such words could be consigned, together with suggestions for the revision or correction of existing entries. The file was opened as soon as Part I of the Dictionary had been published: indeed Furnivall had started to collect such material even before then,[155] and had never ceased to look out for neologisms in his daily reading. In 1905—by which time the file already occupied many shelves—he had even agitated, unsuccessfully, for the setting up of a fresh programme of reading specifically for the Supplement.[156] For the moment, however, even though the need for a Supplement was becoming ever more pressing, there was no time to do more than maintain the growing file: all available lexicographical effort had to go into the push towards Z.

Unfortunately, 1912 brought a fresh set of obstacles to this push. The first came in January, when Bradley, who had apparently been driving himself too hard, succumbed to an attack of carbuncles, which for a while confined him to his bedroom, incapable of

---

[154] It was welcomed, for example, by the distinguished English scholar G. C. Macaulay as 'the best thing of the kind that has appeared' (*Modern Language Review* 7 (1912) 561).

[155] See above, p. 179. Furnivall's conception of the Dictionary had included the need for supplementation as early as 1877 (MP 24 Oct. 1877 FJF to JAHM: 'We shall want a 2-vol. Supplement by the time the 4 vols. of Dicty are out'). The earliest reference to the maintaining of a file of material for a Supplement by the lexicographers themselves that I have been able to find dates from 1891 (SL 15 July 1891 Doble to HB), although Charlotte Brewer is surely right in suggesting (2007: 28) that it must have started in the 1880s.

[156] MP 7 July 1905 JAHM to FJF, 14 Oct. 1905 FJF to JAHM. Murray keenly felt the lack of Furnivall's contributions, and in 1912 appealed to the Philological Society for a volunteer to scour the daily papers for neologisms: 'the whole terminology of Aeroplanes & Aeronautics is wanting. Also the recent terms of Electricity, Town planning, etc.' (MP notes for 1912 Dictionary Evening).

speech. An attempt to get away to Devon for a rest cure was thwarted when Bradley's wife, always in delicate health, was found to require an operation to remove an abscess on her jaw.[157] It was clear that a more substantial break was needed, and the Delegates granted him leave of absence (and a subsidy of £100) to spend the summer months in Canada, visiting his daughter and son-in-law; although this trip also had to be curtailed because of his wife's health, Bradley does seem to have benefited from the holiday. During his absence Craigie had supervised his assistants in the Old Ashmolean, while also maintaining his own output at a respectable level; Onions once again came into his own, bringing his particular skills to bear on the material for *set*, the entry for which was to be the largest in the whole Dictionary.[158] There were also problems for Murray: in March illness struck his oldest and most trusted assistant, Charles Balk, who from May began working only alternate weeks. Murray was already short-staffed, having lost the excellent George Friedrichsen in 1911 and been unable to find a replacement, despite having (as he lamented to Skeat) 'tried every professor of English from Uppsala to Freiburg & Vienna'. Murray's personal response to the situation was characteristic, as well as illustrating the contrast between his and Bradley's constitutions: he once again adopted a punishing work schedule, regularly working from 6 a.m. to 11 p.m. and putting in between 84 and 90 hours a week.[159] As a result, even though he allowed himself a fortnight's summer holiday in the Lake District, he was able to issue 284 pages of T during 1912, equal to more than the published outputs of Bradley's and Craigie's staffs combined: a particularly impressive achievement given that this included the whole of *Th*, with the difficult group of demonstratives (*that, then, there*, and the like).[160] In July, impressed with his own progress, he wrote optimistically to Skeat about the prospects for completion: 'we may, I think now, reckon that the end of 1916 will see the Dictionary finished. If I live to then, I shall be 80, and it will also be my Golden Wedding; let us hope that the Grand Conjunction of all these cycles will really take place.'[161]

But not even Murray's enormous personal effort could compensate for the serious shortfall in manpower, notwithstanding the boost of Onions's return to work on the Dictionary. The tally of pages actually edited during the year—a better indicator of

---

[157] OED/B/3/2/5 1 Feb. 1912 E. K. Bradley to Cannan, 6 Feb. 1912 HB to Cannan, 11 Mar. 1912 Cannan to W. Osler.

[158] OD 17 May 1912. Onions's work on *set* even impressed Murray, who sent him a note expressing 'great appreciation of the arrangement, & the mastery of difficulties. I have seen no better treatment of a long word' (OED/B/3/4/3 undated note JAHM to CTO). The entry for *set* remained the longest in the Dictionary until 2011, when the even longer revised entry for *run* was published in *OED Online*.

[159] MP 28 Sept. 1912 JAHM to Skeat, 8 Dec. 1912 JAHM to W. Stathers, 9 Apr. 1912 J. G. W. MacAlister to JAHM, 28 Sept. 1912 JAHM to Skeat.

[160] Preliminary drafting of the more difficult entries in *Th* was apparently shared between Arthur Maling and George Friedrichsen.

[161] MP 22 July 1912 JAHM to Skeat. Murray's eightieth birthday had been a figure to aim for as early as 1908, when Sir William Osler, the Regius Professor of Medicine, observed to a friend that the University paid his salary to keep Murray alive until then 'when the Dictionary will be finished' (recounted in Sutcliffe 1978: 154).

productivity than the published sections—which had risen to just over 470 in 1911, fell back below 450 in 1912. The project continued to lose some of its most valued helpers: Skeat, whose support for the Dictionary and its Editors in so many ways places him alongside Furnivall and Henry Hucks Gibbs, died in October, and only weeks later Edward Arber, Murray's great friend (and the man who had introduced him to Onions), was knocked down by a taxi, dying on his way to hospital. Towards the end of 1912 Murray seemed to have found at least a partial solution to his understaffing problem, as he took on two new assistants, but once again they failed to stay the course: first T. Z. D. Babington, recruited fresh from studying English at Magdalen College before he had even taken his degree, who left before the end of the year to take up a professorship at Rangoon, and then Eduard Brenner, an older and in fact already well-thought-of German Anglo-Saxon scholar, who however only stayed until the following summer. Babington was soon replaced, at the suggestion of Murray's friend President Warren of Magdalen, by another young Magdalen man, G. G. R. Greene,[162] whose stint of work for the project was to be curtailed for a different and unforeseen reason. Worst of all came the resignation of Charles Balk in October 1913, apparently in order to concentrate on a book of his own on which he had been working for some time. There is some suggestion that his fellow workers in the Scriptorium were not sorry to see him go: Murray later confided to Cannan that 'Mr Balk's return would be very disagreeable to every one', and attributed his assistants' having 'worked like Trojans' to complete the section *Trink–Turn-down* to their being 'desirous of showing me that we could get on without him'.[163] But his departure further depressed the output of Murray and his staff, which in 1913 fell to its lowest level for many years. Murray continued to be optimistic: in the spring of 1913 he repeated in an interview the prediction he had made privately to Skeat a year earlier, that 'in all human probability' the Dictionary would be completed in time for his eightieth birthday.[164]

It was becoming clear, however, that something more than optimism would be required if Murray's 'Grand Conjunction' was to be achieved. Bradley and Craigie had of late been luckier with their assistants than Murray—neither of them had lost anyone since the departure of Rope in 1910—and some more of the special preparatory work done on particular ranges of words by Onions, this time in *sh-*, had boosted Bradley's 1913 tally to his highest figure for some years; but the combined total output of the three Editors for the year was again low (around 460 pages). More worryingly, signs had

---

[162] Magdalen College archives, ref. PR/2/17 (President Warren's notebooks), p. 458. Greene began work in January 1913.

[163] OED/B/3/2/7 24 May 1915 JAHM to Cannan. Balk's departure had a tragic postscript: on 3 December 1915 his body was found in a stream by Port Meadow, with notes which left no room for doubt that it was suicide. His book, which had been at the printers when war broke out, was published posthumously by his family in 1922; entitled *Life is Growth*, it comprised an extended meditation on the meaning of life and on Scripture as a guide to action. His conclusions seem to have increasingly oppressed him; one of the suicide notes laments 'What good growth have I failed to further, and what evil growth have I in many cases furthered! [. . .] I have come to think when it was too late, except to show me how wrong my life had been' ('Sad Death of Mr. C. G. Balk', *Oxford Chronicle* 10 Dec. 1915, p. 7).

[164] Untraced interview in the *London Post* of March 1913, quoted in *Periodical* Apr. 1913, p. 162.

FIGURE 24   William Craigie photographed in the Old Ashmolean, *c*.1914.

begun to appear that even Murray's extraordinary constitution had begun to fail: in May he had confided to his son Aelfric that 'that feeling comes over me strongly at times, when I am not quite well'.[165] He was becoming more subject to colds, and took longer to recover from them; he had also suffered from some kind of internal strain ever since his last Continental holiday in 1904. In Cambridge in June, presenting him for an honorary Litt.D., the university's Orator spoke for many when he wished him to be granted 'the years of venerable Nestor' and thus see the great work through to completion;[166] but only a few weeks later he was again confined to bed for several days, with 'painful rheumatic stiffness' in the head.[167] (He was by no means a broken man, however, and by the time of the family holiday in Wales in August was once again climbing mountains.)

Evidently the editorial team needed strengthening at the highest level; and the person most obviously fitted for promotion was Charles Onions. In June the suggestion—apparently from Onions himself—that he be allowed to take on a section, or sections, of the Dictionary as an independent Editor was approved by the Delegates, but it was only

[165] 2 May 1913 JAHM to Aelfric Murray (quoted in *CWW* p. 309).
[166] *Cambridge University Reporter* 14 June 1913, p. 1293 (Latin: *venerabili Nestoris annos*). Bradley also received two honorary doctorates in 1913, from the universities of Durham and Sheffield.
[167] HJRM p. 255; 19 July 1913 JAHM to 'Dr. Poole' (BodL shelfmark 30254 c.2, f. 17).

FIGURE 25   Charles Onions photographed in the Old Ashmolean, c.1914.

in January 1914 that he actually started work, on the range *Su–Sz*.[168] In February, rather surprisingly, the move received the Delegates' approval for a second time; and the fact that shortly before their meeting a testimonial was submitted to the Vice-Chancellor, setting out Onions's abilities and achievements but signed only by Bradley and Craigie, suggests that Murray may have been against the appointment.[169] Could it be that Murray still regarded Onions's unmentionable indiscretion of 1899 as disqualifying him from holding such a position? Or was he simply restating his well-known doubts as to the efficacy of multiplying editorial teams as a means of accelerating progress?

Opposition notwithstanding, from March 1914 there were at last four streams of copy flowing into the printing offices—Onions's a small trickle, as was only to be expected from a new Editor with only two assistants.[170] Murray was in any case too busy to protest with much vigour, engaged as he was in the enormous struggle to get

---

[168] FC 5, 26 June 1913, 22 Jan. 1914. In a curious repetition of what had happened in Craigie's case, Onions was only elected a member of the Philological Society a few weeks before starting work as Editor (PSOM 5 Dec. 1913).

[169] OED/B/3/2/6 typed copy of testimonial, marked 'Original sent to V.C. 13 Feb. [19]14'; OD 20 Feb. 1914.

[170] In addition to the ever-faithful Birt—who had also worked with Onions on the *Shakespeare Glossary*—there was now Percy Dadley, who had transferred from Craigie's staff (FC 22 Dec. 1913).

train

The writer and suffragette Beatrice Harraden (1864–1936) achieved a certain degree of fame with her debut novel *Ships that Pass in the Night* (1893), a love story set in a Swiss tuberculosis sanatorium. None of her later books were as successful, and she remains a minor figure among the writers of her time. It is tempting to attribute the fact that several of her novels are quoted in the first edition of the *OED* to her friendship with Frederick Furnivall (whom she referred to as 'Ferney': Munro et al. 1911: 68). It seems to have been Furnivall who arranged for her to visit Murray in his Scriptorium; and what she saw there subsequently found its way, in bizarrely transmuted form, in her 1906 novel *The Scholar's Daughter*, several of whose principal characters are at work on 'a dictionary which was to be the abiding pride of the Anglo-Saxon race'—in fact a thinly disguised version of the *OED*. Murray himself appears as 'Professor Grant', whose daughter Geraldine is the 'scholar's daughter' of the title. One can hardly imagine Murray approving of such a novel, whatever its storyline; his disapproval will surely have been intensified by the fact that, in Harraden's highly coloured tale, Professor Grant's wife, Charlotta, has left him and become a famous actress, while he has become a man who 'doesn't care for women—or for anything, indeed, except dictionaries', but who is dramatically reconciled with Charlotta on the final page. The novel's vignettes of the work of Professor Grant and his assistants include details which must have been drawn from Harraden's visit, although she has relocated the Scriptorium to 'a picturesque old manor house [...] in the heart of the country'. It is perhaps not surprising that only a handful of quotations from *The Scholar's Daughter* appeared in the *OED*, only one of which was published before Murray's death. It is an innocuous enough quotation ('My uncle thought I'd better train to be a doctor'), and Murray may even have failed to notice it among the copy presented to him for the verb *train* by his assistant Arthur Maling. Two quotations (for *suet pudding* and *surmise*) subsequently appeared in two of the first fascicles to be edited by Onions, and one found its way into the entry for *work* (verb), in the very last portion of the Dictionary to be completed.

his latest double section finished in time to be issued in June as announced; and, for the first time, he was having to do so without the help of Balk, whom he had so far been unable to replace. With a prodigious effort he finally signed off the last page of the 136-page section *Traik–Trinity* on 25 May; but the strain proved too much, and on the following night he was seized with violent abdominal pains. Appendicitis—of all things—was feared, or the bowel cancer which had killed Furnivall; but his doctors diagnosed obstruction of the bowel.[171] He responded to treatment, and was able to travel to Bournemouth to be with his wife, who was there recovering from another eye operation; but upon returning to Oxford—and, unwisely, travelling to London the day after his return to speak at a Philological Society Dictionary Evening—he relapsed.

[171] OED/B/3/2/6 27 May 1914 JAHM to Cannan.

Sir William Osler, called in once again as consultant, now diagnosed prostate trouble; his illness, or possibly the X-rays prescribed to treat it, left him unable to do much work for several months. Bradley was also troubled with ill health during the year (as was his wife), which obliged him to take lengthy breaks in the spring and autumn.[172] A welcome morale-boost for both men came with the decision of the University— long hoped for by Murray—to confer upon each of them the degree of D.Litt. *honoris causa*, although as Murray observed to his wife, the decision may have come about at this time because of fears that he might not survive, and would have to be made 'a post-mortem doctor'. Onions was also awarded an honorary MA, just in time for the publication of his first section (*Su–Subterraneous*).[173]

In addition to the health problems of the Dictionary's two senior Editors, there were further departures in the first half of 1914—Charlton Walker and George Carline from Bradley's staff, and Frederick Ray from Craigie's. The prospects for Murray's 'Grand Conjunction' were thus already looking extremely gloomy even before August, when the outbreak of war and the ensuing general mobilization reduced the available manpower still further. Craigie's assistant E. N. Martin signed up almost immediately with the Queen's Own Oxfordshire Hussars, the first Territorial unit to see action; G. F. Maxwell, who had only joined his staff in 1913, apparently left around the same time. Two other recruits followed at the end of 1914, G. G. R. Greene from Murray's staff (Royal Army Medical Corps) and J. W. Birt from Onions's (Oxfordshire and Buckinghamshire Light Infantry). Birt rose to the rank of sergeant, and became known within his battalion as 'a pillar of reliability',[174] but was gassed in 1918, resulting in permanent chest problems.

The remaining lexicographers pushed on doggedly. In October Craigie, who had in fact been making good progress during the year, informed Cannan that he was nearing the end of *Sq*; with the rest of S already allocated to Bradley and Onions (Bradley had taken *St*), where should he go next?[175] It was decided that he should move on to the letter V, on the basis that U, as well as the remainder of T, were still expected to be done by Murray: a striking vote of confidence in his chances of a full recovery. From the start of 1915, indeed, he did regain some strength, although he apparently recognized that the ridiculously long working hours of the past were no longer to be repeated: Harold Murray observes that at last 'he had to come down to a reasonable idea of a day's work', and to lay aside Dictionary work in the evenings.[176]

But there was no escaping the fact that progress, across the project, was now drastically slowed: the page totals for the first three months of 1915 were down by nearly

---

[172] HJRM pp. 255–6; *CWW* p. 310; OED/B/3/2/6 31 Aug. 1914 HB to Cannan.

[173] MP 4 Nov. 1914 JAHM to Hilda Murray (lost; quoted in *CWW* p. 293); information from OUA. Bradley, at his own request, received his degree on 17 November, three days later than Murray, so that the maximum honour could be paid to the chief Editor (*Times* 24 May 1923, p. 13); Onions, presumably for a similar reason, received his MA on 10 November.

[174] Rose (1920: 210).

[175] OED/B/3/2/6 15 Oct. 1914 WAC to Cannan.

[176] HJRM p. 258.

a third on the corresponding period of 1914. This was an inevitable consequence of the reduction in editorial staff, and of reduced numbers in other departments of the Press; there was also the fact that it was no longer possible to consult scholars in Germany and elsewhere, as all three Editors had long been in the habit of doing, particularly in regard to difficult etymologies. Murray's next section, which had been announced for 1 April, had to be put back until the following quarter; the double section *Spring–Standard*— containing, unusually, the work of two Editors—was issued in its place.[177] Murray in fact put the finishing touches to *Trink–Turn-down* in May; Cannan, offering his congratulations, suggested that a proper holiday would be in order, but Murray would have none of it.[178] He was already thinking about how to deal with the letter U, and in particular with the alarming body of accumulated evidence for words beginning with the prefix *un-*: 'It is not an easy job,' he had commented to his son Wilfrid in March, 'but I have thought a good deal about it and think myself more capable of tackling it with less un-preparedness and un-wisdom than any one else; but it will need skilful arrangement to keep the un-bounded prefix within bounds.'[179] He was also once again preoccupied with money matters, and in June wrote to the Delegates to complain that the wartime increase in income tax had left him out of pocket.[180]

It fell to Bradley to put a brave face on things in his report to the Philological Society. He claimed that the output from the four editorial teams (presumably during the preceding twelve months) had been 448 pages, 'nearly as usual' in spite of 'numerous obstacles and the difficulties of the Press';[181] but the monthly figures reported to the Delegates continued to tell a different story. Onions had at least managed to enlarge his team by the appointment of a young Scot, W. J. Fortune, and an even younger local lad, H. R. Simpson; but, as ever, new assistants took time to train, and the fourth Editor was still only contributing a tiny number of pages to the total.

As luck would have it, it was at this precise moment that the opportunity was taken, for the first time, to photograph all the Editors with their staffs. An unknown subscriber had suggested to Humphrey Milford that the *Periodical* could publish the Editors' portraits; Milford persuaded Cannan that a picture spread might have some publicity value; and arrangements were made for photographers to visit the Scriptorium and the Old Ashmolean in July.[182]

It was to prove an unrepeatable opportunity. On Saturday 10 July Murray was photographed in the Scriptorium with his assistants (see Figure 26); probably at the

---

[177] The cover copy of Onions's section of *Su–Subterraneous* included an announcement that a section of Murray's part of Volume X would be available on 1 April. Instead, on 25 March a section was issued containing Craigie's entries for *Spring–Ss* and Bradley's for *St–Standard*.

[178] HJRM p. 259 (quoting a lost letter from Cannan, dated May 1915).

[179] Quoted in Murray (1943: 124–5).

[180] FC 10, 23 June 1915. The Delegates were obliged to explain, regretfully, to Murray that they were unable to compensate him for loss of income resulting from government policy.

[181] PSOM 4 June 1915.

[182] ML 23 June 1915 HSM to Cannan.

FIGURE 26   James Murray photographed in the Scriptorium on 10 July 1915 with his assistants: (back row) Arthur Maling, Frederick Sweatman, F. A. Yockney, (seated) Elsie Murray, Rosfrith Murray.

same time a photograph of the rest of the staff—Bradley, Craigie, Onions, and their assistants—was taken outside the Old Ashmolean (see Figure 27). The photographer was engaged to return on the Monday to take an individual portrait of Murray; but on the Sunday, unusually, Murray was too tired to attend church, and when he went into the Scriptorium on Monday morning he felt unwell and returned to his house, where he was discovered to be suffering from pleurisy. The photographer was put off for a week, but Murray's final portrait photograph was never to be taken. He died of heart failure on 26 July.[183] (The last Dictionary entry in which Murray's handwriting can be seen in the copy, poignantly, is that for *twilight*. Corrections in the hand of Craigie, who took over as supervising Editor, appear from *twine* onwards.) Throughout his final illness he had remained keenly interested in the Dictionary, constantly asking whether reviews of his latest section had appeared. He would no doubt have bridled at the repetition, in the notice in *Notes & Queries*, of the old charge that the selection of quotations 'may represent, a thought too exhaustively, the modern newspaper press',

[183] HJRM p. 259; *CWW* pp. 311–12.

FIGURE 27   Bradley, Craigie, and Onions photographed with their assistants in July 1915 outside the Old Ashmolean: (back row) Wilfred Lewis, W. J. Fortune, George Watson, Eleanor Bradley, Mrs E. R. Powell, P. T. J. Dadley, H. R. Simpson, Henry Bayliss; (seated) Walter Worrall, C. T. Onions, Henry Bradley, William Craigie, L. F. Powell.

though the final comment ought to have mollified him: 'It is impossible in the short space at our disposal to exhaust a thousandth part of the good things Sir James has put before us.' He was spared the sight of Fennell's review in the *Athenaeum*, though he might have liked to see his old enemy single out so many entries for praise.[184] More praise came from Bradley in a fitting tribute, reproduced in the *Periodical* in September:

Almost within a week of his death he was still hard at work, showing, as Dr. Bradley wrote of a visit made to him, 'not a little of the zest and mental lucidity that I remembered of old'. In the preceding months, while barely convalescent from an illness that seemed to bring him to the gates of death, he had prepared, and at the appointed date [...] published, his usual 'double section'. 'The words contained in it', Dr. Bradley says, 'present an extraordinary number of

[184] *Notes & Queries* 24 July 1915, p. 79; *Athenaeum* 31 July 1915, pp. 71–2. In fact it is possible that by this time there had been a reconciliation between the two men: see Ogilvie (2012: 128) for a discussion of a letter of Murray's in the *Athenaeum* of 20 Oct. 1900 in which he acknowledges help from Fennell (in regard to the etymology of *jade*) with surprising warmth.

difficult problems, which are handled with the editor's characteristic sagacity and resource; the section is a piece of his work of which he might be proud.' [...] Sir James Murray at the beginning laid the lines and drew the plan; in the prosecution of the work, when it became clear that it must be shared, his amazing capacity for unremitting labour enabled him to take more than an equal part [...]. He will not write the last pages, but more than that of any other man his name will be associated with the long and efficient working of the great engine of research by which the Dictionary has been produced.[185]

The fact that this tribute appeared alongside the two July group photographs would no doubt have pleased Murray, in that they stressed—as he was often at pains to stress—the collective nature of the work on which he had been engaged for four decades. But Bradley was surely also right to place emphasis on Murray's own unique contribution. His name has become indelibly associated with the first edition of the *OED*, and deservedly so; he brought to the task a unique combination of prodigious linguistic (and specifically lexicographical) gifts, extraordinary energy and industry, and a powerful sense of commitment to and identification with the Dictionary. He could at times be a difficult man; but almost always this could be explained as an expression of his passionate determination that the Dictionary should be as good as it possibly could. For him his work was a God-given vocation; he had come to believe that the whole course of his life had been designed to prepare him for the position of Editor, and perhaps it was only his strong sense of vocation which sustained him through the long years of effort. It now remained to be seen how well the 'great engine of research' which he had built and directed could be driven to its destination by his successors.

---

[185] *Periodical* Sept. 1915, p. 201. The tribute was also printed in Bradley's section *Standard–Stead*.

8

After twilight: 1915–1923

Discussions must presumably have taken place at the Press during Murray's final illness, if not before, of the question of how the compilation of the Dictionary might have to be reorganized in the event of his death; but no formal record survives of any firm plans. Indeed, although Cannan was authorized to 'take all necessary steps' when the Finance Committee met on 30 July, he initially even hesitated over such basic questions as whether Murray's staff should continue to work in the Scriptorium.[1] In fact the remaining Editors, with their depleted staffs, were obviously in serious need of reinforcement, especially Onions, whose new assistants Fortune and Simpson left around this time—probably to join up—and who declared himself desperately in need of '[a]n experienced preparer of "copy" '; and in September Maling, Sweatman, Yockney, and Murray's daughters Elsie and Rosfrith were transferred to the Old Ashmolean.[2] There was also the matter of the Scriptorium's inanimate contents: the disposal of the slips, the many valuable books, and even the bookshelves was carefully considered, in consultation with Lady Murray and her son Oswyn. By early November Lady Murray could report to Cannan that the pigeonholes and shelving from the Scriptorium 'fit the room in the old Ashmolean, as if they had been made for it'.[3]

Amid all the disruption, all the various stages of work on the Dictionary, from the preparation of copy for the printer to the publication of completed sections, continued. Murray had already begun to finalize the copy for the final section of T, and the work needed to complete it was carried out by his former staff before being revised by Craigie; copy for T continued to be passed to the printer as it was ready, with batches sent on 28 and 29 July, just as they had been on the 20th and 22nd. After a hiatus in

[1] FC 30 July 1915; OED/B/3/2/7 7 Aug. 1915 Cannan to Oswyn Murray.
[2] OED/B/3/2/7 14 Aug. 1915 CTO to Cannan; FC 15 Sept. 1915. All the assistants were assigned to Onions, although Rosfrith Murray seems to have carried on her general role correcting bibliographical references for all of the Editors (OED/B/3/2/8 undated notes by Cannan recording reallocation of staff).
[3] OED/B/3/2/7 5 Nov. 1915 Ada Murray to Cannan. It is not known what use the Murray family made of the now vacant Scriptorium.

The Making of the *Oxford English Dictionary*. First edition. Peter Gilliver.
© Peter Gilliver 2016. First published 2016 by Oxford University Press.

August, this resumed on 9 September, when Murray's assistants can barely have settled into their new workplace. On 30 September Frederick Sweatman reported to Cannan that 'we have worked hard since Sir James' death, and probably the last of the copy for T will be sent to press next week'.[4]

However, even with the influx from 78 Banbury Road—and a further recruit to Craigie's team in September in the form of his sister-in-law Isabella Hutchen—the headcount in the Old Ashmolean was insufficient to maintain the necessary throughput of copy.[5] Bradley in particular, struggling with the many difficult words in *St*, was seriously slowed by having to prepare much of the copy from scratch himself; his total for August 1915 was a mere 3 pages (although he was at least able to make the 'splendid boast' to Cannan that he had managed to bring his Webster scale down to five and a third, the lowest achieved by any Editor for some years).[6] He gratefully accepted an offer of help from a young New Zealander, Kenneth Sisam, who had come to Oxford as a Rhodes Scholar in 1910 and so distinguished himself as a medievalist and Anglo-Saxon scholar that he had begun lecturing while still studying for his B.Litt. degree; Sisam joined Bradley's staff in October but left early in 1916, although this by no means marked the end of his contribution to the project.[7] Onions's progress would soon also be slowed by his involvement with another Press project: *Shakespeare's England*, a celebratory collection of articles on various aspects of life and thought in the age of Shakespeare, which was languishing without an editor following the resignation of Sir Sidney Lee. Onions was engaged as editor with a view to getting the book published in time for the tercentenary of Shakespeare's death in April 1916; the assistants Dadley and Yockney were also drafted in to help.[8]

In November Cannan began to prepare for a full review of the Dictionary's progress by the Delegates. For an estimate of the amount of work remaining he turned to Craigie, who seems to have taken over from Murray as the project's preparer of such figures, and who presented Cannan with the dispiriting assessment that the remaining parts of the alphabet would occupy 32 single sections.[9] The implications were clear, and serious: the four reduced staffs had managed rather less than a double section

---

[4] OED/B/3/2/7 30 Sept. 1915 Sweatman to Cannan.

[5] Also recruited at this time, apparently on Craigie's initiative, was a Belgian refugee, L. J. Pallemaerts, who was tasked with interfiling the collection of quotations which had accumulated at the Scriptorium for use on the Supplement to the Dictionary with a similar file which had now built up in the Old Ashmolean (OED/B/3/2/15 12 Jan. 1926 WAC to RWC). He continued to work on the Dictionary until the end of 1917, though whether exclusively on this task is not clear.

[6] OED/B/3/2/7 3 Nov., 2 Sept. 1915 HB to Cannan.

[7] OED/B/3/5/14 14 Aug. 1915 KS to HB; OED/B/3/2/14 9 Oct. 1925 KS to RWC. Sisam drafted entries in the range *step–stiff*, but gave up the work in early 1916; in the summer of 1917 there were hopes that he would resume, but this never came to pass (Ker 1972: 415–16). He later commented acerbically that the time he spent working on the Dictionary 'opened [his] eyes to the amount of time that can be virtuously wasted' (PBED 12944 25 June 1941 KS to C. Bailey).

[8] FC 16 Dec. 1915; *TPS* for 1917–20, p. 7. Lee, who had been dividing his time between the *Dictionary of National Biography* and several other projects, resigned in 1914; Onions seems to have turned the project around, and the book appeared on time (Bell 2013: 355). It also included a contribution from Bradley, in the form of an article on 'Shakespeare's English'.

[9] OED/B/3/2/7 30 Nov. 1915 Cannan to HSM.

between them in each of the first two quarters of 1915, with a further drop to barely 100 pages in the third quarter, and now with only three teams, the efforts of one of which were to be largely diverted elsewhere, the completion of the Dictionary—and the end of expenditure for the Press—was some years away. Cannan expressed his concern formally in a note to the Editors. The note has not survived, but the reply has: a carefully argued statement, signed by Bradley, Craigie, and Onions, pointing out that the slowing of progress in recent years could not be attributed simply to the reduction in staff numbers.[10] The two other causes which the Editors cited were a rise in editorial standards compared to the earlier parts of the Dictionary, 'necessitating more research and verification', and the constant increase in the amount of material to be assessed, including evidence for words and usages which had become current in recent years.

This does rather sound like the Editors digging their heels in; but they did also make some positive suggestions. Enclosed with the letter was a draft of a memorandum for possible distribution to all the assistants, emphasizing the need to make good progress and reminding them of a few time-saving measures; and the suggestion was also made that help be sought 'from two members of the former Scriptorium staff,—from one especially in the preparation of certain classes or groups of words'. This seems to be a reference to the scientific expertise of Arthur Maling, now a member of Onions's staff, who in fact had already begun to work on ranges of entries in *St*, where Bradley and his assistants were working.[11] The experiment was continued—and not only with scientific words: he dealt with such items of general vocabulary as *stir* and *stone*, for example—and Bradley acknowledged Maling's work on 'certain portions' of *St* in the 1919 preface to the half-volume *Si–St*, although Maling does not seem to have done similar work for Craigie in V. It is not clear whether the idea of an exhortatory memo to the staff was also taken up;[12] however, the staff did receive a different reminder of the premium placed upon productivity. Looking at the progress figures reported for the year by the three Editors, Cannan concluded that, although none of them had managed to get through 12 pages of Webster (now the minimum required to secure a bonus), Craigie—and, by implication, his staff—had only missed it because of the time spent by Craigie on the completion of T; accordingly, only Craigie's staff were awarded bonuses. In fact it seems unlikely that anyone will have felt hard done by, as most of the other assistants received comparable payments at the end of the year—Murray's former staff in recognition of the particular difficulties they had faced during their Editor's illness and following his death, and Bradley's for long service—and Watson and Dadley received salary increases; but the implicit message will not have been missed.[13]

---

[10]   OED/B/3/2/7 8 Dec. 1915 HB/WAC/CTO to Cannan.

[11]   The entry for the rare geometrical word *steregon* shows signs of having been revised by Maling, as do the scientific entries immediately following it; the definitions of *stereo*, and many of the words beginning with this prefix, are all drafted in Maling's hand. The bundle of slips containing these entries was sent to press on 3 December 1915.

[12]   Cannan certainly took the suggestion seriously: what appears to be a draft of such a memo to the assistants is preserved in OUPA (OED/B/3/2/7, c.10/11 Dec. 1915).

[13]   FC 16 Dec. 1915. Various notes by Cannan and the Editors regarding bonuses for 1915 are in OED/B/3/2/7.

The same review of salaries also saw a change in Bradley's position. From the start of 1916 he was paid £550 per annum, an increase of £50, in recognition of his role as the senior surviving Editor. He had raised this matter with Cannan in November, with quite extraordinary diffidence, despite the fact that he had received no increase in salary since his appointment as second Editor in 1888; it seems that it was only his concern to make adequate provision for his family that finally persuaded him to ask the Delegates to consider his case. In communicating their decision to Bradley, and recognizing 'the distinction of [his] contribution to the Dictionary', Cannan nevertheless did not miss the opportunity to 'lament the smallness of output'. No doubt Bradley took the hint, powerless though he may have been to do much about it.[14]

By way of confirmation that the project had now moved into a new, slower rhythm, the sections published in the four quarters following the death of Murray were all single sections: the first time this had happened for nearly twenty years. Murray's final section, *Turndun–Tzirid*, was finally published in March 1916. The slower progress was hardly surprising, given the project's depleted resources—not to mention the shortages and difficulties endured by the Press generally during the war years[15]—and also the continuing exceptionally challenging nature of the words in *St*: Bradley, looking back on the year's work in December 1916, asserted that no previous part of the alphabet had presented 'such a long unbroken succession of difficult words as we have had lately. It is in words of this kind that the existing dictionaries offer least help, and progress cannot be rapid.' To make matters worse, the material for *St* had not been sub-edited since the early 1880s, making the incorporation of later accessions an enormous additional task (although Craigie's assistants apparently gave some help in pre-processing at least the Old and Middle English materials).[16]

---

strafe

War is almost always a powerful driver of lexical innovation, and the First World War was no exception. Among the many new words and senses noted in 1916 by the veteran sub-editor William Robertson Wilson (who was also a prolific contributor of quotations) was the word *strafe*, which came to his attention when he read the following sentence— strikingly light-hearted given the circumstances—in a letter sent by an unnamed correspondent writing from the Front: 'There is not much Hun artillery fire, but as our guns strafe them well every day, I expect they will wake up and return the compliment.' A slip of paper bearing this quotation reached Oxford a few months later, as did another example of the word spotted by Wilson in the *Daily Mail* of 1 November 1916. At this point

Continued ➤

---

[14] OED/B/3/2/7 3 Nov. 1915 HB to Cannan; OD 19 Nov. 1915; OED/B/3/2/7 23 Dec. 1915 Cannan to HB.
[15] For the effect of the First World War on the Press see Whyte (2013: 72–6).
[16] OED/B/3/2/8 22 Dec. 1916 HB to Cannan, 29 Dec. 1916 WAC to Cannan.

work on the relevant section of *St* was well advanced, but even though the *OED*'s editors were generally cautious about including slang words of recent coinage—on the grounds that it was difficult to judge which would survive—Henry Bradley decided he would take a risk and include an entry for *strafe*. He later recalled (*Periodical* Feb. 1928, p. 24) that he had been 'rather challenging criticism' in doing so, and indeed following the publication of *Stillation–Stratum* in December 1917 at least one reviewer commented on its inclusion in terms which suggested that it might be regarded as premature: 'Dr. Bradley has not been able to resist the claims of the one German word which has become current among the crowd during the War' (*Notes & Queries* Mar. 1918, p. 90). However, he was vindicated in his decision, as the word went on to become firmly established in English, originally meaning 'to punish' (with allusion to its origin in the German slogan 'Gott strafe England', which became widely used as a greeting during the war, especially in Austria) but later also 'damage, injure' or 'attack'; it is now most commonly used specifically with reference to machine-gun fire from low-flying aircraft, a significant semantic shift which its German counterpart has not undergone. In 2014 a revised version of the entry was published in *OED Online*, including slightly earlier evidence of the word's use in English—the word can now be traced back to the summer of 1915—though the sardonic 1916 quotation from 'MS *Let. from Front*' was retained.

In spring 1916 the Press compiled and issued a new prospectus for the Dictionary: notwithstanding the lexicographers' struggles, it was evidently felt to be a good idea to proclaim afresh the project's achievements.[17] The main intention was of course promotional, but there is also a strong sense of a desire to celebrate, in the midst of war, a project which was now firmly established as an endeavour of national importance. The resulting pamphlet, entitled 'The Oxford Dictionary: A Brief Account', was issued in April, and subsequently incorporated into the Press's General Catalogue; it included a history of the Dictionary and a statement of the project's current position, and made favourable comparisons with the progress of some of the Dictionary's European counterparts.[18]

Further cause for celebration came in June with the election of Bradley to a fellowship at Magdalen College; this was accompanied by a handsome stipend, which greatly eased his financial position.[19] Craigie also had things to celebrate: not only

---

[17] Although the authorship of the pamphlet is unclear, the responsibility for the final form of the text seems to have rested with Cannan. A proof, dated 21 Mar. 1916, is preserved at OED/B/3/2/8.

[18] *Periodical* Apr. 1916, p. 36. The General Catalogue was issued in November 1916; an updated version of the pamphlet was issued in 1917 by the Press's New York office. The historical portion of the pamphlet was largely drawn from an earlier, now extremely scarce pamphlet of 1913 entitled 'A Brief Account of the Oxford Dictionary' (copy in OUPA at OED/B/3/2/6).

[19] Bradley described Magdalen as '*the* college of all others to which I should prefer to belong' (2 July 1916 HB to Reginald Lennard, quoted in Bridges (1928: 46–7): perhaps in part a reflection of the relationship which the Dictionary had built up through Murray's friendship with the College's President, Herbert Warren. His election was supported by an impressive list of testimonials from such figures as Robert Bridges (the Poet Laureate) and Joseph Wright (Magdalen College archives, ref. CMR/1/19/1 (report of committee 14 June 1916)).

did he produce a double section, *V–Verificative*, in October, but he also took up the newly reconstituted Rawlinson and Bosworth professorship in Anglo-Saxon.[20] The latter, welcome as it was in terms of recognition of Craigie's abilities, brought its own problems, in that his professorial responsibilities would inevitably divert more of his energies away from the Dictionary. There was compensation for this, of a kind, with the return of Onions from his work on *Shakespeare's England*; but the demands of the war effort would soon make further inroads on the project. By the end of the year Dadley, Powell, and Yockney had left, Powell and Yockney to do war work at the Admiralty, Dadley to join up. This left Craigie with only George Watson, his most senior assistant, Mrs Powell (formerly Ethelwyn Steane: she had married her fellow assistant Lawrence Powell in 1909), his sister-in-law Miss Hutchen, and young Edgar Martin, who had apparently returned to Dictionary work in the summer. It was clear, moreover, that Watson was unlikely to remain on the staff for much longer: conscription, which had been introduced in January for single men aged 18–41, had been extended to married men a few months later.

In December 1916 Craigie returned to the question of the amount of work remaining. Perhaps conscious of the alarm his assessment of the previous winter had caused, and notwithstanding the project's still very limited resources, he managed to be remarkably optimistic.[21] Bradley was already pencilled in as moving on to W once he had finished *St*, probably by the start of 1918, and Craigie would join him on that letter once he had finished both V—which he anticipated finishing in early 1917—and U, which he predicted would be 'easier than either S or W'. He evidently had no idea at this stage of the trouble that U would cause. Onions, meanwhile, would finish off the end of S, and then join Craigie and Onions on W. Thus it was possible, he declared, to envisage completion of the Dictionary by 1920, and to set up a succession of milestones (fixed with reference to the remaining pages of Webster) towards this goal. He proposed, as an efficiency measure which had already worked in *St*, that someone should be engaged specifically to work in advance on the Old and Middle English material in W; preliminary work of some sort apparently began almost immediately, although it is not clear who was involved.[22]

Craigie's optimism is even more remarkable when it is borne in mind that in December 1916 he already knew that he was due to lose the assistant on whom he depended most heavily. Sure enough, in February George Watson left the Dictionary, to join the Devonshire Regiment. He was soon on active service in France, but, remarkably, he continued to do work for Craigie, correcting proofs at the front, and

---

[20] Craigie had been appointed to the newly reconstituted professorship in November 1915, but only took up his responsibilities on 1 October 1916, as the post was suspended for the academic year 1915–16 (*Times* 20 Nov. 1915, p. 4). On his taking up the professorship his salary as Editor was reduced to £450 (OD 20 Oct. 1916).

[21] OED/B/3/2/8 16, 29 Dec. 1916 WAC to Cannan.

[22] Craigie's report to the Philological Society in April 1917 refers to 'work [...] being done to facilitate the preparation of [W] when the time comes' (*TPS* for 1917–20, p. 15).

even, on one occasion, in a captured German dugout, with a pencil in one hand and a candle in the other which frequently had to be blown out for fear of attracting enemy aeroplanes: surely one of the most spectacular acts of devotion to the project in its entire history.[23] Even such heroic efforts, however, could not compensate for his absence from the Old Ashmolean, and with Craigie down to only three assistants, two of whom were part-time, it was inevitable that his output would drop sharply. Onions also fell behind schedule—it was not until early 1919 that he sent the last of S to the printers—and Bradley and his assistants (all of whom remained with him throughout the war) continued to struggle with some exceptionally difficult material: far from finishing *St* in early 1918, they sent the last of it to the printers only a couple of weeks before Onions reached the end of S. During 1917 the quantity of copy sent to the printers by each Editor fell below 9 pages per month; however, in spite of the low productivity, the Press once again awarded 'War Bonuses' to the staff, as they had done in 1916 and would again in 1918.[24]

Progress towards actual publication was of course not solely dependent on editorial capacity, and by early 1917 the pinch was being felt in other quarters. Thanks to a shortage of composing staff and machine-men, a large amount of copy for V had to wait for months before the printers could deal with it; and in March a shortage of the heavy paper used to make covers for sections led to the first interruption in the pattern of quarterly issue since its inception. The Press decided to delay publication of what could have been a single section, or more, of printed and finalized material in *St*. Milford wrote with grim humour of his disappointment that 'an incidental war' might stop the progress of the Dictionary; but of course the difficulties were more than 'incidental'.[25] Only the spring quarterly issue was missed in 1917, but the following year saw only one rather short double section published: Onions's *Supple–Sweep*, issued in March. A few weeks later Onions himself left the project, having been summoned to the Admiralty, where his linguistic expertise may well have been put to good use in Room 40, the Admiralty's cryptographic unit.[26] Such reduced circumstances were no doubt accepted as in the national interest, at a time when the war effort was becoming all-consuming; certainly the situation does not seem to have been considered sufficiently

---

[23] *Periodical* 15 Apr. 1918, p. 232. This version of the anecdote does not name Watson, but he is identified in numerous later sources (e.g. Mathews 1985: 217).

[24] FC 18 Dec. 1916, 21 Dec. 1917, 20 Dec. 1918.

[25] *TPS* for 1917–20, p. 15; PSOM 1 June 1917; OED/B/3/2/8 10 Mar. 1917 HSM to Cannan. All the sections published during the remainder of the war were made double sections, thereby saving on the paper used for covers. Another sign of the privations of the home front may be seen in the noticeable increase, during the war years, in the extent to which the copy for Dictionary entries was written on re-used paper, including Dictionary proofs, envelopes, and even chocolate wrappers (see Figure 28). For an exploration of the varied interests of Arthur Maling, seemingly the most conscientious recycler, as revealed in the paper he brought in, see Gilliver (2005).

[26] FC 24 June 1918; additional information from Paul Gannon. The possibility that Craigie might also be called up was mentioned, but in the event he was exempted because of his professorial responsibilities; Bayliss, despite being nearly fifty, was now also eligible for war service, but the Vice-Chancellor succeeded in securing an exemption for him too (OED/B/3/2/8 18 June 1918 WAC to Cannan; FC 29 July 1918).

FIGURE 28   Versos of slips from Dictionary copy for words in W, showing recycled paper brought in by Arthur Maling, including (left to right) the dust jacket of an Esperanto translation of the play *Box and Cox*, the covers of some piano music, a promotional brochure for Letchworth, and the wrapper of a bar of chocolate (one of several varieties to be found among the copy slips).

serious to be discussed by either the Delegates or the Finance Committee. In any case, the Press's acquisition of the *Dictionary of National Biography* in 1917 must have given them much else to think about.[27]

The fact that, in late May 1918, Craigie ceased to supply copy to the printers altogether might be supposed to mark a further retrenchment; but this was merely an indication that he and his remaining assistants—joined, for a time, by his wife[28]—were directing their efforts elsewhere. Since the previous year they had begun to do some preparatory work in the letter U, Craigie having decided that this would be the best way of facilitating rapid progress through what he had predicted should be a straightforward letter. Straightforward from a philological point of view it certainly was, containing as it did relatively few words with a difficult etymology or sense history; but in another respect it would prove to be anything but straightforward. The problem was apparent from the

[27] For a full account of the transfer of the *DNB* to OUP, and of the earlier and later history of the *ODNB*, see Faber and Harrison (2002).

[28] Craigie acknowledges the work done by his wife on 'rearrangement' of material in his Preface to the letter U; she later proudly recalled this as 'her "war work"' (Wyllie 1961: 280).

most cursory glance at the materials: their scale, and in particular the vast quantity of material for words beginning with *un-*. Craigie had dealt with major productive prefixes before, notably *non-* and *re-*, but nothing compared with the capacity of *un-* to generate new (and, on the whole, not particularly interesting) formations. Moreover, the prefix's position near the end of the alphabet had maximized the time during which materials could accumulate. (Strictly speaking there were two distinct prefixes, one representing 'negation', as in *unkind*, and the other 'reversal or deprivation', as in *unlock*.) The result, as Craigie reported to the Philological Society, was a problem 'different from anything which has yet occurred in the course of the Dictionary': how could this voluminous portion of the lexicon be kept within reasonable bounds?[29] The problem was to prove an exceptionally intractable and painful one.

The Armistice must have lightened the hearts of the Dictionary workers as it did everyone else in Britain; a further boost to morale came a few months later with the return of various individuals from active service. Onions returned to the Dictionary in January 1919, as did Watson in March; Birt resumed work in May, and Powell rejoined his wife in the Old Ashmolean in September. There was also a new face: early in 1919 Bradley's staff was augmented by a former student of Craigie's, J. R. R. Tolkien, also fresh back from active service. His expertise in Old and Middle English suited him well for preparatory work on some of the Germanic words in W, as proposed by Craigie in 1916, and he was also soon drafting entries alongside Bradley's other assistants.[30] The renewal of manpower soon bore fruit: in his report to the Philological Society in March 1919 Onions was able to announce that he had sent the last of the letter S to the printers, so that the Dictionary was at last complete from A to T: or, at least, would be when the final sections of S (Bradley's *Stratus–Styx* and Onions's *Sweep–Szmikite*) were published.[31] With U and W both already in hand—though both would take longer than expected—Onions now moved ahead to X, Y, and Z.

With the reaching of this milestone, and the resumption of something like a normal routine, Craigie was in a mood to look to the future when his turn came to address the Philological Society in April.[32] Now that only something like one-sixteenth of the Dictionary remained to be published, he declared, it was time to think about what should be done next; indeed, he had been doing some thinking himself. The first requirement was of course a supplement to the Dictionary itself, to include corrections, new words and meanings, and antedatings; but even after both this and the main Dictionary were complete, 'English Lexicography will not be ended [...]. Each definite period will need special study and so a special dictionary for each

---

[29] *TPS* for 1917–20, p. 15. I have written elsewhere about Craigie's difficulties with *un-*: see Gilliver (2007).

[30] For a fuller account of Tolkien's work on the Dictionary see Gilliver et al. (2006).

[31] PSOM 7 Mar. 1919. Onions's report was delivered by the Society's Secretary, Leonard Wharton, as Onions himself was prevented from attending by illness.

[32] PSOM 4 Apr. 1919. An updated version of part of this address was later published in the Society's *Transactions*: see Craigie (1931).

period.'[33] He then went on to enumerate the various period dictionaries that he thought were needed. There should be dictionaries dealing with Old English, Middle English, and 'the inexhaustible riches of the virgin Tudor & Stuart periods' (regarding the last of which he lamented that 'handfuls' of material had been left out of the *OED* for want of space); the period 1675–1800 he saw as 'less remarkable linguistically', and perhaps not warranting its own dictionary; and for the period from 1801 onwards, which was characterized by an upsurge in technical vocabulary and the revival of older terms, he proposed '[a] dictionary fully devoted to definition [...] on Littré's scale, for written & spoken English of [the] whole English speaking world'. Finally, there was the older Scottish period—from the fourteenth to the seventeenth centuries—which, as a distinctive variety of English, merited its own dictionary; indeed Craigie had already begun to work at this project himself.[34] As if all of this historical lexicography was not enough, he was also closely involved in a proposal made in 1919 to publish a series of bilingual dictionaries, based on a standard wordlist. A version of this list was prepared in the Dictionary Room, and early consideration was given to Spanish and Serbian dictionaries, but nothing was ever published.[35]

Alluring as these visions of the future might be, the immediate focus of attention had to be the completion of the *OED* itself; and for Craigie this meant the letter U, on which he had now begun work in earnest. Material for the first few pages of the letter had already gone to the printers by the time of his report to the Philological Society, but the real difficulty, as he explained, lay with the *un-* material, amongst which were a large number of 'casually coined words of no permanence', which could hardly be ignored, despite their marginal interest, because they had attained some prominence through being used in well-known poems or other literary texts, or because they had been documented by earlier dictionaries. (In fact a large number of the most marginal words were excluded; Craigie's criteria for doing so are not stated in his published text, but the fact of being attested only by a single quotation dating from 1890 or later seems often to have been taken as marking a word (in the absence of any mitigating factors) as a possible candidate for omission. A few of the 'marginal' items were included within the prefix entries for *un-*, as illustrating the continuing productivity of various types of formation, but all were noted as having a first quotation dating from before 1890.[36])

---

[33] The idea of separate dictionaries for particular periods of English dates back to long before 1919. Craigie himself later recalled having outlined the concept during a lecture to the English Association in 1915 (Craigie 1941: 267); even earlier, in a lecture given in 1905, Henry Bradley had briefly touched on the idea of 'dictionaries [...] of the various successive stages' of the language (Bradley 1906: 314, cited in Aitken 1987: 112).

[34] Further on this project, which was eventually to become known as the *Dictionary of the Older Scottish Tongue*, see Chapter 10.

[35] Correspondence about these projected dictionaries, mainly 1919–23, is preserved in CPED 1016.

[36] Craigie's approach to *un-* may be compared to the less exhaustive treatment he had opted for at *re-*; a note by him in the entry for that prefix observes that '[t]he extent to which this prefix was employed in English during the 19th c[entury], and especially during the latter half of it, makes it impossible to attempt a complete record of all the forms resulting from its use'.

For the most straightforward words that were included, a full definition could arguably be dispensed with—a cross-reference to the relevant subsense of the prefix entry would suffice—but even with this minimal treatment, these words threatened to take up an alarming amount of space, especially if they were entered in their proper alphabetical position, a treatment which was preferable to including them as sub-lemmas within the main prefix entries in that it made them easier for the reader to find. Craigie had accordingly begun to contemplate what '[n]ew typographical devices' might be used to present the necessary information in the smallest possible compass, and now broached the subject of 'typographical condensation' with Cannan, warning that 'unless something drastic is done, either the scale will be very high, or a large number of words will not be found where they would naturally be looked for.'[37]

In the end he devised, and secured approval for, a method of 'condensation' which represents the first significant change in the typographical design of the *OED* since James Murray's experiments in the 1880s. Every word meriting an entry but needing no more by way of definition than a cross-reference to a sense of *un-* was given a headword in small type (and in ordinary bold face, rather than the Clarendon type used until now for all headwords), with the quotation evidence run on without a line break; and where two or more such words were adjacent, they were all run together in a single paragraph of continuous text. The new style achieved both compactness and ease of findability—although the usual system of entering less important words as sub-lemmas under their parent prefixes would have been more compact still—and Craigie was evidently sufficiently taken with it to use it again, or advocate its use, in relation to the prefixes *under-*, *up-*, and *well-*.

By the end of July 1919 copy as far as *Unattaint*, prepared in the new format, had arrived at the printers. But scale rapidly showed itself to be a problem. All of the Editors, including Murray in his last years, had long been exceeding the old limit of eight times Webster; Murray's final letter, T, had ended up with a Webster scale of 12, and this seems gradually to have been accepted as a new realistic figure.[38] In September, however, projections drawn up for Cannan for the remaining letters of the alphabet were accompanied by Onions's comment that 'The scale of *un-* seems likely to vary considerably; thus from *unappropriate* to *unattentive* occupies ¼ of [a] col. in Webster and makes 16 of ours, a scale of 64.' Only slightly less alarming was the figure of 16 given as the overall scale for the portion of U that was now in type. Onions also had troubles of his own: in October he reported that the absence of Sweatman following a serious accident had 'upset [his] programme of output' for the year, and was 'likely to result in a six months' drag'.[39] In the event Sweatman seems to have recovered fairly quickly, but the hiccup can hardly have been good for the nerves of the Delegates. Within a few months Onions was to lose another experienced assistant, when Elsie

---

[37] OED/B/3/2/8 23 Apr. 1919 WAC to Cannan.

[38] The regular spot on the agenda of Delegates' meetings at which the progress of each Editor (and his scale compared to Webster) was reported had been quietly dropped in November 1915.

[39] OED/B/3/2/8 29 Sept. 1919 CTO to Cannan; 23 Oct. 1919 CTO to RWC.

Murray left for South Africa to stay with her brother Wilfrid. Initially this was for health reasons, but in fact she never returned to Dictionary work: in September she married a South African farmer, Alexander Barling.[40]

As if this were not enough, Bradley had found himself forced to delay sending copy to the printers for longer than usual. Some of the older Germanic words were so variable in their spelling that further evidence for a word might turn up (filed under a different form of the headword) long after the relevant entry had seemed finished: the verb *wade*, for example, had various inflections beginning with *wo-*, quotations for which, if filed under this spelling, would be separated from the main evidence for *wade* by some thousands of slips. It was obviously quicker and cheaper to take account of such new material when the entry was still a pile of slips than it would be to make the necessary corrections in proof. Bradley was careful not to let the stock of material waiting to be typeset get so low that there was a danger of the printers running out of copy; but his approach nevertheless represented an uncomfortable paring of margins.

It seems unlikely, however, that Bradley's note to the Secretary of 16 December describing this difficulty—offered by way of explanation when it had become apparent that only one sheet (8 pages) of W would be 'passed for press' before the end of 1919[41]— was given much immediate consideration, for the simple reason that its intended recipient had died the previous day.

The unexpected death of Charles Cannan, after a short illness, could well have dealt a serious blow to the Dictionary. As it was, his place as Secretary was taken by Robert Chapman, whose years of apprenticeship as Assistant Secretary, not to mention his long-standing interest in the Press's lexicographical projects, stood him in good stead to maintain continuity.[42] He does indeed seem to have hit the ground running: within days of his formal appointment as Secretary he was asking Bradley and Craigie to set down their thoughts as to what projects the *OED* lexicographers might turn to once they had finished the main dictionary, in regard both to 'the great work itself' and to 'the creation of new works on the old foundation'.[43] He did not receive an immediate reply; but the current state of the project, in particular the continuing excessive scale of *Un-*, was soon clamouring for his attention. On 16 March he received a report from Onions of 'N.E.D. Progress to Date' which showed that Craigie's treatment of U (which had now reached *Uncut* in proof) was now exceeding Webster by a factor of 18½.[44] Craigie would soon give his reasons for disregarding Webster as a yardstick,

---

[40] FC 4 Mar. 1920; Ruthven-Murray (1986: 90).

[41] OED/B/3/2/8 16 Dec. 1919 HB to 'Secretary'.

[42] Chapman's involvement in several of the Fowler brothers' dictionaries, both before and after his appointment to the Secretaryship, is well documented in McMorris (2001). He is probably best known today for his work on Johnson, Jane Austen, and Trollope.

[43] OED/B/3/2/9 26 Jan. 1920 RWC to HB. A corresponding letter to Craigie does not survive, but it is clear that a similar question was put to him.

[44] OED/B/3/2/9 16 Mar. 1920 CTO to RWC. Bradley and Onions were managing Webster scales of 15 and 12.6 respectively at this point.

but Chapman's reaction—like that of some of his predecessors when first confronted with unwelcome news from an editor of the Dictionary—was that he knew better. He immediately wrote to Percy Matheson, a classicist and historian and a member of Finance Committee, enclosing the 'revelations of C.T.O. very secret': the excessive scale in *Un-* was 'not due in the main to heaps of words not in Webster, but it is alleged [presumably by Onions] to inadequate condensation of copy. I am bound to say that the treatment of *uncertain* and *uncouth* seems to me not only excessive but illegitimate; the divisions don't correspond to real differences of sense.' Anticipating the troubles to come (and showing his familiarity with the project), Chapman insisted that 'we must make a stand against laxity *in extremis*. Craigie has always been reputed the practical thrifty editor, which makes it the more surprising.' He also immediately contacted the Press's Controller (the man in charge of printing operations), Frederick Hall, asking how far the material had been set up in plates. After a flurry of further memos, and a meeting of Finance Committee, Chapman instructed Hall 'The scale is impossible— you had better plate no more before the Easter holiday.' On the same day, still not quite able to believe the magnitude of the problem he had inherited, he wrote to Craigie: 'The printers allege that the scale of U is 19. Can this be possible? I had hoped for a reduction of scale in Un-.' Craigie was not reassuring: the scale was 'between 18 and 19, and I see no way "on historical principles" of reducing it on Un-. [...] It was clear from the first that the scale of Un- would be exceptional; hence the new devices in printing, & the omission of definitions wherever possible.' With this letter Craigie enclosed some proofs, which indeed showed 'how useless Webster has become as a standard': in the range from *uncommunicativeness* to *unconcernedly* Webster listed only 11 words, whereas the *OED* proof had entries for over 100.[45]

This was too much for Chapman. He summoned Craigie to a meeting with himself and the two Delegates D. H. Nagel and Sir Walter Raleigh, with a note whose sense of crisis is palpable: 'This is very serious. $21 \times 18 = 378$, which is in the neighbourhood of £1500 for composition corrections and plates alone.'[46] Craigie's response shows his unwillingness to go over old ground: 'I had several talks with Cannan [about the difficulties of U]. It will be very difficult to make any important reduction of the scale without some serious departure from the methods hitherto followed in the Dictionary.'[47] But Chapman briefed both Nagel and Raleigh carefully for the meeting: not only had both Matheson and David Nichol Smith (Goldsmith's Reader in English, and Raleigh's successor as the Press's principal adviser on English literature) inspected the proofs and found the treatment 'very excessive on its merits', but even Onions

---

[45] OED/B/3/2/9 16 Mar. 1920 RWC to P. Matheson; 17 Mar. 1920 RWC to F. Hall; 24 Mar. 1920 RWC to Hall, RWC to WAC; 25 Mar. 1920 WAC to RWC.

[46] OED/B/3/2/9 26 Mar. 1920 RWC to WAC (marked 'Urgent'). David Nagel was a distinguished chemist, and Walter Raleigh had held the chair of English literature at Oxford since its foundation in 1904.

[47] OED/B/3/2/9 26 Mar. 1920 WAC to RWC. In fact Chapman was always dubious about this; he later suggested that whatever approval Craigie had secured from Cannan 'cannot have been with knowledge (on C.C.'s part at least) of all the facts' (OED/B/3/2/10 24 Feb. 1921 RWC to T. B. Strong (Bishop of Ripon)).

'privately holds, very strongly, that in such words one quotation per century is quite enough.'[48] In several cases more quotations were given for the negative beginning with *un-* than had been given for the corresponding positive: 40 quotations for *unconcerned*, for example, compared with 12 for *concerned*, 22 for *unconstrained* as against 13 for *constrained*, and so on.

The meeting was fixed for Monday 29 March. Two days earlier, however, Craigie dropped a bombshell. In a long letter to Chapman he set out his view of the situation, including an assessment of how much longer U might take, and suggestions as to how the remainder of W might be divided up when all three editorial teams were available to tackle it. He considered it 'unlikely that the whole of U can be in type before the autumn of 1921'—whatever ways were found to reduce the scale ('and I am open to any practical suggestions on this point'), or to accelerate the printing. He went on:

By 1 Oct. 1921, however, at least half of W should be completed, and the preliminary work done for most of the remainder. In view of this, I should for the present like to regard the end of U as a point beyond which my regular work on the Dictionary might be materially diminished. I find it increasingly difficult to combine the satisfactory discharge of professorial and other duties with the regular and close attention to details which the Dictionary requires, unless I sacrifice all other interests and cease to keep up correspondence with scholars [...]. I also now have on hand considerable collections of material connected with my own special studies, and am desirous of setting to work on these as soon as possible.[49]

Of course Craigie had for some time interested himself in other projects besides the *OED*; but until the appearance of this letter there is no evidence that any of these other claims on his attention were in any danger of displacing the Dictionary as his chief priority. Now, however, it must have been clear to Chapman that Craigie was dangerously close to losing patience with the whole enterprise. The stakes could hardly have been higher.

No records of the meeting survive, but it does seem that Craigie agreed to do what he could. The following day he informed Chapman that he had 'given instructions for the severest possible pruning of the next make-up [...] and will submit this for consideration before returning anything further to the printers'; he even asked the printers to return the copy for the prefix *under-* (which was proving to be similarly expansive) so that that material, too, could be reviewed. He also sent Chapman a careful consideration of how the Dictionary's human resources might be deployed after completion, regarding which he envisaged three projects: a Supplement, which he felt should be 'reduced to the narrowest limits'; an already projected bibliographical work provisionally entitled 'Records of English Literature', to which he thought some of the Dictionary's assistants would be well suited (and on which his sister-in-law had already done some work); and, most ambitiously, an 'Oxford Dictionary of Modern English' (something like the

---

[48] OED/B/3/2/9 26 Mar. 1920 RWC to D. H. Nagel.
[49] OED/B/3/2/9 27 Mar. 1920 WAC to RWC.

'Littré-style' dictionary of the nineteenth and twentieth centuries which he had proposed to the Philological Society), for which he saw Onions as an ideal editor.[50]

Chapman declared himself delighted with this 'masterly disquisition on the future';[51] but it would be some time before he could concern himself with anything other than the Dictionary's present difficulties. In April Craigie sent him 'a specimen of cutting-down [...]. It takes a good deal of time, and would give the printer a good deal of work, without effecting such a reduction of scale as you would like to see.' Chapman recognized that Craigie was doing his best, and replied in as encouraging a tone as he could manage: 'I can see how troublesome and vexatious the process of cutting in proof must be and when it is done it is as you surmise very far short of what I should like! But I am sure it is well worth while even so.' The two men met again on 22 April, and Craigie was persuaded to squeeze things even further.[52]

There now followed a period during which the work of the Editors, particularly their scale compared to Webster, came under unprecedentedly close scrutiny: closer, indeed, than in the worst days of the crisis of 1896. Chapman arranged to be informed of the estimated scale of each batch of copy as it came in; composition would not proceed without his explicit approval. Chapman knew exactly what he was doing, and commented wryly to Hall: 'I am frightening the editors.'[53] Not that the scare tactics operated equally on all three: although Hall prepared estimates of scale for each batch of copy submitted by Bradley, Craigie, and Onions throughout the next few weeks, Chapman authorized him to 'go ahead [...] with Bradley generally unless I say stop'. The fact that all three Editors (to each of whom Chapman passed on copies of his own figures) were regularly failing to come anywhere near a scale of 12 must have left Craigie feeling particularly hard done by.[54]

It could be argued that both Bradley and Onions were also working on letters which were particularly liable to require lengthy treatment. Bradley made just this point to Chapman: 'I am afraid my "scale" will not show any improvement at present [...]. W is the *first* letter that has *no* Greek and Latin derivatives. It is on the classical words that space can be saved; when we have the luck to get a run of them the scale goes down.' Onions, too, was dealing with a letter without any significant Greek or Latin content, which gave him little cause for optimism: 'on the whole stretch X–Z we

---

[50] OED/B/3/2/9 30 Mar. 1920 WAC to RWC; 30 Mar. 1920 WAC to [RWC]. Bradley had also written to Chapman with his thoughts on the future, but these amounted to little more than an admission that it was hard to say what could or should be done with the materials which had accumulated with a view to use in a Supplement to the Dictionary until they had been thoroughly assessed (OED/B/3/2/9 2 Mar. 1920 HB to RWC).

[51] OED/B/3/2/9 30 Mar. 1920 RWC to WAC. Brewer (2007: 27) cites this letter as an example of Chapman's ability to come up with 'carefully worded responses [to Craigie's proposals] which flattered while surrendering little'.

[52] OED/B/3/2/9 7 Apr. 1920 WAC to RWC, 21 Apr. 1920 RWC to WAC.

[53] OED/B/3/2/9 22 Apr. 1920 RWC to F. Hall.

[54] OED/B/3/2/9 3 May 1920 RWC to F. Hall. Craigie had reported to the Philological Society that the scale was now 'fifteen times [Webster] at the lowest' (PSOM 9 Apr. 1920).

may be able to average out at 12, but in any selected bit of Y we may reach 20 at any moment.'[55]

Craigie was now running out of options. On 10 May he admitted to Chapman that he was 'at a loss to know what can profitably be done to reduce the scale of *Under-*, which so far comes to an average of 16 […] only extensive omissions of minor words, or combination of distinct senses, can alter the situation appreciably. I have already omitted a considerable number of special terms which are treated at length in the American dictionaries, and I think it unadvisable to go very far in this direction.' Of course it was the expense that was of most concern to the Press; and Craigie had begun to wonder whether an appeal for funds from some external source might improve matters. He asked Chapman for an estimate of production costs for U, and of the likely increase in these if the scale compared to Webster were to slip from 12 to 16. He already had an external source in mind: a personal connection with George MacLean of the American University Union in Europe led him to be optimistic that funds might be raised in the United States. Chapman obliged with some figures: the extra cost, he estimated, of producing a U volume on a scale of 16 rather than 12 would hardly be short of £1,000. '[I]t would be very suitable if someone would come to our assistance with a really handsome grant in aid […] and there is no better insurance of immortality.' Meanwhile, under pressure from Hall, Chapman eventually allowed composition of *under-* to proceed—but he was determined to keep a tight rein thereafter: 'dont go on to *Une* without getting scale approved by me, please.'[56]

Matters deteriorated drastically, however, long before Craigie reached *une-*. On 17 May he wrote in some alarm to Chapman:

I enclose a comparative statement of the Dictionary material compared with 5 lines of Webster [namely the entries for *undeserver* and *undesigning*]. I have reduced the Dictionary entries and quotations to a very low point, and the scale remains at about 48! The whole of the next column of Webster is similarly out of all relation to the actual number of words, and any natural treatment of these would give a scale anywhere between 30 and 40.[57]

After a crisis meeting with Chapman, Craigie spent a week analysing the materials in a range of *und-* which corresponded to one and a quarter columns of Webster. Try as he might, the scale remained horrendously large. His letter reporting this in detail to Chapman is worth quoting at length.

I have spent about a week in reducing a portion of U to the lowest limits of natural compression. This portion covers 1¼ columns in Webster; the reduced copy for the printers is sufficient to fill about 40 columns of the O.E.D., which gives a scale of 32. By inclusion of the next column of Webster (which contains *Undulation* and *Undulatory*) the scale for 2¼ columns would fall to 21,

[55] OED/B/3/2/9 12 May 1920 HB to RWC; 8 May 1920 CTO to RWC.
[56] OED/B/3/2/9 10 May 1920 WAC to RWC; 13 May 1920 RWC to WAC; 11 May 1920 RWC to F. Hall.
[57] OED/B/3/2/9 17 May 1920 WAC to RWC.

but would be followed by an immediate rise which I cannot at present estimate exactly. These facts lead me to make the following remarks and suggestions [...]

1. No reduction of the greater portion of U to a normal scale can be effected by ordinary methods of condensation. To bring it down even to a scale of 12 would imply the abandonment of principles which have been observed from the beginning of the dictionary, and would involve arbitrary selection of the words to be recorded and illustrated, as well as an imperfect presentation of the history of those included. The result of this would be to lower the standard of the dictionary in two ways. In the first place, it would be necessary, both for the saving of space and for the sake of consistency, to omit many words which are of minor importance, but are already recorded and illustrated in previous dictionaries. In the second, the Dictionary could no longer be regarded as a complete record of the language, and it would assuredly be felt that this portion of it was imperfect and unsatisfactory. [...] (As an example of the difficulty of omitting even insignificant words, it may be mentioned that the passage containing Ruskin's *undisappointable* has been sent in by five different readers. Lowell's *undisprivacied* (besides being recorded in the Century Dict.) is the subject of a long note in Fitzedward Hall's 'Modern English' and is specially mentioned by W. D. Howells in commenting on Lowell's language.)

2. At least two-thirds of the work required to prepare U for the printers has already been done. Strict reduction of the prepared copy to the lowest possible scale can be effected by a certain amount of time being spent on it; but to re-cast the main portion of it, so as to produce something like the normal scale of earlier letters, would involve additional labour and time [...]

3. That the increased scale of U (as also of W) is due to natural causes appears clearly from a comparison of these letters in the standard *Deutsches Wörter-buch* with earlier portions of the same work. [...]

4. As the problem is ultimately one of expense, I would suggest that the first consideration should be how to meet this without impairing the quality of the last volume of the Dictionary. It is obviously impossible to do so on a commercial basis, as the cost of volume X. would be out of all proportion to that of the earlier volumes. The alternative is an endeavour to obtain the necessary funds from other sources by private or public appeals for support [...] A sufficient amount of outside aid would enable the Dictionary to be completed in a worthy manner, and without the feeling that the work was being done at rates no longer adequate to the changed conditions of the times. (In my own case the probability is that the salary now paid has no more than half the net value it had in 1916.)

5. If these proposals are to be acted upon, it will be necessary to do so as promptly as possible [...]. The situation as regards U is such that further copy cannot be sent to the printers until the question is settled.[58]

---

[58] OED/B/3/2/9 31 May 1920 WAC to RWC.

This letter sets out clearly and vividly the practical difficulties; but it is noteworthy that Craigie chose to bring up the question of his own salary and of the payment of other Dictionary staff. It seems that, while fully understanding the Delegates' reasons for being unable to allow things to proceed as they were, Craigie felt that the Press was not doing all it could to help.

Chapman circulated Craigie's letters of 17 and 31 May to the Delegates, but supplemented these with a considerably longer memorandum of his own, in which a number of further points are made. His estimate of the increased cost of producing U on a scale of 16 times Webster as opposed to 12 was now (for good reasons) much larger—the excess being more like £2,700. In a section headed 'Possible Retrenchment', after conceding the particular difficulties experienced by Bradley and Onions in W and Y, he declared: 'The obvious view is that *Un*, as duplicating a large part of the rest of the alphabet, lends itself to condensed treatment.' After noting five qualifications to this view—including the fact that not all *un*-words have obvious meanings and that many of them are historically more important than the corresponding positives—he concluded:

Nevertheless those Delegates who have examined the proofs, and those by whom they have been advised, are of opinion that the treatment is too liberal. Dr Craigie allows that there is force in the criticism, and is prepared to make [...] substantial reductions. To go further, and make a definite departure of method, on the ground of financial necessity and of the inferior importance of this part of the alphabet, would no doubt be defensible [...]. But the practical difficulties of carrying out such a policy are serious [...]. Dr. Craigie [...] is convinced that it would retard the completion of the work, which as he points out would swell the editorial expenses.

The memo ends with a list of specific instances, taken from proofs of entries in *unc-*, of treatment which Chapman regarded as too expansive.[59]

The stage, then, was set for what Chapman called 'a full-dress debate'.[60] The Delegates resolved 'not to press for any departure from the methods of the Dictionary, but to urge Dr. Craigie to keep Un- words within the narrowest possible limits (especially of quotations).' They also decided against a public appeal for funds, but encouraged Craigie to make any private approaches as he saw fit.[61] The Delegates' formal resolution was, of course, couched in such general terms as to be useless as far as practical guidance was concerned; Chapman went a little further in his own communication to Craigie, presumably with the approval of at least some of the Delegates (e.g. 'your device of "freq. in 17 C" was thought very helpful, and it was suggested that (e.g.) s.v. *unadequate* [...] not many quotations are required and that the two of 1644 and 1651 ought certainly

[59] OED/B/3/2/9 Copy of 'Memorandum for the Delegates', signed by RWC and dated 2 June 1920.
[60] OED/B/3/2/9 7 June 1920 RWC to Sir W. Raleigh.
[61] OD 11 June 1920. Craigie was also asked to convey the Delegates' views to Bradley and Onions (OED/B/3/2/9 14 June 1920 RWC to WAC).

[to] be cut down'), but on the whole there was very little by way of specific suggestions as to how the scale was to be reduced.[62] He also made a worrying reference to the possible 'gradual restriction of the staff' as the Dictionary approached completion. (At the same time, however, there was good news for the staff as far as remuneration was concerned: it was decided to abandon the scheme of bonus payments for productivity in favour of regular salaries.[63] Perhaps this was simply a way of acknowledging that, with the Webster scale running so high, there was no chance of anyone making enough progress through the pages of Webster to earn a bonus.)

Following the Delegates' meeting the embargo on composition of *Un* was lifted, but Chapman did not take his eye off the ball—the Webster scales achieved in each range continued to be reported to him, and to the Editors—and the figures were not encouraging: between June and September several ranges in both U and Y exceeded a scale of 30.[64] However, the matter seems to have been allowed to ride over the Long Vacation. Chapman in any case had other preoccupations, including the Bradley family's need for new accommodation,[65] the implications (in terms of salary and reduced availability for Dictionary work) of Onions's appointment to a University lectureship in English,[66] and a potential dispute with the manufacturers of Vaseline over Craigie's entry for the word. He had also begun to wonder what could be done by way of securing a fitting honour—a knighthood, or perhaps even the Order of Merit—for Bradley, who was now approaching his seventy-fifth birthday; a chance meeting with Herbert Fisher, the Minister of Education, afforded him an opportunity to point out that it might be unwise to delay such recognition until the completion of the Dictionary. He followed this up with an approach to the well-connected Herbert Warren of Magdalen, and continued to worry away at the question, but without immediate result.[67] Such things took time; but how much time was there?

---

[62] Comments of the type '(Freq. in 17th c.)' had been included in a few Dictionary entries from Volume I onwards; they first appear in U at *undauntable* and *undauntedness*, but are hardly used often enough to make much of a difference to scale.

[63] FC 24 June 1920.

[64] OED/B/3/2/9 14 June 1920 RWC to F. Hall; 25 June, 7, 9, 21 July 1920 Hall to RWC; 25 Sept. 1920 RWC to 'The Editors'.

[65] It seems that Bradley's current residence was to be put up for sale; the Delegates agreed to purchase a lease on 173 Woodstock Road and rent it to Bradley and his family, 'to avoid leaving the old people in the street' (OED/B/3/2/12 24 May 1923 RWC to H. Warren).

[66] There seems to have been some expectation that Onions might be appointed to the Merton chair in English, which had been left vacant since the death of Arthur Napier in 1916 (OED/B/3/2/9 21 July 1920 W. Raleigh to RWC), but in the event this went to H. C. Wyld, professor of English at Liverpool and a distinguished philologist, who in fact went on to produce a substantial English dictionary of his own (*The Universal Dictionary of the English Language*, 1932). Onions's lectureship came with a stipend of £150; he was guaranteed a total salary 'from University Sources' of £750, after he had apparently made representations to Chapman about financial difficulties (OED/B/3/2/9 RWC note on meeting with CTO 27 July 1920; 30 Sept. 1920 RWC to CTO). It should not be overlooked that Onions, like Murray, raised a large family: by this point there were seven children, who would eventually be joined by three more.

[67] OED/B/3/2/9 copy of letter 17 July 1920 RWC to Herbert Fisher; draft letter 3 Nov. 1920 [RWC] to Warren.

The start of Michaelmas term brought the uneasy calm over scale to its inevitable end; the spotlight now fell once again on Craigie, as both Bradley and Onions had

---

Vaseline

The practice of giving a new name to something for commercial reasons stretches back centuries, and some of these names appeared in dictionaries long before the *OED* (whose first published entry for such a word seems to be that for *antigropelos*, a name for a kind of waterproof leggings, although this is described as '[o]riginally, a proprietary name', having subsequently passed into general use). However, during the nineteenth century the idea that such a name could be regarded as a type of property began to take hold, and in due course this began to have significant implications for lexicographers. The Trade Marks Registration Act of 1875 enabled individuals and companies to register a name, and to seek to prevent anyone else from using that name to 'pass off' their own goods as being those of the registered owner. One such case, which reached the High Court in 1903, involved the use of the word *tabloid*, which the manufacturing company Burroughs, Wellcome & Company (who had registered it in 1884) sought to prevent others from using; by the time Murray came to prepare an entry for the word in 1909 he had already received many letters from Burroughs, Wellcome as part of their efforts to protect their rights, and the exact form of the entry was carefully discussed with lawyers before publication. Subsequently other proprietary names became the subject of similar correspondence, often involving demands that the name of a manufacturer be included in the entry in question (as it had been for *tabloid* when it eventually appeared in 1910).

In May 1920 the Chesebrough Manufacturing Company, who manufactured petroleum jelly under the name *Vaseline*, complained to the Press about the *OED* entry for *petrolatum*, which was described as 'the official name in U.S. Pharm[acy] for pure vaseline'. They went on to complain about the failure of Craigie's entry for *Vaseline*, which had been published in 1916, to mention their association with the product, and ultimately secured an undertaking that the entry would be amended. A correction was made in the original plate, adding the information that *Vaseline* was 'a proprietary term, introduced by R. A. Chesebrough in 1872': one of the very rare occasions on which the published text of the Dictionary has been subsequently altered in response to an approach from an external party. The amendment was retained when the Dictionary was reissued in 1933. (No change was made to the entry for *petrolatum*.)

By the time the second Supplement began to be compiled there were many more such names in circulation, and correspondence between lawyers and the compilers of dictionaries regarding the proprietary status of a particular term had become a regular occurrence. After taking advice, Robert Burchfield published a disclaimer in Volume I of the Supplement, noting (p. xxiii) that some words were included 'which are or asserted to be proprietary names or trade marks', and stating that '[t]heir inclusion does not imply that they have acquired for legal purposes a non-proprietary or general significance nor any other judgement concerning their legal status.' (He went on to publish an extended discussion of the subject in Burchfield 1973b: 15–22.) Similar statements have subsequently been included in most Oxford dictionaries, and a version of the disclaimer can be found in *OED Online*.

reached material which proved susceptible of much greater concision.[68] Chapman did his best to be light-hearted in his remonstrance with Craigie over some recent proofs in *unc-*:

I am afraid you will accuse me of damnable iteration; but I am bound to say I still think we are spilling more treasure than we ought over some of the Un words. [Various comments on *uncouple* and adjacent words follow.] When I come to *uncounteracted* and *uncounterbalanced* I am moved to tears. It is so unavoidably unreadable and unentertaining. The financial and industrial stringencies which we had before us a few months ago have altered only to become worse; and I am more than ever uncomfortable—so you wont think me unreasonable.

He sent a copy of these comments to the recently appointed director of the *Dictionary of National Biography*, Henry Davis, accompanied by further mild remonstration: 'Raleigh and Nagel and I had a go at him some time ago, and I wrote him a grandis epistola from the Delegates; but the little man bobs up again in another place. [...] He has fixed ideas about the methods of the Dictionary, and cant see that they are stultified by strict application to this dreadful material.'[69]

Craigie, unsurprisingly, was not disposed to make a light-hearted reply to Chapman's comments. He pointed out that the proofs Chapman had criticized were for material that had already been in type by the end of March; and suggested that, if further compression was really required, 'some disinterested outsider' could be asked to read the proofs with this specific aim. Chapman duly asked D. G. Hogarth, the distinguished orientalist (and Delegate), to comment on a range of proofs, but only after he had tackled the material himself and, as he put it, 'made a bloody mess'. Both men suggested extensive excisions; Craigie's response to their combined comments is not preserved. Davis undertook to speak to Craigie himself, as a comparatively independent figure, on the subject of scale, but it is not clear whether he ever did so: the last mention of this is a brief chivvying note sent by Chapman in November, only a few days before he left for a business trip to New York.[70] (While there Chapman was contacted by George MacLean of the American University Union, who gave him the discouraging news that the Union, although sympathetic, was not in a position to solicit contributions to *OED* production costs.[71])

Thus it was the Assistant Secretary, John Johnson, who on 2 December received news from Craigie of a new perspective on the *Un-* crisis. Craigie had discovered

<hr/>

[68] OED/B/3/2/9 22 Oct. 1920 RWC to CTO (on achieving a scale of 6.57 in the first part of Z: 'Incredible!'), RWC to HB (with 'Congratulations' on achieving 11.25 on *warrenage–warstel*).

[69] OED/B/3/2/9 9 Oct. 1920 RWC to WAC, RWC to H. W. C. Davis.

[70] OED/B/3/2/9 13 Oct. 1920 WAC to RWC; [n.d.] D. G. Hogarth to RWC; 16 Oct. 1920 RWC to WAC; 20 Oct., 20 Nov. 1920 RWC to Davis.

[71] OED/B/3/2/9 21 Dec. 1920 George MacLean to RWC. Further efforts to secure external funds—even from the London livery companies—continued for a few months, but without success (OED/B/3/2/10 9 Nov. 1921 J. R. H. Weaver to RWC).

that there were in fact excellent grounds for regarding the 1864 edition of Webster as offering no guidance as regards the scale of *un-*. While in most respects the 1864 Webster text was an expanded version of that of the 1847 edition, in the later part of *un-* there had been a considerable reduction in the number of words covered: in the range *unfold* to *unfortified*, for example (the copy for which Craigie had just sent to the printers), where the 1847 edition listed 32 words, the 1864 edition had only 7, occupying one-third of a column instead of three-quarters. (Perhaps the editors of the 1864 edition had come under similar pressure to limit scale in the course of their work on *un-*, and had eventually succumbed.) More detailed investigation confirmed Craigie's findings, as he triumphantly reported to Johnson: the 'wholesale excision of words beginning with *Un-*, regardless of their standing in the language' in the 1864 edition of Webster had definitely given a false guide for the *OED*; in fact, using the 1847 edition as a baseline, the part of *un-* already in type (which now reached *unfished*) represented a scale of something between 10 and 12 times Webster.[72] Craigie clearly felt that he was off the hook.

Chapman, however, was having none of it. He knew all too well the ruinous financial consequences of allowing *Un* to expand to such a scale; and upon his return from America he once again tried to enlist the help of an independent but authoritative figure in bringing Craigie to heel. He wrote to Henry White, the Dean of Christ Church, setting out his view of the situation:

Un. is full of nonce words, and you can make a hundred while you shave (Craigie alleges that he has left out far more than he has put in; but he has included *uncusped* because it is in Ruskin). [...] We have all had a go at it—Raleigh, poor Nagel, Hogarth, Davis, all convinced that it could and should be reduced [...] On the merits of the case Onions (this for your very private ear) is entirely with us (Bradley wont give an opinion). [...] I hope you will take a firm line. Craigie wont suspect You, as he doubtless suspects me, of being an enemy to research.[73]

On 20 January the Finance Committee were informed of the failure of MacLean's appeal for external funding, and 'considered the necessity of retrenchment in scale [in U], having regard to the improbability of any financial help from without'; and a week later the Delegates resolved 'to inform Dr Craigie that drastic reduction of the present scale of words in Un- is [...] both necessary as an economy and desirable in itself'.[74]

Would this be the last straw for Craigie? Chapman invited him to a meeting to discuss the Delegates' instruction. Craigie's reply must have puzzled him: 'I suppose you have seen my letter about the scale of Webster 1864 [...] However, I have another suggestion altogether for dealing with the problem.'[75]

[72] OED/B/3/2/9 2, 21 Dec. 1920 WAC to Johnson.
[73] OED/B/3/2/10 14 Jan. 1921 RWC to H. White.
[74] FC 20 Jan. 1921; OD 28 Jan. 1921.
[75] OED/B/3/2/10 31 Jan. 1921 RWC to WAC; 1 Feb. 1921 WAC to RWC.

Craigie's suggestion was indeed entirely novel. Following their meeting on 4 February, Chapman wrote cryptically to the Controller: 'A change of plan has become necessary. Please therefore (1) Stop composition of U altogether [...] (2) Page [i.e. make up page proofs] up to [page] 192 as expeditiously as possible [...] (3) Page nothing beyond.'[76] A longer letter to White, Davis, and Milford was more forthcoming. The proposal, which Chapman described as 'not altogether unsatisfactory; though it is rather an evasion than a solution',[77] was as follows. Craigie had now edited the copy for the whole of *un-*, on slips, and considered himself satisfied with his work—to the extent that he was prepared to wash his hands of it. Nearly enough of U was now in page proof to make a triple section of 192 pages; this represented an expansion by a factor of over 18 compared to Webster 1864, but the entries in it had been compressed as far as Craigie was willing to go. This was also true of the rest of U, which Craigie anticipated that he and his staff would finish (on slips) by July (leaving all further work on the remainder of *un-* for the present); whereupon, he proposed, his assistants could move on to do useful initial work in any part of W that still remained to be tackled (Onions, having now sent the last of Z to the printers, had made a start on the very difficult series of words beginning with *wh-*)—while he himself would embark on something entirely different: a trip round the world. He had received invitations to give lectures in Romania, India, and the United States; the opportunity to take these up presented by what was arguably a natural break in his work on the Dictionary must have seemed too good to miss, especially given his evident disenchantment with the struggles over U. Meanwhile, the remainder of U existed in the form of edited slips; transforming these into copy could wait until one or other of the Editors—and the Press—had the stomach to continue with it. Chapman's observation on the task of keeping to a reasonable Webster scale for what remained of U—which, as Craigie had discovered, was much more difficult[78]—is illuminating: 'It is all the more important that Craigie should hand over to some more docile editor.' Davis, replying in general support of Craigie's proposal, wrote that whoever was to edit the remainder of U 'ought to be a person of high repute, as Craigie's friends will probably be on the war-path when the later (abbreviated) sections of Un- appear & have to be reviewed'; and Milford commented that 'the difference of scale [between the earlier and later parts of U] will have to be carefully masked; and Craigie must be told not to blab?'[79]

Craigie obtained a year's leave of absence from his professorial duties (Onions was appointed as his deputy, presumably at some cost to his availability for Dictionary work).[80] In April, reporting to the Philological Society on progress—including the

[76] OED/B/3/2/10 4 Feb. 1921 RWC to F. Hall.

[77] OED/B/3/2/10 4 Feb. 1921 RWC to White, Davis, and HSM.

[78] The discrepancy between the 1847 and 1864 editions of Webster became greater still as the end of the letter U was approached.

[79] OED/B/3/2/10 6 Feb. 1921 Davis to RWC; 7 Feb. 1921 HSM to RWC.

[80] Minutes of Board of Faculty of Medieval and Modern Languages and Literature (OUA: ref. FA/4/10/1/1); Onions is described as Craigie's deputy during 1921/2 in the record of payments to him as Professor (OUA: UC 6/2/10–11, 6/3/1–3).

zyxt

The final page of the first edition of the *OED* is, unsurprisingly, devoted to words beginning with *zy-*. The last regular entry is a brief one for the word *zymurgy* ('the practice or art of fermentation'), but this is followed by a series of cross-reference entries, of a kind that had been used throughout the Dictionary, directing the reader who has looked up one of the less common spellings of a word to the form under which the word has been entered. The last of these—which reads '*Zyxt*, obs. (Kentish) 2nd sing. ind. pres. of SEE *v.*'—was to acquire considerable prominence following the publication of the section *XYZ* in 1921: far more prominence than the last 'real' word, *zymurgy*, and rather more prominence than might ever have been expected of an obscure variant of the word which might be more conventionally rendered '[thou] seest' (or, in modern English, '[you] see'). The revelation by Craigie at a Philological Society meeting that *zyxt* was to be the last word in the Dictionary (PSOM 1 Apr. 1921) was reported by several newspapers some months before the section was published. Those not *au fait* with the peculiarly irregular progress of the Dictionary through the last few letters of the alphabet would not have appreciated that the end of Z did not mean the end of everything; thus it was understandable, though of course incorrect, for the *Daily Mail* to print an item on 5 April under the heading 'Zyxt. Oxford Dictionary Finished After 40 Years.' The word's celebrity even led to the appearance of a brand of soap under the name *Zyxt*, no doubt intended to be thought of by customers as 'the last word' in soap. The soap seems to have been fairly successful, although the manufacturers (John Knight Ltd.) did report 'uncertainty [among customers] in pronouncing its name'—a difficulty which the company's enterprising sales director addressed by devising 'what is known as a slogan, which runs as follows:– "Dirt, however firmly fixed, Promptly disappears with 'Zyxt'"' (report of the company's AGM in *Times* 22 Feb. 1930, p. 20).

In fact the *OED* entry for the verb *see*, while it mentioned *zyxt* as a variant form, included no quotation illustrating it. The only text known to use the spelling is the fourteenth-century moral treatise *Ayenbite of Inwyt* (Remorse of Conscience), by the (distinctively Kentish) writer Dan Michel of Northgate; it occurs twice in his text, in the prefixed form *y-zyxt* or *yzyxt*, as in the following: 'Nou þou yzyxt wel hou þis uerste word is zuete'—which might be rendered in modern English as 'Now you see well how sweet is this first word.'

exciting news that the whole of Z was in type, right down to the final word *zyxt*—he announced the decision to suspend further work on U, which was now in type as far as *unhealthiness*. In a final parting shot to Chapman, he estimated that the whole of the letter U (all of which now existed in rough draft on paper) would run to something like 500 pages. 'How this can be materially reduced', he admitted, 'without complete re-working and extensive omissions, not merely of quotations but of words, is a question of which I do not see the solution. Perhaps time may solve it.'[81] He left England in July,

[81] PSOM 1 Apr. 1921; OED/B/3/2/10 7 June 1921 WAC to RWC.

FIGURE 29   The Dictionary staff photographed outside the Old Ashmolean, *c*.1921.

and by September had reached Bucharest;[82] in October he visited Greece and Egypt; in December and January he was in Calcutta (where he was awarded an honorary doctorate); and in due course he visited China, Japan, and the United States. 'What he wants to do when he comes back', Chapman had commented, 'is not clear.'[83] Was this temporary separation to become permanent?

In the second half of 1921 progress in the Old Ashmolean (see Figure 29) slowed to a crawl. Craigie's own team was further diminished within weeks of his departure by the loss of both Lawrence Powell, who had been appointed Librarian of the Taylorian Institution, and Isabella Hutchen, leaving only George Watson to soldier on.[84] Bradley was, as it were, becalmed in *water*, with its endless compounds, and Onions was still making heavy weather of *Wh*. Over a year had gone by since the publication of Craigie's section of V—the only section to be published in 1920—and doubts were beginning to be expressed publicly about the completion of the Dictionary, which Bradley did

---

[82] CP55/11 ff. 3–4 14 Sept. 1921 WAC to Johnson. Craigie's activities during his travels were by no means confined to Dictionary-related business: while in Romania he organized a summer school in English (*Journal of International Relations* 12 (1922), 558), and he gave a number of lectures on the merits of a system for representing pronunciation which he had devised for use by foreign learners of English, first set out in Craigie (1917) and subsequently used in a series of readers published at Oxford and elsewhere.

[83] OED/B/3/2/10 4 Feb. 1921 RWC to H. White.

[84] FC 27 July 1921.

his best to allay by telling the Philological Society that a triple section of U, a sizeable portion of W, and Onions's now completed XYZ would 'come out all in a burst'.[85] They did, on 6 October, amounting to over 400 pages; but this left hardly any finished text in hand.[86]

In the autumn of 1921 the prospects for completing *OED* receded still further, thanks to a crisis in another of the Press's lexicographical projects. The editor of the Abridged, William Little, became seriously ill, and by December it became necessary to consider transferring the editorship to someone else.[87] The work involved in completing Little's text would itself be considerable—his draft extended as far as the end of the letter T—but in addition the whole text had to be brought up to date: notwithstanding the implication of the title 'Abridged', it was obviously desirable that the new dictionary should be more up to date than its notional parent, parts of which of course did not include any of the lexical innovations of the last four decades.[88] Little had dealt with some of the most obvious omissions, such as *appendicitis*, but much remained to be done. Onions, one of the few individuals really qualified to take on the task, agreed to do so, but pointed out that to facilitate the updating process it was now more desirable than ever that the *OED*'s accumulated Supplement material should be put into proper order.[89] Work on this intimidating task—an assessment made by Sweatman gave the extent of the file as 80 linear feet, which Onions estimated would take three months to sort—seems to have begun immediately.

William Little died on 14 January 1922. In February the Delegates were informed that 'arrangements had been made for the continuance of the work under Mr Onions's directions, and that the parts now being printed are as far as possible being brought up to date'.[90] Onions and his staff now devoted half their time to work on the Abridged; Onions estimated that this would reduce his output of *OED* copy to a rate of 8 columns of proof (less than 3 pages) per fortnight.[91] At this point Bradley, although at work, was in fact recovering from a broken rib, which had left him with 'a considerable amount of pain, which interferes sadly with my speed of work'.[92] In the event Bradley's output for most of 1922 only averaged about 8 columns per fortnight, and Onions fell far short

---

[85] PSOM 3 June 1921.

[86] There were also difficulties on the printing side, as the Press nearly ran out of coal because of a national miners' strike and had to introduce short-time working; this was followed in the summer of 1922 by a one-month printers' strike over reduced wages (Belson 2003: 321–2).

[87] ML 28 Nov. 1921 HSM to RWC; FC 1 Dec. 1921.

[88] OED/B/3/2/11 notes by RWC 'The Future of the Oxford Dictionaries', dated 16 Apr. 1922.

[89] OED/B/3/2/10 14 Dec. 1921 CTO to RWC. Onions had pointed out the desirability of sorting the Supplement materials a year earlier (OED/B/3/2/9 7 Sept. 1920 CTO to RWC), but nothing had been done.

[90] OD 10 Feb. 1922.

[91] OED/B/3/2/11 20 Apr. 1922 CTO to RWC. Onions was also now trying to squeeze in two other lexicographical tasks: scrutinizing the text of the new *Pocket Oxford Dictionary*, which Henry Fowler was now compiling, and commenting on a new version of the *Concise* being prepared for the American market by George Van Santvoord (OED/B/3/2/11 5 Oct. 1922 CTO to RWC). Remarkably, this project never reached publication—the costly decision to abandon it was finally taken in 1929—although an Americanized version of the *Pocket* dictionary did appear in 1927.

[92] 10 Apr. 1922 HB to Bridges (quoted in Bridges 1928: 46); OED/B/3/2/11 28 Apr. 1922 HB to RWC.

of this. It is hardly surprising that no sections of the Dictionary were published in the whole of 1922.

Notwithstanding the slow progress of the *OED*, Chapman now began to give serious thought to the lexicographical future, and in particular to what projects the Press might contemplate once the main Dictionary and the Abridged were complete. In April 1922 he drafted a substantial document entitled 'The Future of the Oxford Dictionaries'; it is not clear whether this was ever submitted to the Delegates, or even informally discussed with interested parties, but it presents a fascinating survey of the Press's various current lexicographical projects, how they interacted with each other, and what might be done next.[93] Particularly significant are two ideas which were to become key elements of Chapman's thinking over the next decade and more. One was Craigie's suggestion of a substantial dictionary of modern English, which had evidently taken his fancy ('a dictionary with the qualities which made the Concise D. unique at the time of its publication [...] but on a larger scale'), and which he saw as likely to bring far more of an income than the various specialist historical dictionaries for which calls were now beginning to be made. The other was Chapman's proposed solution to the growing problem of keeping all of the Press's dictionaries up to date. Henry Fowler, now hard at work on the *Pocket Oxford Dictionary*, was accumulating corrections and additions for incorporation in the *Concise*, but he was no longer a young man, and could hardly be expected to continue doing this indefinitely; the text of the Abridged was in need of updating even before it had been published; and of course there was the still inchoate Supplement to the main Dictionary. Chapman could see that in a few years the Press would be in possession of 'some half-dozen distinct dictionaries, all of which will continue to grow obsolete in different degrees'. The best way to keep up with rival publications, he concluded, would be to emulate some American dictionary publishers, and 'keep a regular organization at work': a small team of lexicographers based in Oxford, preparing materials for use in the updating of all of the Oxford dictionaries, up to and including the Abridged (he was not ready to contemplate revision of the *OED* itself). He mentioned to Henry Fowler his sense that 'we ought to "keep tab" [on the language] or continuity will break. No one else will do it'; and he regarded Onions as 'fully capable of keeping all the strings in his hands', and therefore as the best man to run this enterprise. He was also aware that Fowler was one of the few people who was already making a systematic effort in this direction—whereas the *OED*'s Editors and staff were, he thought, 'too deep in the fifteenth century to have much time for modern collections'. Fowler was soon being supplied with slips on which he could record his lexical observations, and his brother Arthur soon joined in.[94]

In September, as Chapman was discussing the future with the Fowlers, Craigie returned to Oxford. Chapman must have been relieved to be able to report to the Finance Committee 'Dr. Craigie's willingness to resume work on U, at least for one year'—especially in view of the lack of progress made by George Watson in Craigie's

---

[93] OED/B/3/2/11 (dated 16 Apr. 1922).
[94] OED/B/3/2/11 14 Sept. 1922 RWC to H. W. Fowler; 10 Oct. 1922 RWC to F. Hall; 26 Oct. 1922 H. W. Fowler to RWC; 6 Nov. 1922 A. J. Fowler to [RWC].

absence: no further *U* copy had been sent to the printers, who in October took delivery of the first batch of *Uni-* after having received at least the first part of *Unh-* in January 1921, long before Craigie's departure. Craigie's suggestion, also reported to the Finance Committee, 'that his remuneration for the year should be £500' might seem reasonable enough: after all, his previous salary had not been far short of this. However, rather than rubber-stamping the proposal, the Committee decided to ask Craigie to estimate just how much of his time he was going to be able to give to the Dictionary during the upcoming academic year. This may simply reflect an acceptance that Craigie's academic responsibilities would continue to make demands on his time (the fact that Onions was similarly asked for an estimate tends to support this hypothesis); but there may have been good reason to suppose that Craigie was likely to find other projects to distract him. Onions supplied the requisite estimate, but Craigie informed the Delegates that he was unable to provide one at present, declaring instead that he would 'correct a portion of the proofs of U and to find out what time it takes, with a view to an arrangement'—a long way short of a return to normal. The Finance Committee, in turn, elected to be correspondingly non-committal on the subject of salary: the minutes record no decision regarding what payment Craigie should receive.[95]

Some, at least, of Craigie's reasons for not committing himself were soon to become apparent. He had also been thinking, once again, about the future, but in terms very different from Chapman's. In a memorandum submitted for consideration by the Delegates, Craigie set out the view of the world of English scholarship, as he saw it (and had experienced it during his recent travels), as to where effort should be directed once the *OED* was complete.[96] Unsurprisingly, his recommendation was for period dictionaries of the kind that he had proposed to the Philological Society three years previously, now reduced to three: for Middle English, for Tudor and Stuart English—or Early Modern English, as it would soon become known—and for Older Scottish (the need for a new dictionary of Old English being regarded as less pressing since T. N. Toller's supplement to his and Joseph Bosworth's *Anglo-Saxon Dictionary* had appeared in 1921). The last of these three he proposed to undertake himself, drawing on both the *OED*'s own considerable body of evidence—by no means all of which had been used in the published text—and the additional collections already being made by voluntary workers in Scotland.[97] For the other two dictionaries, Craigie had a bold suggestion for lightening the burden on the Press: much of the work, both of collecting quotations and of drafting entries, could be done by appropriately trained students and faculty staff in the English departments of universities around the world. Indeed, he had already sounded out some American universities about the idea, and met with a favourable response; he was also optimistic about the chances of obtaining American funds to maintain the small permanent editorial staff that would be needed at the heart

---

[95]   FC 28 Sept., 12 Oct. 1922.

[96]   OED/B/3/2/14 typed copy of WAC's memorandum, undated but evidently that presented at the Delegates' meeting of 20 Oct. 1922.

[97]   According to Dareau (2002: 209) the collection of quotations for *DOST*, by Isabella Hutchen and others, began in 1921, at Craigie's instigation.

of each project. His reason for putting the matter to the Delegates now was to secure their approval for the use, where appropriate, of the *OED*'s own collections of material by each of the period projects. Interestingly, he now regarded the idea of a substantial new dictionary of modern English, of the kind that had so enthused Chapman, as 'a question for the future'; perhaps even more surprisingly, he declared that until the *OED*'s 'defects'—by which he meant its lack of detailed coverage of the English of the various periods—had been addressed through the compilation of appropriate period dictionaries, a Supplement to the main Dictionary would be of little value to academia, and might even make matters worse (in giving scholars two places to look instead of one).

How much of a surprise all of this was to the Delegates, or to Chapman, is not clear. Chapman had referred to Craigie's interest in a dictionary of Tudor English in his April 1922 notes, as well as the fact of scholarly interest in a new dictionary of Middle English; but no records survive to show that anyone was expecting Craigie to come up with proposals of such elaborateness and magnitude. On the other hand, it seems that he was not asking for the Press to back any of the new schemes with its own money, merely to give its blessing in principle to any steps he might take. In the event the Delegates decided that applications for the use of *OED* materials would 'receive favourable consideration'.[98] Perhaps they felt that, given the unlikelihood of any institution coming forward to take on any of these laudable but expensive schemes, such approval in principle was a safely non-committal response to Craigie's visionary scheme.

More pressing was the question of a Supplement for the main Dictionary. Chapman, and presumably the Delegates, were in no doubt that one was needed, in spite of Craigie's comments; the problem was what form it should take. Chapman, with his own sights firmly fixed on the future development of English, suspected that within the Old Ashmolean, even those who did accept the need for a Supplement were inclined to regard it more as a means of completing the record of the past, 'digging back into the 15 Century' for antedatings and the like. He decided that the time had come for a serious conference (insofar as Oxford did such things) on the matter. He arranged for a dinner to be held at Oriel College, at which the three Editors, together with two Delegates (Percy Matheson and Norman Whatley) and two key professorial colleagues (Nichol Smith and the English scholar George Gordon), could, as he put it to Matheson, 'stretch our legs a bit over the future of the Dictionary'.[99]

Chapman's letter to Matheson shows his continuing impatience with the Oxford editors' tendency to 'go off at once to the thirteenth century and the quotations that might have been printed proving "earlier use" etc. etc.' when asked for their ideas about a Supplement. More interesting is an inspiration of Chapman's own:

[98] OD 20 Oct. 1922.
[99] OED/B/3/2/11 28 Sept. 1922 RWC to H. W. Fowler; 15 Nov. 1922 RWC to P. E. Matheson. Chapman was, like Craigie, a graduate of Oriel; Craigie had, moreover, been a fellow of the college since 1918.

I have just thought of an effective analogy. Ought we not to do what Lee did with the D.N.B. and produce a supplement to rectify the anomalies which arise from periodical publication— i.e. make the Dictionary what it would have been if it had been published at a blow in (say!) 1925? Lee added the people who had died during the course of publication; why not add the words that have been born in the course of publication? Some new *senses* would have to be recognized as well […] but that is a minor matter.

On hearing of Chapman's idea, Milford immediately wrote in support: 'excellent. If that plan can be brought off it will solve all problems.'[100]

And, in the event, the lexicographers agreed with him, as did everyone else who attended the dinner at Oriel on 25 November. A bad cold prevented Bradley from attending, but all the other invitees were there. Chapman opened proceedings by setting out his own views in a paper; he reported to Bradley that there was 'general agreement on the essential points—that it is necessary to produce a supplement which will bring the Dictionary up to a uniform terminus, and that it is desirable and practicable to look forward to a certain amount of continuous activity even when the Dictionary and its "unifying" supplement (if any) are completed. […] We did not touch questions of supplementation revision or other rehandling of the Dictionary *as a whole*.' The idea of 'maintaining a modest staff to deal with the language' received strong support, particularly from Gordon; but this was a matter for the future.[101]

The dinner seems to have put all parties in a better humour, at least. Chapman commented to Milford: 'We are all very cordial (there is a little of the '70 port left, which I persuaded the Common Room man to produce) […] Craigie is correcting some proofs of U, and I think he will finish.' Chapman wrote up his paper as a memorandum for the Delegates; his covering note supplied some additional practical details, including some comments about the latest estimate for the time to completion which vividly demonstrate the continuing fragility of any projections:

The estimate that the Dictionary can be finished (without supplement) in three years assumes the continuance of Dr. Bradley's share in the work and the resumption of Dr. Craigie's. It is to be hoped that Dr. Bradley, who has finished *Wa* and reached *weather*, may be able to finish *We*. But he was born in December 1845. Dr. Craigie is now correcting proofs of *Un* as far as his preoccupations (permanent and temporary) allow, and it is hoped that an arrangement will be reached by which he will undertake at least to complete *U*. But if Mr. Onions *should* unfortunately be left alone to the task of completion and supplementation (if any) together with that of keeping the Abridged Dictionary in motion, it is obvious that he would have heavy work before him.[102]

Talk of Onions being 'left alone' might seem premature; in fact it was nothing of the kind. Chapman's memorandum was frank enough about the possibility of Craigie

[100] OED/B/3/2/11 16 Nov. 1922 HSM to RWC.
[101] OED/B/3/2/11 29 Nov. 1922 RWC to HB; 30 Nov. 1922 RWC to HSM.
[102] OED/B/3/2/11 Memorandum 'for the Delegates', 15 Dec. 1922. This is an expanded version of the paper which Chapman read at the Oriel dinner.

leaving the project once he had finished *U*; what it failed to mention was the lack of progress he was making even with that, presumably because of his 'preoccupations'. On 12 January 1923 the Delegates attended a 'Teaparty'—unlike most tea parties in having a formal agenda, on which the *OED* and the *DNB* were the main items—at which, as Chapman reported to Milford, 'discussion raged mainly round the continuation or non-continuation of Craigie'; he had returned no proofs since November, and his wife had reportedly intimated that he had 'given up Dictionary work'. Although Chapman's suggestions for the form of the Supplement were 'agreed on all hands', concern about the Editorship was acute—and not only in respect of Craigie. Chapman went on: 'I have told Onions to cast about in his mind for someone capable of taking charge of a piece (he agrees that if H.B. finishes *We* we shall be lucky) [...] W.H.F. [*sic*, i.e. H. W. Fowler] I fear is too old [...]. Tolkien hasn't (yet) enough driving power—besides he has a job.'[103]

The extent to which Craigie considered himself to be an Editor of the *OED* at all at this point is debatable. He was, after all, still not being paid for the work he was doing on U. In March Chapman reported hopefully that he '*seemed* to look forward to working at [the Dictionary]' once his temporary responsibilities as acting treasurer of Oriel College—which were drawing more of his time away from lexicography than usual—came to an end. There was also (relatively) good news on the subject of the scale of the Dictionary, which it seems had once again begun to exercise the Delegates: Craigie calculated that 'the scale from Unforeseen to Unlevel is 12⅔ on the genuine unabridged Webster of 1847, and only 15 on the arbitrarily reduced edition of 1864'—hearteningly low figures compared to those being contemplated in the worst days of 1921.[104] These calculations accompanied a new suggestion from Craigie as to payment, namely that he receive a retaining fee, to be adjusted later to take account of work actually done. This idea found favour, and on 18 May the Delegates finally agreed to award Craigie a salary of £200 for the year ending 25 October 1923.[105] They also approved publication of two sections of W, the first new sections since October 1921. At last, it seemed, the project was moving forward again. But within days of the Delegates' meeting fate struck another blow, from which the Dictionary would never fully recover.

[103] OED/B/3/2/11 29 Dec. 1922 RWC to L. R. Farnell (as Vice-Chancellor); OED/B/3/2/12 16 Jan. 1923 RWC to HSM. Tolkien was now Reader in English Language at the University of Leeds.

[104] OED/B/3/2/12 13 Mar. 1923 RWC to HSM, 22 Mar. 1923 WAC to RWC (incomplete). Craigie deputized as treasurer in 1922–3, having served the college as auditor in 1920 and 1921 (information from Rob Petre).

[105] OD 18 May 1923.

9

Limping over the finishing line: 1923–1933

ON 21 May 1923, in the middle of writing a letter to his daughter, Henry Bradley suffered a serious stroke. The following day, after a visit from the new Regius Professor of Medicine, Sir Archibald Garrod (who like his predecessor William Osler seems to have been expected to keep an eye on the health of the Dictionary's Editors), there was some hope of his regaining consciousness; but these hopes soon faded, and he died on 23 May.[1] His death came as a terrible shock, despite his age. He had not been unwell; the only sign that anything might be amiss was his complaint to his friend Robert Bridges a week or so earlier of 'an unaccountable indisposition to work which he had never known before'.[2] His contribution to the Dictionary—second only to Murray's—and his numerous other publications in other fields, which he had, unlike Murray, continued to produce throughout his period as Editor, were celebrated in numerous obituaries, which were also marked by warm general tributes. Herbert Warren's, in the *Times*, was typical: he quoted Sir Walter Raleigh's description of him as 'the scholars' scholar, in points of English scholarship the ultimate appeal', and mourned the passing of 'the most simple, amiable, and natural of men'. To Warren's (anonymous) text the *Times* added a striking tribute from Chapman:

Only his peers can judge Bradley's work on the Dictionary. They are unanimous that it places him in the first rank of all scholars, not only of his time, but of all time. [...] [G]reater powers than Bradley's of learning, of insight, and of discrimination have not been given to the study of a language.[3]

---

[1] OED/B/3/2/12 22 May 1923 Eleanor Bradley to RWC, 26 May 1923 RWC to T. N. Toller.
[2] Bridges (1928: 50).
[3] *Times* 24 May 1923, p. 13; OED/B/3/2/12 24 May 1923 RWC to HSM. Another affectionate tribute was paid by Tolkien, who wrote of his gratitude for the time he had spent working 'under his wise and kindly hand', and evocatively recalled him at work in the Dictionary Room, 'that great dusty workshop, that brownest of brown studies [...] momentarily held in thought, with eyes looking into the grey shadows of the roof, pen poised in the air to descend at last and fix a sentence or a paragraph complete and rounded, without blot or erasure, on the paper before him' (Tolkien 1923: 5).

An immediate concern was the lack of adequate provision for Bradley's widow. It seemed that Bradley's estate was unlikely to amount to more than £3,000:[4] although in recent years his income had been good—£550 a year as Editor, a Civil List pension of £150, and a stipend from Magdalen which had risen to £400 by the time of his death[5]—various expenses, notably the cost of treating his wife's frequent illnesses, had made it impossible to save much, and none of the children would be able to afford much to support their mother. Murray's old friend and colleague Joseph Wright, who had been involved in the (successful) effort to secure for Lady Murray a continuation of her husband's pension, had also warned of the need to take action quickly if anything similar was to be done for Mrs Bradley. Following representations made by President Warren of Magdalen and others, in due course a pension of £75 was secured for her; the Press also paid £120 for books being used in the Old Ashmolean which had belonged to Bradley, and (more valuably) permitted Mrs Bradley to stay in the house at 173 Woodstock Road rent-free until Michaelmas, thus giving her and her daughters more time to find another house.[6]

Bradley's death may well have deprived him of something else which Warren had for some years—at Chapman's prompting—been attempting to secure for him, namely a knighthood.[7] Warren had continued to make efforts in this direction, through two changes of Prime Minister, and had expressed optimism to Chapman (in characteristically indirect fashion) as recently as March: 'I have not been negligent about the matter you wot of. I wrote to the new Prime Minister [Stanley Baldwin] I have now made another *demarche*.'[8] Whether Bradley's name was indeed put forward for the King's 1923 Birthday Honours List is now academic; at the time of his death he remained plain Doctor, although of course this was itself an honorary title several times over.

Meanwhile: what was to be done with the Dictionary? Bradley's assistants were masterless, as Murray's had been in 1915, and this time it would not be a matter of quickly completing the alphabetical range in hand and then reallocating staff to the other Editors, as only a very small part of *We* had gone to the printers, and neither Craigie nor Onions was in a position to take on extra work. Nor was there any obvious external candidate to put in charge of the decapitated team. The question therefore arose whether any of the existing assistants could manage the task; and Chapman's eye fell on Walter Worrall, the longest-serving of Bradley's assistants. On 6 June he wrote to Onions:

Worrall seemed very low this morning—'no music left'—'would be the end of *him*' etc. But presently asked if he might send back some first proof. I said yes why not? at which he brightened up a bit. We must try to coax him on.[9]

---

[4] OED/B/3/2/12 24 May 1923 RWC to T. H. Warren.

[5] Information from Robin Darwall-Smith.

[6] OED/B/3/2/12 2 June 1923 RWC to J. Wright; FC 29 June 1923; OED/B/3/2/12 copy of receipt to Mrs E. K. Bradley, dated 14 July 1923. Mrs Bradley died in 1932.

[7] See above, p. 348.

[8] OED/B/3/2/12 14 Mar. 1923 Warren to RWC.

[9] OED/B/3/2/12 6 June 1923 RWC to CTO.

The coaxing had its effect. On 25 June, his confidence bolstered by Craigie's advice, Worrall formally applied to take on full responsibility for the remainder of *We*. He felt obliged to mention his health problems—'chronic neuralgic headache, which 38 years' constant lexicographic toil seems to have rendered deepseated in character'—and feared that the extra responsibility might bring on a breakdown. Chapman consulted Craigie forthwith, and wrote approvingly to Onions of Craigie's suggestion that 'Wavy–Wez should be "edited by H.B. & W.W."' and that he could act as a consultant on points of difficulty, and 'generally [...] keep his eye on the section and see that W. does not take an inordinate time. [...] The more we get from W.A.C. the better.' He also mentioned the good news that Craigie was contemplating taking on part of W himself.[10] Onions, who had gone to Aberystwyth to examine for the University of Wales, wrote expressing general approval; however, he mentioned two qualifications. One was that the unpublished portion of U might take Craigie longer than anticipated, perhaps another two years: 'there are heavy patches after *Un-*, viz. Up–Upward, Use–Usury, Utter.' His other comment is rather more enigmatic:

The continuation of the editorial tradition will not tolerate mere editorial *supervision*. Only regular attendance at the editorial desk can maintain efficiency of execution and—a necessary thing to add in view of the experience of these latter years, and given certain individual conditions—staff discipline.[11]

This may merely have been an allusion to the difficulties caused by Craigie's semi-detachment from the project, but it is hard not to read into it some reflection of other issues: perhaps a (supposed) tendency to malingering on the part of one or more of the assistants?

Whatever Onions's misgivings were, the Delegates agreed to allow Worrall to make a trial as a title-page (joint) Editor; however, they took the view that, rather than increase his salary forthwith, it would be wiser to offer the prospect of an honorarium on the publication of the section. Worrall was happy to accept the Editorship on these terms.[12]

In October Onions was elected to the fellowship at Magdalen left vacant by Bradley's death. Much, no doubt, to the relief of the Press, Craigie also announced that he was willing to rededicate his time fully to the Dictionary; the Finance Committee duly voted to restore his salary to its former level of £500 a year with effect from November, 'on the basis of a 24 hours week extending over some ten months of the year'. Onions, meanwhile, confirmed that he would continue to be able to average something over 6 hours per day on the Dictionary, also extending over 10 months of the year; he also had the good news that he was giving up his Oxford examining

[10] OED/B/3/2/12 25 June 1923 Worrall to RWC, 26 June 1923 RWC to CTO; 25 May 1923 RWC to L. R. Farnell (as Vice-Chancellor).

[11] OED/B/3/2/12 27 June 1923 CTO to RWC.

[12] FC 29 June 1923; OED/B/3/2/12 5 July 1923 Worrall to RWC.

responsibilities. At this point Onions was being paid £50 a month, considerably more than Craigie.[13]

The ink was barely dry on Craigie's new agreements with the Delegates when his wanderlust struck again. In November he informed Chapman that he would be spending the summer of 1924 at the University of Chicago, to teach during the summer session. This was bound to detract from the time he could devote to the Dictionary. In a note to Craigie Chapman diplomatically wrote that he was 'both glad and sorry about Chicago. But you will be able to keep your staff employed all right. *What do you say about Worrall's piece?*'—this last presumably a request for an assessment of Worrall's efforts to date in *We.* Craigie's reply included the suggestion that he 'take [*We*] in hand, on the plea that it is wanted as soon as possible', from which it appears that Worrall had so far made little progress.[14]

Chapman's philosophical reaction to Craigie's news about Chicago was not shared by everyone. Milford told him of the anger of Kenneth Sisam (now back at the Press as Junior Assistant Secretary, after some years in London working for the Ministry of Food) and others at the news: Chapman's response, which also neatly summarizes the other problems besetting the project, was that

abusing the publisher won't raise Murray and Bradley, nor restrain Wanderlust in Craigie, nor reduce the extent of Onions's family, nor make W an easy letter, nor make it possible to create fresh editors for the last five yards (say) of the Hundred. (I admit that a metaphor from sprinting may be used against me.)[15]

A minor incident which also occurred in November might be seen as light relief, although in the event all parties at the Press took it fairly seriously. The *Daily Mail* published a brief item reporting that 'it is probable that 1924 will see the finish of the dictionary'.[16] The item, which also mentioned plans for a Supplement to include 'new words, such as appendicitis and radium', generated a certain amount of interest; Chapman consulted both Craigie and Onions about what might be said in response. This resulted in a letter, which Chapman offered, not to the *Daily Mail*, but to Bruce Richmond, editor of the *Times Literary Supplement*, and which was ultimately published in both the *Times* of 20 November and the *TLS* of 29 November. The letter set out the facts regarding where the Dictionary now stood, 'in view of unauthorized statements'; Chapman prudently gave no definite completion date, but offered at least the hope 'that before very long it will be possible to say that this country has produced

---

[13] Minutes of Magdalen College Governing Body meeting of 9 Oct. 1923 (Magdalen College archives, ref. CMM/1/8); FC 26 Oct. 1923; OED/B/3/2/12 24 Oct. 1923 CTO to RWC.

[14] OED/B/3/2/12 14 Nov. 1923 RWC to WAC, 15 Nov. 1923 WAC to RWC.

[15] OED/B/3/2/12 15 Nov. 1923 RWC to HSM.

[16] The article, headed 'A 67-Years Task', was apparently the result of a reporter's misunderstanding of a reply to his telephone call to the Press (OED/B/3/2/12 14 Nov. 1923 RWC to HSM).

the largest and most authoritative linguistic dictionary, as it has produced the largest of all collections of national biography'.

Unfortunately, Worrall was continuing to struggle under the burden of his new responsibility. The job of Editor entailed both the preparation of copy and the correction of proofs; it would seem that Worrall was concentrating on the latter at the expense of finalizing further copy for the printers. Bradley's last bundle of copy, ending with the noun *weigh*, had been passed to the printers on 4 May; and he had done some work on a few entries beyond that. Months now went by without any further copy being sent; Craigie was urged by Chapman to do whatever he could to coax Worrall into greater productivity, but expressed doubts as to his ability to cope with the two streams of work, and offered to take over the preparation of copy. This came as a great relief to Chapman (and to Sisam, who scribbled 'I have jumped at this' on Craigie's letter); lamenting that 'Worrall can't or won't take charge', he accepted Craigie's proposal to 'get him and his staff into order'.[17] Within a week copy for *We* began once more to arrive at the printers. A single consignment of copy, delivered to the printers on 13 February 1924, apparently contains the whole of Worrall's output as Editor up to this point, and it did not amount to much. The slips bearing the definitions for *weigh* (verb), and the top slips for a few of the small entries immediately following, are in Worrall's hand, as are some of the subsenses of *weight* (noun) (which Bradley had begun to work on before his death), but Craigie's hand may be seen even in these entries; and in all the entries that follow, beginning with *weight* (verb), it was Craigie rather than Worrall who corrected the first drafts (all by Lewis and Bayliss). Thus Worrall had so far 'taken charge' of an alphabetical range which eventually occupied a scant four printed pages of the Dictionary.

Of course Craigie's recruitment to this cause would have a cost, namely further delay in completing the remainder of U. However, having been told by Craigie that this was all in proof, Chapman was confident that Craigie could 'keep it going', and still anticipated an early date for the completion of the double section *Unright–Uzzle*. This would, once again, prove optimistic; but at least the throughput of material in W improved, with the printers taking delivery of copy as far as *well* by early June.[18]

At the same time that Craigie was taking on this extra responsibility, Chapman was attempting to spread the burden of work on the Abridged, which threatened to take up rather too much of Onions's time. In 1923 he had persuaded Henry Fowler (now hard at work on his most famous work, *Modern English Usage*) to consider completing the task of abridging the published text of the main Dictionary, leaving Onions and his assistants to incorporate new material. In November a specimen of Fowler's work had been passed to Onions, whose comments on it, however, were distinctly unfavourable:

---

[17] OED/B/3/2/12 10 Dec. 1923 RWC to HSM; OED/B/3/2/13 2 Feb. 1924 WAC to RWC, 4 Feb. 1924 RWC to WAC.

[18] Worrall was at least permitted the privilege of giving a report on the Dictionary, as the four principal Editors had done before him, to a meeting of the Philological Society (PSOM 6 June 1924).

'I think you would find his contribution to the work very costly, and I should not look forward with pleasure to the conclusion of the *Abridged* if he had the preparation of any part of it.' Sisam's assessment was more positive, but for various reasons Fowler was unable to start work on the Abridged in earnest for another two years.[19]

Early in the Long Vacation, shortly after Craigie's departure for Chicago, a booksellers' conference brought Milford to Oxford, and afforded an opportunity to discuss various Dictionary-related matters. Output was down thanks to Craigie's absence; Onions was still producing copy for *Wi*, but U had turned out to be less far advanced than Craigie had suggested—not all of it was even in proof. (A double section, *Unforeseeing–Unright*, was published at the end of July, the first section to be published since *Wash–Wavy* over a year earlier, and no doubt something of a relief to the Dictionary's subscribers; but of course it represented copy which had been prepared long before.) It was agreed that better progress needed to be made. The subject was evidently raised in the Old Ashmolean; whether it was Onions or some other lexicographer who decided to inform Craigie of this is unclear, but the consequence was the arrival of a letter from Craigie in Chapman's office on 25 August. Perhaps it was as well that Chapman was on leave when it arrived, for it was easily Craigie's most bad-tempered letter to date.

I learn from the Dictionary Room that the various staffs have been invited to offer suggestions as to the best means of furthering the progress and hastening the completion of the Dictionary. I am glad to hear of this, as I think it a very necessary step with regard to both sections of W., but it seems to me superfluous in my absence to extend the enquiry to U. Not only can the Staff do nothing in the matter without consulting with me, but for some time past the only delay in the progress of that letter has lain at the Press. As soon as the printers regularly use up copy and proofs more rapidly than I and Watson can supply them, it will be time to consider whether anything more can be done. [...] I have no doubt whatever that my staff would be willing to make any special exertions that might be asked from them, but what I might be able to do is quite another question. I am no longer so free in respect of my time as I was four years ago, nor have I been at all encouraged by recent experiences of Oxford and its ways. As the representations of myself and others have so far produced not the slightest effect, I propose, immediately on my return, to draw up another memorandum on the question of the Dictionary and the Professorship, and to send a copy of this to each of the Delegates. On the reply which may be given to it within the next month or two, a good deal will depend.

In the meantime, the progress of U is entirely a matter for the printer, whose attentions will be appreciated by all of us.[20]

The report from Craigie's Oxford 'mole', presumably Watson, had brought to the surface a whole set of interrelated frustrations. It is not clear whether 'Oxford and its ways' is a reference to the (to Craigie) inadequate response of the Delegates to his 1922 proposals regarding period dictionaries, or to his continuing dissatisfaction with the salary he

---

[19] SOED/1924/2 12 Jan. 1924 CTO to KS. See also McMorris (2001: 173–4).
[20] OED/B/3/2/13 12 Aug. 1924 WAC to RWC.

received from the University for performing what still amounted to considerable duties as Professor, including lecturing for six hours a week.[21] Perhaps, indeed, it is anachronistic to regard Craigie as having separate grievances with the Press and the University: so far as he was concerned, it was a single body which, having appointed him to both academic and lexicographical positions, would neither pay him properly nor comply with his ideas of how things should be done.

In Chapman's absence, Sisam decided that this required an immediate response. By return of post he wrote a letter which was clearly designed both to soothe and to clarify.[22] He explained that the matter of progress had been raised with Onions, who was 'asked to urge his staff to make all the progress they could, and the question of your staff was expressly reserved for your return and remains reserved. I think there must be some misapprehension. Onions would no doubt speak openly on a matter which requires no secrecy, but I cannot see how he could fail to tell your staff that their case awaited your return.' He also reported on the decisions taken regarding two other projects: 'It was agreed that [...] some extra help should be produced for the Abridged; and that a promising assistant, Miss Senior of Leeds, should be engaged to work on the Supplement material, until the other staffs are freer.' Finally, Craigie's allegation regarding the printers' slowness with U had already been dealt with: following fresh instructions to the printer from Chapman, 'we are regularly crying out for copy for all sections'.

On his return to Oxford, Chapman wrote to Craigie himself, as diplomatically as he could, but clearly in some exasperation. (His annoyance is more evident in a letter written the same day to the Delegate David Ross, in which he describes Craigie's threat to write to the Delegates as 'useless pamphleteering', which would 'alienate whatever sympathy for him remains (if any)'.) Chapman delicately suggested to Craigie that, having volunteered to help push the remainder of We through to publication, he would stand a better chance of improving his financial situation by showing some results on this front than by 'launching further memoranda'.[23]

Shortly after this, Craigie also returned to Oxford, whereupon relations rapidly deteriorated. A meeting of the Finance Committee on 29 September discussed '[Chapman's] letter to Dr. Craigie 25 September, Dr. Craigie's reply of the same date received 27 September and his further letter to Dr. Craigie 27 September';[24] the Committee seriously considered withholding Craigie's quarterly £125 salary cheque, but in the event gave him the benefit of the doubt. But before the end of the day a further letter arrived from Craigie, written that morning, whose contents ('communicated to

---

[21] OED/B/3/2/13 13 Oct. 1924 RWC to D. G. Hogarth. The University had agreed to increase his professorial salary to £650; Craigie evidently regarded the figure as having been effectively limited by the fact of his remuneration as Editor being taken into account. His wife was later reported as saying 'it was as if the university had said "your husband may do two jobs, if he so chooses, but he is only to get one salary"' (Wyllie 1961: 282).

[22] OED/B/3/2/13 25 Aug. 1924 KS to WAC.

[23] OED/B/3/2/13 15 Sept. 1924 RWC to W. D. Ross, RWC to WAC.

[24] FC 29 Sept. 1924.

Professor Ross by telephone' after the meeting) caused them to reverse their decision. Craigie's behaviour must have occasioned serious irritation to warrant such a punitive measure. Whether this related to his rate of progress in U or W or to other matters is unclear, as none of the letters mentioned survives.

After writing his letter on 29 September, Craigie had departed for Scotland, to drum up support for the two Scottish components of his grand scheme of dictionaries. He gave several lectures on 'The Study of the Scottish Tongue', and issued appeals for volunteers to help with his own projected 'Dictionary of Middle Scots' and, especially, with the fledgling project to compile a dictionary of modern Scots.[25] Only a few days after his departure Onions added to Chapman's woes with a report that Worrall's work in *Well* was ballooning in volume to an extent that dwarfed the worst excesses of *Un*: '8 columns of our Dict. to 5 lines of a column of the old Webster.' A few days later Sisam confirmed that the Webster scale for the section of *We* printed in September was 48; the fact that Craigie had advised Worrall to model his treatment of the compounds of *well-* on Craigie's own work in *un-* perhaps makes the extravagant scale rather less surprising. Craigie's explanation that this was once again a consequence of the reduction in coverage in the 1864 Webster (which, as with *un-*, was significantly shorter than in the 1847 edition) cut no ice with Sisam, who grumbled, 'Quotation on this lavish scale was never allowed by Bradley.'[26]

So there was plenty to discuss with Craigie upon his return from Scotland. The main difficulty seems to have been how he should be paid for work done during the summer. He had been absent for at least some of June, but felt that he had done what the agreement required down to the end of that month; thereafter, he seems to have conceded that his output had so far been short of expectations. His suggestion that for the second half of the year his payment could be calculated on the basis of output rather than hours worked was rejected by Chapman as fraught with difficulties. Eventually it was agreed to pay him £80 and £150 for the third and fourth quarters of the year respectively: overall only fractionally less pro rata than his nominal salary of £500. There was also the offer of £50 'for services in prosecuting *We* (if results shall justify such a payment)'—the incentive that Chapman had promised for hurrying Worrall along.[27]

Such a system of one-off payments, rather than an ongoing contractual arrangement, shows that there was now considerable doubt about Craigie's long-term commitment to the Dictionary. It was already known that he intended to return to Chicago in the summer of 1925;[28] at least he was planning carefully for this absence, no doubt anxious to avoid a repetition of the disagreements over work and payment. He was advised by Chapman to concentrate effort on completing the copy for U before he left—which,

[25] *Scotsman* 1 Oct. 1924, p. 8, 3 Oct. 1924, p. 3.

[26] OED/B/3/2/13 extract from a letter 2 Oct. 1924 CTO to [RWC?]; 10 Oct. 1924 KS to RWC, 11 Oct. 1924 RWC to KS; 15 Oct. 1924 WAC to RWC, KS to RWC.

[27] FC 24 Oct. 1924.

[28] OED/B/3/2/13 copy of letter 13 Oct. 1924 RWC to D. G. Hogarth, annotated (possibly by RWC) 'He expects to go to America again next year'.

despite earlier reports that it was more or less finished, promised to be a tall order.[29] As for *We*, Chapman saw some grounds for optimism: 'From a long talk I had with Worrall […] I am encouraged to hope that he has found his feet and will not have the same reluctance as he at one time had to pass a sheet for the press.'[30] Certainly Worrall's work on copy was continuing to produce output, although still at an appalling scale: his portion of *Well* eventually occupied over 20 pages, compared to a single column in Webster, a scale of more than 60. The absence of comment suggests that by this stage Chapman was past caring.

The need for Worrall to pull his weight was now greater than ever; for in October the true extent of Craigie's disillusion with Oxford became clear. It was announced on 17 October that he had accepted the offer of a professorship in English at the University of Chicago, on the understanding that he would begin work on a historical dictionary of American English.[31] The breach with Oxford was not to be total, as Craigie would be able to work on *OED* proofs in Chicago—and, he hoped, help Worrall to prepare the etymologies in *We*—and he also planned to make extended visits to Oxford in the summer months; but it is hard to disagree with Onions's description of his impending departure as 'the third great blow to the N.E.D.' after the deaths of Murray and Bradley. He gloomily forecast that the Dictionary might now take another five years to complete.[32]

The end of the Dictionary was, nevertheless, near enough that it was now beginning to be necessary to plan the allocation of the remaining copy so as to avoid any one assistant running out of work, while at the same time continuing with work on the Abridged, and with the preliminary sorting of material for the still inchoate Supplement. Eventually it was provisionally agreed that, once *We* was finished, Worrall, Bayliss, and Lewis would divide *Wo* between them, with Worrall passing his own copy to the printers, while Onions and Maling continued drafting copy in *Wi*. Craigie, ever the optimist, foresaw 'every chance of bringing the end of the Dictionary well within sight in the course of the next year'.[33] The question of a cheap reissue of the Dictionary— something that was expected to do particularly well in the American market—was also beginning to be seriously discussed: in May it was decided (by Chapman and several visiting representatives of the Press's New York office) that the print run for this still theoretical work should be at least 10,000.[34]

---

[29] OED/B/3/2/13 15 Nov. 1924 WAC to RWC.

[30] OED/B/3/2/13 21 Nov. 1924 RWC to WAC.

[31] The *Chicago Daily Tribune* reported the appointment on 18 October, under the impressively American headline 'Midway Signs Limey Prof. to Dope Yank Talk'. Further on the genesis of what later became the *Dictionary of American English* see Adams (1998).

[32] PSOM 6 Mar., 5 June 1925.

[33] OED/B/3/2/14 14 May 1925 WAC to RWC.

[34] PBED 12962 4 May 1925 RWC to HSM. The idea of a reissue of the Dictionary had in fact been proposed as early as 1913 (OED/B/3/10/4 19 Mar. 1920 RWC to Controller, citing untraced earlier correspondence); in 1920 Chapman had consulted Onions about how best to divide the reissue into twelve rather than ten volumes (OED/B/3/10/4 18 Mar. 1920 RWC to CTO).

On 1 June Chapman threw an informal 'tamasha' or tea-party (with tennis and bowls) for all the Dictionary staff, which will also have served as a farewell party for Craigie: the Dictionary's third Editor sailed for America in early July, having resigned his Oxford professorship.[35] (J. R. R. Tolkien was elected as his successor; Sisam, perhaps surprisingly, was also a candidate, and was only beaten by Tolkien to the appointment on the Vice-Chancellor's casting vote.[36])

Progress in Oxford following Craigie's departure soon fell short of expectations. Indeed, it had not been good in the first part of the year: the amount of the letter W completed in the first five months corresponded to only one and a half pages of Webster. The remaining portion of *Wi* continued to be extremely tough going, and both Lewis and Bayliss now had to be drafted in to help with it. Worrall was also once again becoming bogged down. Craigie, writing from Harvard where he was teaching at a summer school, found it hard to believe Chapman's report that he was still working at *wet*: 'I thought that he had plain sailing before him when I left [...]. At this rate it will take some months to get the last of *We-* into its final state.'[37]

By the time Craigie wrote these words the bundle *Wet–Wezzon* had arrived at the printers; but overall output was worryingly low, and continued to be so into the autumn. What was worse, no section had been published since *Whisky–Wilfulness* in November 1924, a hiatus of the kind which went down badly with Dictionary subscribers. It was true that a double section of U would soon be ready, but this could make for difficulty later in that the remainder of the letter was likely to amount to a rather unsatisfactory fragment. Consultation with Onions as to what of W was ready for publication now revealed a chaotic state of affairs resulting from imperfect implementation of the plan he and Craigie had devised. Although Worrall, Bayliss, and Lewis were all still working on *We*, they had all diverted some of their effort to other parts of the letter: Worrall had made a start on *Wo* (and was making heavy weather of the word *woe*), Lewis was helping Onions with *Wi*, and Bayliss had been doing work in both *Wi* and *Wo*. To publish later sections of W when *We* remained incomplete would only confuse the public; accordingly, it made no sense to divert effort away from the one part of W that ought to be finalized as quickly as possible. Chapman, evidently astonished that the lexicographers could be so oblivious of the need to publish, exhorted Onions (and by implication all the assistants) to 'concentrate [on *We-*] in God's name'.[38]

From around this time the figure of Kenneth Sisam (Figure 30) begins to play a more prominent part in the story of the Dictionary. Sisam had of course worked briefly as Bradley's assistant during the war, and had always taken an interest in the project; in 1922—when he returned to OUP as Junior Assistant Secretary—he seems to have taken on a regular editorial role, commenting on bundles of Dictionary copy

[35] OED/B/3/7/4 26 May 1925 RWC to WAC and CTO. Craigie took up his professorial post in Chicago on 1 October (information from Alice Chandler).

[36] Carpenter (1977: 114–15).

[37] OED/B/3/2/14 3 June 1925 KS to RWC (with annotation by RWC 7 July), 3 Aug. 1925 WAC to RWC.

[38] OED/B/3/2/14 7 Oct. 1925 CTO to [RWC], 8 Oct. 1925 RWC to CTO.

FIGURE 30   Kenneth Sisam.

before it went to press.[39] In the autumn of 1925 he provided Chapman with a detailed memorandum setting out—as Chapman himself had done in a similar document three years before—various issues relating to the *OED* and related projects.[40] It must have made painful reading. The combined output of both staffs during the financial year 1924–5 amounted to 526 columns (175 pages) of printed text—barely half what had been achieved in the year chosen by Sisam for comparison, 1914–15 (when work was being done on *St* and *Su*). This was despite the fact that the words being worked on during the year by Craigie's staff constituted much more straightforward material (lexicographically at least). The drastically reduced output also meant that the Press was getting much poorer value for money: Sisam calculated that the editorial cost of work on *We* and *Wi* in 1924–5 amounted on average to £9 per column of printed text—nearly four times the equivalent figure for 1914–15. In contrast, the work of Craigie and his assistants in *Un* and *Up* worked out at less than £4 per column; even allowing for the relative straightforwardness of their material, Sisam still felt that Craigie's staff was more economical.

In analysing the causes of the drop in output, Sisam could draw on his own experience of work on the Dictionary; the result is most informative about editorial practices. Of course part of the reduction could be attributed to the difficulties caused by Craigie's departure; but Sisam identified four other 'special causes'. Firstly, it was more efficient to have a relatively high proportion of staff doing what he called 'first-copy preparation'—i.e. the first attempt to convert the mass of evidence for a word into a bundle of copy ready to be typeset. Secondly there was 'Checking and Revision'—i.e. the verification of quotations (mainly done in the Bodleian Library), and the reviewing of draft editorial text—of which Sisam observed that '[t]here is no point where more time can be frittered away with less practical result [...] and I can't help thinking that

---

[39] Sisam's comments on Onions's copy for W, dating from 1923, survive (OED/B/3/3/3); it seems reasonable to infer that he began this scrutiny of the copy a year earlier, as it is in 1922 that the bundles of copy, which up to this point bear only the stamp 'Received & Entered at the University Press', now begin to show an additional stamp indicating that they were first being taken to the Secretary's office.

[40] OED/B/3/2/14 9 Oct. 1925 KS to RWC.

there has been time wasted, because there was not enough pressure of work.' Thirdly, there was the extent to which an Editor could maintain pressure on his staff by being constantly ready and waiting for more copy to finalize. Onions, of course, had the additional burdens of work on the Abridged, not to mention his teaching obligations; but even without these, Sisam argued, 'it is the man who has the next word wanted that pushes along, and the longer the line of assistants under one editor, the more distant is the day of reckoning on the average, and so the less the exertion of each.' The size of Onions's staff, in other words, was actually inhibiting productivity. Finally there was the similar pressure that could be exerted by the printer, by constantly 'pulling on the editors for copy, revises and press proofs; and the quicker the single sections are printed and published, the less time will be frittered in looking at them.' Sisam also took a careful look at the other projects which were now taking up rather too much of the lexicographers' time. He was profoundly sceptical about the likely commercial value of the Supplement; and he now began to wonder 'whether it might not be better to finish N.E.D. and blow the trumpets without a Supplement', rather than regarding the completion of the Supplement as the point at which to aim for maximum publicity.

What comes through most strongly in Sisam's analysis is his advocacy of proper planning. In assessing the work remaining to be done to complete the main Dictionary—his estimate was that 'the whole thing could be finished up by Christmas 1926 if enough heart were put into it'—he emphasizes the need to have 'a programme for every member of the staff. The greatest waste of time is due to there being no clear programme either for whole staffs or individuals in a subject where there is no natural limit (except life) to the time that they may spend.' Significantly, he also voiced concerns about what was going on across the Atlantic. He recommended offering Craigie an attractive payment for undertaking to 'polish off' a substantial portion of the remaining text, as he was in a position to 'do a lot of harm or good in U.S.A. just as N.E.D. is finishing [...] If Craigie gets a part of his American Dictionary out before the smaller N.E.D. [i.e. the Abridged] is ready, its sale in U.S.A. will suffer, and the nearer his projects come to realization, the more difficult it will be to sell N.E.D. there.' Sisam evidently now regarded Craigie as by no means certain to do what was best for the Dictionary without a financial incentive, and even as capable of sabotage.

Meanwhile, in Chicago Craigie was also once again ruminating upon the future, along rather different lines from Sisam. His main preoccupation was with his grand vision of a family of period and regional dictionaries; and in October, much as he had threatened to do a year earlier, he prepared a formal memorandum for the Delegates on the subject.[41] Things had certainly moved on in the three years since he had last memorialized them: there were now four projects on which a real start could be said to have been made. In addition to the dictionary of American English, under the auspices of the University of Chicago, and the considerable quantity of material for a dictionary of older Scots which he had now accumulated—and was proposing to

---

[41] OED/B/3/2/14 19 Oct. 1925 WAC to RWC (enclosing copies of the memorandum for the Delegates).

work on himself—the Scottish Dialects Committee was now organizing the collection of material for a dictionary of modern Scots,[42] and a committee had been set up by the Modern Language Association of America with a view to the compilation of a dictionary of Middle English. The memo expanded upon an idea which had been present in his earlier memo of 1922, namely that the relevant components of the materials collected for the *OED* might be made available (under suitable conditions) for the use of each of the other projects. The compilation of these new dictionaries was, Craigie argued, the best way to make use of the materials that had accumulated in Oxford, and should be seen as a necessary first step before either a Supplement or a complete revision of the Dictionary could be contemplated. His covering note to Chapman also hinted that there could be reciprocal benefits, in terms of sharing the materials collected by all parties, if the Press chose to become a collaborator in any of these projects.

It might be wondered how on earth Craigie was hoping to find the time to compile a large dictionary of Older Scots alongside all his other commitments. In fact the burden of his Chicago professorship was lighter than might be imagined: as he had earlier explained to Leonard Wharton, Secretary of the Philological Society, 'I am not put down for any formal lecturing [in 1925–6], but for a course on "Making a Dictionary" and a "Middle English Seminar". This ought to give good opportunities for getting work done.'[43] By October 1925 he was indeed getting work done, as he told Wharton: 'The plans for the dictionary of American English are taking shape [...] I have [...] already five graduate students and one professor working with me twice a week to learn dictionary methods. I also have ten graduates studying Middle English, and expect to employ them on the Scottish dictionary after the New Year.'[44]

Craigie's correspondence with Wharton was very far from being a matter of simply keeping in touch with an old friend. There had long been support within the Philological Society for his ideas about period dictionaries; indeed in 1923 the Society had passed a resolution supporting both the period dictionaries scheme in general and the idea of involving American academics in the work.[45] He was now asking for more explicit backing; indeed he even sent Wharton a form letter of support, suggesting that he 'obtain the signatures of the President and other members of Council to a letter in some such terms'. The response Craigie hoped for was some time in coming, but letters of support did emerge, identical to that sent to Wharton, from both the MLA and the University of Chicago.[46]

---

[42] Further on the activities of this committee, see p. 417.
[43] PS(m) 30 Apr. 1925 WAC to L. C. Wharton.
[44] PS(m) 17 Oct. 1925 WAC to Wharton.
[45] PSOM 6 Apr. 1923. Following this meeting a pamphlet inviting offers of help with the 'Period Dictionaries Scheme' had been produced for distribution at a conference of teachers of English held in New York in June 1923 (copies preserved at OED/B/3/2/15).
[46] OED/B/3/2/14 20 Oct. 1925 C. F. Emerson and Clark S. Northup to the Delegates, 23 Oct. 1925 Max Mason and John M. Manly to Delegates.

Craigie's memo was also of course in circulation in Oxford among various interested parties; and the initial reactions were rather more mixed. The Vice-Chancellor, Joseph Wells, thought it 'most interesting';[47] other Delegates were alarmed by it. Onions's response smacks less of outright opposition than of irritation at an incompletely thought-out scheme, in particular with reference to the practicalities:

'To carry out the redistribution of the Oxford material would be a simple task', says Craigie. Simple, no doubt; but has any calculation been made, can any calculation be made, of the time necessary for one or two assistants to sort and distribute among the centuries a mass of something like 5000000 slips?

Onions was here writing from recent experience: the sorting of 80 feet of material for the Supplement had only recently been completed, after a year of work.[48] But worse criticisms of Craigie were abroad. Word had reached Chapman that he 'got his position in America largely by hinting at the treasures of material he can bring over, and that he is now called upon to deliver the goods'; Chapman must have either believed this to be true, or at least been sufficiently fed up with Craigie to pass on unfavourable gossip. Despite such ill feeling, he considered it impolitic to reject Craigie's proposals outright, as the various dictionary projects would almost certainly go ahead however Oxford responded, and 'we shall not strengthen ourselves by merely behaving like Lodge and Borah. On the other hand we can, & should, make it [i.e. the granting of access to the materials] appear both difficult & magnificent, and exact all there is to exact in return.'[49]

In the event the formal response of the Delegates was broadly positive. Chapman informed Craigie that they were 'favourable to the principle' of dividing up the material, subject to a number of reservations designed to safeguard their interests, including the right to publish the dictionaries in question outside North America.[50] There were also important limits on which material could be used: the whole of the so-called 'Supplement material' would not be made available (unsurprisingly in view of the continuing lack of clarity regarding the scope of any Supplement), nor would the materials relating to the unpublished portions of U and W. Finally there was the practical stipulation that the work of separating out material would have to be done at the expense (including transportation and insurance costs) of the period dictionary projects themselves, though under Oxford's direction.

A minor obstacle to the smooth progress of Craigie's proposals emerged at the end of the year, when Onions learned that the Philological Society had given similar 'in principle' approval, and appointed an investigatory Committee, without consulting him—despite the fact that, quite apart from his role as Editor, he was a Vice-President of

[47] OED/B/3/2/14 4 Nov. 1925 J. Wells to RWC.
[48] OED/B/3/2/14 12 Nov. 1925 CTO to RWC; notes 11 Nov. 1925 by CTO on 'Supplement material'.
[49] OED/B/3/2/14 13 Nov. 1925 RWC to HSM. Lodge and Borah were two famously isolationist American senators.
[50] FC 26 Nov. 1925; PS(m) 17 Dec. 1925 RWC to WAC.

the Society. Ruffled feathers were smoothed following a meeting of the Society, attended by Onions (whom Chapman urged to 'exhibit unmistakeable signs of complete harmony' with Craigie); the Society gave general approval to the proposals, though Wharton did raise some queries in relation to copyright.[51] In fact when Chapman's letter reached Craigie in early January, he seems to have been more or less satisfied, quibbling only the question of the 'Supplement material', access to which he felt was essential—and to which he felt that he had some claim, not least as someone who had contributed considerably to the materials himself. He also complained of being kept in the dark as regards what plans were being made for the Supplement; Chapman reassured him that he had not been excluded from any significant decisions, while observing to Milford that even if anything had been done without Craigie—which he denied—then 'if he has long periods of absence he must expect things to happen'.[52] In any case, although the work that had been done on rationalizing the materials for the Supplement had led to some renewed thinking, nothing more definite had been decided about the form it should take.[53]

All this was of course simply a distraction from the task of completing the Dictionary. Onions's output remained steady: in the last two months of 1925 he sent 8 pages of *Wi* to the printers.[54] Craigie, too, was keeping his hand in, mainly with work on *We*. Worrall had been instructed to manage the correction of proofs without reference to Craigie whenever possible, which ought to have improved his rate of progress; but, as Craigie wrote in November, 'the trouble is that all his proofs come so slowly. The one I had the other day has actually been in type since April.' Worrall was not the only one experiencing problems: Craigie reported to Chapman in December that Watson had been having 'difficulties in managing the staff', which he asked Chapman to address by issuing him with an authorizing note, thereby putting Watson 'in a position to insist on regular attendance in order to get the full amount of work done'.[55] Craigie also suggested rewarding Watson for his exceptional efforts on U; but Onions advised against this, revealing a rather different assessment of Watson's abilities, and a rare glimpse of group dynamics in the Old Ashmolean:

The sacrifice of holiday and working overtime [...], however laudable in itself, places at a disadvantage fellow-workers who are not doing the same but are expected to keep pace, and feeling is consequently aroused. [...] Watson, beginning as a mere proof-corrector, has by sheer industry and mechanical efficiency, arrived at a competence of a particular kind in preparing copy (which remains essentially unscholarly,—I have the contrast of Worrall & Maling in

---

[51] OED/B/3/2/14 21 Dec. 1925 L. C. Wharton to CTO, 23 Dec. 1925 CTO to RWC, RWC to CTO; OED/B/3/2/15 16 Jan. 1926 Wharton to Delegates.

[52] OED/B/3/2/15 12 Jan. 1926 WAC to RWC, 28 Jan. 1926 RWC to WAC; PBED 8670 28 Jan. 1926 RWC to HSM.

[53] The notes made by Onions in November (see p. 374 n. 48) reported that the materials for the range *A* to *aero* had been 'minutely examined & compared with the printed Dictionary', and that a provisional selection had been made in line with the idea of an ' "integrating" Supplement'.

[54] Work on the Dictionary does not appear to have been affected by the printers' strike at OUP in November 1926 (see Maw 2013a: 233).

[55] OED/B/3/2/14 7 Nov., 9 Dec. 1925 WAC to RWC.

my mind) [...] I do not find that he has a grasp of philological principles beyond what other assistants have acquired; his patent inability to understand phonetics is a hindrance not only in this but in the handling of our pronunciation system.

This will give an indication of the kind of preparation he is capable of in WR, full of course of philological problems, where the expert can at once give a direction [...] while the inexpert may *bombinare* [Latin: buzz, bumble] long & aimlessly. If W[atson] is to go on with WR [...] he must be somehow dissuaded from the fussy and feverish activity so evident of late and so obviously productive of irritation in the rest of the staff [...] his work at the moment on WR is chaotic.[56]

Sisam's take on the situation, however, was quite different:

I think there is some case for Watson (my opinion of his philology is higher than Onions', and only Maling equals him in the ability to keep going). But the main consideration is to keep Craigie sweet by any means during the next five years, during which he could do us a great deal of harm both financially and in reputation. [...] For this purely political reason I think Watson ought to go on with *Wr-* [...].[57]

Chapman took Sisam's advice, and Watson—who had, after all, 'succeeded where Worrall failed'—was duly paid £20 'for his special services on *U* in Dr. Craigie's absence'.[58] Further evidence of Worrall's 'failure' was soon forthcoming: in May Onions explained that his progress now that he had made a start on *Wo* was not what it might be because '*woe* will hold me up because, though appropriated [by Worrall] months ago, it has not been prepared, and I shall have to do it nearly all myself'.[59]

[56] OED/B/3/2/14 30 Dec. 1925 CTO to RWC. Onions later offered Chapman concrete evidence of Watson's philological shortcomings: 'Worrall has been saving U from some serious negligences and ignorances by his vigilances over the proofs. An instance came under my notice a few days ago, when I caught sight of *ūltrā* so marked in the final stage of a sheet. This is one of a series of "longs" [i.e. vowels inappropriately marked as long with the macron symbol ⁻] which Watson had taken from a Latin Gradus (e.g. *ūsūrpāre*)! But Worrall has been instrumental in getting worse things removed. After all, he and Maling are the only two scholars on the staff' (OED/B/3/2/15 6 June 1926 CTO to RWC).

[57] OED/B/3/2/14 31 Dec. 1925 KS to RWC. Craigie's reputation in America was certainly growing, and not merely in academic circles. His appointment by Chicago, with a remit to edit a dictionary of American English, had been widely reported; on 27 November 1925 he gave a radio broadcast about the project (subsequently printed in the *Bulletin of the Modern Humanities Research Association*), and at a meeting of the Modern Language Association in December he publicized the Press's decision to allow the unpublished *OED* materials to be made use of by the various period dictionary projects (Long 1926: 439). It was at this time that he was also appointed 'Director of Research' for the American Dialect Society's own proposed 'American Dialect Dictionary' (*PMLA* 40 (1925), Appendix, p. x). This project, which Craigie conceived as complementing the historical dictionary of American English just as the *English Dialect Dictionary* complemented the *OED* (Craigie 1925: 318–19), seems eventually to have foundered in the 1930s, although another initiative from the same source eventually bore fruit several decades later in the form of the *Dictionary of American Regional English*.

[58] OED/B/3/2/15 7 Jan. 1926 RWC to CTO; FC 26 Feb. 1926.

[59] OED/B/3/2/15 22 May 1926 CTO to RWC. Some words, of course, would be a long job for anyone: Onions also noted that the word *with* 'will have taken Maling nearly 2 months & will probably need a month's revision by me'.

Political and practical difficulties in the Old Ashmolean notwithstanding, the end of the project was at last heaving into view. In January 1926 it was agreed that Craigie should edit *Wr* during his summer visit to Oxford, and that Watson and his other Oxford assistants should work the material up for him, while Onions and the rest of the staff completed *Wi* and *Wo*; and a temporary halt was called to all work on the Abridged, so that effort could be concentrated on the main Dictionary.[60] In a memo written on 14 June—barely a month after the end of the General Strike—Chapman estimated that the main Dictionary would be completed in 1928: apparently the first time the right date appears in anyone's predictions.[61] And after the Chicago summer term had ended, Craigie returned to Oxford for three months of work. By good fortune or design, this coincided with the publication—at last—of some actual Dictionary text. Three sections, in fact: *Unright–Uzzle* on 29 July, and *Wavy–Wezzon* and *Wilga–Wise* on 12 August.[62] The Prefaces to the first and second of these gave public recognition, in their different ways, of the special contributions of Watson and Worrall. Craigie, writing the Preface for the whole of U in Chicago in March 1926, acknowledged that 'in the later portion of the letter Mr. Watson's services have been of special value both for the progress and the completeness of the work'; in *Wavy–Wezzon*, by contrast, it was simply mentioned that the articles drafted after Bradley's death, 'after the usual preparation by [Bradley's] staff, have been edited by Dr. Craigie with the co-operation of Mr. Worrall'. When, in November 1927, Craigie and Onions jointly drafted the Preface for the whole of W, this acknowledgement was slightly expanded—Worrall was noted as having 'specially prepared portions of *We* and *Wo*'—but this was of course far less than the co-editorship with Bradley which had originally been envisaged. It seems a pity that a man whose service to the Dictionary eventually extended to 48 years should end up with so little recognition; but it cannot be denied that he had his chance.

Craigie returned to Chicago in September after a most productive summer, having sent the equivalent of over 20 pages of *Wr* to the printers; he told a specially convened meeting of the Philological Society that the Dictionary might be finished 'by next Spring'.[63] The fact that within days of his departure Onions raised concerns about the quality of the work—specifically in regard to scale, which at over 24 times Webster was far in excess of the scale he and his staff had been achieving—might lead one to suspect some kind of resentment at Craigie's having (as it seemed) swanned in, done his quota, and then returned to his pet projects. Sisam's comment to Chapman indicates that at this stage there were other priorities: 'Don't let's start this hare again! The thing is to get finished, & if Onions can make as good pace by going to the same scale—by all means

---

[60] OED/B/3/2/15 8 Jan. 1926 RWC to WAC, 11 Jan. 1926 KS to John Johnson (as Printer).

[61] OED/B/3/2/15 14 June 1926 RWC to G. W. S. Hopkins and HSM.

[62] The published portion of the alphabet was now continuous to *Wise*, leaving only the gap from *Wise* to the end of W.

[63] PSOM 3 Sept. 1926.

persuade him—it will be much more economical.'[64] Chapman agreed, and advised Onions not to worry; but it was clear that there was more than simple animosity at work. Onions replied:

I shall find the most serious opposition to a policy of letting the scale rip in my staff, especially Maling & Sweatman, for whom an excessive scale is synonymous with bad lexicography. [...] An excess of copy means excess of time in its handling at every subsequent stage. And the mischief does not end there: it is carried on to the Abridged. The letter N [also edited by Craigie] is already giving trouble on account of excessive subdivision.[65]

He also pointed out that the final volume of the Dictionary was already of immense proportions, another reason for striving to keep scale within reasonable limits. Finally, there was a new proposal:

I have been lately wondering whether, when the Dictionary is finished (? end of 1927), two (say) of the staff should be detailed to collect material with a view to the entire revision of the first two volumes. This need not interfere with the progress of the 'integrating' Supplement, which will, I suppose, be put in full swing at once.

Onions's observations did not stand a chance against Sisam, who provided Chapman with detailed figures showing the appalling slowness, and expense, of Onions's team as compared with Craigie's. Onions 'with 6 experienced men and a reserve of ladies' was managing 200 slips of copy per week, as compared with Craigie and Watson, who were producing 500 with only Rosfrith Murray and Mrs Powell to help them. (Murray's Scriptorium in its heyday had managed 800 slips a week.) The disparity in costs was worse: £10 per column of Onions's text in wages alone, as compared with £2 per column for Craigie. Given these figures, Onions's proposal that his methods were preferable was unlikely to cut much ice, although Chapman reassured him that he was right in principle to set such store by condensation. As for the idea of embarking upon a wholesale revision, Sisam demonstrated that this could hardly cost less than £150,000, and at present rates would probably take 75 years. Such a prospect evoked a nightmare vision of the future:

Perhaps after 20 years of revision there will be in one room of the Delegates' asylum a band of grey-haired and well-fattened lexicographers, gibbering with delight over the last refinement of their craft, whereby the scale as compared with 1 page of Webster has been reduced to nil; and in another, too worn and broken to need a padded cell, the Secretariat, moaning 'Onions, give me back my millions'.[66]

---

[64] OED/B/3/2/15 21 Sept. 1926 CTO to RWC, 22 Sept. 1926 KS to RWC. Onions reported that in *Wh* and *Wi* he had managed to keep his own scale down to less than 14, 'in spite of *what, who*, etc., *will*, and the cruel demands of a series of big words in *white, win, wind, wine* ...'.

[65] OED/B/3/2/15 23 Sept. 1926 RWC to CTO, 18 Oct. 1926 CTO to RWC.

[66] OED/B/3/2/15 20 Oct. 1926 KS to RWC.

Evidently no action was taken to curb the scale of *Wr*, which eventually worked out at 59 printed pages in total, exceeding Webster by a factor of over 20.

Meanwhile, back in Chicago, Craigie had made progress on another front: securing the funds to pay for the extraction of material from Oxford for the period dictionaries. In November he wrote to Chapman with the news that he expected to be free from teaching obligations in the spring of 1927, and hoped in consequence to come over and supervise the start of the extraction process. He also mentioned another request, from a rather different quarter: Thomas A. Knott, the editor of the latest edition of Webster's Dictionary, had expressed an interest in acquiring any 'modern material which is of no special value for the O.E.D.', such as the mass of newspaper cuttings which had been contributed over many years by Furnivall and the former sub-editor William Robertson Wilson.[67] Neither Chapman nor Sisam thought much of the idea that such material should be made available to a purely commercial enterprise; and in any case the material was bound to be wanted for the Supplement.[68] Nothing more came of Knott's request.

All eyes were now firmly fixed on the finishing line. For various reasons—particularly the need to plan publicity—a definite timetable for completion was crucial. Craigie arrived in Oxford on 5 April 1927, and the following day he, Onions, Chapman, and Sisam met to map out the remaining work in detail.[69] It was decided that, with historical neatness, the finishing touches to the text should be made on 7 January 1928—70 years to the day from the passing of the Philological Society's resolutions 'relating to the undertaking of a New English Dictionary'. Onions was to take editorial responsibility for the first part of the final section, and the remainder (starting at *worm*) was assigned to Craigie, who would aim to finish as much as possible of his portion before he returned to America, leaving Onions to deal with any outstanding queries.

An agreed plan of work was, of course, welcome. Considerably less welcome was Craigie's announcement that he had secured an assistant professorship in Chicago for Watson, so that he could help with the dictionary of American English, starting in the autumn; Sisam lamented to Chapman that this would mean 'the removal of our one pace-maker'. Craigie also had suggestions to make about a large-scale Supplement, along the lines that Onions had proposed in October. Evidently both Editors believed that something substantial was needed—approving comparisons were apparently drawn with the supplement to Godefroy's *Dictionnaire de l'ancienne langue française*, which was as big as the parent dictionary—but, to Sisam's relief, Craigie was prepared to regard this as a project that would only be practicable after the completion of the period dictionaries; and he was persuaded of the merits of the 'very short supplement of essential things, to be issued in about three years' time' on which most parties were now agreed. This Supplement was to contain a bibliography of sources quoted in

---

[67] OED/B/3/2/15 29 Nov. 1926 WAC to RWC. These newspaper cuttings occupied about 16 feet of shelving, or 35,000 slips (OED/B/3/2/16 22 Apr. 1927 Sweatman to WAC).

[68] OED/B/3/2/15 17 Dec. 1926 KS to RWC.

[69] OED/B/3/2/16 1 Apr. 1927 RWC to CTO, 6 Apr. 1927 KS to Johnson (as Printer).

the main Dictionary, a historical account of the project, as well as dictionary articles for 'essential [new] words, e.g. *radium*' and 'essential Americana'—the latter being something that Craigie was happy to undertake. He was also now keen to commence the extraction of material for the period dictionaries, which it seems clear were now where his heart really lay. Sisam still had considerable confidence in Craigie's 'executive efficiency', but marvelled at his capacity for combining this with 'so many vague and grandiose schemes'.[70]

The Dictionary's Editors and publishers were also now beginning to give serious thought to what lay beyond the finishing line for those who, as it were, were still running the race. Further conferences were held to consider how the remaining assistants were to be deployed—or, indeed, whether their services could usefully be retained—as they reached the end of what they could do for the main Dictionary.[71] Sisam's notes on the first of these meetings include some ruthlessly businesslike assessments of the abilities of these individuals (or 'the toil-worn remnants', as he described them):

Miss Senior has had 2 years on [sorting materials for the] Supplement with little concrete result. Birt has no educational qualifications, & cannot prepare copy. [...] ? Whether it would not be wiser even now to see if he could not train for a printer's reader's job? Apart from use to Onions, he is no use to the Office. [...]
[O]n [other] staff there were these views:–
That Mrs Powell & Miss Murray, after doing any work for Craigie [i.e. separating out material from the files to be sent to America], might be dropped, the one because she is married, the other because she ought to be.
That Worrall must go.
That Lewis ought to go to some secluded library.
That Sweatman was too slow to be employed economically when his 6 months [i.e. the time during which there was expected to be work for him on the main Dictionary] is up.
That Bayliss was also slow, but might be employed for a few years on odd jobs.
Miss Bradley might slip away (but might also be the rough worker for Supplement).
All very melancholy.

Two other assistants, George Watson and Arthur Maling, received more favourable assessments. Watson Sisam considered to be 'the only man economically employable', but he was soon to leave for Chicago; Maling was evidently considered to be a good worker—and was in any case 'too old to become a burden'—and was earmarked to work on 'big & scientific words' for the Supplement. Completing the list was a Miss Savage, who had been taken on to work on the Abridged but who was due to leave shortly to get married.

[70] OED/B/3/2/16 23 Apr. 1927 KS to RWC. Craigie's attempt to persuade the Press to undertake the compilation of the dictionary of Early Modern English was unsuccessful.
[71] PBED 3974 12 May 1927 KS to RWC; OED/B/3/2/16 file note 25 July 1927 by KS.

The share to be taken by the two Editors in the 'short' Supplement was now becoming clearer. Craigie had already indicated his interest in dealing with items of American vocabulary, and it was now agreed that his entries for these would be interfiled with other material as it was prepared in Oxford by Onions, assisted by Maling and Lewis. Bayliss and Sweatman would compile the bibliography under the supervision of Onions, now identified as the Supplement's principal Editor. Work on one further small component—the list of 'Spurious Words' which had been promised by Murray nearly forty years before[72]—was postponed for the time being, although Sisam (never one for optimism where Onions's speed was concerned) anticipated that 'Craigie will have to pull it out of the fire in the end'. Rosfrith Murray and Mrs Powell would tackle the complex task of extracting various categories of slips from the files for Craigie (both in respect of his work on the Supplement 'Americana' and his period dictionary projects), while Birt and the Misses Senior and (for a time at least) Savage would work on the Abridged, again under Onions's direction. There was also general agreement that the Supplement had to be finished within two years, although by the time the Delegates came to give their approval this had been modified to an undertaking to have 'the whole [...] ready for printing by 31 December 1929'.[73] No explicit provision was made for Walter Worrall; nor for Eleanor Bradley, who however began to work more irregular hours around this time, as more of her time was required to look after her mother.

By this point very nearly all of the remaining copy for W had gone to the printers. The very end of W—the entry for *wyzen* (a variant of the dialect word *weasand*)—had been dispatched in February; all that now remained was a a small portion of *Wor*. It was noted by Falconer Madan, an old friend and helper of the Dictionary, that 'Onions took the *last* piece of "copy" for the Oxf. Eng. Dict. to the Press on Thursday last *July 28 1927*: it was in the word *WORK* [see Figure 31]—not a bad parable.'[74]

For the remainder of Craigie's stay in Oxford, he divided his time between tasks directly relating to the *OED*—including reading proofs (his own and Worrall's) and supervising the early stages of work on the Bibliography—and the extraction of 'period' material. He secured permission to extract quotations relating to Scottish and American vocabulary from the 'Supplement' files, and from the Dictionary's 'rejected' slips, and by the time of his departure for America extracted material for the letters A–D was ready to be sent to Chicago.[75]

[72] See above, p. 221.
[73] OD 18 Nov. 1927.
[74] Note by Madan, dated 30 July 1927 (BodL shelfmark 30254 c. 2, f. 20).
[75] OED/B/3/2/16 copy of letter 12 Sept. 1927 WAC to RWC; 17 Aug. 1927 KS to WAC. Before the end of the year Craigie had persuaded the University of Chicago to undertake publication of the Scottish dictionary as well as the American one (archives of University of Chicago Press (Chicago University Library), minutes of Publication Committee 17 Nov. 1927); he also had permission to extract Middle English material from the 'rejected' slips, but extraction of these does not appear to have begun until 1929 (CPED 611 21 June 1929 C. C. Fries to KS).

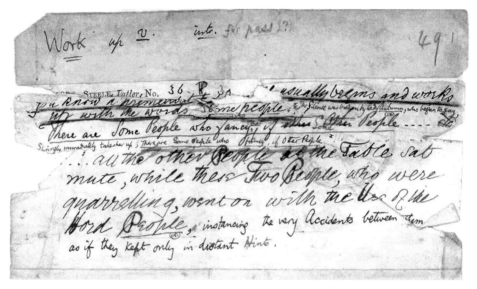

FIGURE 31   The final slip in the last bundle of Dictionary copy to go to the printers in July 1927: a quotation for the phrasal verb *to work up* (the last quotation in the entry for the verb *work*). The handwriting of the original contributor appears to be that of the sub-editor C. B. Mount, who died in 1916.

One last conference took place on 7 September, a week before Craigie's departure. By this stage Sisam could record with satisfaction that 'of the main Dictionary everything is in type except three prefaces [for individual sections] and the dedication, which are in hand'.[76] There was also more detail on the content of the Supplement: the main text would include 'primarily words and senses that have gained importance since 1880, and only secondarily such important omissions of words as may come to light without special research'. Both Editors had now accepted that corrections, as distinct from additions, would have to wait for now.[77] Maling and Lewis had in fact begun to prepare copy in August, and it was anticipated that a specimen would be produced at the end of the year; and Sweatman and Bayliss were progressing with the Bibliography.

Significantly, Craigie still saw this Supplement as very much an interim work. In a report to another specially convened meeting of the Philological Society he referred to it as containing merely 'inevitably necessary addenda', in contrast with another, 'more serious' Supplement which would harvest the fruits of the period dictionaries. To Chapman he was even more explicit, referring to them as the 'First Supplement' and 'Main Supplement', and even suggesting that the Delegates might pay him for work on

---

[76]   OED/B/3/2/16 file note 13 Sept. 1927 by KS (incomplete).
[77]   PBED 3974 29 June 1927 WAC to KS.

the latter.[78] Whatever Chapman thought of this idea, he was probably relieved that at least Craigie was still prepared to contemplate the prospect of an ongoing financial arrangement with the Press.

There was, of course, more work to be done on the main Dictionary after the departure of Craigie (followed, a few weeks later, by Watson). Although some hiccups were perhaps to be expected now that the two Editors were once more separated by the Atlantic, at this late stage any problem must have been viewed with alarm. In October Onions reported the news from Craigie that revises of Worrall's work, which he had been expecting to receive in Chicago, had dried up; the reason being that someone, unaware of Craigie's departure, had continued to send the proofs to his Oxford address. Craigie was still experiencing delay in the receipt of proofs in late November; but at last, on 5 January 1928—two days before the anniversary date which had been decided upon the previous April—Onions passed for press the concluding sheets of the Dictionary.[79] Sisam composed a short 'Carmen editorum superstitum in fine operis' to mark the occasion, with lines for Craigie and Onions.[80] Not, of course, that Craigie was around to perform his part; and in any case the proper celebrations were still to come.

Preparations for the completion, including the celebrations, had long been in hand. Detailed discussions had been taking place for months regarding such matters as pricing, binding, and—a very tricky point—the dedication of the completed Dictionary.[81] In February negotiations began in earnest on the matter of the awarding of honorary degrees at Oxford: Craigie and Onions were indisputable candidates, but Chapman also asked Onions (and presumably also Craigie) to consider whether any of the assistants might merit an honorary MA.[82]

Upon the completion of the main Dictionary, two of the oldest and longest-serving assistants, Arthur Maling and Walter Worrall, seem (each in his own way) to have lost the will to carry on. In the case of Worrall it had been apparent for some months that he hardly seemed to know what to do with himself. Neither did his masters. Sisam's readiness to see him go has already been mentioned, and Chapman seems also to have regarded him as little more than a liability: 'his influence is bad in itself,

---

[78] PSOM 9 Sept. 1927; OED/B/3/2/16 copy of letter 12 Sept. 1927 WAC to RWC.

[79] OED/B/3/2/16 21 Oct. 1927 CTO to KS, 28 Nov. 1927 WAC to KS. A note from Onions announcing the completion was read out at a meeting of the Philological Society the following week (PSOM 13 Jan. 1928).

[80] 'Song of the editors still standing at the end of the work'. Preserved in OED/B/3/2/16.

[81] After much discussion of the idea of re-dedicating the Dictionary to King George V, it was eventually decided that it should simply be 'presented' to him (as formally stated on a special introductory page), to avoid any hint of slighting the memory of his grandmother, to whom it had of course been dedicated in 1897.

[82] OED/B/3/2/17 11 Feb. 1928 RWC to CTO. Chapman had in fact raised the matter with the Vice-Chancellor nearly a year earlier (OED/B/3/2/16 2 Apr. 1927 RWC to F. W. Pember), not long after the former Dictionary assistant L. F. Powell had been awarded an honorary MA; Powell's work on the Dictionary was mentioned by the Public Orator on that occasion, although the honour was mainly in recognition of his work at the Taylorian Institution.

& his superannuation may well have a stimulating effect on the general output.'[83] At a December meeting of the Finance Committee he calmly reported that 'it seems desirable that Mr. Worrall should at an early date cease to be regularly employed on the Dictionary, but that he might do piecework at home'. By January Worrall himself had begun to worry; he wrote to Chapman, rather plaintively asking 'what I am to do now that the work which has kept me occupied for over 42 years has come to a happy end'.[84] It was now decided to pension him off at £2 a week, after 3 months' notice. Chapman's letter communicating the Delegates' decision to Worrall is striking for the absence of any mention of health, or any good wishes for the future. Maybe this was considered inappropriate given the hopes that Worrall would continue to do piecework, but something a little more friendly in tone might have been expected. The decision certainly came as a shock to Worrall, who in fact did do piecework for the Supplement—both compiling copy and reading proofs—for several years.[85]

Maling, by contrast, did manage to make something of a fresh start after finishing work on the main Dictionary: he had been put to work on the Supplement in August, and returned to work after Christmas—on words beginning with *anti-*—apparently as normal. But he was now an old man, prone to attacks of rheumatism, and after only one day's work in January his health—described as 'precarious' by Onions as long ago as 1922[86]—finally gave way. After three weeks of treatment he remained unable to return to work.[87] In April Chapman wrote to the Vice-Chancellor apparently proposing a radical form of therapy: 'We think that A. T. Maling, M.A. Cantab., the senior assistant on the Dictionary, might very suitably be made M.A. honoris causâ. He is a good scholar and has done a great deal for the Dictionary. [...] Recognition might give him a new lease of life.'[88] This seems to have been Chapman's idea, as there is no evidence that Onions had already suggested him as a suitable candidate for such an honour; he was indeed the 'senior assistant', but only because Worrall had retired. In any event, the prospect of recognition failed to have the desired effect: Maling never recovered sufficiently to return to work, and following medical reports he, too, was pensioned off.[89] In due course he did receive his honorary MA, at a ceremony a week after the main occasion on 5 June.[90] But his illness and retirement were nothing short of disastrous for the Supplement; already in April Sisam was admitting to Craigie that 'the rate of progress causes me great anxiety'.[91]

---

[83] OED/B/3/2/16 20 Dec. 1927 RWC to HSM.

[84] FC 23 Dec. 1927; OED/B/3/2/17 17 Jan. 1928 Worrall to RWC.

[85] FC 26 Jan. 1928; OD 27 Jan. 1928; OED/B/3/2/17 28 Jan. 1928 RWC to Worrall, 30 Jan. 1928 Worrall to RWC. See also Gilliver (2010c).

[86] OED/B/3/2/11 5 Dec. 1922 CTO to [RWC].

[87] OED/B/3/4/23 28 Jan. 1928 Maling to CTO.

[88] OED/B/3/2/17 27 Apr. 1928 RWC to F. W. Pember (as Vice-Chancellor).

[89] FC 31 May 1928; OD 1 June 1928.

[90] *Times* 13 June 1928, p. 17.

[91] PBED 3974 4 Apr. 1928 KS to WAC.

It might be wondered whether any of the other assistants had been considered eligible for an honorary degree. The thought occurred to Falconer Madan, who urged Chapman that the University should not forget 'the minor labourers who have borne the burden and heat of the day. Such are people like Worrall, Bayliss and Sweatman, to name three only. Could they not [...] share with Mr Maling (?) the privilege of an "Hon. M.A."? [...] only you and a few others like myself appreciate the aid rendered by the lesser folk of the O. E. D. in its harder times.'[92] In the event none of those whom Madan referred to as 'the "Little People"' received such recognition; none, however, seem to have begrudged Maling his honour, being apparently content in their own knowledge of the part they had played in what was now being recognized on all sides as a stupendous achievement. (Another group of often overlooked Dictionary workers also received some public recognition at this time, namely the compositors. As luck would have it, January 1928 saw the retirement of James Gilbert, who had begun setting type for the Dictionary in 1882—fairly early on in the letter A—and had gone on to set more of it than anyone else; a report of his retirement was picked up by the national press.[93])

In fact a crescendo of press attention was now beginning to build. Chapman, well aware of the importance of good news management, arranged for various pieces of information to be released to the press—the publication date of the final section (19 April), the information that the Dictionary would be presented to the King, and the news that the Goldsmiths' Company would be hosting a special celebratory banquet—together with a tiny pamphlet he had composed containing 'Some Facts and Figures' about the great work.[94] A special number of the *Periodical* was issued on 15 February emblazoned with the words 'The Oxford English Dictionary Completed' on the cover, with articles on various aspects of the project, the contents of which were reproduced in countless newspapers both in Britain and throughout the world. The *New York Times*, slightly jumping the gun, printed a report on New Year's Day that the entire Dictionary was 'now completed and in the printer's hands', having cost a quarter of a million dollars; the Vice-President of OUP's American Branch, Geoffrey Cumberlege, capitalized on this with a corrective letter pointing out that $250,000 was merely the cost of the Dictionary's final volume, whereas the total cost of the project would exceed $2,000,000 (roughly £400,000).[95] The figure for sales was not publicly mentioned, but by 1928 total receipts stood at a little over £100,000: a substantial amount, but one which emphatically confirmed the Dictionary's status as an 'unremunerative'

---

[92] OED/B/3/2/17 25 May 1928 F. Madan to RWC.

[93] *Clarendonian* Fourth Quarter 1927, p. 76; *Observer* 12 Feb. 1928, p. 22.

[94] OED/B/3/2/17 3 Jan. 1928 RWC to HSM. A copy of the pamphlet, and Chapman's draft text, are preserved in OED/B/3/2/16.

[95] *New York Times* 1 Jan. 1928, section 3, p. 1, and 15 Jan. 1928, p. 55. The special issue of the *Periodical* gave the lower figure of £300,000 (a little under $1,500,000) as an estimated figure for the total outlay.

publication from a purely monetary standpoint.[96] Its value to the Press in other terms was of course incalculable; it would be several decades before expressions such as 'flagship product' would come into use, but a flagship the *OED* unquestionably was.

Publication day, 19 April, was marked by special events on both sides of the Atlantic. In Oxford the Bodleian Library opened an exhibition illustrating the history of English dictionaries; the catalogue included a foreword by Onions, who also wrote a celebratory article in that day's *Times*. Few would argue with his opening words: 'This year, whatever else it may be, is the Year of the Dictionary.'[97] Plaudits began to pour in from all quarters, including a telegram from the editors of the Dictionary's Dutch counterpart, the *Woordenboek der Nederlandsche Taal*—still some decades from completion—offering 'fraternal congratulations'.[98] Meanwhile, Craigie was in Washington: it had been decided that, in addition to the formal presentation of the Dictionary to King George V,[99] a copy should also be presented to President Coolidge (ironically a man of notoriously few words). Craigie travelled to Washington to make the presentation in person, an event which was widely reported.[100] American interest in the Dictionary was considerable, and the work was selling briskly; so briskly, indeed, as to cause the Press's New York office some difficulty. An order from the vice-president of General Motors, John J. Raskob, for 27 sets specially bound in full leather (at $1,200 apiece), and another enquiry from 'one Chicago millionaire who may want 50 sets for his friends', led to some anxious exchanges between New York and London, to ensure that stocks were adequate to meet the demand.[101]

The event requiring the most elaborate planning was of course the dinner in Gold-smiths' Hall on 6 June. The initial approach to the Goldsmiths' Company, whose con-tribution to the costs of Volume VI gave them a special connection with the Dictionary, had been made in June 1927;[102] the construction of the guest list and seating plan entailed a great deal of diplomacy and checking of protocol. With space to seat just short of 150 men—women were excluded from the Hall by the rules of the Company—careful calculations had to be made as to just who among all the various constituencies could be invited: an international selection of prominent figures from the worlds of

---

[96] A figure of £116,574 for income/sales to 1928 is given in some calculations prepared for in 1992 by the OUP accountant Hugh Smith (preserved, with covering memo 21 Sept. 1992 C. K. Hall to W. R. Andrewes, in OUPA(u)). For further discussion of *OED* finances see Raff (2013: 202–3).

[97] *Times* 19 Apr. 1928, p. 10.

[98] OED/B/3/2/17 transcript of telegram received 19 Apr. 1928.

[99] The complete Dictionary was not presented to the King, as each volume had been presented to the Royal Library at Windsor as it appeared. However, on 21 March Onions and his wife apparently attended a garden party at Buckingham Palace, at which a presentation of some sort may have been made, perhaps of a volume containing the new dedication, which had been printed in gold for the King's copy (OED/B/3/2/17 17 Mar. 1928 RWC to HSM; ML(B) 20 Mar. 1928 HSM to G. F. J. Cumberlege).

[100] ML 3, 15 May 1928 HSM to RWC.

[101] ML 2 Apr. 1928 HSM to RWC (declaring 'Cheers for General Motors!' and enclosing copy of letter of 23 March from Cumberlege, which concludes 'Alleluia!'), 11 Apr. 1928 HSM to RWC.

[102] OED/B/3/2/16 23 June 1927 HSM to RWC.

philology, literature, publishing, politics, and of course journalism, as well as all the individuals who had actually played a significant role in the creation of the Dictionary itself, not least its staff. (The Dictionary's 'ladies'—both those who had actually worked on the text, and figures like Lady Murray and the wives of both surviving Editors—were permitted the doubtful pleasure of sitting in a small minstrels' gallery and, in the words of one woman who declined the invitation, 'watch[ing] the men eat'.[103])

There were particular problems in relation to Viscount Cave, Lord Chancellor and also Chancellor of Oxford University. He was of course on the guest list—indeed it was hoped that he would make one of the numerous speeches—but by late February he was gravely ill, and plans were soon being made for the Vice-Chancellor to speak in his stead if necessary.[104] Lord Cave died on 29 March. This might have been merely unfortunate, but the decision of the University to allow nominations for the new Chancellor until 7 June (with an election on 16 June) made matters considerably more awkward. The timing meant that even though Lord Grey—who by common consent was to be nominated unopposed—had been invited, protocol demanded that he not be seen to be acting as Chancellor. In the event an awkward situation was avoided when it was discovered that he was after all unable to attend. Another late withdrawal from the list of speakers was Lord Balfour, who had been due to propose the toast to the University of Oxford.[105] This left, of those speakers not directly connected with the University or the Company, only the Prime Minister, who of course could not guarantee his attendance.

It was Oxford's Vice-Chancellor, Francis Pember, who presided over the ceremony in the Sheldonian Theatre on 5 June at which honorary doctorates were to be conferred on five Dictionary figures: Craigie (who had also been elected an honorary fellow of Oriel College a few weeks earlier), Onions, Milford, Chapman, and John Johnson, the Printer to the University. The occasion was somewhat marred by an event unprecedented in living memory: a protest against the conferment of degrees upon several of the honorands. Lewis Farnell, the Rector of Exeter and a former Vice-Chancellor, rose to oppose the awarding of honorary doctorates on two separate grounds. Firstly, when such degrees had been instituted at Oxford it had been agreed that they should only be awarded to those who were not resident members of the University (and who therefore could not proceed to a degree in the usual way); according to this principle, all the Dictionary honorands except Craigie were ineligible. Secondly, it was also a matter of principle that such doctorates should only be awarded to individuals who had distinguished themselves through their scholarly work; and in relation to the *OED*—whatever their other literary attainments—Chapman, Johnson, and Milford,

---

[103] Bailey (1985: 201), quoting Agnes Carswell Fries (wife of Charles C. Fries: see p. 389). For more on the Goldsmiths' Hall dinner see Brewer (2007: 5–7).

[104] OED/B/3/2/17 24 Mar. 1928 RWC to Sir William Pope.

[105] OED/B/3/2/17 12 May 1928 RWC to F. W. Pember; 16 May 1928 G. R. Hughes to RWC.

as officials of the Press, could not be said to fall in this category.[106] The matter was not pressed to a vote, and the degrees were awarded as planned (following 'a witty and eloquent *Epilogus* in Terentian iambics' composed for the occasion by the Public Orator[107]); but the protest was widely commented on in the press, and must have been a considerable embarrassment.

On the following day the Goldsmiths' Hall dinner took place without mishap. The Prime Minister did not let the Dictionary down: he attended the dinner, and toasted 'the Editors and Staff of the Oxford English Dictionary' with an eloquent speech. Craigie responded; the Prime Warden of the Goldsmiths' Company, Sir William Jackson Pope, proposed the health of the University; and the Vice-Chancellor responded. A commemorative pamphlet was printed containing the text of all four speeches; that by the Prime Minister was also issued separately.[108] The week of celebrations continued on 7 June with the awarding of another doctorate to Craigie, this time by the University of Cambridge; and in July Onions, though of comparatively brief standing as Editor, was also honoured by a younger university, when Leeds awarded him a D.Litt. Even James Murray had a share in the honours: a special medal was struck in his honour by the British Academy, of which he had been a founding Fellow, and presented to his eldest son, Harold.[109]

The question of honours from the nation was another matter. Chapman had been anxious to secure the inclusion of Craigie and Onions in the King's Birthday Honours List, and Lord Cave's support had been enlisted; but by the time of his final illness he had not yet raised the matter with the Prime Minister. Writing to the Vice-Chancellor in some agitation on the day after Lord Cave's death, Chapman recalled a letter in which he had 'agreed that knighthoods for C[raigie] & M[ilford], & a minor honour for O[nions], were suitable'—but the letter could not be found.[110] The Vice-Chancellor was informed by Lord Cave's Private Secretary that the Minister of Education, Lord Eustace Percy, 'ha[d] the matter in hand'; but the matter proved not to be as well 'in hand' as it might have been. Craigie was duly knighted, on 28 June, but Onions did not receive his 'minor honour' (a CBE) until 1934, and Milford's knighthood was not to be awarded until 1936.[111]

---

[106] Although Farnell is quoted in contemporary press reports as having stated both objections, the point relating to resident membership of the University is not mentioned in his own fairly full account of the episode in his memoirs (Farnell 1934: 321–3). This point was certainly made through official channels: according to the distinguished classicist G. B. Grundy, who wrote separately to the Press, this was his own reason for signing the letter of protest which had been sent to the Vice-Chancellor (OED/B/3/2/17 fragment of letter 4 June 1928 G. B. Grundy to [?RWC]).

[107] Quoted in full in *Times* 6 June 1928, p. 21.

[108] Copies preserved at OED/B/3/2/17.

[109] *Manchester Guardian* 3 July 1928, p. 10; *Observer* 22 July 1928, p. 19.

[110] OED/B/3/2/17 26, 30 Mar. 1928 RWC to F. W. Pember.

[111] Chapman later learned the truth about what had happened to the 1928 proposal to honour all three men. In 1932 he was informed by Sir Patrick Duff, the Prime Minister's private secretary, that it was a simple case of quotas: such were the difficulties of 'trying to get in even one representative of each important feature of public life and public services' that it had only been possible to give one honour out of the three proposed (OED/B/3/2/21 24 Nov. 1932 Duff to RWC).

The completion of the first edition of the *OED*, then, afforded many opportunities to celebrate the achievement, and to look back over seventy years of toil. But amid the atmosphere of retrospection, the lexicographers themselves, and their publisher, were of necessity pressing forward, or at least attempting to, with the next challenge, namely the Supplement. Indeed, the prospect of this new work had featured prominently in coverage of the completion of the Dictionary, not least because of the Delegates' decision (taken some months earlier) that a copy of the Supplement would be given free to every holder of a complete set of the Dictionary.[112]

In Chicago, at least, good progress was being made. Already by April Craigie had worked through a substantial proportion of the material that had been sent over from Oxford, and was hopeful of being able to bring the American entries for A–C at least with him in June.[113] This was all the more impressive when it is borne in mind how much else Craigie was attempting to do simultaneously. In addition to his work on the two 'Chicago' projects, the Older Scottish dictionary and the 'Historical Dictionary of American English', he was also involved in two of the other proposed period dictionaries, both of which had now progressed as far as the appointment of an editor: Clark S. Northup of Cornell University for Middle English, and Charles C. Fries of the University of Michigan for Early Modern English. As Craigie pointed out to Chapman, this left the way clear for OUP to concentrate on a dictionary of modern (in this context meaning post-1700) English, this being in Craigie's view 'the only one of [the period dictionaries] that might be a source of profit in the end'. Chapman's view of what kind of dictionary of modern English might be profitable was rather different; certainly there was no enthusiasm in Oxford for starting a new dictionary on anything like the scale of the other members of the 'period' family.[114]

Extraction of relevant material from files in Oxford, as begun by Craigie in 1927, was of course crucial to the various period projects, and this work was resumed in the summer of 1928 by Fries, with the help of some of the female Dictionary assistants. This turned out to be rather more of a disruption to the work going on in the Old Ashmolean than expected: Onions later complained that Fries had brought his entire family into the Dictionary Room—with the children sometimes playing trains on the floor—and made a habit of bringing in visiting American colleagues.[115]

In view of such distractions—and the fact that they were trying to edit the Abridged at the same time—it is hardly surprising that Onions and his assistants soon fell far behind Craigie (who in any case was only tackling a relatively small component of the vocabulary). Although copy had begun to go to the printers from the Old Ashmolean

[112] OD 18 Nov. 1927.

[113] PBED 3974 30 Apr. 1928 WAC to KS.

[114] CPED 611 5 Dec. 1927 WAC to RWC. This is not to say, of course, that the Press had no interest in the idea of a substantial dictionary of modern English. Discussions had been going on with Henry Fowler for some time about a possible 'Quarto Dictionary'; this project is further discussed in the next chapter.

[115] CPED 611 28 Jan. 1929 CTO to RWC. Some reminiscences of the several visits made by the Fries family to Oxford appear in Fries (1987).

in February, by the time of the Goldsmiths' dinner in June this work had only reached the word *amoralist*.[116] The lengthy absence of Maling—now declared 'a complete invalid' by his doctor[117]—was partly responsible, but there was also the fact that the other Dictionary veterans on Onions's staff were slow workers. Sisam, reporting to Chapman in April on progress (or lack of it), lamented the absence of Watson, who 'would have been worth £1000 a year to us now'. The slow pace was particularly worrying because Onions's assistant Jessie Senior had spent two years working on the material in A and B with a view to facilitating preparation of copy. At the end of June Onions also lost a key assistant on the Abridged, Miss Savage.[118]

The need to inject some additional productivity into the Old Ashmolean was becoming acute. A suggestion by Craigie that the Press seek to acquire 'an assistant trained in some business school of lexicography, Pitman's or Cassell's or Chambers' led to Milford putting out feelers to other London publishers; Sisam also tried the familiar route of asking suitably placed academics to recommend likely young men and women.[119] Approaches to W. F. Mainland, a promising Scottish Germanist, and Margaret Wattie, an Oxford English graduate who had spent some time working for Craigie in America, came to nothing, as did discussions with Ernest Ogan, at that time the effective editor of the multi-volume *Waverley Children's Dictionary*.[120] At last, in November, Onions secured the services of Elaine Clark, another Oxford graduate; Sisam dismissively referred to her as 'rather a rabbit' (although acknowledging that she came with good credentials), and Onions initially found her 'ineffective', but in due course she proved a reliable worker. In any case, Onions could ill afford to reject her: even before she was able start work, he had lost another assistant, Sweatman, who was signed off for two months with heart trouble.[121] This left only six of the pre-1928 assistants in the Old Ashmolean (Lewis, Bayliss, Rosfrith Murray, Mrs Powell, and Birt, joined on an irregular basis by Eleanor Bradley), none of them particularly fast workers; even with the help of the Misses Senior and Clark, and the piecework being done by Walter Worrall, this was not enough to achieve satisfactory progress on the Supplement *and* the Abridged. Thirty pages of A were now in type, as Onions reported in December in a promotional article about his work;[122] impressive though this might seem, it was arguably very little to show for what was rather more than

---

[116] Supplement copy and proof dates were logged in various booklets preserved in OUPA (OED/B/3/10/4, OED/B/5/7/3).

[117] OED/B/3/2/17 2 June 1928 A. G. Gibson to RWC.

[118] OED/B/3/2/17 3 Apr. 1928 KS to RWC; PBED 3974 4 Apr. 1928 [KS] to WAC.

[119] OED/B/3/2/17 6 July 1928 KS to HSM.

[120] OED/B/3/2/17 11 May 1928 [KS] to CTO, 27 June 1928 [KS] to W. F. Mainland; OED/B/3/4/34 28 May, 4 Aug. 1928 M. Wattie to CTO, OED/B/3/2/17 [?] to RWC, 9 Nov. 1928 CTO to KS. Ogan had a meeting with Chapman in October, but appears not to have been formally offered work (OED/B/3/2/17 20 July 1928 'H.T.B.' to [RWC], 29 Oct. 1928 [RWC] to E. G. Ogan).

[121] OED/B/3/4/9 8 Nov. 1928 KS to CTO, OED/B/3/2/17 14 Nov. 1928 CTO to RWC; OED/B/3/3/1 13 Nov. 1928 RWC to CTO.

[122] Onions's piece, written at Chapman's request, appeared in the *Manchester Guardian* on 27 Dec. 1928 (p. 9).

six months' work, and Sisam regarded it as evidence that Onions was 'settling down for an 8 or 10 years' job [...] the Supplement itself will be out of date when it appears [...] and the Dictionary will be a distant memory by the time we are able to make the reissue.' This last point was now becoming urgent because stocks of the main Dictionary were running low; the Press could not afford to let it go out of print, for fear of damaging its reputation, and would therefore have to start work on the huge task of producing the long-planned cheap reissue. And if the reissue were to appear without an accompanying Supplement, this would lay the main work open to renewed criticism on grounds of not being up to date.[123]

In January 1929 the staffing situation—which even Onions admitted was now 'grow[ing] desperate'[124]—was somewhat improved by the acquisition of another 'rabbit': Monica Dawn, who like Jessie Senior was a graduate of the Leeds University English department, where the former Dictionary assistant J. R. R. Tolkien had apparently given her special training in the work.[125] She was to be joined in July by another former pupil of Tolkien's, Stefanyja Olszewska, who effectively replaced Rosfrith Murray when the latter gave up Dictionary work, thereby bringing to an end the Murray family's direct involvement with the project after over half a century.[126]

The spring of 1929 brought another new recruit to the Old Ashmolean, who was to play an important part in the history of the Supplement and beyond. In April Sisam, still convinced that the staff needed further expansion, heard from the patristic scholar—and lexicographer[127]—Alexander Souter about a pupil of his who Souter thought might be suitable material: James McLeod Wyllie, who had just taken a first-class degree in classics from Aberdeen. Following an interview, Sisam was sufficiently impressed that he offered Wyllie a year's trial on the Supplement, at a salary of £250.[128] In fact he envisaged a rather more substantial role for him than that of merely another assistant: as he explained to Craigie, he was hopeful that, after some initial training, Wyllie would be 'fit to do some independent work. I fear it would be useless to put him into the routine machinery, from which he might never emerge [...] I think we can offer him good prospects if he will learn the executive as well as the reflective art.'[129] Sisam

---

[123] PBED 3974 7 Dec. 1928 KS to RWC; OD 31 May 1929.

[124] OED/B/3/2/18 15 Jan. 1929 CTO to RWC. By this time Sweatman had returned to work, but he was unable to work at full strength.

[125] OED/B/3/2/18 14 Jan. 1929 E. V. Gordon to KS; PSOM 7 June 1929.

[126] OED/B/3/2/18 17 June 1929 R. Murray to RWC, 26 June 1929 CTO to KS. Rosfrith Murray and her mother had decided to leave Oxford to go and live with Rosfrith's brother Harold in Sussex. On their departure Lady Murray arranged for the original pigeonholes which Herbert Coleridge had commissioned in 1860 to be given to the Press, where they are still preserved; some of the tables from the Scriptorium were also sold to Charles C. Fries, who in the summer of 1929 returned to Oxford to continue the extraction of material for the various period dictionaries (CPED 611 21 June 1929 C. C. Fries to KS).

[127] Souter had already compiled a successful *Pocket Lexicon to the Greek New Testament* (1916) for the Press, which had been reprinted many times. He had also known Murray, and had visited him on several occasions (OED/C/6/1/1 29 May 1971 G. W. S. Friedrichsen to RWB).

[128] PED/B/3/2/18 [23 Apr. 1929] J. M. Wyllie to [KS], 26 Apr. 1929 KS to Wyllie, 7 May 1929 Wyllie to KS, 9, 24 May 1929 KS to Wyllie.

[129] PBED 525 15 May 1929 KS to WAC.

planned to entrust Wyllie's training to Craigie during the latter's annual extended visit to Oxford; his confidence in Craigie's ability to take a practical approach to getting the work done contrasts starkly with his view of the 'reflective' Onions, who was not even informed of Wyllie's appointment until a week before his arrival. To add insult to injury, Onions was asked to find Wyllie work to do for his first month, as Craigie had arranged to travel to Romania before coming to Oxford, and would not be able to start working with the new recruit until August.[130]

A few days after Wyllie's arrival Onions submitted another depressing progress report, confirming Sisam's worst fears that he was digging in for the long haul. As far as the main text of the Supplement was concerned, the report predicted completion of rather less than A–C by the end of the year—and that only in manuscript, with the various stages of proof correction still to come—while the proofs of the bibliography, to Sisam's horror, were still being heavily corrected after two years' work ('a disgrace. Had Craigie stayed, it would have been finished in nine months'). Remarkably, only a few weeks earlier Onions had reassured Chapman that the existing staff was 'adequate to the regular supply of copy & the working-off of proofs'. The Editor of the Supplement and his publishers clearly had very different views about adequacy. Sisam—who was increasingly being left by Chapman to manage the Supplement as he thought best— concluded that without 'a radical change' the Press could not contemplate starting to print the reissue (which, because of the prohibitive costs of storing the stock of such a vast printing job, would effectively commit them to a particular completion date for the Supplement). He proposed that as soon as Craigie arrived there should be 'a conference with only one point "What steps will bring this Supplement to an assured conclusion in September 1931" '; and it was clear that his preferred 'radical change' was the assignment of Wyllie to edit a separate section of the alphabet, under Craigie's supervision if necessary.[131]

By the time the conference took place, in early September, Chapman and Sisam had raised the stakes by formally authorizing the commencement of work on the printing of the reissue, making completion of the Supplement by 1931 imperative.[132] As this was clearly unachievable under the present regime, it was agreed that Wyllie—who seems already to have been showing considerable ability—should, on a trial basis, commence preparation of the materials for the letter L, apparently on the understanding that final approval of the text was to be the responsibility of Craigie, whose editorial role in the Supplement was thus significantly enhanced, to something like parity with Onions. Wyllie was to be assisted in the task of preparation by Bayliss, whose main responsibility up to this point had been to deal with the dispatch and return of Craigie's proofs.[133]

---

[130] OED/B/3/2/18 25 June 1929 KS to CTO. Wyllie started work on 1 July, the same day as Onions's new assistant Stefanyja Olszewska.

[131] PBED 3974 11 June, 11 July 1929 CTO to RWC, 12 July 1929 KS to RWC.

[132] PBED 12962 order to Printer to reprint 10,000 copies of 'NED Re-Issue 12 volumes', dated 20 Aug. 1929.

[133] PBED 3974 5 Sept. 1929 WAC to KS, 19 Mar. 1930 [RWC] to HSM.

Onions could be forgiven for feeling some resentment at the opening of a second front, with its implied criticism of himself and his staff. Certainly he seems to have been all too ready to raise objections to the new man's approach. When Wyllie consulted him about some slips in L which had not been sorted at all, and which he thought could be sorted for him by some other assistant, Onions's response was to suggest that sorting them himself would be a useful training exercise, and to comment to Sisam on how other recent accessions to the staff had 'buckled to & made good, liking the rough work with the smooth without a murmur, counting it a privilege to be doing the job at all'—strongly implying that he regarded Wyllie as seriously deficient in this respect. Sisam, however, retorted that with time at such a premium he did not regard basic sorting as a good use of Wyllie's time, and that it would even be acceptable to pay someone else to do this.[134]

Another troublesome initiative of Wyllie's, which led to further friction, arose out of his assessment that the material in L—and, indeed, in various other parts of the alphabet—was so sparse and incomplete that it was not efficient for him even to start preparing copy from it. The materials were certainly patchy, assembled as they were from the ad hoc gleanings of a random selection of individuals working without any direction; their inadequacy had in fact been noticed by both Craigie and Onions as soon as they had moved out of A, which for some reason was rather fuller. Craigie, indeed, had admitted that this might go some way to explaining Onions's slow progress.[135] However, the two Editors differed markedly as to the best way of dealing with this. For Craigie '[t]he great question [was] how to make the best of the situation'; and this could be done by taking whatever material there was and working it up into as complete a form as possible, making notes on what additional information or evidence was required which could be dealt with in due course. He favoured the idea that several assistants could each be assigned a letter or letters on this basis, as a means of making quick inroads on the whole alphabet, and bringing significant gaps to light which could then be addressed. Onions's approach, by contrast, was to work steadily through the material, making it as complete as possible—conducting research in the Bodleian Library and elsewhere if necessary—before moving on. Sisam, who after all had some experience of the work, had long ago spotted a disadvantage of this method, namely the temptation for assistants to spend more and more time on research, which they found more appealing than the 'hard and steady work' of preparing copy in the Old Ashmolean (and also because it enabled them to escape Onions's rather strict supervision for a while).[136]

---

[134] OED/B/3/2/18 21 Sept. 1929 CTO to KS, 23 Sept. 1929 [KS] to CTO.

[135] PBED 525 8 June 1929 WAC to RWC; PBED 3974 4 Dec. 1929 KS to RWC, 19 Mar. 1930 [RWC] to HSM.

[136] PBED 3974 typed note (undated; probably by WAC) 'Recommendations for Staff Work on the Supplement', 20 Jan. 1930 KS to RWC; OED/B/3/2/17 3 Mar. 1928 KS to RWC. Sisam had recently drawn attention to the effect on progress of Mrs Powell's 'drifting more & more into the Bodleian' (OED/B/3/2/18 25 June 1929 KS to RWC). Onions was notorious for expecting high levels of attendance: it was said that his staff would conceal their dental appointments and other absences from him by timing them to coincide with occasions when he left the Dictionary Room to give lectures (anecdote reported by Eric Stanley, given in Ogilvie 2008: 38).

There were at least two ways of making good the deficiencies of the evidence in the Supplement files, and Wyllie was keen to do something about both. One was to carry out some systematic reading of suitably chosen sources; he embarked on some reading of his own, and in December presented Onions with 1,000 slips from recent texts on education and psychology. Onions took exception to Wyllie's request to have these sorted into the main sequence of slips, as many of the slips were for items which he regarded as too marginal to be included, and complained to Chapman about the time that would be wasted by 'the filing of unnecessary material'.[137] Wyllie also began to seek out other people willing to undertake reading of this kind on a voluntary basis; the prospect which this offered of improving the quotation evidence at negligible cost appealed to the Dictionary's publishers, but Onions maintained that amateur reading of this kind was all too liable to produce much useless material, which nevertheless had to be filed. He was no doubt speaking from experience, but against this might be set the material which had been collected in just such an 'amateur' fashion by Furnivall and Robertson Wilson, which he had in fact publicly acknowledged as of enormous value to the Supplement; indeed he had invited members of the Philological Society in 1928 to contribute in very much this manner.[138] His strictures about Wyllie's reading perhaps reflect his unease about the lack of control he had over the young man from Aberdeen.

Another, arguably complementary approach to the matter of inadequate evidence was to issue 'desiderata lists' for words already under consideration, as the Dictionary's Editors had regularly done in the past. Chapman had suggested reviving this practice as early as June 1928, and lists began to appear in the *Periodical* almost immediately (and subsequently in other publications such as *Notes & Queries*).[139] Wyllie soon set about compiling a list for L, but he seems to have adopted a much more rough-and-ready approach than Onions: his lists included many comparatively marginal items, such as simple compounds, many of which would ultimately fail to be included, whereas Onions tended to include only those items which he was fairly sure would be included.[140] Onions was also unhappy that the inclusion of too much from other parts of the alphabet would necessitate the postponement of some of his own desiderata for C. It might be supposed that this sort of thing could be sorted out by discussion between the two men; just how far relations between them had deteriorated may be

[137] PBED 3974 4 Dec. 1929 CTO to RWC, KS to RWC.

[138] PSOM 1 June 1928, 7 June 1929. Robertson Wilson died in October 1929; the *Periodical* described him as having 'easily surpassed' all other readers except Furnivall in the volume of modern material which he supplied (15 Feb. 1930, p. 28). The published Preface to the Supplement also mentions Furnivall and Robertson Wilson in the first rank of those acknowledged as contributing quotations, along with the former Dictionary assistant Henry Rope, now a Catholic priest.

[139] OED/B/3/3/1 23 June 1928 RWC to CTO; OED/B/3/2/17 3 Aug. 1928 CTO to KS (enclosing a first list of desiderata, running from *A.B.C. shop* to *amoral*).

[140] In a sample of the list which appeared in the *Periodical* of February 1930, roughly half of the words in L were omitted from the Supplement as finally published, including such items as *lake-bound, lake-girt, lakemanship,* and *la-la* (verb), whereas the figure for the C words in the list is more like 10%. Wyllie was also careless: his list includes *lantern-slide,* which had already been given in the main Dictionary.

judged from the fact that in March 1930 Onions felt it necessary to take the matter up with Craigie in Chicago as 'a matter of internal discipline'. He complained indignantly to Chapman that he was 'still uninformed whether Mr Wyllie takes his instructions from [Craigie] or not. In the whole matter of this man's appointment I think I have not been treated with common consideration, since his position in this room has never been defined to me.'[141]

There may well have been some justification for Onions's sense of grievance. Chapman was aware that Wyllie could be difficult to get on with: 'no one', he told Onions, 'knows better than I the raw, secretive aggressive Scotch boy; for I was brought up with lots of him.' However, it was undeniable that Wyllie, whatever his personal shortcomings, was impressing his employers—and Craigie—with his industry and initiative. By this stage, in response to a suggestion from Sisam—who was providing on-the-spot advice to supplement what he received from Craigie—he had made a start on some other letters of the alphabet, rather than allowing himself to be held up in L by lack of material for particular words; and for Onions to criticize someone who was so conspicuously making just the kind of progress which schedules demanded, and which he and his assistants were failing to make, was to say the least impolitic. Even the usually urbane Chapman allowed a note of steeliness to creep into his responses. '[T]he production of a supplement in the time, and at the cost, which the experience of A–C suggests,' he warned Onions, 'is not compatible with the declared policy and the known programme of the Delegates. There is no going back on this. The Dictionary *is* going out of print; the Reissue *is* being printed; and the Delegates could not justify to themselves or to the University the cost (in time and money) of proceeding at the pace which A–C suggests.' He reminded Onions of his 'declared willingness to cut your coat according to your cloth' in regard to the concept of a 'scratch' Supplement; and dryly commented that 'the story of Wyllie, so far, reminds me of the story of Watson; and it will not be denied that Watson hacked his way through a heap of stuff.' The sense of two camps—the Onions camp and the Craigie–Wyllie one—is palpable. Referring to the importance of maintaining a consistency of treatment throughout the text, Chapman suggests that 'even if you (with a reduced staff?) should secure that *your* part is up to your standard, I think it would be no matter of satisfaction to you to contemplate a ragged whole'.[142] The reference to a 'reduced staff' was not lost on Onions, who, in a memo reminiscent of Murray at his most uncompromising, fiercely defended both his staff ('no more devoted workers could be found') and his methods, which he described—in implied contrast to Wyllie's—as having been 'perfected by experience', and which he regarded as the absolute minimum that was required if he was not to produce 'something that will be the laughing stock of the world'.[143] The memo, incidentally, also makes a curious comment about Arthur Fowler, Henry's

[141] PBED 3974 22 Feb. 1930 WAC to KS, 11 Mar. 1930 CTO to RWC.
[142] PBED 3974 12, 14 Mar. 1930 RWC to CTO.
[143] OED/B/3/10/1 17 Mar. 1930 CTO to RWC.

brother, who had been sending in quotations for the Dictionary at least since 1922, and had shown a good eye for new words. From 1929 Chapman had taken the unusual step of paying him for his contributions; Onions now described him as being 'under [Chapman's] protection'. Whether or not he knew how much Arthur Fowler was being paid—in fact the rate was a guinea per hundred slips—he may perhaps have felt that the money could be better spent in other ways.[144]

It was time for some straight talking. The seriousness of the situation was made abundantly clear to Onions at a meeting with Chapman and Sisam: he was informed that 'progress in the alphabet must be accelerated or the Delegates will be compelled to find a new secretary and a new editor'. Now 'thoroughly frightened' (as Chapman described him to Milford), he agreed to try to produce a plan of work for his own staff that would see copy as far as the end of K completed by the end of March 1931, and was persuaded to accept, even if he did not agree with, the idea of soliciting more help with reading from the general public.[145] (He immediately put this idea into practice, using a letter to the *Times* about the expression 'Celtic fringe' as an opportunity to make a general appeal for help.[146]) Wyllie, meanwhile, was authorized to continue with his work of 'mapping out' material in the rest of the alphabet; he was evidently not expected to be producing fully drafted copy for the printers yet, although Sisam was hopeful that intensive coaching from Craigie in the summer might pay dividends. The likely size of the Supplement was now thought to be about 1,000 pages, nearly three times the size that Sisam had estimated only nine months earlier.[147]

Relations between Craigie and Onions may have been going through their own rough patch, to judge from a minor incident around this time involving the word *Chicago*. In the first part of the alphabet the two Editors had been producing separate sets of galley proofs, which were then merged into a single sequence at the revise stage: an extremely inefficient mode of working, as might have been foreseen, and one which was discontinued in the spring of 1929 in favour of combining the two streams of copy before they went to the printer. Although Craigie was of course responsible for American vocabulary, from time to time Onions would include an American item in his own copy;[148] and one such word was the verb *Chicago*, included without quotations and defined as synonymous with the American slang term 'to skunk' (i.e. to prevent

---

[144] OED/B/3/2/11 6 Nov. 1922 A. J. Fowler to [RWC] (with 'some references for new words'). The first payment to Fowler for quotations was in July 1929 (information from OUP Publishing Business Cash Books (OUPA; hereafter 'OUP cashbooks')); payments were also made to a small number of other individuals, including Hilda Jenkinson, a Somerville College graduate who carried out various small tasks for Onions, and a Miss Cruickshank whose services as a reader had been secured by Wyllie. In the Preface to the Supplement Fowler and Mrs Jenkinson are mentioned as having been 'specially engaged to read modern literature and technical works' (p. vi).

[145] PBED 3974 19 Mar. 1930 [RWC] to HSM, 24 Mar. 1930 [RWC] to CTO.

[146] 'New Words for the "O.E.D."', *Times* 24 Mar. 1930, p. 15.

[147] PBED 3974 5 Apr. 1930 [KS] to WAC, 12 July 1929 KS to RWC.

[148] He later mentioned '[t]he articles *bromide, dope,* & *graft*' by way of other examples of his contribution to the American component (OED/B/3/10/4 4 May 1933 CTO to KS). For more on *graft*, which Craigie felt Onions had treated too fully, see Brewer (2007: 45).

one's opponent from scoring any points).[149] Craigie was evidently irritated when he encountered this entry in the proofs—as Onions surely might have expected—and complained to Sisam, both about the word itself (which he thought might 'lose him his job, or place him at the mercy of Big Bill or the gunmen') and about the apparent expectation that he and his assistants would do the work of seeking out the requisite quotation evidence.[150] In due course Onions was persuaded to delete the entry; as Chapman commented wryly to Sisam, '*Delenda est Chicago*. Skunk is—or so he now says—but a pleasantry; but the Scotch are not always good at that kind of joke.'[151]

There were also continuing difficulties with another Scot. Wyllie responded well to coaching during the summer, and was authorized to undertake the task of finalizing copy for the printer under Craigie's 'general direction' (for which his salary was increased to £200); but his working relationships with the rest of the staff had deteriorated so drastically—Sisam later referred to 'steady obstruction' and 'freezing out'—that in August it was agreed to take the extraordinary step of allowing him to move back to Aberdeen.[152] To do this he would of course have needed to have access to the materials on which he was working; the Press's willingness to take on the cost and trouble of arranging for slips to be sent to and from Scotland is a striking indication of the faith that was now placed in him (and also of how intractable his interpersonal difficulties must have been thought to be). The fact that a portion of the Supplement was drafted in the land of James Murray's birth is also not generally known.[153]

In the summer of 1930 there was another departure, which had its inevitable impact on Onions's progress. Stefanyja Olszewska, who had become a valuable member of his staff, had secured a lectureship at the University of Reading, and left at the end of July; it proved easy enough to replace her—a Miss Evelyn Lee, classmate of Monica Dawn's at Leeds, was appointed before she had left—but, as ever, the training of a new assistant made inroads on the time of both the Editor and his assistants. Another Leeds graduate, Stella Mills, who came with a recommendation from Tolkien, was taken on

---

[149] A copy of Onions's proof, dated 9 Nov. 1929, is preserved at OED/B/3/2/19. The term evidently owes its origin to the popular explanation of the place name *Chicago* as having the original meaning 'place of the skunk'.

[150] PBED 3974 22 Feb. 1930 WAC to KS, 14 Mar. 1930 [RWC] to CTO. 'Big Bill' Thompson, the notoriously corrupt mayor of Chicago, was well known to have the support of Al Capone.

[151] OED/B/3/2/19 5 May 1930 RWC to KS. Sisam's Latin phrase ('*Chicago* is to be deleted') is a jocular echo of *Delenda est Carthago*, supposedly a favourite phrase of the Roman orator Cato the Elder.

[152] OED/B/3/2/19 14 Aug. 1930 KS to A. E. Durham; PBED 3974 12 Feb. 1931 [KS] to RWC. Wyllie had in fact been awarded a fellowship by the University of Aberdeen to work on a lexicon to the works of Sallust which he had started the previous year; he moved north on 20 September, and Sisam arranged for him to work in the library of King's College (University of Aberdeen, minutes of the Senatus Academicus, 27 May 1930; PBED 3974 29 Aug. 1930 [KS] to W. D. Simpson). Wyllie gave the manuscript of the completed Sallust lexicon to the Bodleian Library in 1949.

[153] Wyllie's first batch of proofs, for the start of the letter L, was sent out to him on 1 November 1930. The acknowledgement to William Simpson that eventually appeared in the Preface to the Supplement (p. vi) seems to imply that Wyllie also prepared the copy for some entries in N and O while in Aberdeen.

in November, but was assigned to work on the Abridged, which Onions was struggling to keep going alongside the Supplement.[154]

November also brought a rather more serious blow to progress in the form of the breakdown of Henry Bayliss's health: he was found to have developed a serious heart condition and now had to abandon work on the Dictionary.[155] This was disastrous for the Craigie–Wyllie side of the project: quite apart from Bayliss's own useful (if slow) lexicographical work—it had been agreed that he should tackle the letter P, on much the same basis as Wyllie—he had also been responsible for the smooth flow of proofs and other material to and from Oxford, a task rendered still more important now that the operation had a Scottish as well as an American component. By January it was clear that a replacement was urgently needed; Sisam contacted a woman named Dorothy Marshall, who had earlier applied speculatively for work, and also wrote to Wyllie, to ask whether under the circumstances he would be prepared to return to Oxford for a month to train her. Both parties proved willing, and it was arranged that Miss Marshall would start on 6 February. Craigie was pleased to hear of Wyllie's return, but gloomily predicted that he would be 'handicapped [...] by lack of any co-operation'.[156]

Apparent confirmation of this prediction came as soon as Wyllie arrived in the Old Ashmolean. Sisam had reminded Onions that he would need some space in the Dictionary Room, but when he arrived he found only 'a peculiarly dirty table' placed between the position occupied by Eleanor Bradley—who now only worked about 3 hours a week—and the absent Bayliss, whose books and papers had not been touched; nor was Wilfred Lewis prepared to budge, 'because it would alter his light'. (In fact Lewis was doing much of his work at home, as he too had been troubled with ill health, but Onions was evidently still inclined to place his working preferences ahead of Wyllie's.) Wyllie, having spoken to Eleanor Bradley about the possibility of using some of her space, and (according to him) secured her 'unenthusiastic assent', then moved her things to the other end of the room; when she next returned to work there was, as Sisam reported angrily to Chapman, 'a general scene [...] it is all like an infant school.' The dispute about where Wyllie should sit was to drag on, incredibly, until the summer; Sisam was evidently right about the 'obstruction' and 'freezing out'.[157] However, he rejected the idea of finding separate accommodation for Wyllie, Bayliss (who at this stage was still expected to recover), and Miss Marshall, as a needless additional expense and likely to impede progress.

---

[154] OED/B/3/2/19 30 June, 26 July 1930 CTO to RWC, 11 Aug. 1930 CTO to KS; OED/B/3/10/1 12 Nov. 1930 CTO to RWC.

[155] OED/B/3/2/19 25 Nov. 1930 W. Torrance Smith to RWC; OED/B/3/2/20 12 Jan. 1931 A. G. Gibson to RWC.

[156] OED/B/3/2/20 7 Jan. 1931 [KS] to D. Marshall, [KS] to Wyllie, 17 Feb. 1931 KS to A. E. Durham; OED/B/3/10/3 26 Jan. 1931 WAC to KS.

[157] PBED 3974 12 Feb. 1931 [KS] to RWC; OED/B/3/10/3 21 Feb. 1931 CTO to RWC, 14 July 1931 WAC to KS ('The claim to a particular table has always been an obsession with some of the assistants').

One option for housing Wyllie which may well have come to mind was unfortunately no longer available: the Scriptorium at 78 Banbury Road was no more. It had survived the departure of Ada Murray and the last of her family—she had moved out in 1929—but the latest occupant of Sunnyside, the American historian Robert McElroy, had decided, apparently sometime in 1930, to demolish it.[158]

Disputes about space in the Dictionary Room notwithstanding, Wyllie agreed to extend his stay in Oxford beyond the month originally planned. He was soon pushing on into N and O, and by March was confidently predicting to Sisam that he would reach the end of the alphabet by the following spring.[159] Onions had less encouraging news: by the start of May he had only sent material to the printers as far as *Ferris*. The letters G–J were all at least partly in an advanced state of preparation by his assistants, but he was still waiting to receive 'Americana' from Craigie for most of this range. An urgent request to Craigie elicited the tart comment to Sisam that 'as it has taken [Onions] seven months to advance his proofs from *E* to *Fe*, I naturally have not been setting aside other work for the sake of pushing on with this'; but it was evident that Craigie was beginning to find it difficult to keep both Wyllie and Onions supplied with fully processed American material, now that work on the *Dictionary of the Older Scottish Tongue* was gathering pace. He resorted to sending some 'raw' quotation slips, without accompanying editorial text, which of course simply transferred some of the editorial burden to the British side.[160] Onions also had other problems: Bayliss was still absent, and neither Birt—constantly liable to chest problems after his wartime experiences—nor the convalescent Lewis could take on any additional work. However, he refused to admit that the agreed schedule was seriously at risk, observing rather grumpily to Chapman: 'The programme for the "mapping out" of the copy to the end of K by the end of June will probably (or possibly) be completed. At all events that is the goal we have set before us during the year.'[161] This vague assurance was in stark contrast to the detailed calculations which Wyllie had provided to back up his March forecast; planning of that kind was, unfortunately, not in Onions's nature.

Wyllie's decision to stay on in Oxford must have been welcome to Sisam, who continued to be impressed by his efficiency, initiative, and methodical approach. He wrote approvingly to Craigie of his 'great ability', and his constant devising of 'plans for saving time, cutting down unnecessary operations, etc.'; and he even began to consider how to make the best use of this promising lexicographer once the Supplement was finished. New dictionaries of both English and Latin were in the offing: Henry Fowler was just beginning to work in earnest on a 'Larger Dictionary of Current English' (also known as the 'Quarto'), and Wyllie's former tutor Alexander Souter had been working

---

[158] OED/B/3/10/3 26 Jan. 1931 WAC to KS (with a pencilled note by Arthur Norrington that the Scriptorium 'was still standing 12 months ago'). The site of the Scriptorium is now a sunken garden, with a commemorative stone plaque recording its former function.

[159] OED/B/3/2/20 27 Mar. 1931 Wyllie to KS.

[160] OED/B/3/10/3 4 May 1931 CTO to RWC, 11 May 1931 WAC to KS, 18 May 1931 KS to RWC.

[161] OED/B/3/4/4 27 Apr. 1931 CTO to WAC, OED/B/3/10/3 5 May 1931 CTO to [RWC].

for some time on a 'Concise Latin Dictionary'. It was a smaller version of the latter—'a *Little Latin Dictionary* [...] similar in plan and size to L.O.D.'—for which Sisam now began to pencil Wyllie in.[162]

There was arguably good reason for Sisam and Chapman to think more highly of Wyllie, and his mentor Craigie, than of Onions when it came to matters of planning and organization of work. The same was not true of editorial questions—Onions's portions of the main Dictionary had, after all, been thoroughly satisfactory—but even here it seems that Onions sometimes found himself marginalized. An interesting illustration of this which arose around this time concerned the words *Lesbian* and *Lesbianism*. In April Onions complained to Chapman that these words had been 'deliberately excluded' by Craigie, despite the fact that they were in the 1929 edition of the *Concise*; this caused him to 'wonder what else is going to happen. *Lesbianism* is no doubt a very disagreeable thing, but the word is in regular use, & no serious Supplement to our work should omit it.' (Onions presumably had good reasons for attributing the exclusion of the words to Craigie, but it is interesting that both words are absent from the copy sent to the printer, for which at this point Wyllie was responsible.) Despite his protestations—and Chapman's own view that exclusion would be 'very silly'—Onions was informed that 'he had better not interfere if C[raigie] has really made up his mind': another uncomfortable reminder for the Supplement's Oxford-based Editor that the Press was willing to allow his views to be overruled.[163]

---

moron

On the completion of the first edition it was noted (*Periodical* Feb. 1928, p. 18) that the Dictionary 'has not attempted to rival some of its predecessors in deliberate humour or sarcasm [...] Such rare occasions for a smile as may be found in it are unintentional.' There is some evidence that William Craigie, at least, would have been happy to see a bit more humour in its pages. James Wyllie, in the effusive obituary he wrote for his lexicographical mentor, claims that on being shown a Supplement entry he had drafted which included humour of a kind, Craigie expressed his approval, and commented that 'there [was] far too little of this kind of thing in the dictionary' (Wyllie 1961: 287). The 'kind of thing' was Wyllie's entry for the word *moron*, which included among its illustrative quotations the following quatrain: 'See the happy moron. He doesn't give a damn. I wish I were a moron.

Continued ➤

---

[162] OED/B/3/10/3 13 Apr. 1931 [KS] to WAC; OD 1 May 1931; CPED 883 27 May 1931 [KS] to RWC. 'L.O.D.' was the *Little Oxford Dictionary*, which had been published in 1930. Following the death of the main compiler, George Ostler, in 1929, this was seen through the press by Onions's assistant Jessie Senior, who contrived to fit in her wedding during the same period, as well as continuing to work on the Abridged. As Jessie Coulson she would go on to become a prolific Oxford lexicographer: see Chapters 10 and 11.

[163] OED/B/3/2/20 10 Apr. 1931 CTO to RWC, 15 Apr. 1931 RWC to [KS] (both more fully quoted in Brewer 2007: 49). Entries for both words were included in the revised Supplement in the 1970s.

My God! perhaps I am!' (Wyllie had taken the quotation himself from a 1929 issue of the journal *Eugenics Review*, but the verse can be traced back to 1927; it has sometimes been attributed to Dorothy Parker, but it has not been found in her writings.) When the entry came to be revised for the second Supplement, this quotation was not included; it may have been that Burchfield did not share Wyllie's (or Craigie's) sense of humour, or he may simply have decided that the history of the word could be better illustrated by a different choice of quotations. The latter seems more likely, as in fact the quotation had already been reused in another Supplement entry, namely that for the phrase *not to give a damn*. Burchfield certainly had a sense of humour, like most lexicographers, although he generally refrained from deploying it in the writing of *OED* definitions. A possible exception is the definition of *bandersnatch* in Volume I of the Supplement ('A fleet, furious, fuming, fabulous creature, of dangerous propensities, immune to bribery and too fast to flee from'); it seems likely that Burchfield intended this to be humorous.

Sisam's confidence in Craigie's Oxford protégé, Wyllie, may have been dented by a minor incident in June 1931, once again involving Wyllie's relationship with a colleague. Dorothy Marshall—who, according to Sisam, had a 'reputation for steadiness'[164]—had become extremely perturbed by Wyllie's attitude to her working hours, which she had understood were flexible provided that she put in the requisite 40 hours per week, but which he felt should be 'as strictly fixed as in a commercial concern'. She took the unusual step of writing to Sisam about Wyllie's attitude, which at times 'bordered on the insulting'. A meeting with Sisam seems to have smoothed matters over, but with knowledge of Wyllie's subsequent history it is tempting to see the incident as a warning that should not have been missed.[165]

Also in June, the activities of another of Oxford's difficult characters precipitated an uncomfortable public debate about whether the lexicographers were to be allowed to remain in the Dictionary Room at all. For some years Robert Gunther, a distinguished scientist and fellow of Magdalen (and a vigorous controversialist), had been conducting what amounted to a one-man campaign to restore the Old Ashmolean building to its original function as a museum, specifically one for scientific instruments.[166] In 1924 he succeeded in persuading the University to make available two rooms on the upper floor of the building to house a newly acquired collection of instruments; he was duly installed there as curator, but continued to agitate to have the rest of the building (the basement of which had come to be used by the Bodleian Library) given over to the

---

[164] OED/B/3/10/3 16 Mar. 1931 [KS] to WAC.
[165] OED/B/3/2/20 3 June 1931 D. Marshall to KS, 5 June 1931 [KS] to Wyllie. Relations between Wyllie and his assistant were still fragile a year later, as may be seen from a letter from Dorothy Marshall to Sisam, in which she refers to 'using the Bodleian' and 'private conversation in work hours' as having been the cause of 'difficulties', but also asks Sisam to assure Wyllie that she has 'no deliberate intention of defying him' (OED/B/3/2/21 6 June 1932 Marshall to KS).
[166] For more on Gunther and the Old Ashmolean see Gunther (1967) and Simcock (1985).

same purpose, having become convinced that the permission granted to the Press in 1900 to use the building for the Dictionary was of questionable validity. In June 1931 the Friends of the Old Ashmolean (of which Gunther was a prominent member) issued a strong protest against a recent report by the Bodleian Commissioners, which had recommended that space in the Old Ashmolean should continue to be reserved indefinitely for 'large co-operative enterprises' like the Dictionary;[167] and this was swiftly followed by a petition to the University's Hebdomadal Council, signed by over 100 members of Congregation, proposing (inter alia) that the floor of the Old Ashmolean that housed the Dictionary Room should become 'a public gallery available for temporary exhibitions and lectures'.[168] In the leisurely manner of these things, the Delegates of the Press were not invited to comment until November; they reasserted their right to the use of the Old Ashmolean, which was to remain a home for their lexicographers for many years to come, and Council resolved in due course to 'take no further proceedings in the matter', but the publicness of the debate—the matter was discussed in the local and national press—will not have helped to allay any feelings of insecurity among the occupants of the Dictionary Room.[169]

By this time it was also abundantly clear that Onions would fail in his undertaking to complete A–K by the end of June; by the start of the month the copy sent to the printers had only reached *fire*. A new schedule was evidently called for. The one which Sisam now drew up envisaged Onions completing 650 slips of copy per week, and sending the last of his part of the alphabet to the printers by September, while Wyllie's target was to be 350 slips a week: a challenging enough figure given that he was still practically working single-handed (hopes that Bayliss would return to work were fading, and Miss Marshall was still very much at the apprentice stage). Wyllie evidently relished the challenge, and was soon reporting proudly that he was ahead of schedule, while Onions quickly fell so far behind that the printers began to grow short of copy.[170] In July he took on a new part-time assistant, J. L. N. O'Loughlin, but this was of course likely to reduce rather than increase output in the short term.[171] Sisam also

[167] *Library Provision in Oxford* (report and recommendations of the commission appointed by the Congregation of the University, 1931), p. 63. The protest of the Friends was reported in the *Times* of 2 June 1931, p. 11. In fact the matter had been raised in 1928, as the first edition was approaching completion; the Delegates had made it clear, no doubt to Gunther's disappointment, that they wished to retain the ground floor of the Old Ashmolean 'for work on the N.E.D. the D.N.B. and other similar enterprises' (OD 1 June 1928).

[168] The petition is reprinted in Gunther (1967: 422–4).

[169] OD 13 Nov. 1931; *Oxford University Gazette* 27 Jan. 1932, p. 288. The Delegates were carefully briefed by Chapman, as is seen from a memorandum prepared for them by him on 16 November (OED/B/2/4/9), which lists in some detail the particular reasons why the *OED* staff should remain exactly where they were (and suggests that the resolutions contained in the petition, 'if they do not conceal, certainly do not reveal all the motives which lie behind them').

[170] OED/B/3/10/3 22 June 1931 [KS] to CTO, [KS] to Wyllie; OED/B/3/2/20 3 July 1931 KS to RWC, OED/B/3/10/3 21 July 1931 Wyllie to KS, 29 July 1931 KS to RWC.

[171] OED/B/3/2/20 29 July 1931 CTO to RWC. O'Loughlin, an Oxford English graduate, had in fact attracted both Craigie's and Onions's attention within months of completing his degree (OED/B/3/4/2 4 Oct. 1930 WAC to CTO); at the same time he was also engaged to teach in the University's English school.

began to be concerned that Onions would soon be overstaffed: once the last piece of copy had been sent in, it would be extravagantly expensive to keep everyone engaged on proofreading. Nor could anyone be redeployed on the Abridged, for which the copy was—at last—complete.[172]

Sisam need not have worried about the lexicographers running out of work. On 28 July Wyllie wrote to him with a revised and considerably gloomier estimate of the time needed before the last section of Z could be put in the printer's hands. He was still confident of being able to draft copy at a good rate, but 'secondary matters' (such as the incorporation of Craigie's American material, research into particular words, and the reading of proofs) were taking longer than he had previously anticipated; the upshot of which was that—apparently even taking into account the return of Craigie to Oxford for another extended stay—he could not see how he could complete his allocated letters in less than 100 weeks.[173] This was bad enough news; worse was the continuing failure of Onions to stick to the programme of work agreed with the printers. This applied not only to his copy—which by mid-September was averaging only 200 slips a week—but also to proofs: the limits of the amount of type available meant that the signing off of corrected proofs (which freed up type for fresh composition) had to be kept up alongside the completion of primary copy. The printer's summer programme, which of course included proofs of the Abridged as well as the Supplement, had fallen victim to the temporary disappearance of Onions's entire team, who it seems had all taken their holidays at the same time. An urgent request for more copy from Chapman, declaring that 'all the Printer's arrangements and our publishing plans are in jeopardy', elicited another 640 slips from Onions; at this point Wyllie was in Scotland getting married.[174] A week later Johnson, the printer, was still complaining of the havoc being wrought on his schedule by the irregular supply of copy. The situation was once again becoming desperate.[175]

During September and October Onions, Chapman, and Sisam explored various possible ways forward.[176] The idea of encouraging assistants to move faster by threatening to move them on to piecework ('the fate of Worrall–Bayliss') was mooted; but in fact they had already prepared preliminary drafts of a great deal of material, which was now awaiting review by Onions. The essential problem was agreed to be—in an echo of language used over forty years earlier by Murray—the 'bottle-neck' represented by Onions himself, as the person across whose desk all of the text

[172] OED/B/3/2/20 3 July 1931 KS to RWC.

[173] OED/B/3/10/3 28 July 1931 Wyllie to KS.

[174] OED/B/3/10/3 29 July, 15 Sept. 1931 KS to RWC, 15 Sept. 1931 [RWC] to CTO, 16 Sept. 1931 KS to RWC. In August Sisam claimed to have secured Onions's agreement that an even higher figure of 1,000 slips a week was at least possible, although he described this to John Johnson as 'a lexicographer's promise', and unsurprisingly it was never achieved (OED/B/3/10/3 6, 11 Aug. 1931 [KS] to Johnson, 15 Sept. 1931 KS to RWC).

[175] OED/B/3/10/3 22 Sept. 1931 Johnson to RWC.

[176] OED/B/3/10/3 28 Sept. 1931 RWC to KS (reporting on a 'heart-to-heart talk' with Onions), 29 Sept. 1931 KS to RWC, 12 Oct. 1931 KS to RWC, 14 Oct. 1931 KS to RWC (with notes on 'Yesterday's conference').

had to pass; and his estimate of the maximum capacity of this bottleneck was 450 slips a week (Sisam predicted that 'this neck will get narrower'). The 'Craigie–Wyllie policy'—namely a narrower inclusion policy and a much more limited approach to research—was held up as a way of getting through the alphabet more quickly, and in less space; but there was clearly a limit to how far Onions could bring himself to go in this direction.[177] Instead, it was agreed to consider whether the bottleneck could effectively be widened by creating a separate unit within Onions's staff, headed by O'Loughlin, who was showing promise; Onions could take the same kind of advisory/supervisory role with O'Loughlin that Craigie had with Wyllie. On this basis Sisam was strongly of the opinion that Onions should be able to get through as much as 700 slips a week—and could therefore take on some other letters of the alphabet, thereby reducing Wyllie's allocation of work. He accordingly drew up a new programme, under which Onions (and O'Loughlin) would undertake S–T as well as the remaining portion of G–K, and Wyllie (supervised by Craigie) the rest of the alphabet, with a date of 1 December 1932 for final handover of copy: this made publication in the spring of 1933 at least plausible.

No sooner had the new arrangements been put into operation when another component of the delicately balanced system ran into difficulty: the supply of 'Americana' from Chicago was drying up. Craigie had for some time been finding it hard to keep up with the two streams of copy in Oxford, and now both Onions and Wyllie found that they had got through everything he had sent. This meant that American material would once again have to be incorporated in proof, which of course was far less efficient than adding it into the copy.[178] This was not a permanent failure— Craigie managed to catch up almost immediately—but during the remainder of work on the Supplement he was only intermittently able to provide copy in time for it to be incorporated.

At the start of 1932 Onions made significant modifications to his method of working, in an attempt to widen the bottleneck. Under what he called the 'New Model', some of his assistants were now permitted to revise some entries in H–K to the point where Onions could allow them to go to the printers with only the lightest modifications; these entries now formed a new third stream of copy, beginning with the letter I and moving on to S. O'Loughlin was among these trusted assistants, but was apparently still not entrusted with a 'unit' of his own as such. The resulting increase in throughput was barely detectable by the time of the next conference, at which Onions's rate was reported as only 475 slips a week, well short of what the programme required: 'June turns to December,' fretted Sisam, 'and December to June.' Wyllie had been

---

[177] When the question of inclusion had been touched on two years earlier, Onions had quite reasonably pointed out that the 'esoteric terms of science and medicine' which he was including in such numbers were 'precisely the class of word that the Supplements of other big dictionaries are careful to include', and that he had excluded hundreds of such entries which could be found in other dictionaries (OED/B/3/10/1 17 Mar. 1930 CTO to RWC).

[178] OED/B/3/10/3 typed extract of letter 3 Nov. 1931 KS to WAC.

(as ever) making good progress—now with some help from Bayliss, who had recovered sufficiently to do some piecework—and was still on course to meet the deadline.[179]

Indeed, now that this deadline was less than a year away, the question of what Sisam referred to as 'a demobilization programme', to which he had already given some thought, was becoming urgent: a programme, that is, indicating what work—if any—the various occupants of the Dictionary Room could most usefully be assigned to once the Supplement (and the Abridged) no longer required them. Even Onions's future had to be considered; he was apparently considering an etymological dictionary of French. Wyllie Sisam still had in mind for work on a small Latin dictionary, perhaps preceded by work with Souter on a larger work now being conceived as a replacement for Lewis and Short's great dictionary of the language. With the exception of Jessie Coulson and Elaine Clark—'[t]he only other meritorious and performing persons' according to Sisam—the remaining staff would soon have to be given notice as work ran out, with the older assistants presumably under consideration for a pension of some kind. In fact Mrs Coulson, in whom Sisam evidently now had considerable confidence, was now working on a specimen for a new project, a dictionary with substantial encyclopedic content; and Miss Clark's abilities warranted recommending her to 'the Americans'—now not only Craigie at Chicago, but presumably also the Middle English and Early Modern English dictionary projects in Michigan.[180]

First, however, the Supplement had to be finished. For Sisam, with his eye on the accumulating stocks of printed sheets and other material for the reissue of the main Dictionary, publication in 1933 was crucial, and it was essential that the lexicographers stuck to the schedule that led up to this; and anything that would help them do so began to look acceptable. He recruited Mrs Coulson, who was already reading Onions's Supplement proofs, to do the same for Wyllie;[181] discussing with Craigie how best to coordinate his work on American material, he encouraged him to pick out only the most obvious items in the latter part of the alphabet, remarking that 'we are now probably losing more time by delay than we could possibly make good by thoroughness'; and in March, following a comment from Onions that only 'under the most favourable circumstances' would his assistants be able to help him to get

---

[179] OED/B/3/10/4 20 Jan. 1932 KS to RWC, 26 Jan. 1932 [KS] to WAC, 8 Feb. 1932 CTO to KS. Strangely, at the time of the conference Sisam was still unclear as to whether the proposed new unit had been set up; impatient at O'Loughlin's failure to make a significant impact, he suggested that 'his addition to the staff has produced no practical benefit (except to himself), and he might as well be dropped again'. Fortunately for O'Loughlin, Onions's view of his work seems to have been more favourable, and he retained his job.

[180] OED/B/3/10/3 14 Oct. 1931 KS to RWC. For the later history of Coulson's encyclopedic dictionary project, and of the two projects based at Michigan, see Chapter 10.

[181] OED/B/3/10/4 extract from a letter 26 Jan. 1932 [KS] to Mrs Coulson. This was partly to address Onions's continuing complaints about errors in Wyllie's proofs, which might sometimes descend to the level of sniping—he was to comment to Sisam that 'there is such a thing as invincible ignorance'—but which Sisam recognized as justified in some respects. It could also be argued, however—and Sisam did so—that when Wyllie's early proofs were being adequately read by others for the more straightforward type of error, it was a waste of Onions's time to do the same (OED/B/3/10/4 26 Apr. 1932 [KS] to Wyllie, extract from letter 28 Apr. 1932 CTO to [KS]).

S and T into proof on time—which Sisam interpreted as a hint that some kind of financial incentive was needed—the offer of a bonus for completion of copy by the end of the year was quickly approved. Even the decision of Bayliss (who had lately been doing useful work verifying quotations for Wyllie) to leave Oxford for good, following a family bereavement, was not allowed to stand in the way of progress: Sisam found a replacement in the form of a Mrs Janet Heseltine, whose good work at the British Museum soon made up for Bayliss's absence. In April the Dictionary Room was much depleted by illness, with Sweatman, Miss Lee, and Miss Marshall signed off, but somehow the printers were kept supplied with copy.[182]

The next few months saw smooth progress: so smooth, in fact, that by August the question of 'demobilization' could no longer be avoided. All of the more junior assistants were advised that they should 'look out for themselves'; indeed, before the end of the month two of them, Miss Clark and Miss Dawn, had found alternative employment. The already tight schedule was squeezed by their departures, both in September, but apparently not to breaking point. Even Sisam was at last prepared to be optimistic. 'If Onions, Craigie, and Wyllie can keep going for a few months more,' he declared to Chapman, 'we have come to the end of the long process of fitting jury-masts, patching sails and splicing broken ropes.'[183] Craigie had as usual been back in England for the summer; Wyllie had by this stage sent most of R to the printers, and was soon able to spend more of his time helping out with S and T. The Abridged was also now becoming a focus of attention: an announcement in early July that it would be published in the spring had generated considerable interest. It had now, after some discussion, been renamed the *Shorter Oxford English Dictionary*: a compromise title, which while less than ideal—John Johnson worried that it 'sin[ned] against the first psychological principle of nomenclature', and that 'the one word "Shorter" will kill actually half the sale'—was considered preferable to any of the alternatives suggested.[184] Publication was now fixed for February. There was also discussion over the title page, on which it was eventually decided to credit Henry Fowler and Jessie Coulson alongside William Little, with Onions described as having 'revised and edited' the whole.[185]

---

[182] OED/B/3/10/4 26 Jan. 1932 [KS] to WAC, 9 Mar. 1932 CTO to KS, 10 Mar. 1932 [KS] to HSM and RWC; FC 18 Mar. 1932; OED/B/3/10/4 21 Mar. 1932 [KS] to Wyllie, 4 Apr. 1932 [KS] to Mrs Heseltine; OED/B/3/2/21 extract from a letter 5 Apr. 1932 KS to WAC; OED/B/3/10/4 7 Apr. 1932 D. E. Marshall to KS, 11 Apr. 1932 CTO to KS.

[183] OED/B/3/2/21 29 Aug. 1932 KS to A. E. Durham, CTO to KS, OED/B/3/10/4 19 Sept. 1932 KS to RWC.

[184] SOED/1932/3,8 25 Aug. 1932 Johnson to RWC, 30 Aug. 1932 KS to Hugh Last. Among other titles considered were 'Intermediate', 'Historical', and 'Scholars'' (SOED/1932/2 12 May 1932 [RWC] to HSM). Humphrey Milford pointed out that if 'Shorter' was chosen, 'we fear that you will have to put "English" after "Oxford"', presumably in order to avoid the unfortunate abbreviation *S.O.D.* (ML 10 June 1932 HSM to RWC).

[185] SOED/1932/14 18 Oct. 1932 CTO to [RWC?]. Onions, who actually thought that it would be best not to mention any individuals on the title page, insisted that Jessie Coulson should have at least equal billing with Fowler, as she had prepared more of the text than he had, and had had to revise much of his material 'in every detail'.

Late November saw Onions quoting Psalm 119—the longest, of course—to Chapman: 'I saw that all things come to an end.'[186] The sense of winding up was indeed palpable. Dorothy Marshall had left, as well as the Misses Clark and Dawn, and a staggered set of departure dates was now drawn up for most of the other assistants, with Eleanor Bradley gone by the end of the month, Mrs Powell and Miss Lee going at the end of December, and O'Loughlin and Mills a month later.[187] Sweatman, Lewis, and Birt would be needed for a few months longer, for the mass of proofreading and other tidying-up that still lay ahead; the two older men could look forward to receiving some kind of pension, but the future was rather more uncertain for Birt, now in his forties and with a chronic chest condition. Wyllie, with the prospect of new projects in Latin lexicography before him, had little to worry about; and Onions, who was now 59, was ready to contemplate retirement, although of a fairly active kind, involving the compilation of any of various possible new dictionaries, of which the most feasible seemed to be a new etymological dictionary of English (although, as Chapman bluntly observed, '[t]he difficulty is to see how anything you can produce would pay its way').[188]

In the event both Onions and Wyllie were able to meet the agreed deadline for final handover of copy (and thereby secure bonuses for themselves and various assistants). Wyllie sent in X, Y, and Z on 22 December, and the last batch of S was dispatched the following day, T having been completed a fortnight earlier.[189] There was, however, one remaining component of the copy which was still incomplete; and the fault lay with Craigie, who—immersed as he was in his various other projects—had fallen seriously behind with his American material. Much of S–Z had gone to the printers without his contribution, and as late as April 1933—even after the dispatch of an urgent telegram to Chicago—he was still apologizing for the non-delivery of parts of S, T, and W. The last of his entries began to make their way across the Atlantic in early May, by which time most of S, and a third of W, was in the second round of proofs.[190] Craigie sought to lay part of the blame for the delay on his two senior assistants in Chicago, George Watson and Mitford Mathews, to whom he had apparently found it impossible to delegate the task of preparing material for Oxford. Onions—who suspected Craigie of being 'unable to delegate anything'—was unimpressed: 'If you cannot clear Sp–T before the end of this month, we must just dree our weird [i.e. submit to our fate].' Sisam, unsurprisingly, simply urged Craigie to cut whatever corners he had to, particularly as he had also undertaken to write the substantial Historical Introduction that was to be printed in both the Supplement and the reissue of the main Dictionary. He was

---

[186] OED/B/3/2/21 26 Nov. 1932 CTO to RWC.

[187] OED/B/3/2/21 file note 30 Nov. 1932 by KS (regarding a conference held on 29 November). Some assistants were retained for a few weeks after the end of their work on the Supplement, for various tasks relating to the conclusion of work on the *Shorter*. Eleanor Bradley subsequently devoted herself to looking after her mother, but continued to take an active interest in the Dictionary.

[188] OED/B/3/2/21 5 Dec. 1932 RWC to CTO.

[189] FC 22 Dec. 1932.

[190] OED/B/3/10/4 18 Nov. 1932 Wyllie to KS, 19 Nov. 1932 WAC to KS, WAC to CTO, copy of telegram 3 Apr. 1933 KS to WAC, 4 Apr. 1933 WAC to KS, 15 May 1933 WAC to KS.

also more sympathetic to Craigie's difficulties in finding time for the Supplement: 'the right thing to do is to do what you can over the remainder of the field quickly without any regard to counsels of perfection. The Supplement, after all, is avowedly a scratch supplement, and it is no use trying to make it complete or to make some parts complete and leave the others blank.' Sisam also revealed a remarkably positive view of Craigie's contribution to the project: 'I know you will be relieved to see the end of an enterprise which you have had to rescue so often!'[191] Onions, still struggling to deal with the delayed consignments of American material, would no doubt have taken issue with this assessment. Craigie's desertion of the main Dictionary for Chicago at a crucial juncture had, it seems, been forgiven and forgotten.

Despite Watson's evident failings in respect of the Supplement, his was one of the two names which were now being put forward as suitable candidates for an honorary degree on the occasion of completion of the Supplement, the other name being Wyllie. Both suggestions seem to have come from Chapman, but were warmly supported by Craigie, who in his letter of recommendation asserted that '[i]t was only through [Watson's] mastery of the dictionary technique that it was possible to finish the Dictionary in the beginning of 1928', while Wyllie 'has distinguished himself by the quickness with which he has mastered the complicated details of the work, by his knowledge of the best means of obtaining necessary information, and by ability to convert the raw material into copy for the printer without loss of time [...] I am convinced that he has quite exceptional qualifications for lexicography.'[192] In the event only Watson's name was put forward for an MA: in discussion with George Gordon, President of Magdalen, who would in due course formally propose Watson for his degree, Chapman concluded that it would be better if Wyllie waited, on the basis that his anticipated future lexicographical endeavours might well earn him a higher degree (and that the fact of having already received an honorary MA might hold him back from this).[193] Watson's MA was conferred in the Sheldonian Theatre on 16 May. Onions does not seem to have proposed that any of his assistants should be similarly honoured; what he thought of awarding a degree to Watson—whose work on the main Dictionary, it will be remembered, he considered to have been 'essentially unscholarly', and who had apparently contributed hardly anything to the Supplement—can only be guessed at. We do know that he later considered Craigie's insistence on making particular mention of the contributions of Watson and Mathews in the Preface to the Supplement to be 'all very comical'.[194] He himself would receive recognition of a different kind in the New Year's Honours List of 1934, when he was made a CBE.

---

[191] OED/B/3/4/4 13 Apr. 1933 CTO to WAC; OED/B/3/10/4 14 Mar. 1933 CTO to KS, 13 Apr. 1933 [KS] to WAC.

[192] OED/B/3/2/21 17 Nov. 1932 RWC to KS, 20 Dec. 1932 WAC to RWC.

[193] OED/B/3/2/22 11 Jan. 1933 RWC to G. S. Gordon, 30 Jan. 1933 Gordon to RWC.

[194] OED/B/3/10/4 1 Aug. 1933 CTO to RWC. Onions noted that he had 'not seen a dozen slips' for the Supplement in Watson's handwriting, and that he had been told that Watson was 'useless to Craigie' in this regard (OED/B/3/10/4 [17 July 1933] CTO to RWC).

In the spring of 1933 there was plenty for the printers to be getting on with besides the Supplement itself. The *Shorter*, published on 16 February, had proved a tremendous success; even before publication arrangements were being made for a second impression of 10,000 copies, almost all of which were snapped up before the end of the month.[195] An even bigger task was the reissue of the main Dictionary (which was at last to bear the official title of *Oxford English Dictionary*[196]); Chapman and Sisam had evidently rowed back on the original schedule, drawn up when publication of the Supplement was expected in 1932, but work on the reissue had nevertheless been going on for some time. It had been decided to make it a corrected reissue, but the corrections—which had to be made on the printing plates themselves—were of necessity few and very minor; indeed, it is impressive that Onions and his staff were able to fit in the task of correcting the plates at all, given their other commitments.[197] The print run for the reissue was 10,000, so that 10,000 copies of the Supplement would have to be printed to be sold as part of this; in addition, Sisam proposed printing another 6,000 in the slightly different form suitable for separate sale. Both forms of the book included, in addition to the 867 pages of entries, the massive Bibliography, and the long-promised list of 'Spurious Words';[198] there was also the Historical Introduction (included in the separate form of the Supplement, and in Volume I of the reissue), written mainly by Craigie, and giving the fullest account yet published of the history of the Dictionary.[199]

By May, although a substantial amount of proof correction remained to be done, the main body of the Supplement was at last nearing the point of no return. One of the very last entries to be added was that for *body-line bowling*, which the publicity-conscious

[195] ML 14, 28 Feb. 1933 HSM to Secretary. The first impression seems to have been of 5,000 copies (ML 31 Jan. 1933 HSM to RWC).

[196] Quite apart from the fact that this was the title by which the Dictionary was now probably best known, there were now other 'New English Dictionaries' in circulation, notably one edited by Ernest Baker and first published by Cassell in 1919. Sisam proposed that the Press should 'distinguish the *Reissue* by calling it the *Oxford English Dictionary*, a copyright title which others can hardly steal once we appropriate it' (OED/B/3/10/4 1 Nov. 1932 KS to CTO). The ten volumes of the original Dictionary had varied considerably in size, with Volumes IX (*Si–Th*) and X (*Ti–Z*) each divided into two Parts which themselves were much the same size as the earlier complete volumes; there was evidently a desire to preserve, if only by means of a fiction, the commitment made in 1896 to keeping the Dictionary within ten volumes.

[197] Printing of the reissue began early in 1930 with the letter B (PBED 12962 10 Feb. 1930 [KS] to CTO).

[198] The version forming part of the reissue also included five pages of 'Additions and Emendations', cumulating the various addenda and corrigenda that had been issued with individual Parts and Sections.

[199] A briefer historical account had appeared in 1928 in the special issue of the *Periodical* marking the completion of the main dictionary. Soon after this an unnamed reader had urged the Press to publish a book about the Dictionary, but the idea had been dismissed by Sisam as 'an unusually vain project' (OED/B/3/2/17 25 June 1928 [KS] to 'H.T.B.' and HSM). In 1931 Harold Murray completed a memoir of his father, which naturally included a fairly full account of the history of the Dictionary, and submitted it the Delegates, but it was politely rejected. Onions was very dismissive of it: 'I didn't *read* it. A glance or two convinced me that it was such that only a heavy bribe would induce me to read it' (OED/B/3/4/4 29 May 1931 CTO to RWC; OD 15, 29 May 1931). A photocopy of one version of this memoir is in OUPA.

Sisam was keen to include 'to please the reviewers'. Despite the fact that the letter B had long been signed off, Onions contrived to squeeze it in, a task which necessitated the excision of two lines from the other material added to the entry for *body*.[200] Other very recent additions included *swimming-pool* and *technocracy*, both attested from 1932 (although both have now been antedated to before 1900).[201] May also saw some rather unseemly argument over the form of the Supplement's title page, with Onions maintaining that the distinct contributions of the two Editors should be clearly indicated (Craigie, as well as contributing the American material, had ultimately been responsible for L–R and U–Z, although Wyllie had of course done much of the work in these letters). In the end the two names were simply placed side by side, with a more detailed account of their respective contributions being given in the brief Preface.[202] The work of all the various assistants was also acknowledged in the Preface, including Walter Worrall, who had in fact made a substantial contribution to the Supplement despite having left the staff at its outset: entries in his hand feature prominently in the copy for many letters of the alphabet. He was now 71, and suffering from permanent headaches; as he commented in a melancholy note to Onions, 'it looks as if my time for work was over. If I *do* manage to get away from Oxford, I want simply not to think about it.'[203]

It is some tribute to the control exercised by the Press's senior figures over information that even at this late stage some key facts about the publication of the Supplement, and even the very fact of the Reissue's existence, were still not publicly known. During May word of the Reissue began to leak out, apparently as a result of a breach of confidence by Heffers (the biggest bookseller in Cambridge), but the Press remained tight-lipped throughout the summer.[204] It was only in September—when the last printing plates for the Supplement were finally signed off—that the publication of both Reissue and Supplement was formally announced, with a scheduled date of 14 November; the offer to supply a copy of the Supplement free to all subscribers who possessed the whole of the main Dictionary was restated, and widely praised. Privileged information was carefully released through trusted channels: a selection of some of the more noteworthy additions in the Supplement, compiled by Onions and Wyllie, was supplied to the *Times*, which responded with an enthusiastic leader, acclaiming 'the completion, for

[200] OED/B/3/10/4 5 May 1933 KS to CTO, 12 May 1933 CTO to RWC. The England cricket team's controversial use of body-line bowling during their tour of Australia in 1932–3, specifically as a means of combating the batting of Don Bradman, had been much discussed in the press; the New Zealander Sisam evidently also derived some mischievous pleasure in ensuring that the Australians were 'represented by their latest coinage'.

[201] For some other suggestions for last-minute inclusion which failed to make it, including *escapologist*, *Fianna Fail*, and *group movement*, see Brewer (2007: 62–3, 72–3).

[202] Correspondence about the title pages (9–15 May 1933) is at OED/B/3/10/4.

[203] OED/B/3/4/35 note (undated, evidently summer 1933) Worrall to CTO. When Worrall died in 1943 the Press contributed towards the costs of his funeral (FC 30 Nov. 1943).

[204] OED/B/7/5/2 19 May 1933 [KS] to Cumberlege, 11 Sept. 1933 [KS] to F. Hobbs.

FIGURE 32   The 1933 reissue of the Dictionary in twelve volumes, with the Supplement: a promotional image from the *Periodical* of March 1934.

some years at least, of the noblest monument of philological learning ever set before the world'.[205] Particular mention was made of the Supplement's American component, but it was also remarked with approval that the separate dictionary which Craigie was compiling in Chicago would be confined to 'usages specially American': a useful pre-empting of the potential threat posed by the *Dictionary of American English*, evidently showing the guiding hand of Chapman, who had been concerned about the possibility of competition. An elaborate 8-page prospectus was prepared, with specimen pages (the two chosen to illustrate the Supplement were one showing the numerous new entries in *aero-* and another showing *radio-activity* and *radium*). At Sisam's behest, the Press's publicity made extensive use of the phrase 'without a rival or the prospect of a rival', chosen as a subtle way of putting Craigie's American dictionary further in the shade.[206]

All this careful promotion of the Supplement, and the reissued Dictionary (see Figure 32), did generate a substantial and favourable response, with numerous positive articles in the public prints. However, the level of interest was distinctly muted compared with that of 1928. This may have been partly due to the fact that 1933 had already seen

[205] OED/B/3/10/4 18 Sept. 1933 [KS] to CTO, [KS] to Wyllie; *Times* 21 Sept. 1933, p. 11.
[206] OED/B/7/5/2 18 Sept. 1933 [?] to G. W. S. Hopkins and HSM.

the—much-acclaimed—publication of one large historical Oxford dictionary; no doubt it can also be partly attributed to the difficult economic situation. When it came to planning an event to celebrate publication, however, it was apparently not the Great Depression but Oxford politics which led to misgivings about staging anything as lavish as the great banquet of 1928. The Press was at this time under an uncomfortable degree of scrutiny from the University, within which there was some feeling that the Press should be brought under tighter control; undue extravagance, Chapman worried, might be a pretext for 'ill-informed (and/or malicious) criticism *intra muros*'. Fortunately the Press were saved from such embarrassment by the Goldsmiths' Company, who offered to host a luncheon at their own expense, to be held on 21 November.[207] Even this more modest event nevertheless required careful planning, as regards both the guest list and the choice of speakers; it was eventually decided that the main speeches (a toast to 'The Editors and Staff', and a response) should be given by George Gordon of Magdalen and—perhaps surprisingly—Craigie, who had made this year's visit to England rather longer than usual.[208] Gordon, in a witty speech, acclaimed 'the riotous, "riproarious", linguistic wealth of the industrial, scientific, artistic, literary, and social and colloquial life, not only of England, but of all the English-speaking countries, during the last half-century' that could be found within the Supplement's pages; his musings on what might be deduced about contemporary culture from the words included echoed a popular theme among reviewers, one of whom described the book as 'the epitome of our generation'. Craigie, responding, spoke generously—as well he might—of Onions and Wyllie, 'on whom the burden [of compilation] has chiefly fallen', and warmly acknowledged the work of all the assistants, while also taking the opportunity to mention his own continuing work in Older Scots and American English.

Nor was Craigie the only person looking forward. The completion of the Supplement unquestionably marked the end, for the foreseeable future, of the adventure in English historical lexicography on which the Press had embarked in 1877; no further Supplements were in prospect, so that, as Chapman remarked to the Vice-Chancellor of Oxford University, F. J. Lys, 'we are saying *finis coronat opus* [...] the New English Dictionary on Historical Principles does necessarily come to an end, and it may be doubted if such a comprehensive work, attempting to cover the whole vocabulary from the beginnings, can ever again be attempted.'[209] In more practical terms it was the end, too, for most of the remaining Oxford lexicographers: from January 1934 Onions, Sweatman, and Lewis began to draw a pension rather than a salary, and Birt

---

[207] OED/B/3/2/21 21 Dec. 1932 [RWC] to Sir Henry Miers; PBED 12962 10 Apr. 1933 RWC to KS. Further on the dispute over the management of the Press see Whyte (2013: 83–7).

[208] For more on the luncheon see Brewer (2007: 63–4). The speeches are fully reported in the issue of the *Periodical* for 15 March 1934, much of which was given over to a celebration of the Dictionary and Supplement.

[209] OED/B/3/2/22 31 May 1933 [RWC] to F. J. Lys (as Vice-Chancellor). *Finis coronat opus*: the end crowns the work.

also ceased to be a paid employee.[210] But in other directions new vistas were opening up, and indeed had already begun to be explored. As Charlotte Brewer has observed, 'Oxford dictionary-making did not come to a halt in 1933; it merely assumed a different face.'[211] An investigation of the features of this new face—or faces—forms the subject of the next chapter.

---

[210] Information from OUP cashbooks. Efforts were made to find other employment for the various assistants, including cataloguing work at the Bodleian for Sweatman and Lewis—and also for Worrall—and secretarial work in the University Proctors' office for Birt (OED/B/3/2/22 7 Apr. 1933 RWC to Edmund Craster, 8 June 1933 RWC to KS). Sweatman and Birt in fact went on to assist Onions in his other lexicographical projects, including his etymological dictionary and the second edition of the *Shorter*.

[211] Brewer (2007: 75).

10

Interregnum: 1933–1957

I T is impossible to give a tidy account of the next phase in the history of the *OED*. There is no longer a single path to follow; instead, several different projects, or groups of projects, each of them a continuation in one sense or another of something which began before the completion of the 1933 Supplement, must be considered in turn.

The projects which most obviously continued the kind of historical lexicography which the *OED* itself embodied were those which aimed at the compilation of period and regional dictionaries, as conceived by Craigie in the grand vision he had first proposed to the Philological Society in 1919 and its subsequent elaborations.[1] By 1933 five of these projects were under way: two of them, remarkably, under the editorship of Craigie himself. Three parts of what had come to be known as the *Dictionary of the Older Scottish Tongue (DOST)*,[2] extending well into the letter B, had appeared, the first of them in 1931; the University of Chicago was the publisher, having entered into an agreement with Craigie in 1929, although the actual printing was carried out at Oxford by the University Press, who also retained the right to sell the dictionary outside North America.[3] No doubt to Chicago's frustration, none of the *Dictionary of American English (DAE)*, arguably the principal original justification for Craigie's professorship, was yet ready for publication, despite reports as early as 1930 that '[a] beginning has already been made to the actual assembling [of the dictionary] for the press'.[4] It seems that, notwithstanding the more than 400,000 quotations now accumulated at Chicago (including over 200,000 from the files of the *OED*), Craigie

---

[1] These projects are surveyed in Adams (2009) and Bailey (2009).
[2] The history of *DOST* has been thoroughly documented by Margaret Dareau and others: see Dareau (2002) (much of the content of which was also published in volume XII (2002) of the dictionary itself), Dareau (2005), and also Dareau and Macleod (2009), which also gives an account of the *Scottish National Dictionary* (see further p. 417).
[3] Dareau (2002: 210). Correspondence (Feb.–Dec. 1930) regarding OUP's rights to sell *DOST* outside North America is preserved at PBED 8670.
[4] Gates (1930: 36).

The Making of the *Oxford English Dictionary*. First edition. Peter Gilliver.
© Peter Gilliver 2016. First published 2016 by Oxford University Press.

still regarded the corpus of evidence as insufficient.[5] In the spring of 1934 he was certainly giving *DAE* his full attention—he even warned Chapman to expect the delivery of the first batch of copy to Oxford 'within a week or two'—but in the event it was not until 1936 that the first section of the dictionary appeared.[6] By this time the 69-year-old Craigie had resigned his professorship and returned to England, to pursue an active retirement from the Oxfordshire hamlet of Christmas Common, near Watlington; an American co-editor, James Hulbert, had been appointed to oversee things from the Chicago end. For this project a very different publication model had been adopted, in that by the time of Craigie's departure the preparation of copy for the entire dictionary was deemed sufficiently complete that subscribers could be promised regular publication of sections: a promise which was honoured, war notwithstanding, eight years later with the publication of the twentieth and final section (*Virginian dogwood* to *zu-zu*) in 1944. Although in the end the University of Chicago opted to print *DAE* in America, OUP retained an interest in the form of non-American sales rights, this having been a condition required, in one form or another, of all the projects to whom the Press agreed to make subsets of the *OED*'s quotation files available.

Two other period projects which had also been recipients of large contributions of evidence from the *OED*'s files were now based at the University of Michigan in Ann Arbor.[7] The more advanced of the two during the early 1930s was the projected dictionary of Early Modern English, under the editorship of Charles Fries, who had gone so far as to produce and circulate a specimen entry (for the word *sonnet*) in 1932,[8] and who in 1934 began editorial work in earnest with the compilation of entries in the letter L. In 1935 Michigan entered into an agreement with OUP, envisaging an 8,000-page dictionary, in eight volumes, to be complete by 1 January 1946, with the Press undertaking the bulk of production costs on the understanding that printing and publishing were to be reserved to them. Batches of copy for the new dictionary immediately began to arrive in Oxford, and in 1936 a prospectus for what came to be known as the *Early Modern English Dictionary* (*EMED*) was printed, including a 14-page specimen of dictionary entries.[9]

---

[5] Craigie listed various categories of vocabulary for which he felt his material was 'most defective' in a renewed appeal for help in collecting evidence (Craigie 1933b).

[6] PBED 12858 19 Mar. 1934 WAC to RWC; *Chicago Daily Tribune* 8 Sept. 1936, p. 25.

[7] For more on the histories of these two projects see Bailey (1980), Bailey (1985), and Lewis et al. (2007). See also Kuhn (1982) for a detailed account of compilation methods on the *Middle English Dictionary*.

[8] The specimen entry was reprinted in *PMLA* 47 (1932), pp. 894–7, as part of a joint report by Fries and Craigie on the progress of the various period dictionaries.

[9] CPED 611 telegram 10 Dec. 1935 Fries to KS (reporting the approval of the agreement by the University of Michigan's 'Dictionary Committee'); Bailey (1985: 183). Due to an administrative error the Press did not receive formal approval of the agreement in its final form until February 1937, although it was evidently regarded as effectively in place by the spring of 1936, when Michigan sent its first annual contribution towards publication costs (CPED 611 9 May 1936 Fries to KS, 6 Feb. 1937 A. Ruthven to KS, 12 Feb. 1937 Fries to KS). Copies of the 1936 prospectus are preserved in OUPA (CPED 609, 610).

Ann Arbor was also now the home of the *Middle English Dictionary* (*MED*), which had moved there in 1930 after some years of poor progress and financial difficulty at Cornell. Michigan had appointed a new editor from among the faculty, Samuel Moore, who realized that the corpus of evidence—which included over 400,000 slips from Oxford—needed to be enlarged still further, and launched an ambitious reading programme.[10] His unexpected death in September 1934, following an operation, was another blow to progress: he had got as far as discussing typography with OUP, which had produced two specimens, and he had even raised the subject of making this another joint Oxford–Michigan venture during a visit to England in the summer of 1934.[11] His successor, Thomas Knott, had the excellent credentials of having just seen through to publication (as general editor) the impressive second edition of *Webster's New International Dictionary*.[12] He worked closely with Fries to find ways in which the two historical projects could cooperate, minimizing duplication of effort. Preparation of copy was well under way by the end of 1935, and in 1937 a specimen was printed at Oxford, much along the lines of that for Fries's Early Modern English project, although the Press had not as yet made any firm commitment to publish *MED*.[13] However, over the next few years both of the Michigan-based projects were afflicted by various problems, involving funding difficulties, criticism of editorial policy and practice from various quarters, and some serious clashes between members of the editorial teams. In 1938 work on *MED* was suspended in order that the combined staffs of the two projects could concentrate on *EMED*; and then in the spring of 1939 Michigan decided instead to suspend work on *EMED* so that the by then limited resources available could be concentrated on *MED*. In fact work on the compilation of *EMED* was never resumed, making this the only one of the 'period dictionaries' projected by Craigie never to have come to fruition.[14] Editorial work on *MED* continued throughout the war, although not always smoothly by any means; Knott, whose editorship remained controversial, suffered from increasingly poor health, and died in 1945, to be succeeded—after a brief caretakership under Hereward Price, Murray's erstwhile assistant in the Scriptorium, who had worked on both Michigan

[10] Lewis et al. (2007: 3). The slips given by Oxford included material from the files accumulated for work on the Supplement—some of which had been accumulating for decades (see above, p. 319)—as well as those relating to the main Dictionary; extraction of 'Supplement' material was still ongoing in 1934, though it may have begun as early as the summer of 1932 (CPED 172 1 June 1932 WAC to KS; OED/B/3/2/23 30 Oct. 1934 Eleanor Bradley to KS).

[11] Lewis et al. (2007: 31); CPED 172 18 July 1934 [KS] to Moore. Copies of the 1933 and 1934 specimens are preserved in CPED 172; they are more dummies than specimens, in that the copy used is simply the Middle English content of a sequence of *OED* entries, rather than actual *MED* text, the editorial work on which had hardly begun.

[12] The first edition of *Webster's New International* had appeared in 1909; the second, published in 1934, soon became 'the most prestigious dictionary in America' (Landau 2009: 214). Knott had in fact been approached as a possible editor of *MED* in 1930, but had declined, regarding himself as committed to the Webster project (Adams 2002: 97–8).

[13] 'Middle English Dictionary Annual Report' dated 1 Nov. 1935 (copy in CPED 172).

[14] In 1965 there was a revival of interest in the project when R. C. Alston of the University of Leeds issued a draft proposal for a Dictionary of Tudor English, which envisaged making some use of Michigan's materials, but this came to nothing, mainly because of failure to secure financial backing (Aitken 1987: 97). Finally, the project's data came to be of use to the *OED* itself decades later: see below, p. 559.

dictionary projects since 1929—by the Austrian émigré Hans Kurath.[15] It was only under Kurath that *MED* at last began to be published, ultimately by the University of Michigan; the first fascicle appeared in 1952, and the last in 2001.

Across the Atlantic, another project nourished by evidence from the *OED* files, though on a more modest scale, was the *Scottish National Dictionary* (*SND*), the pre-eminent dictionary of modern Scots.[16] The project's origins went back to 1907, when Craigie—who unsurprisingly also figures prominently in the *SND*'s history—gave a lecture to the Dundee branch of the English Association, which seems to have led directly to the setting up of a Scottish Dialects Committee and the commencement of a programme to collect dialect material. Craigie saw the idea of a dictionary of modern Scots as complementary to his own work on older Scots; his assistant George Watson soon emerged as a fellow enthusiast, and already by 1916 he was envisaging Watson as a possible editor of the modern dictionary, or at least as 'a kind of connecting medium' between the two (still theoretical) projects. In 1925 the Scottish Dialects Committee made a formal undertaking that modern Scots would receive lexicographical treatment on a scale comparable with *DOST*; and Craigie began to discuss the extraction of quotations from the *OED*'s files with William Grant, convener of the Committee (and soon to be the dictionary's editor)—before he had even secured the agreement of the Delegates to the release of material for the various period projects.[17] The volume of modern Scots quotations among the *OED* materials was considerably less than that for the dictionaries of earlier periods—of the order of tens, rather than hundreds, of thousands—but they still constituted an important component of the *SND*'s corpus of data. Of rather more value was the contribution of George Watson, who not only helped to extract the *OED* quotations, and arranged for their dispatch to Grant, but also donated a large collection of quotations that he had himself collected, and, as Craigie had envisaged, continued to act as a useful link between the two Scottish projects, even after his move to Chicago.[18] 1929 saw another important step, with the setting up of the Scottish National Dictionary Association, and in 1931 the first fascicle was published.

[15] Price's career after his departure from the *OED* had been a remarkable one. He emigrated to Germany to pursue his studies, becoming Lektor in English at Bonn University; he married a German wife in 1911 and became a German citizen, and was conscripted into the German army in 1915. While fighting on the Eastern Front he was captured by the Russians and imprisoned in Siberia, but escaped overland to China, where he was for a time sheltered by Murray's son Jowett, then a missionary in Tientsin. He returned to Germany—where he compiled a two-volume German–English dictionary of economic vocabulary—and in 1929 travelled to Michigan to take up a professorship of English, working thereafter on both *EMED* and *MED*. His wartime experiences are recounted in a colourful memoir, *Boche to Bolshevik* (1919). Price seems to have been an important source of information for Oxford about developments in Michigan after Craigie's return to England, judging from the correspondence preserved in OUPA (CPED 173, 613).

[16] For a full account of the history of *SND* see Macleod (2012). Much historical information about both *DOST* and *SND* can also be seen online at the website for both of these dictionaries, www.dsl.ac.uk.

[17] NLS Acc. 9448/245 28 Jan. 1916 WAC to W. Grant; Acc. 9448/245 18 Sept. 1925 WAC to W. Grant. I am grateful to Susan Rennie for sharing with me her notes on the *SND* papers.

[18] NLS Acc. 9448/230 21 Oct. 1927 Watson to Grant. Watson estimated that his own collections amounted by this time to 14,000 quotations; the *OED* quotations for the range A–E amounted to about 10,000 (NLS Acc. 9448/245 2 Sept. 1927 WAC to Grant).

From this time relations between the project and Craigie cooled somewhat, partly because of disagreement over the use of the word 'National' in the dictionary's title, which could be taken as implying precedence over *DOST*; but ultimately such scruples did not prevent him continuing to support the project, lobbying for funding, and advising on various editorial matters. The dictionary survived various vicissitudes, including war and the death of Grant in 1946; it was completed, under Grant's successor David Murison, in 1976.

The first steps in the conception of the *Dictionary of Old English* (*DOE*) were not taken until the late 1960s, when Angus Cameron and C. J. E. Ball began to formulate plans, and thus the project arguably belongs to the next chapter, but for completeness it is included here as the last of the period dictionaries to benefit from quotations taken from the *OED* files. The contribution made by *OED* to *DOE*, as far as quotations are concerned, is much less than that for any of the other period dictionaries—so much less, in fact, that some accounts of *DOE* fail to mention it at all—but a small number of *OED* quotations were indeed sent to the University of Toronto, where *DOE* has been (and is still being) compiled.[19]

From this brief account it will be apparent that the materials collected for the first edition of *OED* and the 1933 Supplement yielded editorial nourishment to a number of lexicographical endeavours outside Oxford, some of which also benefited from a more direct contribution from *OED* lexicographers, and most of which retained a connection with OUP as far as printing or publication, or both, was concerned. In Oxford itself there was also an ongoing strand of lexicographical activity which could claim some continuity with the work that had been completed in 1933. The most notable evidence of this continuity was to be found in the Dictionary Room. Robert Gunther, so long deprived of the chance to take over the Old Ashmolean as a home for the University's collection of scientific instruments, might reasonably have supposed that with the completion of the Supplement the Dictionary Room would become available for this purpose; and indeed in June 1933 he had already begun renewed agitation on the subject. However, his efforts (and those of many other Oxford figures whom he succeeded in recruiting to the cause) continued to be frustrated for nearly another decade: the room remained a home for lexicographical activity until the spring of 1941, when space was found in the Old Schools Quadrangle of the Bodleian Library.[20]

The main focus of this lexicographical activity, however, was not English, but Latin; and the figure at the centre of this activity was James Wyllie, who was now firmly signed up to work on the large-scale Latin dictionary which the Press had decided to undertake,

[19] Robert Lewis and Antonette diPaolo Healey, personal communication. Further on the history of *DOE* see Cameron (1983) and Adams (2009: 345–51).

[20] OED/B/3/3/1 6 June 1933 RWC to CTO; OD 12 Nov. 1937; BodL Library Records d. 26, 'Report of the Building Committee to the Curators', 10 May 1941; Gunther (1967: 217). Originally the Schola Naturalis Philosophiae had been earmarked for this purpose, but in the end it was decided to use the Schola Logicae instead, initially as a temporary measure until the requisite alterations could be made to the Schola Naturalis Philosophiae (then known as the 'Chinese Room' because of the Chinese materials kept there); these alterations never took place.

and who had already started work in earnest in September 1933, as a full-time assistant to the principal editor Alexander Souter (who however remained at Aberdeen). He was also starting work on a small Latin dictionary, and by the end of the year had produced a specimen page (which Sisam described as 'extraordinarily concise & business-like').[21] For Sisam the redirection of some of the Press's unrivalled lexicographical resources, human and otherwise, into a new language, made perfect sense: the *Oxford Latin Dictionary* (*OLD*), as it would soon come to be known, was 'the best big project we can undertake— it keeps up our strongest special line—lexicography; gives us a hold on school Latin dictionaries, and keeps a nucleus [of] staff usefully employed in the Dictionary Room.' Equally clear to Sisam, and to others, was the central role to be played by Wyllie in this work, and indeed his importance to Oxford lexicography generally. His performance since his arrival on the Supplement had been consistently impressive, notwithstanding the occasional episodes of friction with colleagues, and he had thrown himself into his Latin work with similar enthusiasm and initiative. Sisam, taking the long view, was particularly delighted to have found a lexicographer who was both able and young:

He is undoubtedly a great performer in lexicography, versatile, and with a natural gift for planning his work to a programme. We shall need him in the future to keep up and extend our various dictionaries, Latin and English, when Fowler is gone [...]. Onions (59) is not best at routine work that must pay its way and be done to a stern programme.[22]

The programme of 'keeping up' the various English dictionaries was of course already well under way. The second edition of the *Concise* had appeared in 1929 edited by Henry Fowler, who by then was also hard at work on the proposed new 'Quarto' dictionary of modern English, and who in 1931 recruited his friend Herbert Le Mesurier, a retired British army officer, to help in the compilation of this dictionary.[23] In 1933, when it was decided that new editions of—or at least substantial addenda to—both the *Concise* and the *Pocket* were called for, Fowler proposed that Le Mesurier should take these on; the fact that Wyllie was commissioned to write reports on the planned revision of both dictionaries in the summer of 1933 is a striking indication of the trust already placed in him. From September 1933 he began to be paid a regular retaining fee for work done in respect of both the *OED* and the whole family of smaller English dictionaries, including the *Little Oxford*—soon to appear in a second edition edited by Jessie Coulson—and the 'Quarto'.[24] The new editions of the *Concise* and the *Pocket* appeared in 1934; sadly, Fowler, whose health had broken down in 1932, did not live to see them. He died on

---

[21] CPED 883 27 Dec. 1933 KS to ALPN.

[22] PBED 12941 memo by KS, 21 Dec. 1932. Such glowing commendations were not unusual: a few weeks later Sisam was describing Wyllie as having 'proved himself to us and to Craigie the most promising young English lexicographer we have come upon' (PBED 12940 24 Feb. 1933 [KS] to H. Stuart Jones). For a full account of the compilation of *OLD* see Stray (2012).

[23] McMorris (2001: 201).

[24] L.B.7210 5 July 1933 Wyllie to KS; McMorris (2001: 211); OUP cashbooks 14 July, 30 Sept. 1933.

26 December 1933, and his brother Arthur, jointly with Le Mesurier, took over the editorship of the 'Quarto'—or, as it would soon be known, the *Oxford Dictionary of Modern English (ODME)*.[25] This rapidly became one of the Press's most important and ambitious new lexicographical ventures: a large dictionary (planned to be 1,500 pages long) which was to map, with the aid of a liberal selection of quotations, 'the potential vocabulary of well-educated "Englishmen" who had read widely in the literary classics and were hence well acquainted (perhaps wished to be better acquainted) with a huge hinterland of historical literary language'.[26] Such a book, it was felt, could occupy valuable—and as yet unoccupied—ground in the marketplace for dictionaries, which was becoming increasingly crowded, although Oxford's existing titles, backed as they were by the reputation of the *OED* itself, were all doing well in their respective markets.

Wyllie's Oxford location made him a natural choice as a kind of central clearing-house for correspondence with those working on the various individual dictionaries, almost all of whom were based elsewhere.[27] Each of the published dictionaries generated a stream of correspondence from the public, pointing out errors and omissions, which of course needed to be considered by the relevant editor but might also have implications for other members of the Oxford 'family', and proper coordination of these streams of information would facilitate the process of keeping all the dictionaries up to date. There was also a significant stream of correspondence relating to the *OED* itself. Notwithstanding the Press's decision that '*finis coronat opus*'—and the understandable reluctance of anyone to give serious thought to revising the Dictionary, or even expanding its Supplement—members of the public continued to write to 'The Editor' of the *OED* with observations about entries which they considered in need of correction or supplementation, or about the language in general. Initially, at least, correspondence of this nature was answered by Sisam, but he would regularly pass on any relevant information (sometimes via Le Mesurier) to Wyllie, who noted such information— whether it came to him by this route, or through correspondence with an editor of one of the smaller dictionaries—in a copy of the Dictionary and Supplement in the Dictionary Room.[28]

---

[25] OD 19 Jan. 1934. A full account of the history of the 'Quarto' is given in Brewer (2008); see also McMorris (2001: 184–215).

[26] Brewer (2007: 79).

[27] Le Mesurier was based in Exmouth (Devon), Arthur Fowler in Hinton St George (Somerset), and Jessie Coulson in Teddington (Middlesex). The one exception was Frederick Sweatman, veteran of the Scriptorium and erstwhile member of Onions's staff, now in his sixties and technically a pensioner, whom Sisam set to work (under Onions's supervision) compiling a list of small revisions to the *Shorter*, primarily by scanning the 1934 *Webster's New International* (ODME/7/105 14 May 1935 [KS] to Le Mesurier). He died unexpectedly in August 1936, only a few weeks before the publication of the new edition, in which several thousand additions and corrections (including such recent items as *electronic* and *Nazi*) had all been squeezed into the main text without increasing the page count.

[28] This process had started already by December 1933 (OED/C/2/1/5 13 Dec. 1933 KS to Wyllie). Le Mesurier maintained similar files for use in the revision of the *Concise* and the *Pocket*, and as a resource in the compilation of the 'Quarto'.

Information gathered from unsolicited correspondence did not of course constitute an adequate basis for keeping the various dictionaries up to date. The need for some kind of apparatus for the monitoring of ongoing developments in the language had been recognized as long ago as 1922;[29] and in 1935 the importance of maintaining 'some skeleton organization to watch and record the growth and change of the language' was restated by Chapman in an important discussion document, printed for private circulation among the Delegates and a few other privileged individuals, entitled 'The Oxford English Dictionary and its (Oxford) Children'.[30] This document goes into some detail about the *Oxford Dictionary of Modern English*, which was evidently the most important project in English lexicography in which the Press was then engaged; but it also summarized what was being done to monitor the language, including a description—and implicit endorsement—of Wyllie's work in the Dictionary Room, which amounted to the maintenance of a database for use in the revision of the *OED* itself, even though the document also made it clear once again that no editorial work on the *OED* or the Supplement was planned. Chapman's view was that 'we are perhaps doing as much, in general collection, as can usefully be attempted'; and, while noting that various individuals were necessarily accumulating information in various places, and that an absolutely uniform method of data collection was unfeasible, he '[did] not think it will at any stage be very difficult to adapt the material to any likely use'.

The 'general collection' mentioned by Chapman was a much more modest affair than the kind of large-scale extraction of quotations, carried out by a large body of contributors, that had formed the raw material for the first edition of the Dictionary. The prevailing view was that it was better to rely on the evidence sent in by 'a few Heaven-sent enthusiasts' who had a good sense of what was wanted than to take delivery of a vast volume of quotations of very variable usefulness; so that, instead of launching a public appeal of any kind, it was more a matter of 'taking opportunities of informing people of our plans and inviting their help', an informal mode of solicitation which also usefully maintained the 'general impression that Oxford is still an active lexicographical machine'. Among this band of 'enthusiasts' were several former Dictionary assistants who had formed an incurable habit of sending in quotations from their general reading, including Henry Bradley's daughter Eleanor (whose quotation slips 'though few [were] remarkably good'); Chapman, Sisam, and Le Mesurier did likewise, and various members of this group made a more systematic trawl of particular periodicals (Le Mesurier, for example, carefully read issues of *Nature* for scientific vocabulary, as well as reading the *New York Times* once a week). There were also other individuals with a good track record of sending in valuable material, such as T. G. Phillips, a Methodist minister who had been contributing to

---

[29] See above, p. 359.
[30] Several drafts of Chapman's text, the earliest of which seems to date from the start of October 1935, are in OUPA (ODME/7), together with comments from Onions, Le Mesurier, and others (Wyllie was apparently also shown an early version), and copies of the printed pamphlet, dated October 1935, one of which is annotated with a list of 25 recipients.

the Dictionary at least since 1928;[31] new recruits to this informal group of volunteers included the historian Veronica Ruffer, who wrote offering to contribute early in 1936 and whose quotations Wyllie was soon commending for their quality.[32]

It is clear that by the time Chapman's pamphlet appeared Wyllie had become a key figure in the Press's various lexicographical activities. As far as the *Oxford Latin Dictionary*—which, by general agreement, remained the main focus of his efforts—was concerned, although he was nominally only the assistant editor, with Souter as editor, he was taking the leading role in almost every aspect of the project, which was at this point still at the stage of collecting quotation evidence. In April 1935 a substantial increase in his *OLD* salary[33] showed the Press's recognition of his value to the project; but in fact other factors lay behind the increase. Sisam already had it in mind that once *OLD* was finished Wyllie should resume full-time work in English lexicography. He regarded the ten years that *OLD* was scheduled to take as quite long enough for him to be spending away from the Press's English dictionaries, not least as by then he would be 'the only trained man available to look after them'; indeed he regarded Wyllie as 'a person necessary to the future of the Delegates' dictionary enterprises generally'. In fact he was more than a little anxious that he might be tempted away by lucrative offers from other publishers—a loss which would be effectively irreparable—and was determined to give him sufficient financial security to prevent this.[34] In addition to his *OLD* salary, and £100 a year for work on a 'Little Oxford Latin Dictionary', there was also the £50 he received each year for his work in respect of various of the Press's English dictionaries; initially five were specified (the *Shorter*, the *Concise*, the *Pocket*, the *Little*, and *ODME*), but subsequently most of these were covered by a more general payment for 'Dictionary Collections'. He was also paid consultancy fees in connection with various other dictionaries, including several reports on the encyclopedic dictionary being compiled by Jessie Coulson, and even a projected German dictionary.[35] A further important symbol of recognition came in February 1936 when the degree of MA was conferred on him. Although this was an MA by decree, rather than an honorary degree of the kind that had been conferred on various other *OED* lexicographers, Wyllie certainly regarded it as 'a vote of confidence from the Clarendon Press', and was careful to thank Chapman for his part in securing it. After receiving his degree he was invited to become a member of Balliol College.[36]

---

[31] OED/B/3/4/27 18 Mar. 1928 T. G. Phillips to RWC. Phillips continued to send in quotations until the late 1930s.

[32] OED/C/2/1/6 17 Mar. 1936 V. Ruffer to 'Dear Sir', 4 Apr. 1936 [Wyllie] to Ruffer; OED/C/2/1/8 20 Apr. 1937 [Wyllie] to Ruffer.

[33] From 1 April 1935 Wyllie's salary for his work on *OLD* went up by £50 to £400; this was to be followed by an annual series of increases of a further £25 (FC 28 Feb. 1935).

[34] PBED 12941 memo by KS on *OLD*, dated 17 Apr. 1935; 20 Feb. 1935 KS to RWC.

[35] All information from OUP cashbooks. Wyllie was paid for several reports on Coulson's dictionary in 1935–7, and on 3 May 1935 for an assessment of the likely scale of a German dictionary by H. F. Eggeling.

[36] PBED 12941 28 Feb. 1936 Wyllie to RWC. The degree was conferred by decree of Congregation on 25 February 1936. Wyllie's admission to Balliol took place on 13 May, as noted in a summary of recent College Meetings dated 20 May (Balliol College archives); it is not clear what 'membership' of the college entailed, but it is likely to have entitled him to certain dining rights and probably the use of the Senior Common Room.

Valuable as Wyllie's contribution was to the Press's various English dictionaries, he was not the editor of any of them. Neither was he the Editor of the *OED*; but in view of the fact that he maintained, and had largely devised, the machinery for keeping track of possible revisions and additions, he might reasonably be said to be the lexicographer most closely associated with the *OED*, at a time when the project was more or less in a state of suspended animation. He himself was of course acutely conscious of the continuing presence of the two men who had, in their time, been titular Editors of the Dictionary, and he had a particular respect for Craigie; but from 1936 he does seem to have begun to identify himself strongly with the Dictionary. His position is well illustrated by a letter written in 1936 in response to a query from a Philadelphia attorney about the meaning of the word *house*. After first pointing out that at present 'there is no official editor of the New English Dictionary' (the original letter was in fact addressed to Sir James Murray!), he suggests that Craigie or Onions would be the best people to apply to for an opinion; but he goes on to offer his own view, and signs himself 'Acting Editor of the Oxford English Dictionary'.[37] It is unclear whether he had any authority to use this title, but it may perhaps reflect his sense of being the sole tender of the flame, notwithstanding the presence in or near Oxford of both Craigie and Onions, as the former (now returned from America) was now largely taken up with his work on *DOST* and *DAE*, while the latter was immersed in his work on the *Oxford Dictionary of English Etymology*, not to mention the distractions of life as a fellow of Magdalen College.

For Wyllie, indeed, tending the flame involved more than maintaining a file of revisions and additions and dealing with correspondence. From time to time he would carry out research into the history or meaning of a word, to an extent that went well beyond what an entry in any of the smaller dictionaries might need (though it was often a query relating to such a dictionary, most commonly *ODME*, which prompted it). Sisam and Chapman were aware of Wyllie's inclination to pursue such matters, and of the risk that such profusion of historical detail might become a distraction for Le Mesurier; Sisam undertook to remind Wyllie that 'we are, at the moment, concerned in recording what comes to our notice for O.E.D. correction, not in searching for it'. Wyllie, however, persisted: as he explained to Le Mesurier in relation to his (successful) efforts to track down the coinage of the word *epiloia*, 'The investigation has been quite exciting and useful, for it keeps one in training for this sort of work.'[38] Hard at work on the *Oxford Latin Dictionary* he might be, but he was certainly managing to remain active in English lexicography.

The start of 1937 marked a turning point for *OLD*: in January, Wyllie at last began to prepare actual dictionary entries, rather than simply collecting and organizing quotations. He also chose to see it as something of a turning point for himself

---

[37] OED/C/2/1/7 19 Oct. 1936 E. J. McDermott to JAHM, 28 Oct. 1936 [Wyllie] to McDermott.
[38] ODME/7/226 1 Nov. 1935 KS to RWC; OED/C/2/1/6 6 Feb. 1936 [Wyllie] to Le Mesurier. An entry for *epiloia* (an inherited condition affecting the brain) was not added to the Dictionary until 1993.

personally. For some time he had been concerned that his salary was not sufficient to allow him to maintain what he regarded as an adequate standard of living for himself and his family (he now had a daughter and two sons); and now he confirmed Sisam and Chapman's worst fears by announcing that he had begun to think of looking elsewhere for more remunerative employment. At the end of January he travelled to Aberdeen, ostensibly to discuss the first few specimen entries of *OLD* with Souter, but also, it seems, to explore other employment options; and on his return he presented Chapman with a formal statement of his dissatisfaction with the present arrangements.[39] Chapman, now thoroughly alarmed, hurriedly prepared a report on the situation—essentially an update of his 1935 pamphlet—in which he contrasted the large number of English dictionaries which 'will or may need and deserve revision to keep them up to date' with the extremely limited supply of lexicographers having the combination of competence and (relative) youth needed for such work: the only figure other than Wyllie who was anything like fully trained was Jessie Coulson, whose work on her encyclopedic dictionary Wyllie was still regularly reviewing and commenting on in detail. Chapman concluded by restating his and Sisam's opinion of Wyllie, a man of 'qualities altogether exceptional', likely to 'be for life a scholarly compiler of great value, comparable with Murray himself'—but only 'if his services are retained'.[40] The Delegates took the hint, and promptly authorized an increase of £100 in his *OLD* salary, another £100 a year for work on a Latin dictionary for schools—a revamped version of the small dictionary he had been working on for some time—and further 'suitable remuneration' (a figure of £100 a year was quickly agreed upon) for 'general care of and advice on English and other dictionaries' done in his spare time; Wyllie was also assured that the Delegates 'do not look upon the completion of [*OLD*] as an end of your service, but anticipate that there will be other lexicographical enterprises for you to work on when your time is available'.[41] (One more such lexicographical enterprise was already clamouring for his attention: an entirely new English dictionary for the schools market, to be edited by his friend and fellow Aberdeen graduate Thomas Henderson, and to which he provided considerable input.[42]) On the Latin side of things a large imponderable remained, namely just how much of his time Souter would devote to lexicography when he retired (as he was expected to do later in the year); but as far as the practical aspects of organizing the work were concerned, Wyllie was already in effective control.

---

[39] PBED 12942 4, 28 Jan. 1937 Wyllie to KS; WP undated memorandum, c.Feb. 1937, headed 'Suggested Revision of Agreement between the Clarendon Press and J. M. Wyllie'.

[40] OUPA(u) report by RWC on 'Oxford Dictionaries', dated 22 Feb. 1937.

[41] FC 4 Mar. 1937, OD 5 Mar. 1937; WP 9 Mar. 1937 KS to Wyllie.

[42] The Press had been contemplating the idea of a school dictionary at least since 1930; Henderson, an experienced schoolmaster, was apparently recommended as a compiler by Wyllie (WP 17 Mar. 1937 Wyllie to Souter). After a promising start, the project was interrupted by the war; Henderson subsequently became involved in educational administration, and after various further false starts, in 1951 Dorothy MacKenzie, wife of a Falkirk headmaster (and another suggestion of Wyllie's), took on the dictionary, which was finally published as the *Oxford School Dictionary* in 1957 (details in PBED 3828, 3850).

By contrast, it could be said that as far as the *OED* was concerned there was nothing to control. Chapman noted in his report that the Supplement was 'rapidly going out of date', but reiterated his view that as things stood there was no realistic prospect of revising it, let alone the main Dictionary, in the foreseeable future. Wyllie, admittedly, seems to have taken a different, or at least a longer-term view, as is seen from the fact that he continued to maintain his database of revisions and additions—initially referred to as the 'O.E.D. Collections'[43]—and was also collecting quotations for the *OED* from his own reading;[44] but Latin lexicography, already officially his main activity, was beginning to demand more and more of his attention, particularly after Souter's arrival in Oxford in the autumn of 1937. Unfortunately, it soon became apparent that Souter, despite his undoubted eminence, was—in Wyllie's opinion, but also in the view of other scholars consulted by the Press, including Craigie—simply not up to the job of compiling entries for the dictionary.[45]

In January 1939 the problems with *OLD* came to a head. Souter was informed that the specimen entries he had produced were 'radically and incurably unsound', and that his position as editor of the dictionary was no longer tenable. After a great deal of difficult (and secret) negotiation, a solution was arrived at which allowed Souter to avoid public humiliation: he would redirect his efforts towards the compilation of a separate, supplementary glossary of 'Later Latin' (i.e. the Latin of the early post-classical period, on which he was an authority), and in consequence cease to compile any entries for *OLD*.[46] Further negotiations eventually culminated in July in the formal replacement of Souter as editor by a pair of 'Co-Editors': Wyllie and (as 'senior Co-Editor', though in practice his was a largely supervisory role) the classical scholar Cyril Bailey, who as a Delegate of the Press had long taken a close interest in *OLD*.

In the midst of such turbulence it is hardly surprising that no plans of any kind were being made for the future of the *OED*. However, it is also very clear that as soon as a return, in any form, to work on the *OED* began to be contemplated, Wyllie's involvement would have been taken as read, given his position at the heart of the Press's dictionary publishing—with a finger in almost every lexicographical pie—and the respect which senior Press figures had for his abilities.[47] That, at least, was surely the situation until the spring of 1939; but at this point a troubling new factor entered the picture. It had been apparent almost from the start of Wyllie's work on the Supplement

[43] Brewer (2007: 279 n. 58) notes Sisam's use of the heading on some memos from 1937; it does not, however, seem to have persisted as a formal title, and 'Dictionary records' and 'O.E.D. records' also occur (e.g. PBED 12948 1 July, 30 Nov. 1938, 9 Jan. 1939 [KS] to Wyllie).

[44] WP 3 Oct. 1939 Wyllie to KS.

[45] Stray (2012: xiii).

[46] PBED 12944 10, 24 Jan. 1939 [RWC] to C. Bailey. Souter's *Glossary of Later Latin* was eventually published in 1949, a few weeks after his death; it had originally been conceived as a supplement to the main work.

[47] Wyllie was, for example, described by Sisam as 'our best young man on principles' in a letter to the editors of *EMED* in 1938, accompanying a detailed report on that dictionary which Sisam had commissioned from him (CPED 613 7 July 1938 [KS] to Knott and Fries).

that he could be a difficult person to deal with; there had been Onions's complaint of his insubordination over the matter of desiderata lists in 1930, the unseemly squabble over desk space in the Old Ashmolean a year later, the occasional episodes of friction with his junior colleague Dorothy Marshall, and perhaps more recently the departure of another assistant, Bertha Colman, in 1936 after only a few months in the Dictionary Room.[48] It is perhaps only with hindsight that the pattern formed by these incidents might seem to suggest something more than the acceptable failings of the 'raw, secretive aggressive Scotch boy' that Chapman had pigeonholed Wyllie as in 1931. There is, after all, in Oxford as much as (if not more than) elsewhere, a long tradition of tolerating the eccentricities of a scholar who is capable of good work; and it would have been understandable if Chapman and Sisam, convinced as they were of Wyllie's importance to their plans, had persuaded themselves that such incidents as they were aware of were evidence of no more than manageable eccentricity. Be that as it may, from the start of March 1939 Wyllie's 'difficultness' began to take on aspects of something more like paranoia.

Wyllie was in the habit of meeting Sisam on Mondays to talk about dictionary matters, when the problems of *OLD* must have provided much of the matter for discussion. It was at one such meeting, on 27 February, that Sisam told him, informally, that Souter had been persuaded to step aside—but on terms which could not have been better calculated to touch one of Wyllie's rawest nerves: the feeling of not being properly recognized. Not only was Wyllie convinced of Souter's utter incompetence in matters lexicographical: he also felt that he had failed to discharge his responsibilities right from the earliest years of the *OLD* project, when Wyllie had done much of the early planning and taken the lion's share of responsibility for organizing the collection of quotations. He now learned, to his horror, that—perhaps to sweeten the pill of having to relinquish the editorship—Souter had been given an assurance that in the (as yet unwritten) preface to the dictionary he would be given full credit for the part he had played in planning and organizing the project during its early stages. To many people this might not have mattered—the actual writing of the preface lay some years in the future, after all—but unfortunately it mattered a great deal to Wyllie, who still carried a strong sense of grievance about the wording of the preface to the 1933 Supplement to the *OED*, where his contribution had been stated in terms which he felt did him less than justice.[49] The idea that a similar injustice was now to be inflicted upon him was, it seems, too much to bear; and on 4 March he wrote the first of what was to be a flurry of angry letters to Sisam and Chapman, demanding clarification of what undertakings had been given to Souter, what his own exact position and responsibilities were to be, and so on.[50] Wyllie's relations with Sisam were never to recover from this episode; it is

---

[48] PBED 12944 30 Jan. 1936 B. Colman to KS. Mrs Colman had started the previous October, apparently as a clerical assistant, working mainly on *OLD*.

[49] The preface described Wyllie as having 'prepared for the printer' the entries in Craigie's portion of the text.

[50] PBED 12930 4 Mar. 1939 Wyllie to KS.

probably fair to say that he never trusted him again. His outburst forced various senior figures involved to recognize that the person who had long been regarded as the Press's most able lexicographer was also capable of behaviour which suggested some kind of mental imbalance. Chapman warned him that he and Sisam had been 'disturbed and alarmed by his vexing himself and us in this way'—ironically at the precise time when the delicate negotiations with Souter seemed to be going well—and Cyril Bailey became convinced that Wyllie 'cannot be trusted to take charge [of OLD], being the victim of delusions'.[51] In this context the decision to appoint Bailey as co-editor jointly with Wyllie, rather than simply arranging for Wyllie to take Souter's place, becomes more understandable. It also afforded a means of addressing yet another problem, namely the breakdown of relations between Wyllie and another OLD assistant, a Jewish refugee from Germany named Charles (Karl) Brink, who had joined the staff in 1938, and whose relationship with Wyllie had deteriorated to the point where he declared himself unable to continue to work under him.[52] It was decided that with the appointment of two co-editors the staff could be split into two, working in separate locations; and so, on 28 July, Brink and some of his colleagues were transferred to rooms in 40 Walton Crescent, a house adjoining the Press's main site in Walton Street, which would go on to become a home for lexicographical activity of one kind or another for much of the next three-quarters of a century.

Thus at the outbreak of the Second World War the OED continued to be in a state of suspended animation, without immediate prospects of resuscitation. The public continued to write in, often to 'The Editor' of the Dictionary, with occasional suggestions, comments, and corrections, which continued to be acknowledged—most often by Sisam—and which Wyllie, notwithstanding his many distractions, continued to file for future use; but the possibility of doing anything with the 'O.E.D. Collections' must have seemed remote indeed. One such letter of Sisam's, written in January 1940, summarizes the situation:

We see no prospect of a new Supplement [...] As for the main work [...] a thorough revision would probably cost half a million pounds, even if the staff could be obtained. [...] So I expect the great work will stand for at least half a century.[53]

The comment about the scarcity of suitable staff would have been heartfelt: in addition to the question-mark that now stood over Wyllie's reliability,[54] the Press's dictionary

---

[51] PBED 12942 14 Mar. 1939 [RWC] to KS; PBED 12933 30 May 1939 RWC to KS. Wyllie was also encouraged to consult a specialist at the Press's expense, possibly a psychiatrist (PBED 12949 4 July 1939 RWC to KS); it is not known whether he did so.

[52] PBED 12933 18 May 1939 Bailey to RWC.

[53] PBED 12948 4 Jan. 1940 [KS] to D. V. Glass (who had written with information about the origins of the term neo-Malthusian).

[54] Wyllie was at least continuing to be do useful work in English as well as Latin lexicography: in January 1940 he read and commented on another section of Jessie Coulson's encyclopedic dictionary, and in March he reinvestigated the origins of Very light (a name for a kind of flare), in response to a letter querying the information given in the Supplement (OED/C/2/1/12 12 Jan. 1940 [Wyllie] to KS, PBED 12948 12 Mar. 1940 Wyllie to KS).

plans were having to be adjusted to take account of the loss of Arthur Fowler, who had died on 24 October from lung cancer; less than two months later Le Mesurier was also dead. (Fortunately work on *ODME* could continue, as Le Mesurier had been joined in Exmouth by a Scottish schoolmaster named Edward McIntosh, who had initially been recruited for work on *OLD* but who had been diverted to *ODME* early in 1939 when Arthur Fowler became ill. He also took over responsibility for the *Concise*.[55]) In the summer of 1940, apparently as an escape from the *OLD* and its troubles, Wyllie volunteered for active service, leaving the Old Ashmolean practically empty of lexicographers.[56] The coma had, if anything, deepened still further.

Only a few months later, however, there were signs of life from a rather unexpected quarter, and for an unforeseen reason. Both of the *OED*'s former Editors were of course still lexicographically active, and in touch with various figures at the Press; in fact 1940 had seen both Craigie and Onions discussing a new specimen of the *Middle English Dictionary* with Sisam.[57] Craigie's position in relation to *MED* seems to have been that of a consultant, for which he received an annual fee from the University of Michigan; but in the spring of 1941 the authorities at Michigan came to the conclusion that, because of the vulnerability of Allied convoys in the Atlantic to attack, various categories of material had become too valuable to risk sending by mail, and that accordingly they would have to terminate their arrangement with Craigie for lack of anything he could work on.[58] Alarmed at the prospect of a significant reduction in his income, Craigie visited Sisam to propose a project for which, he hoped, the Press might be able to pay him: the task of 'put[ting] all his collections for supplementing O.E.D. into shape'.[59] The fact that he had accumulated his own collection of such material—quite separate from the 'O.E.D. Collections' in the Old Ashmolean—would have been no surprise: he had, after all, been working for many years on two dictionaries which extensively supplemented *OED*. It was also to be expected that he, like many of his former colleagues, had never kicked the habit of making notes of lexical data encountered in any context. Sisam's initial response was that any work towards a new or revised Supplement, let alone a full revision of the Dictionary, would have to wait until after the war; but within a few weeks he had changed his mind. Perhaps Craigie had persisted with his suggestion; it may also be relevant that at just this time a new volunteer, Sir St Vincent Troubridge, had begun to send in some impressive new quotation evidence, drawn initially from his careful reading of eighteenth- and nineteenth-century material relating to the London theatre but eventually extending considerably. It may have been borne in on Sisam, as he contemplated Troubridge's material—and the occasional

---

[55] ODME/9/234 14 Dec. 1938 [KS] to Le Mesurier, OED/C/2/1/12 1 Mar. 1939 Le Mesurier to Wyllie.

[56] Wyllie's pay records suggest that he ceased his regular lexicographical work at the end of July 1940.

[57] CPED 173 28 May 1940 Eleanor B. Stuhlmann to KS, 21 June 1940 [KS] to CTO, 19 July [KS] to T. Knott.

[58] CPED 173 10 Apr. 1941 Knott to KS, 15 May 1941 [KS] to Knott.

[59] PBED 12869(I) File note by KS, 25 June 1941. Craigie also suggested, as an alternative, that he might prepare a supplement to Cleasby and Vigfusson's great dictionary of Icelandic.

accessions from other sources, such as the periodic parcels of quotations still being sent in by Eleanor Bradley—that it might not be such a bad idea to consider what was eventually to be done with it all.[60] Be that as it may, Craigie had soon gone beyond starting to put his materials in order. In August he began to write what would become a 'Tract' for the Society for Pure English, entitled 'Completing the Record of English', in which he demonstrated, with numerous examples—many of them collected by his former *OED* colleague Wilfred Lewis, now well into his seventies—that much could be added to the Dictionary's record of the general vocabulary even of modern (by which he seems to have meant post-1600) English, quite apart from the additional information being brought to public attention in the fascicles of period and regional dictionaries like *DAE* and *DOST*.[61] At much the same time he wrote a rather more businesslike memorandum for Sisam, which at last addressed from a practical point of view the question of how the Press might embark on the next phase of the *OED* project.[62] The memorandum, headed 'O.E.D. Supplement 2', envisaged an expansion of the 1933 Supplement, specifically in order to 'make more complete the record of such words, compounds, collocations, and phrases, as have been current at any time since 1600', and of course to add items not currently recorded. A particular focus on items 'in common use in the modern period' was advocated; and Craigie was keen to find a way of linking the *OED* with the other historical dictionaries, by referring the reader to *DAE* or *DOST* for fuller illustration, rather than simply copying their findings into the main work.

There were other practicalities to consider. The Press's printing facilities were so taken up with war work for the government that there was little chance of actually printing anything that Craigie might produce; indeed it was not long before printing of 'all dictionary and difficult work'—including *DOST*, for which Craigie was also preparing copy—was suspended 'for the duration'.[63] Craigie was well aware of this, and had reassured Sisam that he had in mind a method of working that would allow the material to be kept in a form ready to be printed immediately as soon as it was possible to do so. He continued to work intermittently on his Supplement material for the remainder of the war, benefiting greatly from the new material being sent in by St Vincent Troubridge, whose contributions were such that he contemplated marking Troubridge's quotations so as to acknowledge their source.[64] Onions, too, maintained

[60]   ODME/10/87 1 May 1941 [KS] to McIntosh, ODME/10/103 copy of letter 18 July 1941 [KS] to McIntosh. Troubridge also published a selection of his findings in a series of articles for *Notes & Queries*, long a journal of choice for such matter, beginning on 30 August 1941 (pp. 116–18).

[61]   PBED 12869(I) extract from letter 21 Aug. 1941 WAC to KS, 28 Aug. 1941 [KS] to WAC; Craigie (1941). The 'Tract', although dated 1941, was eventually published early in 1942. For more on the activities of the Society for Pure English, to whose 'Tracts' Bradley, Craigie, Onions, Sisam, Chapman, and Henry Fowler all contributed, see Ogilvie (2012: 148–52).

[62]   PBED 12869(I) 14 Oct. 1941 WAC to KS.

[63]   PBED 8670 copy of letter 30 Dec. 1942 KS to D. H. Stevens. On printing at OUP during the Second World War, see Whyte (2013: 93–4), Maw (2013a: 242–3).

[64]   PBED 12971 1 July 1942 [KS] to Troubridge.

an awareness of new words and meanings which merited a place in the *OED*, not least through his work revising and expanding the Addenda to the *Shorter* (an enlarged version of the original Addenda had appeared in 1939 and a still larger one in 1944[65]); he was also interested in revisions and corrections to the main Dictionary. Word of a list of such corrections reached Sisam in August 1943, although it seems that Onions was too busy with other work—including University teaching commitments and his still unfinished etymological dictionary—to put his *OED* materials in order.[66] Nor was there any suggestion that either his or Craigie's collections should be combined with the 'O.E.D. Collections', which Sisam was doing his best to maintain in Wyllie's absence.[67]

By January 1945 Craigie estimated that his collections, augmented by Troubridge's contributions—and with much more still to be added from *DAE* and *DOST*—amounted to something over 17,000 quotations that could usefully supplement the record of *OED* and the 1933 Supplement. He had not in fact begun to work up the material into publishable form, but he was now keen to do so, and if possible to see it published, under 'some such title as "Addenda to the Oxford English Dictionary, by…"'. Sisam cautioned that continuing wartime constraints made publication in the near future unlikely; but he encouraged Craigie to prepare the material, assuring him that it 'would be used at the first opportunity', perhaps suitably augmented by contributions from Onions and from the collections for *ODME*.[68] The first opportunity, however, was unlikely to occur very soon: printing activities were now even further curtailed by paper rationing, which continued for some years after 1945. 'Addenda' to the *OED*, let alone a new Supplement, would have to wait.

The end of the war of course saw the resumption of many interrupted activities, and the return of many people to Oxford. Among those who did not return immediately, however, was one person who might have been expected to play a key role in anything relating to the future of the *OED*, as well as the Press's other lexicographical projects: James Wyllie. The erstwhile so-called (by himself) 'Acting Editor' of the *OED* had certainly had an interesting war. Having gone into the Royal Artillery upon joining up, early in 1942 he was transferred to intelligence work, and soon thereafter moved to Bletchley Park to become part of the highly secret Ultra project to break the Enigma and other codes being used by German, Italian, and Japanese forces. He even managed to combine lexicography with his cryptography: not only did he continue to do lexicographic work for Oxford—he supplied comments on new dictionary proposals, including a dictionary of Turkish, and began work on a new and ambitious dictionary

---

[65] Although the version of the *Shorter* which appeared in 1944 was described as the 'third edition', only space-for-space corrections were made to the main body of the text.

[66] PBED 12869(I) 4 Aug. 1943 KS to J. B. Leishman.

[67] For example PBED 12948 21 Oct. 1940 [KS] to O. F. Morshead (acknowledging information about the bookbinding term *azured*: 'We are always glad to have new matter for our O.E.D. files'); ODME/10/234 7 July 1944 [KS] to Eleanor Bradley (thanking her for her latest batch of quotations: 'We can't make present use of earlier examples for O.E.D., but like to have any that are considerably earlier in our correction file').

[68] PBED 12869(I) 17 Jan. 1945 WAC to KS, 18 Jan. 1945 [KS] to WAC.

of synonyms—but he also compiled a 'Cryptographic Dictionary' of the jargon used by the codebreakers themselves.[69] He also recruited two of his Bletchley colleagues, C. T. Carr and John Chadwick, into lexicographical work (respectively English and Latin) for the Press.[70] He had maintained some contact with *OLD* during the war, through his occasional visits to Oxford as well as by correspondence. However, early on in the war he had formed the idea of moving back to Scotland—he later claimed that it was mainly out of 'a desire to get away from Sisam'[71]—and in the spring of 1945 he began to negotiate the purchase of a house in his native Kincardineshire; he insisted that he would be able to carry out his part of the compilation of *OLD*, and to do what was required in respect of other dictionary projects, at least as effectively from Scotland as he would if based in Oxford. Sisam—now Secretary to the Delegates, having succeeded Chapman in 1942—was evidently prepared to accept this rather unorthodox arrangement; he also asked Wyllie to go to Exmouth in December, to re-establish contact with McIntosh and to assess the situation with respect to *ODME* and the other dictionaries for which McIntosh had responsibility.[72] Wyllie was also continuing to work closely with Carr on the encyclopedic dictionary, and to work on his own dictionary of synonyms.[73]

With so many other things to occupy his time, it is perhaps not surprising that Sisam did not seek to involve Wyllie in Craigie's preliminary work towards a new Supplement. Wyllie, however, had retained his preoccupation with the relationship between *OED* and the various smaller dictionaries, and the importance of keeping all of them up to date; and on his return to Scotland from Exmouth he informed Sisam of his intention to 'start right away to collect new materials for all dictionaries on the scale of a new supplement to OED (1933–60) so that we may keep in touch with current developments of the common language'. He also anticipated that the new *OLD* assistant, Elizabeth Meldrum, who was about to join him in Scotland

[69] OUP/C/3/11/2 18 Jan., 3 July 1942 Wyllie to KS, ODME/10/156 23 Apr. 1942 [KS] to McIntosh ('He is now working in an Intelligence department—all very mysterious'). Wyllie began to be paid for his work on the synonym dictionary in the autumn of 1942 (OUP cashbooks). His 'Cryptographic Dictionary' is preserved in the American National Security Agency's Historic Cryptographic Collection (Record Group 457, Box 1413, ref. NR 4559); a version of this is available online at www.codesandciphers.org.uk/documents/cryptdict. For a brief reminiscence of Wyllie's work at Bletchley Park by a former colleague, William Tutte, see Copeland (2006: 352–69). He had been providing OUP with comments on bilingual dictionary proposals at least since 1941, and continued to do so until late 1953 (information from James Wyllie, junior).

[70] OID/1/37 18 Apr. 1945 Wyllie to KS; PBED 12942 17 Sept. 1945 Wyllie to KS. Carr was taken on as a new editor of the projected encyclopedic dictionary, which Jessie Coulson had been obliged to abandon towards the end of the war. Chadwick, after returning to Cambridge to complete his degree, joined the staff of *OLD* in 1946.

[71] PBED 12933 'Memorandum on the relations between the Clarendon Press and J.M.W. with particular reference to the O.L.D.', Oct. 1953, p. 8.

[72] ODME/10/256 28 Dec. 1945 [KS] to McIntosh. The compilation of *ODME* had at last reached *Z* in October, but as was to be expected with a text which had been so long in gestation, the early part was much in need of revision and updating (ODME/10/253 extract from letter 12 Oct. 1945 KS to McIntosh).

[73] CPGE 364 (*passim*, 1944–5). There was also another new project, for a 'popular' book on common errors in English, which had grown out of some work he had done correcting naval artillery manuals, but which seems to have come to nothing.

would spend some of her time working on English dictionaries. In the event she was hardly to have a chance to do so: in March 1946, less than three months after her arrival, Wyllie dismissed her, apparently because she aspired to work on *OLD* at a more advanced level than he thought her capable of. His tendency to be suspicious of the abilities, or motives, of others had evidently survived the war: by the autumn of 1946 Sisam described him as being convinced that '[e]verybody he deals with is either incompetent or dishonest', and despaired of the prospects for training new assistants for *OLD* in such an atmosphere of mistrust.[74]

---

chalcenterous

Almost certainly the adjective most famously associated with lexicographers is *harmless*; indeed, Samuel Johnson's phrase 'harmless drudge' can even be used without further explanation to refer to a lexicographer, so famous has his definition become. However, one adjective which is first recorded in the mid-twentieth century has come to be applied more to lexicographers than to anyone or anything else. The first recorded user of the word in English is R. W. Chapman, who in 1946 observed, in a review of two other dictionaries, that attempting to produce something comparable to the *OED* in the present age, with its proliferation of neologisms, 'might well deter the most chalcenterous Scotsman who may hereafter seek the shelter of Oxford' (Chapman 1946). He did not claim credit for the word, however; he subsequently (Chapman 1948: 12) described it as 'common "Greats" slang' (i.e. used by those studying classics in Oxford), and recalled having heard it used by the Oxford philosopher J. A. Smith (1863–1939) to describe 'a lexicographer who had conspicuously earned the title'. The word, which Chapman glossed as 'brazen-gutted', derives from a Greek equivalent, χαλκέντερος, which had been used (in a Byzantine encyclopedia called the Suda) to describe the prodigiously industrious first-century BC scholar and grammarian Didymus, who had reputedly written over 3,500 books. The most likely candidate for Smith's application of the word is surely his fellow Scot James Murray, who in addition to being phenomenally industrious must have had a remarkably robust constitution to have worked such long hours in his notoriously cold and damp Scriptorium. Although the word has not been found in Smith's published writings, the alternative adjective *chalcenteric* has been used by classicists at least since 1826, when an article in the Cambridge journal *Museum Criticum* refers to '[the Byzantine scholars] Michael Psellus, Moschopulus, and their Chalcenteric brethren'.

Robert Burchfield's attention seems to have been drawn to these words at a late stage in the preparation of Volume I of the Supplement, and an entry was added in proof. He also took up the word *chalcenterous* himself, writing in a book review that '*Homo lexicographicus*

Continued ➤

---

[74] WP 12 Dec. 1945 Wyllie to KS; PBED 12943 30 Mar. 1946 Wyllie to KS, 26 Nov. 1946 [KS] to Bailey. It should perhaps be mentioned that around this time Wyllie began to become more involved with the *Scottish National Dictionary*: he became a member of its Executive Council in 1946, and went on to give help and advice for several years (Macleod 2012: 150).

is a chalcenterous subspecies of mankind' (*New York Times Book Review* 26 Nov. 1972, p. 22), and using it elsewhere in his writings; other lexicographers followed suit, including John Sykes (who used the word in relation to Johnson, Noah Webster, and Murray: *New York Times* 7 Sept. 1976, p. 33) and the Australian Bill Ramson (who contrived to insert the word, again referring to Murray, in a review of *OED2*: *Sydney Morning Herald* 1 Apr. 1989, p. 87). In 1999 it was even applied to Burchfield himself: the citation in which John Simpson was presented for an honorary doctorate from the Australian National University mentions his having worked 'under the chalcenterous New Zealander, Robert Burchfield' on the Supplement (copy of citation in OUPA).

1946 did at least see continuing progress with the putting in order of Craigie's materials for a new Supplement;[75] but nothing was printed. Indeed, over the next few years the Press's main preoccupations in the area of English lexicography continued to be the other dictionaries in course of preparation, especially the 'Encyclopaedic'—to which Wyllie continued to devote substantial time and effort—and *ODME*. (Incidentally, the Oxford 'centre of operations' for these projects, such as it was, moved once again during the year: a room in the New Bodleian building became available, and the contents of the 'Dictionary Room' were moved there from the Old Schools Quadrangle in the autumn.[76]) There must have been some frustration at the continuing absence of anything in print to show for the decades of work that had gone into these two projects, not to mention the failure of Edward McIntosh to produce anything more than expanded addenda and minor revisions to the established smaller dictionaries.[77] Chapman, now retired from publishing, voiced his own frustration in an anonymous review of a new small dictionary published by Odhams Press (which he described as 'the first of our post-war dictionaries'). Although the product of a rival publisher, this was, as Chapman noted, something of an 'Oxford' dictionary, as a large part of the compilation had been carried out by J. L. N. O'Loughlin, who as an assistant working on the 1933 Supplement had received his training from Onions; but that was no comfort to the Press. Chapman took the opportunity to make approving comments about Onions's latest set of addenda to the *Shorter*, which had appeared during the war, but he also provocatively characterized the lack of other new editions of the Oxford dictionary family as 'famine in the midst of plenty'; he went on to grumble that the main *OED* 'has received no augmentation since the Supplement of 1933', and concluded by issuing a curious call to arms: 'The six years' war has yielded new and inspiring proof of the vitality of the language in every continent. May its lexicographers rise to their occasion.'[78] Over the

[75] See Brewer (2007: 134) (who notes the further assistance provided by the elderly Wilfred Lewis).
[76] PBED 12929 report on *OLD* for 1946.
[77] The third and fourth editions of *POD*, with corrections and expanded addenda, had appeared in 1941 and 1943 respectively, and a version of *COD* with similarly revised addenda in 1944. Jessie Coulson had produced a third edition of the *Little* along similar lines in 1941.
[78] Chapman (1946).

FIGURE 33   James Wyllie at work in the Dictionary Room in the 1940s.

next few years there was little outward sign of the call having been taken up: it was not until 1951 that a fully revised and reset edition of the *Concise* appeared, and *ODME* and the 'Encyclopaedic' continued to languish.

Neither was there any sign of new developments as far as the *OED* was concerned, although various interested parties continued to amass material. The death of Wilfred Lewis in 1947 seems to have put a stop to the organization of Craigie's materials (as considerably augmented by St Vincent Troubridge);[79] but new contributors continued to turn up, such as Atcheson Hench, a professor of English at the University of Virginia (and former contributor to the *Dictionary of American English*), who first made contact with Sisam during the war and who would continue to send in quotations to the Dictionary over three decades. Some contributors could claim an existing connection to the project, like the former assistant Henry Rope, who had contributed many quotations to the 1933 Supplement and who would continue to do so for even longer than Hench.[80] And of course there was Wyllie, who had been making his own collections for some time. His efforts in this area had been galvanized by reading some of the copy for *ODME*, which convinced him that a considerable injection of quotations from twentieth-century writers was needed (*inter alia*) to bring this long overdue text into something like publishable form; and he promptly set about recruiting readers to collect suitable quotations.[81] In the summer of 1948 he did at last move back to Oxford (see Figure 33), for the good of his wife's health; and in March 1949 Arthur Norrington—the new Secretary to the Delegates, following Sisam's retirement in 1948—at last formally appointed him sole editor of *OLD*. Strangely, however, he had

---

[79] It was some years later that OUP finally acquired the portion of Craigie's materials that he had managed to put in order, which only reached as far as the letter C (PBED 12869(I) 29 Apr. 1954 DMD to ALPN and CHR).

[80] PBED 12971 12 Aug. 1945 Hench to KS; PBED 12869(I) [4 Oct.] 1948 H. E. G. Rope to [?].

[81] ODME/11/12,21 22 Jan., 24 Feb. 1948 Wyllie to DMD.

actually been asked to reduce the amount of time he spent on Latin lexicography, so that he could make more progress with another English project: his own self-devised dictionary of synonyms, on which he was now asked to spend half his time, apparently with a view to producing a publishable text by 1950.[82] He was still providing detailed criticism of the 'Encyclopaedic'—in addition to training a new lexicographer, Patrick Stewart, who was being tried out as a possible assistant to McIntosh on *ODME*— and was regularly asked for his comments on addenda to the smaller dictionaries.[83] Although Stewart showed initial promise, by early 1949 it had become clear that he was unable to continue with the work, and a few months later C. T. Carr was persuaded to take his place.[84] Interestingly, Carr, like Wyllie, identified the need for a programme of reading contemporary sources to collect quotations for use in *ODME* entries. A group of readers was soon assembled for the purpose; much of the reading was organized from the Press's London offices by Raymond Goffin, an English scholar in his own right—with a particular interest in Indian English—as well as a Press employee of long standing.[85]

Wyllie's particular interest in identifying new words and meanings was highlighted by an article in the *Times* in January 1949, which described his daily examination of the paper for this purpose, noting that when he had finished marking the new usages in a copy 'the page was almost as red as it was black and white'.[86] Curiously, however, he was described only as 'an Oxford lexicographer', and no mention was made of any of the projects on which he was engaged for the Press. This may have been coincidence, but there is some suggestion that around this time his allegiance had become somewhat mixed. Always prone to money worries—particularly in regard to paying for his children's education—in the autumn of 1948 he had entered into negotiations with representatives of the *Encyclopaedia Britannica* about the possibility of editing a dictionary for them. No actual editorship ensued, but for the next two years he did contribute material on 'New Words and Meanings' to the *Britannica Book of the Year*. He also accepted an invitation

---

[82] PBED 12929 quarterly report on *OLD* by Wyllie, dated 2 July 1948.

[83] It was also around this time that Wyllie began work on another book of his own: an exposition of the theory and practice of lexicography. He subsequently sought—apparently successfully—to interest OUP in publishing it, but no publication ever emerged: it seems that sometime in 1953 he came to the conclusion that he could not expound his preferred lexicographical 'system' when the dictionary which represented the fullest implementation of this system, namely the *Oxford Latin Dictionary*, was experiencing such severe difficulties (WP 9 Nov. 1948, 30 Jan. 1951, 22 Apr. 1953 Wyllie to P. C. Schoonees).

[84] ODME/11/151 7 July 1949 DMD to ALPN. Stewart, who had been paralysed from the waist down by a wartime injury, was also a co-founder of the National Association for the Paralysed. The 'Encyclopaedic' dictionary project remained unfinished for some years longer; it was eventually published in 1962 as the *Oxford Illustrated Dictionary*.

[85] OED/C/2/1/15 21 Sept. 1949 DMD to Wyllie. Goffin's 'Some Notes on Indian English' had been published by the Society for Pure English in 1934. For his earlier career in India see Chatterjee and Murray (2013: 657–8).

[86] *Times* 10 Jan. 1949, p. 6. Wyllie later recalled how the article had come about: upon finding, after his move to Oxford, that his local newsagent was unable to supply him with a daily copy of the *Times*—a consequence of paper rationing—he wrote to the editor explaining its value to him as a source of new words, whereupon a journalist was dispatched to Oxford to interview him (Wyllie 1967, inside front cover).

from Eyre and Spottiswoode to prepare a revised edition of their *Pocket Pronouncing Dictionary*, which appeared in 1952 but (at his insistence) without his name attached.[87] More explicit evidence that he was prepared to act other than in the best interests of the Press and its projects may be found in a letter sent to McIntosh a few days after the appearance of the *Times* article with a list of the latest neologisms he had encountered in his reading, in which he asks McIntosh not to send the whole list to the Press, 'nor indeed [to] go out of your way to call their attention to your having it; we must keep some things in our own hands.'[88] This seems particularly odd given that Wyllie had been asked by Dan Davin—recently appointed as Assistant Secretary to Norrington—to suggest possible recruits to the *ODME* reading programme.

At the same time, however, Wyllie appears to have been identifying himself more closely with the *OED* than ever. In the spring of 1949 he even seems to have improvised some 'Oxford English Dictionary' letterhead, by taking some of the *Oxford Latin Dictionary*'s stock of notepaper and using a rubber stamp to substitute 'English' for 'Latin'.[89] And, despite the fact that no definite project to revise either the main Dictionary or its Supplement was in prospect—as is clear from an internal memo of October 1949 listing 'Oxford Dictionary Projects', which made no mention of the *OED*[90]—he saw fit to describe himself to a potential reader as 'not too old to look forward to doing a major revision, or a bringing up to date of the OED after the Latin Dictionary is finished'.[91] In fact he was still doing a great deal for many of the Press's dictionary projects, and his stock was still high with some senior figures at the Press. The description of him by Davin as 'our expert on lexicographical matters' is not untypical, and suggests that he had some justification in regarding himself as 'Lexicographer to the Clarendon Press', a title which he began to use around this time,[92] although there is no evidence that such a title was ever formally conferred. At the same time he continued to be a problematic figure, with a manner which some people found difficult to deal with: in October 1948, for example, he was allegedly barred from the senior common room of Balliol College.[93] The tone of some of his letters attacking what he saw as declining standards in some of the Press's lexicographical work could certainly be abrasive, even stinging, as in the following

---

[87]   Information from James Wyllie, junior.

[88]   OED/C/2/1/15 31 Jan. 1949 Wyllie to McIntosh.

[89]   The improvised letterhead can be seen on correspondence (about the meaning of the expression *dyed kippers*) dating from March 1949 in OED/C/2/1/15.

[90]   CPGE 226 28 Oct. 1949 [DMD] to G. F. J. Cumberlege.

[91]   OED/C/2/1/15 18 May 1949 [Wyllie] to S. Gray.

[92]   The title appears, for example, against Wyllie's name in the *Britannica Book of the Year*. He later also made the curious claim (in the course of a discussion of the meaning of the word *petroleum*) that he was 'the person who is responsible for bringing OED definitions of technical terms up to date' (WP 19 May 1951 Wyllie to Canadian Pacific Railway): curious because at this point no means of bringing any entries in the *OED* 'up to date' was in prospect. In the same letter he also asserted that his definitions 'would normally be quoted as the official views of the Clarendon Press'.

[93]   As stated by Wyllie in a letter to the Delegates of 6 May 1954 (untraced), quoted in Wyllie (1965: 107). The reason for his exclusion is not known; it is not mentioned in the minutes of Balliol College Meetings around this time.

remark made to Davin in 1949: 'It may well be my fault that I have never pointed out to you that competent and responsible lexicography can only be done by a lexicographer. May I do so now? And may I add that if you think work of this quality is not beneath your notice, our conceptions of lexicography must be radically different?'[94] It says much for the willingness of the Press to give Wyllie credit for his abilities, notwithstanding the friction that sometimes seemed to surround him, that in March 1950—after he had again expressed dissatisfaction about his position and remuneration—the Finance Committee approved an increase of £200 in his annual salary, notwithstanding the fact that the slow rate of progress on *OLD* was giving serious cause for concern.[95] Interestingly, the letter informing him of the increase emphasized the Press's keen anticipation of the completion of *OLD*, 'not only for the sake of the work itself, but in order that other lexicographical projects may be undertaken'. If this is a veiled reference to the next phase (whatever form it might take) of work on the *OED*, then it could be regarded as evidence that senior figures at the Press shared Wyllie's view of himself as the only possible person to take on this work; on the other hand, the steady flow of awkward incidents may have given them pause.[96]

As for any possible involvement of Craigie or Onions—now respectively 83 and 77, and much taken up with other projects—in any such next phase of the Dictionary's history, it would have been understandable if they had ruled themselves out; but this was not the case. In the spring of 1951 Onions, increasingly exercised by the 'hosts of wrong definitions, wrong datings, and wrong cross-references' in the main text of the Dictionary, tackled Davin on the subject of how these might be put right in a fresh printing, and even had some 'radical suggestions for the typography'.[97] Whatever Davin or Norrington thought of Onions's ideas, it was increasingly accepted that it would soon no longer be possible to postpone a decision regarding the future of the *OED* any further. Both it and the Supplement were unquestionably beginning to show their age (a fact to which the various new editions of the *Concise*, *Pocket*, and *Little* only served to draw attention); the effect would only become more noticeable over the few years it was expected to take to use up the remaining stocks of the 1933 reissue.[98] To embark on a fresh printing at that point, of a book of which even the newest portion would then be nearly thirty years old, was hardly satisfactory from the point of view of maintaining the Press's reputation for lexicography which was up to date as well as authoritative; but if anything else was to be done—whether an expanded Supplement or some kind of revision of the main text—then work would have to begin long before that. Writing

[94] OED/C/2/1/15 25 May 1949 Wyllie to DMD.

[95] PBED 12949 13 Feb. 1950 Wyllie to ALPN; FC 28 Mar. 1950. By this stage the Finance Committee had become the Press's general management committee, with the Delegates (to whom it officially reported) usually—but by no means always—accepting its recommendations (Nicholls 2013: 113).

[96] WP 29 Mar. 1950 ALPN to Wyllie.

[97] SOED/1951/14/3 24 Mar. 1951 CTO to [DMD].

[98] According to an estimate drawn up by Davin in 1952, assuming annual demand of 500 copies, there was about six years' worth of stock left (ODME/22/331 20 June 1952 [DMD] to C. Batey).

to another *OED* veteran, G. W. S. Friedrichsen, Davin admitted: 'we are beginning to get anxious over O.E.D. and we may have to look before long for someone to edit a new supplement.' There was some hope that Friedrichsen—now a Gothic scholar of some repute, based in Washington, DC, who had recently undertaken to revise the etymologies in the *Concise*—might be persuaded to return to Oxford with a view to taking on a prominent role in this task, perhaps in the first instance by making an assessment of the separate collections of relevant material now held by Craigie, Onions, and the Press. Both he and O'Loughlin—who was now also in America, working for the British Information Services in New York—were highly rated by Onions; but although both men continued to be mentioned in discussions as possible key workers on a new Supplement, for the time being they both remained on the wrong side of the Atlantic.[99]

Even without any firm decision as to who should be the editor (or editors) of the new Supplement, there was much to discuss. As with its 1933 forebear, there was the question of whether it should include corrections or revisions to the main text of the Dictionary, as well as entries for new words and usages. (Only Onions seems to have been prepared even to contemplate actual recasting of the main text; and even he will have recognized that the enormous cost and scale of such an undertaking placed it out of practical consideration.) As soon as such matters began to be considered in earnest, however, it quickly became apparent that there was little chance of getting even a severely limited Supplement ready for publication before the stocks of the 1933 reissue ran out.[100] In September 1952 Sisam, now retired to his beloved Scilly Isles but also enjoying an active role as an *éminence grise*, contributed a typically clear-headed and practical memorandum, which subsequently formed the basis of much of the discussion.[101]

Sisam's memorandum posited the new Supplement—or, rather, the collection of material for one—as a key element in the future success of all of the Press's English dictionaries, which together now amounted to an important factor in the Press's overall success.[102] He noted how all of the smaller dictionaries derived their success, in the first instance, from 'high-class editing of the materials presented in O.E.D.'; without adequate collection of more such material—which in the first instance meant quotation evidence documenting recent developments in the language—subsequent editions of the *Shorter*, the *Concise*, and the like would inevitably deteriorate in quality. Once such materials

---

[99] PBED 3967 6 Apr. 1951 [DMD] to Friedrichsen; PBED 23428 extract from letter 20 June 1951 DMD to CTO; PBED 12860 20 Aug. 1940 CTO to KS.

[100] PBED 12869(II) 1 July 1952 ALPN to DMD.

[101] The memorandum, entitled 'English Dictionaries', is discussed in detail in Brewer (2007: 136–42); a copy is preserved at PBED 12869(I). Burchfield (1989: 4) dates the memorandum 28 September 1952.

[102] Annual sales of the *Concise*, *Pocket*, and *Little* dictionaries had consistently measured in the tens of thousands (for each title) throughout the 1930s and 1940s, with occasional excursions into six figures, while the *Shorter* also steadily sold thousands of copies per year; from 1950 sales increased significantly, with aggregate figures for the four titles approaching half a million by 1952/3; by 1953 income from OUP's English dictionaries was estimated as amounting to 'at least a third' of the total for the entire Press (GF28/181 9 Oct. 1953 ALPN to DMD; other figures extracted from this file). Further on OUP's dictionary sales in the early 1950s see Nicholls (2013: 116–17).

had begun to be collected, they should immediately be made use of in the revision of the smaller dictionaries; this method of working would have the advantage that, by the time these new lexical developments were presented to the public in the new Supplement, Oxford's own smaller dictionaries would have 'sucked it dry' before any of it could be made use of by competitors. Sisam had some definite recommendations in regard to the Supplement itself—he envisaged an expansion of the 1933 text by perhaps 400 pages devoted to 'new words, important new meanings, and phrases' rather than to corrections of the main Dictionary,[103] with a finishing date of 1965—but the first priority, in his view, was the setting up of a proper system for the collection of evidence. He proposed two quite different approaches to the collection of, on the one hand, scientific and technical vocabulary, and, on the other, general vocabulary, 'such as one might find in a *Times* leader, or good literary work'. For the former, which he regarded as much more straightforward, selections could be made from existing specialist dictionaries, perhaps by consultants engaged for particular subject areas, with assistance if possible from learned societies and relevant institutions ('the R.H.S. [might watch] over Horticulture; the B.B.C. over Wireless and Television', and so forth). General vocabulary was more difficult: the only way to identify significant innovations was to look for them directly, in other words to read and excerpt general works by much the same method as had been used to collect evidence for the original Dictionary. Moreover, anyone undertaking such reading would have to be sufficiently familiar with what was already in the *OED* not to waste too much effort collecting examples of items which were already included. In assembling a group of volunteer readers for this task, Sisam suggested that a start could be made with figures already known to the Press, and that this could then be augmented as other suitable individuals came to light, perhaps as a result of appeals in the public prints. (He seems to have been unaware of the programme of reading already under way for *ODME*.) American vocabulary 'of a certain status and permanence' should be included; and for the other parts of the English-speaking world, he had the novel idea that 'a discreet professor' in each country should be asked to find a student who could prepare 'a thesis on *local* new words'.

The selection of the right figure to edit this new Supplement, and to oversee the dissemination of the new material into the smaller dictionaries, was obviously an important matter, although perhaps less urgent than the setting up of a reading programme. Tellingly, having characterized this figure in his memorandum as an 'editor with scholarship and initiative as well as industry', Sisam went on to declare that there was 'none available within the business'; which implicitly excluded Wyllie from serious consideration. Perhaps this was to be expected given Sisam's long and bruising experience of Wyllie; Norrington was less sure. 'I do not expect Sisam to agree,' he told Davin, 'but I am convinced that Wyllie is the best choice for Editor.

---

[103] In a subsequent letter Sisam restated more firmly the view that corrections to the main Dictionary should not form part of the Supplement, noting that, quite apart from the effort required to produce a really adequate body of corrections, this work would be of no benefit to the other Oxford dictionaries. He described the material collected by Craigie and Onions for this purpose as 'in no way urgent or profitable [...] I shouldn't use them until you had nothing better to do' (PBED 12869(I) 13 Oct. 1952 KS to DMD).

He is much the best definer—and indeed all-round lexicographer—that we know of, apart from the over-age Craigie and Onions. As it turns out, it is lamentable that he was ever involved in *Latin* lexicography, and the sooner he gets back to English the better.' He also recognized the particular difficulties attendant on Wyllie's personal identification with the *OED*, predicting that 'the knowledge that somebody else will edit O.E.D. Supplement, or the avoidance of a decision on this point, will ruin Wyllie, and probably ruin O.L.D.' He expressed similar views to Sisam, who responded with a more nuanced assessment:

Nobody is more competent to edit this Supplement than Wyllie if he could be got back to the frame of mind in which he did so much for the first Supplement i.e. do what he is told to do, instead of throwing away all that others have done and starting afresh on different lines. [...] The trouble is that he hates everybody else's work.

In fact it was generally recognized that, with the Latin dictionary entering a new and critical phase, Wyllie could not be spared for work on the Supplement for the next five years in any case. Fortunately there was more general agreement that Raymond Goffin—who as it happened was approaching retirement from his London post— might well be a suitable person to supervise the collection of general quotations.[104]

Despite Sisam's misgivings, it was not long before Wyllie was agreed upon as the only possible candidate for the job of editing the new Supplement, although it was not until May 1953 that the plan, and the idea of engaging Goffin to organize the collection of materials, was discussed with him.[105] By this time Wyllie was immersed in the preparation of the first batch of printer's copy for *OLD*, it having at last been agreed to commence composition, a move for which he had been pressing for some time.[106] He expressed himself in agreement, and the slow process of formally presenting the plan to the Delegates began. The possibility that work on the new Supplement might soon be under way began to affect various ongoing activities, such as the acquisition of books 'for the use of' the *OED*, which had been going on in a desultory fashion ever since the completion of the 1933 Supplement: Davin, sending Wyllie a copy of a new dictionary of psychiatric terms which the Press's New York branch had just published, now specifically envisaged it being made use of 'when the supplement is being revised'. Wyllie agreed that the book would be useful, as well as commenting—with what would soon seem a strange irony—that it shed 'a new if somewhat lurid light on human nature'.[107]

When, on 20 July 1953, the Delegates at last came to give full and formal consideration to the matter of the Supplement, they had the benefit of a detailed memorandum on the

---

[104]   PBED 12869(II) 7 Oct. 1952 ALPN to DMD; 10 Oct. 1952 KS to DMD; 22 Oct. 1952 Goffin to ALPN.
[105]   PBED 12869(II) 1 May 1953 DMD to ALPN.
[106]   Stray (2012: xiv and n. 31).
[107]   PBED 12869(I) 16 May Wyllie to DMD, OED/C/2/1/15 16 July 1953 DMD to Wyllie, 20 July 1953 Wyllie to DMD. The acquisition of books for the *OED* library in the period 1935–53 is discussed in Brewer (2007: 84, 279).

subject, carefully prepared by Davin.[108] It was agreed that the time was now right—if not long overdue—to start work in earnest on a revised Supplement, to be issued following the reprinting of the main Dictionary, which it was now thought would be needed in six or seven years' time. The Delegates endorsed the scheme of engaging Goffin to start work on 'the material already assembled', in consultation with Wyllie, who it was anticipated would take charge as editor, but only once he was sufficiently free from the demands of *OLD* to do so. They were even prepared to take a broader view of the Press's lexicographical future, something which both publishers and lexicographers had long hoped for: Norrington was tasked with drawing up 'plans for the establishment of a permanent staff and the training of a young lexicographer', with a view to 'the maintenance of the Delegates' English Dictionaries'. There was, however, some reluctance to give up on the idea of a Supplement containing revisions and corrections as well as additions, and Davin and Norrington were requested to report back on what was feasible in this regard.

The ink was hardly dry on the Delegates' minutes when they were given a fresh reason to wonder about the wisdom of putting their faith in Wyllie: the dismissal of another member of the *OLD* staff, less than a year after his appointment. The circumstances this time were particularly alarming. Professor John Craig, a distinguished classicist some twenty years Wyllie's senior, had been taken on in 1952 following his retirement from the chair of Latin at the University of Sheffield. Wyllie now wrote to inform him that his employment was to cease at the end of September, claiming that he was forced to take this action because of Craig's behaviour, which amounted to 'deliberate rudeness' and 'rowdyism' (including 'suggestions of a resort to physical violence'), and because he believed Craig had given outsiders 'a very unfavourable account of the conditions under which [Wyllie's] staff work'.[109] There is unfortunately no indication of what had brought about this alleged behaviour; but it must surely have placed an even bigger question mark over Wyllie's ability to manage whatever new team would be required to compile the new Supplement.

This alarming incident, however, was to pale into insignificance beside the catastrophe that overtook Wyllie a little over two months later. There is no mention of this in the official minutes of the next Delegates' meeting, held at the start of the following term, but the initials 'J.M.W.', written on Norrington's copy of the agenda, suggest that there was something about him that needed to be reported.[110] There certainly was. At the start of October all of Wyllie's preoccupations—his worries about money, his frustration at what he saw as a lack of clarity in his role within the Press, and his suspicions about the actions of Sisam and others—seem to have come to a head in some way; and the strain proved too much. During the weekend of 3–4 October he worked, apparently solidly, on a 19-page memorandum setting out his view of 'the relations between the Clarendon Press and J.M.W. with particular reference to the O.L.D.': an extraordinary diatribe directed largely against Sisam, whom he accused

[108] OD 20 July 1953.

[109] PBED 12947 draft letter 22 July 1953 [Wyllie] to J. D. Craig (with a covering note from Norrington, dated 23 July, recording that he agreed to Wyllie's sending the letter).

[110] ALPN's agenda book for Delegates' meetings, 16 Oct. 1953 (in OUPA).

of having systematically plotted to undermine and marginalize him over many years, and appealing to Norrington to take action to bring 'this nightmare of uncertainty, fear, humiliation, and slander' to an end. On the completion of this memorandum he underwent what he regarded as a transcendental religious experience, but others might see as the beginnings of a serious mental breakdown.[111] He later described it as the moment when God 'suddenly created in me a clean heart and renewed a right spirit within me', to be followed a few days later by being 'wakened from sleep and compelled to write words which were not my words in a note-book', the first of many occasions on which this was to happen.[112] On 12 October attempts were apparently made to have him admitted to the Warneford Hospital, a local psychiatric institution, but he escaped, going instead to Scotland, where he spent ten days discussing various dictionary projects with various key individuals.[113] Remarkably, he managed to preserve a semblance of normality in some parts of his working life—he attended a meeting of the Latin Dictionary Committee on 5 October, for example, and nothing untoward is recorded in the minutes—but something was clearly terribly wrong. Following his return to Oxford, on 23 October a second attempt to detain him in the Warneford was successful. Writing to C. T. Carr (one of those visited by Wyllie during his Scottish tour), Davin described it as 'a very sad affair. We do not know when or in what state he will emerge [from hospital] and we are trying desperately to think how we shall adjust ourselves to the loss, even temporarily, of such a brilliant lexicographer.'[114] In fact Wyllie left the Warneford on 7 November, and, almost incredibly, resumed work on *OLD* immediately. Norrington described him as having been 'in consistently good, or even exuberant, form since he emerged', and in January 1954 Davin noted that he was 'much more like his old self', despite the occasional 'gnomic utterance one finds slightly disturbing'. Evidently all parties were desperate to believe that what had happened had been merely some kind of aberration. A formal report on Wyllie's mental state, delivered to the Delegates in February, apparently gave credence to this view.[115]

But it was too good to last. Wyllie's mystical visions had continued unabated, and in March he became convinced that he must dedicate himself to communicating the

[111] The original of the memorandum, with its covering letter to Norrington stapled to it, is in OUPA (PBED 12933). Wyllie later retyped the memorandum on several occasions, and in 1959 published it under the title 'The Unanswered Memorandum, or the Clarendon Press Shown Up'.

[112] Quotations taken from a typed document headed 'Truth, or The Way of Peace; Communication No. 1: The Secret of Happiness', dated 24 April 1954 (copy in PBED 12933, which also contains earlier and later drafts). In this document Wyllie claims that he had been vouchsafed revelations from God on 'sundry previous occasions'.

[113] A copy of Wyllie's typed 'Report of a Lexicographical Tour in Scotland (in so far as it concerns the Clarendon Press)', dated 22 Oct. 1953, is preserved in WP; projects mentioned include *DOST*, *SND*, *ODME*, the school dictionary then being edited by Dorothy MacKenzie, the encyclopedic dictionary, and *OLD*.

[114] ODME/12/60 30 Oct. 1953 [DMD] to C. T. Carr. Wyllie remained in the Warneford from 23 October until 7 November; according to one letter written by him while in hospital (dated 31 Oct. 1953; PBED 12933), he even did some lexicographical work while still a patient, including reading and excerpting quotations from a book.

[115] PBED 12933 Note by ALPN headed 'O.L.D.', dated 15 Dec. 1953; ODME/12/64 5 Jan. 1954 [DMD] to Carr; FC 23 Feb. 1954.

substance of his revelations to the world. A letter (on *OLD* letterhead) to the Prime Minister, offering to disclose to him the means whereby mankind could be enabled 'to control the destructive forces which the advance of science has placed in his hands', seems to have been one of the earliest public manifestations of this.[116] He then informed Norrington that he wished to take a year's sabbatical in order to 'change the nature of mankind'. Even more disturbingly, Norrington received a near-midnight visit at which Wyllie gave him a draft of a document entitled 'The Truth', intended for public circulation, in which he set out something of what had been revealed to him—namely that the human body could, if the endocrine glands were properly adjusted, produce 'a subtle lubricant, the elixir of life', the virtues of which were such that all pain and disease could be eliminated, and that universal achievement of the beatific state conferred by the correct tuning of the 'endocrine orchestra' constituted 'the perfect and only feasible answer to war, hydrogen bombs, and all other forms of frightfulness'—and exhorted all his readers to spread this wisdom and thereby 'touch off the greatest "chain-reaction" of love the world has ever seen'.[117] Finally, just before Easter, he perturbed a number of his lexicographical colleagues in the Bodleian by announcing that their work was 'unimportant compared with the message he has to give the world'.[118]

Such actions could not be ignored. As his erstwhile colleague John Chadwick later put it, 'no organisation, be it never so academic, can continue to tolerate an employee who uses his time to vilify his employers and propagate a quasi-religious dogma.'[119] It was now impossible to avoid the awful conclusion that the editor of the *Oxford Latin Dictionary*, and the only known person with the necessary expertise and experience to undertake the new Supplement to the *OED*, had become incapable of fulfilling either of these roles. Accordingly, on 15 April Norrington instructed Wyllie to take three months' leave, urging him to take a complete break; and when Wyllie insisted on continuing with his great mission, and sent a letter to each of the Delegates, formally requesting a year's leave—and enclosing, for their information, copies of both his massive October memorandum and a revised version of the document he had given Norrington (now entitled 'Truth, or The Way of Peace; Communication No. 1: The Secret of Happiness')— the Delegates decided that enough was enough. On 30 April they resolved that he should be immediately relieved of his duties as editor of *OLD*, although it was agreed that his salary should be paid until the end of September.[120] It is testimony to the

---

[116] PBED 12933 typed copy of letter 31 Mar. 1954 Wyllie to Sir Winston Churchill. The original of this letter has not been traced.

[117] Quotations taken from an undated early draft (apparently the version given to Norrington), preserved in PBED 12933.

[118] PBED 12933 Notes by ALPN for the Delegates' meeting of 30 Apr. 1954.

[119] PBED 12933 unpublished typescript draft of an obituary of Wyllie. This remarkably sympathetic memoir, which Chadwick submitted to OUP in 1972 but decided not to publish, is discussed, with some lengthy extracts, in Brewer (2007: 88–91).

[120] PBED 12933 15 Apr. 1954 ALPN to Wyllie; OD 30 Apr. 1954. Some quotations in this paragraph are taken from Norrington's notes for this meeting.

confidence of Norrington and others in his abilities—or perhaps to their desperation to salvage something publishable from the disaster—that even in these extraordinary circumstances the possibility of Wyllie's continuing to work on his projected dictionary of synonyms was seriously entertained; it was now recognized that he simply could not be trusted to work as part of a team any longer, but as a 'lone wolf' he might be capable of something productive. There was also concern to ensure that his wife and children were adequately provided for. Wyllie's own response to the letter terminating his editorship of *OLD* was to observe that, while he doubted the wisdom of the Delegates' action, his dismissal from this specific post seemed to him to leave open the question of his 'basic appointment', which he claimed was 'as the Press's lexicographer'. Of course no such post existed; and in any case he was soon insisting that he was not prepared to consider any form of employment by the Delegates other than as editor of *OLD*.[121] His campaign to be reinstated became indissolubly bound up with the more general expression of his grievances against the Press, and with the promulgation of his mystical revelations. Further letters to the Delegates were followed by open letters to the world at large and, over the course of the next decade or so, by a series of self-produced pamphlets, some appearing under the name of the 'Barras Seer', the best known of which is probably that entitled 'The Oxford Dictionary Slanders: The Greatest Scandal in the whole History of Scholarship', which appeared in 1965.[122]

Wyllie managed to obtain a post as a Latin master at a school in Scotland, which he took up in September 1954; this was followed by a sequence of other teaching posts. His dismissal did not mark the end of his lexicographical activities: he did resume work on the synonym dictionary for a while, and in fact worked on it intermittently for the rest of his life, although nothing was ever published, and for several years—starting almost immediately after he had ceased to be formally employed by the Press—he supplied definitions and quotations to the American lexicographer (and former Craigie pupil) Clarence Barnhart.[123] He remained in intermittent contact with the Press, but he was never again to make any significant contribution to any of its dictionaries: a tragedy for a man who had contributed so much over the preceding two decades, and a terrible loss to both Latin and English lexicography. A member of the *OLD* staff, Peter Glare, was put in charge of that dictionary,[124] and the senior figures at the Press now began to consider what was to be done about the still inchoate Supplement to the *OED* now that its intended editor had so dramatically left the scene. (Another departure which

---

[121] PBED 12933 3 May 1954 Wyllie to ALPN; duplicated letter 9 June 1954 ALPN to [Delegates].

[122] The bibliography of these pamphlets is complex, as several of them appeared in more than one edition or impression. Many of them are scarce; good collections are held by the Bodleian Library, the University of Aberdeen, and the National Library of Scotland.

[123] PBED 12947 fragment of letter 10 Dec. 1954 WAC to [?] (quoting Barnhart's comment that '[t]he fact that [Wyllie] has set out to reform the world will not bother me if he can write good dictionary definitions'); WP 6 Apr. 1957 Wyllie to C. Barnhart (citing 'general exhaustion' as his reason for discontinuing his dictionary work).

[124] Despite the decades of work which had already gone into *OLD*, the first fascicle was not published for another fourteen years. The dictionary was finally completed in 1982.

should be noted is that of Arthur Norrington, who later in 1954 relinquished the Secretaryship to become President of Trinity College; he was succeeded as Secretary by the classicist Colin Roberts.)

Discussions about the Supplement had not of course gone into suspended animation during the period of Wyllie's breakdown and departure. Already in October Davin had suggested that, for the kind of consultancy that Goffin was likely to need when he began his work of collecting evidence, it might be necessary to turn to Craigie and Onions rather than to Wyllie. While no doubt as conscious as ever of the need for revision as well as supplementation, the Dictionary's former Editors seem to have accepted the practicality of the view that the scope of the new work should be limited to new words and senses that had entered the language since 1930, much as Sisam's 1952 memorandum had advocated.[125] Norrington and Davin could thus report to the Delegates that this was now the considered view of all relevant parties; this they did in June 1954, in a memorandum[126] which also put forward the names of four men who might, either now or in a few years' time, be capable of taking on the post of editor. Their first choice was Friedrichsen, 'probably the best man after Wyllie', who they still hoped could be enticed over from America by a suitable salary, although at nearly 70 he might not have the years ahead of him that the job required; Glare might also be suitable once he had completed *OLD*; and two academics, Norman Davis and Eric Dobson, were also mentioned as 'of the right quality', though untrained lexicographically, and probably impossible to tempt away from their current posts. The memorandum envisaged the engagement of an editor only after a suitable body of evidence had been accumulated; it was the collection of data, Norrington and Davin felt, that was most urgent, and a start on this should be made as soon as possible. The Delegates gave their blessing to the engagement of Goffin on this work when he became available; but they decided that the search for an editor should begin forthwith.[127] On 29 June Davin contacted Davis, who was at this time professor of English language at Glasgow University, about the editorship, and was pleasantly surprised to find that he was 'by no means disposed to turn the idea down out of hand'.[128] In fact Davis was very much a known quantity: like both Sisam and Davin, he was a New Zealander, and had come to Oxford as a Rhodes scholar, where he had studied under Tolkien. Onions considered him 'a first-class philologist' (and, tellingly, 'very sane'), and Sisam declared that there was 'no more promising man for the experiment'. Moreover, he had been making a modest contribution to other Oxford dictionaries for some years, such as supplying quotations for *ODME*, to which task he had been recruited by Davin in

---

[125] PBED 12869(II) 28 Oct. 1953 DMD to ALPN; OED/C/2/1/17 27 Oct. 1953 DMD to ALPN; PBED 12869(I) 29 Apr. 1954 DMD to ALPN and CHR, 5 May 1954 CHR to DMD.

[126] A copy of the memorandum is in PBED 12869(I).

[127] OD 11 June 1954; PBED 12869(II) 6 July 1954 [DMD] to KS. Sisam was unenthusiastic about Eric Dobson, then an English lecturer at Oxford, as a possible editor (PBED 12869(II) 10 July 1954 KS to DMD). Dobson went on to become Professor of English Language at Oxford, and an authority on the history of English pronunciation.

[128] PBED 12869(II) 30 June 1954 DMD to ALPN. Norrington annotated this letter 'We *must* get him'.

1949.[129] Davis's initial favourable response led to a more definite offer in the autumn, with the handsome salary of £2,500, but in the end he decided that after all the job was not for him, essentially because he had concluded on further consideration that the freedom and variety of his present job was preferable to the anticipated 'daily grind' of lexicography. 'I don't know whether I am right or not,' he told Davin, 'and I may live to regret it; but "No" it is, thank you very much.'[130] So it was back to square one, although Davis (who in 1959 took up the Merton chair in English Language and Literature at Oxford in succession to Tolkien) was to become a valued adviser on *OED* matters. He was consulted, for example, about the next two names to be suggested, both apparently in the capacity of 'a young scholar [...] who could be trained as a Lexicographer at the Delegates' expense', this being now recognized as probably the best that could be hoped for in the absence of any candidate who was already fully capable. He was dismissive of Peter Goolden, an Old English scholar and former pupil of his; O'Loughlin, who now once again came up for consideration, received a more favourable assessment, but discussions came to nothing.[131]

By the spring of 1955 the search for someone to edit the Supplement was becoming somewhat desperate. To make matters worse, there was now also a need for someone to prepare a new edition of the *Shorter*: this was something that it had been expected Onions would do, but he had now declared himself out of the running, so that a successor would have to be found.[132] Craigie, too, was now getting too old for such work, and had even given up work on his beloved *DOST*.[133] Very much the same combination of skills was required in the editing of both a new *Shorter* and the revised Supplement, but could one person be found who was capable of doing both jobs at the same time? The next person to come up for serious consideration, in the summer of 1955, was another New Zealander, Alan Horsman, an English scholar at Durham University, whose edition of the diary of the nineteenth-century New Zealand statesman and poet Alfred Domett had just been published by the Press, and who had now begun editing a sixteenth-century text.[134]

---

[129]   PBED 12869(II) 8 July 1954 DMD to ALPN, 10 July 1954 KS to DMD; ODME/11/219 12 Oct. 1949 DMD to ALPN.

[130]   OD 29 Oct. 1954; PBED 12869(II) 8 Nov. 1954 Davis to DMD.

[131]   OD 12 Nov. 1954; PBED 12869(II) 29 Mar. 1955 DMD to CHR. Further correspondence with and about O'Loughlin, who visited the Press in April 1955, is in PBED 12869(II).

[132]   CPGE 226 14 Jan. 1955 [DMD] to J. L. Austin. The final impression of the *Shorter* to appear under under Onions's editorship—a reprint of the third edition of 1944 with newly revised Addenda—was published in the spring of 1955.

[133]   Since 1948 Craigie had been assisted in his work on *DOST* by A. J. Aitken, who in 1955 formally took over as editor. The project was to continue for most of the next fifty years, seeing several further changes of editor and surviving various funding and publication difficulties; the final fascicle was published in 2002 by OUP (the University of Chicago withdrew as publisher in 1981; Aberdeen University Press took over until 1994).

[134]   Some of the information given in the following paragraphs in relation to Alan Horsman's involvement with the Supplement is taken from personal communication with Professor Horsman, the first of many individuals whose reminiscences I have been able to draw on in this and the ensuing chapters, as noted in the Preface.

Horsman, too, responded favourably, to the extent that definite plans began to be made to engage him for a year's trial, starting the following autumn.[135] In November a formal offer of the editorship was made, and Goffin was installed in 40 Walton Crescent—where some of the *OLD* staff had once been accommodated—to begin his preparatory work.[136]

Davin drew up a memo for Goffin, setting out in detail the task which he was expected to carry out, which had now developed into something more elaborate than simple data collection. His principal aim should be to compile a 'word-list', in other words a list of lexical items for the soon-to-be-appointed editor to work through; and the first task which he seems to have set himself was to find out what existing materials could be brought together to form the basis of such a list, rather than setting up a programme for the collection of new quotations on the traditional model. There was quotation material from various sources to be assembled (or, as he later recalled, 'discovered and garnered from odd hide-outs all over Oxford'[137]); but arguably even more valuable than quotations for the assembling of a wordlist were the lists of items that had been and were being added to the Press's various smaller English dictionaries, and he was soon in regular correspondence with Carr and McIntosh. Meetings were also arranged with Craigie and Onions, so that they might give him the benefit of their experience.[138]

A document compiled by Davin for Horsman's benefit in July 1956 gives a useful summary both of what Goffin had been able to achieve and of how the project was now conceived.[139] The scope and extent of the Supplement was still very much as Sisam had envisaged in 1952: an expansion of the 1933 volume by 400 pages, roughly equivalent to 12,000 entries, dealing with post-1930 developments in the language (plus corrections to the 1933 text). It was anticipated that the bulk of the new vocabulary was likely to be technical, in consequence of the ever-increasing pace of scientific innovation, which brought wave after wave of specialist terminology into general use; identification of the technical items to be included was to be achieved by combining a list of the words to be found in a few standard reference works with the suggestions of selected experts in particular fields. For items of general vocabulary, a programme of reading—carried out initially by a small group of volunteers of known ability, to be expanded in due course—would be necessary. There was also specific provision for the collection of American and Commonwealth lexis: for the former there were

---

[135] PBED 12869(II) 25 Aug. 1955 DMD to CHR, 28 Aug. 1955 E. A. Horsman to DMD, 17 Nov. 1955 [DMD] to N. Davis; OD 25 Nov. 1955. There was initially some suggestion that Horsman should be appointed alongside another individual, with a view to their working as joint editors; various names were considered for this joint post, including M. L. Samuels and John Bromwich, but no appointment was made (correspondence in PBED 12869(II)).

[136] PBED 12869(I) 28 Oct. 1955 [DMD] to Goffin; OD 25 Nov. 1955. Goffin became available for work in Oxford on 1 November 1955, although technically he did not retire from his London post until the following April.

[137] OUPA(u) (RWB papers) 3 Dec. 1969 Goffin to RWB.

[138] PBED 12869(I) Report by Goffin, dated 14 Nov. 1955; 16 Nov. 1955 [DMD] to WAC, [DMD] to CTO.

[139] PBED 12869(I) Report on 'O.E.D. Supplement n/e', dated July 1956.

various individuals known to be ready to help, some of whom had built up their own collections, while for the latter it was hoped that useful input could be obtained from various universities with which the Press had good contacts. For the collection of evidence for general vocabulary the report gives an interesting list of likely helpers, including dictionary veterans Carr, Friedrichsen, and O'Loughlin but also Sir Ernest Gowers and the literary scholar J. E. Butt. Goffin had also begun to correspond with his friend Michael West, a pioneering teacher and lexicographer of English as a second language, who soon became a valued contributor of quotations for the Supplement; but there is no evidence that he had yet done anything by way of setting up a full reading programme in the *OED* tradition.[140]

At the end of July Horsman arrived in Oxford, and Davin sought to set up meetings with the three lexicographers who might be expected to have most to offer him by way of advice: Craigie, Onions, and the editor of *OLD*, Peter Glare. All three men agreed to meet him: Onions rather more unwillingly than the others, describing himself as 'rather weary', and having 'no enthusiasm' for the Supplement as it was now conceived. He suggested that Horsman could usefully do some 'prep.' before meeting him, by carrying out a careful comparison between some surviving batches of printer's copy for the 1933 Supplement and the corresponding printed pages.[141] Everything was now gearing up for the start of work in earnest on what was to be Horsman's Supplement. But no sooner had he arrived in Oxford when the fledgling project suffered another setback: he was offered, and accepted, the English chair at Otago University, an appointment which allowed him to fulfil his long-held desire to return to New Zealand. He would not be taking up the new post immediately, but the appointment set a definite terminus to his work as editor of the Supplement. 'So once again,' lamented Davin to Norman Davis, 'we are adrift.'[142]

By great good fortune, however—and through another application of the networking skills of what its members would come to refer to as the 'New Zealand mafia'—a new candidate for the editorship was quickly found. Indeed, on the same day that Davin wrote to Davis, he had arranged to have a word with another New Zealand Rhodes scholar, who had in fact also applied for the Otago post. Robert Burchfield (already known as 'Bob' to Davin, whose idea it seems to have been to approach him[143]) had studied at Magdalen College after graduating from Victoria University College in

---

[140] For more on Michael West, whose *New Method English Dictionary* (1935) has been claimed as the first ever monolingual dictionary for learners of English, see Smith (2003). Goffin's correspondence with West is preserved in OED/C/2/3/3.

[141] PBED 12869(II) 31 July 1956 [DMD] to WAC, [DMD] to CTO, [DMD] to Glare, 1 Aug. 1956 WAC to DMD, Glare to DMD, 3 Aug. 1956 CTO to DMD.

[142] PBED 12869(II) 1 Nov. 1956 [DMD] to N. Davis. The decision to accept the Otago chair was apparently not an easy one: Goffin later recalled Horsman's 'agonizing doubt [...] he was a genuine lover of words, & he would dearly have liked to stay' (OUPA(u) (RWB papers) 3 Dec. 1969 Goffin to RWB).

[143] PBED 12869(II) 1 Nov. 1956 [DMD] to CTO: 'The only name that occurs to me is Burchfield.' Burchfield himself apparently credited Onions with having first suggested him (Elizabeth Burchfield, personal information).

Wellington, and had gone on to take up various lecturing posts at other Oxford colleges. While at Magdalen he had come to know Onions, who was sufficiently impressed with his abilities to declare to Davin that he 'would do admirably', and who followed this up with a warm testimonial, identifying '[h]is interest in problems of language and his capacity for hard and persistent work' as the only crucial qualifications, and noting that his lack of actual lexicographical experience was something he shared with 'all the recruits to the staffs of the Oxford Dictionary whom I can remember being engaged during the past sixty years [...] It is a craft by itself, and solvitur ambulando.'[144] Davis concurred, while acknowledging that with Burchfield's still relatively lowly academic status and lack of experience he was 'clearly not ideal'; he had 'a high opinion of his practical good sense and punctual execution of whatever he takes on'. Sisam confirmed that he was 'well trained in philology, conscientious in his work, & as businesslike as you could expect'; he recognized that he would need training, 'which, since Wyllie's aberration, [the Press has] nobody to give', and suggested that he might come to the Scillies and receive whatever training he himself could provide.[145] For his part, Burchfield quickly declared himself willing to accept the job (and for a salary of £1,500, significantly less than Horsman had been offered); and this time there was to be no pulling out.[146] The Delegates, relieved to have found a replacement for Horsman so quickly, agreed to make a formal offer, and it was settled that he would take up the editorship in the summer of 1957, when his teaching post at Christ Church ended.[147] The completion date for the new Supplement was now projected to be 1967.

Horsman was not held to his original commitment of a full year's work on the Supplement, but was allowed to leave in the spring of 1957, in time to take up his New Zealand post before the second term of the year began. For the remainder of his time in Oxford he continued to carry out preliminary work.[148] For the wordlist of items to be included in the new Supplement he and Goffin ultimately identified about a dozen different sources, including various non-OUP publications monitoring new

---

[144] PBED 12869(II) 2 Nov. 1956 DMD to CHR, 13 Nov. 1956 CTO to DMD. On Burchfield's work with Onions in the years preceding his appointment, see Burchfield (1987a: 12).

[145] PBED 12869(II) 3 Nov. 1956 Davis to DMD, 8 Nov. 1956 KS to DMD. Sisam also suggested three months' apprenticeship on DOST under Craigie, in whose abilities to inculcate 'the qualities & practical methods needed in a Supplement' he still had great confidence. Craigie, however, was no longer up to such a task, and in fact his faculties seem already to have begun to fail him: already in 1955 a neighbour in Watlington had reported him as having suffered a number of falls, and his memory as being 'not what it was' (NLS MS.9987 f. 193 15 May 1955 John Munro to CTO).

[146] As Charlotte Brewer has noted (2007: 151), there was to be another pulling-out from an Oxford lexicographical project only a few months later: in August 1957 C. T. Carr finally gave up on the Oxford Dictionary of Modern English, declaring that lexicography 'gets one down after years of labour', and that 'I don't want to get myself in the same state as Wyllie'. Hope lingered for another decade that something publishable might be salvaged from the project, into which the Press had poured considerable quantities of effort and expectation since its first stirrings in the late 1920s, but in 1970 the surviving files were finally consigned to the OUP archives.

[147] OD 16 Nov. 1956, OED/C/2/2/2 19 Nov. 1956 DMD to RWB.

[148] Horsman's work is summarized in his progress report, dated 19 Mar. 1957 (copy in PBED 12865(I); original in OUPA(u) (RWB papers)).

developments in the language (such as the *Britannica Book of the Year*, to which Wyllie had contributed, and the 'Among the New Words' columns in the language journal *American Speech*) as well as several of the Press's own published and unpublished dictionaries. The large body of slips which had been excluded from consideration for the 1933 Supplement, as being outside its terms of reference, was re-examined, and proved to contain a number of items which it was now clear should be added.[149] Valuable collections had also been contributed by other individuals, including St Vincent Troubridge, and also H. S. Bhide, an Indian correspondent who had sent in thousands of suggested corrections and additions to the *OED* since 1941, and whose Ph.D. thesis for the University of Bombay, consisting essentially of a dictionary of English neologisms in *OED* style, had been examined by Onions.[150]

There were also, of course, the '*OED* Collections' maintained by Wyllie and others over the years. Horsman reported that he had incorporated '[m]ost of the material in J. M. Wyllie's files', but it is not entirely clear that he or Goffin will have known where all of Wyllie's materials were, nor does Burchfield seem to have been told much about them. According to an account of Wyllie's lexicographical activities prepared sometime in the late 1940s,[151] all his work on English dictionaries was being done at his home—because all the hours when the Dictionary rooms in the Bodleian were open were devoted to work on *OLD*—and 'a considerable amount of material' relating to the English component of his work was accordingly kept at home for his convenience. Owing to the extremely difficult circumstances under which Wyllie's employment had come to an end, it is not at all clear that all of these materials were retained by OUP. A portion of them, fortunately, did reach the Press after his death, namely a collection of some thousands of quotation slips, apparently mostly collected by Wyllie himself during the late 1940s and intended for eventual use in the revision of the *OED*; some of these slips were given to the Press in 1972, but were mistakenly filed with material for his synonym dictionary, and their value for *OED* purposes was only recognized in 1978.[152] In 2011 another component of the same collection of slips was identified among the papers still held by the Wyllie family, and was by them generously returned

---

[149] Interestingly, at around this time the Press was approached by Mitford Mathews, of the University of Chicago, about the possibility of acquiring (presumably for payment) the collection of over 100,000 quotations which had been built up by Craigie for the *Dictionary of American English*. However, examination of a small sample of slips suggested they would be of little use, and the collection remained in America (correspondence (Feb. 1957) in PBED 12865(I)).

[150] Bhide numbered his submissions individually; the earliest to survive, dating from 17 Sept. 1941 and numbered 53–60, are preserved in PBED 12948. Many of his quotations were passed on to the editors of *ODME*. His contributions were of variable quality: Davin, commenting on one batch in 1949, described him as a 'gadfly' who had 'wasted a good deal of our time in the past' (SOED/1949/4/3 3 Feb. 1949 DMD to R. H. Hawkins). His dissertation, 'A study in the development of the English vocabulary', remains unpublished. Troubridge had renewed contact with the Press in February, with an anxious enquiry as to the fate of the quotations he had sent to Craigie in the 1940s (OUPA(u) 22 Feb. 1957 Troubridge to the Editors of the *Shorter OED*).

[151] Preserved in WP.

[152] PBED 12933 9 Jan. 1972 David Wyllie to CHR; OUPA(u) undated report (c.Jan. 1978) by Joyce Hawkins.

to Oxford, where it has now been incorporated into the slip files now being made use of in the ongoing process of revising the Dictionary. These salvaged remnants notwithstanding, it nevertheless seems likely that a significant part—maybe even the majority—of the evidence which by the 1950s had been collected for eventual use in the revision or supplementation of the *OED* was never retrieved for use either by Horsman or by his successors.[153] The loss of such material, if it was indeed lost, must be one of the most disastrous consequences, for Oxford lexicography, of the rift between Wyllie and the Press.[154]

Working from all of the materials that were available to him, Horsman could begin to compile his wordlist; and it was clear that constraints of space and time required the list to be quite selective, certainly in regard to more technical vocabulary. He realized that in many cases a decision about whether to include a particular item would ultimately have to depend on an assessment of the quotations sent in, rather than finding quotations to match a chosen item. Unless a competent band of outside readers was built up soon, he concluded, the editor of the Supplement was likely to find himself forced by time constraints to compile a work 'which in its latest entries was a mere hodgepodge of other dictionaries', and possibly even without proper illustrative quotations.[155] He also advised that, what with the economic and social changes that had taken place since the great voluntary reading programmes of the past, it might now be necessary to offer payment (perhaps in OUP books) for reading. Following his departure a leaflet intended to bring in new readers—though without any mention of payment—was drafted and circulated to interested parties; however, following criticism from various quarters (including Burchfield, who begged Davin to wait until he was installed in post before launching any such major initiative), it was decided to hold off from a public appeal for the moment.[156]

And thus it was that the next phase in the history of the Dictionary began in earnest when Burchfield arrived at the Press on 1 July 1957, marking almost exactly the centenary of the formation of the Philological Society's Unregistered Words Committee: 'a cherished coincidence', as he observed soon afterwards.[157] In a later account he vividly evoked his sense of setting out into unknown territory, echoing (as Charlotte Brewer has noted) James Murray's famous reference to 'pioneers [in] an untrodden forest': he likened his arrival in 40 Walton Crescent to 'arriving in a new

---

[153] One valuable resource which does not seem to have survived is Wyllie's own annotated copy of the *OED* and the 1933 Supplement (referred to above, p. 317).

[154] Here may also be a suitable point to mention that Wyllie gave another collection of slips to the Press in 1962; these were a collection which had been given to Craigie by an American scholar, and which had by some means passed to Wyllie. The slips were assessed as being likely to be of use in the revision of the main Dictionary, rather than the preparation of the Supplement; the Press agreed to take them, and in recognition of their value to cancel the balance of Wyllie's debt to the Press on account of a loan which had been made to him to help with the purchase of his house in Oxford (WP 16, 25 May 1962 CHR to Wyllie).

[155] Quotation from Horsman's 19 Mar. 1957 progress report.

[156] The draft leaflet, and responses to it from Burchfield and others, is in PBED 12865(I).

[157] Burchfield (1958: 229).

colony and finding a log cabin to house me but no other resources except a rather superior Man Friday [namely Goffin] to assist me'.[158] The evocation perhaps does less than justice to the preparatory work done by Horsman, Goffin, and others; but it was certainly true that, more than any of his predecessors since Murray, Burchfield would have to work things out for himself.

[158] Burchfield (1984: 115–16); the parallel with Murray is noted in Brewer (2007: 152). Cf. also Burchfield (1987a: 13): 'It quickly dawned on me that I would simply need to organize the whole project myself from scratch.' He and Horsman never discussed any matters relating to the Supplement, according to Horsman, who attributes this perhaps surprising lack of communication to the fact that both men were 'in some degree preoccupied, Bob with the job he was leaving and I with the one to which I was going' (personal communication, 26 Sept. 2011).

11

Learning to swim (again):
1957–1972

Burchfield frequently recounted the story of his first day as Editor of the Supplement, when, having expected to receive instruction in how he should set about his task, he was disconcerted to find himself left to his own devices, and spent much of the day systematically reading his copy of the *Times* and noting the enormous number of words and meanings not recorded in either the *OED* or the 1933 Supplement.[1] Of course he was not entirely alone: there was Raymond Goffin, at work alongside him on various aspects of data collection as he had been for some months (not to mention various individuals working on other Press projects in 40 Walton Crescent, and indeed the building's caretaker and his family). But it is certainly true that there was, effectively, nobody who could tell him what he needed to know; and that, as he fully appreciated, was a lot. As he later recalled: 'I had never defined a word in my life and, as a closet scholar and university lecturer, had no experience of the kind of organization needed to establish and maintain a whole department of scholars.'[2]

Davin was of course aware of the need to put Burchfield in touch with anyone who could help, and indeed had already proposed a visit to Kenneth Sisam; Onions could also be counted on for guidance. Craigie was by this stage not up to providing much by way of training, although the two men did meet.[3] Arrangements were made for a trip to the Scillies, and a formal meeting with Onions; in the meantime, Burchfield familiarized himself with the contents of various Press files about the proposed Supplement, including Sisam's 'splendidly autocratic' memorandum of September

---

[1] Published accounts include Burchfield (1969) and Burchfield (1987a). Curiously, not a single quotation from the 1 July 1957 issue of the *Times* found its way into the text of the Supplement as eventually published.

[2] Burchfield (1987a: 13).

[3] Elizabeth Burchfield, interview with author, 22 Aug. 2012.

The Making of the *Oxford English Dictionary*. First edition. Peter Gilliver.
© Peter Gilliver 2016. First published 2016 by Oxford University Press.

1952.[4] He also worked closely with Goffin on various ongoing tasks, such as writing requests for information about particular words which it had already been decided to include,[5] and corresponding with individuals who had already offered, or might be willing to contribute, quotations. He had already realized the need for increased effort in regard to the latter: as he wrote to St Vincent Troubridge, 'it is quite clear that the production of the Supplement will only be possible if we can persuade a great many more people to start hunting for quotations.'[6] This requirement had been highlighted by Alan Horsman in his valedictory report, but it seems that little had so far been done about it.

On 1 August Burchfield met Onions for the scheduled 'conference' (as his notes on the meeting describe it).[7] Onions was, as might be expected, full of advice: he recommended, for example, that in choosing assistants Burchfield should avoid 'men with degrees, or anyone seeking advancement or higher pay', and he advised against consulting professionals about a word until all other resources had been exhausted.[8] He also suggested that entries in the 1933 Supplement which simply recorded earlier American evidence for items which were already in *OED* might be omitted: arguably an implied criticism of Craigie, as such entries were generally his work.[9] But Onions also had his own preoccupations. He favoured the idea of founding a new journal to which scholars could send findings that might be of use—apparently on the model of *American Speech*, whose articles documenting American neologisms Horsman had already made use of—but only if its scope embraced anything of potential relevance to the revision, as well as the supplementation, of *OED*. Wholesale revision of the Dictionary was, understandably, a matter still close to Onions's heart, and a theme to which he would continue to return.

The following day Burchfield, evidently galvanized by these discussions, made contact with Onions's former assistant Stefanyja Olszewska (now married to Alan Ross, the professor of linguistics at Birmingham), and persuaded her to read *Notes & Queries* and the *Times* for Supplement purposes; and he wrote to the Press's two other editors of English dictionaries, Carr and McIntosh—unaware that Carr was on the point of abandoning *ODME*—introducing himself and undertaking to help the smaller dictionaries keep up to date with the vocabulary being considered for the Supplement

---

[4] Burchfield (1989: 4). Burchfield had been sent Davin's July 1956 plan for the Supplement some months earlier (OED/C/2/2/2 19 Nov. 1956 DMD to RWB).

[5] Some letters of 1957 to and from Burchfield about particular words are preserved in OED/C/2/8.

[6] OED/C/2/9/1 18 July 1957 [RWB] to Troubridge.

[7] Preserved in OED/C/2/2/2, as are Burchfield's notes on his visit to Sisam a few days later. Of course Burchfield's consultation with Onions was not confined to this single occasion, but the meeting on 1 August seems to have had particular significance: perhaps it was arranged as a kind of informal review of Burchfield's first month.

[8] Compare his earlier identification of Murray as the Editor most inclined to consult specialists (see p. 268 n. 20).

[9] Thus, for example, the Supplement entry for the noun *accost* (defined in the first edition as 'Address, salutation, greeting') simply gives two earlier quotations from John P. Kennedy's *Swallow Barn*. In fact Onions's suggestion was taken up, and these, like many other such quotations, were omitted from the revised Supplement. The first of these quotations has been reinstated in the course of revision, and appears in the entry in *OED Online*.

by sending them 'bulletins' from time to time. The first of these bulletins, with three pages of information on words ranging from *agent provocateur* to *water-bloom*, was also completed on 2 August, and immediately sent out.[10]

Burchfield's discussions with Kenneth Sisam were necessarily more protracted, involving as they did a trip to the Scillies lasting several days. Perhaps unsurprisingly in view of some of the past friction between the two men, Onions had been doubtful of the value of a visit to Sisam until Burchfield had been able to gain some 'practical experience', by having a go at drafting some dictionary entries;[11] however, he may not have expressed his doubts to Burchfield directly, and Burchfield certainly took careful notes of Sisam's advice.

Sisam likened the task which Burchfield faced to swimming the Channel, an image powerful enough to be recalled three decades later: 'make the crossing before the tide turns or you will never get across.'[12] His advice has the unmistakable ring of the pragmatic publisher rather than (indeed in opposition to) the scholar striving after perfection: 'A workmanlike Suppl[ement] is better than a perfect one which is unpublished. The Delegates are interested in performances, not in excuses.'[13] He repeatedly stressed the importance of setting limits of time and space, and of sticking to them (or at least of not missing them by much: 'Say 7 years and get [it] out in 10'). Of course he had first-hand experience of the difficulty of maintaining progress on a large-scale lexicographical project, and he warned of the inability of editors to meet deadlines without being closely monitored, noting that Onions had been 'one of the worst' in this respect; he did, however, acknowledge Onions's expertise in the minutiae of lexicography, and advised consulting him as much as possible about writing definitions, something of which Burchfield had no experience whatsoever. In this, as in so many other aspects of the 'swimming' that lay ahead, he was a complete novice, with few coaches to turn to for training.[14]

The discussions with Sisam also formed the basis of a number of recommendations which Burchfield made in a report which he prepared immediately upon his return from the Scillies.[15] The report is both businesslike and impatient. Burchfield was 'anxious to make things move'; he complained that too much time had been spent on 'preliminaries' like the compilation of wordlists from other dictionaries, which (as his reading of the *Times* on his first day had shown him) fell far short of identifying the range of vocabulary that the Supplement needed to include. His four main recommendations

[10] PBED 12866 2 Aug. 1957 RWB to P. J. Spicer (re Stefanyja Ross); PBED 12865(I) 2 Aug. 1957 [RWB] to Carr; PBED 12865(II) 2 Aug. 1957 [RWB] to McIntosh. The 'bulletins' had their forerunners in the form of a series of lists of new words spotted in various sources (referred to internally as 'budgets') compiled by Davin and sent to McIntosh, Onions, and Goffin; copies of several 'budgets', dating from 1955–7, survive in OUPA(u). Copies of Burchfield's 'bulletins', issued between 1957 and 1959, are in OED/C/1/3/1.

[11] PBED 12865(II) copy of letter 15 June 1957 CTO to DMD.

[12] Burchfield (1984: 116).

[13] OED/C/2/2/2 notes by RWB on 'Points made by K.S. 12–15 Aug. 1957'.

[14] Henry Fowler's description of the work of compiling the *Concise Oxford Dictionary* as 'plunging into the sea of lexicography without having been first taught to swim' (preface to second edition, 1929) was later quoted with feeling by Burchfield himself (1979: 13).

[15] Preserved in PBED 12865(I), dated 20 Aug. 1957.

were: to engage additional staff immediately (Sisam had advised 'two good girls of clerical type', and he also needed a secretary); to find other ways of coordinating between different dictionary projects (beyond his planned 'bulletins' to Carr and McIntosh), with a view to making 40 Walton Crescent 'a kind of lexicographical headquarters'; to establish a space—ideally within the pages of *Notes & Queries*—for the publication of material likely to be of use in compiling the new Supplement (evidently a reconsidered version of the earlier idea of a journal along the lines of *American Speech*); and to recruit a network of experts to give specialist advice in particular scientific subjects. He also proposed printing a pamphlet about the Supplement, along the lines of the one which had been drafted in the spring, so that copies could be sent to interested parties, though there is no suggestion of mass distribution on the lines of some previous appeals. There is a strong sense of a contained, limited project, still with a target completion date of 1967.

One respect in which Burchfield was determined not to be limited—certainly not to the extent apparently favoured by Sisam—was in the range of vocabulary that should be considered eligible for inclusion. In the coverage of scientific terms he regarded Sisam's view that they should be included 'only in so far as the words could be explained to an intelligent layman' as inconsistent with the comprehensive coverage of the technical terminology of earlier periods (medieval alchemy and the like). As for the Englishes of America and the Commonwealth, he was evidently taken aback by his fellow New Zealander's recommendation that the criterion of inclusion should be 'reasonable currency in the UK'—an approach which he later described as having 'all the classical hallmarks of Dr. Johnson's *Dictionary of the English Language*'.[16] His own preference for a less insular approach may be seen in the request which went out to the Press's various overseas branches early in September, asking for lists of words meriting inclusion in both the Supplement and the new edition of the *Concise* which McIntosh was preparing.[17] September also saw the preparation of the proposed pamphlet about the Supplement. A proof was sent for comment to Onions, whose criticisms were mainly directed at a section (subsequently excised) seeking to steer contributors away from particular categories of vocabulary; Onions felt that such questions of selection should be left to the editor.[18] Sadly, the pamphlet could not be similarly sent to Craigie:

---

[16] Burchfield (1984: 116–17). Sisam was not opposed to the inclusion of non-British vocabulary, as is clear from his recommendations regarding the Supplement in 1952 (see p. 331); but, like the compilers of the first edition, who were happy to include lexical items from all over the English-speaking world, he seems to have taken a 'Britocentric' view of the language, according to which the 'core' of the language, as represented on Murray's famous diagram, was standard British English. As Weiner has observed, '[t]he idea that there could be regional standard forms of English was never seriously entertained' by the editors of *OED1* (Weiner 1986: 261). Whether Burchfield had yet embraced a genuinely polycentric model of English is doubtful, as it was only in the 1960s and 1970s that such ideas became widely accepted (see e.g. McArthur 2012: 446–9). On Burchfield's own later 'Britocentrism' see below, p. 504.

[17] PBED 3958 5 Sept. 1957 [DMD] to C. C. Johnson (Toronto) (copied also to the Australian, New Zealand, and South African branches).

[18] Copies of the proof (stamped 11 Sept. 1957), including one with Onions's comments, are in OED/C/2/2/2, as is a revise stamped 23 September.

he died on 2 September, bringing to an end over half a century of remarkable and wide-ranging lexicographical endeavour. The presence of Wyllie among the mourners at his funeral must have been an uncomfortable reminder of what might have been.[19] Some of the books and materials amassed by Craigie during his long, and lexicographically enormously productive, life were passed on to the Press, though not, it seems, his own annotated copy of the *OED*, which would surely have been of substantial use even if much of what it contained related more to the revision of the Dictionary than to its supplementation.

October saw the arrival of the first of the additional assistants that Burchfield had asked for, although Jennifer Dawson, a talented history graduate from St Anne's College, promised to be rather more than a 'good girl of clerical type'. It also saw the process of data collection gathering pace on various fronts. Burchfield gratefully accepted an offer from Michael West to read issues of *New Scientist*, a journal which he had already found a valuable source for scientific vocabulary, and similar work was being done with back issues of the journal *Nature* by Michael Wood, an experienced Press editor of scientific books (whose services as an adviser to the Supplement on science matters had been retained some months earlier).[20] Burchfield also succeeded in recruiting Eric Stanley, an old Oxford friend now studying under Stefanyja Ross in Birmingham, to join the growing band of readers; Stanley in turn recruited other readers from among his Birmingham acquaintances.[21] In November Roland Auty, a Faversham schoolteacher who in January had written to Oxford with a list of words which he had noted were missing from the *Shorter*, was persuaded to start reading a selection of books by modern authors; he would go on to be one of the most prolific of all readers for the new Supplement.[22] Over the next three months the services of another dozen or so readers were secured, the majority of whom turned out to be happy to do the work for nothing, although Burchfield was authorized to offer modest payment, and in fact did so for many years, as well as rewarding some of the best of the volunteers with gifts of books.[23] By January something like 500 quotations were arriving every week.

---

[19] Mathews (1958: 55).

[20] OED/C/2/3/3 8 Oct. 1957 [RWB] to M. West; OED/C/2/5/77 19 Sept. 1957 [RWB] to Stefanyja Ross, PBED 12865(II) 8 Feb. 1957 [DMD] to A. M. Wood.

[21] OED/C/2/2/2 28 Oct. 1957 E. G. Stanley to RWB; OED/C/2/5/84 24 Dec. 1957 [RWB] to Stanley.

[22] OED/C/2/9/1 18 Jan. 1957 R. A. Auty to 'Dear Sir', OED/C/2/5/1 21 Nov. 1957 [RWB] to Auty. In fact Auty had first shown his interest in contributing to dictionaries two decades earlier, when he wrote suggesting some additions to a dictionary of cricketing vocabulary—compiled by the former *OED* assistant Wilfred Lewis—which OUP had published in 1934 (ML 11 Jan. 1938 HSM to Auty). He retired from teaching in 1958, enabling him to devote more time to reading for the Supplement.

[23] The usual rate offered was 7s. 6d. per hour, although some potential readers declined this (correspondence in PBED 12865(II)). Among the unpaid readers was another veteran from pre-1933 days, the former Mary Savage (now Mrs Alden), who had worked on the first edition of the *Shorter* and who had kept in touch with Onions and with Oxford dictionaries; at the time when Burchfield first approached her she was doing freelance work on two of the Press's smaller dictionaries (OED/C/2/3/1 12 Oct. 1957 Mary Alden to RWB). She had also been secretary of the Society for Pure English, and edited the *Odhams Concise English Dictionary* (1956).

In addition to the collection of data by individuals, access was gained to some existing substantial collections. A long-delayed reply from Atcheson Hench, to whom Burchfield had written in July, brought a renewal of his offer to make available his own quotation files on American usage, amounting to some 15,000 slips.[24] In the end it was decided to make only selective use of these; but a similar offer from another American who had worked under Craigie in Chicago was taken up. Clarence Barnhart's offer of access to some of the quotation material collected for the Thorndike–Barnhart series of dictionaries, in return for access to Oxford's quotation files, had first been made five years previously, and an agreement to limited exchange of materials had been drawn up, although it is not clear that Barnhart ever invoked it.[25] Burchfield, alerted by Davin to the existence of the arrangement, now asked whether Barnhart could send quotations from a run of *Science News*, a periodical recently established by Penguin Books; Barnhart readily agreed to this request, and to others made subsequently, eventually sending some 4,500 slips from various sources (some of which, ironically, had been supplied to Barnhart by Wyllie).[26] Both Hench and Barnhart remained stalwart supporters of the Supplement for many years. There was also more to be gleaned from the unused material left over from the 1933 Supplement than had so far been extracted, and Burchfield embarked on a full-scale reorganization and sifting of this large body of slips.[27] It was already becoming clear, however, that the volume of new vocabulary coming to light by these various means was far in excess of what could be included in the new Supplement if it was to be completed by 1967. Methods of selecting the most suitable material—or, as he put it to his former Christ Church colleague W. H. Auden, 'ingenious traps which catch the large but let the little pass'—would have to be devised.[28]

By late January 1958, with just over six months of experience under his belt, Burchfield decided that it was time to write his first formal review of progress.[29] He may have been encouraged to make such reports—which appear with reasonable regularity from this point—by Davin or other senior figures at the Press, and of course he had Horsman's report of the previous March as a model; they are certainly evidence of his determination to take an organized approach to the project, despite his lack of experience of running anything of the kind. From this first report it is clear that the main effort was now decidedly focused on the collection of quotations. Various periodicals were now being read regularly, including specialist titles like the *Lancet* and *Social Service Quarterly* as

---

[24] OED/C/2/5/86 31 July 1957 [RWB] to Hench, 6 Oct. 1957 Hench to RWB, 22 Nov. 1957 [RWB] to Hench. Burchfield's probably approached Hench in consequence of encountering earlier inconclusive correspondence with Davin in Press files (May–July 1956; now in PBED 12869).

[25] Correspondence (Sept. 1952–Apr. 1953) preserved in OED/C/2/11/1.

[26] OED/C/2/11/1 18 Dec. 1957 RWB to DMD.

[27] OUPA(u) 23 Jan. 1958 [RWB] to Mr. Carr.

[28] OED/C/2/1/20 14 Dec. 1957 [RWB] to W. H. Auden. Auden had sent in a quotation from John Aubrey for the adjective *unkiss*, which Burchfield regretfully rejected as falling outside the scope of the Supplement; in fact the quotation was already in *OED* under the headword *unkissed* (where Aubrey's word had been interpreted as a variant spelling).

[29] PBED 12865(II) 26 Jan. 1958 RWB to CHR/DMD.

well as general newspapers and magazines; twelve readers had also been found to read through the works of specific authors, including T. S. Eliot, Robert Graves, and Winston Churchill. (There is no mention of contributors from overseas; it seems that nothing had yet come of the appeal to OUP branches beyond the identification of a few individuals.) The processing of the 1933 Supplement quotations was also yielding dividends, including some early evidence for such words as *schizophrenia* and *usherette*. Burchfield was also about to revive the old system of sending out 'desiderata lists' with issues of the *Periodical*; the first such list would be heralded by an article about the project in the summer issue. Limited in circulation though this (now quarterly) Press journal might be, its contents tended to get picked up by other publications, so that the decision to feature the Supplement marked a new departure as far as publicity was concerned.

In fact there were already a few signs of increasing public interest, perhaps in consequence of the October pamphlet (which was now getting wider distribution). Perhaps surprisingly, not all opportunities for publicity were yet regarded as welcome: when Burchfield learned that a reporter from the *Oxford Mail* (who had interviewed him) was writing an article about the Supplement, he informed the newspaper's editor that 'we should prefer not to have such an article published at this stage. It would no doubt be noticed by London papers, and we are not yet sufficiently organised to be able to cope with the work which would result.'[30] An article in 'a year or two', he suggested, might be desirable. On the other hand, when a columnist in the weekly journal *Engineering* wondered 'whether there is any special agency for keeping the *Oxford Dictionary* primed on new words', Burchfield wrote a letter encouraging readers to contribute to the Supplement.[31]

However, the project was now beginning to be seriously understaffed. Useful though Jennifer Dawson was proving to be, it was evident that her fragile state of health would prevent her from being as much help as he had hoped; and Burchfield had increasingly come to look on the 66-year-old Goffin, with his four-day week whose days ended at 5 o'clock, as what would now be called 'legacy staff', capable of some useful work but not really what was needed. He therefore still felt that, as he wrote in his report, '[his] main assistants have yet to be found'. His urgent need for secretarial help was met quickly enough, but editorial assistance proved harder to locate (and more than a straight replacement for Dawson was needed).[32] Two women, Sally Hilton and Joyce Hawkins, were eventually appointed, to start in September.[33] A potential short-term staffing crisis in July, resulting from the realization that Jennifer Dawson could not

[30] OUPA(u) 16 Jan. 1958 RWB to Editor, *Oxford Mail*.

[31] *Engineering* 24 Jan. 1958, p. 119. Burchfield's letter appeared in the 7 Feb. issue (p. 163), and numerous readers volunteered their services as readers (correspondence in OED/C/2/7/4).

[32] The secretary, Caroline Webb, started in mid-February; before this Burchfield seems to have borrowed secretarial help from elsewhere in the Press.

[33] OED/C/6/3/1 20 May 1958 [RWB] to KS. Correspondence about applications for these posts, which were handled by the University Appointments Committee, is preserved in PBED 12865. Hawkins had some experience in lexicography, having previously worked on the *Patristic Greek Lexicon* (which was eventually published in 1961).

continue her work for much longer—she eventually left in August[34]—was averted by the unexpected expedient of engaging the services, more or less full-time, of Onions's son Giles, who had been produced 'out of the air' by his father as a possible reader (he had helped in the compilation of the most recent set of Addenda for the *Shorter*), and who had gone on to do excellent work in seeking out antedatings for words included in the draft of the first desiderata list for the *Periodical*.[35] The immediate need for additional personnel came to an end with the arrival of Hilton and Hawkins in September, but Burchfield was so impressed with Giles Onions's work that he arranged to retain his services; he continued both with general reading and with antedating of items on pre-publication versions of the *Periodical* desiderata lists for the next two years.

Autumn 1958 marked a definite gearing up on several fronts. In addition to two new editorial assistants, in October Burchfield acquired a second secretary, Betty Jennison, who would also go on to provide some editorial help. He was also encouraged to find individuals who could check quotations and conduct research in the Bodleian and the British Museum—in keeping with Sisam's dictum that it was more efficient to engage separate researchers than for those drafting entries to carry out their own research—and Elizabeth Brommer, who had previously worked as a librarian in the Press's London offices, was engaged half-time as the project's first London researcher.[36] The first desiderata list, issued with the *Periodical* in September and covering words from *A* to *akka*, proved a great success: only a week later more than a tenth of the 700 items listed had been improved by material sent in.[37] (Interestingly, this first list, like James Wyllie's list for L in 1930, included a substantial number of items—roughly a quarter of the total—that would ultimately not make it into the published text. Later lists included a diminishing proportion of unused items.) The list was also effective in generating publicity, including a 'fourth leader' in the *Times* entitled 'Hunting the Word' which anticipated that a 'large field of enthusiastic amateur followers' would respond to the Dictionary's 'loud "Halloo"' and start to hunt down the words on the list.[38] The list—or possibly the earlier pamphlet about the Supplement—even reached Broadmoor, where a patient, Arthur Graham Bell, responded, as Dr Minor had over half a century before, with the first of a steady (if not especially valuable) series of observations about new words that was to continue for the next eight years.[39]

---

[34] She continued to read and supply quotations for the Supplement for the next three years, including a brief period in summer 1959 when she returned to work in Walton Crescent. She went on to be a novelist, probably best known for *The Ha-Ha* (1961), an exploration of schizophrenia.

[35] OED/C/2/5/70 21 May 1958 RWB to DMD, file note by RWB 12 July 1958; PBED 12866 21 July 1958 RWB to CHR/DMD.

[36] OUPA(u) file note by RWB 26 Sept. 1958. Elizabeth Brommer started work in January 1959 (correspondence in OED/C/2/5/10).

[37] PBED 12865(II) 22 Sept. 1958 RWB to CHR/DMD/John Bell.

[38] *Times* 15 Sept. 1958, p. 9.

[39] Correspondence with Graham Bell—whom Burchfield noted on one 1965 letter as 'Not one of our favourite correspondents'—began in October 1958, and is preserved in OED/C/2/5/31. Nor was he the last Broadmoor patient to send in quotations: one J. B. T. Norris began to contribute sometime in the 1960s, and was given a copy of Volume I of the Supplement in recognition of the usefulness of his material (OUPA(u) 9 Jan. 1973 RWB to Norris). He continued to send in quotations until 1986 (OED/C/2/3/8 23 Aug. 1986 Norris to 'Dear Madam') by which time he had been released from Broadmoor. He died in 2005.

Fortunately, other new readers would prove to be more valuable; few more so—and none more prolific—than Marghanita Laski. This remarkable woman, then already well known as a writer, critic, and broadcaster, first made contact with Burchfield in December 1958 after seeing a copy of the second *Periodical* desiderata list, and went on to contribute the staggering figure of a quarter of a million quotations over the next thirty years, during the course of which she also helped and campaigned on behalf of the Dictionary in other ways, taking full advantage of her position as a journalist and a prominent figure in 'literary London' to do so. Another prolific and greatly valued reader whose first contributions date from this time is Roland Hall, a young philosophy lecturer then teaching at Queen's College, Dundee, whose connection with the Dictionary would continue for even longer than Laski's.[40]

Laski and Hall were only two of the 'stars' of a body of readers and contributors that already numbered over 100,[41] and which was now beginning to include contributors from overseas: both volunteer readers on a small scale, like Rosalind Meyer of Victoria (Australia) who had responded to an appeal in the Melbourne *Age*,[42] and scholars engaged in substantial research on particular varieties of English, such as Harry Orsman, who contacted Burchfield to offer the fruits of the reading he had begun in relation to his own Ph.D. thesis on New Zealand English—eventually amounting to 12,000 quotations—and William S. (Bill) Ramson, researching Australian English in Sydney, who was contacted in March 1959, visited Oxford in April, and immediately began to send in contributions.[43] Ramson continued to help the *OED*, as a reader and a consultant, for the next half-century; he later became the editor of the *Australian National Dictionary*. For South African English, help was forthcoming from C. P. Swart and Nicolaas van Blerk, who were identified as a possible helper by OUP's South African office. Van Blerk, one of the co-editors of a new historical dictionary of Afrikaans being compiled at Stellenbosch, proved to be exceptionally useful; by December 1958 he had already begun to supply what Burchfield described as 'fully edited' entries for items of South African English, complete with quotations, and the idea began to materialize that he might visit Oxford for a few months and prepare draft entries for many, perhaps most of the South African items likely to be included. Burchfield now contemplated tackling other varieties of World English in the same way, if suitable specialists could be found and persuaded to visit Oxford. He was well aware that there was far more such material than could possibly be accommodated within the new Supplement's anticipated limits, and envisaged setting an 'arbitrary numerical restriction' for each regional variety.[44]

---

[40] OED/C/2/5/42 6 Dec. 1958 M. Laski to RWB; OED/C/2/5/33 22 Dec. 1958 R. Hall to 'Dear Sir'. For more on Laski's contribution to the Dictionary see Brewer (2007: 161–3). Roland Hall has become one of the most durable of all the Dictionary's contributors: at the time of writing he is still acting as a consultant for philosophical vocabulary.

[41] *Oxford Mail* 10 Oct. 1958, p. 8.

[42] OED/C/2/6/4 6 Feb. 1958 Rosalind S. Meyer to RWB.

[43] Correspondence preserved in OED/C/2/5/75. Ramson had studied at the same New Zealand university as Burchfield before embarking on research into Australian English in Sydney,

[44] OED/C/2/6/16 7 May 1958 [RWB] to Orsman.

Notwithstanding the reference to 'fully edited' entries, it was to the collection of quotations, rather than editing, that the vast bulk of effort was still directed. This is not to say, however, that editorial matters had been entirely set on one side. By the autumn of 1958 work had begun on a specimen page of entries, covering a range of words in *ac-*.[45] Burchfield also mentioned the drafting of entries being carried out by his assistants Hilton and Hawkins when Godfrey Smith, a columnist for the *Sunday Times*, visited 40 Walton Crescent in January 1959. The article which subsequently appeared made no mention of the drafting of entries, although it did give some details of the work being done both by Burchfield and his staff, in their 'rather shabby villa in an Oxford back street', and by those collecting quotations for the Supplement, whose numbers Smith encouraged his readers to join by sending in antedatings of items on a short list of 'particularly knotty words' in A.[46] The article was a great success: in addition to eliciting a number of useful antedatings for items on the list—which was followed by several other lists in subsequent months[47]—it generated a significant amount of publicity, including an approach from the BBC to make a short television feature about the Supplement and other members of the Oxford dictionary family.[48] The feature was broadcast as part of the 'Tonight' programme on 11 February, and included footage of the now 85-year-old Charles Onions, as well as of Burchfield (see Figure 34) and Sally Hilton.

April brought another of Burchfield's progress reports, some fifteen months since the previous one.[49] Burchfield was keen to expand: his report included a proposal to recruit three new assistants, including one with a specifically scientific focus—the first in the history of the Dictionary. Such an expansive vision might seem ambitious when his team had still only produced two or three pages of edited entries—and the projected specimen page was still not ready—but Burchfield seems to have been confident that his proposals would be accepted. His confidence may have stemmed partly from his good working relationship with his fellow New Zealander Davin; but he also knew that he could count on the support of John Brown, the Press's London publisher, who had declared in January that 'a great deal of money should be found' to keep the *OED* up to date, 'because the reputation and the income of the Press depended primarily upon it and the derivative works'.[50] Brown had also put forward the idea that, in view of the amount of scientific vocabulary that the reading programme was bringing to light, the Press might consider producing a scientific dictionary drawing on this material, to

---

[45]   OED/C/2/9/2 28 Oct. 1958 Joyce Hawkins to J. Cunningham.

[46]   OUPA(u) note by RWB 14 Jan. 1959 on Smith's visit; Smith (1959).

[47]   By April about a third of the 47 items that had appeared in the first three *Times* lists had been antedated (OED/C/3/2/7 23 Apr. 1959 RWB to CHR). Two similar initiatives in other publications proved less successful: both the *Journal of the Royal Aeronautical Society* and *Africana Notes and News* published a few appeal lists, but neither elicited much in the way of useful results (PBED 12871(I) Annual Report for 1959 and 1960).

[48]   PBED 12871(I) Annual Report for 1959. No recording of the 'Tonight' programme has been traced.

[49]   PBED 12870 Report by RWB, 18 Apr. 1959.

[50]   OUPA(u) note by RWB 22 Jan. 1959 on a meeting with the Publisher.

FIGURE 34   Robert Burchfield on the occasion of his first appearance on television, November 1958.

be published in advance of the Supplement proper. The proposed new science assistant was seen as a possible future editor of this dictionary; another of the new posts was for a researcher to work on quotations in Oxford's libraries in the same way as Elizabeth Brommer at the British Museum, who also agreed to increase her hours. In fact two new researchers—one in Oxford and one in London—were soon found, and in June a start of some kind was made with the drafting of entries, which Sisam had been urging as 'the sure way to progress', but for which Burchfield and his staff had so far been able to spare little time; the lion's share of this work was done by Goffin, whose time seems to have been less taken up with other activities. By late July over 200 entries could be described as 'in a more or less finished state'. 'It is very exciting', Burchfield wrote to Stefanyja Ross, 'to be able to walk after having crawled for so long.'[51]

---

[51] OED/C/6/3/1 20 Feb. 1959 KS to RWB; OED/C/2/5/77 27 July 1959 [RWB] to Mrs A. S. C. Ross.

Interestingly, the provisional selection of lists of words for inclusion, and their publication in the *Periodical*, was running far ahead of the actual drafting of entries: the list published in summer 1959 extended as far as *colour triangle*. Indeed, from a letter to another new contributor, the chemist Edward de Barry Barnett, it would appear that some kind of preliminary selection of words had already reached E by May 1959.[52] Meanwhile, the collection of quotations was proceeding apace: having been given financial approval to build up his team of readers, Burchfield was now taking delivery of about 1,500 quotations a week, in addition to the many quotations collected by himself and his staff (who were all still participating in reading work). It was clear that the space available in 40 Walton Crescent would soon be inadequate to house the growing project—together with the proposed science dictionary and other dictionaries that Burchfield ultimately hoped to bring to Oxford—and negotiations were under way to acquire the adjoining house.[53]

Amid all this burgeoning activity it is perhaps surprising to find that Burchfield himself was still taking on additional work. In June he became joint editor (with J. C. Maxwell) of *Notes & Queries*, with responsibility not only for content relating to English language and lexicography—which of course gave him control of the kind of forum for presentation of material relevant to the Supplement that had been desiderated in 1957—but also for contributions on medieval literature. As it turned out, although the journal published numerous articles about English lexis during the three years of his editorship, most of the contributions were beyond the agreed scope of the Supplement, in that they mainly dealt with antedatings of existing words and senses and with items found in nineteenth-century or earlier sources, although it occasionally proved possible to improve on inconclusive research about a word by publishing the interim findings and thereby provoking others to work at it.[54] Burchfield was also increasingly called upon, much as Wyllie had been, to report on proposals submitted to the Press for dictionaries and other books.[55] He somehow managed to combine all of this activity with his academic duties: his teaching post at Christ Church had ended before his appointment to the Editorship, but he still held a lectureship at St Peter's Hall (soon to become St Peter's College), which required him to teach various courses to

[52] OED/C/2/3/1 22 May 1959 [RWB] to E. de Barry Barnett. Barnett proved adept at seeking out antedatings of words in the lists, and often suggested additional items for inclusion; he continued to send in contributions until his death in March 1961.

[53] OED/C/2/2/2 note by RWB 26 May 1959; OED/C/6/3/1 25 June 1959 [RWB] to KS.

[54] An example is Elizabeth Brommer's article on *astronaut* and *astronautics* (Aug. 1960, pp. 312–13 and 283), in response to which a 48-year antedating of her first quotation for *astronaut* (1880 from 1928) was sent in by Roger Lancelyn Green. Burchfield himself occasionally wrote articles for inclusion, as for example the two appeals which appeared in the July/August 1959 issue (pp. 290–1), one for additional information about the words *all-rounder* and *all-roundness*, the other for copies of various scarce publications wanted for the library in 40 Walton Crescent. Longer lists of desiderata began to appear in June 1961.

[55] The earliest such proposals for which correspondence (preserved in OUPA(u)) survives date from early 1958.

English undergraduates (he regularly gave tutorials in his office in Walton Crescent).[56] He was also still helping with the administration of the Early English Text Society. It is little wonder that he soon acquired a reputation as something of a workaholic.

In September the Press's attention was drawn to one of its other dictionaries in the most dramatic and unwelcome fashion, and with the apparent consequence of yet another additional task for Burchfield. It is unusual for a dictionary to be the cause of an international incident, but on 11 September this is precisely what happened, when the government of Pakistan announced that it was banning the fourth edition of the *Concise* throughout the country, and took steps to seize all copies of the book. The reason was that violent exception had been taken to the dictionary's entry for *Pakistan*, apparently because it could be understood as stating that Pakistan was part of India.[57] Two months later the ban was lifted following an undertaking from OUP to issue a correction slip for all copies of *COD* sold in Pakistan. It was decided, however, that Burchfield would vet McIntosh's copy for the new edition of the *Concise*, now in preparation. Burchfield took the task seriously, and also took the opportunity to impose some stylistic and policy changes on the text, thus taking coordination between Oxford dictionaries to a new level.[58]

Autumn also brought other problems. Joyce Hawkins was off sick for several weeks in October; it was also proving less than straightforward to find a person to fill the new vacancy for a science editor, which had been advertised in August, and it was agreed to use external consultants for scientific vocabulary rather than an in-house editor for the time being. Suitable specialists were soon found in several fields, including aeronautics, biochemistry, metallurgy, and (courtesy of the reader Roland Hall) philosophy.[59]

Still, by the end of the year Burchfield could report some steady progress. He now had some fifty external readers, and the total number of quotation slips in 40 Walton Crescent—including a proportion of those left over from the 1933 Supplement, which were still in the process of being brought in and sorted—stood at around 100,000.[60] (Marghanita Laski headed the list of contributors, with 8,600 quotations in her first year.) Preliminary selection of items for inclusion, in the form of the *Periodical* lists, had reached the end of G (though it was now recognized that this first sequence of items

---

[56] Burchfield became a fellow of St Peter's College in 1963.

[57] The incident is recounted in Burchfield (1978a). OUP had received letters objecting on various grounds to the entry for *Pakistan* inserted in *COD* by McIntosh at least since 1954; a common complaint, and the basis of the action taken in 1959—following renewed discussion of the matter in the Pakistani press—was that the definition referred to Pakistan being 'in India', by which McIntosh maintained that he had meant only that it was in the large geographical region which has commonly been referred to as India, rather than the sovereign state of the same name.

[58] OUPA(u) note by RWB 5 Nov. 1959; 11 Nov. 1959 [RWB] to DMD (with report on the first 64 pages of the new *COD*; reports on subsequent sections followed).

[59] OED/C/2/2/2 7 Oct. 1959 Hawkins to RWB, PBED 12870 14 Oct. 1959 RWB to CHR/DMD; OUPA(u) note by RWB 12 Nov. 1959.

[60] PBED 12871(I) 'Annual Report' for 1959 (sent to CHR/DMD 29 Jan. 1960). The report does not give a total for the number of quotations collected, but a rough figure of 100,000 can be inferred from elsewhere. An article in the *Evening Standard* of 2 Mar. 1960 (p. 14) gives the total as 'up to 100,000'.

would have to be added to, and a second A–Z sequence was anticipated). There were now over 1,000 draft entries in A–C, of which about 200 could be said to have been finalized.

The New Year brought another specialist to Oxford, in the form of Nico van Blerk, who arrived on 1 January to prepare entries for South African words; during his four months' stay he reached the letter S, thus providing a 'splendid nucleus' for the Supplement's quota of South African vocabulary.[61] It is not clear how 'finished' these entries were; they, and the other entries already prepared, could only be described as 'finalized' in a provisional sense, since many questions of editorial style had still to be settled. The basic principle—that entries should in general conform as closely as possible stylistically to entries in the first edition and the 1933 Supplement—was clear enough, but putting this principle into practice brought up all kinds of editorial issues, for the resolution of which Burchfield could draw on neither written guidelines nor any accumulated body of knowledge about how his predecessors had dealt with such things, except insofar as this knowledge resided in the memory of Onions, whom Burchfield was constantly consulting. At times he was cycling to the Onions family home in North Oxford almost daily to consult him about editorial matters.[62]

It would appear that very little, if any, actual editing of entries, other than those drafted by van Blerk, went on during much of 1960; Burchfield's report on the year describes it as 'the last full year of reading and collecting before the editing is put in hand', and makes no mention of the preparation of any entries apart from the South African material. A new assistant, Tony Augarde, was identified by Burchfield from among his students at St Peter's, and joined the staff in August after graduating—effectively replacing Sally Hilton, who left in July to get married—but he too was set to collecting quotations rather than drafting entries.[63] Quotations continued to be collected at a great rate, with Laski and Auty heading the lists of individual contributors (with 12,000 and 9,000 quotations respectively during the year), and an impressive overall total of 250,000 by the end of the year; and the *Periodical* wordlists continued to make progress through the alphabet, reaching *science fiction* with the last list of the year.[64]

Burchfield estimated that when the *Periodical* lists reached Z they would amount to about 10,000 items. If he was still regarding himself as bound by the overall figure of 12,000 given in Davin's 1956 memo for Alan Horsman, this left room for a further 2,000, which a second traverse of the alphabet would surely surpass; but although no

[61] PBED 12871(I) Report by RWB, 31 Jan. 1961, on 'Progress in 1960'.

[62] Giles Onions's recollections of Burchfield's frequent visits are recorded in Ogilvie (2012: 155); Burchfield himself later recalled seeing 'a great deal of' Onions during the early years of his editorship (Burchfield 1989: 6). Topics discussed included the use of the symbol ‖ ('tramlines') to identify incompletely naturalized foreign words (Ogilvie 2012: 160–1) and the system to be used for representing pronunciation (OED/C/4/2/1 file note by RWB 25 Feb. 1960).

[63] OUPA(u) 15 Aug. 1960 Augarde to RWB. Augarde recalls that his first job was to copy out entries from W. S. Sharps's *Dictionary of Cinematography and Sound Recording* onto slips (interview with author, 18 Jan. 2012).

[64] PBED 12871(I) report by RWB, 31 Jan. 1961, on 'Progress in 1960'.

specific increase beyond the 1956 figure seems to have been approved, a comment in his report that the new material was likely to be in a ratio of 'roughly 1:1' to the 1933 text suggests he may have accepted that the new Supplement was going to be substantially larger than originally planned. Whether the apparent lack of any serious questioning of this expansion should be attributed to the Press's being in a strong enough financial position to accept it without a murmur, or simply to Davin's determination to back the man he had chosen for the job,[65] is unclear. Enlarged though the Supplement might now have become, however, it was still conceived as a project with limits: Burchfield's report listed a number of readers whom he planned to make use of after the current programme of reading was completed, '[t]o keep things "ticking over" for any future Supplements', and also mentioned the idea of continuing to scrutinize current periodicals for words coined in 1961 or later, 'for inclusion in the *next* Supplement'.[66]

The question of which words should be included in the current Supplement, however, was still an open one, and attention was focused on one particular lexical category in November 1960 in an unexpected way. It was well known that a number of 'four-letter words' and other taboo items had been omitted from the first edition of the Dictionary; and already in 1959 Burchfield had persuaded Davin (who had initially hoped otherwise) that there was 'no place' in the new Supplement for such material, on the pragmatic grounds that his small editorial team, focused on the English of the last few decades, was simply not in a position to deal adequately with the literature of earlier centuries.[67] However, the question was reopened by the conclusion of the celebrated prosecution of Penguin Books under the 1959 Obscene Publications Act for their publication of an unexpurgated edition of *Lady Chatterley's Lover*. The trial had already engendered public discussion of the once-taboo words used in D. H. Lawrence's novel, and the question was beginning to be asked whether the most notorious of these, *cunt* and *fuck*, were to be included in the Supplement.

The matter seems to have been brought to a head by an enquiry to the Press's London office from a news agency as to whether the 'not guilty' verdict (delivered on 2 November) would lead to the words being included. John White, the Press's head of publicity, under pressure to give an answer without being able to consult the Oxford offices, responded to the effect that it would not, declaring that the verdict was 'not relevant to the kind of considerations that prompt inclusion or omission'. Following an apologetic note from White explaining what had happened, Burchfield prepared

[65] Davin's biographer observes: 'Once he judged someone competent to write a particular book, or to carry out a particular task, that person had his wholehearted support' (Ovenden 1996: 290).

[66] The idea that there might be a 'next' supplement was to persist for some years, although Burchfield was soon referring to the needs of such a project as 'somewhat "academic"' (OED/C/2/5/2 24 Oct. 1964 [RWB] to R. Quirk).

[67] OUPA(u) note by RWB 24 Nov. 1959 on a meeting with DMD. The discussion was apparently prompted by the draft of an article for the London *Evening Standard* by the journalist Richard Findlater, which eventually appeared on 2 March 1960; a draft paragraph dealing with obscenities was removed at Burchfield's request, on the grounds that the policy for such vocabulary had not been finalized (OUPA(u) 24 Nov. 1959 [RWB] to R. Findlater).

a discussion document on 'Four-Letter Words and the Oxford Dictionaries'.[68] (The reference to 'Dictionaries' in the plural is significant: the issue was of course relevant to all of Oxford's English dictionaries, several of which were in the process of being revised, and Burchfield—and, evidently, others—took the view that it was his job to set out a general position, not just for the specific project for which he had direct editorial responsibility.) He restated 'the case against inclusion' (which he conceded as being 'not necessarily decisive') under three heads: the first edition of *OED* had excluded many such words, and if the two words currently under discussion were to be included, then many others would need to be as well; the gaps in the historical record of such words made for particular difficulties in their historical treatment; and they were in any case already adequately treated in standard dictionaries of slang. His preferred course—a significant, though probably reluctant, shift from the position he had taken a year earlier—was to include a brief entry for two (or possibly more) words in the new edition of *COD* currently in preparation, and then give the historical evidence ('in so far as it is possible to collect examples') in the Supplement for each of the items given in *COD*. As the publication of a new edition of the *Concise* was a more immediate—and of course more commercially sensitive—prospect than the appearance of the Supplement, Davin consulted the Press's branches in other parts of the English-speaking world; he also took the opportunity to canvass views on the inclusion of four-letter words in a new edition of the *Shorter*, whenever that might appear. (His letter to the branches gives an additional, somewhat Jesuitical reason for not including these words in the Supplement, namely that entries for words which should have been included in the first edition had no place in the Supplement, it being 'not the policy of the Supplement to correct the main dictionary'.) The uniform reaction of the branches was one of horror at the damage that the inclusion of such words in *COD* was likely to do in markets where the dictionary was heavily purchased for school use, or where conservative views prevailed, and McIntosh was duly informed that there should be no such provocative entries in his new *Concise*.[69] As far as the Supplement was concerned, however, the issue seems to have remained unresolved; but then there was no need to make a firm decision until much nearer publication.

By the beginning of 1961 Burchfield seems to have been ready at last to make a start in earnest on drafting entries. He began by selecting a series of pages of the 1933 Supplement, scattered across the first half of the alphabet, presumably as a means of exploring how the source text—and, especially, the challenges posed by the addition of further entries to it—varied; working through these would also have been as good a way as any of training himself to a point where he could instruct his assistants in the task. His own working copy of the 1933 Supplement[70] is marked up with the dates

---

[68] PBED 12870 5 Nov. 1960 J. White to CHR, 5 Nov. 1960 RWB to CHR (with accompanying document 'Four-Letter Words and the Oxford Dictionaries').

[69] CPGE 226 22 Nov. 1960 [DMD] to New York Branch, copied to other branches (replies from branches also in this file); 5 Jan. 1961 [DMD] to McIntosh.

[70] The volume is preserved in OUPA.

at which these sample pages were completed, beginning with page 5—covering the words *acrochordite* to -*ad* (suffix)—which is marked 'This page drafted Jan. 1961'; this was of course the range of specimen entries on which work had started over two years earlier, and was followed over the next eight months by pages in F, B, M, D, L, G, C, E, H, and I. A small number of additional new items were added to those which had already been identified (and printed in the *Periodical* desiderata lists), as may be seen from the series of further short lists which now began to appear in *Notes & Queries*, just as the *Periodical* lists were approaching Z.[71] By September, as planned, the main bulk of the programme of directed reading was complete, although eight external readers were retained, to provide additional quotations for both the current Supplement and 'any future Supplements'; the quotation files were now estimated to contain somewhere between a third of a million and half a million slips.[72] Also in September Burchfield was joined in drafting by Tony Augarde; his more experienced fellow assistant, Joyce Hawkins, did not commence drafting until 1962.[73] (Raymond Goffin, incidentally, was no longer part of the team, having finally retired at the end of 1960.) Finally, in the autumn, Burchfield brought the sequence of sample pages to an end, evidently now confident enough to begin the main editorial 'pass' through the alphabet. Work on page 1 of the 1933 text was marked as complete in November, and page 2 (*aboideau* to *acatholic*) in December.

But the new year brought a change of plan, and for a most unwelcome reason. In September 1961 an event took place on the other side of the Atlantic which was to have profound implications for the Supplement project: the publication of the third edition of *Webster's New International Dictionary*, a long-anticipated revision of the 1934 edition. The fact that the new edition was in preparation, and its likely scale, would have been well known long before publication, and some ripples from the controversy which it generated in America—mainly on account of its determinedly descriptivist stance, which provoked considerable hostility—would quickly have reached British shores, although it was only following its British publication date, 27 February 1962, that the British press accorded it extensive coverage.[74] This coverage, moreover, was largely favourable. (At least two British reviewers, Randolph Quirk and Alan Ross, were known to Burchfield, and may have communicated something of their opinions

---

[71] The first of the new lists, for words from *acrophonic* to *actuary*, had appeared in *Notes & Queries* in June 1961. The last 'regular' desiderata list (*U* to *zwitterionic*) appeared with the autumn 1961 issue of the *Periodical*; a note in this list makes it clear that the idea of a complete second alphabetical sequence of lists in this format had been abandoned.

[72] The figure of 340,000 is given in a draft of Burchfield's progress report for 1961 (OED/C/2/2/2; no finalized report for 1961 has been found). A report prepared in July 1962 (see p. 471 n. 79) states that the total by the end of 1961 was 'about half a million'.

[73] The delay seems to have had something to do with uncertainties about Hawkins being able to continue with her work. The problem seems as likely to have been itchy feet as any health-related matter: in January 1962 she considered, but eventually turned down, a job on the *Encyclopaedia Britannica* (correspondence in OUPA(u)).

[74] An early British notice of the new dictionary appeared in the *Bookseller* of 9 Sept. 1961 (pp. 1370–2). For a full consideration of the 1961 Webster dictionary and its reception, see Morton (1994).

to him, even if they did not send him advance drafts of their reviews, both of which appeared in March.[75])

As Burchfield later recalled, the new dictionary 'released for public inspection an unprecedented number of current English words', making it clear that he 'had seriously underestimated the task of collecting modern English vocabulary wherever it occurred'.[76] A Supplement based on the materials collected to date would, he realized, compare very poorly with this new American work. On the other hand, a more generous inclusion policy had obvious implications in terms of extent, cost, and timescale. At any event, it was clear that the work of compiling the new Supplement, for which a pattern had only just been established, would need to be reconsidered, and possibly changed radically. The routine of working through the pages of the 1933 Supplement from the beginning was broken off at the end of page 2—in the event page 3 would not be tackled for over a year—and, instead, Burchfield resumed his sampling of pages from this text, but now with a new focus. Among the ranges now selected for attention was one which included the prefixes *aqua-* and *aqui-*, and also a group centred on *electric*; these were followed in the next few months by ranges containing the prefixes *astro-*, *macro-*, *meta-*, *micro-*, and *radio-*.

The most likely explanation for this second sampling phase is that the generous coverage given in Webster to new words formed on prefixes like these, which were emerging in such profusion in science and technology, made it strongly desirable that Burchfield should work out how to deal with them. There may also have been other selection criteria in operation: the range *lo* to *lock-up*, for example, which was worked on in March, contains no important prefixes. But scientific lexis was certainly receiving a great deal of attention. Furthermore, the editorial team would need to be augmented if it was to cope with an influx of such vocabulary; after all, neither Burchfield nor Augarde nor Hawkins had any scientific background. And so in February Leopold Firnberg, a retired telecommunications engineer who had been reading for the Supplement since early 1960, was engaged to work part-time on entries for terms in electronics and related fields.[77] Strangely, there is no sign of one other response to the appearance of the new Webster dictionary which Burchfield mentions in his 1984 account, namely a 'vastly expanded reading programme'; from correspondence with those external readers who continued to send in quotations after September 1961 it would appear that the programme of directed reading was not formally revived or

---

[75] *New Statesman* 2 Mar. 1962, pp. 304–5 (Quirk); *Guardian* 9 Mar. 1962, p. 7 (Ross). Burchfield himself reviewed the dictionary for the *Review of English Studies* in 1963; his review is far from offering undiluted praise—he deplores the over-generous coverage of new words of marginal significance, notes flaws in the coverage of Australian and New Zealand English, points out some notable omissions, and criticizes various other aspects of policy and presentation—but concludes by congratulating the editor and staff on having assembled 'a register of present-day English vocabulary which will be of service for many years to come' (Burchfield 1963: 323).

[76] Burchfield (1984: 117).

[77] Correspondence with Firnberg, beginning in January 1960, is preserved in OED/C/2/5/25.

enhanced, and although texts continued to be sent out to these readers, the selection of texts shows no particular bias in favour of science or indeed in any other direction.[78]

In July Burchfield completed a report, apparently for the benefit of Davin and Roberts (who may well have commissioned it), in which he set out in some detail the project's history, present state, and future prospects.[79] The report conveys a clear impression of orderly progress: while acknowledging that various imponderables make the feasibility of publication in 1967 as originally planned 'an open question', Burchfield does not anticipate significant delay beyond this date. His estimate of the likely extent of the new material—'about three-quarters' that of the 1933 text—is actually smaller than the one given eighteen months earlier, although the figure for the number of new items to be included, 30,000, is significantly larger than anything given previously. The only reference to Webster is in a section on scientific vocabulary, where Burchfield declares that, while aiming to be as generous as the editors of *OED1* in his inclusion of scientific terms, he will not be 'filling the Supplement in Webster-like fashion with neologisms of doubtful permanence and rapidly changing sense'. He declares his intention to 'use "etc." freely' as a way of keeping coverage of words formed on common affixes like *electro-* and *tele-* within reasonable limits, this being preferable to the voluminous treatment of such formations given in Webster, whose approach in this area he clearly wishes to characterize as inappropriate for a dictionary like the *OED*. The aim of the report, in short, is clearly to demonstrate, as Burchfield writes in his closing paragraph, that 'the preparations [for publication] are well advanced, and that my staff and I are proceeding with all possible speed while endeavouring to maintain the high standard set by the O.E.D. itself'.

Perhaps, however, the report should not be taken entirely at face value. Was Burchfield's determinedly upbeat assessment a response to expressions of concern that things might not be going entirely to plan? The impression that he may have been aware of the possibility of criticism, and the need to address or pre-empt it, is reinforced by a covering note sent with the report, in which he declares that he would 'welcome suggestions which will hasten the appearance of the Supplement or contribute to its quality'.[80] Perhaps his employers had simply been anxious for reassurance that, halfway through its original ten-year lifespan, the project was still on track, and had not gone the way of other large-scale dictionary projects of whose history they were only too well aware. The appearance of a new potential source of delay and expansion, in the form of the 1961 edition of Webster, might well have added to their anxiety.

---

[78] Burchfield (1984: 117); correspondence with readers in OED/C/2/3/1–3. Cf. Burchfield (1973c), whose account of the collection of quotations since 1957 makes no mention of Webster's Third, commenting only (p. 99) that '[s]ince 1961 we have proceeded with further gap-filling and topping-up reading, with an average annual output of rather more than 50,000 quotations'.

[79] PBED 3977 Report by RWB, dated 11 July 1962, on 'O.E.D. Supplement: New Edition'. This report is discussed in some detail in Brewer (2007: 158–66).

[80] PBED 12871(I) 23 July 1962 RWB to CHR.

Whether or not Burchfield's report was deliberately framed to convey a specific impression, it affords an opportunity to explore in some detail the state of the Supplement, and of the views of its editor, five years after he had started work. One thing which becomes immediately apparent is that Burchfield was firmly wedded to the idea that 'literature', in some sense, should be well represented in his text. This is strikingly conveyed by the terms in which he criticized the evidence on which the 1933 Supplement—compiled as it had been from the materials immediately to hand— was based: it suffered 'the defect, in a literary instrument, of not being based on a proper reading of the main literary works of the period 1884–1930'—that is, the period of compilation of the first edition of the Dictionary.[81] The remedy he had decided upon was that the works surveyed by his readers should include a generous helping of 'literary works' dating from the late nineteenth and early twentieth centuries; these were listed alongside '[t]he main literary works of the period 1930–1960' as key elements of the reading programme that had just been completed. The rest of the main reading effort had been directed at four other categories: '[a] selection of important scientific and technical works' of the period 1930–60; a broad range of periodicals of all kinds from the same period; 'the main Commonwealth sources', also from the mid-century; and current newspapers. In addition to this reading of primary sources, a great deal of secondary material had been mined for suitable vocabulary, including journals and other academic sources dealing directly with English lexis—which readily yielded quotations and other information which could be made use of directly in the compilation of entries—as well as glossarial sources of various types (the contents of two dictionaries of 'new words' had been carefully trawled, as had several slang dictionaries compiled by Burchfield's fellow New Zealander Eric Partridge).

Notwithstanding the substantial 'literary' component of this raw material, it was clear that the majority of the new items in the Supplement would be of a type which would not be regarded as forming the common currency of what was usually meant by 'literature'. The material drafted so far suggested that 'roughly 50%' of the new items would be 'technical or scientific' (even if the supposed excesses of Webster in this regard were to be avoided). There was, moreover, no mention of Sisam's concept of intelligibility of definitions to the 'intelligent layman' as a criterion for selecting what to include. The approach to American English was likewise more inclusive than Sisam had envisaged: not only would 'U.S. vocabulary that had become established in this country' be included, but also a selection of items 'more or less restricted to the United States but encountered in American fiction, at the cinema, and elsewhere, as *comfort station, motorcade*, etc.'—although, rather quaintly, the use of restrictive labels was proposed 'so as not to suggest that Hollywood, Jazz, etc., terms are necessarily part of the *standard* vocabulary of educated Americans'. The number of such specifically

---

[81] The expression 'literary instrument' is an odd one in this context—it is more usually used of a particular language or idiom, considered in respect of its suitability as a vehicle for the composition of literature—but in his characterization of this 'defect' it is clear what he meant: 'Kipling, Conrad, Henry James, Shaw, Arnold Bennett, and other writers who flourished after 1890 are hardly represented at all.'

American terms, however, was to be 'relatively small', as was the number of items from the various Englishes of the Commonwealth: Burchfield anticipated finding room for 500 items of Australian English—which he believed to be particularly productive of new vocabulary—300 each from New Zealand, Canada,[82] and South Africa, and 'a few' from India and the Caribbean. Although the report makes no specific mention of 'future Supplements', its use of specific figures such as these, and its general tone, conveys a strong sense of a project still seen as having strict limits.

One figure which is curiously absent from the report is that for the number of entries now completed. Indeed, it might seem strange that, although work was proceeding 'with all possible speed', Burchfield cautioned that it would not be until late 1963 at the earliest that he would have enough material to ensure a continuous supply of copy to the printers. Perhaps the ongoing work on specimen pages, and the new attention being paid to scientific vocabulary, were causing him to question whether his existing editorial team would be able to meet the expectations placed upon them. After all, he still only had one part-time assistant with any specific scientific expertise; even with the benefit of a full set of consultants in all relevant disciplines—which had yet to be assembled—he might reasonably have wondered whether this would be sufficient.

Just as likely, however, his own capacity to get through the work, alongside all of his other activities, may have been giving him pause. In a memo to Davin, sent a few days before he submitted his July report, he mentions that in the past few months he has been asked to consider taking on several other lexicographical projects 'some time or other', including a supplement of New Zealand words for inclusion with the next edition of *COD*, etymological work on a proposed dictionary of surnames, and, extraordinarily, the wholesale revision of the *Shorter*: a task whose increasing urgency was generally recognized—for the latest reprint of the current edition a number of plates were now so worn as to require replacing, and of course the text was badly in need of updating—but one which Onions could hardly perform.[83] It had also been suggested that Burchfield's assistance might be needed in order to bring Onions's long-gestating etymological dictionary to publication. In the event it was agreed that Burchfield would give up his co-editorship of *Notes & Queries* and his administrative work for the EETS with a view to freeing up his evenings for work on the *Shorter*, which he would begin to tackle in January 1963 with the staggeringly optimistic aim of completing a new edition in five years.[84]

[82] Interestingly, in an article published only the previous year, Burchfield had declared that, in view of the historical dictionary of Canadian English then in preparation (it would be published in 1967 as *A Dictionary of Canadianisms on Historical Principles*), he would be 'restrict[ing] the Canadian section [...] to words which have passed into general use outside Canada' (Burchfield 1961: 48). It is not clear whether he had yet abandoned this policy.

[83] PBED 3977 reprint order (31 Jan. 1962) for 60,000 (later increased to 70,000) copies of *SOED*; 11 July 1962 [DMD] to John Brown; OED/C/2/2/2 13 July 1962 RWB to DMD.

[84] PBED 3977 25 July 1962 DMD to CHR. The series of desiderata lists printed in *Notes & Queries* came to an end with Burchfield's departure as joint editor; he was succeeded in January 1963 by Eric Stanley.

By September Burchfield and his assistants had prepared copy corresponding to a full 40 pages of the 1933 Supplement, and he proudly reported to Davin that, with Augarde, Hawkins, and Firnberg all now drafting, progress was 'now very rapid'. It was now, he suggested, time to produce a printed specimen, which could form the basis of a request to various interested parties for detailed comment on the approach being taken.[85] He selected the range *lo* to *lock-up*—a range corresponding to a single page of the 1933 text—and a three-page specimen was printed, suggesting an expansion ratio rather larger than his July report had stated, even on a range of words which contained a rather low proportion of scientific vocabulary. It was not until January 1963 that copies of the specimen were sent out for comment, apparently because of Davin's slowness in providing initial feedback on an early version. The Delegates also received copies at the same time, together with a shortened version of Burchfield's July report.[86]

The response to the specimen was generally very favourable. Burchfield had specifically requested comment on his treatment of the material from the corresponding page of the 1933 Supplement (he had retained every entry from the original text, but occasionally omitted a quotation where an earlier one was now available or where it had otherwise been rendered superfluous); this approach was declared satisfactory by most of those consulted, although Eric Stanley queried whether the new Supplement could be said to render its predecessor entirely redundant if it did not repeat every quotation (or at least every quotation not given in Craigie's *Dictionary of American English*, as many of the American quotations in the 1933 Supplement of course had been).[87] Burchfield's new entries met with widespread approval, as did the general style of presentation, which was of course very close to that of the 1933 text, although not quite identical: the Clarendon typeface formerly used for headwords had been abandoned, and all lemmas were now given a lower-case initial unless the word in question generally took a capital.[88]

Encouraged by these endorsements, Burchfield decided that there was no need to tackle any more sample pages; he and his staff—newly augmented by Jill Gifford, a Birmingham English graduate[89]—returned to working through A. However, it was soon clear that, although progress may have been rapid when measured by the rate of entries produced, by the measure that really mattered—traversal of the alphabet—it

---

[85] PBED 12871(II) 15 Sept. 1962 RWB to DMD.

[86] OUPA(u) (RWB papers) 20 Oct., 12 Nov. 1962 RWB to DMD; PBED 12871(I) 23 Jan. 1963 [CHR] to Delegates. The individuals asked for comment on the specimen include Onions, Goffin, Sisam, Friedrichsen, Michael Wood, Norman Davis, J. C. Maxwell, Randolph Quirk, and Eric Stanley (correspondence in PBED 12871(I) and OUPA(u) (RWB papers)).

[87] OUPA(u) (RWB papers) 5 Feb. 1963 E. Stanley to DMD.

[88] The idea of downcasing lemmas had been proposed as long ago as 1956 (in Davin's report on 'O.E.D. Supplement n/e', cited above, p. 447 n. 139), and was no doubt discussed before that, as the Press received a steady trickle of complaints from the public about the use of capitals.

[89] Interestingly, one of Gifford's first tasks was to make quotation slips for all of the headwords in *Chambers's Technical Dictionary*, a recent dictionary of scientific terminology, evidently in order to bolster what was still felt to be inadequate coverage of such material in the Supplement's files (Jill Cotter (née Gifford), personal communication).

was falling far short of what was needed in order to complete the text by anything like 1967. A key part of the problem was the continuing inflow of new quotation evidence from external readers, which constantly increased the number of items that had to be considered for inclusion: even if the number of items actually included remained fixed, assessment of each candidate took time. Realizing that firm action was needed, in April Burchfield advised his readers that as from 1 June the quotation files would be effectively closed to new material. Some new quotations would of course continue to arrive, including some that would be found useful, but as he explained to Marghanita Laski, the bulk of any new material would now be placed in a new file 'intended to be the starting-point for the third supplement', to be tackled by a putative successor editor in about thirty years' time.[90] To be contemplating a third Supplement before any of the second Supplement had gone to press might seem premature, but it is indicative of Burchfield's continuing determination to set limits to the current project. It is therefore perhaps surprising to find him writing to Auty, another of his most prolific readers, later that year with a request that he should make a start on Joyce's *Ulysses*, which he described as the book 'most urgently' demanding to be read; and even more surprising that he instructed Auty to read it by 'what I have called the "fine-tooth comb method" of reading, as you know that we want every crumb from it'.[91]

The drafting of entries continued steadily throughout 1963 and 1964. The work was still done entirely on paper slips; printing of entries would only start when a substantial quantity of copy had been prepared. The staff expanded further during this time, with Eric Dann becoming a new assistant in Walton Crescent in late 1963, and Norman Sainsbury and Elizabeth Livingstone swelling the team of library researchers in Oxford from about the same time; Sainsbury, who gave part-time assistance (he was also Keeper of Oriental Books at the Bodleian Library), subsequently also became the project's first bibliographer. Burchfield also acquired two part-time assistants, Anne Wallace-Hadrill and Jelly Williams, to help with his work on the *Shorter*, which by the end of the year had progressed far enough for a specimen to be commissioned.[92] In the summer of 1964 the editorial strength received a further temporary boost when the New Zealander Phyllis Trapp arrived, having been invited to deal with New Zealand vocabulary much as Nico van Blerk had earlier done for South African English, a task which she completed in July 1965.[93]

By September 1964, encouraged by the rate at which completed entries were being prepared, Burchfield predicted that copy for the whole of the letters A to D would be ready for press by the end of 1965.[94] This prediction would turn out to be hopelessly optimistic, but a substantial body of drafted material was certainly building up. By way

[90] OED/C/2/5/43 23 Apr., 8 May 1963 [RWB] to Laski.
[91] OED/C/2/5/2 11 July 1963 RWB to Auty.
[92] Correspondence about these appointments in PBED 12871(II) and OUPA(u).
[93] She was the sister of the literary scholar J. B. Trapp, a friend of Burchfield's who had been a valued reader for the Supplement for several years.
[94] PBED 12871(I) 17 Sept. 1964 RWB to CHR/DMD.

of preparation for the start of typesetting, a second specimen was now prepared, this time for a range in A that was specifically chosen for its high proportion of scientific vocabulary (including the prefix *astro-* and the words *atom* and *atomic*). Again the range corresponded to a single page of the first Supplement, but this time the additions to the 1933 material were so extensive that the original single page expanded to seven. The high science content warranted a different approach in the preparation of the specimen: scientific entries were first submitted to various specialist consultants, and then in March 1965 the seven printed pages were sent out for general comment, mainly from the various people who had commented on the earlier one.[95] The general response was once again favourable. A notable exception was Sisam, who complained of the 'profuseness' of the specimen, in regard to both generosity of inclusion and overall scale, and recommended 'more severe editorial pruning'; but his seems to have been a lone voice, and Burchfield now felt confident enough to dismiss many of his criticisms with some asperity, arguing that Sisam might now be capable of being 'on the wrong side of infallibility in matters of doctrine at the O.E.D. level'.[96]

By the time these discussions were taking place the copy for something over 40 pages of the new Supplement was already ready to go to the printers, with another 40 only awaiting bibliographical standardization by Sainsbury (who as a part-timer was, unsurprisingly, finding it difficult to keep up), and the preliminary drafting of entries running far ahead beyond the letter A. Finally, on 27 May 1965, the first batch of copy was at last delivered to the printers. Sadly, Charles Onions, the last surviving Editor of the first edition, did not live to see the first proofs of the new Supplement: he died on 8 January 1965.

During the rest of 1965 Burchfield managed to keep to the schedule he had drawn up for the delivery of copy to the printers, with two further quarterly batches handed over in August and November, taking the text to the end of the letter A. However, by the end of the year the amount of printed galley proof reached only as far as the word *acriflavine* (equivalent to roughly sixteen pages).[97] Burchfield does not appear to have been unduly concerned by this extremely slow start by the printer, at least to judge from his annual progress report, where the only problems mentioned relate to bibliographical matters and to the verification of quotations. Indeed, he remained remarkably optimistic, predicting that 'if we can keep to the schedule now drawn up the whole of the material will be at press by the end of 1970'. This was of course a significant retrenchment from the original publication date of 1967, but still offered a not too distant prospect of publication, and one which Burchfield evidently expected to be regarded as satisfactory. He could also point to good progress in the preparation of entries by his staff, with copy ready for the printers extending to *bald*, and preliminary drafting in the middle of F. (The work of drafting entries was also being carried out by at least one individual working out-of-house: Roland Hall, who had been acting as a consultant in philosophy and psychology for several years, was now compiling fully-fledged entries.) Useful work on other fronts was done during

---

[95] Correspondence in OED/C/2/4/1 and PBED 12871(I).

[96] PBED 12868 12 Mar. 1965 KS to DMD (with annotations by RWB).

[97] OED/C/4/2/1 31 Dec. 1965 RWB to CHR/DMD reporting on 'Progress in 1965'. Copies of Burchfield's progress reports for 1966, 1967, 1968, 1969, and 1970 are also to be found in this file.

the year, including the incorporation into the Supplement's reference library of 1,000 books from the days of the first edition—retrieved from storage during the summer—and the receipt of another 31,000 quotations. More than two-thirds of the new quotations came from the reading of just three individuals, with Marghanita Laski for once coming third in the roll of honour for the year, behind Roland Auty and another prolific retired schoolmaster, Wilfred Kings.

There is no suggestion in Burchfield's report that the new quotations are to be filed for use in a 'third supplement', an idea of which no more is heard henceforth. In fact, although the report gives no estimate of the size of the Supplement on which he was presently engaged, Burchfield's conception of the work had enlarged considerably. A few weeks before submitting his report he had floated the idea—which was soon rejected—of publishing the text in nine fascicles of about 300 pages each, implying a total extent of 2,700 pages. It was clear that there could no longer be any question of containing the text within the covers of a single volume.[98] The estimate of 2,700 pages—based as it appears to be on the expansion factor to be seen in the (very small) amount of galley proof so far produced—also suggests that Burchfield may not yet have grasped an important fact about the work of revising the Supplement: namely that, because the beginning of the alphabet in the 1933 text was much fuller than the end (reflecting the period of time since publication of the first edition), the expansion factor was likely to increase as work progressed. His failure to appreciate this is all the more surprising when it is remembered that specimen pages from all over the alphabet had already been worked on. The amount of material added to a page like that containing the range *Tannaite–taster*, for example, must surely have been noticeably more, in terms of the number of slips, than that added to a page in A or B, even without the more definite evidence of a printed proof. (In the event this range was to cover 13 printed pages of the new Supplement, although this of course included extensive additional material added subsequent to the original work on the page.) The need for a yardstick other than the 1933 text had in fact been pointed out by Sisam as early as 1952; it was unfortunate, to say the least, that what was really a fairly obvious point had been lost sight of.[99]

---

[98] PBED 12868 18 Oct., 21 Nov. 1965 RWB to DMD. In fact the idea of publication in fascicles had been briefly considered in 1957: it is mentioned (and rejected) in Burchfield's notes on his visit to Sisam. Burchfield later recalled that his interest in reviving the idea was prompted by concern at the effect on the morale of his staff of the receding prospect of publication of their work (Burchfield and Aarsleff 1988: 50); he may also have been influenced by the recent decision to publish the *Oxford Latin Dictionary* in fascicles (OD 15 May 1964), although the first fascicle of *OLD* did not appear until 1968.

[99] PBED 12869(I) memorandum by KS on 'English Dictionaries', Sept. 1952 (see p. 438 n. 101): 'the proportion of each letter [of the new Supplement] should be roughly calculable (not, of course, by reference to [the] existing Supplement, which is wedge-shaped).' Even a year later Burchfield seems not to have grasped the implications of the 1933 Supplement's 'wedge' shape: his progress report for 1966 looks forward to reaching the end of the letter G during 1967, which 'will bring the drafting [of entries] to the half-way point (in the 1933 Supplement G ends at p. 440 of an 867-page work)'. It is conceivable (as suggested in Brewer 2007: 171) that Burchfield may here have been deliberately avoiding a full discussion of scale with his publishers, but there is now anecdotal evidence to suggest that even in the 1970s he still had not fully grasped the scheduling implications of the 1933 'wedge' (N. Wedd, interview with author, 21 Dec. 2011; A. Hughes, interview with author, 3 Feb. 2012).

Any of the Editors of the first edition of the Dictionary, of course, could have told Burchfield how important it was to have reliable estimates of scale. They might well also have urged upon him the importance of coordinating progress across the various separate streams of material (copy, galley proofs, revises, page proofs) once printing had started; but Burchfield seems to have been content to allow these processes to take place at very different speeds. The state of play at the end of 1965, with preliminary drafting in F, finalization of copy in B, and only a few dozen columns of galley proof, has already been mentioned; a year later preliminary drafting was in G, the copy ready for press had reached the word *choky*, and, extraordinarily, the production of galley proofs, extending to *alignment*, had still not reached the end of the first consignment of copy sent to the printers in May 1965. Burchfield was, unsurprisingly, dissatisfied with this rate of progress on the part of the printer, and asked for the rate of production of galleys to be doubled. But he was also forced to acknowledge that the production of copy by his own staff was falling short of what was needed, noting that if they continued to manage no more than 100 pages of the 1933 Supplement—still his standard unit of measurement—per year, then the copy for the revised edition would not be completed until 1973: a three-year slippage from only a year earlier.

At least Burchfield could point to having had to cope with some unanticipated additional drains on his editorial resources. He and his staff had been asked to prepare a glossary of items of Australian and New Zealand English, for planned inclusion in forthcoming editions of some of the Press's smaller dictionaries,[100] and a significant amount of his own time had had to be devoted to seeing the text of the *Oxford Dictionary of English Etymology*—left nearly complete by Onions at his death— through to publication. In the latter task he worked closely with Friedrichsen, who was now also providing revised etymologies for the *Shorter*. Burchfield was becoming acutely conscious of the effect on the Supplement of such diversions of effort into other projects, but was for the moment resigned to them, although he did formally register with Davin the desirability of freeing himself and his staff from such distractions.[101] 1966 also saw an expansion in the Supplement's team of library researchers, to meet the increasing need for quotations from sources not available in Oxford and London to be checked; Adriana Orr, based in Washington, became the project's first regular American researcher, with others in Australia and New Zealand also providing a similar service from time to time.

Among the entries sent to press during 1966 were two which brought up, once again and now with greater urgency, the question of what was to be the Supplement's policy on the inclusion of obscene and taboo language—or, as Burchfield put it in a letter to Stefanyja Ross, 'the establishing of the decency line'. The entries in question were those

---

[100] Correspondence in PBED 3955. The original idea was to produce an Australian and New Zealand supplement which could be included as end matter with various dictionaries, including *COD*, *POD*, and the *Oxford Illustrated Dictionary*, but in the event it only appeared in the fifth edition of *POD*, which was eventually published in 1969.

[101] PBED 12868 29 Dec. 1966 RWB to DMD.

for *bugger* (noun and verb), drafts of which he sent to Ross and Eric Stanley in order to elicit their views on where this line should be drawn. Both responded by strongly advocating comprehensive inclusion; Davin, consulted in turn by Burchfield—who delicately noted that '[t]he real difficulty will come when we get near to the end of the letter C'—also favoured an inclusive policy.[102] The boundaries of 'acceptable' language were evidently changing: in 1965 George Garmonsway's *Penguin English Dictionary* had included entries for both *cunt* and *fuck*, the first general English dictionary to do so. In August, as if to provide confirmation of the changing climate, an article appeared in the *New Statesman* which declared the *OED*'s omission of 'the universally known sexual words' to be 'curiously mealy-mouthed and prissy', and called on OUP to rectify the omissions.[103] The final decision about the two most contentious four-letter words would not be taken until 1968, when draft entries for both words were submitted to the Delegates for consideration; but by then the matter was a foregone conclusion, and the Delegates seem to have had no hesitation in endorsing the proposed inclusive policy.[104]

1967 was, of course, the year in which it had originally been hoped to publish the new Supplement; Burchfield confided to Marghanita Laski, as the 'dreaded day' of 1 July— the tenth anniversary of his appointment—approached, that thereafter 'my conscience at not having finished the dictionary will get worse'.[105] But, remarkably, there seems to have been very little to goad him beyond his own conscience. If senior figures at OUP were seriously worried by the constant pushing back of the project's end date—as well they might be—there is no sign of it. There must surely have been some informal conversations about rates of progress, but the lack of a formal record of anything of the kind is striking. It should perhaps be borne in mind that the last system for producing *OED* text had ceased to operate over thirty years earlier; the fact that Burchfield had at last set another such system in motion, and that it appeared to be generating text of the kind and quality required, may have been such a relief that there was felt to be no need, for the time being at least, to subject it to constraints of time and extent.

There certainly appear to have been no drastic changes of direction over the next few years, to judge from the annual reports which continued to appear. Copy continued to be produced in varying quantities, as did various stages of proof; and if output was less than might have been expected, an explanation was usually to be found in the effort which it had proved necessary to divert to other projects, including new editions and new impressions of other dictionaries. Indeed, during these years the Press seems

---

[102] OUPA(u) 31 Mar. 1966 [RWB] to Ross, [RWB] to Stanley (with their replies), 2 May 1966 RWB to DMD (with annotations by DMD).

[103] Brien (1966).

[104] OUPA(u) 5 Jan. 1968 [DMD] to Delegates; the responses of various Delegates, all favouring inclusion, are also in this file. The policy proposed envisaged inclusion of the words in the *Shorter*, but not in the smaller dictionaries; in fact both *COD* and *POD* included both words in their sixth editions (1976 and 1978 respectively). Burchfield (1972) recounts the sequence of events leading up to the decision, as well as the curious postscript that the proposed inclusive policy was publicized in 1969 in the pages of the 'alternative' magazine *Oz*, which published an exchange of correspondence between Davin and its editors.

[105] OED/C/2/5/43 29 June 1967 [RWB] to Laski.

increasingly to have looked on its lexicographers, formally engaged on a particular project though they might be, as together forming a single resource to be deployed according to whichever dictionary or dictionaries required their skills. Looked at from the perspective of the Supplement alone this might have its drawbacks, but the needs of a single project were necessarily subordinate to the Press's business aims across the whole range of English dictionaries, and a flexibly deployable pool of lexicographical effort of this kind had long been considered highly desirable. (Another consequence of the interconnectedness of all these projects is that it becomes increasingly difficult to maintain an exclusive focus on the story of the *OED*: the constant redeployment of staff—including figures with key roles in the history of the *OED*—between projects, and the other ways in which events relating to one project can have knock-on effects elsewhere, mean that in order to give a full account of the *OED*, and its Supplement, it is frequently necessary to include a great deal about developments involving one or other of the Oxford dictionaries, any one of which arguably deserves a history in its own right.)

Redeployment of effort in favour of the Supplement, and to the detriment of the *Shorter*, took place in 1966 and 1967. In fact work on the *Shorter* had already been scaled back long before then, as it became apparent that it would not be practicable for Burchfield to attempt the preparation of fully revised entries concurrently with the editing of the Supplement; and in the summer of 1967 it was reluctantly decided to abandon full-scale revision in favour of a re-setting of the existing text—incorporating Friedrichsen's revised etymologies—with a revised set of Addenda, to be prepared from Supplement materials at some later date. The full revision, the need for which was still recognized, was rescheduled to start around 1977.[106] Both Jelly Williams and Anne Wallace-Hadrill were reallocated to the Supplement, although the latter returned to work on the Addenda for the *Shorter* in 1968, alongside Jessie Coulson, who had rejoined the staff in Walton Crescent in 1967.

One rather drastic redeployment took place in December 1967, when Joyce Hawkins abruptly ceased to work on the Supplement. The precise circumstances—referred to darkly by Burchfield as 'a tangled story'—remain unclear, but Hawkins seems to have become increasingly dissatisfied with the nature of her work, notwithstanding her abiding passion for lexicography in general, and there had also been quarrels with other members of staff, as a result of which Burchfield had begun to have doubts about her ability to work harmoniously with her colleagues.[107] These doubts now suddenly— perhaps following some further, unrecorded incident—became a conviction that it would be impossible for Hawkins to continue working at 40 Walton Crescent. Fortunately an alternative application of her unquestioned lexicographical abilities was very quickly found, namely work on the new edition of the *Oxford Illustrated*

---

[106]   PBED 3977 17 May, 31 July 1967 RWB to DMD.
[107]   OED/C/2/5/44 28 Dec. 1967 [RWB] to M. Laski; Jill Cotter, interview with author, 26 Mar. 2013. The date of Hawkins's departure is variously given as 18 and 20 December.

Dictionary, which was being prepared literally next door at No. 41. She went on to become one of the most able of all compilers of 'small dictionaries', producing over a dozen titles for OUP before her retirement in 1991.

Hawkins's departure must have been a significant loss to the Supplement; however, the project's staff was better able to cope with it than it would have been a year or two earlier. In addition to Jessie Coulson, 1967 had seen the arrival of another new assistant, David Clegg—although he was to leave after barely a year—and also of another distinguished name in lexicography (and other fields): that of John Bradbury Sykes, an astrophysicist and Oxford mathematics graduate whose remarkable facility for languages had earned him the position of head of the translations office in the library of the Atomic Energy Research Establishment at Harwell. Having started some years earlier, like so many others, as a contributor of quotations, in 1967 he began—while continuing with his work at Harwell—to come into Walton Crescent on Saturday mornings to write definitions of technical vocabulary, an area where Burchfield evidently still felt under-resourced.[108] Thus began a brilliant career in Oxford lexicography that lasted almost three decades, during which Sykes contributed an enormous amount to the Supplement but also to several other titles, notably *COD*, while still continuing to be an important figure in the world of professional translation (as well as achieving a different kind of fame through his repeated winning of the *Times* crossword competition).

A discernible raising of the Supplement's public profile can also be dated to around this time. This can partly be accounted for by Burchfield's excellent working relationship with Elizabeth Knight, the person in OUP's London office charged with promoting reference works (the two had first worked together on Onions's etymological dictionary); but some credit should also be given to the efforts of Marghanita Laski— although it has to be said that her pen was not always wielded to the Press's liking. In 1968 she wrote a series of articles for the *Times Literary Supplement* about the reading she did for the *OED*[109]—which in her case meant not just the Supplement, but also the full-scale revision of the Dictionary, an event to which she eagerly looked forward, and for which she was quite prepared to lobby. Early in 1967 she made a public call for OUP to commit itself to embarking on revision in time to bring out the first part of the new edition in time for the centenary of the appearance of Murray's first fascicle in 1884;[110] a few months later she repeated the call in a written submission to the Waldock Committee, which had been appointed by Oxford University to investigate OUP's operations and its relationship to the University, declaring that her thorough familiarity with the *OED* had shown it to be 'more outdated than any dictionary purporting to be authoritative has any right to be', and that full-scale revision was to be preferred to 'tinkering at the task with [...] Supplements and Shorter Dictionaries'. Davin and Burchfield did their

---

[108] OUPA(u) 24 Aug. 1967 J. L. Ashton to Sykes.
[109] Eight of Laski's articles appeared in the *TLS* between 11 Jan. and 31 Oct. 1968.
[110] Laski (1967).

best to disabuse her of these hopes, the former warning her that she could hardly expect to see revision commence during his, her, or Burchfield's lifetime, but she continued to ride her hobby-horse, mischievously referring in the first of her *TLS* articles to 'the Great Jubilee when a revision of the whole dictionary is set in hand', which some at OUP feared might be taken as an insider's confident assertion that revision would begin in 1978, the year when the Press planned to celebrate its quincentenary. By the summer of 1968 Burchfield had begun to worry that it might be 'beginning to look to outside readers as if this is Miss Laski's Dictionary'; but the personal interest she took in the project, and the publicity which resulted, unquestionably did far more good than harm.[111]

One of the most beneficial consequences of Laski's journalistic efforts on behalf of the Supplement came in the form of a letter from Philip Gove, the editor of *Webster's New International Dictionary*, who was prompted by reading her first *TLS* article to write to Burchfield with an offer he had been considering for some time, namely to make the quotation files of Merriam-Webster (the publishers of the *New International* and numerous other dictionaries) available in some way to the compilers of the Supplement. Burchfield gratefully accepted this generous offer, and soon lists of requests for antedatings were regularly being sent to Springfield, Massachusetts, for about a third of which the Merriam-Webster files were able to provide earlier evidence, often of a kind which would have been impossible for the Supplement's own library researchers to track down.[112] A cordial relationship developed between the two projects which was to last for nearly a decade; such collaboration between competing dictionary publishers is rare indeed.

1968 also saw significant consolidation and expansion of the lexicographical enterprise over which Burchfield presided. A resurgence of interest in the idea of a dictionary of scientific vocabulary, which had lain dormant for some time, led to approval being given for the recruitment of two more scientists, of whom one, Alan Hughes, took up his post in October (the other, Elizabeth Price, did not start until the following January), although it was understood that work on this dictionary could hardly begin until the Supplement was approaching completion. Two additional American library researchers were also taken on, and in a new departure Frances Williams, an experienced proofreader, was engaged specifically to help with this component of the work.[113] Consolidation, in the form of the bringing of the *Concise* and the *Pocket* under the roof of 40 Walton Crescent, took place rather sooner than expected following the withdrawal of McIntosh through illness early in the year. It had

---

[111] OED/C/2/5/44 30 Nov. 1967 Laski to P. A. Gore, 29 Dec. 1967 J. White to RWB, 4 Jan. 1968 [RWB] to White, 18 June 1968 RWB to DMD. The exchange of memos about the 'Great Jubilee' occurred before Laski's article was published; she regularly submitted early drafts of her articles about the Dictionary to Oxford for comment, and indeed had sounded Burchfield out on the idea of writing them.

[112] OUPA(u) 22 Jan. 1968 P. B. Gove to RWB.

[113] PBED 23306 4 May 1968 CHR to RWB/DMD/J. L. Ashton; OUPA(u) 23 July 1969 [RWB] to J. L. Ashton; OUP *Record* No. 13 (Dec. 1968), p. 2. Another new assistant, Robin Dixon, started in September, effectively replacing David Clegg.

been anticipated that he would probably retire following publication of the new edition of *POD* on which he had been working for some time, but in the event he was unable to finish seeing it through the press; the commercial importance of this new edition was sufficient to warrant diverting some of Burchfield's own effort into completing the task (with the assistance of Joan Pusey, whose main assignment was the revision of the *Oxford School Dictionary*).[114] Burchfield could now regard himself as having charge of considerably more than just the Supplement; his new role is reflected in the fact that his 1968 report is headed 'Oxford Dictionaries in 40 Walton Crescent', and dealt with the *Shorter*, the *Concise*, the *Pocket*, the *Oxford Dictionary of English Etymology*, and the projected science dictionary. The Press had long sought someone capable of shouldering this considerably enlarged burden, and Burchfield was evidently quite happy to do so. The consequences in terms of the progress of the Supplement were, however, only too clear: the amount of copy prepared for press during the year was less than half that for 1967, and the correction of galley proofs had only just reached the beginning of B.

It might be thought that there was more than enough to be getting on with in Oxford; but in the summer of 1968 Burchfield made what was the first of many trips abroad in an 'official' capacity. There were of course perfectly good business reasons for a visit to North America, but it is tempting to discern in his extensive itinerary something of a 'grand progress', or a deliberate effort to boost his international profile as a significant figure in the world of lexicography. During June and July he visited three significant lexicographical centres of activity in New York—Random House, the *American Heritage Dictionary*, and Clarence Barnhart's offices in the Bronx—as well as Merriam-Webster in Springfield, Massachusetts, the *Middle English Dictionary* in Ann Arbor, the *Dictionary of American Regional English* in Madison, Wisconsin, Mitford Mathews (Craigie's former assistant, now one of the grand old men of American lexicography) in Chicago, Friedrichsen and the Supplement's American library researchers in Washington, and OUP's Canadian headquarters in Toronto.[115] This transatlantic odyssey may have afforded excellent opportunities for publicity and networking, but Burchfield's absence must surely have made a further dent in the Supplement's output for the year.

The further receding of any prospect of a completed Supplement may help to explain why the Press responded so enthusiastically to an idea for exploiting the text of the *OED* itself in a new way, which was first brought to the attention of OUP's New York office in September 1968. Albert Boni, a flamboyant and innovative American publisher, had developed a technique for making micrographic reproductions of large reference works; he now approached the Press with a proposal to produce a two-volume version of the first edition of the Dictionary, which could be sold for a fraction

---

[114] PBED 3978 5 Jan. 1968 DMD to CHR/P. J. Spicer/J. L. Ashton. The new edition of *POD* was published on 1 May 1969.
[115] OUP *Record* No. 13 (Dec. 1968), p. 14.

of the price of the full-size twelve-volume edition (another reprint of which was in progress). Senior figures at the Press were already aware of the attractions of the idea of issuing a cheap edition of the *OED*—in fact an offer from Sphere Books to produce a paperback edition (which would have run to over 50 volumes) had been turned down less than two years earlier—and the new proposal had obvious advantages.[116] After some initial discussions with Boni it was decided that, rather than licensing Boni's company to produce a small-print edition, the Press would have a go at doing so itself. An indication of the anticipated returns from the venture may be gained from the fact that the Delegates authorized the expenditure of £105,000 on it.[117] In the event it would be more than two years before what became known as the *Compact Oxford English Dictionary* was published; but this was still some years ahead of even the most optimistic predictions for the appearance of the Supplement, for which the publicly admitted completion date was now 1975.[118]

A desire to accelerate production must surely account for the further expansion of the staff during 1969. Elizabeth Price, who joined the staff in January, was followed by four more assistants during the year. An important addition to the science team was Sandra Raphael, a former librarian of the Linnean Society; the other arrivals included a bibliographer, Michael Grose—whose skills were sorely needed, as the project had been without anyone to fulfil this role since the resignation of Norman Sainsbury in 1966—and a young modern languages graduate from Magdalen College named Julian Barnes.[119] By the time the year's last recruit, Deirdre McKenna, arrived in September, Burchfield found himself with fifteen people under his direction in 40 Walton Crescent (see Figure 36) and nearly as many again out-of-house.[120] What with coordinating the work of this group of people (and that of the project's external consultants), not to mention the demands made on his time by various other Oxford dictionaries, it is easy to imagine him sometimes finding that he had precious little time for doing any editing.

The slow rate at which completed printed pages of the Supplement could be produced brought additional concerns, which increasingly preoccupied Burchfield during 1969. For one thing, it was frustrating for both him and his staff that, as they began the fifth year since copy had begun to go to press, the prospect of their work being placed before the public was still so remote: 'we are aching', he wrote, 'to give the *coup de grace* to this very sizable portion of the dictionary.' For another, there was the question of datedness. If the whole Supplement remained unpublished until 1975, then the earliest parts of the text—which had now passed the whole of the cycle of

---

[116] PBED 12875 11 Sept. 1968 W. Oakley to J. R. B. Brett-Smith (president of OUP's New York business); FC 25 Apr. 1967. A previous reprint of the first edition, the first since the 1933 Reissue, had taken place in 1958–61 (OUP *Record* 3 (Dec. 1958), p. [2]). There would be one final reprint in 1978.
[117] OD 4 Feb. 1969.
[118] OUPA(u) 13 Feb. 1968 [RWB] to DMD and attached notes.
[119] Correspondence about these appointments in OUPA(u).
[120] OED/C/4/2/1 3 Sept. 1969 [RWB] to CHR.

proofing and correction and could no longer be altered—would look considerably less up-to-date than had been hoped; 'faint traces of datedness' could already be discerned in A. For example, the attention drawn in 1969 to the Caribbean island of Anguilla by international events came too late for *Anguillan* to be included in the Supplement.[121] For these and other reasons—not least the chance for the Press to get some financial return for its large investment in the project at an earlier date—the idea of publishing the two volumes separately, at different times, now began to look distinctly attractive. Burchfield made a formal proposal for staggered publication in September, and by November this had been approved, with publication of Volume I—extending as far as the end of J—provisionally scheduled for autumn 1971 or spring 1972. This promised to fit in well with plans to publish the *Compact OED* in the spring of 1971, in that the publicity generated by the latter might help to boost interest in the new work.[122]

It was clear, however, that getting everything ready to publish a volume in two years was going to be a challenge; effort would have to be concentrated on the generation and finalization of printed pages—remarkably, not a single page of the text had yet been fully signed off for press—while still maintaining some kind of forward progress through the alphabet in the production of copy. Burchfield drew up a tough schedule for himself and his staff, and sought to streamline the production process by, for example, limiting as much as possible the insertion of additional words or senses at the galley-proof stage, and imposing firm restrictions on activities such as systematic reading which were not directly related to the main task in hand. Remaining external readers like Marghanita Laski were also firmly told that further incoming quotations relating to Volume I simply could not be taken into account.[123]

Unfortunately, despite everyone's best efforts, the schedule very quickly began to slip. In fact it was the Press's printers who found themselves unable to keep up, evidently because of having to spread compositorial effort across four separate dictionaries (the Supplement, the *Oxford Latin Dictionary*, the reset *Shorter*, and a new Turkish dictionary). By March 1970 there were simply not enough Supplement proofs available to keep Burchfield's proofreaders occupied, and it had become clear that some of the typesetting would have to go to an outside printer. '[I]t is a pity', Burchfield grumbled, 'that we have to fall back on outsiders for dictionaries of all things.'[124] The printing company William Clowes & Sons was engaged to set the letters E–J, and was soon producing pages which perfectly matched those produced in Oxford. But it proved impossible to catch up with the original schedule, and it soon became clear that publication before the end of 1971 was no longer realistic. Progress was further affected

---

[121] PBED 12867 29 Sept. 1969 RWB to CHR/DMD. In March 1969, following Anguilla's unilateral declaration of independence and the subsequent expulsion of a British emissary, the British government had sent several hundred troops and police officers to the island, provoking international criticism.

[122] PBED 12867 24 Nov. 1969 CHR to DMD; PBED 12875 15 Dec. 1969 [CHR] to Brett-Smith.

[123] OED/C/4/2/1 notes by RWB, 8 Jan. 1970, of a meeting with senior members of his staff; 8 Jan. 1970 RWB to Augarde and eight others re 'Reading of Sources'; OED/C/2/5/44 9 Jan. 1970 [RWB] to Laski.

[124] OED/C/4/2/1 file note by RWB 13 Mar. 1970; PBED 12867 16 Mar. 1970 RWB to CHR, DMD, and T. Chester.

by staff changes: Elizabeth Price had left in November 1969, and Robin Dixon left the following July, and although several additional staff were taken on during 1970, they of course would take time to train. One of the new arrivals, another English graduate from St Peter's named Paul Davenport, was taken on in anticipation of the loss of Julian Barnes, who despite being regarded by Burchfield as the most promising of his younger assistants had indicated that he was dissatisfied with his position and had begun to apply for posts elsewhere; in fact Barnes—who was even offered the editorship of *COD*, a new edition of which was now recognized as needing to be set in motion—did not leave the project for another two years.[125]

Already by October Burchfield was ready to admit in public that even 1972 was now only 'hoped' to be the year when Volume I would be published.[126] The scale of the Supplement had also expanded again: by December it was being described as a 3,600-page work, to be issued in 'two, or perhaps three volumes', of which the first would appear 'toward the end of 1972'.[127] The situation was set out more fully in Burchfield's end-of-year progress report, in which he acknowledged that completion of A–J in time for publication in 1972 was no longer feasible, and recommended that the first volume cover the shorter—and manageable—range A–G, with the second and third volumes (covering H–P and Q–Z respectively) to follow as soon as possible therafter.

Some observers might have regarded such revisions to the scheduling and planned extent of the Supplement, so late in the day, as evidence of mismanagement; but there is nothing in the surviving record to suggest that at this stage anyone was seeking to criticize, let alone censure, Burchfield's management of the project. Indeed the work of 'the Oxford English Dictionaries' was specifically mentioned, in a document considering possible economies that might be made in OUP's publishing business, as being an enterprise 'on which much of the future prosperity of the Press may depend', and consequently an area which should not be subject to cutbacks, even at a time of widespread uncertainty and some apprehension about the state of the economy. It appears that the Delegates recognized the value, commercial and otherwise, of these major lexicographical projects—including the reset *Shorter*, which by the end of 1970 was also badly behind schedule—and accepted that, if such things were worth doing, they were worth doing properly; but they were perhaps beginning to find it difficult to hold their nerve.[128]

However, things did at last seem to be running, if not actually to schedule, then at least not so seriously behind it as to push a 1972 publication date for Volume I beyond

[125] OUPA(u) 4, 15 May 1970 RWB to DMD/J. L. Ashton. The editorship of *COD* (and *POD*) was subsequently offered to, and accepted by, a linguist and translator named Peter Stabler; however, he left after a few months, having only produced an expanded set of *COD* addenda (PBED 3965 9 June, 19 Nov. 1970 RWB to DMD).

[126] *Library of Congress Professional Association Newsletter* Oct. 1970, p. 3 (where Burchfield's comment, given in a lecture at the Library, is reported). This transatlantic trip was occasioned by an invitation to Burchfield to a conference at the University of Toronto, to take part in preliminary discussions about the proposed new *Dictionary of Old English*.

[127] *Oxford Times* 25 Dec. 1970, p. 5.

[128] GF19/101 25 Jan. 1971 [CHR] to Delegates.

the bounds of possibility. There was even time for Burchfield to attend a conference in Florence in May 1971—a grand 'Round Table Conference' of historical lexicographers, attended by representatives of other great European dictionary projects—at which he distilled some of his experiences of the preceding decade and a half into a short paper, 'Some aspects of the historical treatment of twentieth-century vocabulary',[129] some parts of which subsequently found their way into his Introduction to Volume I. Shortly after his return from Florence the last bundles of copy for G were sent to press. By this point the bulk of editorial effort was concentrated on proofreading, though some drafting of entries for what would now be Volume II continued (building on the work that had already been done on the now postponed range H–J).

July brought a notable observation from Burchfield's old friend Eric Stanley, who had been reading proofs since they first began to appear, and who in 1963 had queried the practice of dropping some of the quotations from the 1933 Supplement. He now noticed that, in addition to quotations, complete entries were now occasionally being omitted. It is not clear how long this had been going on—the omitted entries begin with *abactinally*, on the very first page of the 1933 text—but the reason seems to have been that Burchfield had come to the conclusion that some of the 1933 items were of such marginal significance that he could not afford to allow them to take up space, or editorial effort, which he would rather bestow on some of the innumerable other items clamouring to be included; 'I cannot believe', he insisted, 'that any user of the new Supplement will regret their absence—all very trivial items.'[130]

One other publication schedule which had slipped slightly was that for the *Compact OED*. It had been planned to issue this in the spring of 1971, but various difficulties led to it being rescheduled to October. Some of the problems related to production— not so much of the book itself as of the accompanying magnifying glass and box— but there had also been protracted and sometimes rather bad-tempered negotiations with Albert Boni, who was fiercely proprietorial about what he understandably felt to have been his idea. Eventually matters were settled, if not amicably then at least without resort to legal action; although the strikingly prominent acknowledgement of OUP's indebtedness to Boni 'for the suggestion of this latest edition', and of his having

---

[129] Burchfield (1973a).

[130] OED/C/2/5/84 21 July 1971 E. G. Stanley to RWB, 23 July 1971 RWB to Stanley. The omitted items do indeed seem on the whole to have been trivial, to the extent that their absence passed unnoticed by most reviewers of all volumes of the Supplement (Meier 1979 is a rare exception). Ogilvie (2012) provided the first detailed analysis of any of these omissions, looking specifically at loanwords and World Englishes; by the time this critique appeared, however, it had already been decided that all such omissions would be reinstated in the preparation of *OED3* (see below, p. 557).

Preliminary findings from the gradual implementation of this policy of reinstatement tend to confirm that the vast majority of the items omitted were indeed marginal. Out of a sample of 40 reinstated items, taken from two short ranges in A and P (*abolitional* to *across* and *painterish* to *pantherishly*), 29 are now explicitly labelled (with *Obs.*, *rare*, or similar) to show restricted currency, and a further 8 items would almost certainly have been had they not been embedded within broader coverage of a lexical item (unpublished paper 'From "ingenious traps" to "editability": framing inclusion policy in the second Supplement to the *OED*', presented by the author at the DSNA meeting in Athens, Georgia, May 2013).

FIGURE 35   A page of the Compact edition of the *OED* (first edition).

'pioneered this method of publication', which eventually appeared on a separate page following the title page of the new book perhaps gives some indication that matters had not gone entirely smoothly.[131] The book (see Figure 35) proved to be a tremendous success, both in direct commercial terms—approximately 25,000 copies were sold in the first year, many through a highly successful deal with the Book of the Month

---

[131]   Correspondence relating to the *Compact* is preserved in PBED 12874-5.

Club,[132] and it continued to sell well thereafter—and, as anticipated, as a generator of advance publicity for both the Supplement (for which publication was now fixed for October 1972) and the new reset *Shorter*. It is also worth pointing out that the new format brought ownership of a complete copy of the Dictionary within reach of thousands of individuals who could never have afforded the full-size version.

The schedules for production of these important titles, however, remained highly vulnerable. February 1972 marked something of a crisis for the *Shorter*—now under Jessie Coulson's direction—when it was realized that work was not proceeding fast enough to ensure publication in 1973 as now planned. It was agreed that as soon as the proofs of Volume I were completed Burchfield would take back the *Shorter* fully into his own control, and several other members of the Supplement team would be reassigned to work on various aspects of the book, particularly its expanded Addenda, which were in danger of looking seriously out of date unless some extensive revision took place.[133] These moves, while not directly affecting the publication schedule for Volume I, were of course bound to hold back progress on Volume II.

Another illustration of the conflicting claims of different dictionary projects was the appointment of John Sykes to the editorship of both *COD* and *POD*, which took place in September 1971. This coincided with his becoming a full member of staff for the first time—previously his other work had only left him free for lexicography on Saturday mornings—but his new responsibilities meant that he was now less available for work on the Supplement. A few months after taking up this post he was also formally appointed to the position of 'Deputy Chief Editor' of the Oxford English Dictionaries.[134] (Burchfield had of course been recognized as being in overall charge of the other dictionaries for some years; it seems to have been only with the appointment of a Deputy that the title 'Chief Editor' became necessary.)

Finally, in April 1972, the last pages of Volume I were signed off for press. The completion of editorial work on the volume coincided with the beginnings of a crescendo of publicity for the long-anticipated work, with well over 100 copies sent out for review.[135] Unfortunately it also coincided with publicity of a more unwelcome kind. In late April an ongoing campaign by a Salford businessman, Marcus Shloimovitz, against the inclusion of what he regarded as defamatory definitions of *Jew* in various dictionaries was taken to a new level when he took out a writ against the Clarendon Press.[136] He eventually lost his case in the High Court in July 1973, but the action attracted a great deal of attention, with Burchfield at one point becoming one of the

---

[132] OED/C/4/2/1 22 Oct. 1972 RWB to DMD.

[133] PBED 12876 14 Feb. 1972 RWB to DMD.

[134] OUPA(u) (RWB papers) 27 May 1971 J. L. Ashton to J. B Sykes; OUP *Record* 16 (Dec. 1971), p. 6; OED/C/4/2/1 staff list for 'The Oxford English Dictionaries', dated May 1972 (listing Burchfield and Sykes as Chief Editor and Deputy Chief Editor respectively).

[135] Publicity correspondence and clippings in OED/C/5/4/10.

[136] *Guardian* 28 Apr. 1972, p. 7. An account of Shloimovitz's campaign, and some earlier protests—dating back to the 1920s—about dictionary definitions of *Jew*, is given in Burchfield (1978a).

few lexicographers ever to receive a death threat.[137] The matter had implications beyond Oxford: in June, while attending an international conference on English lexicography in New York, Burchfield sounded out other lexicographers about their response to 'the various pressure groups that plague the dictionary houses' (and was reassured: most expressed their determination to resist any pressure to remove such items from their dictionaries).[138] The trip to New York was useful in other respects, enabling him to brief OUP's New York sales conference about the Supplement; he repeated the briefing in Oxford a few weeks later.[139] OUP was evidently giving serious attention to what was bound to be a publishing event of exceptional significance; a special 'Supplement' postmark was even arranged for all of the Press's outgoing mail, with the publication date, 12 October, shown prominently. A demanding promotional itinerary was drawn up, taking Burchfield to America in time for their slightly later publication date in November, and continuing with a tour of the Far East. More domestically, two events were held at St Peter's College on publication day itself: a drinks party for the staff, senior Press figures, and various other helpers, followed by a formal dinner for a more select list of guests. Among those attending the celebrations was Henry Bradley's former assistant J. R. R. Tolkien, now a venerable Oxford figure, whose writings were quoted in Volume I for words from *barrow-wight* to *grass-clipping*, and whom Burchfield had already consulted about the definition of *hobbit* for what would now be Volume II.[140]

Sadly, some people who had been closely involved with the Supplement did not live to see its first instalment. One dramatic absence was that of Elizabeth Brommer, the longest-serving of the London team of library researchers, who had dropped dead from a heart attack in the British Museum reading room in May.[141] Some of the most important contributors of quotations, including St Vincent Troubridge and Roland Auty, had not lived long enough to see the fruits of their labours in print. Two older figures who will have been missed in very different ways were Kenneth Sisam and James Wyllie, who had both died in 1971, the latter in a traffic accident. Also absent, though still very much alive, was Julian Barnes, who had finally left the staff in April.[142] One indication that OUP was now experiencing straitened financial circumstances is given by the fact that a ban on new appointments was now in place; however, it proved possible to make good the loss of

---

[137] A photocopy of one such threatening letter, apparently sent from Chicago in July 1973, is preserved in OUPA(u) (RWB papers).

[138] OED/C/4/2/1 15 May 1972 [RWB] to DMD; OUPA(u) 13 June 1972 [RWB] to DMD/B. L. Philips.

[139] PBED 12873 12 June 1972 RWB to CHR/DMD; OED/C/4/2/1 notes by RWB for a talk given at the Oxford sales conference on 28 June 1972.

[140] ML/57 11 Sept. 1970 Tolkien to RWB.

[141] It was not long after Brommer's death that George Chowdharay-Best (1935–2000) began to do some freelance library research for Burchfield. He was to go on to become one of the Dictionary's most durable London researchers, working on into the 1990s, although he did not formally become a member of staff until 1984.

[142] One of Barnes's last assignments was to make recommendations regarding the fate of the main body of the collection of slips from which the first edition of the Dictionary had been compiled (OUPA(u) 25 May 1972 RWB to CHR (enclosing Barnes's report, which Roberts describes as 'admirable & convincing')). Thankfully for future historians, the slips were deposited in the Bodleian Library, where they remained until reclaimed by OUP in the 1990s.

Barnes—and of Anne Wallace-Hadrill, who also left in April—by transfers from elsewhere in the Press. Nor does the ban seem to have been applied with absolute consistency, as a new science editor, Andrew Buxton, was recruited externally in August.[143]

The publicity for Volume I was skilfully coordinated by Elizabeth Knight, with full cooperation from Burchfield, whom journalists soon found to be an enthusiastic and communicative interviewee. A press release[144] which Knight and Burchfield worked on together, and on which much of the newspaper coverage drew heavily, highlighted various features of the new book: the thoroughness with which the output of the twentieth century's greatest writers—including scientific luminaries such as Ernest Rutherford and Julian Huxley as well as literary figures like Yeats and Eugene O'Neill—had been gone through; the geographical spread of its vocabulary across the whole English-speaking world; the range of fields and subjects covered, from computing and space terminology to the slang of hippies and surfers; and, of course, its inclusion of the two notorious four-letter words. As with *body-line bowling* in 1933, Burchfield was keen to squeeze in some very late additions, including the verb *Doppler-shift* and the noun *float* in the topical sense 'an operation of floating a currency', for both of which his earliest evidence dated from 1971; and there were even several quotations from 1972, such as those for the verbs *garage* and *get back at*. The press release acknowledged the contribution made by the many external readers in amassing the million-and-a-half quotations so far collected; it also noted that the project had cost OUP over a third of a million pounds to date, and—still showing remarkable optimism—anticipated that two further volumes, bringing the Supplement to completion, would be published in 1975 and 1977 respectively.

Among those who were presented with a copy of Volume I ahead of publication was Marghanita Laski, whose contribution was fully and fittingly acknowledged in its introductory matter. She wrote to thank Burchfield both for the gift—on receipt of which she 'almost cried'—and for 'what has been now fourteen years of sheer delight', and predicted that the new Supplement would 'remain the standard by which future dictionaries are judged'.[145] The gratification felt by Burchfield at this typically warm and effusive letter, however, will have been considerably lessened by his prior knowledge of another letter which appeared in the *Times Literary Supplement* the day after publication, in which she remounted her old hobby-horse of calling for the revision of the Dictionary.[146] The timing might seem unfortunate in the extreme, though given Laski's involvement with the literary and journalistic world it is more likely that she deliberately chose her moment to give her point maximum impact. Her letter acclaimed the 'magnificent' Supplement, but placed it in stark contrast with the Dictionary itself, which while 'still—just—a working tool that is deservedly a world-famous glory of English culture', was, she argued, obsolete in so many respects that wholesale revision

---

[143] OUP *Record* 17 (Dec. 1972), p. 3.
[144] Copy preserved (together with a first draft by Knight) in OED/C/5/4/10.
[145] OED/C/2/5/45 7 Oct. 1972 Laski to RWB.
[146] PBED 17948 5 Oct. 1972 E. Knight to DMD (with annotation by RWB), giving advance warning of Laski's letter, which appeared in the *TLS* on 13 Oct. 1972 (p. 1226) under the heading 'Revising OED'.

FIGURE 36   Supplement staff at work in the quotations room at 40 Walton Crescent, July 1972: (left to right) Jelly Williams, Robert Burchfield, Michael Grose, Eric Dann, Tony Augarde.

was urgently needed, if it was not to become 'a magnificent fossil'. She acknowledged that the likely cost of such a revision might account for OUP's failure to undertake it, but now proposed the establishment of 'a publicly supported perpetual Trust', by which the revision of the Dictionary on a continuous basis could be undertaken.

Burchfield angrily drafted a response just before setting off on his international promotional tour. It was never printed, but it contents clearly show his irritation. 'It is a strange way', he wrote, 'to applaud an athlete by telling him one-third of the way through a long-distance event that he should brace himself for the marathon.'[147] The reference to a 'magnificent fossil' had evidently been particularly wounding; his retort was that the unrevised Dictionary 'has been purchased in its Compact form by some 25,000 individuals or institutions in the last twelve months or so. Some fossil!' He also pointed out the impossibility of committing the Press to the project of revising the Dictionary when other concerns—including not only the completion of the Supplement itself, but the projected historical dictionary of scientific terms and the long-delayed revision of the *Shorter*—showed every prospect of keeping all of the Press's lexicographical capacity fully occupied for many years to come. In fact this view of the medium-term future of Oxford's English dictionaries would prove to be wrong in several respects; and the thoughts of various figures at the Press, including even Burchfield himself, would turn to the subject of revision long before the Supplement was complete.

---

[147] OED/C/4/2/1 22 Oct. 1972 RWB with draft letter. In the event all that appeared in the *TLS* from Burchfield was a letter in the 27 October issue, responding not to Laski's letter but to another which had appeared in the 20 October issue on the subject of the treatment of four-letter words in earlier dictionaries. The latter issue had also carried a letter from Burchfield's fellow lexicographer A. J. Aitken, casting doubt on the chances of securing public funds for a project such as that proposed by Laski.

12

Second Supplement to Second Edition: 1972–1989

ALTHOUGH much of the period covered by this chapter, even more than its predecessor, might be referred to as 'the Burchfield years', such a description would seriously misrepresent the collective nature of the enterprise which the *OED* had now become. That being said, Burchfield's pre-eminent position can hardly be denied. He was, after all, in sole charge of the Dictionary, as no individual had been since Henry Bradley took up his position as the Dictionary's second Editor in 1888. This had of course been the case since 1957; but with the publication of Volume I of the Supplement Burchfield's profile seems to have grown, both inside and outside the Press. Internally he now presided as 'Chief Editor' over all of the other dictionaries being worked on in Walton Crescent, now including the *Concise* and the *Pocket* as well as the *Shorter*; and externally he was increasingly coming to be identified as the public face of 'Oxford Dictionaries'. Press coverage of Volume I of the Supplement did generally acknowledge the part played in its compilation by both the in-house staff and the network of readers; but it was Burchfield alone who in 1972 took on the role of international lexicographical ambassador for Oxford, with a round-the world trip which began with a press conference in New York on 1 November (the day before publication day in the US) and which over the next four weeks took him to Japan, Korea, and various other destinations in south-east Asia. His time in Japan—where he gave several lectures—made a particular impression on him, with 'a deputation of Japanese at hand at every turn', as he told Davin, 'bowing, complimenting, expressing admiration for the O.E.D., or Oxford, or whatever'.[1]

There was also admiring press coverage at every turn, both in America and in the Far East, which pleasingly complemented the steady flow of laudatory notices which had

---

[1] CPGE 227 17 Nov. 1972 RWB to DMD.

appeared in the British press since publication.[2] One of the very few critical voices was Kingsley Amis, who in a review in the *Observer* wondered whether the Supplement was in various ways 'fatter than it ought to be', criticizing in particular its generous treatment of proper names, while at the same time noting some significant omissions from the slang of both sex and 'the pot-and-pop scene'. His main complaint, however, was that too many infelicities of language had been included without critical comment; his review listed a rather odd selection of what he regarded as 'uncensured barbarities', including the linguistic term *disambiguate*, Gerard Manley Hopkins's coinage *elisionable*, and even the use of *fund* as a verb. A waspish letter from Burchfield, published the following week, in response to what he called Amis's 'whiff of grapeshot', sought to dismiss his 'lazily [...] aimed' shots, pointing out that dictionaries like the *OED* were 'not normative in the way Mr Amis would wish'; but the fact that he felt it necessary to repeat the dismissal at his New York press conference suggests that the criticism, like Marghanita Laski's comments about revising the Dictionary, still rankled.[3] It seemed that, like James Murray before him, he could sometimes overreact to adverse comment.

On his return to Oxford Burchfield was unable himself to return to work on the Supplement straight away, as there was still work to do on the new Addenda for the *Shorter*; but the initial drafting of entries had continued throughout 1972, and by the second week of the new year—when Burchfield could declare himself and his senior assistants free to resume work on Volume II—his junior staff were working in L and M. Fresh copy for the letter H began to flow to the printers again in March.[4] In fact a sizeable portion of H had been worked on up to galley proof stage between 1968 and 1970, reaching *Hollander* before the endpoint of Volume I was redrawn. Entries could of course be added to the text at the proof stage, and among those added in H were a number of Japanese words thrown up in the course of an investigation of likely sources which Burchfield had instigated in anticipation of his visit to Japan.[5]

After all, the Supplement's quotation files were very far from closed: quite apart from the continuing steady flow of new quotations from the project's regular readers, new areas of lexis which Burchfield felt had been insufficiently thoroughly trawled would continue to crop up from time to time, and the fruits of a programme of dedicated reading would be added to the files, often with a by-product in the form of an article—effectively a supplement to the Supplement—about the vocabulary in question. Some of these seem simply to have occurred to Burchfield by chance, like the Japanese

---

[2] Notices appeared, for example, in the *Times*, *Guardian*, and *Daily Telegraph* on publication day (12 October), and in the *New York Times* on the following day; others followed in the *Economist*, the *Sunday Telegraph*, and the *Sunday Times* during the next fortnight.

[3] *Observer* 15 Oct. 1972, p. 39, 22 Oct. 1972, p. 14; OUPA(u) (RWB papers) typed text of RWB's opening statement for the New York press conference.

[4] OED/C/4/2/2 9 Jan. 1973 RWB to [staff]; PBED 17949 20 Mar. 1973 RWB to T. Chester.

[5] Entries for *hakama*, *hanami*, *hanashika*, *haniwa*, and several other words in H were added in proof. A number of Japanese loanwords which had come to light too late to be included in Volume I were published in the form of *OED*-style entries in Burchfield and Smith (1973–4).

project, and another project examining the prosodic terminology of Anglo-Saxon scholars;[6] others look rather more like responses to particular criticisms of Volume I. For as time went on a few other critical voices joined Kingsley Amis's 'whiff of grapeshot', although overall the vast bulk of reviews continued to be favourable.

Another notable early critic was A. J. Aitken, whose mainly very positive review in the *Times Literary Supplement* showed a fellow lexicographer's understanding of the conflicting demands placed on Burchfield and his team, conceding that those few respects in which he had found Volume I to be 'short of perfection' were entirely understandable given that it had issued from 'a publishing house with limited resources and a staff of twenty or so—quite modest for such an enterprise'.[7] His specific criticisms with regard to coverage were that sources for 'the literary English of Black Africa, of the Caribbean, and, nearer home, of Scotland' had been inadequately scrutinized; he also mentioned a few slang terms which had been overlooked (including *acid* in the 'LSD' sense, which had also been mentioned by Amis). Burchfield's response to the criticisms about coverage can be seen in the appearance of new texts from the areas mentioned by Aitken among the quotations appearing in Volume II as eventually published: thus the Nigerian writer Chinua Achebe is first quoted at *iron horse*, and other quotations by him appear fairly regularly thereafter; quotations from novels by the Caribbean writers Samuel Selvon (*A Brighter Sun*) and Sylvia Wynter (*The Hills of Hebron*) begin to appear from H onwards, as do examples from Caribbean newspapers such as the *Trinidad & Tobago Express*; and works by the Scots Neil M. Gunn and George Mackay Brown begin to make their appearance.[8] Burchfield also sought to respond to the surge of interest in the English of black Americans by initiating fresh reading in this area,[9] resulting in the addition (sometimes in proof) of entries for items such as *heah* and *homeboy*. Another published response to criticism, supplying entries for some of the specific items in A–G whose absence had been noted in reviews (including *acid*, and also *Afro*, *Beeb*, *bovver*, and *Chomskyan*), appeared in a New Zealand journal.[10]

Even without these small augmentations of the Supplement's scope, it would surely have been difficult enough to maintain the lexicographical throughput required to finish another volume by 1975; and within months the rate of progress was again giving cause for concern. In particular the project's team of scientists was finding it hard to keep working ahead of

---

[6] Work on this project, resulting in a contribution to a Festschrift for the Old English scholar John Pope (Burchfield 1974b)—again in the form of a collection of *OED*-style entries—seems to have begun before the publication of Volume I, although corresponding entries only began to be added to the Supplement (initially once again in proof) in Volume II, beginning with *half* (a half-line of verse) and various *half*-compounds.

[7] Aitken (1973).

[8] Caribbean and Scottish vocabulary were both specifically mentioned by Burchfield in his Preface to Volume II of the Supplement as having received 'somewhat more attention' than hitherto.

[9] OED/C/2/5/4 7 May 1973 [RWB] to C. L. Barnhart.

[10] Burchfield (1974a). Most, though not all, of the items noted in this article were subsequently added to *OED2* in 1989.

Burchfield's own editing[11]—something that was to be a recurring problem—and there was also a shortfall of bibliographical effort (the project's bibliographer, Michael Grose, left at the end of 1972, to be replaced two months later). As early as March Burchfield was having to ask some of his scientists to consider working overtime;[12] and by early September it was impossible to avoid the conclusion that Volume II would not be ready for publication by 1975. It is interesting to see how 'joined-up' OUP's forward dictionary publication schedule had now become: it was recognized that, if there was to be no Supplement volume published in 1975, some other new Oxford dictionary would have to be identified that could be published during the year instead, thereby helping to maintain OUP's profile. (For 1973 there was the new *Shorter*, which was at last now ready; though not a full revision, it could boast fully revised etymologies throughout, and a much expanded set of Addenda, and was published in October. For 1974 there was Joan Pusey's new edition of the *Oxford School Dictionary*, which was on schedule.) The *Oxford Children's Dictionary* was pencilled in as a rather inadequate replacement for the Supplement, and the publication date for Volume II was allowed to slip to 1976.[13]

Within weeks the feasibility of even this target was beginning to look doubtful, and Burchfield carried out a major reorganization of working practices, with clearer

---

insinuendo

Burchfield admitted to Marghanita Laski in 1977 that he had 'found [himself] not believing in an unqualified descriptivism as 1976 proceeded' (OED/C/2/5/46 18 Feb. 1977 [RWB] to Laski); he assured her of his intention to 'continue to make value judgements in the dictionary on all kinds of matters, and we'll see what happens'. Indeed, a number of entries in the second, third, and fourth volumes of the Supplement contain observations by Burchfield—signed 'Ed.'—which clearly fall into this category, from *insinuendo* (described as 'A tasteless word') to *supportive* ('An unnecessary formation, since the shorter *supportive* is completely established'). He acknowledged this change of approach in the preface to Volume III, where he comments (pp. v–vi) that 'here and there in the present volume I have found myself adding my own opinions about the acceptability of certain words or meanings in educated use'. In fact such expressions of opinion can be traced back before 1976: the comment about *insinuendo* is present in a bundle of copy which went to

Continued ➤

---

[11] In fact the scientists started work on Volume II at an additional disadvantage: their drafting of entries in H in 1968 and 1969 had been slowed by the requirement to spend part of their time reviewing and revising some of the scientific entries from the first half of Volume I which had been written by non-scientists (OUPA(u) (RWB papers) 18 Apr. 1974 Alan Hughes to [RWB]).

[12] I am grateful to Alan Hughes for supplying this and many other details from the notes made in his work diary. Elizabeth Burchfield has also kindly made available to me her husband's work diaries from the 1970s and 1980s.

[13] OUPA(u) (RWB papers) file note by RWB 6 Sept. 1973. In the event the *Children's Dictionary* did not appear until 1976; instead, 1975 saw the publication of a well-reviewed new edition of the *Oxford Illustrated Dictionary*.

the printers in September 1973. Evidence of prescriptivism in the *OED* can of course be traced back long before this: the views of Murray and his fellow Editors regarding notions of 'correctness' in language are reflected in their frequent use of labels such as 'erron[eous]', and of the paragraph symbol (¶) to mark 'Catachrestic and erroneous uses, confusions, and the like' (Murray 1884: xi). Similarly, the comment 'Now regarded as incorrect' appears in various entries, for example at the use of the verb *substitute* to mean 'replace', although this is arguably simply a statement of what was believed to be prevailing opinion, with no intended editorial endorsement. There are also more nuanced comments such as 'commonly avoided by good writers' (for the use of *female* to mean 'woman'), where the reference to 'good writers' may reflect the widely accepted contemporary view that 'good' writing (as found, for example, in the work of prestigious authors) was something that could readily be distinguished from bad or merely average writing (as found in popular fiction, newspapers, and the like); in this context such a comment may be simply an observation drawn from the available quotation evidence, assessed with reference to this distinction. All of these aspects of editorial practice were continued by Burchfield, who, for example, described the use of *agenda* as a singular as 'now increasingly found but avoided by careful writers', and marked the similar use of *data* with the paragraph symbol. His readiness to declare his own personal opinion on what are essentially matters of taste, however, marks a new departure, and arguably places him in conflict with his predecessors; Herbert Coleridge, after all, had asserted over a century earlier that 'the mere merit of a word in an artistic or æsthetic point of view is a consideration, which the Lexicographer cannot for a moment entertain'. It is also worth pointing out that both Burchfield and his predecessors were the recipients of widely varying advice, from reviewers and correspondents of all kinds, about the degree of prescriptivism that was considered appropriate in the Dictionary. (For a fuller discussion of the prescriptivist–descriptivist spectrum as reflected in the *OED* during its history, see Brewer (2010).)

demarcation between the drafting of entries and research in Oxford's libraries.[14] (During the course of work on Volume I staff had been allowed to do some of their own library research—checking quotations, antedating, and the like—and had even been granted access to some of the Bodleian's bookstacks; under the new dispensation, while scientists continued to do this, other drafters were now expected to commission much or all of their research from others rather than doing it themselves.) Problems with throughput of science material persisted, however, perhaps unsurprisingly given that the available manpower remained unchanged.

Such matters were, of course, not discussed publicly; but there were also battles to be fought on more public fronts. Marcus Shloimovitz eventually lost his action against the Clarendon Press over the word *Jew* in July 1973, but the case received a steady flow

---

[14] OED/C/4/2/2 6 Nov. 1973 RWB to staff.

of press coverage, with occasional flare-ups. One of these resulted from an ill-judged barb aimed at David Guralnik, editor-in-chief of the Webster *New World* series of dictionaries, in the course of a paper which Burchfield had been invited to give to the Philological Society in June. In his wide-ranging paper, entitled 'The Treatment of Controversial Vocabulary in *The Oxford English Dictionary*', Burchfield examined various categories of vocabulary which lay 'on or near the admission/exclusion boundary' in the *OED* and its Supplements, including racially and religiously sensitive terms. His observations about this category included extracts from the material he was proposing to include in his update to the entries for *Jew* and related words; more provocatively, he criticized Guralnik's exclusion of some words of this type from a 1970 edition of one of his dictionaries, decrying his approach as 'Guralnikism, the racial equivalent of Bowdlerism'.[15] It would have been easy enough to justify his own descriptivist approach without making such an *ad hominem* attack, which unsurprisingly provoked Guralnik into a vigorous defence of his approach, and no doubt lost Burchfield other friends.[16] Fortunately there were other more straightforward opportunities for publicity, such as the National Scrabble Championships, at which Burchfield was invited to be a judge, and another competition run by Mars (the confectioners) in which *COD* was the nominated dictionary authority.[17] John Sykes could also attract publicity—coverage of his successful defence of his title in the *Times* crossword competition highlighted the fact that he was an Oxford lexicographer—but Burchfield was distinctly unenthusiastic about letting his Deputy Chief Editor do too much formal publicity work, and in fact asked him not to accept invitations to give public talks on his lexicographical work, following one given in London in May, apparently regarding him as dangerously naïve about such matters.[18]

The spring of 1974, with all the continuing preoccupations of work on the Supplement and the challenges of keeping to the schedule for Volume II, might seem a strange time to be thinking about how to go about the much bigger task of revising the *OED* itself; but the question of revision was very much on Burchfield's mind. He had been invited to give a public lecture at the University of London's Senate House in March, and various topics had been suggested, including—an idea of Davin's—'problems involved in revising O.E.D.'[19] There will have been more to this suggestion than a desire to respond more fully to Marghanita Laski's 'magnificent fossil' remarks. Other commentators on the new Supplement had seen fit to draw attention to the need for extensive revision of the

---

[15] Burchfield (1973b: 1, 22). The paper, which was delivered in early June 1973, made no explicit reference to the ongoing lawsuit, but inevitably press reports of it made the connection.

[16] Letter in *New York Times* 21 June 1973, p. 40. This is a shorter version of the letter which Guralnik submitted to the London *Times*, in response to a report of Burchfield's Philological Society paper which had appeared in the *Sunday Times* on 10 June; extracts from the longer letter, which also criticizes Burchfield's treatment of *dago* in Volume I as inadequately labelled for offensiveness, are quoted in Guralnik (1974).

[17] OUP *Record* 18 (Dec. 1973), p. 3.

[18] OUPA(u) (RWB papers) 16 May 1973 RWB to DMD.

[19] OUPA(u) (RWB papers) file note by RWB 6 Sept. 1973.

main *OED* text, such as the writer in the *Yale Review* who had expressed regret at the exclusion of early antedatings, and the absence of corrections to *OED*'s etymologies; and in January 1974 another decision regarding one particular aspect of revision was criticized in *Notes & Queries*, in a review of Volume I by the distinguished linguist Barbara Strang. Although Strang began and ended her review in thoroughly laudatory terms, she contrived in between to make a number of serious and carefully argued criticisms, of which the first concerned the decision to regard pre-1820 antedatings as out of scope.[20] Such comments effectively questioned some of the decisions taken regarding the boundary between supplementation and revision, and the March lecture provided an opportunity to review these. Ultimately Burchfield chose a more general title, 'The O.E.D. in 1974', and dealt with several other topics besides revision, including the work that had been undertaken to improve coverage of Black English and a detailed account of the process of selecting items for inclusion in the Supplement; but the subject of revision featured prominently. Burchfield had apparently even gone so far as to begin collecting the material that might be needed for the revision of at least one sample entry; but his conclusion was that any thoughts of full-scale revision simply had to be set aside as impracticable, or at least not to be seriously contemplated until work on various other dictionaries, on which such revision would heavily depend— principally the period and regional dictionaries envisaged by Craigie in 1919—had progressed.[21] Marghanita Laski, who attended the lecture, was so convinced by his arguments that she even offered to issue a public retraction of her call for revision of the Dictionary (an offer which was politely declined).[22] Burchfield could hardly hope to silence rumblings about revision entirely, but his lecture does seem to have kicked the issue into the long grass.

After all, the Supplement provided quite enough work to be going on with; and by April 1974, when Burchfield conducted a formal review of progress, it was clear that

[20] Robinson (1973); Strang (1974). It is not clear when Burchfield took the decision to exclude pre-1820 antedatings, which he justified (Introduction to Vol. I, p. xv) on the grounds that 'the systematic collection of such antedatings could not be undertaken at the present time'. The 1933 Supplement had in fact given a large number of antedatings in this category, but almost all of them were of American usages, for full coverage of which it could be argued—not entirely convincingly—that the reader could or should consult the *Dictionary of American English* (cf. p. 474).

Strang's other main criticism focused on what she argued was the Supplement's inadequate coverage of the technical vocabulary of non-scientific subjects; the review includes extensive notes on a number of words which had been omitted from Volume I (or on which more information could have been given), taken mainly from the field of horsemanship but also from pottery, linguistics, and general colloquial usage. She also expressed regret at Burchfield's declared decision (Introduction to Vol. I, p. xiv) to shift from the 'total literary inclusiveness' of the first edition to a policy of only 'liberally representing' the vocabulary of distinguished authors.

[21] Notes and an incomplete text for Burchfield's lecture survive in OUPA(u) (RWB papers), together with a letter from Richard Bailey of the *Middle English Dictionary* responding to a request from Burchfield for any material in the *MED* files that might be relevant to a revision of the entry for the word *actional* (19 Feb. 1974 Bailey to RWB). The lecture remained unpublished, though a revised version of the section dealing with approaches to revising the Dictionary did eventually appear (Burchfield 1977a), as did a version of the discussion of inclusion policy (Burchfield 1975: 355–6).

[22] OED/C/2/5/45 29 Mar. 1974 Laski to RWB, 5 Apr. 1974 [RWB] to Laski.

something would have to be done about the mismatch between the capacity of the main body of editorial staff—now mainly working in O—and the team of scientists, who were still labouring in L. Publication before the end of 1976, which seems by now to have become an immoveable target, necessitated the drawing up of a tough schedule: not a new schedule, apparently, but—remarkably—the first formal forward schedule for Volume II to be issued to the staff. The scientists protested, not unreasonably, that this schedule placed excessive demands on them, in that they were now to be required to progress through the alphabet at something like three times the rate they had achieved in the previous year.[23] Scientists were encouraged to delegate more of their research to library workers, but it was obvious that what was really needed was additional staff; unfortunately a ban on new appointments seems to have been in operation at OUP, on account of the continuing difficult economic conditions. (Vacancies caused by staff leaving could still be filled; this was just as well, as two members of staff left in April.) Efforts to make some kind of informal arrangement with a recent Oxford chemistry graduate (who had done some vacation work on the Supplement as an undergraduate) came to nothing. The retirement, at the age of 80, of the part-time science editor Leopold Firnberg might have been expected to exacerbate the situation; but following the appointment of a (numerical) replacement in the form of a new science library researcher, Claire Nicholls, and increased quantities of overtime, science scheduling difficulties ceased to be a major concern, for the time being at least.[24]

By the end of November—when Burchfield's preparation of copy for press had reached the end of L—it had become apparent that, such was the volume of material being produced, a volume covering the whole of H–P was likely to be unfeasibly large. From the point of view of getting Volume II out on schedule this was actually good news, in that if the endpoint of the volume was brought back to somewhere in the middle of P, this would reduce the amount of work left to do, at every stage, and keep publication in 1976 within the bounds of possibility. There were obvious implications in terms of the work outstanding thereafter, but such was the importance of keeping to the 1976 target that approval for this change was quickly secured, with *Ph* pencilled in as the new starting point for Volume III: a point which, pleasingly, some drafters—though not the scientists—had already reached by the end of the year.[25]

1974 was also notable for the arrival as assistants on the Supplement of Robert Allen and Lesley Burnett, who would both become important figures in Oxford lexicography. Within only a few months of their appointment—in May and August respectively—plans were being made for them to be released from preparing the first drafts of entries in order to assist Burchfield with the editing of the remaining material for Volume II. This may have been a matter of necessity, as Burchfield realized that he was going to

[23] PBED 17949 16 Apr. 1974 RWB to Supplement staff; OUPA(u) (RWB papers) 18 Apr. 1974 A. Hughes to [RWB].
[24] OUPA(u) (RWB papers) 10 June 1974 A. Hughes to RWB; PBED 17949 2 Dec. 1974 RWB to DMD; OED/C/4/2/2 3 Jan. 1975 RWB to Supplement staff.
[25] PBED 17949 2 Dec. 1974 RWB to DMD.

need to delegate tasks in order to have sufficient time for editing and proof correction; but it was certainly true that a strong team of lexicographers was building up in Walton Crescent. Of course, in addition to the promising newcomers, there were more senior figures like Augarde and Sykes, both of whom had deputized to some extent for Burchfield during the summer of 1974, when he disappeared for another round-the-world tour, giving lectures or visiting OUP branches in the southern United States, New Zealand, Australia, Indonesia, and South Africa. Curiously, although Sykes was Burchfield's formal deputy during this six-week period, he was told to refer media enquiries to other Press figures rather than dealing with them himself: it seems he was still regarded as not to be trusted with such matters.[26]

1975 began with a most welcome boost on the PR front, with the announcement in the New Year Honours List that Burchfield had been made a CBE. At his investiture in February he secured the Queen's approval of the idea that the Supplement should be dedicated to her, as the first edition of the Dictionary had been dedicated to her great-great-grandmother.[27] Two other prestigious events followed for him in February: dinner at 10 Downing Street with the Prime Minister of New Zealand, and a paper given by invitation at the Royal Society of Arts, following which he was made a Fellow of the Society.[28] Two months later he was able once again to indulge what seems to have become a taste for international lecturing, with a paper given at the University of Münster.[29] There were also radio talks and a steady stream of newspaper mentions of the Supplement or its Editor or both, and in the autumn TV cameras even descended upon the lexicographers in Oxford, for a programme for schools entitled 'The Unknown Best-Seller'.[30]

Behind this flourishing public image there were difficulties back in Walton Crescent; and now it was Burchfield himself who was struggling to keep up. Unable to complete printer's copy at the rate needed by the schedule, he was obliged to move the endpoint of Volume II again, first to the end of O, then to the end of N.[31] The alternative, of allowing the publication date to slip back to 1977, was considered but rejected, although it would now have been less awkward for the Press were this to happen, with three other dictionary titles scheduled for publication in 1976, including John Sykes's new *Concise*. Even with this shorter alphabetical span, such was the volume of material being produced that there was no danger of the volume being too short; in fact the

---

[26] OUPA(u) (RWB papers) 7 June 1974 [RWB] to DMD. In other respects, however, Burchfield was happy for Sykes to deputize for him: later that year he began to spend Tuesday and Thursday mornings at St Peter's—in order to do the teaching which he had previously squeezed in between work and dinner—and arranged for Sykes to be 'in charge' during his absence from the office (OUPA(u) (RWB papers) 26 Oct. 1974 RWB to DMD).

[27] OED/C/4/2/2 [12 Feb. 1975] [RWB] to DMD. It was only with the appearance of Volume II, with a special page announcing it, that the dedication became public knowledge.

[28] OED/C/2/5/84 19 Feb. 1975 [RWB] to E. Stanley; Burchfield (1975).

[29] The Münster paper is preserved in OUPA(u) (RWB papers); it includes a section entitled 'Impossibility of revising the *O.E.D.*', based on part of his London University lecture of 1974.

[30] Correspondence about the programme, which was broadcast in June 1976, is in OUPA(u).

[31] PBED 17949 16 Apr. 1975 RWB to T. Chester; OED/C/4/2/2 22 May 1975 DMD to RWB et al.

entries in Volume II as eventually published run to 1,282 pages, less than 50 pages shorter than Volume I. Interestingly, the number of lexical items covered in Volume II is significantly down: approximately 35,000, as against nearly 46,000 in Volume I.[32] Individual entries were, it seems, being allowed to become longer, mainly through the inclusion of a more generous selection of quotations. It is true that some of the entries in Volume I had been rather thinly illustrated, for the same reason as for the earliest sections of the first edition, namely lack of available quotations, but the risks—in terms of pressure on space—of going too far in the opposite direction should have been clear.

In October a temporary halt was called to drafting—now well into *Pr*—so that effort could be concentrated on proofreading.[33] In fact the available effort had diminished alarmingly: four members of the Supplement staff left in as many months. This was a source of some frustration to Burchfield, who complained that '[t]he soaring unemployment figures might lead one to expect that staff movements would be minimal';[34] but it is some measure of the importance ascribed to the Dictionary Department by OUP that, even in what was another exceptionally difficult year economically, six new appointments were made to the Supplement's staff (one of whom, Joan Pusey, fresh from editing the *Oxford School Dictionary*, was admittedly hardly a newcomer).

During the early part of 1976 newcomers and old hands alike—the former further augmented by another new recruit, Edith Rogerson, in January—were kept busy reading proofs for Volume II, the last of which were signed off in early May.[35] The publicity machine swung smoothly into operation in preparation for publication, now set for 4 November. This time the new Supplement volume had to compete for attention with the new *Concise*, published in July, which generated its own storm of (overwhelmingly positive) publicity, with John Sykes at its centre, whose crossword-solving prowess sometimes seemed to interest his interviewers as much as his lexicographical skill.[36] In fact the appetite of the media for material about dictionaries was by no means exhausted by the extensive coverage of *COD*, and Volume II received a healthy crop of favourable reviews, and much other positive publicity besides. Even the Queen was pleased: a letter acknowledging receipt of specially bound copies of Volumes I and II records her pleasure at possessing 'the first half of your record of the English language in the twentieth century'.[37] (Burchfield himself had another reason

---

[32] Counting 'items' in dictionaries is notoriously difficult. Volumes I and II contain (according to figures given in their prefatory matter) 17–18,000 and 13,000 entries respectively, but as each sense and compound of a headword constitutes a separate piece of lexicographical work, with its own paragraph of quotations, my figures for 'lexical items' are arrived at by adding those given for senses and compounds (or 'combinations').

[33] OED/C/4/6/3 log of bundles handed out to drafters, 1974–83.

[34] OUP *Record* 20 (Dec. 1975), p. 5.

[35] OUPA(u) (RWB papers) notebook recording progress of Volume II, 1973–6.

[36] Among the many interviews with Sykes which mentioned both areas of expertise was one with the impressively contrived title 'A British Concise Dictionary Editor, Finding Good Hunting In Judiciously Knowing Lexicography, Muses Nightly Over Puzzle Questions, Revealing Sensitivity To Uncommon Verbally Wayward Xenogamy, Yielding Zymosis' (*New York Times* 7 Sept. 1976, p. 35).

[37] OED/C/5/4/10 photocopy of letter 1 Nov. 1976 Martin Charteris (Buckingham Palace) to GBR.

to celebrate: on the day after publication he and Elizabeth Knight, assiduous promoter of all of Oxford's dictionaries, were married in London, his first marriage having ended in divorce earlier in the year.)

Of course two volumes should have constituted two-thirds, not a half, of the completed Supplement; but the implications of the shortened alphabetic span of Volume II now had to be acknowledged. Quite when the need for four volumes was first formally recognized is not clear, but it was referred to publicly at least as early as June 1976.[38] The press release for Volume II[39] declared that Volumes III and IV were expected to appear in 1979 and 1982 respectively; this bespoke exceptional optimism, given that drafting had only just started on the letter R and that Burchfield's own preparation of copy for the printer was a long way from finishing O. The optimism is even more remarkable when it is borne in mind that since July Burchfield had taken on yet another responsibility: in addition to English dictionaries, he was now to be responsible for the planning of the Press's growing family of bilingual dictionaries.[40] He—or rather the Supplement—had also lost his most experienced colleague, Tony Augarde, who moved over to work with John Sykes on the *Pocket* and the other smaller dictionaries. Admittedly there was one new and promising assistant in the shape of John Simpson, an English graduate from York University who had joined the project in August after completing an MA at Reading, but new staff generally took some months to get up to speed. At least he could still rely on Alan Hughes and Sandra Raphael to bring the science and natural history entries to a point where he needed to do little or no further work on them; in fact he had taken a fairly 'hands-off' approach to the editing of this material for some time. He could also ill afford to spend time training new staff; for this, fortunately, he could rely on Allen and Burnett, who seem to have taken a more systematic approach to the task than hitherto (though there was, as there always has been, a substantial degree of 'learning on the job').[41]

He had also begun to rely on the same two lexicographers to re-edit the entries drafted by colleagues, so that when the copy reached him for final editing it was in a highly polished state, enabling him to work through it relatively quickly. In fact the re-editing—sometimes involving making only minor changes, sometimes closer to redrafting from scratch—was soon producing material of such consistently good quality that often only the lightest of editorial touches was required from Burchfield himself. Allen and Burnett also took on the task of sorting the quotation files, identifying material to be distributed to staff for drafting. The system for generating the text of the Supplement was thus becoming less centralized than it had been in the

[38] Davie (1976).

[39] A copy is preserved in OED/C/5/4/14.

[40] Oxford Dictionaries staff newsletter (hereafter 'Dictionaries newsletter') 6 Sept. 1976. The first of these internal newsletters, originally intended as a means of keeping far-flung members of Dictionary staff in touch with the main group at Walton Crescent, appeared in July 1976; they continued until 1984 (copies in OUPA(u)).

[41] A set of 'drafting notes' prepared by Allen in December 1975, evidently for training purposes, survives in OUPA at OED/C/4/1/6, along with some guidelines dating from a few years earlier.

early days of Volume I:[42] a change which reflects the size and strength of the team with which Burchfield now found himself surrounded, even if it was partly driven by his need to free up time for other work.

Perhaps surprisingly, the Supplement's editorial policy was still subject to reconsideration and modification even as the editing of the second half of the text began. Of course modifications could constantly be made to the range of vocabulary covered by feeding material from what were felt to be neglected areas into the ongoing reading programme, and this continued to happen—sometimes on what seemed to some of Burchfield's colleagues to be a rather haphazard and reactive basis. For example, the fact that quotations from various South Carolina newspapers began to appear in Volume II is due to Burchfield's having picked some up while lecturing there in 1974; and after he developed an interest in the slang of Citizens' Band radio and the terminology of the oil industry, items from both fields began to appear with unprecedented frequency in Volume III.[43] However, notwithstanding such new forays into remoter lexical regions, Burchfield had come to the conclusion that there was now 'a danger that the proliferating English of the periphery may obscure the descriptive picture of the centre of the language'—and that it was, after all, in British English that this centre could be most clearly discerned. With a view to redirecting some effort towards what he chose to call 'Core British English', he commissioned Allen and Burnett to organize reading that would enrich the quotation files in various domains within this 'core'.[44] This particular initiative does not seem to have led to anything; but the consignment of non-British varieties of English to a 'periphery' may surprise some who have read of Burchfield's enthusiastic championing of the geographical diversity of English. In fact his continuing interest in recording non-British regional varieties, as well as being reflected in the pages of the Supplement, is evident in his involvement in the planning of various new regional historical dictionaries; among these was a projected dictionary of Australian English, for which he flew to Australia in December 1976 to give advice during the early planning stages.[45]

---

[42] The Introduction to Volume I (pp. xvi–xvii) gives an account of the earlier interaction of editorial processes, up to the delivery of copy to the printer; Burchfield is shown as solely responsible both for preliminary sorting of the quotation files—the stage at which suitable items were selected for inclusion—and for final editing, although he had experimented with delegating the former to Tony Augarde as early as 1965 (OED/C/4/2/1 30 Sept. 1965 RWB to Hawkins and Augarde). Work on proofs had of course been a shared task from an early stage.

[43] In April 1976 Burchfield was disconcerted by being asked about CB radio—of which he knew nothing—while lecturing in the States (Davie 1976). Oil terminology was thrust into British consciousness during the 1970s by the burgeoning North Sea oil industry; Burchfield visited a land-based oil rig in Wiltshire in 1975, and instituted an extensive reading programme for the subject at the same time, resulting in another article containing *OED*-style entries (Burchfield 1977b), of which only those in the range O–Z were included in the Supplement.

[44] *Times* 3 Nov. 1976, p. 5 (quoting RWB); OED/C/4/2/3 22 Nov. 1976 RWB to REA/LSB.

[45] Burchfield had been corresponding regularly with many of the key figures in Australian lexicography, including some of the prime movers of the *Australian National Dictionary*, since the late 1950s. For more on the history of this dictionary see Ramson (2002), ANDC (2013) (which includes a reminiscence by John Simpson about his own contribution to the *AND*), and Laugesen (2014).

Burchfield's distaste for the 'non-central' tendencies of American English was made startlingly clear in a radio talk which he recorded shortly before departing for Australia. He had been asked by the BBC to review a recently issued British printing of *Webster's New International Dictionary*; having explained that this was not, as the BBC had thought, a new edition, he agreed instead to speak more generally about the place held by this dictionary in modern lexicography, notwithstanding its stormy reception. In this talk, which was to be entitled 'That Other Great Dictionary', Burchfield argued that the opprobrium heaped upon Webster's Third was undeserved, in that the real problem lay with 'the meretricious tendencies in American English itself', which the dictionary's compilers had simply described as they found it: he regarded the American language of the mid-twentieth century as having entered 'a much more strident stage, marked by brash innovation of vocabulary at various levels of society, by an abandonment in many quarters of any concept of well-formedness for words and sentences, by an invasion of the central area of traditional American English by the language of the technologists, by the syrupy double-talk of politicians and strategists, and by the unacceptable or non-standard grammar of the speech of certain ethnic minorities'. These developments, he claimed, threatened to make American English 'an increasingly unappealing model for people at a distance'.[46] Ironically in view of subsequent events, Burchfield praised the dictionary itself for its 'meticulous scholarship' and confined his actual criticisms of it—which he had set out at much greater length in a review published over a decade earlier[47]—to a small section of his talk. He was somewhat taken aback to be informed by the BBC that they had changed the advertised title of the talk to 'An Enemy of Good Language?', a title which arguably rather missed its point and which he feared might cause offence.[48] Pleas to revert to the old title were unavailing, and Burchfield's fears were realized: on his return to Oxford in January 1977 he found a furious letter from William Llewellyn, the president of G. & C. Merriam, who had not heard the talk but had been informed (incorrectly) that Burchfield's 'general distaste for American English' had led him to review the dictionary unfavourably. Llewellyn's response—unchanged even after several exchanges of letters with Burchfield (in which it is admittedly all too easy to discern two strong personalities both refusing to make concessions)—was to withdraw from the collaborative relationship between the two dictionary projects that had obtained since 1968, whereby batches of words to be included in the Supplement were checked in the Merriam-Webster files for antedatings and other useful evidence.[49] Burchfield later described this as 'a grievous blow',[50] and the loss of access to these files

---

[46] Quotations taken from the published version of the talk in Burchfield (1977c).
[47] See p. 470 n. 75.
[48] OUPA(u) (RWB papers) 3 Dec. 1976 P. Rogers (BBC) to RWB.
[49] The correspondence is preserved in OUPA(u). As a postscript to this episode it may be mentioned that in 1986 an attempt to re-establish the collaborative relationship was made by Tim Benbow, who visited the Merriam-Webster offices, but without success (OUPA(u) 29 Apr. 1986 TJB to RDPC/RWB/JAS/ESCW).
[50] Preface to Volume III of the Supplement, p. vi.

must unquestionably have made the task of establishing reliable first dates for items of American English, and some others, significantly more difficult.[51]

Burchfield's observations about American English were, of course, not the first of his publicly expressed opinions to have unfortunate consequences. It does seem, however, that he was becoming increasingly ready to write and speak, not only about the *OED* and its Supplement, but also about other language-related matters. Indeed it could be argued that by 1976 he had become a more widely heard and published commentator than any of the *OED*'s previous Editors, with a steady stream of public lectures, radio broadcasts, journal articles, and reviews. His close relationship with— and now marriage to—one of OUP's most experienced and effective publicists may help to account for this burgeoning public profile. It is tempting to suppose that he had begun to take rather too seriously the title of 'custodian of the English language' which his colleague at St Peter's, Francis Warner, had taken to using when introducing him to guests;[52] there may also simply have been an increasing public appetite for authoritative comment of the kind that Burchfield was able (and willing) to supply.

It is also possible to discern a reluctance on his part to leave any criticism of the Dictionary or the Supplement unchallenged. A case in point, and a glimpse of another apparent policy shift and what may have caused it, is provided by Burchfield's review of Raymond Williams's influential book *Keywords*, which appeared early in 1976.[53] Burchfield was evidently irritated both by the book—which discusses the history and cultural significance of some 110 words—and by some of the comments made by its reviewers, including Philip Toynbee's assertion that the *OED*'s compilers 'were signally out of touch with demotic usage'; his own review suggested that Williams's selection of words had been ideologically driven, and dismissed his treatment of them as 'obviously derivative', with little or nothing to add to what is said in the *OED*. However, he also declared that, as a response to Williams's 'timely reminder', the remaining two volumes of the Supplement would include, 'in addition to the new senses [of words], fully updated entries for social, cultural, and political words' of the kind considered in *Keywords*. In fact replacement definitions had occasionally featured in the Supplement from the beginning—as, indeed, they had in its 1933 predecessor—mainly as a means of correcting errors; but to embark on this kind of updating of culturally significant words on a large scale would be a significant shift towards exactly the kind of full revision which had always

---

[51] During 1977 Burchfield organized some extensive reading of American sources, no doubt with a view to at least partly ameliorating the effects of the loss of access to the Webster material (OED/C/2/5/46 20 Jan. 1978 [RWB] to M. Laski). He was also fortunate in having received a gift from Atcheson Hench of more material from his extensive files of American newspaper quotations, although delivery problems meant that many of the slips failed to reach the files in Oxford in time to be utilized in the relevant entries (correspondence in OED/C/2/5/86,87). Deficiencies in the range of American sources read for the Supplement were later commented on by Spevack (1990). Oxford's lexicographers also had another reason to be grateful to Hench, in the form of a pair of seats purchased with a gift of money from him for use in the garden outside 40 Walton Crescent (PBED 17948 26 Sept. 1972 RWB to CHR); one of these, sometimes referred to as the 'Hench bench', is still in use.

[52] Burchfield (1975: 357).

[53] Burchfield (1976).

been declared to be out of scope. Such a shift would, moreover, entail extensive and time-consuming additional reading: there were of course no large machine-readable English corpora from which the sort of information needed for revision could be distilled, and the Supplement's existing quotation files had been generated by a reading programme focusing on words and meanings that were *not* already covered in the Dictionary. And, indeed, Burchfield seems to have thought better of this idea: while many entries for culturally prominent words contain lengthy, sometimes discursive additions, only one such entry in Volume III, namely that for *peasant*, is presented in a form which could be said to constitute a 'full updating' of the type suggested.[54]

1977 saw the arrival in the Dictionary offices of a new kind of distraction, namely industrial unrest. In March, apparently for the first time, members of the Dictionary Department staff went on strike, as part of a dispute at OUP over working hours which had been rumbling on for some time. The strike lasted only one day, but a work-to-rule—which went on for rather longer—was bound to have a serious effect on projects which depended to a significant extent on overtime. The Supplement was certainly affected; just as serious, if not more so, was the effect on the new edition of *POD*, on which John Sykes had begun work after completing *COD* in 1976. Sykes found himself unable to complete the copy for *POD* in time for his original handover date in June, owing partly to the fact that several of his staff were working to rule, and partly to his having to spend time helping out with the recently commissioned *Oxford Junior Dictionary*. In the end Sykes only missed the *POD* deadline by a couple of weeks.[55] Burchfield, however, was becoming increasingly dissatisfied with his Deputy Chief Editor, complaining that the pressure of work on *POD* prevented him from deputizing—resulting in a falling-behind with Burchfield's own work on the Supplement—and that Sykes seemed incapable either of pushing his staff hard enough (although he readily acknowledged 'the superlative discipline he imposes on himself') or of refusing requests for help from other quarters.[56] It cannot have helped that the new *Concise* had been the subject of another potentially disastrous dictionary-related international protest, this time over its entries for *Palestinian* (one meaning of which was given, inexplicably, as '(person) seeking to displace Israelis from Palestine') and *Jerusalem* (described, rather less contentiously—though still unsatisfactorily in some quarters—as being 'in Israel'). Following protests from various groups, and even calls for a boycott of OUP books in Egypt, the Press undertook to insert suitably modified entries in the next impression; this was inevitably followed by counter-accusations that it had caved in to political pressure.[57]

---

[54] Lesley Brown recalls being tasked with collecting large numbers of quotations for *peasant* in this connection, as part of a 'Keywords-related' reading programme which also involved several other colleagues (personal communication, 8 Oct. 2014).

[55] PBED 3962 20 May 1977 RWB to DMD; OUPA(u) 18 July 1977 RWB to DMD. The new edition of *POD* was finally published in July 1978.

[56] OUPA(u) (RWB papers) 18 July 1977 RWB to DMD.

[57] Papers preserved in OUPA(u); the incident is recounted in Burchfield (1978a). Although this matter was arguably Sykes's responsibility, Burchfield took charge of dealing with the voluminous correspondence.

Rather more person-hours—running into person-months, in fact—were being lost to the Supplement because of the needs of other dictionary projects. Three Supplement editors took part in the preparation of a new edition of *Hart's Rules*, and two others spent several months 'anglicizing' the text of the *Family Word Finder*, an American synonym dictionary originally published by Reader's Digest.[58] Effort could be diverted in the other direction as well: Julia Swannell, who had been recruited in 1976 to work on *POD*, moved over to the Supplement in July, although only a few months later she returned to work on the smaller dictionaries, this time as editor of the next edition of the *Little Oxford*.[59] It should be mentioned that 1977 also saw the arrival of another important member of the next generation of Oxford lexicographers, in the form of Edmund Weiner, an English graduate from Christ Church, who joined the staff of the Supplement in July.

---

inquorate

In general, if a word is entered in a dictionary, it is reasonable to expect to find it entered under its initial letter. The fact that readers wishing to find *inquorate* in the *OED* Supplement would need to look under Q is a curious consequence of the chronology of the word's arrival in the language. Its antonym, *quorate*, seems to have come to the attention of the compilers of the Supplement in 1972, when an enquiry was received in relation to the use of the word in a draft of the constitution of an international body. By this point (according to a note in the superfluous material for the Supplement entry for the word) three quotations for *quorate* had already been collected, the oldest dating from 1969, and it seemed likely that an entry would be drafted when Q was reached. In contrast, there was no evidence for *inquorate* when the relevant portion of the letter I was reached a few months later, and no entry for the word was drafted. However, on 13 May 1974 John Sykes noted an instance of the word in an article in the *Times*, and wrote out a quotation slip for the departmental files; it was of course too late for inclusion in the Supplement, but the evidence might perhaps be of use to another dictionary. The profile of both words was on the rise, however—there were significant numbers of examples of *inquorate* to be found in contexts relating to British student politics, for example—and by 1977, when an entry for *quorate* came to be drafted for Volume III of the Supplement, a convenient way was found of remedying the (understandable) absence of *inquorate* from Volume II, namely the inclusion of both words in the same entry under Q, still with John Sykes's 1974 quotation as the earliest available example (although in fact *inquorate* can now be traced back to the 1960s). It was not possible, however, to insert even a cross-reference retrospectively in Volume II, so that readers looking up *inquorate* in its expected place were left in ignorance. It was only in 1989, with the creation of the second edition, that an entry for *inquorate* could be moved to its expected alphabetical place. (Of the two entries, only that for *quorate* has so far been revised for the third edition; the word's history has now been extended back to 1893, when W. E. Gladstone recorded in his diary that a meeting was 'non quorate', although both words do seem to have been little used before the late twentieth century.)

---

[58]   *Hart's Rules*: see PBED 9306. *Family Word Finder*: correspondence file in OUPA(u).
[59]   PBED 3994 25 Nov. 1977 RWB to DMD.

Disruption on a smaller scale, and for a much more welcome reason, occurred in the autumn. The space available in Walton Crescent had become increasingly cramped in the two decades since Burchfield and his first assistants had moved into No. 40; even with expansion into No. 41, which had become a home for some of the smaller dictionaries, it had been clear for some time that more spacious accommodation was needed. The need became still more pressing as OUP's bilingual dictionary programme began to expand. (David Evans arrived in March 1977 to begin work on a new Swedish–English dictionary, and the decision by the Press to take over a large unfinished German dictionary from the publisher Harrap created the need for further space.[60]) In April, after protracted lobbying, approval was at last secured for the whole Dictionary Department to move into a handsome Georgian house owned by the University in St Giles', a broad avenue a short distance away from the main OUP site. The move, entailing the transfer of hundreds of books and hundreds of thousands of slips, had to be carefully planned, but everything went smoothly, and by 9 September everything was in its new home. Everyone was delighted with No. 37a St Giles', which was to be the principal home of the Dictionary Department for a decade and a half; Burchfield wrote happily that 'Curzon's "engine of research" […] has never been better housed in the period of nearly a century during which the OED has belonged to OUP'.[61]

The move to St Giles' was swiftly followed by another misadventure, this time one which arguably posed a commercial threat to the entire range of Oxford dictionaries. The British dictionary market had become increasingly competitive during the 1970s, and rumours reached OUP that Pergamon Press, another Oxford-based publisher (though one relatively new to the sector), was preparing to issue a dictionary for schools—with the title 'Pergamon Oxford Perfect Spelling Dictionary'.[62] The prospect of another publisher starting to use the words 'Oxford' and 'dictionary' in titles which could compete with OUP's products was extremely disturbing, but one which it was decided could be legally challenged on the basis that it was an attempt at 'passing off', even though the University had not registered 'Oxford' as a trade mark. The challenge was ultimately successful, and OUP were awarded an injunction against Pergamon; the book was withdrawn, and subsequently issued under the less troublesome title *The Pergamon Dictionary of Perfect Spelling*.[63] But of course the preparation of the Press's case was a further time-consuming distraction.

What made the whole matter infinitely worse was that in September, only days before the first court hearing, Burchfield discovered that a lexicographer in his own department had been involved in the preparation of the rival dictionary. The culprit—if that is the right word for someone whose very innocence often seemed to be what landed him in trouble—was John Sykes. In July 1976 he had been approached with

---

[60] Dictionaries newsletters 19 Apr., 1 June 1977.
[61] OUPA(u) 12 Sept. 1977 RWB to GBR/DMD.
[62] OUPA(u) 22 Aug. 1977 M. Cowell to RWB.
[63] The case was only settled in the Court of Appeal on 18 October (*Solicitors' Journal* 121 (1977), p. 758).

some general lexicographical questions by the daughter of Robert Maxwell, the owner of Pergamon, who was editing the dictionary; he had answered these and other questions, no doubt out of courtesy—and always making it clear that he was acting in a private capacity—but had not seen fit to mention the matter to Burchfield. It was only when he was sent a copy of the book that he learned that it had been given the problematic 'Oxford' title. He now went to Burchfield and told all; and Burchfield promptly exploded. He wrote in furious terms to Davin, pointing out that there was now a risk that Sykes's involvement might seem to imply that the Press had known about the dictionary all along and was therefore being malicious by only serving the writ on the eve of publication.[64] In fact he had for some time been expressing dissatisfaction, not just with Sykes's naïvety and lack of media savvy, but also with his lexicography. He now began to ask how much longer he could put up with someone he regarded as so thoroughly unsatisfactory as a Deputy Chief Editor—or, rather, as a joint Deputy, as in fact Burchfield had already instituted a reorganization under which Sykes was to share this title with Sandra Raphael.[65]

Sykes now offered to relinquish his Deputy Editorship entirely, an offer which Burchfield was evidently only too glad to accept; a further reorganization followed, under which Raphael became Assistant (not Deputy) Chief Editor.[66] Sykes also had a new and perhaps rather surprising project to work on: he had been tasked by Burchfield with seeing what, if anything, could be made of the materials for James Wyllie's unfinished dictionary of synonyms, which had passed into OUP's possession after Wyllie's death.[67] The synonym dictionary market was an important one, and one in which the Press may have been seeking a foothold; but it is hard to believe that anyone could really have regarded the elaborate materials left by Wyllie as the best place to start. There was also work to be done on other small dictionaries, including the revision of the *Little Oxford* and the preparation of a new, still smaller dictionary conceived as a competitor to the successful Collins *Gem*; but these projects were entrusted to Julia Swannell and Sandra Raphael respectively, Burchfield having evidently taken the view that work on the distinctly problematic Wyllie materials was the most suitable task for Sykes—along with helping out with a backlog of library research on scientific entries for the Supplement. It is hard not to see this diversion into more low-profile work as something of a humiliation for Sykes, who had after all produced successful new editions of two of OUP's most important dictionaries; but while his considerable lexicographical skills, and his remarkable range of linguistic and other abilities, were widely recognized, the combination of these with a degree of innocence in other matters seems to have left Burchfield at a loss as to what to do with him.

---

[64] OUPA(u) (RWB papers) 23 Sept. 1977 RWB to DMD.
[65] Dictionaries newsletter 26 Sept. 1977.
[66] OUPA(u) (RWB papers) 7 Nov. 1977 RWB to DMD.
[67] OUPA(u) file note 30 Apr. 1971; OUPA(u) 18 July 1977 RWB to DMD.

Also hard on the heels of the move to 37a St Giles' came a new challenge for all of its lexicographers, this time in the administrative sphere: OUP was in the process of implementing a job evaluation system. This meant that each separate job within the department had to be provided with a formal job description so that this could be evaluated and assigned a pay grade. Unfortunately, the first set of job descriptions ended up being so badly misunderstood by those charged with evaluating them that the gradings which emerged from the exercise simply did not match the actual importance of particular jobs, thus necessitating the wholesale rewriting of descriptions so as to convey the significance of each job more clearly. It was not until April 1978 that a satisfactory set of gradings was arrived at.[68] Sorting out such matters took considerable time and effort which could ill be spared from lexicography.

The same could surely be said of some of the continuing flow of public speaking engagements, broadcasts, and interviews, which in 1977 included a talk to the Oxford Book Association on 'The Joys and Tribulations of Lexicography', an international lexicography conference in Leiden (the successor to that held in Florence in 1971), a lecture at a Goldsmiths' College summer school (for the second year running), and another conference in Augsburg at which Burchfield spoke on 'The Authority of the *OED*'. He was no doubt helping to maintain the public profile of the Oxford Dictionaries, and thus the authority of OUP as a dictionary publisher, through these engagements, but it cannot be denied that they took him away from his desk. There may of course have been many other requests for interviews and articles which he turned down; but one suspects that others in his position might have turned down, or delegated, more. There are, admittedly, some signs of delegation in 1978, when Robert Allen gave a lecture on English usage in Cambridge—subsequently reprised in Zürich—and Lesley Burnett and Sandra Raphael presented papers at a lexicography seminar organized at the University of Exeter.[69]

Certainly the effect of all of these many distractions on the progress of the Supplement was disastrous. By the end of 1977, when the bulk of Volume III should surely have reached at least the stage of first proof, the copy dispatched to the printers had only reached *park*, and not a single corrected galley proof had been returned.[70] Of course schedules for the Supplement had to be considered alongside those for all the other dictionary projects now being tackled by the occupants of 37a St Giles'. Indeed it is hardly surprising that the task of juggling the department's unprecedentedly large and flexible array of editorial resources between so many different dictionaries, in response to changing business priorities and the overrunning of one project or another, continued to be an endlessly frustrating one; nor that the Supplement continued to lose out from time to time in the battle for resources, with the inevitable consequence of further pushing back of the date for its completion. (By May 1978 the

[68] Dictionaries newsletters 26 Sept. 1977, 17 Apr. 1978.
[69] OUP *Record* 23 (Dec. 1978), p. 7.
[70] OUPA(u) (RWB papers) notebook recording progress of Volume III, 1977–81.

scheduled publication date for Volume III had slipped to March 1980; this became 'late 1980?' by December—by which time drafting, at least, had reached *Sk*, and was therefore significantly past the start of Volume IV—and by the following March the provisional date was 1981.[71]) If the only way of ensuring publication of a particular title by a particular date was by seconding staff from another project, then choices had to be made in the light of OUP's overall publishing needs rather than by always privileging one project over all the others. Burchfield no doubt accepted this in principle, but he does seem to have regarded the various smaller dictionaries, whatever their commercial importance—which in some cases was considerable—as in some sense of lesser value than the Supplement, as is seen from his later description of the task of allocating resources to different projects as 'a distraction of indescribable proportions from my main work on the *Supplement to the OED*'.[72]

He could also make mistakes in his assessment of who might be suitable for which project. The skills required to prepare historical entries for the Supplement were not the same as those required to edit a small dictionary of current English; and in March 1978, after some months attempting the latter—having been assigned to the editorship of the new 'miniature' Oxford dictionary (eventually published as the *Oxford Minidictionary*)—Sandra Raphael came to the conclusion that she was not cut out for it, and formally indicated her wish to withdraw from the work, and indeed from administrative responsibility for smaller dictionaries generally.[73] The new dictionary was subsequently reassigned to Joyce Hawkins, whose track record with small dictionaries was already established, and she and Tony Augarde took over the management of this and some other dictionaries; Raphael returned to editing natural history items for the Supplement, and to her former title of Senior Editor. This left Burchfield with neither Deputy nor Assistant Chief Editor; perhaps the role was an impossible one to fill.

1978 was a year both for looking back and looking forward. For OUP as a whole it was a year of retrospection, as the Press celebrated the 500th anniversary of the start of academic printing in Oxford; as part of the quincentenary celebrations, much was of course made of the *OED*, which had now been associated with the Press for a fifth of those 500 years, and interest in which had been further stimulated by the publication of Elisabeth Murray's acclaimed account of the life and lexicographical achievements of her grandfather James Murray. The Dictionary and its offspring featured in a BBC documentary about the Press, broadcast on 24 March, and the history of the Press's English dictionaries was also the subject of a specially designed set of exhibition panels, several copies of which were sent round the world; Burchfield flew to New York in March to take part in a celebratory lecture series at the Pierpont Morgan Library, where he spoke on the Fowler brothers. In June he paid a visit to 78 Banbury Road, now the home of

---

[71] OUPA(u) 31 May 1978 RWB to DMD; OUPA(u) progress reports for 4 Dec. 1978, 5 Mar. 1979.
[72] Burchfield (1989: 15). Some former members of the Supplement staff recall Burchfield as 'look[ing] down on', or even having 'disdain' for, the smaller dictionaries (interviews with author, 2010 and 2012).
[73] OUPA(u) 21 Mar. 1978 Raphael to RWB.

the writer and popular anthropologist Desmond Morris, who showed him his own fine collection of dictionaries, and also gave him (in exchange for a copy of the latest *COD*) a child's hoop which he had unearthed in his garden, and which was identified by Elisabeth Murray as almost certainly the hoop that her father and his brothers and sisters had played with when they were not sorting Dictionary slips. The hoop subsequently made its way to the Dictionary Department, and still forms part of the Dictionary's 'archives'.

Burchfield recounted his visit to 78 Banbury Road, and his having stood on the 'sacred spot' where the Scriptorium had once stood, in a lecture at the American Library Association's annual convention in Chicago in June, which as well as proving to be the occasion of one of his most controversial public utterances also looked forward beyond the completion of the Supplement. The controversy related to Burchfield's perhaps unwise assertion that American English and British English, 'separated geographically from the beginning and severed politically since 1776', were becoming increasingly dissimilar, and in another 200 years would become mutually unintelligible.[74] His remarks were widely reported—in some cases approvingly, in other cases disbelievingly—on both sides of the Atlantic. Far more important, however, in Burchfield's own view was his conclusion that a new period dictionary was needed, namely one devoted to the English (of Britain, America, and the rest of the world) of the eighteenth century; this, he declared, was the project that he himself would like to move on to once the Supplement was finished.[75]

Important though this conclusion may have been to Burchfield himself, OUP seems to have shown no appetite for a new historical dictionary of this kind, and nothing further was heard of the eighteenth-century project.[76] There were, however, two other important new lexicographical ventures which the Press was now seriously contemplating. Between them they were expected to absorb a substantial part of the Dictionary Department's headcount as lexicographers became available through being released from work on the Supplement or other projects; indeed, they were clearly envisaged as forming the Department's key projects in the post-Supplement period, a period which seemed at last to be coming into view. Both were seen as of sufficient importance to justify such substantial investment of resources. One was the long-overdue full revision of the *Shorter*, much of the main text of which had now remained to all intents and purposes unchanged for forty years; this promised to be nearer fifty by the time a new edition was ready, and the need to make a start on this as soon as possible had long been recognized.[77]

---

[74] The lecture was subsequently published (Burchfield 1978b); the original text survives in OUPA(u) (RWB papers). The specific assertion about mutual unintelligibility seems to have been made at a press conference following the lecture.

[75] OUPA(u) 5 Apr. 1978 RWB to DMD/RAD.

[76] It also appears to have been around this time that the idea of a historical dictionary of scientific vocabulary—which Burchfield had described a year earlier as 'still very much "on"' (OUPA(u) 16 Feb. 1977 [RWB] to David Elder)—was finally abandoned.

[77] John Sykes had at one point been pencilled in as a possible editor for *SOED* (OUPA(u) file note by RWB 7 Sept. 1976).

The other project had arisen out of a growing awareness that booksellers were keen to have—and OUP's sales force was keen to offer—an English dictionary intermediate in size between the *Concise* and the *Shorter*. In some respects the envisaged new dictionary resembled the ill-fated 'Quarto' dictionary begun by Henry Fowler half a century earlier, and for a time it was even given the same name ('The Oxford Dictionary of Modern English'); but this was to be an entirely new dictionary, written from scratch by selected members of the Dictionary Department, with Burchfield himself taking charge of the overall editorial policy. In a conscious echo of the title of Samuel Johnson's famous dictionary of 1755, it was soon retitled 'The Oxford Dictionary of the English Language'.[78] It was also envisaged—at least by Burchfield—as Johnsonian in other ways: he subsequently characterized it as a '20th c[entury] equivalent of Dr. Johnson's dictionary', with the individual senses of words illustrated by 'quotations from named writers, especially writers of distinction, of the present century'—for which a special reading programme was to be set up—and prescriptive guidance on usage where relevant.[79]

Whether or not this was the kind of dictionary that OUP really wanted or needed, Burchfield's ideas about *ODEL* suggest that his views regarding the function of the lexicographer, or at least of those dictionaries with which he was most directly involved, were no longer as neutrally descriptivist as they might seem to have been during the early years of his Editorship. Of course, he had always viewed the landscape of the English language as something other than a featureless plateau, making him perhaps less 'neutral' than some: his concern that the vocabulary of 'literature'—however defined—should be well represented in the Supplement is already evident in his earliest recommendations about a reading programme. But during the 1970s he does seem to have become more favourably disposed to at least some forms of prescriptivism.[80] It is hard to account satisfactorily for this shift. Given the language in which he later wrote of what he regarded as the most extreme advocates of descriptivism—'scholars with shovels bent on burying the linguistic past and most of the literary past and present [...] who believe that synchronic means "theoretically sound" and diachronic "theoretically suspect"'[81]—one might suppose that his antipathy towards the supposed excesses of these scholars had led him to take up a more directly contrary position; he certainly saw himself as not alone in doing so, and explicitly associated himself with some of the newspaper and magazine commentators who 'seemed to believe that the English language itself was in a period of decline'.[82] He will also have been aware—probably ever-increasingly so—of the widespread view that the 'custodian of the English language' was, or was

---

[78] Correspondence about the project is preserved mainly in a single file in OUPA(u).

[79] OUPA(u) file note by RWB 25 Feb. 1981, 15 July 1981 RWB to J. K. Cordy.

[80] Burchfield had also begun to find opportunities for prescriptive comment—and indeed for the expression of his own personal views—in some Supplement entries: see p. 496.

[81] Preface to Vol. IV of the Supplement, p. x.

[82] Preface to Vol. III, p. v.

expected to be, its arbiter as well. However, there was never any question of departing from the general principle that the *OED* and its Supplement should describe, rather than influence, the language it sought to document, whatever might be considered appropriate elsewhere.

It was anticipated that the first people to become available for work on *ODEL* would be John Sykes—now released from the synonym dictionary project, which had been abandoned as a hopeless case—and Tony Augarde, while Lesley Burnett was to make a start on the new *Shorter* in January 1979.[83] In the event, however, 1979 saw an upsurge in the demands of various other shorter-term lexicographical projects; indeed, as Burchfield tartly commented, his report on the dozen or so projects which had occupied the Department during the year 'could be subtitled "reasons for not starting on S.O.E.D. and O.D.M.E. in 1979"'.[84] It had now been decided that Volume III of the Supplement—which had also suffered some 'sapping of strength'—should end at *Scz*, instead of *Sh*, which had been the provisional endpoint for some time. Even with this reduction in alphabetical span, Volume III was to be the fattest of the Supplement's four volumes, with 1,579 pages; and also the most expansive as compared to the first edition, with each page corresponding to only 1.85 pages of the first edition (the equivalent figures for Volumes I and II had been 3.70 and 2.26). The expansion can largely be attributed to the increasing tendency towards generous provision of quotations; Burchfield later recalled this as being one of the main ways in which the Supplement had diverged from the first edition, in that while the latter had generally aimed at one quotation per century, '[w]e have moved towards a policy of including at least one quotation per decade'.[85] In Volume IV a deliberate effort to curb this tendency by Simpson and Weiner—who by that stage were re-editing drafted entries ahead of Burchfield[86]—achieved a retrenchment, with each page corresponding to 3.36 pages of the first edition.

By the start of 1980 drafting of entries for Volume III was complete, apart from the botanical and zoological entries (which were entrusted to a single editor, Sandra Raphael, as the only person deemed fully qualified to tackle them); but Burchfield's own final editing was some way off the end of P. There were also other significant distractions during the year, including a trip to China for Burchfield, and a month-long project to monitor the use of English on the BBC's radio networks, at their request, resulting in the production of a 24-page pamphlet offering guidance on matters of

---

[83] OUPA(u) file note by RWB 8 Nov. 1978.

[84] OUPA(u) 2 Jan. 1980 RWB to RAD/J. K. Cordy. Among the dictionaries mentioned in Burchfield's report are the *Oxford Paperback Dictionary* (a new title by Joyce Hawkins, which went on to be extremely successful), the fifth edition of *LOD*, the *Oxford Dictionary for Writers and Editors* (*ODWE*), the *Minidictionary*, the *Concise Oxford Dictionary of Proverbs*, the *Oxford Intermediate Dictionary*, the seventh edition of *COD*, the *Oxford–Duden Pictorial German–English Dictionary* (an innovative joint venture with a German publisher), the *Pocket Oxford English–Russian Dictionary*, the *Oxford Australian Junior Dictionary*, and Americanized versions of the *Paperback* and of the *Oxford Illustrated Dictionary*.

[85] Burchfield (1987a: 19).

[86] John Simpson, interview with author, 5 Feb. 2014.

pronunciation and usage.[87] The Supplement also lost an able lexicographer in David Howlett, a member of the staff since 1975, who left to take up the editorship of another large-scale historical dictionary project, the *Dictionary of Medieval Latin from British Sources*.[88] The Department suffered a more shocking loss in October when Nigel Rankin, who had joined the staff in 1976 to work on an English–Russian dictionary, and who had also contributed to some Supplement entries for words of Russian origin, died from injuries sustained in a traffic accident.[89] Finally, trade union activities once again became a source of frustration for Burchfield, who complained in his report that several members of the Department had taken on 'time-consuming office-holding [union] posts'; this of course they were entirely entitled to do, but for Burchfield—who disliked his staff even joining the union—it amounted to a betrayal of their proper responsibility to their lexicographical work. In December he even went so far as to threaten to cancel the impending promotion of a member of the Supplement staff who had had the temerity to allow himself to be elected as chairman of the union group within OUP, until it was pointed out to him that behaviour of this kind was the one thing guaranteed to bring staff out on strike.[90]

Burchfield's attitude to trade unions will hardly have been softened by the next problem to afflict the progress of the Supplement: industrial action by print unions in the spring of 1980, which held up the work being done on Volume III by Clowes of Suffolk. Coming as it did only weeks after Burchfield had put in place a new and demanding schedule designed to 'take Volume 3 by the scruff of the neck' and get it published before the end of 1981, this new delay must have been particularly galling. Considerably more serious, however, was the news which reached Oxford in July: Clowes, who had already typeset the letters O and P, were to close down their hot-metal department.[91] The ensuing search for a replacement printer—Latimer Trend of Plymouth was chosen—and the reallocation of the remaining typesetting between them and OUP's own printing division, resulted in a delay of something like six months.[92] The Press

---

[87] Burchfield et al. (1979). During Burchfield's China visit outline agreement was reached on a collaborative Chinese–English dictionary, which however later had to be shelved due to disagreement about marketing arrangements (FC 29 May 1979).

[88] The *DMLBS* could trace its origins back over sixty years (and in fact to a proposal by a valued contributor to the first edition of the *OED*, R. J. Whitwell); the collection of quotations had begun in the 1920s, but it was not until 1975 that the first fascicle of dictionary entries was published. Howlett was succeeded in 2011 by Richard Ashdowne, under whose editorship the dictionary was completed in 2013. For an account of the project see Ashdowne (2014).

[89] Dictionaries newsletter 5 Oct. 1979.

[90] Elizabeth Burchfield, interview with author, 22 Aug. 2012; P. R. Hardie, personal communication.

[91] Most typesetting at OUP was now mechanical, using Monotype machines, in which metal type was cast from molten alloy in response to text typed in at a keyboard; mechanical methods were subsequently superseded by photocomposition and computer typesetting (Maw 2013b: 277–92).

[92] PBED 8293 6 Mar. 1980 RWB to J. K. Cordy; PBED 17907 28 Apr. 1980 RWB to Cordy, 7 July 1980 B. Townsend to RWB; Dictionaries newsletter 1 Oct. 1980. The printing (as opposed to the typesetting) of Volume III (and Volume IV) was moved to East Kilbride in Scotland, a financially astute move which took advantage of a government scheme for encouraging investment in areas suffering industrial deprivation.

was also experiencing real financial difficulty, as it struggled to cope with the effects of the publishing recession; although there were no redundancies in the Dictionary Department, it could not remain insulated from such difficulties, and Burchfield and his senior editors were soon having to contemplate a future in which 'natural wastage' would be allowed to effect a reduction in Departmental headcount (then standing at around 30) by two or three posts a year for several years to come. In such circumstances, the fact that work did at last begin on the revision of the *Shorter* during 1980—Lesley Burnett began work in April, with William Trumble as her chief science editor—is a striking indication of the importance that this project was recognized as having for the Press. Work on *ODEL*, under Tony Augarde, did not get under way until the following March, but this was another vote of confidence in the future.

A good illustration of the interrelatedness of the Dictionary Department, and the way in which the whole of the staff sometimes had to be regarded as a single resource to be redeployed as necessary, came in the spring and summer of 1981. When John Pheby resigned from his position at the head of the Department's group of German lexicographers, in order to take up a position in Berlin, John Sykes was invited to take his place, as the most suitably qualified person available; the job could not really be combined with that of editor of *COD* and *POD*, so that position was in turn taken up by Robert Allen, who had only just started work alongside Lesley Burnett on the *Shorter* following the completion of work on *ODWE*.[93] The unavailability of Allen for Supplement work had a knock-on effect on the progress of Volume III, the last batch of copy for which Burchfield sent to press in April. (Following the departure of Burnett and Allen, John Simpson and Edmund Weiner were promoted to senior positions on the Supplement staff, taking over from them both as sorters of the quotation files—and therefore as distributors of material for drafting to the other staff—and as re-editors of some draft Supplement copy; they also took over the handling of galleys and page proofs.[94]) Another, tragic loss came only two months later when Gordon Murray, who had been a member of the Supplement's science team since 1977, died of cancer aged only 32. The loss of such a young colleague was deeply felt by his fellow lexicographers; it was also a loss in a particularly vulnerable part of the project, and under the circumstances it is perhaps not surprising that approval was obtained to replace him, and a new science researcher joined the staff in October. Another new arrival during the year was Richard Palmer, a classicist who transferred to the Supplement following the completion—at last—of work on the *Oxford Latin Dictionary* (and whose arrival could be countenanced as not being an increase in the Press's headcount).[95]

---

[93] Dictionaries newsletter 12 June 1981; OUPA(u) (RWB papers) 27 Aug. 1981 RWB to RAD. Sykes had just completed editorial work on the seventh edition of *COD*, but it was left to Allen to see it through the press. A corrected reprint of *POD*, with new Addenda, also appeared in September 1981.

[94] Dictionaries newsletter 16 Feb. 1981; John Simpson and Edmund Weiner, personal communication.

[95] Dictionaries newsletters 13 Apr., 12 June 1981.

The autumn of 1981 also saw another change of personnel at a higher level, and one which would be significant for the *OED* in various ways. The general and reference division of OUP, which published all of the Oxford dictionaries and much else besides, had been headed since Dan Davin's retirement in 1978 by Robin Denniston, his successor as the Press's Academic Publisher, who subsequently delegated some of the responsibility to his colleague John Cordy; the reference books portfolio now passed to Richard Charkin, who had come to the Press in 1975 (from Pergamon Press, as it happens) as a science publisher. In view of the hostility which subsequently developed between the two men, it is remarkable that Burchfield's initial impressions of Charkin were extremely favourable. Burchfield wrote to Byron Hollinshead, president of OUP's New York branch, of the 'very impressive start' Charkin had made, and welcomed Charkin's pledge to protect him from what he called 'the devastating bureaucracy of the Walton St. publishing side [of OUP]'.[96] More significant, however, for the future of the *OED* was Charkin's enthusiasm for and knowledge of new technology, and information technology in particular. Computers had been having a significant impact in publishing for some years; interest at OUP in the potential of computers for specifically lexicographical purposes can be traced back at least as far as 1967, when it had been proposed to make use of computers in the compilation of the bibliography for the Supplement, although it was decided, probably rightly at the time, that this approach offered no advantage over conventional methods, and the idea was dropped.[97] Burchfield and his colleagues had long been in touch with researchers outside Oxford with ideas about some of the many possible lexicographical applications of information technology, including computer-based storage and even compilation of dictionaries; for example, both the *Dictionary of Old English* and the *Dictionary of American Regional English* had made extensive use of computers since their inception. However, Burchfield's comments on receiving news about the computerization of aspects of the work of *DARE*, a few months before the Supplement bibliography project, suggest that he did not share the enthusiasm of these other projects: 'a good deal of lexicographical material has been fed into the computers in recent years but no dictionary has yet come out at the other end. Our view here is to let the prickly problems of theory be settled first by others and we shall come in somewhat later. In practice I have resolved to go into the whole question as soon as the O.E.D. Supplement is finished.'[98] Interest in the potential of the new technology, however, continued to grow, and in 1977 Burchfield went so far as to arrange for the appointment of Joyce Hawkins as the Dictionary Department's 'Computer Liaison Officer'.[99]

---

[96] OUPA(u) 14 Oct. 1981 RWB to B. Hollinshead; OUPA(u) (RWB papers) 15 Oct. 1981 RWB to D. C. Cunningham.
[97] OUPA(u) 6 Oct., 14 Dec. 1967 RWB to T. Howard-Hill.
[98] OUPA(u) 4 Jan. 1967 RWB to J. R. B. Brett-Smith.
[99] Dictionaries newsletter 28 Dec. 1977.

By 1981 a number of other ideas were in the air. In June the Department's first computer terminal was installed, initially only as a means of accessing the University's computing service in connection with a project to use new scanning technology to create machine-readable copies of a selection of texts. These were envisaged principally as a supplementary source of illustrative quotations (in addition to those collected via a conventional reading programme) for *ODEL*, though in due course they would also prove to be of use for the Supplement.[100] The arrival of this terminal was soon followed by a proposal to install the equipment needed to access some of the increasingly wide range of databases now available 'online' (i.e. accessible via the telephone network), the value of which as sources of quotation evidence for dictionaries had been recognized for some time.[101] At the same time approval was secured for the acquisition of a minicomputer for use in compiling some of the Department's smaller dictionaries.

Grander, though sometimes nebulous, visions of the future—specifically in relation to the *OED*—were also heaving into view. In today's world of instant access to comprehensively searchable databases of all kinds, it is easy to forget how difficult it was for anyone other than a computing specialist even to imagine what it meant to convert a large text into electronic form, let alone grasp what could be done with the result. One relatively simple—though challenging—computer-based idea was mooted by Robin Denniston in a letter to a contact at the legal publishers Butterworths in October: namely that, when the fourth and final volume of the Supplement was published—which at this stage was expected to be in 1985—the four-volume Supplement and the original *OED* could be made 'available on line [*sic*] for professional use'. He felt that this might be a logical next step, given that 'no further revisions or Supplements [to the Dictionary] are planned'.[102] But Richard Charkin, ever an innovative publisher, was already imagining new things that could be done with these texts. Since the entries of the Supplement were presented in the form of additions to the original text of the Dictionary—with specific directions as to how the new material was to be incorporated—would it be possible to carry these directions out, and create a single integrated text? Initially he and Denniston conceived of doing this by traditional methods—or, as Denniston called it, 'the biggest scissors-and-paste job in history'[103]—but Charkin now began to wonder whether the same goal could be achieved by electronic means: would it be more practicable to manipulate entries on-screen than on paper? From this bold new conception it was only a short step to

---

[100] OUPA(u) (RWB papers) notebook recording progress of Volume III.

[101] OUPA(u) file note by RWB, 15 Feb. 1982.

[102] PBED 17907 12 Oct. 1981 RAD to Gordon Graham. At this point Butterworths were among the bigger British players in the world of online databases through their links with the American firm Mead Data Central, who owned the important legal and newspaper databases Lexis and Nexis.

[103] Quoted on p. 379 of Weiner (2009), a full account of the computerization of the *OED* on which I have drawn freely in the following pages; see also Weiner (1987). The history of the project is also fully told in the preliminary pages of *OED2*.

thinking what had long been regarded as unthinkable: could the integrated text thus created become the basis of a continuously revised database?[104]

In March 1982, just as the final proofs of Volume III of the Supplement were at last being signed off for press, Charkin placed this visionary prospect before Burchfield.[105] Electronic publishing was in its infancy, but Charkin had grasped the potential of a single integrated Dictionary database in electronic form: it might prove to be saleable in its own right, but it could also form the basis for an ongoing programme of revision, the fruits of which could perhaps be made available piecemeal—perhaps in the form of fascicles, or one letter at a time—until eventually the whole alphabet had been worked through, whereupon the Press would be in the position of having a new edition of the *OED* for sale, potentially in multiple formats. A further attraction for OUP of this vision of the future was that the revision programme could, he believed, be carried out by a much smaller team than the current Supplement staff, which was still more than twenty strong; the Press's continuing financial difficulties made it imperative to find ways of reducing the Dictionary Department's massive overheads, by redeploying lexicographers onto more rapidly profitable projects if not by dispensing with them altogether. (The making of substantial economies may in fact have been a primary motivation for Charkin's line of thinking: it has been claimed—by Charkin himself—that he was tasked on his appointment with 'overseeing the gradual whittling down of the OED department', although he rapidly came to appreciate the importance of keeping OUP's lexicographical powerhouse adequately funded.[106]) With hindsight Charkin's proposal that an adequate revision programme could have been sustained by a staff of five suggests a failure to grasp what revision would involve; but then this was a matter about which nobody really knew. That being said, Burchfield knew enough to express doubts about whether staff savings on this scale could be made. He did, however, respond positively to Charkin's ideas about what he recognized was a 'very important matter', and immediately commissioned Lesley Burnett and John Simpson to investigate and report on key aspects of the project, including how what would now be called the digitization of the text could be achieved, and the range of ways in which *OED* text was now in need of revision.[107]

[104] OUPA(u) report by Julia Swannell 21 Dec. 1981 (noting Charkin's having 'looked forward [at a seminar ten days earlier] to the OED being available for sale in electronic form, and to supplements and revisions being made continuously'). A strange precursor to this proposal had in fact been made nearly three years earlier, when the senior OUP figure John Brown had suggested to Burchfield that the optical character recognition technology that was being used to convert the British Library's massive General Catalogue of Printed Books might be applicable to the *OED* and its Supplements. The idea's time had evidently not yet come; Burchfield thought not, at any rate, commenting that he did 'not think Optical Character Recognition and the revision of OED are reconcilable' (OUPA(u) 29 Jan. 1979 Brown to RWB, 30 Jan. 1979 RWB to Brown).

[105] PBED 17907 10 Mar. 1982 RDPC to RWB.

[106] OUPA(u) draft of a paper delivered by RDPC in Philadelphia Nov. 1984.

[107] PBED 17907 17 Mar. 1982 RWB to RDPC. Copies of the reports by Burnett and Simpson, dated 24 Mar.–1 Apr. 1982, are preserved in OUPA(u).

The next step was to approach the Delegates of the Press.[108] It was some years since they had last concerned themselves formally with the *OED*, but this was a momentous matter. It was not simply that the Dictionary was a flagship publication, and one whose importance for the Press's reputation as a dictionary publisher—and, indeed, as a publisher generally—was such that decisions about its future had to be taken with great care: there was also the matter of the likely cost of the computerization project, which it was already clear would be on such a scale that appeals to external bodies for funding would have to be considered. (Initial ideas about the likely costs had already had to be revised upwards once it was realized that direct electronic capture of the text by means of optical character recognition was beyond the current limits of the technology—the typographical complexity of Dictionary pages was too great—and that the entire text would therefore have to be keyed manually.) A further consideration was that in 1983 fifty years would have elapsed since the reissue of the first edition of the Dictionary: an anniversary which brought with it the possibility that parties other than OUP who wished to exploit the text commercially might claim that it was no longer in copyright, making it highly desirable to find a way of unambiguously reasserting the Press's claims to the text.[109] The Delegates evinced considerable interest in the proposals presented to them by Charkin, and initial feelers were put out towards various institutions which might be interested in contributing, or even collaborating. It was clear that it would be some time before the project reached the point where substantial editorial involvement would be required, but Edmund Weiner—who at this point had been seconded from the Supplement to work on a new usage guide, subsequently named the *Oxford Miniguide to English Usage*—was tentatively identified as the right person to be 'lexical supremo' when the time came, with input on technical matters from Julia Swannell, whose grasp of computing matters had led to her appointment as the Department's Computer Resources Editor.[110]

Notwithstanding all of this contemplation of the future, there was still plenty to do as far as the main project in hand was concerned. Publication of Volume III of the Supplement took place on 15 July 1982, attended by another wave of publicity (see Figure 37); it had been arranged that the new *Concise* should appear on the same day, but most of the publicity focused on the Supplement. Burchfield himself figured prominently, taking part in a high-profile interview with Bernard Levin on BBC TV in the week of publication, and featuring in various other interviews over the next several months. He also participated in another public spat, this time with the professor of general linguistics at Oxford, Roy Harris, who used his review of Volume III in the *Times Literary Supplement* as a platform to mount various attacks on the methodology

[108]   FC 25 May 1982, OD 8 June 1982.
[109]   In fact news reached Oxford only a few months later of an attempt to produce a pirated edition of the 13-volume *OED* (including the first Supplement) in Korea, which the Press managed to prevent (FC 31 May, 20 Dec. 1983).
[110]   FC 30 Nov., 21 Dec. 1982; OUPA(u) (RWB papers) 2 Aug. 1982 RWB to RDPC. Documentation of this early phase of the computerization project is preserved in OUPA(u).

FIGURE 37   Robert Burchfield and the Supplement staff on the steps of the Radcliffe Camera, Oxford, July 1982.

of the *OED* itself, including its favouring of printed sources, and indeed the very basis of its historical approach, which he described as representing 'the fossilized epistemology of a bygone era'. The next week's issue included a counterblast from Burchfield, dismissing Harris's criticisms as simplistic and misguided. Other reviews of Volume III were once again generally favourable; one notable partial exception was that by the former staff member Julian Barnes, now beginning to make his name as a novelist, who while acknowledging that it was 'magnificent, scholarly and impressive', pointed out various errors and omissions, noting that 'when there are blackheads on the brow of Nefertiti, we shouldn't pretend they are beauty-spots'.[111]

A radio interview on 3 June, marking the centenary of James Murray's first delivery of *OED* copy to the printers, prompted a remarkable—though sadly brief—connection to the days of the first edition: the Department learned that John Birt, Onions's veteran assistant, was still alive, though he was in poor health, and in fact died the following month, at the age of 91. Mention should be made here of an even longer-lived veteran of the Murray years, Father Henry Rope, who had died in 1978 aged 97, having continued to send in quotations well into his tenth decade.[112]

The longevity of at least some lexicographers has been commented on by many, including Burchfield himself, who however wrote of being 'haunted' by the fact that 'many fail to complete their course'.[113] On 30 June 1982 he was given a surprise lunch to mark the twenty-fifth anniversary of his entry into lexicography; this was indeed an occasion for celebration, but his enjoyment will surely have been mingled with the painful awareness that, even fifteen years after the original scheduled publication date, the Supplement was still incomplete.[114] Volume IV was of course well under way by this stage, with drafting of S and T already finished, and copy sent to the printers as far as *shiny*, but publication by the agreed date of 1985 was going to be extremely tight. The resources of the Department as a whole were also at full stretch, with little prospect of expanding them; indeed, there seemed every likelihood that they would be reduced. Apprehensions about this became acute only days after the anniversary lunch when it became generally known that Sandra Raphael was to be made redundant once her work on natural history vocabulary for the Supplement came to an end in January 1983.[115] This was something rather more complex than the economizing measure it might appear, coming as it did at the end of a long-running clash between Raphael and Burchfield over her role and the value of her work; but the news of her redundancy was bound to be unsettling. Reassurance of a kind was secured at a meeting between Charkin, Burchfield, and the Department's six senior editors, at which it was recognized that staff replacements would need to be guaranteed if all current publishing targets— which included publication of the new *Shorter* in 1990 or 1991—were to be met.

---

[111] Harris (1982: 936); Barnes (1982: 20).
[112] Dictionaries newsletters 14 June 1982, 22 Oct. 1976, 17 Apr. 1978.
[113] Burchfield (1989: 9).
[114] Dictionaries newsletter 12 July 1982.
[115] OUPA(u) (RWB papers) file note by RWB 7 July 1982.

The fact that only two months after this meeting the Department was asked to find the resources to work on a new title (an 'anglicization' of another American reference work from Reader's Digest) illustrates how fragile such assurances were likely to be.[116] Charkin was firmly committed to the view that it was essential for OUP to keep the Dictionary Department properly funded, but if a new project—whether conceived by him or anyone else—came into view which offered enticing prospects for the Press in the shorter term, the pressure to divert resources into it could be difficult to resist.

This was no less true of publicity than it was of lexicographical work. It was of paramount importance to OUP that it should maintain its dominance of the British dictionary market, and while its market share was still in excess of 50 per cent, it had been seriously eroded in recent years, thanks mainly to competition from Longmans and, particularly, Collins, whose new 'collegiate' dictionary (the *Collins Dictionary of the English Language*), published in 1979, had been something of a game-changer with its substantial encyclopedic component.[117] Publicity and public relations played a crucial part in this battle, and even senior members of the Department could find themselves diverted from lexicography into time-consuming PR work if the anticipated benefits for OUP were considered great enough. Thus in January 1983 Lesley Burnett— who in fact had only just returned to the *Shorter* after having been seconded back to the Supplement for nine months, helping to cover for Edmund Weiner's diversion to the *Oxford Miniguide to English Usage*—spent a full week at the studios of Yorkshire Television recording episodes of *Countdown*, a game show featuring word puzzles which had been the first programme to be broadcast on Britain's new national television channel, Channel 4, the previous November. The programme (see Figure 38), which had formed an association with the Oxford Dictionaries from the start, quickly became—and remains—very popular. Burchfield had noted with approval the visible presence of a copy of the *Shorter OED* on set, 'sitting there on display all the time just like the famous Adidas boots on rugby fields'; but progress on the revision of the *Shorter* will not have been helped by Burnett's absence on this and other occasions.[118]

Considerably greater demands were placed on the lexicographers' time two months later by another PR initiative: the Oxford Word and Language Service (OWLS), a free service offering answers—by telephone or letter—to language queries from the public. The service was launched on 10 March 1983 amid a storm of publicity, and was

---

[116] OUPA(u) note 22 July 1982 (recording decisions made at a meeting 21 July), 23 Sept. 1982 RWB to RDPC.

[117] 'Collegiate', a term from American publishing, had come into more general use as a name for a large single-volume desk dictionary intended to meet the needs of college students as well as general readers. Béjoint (1994) discusses the impact of the *Collins Dictionary* on the British dictionary market, in the course of a useful account (pp. 42–91) of English monolingual dictionary publishing since the Second World War.

[118] Dictionaries newsletters 9 Dec. 1982, 10 Feb. 1983. Lesley Burnett had been briefly preceded, as the lexicographer in 'Dictionary Corner', by Joyce Hawkins, and she was succeeded by Julia Swannell later in 1983. Several other lexicographers have followed, although the best-known occupant of the position, Susie Dent, was working on the publication of dictionaries, rather than their compilation, when she first appeared on the programme in 1992.

FIGURE 38   Participants in a 1985 episode of *Countdown*, with Yvonne Warburton (standing centre) as the lexicographer in 'Dictionary Corner' (photograph supplied by Gyles Brandreth, pictured standing to the left of her).

soon averaging twenty to thirty telephone calls a day and a similar number of letters, asking about anything from the pronunciation of *forehead* to the origin of the phrase *sick as a parrot*; fortunately for the lexicographers this soon declined, but the enquiry rate remained substantially higher than it had been previously.[119] It is of course debatable whether the person-hours that went into dealing with these enquiries over the ensuing three decades could have been more effectively deployed, but OWLS was without question brilliantly successful in reinforcing the public image of the Oxford Dictionaries as the first port of call for all queries relating to the English language.

During the first few weeks following the launch of OWLS a large proportion of the queries reaching St Giles'—many more were headed off by Elizabeth Knight from the London office—were dealt with by John Simpson, who had returned to the Supplement a few months earlier after completing the *Concise Oxford Dictionary of English Proverbs*. He also featured in the associated publicity; for example, it was he rather than Burchfield who appeared on the BBC magazine programme *Nationwide*

---

[119] *Christian Science Monitor* 12 Apr. 1983, p. 3.

(inspiring one viewer to send him a model owl to put on his desk). Indeed, Burchfield admitted to finding himself 'rely[ing] on [Simpson] a great deal and more each day as my own schedule is becoming more and more punishing'.[120]

There was indeed a formidable schedule ahead for both Burchfield and the senior editors (mainly Simpson and Weiner, but also Burnett, once again borrowed back from the *Shorter*) who now assisted him with the later stages of the editorial process; and a shortfall in throughput during 1981 and 1982 meant that an average of 10,000 slips of copy would now have to be sent to press each month in order to complete this stage by the current target date of April 1984.[121] At the same time, the schedule for other members of the Supplement team was drawing—at last—to a close. The preliminary drafting of entries was complete to the end of W by July 1983, and the draft copy for the last entry of all, *zzzz*, was completed by Edith Bonner (formerly Rogerson) four months later, an event celebrated with a tea party at Oxford's Browns restaurant.[122] The question of what should be done with the resources engaged in these earlier stages in the editorial process as they came to an end had been carefully considered. A swathe of Supplement editors were reallocated to the *Shorter*, the *Pocket*, *ODEL*, and other projects in January,[123] and others would follow later in the year.

The spring of 1983 saw the computerization project gathering momentum. By March half a dozen or so possible institutional partners had been informally identified, some of them arising by chance personal connections. For example, it was thanks to Michael Brookes, an estates manager for Oxford University who had formerly worked at the University of Waterloo in Ontario, that word of the proposals reached Waterloo's President, Doug Wright, who impressed Charkin with the strong record of his university's computer science department.[124] Similarly, the fact that Rex Richards, a former Vice-Chancellor of Oxford, was also a director of IBM UK facilitated the identification of the appropriate people to contact within IBM about the possibility of collaboration. A document entitled *A Future for the Oxford English Dictionary* was drawn up, combining information about the project with a formal invitation to tender, and approximately 100 copies were sent out. It was arranged that one copy should reach the desk of the Prime Minister, Margaret Thatcher, on the Monday following her victory in the British general election on 9 June, accompanied by a carefully worded letter emphasizing the national importance of the Dictionary; this paved the way for constructive discussions with the Department of Trade and Industry about possible funding, as did a direct approach to Kenneth Baker, the DTI's

---

[120] OUPA(u) (RWB papers) 6 Apr. 1983 RWB to RDPC; Dictionaries newsletter 12 Apr. 1983; OUPA(u) (RWB papers) 17 Mar. 1983 RWB to RDPC.

[121] OED/C/4/2/4 26 Nov. 1982 [RWB] to JAS/ESCW.

[122] Dictionaries newsletter 14 Nov. 1983. In fact the entry for *zzzz*—the conventional representation of the sound of someone snoring—was subsequently recast as a subsense of the entry for the letter *Z*, so that the last entry in the Supplement as eventually published was that for *Zyrian*.

[123] Dictionaries newsletters 9 Dec. 1982, 12 Jan. 1983.

[124] Tompa (1996: 1).

first Minister for Information Technology, by Sir Fred Dainton, another influential figure with Oxford connections.[125]

The demands of computerization—or rather of work on the proposal to computerize—were now beginning to threaten progress on other fronts. By July both Weiner and Simpson were constantly being called to meetings or asked to prepare documents, with inevitable consequences for their work on the Supplement, to the increasing frustration of Burchfield, who finally wrote to Charkin demanding to have prior notice of calls on their time: 'I am losing Edmund over and over again, [...] John looks like being drawn in more and more, and the results on the Volume 4 front are obvious and alarming.'[126] In addition to the perennial problem of juggling manpower between projects, he was evidently beginning to feel 'out of the loop' where computerization matters were concerned. Nor was this the only clash between the two men at this time. An argument about staff salaries, and whether reorganization of the Department could be achieved without further compulsory redundancies (it was), dragged on for several months; Charkin also refused Burchfield's insistent demand that an additional person should be recruited to assist Weiner with work on the forthcoming data capture.[127] Burchfield's honeymoon period with Charkin was clearly well and truly over.

In November the *OED* computerization team—including Charkin and Weiner, and also two key members of OUP's Information Systems group, Ewen Fletcher and Richard Sabido—travelled to the US and Canada for a fact-finding visit to various organizations that had submitted a tender or might otherwise have something to offer. By this stage the clear front runners were IBM and the University of Waterloo—both with much to offer in the area of computing expertise—and, for the actual business of entering the text of the Dictionary and Supplement, the International Computaprint Corporation (ICC), a Pennsylvania-based subsidiary of Reed International. It had also become clear that no single organization could carry out everything OUP needed; the project would have to be a collaboration between two or more parties, with the Press taking on a central managing role. Tim Benbow, the deputy director of the Press's International Division and a man with considerable experience in managing technically complex publishing projects (including the computerization of various reference works), was identified as a suitable person to take administrative charge of what would very shortly become known as the 'New *OED* Project'.

November also marked the completion of the restructuring of the Dictionary Department in readiness for the post-Supplement era (although of course a small group of senior editors, centred on Burchfield himself, remained at work on Volume IV).

---

[125] OUPA(u) 6 July 1983 T. Flesher (Prime Minister's private secretary) to RAD; Dainton (2001: 413–14). Sir Fred Dainton was a former professor of chemistry at Oxford who had gone on to become chairman of the University Grants Committee.

[126] OUPA(u) (RWB papers) 20 July 1983 RWB to RDPC.

[127] OUPA(u) 29 Nov. 1983 RWB to RDPC, 2 Dec. 1983 RDPC to RWB; further correspondence (Mar.–May 1983) about staff salaries and reorganization in OUPA(u) (RWB papers).

The several groups working on the *Shorter*, *ODEL*, and various smaller dictionaries had all now been enriched by the transfer of Supplement staff; there was also to be a new, though initially tiny, project which would carry forward the Supplement's lexicographical approach, and indeed some of its staff, into the new era. The benefit, to all of the smaller dictionaries (up to and including the *Shorter*), of being able to draw on the fully researched historical entries in the Supplement for coverage of the vocabulary of the past few decades was well understood; it followed naturally enough that these other projects might find it useful to draw on something similar in relation to still more recent vocabulary. If the new entries to be used in this way were actually prepared in full *OED* style, like those of the Supplement, they might conceivably be incorporated into the *OED* at some later date (though the exact way in which this might be done, like many other aspects of computerization and what might follow from it, remained vague for the time being); but in the meantime they could form an ongoing database of just the kind of material that the *Shorter*, *ODEL*, and other projects needed to update their headword lists. Thus was born what came to be known as the New English Word Service (NEWS).[128] A start was made in a very small way, with only Edith Bonner (now working half-time) assigned to the work, under the direction of Edmund Weiner when he could be spared from other activities; items were initially identified by searching of some of the departmental quotation files, but there were soon also requests for particular items identified as essential additions for one or other of the smaller dictionaries.[129] The need for a larger team to meet all of the department's needs for coverage of new vocabulary was clear enough, though the resistance of OUP to increasing headcount was also clear.

The start of 1984 saw Weiner moving fully over to the *New OED* project, and indeed moving out of St Giles'; accommodation was found in the Press's main Walton Street buildings so that he could devote himself to the computerization project. Lesley Burnett was drafted in to take his place on the Supplement, once again leaving the *Shorter* without its chief editor. There was even some suggestion of suspending work on the *Shorter* entirely so that effort could be concentrated on computerization, but this was fiercely resisted—particularly by Burnett herself—and work continued, though progress was inevitably very limited.[130]

The date of 1 February 1984 had been earmarked for some time as an occasion for celebration, 100 years after the publication of Part I of the first edition.[131] A coachload of

[128] Its original title was 'Series 4', as the copy for the entries was filed in the Department as a new series of slips alongside three other files, serving different purposes, which had built up during the lifetime of the Supplement (and which had recently been officially named 'Series 1', 'Series 2', and 'Series 3'). The last of these, which had started out as a file of quotations built up for the *Shorter* and *ODEL*, was now designated as the file for all new quotations coming into the Department regardless of which project they were intended for. Dictionaries newsletter 12 Nov. 1982; OUPA(u) announcement (1 Sept. 1983) about 'Series 4'.

[129] OUPA(u) notes (1 Dec. 1983) on 'Additional arrangements' for Series 4.

[130] OUPA(u) notes (19 Dec.) of a meeting held 16 Dec. 1983; OUPA(u) note by RWB 5 Jan. 1984; OUPA(u) (RWB papers) 3 May 1995 RWB to Eric Stanley.

[131] Although the actual anniversary was on 29 January (see p. 176 n. 234).

Oxford lexicographers visited Mill Hill School a few days beforehand to view a special centenary exhibition of *OED* memorabilia and to have lunch with 'the Headmaster, 57 bearers of the surname Murray, a Skeat or two', and various other descendants of individuals who had contributed to the first edition.[132] It had also been the intention to use the occasion to make a formal public announcement about the computerization project, but this had to be postponed because not all of the contracts had been signed and returned.[133] Even a month later, when Burchfield delivered the Threlford Memorial Lecture at the Institute of Linguists—a meditation on the lexicographical labours of the preceding three decades, which he saw as concluding with the publication of Volume IV in late 1985 or early 1986, and a brief glance at the next phase of work which had already begun—he referred only to the prospect of an announcement being made '[i]n the course of this year'.[134] News, however, began to leak out, so that by the time of the official launch of the *New OED* project, which took place at the Royal Society in London on 15 May and received considerable media coverage, many of those attending will already have known some details.

The scale of the new project was undeniably impressive. In order to create an electronic database containing the integrated text of the *OED* and Supplement— from which it was also planned to produce a printed version of the text—350 million characters would need to be keyed and proofread, with additional markup added to the text in order to represent the structure of the entries; the machine-readable text, with its tagging, would then need to be transformed by means of specially written software into a searchable database; and material from the Supplement was to be integrated into the main body of the Dictionary, a complex task requiring a mixture of computational and manual methods. The resulting text would then be typeset and printed. This formidable combination of tasks, described as 'Phase 1', was expected to take four years. 'Phase 2' was more open-ended, but its goals included the publication of the Dictionary in electronic form, and the ongoing revision, updating, and enhancement of the text. (It is worth pointing out that publication of a printed version of the integrated text had not formed part of the initial concept at all, although it rapidly became an important goal, both because of the much-needed revenue that would result—Edmund Weiner later referred to it as 'absolutely necessary to the economic viability of the New OED project as a whole'[135]—and also simply because of the need, in the uncharted and unbounded territory that computerization and revision of the Dictionary represented, for an interim objective that could readily be conceived and planned for.) In order to achieve the first phase, and make the necessary preparations for the second, OUP was now entering into a four-way partnership with IBM UK, ICC, and the University of Waterloo: ICC would undertake the keying of

[132] Dictionaries newsletter 15 Mar. 1984.
[133] OUPA(u) minutes of *New OED* In-house Group meeting 13 Jan. 1984.
[134] Burchfield (1984: 118).
[135] Weiner (1989: 25).

the text, IBM would contribute hardware, software, and personnel to assist with the creation of the database, and the University of Waterloo would conduct research into the electronic handling of large text databases (using the *OED* data as raw material) and make available any software which resulted from this work. The Department of Trade and Industry had also undertaken to make a subvention of nearly £300,000 towards research costs; but the anticipated total cost of the project during its first five years was put at close to £7 million.

Many of the press reports of the launch included quotes from Weiner—now officially designated Editor of the *New OED*—and Benbow as the project's manager, but also, unsurprisingly, from Burchfield. This was not, however, his occasion; indeed, he had become strangely detached from the project (describing his position to one correspondent as 'deliberately standing just a little off-stage').[136] His scepticism about computers may have moderated, but he evidently suspected that they were not for him: a year earlier he had written, with a touch of wistfulness, that the 'Age of Traditional Scholarship' in lexicography was drawing to a close, and that '[i]t will be computers, computers, all the way, from now on [...]. Within the Department the Traditional Scholars will continue to work in a traditional way. Those under or about 30, and malleable, will take over the new technology. They will doubtless be joined by others as time goes on, people from the new generation.'[137] He had proudly brought along to the launch some of the materials of 'Traditional Scholarship', in the form of a bundle of some of the very first slips of copy for the letter A in the first edition of the Dictionary, which had only recently been discovered in OUP's printing section; and when asked whether the vast collection of slips—now numbering more than 3 million—that had been built up for the use of the Supplement would be disposed of when the text was published and computerized, he retorted: 'Never. I don't trust this electronic equipment.'[138]

In any case, there was another lexicographical project dear to Burchfield's heart. Notwithstanding his heavy schedule of work for Volume IV of the Supplement—he was still aiming to prepare 500 slips of copy for the printer every day[139]—he had now become more involved in the preparation of *ODEL*, which under Tony Augarde's supervision was making slow but steady progress (less slow now that he had two other lexicographers to help him). It was therefore all the more of a shock when, at a meeting on 14 June and without warning, Charkin announced that the project was cancelled. He had come to the conclusion that there were cheaper ways of filling the market gap between the *Concise* and the *Shorter* than by writing a completely new dictionary from scratch, and moreover that *ODEL*, with its Johnsonian emphasis on literary quotations, was poorly conceived for this market. Burchfield's sense of outrage is vividly conveyed by his note of the meeting, at which Charkin 'rejected out of hand'

---

136 OUPA(u) (RWB papers) 16 Apr. 1984 RWB to I. Montagnes.
137 Dictionaries newsletter 13 July 1983.
138 Plommer (1984). See also Burchfield (1984: 114).
139 Lewis (1984).

all arguments put forward for continuation of the project.[140] The decision was a shock to the Department as a whole, but Burchfield evidently took it particularly hard. Richard Palmer, who had been due to join the *ODEL* team later in 1984, privately noted the general suspicion that personal motives may have played a part in the decision, commenting that Charkin and Burchfield were 'at daggers drawn' and that *ODEL* had been a 'pet project' of Burchfield's, which he had looked on as 'his swan-song (he retires in 3½ years' time)'. Tellingly, Palmer adds that the announcement had left Burchfield 'visibly shaken [...] his power is no longer what it was.'[141] The project's staff were reassigned to other projects, with Augarde being given temporary charge of the departmental new words programme.

Further reorganization followed, also at Charkin's instigation. The establishment of a board of senior lexicographers to deliberate on editorial matters affecting more than one dictionary, and the creation of a post of departmental manager, charged with organizing meetings of this board and other administrative responsibilities, could be presented as addressing the need to relieve Burchfield of some of his administrative burden, allowing him to concentrate on editorial work; but it might equally be seen as a means of bringing the Dictionary Department more directly under Charkin's control (or, to put it another way, of wresting control from Burchfield). Be that as it may, on 3 September Tony Augarde became departmental manager for the Oxford Dictionaries, and the first meeting of the English Dictionaries Editorial Committee (EDEC) took place a few days later.[142] John Simpson was identified as a suitable person to take over the running of NEWS, and to join the *New OED* project, which it had now been decided should draw on the output of the NEWS team as well as on the text of the *OED* and Supplement.[143]

By the end of 1984 the revision of drafted entries for Volume IV was at last complete. Preparation of copy for the printer—the one component of the compilation process which Burchfield still reserved exclusively for himself—was in W, and although there was still plenty of work to be done on the proofs, it had been decided—with Burchfield's consent, though not, no doubt, his approval—that all other remaining members of the Supplement team, with the exception of the bibliographer John Paterson, could be formally transferred to other activities in the New Year: Alan Hughes to the *Shorter*, and Simpson to the *New OED*, together with Yvonne Warburton, who had joined the Supplement as a library researcher in 1976, and who had the daunting task of organizing the team of freelancers needed to proofread the text produced by ICC's 120-odd keyboarders, working in Florida and Pennyslvania (keying of the text of the *OED* and Supplement had begun in November). These and other editors would continue to

---

[140] OUPA(u) file note by RWB 14 June 1984.
[141] Quoted in Palmer (2006: 23).
[142] OUPA(u) 11 Sept. 1984 Augarde to EDEC members. Tony Augarde went on to compile an *Oxford Guide to Word Games* and the *Oxford Dictionary of Modern Quotations*; he retired in 1991.
[143] OUPA(u) 4 Sept. 1984 TJB to various; minutes of OUP/IBM progress meeting 14 Sept. 1984; minutes of EDEC meeting 11 Oct. 1984.

help out with the remaining work on the Supplement with Burchfield over the next few months, but for the Chief Editor the sense of abandonment was acute: he subsequently described the loss of people to other projects as 'painful beyond description [...] I entered the last few months literally by myself.'[144]

Nevertheless, on 25 March 1985 he put the finishing touches to the copy for the last entry in Volume IV, and in June he signed off his fourth and final Preface, with the announcement that he would now 'retire from the "great theatre" of lexicography' (a reference to the words of George Washington upon resigning his military commission in 1783) in order to devote himself to 'a reconsideration of English grammar'.[145] For there was yet another publishing project now awaiting his attention, even after the abandonment of *ODEL*: a new edition of Fowler's classic *Modern English Usage*, which had long been contemplated—with Robert Allen even pencilled in to tackle it, in conjunction with Weiner and others—but which had been postponed in 1978. Burchfield had agreed with Charkin that this should be a project for his retirement, but the timetable was now brought forward, perhaps as a consolation for the loss of the dictionary that was to have been Burchfield's own 'baby'.[146] Remarkably, he was also managing to fit in the task of editing a version of the *Pocket Oxford Dictionary* for the New Zealand market.[147]

There was to be one last sting in the long tail of the Supplement itself. At the time Burchfield was writing his Preface, the scheduled publication date for Volume IV was March 1986, as it had been for some time; but the final instalments of proofs were dogged by delays on the part of the printer (causing a frustrated Burchfield to liken his position to that of 'a marathon runner who has reached the stadium after 26 miles to be told that I must wait for the stadium to be completed before I run the last 385 yards'), and publication had to be postponed to 8 May.[148] (Tardiness on the part of the printers is understandable in one respect: Latimer Trend had decided to close down their hot-metal department, but agreed not to do so until work on the Supplement was finished. The prospect of being laid off upon the completion of one's current task is hardly an incentive to speed.) The last proof of all was signed off on 16 January 1986.

By this time the *New OED* project had grown and ramified considerably. The year and a half since its public launch had seen developments on a number of fronts, including the establishment of an Advisory Council (chaired by Professor Roger

---

[144] Quoted in Midgley (1986).

[145] Preface to Volume IV, p. xiii.

[146] OUPA(u) (RWB papers) 7, 20 Nov. 1978 RWB to J. K. Cordy, 20 Jan. 1982 RDPC to RWB, note by RDPC 28 June 1984. Burchfield's reference to grammar rather than usage reflects his decision that the writing of a grammar of English would be a suitable preparation for and adjunct to the revision of *Modern English Usage*, although in the event no such book issued from his pen.

[147] The copy for the *New Zealand Pocket Oxford Dictionary* was in fact largely prepared by Julia Swannell, leaving Burchfield only the relatively straightforward task of finalization for press. The dictionary was published in April 1986.

[148] OUPA(u) (RWB papers) 18 Oct. 1985 RWB to RDPC, PBED 15918 29 Nov. 1985 RWB to RDPC.

Elliott) and an Editorial Board (chaired by Burchfield);[149] the formation of a twelve-member computing team, comprising both OUP staff and individuals seconded from IBM (who also donated a mainframe computer for project use); the preparation of an outline system design, and the development of prototypes for key components of this system; the keying and proofreading of nearly two-thirds of the *OED* and Supplement text; and the preparation and distribution of a survey of potential users of an electronic version of the Dictionary (over 1,000 copies were sent out, of which over 45 per cent were returned). John Simpson's NEWS team had also taken on a third editor, Sara Tulloch, and had once again begun to issue 'appeals lists', like the desiderata lists of old.[150] There had also been a small but significant change in the interpretation of the team's acronym. As Simpson explained to Marghanita Laski—whose enthusiasm for collecting quotations had not been dimmed by the completion of the Supplement—NEWS remained very much in demand as a 'service' for the supply of new vocabulary to other Oxford dictionary projects, but he now regarded it as being the 'New English Words *Series*', a body of lexicographical work in its own right; a body of work which, moreover, it had now been decided should be published (or at least some of it) as part of the new integrated version of the Dictionary.[151] Simpson initially gave 1987 as the scheduled date for the publication of this integrated text, but detailed planning work during the summer of 1985 made it clear that 1989 would be a more realistic date.

A number of significant developments had also been taking place on the Canadian side of what was now a thoroughly transatlantic project, bound closer together by a steady stream of visits from Oxford to Waterloo and vice versa (as well as by the still comparatively novel, and restricted, medium of electronic mail). A striking demonstration of the enthusiasm of the University of Waterloo for the project was its establishment—with support from the Canadian government—of a 'Centre for the New *OED*' in January 1985, which provided a focus for research and development connected with the *OED*, and a place where visiting scholars and professionals could meet and work. The most valuable contribution made by Waterloo during this early phase of the project was the development of a parsing program which could convert the keyed portion of the text as supplied by ICC into a combination of text and markup (using a form of Generalized Mark-up Language (GML)) which better represented the *OED*'s entry structure, a necessary prerequisite for the integration of entries from

---

[149] The Advisory Council first met on 27 February 1985; consultation of members of the Editorial Board (which was conceived rather as a group of experts who could be asked for advice on specific matters than as a body meeting regularly) began at around the same time. A separate Japanese Advisory Council was subsequently set up, in recognition of the importance of the Japanese market for the Dictionary and the potential for valuable Japanese technical input, but it only seems to have met once, in September 1988.

[150] The first such list appeared in the May 1985 issue of the *New OED Newsletter*, a new and valuable source of information about the project which had been instituted by Tim Benbow in July 1984, and from which many of the details given here are taken (copies preserved in OUPA(u)).

[151] OUPA(u) minutes of EDEC meeting 9 May 1985, OED/C/2/5/46 28 May 1985 JAS to Laski.

the first edition and Supplement.[152] John Simpson, now finally free from work on the Supplement, spent the last four months of 1985 on secondment to the University of Waterloo, where he gave advice on the lexicographical aspects of the project and taught a graduate course in lexicography; he also gave the opening address at the first of what was to be a decade of conferences organized by the Centre. On his return to Oxford, the importance of NEWS to the *New OED* project, and of Simpson's work as the head of this team, was recognized when he was made Co-Editor of the *New OED*, a title conferred on Weiner at the same time.[153] The two men had been close colleagues for some time, and would go on to make a formidable duo.

---

tribology

In general those who discover a new substance, or identify a new concept, are more than happy to devise a name for it themselves; but sometimes it is felt that this is a matter requiring the expert assistance of a lexicographer. In 1964 Peter Jost, the chairman of a committee of engineers, became aware that the subject with which the committee's discussions were principally concerned—namely the study of lubrication, friction, and more generally of the interaction of surfaces moving relative to one another—was one which lacked a suitable name. He contacted Burchfield to ask for advice; Burchfield in turn consulted the classicist Colin Hardie, who suggested *tribology* (from Greek τρίβος 'rubbing'). In fact there were already a few *tribo-* words in English, the most relevant perhaps being *tribophysics*, coined by the physicist David Tabor in the 1940s as a name for the subject studied by the research group at Melbourne University to which he belonged. Jost disseminated the word among his colleagues, and it soon became established as a name for the new subject. Both words were duly included in Volume IV of the Supplement in 1986.

With the arrival of advance copies of Volume IV of the Supplement in March 1986, everything was now in place for publication. The *OED*, and its Supplement, had in fact been kept in the public eye by a steady stream of articles—some of them written by members of the *New OED* project—reporting on the progress of computerization; but it was clear that the completion of the Supplement, after nearly three decades, was a momentous enough event to warrant considerable attention, even without the aid of OUP's now well-honed publicity machine, operated for the fourth time by Elizabeth Knight. Television crews and interviewers from both sides of the Atlantic descended on 37a St Giles', and publication day itself, 8 May, was marked by several live radio interviews with Burchfield, items in the TV news bulletins, and reports in just about

---

[152] Among those who came to work on the *New OED* project at Waterloo was Tim Bray, one of the original authors of the now widely used XML (Extensible Markup Language) standard, who has said that his work with the *OED* 'was a significant input to the development of XML' (quoted in Simpson 2010).

[153] *New OED Newsletter* Jan. 1986.

all of Britain's national papers. There was also, of course, a party in Oxford, this time on a grand scale: nearly 200 people—current and former staff, readers, consultants, and various other contributors and supporters—congregated in the distinguished surroundings of Rhodes House to celebrate. Media coverage, just as congratulatory in tone as for previous volumes, continued for several weeks. Anthony Burgess's encomium, acclaiming the completion of the Supplement as 'the major pacific event of the year', is typical, as well as furnishing a characteristically Burgessian appraisal of Volume IV's contents: 'I have taken this book like a mistress to bed (a weighty one but handleable) and pored over a great many of the pages, looking for omissions. Nothing is omitted, nothing, however slangy or scabrous or high-tech.'[154]

Another idiosyncratic take on the occasion was provided by BBC TV's 'Bookmark' programme, broadcast on the evening of publication day. In a mocked-up scene, Burchfield, required to open his suitcase as he passed through customs, was revealed to be carrying the four volumes of the Supplement; the customs officer's enquiry as to what he was doing with such a large book was met with the response from Burchfield that it was 'my book. I wrote it.'[155]—a rather unfortunate description of a work which, like its parent Dictionary, was so conspicuously the result of massively collective endeavour, and a comment which will hardly have gone down well with his staff. Nor was it a fair reflection of Burchfield's own view: due acknowledgement is made in his Preface to Volume IV, as it was in its predecessors, of the contributions made by his staff, and indeed by many others. But his own role in the success of the enterprise also merits recognition.[156] He did, after all, achieve the remarkable feat of re-establishing, essentially *de novo*, a lexicographical department within OUP, from which an entire new generation of lexicographers had emerged under his guidance. The plain fact of the Supplement having been carried through to completion, over a timescale and at an expense so very much greater than had originally been contemplated, is also worthy of note. Burchfield's gratitude to the Delegates of the Press for keeping faith with the project is, again, recorded in his Preface; but credit should be given to his own part in convincing them to do so. Many of his former staff recall him as a forceful, autocratic, sometimes irascible figure—'headmasterly' is a word that crops up more than once—even something of a tyrant; but there is also recognition that some of these personality traits may have been useful in getting the Supplement finished, and in heading off some of the occasional threats to other dictionary projects, on those occasions when retrenchment was in the air. 'With a more amenable temperament,' as one former colleague put it, 'he (and the department) might not have survived.' Nor was this aspect of his character the only one which has stuck vividly in the memory:

---

[154] OUPA(u) printout signed by Anthony Burgess [n.d., Sept. 1988]; *Observer* 11 May 1986, p. 25.

[155] The programme does not appear to have been preserved, but the exchange with the customs officer is recorded in a review of the broadcast in the *New Statesman* (16 May 1986, p. 33).

[156] He had already received academic recognition of his achievements in the form of honorary doctorates from the universities of Liverpool and Victoria, awarded in 1978 and 1983 respectively.

others have commented on his ability to charm, and this too may have stood him in good stead when arguing the lexicographers' case.

The weeks following publication offered many further opportunities to try out his charm, as he embarked on one last international promotional tour for the Supplement, beginning in the States and proceeding to Canada and Japan. A keynote event which took place on 29 May—the official publication day for the US—was the celebratory symposium held at the Library of Congress, at which both Burchfield and Weiner gave papers, as did Hans Aarsleff, the distinguished historian of the study of language; between them they surveyed the Dictionary's past (now extending over nearly a century and a half), present, and future.[157] It had also been OUP's intention that the symposium should be the occasion for an exciting announcement about another, entirely new lexicographical initiative: the establishment of a unit for the study—on American soil— of North American English.[158] The idea of setting up a lexicographical unit somewhere in the States, to collect information on American English and use this to supplement and revise the *OED*—and also to liaise with American projects like the *Middle English Dictionary*—had been in circulation at least since early 1985; the concept gained additional credibility from the fact that similar lexicographical units had now been established in both Australia and South Africa, and were both now compiling historical dictionaries of these varieties of English which would in due course be published by OUP.[159] Both New York and Washington had their attractions as possible locations for such a unit, but the research facilities offered by the Library of Congress perhaps gave Washington the edge. An initial informal approach to Daniel Boorstin, the Librarian of Congress, about the idea of housing such a unit in the Library had met with a favourable response, and discussions had gone so well that by November, following a visit to Washington by Benbow, the decision to make an official offer of accommodation was thought to be 'now merely a formality'. However, it was decided—fortunately, as matters later turned out—that after all no public announcement should be made at the May symposium, and that the plan should remain confidential for the present.[160]

The completion of a major project usually brings mixed emotions, and for Burchfield the Supplement was no exception. The sense of achievement must have been enormous, and indeed the sense of relief: 'It is wonderful', he observed, 'to be still alive and to have finished the book.'[161] All the same, the realization that his part in one great stage of the development of the *OED* was now over, and the next stages were in

---

[157] Some of the material presented—though not Weiner's progress report on the *New OED* project— was published in Burchfield and Aarsleff (1988).

[158] For some of the early correspondence about the proposed unit, see OUPA(u).

[159] The *Dictionary of South African English on Historical Principles* was published in 1996 under the editorship of Penny Silva (on whom see also below, pp. 567ff.); she and other members of the Dictionary Unit for South African English (based at Rhodes University in Grahamstown) benefited from close collaboration with OUP lexicographers in Oxford over many years. For more on this dictionary, and the work of the Unit, see Silva (1999).

[160] OUPA(u) 19 Nov. 1985 TJB to GBR et al.; FC 28 Jan. 1986; OUPA(u) 1 May 1986 ESCW to Augarde.

[161] Quoted in Midgley (1986).

the hands of others—and, indeed, that 'his' book had already begun to be digested into a larger text—must have been a melancholy one, especially to someone who so relished being at the centre of things. He did of course have a continuing part to play in the *New OED*, both as chairman of its Editorial Board and as a reader of some NEWS entries for John Simpson; but that was very different from having one's hand on the tiller. A blunt reminder of the fact that the Press's lexicographical priorities lay elsewhere came within weeks of his return from the Far East, when he was informed that his office in 37a St Giles' was needed, and that it was desirable that he should find another office for his work on grammar and usage. Ironically, it was to 40 Walton Crescent—his base during more than two-thirds of his editorship of the Supplement—that he relocated, on 29 August.[162] From here he could continue to function, for a while at least, as an *éminence grise* for Oxford lexicography; but grey was hardly his colour.

An important milestone for the *New OED* project had been passed only a few weeks before Burchfield vacated his office in St Giles'. The keyboarding of the entire text of the *OED* and Supplement was completed in late June, and the equally formidable task of proofreading the keyed text was completed very soon afterwards. By late September work could begin on the further processing—computational and human—that would be necessary in order to transform the database into the version that was to be published, in paper form, in 1989.

This version of the Dictionary had already begun to be referred to informally as the second edition. This would become a controversial designation, for some, of a text which it had been accepted would not be subjected to full-scale revision; but it was already clear that the version of the Dictionary that was to be issued in 1989 would differ in several significant respects from what had been published previously, and that revision of the Dictionary had already begun.[163] Many of the changes resulted not from a decision that a particular type of revision could or should be carried out, but rather from the need to create consistency—or at least avoid distracting inconsistency—in a text which had been amalgamated from components which were themselves inconsistent, both with one another and (particularly in the case of the first edition) within themselves. For example, the fact that the Supplement had discontinued the first edition's policy of capitalizing every headword meant that for every entry—indeed every lemma—in the latter the capital initial had to be reviewed, and downcased unless the word in question normally took a capital. Similarly, the amalgamation of Dictionary and Supplement, and the shifting and altering of some sections of text that this necessitated—when, for example, the Supplement inserted additional senses within the main sequence of senses in a large entry—meant that thousands of cross-references were rendered invalid and would have to be altered. Inconsistent treatment of foreign scripts in etymologies—the first edition had regularly cited foreign words in Cyrillic, Arabic, and other scripts, whereas the Supplement had

---

[162] OUPA(u) (RWB papers) 22 July 1986 RWB to members of EDEC.
[163] A description of these changes is given on pp. xii–xvi of the Introduction to the second edition.

used transliterations—was also eliminated by opting for transliterations for every script other than Greek. These are just some of what might be called 'housekeeping' changes. In addition, one exception was made to the principle of not subjecting any component of the text to thoroughgoing revision: it was decided that the distinctive (and, for many users, difficult) phonetic notation devised by Murray to represent pronunciations, and used throughout the Dictionary and Supplement, would be translated into the widely used International Phonetic Alphabet. This decision was made easier by the fact that a very large part of the work of conversion could be carried out by suitably written software. A large number of small misprints and slips in the text which had come to light as the entries were scrutinized in the course of the integration process were corrected; and, very occasionally, amendments were made to definitions from the first edition when wording was felt to be not merely dated but patently offensive.[164]

Another major feature of the second edition, of course, was the new material being prepared by the NEWS team. A schedule was drawn up for incorporating the new entries into the *OED* database, which required the bulk of them—eventually numbering approximately 5,000—to be fully edited by the end of November 1986; thereafter a few late entries were keyed into the database, but most of the copy subsequently produced by the NEWS team remained in paper form, to be keyed and incorporated into the database at some point after the publication of the second edition. (The idea of publishing the material annually in 'OED Yearbooks' was abandoned after lengthy discussion.) The new entries were of course also available to be made use of by other dictionary projects within 37a St Giles'.[165]

In fact 1986 had been a remarkable year for other OUP lexicographers besides those working on the *OED*. Several other new dictionaries had issued from 37a St Giles', including the sixth edition of the *Little Oxford* (the second to be edited by Julia Swannell) and Joyce Hawkins's new *Oxford Reference Dictionary*. Success in a different sphere—but no less appreciated by OUP—came with the *Griffin Savers Oxford Dictionary*, a version of the *Oxford Senior Dictionary* (a schools dictionary, also edited by Hawkins) which had been made in 1984 for distribution by the Midland Bank as a promotional item for its younger customers, and sales of which topped the million mark during the year. The *Shorter*, though still a long way from publication,

---

[164] The first such entry to be amended in this way was that for *canoe*: the distinction made in the entry between the boat as used by 'uncivilized nations' and that to be found '[i]n civilized use' was felt to be unacceptable. The fact that revisions of this kind were made was publicly acknowledged (see e.g. Berg 1988: 3), although the printed Introduction to the second edition referred only to the correction of 'small misprints and slips' (p. xiv). As John Simpson has recently observed of this 'minor turning point' in the integration process, arguments can be (and have been) made both for and against such revisions; looking at the Dictionary from the viewpoint of the general user, it is hard to argue with his assessment that 'on balance [...] the sort of small-scale, local change we initiated then did more good for the dictionary than harm' (Simpson 2013a: 165–6).

[165] OUPA(u) text of email sent by JAS to Y. L. Warburton 3 Dec. 1986. Materials relating to the yearbook idea are preserved in OUPA(u).

was steaming ahead, with perhaps a quarter of the revised text completed in draft by a now much expanded staff.[166]

The increase in the pace of work on *SOED* had direct consequences for the NEWS team. In the course of their revision of the text, Lesley Burnett and her colleagues were identifying items not covered in the *OED* or the Supplement at a rate which dwarfed the small number of requests coming from those working on the smaller dictionaries. The effect of this on the NEWS workload was maximized by the decision—taken by Burnett in light of the heavy demands posed by all the other aspects of revision—that the *SOED* editors should spend no time working on new items, but simply pass them all to NEWS. A further difficulty for the NEWS editors was that none of them were scientifically trained, which made the preparation of entries for scientific items—of which there were inevitably a great many—particularly time-consuming: an editor without a science background took considerably longer to draft a science item, and much of the resulting material often had to be substantially revised or even rewritten. The time which Alan Hughes—now one of the senior science editors on the *Shorter*, but also of course a Supplement veteran—was able to devote to this was also inevitably limited. These severe limits on the capacity of NEWS to deal with scientific vocabulary had in fact already had an effect on the selection of items for inclusion in the second edition of *OED*: many scientific entries which might otherwise have been added had had to be held back pending their revision by a qualified scientist. The obvious solution, or part of it, was to recruit a scientist to the NEWS team, and approval for this was secured early in 1987. John Simpson was aware, however, that this on its own would not increase NEWS capacity enough to meet all of the requirements being placed upon it, and pressed for further expansion. He was only partially successful: by the end of the year a new general editor and a new scientist had been taken on, but the team had also lost the generalist Eric Dann, who had opted to take early retirement.[167] It was also true that the continuing demands of computerization would limit the resources that could be put into recruitment and training of further NEWS editors.

Plans for expansion on the other side of the Atlantic also ran into difficulties. In December 1986 the Press advertised for the post of Director of the 'Center for North American English', to be based in Washington. However, it now emerged that objections had been raised to the siting of the Center in the Library of Congress, on the grounds that this use of Congressional facilities would amount to subsidizing a non-American publisher at the expense of American competitors, and the offer of accommodation was subsequently withdrawn.[168] The lack of a suitable location for

---

[166] OUP *Record* 31 (Dec. 1986), p. 7.

[167] OUPA(u) 9, 15 Dec. 1986, 2 Feb., 14 July 1987 JAS to TJB. The two new recruits, who both joined the staff of NEWS in September 1987, were Bernadette Paton—who had already been doing freelance work for the project for some months—and the present writer.

[168] For an account of some of the Congressional discussions which took place on the matter, which also reproduces some correspondence with OUP and various American publishers, see *Legislative Branch Appropriations for 1988: hearings before a subcommittee of the House of Representatives Appropriations Committee* (Washington: U.S. Government Printing Office, 1987), part 2, pp. 457–86.

the Center, together with the failure of attempts to raise funds to support it, forced a rethink of the whole proposal; from the discussions emerged the rather less grandiose concept of an American-run reading programme, to be run from a smaller unit housed elsewhere. It was decided that even this more modest enterprise would have to wait.[169]

At least the computerization of the Dictionary was continuing to make impressive progress. Automatic processing of the keyed text, including the integration of first edition and Supplement material to the extent that this was possible without human intervention, was completed by the end of May 1987; a month later the bespoke editing software that would be needed for the next stage—an adaptation of a lexicographical text editing system called LEXX (see Figure 39), developed by the IBM computer scientist Mike Cowlishaw—was ready for use (and had already been christened OEDIPUS, the 'OED Integration, Publishing, and Updating System', by Veronica Hurst, a freelance assistant working on the *New OED* project), and the editing of fully integrated entries could begin. By August the first sections of integrated text were ready to be sent to a typesetting company, Filmtype Services of Scarborough, to be converted into a form from which printed as opposed to machine-readable entries could be produced; the resulting galleys and page proofs were now dealt with by a new team of proofreaders. Simpson and Weiner jointly undertook to read page proofs for the entire 59-million-word text: a mammoth task which has been compared to their both reading the Bible from cover to cover every week for a year. Seeing the whole Dictionary in proof also gave them a thorough knowledge of the whole text in a way that nothing else could have done.

It is worth stressing once again that the pioneering nature of much of this work, and also the volume of data involved, tested the limitations of the available technology, in some cases severely. Full searchability of the complete Dictionary text, for example—something which would now be taken for granted with a database of only a few hundred megabytes—was simply not available. Most of the processing of the text had to be carried out repeatedly on each of forty separate alphabetical ranges or 'tables'; magnetic tapes of data from tables on which integration had already been completed were sent off to Scarborough even as the work of integrating the text in other parts of the alphabet was still going on, thereby introducing a further element of complexity to the task of coordinating all of the different stages of work. Proofreading and integration continued in parallel until the latter task was completed in June 1988. Once proofreading of a range of text was complete, camera-ready copy for printing could be produced; film for printing the 21,730 pages of the second edition then had to be sent to the selected manufacturer, Rand McNally of Taunton, Massachusetts (not OUP's

---

[169] Correspondence preserved in OUPA(u). A small 'consolation prize', in regard to improving coverage of American lexis, came in the form of a collection of tens of thousands of quotation slips amassed by Colonel Albert F. Moe, a veteran amateur lexicographer of American slang and military language (and an occasional correspondent with the *OED*'s lexicographers since the 1970s), donated to the *OED* by his widow (correspondence in OUPA(u)).

FIGURE 39   The early days of the electronic *OED*: (a) photograph of part of the Dictionary entry for *bungler* as displayed on the LEXX editing system; (b) the first edition of the Dictionary on CD-ROM.

own struggling printing department, for whom the awarding of this job to an external printer was a bitter blow). The division of this material into twenty volumes took place at a relatively late stage in the process.[170]

The innovative nature of the work involved in the creation of OED2 was recognized in October when the Dictionary won the British Computer Society's annual Applications Award. This was swiftly followed by another excitingly novel by-product of computerization: a version of the text of the first edition of the Dictionary on two compact discs (CD-ROM technology was still in its infancy, and it was not yet possible to fit all of the text on a single disc, although this was to follow a year later).[171] This was to revolutionize the way in which the content of the Dictionary was to be accessed by readers and researchers. A second instalment of another innovation, older but still impressive, had appeared a few months earlier in the form of the 'Compact' (paper) edition of the entire Supplement, a third volume to accompany the two earlier micrographically printed volumes of the Compact first edition.

Computerization of the OED was soon also directly benefiting another of OUP's English dictionaries. There was considerable pressure to bring publication of the revised *Shorter* forward, and the availability of the text of OED2 in machine-readable form now suggested a possible means of accelerating the editing process. Given that the *Shorter* was, at least in principle, a condensed version of the *OED*, might it be possible to extract a subset of the data contained in the electronic version of the text, containing only those entries—and, indeed, only those components of the entries— that fell within the agreed scope of the smaller dictionary, and for the *SOED* editors to take these automatically extracted and condensed entries as the starting point for their work, rather than writing out revised entries from scratch in the traditional way? An approach was made to the University of Waterloo, whose programmers soon established the feasibility of this radically different methodology; in the course of 1988 a specification for the extraction and pre-processing of what became known as 'subset *OED*' was drawn up and implemented,[172] and editors were trained in new working methods. At the same time authorization was given for the development of a computer system for the use of the *Shorter*, at the cost of nearly £1 million, again with a view to bringing publication forward—1992 was now firmly set as a target date—as well as enhancing the potential for exploiting the content of the new database that was being created.[173]

---

[170] One consequence of this is that some of the early images of OED2 produced for promotional purposes—which continued to appear from time to time even after publication, for example on the cover of the July 1989 issue of the journal *English Today*—showed volumes which never existed; thus, for example, it had been guessed that the words marking the start and end of volume XVIII would be *tarlatan* and *tuzzy-muzzy*, whereas in the event Volume XVIII ran from *thro* to *unelucidated*.

[171] The CD-ROM edition of OED1, which was released in late 1987, was produced for OUP by TriStar, a sister company of ICC.

[172] For a full account of the extraction process, given mainly from a technical perspective, see Blake et al. (1992).

[173] FC 26 Apr. 1988.

Simpson also reorganized the work of the NEWS team, with a view to making the editing of the *Shorter* more efficient. Specific requests from various projects, especially the *Shorter*, had displaced sorting through the quotation files as the main source of items for NEWS to work on; it was now decided to reintroduce sorting, starting at the letter L—well ahead of the point reached by the *Shorter*'s own procedures for identifying new items (such as checking of other dictionaries)—so that entries could be drafted in advance of their being needed by the *Shorter* lexicographers. Sorting under this new system commenced early in 1988.

At this point all of the Dictionary Department's quotation files still only existed in paper form (except, of course, for the quotations which formed part of the *OED* database itself). These files were continuing to grow at a rate of something like 10,000 quotations a month, thanks mainly to an ongoing programme of directed reading (now being administered by Sara Tulloch); and the desirability of embarking on the computerization of this resource—so as to make its contents more fully accessible, for use in a variety of ways—had been recognized for some time. A proposal had even been made, late in 1987, that a start should be made on the task using a standalone IBM PC; this was followed by a detailed feasibility study for a more ambitious project to capture incoming quotations ('Incomings') as a searchable database.[174] However, this coincided with growing interest elsewhere in OUP in the rapidly developing discipline of corpus linguistics, and in exploring what the analysis of a purpose-built corpus of English text could do for lexicography, particularly with reference to learner's and bilingual dictionaries. Such corpora were generally conceived as composed of sizeable samples of text (larger in size than the quotations to be found in the Departmental slip files), taken from a carefully balanced selection of sources.[175] Given the substantial costs which setting up a new corpus of this kind would incur, there seems to have been some reluctance to commit the funds needed for the computerization of Incomings at the same time, and the latter project languished until late 1989.[176]

Even as the first printed volumes of *OED2* had begun to arrive in Oxford, in the summer of 1988, serious thought was beginning to be given to another future enterprise for the Press, and one likely to involve vastly more investment than the creation of a corpus, let alone the computerization of Incomings: the full-scale revision of the *OED*. The project which was to culminate in the publication of *OED2* had involved enormous expense and effort, but it was of course merely 'Phase 1', and in some ways no more than a necessary preliminary to the much bigger task of revising, expanding, developing, and exploiting the integrated first edition and Supplement. Detailed discussion documents about 'Phase 2' began to circulate internally in late

---

[174]   OUPA(u) 3 Dec. 1987 Tim Bray to Sue Bennett, 4 Mar. 1988 R. Akroyd to various.

[175]   The drive to create a corpus of modern British English was eventually to bear fruit in the 100-million-word British National Corpus, a collaborative project involving many organizations and individuals besides OUP. The BNC website (www.natcorp.ox.ac.uk) gives historical and other information about the project.

[176]   See below, p. 553.

1987, and consultation of external parties, including both the Dictionary's Advisory Council and the Editorial Board, followed over the next few months. However, this was a momentous matter, involving many imponderables—and extremely large sums of money—and planning was necessarily a slow and cautious process.

The post-*OED2* stages of the project had, of course, to be planned for in advance. However, there was still the small matter of completing the second edition; and there some ticklish decisions remained. What, for example, should the title page of the new book say? In February 1988 Burchfield—who had finally retired the previous month, having vacated his Walton Crescent office in favour of working from his Sutton Courtenay home the previous September[177]—expressed himself satisfied with the format proposed by Tim Benbow, which closely resembled that eventually used, with the exception of one detail: this 'first version of the "Second Edition"' could not, he felt, be described as having been 'edited by' Simpson and Weiner. While not doubting their competence to undertake the revision of the Dictionary, he felt that 'they should do it first before laying claim to the editorship of a work that has not been re-edited'. In the end it was decided instead to describe *OED2* as having been 'prepared by' its two Co-Editors. Burchfield also felt that the omission of other names from the title page constituted an injustice: as he later lamented to his friend Eric Stanley, 'No one seems to recognize that in editorial terms OED2 = 66% Murray and co-editors, 33% myself, and 1% S[impson] & W[einer].'[178] There was, of course, similar injustice in this equation, concealing as it did the contribution of all lexicographers below the rank of (Co-)Editor; and in fact the part played by Murray, Bradley, Craigie, Onions, and Burchfield himself was fully recognized on a page facing the main title. But he could be forgiven for feeling at least a little rueful that, barely three years after the completion of a project over which he had presided for nearly half his life, the publication which had borne his name was to be merged into a larger whole and, consequently, to cease to exist as a separate entity.[179]

At last, on 8 December 1988, the last page of *OED2* was passed for press, one day ahead of schedule, with manufacture of the last of the twenty volumes completed a few weeks later.[180] It is rare indeed for any dictionary project to be completed ahead of schedule; the completion of this exceptionally large, complex, and pioneering project on schedule *and* within budget was a remarkable achievement, and an impressive testimony to the project management of Tim Benbow.[181] It also represented

---

[177] OUPA(u) 7 Sept. 1987 RWB to Tony Augarde; OUP *Record* 33 (Dec. 1988), p. 39.

[178] OUPA(u) (RWB papers) 4 Feb. 1988 RWB to TJB, 1 Mar. 1990 RWB to Stanley.

[179] Another figure whose role in the creation of *OED2* was generally acknowledged unexpectedly left OUP before its publication. Richard Charkin had of course been the driving force behind so much of the whole *New OED* project during its earlier stages; but by the end of 1988 he was no longer working for the Press, having left in 1988 after the failure of his bid to become Secretary to the Delegates on the retirement of George Richardson. He would continue to be a big player in British publishing, holding directorships with various other publishing houses, including Bloomsbury, whose board he joined in 2007.

[180] OUPA(u) minutes of *New OED* Project Status Review Meetings 14 Dec. 1988, 16 Feb. 1989.

[181] In 1994 Benbow's contribution was acknowledged by the University of Waterloo with the award of an honorary LL.D.

the triumphant culmination of hundreds of person-years of effort on the part of a huge team of keyboarders, proofreaders, programmers, researchers—and of course lexicographers, with Simpson and Weiner at their head—and the vindication of the considerable commitments, financial and otherwise, made to the project by the principal institutional partners.

OUP's commitment to the *OED*, and to other lexicographical projects, was of course ongoing. The first few months of 1989 saw further fresh investment in the Dictionary, even as preparations were being made for the launch of *OED2* in March. In both cases the investment was directed towards activities which would also benefit the Press's other lexicographical enterprises (all of which had now been brought under the overall charge of Tim Benbow as Director, Dictionary Projects). The NEWS team was expanded by the engagement of three new lexicographers, a move designed to help meet the need of the *Shorter* for new entries. At the same time the Press was finally able to appoint a person to man its long-hoped for lexicographical outpost in North America. Following the collapse of the Library of Congress initiative, a base had been found for a more modest enterprise—comprising no more than a reading programme focusing on North American sources—in the offices of the telecommunications research company Bellcore in Morristown, New Jersey; and Jeffery Triggs, a recent graduate from Rutgers University, was appointed to direct operations.[182] (It is worth mentioning that at precisely this time those working for OUP were given a dramatic illustration of the Press's readiness to *dis*invest when it wished: on 31 January 1989 the Delegates decided to close down its ailing printing business, resulting in over 200 redundancies and the termination of an Oxford working tradition several centuries older than that of its English lexicography.[183])

It was extremely important for the Press that vindication of its investment in *OED2* should come in the form of sales of the book as well as critical acclaim; and it was therefore crucial to mount an effective promotional campaign. Fortunately the publicity machine for OUP's dictionaries—now no longer under the direction of Elizabeth Knight, who had retired a few months after the publication of Volume IV of the Supplement—was in excellent working order; and the story of *OED2* would have been impressive enough to generate considerable public interest even without a vigorous campaign. The Dictionary had, moreover, many champions, who required little prompting to enthuse about it. An early gift to the publicists had been provided by Anthony Burgess in September 1988, with the declaration that '*[t]here will be no greater publishing event this century* than the appearance of the new OED'. His endorsement featured prominently in the subsequent publicity, and was widely quoted in the increasingly extensive coverage which began to appear in newspapers and magazines, and on radio and television, all over the English-speaking world as publication day approached.

---

[182] OUPA(u) 17 Mar. 1989 JAS to M. Lesk. Agreement had been formally reached with Bellcore about these arrangements a year earlier (OUPA(u) 25 Mar. 1988 M. Lesk to TJB).

[183] See Phillips (forthcoming). The decision was communicated to the workforce on 1 February.

Sebastian Faulks wrote of 'an extraordinary co-operation of literature and electronics, of history and technology'; William Golding, who was old enough to remember the completion of the first edition in 1928, gave 'a rather awed welcome' to its successor, 'a superb example of organised scholarship'; and Philip Howard declared that the book 'will be remembered and used as long as English is spoken', and that the database was 'a tool of research and scholarship of richness undreamed of in our philosophy until now'. Or, as Richard Boston rather more straightforwardly put it in the *Guardian*: 'damn it, the thing's a triumph. Sound the trumpet, beat the drum.'[184] OUP's marketing department had every reason to be proud of their campaign, the effectiveness of which received external recognition when it was declared the best promotion of the month in a competition sponsored by *Publishing News*. More importantly, nearly a third of the initial print run of 10,000 copies of the 20-volume Dictionary (see Figure 40) were sold in advance of publication.[185]

Celebration of the new Dictonary—now dedicated, like the Supplement before it, to the Queen—continued to build, culminating in a grand luncheon at Claridge's Hotel on 29 March 1989, the eve of the official day of publication. This was a truly splendid occasion: different, certainly, from the great dinner held in Goldsmiths' Hall to mark the completion of the first edition of the Dictionary, but mainly in ways which reflected the social and cultural changes that had taken place over the intervening seven decades. Certainly no expense was spared by OUP (for whom on this occasion there was no Goldsmiths' Company to share the cost). Some 200 guests were regaled with speeches from several luminaries of the world of letters. The extravagant panegyric delivered by Daniel Boorstin, the now retired Librarian of Congress—likening the occasion to 'the revelation of the second edition of the Bible', and acclaiming the *OED* as 'the greatest work of literary scholarship in modern times'—would have carried extra resonance to those who knew of his strong, though ultimately unavailing, support for the proposal to house the Dictionary's North American unit in his institution. Malcolm Bradbury, representing the writing profession, praised the Dictionary as 'a great record of the love affair between literature and its language' (and also mischievously drew attention to the fact that the last word defined in Volume I of *OED2* happened to be *bazoom*); and the English academic Christopher Ricks, flown in from Boston for the occasion, bestowed further encomiums in what was later recalled as a 'virtuoso lexical dance before the ark'. There were also speeches by Benbow and both Co-Editors, by representatives of IBM and the University of Waterloo, and by Oxford University's Chancellor, Lord Jenkins of Hillhead, who saluted the Dictionary as 'at once monumental and intimate, authoritative and infinitely entertaining' (and who enthused more light-heartedly about the book's 'elegant, satisfying chunkiness'). There was praise too for

---

[184] *Independent* 18 Mar. 1989, Magazine, p. 44; *Evening Standard* 16 Mar. 1989, pp. 27, 31; *Times* 18 Mar. 1989, p. 29; *Guardian* 24 Mar. 1989, p. 25.
[185] Information from the 3 April and 27 April issues of 'OED2 News', an irregular internal OUP leaflet summarizing publicity for the Dictionary (copies at OUPA(u)).

FIGURE 40   John Simpson and Edmund Weiner photographed in March 1989 with the twenty volumes of *OED2*.

Burchfield—who presided over the festivities, and who was christened 'the grand old man of English lexicography'—and for all of the thousands who had made contributions, large and small, throughout the project's long history.[186] (One melancholy absence was noted: that of Marghanita Laski, one of the Dictionary's fiercest champions in recent years and its most prolific contributor of quotations, who had died just over a year earlier, having continued to send in quotations until less than a month before her death.[187])

The celebrations would continue for some time to come—including a promotional trip to the United States and Canada in April for Simpson and Weiner, and another to Japan in May—as would the acclamations. The chorus of praise was not entirely unanimous. A review in the *Times Literary Supplement* by Geoffrey Hill—which, strangely, hardly commented on the second edition as such, being mainly concerned with some of the ways in which the Dictionary fell short of an exhaustive guide to the language of Gerard Manley Hopkins—was followed by a series of letters which delivered some rather more hard-hitting criticisms, including the complaint that antedatings and other material for revision which had been sent in over the preceding decades had not yet been acted on, and that those who already owned the first edition and Supplement had no way of acquiring the entries for the 5,000 new items other than by purchasing the whole of *OED2*.[188] John Simpson responded to the first of these by reiterating that revisions of this kind had had to be ruled out of scope because of the magnitude of the other tasks being undertaken, and encouraged readers to continue to send in such material. Rather more trenchantly critical comments were made by Charlotte Brewer in an article in the *London Review of Books* in which she highlighted some of the criticisms that had been made of the first edition and Supplement—and which remained unaddressed in the new edition—and protested that the merging of the two components blurred the distinction between the different layers of editorial material; she ended by questioning the decision to publish the 'provisional' text at this point at all.[189] This, too, elicited a response from Simpson, in which he noted that many of the shortcomings of the Dictionary text were addressed in the preliminary pages of the second edition itself, where, in a section entitled 'The Future of the *OED*',[190] 'the principal aspects of the *OED* on which there is work to be done' were set out at length. It was true that OUP could have elected to postpone publication until all of this work had been completed, and the Dictionary completely revised; instead, the view had been taken that the issuing of *OED2* at this point in the process would best serve 'the needs of the scholarly world, and of all those interested in the minutiae of the language'. A briefer but in some ways more embarrassing critique—delivered, extraordinarily, less

---

[186] *Glasgow Herald* 30 Mar. 1989; *Guardian* 3 Apr. 1989, p. 19 (an edited version of Boorstin's speech); *London Review of Books* 20 Apr. 1989, p. 21; personal recollection.

[187] OED/C/2/5/46 7 Jan. 1988 Laski to S. Tulloch.

[188] *Times Literary Supplement* 21–7 Apr. 1989, pp. 411–14; 28 Apr.–4 May 1989, p. 455; 19–26 May 1989, p. 545; 9–15 June 1989, p. 637; 30 June–6 July 1989, p. 719.

[189] Brewer (1989). Simpson's response to these criticisms appeared in the issue of 9 Nov. 1989.

[190] *OED2* vol. I, pp. lv–lvi.

than a week after publication—came from Burchfield, who in an interview with Israel Shenker expressed regret that the text had not been more extensively revised. While praising the 'computer work', he, like Brewer, wondered '[w]hether the product should have been put out'. The fact that a man in his position should choose to say such things publicly, and to comment more generally on the second edition that '[i]t's one way of doing it', seems to bespeak considerable frustration or bitterness, or both, on his part.[191]

But for the moment, at least, such views remained very much in the minority. Furthermore, the negative points made by the critics were all matters of which Simpson, Weiner, and their colleagues at OUP had long been well aware, and had been publicly acknowledged. Indeed, some of the 'work to be done' was already under way: as had been the case in 1928, the lexicographers had embarked on the next phase in the development of the Dictionary even before the previous phase had been completed. Some of the work in store involved thoroughly familiar territory, such as the drafting of additional new entries, of which there were already several thousand more, beyond those included in *OED2*, awaiting incorporation in some future version of the Dictionary. But the nature of that future version—towards which the second edition was of course no more than a staging-post—was as yet undetermined, and a great deal else besides. A whole new 'untrodden forest', some of which James Murray and his contemporaries would have recognized, but much of which was unknown even to their twentieth-century successors, lay ahead.

[191] Quoted in Shenker (1989: 99). A few other critical notices of *OED2* were to follow, of which perhaps the most remarkable was that by Eric Stanley which appeared in the *Review of English Studies* (Stanley 1990); briefly discussed in Brewer (2007: 228–9). It was remarkable not least for the fact that Stanley (who implied by his careful avoidance of the words 'second edition' that *OED2* was unworthy of the description) was, as he acknowledged, a member of the Editorial Board for the project.

13

Towards *OED3*: 1989–

F OR those on the staff of the *OED* today who were not even born when the second edition was published, at least some of the years following 1989 must seem long enough ago to be written about as history. For those of us (including myself) for whom those two and a half decades are within living memory, however, the detached perspective which the writing of history requires is not available. More practically, the body of archival material relevant to this period becomes increasingly incomplete, and incompletely accessible, as one approaches the present. Nevertheless, I believe it is of some value to set down an account of these years as seen from one contemporary viewpoint, while acknowledging that what follows must be regarded as partial and provisional. The account also, necessarily, takes on more and more of the character of a simple chronicle of events as it approaches the present day.

In some respects, however, 1989 can be straightforwardly regarded as quite a long time ago. After all, the world has changed a great deal in the quarter-century since the publication of *OED2*, and in ways which could not have been foreseen. By a striking coincidence, March 1989—the month of publication of the second edition—was also the month in which a British computer scientist working at CERN in Geneva wrote a paper proposing 'a large hypertext database with typed links'.[1] The internet—as the worldwide network of computer-mediated communication has come to be known—already existed in 1989, but the World Wide Web, as inaugurated by Tim Berners-Lee's paper, was to transform the nature of both research and publishing; and the *OED*, as a large publishing project dependent on extensive research, was bound to be profoundly affected by these developments.

Accordingly, it is hardly surprising that the projection of the Dictionary's future constructed by those within OUP, from the perspective of 1989, went out of date so quickly; but there were other reasons for this besides the advent of the Web. As has

---

[1] Berners-Lee (1999) is one of many accounts now available of the conception and development of the World Wide Web. Berners-Lee's 1989 paper can be read online at www.w3.org/History/1989/proposal.html.

The Making of the *Oxford English Dictionary*. First edition. Peter Gilliver.
© Peter Gilliver 2016. First published 2016 by Oxford University Press.

already been mentioned, discussions about 'Phase 2' of the *New OED* project had been going on since 1987, but the forward planning of such an unprecedented venture was bound to be fraught with uncertainty; in particular, the revision of the Dictionary's text (as distinct from its supplementation) was an activity of which no substantial trial had yet been made. (A very limited pilot study had been carried out in 1987–8 at John Simpson's suggestion, taking a single page of *OED1* (*dogmatize–dogstones*) as its basis and using little more than the resources available within 37a St Giles'.[2]) Nevertheless, a broad outline plan envisaging publication of the third edition of the Dictionary in 2005 was presented to the Press's Finance Committee on 30 May 1989, and duly approved by the Delegates a week later.[3] We may smile now at the idea that anyone could have imagined the preparation of a fully revised edition as taking as little as sixteen years, but really at this point it was hardly more than a guess; or perhaps 2005 was as far into the future as Benbow, Simpson, and Weiner thought they could persuade the Press to commit itself. (The even earlier date of 2000 had been seriously proposed only a few months previously.[4]) It should also be borne in mind that at this point it was still possible to regard the revision of the *OED* as a 'light touch' process, drawing on the work done in the preparation of the new edition of the *Shorter* and making a modest number of further changes. It would soon become apparent, however, that, for the task to be done properly, just about every component of every entry in the Dictionary would need to be subjected to a full re-examination. Be that as it may, a commitment to the idea of revising the Dictionary had been made, at least in principle, and the development of more detailed plans could now proceed in the knowledge that they were likely to be given serious consideration.

Indeed, looking at the other major lexicographical and reference projects which were authorized to 'proceed as planned' at the same Delegates' meeting, it might be supposed that there was an appetite at OUP for seizing every significant opportunity in the field which presented itself. These projects included the ongoing revision of the *Shorter*, the development of an 'Oxford Corpus'—evidently envisaged as an important enabling resource for the new intermediate dictionary which had also been figuring prominently in the Press's plans for some time—and an important collaborative project with the French dictionary publisher Hachette. As if this was not enough, the Delegates had also come to the conclusion that a full-scale revision of the *Dictionary of National Biography* was desirable, and was beginning to consider how the external funding which would be necessary for such a massive undertaking might be sought.

There were, however, very real limits to the Press's enthusiasm for such projects. This was made abundantly clear barely a month later when the Delegates decided that the unfinished German dictionary project which had been acquired by OUP from

---

[2] OUPA(u) minutes of NEWS meeting 4 Nov. 1987. The antedatings and other information collected for this study were eventually given proper consideration when the range of entries for words beginning with *dog-* was revised in 2008–10.

[3] FC 30 May 1989, OD 6 June 1989; copy of plan in OUPA(u) (Secretary's papers).

[4] OUPA(u) 17 Nov. 1988 TJB to *New OED* In-house Group. In fact an option to publish *OED3* in 2000 was investigated in some detail as late as 1991, although the calculations submitted to Finance Committee came with a strong recommendation against it (OUPA(u) (ISA papers) 18 Feb. 1991 ISA to Finance Committee).

Harrap twelve years earlier should simply be abandoned—even though the letters S to Z remained unpublished.[5] Attempts were made to obtain external funding to secure the dictionary's future, but these were unavailing.

Closer to home—for the monolingual lexicographers of the *OED*—the *Shorter* was still giving cause for concern. The importance to OUP of getting this long-overdue member of the Oxford dictionary family out as quickly as possible was well understood, but despite considerable investment, including a new computer system, work was not progressing at the rate necessary to ensure publication in 1992. Early completion of the *Shorter*, together with the preparation of the new intermediate dictionary (provisionally titled the *Oxford Dictionary of the English Language*, the same as Burchfield's ill-fated Johnsonian venture, although it was eventually renamed the *New Oxford Dictionary of English*), now became the key publishing goals, to which other objectives in this sector of the Press's activities had to be subordinated; and this included, it seems, much of what might have been expected to form part of the next phase of work on the *OED*.[6] The compilation of new entries—an activity which had already been aligned closely with the needs of the *Shorter*—continued, but it was to be five years before any start was made on the central new task of revising the Dictionary's existing entries. Even the task of developing more detailed plans for the preparation of the third edition, as carried out mainly by Edmund Weiner with whatever assistance he could get from those other members of the *OED* team not engaged in new-words work, was to proceed painfully slowly; it would not be until February 1991 that the plans—with an envisaged possible cost of over £16 million—were approved by Finance Committee.[7] Indeed, some of Weiner's own time had been commandeered for the use of the *Shorter*. Competition between the *Shorter* and the *OED* for resources was to remain a source of frustration for the next few years.

Which is not to say that there were no significant new developments for the *OED* itself. Work on the development of a CD-ROM of the second edition began soon after the paper version came out; a Dutch company, AND Software, was commissioned to prepare a CD-ROM version of *OED2* which could match the demands of a market which had grown and matured considerably since the pioneering two-disc version of *OED1* had made its appearance in 1987. By the time this new product appeared in 1992 the second edition had also been made available in another format: the micrographically printed 'Compact *OED2*', this time contriving to squeeze nine pages of the 1989 text onto each large page of a single volume, was published in October

---

[5] OD 18 July 1989. One consequence of the termination of the German project was that the *Shorter* regained the services of John Sykes a few months earlier than expected.

[6] The point had already been made some months earlier by Simon Wratten, sales director for the Press's academic division, who invited Benbow to 'consider whether the development of OED 3 should, or needs to be, sacrificed to the more commercially pressing need to publish new SOED and the collegiate dictionary' (OUPA(u) 23 Nov. 1988 Wratten to TJB).

[7] OUPA(u) (ISA papers) 14 Jan. 1991 ISA to Finance Committee; FC 26 Feb. 1991. Finance Committee's recommendation received formal approval from the Delegates on 23 April. The plan nevertheless became known as the '1990 plan', having been submitted in its final form to Finance Committee late in 1990.

1991 (retailing at £150, exactly one-tenth of the price of its full-size counterpart). Both formats sold well, and the CD-ROM went on to win numerous awards.

There was also the matter of finding a suitable publication format for the new items of vocabulary being researched and documented by the NEWS team. Various possibilities for this new material had long been under consideration; at one point it had been proposed that the new entries might be issued in the form of a new OUP journal—an idea which fed into the eventual setting up of the quite differently focused *International Journal of Lexicography*—but eventually it was decided to go for a series of small hardback volumes, each containing a few thousand entries, with a target publication rate of one every two years.[8] Meanwhile, another point in the market for the findings of the NEWS team had been identified: a 'popular' guide to some of the words which had risen to prominence in the most recent decade or so. The *Oxford Dictionary of New Words*, compiled by the experienced NEWS editor Sara Tulloch but drawing on the work of many of her colleagues, appeared with impressive promptness in 1991 and was sufficiently successful to warrant the commissioning of a second edition, which however did not appear until 1997.

One other new strand of *OED*-related activity which got under way in the months following the publication of *OED2* was that presided over by Jeffery Triggs in New Jersey. Triggs's principal brief, as director of the Dictionary's North American Reading Programme, was of course to establish a system for the reading and excerpting of American sources, but arguably at least as important as the quotations which he and his readers began to collect in the summer of 1989 was the fact that from its inception the reading programme stored its results in electronic form. Plans to computerize Oxford's incoming quotations had been in hand since 1987, but by the time Triggs started work there was still no sign of a system for doing this. The steady accumulation of machine-readable *OED* quotations on the other side of the Atlantic gave new urgency to the Oxford end of the project; by November keyboarding trials were under way, and within a few months the Incomings database—still in use today by OUP's lexicographers, with over 3 million quotations and roughly 100 million words—had come into existence.[9] The keying of NEWS entries also began at this time, although the entries continued to be compiled on paper slips.

Meanwhile, the *OED* database itself had not gone into suspended animation. Already during the final stages of the preparation of *OED2*, further work on tidying up the database in various ways, and improving its structure and consistency, had begun; the requirement to supply the CD-ROM developers with a version of the text that was as optimized as possible for electronic searches provided an incentive to continue with this work. A small number of corrections were also made for a reprint of the paper edition in 1991.

---

[8] OUPA(u) 1 Feb. 1991 JAS to TJB, 30 May 1991 JAS to R. Scriven.

[9] OUPA(u) minutes of a NEWS meeting 29 Nov. 1989. Triggs recalls (personal communication) that the first program for creating electronic quotation slips was written for him by Tim Bray at Waterloo.

Notwithstanding all of these various activities, the bulk of the Dictionary Department's lexicographical effort during 1990 and 1991 lay elsewhere. The largest editorial team was that engaged in producing the new edition of the *Shorter*; even this activity could be argued to be 'OED-related', in that the revised (or, in many cases, completely rewritten) entries being produced for the *Shorter* would in turn become a valuable resource to be drawn on when revising corresponding entries in the *OED* itself. However, historical lexicography—as represented by the *Shorter* and the work of the NEWS team—had also to compete for resources with the commercially crucial smaller dictionaries; and the new top priority in this category was the *Oxford Dictionary of the English Language*, on which work at last got under way in 1991, and which was soon drawing editorial effort away even from the *Shorter* and NEWS.[10]

Nevertheless, by mid-1992 the end of editorial work on the *Shorter* was in sight, and thoughts could turn to the redeployment of staff to other projects, including the *OED*, for which the arrival of lexicographers with extensive experience of revising another, closely related historical dictionary was bound to have some advantages.[11] It now became imperative to establish working methods for revision in some detail; as a basis for this, a range of words in *mu-* was selected for trial revision. It had already been decided that revision should start in the middle of the alphabet rather than at the beginning: the part of the Dictionary near the beginning of the alphabet showed clear signs of having been compiled first—entries from the first edition, and to a lesser extent the Supplement, were comparatively sparsely documented with quotations, and the editorial style had not yet settled down—and there were clear advantages in making a start at a point where the editors of *OED1* had fully developed their approach.

It was also time to prepare to publish some of the entries produced by the NEWS team since the appearance of *OED2*. In fact the first volume's worth of such material— for which the title 'OED Additions Series' had been settled on—had been fully edited a year earlier, with publication scheduled for autumn 1992; unfortunately, difficulties on the production side necessitated a postponement to 1993. By the original scheduled publication date enough material was ready to fill a second volume, and both duly appeared in November 1993 as Volumes 1 and 2 of the series, once again co-edited by Simpson and Weiner.[12] The decision to allow each volume to run from A to Z, rather than containing a single alphabetical sequence spread across two volumes, occasioned some bemusement; but it did at least establish the idea that the series was to be used

[10] The initial editor of *ODEL* was Robert Allen, who had begun detailed planning of the project well before his new edition of the *Concise* (the eighth) appeared. However, a dominant role in the project— which was to make extensive and (for OUP) pioneering use of corpus lexicography—was soon taken by Patrick Hanks, the enterprising former editor of several successful dictionaries published by Collins (OUP's main competitor in the dictionary market), who in early 1990, shortly before the publication of *COD8*, was persuaded to join the Press as 'Manager, English Dictionaries'. Allen left OUP in 1991 for a position with the reference publisher Larousse.

[11] OUPA(u) 2 June 1992 TJB to ISA.

[12] OUPA(u) *New OED* status meeting minutes 29 Nov. 1991, *OED* Progress Meeting minutes 26 Oct. 1992.

as a means of making available batches of new entries as they became ready for publication. By publication day over half of the entries that would form the content of Volume 3—scheduled for publication in 1995—had been drafted.[13]

With the completion of editorial work on the *Shorter* in the spring of 1993, and the transfer of editorial staff to the *OED* (as well as to other projects), a new era could begin. (Actual publication of the *Shorter*—a major event for the Press—did not take place until September. The *New Shorter Oxford English Dictionary*, as the new edition was called, garnered glowing reviews, and also sold extremely well, although it seemed unlikely that it would ever recover its costs, now estimated at over £3 million.[14]) Simpson now handed over the day-to-day running of the NEWS team to Michael Proffitt (who had joined the *OED* in March 1989, and who was now newly returned from a secondment working on a new dictionary-cum-thesaurus[15]), leaving him free to work with Weiner—himself only recently released from editorial work on the *Shorter*—and a newly expanded team of lexicographers at putting the policies and procedures for revision, so long in the making, into practice. By March the permanent staff of the *OED* had grown to 21, of whom a third made up the newly formed '*OED* Revision' team; in addition there was also a growing body of casual and freelance workers carrying out ancillary tasks.[16] A few weeks after the transfer of staff from the *Shorter* the new era was marked in another way when the entire Dictionary Department moved out of 37a St. Giles' into offices in the main OUP buildings in Walton Street.

The exploratory work done with the *mu-* sample was really only the start of the enormous task of developing the full range of policies and procedures for the revision of the *OED*: after all, the editing of complete Dictionary entries for words whose history extended across hundreds of years, many with dozens or even hundreds of senses and subsenses, was something which had not been attempted since the completion of the first edition nearly a century earlier (with the minor exception of the two venerable four-letter words added in Volume I of the Supplement). 1993 saw a great deal of detailed investigation of particular points of policy and practice, carried out by senior members of the newly expanded team. It also saw the establishment of the *OED* Advisory Committee, an external body of distinguished linguists and others who could advise on key matters of policy, in some of which OUP as a whole could claim to have an interest, in that the policy decisions made had considerable implications for the progress and finances of

[13]   OUPA(u) *OED* Progress Meeting minutes 13 Oct. 1993.

[14]   OUPA(u) (ISA papers) 15 Feb. 1993 ISA to Group Executive Committee.

[15]   The *Reader's Digest–Oxford Complete Wordfinder*, edited by Sara Tulloch, was published later in 1993. Despite the similarity of title, the book is unrelated to the earlier Reader's Digest *Family Word Finder* (see above, p. 508); it brought together material from the latest edition of the *Concise* and the 1991 *Oxford Thesaurus* compiled by Laurence Urdang.

[16]   OUPA(u) *OED* Status Meeting minutes 26 Mar. 1993. Lesley Burnett—who had now reverted to her unmarried name, Lesley Brown—did not herself transfer directly from the *Shorter* to the *OED*, working instead on a CD-ROM version of the dictionary she had edited. Thereafter she did work briefly on the *OED*, collaborating with Edmund Weiner on modal verbs. She subsequently moved away from OUP, but in 2007 returned to work on the *OED* on a freelance basis.

the project. The committee would continue to play a key role in shaping the Dictionary during 1993–5, but some of the most fundamental policy questions were addressed in 1993. Papers setting out the proposed policy in various areas were presented by Simpson and Weiner, and these were generally endorsed by the Committee; they sometimes also made recommendations in response to particular questions put to them.

Among the most momentous policy decisions taken were those relating to the Dictionary's coverage of earlier periods of English, the scope of its etymologies, and its inclusion policy.[17] The decision that, in view of the existence of (admittedly not yet complete) large scholarly dictionaries of Old and Middle English, it would be acceptable not to attempt exhaustive coverage of the language of these periods relieved the project of the requirement for a great deal of work, much of it requiring specialist skills, although it was agreed that coverage should still extend back to the date of 1150, rather than being brought forward to a later date such as the end of the Middle English period. It was decided to eliminate many of the reconstructed forms commonly found in *OED1* etymologies, a step which it was anticipated might bring a significant saving of effort.[18] Interestingly, the question of the Dictionary's geographical, as distinct from temporal scope proved to be entirely uncontroversial. Weiner, writing while *OED2* was still in preparation, had identified 'the coverage of English before the modern period, and the coverage of the vocabulary of varieties of English other than St[andard] Br[itish] E[nglish]' as two major questions of policy that would confront the (future) revisers and updaters of the *OED*;[19] but by 1993 there was no question that English in all its international variety, and varieties, should be covered as fully as was practicable. At the same time the *OED* could now look to the prospect of an increasingly full set of dictionaries of national English varieties which provided more comprehensive coverage: the historical dictionaries of American English of the mid-twentieth century had now been joined by dictionaries of Australian, Canadian, Jamaican, and other Englishes, and major dictionaries of South African and New Zealand English were in preparation.

Another important policy decision, namely that every lexical item included in any previous version of the Dictionary should be retained in the third edition, had the effect of substantially increasing the estimates of editorial effort. The idea that 'what goes in the *OED*, stays in' is now so firmly established that it is hard to remember that until the prospect of a revised Dictionary was clearly in view it was hardly even a meaningful statement, in that only when a text is revised is there any opportunity for taking anything out.[20] The proposition that all entries should be retained in *OED3*

---

[17] For a fuller account of the issues considered by the Committee see Weiner (2009: 399).

[18] Durkin (1999) provides a full discussion of the etymological component of revision, which has in fact proved to be considerably more demanding than was anticipated in 1993.

[19] Weiner (1986: 260). The approach taken in the preparation of *OED3* as regards coverage of the major varieties of English is further explored in Price (2003).

[20] The idea that inclusion in the *OED* was a permanent matter can nevertheless be traced back at least to 1986, when Burchfield observed in an interview that, unlike other 'temporary' dictionaries, 'the OED never throws any words out' (quoted in Sanoff 1986: 60).

was now formally endorsed by the Advisory Committee, who also agreed that even the items in the 1933 Supplement which had been left out during the preparation of its successor should be reinstated.[21] From this it was clear that the effort involved in fully revising every entry, particularly in the area of scientific vocabulary, would be considerably greater than that envisaged in the 1990 Plan. More generally, it was becoming apparent[22] that revising the *OED* could not be regarded as something that could largely be achieved by drawing on the revision work that had gone into the *Shorter* together with other resources which were either in-house or already existed in a form suitable for easy consultation (such as other historical dictionaries and and the departmental quotation files): only a root-and-branch revision, bringing original research to bear on every entry, would do. In addition, further analysis of the number of new words and senses that were likely to be needed in order for *OED3* to be able to present an adequately comprehensive picture of the language—and the staffing needed to prepare these entries—suggested that previous estimates fell well short of the mark.

The upshot of the Advisory Committee's various recommendations, and of the review of the new words requirement, was a revised plan, envisaging an increase in expenditure of nearly £2 million. This was approved by Finance Committee in December, but on condition—reasonably enough given the magnitude of this commitment—that there should be stringent monitoring of progress.[23] The target publication date was still 2005. It should be remembered that at this stage it was taken as read that work on *OED3* should be directed towards publication of the fully revised Dictionary as a single event, and that no sales income would be forthcoming to begin to recoup OUP's investment while the preparation of the new edition was in progress; the Press's reluctance to allow this prospect to recede further into the future is understandable. Its determination to keep to this timetable is reflected in the decision that the forthcoming wave of new recruits to the project—for it was known that the influx of personnel from the *Shorter* was not enough even to meet the needs of the 1990 Plan—would be appointed on 10-year contracts, rather than as permanent staff. This unprecedented arrangement had the financial advantage that the Press's obligations to the new employees came to an end when the contracts expired, thus relieving it of having to find them alternative employment (or make redundancy payments); of course it also had the disadvantage that, as the end of the period approached, the lack of prospects for these employees might lead them to seek jobs elsewhere. It was also unclear what would be done in the event of the project overrunning significantly.

The project had also undergone a change of leadership. Since 1986 John Simpson and Edmund Weiner had been Co-Editors of the *New OED* project in its various manifestations, including *OED2* and the Additions Series; but it was now decided that

---

[21] OUPA(u) minutes of Advisory Committee meeting 22 July 1993, with accompanying paper 'OED entries: selection criteria'.

[22] Edmund Weiner has credited John Simpson with being the first to realize this.

[23] FC 21 Dec. 1993.

the much more complex enterprise of creating the third edition, and the much larger editorial team which was to carry out this work, would be more effectively led by a single person. Accordingly, on 23 November 1993, John Simpson was given the new title of Chief Editor of the *OED*, with Edmund Weiner taking the position of Deputy Chief Editor.[24] The change had been suggested by Weiner, who in his new role was more free to concentrate on specific key aspects of the revision process, particularly etymology and the treatment of function words and other linguistically difficult vocabulary.

As 1994 began the new project faced exciting, though perhaps also intimidating prospects. With approval of the new Plan had come authorization to make new appointments that would nearly double the size of the staff, and at last the necessary procedures to start revision in earnest were just about in place. It was of course impracticable to take on nearly twenty new lexicographers at once: quite apart from the training load that this would have entailed, there was insufficient office space to accommodate such an influx. Nevertheless, the first round of ten new posts, for which recruitment began in March, represented an unprecedented expansion in OUP's lexicographical manpower. The opportunity to participate in this work, fixed-term contracts notwithstanding, was evidently attractive: by April some 850 applications had been received.[25] The new appointees joined the project in August, several months later than originally planned, due partly to delayed availability of office space and partly to the sheer volume of effort involved in the recruitment process.[26]

The process of collecting raw material for the revision programme was also expanding on several new fronts. Three new reading programmes were launched, to complement the two programmes of reading contemporary material which fed into the Incomings quotation file on both sides of the Atlantic. A new programme of reading of historical texts addressed the need to improve the Dictionary's coverage of the language of earlier periods; separate but closely related to this was a project to read modern editions of historical documents such as probate inventories and household accounts, which had been identified as a fertile source of documentation. Thirdly, and quite different from the other programmes, there was the 'Scholarly Reading Programme', aimed not at collecting primary documentation but at the examination of publications which could be identified as containing information likely to be of value in the revision of *OED* entries: in other words a systematic attempt to trawl the

---

[24] OUPA(u) announcement by TJB 23 Nov. 1993. The title of Chief Editor had also of course previously been borne by Burchfield, for whom however the position was in relation to other dictionaries as well as the *OED*. The reorganization of the Dictionary Department in 1984, a few months after the inception of the *New OED* project, had not been followed by any call for a single person to reassume editorial responsibility for all of the Oxford dictionaries (although Benbow had overall managerial charge as Director of the department). Certainly the planning and compilation of *OED3* was recognized as being quite enough of a responsibility in itself, as indeed the editorship of *OED2* had been for Simpson and Weiner.

[25] OUPA(u) *OED* Progress Meeting minutes 12 Apr. 1994.

[26] OUPA(u) 26 July 1994 TJB to N. Wilson. In the event only nine appointments were made, a tenth editor dropping out at the last minute.

entire body of published research into the English language over the preceding century or so, the findings of which the *OED*'s editors were now at last in a position to be able to consider. As a counterpart to this last reading programme, a formal call for research materials was issued, initially in the form of a letter in the *Times Literary Supplement* and subsequently the *New York Review of Books*; similar letters subsequently appeared in other academic and linguistic journals, and flyers carrying a similar appeal were distributed to major libraries, university departments, and other research institutions. The fact that the *OED*'s lexicographers were now able to respond to observations and criticisms opened up a new channel of communication for anyone who made a discovery about the language in the course of their research: instead of publishing their findings and simply hoping that these would somehow come to the *OED*'s notice, they could now send them directly to Oxford. The response from academia, and from the wider community, was encouraging, and a steady stream of material began to flow into the Dictionary's files. A further valuable acquisition of material arrived in the spring of 1994 in the form of the entire body of material that had been collected for the abortive *Early Modern English Dictionary* project at the University of Michigan, a collection which had of course been built around a core of quotations originally collected for the *OED* itself, and which it was now realized would be of considerable use to the 'mother' project.[27]

Individual quotations had of course long ceased to be the only way to collect evidence for historical lexicography; and out in New Jersey, Jeffery Triggs had started to do something about this for the *OED*. He had found that running the North American reading programme left him with enough time to experiment with some machine-readable versions of complete literary texts made available to him by colleagues at Bellcore, and in 1992 he began to build up a corpus of full-text material from all historical periods. In its first year this had reached 12 million words, and it would subsequently grow to several times this size: tiny by the standards of today's corpora, but vast by the standards of the time.[28] The historical corpus complemented the other searchable in-house collections of text already at the disposal of the lexicographers in Oxford, namely the database of incoming quotations and the body of quotations contained in the *OED* itself. The availability of such resources was to transform the work of revising the Dictionary to an extent which is hard to appreciate in an era when full-text access to a vast range of material is so easy.

[27] The slips were shipped to Oxford in the metal cabinets which had held them in Michigan; these now make an eye-catching feature of the *OED* offices, thanks to the impressive 5-metre-long dragon which had been painted across them in their previous home.

[28] The task of creating suitably tagged versions of historical texts became a collaborative venture which Triggs shared with John Price-Wilkin of the University of Virginia and, especially, the Oxford Text Archive project established by Lou Burnard of the Oxford University Computing Service. Holdings of searchable historical text were further augmented by donations of material from other projects, including the Women Writers Project at Brown University. Triggs (1993); *OED News* Jan. 1996, p. 4; Jeffery Triggs, personal communication. (*OED News*, a more widely circulated successor to the earlier *New OED Newsletter*, first appeared in January 1995 and continued, in paper and online form, for just over a decade.)

It was in the summer of 1994, just before the arrival of the new recruits, that revision of the Dictionary could be said to have got properly under way. A number of alphabetical ranges of entries at the beginning of M had been put through various pre-editorial procedures designed to bring together all of the relevant materials and information from various sources; and in early July John Simpson began to revise a small range of entries beginning with *Macaulayism*.[29] Other members of the team were soon following suit, and by the end of September fourteen pages of *OED2* had passed through 'definition revision'. (Work on scientific entries was scheduled to follow some months behind general revision, and indeed several scientific posts had yet to be filled; a similarly staggered approach was to be taken with etymologies and some other components of the text.) This was undeniably a slow start, and some way behind schedule—the 'milestone plan' drawn up for definition revision had projected that over 100 pages would be completed by this point—but much of the shortfall could be attributed to the delayed arrival of the new staff; there was also the fact that some software for facilitating editorial work had not yet been delivered. Progress with new words had been rather better, and Benbow and Simpson, reporting to Finance Committee in November, felt that they could look beyond the 'start-up phase' to a time when all of the rates specified in the various milestone plans which had been drawn up would be achieved.[30] Excitingly, and perhaps surprisingly at this extremely early stage, there were also some specimen pages—commissioned from an external design consultancy—to look at, designed to show how entries in the third edition might look on paper.[31]

However, within weeks doubts began to be expressed about the achievability of the rates for certain components of revision. In particular, the rate for the revision of general (non-scientific) definitions—a key activity, on which the largest number of editors were engaged—was proving to be unattainable even by the best and most experienced staff.[32] The rate specified in the plans had, necessarily, been based on untested assumptions, and over the next few months the experience of actually doing this work on a substantial scale began to show that nothing like the target rate could be achieved—at least, not without drastically compromising the editorial standards of the work (or, as Simpson bluntly put it, producing 'a pretty shabby dictionary').[33] Inadequate computing support also continued to be a problem; in fact dissatisfaction with the work being done by Reference Computing (the group responsible for supporting both the *OED* and the fledgling project to revise the *Dictionary of National Biography*) led to the engagement of management consultants, and ultimately to the engagement of Ewen Fletcher—who had played a key role in the computerization of the Dictionary in the 1980s—as the

---

[29] OUPA(u) *OED* Editorial Meeting minutes 5 July 1994.
[30] OUPA(u) 14 Nov. 1994 TJB to ISA (with report).
[31] OUPA(u) 28 July 1994 R. Waller (of Information Design Unit) to JAS with two printed specimens. Further correspondence with IDU in OUPA(u).
[32] OUPA(u) *OED* Progress Meeting minutes 7 Dec. 1994.
[33] OUPA(u) 5 Apr. 1995 JAS to TJB.

group's new director early in 1995.[34] To make matters worse, the imposition of a freeze on recruitment across OUP put a temporary halt to the further expansion of the *OED* team (several additional staff had been taken on in the first few months of the year, but other planned-for posts remained unfilled).[35] Even without any additional staff, the project had outgrown the premises that it had moved into in 1993, and in June the *OED*, along with several other lexicographical projects, moved into new offices created in an area of the OUP site formerly occupied by some of the old printing works.[36] The move to new premises was followed by a significant change in working practices, gradually implemented across the project over the next year or so: where editors had previously made their revisions by marking them up on proofs which were then passed to keyboarders, they were now keying them directly. The software used for this had been developed in-house by Reference Computing, as a replacement for the IBM OEDIPUS system; facilities for searching the Dictionary and various other databases were also now 'home-grown', replacing the earlier Waterloo software.

The difficulties caused by not being able to expand the staff as required by current plans now began to be overshadowed by the more serious problem of the extent to which the work of compiling *OED3* was going to require vastly more effort (and therefore time and money) than had been anticipated. A lengthy project review, completed in July, demonstrated convincingly that it would not be possible to complete the third edition by 2005 along the lines of the plan approved in 1993. A new round of replanning was called for: hopefully, this time, based on reliable information about the manpower requirements of all of the different components of the project. It was clear, however, that the costs of a full revision of the Dictionary were going to be much greater than what the Press had so far agreed to countenance.

---

marzipan

In the first edition of the *OED* there was no entry for *marzipan*. Or rather, there was no separate entry for this form of the word, which was simply listed as one of the variant forms—important enough, admittedly, to be given as a second headword form rather than simply as one among numerous variants—of a word which was entered under the spelling *marchpane*, with only a cross-reference at the more familiar modern form ('*Marzepa(i)ne, Marzipan*: see MARCHPANE'). This was a reasonable enough decision when the section *Mandragora–Matter* was published in 1905, as *marchpane* had long been the

Continued ➤

---

[34] OUPA(u) 15 Aug. 1995 ISA to James Arnold-Baker.

[35] OUPA(u) *OED* Editorial Meeting minutes 19 Apr., 17 May 1995.

[36] The new premises were almost entirely open-plan, a prospect which alarmed some lexicographers anticipating a distracting increase in background noise levels. They need not have worried: much of lexicography is intrinsically quiet work, and visitors to the *OED* offices have often commented on the hushed atmosphere.

predominant spelling, with forms beginning *marz-* only found comparatively rarely (although in the published entry Bradley, noting the widespread importation of the confection itself from Germany in recent times, declared that 'the Ger[man] form *marzipan* has at least equal currency with the traditional Eng[lish] form'). It was only when the entry came to be revised in the 1990s that the opportunity came to reconsider the matter; by this time the spelling *marzipan*, and the trisyllabic pronunciation which goes with it, had almost completely replaced *marchpane*, which is now rarely found outside historical contexts.

Although *marchpane* and *marzipan* both derive ultimately from Italian *marzapane*, they can be regarded as distinct words, and in 1995, when revision reached this part of the letter M, it was decided that there should be separate entries for the two forms. At this point it was expected that it would be some years before the revised entries would be published, and of course that they would be published simultaneously (along with the rest of the completed third edition); but in fact the entry for *marchpane* was published online in September 2000, and *marzipan* appeared three months later. The entry for *marchpane* now offers an explanation of how this form of the word came to be so different from its Italian etymon. The first element, as well as showing an English sound change, may have been influenced by the month name *March*, and the second was evidently thought to derive from Latin *panis* or French *pain*. This 'more Anglicized' form of the word certainly seems to have been in more general use in English than the 'foreign-looking' *marzipan*: the form 'marzepaines' is found as early as 1542, in an English translation of Erasmus, but it was only in the nineteenth century that such forms became common. Hardly any of this detail is present in the first edition, where the etymology simply makes the general comment that 'the Eng[lish] forms [of the word] come from various continental sources'. Much of the new information comes directly from primary research carried out by the *OED*'s etymologists, but some draws on the findings of the research into the history of other languages which has gone on elsewhere since 1905.

It is thanks to some of this research that *OED Online* can now offer new information about the ultimate origin of *marzipan* (and its cousin *marchpane*). The original entry described its origin as 'obscure', and merely mentioned that one scholar had 'ingeniously' suggested a link with 'Arabic *mauthabān* "a king that sits still"'. The revised etymology now tentatively derives the word from a Persian or Arabic word *martabān* or *marṭabān* denoting a kind of glazed earthenware jar or pot of a kind formerly used for sweetmeats (it being plausible enough that a word denoting a container could come to be used of the thing contained), which in turn can be traced to the Burmese port of Martaban, which formerly exported sweetmeats to the West in such jars. The suggestion had been made independently by two Italian scholars in 1969 and 1976, and references to their work in the great *Dizionario etimologico della lingua italiana* (Vol. III, 1983) were picked up by the *OED*'s etymologists. The two revised entries thus provide an illustration of how, in etymology as in other aspects of revision, research carried out by scholars elsewhere is combined with original work carried out by the Dictionary's own staff.

It was at this point that a new factor entered the Press's calculations, and one which would transform the fortunes of the *OED* in various ways. By 1995 the World Wide Web was still tiny in today's terms, but its exponential growth, and its likely impact on both commercial activity and academic research, could no longer be ignored. The idea of making the Dictionary available online in some form had been under active consideration for some years: in fact OUP had granted the company Mead Data Central a licence to do so as early as 1990, but they had never made use of it, most likely because of the problems posed by the text's typographical complexity.[37] The widespread availability of Web browsers, and increased bandwidth, altered the situation. In fact Jeffery Triggs, enthusiastic as ever about new technologies, had already set up a prototype *OED* website, complete with a searchable version of the Dictionary text, as early as 1994, making it one of the first few hundred websites in the world. It was still unclear exactly how effectively revenue could be generated from the Web, but new possibilities were unquestionably opening up, including the exciting prospect of using the new website (for which Triggs had wisely registered the domain name of www.oed.com) to make revised entries available long before the completion of the whole Dictionary. These new possibilities needed to be taken into account in any replanning of the project.

The plan which was finally submitted for the consideration of Finance Committee in July 1996 by Ivon Asquith, managing director of OUP's Arts and Reference division, presented three options: to continue with the timetable and budget as approved in 1993, which would involve drastic reduction in the editorial aims of the project, and result in a considerably less than fully revised Dictionary; to bring annual expenditure—at this point running at £1.8 million—down to more acceptable levels, thereby slowing the project down to such an extent that completion of *OED3* would not be achieved before 2023; or to expand the project in order to complete editorial work by 2010, for publication in 2011, to the scholarly standards that had already been agreed.[38] The recommendation, which came with the backing of the Advisory Committee, was for the third of these options, even though it was costed at £34 million, an increase of something like 70 per cent over the 1993 figures. (It should not be overlooked that a fourth option, namely the abandonment of the project, was never seriously considered.) Approval was also sought for the establishment of a system for distributing the *OED* online, which was seen both as a means of generating (admittedly unknown) revenue and as a worthwhile goal in itself.[39]

The response of Finance Committee was to ask for yet another option to be investigated. The fact that it would be necessary to exceed the overall budget of £19.2 million

---

[37] OUPA(u) *New OED* status meeting minutes 31 Aug. 1990; OUPA(u) (ISA papers) 28 July 1995 TJB to ISA.

[38] OUPA(u) (Secretary's papers) 2 July 1996 ISA to Finance Committee with document 'Replanning the Oxford English Dictionary Project' by TJB and JAS.

[39] For a full account of the project to develop an an online publication system for the *OED*, see Elliott (2000).

approved in 1993 in order to complete *OED3* seems to have been accepted, much to the relief of the lexicographers; but at a senior level within the Press there was still a strong desire to retain 2005 as the date of publication (and, in consequence, the date beyond which expenditure on the massive scale required for such work would come to an end). Accordingly, Benbow and Simpson were asked to come up with a revised plan setting out how the third edition could be completed by 2005, drawing on additional resources as needed.[40] This they did; and notwithstanding the practical difficulties with such a foreshortened project—including a 50 per cent increase in office accommodation needs, and a fearsomely challenging training and management burden—in December the decision was made to go for completion by 2005.[41] A round of recruitment to fill vacancies already budgeted for was under way at this point; this was suddenly expanded, and instead of five new appointees, ten new editors were invited to join the project in February 1997.

Remarkably, however, only a month after the new recruits had arrived there was another change of course: in March it was decided to opt after all for completion by 2010.[42] The reasons were various: recruitment to the levels necessary was being constrained by limits on available office space (though the training and supervision of ten newcomers was certainly felt to be enough to be going on with by those involved); it was becoming apparent that there were simply not going to be enough senior lexicographers to carry out the higher-level tasks that would be called for; and, perhaps most significantly, the startup costs for the project to publish the Dictionary online, only now being fully costed, threatened to push total annual expenditure well above manageable levels. Whatever the reasons, acceptance of the unfeasibility of the 2005 timetable came as something of a relief to the Dictionary's senior editorial team.

At the same time that all this planning and replanning was going on, the work of creating the text of *OED3* was of course continuing. From its beginnings at the start of the letter M, by July 1997 first-round revision of general entries had reached *pen*—representing something like one-tenth of the whole text of the Dictionary—and science revision, now working ahead of general revision, had advanced to *plan*.[43] Senior members of the editorial team had recently started to tackle the task of finalizing revised entries for publication. The number of items drafted for *OED3* by the NEWS team had reached 25,000. July also saw publication of another 3,000 of these in the third volume of the *OED* Additions Series, under the editorship of Michael Proffitt; the text of this volume had been largely ready since 1994, but publication had once again been delayed by production difficulties. In fact even before publication it had

[40] FC 9 July 1996.
[41] OUPA(u) (ISA papers) 29 Oct. 1996 ISA to Finance Committee, with revised plan by TJB; FC 3 Dec. 1996.
[42] OUPA(u) (ISA papers) 25 Feb. 1997 ISA to Finance Committee; FC 4 Mar. 1997. The fact that the new staff had been taken on under contracts which terminated in 2004 shows the extent to which this reversal was unanticipated.
[43] *OED News* July 1997, p. 2.

been decided that this would be the last such volume: plans for *OED Online* were now sufficiently definite that further batches of new entries could now be earmarked for online publication.[44]

The approach of online publication was to transform the work of revision just as much as that of the NEWS team, if not more so. Up to this point, in view of the fact that no part of the revised text of the Dictionary was expected to be available to the public until the whole revision programme had been completed, certain aspects of revision had been planned on a very long timescale, with various tasks being left to be tackled at a late stage in the overall schedule. Henceforth it would be necessary to have entries in a state suitable for public viewing much sooner; the publication model which was eventually settled on would provide a new release of alphabetical ranges of revised entries every quarter. (These entries would stand alongside an online version of the unrevised text of *OED2*, which would gradually be superseded by the revised text as this grew quarter by quarter.) The rethink required could be likened to moving from a plan for renovating a car over a period of several years, during which various components might be stripped down or dismantled, to one in which it had to be capable of being driven every three months. The first round of revision of entries might have advanced into P, but it was now going to be necessary to return to the start of M and truly finalize entries for publication. And so in 1997 the staff of the *OED* found themselves once again embarking on a pioneering venture. There were certain to be challenges ahead, but few could have guessed just how turbulent the next two and a half years would be.

One significant change took place in May 1997, with the departure of Tim Benbow as the *OED*'s director. He moved on to other work elsewhere in OUP, and was replaced by Ewen Fletcher, who as well as having charge of Reference Computing had become closely involved with the development of *OED Online*. The new director almost immediately found himself in a position with which his predecessor was all too familiar: failure to make as much progress as had been anticipated. A new set of editorial milestone plans had been drawn up, in line with the 2010 schedule approved by Finance Committee, just before Benbow's departure; and within months significant divergences had begun to appear. Initially the main reason was that some senior staff were not available to do the tasks assigned to them. Edmund Weiner, who it had been assumed would be spending his time finalizing etymologies, was seconded to work on *ODEL*—now at last in its final stages[45]—for ten months, while the senior staff who should have been learning to review the work done by junior revisers, and bring it

---

[44] OUPA(u) *OED* Status Meeting minutes 10 June 1994; correspondence about discontinuation of Additions volumes (Jan. 1997) in OUPA(u).

[45] The new dictionary, now under the editorship of Judy Pearsall—formerly a member of the *OED*'s new words team, recruited alongside Michael Proffitt in 1989—was finally published in August 1998 (as the *New Oxford Dictionary of English*; the 'New' was dropped in later editions). It was a critical and commercial success, and went on to become a key member of OUP's family of English dictionaries, and a version of the text eventually formed the heart of the Oxford Dictionaries website (www.oxforddictionaries. com).

nearer to publishable standard, were temporarily prevented from making much of a start on this, partly by having to spend more time than expected on training the new recruits, and partly by the unavailability of John Simpson to train them in the work because of his heavy involvement in development work for *OED Online*. This admittedly crucial project would go on to draw substantial effort away from the main editorial work on the Dictionary.

Matters were made worse in early 1998 by the sudden imposition of another freeze on recruitment, including replacements for staff departures, which left parts of the project with too few editors to achieve the targets set, even without secondments to *OED Online* work. A drive to reduce costs—the project was running substantially over budget—led to the shedding of some casual workers, some of whom had worked on the Dictionary for many years, and reductions in the amount of both casual and freelance work available. The *OED* was fortunate to escape more painful economies: several staff were made redundant elsewhere in OUP, which was going through a difficult time financially. More seriously, now that a sizeable group of senior editors had begun to tackle the task of reviewing and revising junior editors' work, it was becoming clear that this task could not be carried out at the rate assumed in the new milestone plans (which, as with other activities in earlier plans, were based on only very limited testing).

A new problem with the first-stage revision done by more junior staff also began to manifest itself; paradoxically, it resulted from an improvement in the range of resources available. While OUP's lexicographers had been making use of external full-text databases as a source of quotation evidence since the days of the Supplement, there had been very little to draw on for periods of English earlier than the late twentieth century (a deficiency which the *OED*'s own historical corpus had been designed to address). Now, however, sizeable collections of earlier texts were becoming publicly available via the internet. The first to be extensively used by the *OED* was the University of Michigan's Making of America collection of mainly nineteenth-century material; this was soon joined by Chadwyck-Healey's Literature Online database, containing thousands of literary texts from all periods of English—which came to supersede, in effect, the home-grown historical corpus—and the academic journals archive JSTOR, and other databases soon followed. It might seem obvious that the work of the lexicographers could be improved by being able to bring all of this additional information to bear on the compilation or revision of an entry; but time for the consideration of this kind of new material had not been allowed for in the plans, and in their efforts to take it into account the lexicographers soon found their rates of work for this task also slipping below target. Etymological and bibliographical work were also behind schedule.[46] Alarmingly, the phrase 'out of control' began to occur in discussions of the state of the project among senior management figures at the Press; Ewen Fletcher, in a brutally candid assessment of the situation delivered in

---

[46] Scientific editing received a boost in April 1998 with the transfer of two science editors from *ODEL*.

May, observed that there was 'no credible plan' for revision of the Dictionary, and that major changes would have to be made before one could be produced.[47]

The organizational and administrative changes that were to follow over the next year were indeed radical. By way of refocusing the project on the job of regularly delivering ranges of publishable revised Dictionary entries to the online publication team, the main body of the editorial staff was reorganized into four groups, each combining a variety of functions (general revision, new entries, science) which had each previously been the responsibility of separate teams; each group was to be responsible for dealing with all aspects of the text, other than etymological and bibliographical work, which remained as centralized functions, each carried out by a dedicated team. Every three months, the alphabetical range of text produced by one team would be finalized by John Simpson and handed over for publication. In fact the four-team system did not survive for long, but the system of dividing the text of the *OED* into relatively small batches, to be prepared for publication in sequence, was to prove far more amenable to reliable planning than previous attempts to quantify the task of revising the Dictionary as a whole, and has continued in use, with modifications, down to the present. Indeed, for those currently engaged in preparing *OED3*, it is hard to imagine proceeding in any other way.

The Delegates finally gave their approval to the new dispensation—and to an annual budget of £3 million, to be brought down in future years if possible—on 2 February 1999, and the new four-team structure came into effect on 1 May.[48] By this time primary editing of entries had extended into R, and several thousand of the first entries to have been revised, at the start of M, had also been finalized for online publication; and now the focus of the entire project began to shift back to M, with a view to maintaining a steady flow of finalized entries for *OED Online*. As part of the reorganization Edmund Weiner stepped aside as Deputy Chief Editor; his replacement was the former managing editor of the *Dictionary of South African English*, Penny Silva, who was a familiar face in the Department, having visited the office on several occasions, as well as being a consultant on the *OED*'s South African English entries. Severe financial stringencies nevertheless remained in place, to the extent that some vacancies caused by the departure of existing staff remained unfilled. There was considerable apprehension about the long-term future of the project, and staff morale reached its lowest point for some years.

[47] OUPA(u) 7 May 1998 Fletcher to ISA/M. Richardson.

[48] OD 2 Feb. 1999. In fact much more radical, indeed drastic, measures, including the termination of the contracts of forty casual staff and the imposition of redundancies among the permanent editorial staff, were seriously considered by both senior OUP management and Delegates during 1998/9, in the light of continuing difficult economic conditions—and continuing impatience among senior management with the seeming failure of attempts to bring the project under tight control—and only abandoned after lengthy discussion. Opposition to the retrenchment, on grounds of practicality as well as the potentially disastrous effect on staff morale, was led by the distinguished philologist (and member of Finance Committee) Anna Morpurgo Davies. A desire to avoid further adverse publicity, in the wake of that generated by OUP's controversial decision in November 1998 to abandon the publication of contemporary poetry (for a useful account of which see Sperling 2013: 207), also seems to have been a factor. FC 3 Nov., 1 Dec. 1998, 26 Jan. 1999, OD 24 Nov. 1998, 19 Jan. 1999; related correspondence in OUPA(u) (Secretary's papers, ISA papers, and elsewhere).

By summer there was at least good news to report as regards *OED Online*. Confidence in the ability of OUP and its chosen partner—a Stanford University-based online publishing company called HighWire Press—to solve the formidable technical problems posed by this pioneering project had reached the point where it was considered safe to go public with a publication date; and in July 1999 it was announced that the *OED* would be available online to subscribers from March 2000. The first version would contain the full text of *OED2* and the three Additions volumes, together with a range of 1,000 revised entries. Publication of the fully revised Dictionary by 2010, at an estimated cost of £35 million, was mentioned as still being the ultimate objective, whatever doubts there may have been internally about the achievability of this timetable. The announcement—which was combined with a renewed appeal to the public to send in their observations about the language, under the banner 'Your Language Needs You'—garnered considerable publicity. Autumn saw something of a relaxation of the stringent limits on editorial expenditure with the appointment of a new etymologist in Oxford, and a substantial new investment in the States: the establishment of a North American Editorial Unit for the *OED*, over a decade after the original abortive plans to open such a unit in the Library of Congress. The new unit—initially housed in offices in Old Saybrook, Connecticut, but transferred to Manhattan early in 2001—began life with a single editor, Jesse Sheidlower, who unlike most new appointees had substantial lexicographical experience, having worked for several years as an editor on the Random House *Historical Dictionary of American Slang* (and who had acquired a significant public profile thanks in no small part to his own book *The F-Word* (1995), a scholarly exploration of the history of the word *fuck*).

There was one other important aspect of the reorganization of the project which had been identified early on in Ewen Fletcher's directorship, but which by the winter of 1999 remained unaddressed. The fact that nearly every member of the *OED*'s staff who had been appointed since 1994 had been given a fixed-term contract which terminated well before the (current) planned completion date of 2010 was clearly anomalous, and Fletcher had indicated his desire to rationalize the situation over a year earlier; the same applied to some of the (now admittedly reduced) group of individuals engaged on a 'casual' basis to carry out essential work of a steady, ongoing nature.[49] By mid-December formal steps to convert all fixed-term contracts to permanent ones, and to offer similar terms to most of the casual workers, were at an advanced stage; approval was secured for both of these rationalizations—thereby pushing the editorial employee headcount over 50—a few weeks later.[50]

By the time the good news came through, the project found itself unexpectedly without a director: Ewen Fletcher abruptly left the Press just before Christmas 1999, following a meeting with senior managers. No reason was given, although palpable tensions

[49] OUPA(u) 7 May 1998 Fletcher to ISA/M. Richardson.
[50] Correspondence in OUPA(u).

had been building up both with senior OUP management and within the Dictionary Department for some time. His departure was all the more surprising in view of the fact that the now firmly fixed date for the launch of *OED Online*, with which he had been so closely involved, was less than three months away. Laura Elliott, a senior member of the publication team with over a decade of experience working with the *OED* and other Oxford dictionaries, was now tasked with seeing the project through to launch.[51]

Fortunately *OED Online* was launched into the world without a hitch.[52] On Monday 13 March 2000, in an apt (and shrewdly photogenic) link with the past, Thomas Murray, the five-year-old great-great-great-grandson of the Dictionary's first Editor, became—with a little help from John Simpson—the first public user of *OED Online* (see Figure 41). The official launch took place on the following day, 14 March, a day which Robert McCrum of the *Observer* described as 'deserv[ing] to be compared to 15 April 1755, the publication day of Dr Johnson's Dictionary' as regards its significance for the history of the English language. The first subscribers began to use the Dictionary at one minute past midnight; the computer system coped smoothly with the millions of hits which the website now began to receive, much to the relief of those who had been meticulously testing it for months (but who had not been able to test beforehand for volume of traffic on the day). Media coverage, which had begun weeks before the launch and continued long after it, was comprehensive, international, and overwhelmingly positive, featuring numerous interviews with John Simpson (who in April spent two weeks in the States publicizing the new venture) and many other members of the *OED* team. Reviewers, excited by the possibilities of the new medium as much as the new content, reached for superlatives as enthusiastically as they had for *OED2* in 1989: the *Wall Street Journal* described it as 'a much-needed new-media setting for appreciating the richness and history of the English language', the *Times* rejoiced in 'a browser's paradise', *Nature* acclaimed 'an incomparable monument of scholarship, one of the wonders of our age', the *Guardian* predicted that the *OED* 'will instantly become the internet's biggest, most prestige-laden reference book'.[53] In fact the new content of this newly transformed 'book' was relatively modest: the first alphabetical segment of the revised and updated Dictionary—in effect the first portion of *OED3*—contained only 1,000 entries, extending from *M* to *mahurat* (the latter word being a wonderfully apposite new addition defined as 'an auspicious moment for beginning

---

[51] The overall running of the *OED* project following Fletcher's departure was 'minded' by his former superior, Martin Richardson, in conjunction with Simpson, Weiner, and Penny Silva. After an extensive search for a new director, lasting over a year, the position was taken by Silva (at which point Weiner resumed his position as Deputy Chief Editor); subsequent directors have been Robert Faber—who as director of the *Oxford Dictionary of National Biography* had overseen its publication both on paper (in 60 volumes) and online in 2004—and former *OED* lexicographer (and editor of *NODE*) Judy Pearsall (2011 to date).

[52] Much of the information given here is taken from the account of the launch by Mark Dunn, another member of the publication team, which appeared in the July 2000 issue of *OED News*.

[53] *Observer* 19 Mar. 2000, Review, p. 11; *Wall Street Journal* 23 Mar. 2000, p. A20; *Times* 16 Mar. 2000, p. 19; *Nature* 27 Apr. 2000, p. 925; *Guardian* 11 Mar. 2000, p. 9.

FIGURE 41   Launch of *OED Online*, 13 March 2000: Thomas Murray (holding a photograph of his great-great-great-grandfather James Murray), accompanied by his parents, and John Simpson, in the University of London Library.

an enterprise'), representing less than 0.3 per cent of the alphabet. But it was of course an earnest of things to come; and already by the launch date the next few batches of entries scheduled for online publication in subsequent quarters had been finalized, with work on thousands more well under way. Importantly, subscriptions—mainly institutional rather than individual—for the online Dictionary also began to flow in.[54] The production line for *OED3* had begun.

---

[54] Within four months of launch, subscription income for the year 2000/1 had reached £200,000 (OUPA(u) sales report 27 July 2000). Fittingly, the very first subscriber was CERN in Geneva, the institution where the Web had been born.

EPILOGUE

And the rest, it could be said, is not yet history. The phase of the *OED*'s existence which was ushered in by *OED Online* is still going on: today's team of lexicographers, researchers, and software engineers is simply carrying on the work of preparing the third edition of the Dictionary, very much in the manner and along the lines envisaged at the turn of the millennium. To say that and no more, however, hardly seems right, particularly given that the pace of technological change over the last decade and a half, in publishing as elsewhere, has shown no signs of slowing down. The following account lists what appear to be some of the more significant or memorable events of this period.

One important change which took place almost immediately after the publication of the first batch of revised entries was the formal abandonment, at least for the time being, of any attempt to plan the *OED3* project through to completion.[55] 1999 had seen the main focus shift away from working towards the publication of a fully revised edition in 2010 to ensuring a continuous supply of revised material for online publication; the former objective was now dropped in favour of plans which set targets over a shorter timescale (making them less vulnerable to unforeseeable circumstance). The first such plan, covering three years, was submitted to the Delegates in December 2000, and other three- or five-year plans have followed. The adoption of this approach did not place in question OUP's commitment to the principle that the third edition of the Dictionary should be completed, which has remained laudably firm. As for what might be done when the third edition is complete—when, that is, the whole contents of the database from A to Z have been revised—that is still too distant a prospect for any meaningful plans to be made.

Another early but significant change was the departure, for the first time in the Dictionary's history, from the principle of publishing entries in alphabetical order. The first online release of *OED3* material had included revised and new entries in the same narrow alphabetical range, but although the work of revising existing Dictionary text was still proceeding alphabetically, those editors working with new vocabulary had long been free to prepare entries in any part of the alphabet; and no great leap of the imagination was required to realize that such entries could be published 'out of sequence' online. This had the obvious advantage that new items in parts of the alphabet that were not scheduled to be revised for some time could be documented in a more timely fashion (provided of course that the new entries could be clearly differentiated from the unrevised text around them). Work on preparing the first such batch of out-of-sequence entries for publication began in the summer of 2000, and the

---

[55] FC 19 Dec. 2000.

entries in question duly appeared in June 2001, covering—to take examples from only one field—new words such as *internet* and *webcam*, and new meanings of *browser*, *domain*, and the like (not to mention *web*). In July 2000 the project's new-words editors, who had been dispersed across the four editorial groups in the restructuring of the previous year, were once again brought together in a single team under the leadership of Michael Proffitt, it having become apparent that this work was most effectively carried out by a single group.

Another obvious advantage of online publication was the opportunity to make further revisions to an entry in the light of information which came to light after the publication of a revised version. Two early examples were the mathematical term *Maclaurin's series*, republished within a year of the launch of *OED Online* with earlier quotation evidence discovered after the original revised version appeared, and the new entry *machicote* (a garment worn by some Native American women), which had been labelled as obsolete when first published, but which now includes a twentieth-century historical quotation (and pronunciation information, this being required for all non-obsolete words). John Simpson had written in 1997 of the potential of the online Dictionary to be 'a dynamic document, able to respond to scholarly (and other) discoveries relating to the language far more rapidly than it has been able to in the past',[56] and referred again in his online Preface to the Third Edition of the *OED* as 'a "moving document" '; this concept had now become a reality.

The wider access to the text of the *OED* which online publication has enabled has also wrought a significant change in the outlook of today's lexicographers as they edit the Dictionary's entries. Whereas formerly it could be assumed that the vast majority of readers were from a narrow demographic, namely academics and others with a high level of education—together with people who aspired to something similar—the online Dictionary is now potentially much more readily available to be consulted by users of any educational background or level. Accordingly, while the accuracy, comprehensiveness, and richness of detail which entries need to provide remains unchanged, it has become more important to think about how to present information in a way which can be understood by a broad range of users.

Contributions from the general public, as well as the world of academic research, have continued to form an important part of the range of assets that the compilers of *OED3* can draw upon, and OUP has continued to work at maintaining an active dialogue with the public: a dialogue which has also been beneficial to the Press in other ways. The OWLS enquiry service had become a valuable part of the Dictionary Department's public profile, and May 2001 saw the opening of an online counterpart to it, AskOxford.com; this subsequently became part of the broader OxfordDictionaries. com website.

---

[56] *OED News* July 1997, p. 1.

miserabilistic

The *OED* may have gone online in 2000—thereby becoming a text which partly existed only in electronic form—but it was not until 2001 that its entries began to include quotations from other texts which only existed in this form. Its lexicographers had of course been making use of quotations from electronic versions of texts since the arrival of access to online databases in 37a St Giles' in the early 1980s, and consultation of computer-generated concordances derived from machine-readable texts went back still further; but all of these texts had a paper counterpart, to which it was understood that a quotation could be (and generally was) converted and rechecked. With the rise of the internet, and especially the World Wide Web, the question of whether and how to cite texts which lacked such a counterpart became increasingly urgent: the existence, in electronic form, of a particular quotation at a particular moment in time could now be reliably attested, and might be of value as evidence for a word in the same way as datable printed or written evidence had always been. The problem of the potentially ephemeral nature of websites was addressed by keeping a printout of every web page quoted, made at the point when the quotation was taken, in the Dictionary's files. This policy was first put into practice on 16 November 2001, when John Simpson was revising a range of entries for words beginning with *mis-*; for a number of these words there was no evidence available from conventionally published sources from any point in the last century and more, so that the words in question would have had to be regarded as obsolete were it not for the online evidence of continuing use. Simpson added Web quotations to more than twenty such words on 16 November. The entry for *miserabilistic* is typical: the solitary 1882 quotation from J. W. Barlow's philosophical text *The Ultimatum of Pessimism* was supplemented by a quotation from the website www.secret-passage.com (a personal site created by a New Zealander named Robyn Gallagher) extolling 'the miserabilistic warblings of [the Smiths singer] Morrissey'. This and several dozen other Web quotations were published in *OED Online* in June 2002 as part of the range *mis–mitzvah*.

At the same time it was also decided that quotations from a different part of the internet, namely the collection of online discussion groups known as Usenet, could be used in *OED* entries; moreover, the archive of contributions, or 'postings', to these discussions—which was consultable via the Web—was considered to be sufficiently stable that quotations could be dated according to when the posting was written. The postdating added to the *OED* entry for the rare word *miscoloration*, taken from the newsgroup *sci.chem* and dating from 1990, is typical. Some Usenet postings date back to 1981, such as the quotation which now appears in *OED Online* as the first example of the verb *undelete*. Other, even older electronic sources have subsequently been accepted— such as the 'Request for Comments' documents which began to be circulated on the recently established ARPANET network (a forerunner of the internet) in 1969—and also newer communication channels such as Twitter (the first *OED* entry to include a quotation from Twitter was, appropriately enough, that for the relevant sense of the noun *tweet*, which was published in 2013). In fact any quotation which can be reliably dated, and whose text can be verified, can be used as evidence for an *OED* entry, whether the medium used is paper, electronic, or anything else.

The potential of the Web to facilitate information-sharing in specific fields of a kind which could assist the *OED* very directly was effectively demonstrated by a project set up by Jesse Sheidlower in 2001 to collect evidence for words from the vocabulary of science fiction. A website was set up—initially run out of Sheidlower's New York apartment—where quotation evidence for science fiction terms, and other observations relating to the vocabulary of the field, could be submitted for inclusion in a special database. The *OED*'s own website had provided a general facility for making such contributions since 1999, but the science fiction site had the advantage of offering interested individuals a dedicated location where findings could be shared. The project was a great success, due in no small part to the particular dedication of many fans—some of whom owned or had access to collections of scarce pulp magazines and other elusive quotation sources—and has yielded information of great value to the *OED* in updating and expanding its coverage of science fiction; a

---

agreeance

It very often occurs in English (and other languages) that, out of two or more essentially synonymous words formed by adding different prefixes to a particular word or stem, only one becomes firmly established. One such pair consists of *agreeance* and *agreement*, of which the latter is of course far more common and familiar. The former enjoyed some currency in Scots in the sixteenth and seventeenth centuries, but then fell out of use; accordingly, the entry for the word in the first edition of the *OED*—with quotations ranging in date from 1536 to 1714—marked it as obsolete. In fact at the time (1884) when the entry appeared this was not strictly true, as the word had continued in very occasional use; but this had escaped the notice of the readers for the first edition. The continuing use of the word remained too infrequent to be noticed in dictionaries (other than those which noted its earlier currency in Scots) for another century, although awareness (and disapproval) of its increasing use in Australian contexts in the 1980s led the Australian language commentator Stephen Murray-Smith to include an entry for the word in the second edition of his usage guide *Right Words* (published posthumously in 1989).

It is also not uncommon for a previously little-known word to be thrust into the limelight for quite unforeseeable reasons, as had happened, for example, with *appendicitis* in 1902 (see p. 289). In February 2003 the profile of *agreeance* received a similar boost when it was used by Fred Durst, lead singer of the band Limp Bizkit, in a speech at the Grammy Awards in New York. After his use was criticized by some commentators, Jesse Sheidlower—who was at this time well known as an American spokesperson for the *OED*—was asked for his opinion. His description of *agreeance* as 'a perfectly regular formation' was widely quoted, as was his repetition of the word's definition as given in the *OED* entry, which at this point was essentially unchanged since the first edition. Revision of *agreeance*, and other words from the beginning of the letter A, followed a few years later, and a revised entry for *agreeance* was published in 2012, with additional quotations extending the documented record of the word into the twenty-first century (as well as back to 1525, thanks to an earlier quotation located in the corresponding entry in the *Dictionary of the Older Scottish Tongue*).

spin-off dictionary, *Brave New Words*, appeared in 2007, and the website is still running (www.jessesword.com/sf/home). Other projects, likewise affiliated to the *OED* while independent of it, have appeared subsequently, including a community-based website for the documentation of Philippine English (www.languagecommunities.com) and a dictionary of hip-hop slang (www.therightrhymes.com).[57]

Another important, indeed transformative change for the Dictionary has been the development and implementation of a new computer system to support all of the project's various editorial functions.[58] Well before the launch of *OED Online* the existing suite of in-house software was beginning to show its age: it had after all been designed before the idea of publishing regular updates on the Web had been thought of, and it did not cover all of the editorial activities required by the revision programme as now conceived. In 2002 a team of *OED* lexicographers and software engineers headed by Laura Elliott was tasked with developing a replacement system, in collaboration with an external software company (the French company IDM was subsequently selected). A comprehensive picture of the requirements—and wishes—of users was built up on the basis of detailed interviews with every member of Dictionary staff, carried out by Michael Proffitt, who had been seconded to the development team; the conversion of a large and diverse collection of electronic resources—including the text of the *OED*, the Incomings quotation database, and much else—into the more readily manipulable markup language XML represented a formidable challenge in itself; and a great deal of additional functionality, enabling many more activities to be automated or at least computer-assisted, had to be designed from scratch. The new system, christened Pasadena (see Figure 42), went live smoothly on 15 June 2005.[59] (Shortly before launch the Dictionary staff underwent a reorganization, in which the system of allocating particular ranges of text for revision to particular groups was finally abandoned; Michael Proffitt, now the project's managing editor, was given overall charge of the new structure, with dedicated groups for science editing and general revision as well as new words.)

One far-reaching consequence of the improved control of the *OED* database that Pasadena provided was that it was now feasible to break away entirely from the constraints of alphabetical order. New entries had been being prepared on a non-alphabetical basis since the 1980s, but with better information now available on the status of every entry in the database, the same freedom applied to revision. It could now be decided to revise any entry or group of entries from any part of the alphabet, rather than proceeding alphabetically as had been done since 1994; and in 2006 it was decided to experiment with this, selecting entries for revision out of sequence

---

[57] The Philippine English site was set up in 2013 by Danica Salazar, whose appointment, under the joint auspices of OUP and the English Faculty in Oxford, as a Mellon Foundation Postdoctoral Fellow in English-language lexicography was another new departure. The *Right Rhymes* website was set up in 2014 by Matt Kohl, a former researcher for the *OED*.

[58] For a full account of the development of the new system see Elliott and Williams (2006).

[59] The name was devised by Jeremy Marshall, one of the Dictionary's science editors, and won him a bottle of champagne in an in-house competition. In the tradition of the earlier OEDIPUS (see p. 540 above), it is an acronym, in this case with the whimsical expansion 'Perfect All-Singing All-Dancing Editorial and Notation Application'.

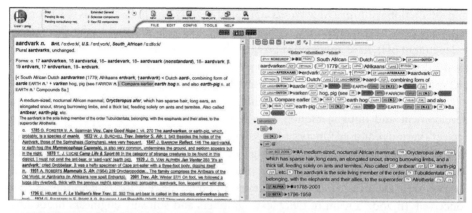

FIGURE 42   Part of the *OED* entry for *aardvark* (a) as shown in the Pasadena entry editor used by *OED* lexicographers, (b) as displayed in *OED Online*.

according to criteria such as evidence pointing to a word having undergone significant lexical development over the past century, or issues within an unrevised entry which particularly called for review.[60] The first such entries were published online in March 2008; and since March 2011, when the final instalment of alphabetically revised entries in R was published, material has been selected for revision entirely on its own merits rather than because of its position in the alphabetical sequence. One consequence is that the Dictionary as published online is something of a patchwork, with the fully revised M–R sequence of entries surrounded by shorter revised and unrevised

---

[60] The rationale for initiating out-of-sequence revision is discussed more extensively in Simpson (2008).

sequences (though with the status of each entry clearly indicated); the patchwork of revised entries will, however, become more and more complete as revision proceeds. Another, literally far-reaching benefit of Pasadena was that the new software made it possible, for the first time, for revision to be carried out by people working outside the *OED*'s main office. An editor now only needs a suitable internet connection to edit the database from anywhere. This has made it possible for revisions to be made directly to the *OED* database from all corners of the globe, as well as making homeworking much easier.

The smaller members of the Oxford family of dictionaries, of course, can be revised from cover to cover more quickly than the *OED* itself; and new editions of all of these dictionaries, from the *Shorter* downwards, have continued to be published, with (for example) the fifth and sixth editions of the *Shorter* appearing in 2002 and 2007 and the eleventh and twelfth editions of the *Concise* in 2004 and 2011. The second edition of the youngest member of the family, the (now no longer *New*) *Oxford Dictionary of English*, appeared in 2003 and the third in 2010. All of these dictionaries were prepared by members of the Dictionary Department, and all were issued in conventional paper form; but the world of dictionary publishing was changing, and electronic versions have become more and more important. Some dictionaries were issued as CD-ROMs; others have been embedded in a wide range of electronic devices; most recently of all, many Oxford dictionaries have been made available as apps for mobile phones and other handheld devices. Most consultations of a dictionary must now take place in electronic form rather than on paper; and it seems increasingly unlikely that there will be significant demand for a paper edition of the *OED* itself when the third edition is completed. (Which is not to say, however, that any definite decision has been taken to abandon print publication, contrary to reports which have appeared in the press from time to time.[61])

In addition to transforming the range of possible modes of delivery for dictionaries, technology has transformed—and is continuing to transform—the means by which dictionary entries are created. Mention has already been made of the explosion of searchable text databases, covering all historical periods of English; such is the coverage of some of these, so fine is the mesh of the 'sweep-net' (to use Trench's metaphor from a century and a half ago) now cast over recorded English—much finer than that achievable by readers working entirely on paper—that it is sometimes possible to have a real sense of being 'in at the birth' of a word or usage. Where a lexicographer was once obliged to make do with the evidence of a handful of slips, suggesting, for example, that a word might have come into use in America in the mid-nineteenth century, a few searches in the relevant newspaper databases can reveal a flood of examples whose chronological and geographical distribution point very precisely to a particular place and date of origin. The fuller historical picture afforded by this greatly enriched evidence base has also made it possible to apply the 'historical principle' of lexicography more rigorously

---

[61] A flurry of reports to this effect appeared following an interview with Nigel Portwood, chief executive of OUP since 2009, in the *Sunday Times* in August 2010, in which he was understood to have forecast that within three decades dictionaries would only exist online.

than ever before, by making it an absolute requirement that senses within an entry—or subsenses within a sense or branch—should be ordered chronologically. The decision to abandon the option, widely exercised in the first edition, of basing the structure of an entry on an assumed chronology of development which is not fully substantiated by the available evidence was made early on during the planning of *OED3*. In many cases the additional evidence now available confirms the sense sequence inferred by the earlier lexicographers; where it does not, as John Simpson observed in 1997, 'the

---

chav

It often happens that a particular word which is of recent coinage, or (more usually) which was previously little known, suddenly comes into widespread use; and such words are often felt to have acquired this sudden popularity because they capture something of the spirit of the times. Such words have often been identified as the 'word of the year' by particular commentators. But it is only since the later twentieth century that the identification of such words has become a matter upon which lexicographers, and other individuals concerned with the monitoring of language, are regularly called upon to pronounce. The practice of making an annual announcement may have started in Germany, where the Gesellschaft für deutsche Sprache has been announcing a 'Wort des Jahres' since they identified *aufmüpfig* (rebellious, insubordinate) in 1971 as capturing the essence of the period's student unrest. The American Dialect Society instituted a 'Word of the Year' in 1991, but it was not until 2004 that Oxford entered the lists—although as early as 1992 a selection of 'words of the year' was nominated by John Simpson. His list includes some words which have unquestionably stayed the course and others which could not be claimed to have secured a permanent foothold in the language (and have yet to make it into the *OED*): *buckyball, carjack, Dianagate* (together with *Threshergate*), *double whammy, ethnic cleansing, grunge, kickstart, Serie A* (and *Serie B*), *subsidiarity*, and *virtual reality*.

The single word nominated in 2004 was the choice of Susie Dent, whose regular appearances in Dictionary Corner on the TV programme *Countdown* had earned her a reputation as a language pundit, and who in her book *Larpers and Shroomers: The Language Report* (which also included a list of other words 'born' in each of the last 100 years) identified *chav* as 'a contender for the word of 2004'. She wrote that the word had very recently come to be widely applied in British use to members of 'a group of people pejoratively described as delinquents or members of an underclass'. Although many of the news stories which picked up on Dent's nomination mistakenly reported that the word had been added to the *OED*, it was only in 2006 that a full *OED* entry was published, tracing the documentary record of the word back to 1998, with a first quotation taken from an online newsgroup. An entry for the much older, and almost certainly cognate, word *chavvy* (of Romani origin, and meaning 'child') appeared at the same time. In 2005, and in several subsequent years, OUP lexicographers nominated two separate 'words of the year', one each for British and American English. One of the most successful nominations of recent years was *selfie* in 2013, a word which genuinely seems to have captured something of the zeitgeist; use of the word has now been traced back to 2002, again in an online source.

discipline of maintaining a chronological ordering raises significant issues of semantic development which would otherwise remain unaddressed'.[62]

In analysing the behaviour of contemporary language, too, OUP's lexicographers— and not just those working on the *OED*—now have access to new tools and resources. Since 2004 they have been able to use an innovative piece of corpus analysis software (Sketch Engine) to interrogate the Oxford English Corpus—launched in 2000 and currently containing well in excess of 2 billion words, enriched with part-of-speech tagging and other metadata—to obtain detailed summaries of the grammatical and collocational behaviour of a word in twenty-first-century English; more recently it has begun to be possible to use the same software to analyse other corpora, including historical material relating to the English of earlier periods.[63] With the aid of all this information it is possible to create dictionary entries of unprecedented richness and detail. This proliferation of information brings its own problems, however: the time available to a lexicographer to work on an entry remains limited, and careful decisions have to be made about which sources of information to consult.

Another type of evidence which the *OED* can draw on is, of course, that to be found in other dictionaries, in particular other historical dictionaries. The number of such dictionaries has continued to increase, and valuable contacts are maintained with many other historical lexicography projects around the world, many of them tracing their origins to initiatives from Oxford, many more consciously following methods similar to those of the *OED*. Links within this scholarly network continue to be maintained and fostered, both through regular communication and by personal contact at conferences and similar occasions. The network acquired a new European dimension with the formation of the European Federation of National Institutions for Language, to the inaugural conference of which in Florence in 2000 John Simpson was invited as a representative of what could be called the United Kingdom's most notable 'institution for language'. *OED* staff have continued to attend and give papers at a wide range of academic conferences and other scholarly gatherings, which have on occasion been co-hosted or supported by OUP.[64]

In 2010 delegates to one such conference,[65] held in Oxford, were invited to OUP to be shown a preview of an extensively revamped version of the *OED* website (see Figure 42), which was formally launched in November 2010. The new website featured many innovations, including new ways of visualizing the information contained in the Dictionary's database, new links between pieces of Dictionary data and various external

---

[62] Quoted in Silva (2000: 93).

[63] For an account of Sketch Engine see Kilgarriff et al. (2014).

[64] One particular scholarly link with the past was renewed in 2000 when Philip Durkin (see p. 585 below) was elected to the Council of the Philological Society; he went on to serve as Hon. Treasurer from 2008 to 2014, the first time in many years that a senior *OED* lexicographer had held office in the Society. Recent papers by *OED* editors published in the Society's *Transactions* include Durkin (1999) and Simpson et al. (2004).

[65] The conference (the 5th International Conference on Historical Lexicography and Lexicology), which took place mainly in St Anne's College, was jointly supported by the Press, the Philological Society, the English Faculty, and the University's John Fell Fund. An exhibition marking the tenth anniversary of *OED Online* was mounted in the Bodleian Library to coincide with the conference.

resources (allowing readers to click through to, for example, a corresponding entry in the *Middle English Dictionary* or OxfordDictionaries.com, or full bibliographical records for many quotations), and a greatly expanded set of public information pages. Another change of considerable significance was the fact that every entry in the online database—whether fully revised or not—was now a copy of the corresponding entry in the working database used by the *OED*'s lexicographers. The significance of this lay in the fact that, ever since the publication of *OED2*, many revision tasks had entailed making small (and not so small) changes across the entire database—notably the correction and standardization of all quotations from a particular textual source, a major activity carried out on a text-by-text rather than entry-by-entry basis—which however could hitherto only be seen in the online database in the entries which had been fully revised: other entries continued to appear in the form in which they had appeared in the second edition. Publishing the working database enabled readers to benefit from all of these small revisions even in entries which were still waiting to be fully revised.

Possibly the most important new feature of the website was the integration into the Dictionary's text of a new set of semantic data derived from the *Historical Thesaurus of the Oxford English Dictionary*, which had been published in book form in July 2009. This unique project,[66] conceived by Michael Samuels of the University of Glasgow in 1965 and carried out there over the next four decades, assigned each word and sense in the *OED* (originally the first edition, later expanded to include more recent material) to one or more positions in a specially devised semantic network, allowing them to be grouped into a hierarchy of synonyms as in any thesaurus, but with the additional feature that synonyms could be arranged into a historical sequence. Embedding this network in the *OED* database created an entirely new way for users of *OED Online* to navigate the Dictionary's contents, by following links between semantically related words. The idea of intermeshing other kinds of text with the *OED* seems likely to provide a fruitful direction for further exploitation of its contents; among the possibilities currently being investigated is that of connecting the Dictionary directly into texts being read on an e-reader, so that all the meanings of a word throughout its history can be looked up at the point where it is encountered.

The 2010 relaunch of the website generated significant publicity. Strangely, however, many of the reports of it which appeared in newspapers around the world appeared under headlines proclaiming a rather different piece of information, namely the fact that the *OED* entry for the word *pavlova* showed as its first evidence for the word a New Zealand publication of 1927.[67] Even more strangely, this information was not

---

[66] For a full account of the project see Kay et al. (2009).

[67] Australian and New Zealand sources might have been expected to cover the story—especially as the question of which country named the dessert has long been a matter of (light-hearted) dispute—but it also featured in the headline of stories about the launch in the *Daily Telegraph* (2 Dec. 2010), the *Independent* (3 Dec.), and the *Irish Times* (4 Dec.).

new, and had in fact been available in the *OED* for decades: the 1927 quotation had been given in the first version of the entry to be published, in the *Supplement* in 1982. This neatly illustrates the impossibility of predicting just how an *OED*-related story will be reported. That being said, the Dictionary's media profile has flourished since the launch of *OED Online*. The regular publication of new batches of *OED3* text, of course, provides a reliable stream of opportunities, but there have also been many other notable occasions when the Dictionary has found itself in the spotlight. It has continued to feature in various TV programmes, including a 2003 BBC documentary entitled 'An A–Z of the *OED*' and two series (broadcast 2006 and 2007) of a BBC programme entitled 'Balderdash and Piffle', in which—in another manifestation of the *OED*'s long-standing practice of appealing for help—findings collected from the public about a selection of 50 words and phrases were reviewed by a panel of three *OED* editors headed by John Simpson (in a manner at times reminiscent of the reality TV programme 'The Apprentice'). Publicity of a rather different kind was generated in 2004 when a quiz team representing OUP—but consisting entirely of people working on the *OED* (three lexicographers, including the author, and a software engineer)—reached the final of *University Challenge: The Professionals* (to be defeated, respectably enough, by the British Library).

A more melancholy event which also garnered some public attention was the death of Robert Burchfield, after a long struggle with Parkinson's disease, on 5 July 2004. In an appreciation published in *OED News*, John Simpson paid tribute to his predecessor's tenacity in steering the *OED* through a challenging period, and his efforts to pass on 'the traditional lore of the Dictionary' and thereby maintain a link with the past; there were also tributes from prominent figures elsewhere in the world of English historical lexicography, including Toni Healey of the *Dictionary of Old English* in Toronto, Bob Lewis of the *Middle English Dictionary* in Ann Arbor, and Graeme Kennedy of the New Zealand Dictionary Centre in Wellington.

In fact it is hard to work on the *OED* without developing some awareness of its past. Today's lexicographers may be using equipment and techniques unimaginable to their predecessors, but on just about every desk in the *OED* office are still to be found the same paper slips that have formed the principal stock in trade of historical lexicography since the days of Trench and Furnivall and Coleridge; some of them, indeed, are in Furnivall's handwriting, still being made use of over a century after his death. The tools may have changed, but the essence of the job remains the same: the lexicographer must survey the available data about how a word has been used over time, and distil this data into a historical account. Many aspects of this process of analysis and synthesis, as it goes on in the offices of the *OED* today, would be recognized and understood by those who have worked on the Dictionary in previous generations; they would surely also have sympathized with our struggles to cope with the deluge of words and of information about them, and to keep up the throughput of work.

---

macadamized

One of the first entries in *OED2* to be revised, in 1994, was that for *macadamized*; the revised entry was also included in the first batch to be published online six years later. When first published, this revised entry included no evidence earlier than the two 1827 quotations which had appeared when the entry first appeared in *OED1* nearly a century earlier (one illustrating the use of the word as applied to roads surfaced with tarmacadam, the other a figurative extension of this meaning 'made level, even, or smooth'). In the decade following the appearance of the entry in *OED Online*, the range of resources— especially full-text databases—available for consultation has increased enormously, making it possible to improve significantly on the findings on which that first version of the *OED3* entry was based. In 2014 a project to revise entries for some words beginning with *un-* led to re-investigation of many of the corresponding unprefixed words which had already been revised. In the case of the entry for *unmacadamized*, first published in 1924 with a first quotation of 1840, research brought to light an example of the word from 1826. While it is by no means uncommon for an *un-*word to be older than its corresponding 'positive' word, the question of whether this was really true for *macadamized* now needed to be re-researched; and in fact one of the various newspaper databases which are now searched as a matter of course yielded a quotation from the *Morning Post* of 2 December 1823: 'The unsightly buildings at the east end..have been removed, and a very handsome avenue formed, leading from Pall-mall to the Park, with a Macadamized road.' The entry for *macadamized* was republished in 2014, with its new 1823 antedating, at the same time as the revised entry for *unmacadamized*. The 'positive' counterparts of many other *un-*words were also antedated during the same revision project. As new resources and new information continue to become available, such re-revisions of published revised entries now make up a significant part of the ongoing work of preparing *OED3*.

One way to end this history of the making of the *Oxford English Dictionary* would be to observe, on the one hand, that this work of making, and remaking, the Dictionary's text is still going on, and seems likely to go on for decades to come, and, on the other, that the future for lexicography, and for dictionaries and how they may be used and exploited, is teeming with new possibilities, which today's generation of editors and publishers are engaging with enthusiastically.[68] But there is an important respect in which an era has very recently come to an end. John Simpson retired in October 2013 (see Figure 43) after over twenty years as the Dictionary's Chief Editor, preceded by nearly another decade as Co-Editor with Edmund Weiner. Throughout this time his quiet, unassuming, sometimes even self-deprecating manner had made it easy to be unaware of the sure hand with which he had guided the Dictionary through

---

[68] An important expression of the *OED*'s, and OUP's, engagement with the future took place on 1 August 2013, when the Press hosted a one-day symposium in Oxford at which approximately fifty invited delegates, specialists in a diverse range of fields, took part in discussions about future plans and possibilities for the Dictionary (www.oedsymposium.com).

FIGURE 43   John Simpson (right) cutting the cake at his retirement, October 2013. Also visible are Judy Pearsall (Director, Oxford Dictionaries) and Edmund Weiner.

a period of extraordinary change, with challenges considerably greater than those faced by Robert Burchfield before him.[69] The challenge of setting out upon the task of revising the text, and of persuading (and re-persuading) senior figures at OUP that this was feasible and that the Press should support it, had been formidable enough; the challenge of reconceiving the whole revision project for online publication was arguably greater still. Through all of this he succeeded in maintaining the Dictionary's scholarly standards, and in developing a team capable of producing work which matched them. In this he was much assisted by Edmund Weiner, who had continued

[69] Simpson's achievement as editor was recognized in the Queen's Birthday Honours in June 2014 when he was awarded an OBE.

to work closely with him long after stepping down as Co-Editor; but Simpson was of course the project's leader, both editorially and in other respects, and he found a way of fulfilling the role which paid dividends, leading less by exhortation or forcefulness than by persuasion (which sometimes seemed more like allowing people to persuade themselves) and by the example of his own editorial work. In fact he was a gifted, instinctive lexicographer, with an uncanny ability simply to see what is worth saying about a word, and to find the right words to say it, combined with a readiness to engage with innovation—crucial during a time of such rapid technological change—and a well-developed awareness of the needs of the ordinary user of the Dictionary. It

FIGURE 44   Michael Proffitt.

was only as his retirement approached that his colleagues realized how alarming the prospect was of doing without him. In fact the transition to the new Chief Editor, Michael Proffitt (see Figure 44), has been a remarkably smooth one, no doubt helped by the fact that he had latterly assumed much of the managerial responsibility for running the project. (He is also helped by having a second Deputy Chief Editor, working alongside Edmund Weiner: Philip Durkin, one of the first recruits to the Dictionary's revision team in 1994, who has also been in charge of the project's etymological work since 1998.)

The question of the *OED*'s philosophy is one which those engaged in its compilation (see Figures 45, 46) rarely have time to contemplate; but in an article written a few

FIGURE 45   The *OED* offices in Oxford, August 2015.

FIGURE 46   *OED* staff in Oxford, September 2015.

months before his retirement John Simpson took the opportunity to explore it.[70] In a new reformulation of the guiding principle of historical lexicography, he observed:

> [the] assumption [...] applied at every stage of the editorial process [is] that there is an incremental and logical progression (of meaning, spelling, pronunciation, etc.) throughout the chronological history of any word, from the earliest times right up to the present day [...] The historical lexicographer's task is to describe each word whilst bearing in mind this concept of incremental logical progression over history.

He also noted, however, that

> the nature of language and of our interpretation of history is such that what appears right, on the best evidence, today may well represent an outmoded view in years to come [...] the output of lexicographical work is temporary—ideally the best that can be achieved at the time of editing and with the materials available.

Surely all of those who have participated in the making of the *Oxford English Dictionary* over the last century and a half would agree, not only that this lexicographical ideal remains worth striving for, but also that there will always be challenges to be faced in attempting to realize it.

---

[70] See Simpson (2013b).

GUIDE TO ABBREVIATIONS
AND SOURCES

ABBREVIATIONS FOR FREQUENTLY MENTIONED
INDIVIDUALS AND ORGANIZATIONS

AJE	Alexander Ellis
CTO	Charles Onions
DMD	Dan Davin
EETS	Early English Text Society
ESCW	Edmund Weiner
FJF	Frederick Furnivall
GBR	George Richardson
HB	Henry Bradley
HC	Herbert Coleridge
HHG	Henry Hucks Gibbs
HSM	Humphrey Milford
ISA	Ivon Asquith
JAHM	James Murray
JAS	John Simpson
JM	John Murray
KS	Kenneth Sisam
OUP	Oxford University Press
PS	Philological Society (of London)
RAD	Robin Denniston
RDPC	Richard Charkin
RWB	Robert Burchfield
RWC	Robert Chapman
TJB	Tim Benbow
UWC	Unregistered Words Committee (of the Philological Society)
WAC	William Craigie

ABBREVIATIONS FOR MANUSCRIPT
SOURCES AND COLLECTIONS

BL	British Library
BodL	Bodleian Library, Oxford
FC	OUP, Minutes of Finance Committee
FL	OUP, letterbooks of Henry Frowde
GL	Guildhall Library, London
HL	Huntington Library, San Marino, California (Furnivall Papers)
JMA	John Murray Archive, National Library of Scotland
JP	Papers of Benjamin Jowett, Balliol College, Oxford
KCLFP	Furnivall Papers, King's College London
ML	OUP, letterbooks of Humphrey Milford
ML(B)	OUP, 'Branch' letterbooks of Humphrey Milford
MP	Papers of Sir James Murray, Bodleian Library
NLS	National Library of Scotland
OD	OUP, Delegates' Order Books
ODA	OUP, Delegates' Agenda Books
OUA	Oxford University Archives
OUPA	OUP Archives
OUPA(u)	Uncatalogued material in OUP Archives: see below
PSCM	Minutes of Philological Society Council meetings (currently on deposit in OUPA)
PSOM	Minutes of Philological Society ordinary meetings (currently on deposit in OUPA)
PS(m)	Philological Society miscellaneous correspondence
SL	OUP, Secretary's letterbooks
SL(P)	OUP, single letterbook described as 'Secretary's Private Letterbook 1901–6'
WP	Papers of James Wyllie (in the possession of James Wyllie, junior)

All archival references are to documents in OUPA unless otherwise stated. A list of currently uncatalogued documents in OUPA which have been cited in the text, with location details, has been deposited with the archivist.

ABBREVIATIONS FOR FREQUENTLY CITED SOURCES

CWW	*Caught in the Web of Words*: see Murray (1977)
HJRM	'Sir James Murray of the Oxford English Dictionary', unpublished typescript (photocopy in OUPA)
ODNB	*Oxford Dictionary of National Biography*

ProcPS   Published proceedings of the Philological Society (used to refer to the printed
records of the Society's meetings, which however are not always called
'Proceedings' as such: e.g. the 'Minutes of Meetings' for Jan 1877 to May 1879,
which appear as an appendix to *TPS* for 1877–9 under that title)

TPS   *Transactions of the Philological Society*

NOTE ON *OED* FASCICLES AND THEIR PREFACES

The separately published instalments of the first edition of the Dictionary are often
referred to as 'fascicles', but the term was not in official use by OUP, nor did the Editors
themselves regularly use it. The first instalments of the Dictionary, which ran to over
300 pages, were referred to as Parts. Part IV (*Bra–Cass*) was also made available in two
instalments (the first for the benefit of those wishing to end their first bound volume
at the end of the letter B), which were called 'Section I' and 'Section II'; the same also
occurred with the Parts *Crouchmas–Depravation* and *Everybody–Field*, and the terms
'section' and 'fasciculus' were sometimes used to refer to these subdivisions of a Part.
In due course 'section' became the standard name for the shorter instalments that
began to be issued from 1894. The usual size for these was 64 or 72 pages; occasionally
there was enough material in hand to allow the publication of a 'double section' of
(approximately) twice as many pages, and even on occasion a 'triple section'. It also
continued to be possible to buy the Dictionary in the form of larger Parts, generally
equivalent in size to five single Sections, and also as volumes or half-volumes. For a full
guide to Sections and Parts, with dates of publication, see McMorris (2000).

Sections and Parts were generally issued with brief prefaces by the relevant Editor;
longer prefaces were also issued for volumes and half-volumes of the Dictionary. This
matter, which contains a great deal of valuable historical information, was omitted from
the 1933 reissue of the Dictionary; its historical interest was, however, recognized during
work on the creation of *OED2*, and a collection of prefaces was reissued in facsimile
by the University of Waterloo in 1987 (Raymond 1987). The compiler of this collection,
Darrell Raymond, subsequently carried out further work to improve the quality of the
facsimiles, and (with help from Steven Wood) located numerous additional prefaces.
The expanded and improved set of facsimiles is available from Raymond's own website
(www.darrellraymond.com/prefaces); he has also kindly allowed copies of them to be
made available via the *OED*'s own website, where numerous other archival documents,
including the prefaces to *OED2* and *OED3*, may also be consulted either in facsimile
or as full text.

BIBLIOGRAPHY

Aarsleff, Hans (1962). 'The early history of the *Oxford English Dictionary*', *Bulletin of the New York Public Library* 66, 417–39.

Aarsleff, Hans (1967). *The study of language in England, 1780–1860*. Princeton, NJ: Princeton University Press. Reprinted in 1983, with a new preface, by University of Minnesota Press/Athlone Press.

Aarsleff, Hans (1985). Review of William Benzie, *Dr. F. J. Furnivall: Victorian scholar adventurer, Victorian Studies* 29, 175–8.

Aarsleff, Hans (1990). 'The original plan for the *OED* and its background', *TPS* 88, 151–61.

Adams, Michael (1998). 'Credit where it's due: authority and recognition at the *Dictionary of American English*', *Dictionaries* 19, 1–20.

Adams, Michael (2002). 'Phantom dictionaries: the Middle English Dictionary before Kurath', *Dictionaries* 23, 95–114.

Adams, Michael (2009). 'The period dictionaries', in Cowie (2009) vol. 1, 326–52.

Adams, Michael (ed.) (2010). *'Cunning passages, contrived corridors': unexpected essays in the history of lexicography*. Monza: Polimetrica.

Aitken, A. J. (1973). 'Modern English from A to G', *Times Literary Supplement*, 26 Jan., 90.

Aitken, A. J. (1987). 'The period dictionaries', in Burchfield (1987b), 94–116.

Aitken, A. J. (1992). 'Scottish dictionaries', in T. McArthur (ed.), *The Oxford companion to the English language* (Oxford: Oxford University Press), 901–3.

ANDC (2013). *Celebrating 25 years of the* Australian National Dictionary. [Canberra]: Australian National Dictionary Centre.

Ashdowne, Richard (2014). 'Dictionary of Medieval Latin from British Sources', *British Academy Review*, Summer, 46–53.

Bailey, R. W. (1980). 'Progress toward a Dictionary of Early Modern English 1475–1700', in W. Pijnenburg and F. de Tollenaere (eds), *Proceedings of the Second International Round Table Conference on Historical Lexicography* (Dordrecht: Foris), 199–226.

Bailey, R. W. (1985). 'Charles C. Fries and the Early Modern English Dictionary', in P. H. Fries and N. M. Fries (eds), *Toward an understanding of language: Charles Carpenter Fries in perspective* (Amsterdam: John Benjamins), 171–204.

Bailey, R. W. (ed.) (1987). *Dictionaries of English: prospects for the record of our language*. Ann Arbor: University of Michigan Press.

Bailey, R. W. (1996). '[The *Century Dictionary*:] Origins', *Dictionaries* 17, 1–16.

Bailey, R. W. (2000a). '"This Unique and Peerless Specimen": the reputation of the *OED*', in Mugglestone (2000), 207–27.

Bailey, R. W. (2000b). 'Appendix III: The *OED* and the public', in Mugglestone (2000), 253–84.

Bailey, R. W. (2009). 'National and regional dictionaries of English', in Cowie (2009) vol. 1, 279–301.

Barnes, Julian (1982). 'The social democratic phase', *New Statesman*, 16 July, 20–1.

Barnhart, R. K. (1996). '[The *Century Dictionary:*] Aftermath', *Dictionaries* 17, 116–25.

Béjoint, Henri (1994). *Tradition and innovation in modern English dictionaries.* Oxford: Clarendon Press.

Bell, Alan (2013). 'Scholarly and reference publishing', in Louis (2013), 325–88.

Belson, Mick (2003). *On the Press: through the eyes of the craftsmen of Oxford University Press.* Witney: Robert Boyd.

Benzie, William (1983). *Dr. F. J. Furnivall: Victorian scholar adventurer.* Norman, Okla.: Pilgrim Books.

Berg, Donna Lee (1988). 'Old wine into new bottles: the potential of an electronic *OED*', in *Papers presented at the 12th Annual Meeting of the Atlantic Provinces Linguistic Association* (Charlottetown: University of Prince Edward Island), 1–10.

Bergheaud, Patrice (1979). 'De James Harris à John Horne Tooke: mutations de l'analyse du langage en Angleterre dans la deuxième moitié du XVIIIe siècle', *Historiographia Linguistica* 6, 15–45.

Berners-Lee, Tim (1999). *Weaving the Web.* San Francisco: HarperSanFrancisco.

Bivens, L. (1981). 'Nineteenth century reactions to the *O.E.D.*: an annotated bibliography', *Dictionaries* 3, 146–52.

Blake, G. Elizabeth, Tim Bray, and Frank W. Tompa (1992). 'Shortening the *OED*: experience with a grammar-defined database', *ACM Transactions on Information Systems* 10, 213–32.

Bradley, Henry (1906). 'The *Oxford English Dictionary*' (paper read in Hamburg, 4 Oct. 1905), *Zeitschrift für deutsche Wortforschung* 7, 311–18.

Brewer, Charlotte (1989). 'Thoughts on the second edition of the *Oxford English Dictionary*', *London Review of Books*, 31 Aug., 16–18.

Brewer, Charlotte (1996). *Editing* Piers Plowman: *the evolution of the text.* Cambridge: Cambridge University Press.

Brewer, Charlotte (2007). *Treasure-house of the language: the living* OED. New Haven, Conn.: Yale University Press.

Brewer, Charlotte (2008). 'The Oxford Quarto Dictionary', *Bulletin of the Henry Sweet Society* 51, 25–39.

Brewer, Charlotte (2010). 'Prescriptivism and descriptivism in the first, second and third editions of *OED*', *English Today*, June, 24–33.

Bridges, Robert (1928). 'A memoir [of Henry Bradley]', in *The collected papers of Henry Bradley* (Oxford: Clarendon Press), 1–56.

Brien, Alan (1966). 'Down with all Bowdlers!' *New Statesman*, 5 Aug., 198–9.

Bromley, J. (1959). *The man of ten talents: a portrait of Richard Chenevix Trench.* London: SPCK.

Burchfield, R. W. (1958). 'O.E.D.: a new Supplement', *The Periodical*, Summer, 229–31.

Burchfield, R. W. (1961). 'O.E.D.: a new Supplement', *Essays and Studies* 14, 35–51.

Burchfield, R. W. (1963). Review of *Webster's Third New International Dictionary*, *Review of English Studies* 14, 319–23.

Burchfield, R. W. (1969). 'O.E.D. Supplement: a dymaxion exercise', *Oxford Magazine*, 21 Nov., 68–9.

Burchfield, R. W. (1972). 'Four-letter words and the *OED*', *Times Literary Supplement*, 13 Oct., 1233.

Burchfield, R. W. (1973a). 'Some aspects of the historical treatment of twentieth-century vocabulary', in *Tavola rotunda sui grandi lessici storici* (Florence: Accademia della Crusca), 31–5.

Burchfield, R. W. (1973b). 'The treatment of controversial vocabulary in *The Oxford English Dictionary*', *TPS* 72, 1–28. Reprinted in Burchfield (1989), 83–108.

Burchfield, R. W. (1973c). 'Data collecting and research', *Annals of the New York Academy of Sciences* 211, 99–103.

Burchfield, R. W. (1974a). 'Acid to Downer: some words for *O.E.D.*', *Words: Wai-te-ata Studies in Literature* 4, 93–6.

Burchfield, R. W. (1974b). 'The prosodic terminology of Anglo-Saxon scholars', in R. B. Burlin and E. B. Irving (ed.), *Old English studies in honour of John C. Pope* (Toronto: University of Toronto Press), 171–201.

Burchfield, R. W. (1975). 'The art of the lexicographer', *Journal of the Royal Society of Arts* 123, 349–61.

Burchfield, R. W. (1976). 'A case of mistaken identity', *Encounter*, June, 57–61.

Burchfield, R. W. (1977a). 'Some thoughts on the revision of the *O.E.D.*', in B. S. Lee (ed.), *An English miscellany presented to W. S. Mackie* (Cape Town: Oxford University Press), 208–18.

Burchfield, R. W. (1977b). 'Names of types of oil wells: an aspect of short-term historical lexicography', in P. G. J. van Sterkenburg (ed.), *Lexicologie: een bundel opstellen voor F. de Tollenaere ter gelegenheid van zijn 65e verjaardag* (Groningen: Wolters-Noordhoff), 71–8.

Burchfield, R. W. (1977c). 'On that other great dictionary', *Encounter*, May, 47–50.

Burchfield, R. W. (1978a). 'The turn of the screw: ethnic vocabulary and dictionaries', *Listener*, 13 Apr., 454–6. Reprinted in Burchfield (1989), 109–15.

Burchfield, R. W. (1978b). 'The point of severance: English in 1776 and beyond', *Encounter*, Oct., 129–33. Reprinted in Burchfield (1989), 116–24.

Burchfield, R. W. (1979). *The Fowlers: their achievements in lexicography and grammar.* London: English Association. Reprinted in Burchfield (1989), 125–46.

Burchfield, R. W. (1984). 'The end of an innings but not the end of the game', *Incorporated Linguist* 23, 114–19.

Burchfield, R. W. (1987a). 'The *Supplement to the Oxford English Dictionary*: the end of the alphabet', in Bailey (1987), 11–21. Reprinted in Burchfield (1989), 188–97.

Burchfield, R. W. (ed.) (1987b). *Studies in lexicography.* Oxford: Clarendon Press.

Burchfield, R. W. (1989). *Unlocking the English language.* London: Faber and Faber.

Burchfield, R. W. (2004). 'Murray, Sir James Augustus Henry (1837–1915)', in *Oxford Dictionary of National Biography*, vol. 39, 933–8.

Burchfield, R. W., and Hans Aarsleff (1988). *The Oxford English Dictionary and the state of the language.* Washington, DC: Library of Congress.

Burchfield, R. W., Denis Donoghue, and Andrew Timothy (1979). *The quality of spoken English on BBC Radio: a report for the BBC.* London: British Broadcasting Corporation.

Burchfield, R. W., and Valerie Smith (1973–4). 'Adzuki to Gun: some Japanese loanwords in English', *The Rising Generation* (Tokyo), Dec. 1973, 524–6, and Jan. 1974, 593–5.

Cameron, Angus (1983). 'On the making of the *Dictionary of Old English*', *Poetica* 15/16, 13–22.

Cameron, Averil, and Ian W. Archer (eds) (2008). *Keble past and present*. London: Third Millennium.

[Campbell, Archibald] (1767). *Lexiphanes, a dialogue*. London: printed for J. Knox.

Carpenter, Humphrey (1977). *J. R. R. Tolkien: a biography*. London: George Allen & Unwin.

[Chapman, R. W.] (1946). 'The world of words', *Times Literary Supplement*, 12 Oct., 492.

Chapman, R. W. (1948). *Lexicography*. London: Oxford University Press.

Chatterjee, Rimi B., and Padmini Ray Murray (2013). 'India', in Louis (2013), 649–71.

Coleridge, Derwent (1860). 'Observations on the plan of the Society's proposed New English Dictionary', *TPS* for 1860–1, 152–68.

Coleridge, Herbert (1859). *A glossarial index to the printed English literature of the thirteenth century*. London: Trübner.

Coleridge, Herbert (1860). 'A letter to the Very Rev. the Dean of Westminster' (dated 30 May 1860), in Trench (1860), 71–8.

Coleridge, Herbert (1861a). 'On the exclusion of certain words from a dictionary', *TPS* for 1860–1, 37–43.

Coleridge, Herbert (1861b). *The Philological Society's New English Dictionary. Basis of comparison. Third period. Eighteenth and nineteenth centuries. Part I: A to D*. London: Emily Faithfull.

Collison, Robert (1966). 'Samuel Taylor Coleridge and the *Encyclopaedia Metropolitana*', *Journal of World History* 9, 751–68.

Congleton, J. E. (1968). 'Sir Herbert Croft on revising Johnson's *Dictionary*', *Tennessee Studies in Literature* 13, 49–62.

Considine, John (2014a). 'The deathbed of Herbert Coleridge', *Notes & Queries*, Mar., 90–2.

Considine, John (2014b). 'John Jamieson, Franz Passow, and the double invention of lexicography on historical principles', *Journal of the History of Ideas* 75, 261–81.

Considine, John (2014c). *Academy dictionaries 1600–1800*. Cambridge: Cambridge University Press.

Considine, John (2015a). 'Historical dictionaries: history and development; current issues', in Durkin (2015), 163–75.

Considine, John (2015b). 'A chronology of major events in the history of lexicography', in Durkin (2015), 605–15.

Cook, Albert S. (1881). 'The Philological Society's English Dictionary', *American Journal of Philology* 2, 550–4.

Cooper, Elena (2015). 'Copyright and mass social authorship: a case study of the making of the *Oxford English Dictionary*', *Social and Legal Studies* 24, 509–30.

Copeland, B. Jack (2006). *Colossus: the secrets of Bletchley Park's codebreaking computers*. Oxford: Oxford University Press.

Cowie, A. P. (ed.) (2009). *The Oxford history of English lexicography*, vol. 1: *General-purpose dictionaries*; vol. 2: *Specialized dictionaries*. Oxford: Clarendon Press.

Craigie, W. A. (1917). *The pronunciation of English reduced to rules by means of a system of marks applied to the ordinary spelling*. Oxford: Clarendon Press.

Craigie, W. A. (1925). 'The need for an American Dialect Dictionary', *Dialect Notes* 5, 317–21.

Craigie, W. A. (1928). *The Oxford English Dictionary: a short account with some personal reminiscences.* New York: Oxford University Press.

Craigie, W. A. (1931). 'New dictionary schemes presented to the Philological Society, 4th April, 1919', *TPS* for 1925–30, 6–11.

[Craigie, W. A.] (1933a). 'Historical introduction', in *OED* (Introduction, Supplement, and Bibliography), vii–xxvi.

Craigie, W. A. (1933b). 'The Historical Dictionary of American English', *PMLA* 48, 956–8.

Craigie, W. A. (1941). *Completing the record of English* . London: Oxford University Press.

[Craigie, W. A., et al.] (1928). 'The making of the Dictionary', *Periodical*, 15 Feb., 3–20.

'Curiosus' (1880). 'A literary workshop', *Notes & Queries*, 2 Oct., 261–3.

Curthoys, Mark (2013). 'The Press and the University', in Eliot (2013a), 27–75.

Curzon, George Nathaniel (1909). *Principles and methods of university reform.* Oxford: Clarendon Press.

Dainton, Fred (2001). *Doubts and certainties: a personal memoir of the 20th century.* Sheffield: Sheffield Academic Press.

Dareau, Margaret G. (2002). 'DOST: its history and completion', *Dictionaries* 23, 208–31.

Dareau, Margaret G. (2005). 'The history and development of *DOST*', in C. J. Kay and M. A. Mackay (eds), *Perspectives on the older Scottish tongue: a celebration of DOST* (Edinburgh: Edinburgh University Press), 18–37.

Dareau, Margaret, and Iseabail Macleod (2009). 'Dictionaries of Scots', in Cowie (2009) vol. 1, 302–25.

Darwall-Smith, Robin (2008). *A history of University College, Oxford.* Oxford: Oxford University Press.

Davie, Michael (1976). 'In the lexicographer's lair', *Observer*, 13 June, review section, 32.

De Quincey, Thomas (1823). 'Notes from the pocket-book of a late opium-eater. No. III: English dictionaries', *London Magazine*, Nov., 493–6.

Durkin, Philip (1999). 'Root and branch: revising the etymological component of the *Oxford English Dictionary*', *TPS* 97, 1–49.

Durkin, Philip (2011). 'An influential voice in the Germanic etymologies in the first edition of the *OED*: correspondence between early editors and Eduard Sievers', in R. Bauer and U. Krischke (eds), *More than words: English lexicography and lexicology past and present: essays presented to Hans Sauer on the occasion of his 65th birthday* (Frankfurt: Peter Lang), 23–38.

Durkin, Philip (ed.) (2015). *The Oxford handbook of lexicography.* Oxford: Oxford University Press.

Eliot, Simon (ed.) (2013a). *The history of Oxford University Press*, vol. 2: *1780–1896*. Oxford: Oxford University Press.

Eliot, Simon (2013b). 'The evolution of a printer and publisher', in Eliot (2013a), 77–112.

Elliott, Laura (2000). 'How the Oxford English Dictionary went online', *Ariadne* 24. Available at: www.ariadne.ac.uk/issue24/oed-tech.

Elliott, Laura, and Sarah Williams (2006). 'Pasadena: a new editing system for the *Oxford English Dictionary*', in Elisa Corino, Carla Marello, and Cristina Onesti (ed.), *Atti del XII Congresso internazionale di lessicografia/Proceedings of the XIIth Euralex International Congress* (Alessandria: Edizioni dell'Orso), vol. 1, 257–64.

Evans, A. B. (1848). *Leicestershire words, phrases and proverbs*. London: William Pickering.

Faber, Robert, and Brian Harrison (2002). 'The *Dictionary of National Biography*: a publishing history', in R. Myers, M. Harris, and G. Mandelbrote (eds), *Lives in print: biography and the book trade from the Middle Ages to the 21st century* (London: British Library/New Castle, Del.: Oak Knoll Press), 171–92.

Farnell, Lewis R. (1934). *An Oxonian looks back*. London: Martin Hopkinson.

Feather, John (2013). 'Authors and publishers', in Eliot (2013a), 321–53.

Field, Jean (2002). *Mary Dormer Harris: the life and works of a Warwickshire historian*. Studley: Brewin Books.

Fleming, R. McClung (1952). *R. R. Bowker: militant liberal*. Norman: University of Oklahoma Press.

Fries, Agnes Carswell (1987). 'Reminiscences of lexicographers', *Dictionaries* 9, 211–17.

[Furnivall, F. J.] (1861). *An alphabetical list of English words occurring in the literature of the eighteenth and nineteenth centuries; and forming a basis of comparison for the use of contributors to the New Dictionary of the Philological Society*, pt 2: *E to L*. Hertford: Stephen Austin.

[Garnett, Richard] (1835). 'English lexicography', *Quarterly Review*, Sept., 295–330.

Gates, Floy P. (1930). 'The Historical Dictionary of American English in the making', *American Speech* 6, 36–44.

Gildersleeve, Basil Lanneau (1880). 'The Philological Society's Dictionary', *Nation*, 15 July, 44. Reprinted in W. W. Briggs (ed.), *Soldier and scholar: Basil Lanneau Gildersleeve and the Civil War* (Charlottesville: University Press of Virginia, 1998), 99–107.

Gilliver, Peter (1995). 'At the wordface: J. R. R. Tolkien's work on the *Oxford English Dictionary*', in P. Reynolds and G. H. GoodKnight (eds), *Proceedings of the J. R. R. Tolkien Centenary Conference* (Milton Keynes: Tolkien Society/Altadena, Calif.: Mythopoeic Press), 173–86.

Gilliver, Peter (2000). 'Appendix II: *OED* personalia', in Mugglestone (2000), 232–52.

Gilliver, Peter (2004). '"That brownest of brown studies": the work of the editors and in-house staff of the *Oxford English Dictionary* in 1903', *Dictionaries* 25, 44–64.

Gilliver, Peter (2005). 'The interests of Arthur Maling: Esperanto, chocolate, and biplanes in Braille', *OED News*, Mar.

Gilliver, Peter (2007). 'The great *Un-* crisis: an unknown episode in the history of the *OED*', in John Considine and Giovanni Iamartino (eds), *Words and dictionaries from the British Isles in historical perspective* (Newcastle: Cambridge Scholars Publishing), 166–77.

Gilliver, Peter (2008). 'The Philological Society's first *New English Dictionary*: Frederick Furnivall's sub-editors and their work', in M. Mooijaart and M. van der Wal (eds), *Yesterday's words: contemporary, current and future lexicography* (Newcastle: Cambridge Scholars Publishing), 67–76.

Gilliver, Peter (2010a). '"Not altogether treated as I should treat it now": James Murray's early editorial decisions for the *New English Dictionary*', in J. Considine (ed.), *Adventuring in dictionaries: new studies in the history of lexicography* (Newcastle: Cambridge Scholars Publishing), 212–37.

Gilliver, Peter (2010b). 'Collaboration, competition, confrontation: the *Oxford English Dictionary*'s associations with other dictionaries, *c.* 1880–1900', in Adams (2010), 57–84.

Gilliver, Peter (2010c). 'Walter Worrall and George Watson: the "nearly men" of the *Oxford English Dictionary*' (paper read at ICHLL in Oxford, 18 June 2010). Available at: ora. ox.ac.uk/objects/uuid:6be52b97-aded-4de7-b42f-856c49f5dea5.

Gilliver, Peter (2011). 'Harvesting England's ancient treasure: dialect lexicography and the Philological Society's first plans for a national dictionary', *Dictionaries* 32, 82–92.

Gilliver, Peter (2013). '*Make, put, run*: writing and rewriting three big verbs in the *OED*', *Dictionaries* 34, 10–23.

Gilliver, Peter, Jeremy Marshall, and Edmund Weiner (2006). *The ring of words: Tolkien and the* Oxford English Dictionary. Oxford: Oxford University Press.

Grimm, Wilhelm (1847). Address about a German dictionary ('über ein deutsches Wörterbuch'), in *Verhandlungen der Germanisten zu Frankfurt am Main am 24., 25. und 26. September 1846* (Frankfurt: Sauerländers Verlag), 114–24. Reprinted in G. Hinrichs (ed.), *Kleinere Schriften von Wilhelm Grimm* (Berlin: Ferdinand Dümmler, 1881), vol. 1, 508–20.

Gross, John J. (1969). *The rise and fall of the man of letters: aspects of literary life since 1800.* London: Weidenfeld & Nicolson.

Gunther, A. E. (1967). *Robert T. Gunther: a pioneer in the history of science, 1869–1940.* Oxford: printed for the subscribers.

Guralnik, David B. (1974). '"Jew" as defamation in the dictionary', *Sh'ma*, 6 Sept., 123–5.

Hall, Fitzedward (1874). 'Dr. Hall on the English language [letter]', *New York Times*, 5 Jan., 4.

Hammond, Mary (2013). 'The London connection', in Eliot (2013a), 277–319.

Harris, Roy (1982). 'The history men', *Times Literary Supplement*, 3 Sept., 935–6.

Heussler, Robert (1981). *British rule in Malaya: the Malayan Civil Service and its predecessors, 1867–1942.* Oxford: Clio Press.

Hinchcliffe, Tanis (1992). *North Oxford.* New Haven, Conn.: Yale University Press.

Hjelmqvist, Theodor (1896). *Modern lexikografi: några anteckningar om de historiska ordböckerna i Tyskland, Holland och England.* Lund: C. W. K. Gleerups Förlag.

Hudson, Derek (1974). *Munby, man of two worlds: the life and diaries of A. J. Munby.* London: John Murray.

Humphreys, Jennett (1882). 'English: its ancestors, its progeny', *Fraser's Magazine*, Oct., 429–57.

Hunter, Joseph (1829). *The Hallamshire glossary.* London: William Pickering.

Hunter, R., W. Hume Elliot, and C. C. Pond (1997). *The life of Robert Hunter (1823–1897).* Loughton: Loughton and District Historical Society.

Kay, Christian, et al. (2009). 'Unlocking the *OED*: the story of the *Historical Thesaurus of the OED*', in C. Kay et al. (eds), *Historical Thesaurus of the Oxford English Dictionary* (Oxford: Oxford University Press), vol. 1, xiii–xx.

Kendall, Joshua (2011). 'A Minor exception: on W. C. Minor and Noah Webster', *Nation*, 4 Apr.

Kennedy, James (1861). *Essays ethnological and linguistic*, ed. C. M. Kennedy. London: Williams & Norgate.

Ker, Neil (1972). 'Kenneth Sisam, 1887–1971', *Proceedings of the British Academy* 58, 409–28.

Kilgarriff, Adam, et al. (2014). 'The Sketch Engine: ten years on', *Lexicography: Journal of ASIALEX* 1, 7–36.

Kirkness, Alan (1980). *Geschichte des Deutschen Wörterbuchs 1838–1863: Dokumente zu den Lexikographen Grimm*. Stuttgart: S. Hirzel.

Kirkness, Alan (2012). 'Deutsches Wörterbuch von Jacob Grimm und Wilhelm Grimm', in U. Hass (ed.), *Grosse Lexika und Wörterbücher Europas: Europäische Enzyklopädien und Wörterbücher in historischen Porträts* (Berlin: de Gruyter), 211–32.

Kirkness, Alan (2015). 'Behind the scenes of Grimms' German Dictionary (1838–1863): a survey of original source materials', in C. Brinker-von der Heyde et al. (eds), *Märchen, Mythen und Moderne: 200 Jahre* Kinder- und Hausmärchen *der Brüder Grimm*, vol. 2 (Frankfurt: Peter Lang), 1063–82.

Knowles, Elizabeth (1990). 'Dr. Minor and the *Oxford English Dictionary*', *Dictionaries* 12, 27–42.

Knowles, Elizabeth (2000). 'Making the *OED*: readers and editors. A critical survey', in Mugglestone (2000), 22–39.

Knowles, Elizabeth (2013). 'Dictionaries and other works of reference', in Eliot (2013a), 601–30.

Kogan, Herman (1958). *The great EB: the story of the* Encyclopædia Britannica. Chicago: University of Chicago Press.

Kuhn, Sherman M. (1982). 'On the making of the *Middle English Dictionary*', *Dictionaries* 4, 14–41.

Landau, Sidney I. (2009). 'Major American dictionaries', in Cowie (2009) vol. 1, 182–229.

Laski, Marghanita (1967). 'Replanting old favourites', *Times*, 9 Mar., 8.

Latham, R. G. (1841). *The English language*. London: Taylor & Walton.

Laugesen, Amanda (2014). 'Dictionaries for a nation: the making of the *Macquarie Dictionary* (1981) and the *Australian National Dictionary* (1988)', *Journal of Australian Studies* 38, 52–67.

Leisure Hour (1883). 'Dictionary making', *Leisure Hour*, June, 362–6.

Lewis, Peter (1984). 'The A to Z marathon that spelt a sentence for life', *Mail on Sunday*, 29 Jan.

Lewis, Robert E., et al. (2007). *Middle English Dictionary: plan and bibliography*, 2nd edition. Ann Arbor: University of Michigan Press.

Liberman, Anatoly (1996). '[The *Century Dictionary*:] Etymology', *Dictionaries* 17, 29–54.

Liberman, Anatoly (2009). 'English etymological dictionaries', in Cowie (2009) vol. 2, 269–89.

Liddell, H. G., and Robert Scott (1843). *A Greek–English lexicon: based on the German work of Francis Passow*. Oxford: University Press.

Littré, Émile (1880). 'Comment j'ai fait mon *Dictionnaire de la langue française*: causerie', in *Études et glanures pour faire suite à l'*Histoire de la langue française (Paris: Didier et Cⁱᵉ), 390–442.

Long, Percy W. (1926). 'The American Dialect Dictionary', *American Speech* 1, 439–42.

Louis, Wm. Roger (ed.) (2013). *The history of Oxford University Press*, vol. 3: *1896–1970*. Oxford: Oxford University Press.

Lowenthal, David (2000). *George Perkins Marsh, prophet of conservation*. Seattle: University of Washington Press.

Luna, Paul (2000). 'Clearly defined: continuity and innovation in the typography of English dictionaries', *Typography Papers* 4, 5–56.

McArthur, Tom (2012). 'English world-wide in the twentieth century', in L. Mugglestone (ed.), *The Oxford history of English*, updated edition (Oxford: Oxford University Press), 446–87.

McConchie, R. W. (1997). *Lexicography and physicke: the record of sixteenth-century English medical terminology*. Oxford: Clarendon Press.

McKitterick, David (2004). *A history of Cambridge University Press*, vol. 3: *New worlds for learning, 1873–1972*. Cambridge: Cambridge University Press.

McKusick, James C. (1992). '"Living Words": Samuel Taylor Coleridge and the genesis of the *OED*', *Modern Philology* 90, 1–45.

McKusick, James C. (2009). 'Coleridge and language theory', in F. Burwick (ed.), *The Oxford handbook of Samuel Taylor Coleridge* (Oxford: Oxford University Press), 572–87.

Macleod, Iseabail (2012). 'Scottish National Dictionary', in Macleod and McClure (2012), 144–71.

Macleod, Iseabail, and J. Derrick McClure (eds) (2012). *Scotland in definition: a history of Scottish dictionaries*. Edinburgh: John Donald.

MacMahon, M. K. C. (1985). 'James Murray and the phonetic notation in the *New English Dictionary*', *TPS* 83, 72–112.

McMorris, Jenny (2000). 'Appendix I: *OED* Sections and Parts', in Mugglestone (2000), 228–31.

McMorris, Jenny (2001). *The warden of English: the life of H. W. Fowler*. Oxford: Oxford University Press.

Madan, Falconer (1908). *A brief account of the University Press at Oxford*. Oxford: Clarendon Press.

March, Francis A. (1860). 'English lexicography', *American Presbyterian Review*, Aug., 444–56.

March, Francis A. (1868). 'The scholar of to-day' (delivered at Amherst College in July 1868), *American Presbyterian Review*, Jan. 1869, 76–93. Reprinted in C. S. Northup, W. C. Lane, and J. C. Schwab (eds), *Representative Phi Beta Kappa Orations* (Boston, Mass.: Houghton Mifflin, 1915), 112–28.

Marsden, William (1834). *Thoughts on the composition of a national English dictionary*. London, 1834: published for the author by Parbury, Allen).

Marshall, Fiona (2006). 'History of the Philological Society: the early years'. Available at: www.philsoc.org.uk/includes/Download.asp?FileID=39.

Martin, G. H., and J. R. L. Highfield (1997). *A history of Merton College, Oxford*. Oxford: Oxford University Press.

Mathews, Mitford M. (1955). 'Of matters lexicographical', *American Speech* 30, 132–6.

Mathews, Mitford M. (1958). 'Of matters lexicographical', *American Speech* 33, 50–5.

Mathews, Mitford M. (1974). Review of *OED* Supplement Volume I. *Modern Philology* 72, 218–21.

Mathews, Mitford M. (1985). 'George Watson and the *Dictionary of American English*', *Dictionaries* 7, 214–24.

Matthews, David (1999). *The making of Middle English, 1765–1910*. Minneapolis: University of Minnesota Press.

Maw, Martin (2013a). 'The printer and the printing house', in Louis (2013), 219–57.

Maw, Martin (2013b). 'Printing technology, binding, readers, and social life', in Louis (2013), 277–307.

Meier, Hans Heinrich (1979). Review of *OED* Supplement Volumes 1 and 2. *English Studies* 60, 648–60.

Midgley, Simon (1986). 'Quest for the longer-lasting neologism', *Times Higher Educational Supplement*, 13 June, 12.

Momma, Haruko (2012). *From philology to English studies: language and culture in the nineteenth century.* Cambridge: Cambridge University Press.

Morris, E. E. (1892). 'Section I. Literature and Fine Arts. Address by the President', in A. Morton (ed.), *Report of the Fourth Meeting of the Australasian Association for the Advancement of Science* (Sydney: published by the Association), 170–84.

Morris, Jeremy (2004). 'The text as sacrament: Victorian Broad Church philology', in R. N. Swanson (ed.), *The Church and the Book: papers read at the 2000 Summer Meeting and the 2001 Winter Meeting of the Ecclesiastical History Society* (Woodbridge: Boydell Press), 365–74.

Morton, Herbert C. (1994). *The story of* Webster's Third: *Philip Gove's controversial dictionary and its critics.* Cambridge: Cambridge University Press.

Mugglestone, Lynda (ed.) (2000). *Lexicography and the* OED: *pioneers in the untrodden forest.* Oxford: Oxford University Press.

Mugglestone, Lynda (2005). *Lost for words: the hidden history of the Oxford English Dictionary.* New Haven, Conn.: Yale University Press.

Mugglestone, Lynda (2007). '"Decent reticence": coarseness, contraception, and the first edition of the *OED*', *Dictionaries* 28, 1–22.

Munro, John, et al. (1911). *Frederick James Furnivall: a volume of personal record.* London: Henry Frowde.

Murray, J. A. H. (1884). 'General explanations', in *A New English Dictionary on Historical Principles. Part I: A–Ant* (Oxford: Clarendon Press), vii–xiv. (Page references for quotations from the 'General explanations' are those relating to their first publication as part of part 1; page numbers in the more generally available 1933 reissue of *OED* are the same plus 20.)

Murray, J. A. H. (1900). *The evolution of English lexicography.* Oxford: Clarendon Press.

Murray, J. A. H. (1957). *Sir James A. H. Murray: a self-portrait,* ed. George F. Timpson. Gloucester: John Bellows.

Murray, K. M. Elisabeth (1977). *Caught in the web of words: James A. H. Murray and the Oxford English Dictionary.* New Haven, Conn.: Yale University Press.

Murray, Wilfrid (1943). *Murray the dictionary-maker: a brief account of Sir James A. H. Murray.* Wynberg, Cape: Rustica Press.

Nicholls, C. S. (2013). 'Oxford University Press, 1945–1970', in Louis (2013), 97–134.

Nowell-Smith, Simon (1968). *International copyright law and the publisher in the reign of Queen Victoria.* Oxford: Clarendon Press.

Noyes, Gertrude E. (1955). 'The critical reception of Johnson's *Dictionary* in the latter eighteenth century', *Modern Philology* 52, 175–91.

Ogilvie, Sarah (2008). 'Rethinking Burchfield and World Englishes', *International Journal of Lexicography* 21, 23–59.

Ogilvie, Sarah (2010). 'The *OED* and the *Stanford Dictionary* controversy: plagiarism or paranoia?', in Adams (2010), 85–109.

Ogilvie, Sarah (2012). *Words of the world: a global history of the Oxford English Dictionary.* Cambridge: Cambridge University Press.

O'Sullivan, Dan (2009). *Wikipedia: a new community of practice?* Farnham: Ashgate.

Ovenden, Keith (1996). *A fighting withdrawal: the life of Dan Davin.* Oxford: Oxford University Press.

Palmer, Bernard (ed.) (2006). *Richard Palmer: a life in letters.* Privately printed.

Passow, Franz (1826). *Johann Gottlob Schneiders Handwörterbuch der griechischen Sprache: Nach der dritten Ausgabe des grössern Griechischdeutschen Wörterbuchs... ausgearbeitet.* 2nd edition, vol. 1: *A–K.* Leipzig: F. C. W. Vogel.

Penhallurick, Robert (2009). 'Dialect dictionaries', in Cowie (2009) vol. 2, 290–313.

Phillips, Angus (forthcoming). 'Closure of the Printing House', in K. Robbins (ed.), *The history of Oxford University Press,* vol. 4 (Oxford: Oxford University Press).

Platt, W. (1910). *James Platt the Younger: a study in the personality of a great scholar.* London: Simpkin Marshall.

Plommer, Leslie (1984). 'Dictionary meets its Waterloo', *Globe and Mail* (Toronto), 16 May.

Powell, E. P. (1879). 'Dr. Murray and the New English Dictionary', *Mill Hill Magazine,* Apr., 179–82.

Price, Jennie (2003). 'The recording of vocabulary from the major varieties of English in the Oxford English Dictionary', in C. Mair (ed.), *The politics of English as a world language: new horizons in postcolonial cultural studies* (Amsterdam: Rodopi), 119–38.

Raff, Daniel (2013). 'The business of the Press', in Louis (2013), 191–216.

Ramson, Bill (2002). *Lexical images: the story of the Australian National Dictionary.* South Melbourne: Oxford University Press.

Raymond, Darrell R. (ed.) (1987). *Dispatches from the front: the prefaces to the* Oxford English Dictionary. Waterloo, Ontario: University of Waterloo, Centre for the New Oxford English Dictionary.

Read, Allen Walker (1937). 'Projected English dictionaries, 1755–1828', *Journal of English and Germanic Philology* 36, 188–205, 347–66.

Read, Allen Walker (1986). 'The history of lexicography', in R. Ilson (ed.), *Lexicography: an emerging international profession* (Manchester: Manchester University Press), 28–50.

Reddick, Allen (1996). *The making of Johnson's Dictionary 1746–1773,* revised edition. Cambridge: Cambridge University Press.

Reddick, Allen (2009). 'Johnson and Richardson', in Cowie (2009) vol. 1, 155–81.

Rennie, Susan (2012). *Jamieson's Dictionary of Scots: the story of the first historical dictionary of the Scots language.* Oxford: Oxford University Press.

Richardson, Charles (1836). *A new dictionary of the English language,* vol. 1: *A–K.* London: William Pickering.

Richardson, Charles (1854). *On the study of language.* London: George Bell.

Ritter, Robert M. (2004). 'The birth of Hart's *Rules*', *Journal of the Printing Historical Society* 7, 36–53.

Robinson, Fred C. (1973). 'A B C D E F G', *Yale Review* 62(3), 450–6.

Rose, G. K. (1920). *The story of the 2/4th Oxfordshire & Buckinghamshire Light Infantry.* Oxford: B. H. Blackwell.

Ross, A. S. C. (1934). Review of 1933 Supplement to *OED. Neuphilologische Mitteilungen* 35, 128–32.

Ruthven-Murray, Peter (1986). *The Murrays of Rulewater.* London: RCS.

Sanoff, Alvin P. (1986). '"All other dictionaries are temporary works"', *U.S. News & World Report,* 11 Aug., 59–60.

Shenker, Israel (1989). 'Annals of lexicography', *New Yorker*, 3 Apr., 86–100.

Silva, Penny (1999). 'Dictionary unit for South African English' (one of a set of papers entitled 'Lexicography in a multilingual South Africa'), *Lexikos* 9, 224–30.

Silva, Penny (2000). 'Time and meaning: sense and definition in the *OED*', in Mugglestone (2000), 77–95.

Silva, Penny (2005). 'Johnson and the *OED*', *International Journal of Lexicography* 18, 231–42.

Simcock, A. V. (1985). *Robert T. Gunther and the Old Ashmolean*. Oxford: Museum of the History of Science.

Simpson, J. A. (2002). 'The revolution of English lexicography', *Dictionaries* 23, 1–15.

Simpson, J. A. (2008). 'Major change in the choice of revised entries published on *OED Online*'. Available at: public.oed.com/the-oed-today/recent-updates-to-the-oed/previous-updates/march-2008-update/.

Simpson, J. A. (2010). 'The OED and innovation'. Available at: public.oed.com/about/the-oed-and-innovation/.

Simpson, J. A. (2013a). 'The spirit of place: five rooms and the *OED*', *Dictionaries* 34, 156–74.

Simpson, J. A. (2013b). 'The *Oxford English Dictionary* and its philosophy', *Philosophy and Technology* 26, 341–8.

Simpson, J. A., Edmund Weiner, and Philip Durkin (2004). 'The *Oxford English Dictionary* today', *TPS* 102, 335–81.

Singleton, Antony (2005). 'The Early English Text Society in the nineteenth century: an organizational history', *Review of English Studies* 56, 90–118.

Skeat, W. W. (1880). 'The Philological Society's New Dictionary', *Notes & Queries*, 5 June, 451–2.

Sledd, James H., and Gwin J. Kolb (1955). *Dr. Johnson's Dictionary: essays in the biography of a book*. Chicago: University of Chicago Press.

Smith, Godfrey (1959). 'The OED from A to Z', *Sunday Times*, 1 Feb., 8, 25.

Smith, Lucy Toulmin (1880). 'The New English Dictionary of the London Philological Society', *Anglia* 3, 413–14.

Smith, Richard C. (2003). 'Introduction', in R. C. Smith (ed.), *Teaching English as a foreign language, 1912–36: pioneers of ELT*, vol. 3: *Michael West* (London: Routledge), ix–xxvi.

Snyder, Alice D. (1940). 'Coleridge and the Encyclopedists', *Modern Philology* 38, 173–91.

Sperling, Matthew (2013). 'Books and the market: trade publishers, state subsidies, and small presses', in P. Robinson (ed.), *The Oxford handbook of contemporary British and Irish poetry* (Oxford: Oxford University Press), 191–212.

Spevack, Marvin (1990). 'The "world" of the Supplement to the *Oxford English Dictionary* (OEDS)', in T. Magay and J. Zigány (eds), *BudaLEX '88 Proceedings: Papers from the 3rd International EURALEX Congress, Budapest, 4–9 September 1988* (Budapest: Akadémiai Kiadó), 237–42.

Spevack, Marvin (2001). *James Orchard Halliwell-Phillipps: the life and works of the Shakespearean scholar and bookman*. New Castle, Del.: Oak Knoll Press/London: Shepheard-Walwyn.

Stanley, E. G. (1990). 'The *Oxford English Dictionary* and Supplement: the integrated edition of 1989 [review article]', *Review of English Studies* 41, 76–88.

Stevens, Mark (2013). *Broadmoor revealed: Victorian crime and the lunatic asylum*. Barnsley: Pen & Sword.

Strang, Barbara M. H. (1974). Review of *OED* Supplement Volume 1. *Notes & Queries*, Jan., 2–13.

Stray, Christopher (2004). 'From one Museum to another: the *Museum Criticum* (1813–26) and the *Philological Museum* (1831–33)', *Victorian Periodicals Review* 37, 289–314.

Stray, Christopher (2010). 'Liddell and Scott: myths and markets', in C. Stray (ed.), *Classical dictionaries: past, present and future* (London: Duckworth), 94–118.

Stray, Christopher (2012). 'The *Oxford Latin Dictionary*: a historical introduction', in *Oxford Latin Dictionary*, 2nd edition (Oxford: Oxford University Press), x–xvii.

Stray, Christopher (2013). 'Classics', in Eliot (2013a), 435–70.

Stray, Christopher, M. Clarke, and J. Katz (forthcoming). *Liddell and Scott: studies of a lexicon*. Oxford: Oxford University Press.

Sutcliffe, Peter (1978). *The Oxford University Press: an informal history*. Oxford: Clarendon Press.

Sutcliffe, Peter (2000). 'The Oxford University Press', in M. G. Brock and M. C. Curthoys (ed.), *The history of the University of Oxford*, vol. 7 (Oxford: Clarendon Press), 645–58.

Thompson, Jane Smeal, and Helen G. Thompson (1920). *Silvanus Phillips Thompson, D.Sc., LL.D., F.R.S.: his life and letters*. London: T. Fisher Unwin.

Todd, H. J. (ed.) (1818). *A Dictionary of the English Language; [...] By Samuel Johnson, LL.D. With numerous corrections, and with the addition of several thousand words*. London: Longman, Hurst, Rees, Orme, and Brown.

Tolkien, J. R. R. (1923). 'Henry Bradley: 3 Dec., 1845–23 May, 1923', *Bulletin of the Modern Humanities Research Association* 20, 4–5.

Tollemache, Lionel A. (1908). *Old and odd memories*. London: Edward Arnold.

Tompa, Frank W. (1996). 'Exposing text: how questions for the OED led to answers for the World Wide Web'. Available at: cs.uwaterloo.ca/~fwtompa/.papers/FriendsLib.pdf.

Trench, Richard Chenevix (1857). *On some deficiencies in our English dictionaries*. London: John W. Parker and Son, 2nd edition (1860), published with 'A letter to the author from Herbert Coleridge, Esq. on the progress and prospects of the Society's New English Dictionary'.

Triggs, Jeffery A. (1993). 'Doing other things with texts: the use of electronic resources in revising the *OED*', paper presented at the Conference on Early Dictionary Databases, Toronto, Oct. 1993. Available at: triggs.djvu.org/global-language.com/triggs/EED.html.

Tuckwell, William (1900). *Reminiscences of Oxford*. London: Cassell.

Weiner, Edmund (1986). 'The *New Oxford English Dictionary* and World English', *English World-Wide* 7, 259–66.

Weiner, Edmund (1987). 'The *New Oxford English Dictionary*: progress and prospects', in Bailey (1987), 30–48.

Weiner, Edmund (1989). 'Editing the *OED* in the electronic age', in *Dictionaries in the electronic age: proceedings of the Fifth Annual Conference of the University of Waterloo Centre for the New Oxford English Dictionary* (Waterloo, Ontario: University of Waterloo, Centre for the New *OED*), 23–31.

Weiner, Edmund (2009). 'The electronic *OED*: the computerization of a historical dictionary', in Cowie (2009) vol. 1, 378–409.

Wheelwright, George (1875). *An appeal to the English-speaking public on behalf of A New English Dictionary*. Privately printed.

Whyte, William (2013). 'Oxford University Press, 1896–1945', in Louis (2013), 59–95.

Winchester, Simon (1998). *The surgeon of Crowthorne*. London: Viking.

Winchester, Simon (2003). *The meaning of everything: the story of the* Oxford English Dictionary. Oxford: Oxford University Press.

Wright, E. M. (1932). *The life of Joseph Wright.* 2 vols. Oxford: Oxford University Press.

Wyllie, J. M. (1961). 'Sir William Craigie, 1867–1957', *Proceedings of the British Academy 47*, 273–91.

Wyllie, J. M. (1965). *The Oxford Dictionary slanders: the greatest scandal in the whole history of scholarship.* Privately printed.

Wyllie, J. M. (1967). *The great betrayal, or the failure of science: part three.* Privately printed.

Zgusta, Ladislav (1989). 'The Oxford English Dictionary and other dictionaries (Aikakośyam)', *International Journal of Lexicography 2*, 188–230.

Zgusta, Ladislav (2006). *Lexicography then and now: selected essays*, ed. F. Dolezal and T. Creamer. Tübingen: Max Niemeyer.

For a further extensive bibliography of *OED*-related material see the relevant pages of the 'Examining the *OED*' website (oed.hertford.ox.ac.uk).

INDEX

For references to the Dictionary before the opening of negotiations with OUP in 1877, see *New English Dictionary*; for references relating to later periods, see under the title of the respective edition (*OED1, OED* Supplement (1933), etc.).

Many individuals contributed to the Dictionary as *readers* (i.e. by supplying quotations); others worked on it as *sub-editors* in advance of the main editorial work; others served as members of the in-house or permanent *staff*. Membership of these groups is indicated, respectively, by the abbreviations (r), (sub), and (s). Those who have served as Editors or Co-Editors of the Dictionary are entered in bold type.

Some topics relating to two or more phases of the project are dealt with under each relevant phase; others are entered separately.

Italic page numbers denote references to illustrations.